Southern Africa

David Else
Joyce Connolly
Mary Fitzpatrick
Alan Murphy
Deanna Swaney

LONELY PLANET PUBLICATIONS
Melbourne • Oakland • London • Paris

SOUTHERN AFRICA

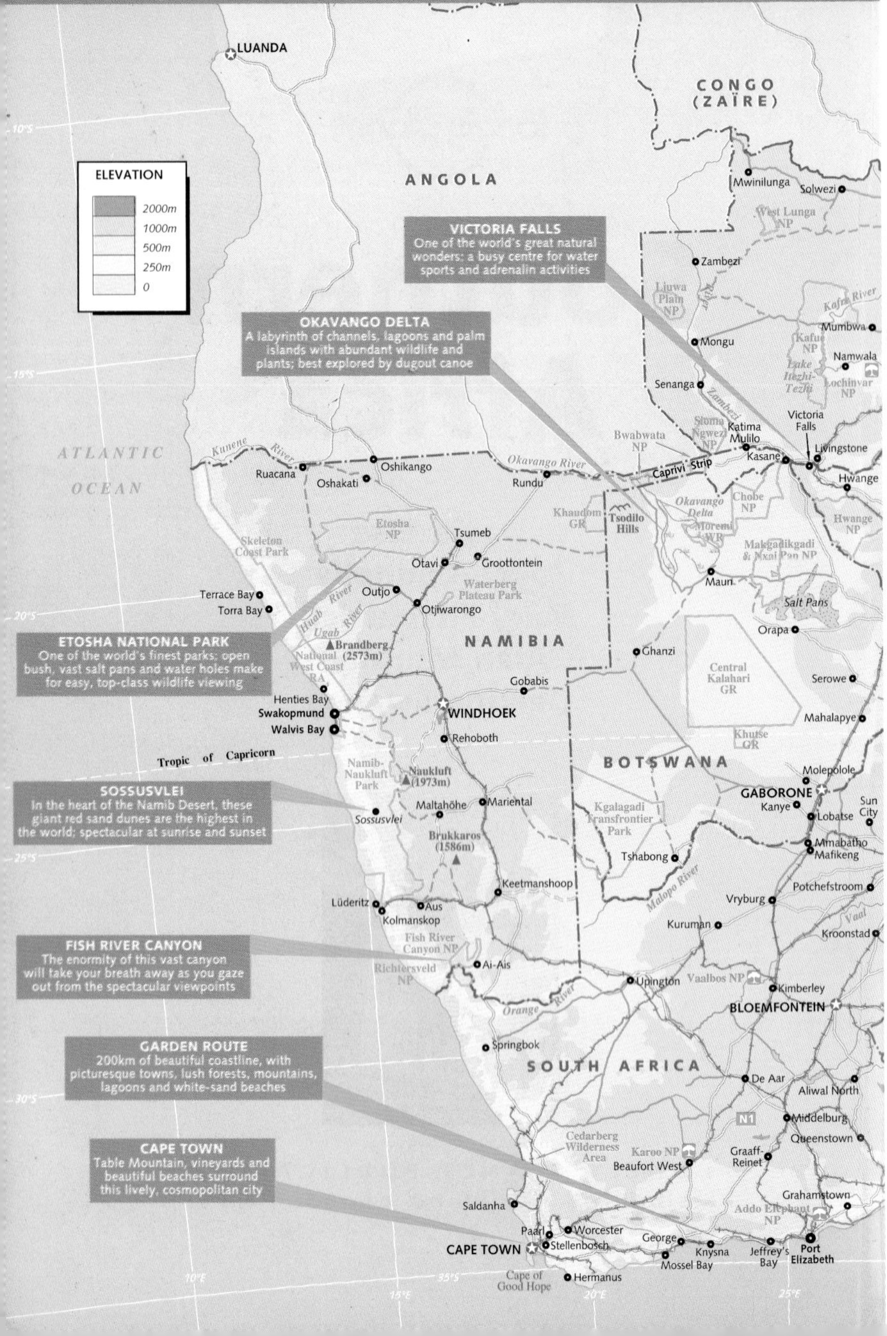

ELEVATION

2000m
1000m
500m
250m
0

VICTORIA FALLS
One of the world's great natural wonders: a busy centre for water sports and adrenalin activities

OKAVANGO DELTA
A labyrinth of channels, lagoons and palm islands with abundant wildlife and plants; best explored by dugout canoe

ETOSHA NATIONAL PARK
One of the world's finest parks: open bush, vast salt pans and water holes make for easy, top-class wildlife viewing

SOSSUSVLEI
In the heart of the Namib Desert, these giant red sand dunes are the highest in the world: spectacular at sunrise and sunset

FISH RIVER CANYON
The enormity of this vast canyon will take your breath away as you gaze out from the spectacular viewpoints

GARDEN ROUTE
200km of beautiful coastline, with picturesque towns, lush forests, mountains, lagoons and white-sand beaches

CAPE TOWN
Table Mountain, vineyards and beautiful beaches surround this lively, cosmopolitan city

SOUTHERN AFRICA

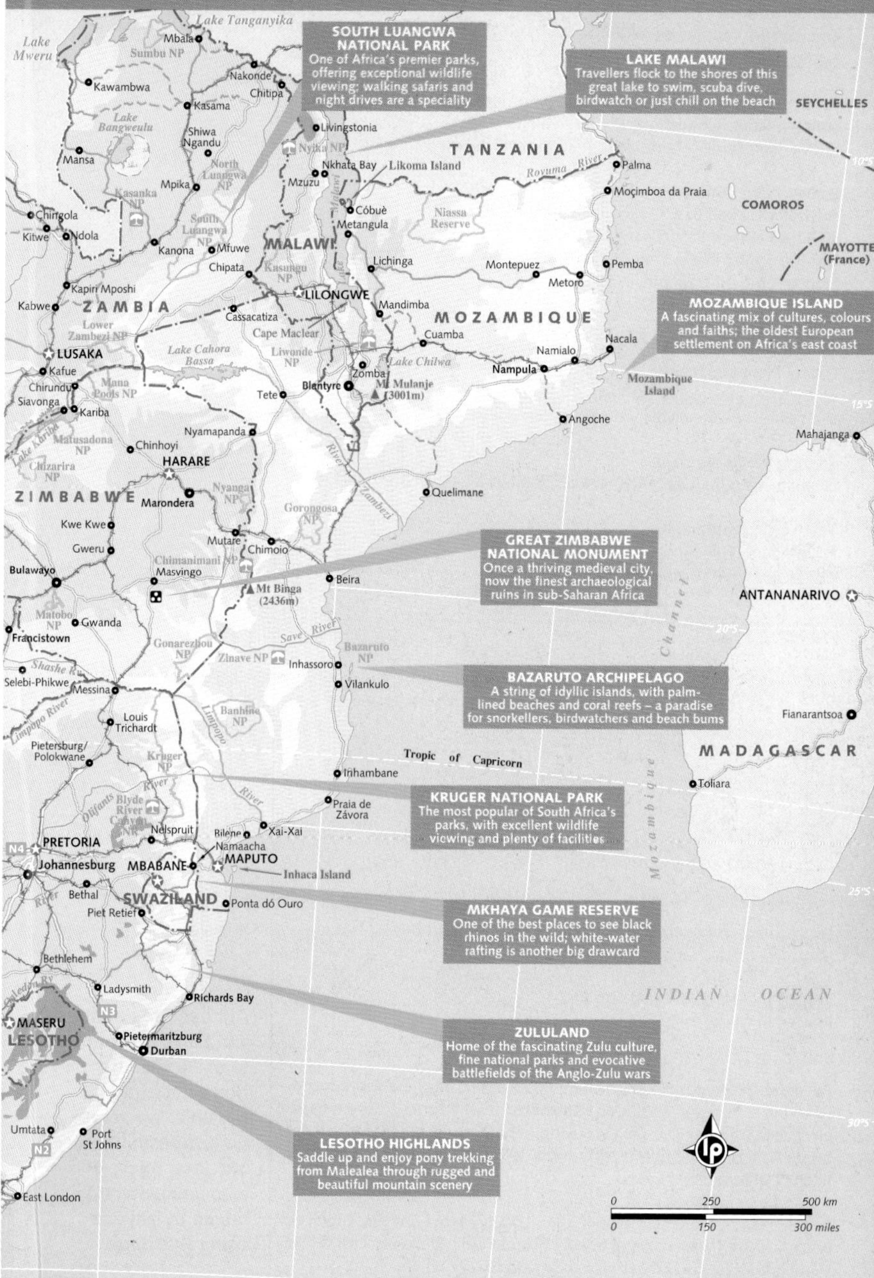

Southern Africa
2nd edition – September 2000
First published – September 1997

Published by
Lonely Planet Publications Pty Ltd ABN 36 005 607 983
90 Maribyrnong St, Footscray, Victoria 3011, Australia

Lonely Planet offices
Australia Locked Bag 1, Footscray, Victoria 3011
USA 150 Linden St, Oakland, CA 94607
UK 10a Spring Place, London NW5 3BH
France 1 rue du Dahomey, 75011 Paris

Photographs
Many of the images in this guide are available for licensing from Lonely Planet Images.
email: lpi@lonelyplanet.com.au
Web site: www.lonelyplanetimages.com

Front cover photograph
Elephant warning sign, Victoria Falls, Zimbabwe (John Borthwick)

Title page photographs
Facing page 104 (Andrew van Smeerdijk)
Facing page 440 (Daniel Birks)

ISBN 0 86442 662 3

Printed by SNP SPrint (M) Sdn Bhd
Printed in Malaysia

Contents – Text

Contents – Maps

INTRODUCTION

FACTS ABOUT THE REGION

BOTSWANA

LESOTHO

MALAWI

MOZAMBIQUE

NAMIBIA

SOUTH AFRICA

SWAZILAND

ZAMBIA

ZIMBABWE

The Authors

David Else

After hitchhiking through Europe for a couple of years, David Else first reached Africa in 1983. Since then he has travelled, trekked, worked and written all over the great continent, from Cairo to Cape Town, from Sudan to Senegal, via most of the bits in between. David has written and co-written many guidebooks, including Lonely Planet's *Trekking in East Africa, West Africa, The Gambia & Senegal, Malawi* and *Africa on a shoestring*. When not in Africa, David lives in the north of England, where he writes most days and escapes quite often to the Derbyshire Dales or mountains of Scotland.

Joyce Connolly

Born in Edinburgh, Scotland, Joyce has been moving from a tender age, including time in Europe where she developed a taste for beer. Fuelled by the travel bug (and beer) she studied to become a professional tourist but instead fell into publishing. The urge to move on kicked in again and she set off to Australia in pursuit of Jason Donovan. She bumped into Jason in Bondi, but fell for another true blue Aussie. Together they made a tent in St Kilda, Melbourne their home before becoming respectable employees of Lonely Planet. Joyce has also contributed to LP's *Victoria* and *Morocco* guidebooks.

Mary Fitzpatrick

A native of Washington, DC, Mary has travelled extensively in Africa, Asia and Europe. Her journeys have taken her on foot through remote Malagasy rainforests, on rickety pick-ups to dusty villages in the Sahel, by dhow to palm-fringed East African islands and on bicycle through Tibet and south-western China. For much of the past six years, she has worked in Africa, including more than three years in Mozambique. Mary has written Lonely Planet's *Tanzania, Zanzibar & Pemba, Mozambique* and *Read this First – Africa*, and has contributed to LP's *West Africa, East Africa* and *Africa on a shoestring* guidebooks.

Alan Murphy

Alan Murphy took off from West Australia for a six-month stint around Europe and the Middle East in 1992. Four years later and after plenty of temp work (which he found as exciting as long-distance bus journeys) he was back on home soil. Alan returned to studies in 1997 and after completing a journalism course he offered his services to Lonely Planet as a trainee editor, graduating 18 months later as an author. Alan enjoys watching Australia flog the opposition in cricket, sniffing out new watering holes, and hopes one day to write a Good Pub guide – a project he began researching years ago.

Deanna Swaney

After her university studies, Deanna made a shoestring tour of Europe and has been addicted to travel ever since. Despite an erstwhile career in computer programming, she avoided encroaching yuppiedom in midtown Anchorage by making a break for South America, where she wrote Lonely Planet's *Bolivia* guide. Subsequent travels led to six more titles: *Iceland, Greenland & the Faroe Islands*, *Tonga*, *Samoa*, *Zimbabwe, Botswana & Namibia*, *Norway*, and *The Arctic*, as well as updates for Lonely Planet's guides to Mauritius, Réunion & Seychelles, Brazil, Madagascar & Comoros, Southern Africa and Russia, Ukraine & Belarus. Her time is divided between travelling, writing and working on various construction projects around her home base in Alaska's Susitna Valley.

FROM THE AUTHORS

David Else

Firstly – a big thank you to my wife Corinne. Although my name goes down as coordinating author of this book, our six-month research trip through the nine countries of Southern Africa was very much a joint project. Corinne wrote several historical, political and background items and (as Dr Corinne Else MB BCh DA) also helped compile the health section.

In the UK, thanks to Roger Gook and Janet McDougal of Footloose Adventure Travel in Ilkley for providing international flight and tour information, and to John Douglas of Malawi Tourism for regular updates.

In Southern Africa, many thanks to the Higgs and Taylor families (KwaZulu-Natal) for friendship, hospitality, an email connection and (most appreciated) a base to come back to at the end of our trip. Thanks also to: Richard Boon (Durban) for help with environmental issues; Tom Crawford (Durban) for automotive advice; Agnes at ZNTB Lusaka; Mark Harvey, Nixon, Gene Pecker, Doris Glasspool, Penelope Mee, Edith Kabalika, Scollie Muswala and Patrick Sakanjole for details on Zambia's rapidly growing safari scene; Gillian Mann and Sarah Markes for a lively introduction to Blantyre nightlife; Carl and Jill Brussow, Jens Haugaard and Sean Conchar for advice on Malawi wildlife and environment; Harriet Chiwaula, National Parks information desk, Lilongwe; Chris and Pam Badger, Rob McConaghy, Lindsay Clark, Katie French, Andrea Bizzaro, Paul and Claire Norrish, Nick Dunba, Mark Sprong, Marga van der Water and Pim Kremer for help and advice in Malawi; Carol Holm-Hansen, Patrick Simkin, Ben and Becks, Jon de St Pear, Joe Claven, Gertjan van Stam, Phil Howard, Louse Kerbiriou and Stephen O'Conner for detailed notes and good stories from all around Southern Africa; plus all the VSOs, gappies and Peace Corps volunteers who were always happy to provide information from very close to the ground. Lastly, special thanks and greetings to all the citizens of Southern Africa who we met during our research trip: It was a pleasure travelling in your land.

Joyce Connolly

Thanks to Reg for letting me share his first overseas trip and Jenny for an interesting car ride and a whole lot more. Big thanks also to Neil Davis and Jim Bath for the bizarre fun in Harare and drowning scenes on the Zambezi; the Walcha rugby team for the road trip and beer for breakfast; Amy Willis for driving me...; Naomi at Shoestrings for the birthday Amurula; Leanda Brass for almost showing me sculpture; Byron for the beach buggy rides and everyone at Hillside for making me too comfortable to leave; and the Australian cricket team for helping me suck up to the boss.

Others to thank are Russell Comfrey and Mike Scott for sharing their safari expertise and knowledge; Sue Nollovu, Bulawayo Publicity Association; Ronald, Victoria Falls Publicity Association; Simba Berejena, Masvingo Publicity Association; the Mutare Publicity Association; Joseph Kutinyu, National Parks and Wildlife Zimbabwe; Elton, Zimbabwe Tourism Authority; Simba & Tafare for sorting us out in Victoria Falls; and Tony for taking us on the biggest wild goose chase.

Finally, thanks to Mick, Lorien and Esther for the girl power; Naomi, Scott and jr (and Ed) for somewhere to write; Deanna for the original text and contacts; David for his ftp patience; Geoff for the job; and everyone else at LP for the support and two years of in-house fun and gossip.

Mary Fitzpatrick

I would like to thank the following people who assisted me while I was researching and writing this chapter: Robin Mason and John Newstead, Julie Harrold and Ted Peck, Renato and Dot Gordon and Sally Henderson, all in Maputo; Isabella Bartlett in Inhambane; Grant and Kirsty, and Joaquim Alberto in Vilankulo; Isabelle Schmidt and family and Arthur Norval in Beira; Jonathan Hubchen, Bertrand, Elsa, Hans and Guy, and Felisberto Elija and Jytte Nhanenge in Chimoio; Sr Simão Fernando and Brian Hilton in Quelimane; Gonçalves Alface, Paula Hall, Gabriele Walz and Dagmar, and Richard and Jacqueline Dove in Gurúè; Edgardo Vosotros in Tete; Sam Connor and Claudia Werner and Dave Lepoidevin in Nampula; Victoria Salinas in Massinga; James and Kyoko Riley and the staff at the Tourist Information Centre on Ilha de Moçambique; Rolf Gsell in Pemba; Ariana Barbosa Lins and Marita and Berndt in Lichinga; Henry, Dr Candido, Paul and Gudweig, Paul and Guga, and Domingas and Lucinda in Lichinga and Meponda; and Daniel Fernandes, Sanchez Varela and Henrique Theodosio Tiago in Mueda.

Special thanks to Sidney Bliss for his generous hospitality in Maputo, and for all the information and assistance provided before, during and after my research. Finally, thanks most of all to my husband Rick for his patience, enthusiasm and support.

Alan Murphy

Firstly my gratitude and thanks to my partner Justine, navigator extraordinaire, whose unwavering support and invaluable research greatly enhanced this project. Also my appreciation to Jules and Dan at Flight Centre for their help with air fares. A special thanks to Stech – the crusader – for his friendship and his tunes. In Pretoria thanks to Algy Vaisutis for his warm hospitality, the use of his telephone and assistance in researching Jo'burg.

Around South Africa thanks to: Sue and Jinty at the tourist kiosk on the beach at Durban; the guides at Robben Island for imparting some of their incredible experiences to me; the people in the tourism industry in South Africa – especially hostels – for all their assistance and advice; and lastly Michael and Monique, a Dutch couple whose company on the road was greatly appreciated. In Swaziland thanks to Vusi for his help in unraveling the mysteries of the MR103. In Lesotho thanks to the elderly gentleman who chased me down the main street of Maseru, for not catching up with me. Finally, thanks to all the travellers we met on the road who took the time to tell us their stories.

Deanna Swaney

Not a day passes in Southern Africa that I don't receive invaluable help and incredible kindness. My most recent update trip would have been considerably less productive without the help and friendship of Sandy & Detlef in Cape Town; Grant & Marie Burton in Calitzdorp; Annmarie Byrne on Mud Island; Colin McVey & Cecilia Mooketsi in Gaborone; Steve Caballero & Sarah in Maun; Tiaan & Sabine in Maun and Sepupa; Susan Sainsbury at Seronga; Ralph and all the folks at Lianshulu; Uwe & Tammy Roth in Kamanjab; Aulden & Rachael Harlech-Jones in Windhoek; Mike Godfrey & Hannah in Windhoek; Marlies Alpers & Ralph Bousfield at Jack's Camp in the Makgadikgadi; Louis & Riette Fourie in Fish River; Frenus & Sybille in Swakopmund; Valerie & Weynand Peypers in Rundu and Grootfontein; Nick Shaxson, for his invaluable help with Angola; and the brothers Willem and Piet Swiegers at Klein Aus.

Also, love and thanks to Earl, Dean, Kim, Jennifer and Lauren Swaney, in Fresno; Rodney, Heather & Bradley Leacock in Colorado Springs; Keith & Holly Hawkings in Anchorage; and to Dave Dault, who most admirably continues to keep things humming back home.

This Book

The first edition of this book was written and researched by David Else, Jon Murray (based on his own research and that of Jeff Williams) and Deanna Swaney. For this edition, David Else coordinated the project, as well as updating the Malawi, Zambia and introductory chapters. Joyce Connolly updated Zimbabwe and Mary Fitzpatrick updated Mozambique. Alan Murphy updated the South Africa, Lesotho and Swaziland chapters, while Deanna Swaney updated Botswana and Namibia.

FROM THE PUBLISHER

This edition was coordinated by Elizabeth Swan (editorial) and Hunor Csutoros (mapping and design). Adam Ford, Bethune Carmichael, Brigitte Ellemor, Evan Jones, Isabelle Young, Justin Flynn, Kerryn Burgess, Susan Holtham, Thalia Kalkipsakis and Virginia Maxwell assisted with editing. Anna Judd, Brett Moore, Katie Butterworth, Lyndell Stringer, Rodney Zandbergs, Sarah Sloane, Shahara Ahmed, Sonya Brooke and Tim Germanchis assisted with mapping. Quentin Frayne prepared the Language chapter, illustrations were drawn by Sarah Jolly, Hunor did the decorative borders and climate charts, and the cover was designed by Margaret Jung. The Wildlife Guide was written by Luke Hunter.

Acknowledgments

Aase Gustavsen, Alexandra & Isabel Finch, Alexandre Coutinho, Allan Tyrer, Amanda Coady, Amber Hughes, Amy Sumner, Andrew McNeil, Andrew Thorburn, Ans Compaijen, Asger Blom, BJ Wakefield, Bruce Bartrug, Bruce Melendy, Carola Zelalia, Charles Radcliffe, Christiane Beck, Christoph Maluck, Cornelie Van der Feen, Craig Smith, Cymen Crick, DL McNamara, DL Scott, D Somerville, Dan Spealman, Dan Stothart, Dan Taylor, Dave Tesh, David & Katherine Sturley, David Carroll, David Edwardes, David Lee, David Thomforde, Debbie McMillan, Debbie Skipper, Doug Smith, Ed Gates, Edith Millan, Edward Willem Spiegel, Eef Barendrecht, Ellis & Ellen Harris, Eric & Charlotte Osgood, Eric Loe, Florian Roser, Gayne C Young, Gerard Doherty, Giavi Lara, Graeme McClimont, Han Michaelsen, Hannah Lewis, Hans Dam Frandsen, Harold Fitzgerald, Haz Griselda, Henk & Ine Hovels, Holger Schulze, Holly Keas, Ilario Lagasi, Irene Shepard, J & R Sherlock, JA Riches, James Eddelston, Jamie Mackenzie, Jan Burgemeister, Jens Ulrik Jensen, Joanna Newton, John W Briel MD, Jonathan Griffin, Jorge Russo, Joseph Copeland, Julien Pioger, Jurgen Nijs, Kara Arkless, Karin Wandschura, Katherine Hubber, Katie Cuddon, Kerina Tull, Kimberly Fisher, Kristin LaRonca, Lilian Noack, Lindsay & Lynda Jeffs, Lisa M Campbell, Loretta Creckendon, Louis Mazel, Lyn Rowley, MF Tang, Marcel Stoessel, Marcello Missiroli, Marcus Phillips, Marilyn Staib, Marja van Weeren Marta Stojek, Maryam Moayeri, Matthias Ripp, Megon Smith, Michel Zbinden, Molly Kleinman, Narelle Neagle, Natalie Wheatley, Nellars Tembo, Nick Meech, Nicole Dyer, Nigel Walder, Pam Currie, Peter Muller-Brunke, Petter Konig, Phil Baker, RW Le Sueur, Ragnhild Kjetland, Ralph Sanders, Richard Bartlett, Richard Hammond, Richard Lambertus, Robin Flood Mardeusz, Robyn Curtis, Rolf Layer, Russ Ty, Ruud van Leeuwen, Sandra Eagon, Sandra Westlake, Sarah Hilton, Steve Buckley, Steve Walker, Tamarra Price, Thomas Pickard, Tim Care, Tim Slingsby, Tom Freeman, Tomaz Vizintin, Ursula Garcia, Ursula Rose, Veronique Leger

THANKS
Many thanks to the travellers who used the last edition and wrote to us with helpful hints, advice and interesting anecdotes.

Foreword

ABOUT LONELY PLANET GUIDEBOOKS

The story begins with a classic travel adventure: Tony and Maureen Wheeler's 1972 journey across Europe and Asia to Australia. Useful information about the overland trail did not exist at that time, so Tony and Maureen published the first Lonely Planet guidebook to meet a growing need.

From a kitchen table, then from a tiny office in Melbourne (Australia), Lonely Planet has become the largest independent travel publisher in the world, an international company with offices in Melbourne, Oakland (USA), London (UK) and Paris (France).

Today Lonely Planet guidebooks cover the globe. There is an ever-growing list of books and there's information in a variety of forms and media. Some things haven't changed. The main aim is still to help make it possible for adventurous travellers to get out there – to explore and better understand the world.

At Lonely Planet we believe travellers can make a positive contribution to the countries they visit – if they respect their host communities and spend their money wisely. Since 1986 a percentage of the income from each book has been donated to aid projects and human rights campaigns.

Updates Lonely Planet thoroughly updates each guidebook as often as possible. This usually means there are around two years between editions, although for more unusual or more stable destinations the gap can be longer. Check the imprint page (following the colour map at the beginning of the book) for publication dates.

Between editions up-to-date information is available in two free newsletters – the paper *Planet Talk* and email *Comet* (to subscribe, contact any Lonely Planet office) – and on our Web site at www.lonelyplanet.com. The *Upgrades* section of the Web site covers a number of important and volatile destinations and is regularly updated by Lonely Planet authors. *Scoop* covers news and current affairs relevant to travellers. And, lastly, the *Thorn Tree* bulletin board and *Postcards* section of the site carry unverified, but fascinating, reports from travellers.

Correspondence The process of creating new editions begins with the letters, postcards and emails received from travellers. This correspondence often includes suggestions, criticisms and comments about the current editions. Interesting excerpts are immediately passed on via newsletters and the Web site, and everything goes to our authors to be verified when they're researching on the road. We're keen to get more feedback from organisations or individuals who represent communities visited by travellers.

Lonely Planet gathers information for everyone who's curious about the planet – and especially for those who explore it first-hand. Through guidebooks, phrasebooks, activity guides, maps, literature, newsletters, image library, TV series and Web site we act as an information exchange for a worldwide community of travellers.

Research Authors aim to gather sufficient practical information to enable travellers to make informed choices and to make the mechanics of a journey run smoothly. They also research historical and cultural background to help enrich the travel experience and allow travellers to understand and respond appropriately to cultural and environmental issues.

Authors don't stay in every hotel because that would mean spending a couple of months in each medium-sized city and, no, they don't eat at every restaurant because that would mean stretching belts beyond capacity. They do visit hotels and restaurants to check standards and prices, but feedback based on readers' direct experiences can be very helpful.

Many of our authors work undercover, others aren't so secretive. None of them accept freebies in exchange for positive write-ups. And none of our guidebooks contain any advertising.

Production Authors submit their raw manuscripts and maps to offices in Australia, USA, UK or France. Editors and cartographers – all experienced travellers themselves – then begin the process of assembling the pieces. When the book finally hits the shops, some things are already out of date, we start getting feedback from readers and the process begins again…

WARNING & REQUEST

Things change – prices go up, schedules change, good places go bad and bad places go bankrupt – nothing stays the same. So, if you find things better or worse, recently opened or long since closed, please tell us and help make the next edition even more accurate and useful. We genuinely value all the feedback we receive. A well-travelled team reads and acknowledges every letter, postcard and email and ensures that every morsel of information finds its way to the appropriate authors, editors and cartographers for verification.

Everyone who writes to us will find their name listed in the next edition of the appropriate guidebook. They will also receive the latest issue of *Planet Talk*, our quarterly printed newsletter, or *Comet*, our monthly email newsletter. Subscriptions to both newsletters are free. The very best contributions will be rewarded with a free guidebook.

We may edit, reproduce and incorporate your comments in all Lonely Planet products, such as guidebooks, Web sites and digital products, so let us know if you don't want your comments reproduced or your name acknowledged.

Send all correspondence to the Lonely Planet office closest to you:

Australia: Locked Bag 1, Footscray, Victoria 3011
USA: 150 Linden St, Oakland, CA 94607
UK: 10a Spring Place, London NW5 3BH
France: 1 rue du Dahomey, 75011 Paris

Or email us at: talk2us@lonelyplanet.com.au

For news, views and updates see our Web site: www.lonelyplanet.com

HOW TO USE A LONELY PLANET GUIDEBOOK

The best way to use a Lonely Planet guidebook is any way you choose. At Lonely Planet we believe the most memorable travel experiences are often those that are unexpected, and the finest discoveries are those you make yourself. Guidebooks are not intended to be used as if they provide a detailed set of infallible instructions!

Contents All Lonely Planet guidebooks follow roughly the same format. The Facts about the Destination chapters or sections give background information ranging from history to weather. Facts for the Visitor gives practical information on issues such as visas and health. Getting There & Away gives a brief starting point for researching travel to and from the destination. Getting Around gives an overview of the transport options when you arrive.

The peculiar demands of each destination determine how subsequent chapters are broken up, but some things remain constant. We always start with background, then proceed to sights, places to stay, places to eat, entertainment, getting there and away, and getting around information – in that order.

Heading Hierarchy Lonely Planet headings are used in a strict hierarchical structure that can be visualised as a set of Russian dolls. Each heading (and its following text) is encompassed by any preceding heading that is higher on the hierarchical ladder.

Entry Points We do not assume guidebooks will be read from beginning to end, but that people will dip into them. The traditional entry points are the list of contents and the index. In addition, however, some books have a complete list of maps and an index map illustrating map coverage.

There may also be a colour map that shows highlights. These highlights are dealt with in greater detail in the Facts for the Visitor chapter, along with planning questions and suggested itineraries. Each chapter covering a geographical region usually begins with a locator map and another list of highlights. Once you find something of interest in a list of highlights, turn to the index.

Maps Maps play a crucial role in Lonely Planet guidebooks and include a huge amount of information. A legend is printed on the back page. We seek to have complete consistency between maps and text, and to have every important place in the text captured on a map. Map key numbers usually start in the top left corner.

Although inclusion in a guidebook usually implies a recommendation, we cannot list every good place. Exclusion does not necessarily imply criticism. In fact, there are a number of reasons why we might exclude a place – sometimes it is simply inappropriate to encourage an influx of travellers.

Introduction

More than anywhere else in Africa, it is the sheer *diversity* of the vast Southern African region that most strikes visitors: from Johannesburg's gleaming high-rise towers to the Okavango Delta's pristine wilderness; Zimbabwe's country towns and Malawi's lakeshore villages to Mozambique's tropical beaches; and Namibia's sand dunes to Lesotho's mountains, and the scenic wonders of Victoria Falls.

You can travel through desert, rainforest, traditional farmland, manicured vineyards, low savanna plains or over high mountain peaks – sometimes several in the same day. You can do this by car, horse, local bus, luxury train or the back of a truck. You may take a large steamboat down Lake Malawi, explore the tranquil waterways of Botswana by dugout canoe or scare yourself silly rafting rapids on the River Zambezi. You will

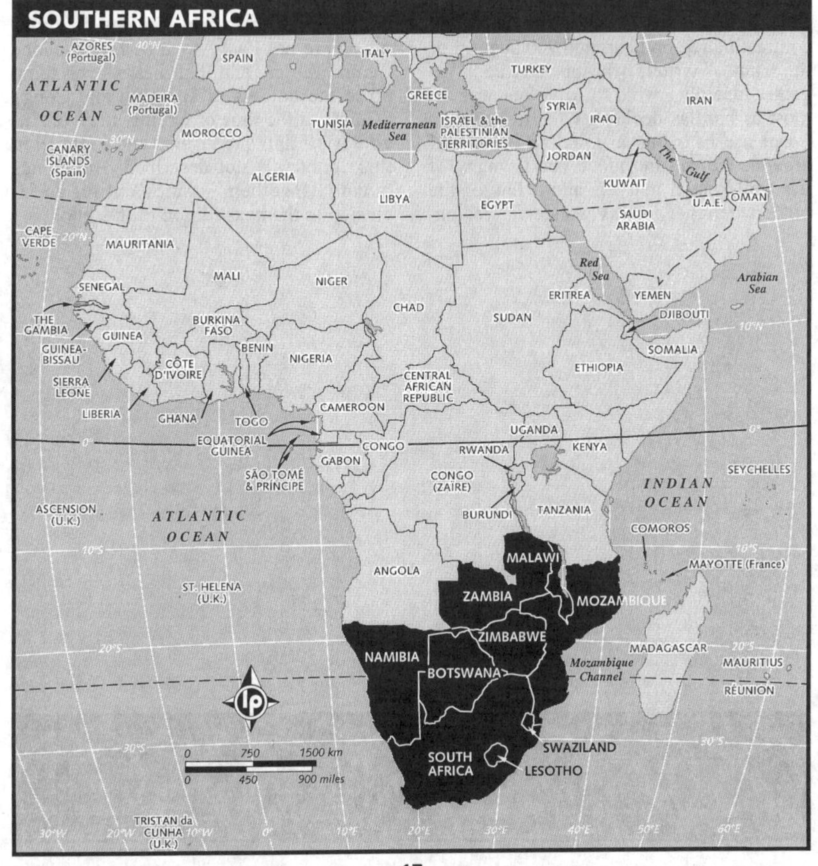

be able to see elephants in the desert or penguins on the beach. You'll pass simple villages with huts of mud and grass, comfortable city suburbs or poverty-stricken townships. The contrasts may be stark, but they are always fascinating.

Add to this the classic African wildlife in national parks and reserves such as Kruger, Chobe, Mana Pools, South Luangwa and Liwonde; the splendidly varied birds and flowers found all over the region; and the cultural richness of peoples such as Zulu, Ndebele, Lozi, Makonde and Himba, and you'll understand why its range of landscapes and attractions make Southern Africa unlike any other part of the world.

This book aims to cover this huge and contrasting region in around 900 pages. For the team of writers who put this book together, deciding what to leave out was almost as hard as deciding what to leave in. So please bear this in mind as you travel around. We can introduce you to many of the well-known marvels and a few of the hidden delights in this wonderful region, and hopefully add considerably to your enjoyment and understanding, but don't lose sight of the fact that the things you discover and the people you meet *without* the help of a book will make your journey through Southern Africa even more rewarding.

Note

The borders of Southern Africa are not firmly defined and vary according to political, economic or zoological use. Some authorities see Southern Africa as the countries below the Kunene and Zambezi Rivers, which is not very helpful as the Zambezi goes through the middle of Mozambique. In this book we have taken Southern Africa to mean all the countries which are not East Africa or Francophone Central Africa, and that means everything up to the borders of Tanzania and Congo (Zaïre). At the time of writing, most of Angola is off limits to visitors and so travel in this country is not described. But things might change here – watch out for an inclusion in the next edition of this book.

Facts about the Region

This chapter describes the more general aspects of Southern Africa. For specifics about individual countries, see the relevant country chapters.

HISTORY

Southern Africa contains many archaeological records of the world's earliest human inhabitants. Controversy among scientists makes it difficult to determine exactly who evolved into whom, and when, but most accept that the first 'hominids' (upright-walking human-like creatures) became established in the savannas of East and Southern Africa nearly four million years ago. Evidence of early hominids over three million years old have been discovered in South Africa's Mpumalanga Province. In Malawi, remains reckoned to be 2.5 million years old have also been found.

Most scientists agree that by about two million years ago, changing climatic and environmental conditions resulted in the evolution of several hominid species, including *Homo habilis* and *Homo erectus*. By about 1.5 to one million years ago, the latter apparently became dominant and developed basic tool-making abilities, evolving into *Homo sapiens* (essentially the same as modern humans). These early Africans lived a nomadic existence, eventually migrating to inhabit other parts of the world, and evolving further into various races according to local factors.

Today, remains of temporary camps and stone tools are found throughout Southern Africa. One archaeological site in Namibia provides evidence that 750,000 years ago these early people were hunting elephant and cutting up the carcasses with large stone axes. By 150,000 years ago they were using lighter spear heads, knives, saws and other tools for various hunting and gathering activities. (Archaeologists classify this period of tool making as the Stone Age, divided into Early, Middle and Late stages, although the term applies to the people's level of technological development, rather than to a specific period of time.)

Early Khoisan Inhabitants

By about 30,000 years ago, the humans in Southern Africa had developed an organised hunting and gathering society. Use of fire was universal, tools were more sophisticated – made from wood and animal products as well as stone – and natural pigments were used for personal adornment. These Boskop people (named after the site in South Africa where their remains were discovered) are believed to be the ancestors of the San people (also called Bushmen), who still exist in isolated pockets today. Physical features of the San include a relatively small build (average males are about 1.3m tall), yellow to light-brown skin, slightly slanted eyes and dark hair growing in 'clumps' of tight curls.

By about 20,000 years ago, the San had made significant progress. Tools became smaller and better designed, which increased hunting efficiency and allowed time for further innovation and artistic pursuits. This stage is called the microlithic revolution because it was characterised by the working of small stones. The remains of microliths are often found alongside clear evidence of food gathering, consumption of shellfish and working of wood, bone and ostrich eggshell.

By about 10,000 years ago, the San began producing pottery. The artistic traditions of these people are also evidenced by the paintings that can be seen today in rock shelters and caves all over Southern Africa (see the 'Ancient Rock Art' section in this chapter). Despite these artistic and technical developments, the San had no knowledge of metal working, and thus remain classified as Stone Age people.

During this same period (around 8000 BC), the San came under pressure from another group called the Khoikhoi (or Khoi-Khoi), known in more recent times as

Hottentots. Their precise origins are uncertain, but most scientists agree that the San and Khoikhoi share a common ancestry, and that differences were slight, based more on habitat and lifestyle than significant physiological features. (The Khoikhoi were more sedentary, which may have allowed them to develop larger physiques.) They also shared a language group, characterised by distinctive 'click' sounds. Today these two peoples are regarded as one, termed Khoisan or Khoi-San, and are found only in remote parts of Namibia and Botswana. (For more information, see 'The San' special section in the Botswana chapter; some details are also given in the Namibia chapter.)

The Bantu Migration

While the Khoisan were developing in Southern Africa, another group of peoples, the Bantu-speaking peoples, had evolved in West Africa. They were larger than the Khoisan, with darker skins. More importantly, by around 3000 to 4000 years ago, they had developed iron-working skills, which enabled them to make tools and weapons. They are therefore classified as Iron Age peoples.

Their skills led to improved farming methods and the ability to migrate into the territory of neighbouring peoples. From West Africa, the Bantu moved through the Congo Basin and reached the plateaus of Southern and East Africa around 2000 years ago. Over the next thousand years the Bantu spread across present-day Uganda, Kenya and Tanzania and migrated south into Zambia, Malawi, Mozambique and several other parts of Southern Africa. For more details, see the boxed text 'The Bantu Migrations' on this page.

In Southern Africa the Bantu seem to have lived in relative harmony with the original Khoisan inhabitants at first, trading goods, language and culture. However, as Bantu numbers increased it appears that the Khoisan were destroyed (by superior weaponry), absorbed (by intermarriage) or forced to retreat to parts of Southern Africa unsuitable for farming and therefore less attractive to the Bantu incomers.

The Bantu Migrations

The Bantu peoples could more accurately be called 'Bantu-speaking peoples' since the word 'Bantu' actually refers to a language group rather than a specific race. However, it has become a convenient term of reference for the Black African peoples of Southern and Eastern Africa, even though the grouping is as ill-defined as 'American' or 'oriental'. The Bantu ethnic group is made up of a great many subgroups or tribes, each with their own language, customs and cultural traditions.

The term 'migration' when used in this context refers not to a specific or sudden upheaval, but to a sporadic and very slow spread over many hundreds of years. A migration in this sense was made up of numerous short moves (from valley to valley, or from one cultivation area to the next), with dominant groups slowly absorbing other groups in the process. The movements inevitably had a knock-on effect too, as groups being invaded from one side expanded in the other direction.

Historians believe that there were at least three main routes followed by the migrating Bantu: some spread from the Congo Basin east to the Tanzanian highlands and the Indian Ocean coast, and then south down the coastal plain through Mozambique and into KwaZulu-Natal; others kept to the higher ground of the interior and spread through western Tanzania into Zambia; while others came south from Congo (Zaïre) directly into Zambia, Malawi, Zimbabwe and western Mozambique.

Early Bantu Kingdoms

A feature of the Bantu culture was its strong social system, based on extended family or clan loyalties and dependencies, and generally centred around the rule of a chief. Some chiefdoms developed into powerful kingdoms, uniting many disparate tribes and covering large geographical areas.

One of the earliest Bantu kingdoms was Gokomere, in the uplands of Zimbabwe. The Gokomere people are thought to be the first occupants of the Great Zimbabwe site, near present-day Masvingo. Between AD 500 and 1000 the Gokomere and subsequent groups developed gold-mining techniques and produced progressively finer-quality ceramics, jewellery, textiles and soapstone carvings. Cattle herding became the mainstay of the whole community.

Arabs & Swahilis

Meanwhile, from the latter half of the 1st millennium, Arabs from the lands around the Red Sea were sailing southwards along the eastern seaboard of Africa. They traded with the local Bantu inhabitants, who by this time had reached the coast, buying ivory, gold and slaves to take back to Arabia.

Between 1000 AD and 1500 AD the Arab-influenced Bantu people founded several major settlements along the coast, from Mogadishu (in present-day Somalia) to Kilwa in southern Tanzania, including Lamu (Kenya) and Zanzibar (Tanzania). In Kenya and Tanzania particularly, the Bantu people were influenced by the Arabs, and a certain degree of intermarriage occurred, so that gradually a mixed language and culture was created, called Swahili, which remains intact today. From southern Tanzania the Swahili-Arabs traded along the coast of present-day Mozambique, establishing bases at Quelimane and Ilha de Moçambique (both still exist and are described in the Mozambique chapter of this book).

From the coast the Swahili-Arabs pushed into the interior, and developed a network of trade routes across much of East and Southern Africa. Ivory and gold continued to be sought after, but the demand for slaves grew considerably, and reached its zenith in the early-19th century when the Swahili-Arabs and dominant local tribes are reckoned to have either killed or sold into slavery 80,000 to 100,000 Africans per year (see the boxed text 'The Horrors of Slavery' below).

Later Bantu Kingdoms

Meanwhile, quite separate from the development along the coast, the Bantu societies in the African interior were becoming increasingly organised. As early as the 11th century, the inhabitants of Great Zimbabwe had consolidated their position and come into contact with Arab-Swahili traders venturing inland from the coast. Great Zimbabwe became the capital of the wealthiest and most powerful society in Southern Africa, its people the ancestors of today's Shona people, and reached the zenith of its powers around the 14th

[Continued on page 24]

The Horrors of Slavery

At the height of slavery in the 19th century, one of the busiest slave-trade routes was from the areas now called Malawi and Zambia, to the coast of Mozambique. Captives taken from the hinterland were brought to trading centres on the western shore of Lake Malawi such as Nkhotakota, Karonga or Salima, from where they would be crammed into dhows and taken across the lake. On the other side, they were marched across Mozambique to the east coast, usually chained to prevent escape. Many also carried elephant tusks, as ivory was another major trade item going from Africa to the outside world. Any slaves too ill to make the journey were simply abandoned. Most died of dehydration or were killed by wild animals.

At the coast, the slaves were once more loaded back into dhows for the hazardous journey north to Zanzibar. They would be packed tightly lying down in several layers in the hold of the boat, jammed in place by the deck holding the layer above. For the duration of the voyage they would have no food or water, and would lie in their own excrement. Those who died (and there were many, particularly if journeys took longer than anticipated due to poor winds), could not be removed until the journey ended. Those who managed to survive were sold once more in the large slave market in Zanzibar and then shipped to places such as Arabia or India, once again in horrific conditions. Estimates vary, but it's reckoned that of all the slaves captured in the interior of Africa, two in three died before reaching their final destination.

ANCIENT ROCK ART

Examples of ancient rock art – usually paintings on the inside walls of caves and overhangs – can be found all over Southern Africa. Their origins are unclear (even dating them is difficult as the process is damaging); however, deposits left in caves and scenes depicted in the paintings indicate that the artists were nomadic hunter-gatherers without knowledge of agriculture or pottery. For that reason, this ancient rock art is thought to be the work of early San people.

Some rock paintings are stylised representations of the region's people and animals, but most are remarkably realistic – all in rich colours of red, yellow, brown and ochre. Common themes include the roles of men and women, hunting and gathering, and natural medicine. There are even examples of trance dancing and spiritual healing using the San life force, known as *nxum*, which was invoked to control aspects of the natural world, including climate and disease. All these things still feature in San tradition.

Animals portrayed in rock art include giraffe, elephant, rhino, lion and antelope, and some experts have suggested that, as with similar cave art found in Europe, perhaps the paintings were intended to magically ensure an abundance of those animals. However, this concept hasn't been noted in any present-day African culture, and there's no evidence of ancient ties with Europe. Furthermore, few of the animals portrayed served as food for the ancient San.

Despite the earliest works having long faded into oblivion, in many areas a dry climate and sheltered position have preserved more recent

RICHARD I'ANSON

Left: San rock painting, Nswatugi Cave, Matobo National Park (Zimbabwe)

paintings. And although no reliable dating method has been devised, anthropological studies have used the content, skill level and superposition of the paintings to identify three distinct stages. The earliest paintings seem to reflect a period of gentle nomadism during which people were occupied primarily with the hunt. Later works, revealing great artistic improvement, suggest peaceful incursions by outside groups, perhaps Bantu-speaking peoples. The final stage indicates a decline; either a loss of interest in the genre, or imitation of earlier works by subsequently arriving peoples.

Pigments used by these ancient artists were applied to the rock using animal hair brushes, sticks and the artist's fingers. Reds were ground mainly from iron oxides, then powdered and mixed with animal fat to form an adhesive paste. Whites from silica, powdered quartz and clays were less adhesive than the red pigments. For that reason, white paintings survive only in sheltered locations, such as well-protected caves.

The most important thing about rock art is that it remains in the spot where it was created. Viewing the work in a 'wilderness art gallery' is so much more poignant than seeing it in a museum, and as well as enjoying the paintings, sensitive observers may catch a glimpse of the inspiration that went into them. Although examples of rock art can be found all over the region, some of the best examples are in Matobo National Park, Domboshawa and Ngomakurira in Zimbabwe; the Tsodilo Hills in Botswana; Twyfelfontein in Namibia; and Giant's Castle Game Reserve in South Africa.

RICHARD I'ANSON

Right: San rock painting, Nswatugi Cave, Matobo National Park (Zimbabwe)

[Continued from page 21]

century. (The history of Zimbabwe is continued in detail in the Zimbabwe chapter.)

To the north of Zimbabwe, between the 14th and 16th centuries, another Bantu group called the Maravi (of whom the Chewa became the dominant tribe) came into Southern Africa from the Congo Basin area. They founded a large and powerful kingdom covering southern Malawi and parts of present-day Mozambique and Zambia. At about the same time the Tumbuka and the Phoka groups migrated into the north of Malawi, although their traditions do not agree on their origins. (The histories of Malawi, Zambia and Mozambique are continued in the relevant country chapters.)

Meanwhile, in present-day Namibia, during the 16th and 17th centuries, another Bantu group called the Herero migrated from the Zambezi Valley. They came into conflict with the San and competed with the Khoikhoi for the best grazing lands. Eventually most indigenous groups (including the Damara people, whose origins are unclear) submitted to the Herero. Only the Nama people, thought to be descended from early Khoikhoi groups, held out. (The histories of Botswana and Namibia are continued in the relevant country chapters.)

The power of the Bantu kingdoms started to falter in the late 18th and early 19th centuries, as two significant events had a tumultuous effect on the whole Southern African region. The first was a major dispersal of indigenous tribes, called the *difaqane*, and the second was a rapid increase in the number of settlers from Europe.

The Difaqane

The *difaqane* ('forced migration' in Sotho, or *mfeqane*, 'the crushing', in Zulu) was a period of immense upheaval and suffering for the indigenous peoples of Southern Africa. It originated in the early 19th century when the Nguni tribes in modern KwaZulu-Natal changed rapidly from loosely organised collections of chiefdoms into a centralised nation of people called the Zulu. Based around a highly disciplined and powerful warrior army, the process began under Chief Dingiswayo, and reached its peak under the military commander Shaka.

Not surprisingly, tribes in the path of Shaka's army fled, and many in turn invaded their neighbours. Some refugees and displaced people travelled great distances, causing waves of disruption and terror throughout Southern Africa. Tribes displaced from Zululand include the Matabele, who settled in present-day Zimbabwe. Another group settled in Malawi and Zambia, where they are now known as the Ngoni. Two notable survivors of the destruction were the Swazi and Basotho peoples; they used the period of unrest to forge the powerful nations that became Swaziland and Lesotho.

The European Settlers

Although there had been a European presence in Southern Africa for several hundred years (see the boxed text 'Early European Settlement in Southern Africa'), 1820 saw a major influx of settlers in the British Cape Colony. Around 5000 individuals were brought from Britain on the promise of fertile farmland around the Great Fish River, but in reality to form a buffer between the Boers (to the west of the river) and the Xhosa (to the east) who were both competing for territory. Within a few years many retreated to safer settlements to pick up the trades they had followed in Britain, and places such as Grahamstown developed into commercial and manufacturing centres.

From this point, European settlement of Southern Africa snowballed rapidly, spreading from the Cape Colony to Natal and later to the Transvaal – especially when gold and diamonds were discovered there. In many cases Europeans were able to occupy land abandoned by African people following the difaqane. (For more detail on this period, see under History in the Facts about South Africa section of the South Africa chapter.)

From South Africa, over the next 100 to 150 years, an ever-increasing number of Europeans settled in areas that became the colonies of Swaziland, Nyasaland (Malawi), North and South Rhodesia (Zambia and Zimbabwe), Bechuanaland (Botswana),

Early European Settlement in Southern Africa

Since the 15th century, Portuguese navigators had explored the west coast of Africa, searching for a route to India and China. In 1486, Diego Cão reached present-day Namibia, where he built a stone cross (at a point still called Cape Cross today). A year later Bartholomeu Dias pushed further south and reached a peninsula that he named Cabo da Boa Esperanca (Cape of Good Hope).

The real breakthrough came a decade later when Vasco da Gama rounded the Cape of Good Hope and sailed north, along the coast of Mozambique, before striking east across the ocean, finally reaching India in 1498.

Despite the strategic importance of the Cape, the Portuguese were not interested in developing a colony there, so contact with the local Khoisan was very limited. However, the Portuguese did establish trading stations on the coast of Mozambique, and along the Zambezi and Save Rivers. Trade with the local Bantu inhabitants was brisk, and imports such as glass beads, guns and cloth were exchanged for exports such as slaves and ivory. Although there was no attempt to colonise the hinterland, Portuguese influence spread deep into Southern Africa.

By the late 16th century, ships from England and the Netherlands were challenging Portugal's monopoly on the trade routes between Europe and the East Indies. In 1647 a Dutch ship was wrecked in Table Bay, just north of the Cape of Good Hope, and the crew were stranded for a year before they were rescued. This inspired the Dutch East India Company (Vereenigde Oost-Indische Compagnie, or VOC) to establish a permanent revictualling base, and a small expedition of VOC employees, led by Jan van Riebeeck, reached Table Bay on 6 April 1652 – a landmark date in the history of South Africa, and Southern Africa as a whole.

Once again, there was no plan to colonise the country but some early arrivals (mostly Dutch, some German) established farms. In 1688 they were joined by about 150 French settlers, and over the next hundred years the European settler population increased slowly. Some settlers rejected VOC rule and moved away from the main Cape settlement. These people were the first of the *trekboers* (pioneer farmers) – isolated, self-sufficient and completely independent of official control.

Inevitably, these early Boers clashed with the indigenous peoples. The Khoisan were driven from their traditional lands, decimated by introduced diseases and destroyed by superior weapons. Most survivors had no option but to work for Europeans – often on terms little different to slavery.

The first major Bantu group to encounter the trekboers were the Xhosa – west of the Great Fish River during the 1770s. Once again, any chance of a peaceful coexistence was short-lived: the first of nine frontier wars between the Boers and the Xhosa broke out in 1779.

As the 18th century closed Dutch power was fading, and in 1795 Britain entered the scene, invading the Cape to prevent it from falling into French hands. They invaded again in 1806, and the colony was permanently ceded to Britain on 13 August 1814. By this time, the Cape Colony (as it was called) comprised 20,000 white settlers, plus 15,000 Khoisan and 25,000 slaves of various origins (including those from present-day Indonesia, Malaysia and Madagascar).

Basotholand (Lesotho), German South West Africa (Namibia) and Portuguese East Africa (Mozambique), changing their nature forever.

After the 1820s

The spread of European settlers and the disruption of the difaqane had a pivotal influence on the colonial and postcolonial histories of all countries in the Southern African region. These are covered separately in the relevant country chapters.

GEOGRAPHY

Africa can be divided into two main geographical regions. 'Low Africa' is the western and northern areas of the continent, mainly between 200m and 1000m above sea level. 'High Africa' is the eastern and southern parts, mainly between 1000m and

2000m. The region covered by this book is in High Africa, but there are no major mountain ranges like the Andes, Rockies or Himalayas. Much of the land is a relatively uniform plateau, although some of Southern Africa's mountains, hills and valleys more than make up in scenic splendour what they may lack in sheer size.

The main Southern African plateau has escarpments on its southern and eastern sides, stretching in a great arc across the region – its most striking section is the Drakensberg Range between South Africa and Lesotho. Below the escarpment, a coastal plain runs all the way around Southern Africa, obvious on the eastern and southern sides, and at its widest in southern Mozambique. On the western side of the region (in Namibia), the coastal plain is narrower, while the divide between the high and the low ground is less distinct.

The highest part of the region is Lesotho (often called the Kingdom in the Sky), and the neighbouring Drakensberg area, where many peaks rise above 3000m. The highest point in Southern Africa, Thabana-Ntlenyana (3482m), is also here. Other highland areas of Southern Africa include the Nyika Plateau (in northern Malawi and north-eastern Zambia), Mt Mulanje (in southern Malawi) and the Eastern Highlands (between Zimbabwe and Mozambique). Lower and more isolated hills (although often no less spectacular) also exist, from the characteristic *inselbergs* (isolated rocky hill) of Namibia or South Africa's Karoo, to the lush Zomba Plateau in central Malawi.

The relative uniformity of the plateau is broken up by several large rivers (see boxed text 'Rivers of Southern Africa') and, most spectacularly, the Great Rift Valley.

The Great Rift Valley

The largest geographical feature to break up the relative uniformity of the Southern African plateau is the Great Rift Valley – a

Rivers of Southern Africa

For visitors to Southern Africa, rivers are major features. They provide the focal point for many major wildlife reserves and for activities such as canoeing, fishing and white-water rafting (for which the region is famous) – these would of course be impossible without rivers.

Most well known of Southern Africa's rivers is the Zambezi, which rises in the far north-western corner of Zambia. Further downstream, it becomes the border between Zambia and Namibia, and (very briefly) Botswana, before plummeting over the world-famous Victoria Falls. Now the border between Zambia and Zimbabwe, the Zambezi is already a giant (and still only a third of its way from source to mouth) as it forces its way down the Batoka Gorge to Lake Kariba.

Beyond Kariba Dam, the major Kafue River adds its waters to the flow, and then the Zambezi runs between Zimbabwe's Mana Pools and Zambia's Lower Zambezi National Parks. The Zambezi is joined by another major tributary, the Luangwa River, and then enters Mozambique and another dam-created lake – Lago Cahora Bassa. Downstream from here, the Zambezi slows and broadens out. The Shire River (which drains Lake Malawi) enters from the north, and the Zambezi crosses the last few hundred kilometres of coastal plain, finally flowing into the Indian Ocean north of Beira.

Other main rivers in Southern Africa are: the Kunene (also spelt Cunene), which forms the border between Angola and Namibia, flowing westwards into the Atlantic Ocean; the Okavango, which rises in Angola and flows eastwards into Botswana's Kalahari Desert, where the waters disperse and form the Okavango (Inland) Delta; the Limpopo, whose various source tributaries rise in Botswana and South Africa, joining to flow eastwards, forming the border between South Africa and Botswana, then Zimbabwe, before entering Mozambique and reaching the Indian Ocean near Maputo; and the Orange, which rises in Lesotho and flows westwards into South Africa (where it is joined by its major tributary, the Vaal), eventually becoming the border between Namibia and South Africa, and flowing into the Atlantic at Alexander Bay.

6500km-long fissure where the continent of Africa is literally 'breaking apart' as huge chunks of land have sunk between giant cracks in the earth's surface. The Rift starts in Arabia, and enters Africa at the Red Sea. South of Ethiopia it splits in two: the eastern branch going through Kenya and Tanzania; the western branch stretching down Lake Tanganyika and into Zambia. The two branches meet in northern Malawi, and the Rift Valley continues down Lake Malawi into Mozambique, ending near the mouth of the River Zambezi. Another branch forms the Luangwa Valley in Zambia.

Beyond the Rift Valley wall, mountains such as Mt Kilimanjaro and Mt Kenya were formed when molten rock erupted through the cracks. In Southern Africa, the mountains near the Rift (such as the plateaus of Malawi) are not volcanic in origin, but were created by localised uplift associated with rift formation.

CLIMATE

This section gives an overview of the climate and seasons of Southern Africa. The climate of each country is described in more detail in the relevant country chapters.

In Southern Africa, summer runs from about November to March/April, while winter is from May to July/August. Spring is from August/September to October, and there isn't really an autumn/fall as in the northern hemisphere. In fact, despite the names, none of the seasons in Southern Africa are as people from the northern hemisphere would expect.

The main factors affecting the climate of Southern Africa are ocean currents. Off the west coast, the Atlantic's Benguela Current (from the Antarctic) brings cold air that rarely turns to rain, and has created the dry Western Cape coast and the deserts of Namibia. Off the east coast, the Agulhas Current brings warm moist air from the Indian Ocean, providing frequent rain for the lush forests of Mozambique and the farmlands of KwaZulu-Natal. Thus, in the eastern and central parts of the region, summer is generally hot and wet, with rainfall from November through February, while summer in the western areas is relatively dry, with limited rainfall. In the east, the rain combined with high temperatures means conditions can be humid, especially on the coast.

By March and April, temperature and rainfall levels begin to drop. In May, winter begins; this period is quite dry, with limited rainfall and cool temperatures (although warmer in low areas and cold on the high ground – South Africa's Drakensberg and parts of Lesotho get snow at this time). Through June and July the weather remains dry, warm on the coast but with a huge range in the interior – from 20°C in the day to below freezing at night.

In August, rainfall is still low, but temperatures start to rise again. Through September and October temperatures continue to rise and the air becomes more humid. Only the higher areas remain cool. In November the rain starts and the Southern African summer begins once again.

The main exception to this overall pattern is the southern part of South Africa's Western Cape Province, which, for various reasons, makes its own rules and gets most rainfall in winter and is dry during the summer (it is therefore called the Winter Rainfall Area; everywhere else is the Summer Rainfall Area).

In recent years the weather patterns all over Southern Africa have apparently become less predictable, with rains finishing earlier and starting later (or sometimes not at all). Some authorities cite a general trend

Climate & Seasons of Southern Africa

Season	Months	Summer Rainfall Area	Winter Rainfall Area
Summer	Nov – Apr	hot & wet	warm & dry
Winter	May – Aug	warm & dry	cool & wet
Spring	Sept – Oct	hot & dry	hot & dry

towards a drier world climate, others hold that Southern Africa goes through dry and wet cycles each roughly seven years long.

For details on how these seasons affect travellers in Southern Africa, see the When to Go section in the Regional Facts for the Visitor chapter.

ECOLOGY & ENVIRONMENT

Environmental issues in Southern Africa are similar to those faced by the rest of the world: habitat and wildlife destruction, alien plant invasion, deforestation, soil erosion, water degradation and industrial pollution are all increasingly pertinent. But when discussing any of these issues, it is important to realise that none can be addressed in isolation. They are all interrelated and linked to wider economic, social and political situations – on a national, regional and global scale.

It is also important to realise that environmental issues are never straightforward. For example, all over Southern Africa, an ever-increasing human population puts great demands on the land and other natural resources. To conserve these resources, the rate of population growth needs to be lowered; however, to suggest that the solution simply involves contraception or a change in cultural attitudes is a narrow view. Environmentalists with a broader perspective see rapid population growth closely linked to social issues such as unemployment, limited education and poor healthcare. Thus, conservation of natural resources must start with tackling the root of the problem – poverty.

Poverty & Resources

One strategy for the alleviation of poverty encourages poor (or Third World) countries to increase economic development to provide income for their citizens, which in turn will lead to a better standard of living, the lowering of birth rates and thus, eventually, to an interest in conservation. Against this, economic development often involves industrialisation – and this can cause its own environmental damage such as air and water pollution.

But even if the Third World's population growth-rate was stabilised, and living standards raised, this is not a solution on its own. If everybody on Earth enjoyed the high standards (ie, high consumption) of the First World countries, the planet's finite resources couldn't support everyone anyway.

This point – that the First World uses more of the earth's resources than the Third World – is often overlooked, especially in areas such as Southern Africa. Instead, 'indigenous' situations are emphasised (eg, wood stoves create deforestation; overgrazing causes soil erosion). However, an urban citizen of the UK, Australia or the USA can consume 50 times more than a poor rural inhabitant of Lesotho, Zambia or Mozambique. This imbalance is ultimately related to all other environmental issues (such as those discussed later in this section) throughout Southern Africa and across the whole world.

The Ivory Debate

A major issue, particularly relevant in Southern Africa, concerns the conservation of the elephant. This is also a good example of how environmental matters are never straightforward. Basically, there are two sides to the argument: one holds that elephant herds should be conserved (or preserved) for their own sake or for aesthetic reasons; the other side holds that the elephant must justify its existence on long-term economic grounds – 'sustainable utilisation' is the buzzword – for the benefit of local people or for the country as a whole. In fact, the same arguments can be applied to most other wildlife resources (preservation versus sustainable utilisation).

Elephant poaching complicates the picture, and since the 1970s various factors have led to a massive increase in elephant poaching in many parts of Africa. By the late 1980s the price of 1kg of ivory (US$300) was three times the *annual* income of over 60% of Africa's population. Naturally, the temptation to poach was great, although the real money was made not by poachers – often desperately poor villagers – but by the dealers, who acted with the full knowledge (and support) of senior government figures. In East Africa and in some Southern African countries – notably in Zambia – elephant populations were reduced by up to 90% in about 15 years. But in some other countries of Southern Africa where national parks or wildlife reserves were well managed – notably Zimbabwe, South Africa and Botswana – elephant populations were relatively unaffected.

In 1990, following a massive campaign by conservation organisations, a world body called the Convention on International Trade in Endangered Species (CITES) banned the import and export of ivory. The closure of this trade, combined with increased funds for law enforcement, was seen as an important step in elephant protection.

Although elephant populations recovered in areas where they'd been previously ravaged, in the well-managed and protected parks of Southern Africa the populations continued to grow, and this created another problem. Elephants eat huge quantities of foliage, and a large herd remaining within an unnaturally small area (even though it may be hundreds of square kilometres) will quickly destroy its surroundings. In the past, the herd would have migrated, allowing time for vegetation regrowth, but with the increase in human population around national parks, this option is increasingly closed off.

Therefore, by their successful protection of a species, the park authorities are now facing the problem of overpopulation. Solutions include relocation (where animals are taken to other areas) and a pioneering contraception project (where breeding cows are injected with a 'pill' equivalent – so no jokes about jumbo condoms please). The alternative is to cull (or 'crop') elephants, sometimes in large numbers. Killing elephants to conserve them seems a bizarre paradox, but illustrates the seriousness of the problem, and at present the other options remain experimental and limited in their effect.

Good management requires money, and in the past, ivory from legally culled elephants could be sold to raise funds. Through most of the 1990s this was not possible because of the CITES ban. Some Southern African countries called for the trade to be legalised again, so that funds from ivory sales could go towards conservation projects to benefit both animals and people. In this way, as unpalatable as it may seem, the elephant herds become a resource with tangible value for each country, thus giving governments and local people an incentive to ensure the elephants' survival.

In March 1999, Botswana, Namibia, South Africa and Zimbabwe were permitted by CITES to resume strictly controlled ivory exports. Despite these measures, opponents of the trade say that elephant poaching has increased in other parts of Africa, as poached ivory can be laundered through the legal trade. This argument seems to carry some weight, as an increase in poaching through 1999 was reported Africa-wide – from countries as far apart at Kenya and Gabon. In late 1999, a Zimbabwean newspaper reported that 84 elephants were illegally killed during that year. Opponents of the ivory trade say this confirms their fears, although the Zimbabwean government attributed the surge to animal rights campaigners lobbying for a reintroduction of the ban. Either way, it is still too early to say if the resumed trade will have an overall financial benefit for the countries of Southern Africa. The ban came under review again in mid-2000, but a push by Botswana, Namibia, South Africa and Zimbabwe for the continuation of an increasingly unrestricted ivory trade was unsuccessful.

Tourism & the Environment

International tourism is another way in which it is hoped the elephant and other wildlife species can be given a use-value in order to ensure their survival (this is often called the 'pay to stay' argument). The idea is that if rich foreigners pay money to come and see the animals, some of this money might find its way back to the local people (or to the country as a whole) and this will encourage wildlife and environmental protection.

Commercial hunting is a form of tourism that can also benefit the wildlife and the local people. In some parts of Southern

Africa, areas of land are set aside for hunting, and big-game hunters are charged 'trophy fees' to shoot the animals. This sounds unacceptable to many people, but the trophy fees are large (thousands of US dollars for animals such as elephants or lions) and a valuable source of income for impoverished areas with no other resources to exploit. Once again, benefits from the wildlife provide encouragement to protect the species and their environment.

It has become obvious over the last decade or so that if there is no benefit for local people, there is absolutely no incentive to conserve wildlife. But in the last few years there has been another crucial shift in the argument: now this perceived benefit is central – it's the only remaining justification for conserving wildlife. Saving animals because it's a nice thing to do simply isn't enough any more. Conservation for its own sake is a luxurious western notion that the people of Southern Africa simply cannot afford.

All over Southern Africa, there are increased moves to involve local people in wildlife conservation schemes. Examples include 'good neighbour' arrangements in countries such as South Africa and Malawi, where villagers on lands bordering parks and reserves are allowed access to gather resources (eg, firewood and thatching grass). Another is the pioneering Communal Areas Management Programme for Indigenous Resources (CAMPFIRE) project in Zimbabwe, where local villagers 'own' the elephants and other animals that inhabit their traditional lands, and can generate funds from controlled hunting or photographic safaris run there. Similarly, in Namibia, the Save the Rhino Trust (SRT) promotes conservation education and public sponsorship of individual animals to provide local people with alternative sources of income. In Zambia, the ADMADE program and the South Luangwa Area Management Unit (SLAMU) scheme allow local people to benefit financially from their wildlife populations, getting a share from revenue paid by tourists and hunters.

Income is also generated by the jobs that hunting and wildlife tourism create, such as guides, game rangers, tour guides and various posts in the hotels, lodges and camps. Further spin-offs include the sale of crafts and curios.

For true success, a balance has to be struck between tourism growth and environmental destruction – in other words, all development has to be sustainable. The real reason for wildlife to be conserved is not for tourists to admire, but so local people can benefit. Wildlife is a resource like oil or copper, and (unlike those) is infinitely more sustainable.

The Down Side of Tourism Although tourism can be an environmental saviour in some instances, it can also have very negative effects. Either way, tourism itself is a major environmental issue (it is one of the largest global industries), and is impossible to ignore.

When a destination cannot cope with the number of tourists attracted to it, great damage can be inflicted on the natural and social environments. A classic example of this in Southern Africa is Victoria Falls, shared by Zimbabwe and Zambia. In 1986 less than 80,000 visitors came to the Falls; by 1999 the figure had increased to around 400,000 – in another 10 years the figure could be more than a million. In response to the influx of tourists, new hotels and lodges are being built or redeveloped on both sides of the Falls and upstream along the banks of the River Zambezi.

Less visible to tourists, but more important, the population of Chinotimba township (on the edge of Victoria Falls town in Zimbabwe) has also increased massively as local people are attracted by work opportunities. The town's water and sewage utilities reportedly can't cope with the increased usage, so pollution ends up in the river. More visible are the vast amounts of plastic and metal rubbish that the burgeoning population generates. Local environmental campaigners say that the increase in river activities (such as white-water rafting) disturbs wildlife and damages the natural vegetation along the banks, and that the woodcarvings for sale on every street corner mean that trees are being destroyed in a large area around the town.

Another issue, one that is particularly relevant for visitors in Southern Africa, is the growth of so-called 'ecotourism' – a term applied to any kind of activity with an environmental connection (however vague), often simply because it's outdoors. The 'eco' tag is blatantly used to make the whole thing feel more wholesome. Even the slightly more specific term 'ecofriendly tourism' is now horribly overused. Don't be fooled by travel companies blithely claiming to be ecofriendly. Activities such as camping, wildlife viewing (by car, foot or balloon) or sightseeing trips to remote or fragile areas can be *more* environmentally or culturally harmful than a conventional hotel holiday in a specifically developed resort. A leading British environmentalist, perhaps surprisingly, reckons that Sun City in South Africa is one of the best examples of ecotourism in the world: 'a purpose-built resort complex, creating 4500 local jobs, and putting wildlife back onto a degraded piece of useless veld'.

If you want to support tour companies with a genuinely good environmental record, you have to look beyond the glossy brochures and vague 'eco' claims and ask what they are really doing to protect or support the environment (and remember that 'the environment' includes local people, as well as animals and plants). These matters are discussed further under Responsible Tourism, in the Regional Facts for the Visitor chapter.

FLORA & FAUNA

As in any other part of the world, the flora and fauna of Southern Africa are determined largely by natural factors such as climate and topography, and by non-natural factors, including human influence. Most of Southern Africa's plant and animal species are widespread throughout the region, although there are several species that occur only in a single country, or even in one very small area.

Mammals and birds are varied and impressive, and are the main reason many visitors come to the region; these are covered in the colour 'Wildlife Guide' and 'Birds of Southern Africa' sections. Reptiles are less of a draw, and so are covered only briefly. The region's fish species are also an attraction – some are listed under Snorkelling and Fishing in the Activities sections of the individual country chapters. For some pointers on watching animals, see the boxed text 'Wildlife Viewing' later in this section.

Vegetation

Southern Africa can be divided into several broad vegetation zones – all quite complex, with firm division lines impossible to draw. There are considerable overlaps, pockets of one zone within another and varying definitions among biologists. The following list of major zones (arranged roughly south to north, and from the coasts to the inland areas) is not exhaustive and, by necessity, is greatly simplified, but it will provide a useful overview.

Southern Africa's most distinctive vegetation zone occurs around the Cape Peninsula and along the south coast of South Africa. This is usually called the **fynbos** zone after the dominant vegetation type (see the boxed text 'Fynbos' in this section for more details). Also here are small pockets of **temperate forest**, where trees such as the large yellowwood, with its characteristic 'peeling' bark, are easily recognised.

The west coast of Southern Africa consists largely of **desert**, forming a wide strip through western Namibia, where annual evaporation exceeds rainfall, which is often less than 100mm per year. Vegetation consists of tough grasses, small bushes and succulents, plus some local specialities evolved to survive in such climates, including the welwitschia and kokerboom (see the boxed texts in the Namibia chapter).

Along the east coast of Southern Africa (mostly Mozambique and South Africa's KwaZulu-Natal), the natural vegetation is often described as **coastal bush** – a mixture of light woodland and dune forest. The warm climate and high rainfall have created pockets of **subtropical forest**, where trees are larger. Palms also occur here, and mangroves grow in some estuaries.

Inland, north of the fynbos, a broad band of **semidesert** stretches through western

South Africa and central Namibia. Although rainfall is higher than in true desert regions, porous rock means there is little standing water and few rivers. The southern part of this zone is called the Karoo semidesert, while the northern section is often called the Kalahari semidesert. Typical vegetation includes various types of grass, plus normally dull-looking bushes and succulents that bloom colourfully after the rains. Much original Karoo vegetation has been destroyed since European settlers introduced grazing animals and various alien plants.

East of the Karoo are the **temperate grasslands** of central South Africa, usually called the 'highveld'. Once again, little original grassland remains as conditions are ideal for cereal crops and much of the area is farmed. At the centre of this zone, roughly coinciding with the borders of Lesotho, is a pocket of high grassland, sometimes defined as a separate zone called afro-montane grassland (more details at the end of this section).

East of the semidesert and north of the temperate grassland is a large area called **arid savanna**, also known as acacia savanna or

Fynbos

The plants of the world are divided into six floral 'kingdoms', including the Australian Kingdom and the Boreal Kingdom (most of Europe, Asia and North America). By far the smallest is the Cape Floral Kingdom, which covers the southern tip of South Africa in a band from Niewoudtville (about 250km north of Cape Town), including Cape Town and the Cape Peninsula, and east to Grahamstown and Port Elizabeth. The major vegetation type here is termed 'fynbos', which is derived from the Dutch for 'thin-bush' – local conditions (including poor soil and frequent winds) meant plants evolved distinctive narrow leaves.

Over 8000 different species of fynbos have been recorded in the Cape Floral Kingdom. All these packed into such a small area make it the most densely speciated plant community in the world. The Cape Peninsula alone (including Table Mountain) contains over 2250 plant species in just 470 sq km – more than the whole of Britain, which is 5000 times bigger. Most species belong to the protea, erica (heather) and restios (reed) families, as well as seven other plant families found nowhere else in the world. More than 70% of fynbos plants are endemic to the area.

Fynbos vegetation is under serious threat from the spread of alien plants such as hakea, pine and Australian wattle. Other significant threats include fire, commercial forestry and the development of housing estates and farms. To protect this unique flora, there are calls to proclaim the Cape Floral Kingdom an internationally recognised Biosphere Reserve.

simply 'thornveld'. This zone includes western-central Namibia, much of Botswana, and the northern parts of South Africa bordering Namibia and Botswana. Trees grow on the grassland, but are widely spaced and dominated by various narrow-leafed thorny *Acacia* species, although some broad-leafed species also occur.

Much of the rest of the Southern African region is defined as **woodland**, or woodland savanna – consisting of mainly broadleaf deciduous trees that grow closer together than in the arid savanna, but do not form a continuous canopy, allowing grasses and other plants to grow between them. (If the upper parts combine to form a continuous canopy – it's forest.) There are three main types. **Dry woodland** covers northern Namibia, northern Botswana, the lower areas of Zimbabwe and the valleys of the Zambezi, Luangwa and Shire Rivers in Zambia and Malawi. The dominant trees are the species *Colophospermum mopane*, and this zone is also called mopane woodland. Also occurring here is the baobab, a classic tree of Africa (see the boxed text 'The Baobab' in this chapter). In areas where conditions are wetter – central Zimbabwe, northern Mozambique and most of Zambia and Malawi – the dominant trees are various species of *Brachystegia* and this zone is often called **moist woodland** or miombo woodland. Belts of dry/mopane and moist/miombo woodland occur together in the noncoastal areas of northern and eastern South Africa and central Mozambique, and the term **mixed woodland** is used. Mixed woodland is also known as 'bushveld', but this is a very loosely applied term.

Small pockets of high ground all over the region have a vegetation zone termed **afromontane**. This occurs most notably in Lesotho and the Drakensberg Range of KwaZulu-Natal, and also in parts of southwest South Africa, the Eastern Highlands of Zimbabwe, and on Mt Mulanje and the Nyika Plateau in Malawi. Characteristic of this zone are wide areas of grassland, or belts of ericas (heathers) and proteas, plus various species, such as helichrysums ('everlastings'), which have evolved to survive the freezing nights and intense daytime sunlight. In these areas, clumps of forest are restricted to valley bottoms and other sheltered spots.

Reptiles

Southern Africa's most notable reptile is the **Nile crocodile**. Once abundant in lakes and rivers across the region, today its numbers have been greatly reduced by hunting and habitat destruction, and it is now classed as 'threatened'.

The Baobab

One of the great symbols of Africa, the baobab tree, with its bizarre appearance, thick trunk and root-like branches, is surrounded by myth and folklore. Stories have been passed down through generations about how the Creator, angry with the baobab, pulled it out and flung it back into the ground headfirst. The San people tell a story about God giving all the animals a seed to plant. The hyaena, angry at being left until last, planted his allocated seed, the baobab, upside down.

Baobabs live for a very long time – often for millennia. Research has shown that they grow fast during their first 270 years, and then slow down. Trees with a circumference of over 30m could be as much as 4000 years old. Calculating the age of these trees can prove to be very difficult, since growth rates vary enormously and the trunk may even shrink during years of drought. Radiocarbon dating is the only reliable method. One of the largest baobabs in Southern Africa has been reported as having a circumference of over 46m – a respectable age by any standard!

The wood of the baobab is very light and almost spongy in appearance. When the tree dies, within a few months it will have rotted down to a mass of fibre. Baobabs produce big, white flowers from October to December, each bloom only lasting 24 hours. They are pollinated by various species of fruit bat and it's interesting to note that the distribution of fruit bats and baobabs throughout Southern Africa is very similar. Baobabs may also be pollinated by ants. Large oval fruits containing seeds are produced in April and May.

The uses of this tree seem endless. Although not suitable for hut construction, the very light, fibrous wood can be used in the manufacture of paper and also as floats for fishing nets. The interior of the trunk frequently dies off, leaving a hollow shell – excellent for use as a water trap, a nesting site for birds and reptiles, a place of refuge for both humans and animals, and as a storage room. The fibrous bark makes a very strong thread, used for making nets, sacks and even cloth.

SARAH JOLLY

All parts of the tree seem to have some nutritional value. Animals, especially baboons and elephants, eat the fruit, flowers and young roots. Elephants also strip and eat the bark. In times of drought they will dig out and eat the inner wood, which has a water content of up to 40%. For people, the fruits are very rich in proteins and vitamins. The seeds can be ground and roasted, while leaves can be cooked and eaten as a type of spinach. The baobab has medicinal uses too: the leaves are used to treat diarrhoea and fevers. The bark can also be used in the treatment of fevers, and was once sold commercially for this purpose.

More modern uses for the baobab include the WWI gun emplacement and ammunition store that was built in the branches of a tree at Karonga in northern Malawi. Finally, we should not forget Major Trollip, who, while stationed at Katima Mulilo in Namibia, installed a flush toilet in his local hollow baobab. It remains there to this day.

Wildlife Viewing

A selection of mammals and birds that you may see in Southern Africa is described in the colour Wildlife Guide. Whether you're viewing from a vehicle or on foot, the following tips will help you get the most out of watching them.

- Wildlife viewing is generally better in the dry season, as the sparse vegetation makes visibility easier and the animals congregate around water sources.
- Early morning and evening are the best times to go out, as this is when most animals are active. First light or at least 30 minutes before sunrise is a good start time, then for the next two or three hours. In the middle of the day cheetahs are often seen hunting; it's also a good time to see giraffes and zebras. In winter, birdwatching is still better in the morning, but can be reasonable all day.
- Don't rush around. Take your time, and get 'tuned in'. Often you first notice one animal, stop the car, and suddenly realise that there are many more in the area. It can be very rewarding to stake out a water hole for several hours and let the animals come to you.
- Warthog, baboon, zebra, giraffe and many antelope species will happily graze together, so if you see one species, there will often be more close by. The presence of feeding herbivores does not preclude the possibility of a predator in the vicinity, so be alert for stalking lions or leopards.
- If you stop to watch animals, and another vehicle has got there first, it's polite to stay back a little and not block their view.
- To avoid scaring off animals, wear neutral or earthy-coloured clothing, keep quiet and don't make sudden movements. Even dangly jewellery or mirror shades can be enough to frighten some animals. It's often no surprise that a truck full of excitable people will come back from a drive having 'seen nothing'.

Female crocodiles lay up to 80 eggs at a time, depositing them in sandy areas above the high-water line. After three months incubation in the hot sand, the young emerge. Newly hatched crocs are avocado green in colour; as they age, they darken to nearly black. Many live to be over 70 years old.

Southern Africa has a complement of both venomous and harmless snakes, but most fear humans and you'll be lucky to even see one. The largest snake – although harmless to humans – is the **python**, which grows to over 5m in length. Another snake worth mentioning is the **puff adder**, which grows to about 1m long. Like all reptiles it enjoys sunning itself, but it is very slow and sometimes stepped on by unwary people before it has had time to wake up and move. When stepped on, it bites. This snake occurs in mountain and desert areas, so take care when hiking, especially in the early morning.

Lizards are ubiquitous in Southern Africa, from the hot and dusty Kaokoveld (Namibia) to the cool highlands of the Nyika Palteau (Malawi), and from the bathroom ceiling to the kitchen sink. The largest of these is the **water monitor**, a docile creature that reaches over 2m in length and which is often seen lying around water holes, perhaps dreaming of being a crocodile. Two others frequently seen are **chameleons** and **geckos** – the latter often in hotel rooms, where they are quite harmless and help to keep the bug numbers low.

Endangered Wildlife

In Southern Africa over the last few hundred years – not coincidentally since Europeans settled in the region – two large mammal species (the blue antelope and the quagga, which may have been a zebra subspecies) have become extinct, as have many smaller mammals, birds and insects. Today, several other animal species face the prospect of extinction in an unnaturally quick time.

The World Conservation Union (IUCN) defines an 'endangered' species as one that is in imminent danger of extinction, and a 'vulnerable' species as one that will become endangered if current trends continue. However, the term 'endangered' is used in this book for both categories, as this is more commonly understood. Under the auspices of the IUCN, several countries have compiled Red Data Books (RDBs) listing in detail their endangered animal species, including mammals, birds, fish, insects, amphibians and reptiles. In the region covered in this book, only South Africa has compiled a complete RDB, but Namibia has a partially complete RDB, and several other countries have lists compiled by nongovernmental bodies (such as wildlife societies) which include most endangered species.

Endangered Mammals One of the most endangered mammal species (and *the* most endangered carnivore) in Southern Africa is the **wild dog** (also called the Cape hunting dog), similar in size and appearance to a large domestic dog – sleek, with long legs, patchy black, yellow and white colouring and large rounded ears. Outside national parks, wild dogs often kill livestock, as their natural prey (small mammals) have already been reduced, so a great many have been shot or poisoned by farmers. They can survive in a wide range of habitats, but their numbers are low, and as they hunt over a very wide area they are only rarely seen.

More high-profile is the **black rhino** – the most endangered animal in all Africa. Their numbers dropped from 60,000 in 1970 to less than 3000 by the end of the 1980s as they were poached for their horn (it is used for traditional medicines in Asia, and for dagger handles in Yemen). The black rhino populations in Southern Africa are relatively high compared to East Africa, as the animal is better protected: Zimbabwe's parks have about 1500, South Africa's have about 750, and Namibia's about 500 (mostly in Etosha National Park), giving Southern Africa an approximate total of 2750. Today there are about 500 other individuals in the rest of Africa. In contrast, the total number of white rhinos in Africa is around 5000, but this species is not classed as endangered as nearly all occur in South Africa, notably Hluhluwe-Umfolozi Park in KwaZulu-Natal, where they breed successfully.

Perhaps the most celebrated species to have been brought back from the brink of extinction is the **mountain zebra**. After being hunted for centuries, by the 1930s only about 10 individuals remained. The Mountain Zebra National Park (described in South Africa's Eastern Cape chapter) was established to protect the species and the population slowly grew again, so that now some have been relocated to other parks and reserves.

Several of Southern Africa's antelope species are endangered, most notably the **roan antelope**, under threat because its natural habitat (grassland) has been taken over by cereal crops. Other endangered antelope include the **oribi**, the **bontebok** and the **suni**.

Other mammals that are endangered include: the **honey badger**, which has taken to eating chickens because its natural prey has been reduced (and so is frequently poisoned by farmers); and the **pangolin** (anteater) and **aardvark** (antbear), which are killed when they eat insects poisoned by insecticides, and by electric fences. Aardvarks are also hunted because their claws are used in traditional medicine.

Smaller, and less well known (and less 'fashionable'), is the **riverine rabbit**, found in South Africa's Karoo. This is actually the most endangered mammal in Southern Africa. Similar to other wild rabbits, this species digs burrows, but as its name suggests, it prefers burrowing in dry river courses and is frequently threatened by flash floods, as well as the destruction of its natural feeding grounds by the continual development of farmland. For smaller mammals, habitat destruction is frequently the reason for their impending extinction, even more so than for the larger mammals, which are also endangered by hunting. For example, most of the natural forests inhabited by the African **red squirrel** in KwaZulu-Natal have been cleared to make room for sugarcane fields or commercial plantations. The **white-tailed mouse** and the **golden mole**, both endemic to Southern Africa, are similarly endangered.

Endangered Birds Top of the list of Southern Africa's endangered birds is the **Egyptian vulture**. This bird lives in East Africa, but occasionally visits Southern Africa and may be seen in Etosha (Namibia) or Chobe (Botswana) National Parks. It is officially extinct in South Africa, where it was poisoned and shot out of existence by ostrich farmers because it preyed on ostrich eggs. Other endangered birds of prey, also threatened by the setting of poisoned carcasses by farmers, include the **Cape vulture**, the **lappet-faced vulture** and the **bateleur**. The **ground hornbill**, a black turkey-sized bird with a prominent red bill, is also threatened by these poisoned carcasses.

The next Southern African bird due for extinction if things continue the way they are is the **blue swallow**. This bird has specialised habitat requirements – montane grassland (see Vegetation under the Flora & Fauna section earlier), which thrives in highland areas with good soil and reliable rainfall, exactly the conditions required for commercial forestry. As more plantations are planted, the grassland disappears, and the blue swallow goes with it.

Also near the top of the list is the **wattled crane**, a tall, long-necked wading bird with characteristic nodes (or wattles) under its bill; it inhabits wetland areas in various parts of Southern Africa. Wetlands are a particularly threatened habitat, as they are drained to provide farming or housing land, flooded under dams, or silted up because of soil erosion. Consequently, the crane has become threatened too. Wattled cranes occur in the Okavango Delta (Botswana) and in parts of Zimbabwe. Only 120 pairs remain in South Africa, and they are occasionally seen in Etosha and parts of Malawi. They also occur in Mozambique's Zambezi Delta, as this habitat has not been denigrated.

Another wetland bird, which occurs notably in the Okavango Delta and Zambezi Valley, is the **African skimmer**. It is also threatened by human intervention, this time by power boats: their wake floods the skimmers' nest sites.

Southern Africa's rarest breeding seabird is the **roseate tern**; its nesting sites have come under increasing pressure from introduced domestic rabbits. The **jackass penguin** is another seabird whose nesting sites are threatened – in this case, by oil spills and refuse dumping; overfishing, causing reduced foodstocks, hasn't helped much either.

The colourful **Cape parrot** is another endangered bird that has a particularly tough time trying to survive. As well as being shot as a scavenger on farms, its preferred forest habitat is being reduced and replaced by crops or commercial plantations. On top of all this, any parrots that manage to survive these threats risk being captured and sold overseas as decorative cage birds.

Why Bother?

With all Southern Africa's massive social and economic problems, it may seem a little inappropriate to worry about cuddly bunnies, a few fish or a flock of ugly vultures, but conservationists argue that the status of endangered species and some of the region's wider problems are inextricably linked. For example, the wattled crane is threatened as its wetland habitat is reduced. And the wetlands are reduced by silting, which is caused by soil erosion due to unsustainable deforestation and farming methods. In other areas, the wetlands are simply drained, and the land used for agriculture. Either way, where the wetlands once acted as giant sponges to control water levels, their demise now means flooding is an increasingly frequent and serious problem throughout Southern Africa.

The major floods in Mozambique in early 2000 were caused by massive amounts of water racing down the Limpopo and Save Rivers from South Africa and Zimbabwe. With no wetlands to slow the deluge, the results were devastating. Therefore, to protect wetlands destructive causes must also be prevented, and the end results will in turn have great benefits for local people. Put very simply, if the wattled cranes are OK then the chances are that a lot of other things will be OK too.

Other Endangered Animals Various freshwater fish in Southern Africa face extinction as their waters become silted up, polluted with industrial and urban discharge or agricultural run-off, or altered dramatically by dams or hydroelectric schemes. Introduced (alien) fish species that prey on indigenous fish, or compete for food, are also a danger, and even alien water plants, which disturb the habitat (for example, by cutting out light or reducing oxygen levels) can have a disastrous effect. Endangered species include South Africa's **Berg River redfin** and **fiery redfin** and Lesotho's **Drakensberg minnow**. Just offshore, the **Knysna seahorse** is also endangered.

Several species of reptile are endangered, most notably the **Nile crocodile** (see under Reptiles in the Flora & Fauna section earlier). Less high-profile cousins of the crocodile, which are in fact closer to extinction, include the **Smiths dwarf chameleon**, whose habitat and range consists of a single mountainside near Port Elizabeth, and the **geometric tortoise**, once threatened by habitat destruction and pet collectors and now protected in a number of private wildlife reserves.

The **Table Mountain ghost frog**, as the name implies, also has a restricted range, and its neighbour, the marvellously named **micro frog**, Africa's smallest at less than 2mm, is threatened by urban development in the Cape Town area.

Of the amphibians, **sea turtles** are endangered in Mozambique, and are also under pressure in South Africa.

National Parks & Reserves

The term 'national park' actually has a very precise definition, but is often used as a catch-all term to include wildlife reserves,

National Parks in Southern Africa

LESSER-KNOWN PARKS

The region's less well-known parks and reserves include some real gems, usually smaller and often quieter than their more famous counterparts, with excellent wildlife viewing and birdwatching opportunities. These include:

Botswana

Makgadikgadi & Nxai Pan – vast and remote, where Southern Africa's last great wildlife migrations are to be found

Malawi

Liwonde – well-managed lowland park, growing in status, with good elephant viewing
Mt Mulanje – the 'island in the sky', with sheer peaks and excellent hiking
Nyika – unique montane grassland area, with endless views and splendid horse riding

Mozambique

Bazaruto Archipelago – tropical reefs and islands, beaches, sailing and diving

Namibia

Waterberg Plateau – a mountain wilderness, with excellent birdlife and walking trails

South Africa

Drakensberg – mountain region, low on 'big game', high on scenery and hiking
St Lucia – coastal wetlands of global significance
Tsitsikamma – coastal park with forests, fynbos, beaches and rocky headlands

Zambia

Kafue – massive and genuinely wild, with an impressive range of habitats and wildlife
Kasanka – pioneering, privately managed park, noted for sightings of the rare sitatunga antelope
Lower Zambezi – spectacular setting, escarpments and plains, plus the great river itself

forest parks, or any state-managed conservation area. Several privately owned reserves also exist in the region. Most parks in Southern Africa conserve habitats and wildlife species and provide recreational facilities for visitors. South Africa's parks are among the best managed in the world, and many others in the region are very good, although in some countries the stand- ards in 'low-profile' parks have slipped considerably.

In parks and reserves that contain large (and potentially dangerous) animals, only visitors in cars are allowed to enter; those without a vehicle usually join an organised safari. In some parks you can also walk, either alone or with a ranger/guide. More details are given under Activities in the Regional Facts for the Visitor chapter.

One feature of national parks that escapes no visitor's notice is that most charge an entrance fee. This can range from less than US$1 to around US$50 per day (see the boxed text 'Park Fees'). Many parks charge a range of prices: foreign visitors pay considerably more than residents or citizens.

This is fair enough, as many local people do not have the spare cash to spend on luxuries such as wildlife viewing, and it's only right that they should be allowed to enjoy their natural heritage without having to fork out the sums most westerners can easily afford (although it seems to go against the grain when diplomats, UN workers and other wealthy expats often pay resident rates too).

Park Accommodation Most parks and reserves contain accommodation, so you can stay overnight and go wildlife viewing during the early morning or evening.

National Parks in Southern Africa

Zimbabwe

Chizarira – a beautiful and little-visited wildlife park
Matusadona – lowland park, with both lakefront and mountain habitats
Nyanga, Vumba, Chimanimani – the Eastern Highlands, with various mountain retreats and activities
Zambezi National Park – near Victoria Falls, accessible and popular

WORLD FAMOUS PARKS

World-famous parks in the region, nearly all with excellent wildlife viewing, include the following:

Botswana

Chobe – particularly known for its large herds of elephants
Moremi – including part of the vast and stunning Okavango Delta

Namibia

Etosha – wide flat pans, water holes and excellent wildlife viewing
Namib-Naukluft – huge orange sand dunes and wild desert mountains

South Africa

Hluhluwe-Umfolozi – close to the Zulu heartland, with many rhinos
Kgalagadi Transfrontier – a wild corner of the Kalahari, with a surprising range of wildlife (also in Botswana)
Kruger – huge, with good facilities and almost guaranteed sightings

Zambia

Luangwa Valley – wild and pristine; still called 'Africa's best-kept secret'

Zimbabwe

Hwange – holds one of the densest wildlife populations in Africa
Mana Pools – on the River Zambezi, where canoe safaris are popular

Park Fees

Many visitors complain about the high prices charged by many national parks in Southern Africa, particularly when facilities are seriously substandard. (The exception is South Africa where parks are well managed, facilities are excellent, and fees are very reasonable.) But there is no reason why tourists from wealthy western nations should come to a developing country and expect everything to be cheap. If national parks can produce revenue, rather than be a drain on limited financial resources, this should be welcomed. The more money visitors pay to see the animals, the greater their commercial value, and the better chance they have of surviving. In some parks, the money you pay is channelled back into management or conservation, or directed to local people who live in the surrounding areas. Unfortunately, in many places the revenue goes to government treasuries, where it gets swallowed up by other schemes or simply 'disappears'. And that's the real issue: paying to enter a national park is fine, but making sure the money goes to the right place is a major problem.

Accommodation ranges from simple camping grounds to luxury hotels (called 'lodges' to make them seem authentic). Prices vary to match the quality of facilities. In some countries you can just turn up and find a place to camp or stay; in other countries reservations are advised (or are essential at busy times).

More details are given in the individual country chapters.

GOVERNMENT & POLITICS

The politics of Southern Africa were dominated through the 1980s by South Africa's declared state of emergency, continued implementation of the apartheid laws and deliberate disruption of neighbouring states. To counter this, the other countries formed the Southern African Development Coordination Conference (SADCC) – unofficially known as the 'Frontline States'. (A notable exception was Malawi, which annoyed the SADCC states, and the Organisation of African Unity (OAU), by refusing to ostracise South Africa. It was well rewarded with valuable trade and aid from Pretoria for doing this.)

Since the 1994 democratic elections, South Africa is back in the fold. Several South African state and private-sector organisations have teamed up with counterparts in neighbouring countries to further trade links and intra-governmental contacts, and South Africa is now a leading member of the renamed Southern African Development Community (SADC). South Africa has also been readmitted to the Commonwealth of former British colonies, which includes most other countries in the region. Intriguingly, Mozambique has also joined the Commonwealth, even though it was never a British colony.

Despite re-entry into the regional government and political scene, South Africa has been accused of not entering fully into the spirit of cooperation. For example, South Africa was initially not keen to join the multi-state African Development Bank (ADB) developmental finance organisation due to concern about alleged mismanagement.

Some commentators applauded the stalling, while others suggested that South Africa should join such pan-African organisations if only to introduce some longoverdue 'house-cleaning'. Following negotiations, South Africa became the ADB's 53rd member in mid-1996.

But while some Southern African countries are unhappy with South Africa's cherry-picking attitude, others are already wary of their big neighbour's level of involvement. By 1999, goods from South Africa were available all over the region, under-cutting the price of local products and putting local manufacturers out of business.

Some countries fear a complete economic and political takeover, and that they will become totally dependent on their former enemy.

ECONOMY

The Figures

When discussing a country's economy the usual unit of measurement is per capita gross national product (GNP), which calculates what a country 'earns' annually, divided by its total population – giving an indication of what each inhabitant produces per year. Of the countries in Southern Africa, the poorest are Mozambique (with a per capita GNP of US$80), Malawi (US$180) and Zambia (US$360), putting them among the 20 poorest countries in the world. Doing a bit better are Zimbabwe (US$610) and Swaziland (US$1210), while the relative high-rollers are Namibia (US$2250), Botswana (US$2800) and South Africa (US$3520). In contrast, most western industrialised nations have per capita GNPs of around US$20,000. In crude terms, the average westerner is at least 10 times richer than most Southern Africans, and over 100 times richer than the poor citizens of Mozambique and Malawi.

Admittedly, per capita GNP is a very blunt instrument, concerned only with economic values. So the United Nations devised the Human Development Index (HDI), which takes account of factors such as life expectancy and education standards, as well as income. Unfortunately, in Southern Africa the results don't change much. Mozambique still comes out as one of the poorest nations in the world, ranking 166th out of 174 countries, closely followed by Malawi at 161st. Other 'low' countries are Zambia, ranked at 146 and Lesotho at 134. The other countries of Southern Africa get 'medium' status – Zimbabwe at 130, Swaziland at 115, Namibia at 107 and Botswana at 97. South Africa is the highest at 89, but to put things in perspective the richest country in the region is on a par with Sri Lanka (90), Paraguay (91), Jordan (87) and the Dominican Republic (88). By contrast, western countries such as Canada, USA, New Zealand, Australia, the UK, Ireland and Germany are all ranked in the top 20.

The Facts

What do these league tables really mean? In human terms this poverty gives a low life expectancy – between 50 and 57 years old in the well-off countries of Botswana, Namibia and Swaziland, as low as 43 to 45 in Malawi, Zambia and Mozambique. In the poorest countries, literacy rates are also very low, especially among women, and between 100 and 200 children in every 1000 die before the age of five – although birth rates are around 3% annually, which makes them among the highest in the world. In nearly all the countries of Southern Africa, unemployment is high and earnings low, so people have no money to buy food and can only grow cereal crops. This means nutritional intakes are low, which makes a large proportion of the population – especially children – susceptible to disease, for which there are very few medical services. It's a depressing scenario, and likely to get worse; the *Economist* in 1997 stated that: 'the gap between Africa and the rest of the world is widening'.

But an even darker picture lies behind the scenes. Along with most other Third World countries, the economies of Southern African nations are dominated, some say suffocated, by debt.

International Debt

It all started in the 1970s. The rise in oil prices meant that commercial banks had spare cash to farm out, so billions of dollars were loaned to developing countries, in Southern Africa and around the world, with little concern for safeguards or collateral. More money came from western governments, the World Bank and the International Monetary Fund (IMF) – all keen for the developing countries to take on loans. Sometimes it went beyond encouragement; often loans were tied to huge engineering projects (eg, dams) or linked to the purchasing of imported goods (eg, armaments), from which the lending countries would benefit. And on top of all this, a lot of money was wasted; spent by dictators on their military, presidential palaces, inefficient nationalised industries or grandiose and unnecessary schemes such as airports and motorways. And millions were simply embezzled – to such a degree that some African rulers joined the ranks of the richest men in the world.

Meanwhile, the prices for Southern African export commodities (such as tobacco in Malawi or copper in Zambia) dropped. The countries of the region were earning less from their exports, and finding it increasingly hard to meet their interest payments. At the same time, the cost of importing western manufactured goods went up, creating an imbalance of trade which still affects many Southern African countries today. For example, the cost of imports in Mozambique, Malawi and Zimbabwe are double what the countries earn from exports.

The Debt Crisis in Africa

Things came to a crunch in the early 1980s, when the term 'debt crisis' was coined. It was a crisis for the African nations who could no longer afford to pay interest, but even more of a crisis for the major banks who stood to lose their money. The world's economy is like a stack of dominoes – if one big bank goes down, it can take many others, and even whole countries, with it. At one stage, the outstanding debt, especially when some Latin American countries famously refused to pay, meant the entire global financial system was threatened with collapse – and that would have hit every stock market, every pension fund and every savings account in the west, from Washington to Alice Springs.

To avert the crisis, several western governments bailed out the banks (with taxpayers' money) while the IMF and other lenders introduced 'structural adjustment' or restrictions on the spending allowed by the debtor countries. In the poorer countries of Southern Africa, this may have controlled corruption and inefficiency among the ruling elite – but only slightly. For the ordinary people, things got worse: their wages went down, the price of food went up, and services such as schools or hospitals were cut.

Despite the economic warning signs, and despite the suffering of the Third World poor, the loans kept going out and the debts kept piling up. Even today, the IMF continues to approve loans – so that interest on other loans can be paid. The World Bank is owed five times more today than it was 10 years ago. And the 'debt crisis' is as big as it ever was.

Opponents of the World Bank, the IMF and other large development organisations point out that, quite apart from human and environmental costs, loans fail on an economic front too. Despite the billions of dollars in development loans that have been pumped into Africa in the last 30 years, most countries are now far worse off economically than they were at independence.

Debt in Southern Africa Today

The debt figures are so high they almost become meaningless. On a global scale, the Third World owes the west over two trillion US dollars, and pays US$700 million interest *every day*. Africa's total debt is around US$350 billion. Of this, Mozambique's debt is almost US$6000 million, Zambia owes over US$7000 million, and South Africa owes US$23,000 million. Even comparatively well-off Botswana owes US$600 million.

In many African countries, around 15% of export earnings go on 'servicing' debt (ie, paying off the interest, not the loan itself). In several Southern African countries the percentage is higher – 20% in Zimbabwe, 24% in Zambia and over 30% in Mozambique. Botswana and South Africa pay out 5% to 10% of total export earnings. Especially in the poorer countries, this means less money gets spent on useful things such as schools and hospitals. In fact, the United Nations Development Program (UNDP) estimates that in 23 African countries, spending on loan repayments exceeds spending on health.

It has become increasingly obvious, and bitterly ironic, that although loans from western governments, the World Bank and other institutions are supposed to help developing nations, in actuality they seem to siphon money *from* the poor countries *to* the richer countries. And while the west benefits, the vast majority of people in Malawi, Zambia, Mozambique and the rest of Southern Africa continue to suffer. This is not to say that government corruption and inefficiency are not major problems in the region, but the outstanding debts that absorb so much money are an undeniably significant factor.

To put the figures in some kind of perspective – while Africa owes US$350 billion, only US$6 billion is required to provide adequate education for children in all developing countries – that's just 1% of what the world spends every year on its militaries. The UN estimates that it would cost roughly US$80 billion to provide universal access to basic social services, and to alleviate income poverty – less than the combined net worth of the world's seven richest men.

The Solution?

There are increasingly loud calls from various charitable, human rights, church and welfare organisations for the western banks and nations to write off Third World loans. They argue that the rich countries will never get their money back (even though the interest paid over the years is many times more than the original debt anyway), and that the interest repayments only stifle Third World economies, encourage political instability and harm the populations. While huge numbers of people in Southern Africa would benefit from this solution, the cost of wiping off most loans would cost western taxpayers around US$3 annually.

In the last couple of years, anti-debt campaigns have been supported by rock stars and other celebrities, so many ordinary people in the west are now aware of the situation, and are calling on their own governments to act. Meanwhile, a debt conference in Nairobi in August 1999, chaired by Botswana's President Mogae, proposed that debts might be lifted if debtor countries guaranteed the money saved would be spent on social projects such as health and education.

In response, some western nations have agreed to write off *some* loans, but others remain resolute that the money must be repaid in full. The IMF and World Bank also indicate that some loans might be written off (if the indebted countries guarantee to put the money saved towards schemes that raise living standards – an issue also fraught with difficulties), but in these poor countries the effects will not be felt for several years. Nevertheless, it's a step in the right direction.

On a personal scale, what can travellers in Southern Africa do? Just being aware is the main thing. See the wider picture. Don't overlook the part your own government or bank back home plays in the enforcement of debt repayments from the developing world. Consider banking or investing with institutions that have ethical policies. And don't be fooled by claims in your home country about loans from western governments, banks and financial institutions 'helping' the poor of Southern Africa. In many cases, they're doing the exact opposite.

EDUCATION

All the countries in Southern Africa have state education systems that follow patterns established by their colonial powers, ie, a primary stage for all children, a secondary stage for most and a tertiary stage for a few academic achievers or for the wealthy.

Officially, those who pass relevant examinations can go to secondary school and university. In reality, which children go to school and how far up the ladder they progress is determined by their family income rather than by academic performance; poor children may not be able to afford school fees or extra items such as uniforms and books, and may be kept away from school to work in the fields or to provide income from other employment.

Across the region, these problems are compounded by restrictions on government revenue available for education. The end result is simply not enough schools to cater for the number of children – particularly in rural areas. Many schools have to operate two 'shifts', with one lot of children studying in the morning, and another in the afternoon. Even so, classes may hold over 100 pupils, sitting three or four to a desk and sharing books and pens. At the same time, teachers are grossly underpaid and become understandably demoralised so that standards slip further. Consequently, literacy rates across Southern Africa are low.

State-funded education in South Africa is slightly different to systems elsewhere in the region. Despite the end of apartheid, there are still effectively two systems – underfunded schools in poor areas where conditions are similar to those in other countries in Southern Africa; and schools with good facilities in wealthier areas, which are similar to schools in western countries. Inevitably, the pupils in poor schools are predominantly black and coloured, and the pupils in the good schools are predominantly white. There is some crossover, and the gap is gradually closing, but there's still a long way to go – it's one of the parity issues that continues to face the South African government.

SOCIETY & CONDUCT

In South Africa and Namibia, two societies and cultures (western and African) run in parallel, and they rarely cross. As you might expect, in a western situation social customs are similar to those in Europe, although often a touch more formal, but at the same time more friendly, than in other parts of the western world. For example, Afrikaners will often shake hands and say their name, even if you're only meeting them briefly. In other Southern African countries, although you will meet people of European origin, the society and culture is predominantly African, and most advice here assumes you're in an African situation.

Behaviour

As anywhere, the best way to learn about a society's conduct is to watch the locals. Don't worry: Africans are generally very easy-going towards foreigners, and any social errors are unlikely to cause offence (although they may cause confusion or merriment). However, there are a few things that are frowned upon wherever you go in Southern Africa. These include: public nudity; open displays of anger; open displays of affection (among people of the same or opposite sex); and vocal criticism of the government or country.

On top of these basics, a few straightforward courtesies will greatly improve your chances of acceptance by the local community, especially in rural areas. Pleasantries are taken quite seriously, and it's essential to greet someone entering or leaving a room. Learn the local words for 'hello' and 'goodbye' and use them unsparingly. For those out of earshot, it is customary to offer a smile and a pleasant wave, even if you're just passing in a vehicle.

Great emphasis is also placed on handshakes. There are various local variations, involving linked thumbs or fingers or the left hand touching the right elbow, which you'll pick up by observation, but these are

Dress Codes

None of the countries in Southern Africa have any specific regulations regarding clothing or behaviour. Malawi used to be a celebrated exception because women visitors were required by law to wear skirts that covered the knees, while men were required to have short hair and tidy beards. The reason for this was partly because many women travellers used to tour Malawi wearing shorts, which offended the locals (men and women) – particularly in the mainly Muslim north, but also in the centre and south where most people are still pretty conservative. The law was dropped in 1994, but although you are now *allowed* to wear what you like, it's still pretty insensitive to wander around with most of your legs showing (although this is no problem on the lake beaches, for hiking or for sports).

For women, the same applies in most other countries in the region: apart from the disrespect you are showing to local sensibilities, you also make things harder for yourself – don't be surprised if kids laugh, adults (men and women) treat you with disdain and some young guns see you as easy prey. From a practical point of view, keeping reasonably covered with loose-fitting clothes also helps prevent sunstroke.

Men should also consider what they wear. Look around: the only people wearing shorts or tatty clothes are kids, labourers or the poor. Then ask yourself why some officials and other locals treat scruffy, bare-legged travellers with contempt.

reserved for informal occasions (not greeting officials). A western handshake will do fine in most situations. Sometimes, people who know each other continue to hold hands right through their conversation, or at least for a few minutes.

As in most traditional societies, older people are treated with respect. Teachers, doctors and other professionals (usually men) receive similar treatment. Likewise, you should always be polite to people in authority – immigration officers, government officials, police, and village chiefs (also usually men) – even if they seem awkward or unpleasant. It is one thing to stand up for your rights, but undermining an official's authority may only serve to waste time, tie you up in red tape and inspire closer scrutiny of future travellers. Having said that, officials are normally courteous and fairly efficient, sometimes even friendly. On your side, manners, patience and cooperation will nearly always get things off to the right start.

Children rate very low on the social scale, and the status of women is only slightly higher. For example, an African man on a bus might give his seat to an older man, but not normally to a woman, never mind that she is carrying a baby and luggage and minding two toddlers. In traditional rural areas, women are expected to dress and behave modestly, especially in the presence of chiefs or other esteemed persons. Visitors should act in the same way.

When visiting rural settlements, go first to the chief to announce your presence and request permission before setting up camp or wandering around. You will rarely be refused. (In South Africa particularly, but also in some other countries in the region, rural settlements may be apartheid-style townships, and very different rules apply here.)

Eating

Most travellers will have the chance to share an African meal sometime during their stay and will normally be treated with embarrassing honour. Although concessions are sometimes made for foreigners, table manners are probably different from what you're accustomed to. Before eating, diners may pass around a bowl of water for washing hands. If it comes to you first and you're not sure of the routine, indicate that the bowl should be passed to the head of the family.

A stiff porridge made from maize flour is the main component of nearly every meal. It is taken with the right hand from a communal pot, rolled into balls, and dipped in a sauce or 'relish' of meat, beans or vegetables.

Gifts

In some African societies, it isn't considered impolite for people to ask for things; but likewise it isn't rude to refuse. So if a local asks for your watch or camera, say 'no' politely, and all will be fine. Reciprocation of kindness is OK but guilt-ridden indiscriminate distribution of gifts from outside, however well intentioned, tends to create a taste for items not locally available, erodes well-established values, robs people of their pride and in extreme cases can create villages of beggars.

On the other hand, when you're offered a small gift, which you're sure the giver can afford, don't feel guilty about accepting it; to refuse it would bring shame on the giver. To politely receive a gift, local people may accept it with both hands and perhaps bow slightly, – the equivalent of saying 'thanks'. Spoken thanks are uncommon, so don't be upset if you aren't thanked verbally. In fact, Africans tend to think westerners say 'thank you' too often and too casually.

Photos from Home

Lone travellers may be looked upon with suspicion – women because they should be at home rearing families and men because, in some countries, white foreigners recall the days of South African spies. It may help to carry photographs of your family or evidence of a profession unlinked to espionage. Photos of home are also very useful conversation-openers.

It is impolite to scoff food, as your hosts may feel they haven't provided enough. For the same reason, it is polite *not* to be the one who takes the last handful from the communal bowl. If your food is served on separate plates, and you can't finish your food, don't worry; again this shows your hosts that you have been satisfied. The bowl is passed around again for hand washing, then jugs of water or home-brewed beer may be passed around from person to person. It is not customary to share coffee, tea or bottled soft drinks.

RELIGION

Most people in Southern Africa follow Christianity or traditional religion, often combining aspects of both. All the western-style Christian churches are represented (Catholics, Protestants, Baptists, Adventists etc) – most of which were introduced in colonial times by European missionaries. Many indigenous Christian faiths have also been established, ranging from a small congregation meeting in a simple hut to vast organisations with millions of followers such as the Zion churches in Zimbabwe and South Africa.

Islam is followed in some parts of the region. In South Africa, people brought by the colonial authorities from India or Malaysia carried their religion with them. In Malawi and on the coast of Mozambique, Islam was originally introduced by Swahili-Arab slave-traders.

There are many traditional religions in Southern Africa, but no great temples or written scriptures. For outsiders, beliefs can be complex (and to the western mind, illogical) as can the rituals and ceremonies that surround them. Most traditional religions are animist – based on the attribution of life or consciousness to natural objects or phenomena – and many accept the existence of a Supreme Being, with whom communication is possible through the intercession of ancestors. Thus, ancestors play a particularly strong role. Their principal function is to protect the tribe or family, and they may on occasion show their pleasure (eg, a good harvest) or displeasure (eg, a member of the family becoming sick).

MITCH REARDON

A Zulu *sangoma* (witchdoctor) in KwaZulu-Natal, South Africa

Witchcraft

Within many traditional African religions, there is a belief in spells and magic (usually called witchcraft), which is a complex subject, and hard for westerners to appreciate or understand. In brief simplistic terms it goes like this: physical or mental illnesses are often ascribed to a spell or curse having been put on the sufferer. Often, a relative or villager is suspected of being the 'witch' who placed the curse, usually for reasons of spite or jealousy. A traditional doctor, also called a diviner or witchdoctor, is then required to hunt out the witch and cure the victim. This is done in different ways in various parts of the country, and may involve the use of herbs, divining implements, prayers, chanting or dance. Services do not come free of charge, and many witchdoctors demand high payments – up to US$20, in countries where an average month's earnings may be little more than this. It's a sad fact that the 'witches' who are unearthed are frequently those who cannot defend themselves – the sick, the old or the very poorest members of society. There are even reports of very young children being accused by witchdoctors of harbouring evil spirits.

LANGUAGE

Many indigenous languages are spoken in Southern Africa. However, English is widely spoken in all countries covered by this book (except Mozambique), and widely used in commercial or government situations. Despite its colonial overtones, English is also the official common language in most countries because it is seen as neutral, and not favouring any local language group. More details on languages (and the people who speak them) are given in the individual country chapters, and in the Language chapter at the end of this book.

Regional Facts for the Visitor

This chapter describes the more general aspects of travel in the Southern African region. For specifics about travel in the individual countries, see the relevant chapters.

HIGHLIGHTS

At the risk of creating controversy, we have chosen a selection of major highlights that many people travelling in Southern Africa rate as absolute must-sees. These include, in South Africa, the lively cosmopolitan city of **Cape Town** and the national parks and wildlife reserves in **KwaZulu-Natal**. The **mountains of Lesotho** (called the Drakensberg Range on the South African side) are another spectacular natural highlight, and in Swaziland, the **Mkhaya Game Reserve** is the best place in the region to see the rare black rhino. In Namibia, the perfectly sculptured sand dunes of **Sossusvlei** and the wide open spaces of **Etosha National Park** attract many visitors. In Botswana, the **Okavango Delta** and the neighbouring **Chobe National Park** and **Moremi Wildlife Reserve** are world-renowned wildlife areas. Probably the region's most famous highlight is **Victoria Falls** (between Zambia and Zimbabwe), as is the **River Zambezi**, which flows through these two countries as well as Mozambique. The national parks of Zambia are major highlights, with **South Luangwa** among the best in Africa. Malawi is defined by **Lake Malawi**, one of the most beautiful sections of the Great Rift Valley, while the **Great Zimbabwe Ruins** are the cultural soul of Zimbabwe, and the finest archaeological site south of the Sahara. The great highlight of Mozambique is its coastline, but most people rate the **Bazaruto Archipelago** as the jewel in the crown here.

Most of these highlights are also indicated on the colour regional map towards the front of this book, and some more ideas are given in the following Suggested Itineraries section. Of course, you could have an enjoyable or rewarding trip in Southern Africa without seeing any of these highlights. In fact, some people might avoid them precisely because they *are* listed in this book! But many of the highlights we mention are unique and particularly fascinating, and it would be a shame to travel in the region without seeing any of them.

For more inspiration, see the Highlights list at the start of every country chapter.

SUGGESTED ITINERARIES

Southern Africa is a large and diverse region, and where you go and what you do depends on available time and money. The main factor affecting the number of places you can reach will be your form of transport. Many travellers use buses and trains for their entire trip, and can get to most places this way, at fairly low cost, albeit sometimes quite slowly. A rental car cuts these delays; it's also near-essential for getting into some national parks, but is more costly. Many travellers combine public transport with a few days or weeks in a rental car, sometimes teaming up with others to split the costs. There is also a small but growing number of travellers who buy a car in South Africa, use it to tour the region, then sell it. For more details, see the Getting Around the Region chapter and Getting Around sections in the individual country chapters.

Whatever transport you choose, if you've got plenty of time, then naturally you can visit and see numerous places. If your time is limited, it would be far better to visit just one or two places rather than rushing around to fit a lot in, and only skimming the surface.

Two to Three Weeks

It's unlikely that visitors from Europe or further afield will come to Southern Africa just for one week, but for 10 days or two weeks a tour might include: Zimbabwe's Victoria Falls, combined with Botswana's Okavango Delta or Chobe National Park, or with one or two parks in Zambia such as Kafue or Lower

Zambezi, or with Mana Pools, Hwange or Matobo National Parks in Zimbabwe.

Another option for two weeks might be South Africa's Western Cape, or the parks and coast of KwaZulu-Natal, possibly combined with a few days in Lesotho, Swaziland or southern Mozambique. Malawi is a compact country that lends itself to a two-week visit, possibly combined with a visit to Zambia's South Luangwa National Park.

One to Two Months

With one month to travel, your possibilities increase to three or four of the options listed earlier. If you've got two months and your own set of wheels, you could probably do them all at a rush. By using public transport (maybe including a regional flight), you could still see a good selection in the same length of time. In the Three to Six Months section we suggest a 'grand tour', but if you've only got half this time, consider half or one-third of the circuit – it's still an excellent trip.

Three to Six Months

With three months you could link all the suggestions outlined earlier, and spend a bit longer in each place or add on a few extra side trips. Some more detailed itineraries for each country are included in the relevant chapters. Not many visitors to Southern Africa will visit every country in the region, and for the lucky few who can get everywhere there are endless options; however, the following outline will be a useful guide.

A grand tour of the entire region would take a minimum three months by car, and four to six months by public transport, although you can of course always trim or add sections to reduce or increase the duration of your trip. This suggested itinerary starts in Johannesburg (Jo'burg), but takes in several other large cities and capitals where you might just as easily start and finish your trip.

Begin by flying to South Africa – you'll probably land at Jo'burg, from where you can head east through Zululand and/or Swaziland (with a visit to the Drakensberg Range) to reach Durban. Alternatively, go south to Bloemfontein and into Lesotho near Maseru (possibly crossing the country to descend Sani Pass, in the southern Drakensberg, to reach KwaZulu-Natal) and then on to Durban. Another option is to fly from your home country direct to Durban.

From Durban or Bloemfontein visit some resorts on the KwaZulu-Natal south coast, or the Eastern Cape and the Wild Coast, including the backpacker-friendly Port St Johns. Then travel along the Garden Route (with possible excursions to the Karoo or Settler Country towns such as Grahamstown) to reach Cape Town.

From Cape Town head north up the Western Cape coast into Namibia. Note, however, that this country is hard to get around by public transport and independent travellers using buses and trains will need considerable persistence to reach the main places of interest. However, rental cars are an option for some, and various tours of the country can be arranged in Windhoek (or at Victoria Falls in neighbouring Zimbabwe). If neither of these options appeal, you may be better off going straight to Botswana or Zimbabwe from South Africa.

If you go to Namibia, the main highlights are conveniently arranged in a south-north line: Fish River Canyon, Lüderitz, Sossusvlei sand dunes, Naukluft Mountains, Skeleton Coast, Kaokoveld and Etosha National Park. From Etosha, travel along the Caprivi Strip to reach Kasane (on the River Zambezi) from where you can either go south to Maun (gateway to the Okavango Delta) or east to Victoria Falls.

If you skipped Namibia, you can go from South Africa (via Mafikeng) to Gaborone (Botswana) and then to Francistown (via Mokolodi Nature Reserve and/or Serowe). From Francistown you can either travel north-west to Maun, from where you can reach the Okavango Delta, or go north-east to Bulawayo in Zimbabwe (with a side trip to Matobo National Park), and then to Victoria Falls.

Victoria Falls is a major regional hub for tourists. Apart from the splendid falls itself, attractions include boat trips, white-water

The Total Eclipse in Southern Africa

A total solar eclipse (when the moon passes in front of the sun, obscuring it all, and casting a shadow on a part of the earth's surface) will occur in Southern Africa on 21 June 2001. The path of totality (the band formed as the shadow moves across the earth) passes through Angola, south of Luanda, through Zambia, north of Mongu and over Lusaka, through the northern tip of Zimbabwe, and through Mozambique north of Beira. The shadow will cross the African mainland between 12.35 and 13.25 GMT/UTC – 2.35 pm to 3.25 pm locally. The actual eclipse at any point along the path of totality between Zambia and Mozambique will last from four to 3½ minutes.

Eclipses of this sort happen less than once per year, but are sometimes in inaccessible areas or obscured by bad weather conditions. The weather in Southern Africa in June is likely to be very good, and may offer one of the best total eclipse viewing opportunities for many years anywhere in the world. Camps and lodges in national parks in the path of totality (including Kafue and Lower Zambezi in Zambia) were reported to be fully booked for the eclipse period by mid-1999.

Another eclipse will pass across Southern Africa (through south-western Zambia, Namibia's Caprivi Strip, north-central Botswana and northern South Africa) early in the morning of 4 December 2002. This eclipse will last for about one minute, and viewing conditions are unlikely to be as good.

For more details on eclipses, and how to see them, check the following Web sites:

http://sunearth.gsf.nasa.gov/eclipse
www.holeinthesky.com

rafting and bungee jumping. From Victoria Falls, travellers without wheels can arrange safaris (from cheap to luxurious) into Namibia, Botswana, Zambia or Zimbabwe.

Onwards from Victoria Falls, you can travel towards Malawi, going through Zambia via Livingstone and Lusaka (from where you can reach Kafue and Lower Zambezi National Parks) and Chipata (jumping-off point for the South Luangwa National Park). Alternatively, head for Malawi through Zimbabwe, via Bulawayo or Kariba, to reach Harare (side-tracking into the Eastern Highlands) and crossing western Mozambique via Tete.

In Malawi, highlights include several wildlife reserves, the lake and Mt Mulanje, and the country can be neatly toured in an elongated loop.

If you flew into South Africa, you might decide to end your tour by flying out of Lilongwe, or you could go to Harare and fly out from there.

Alternatively you could visit Mozambique crossing into the north of that country from Malawi or into the central region from Mutare (Zimbabwe). Many of Mozambique's highlights are on the coast and from Beira you can follow the coast southwards to Maputo, and then into South Africa – via KwaZulu-Natal, Swaziland or Lesotho if you missed them at the start of the trip – and then head for Jo'burg and the long flight home.

PLANNING

Planning for your trip can be almost as exciting as taking it. Just think of all those colourful maps and guidebooks, fancy travel gadgets, exotic vaccinations and relaxing conversations with travel agents!

Planning is important too: it should make your trip more pleasurable, and help you avoid much of the hassle that often goes with arriving in new places.

When to Go

Assuming that most people find rain and cold a downer, the beauty of Southern Africa's climate pattern is that at any time of year there's normally somewhere dry and warm. However, generally speaking, a visit between April and August will be most rewarding weather-wise, although March and September are usually fine, and February or October are still OK in some areas. In the

Winter Rainfall Area, November to March is the most pleasant time to visit. (For more details see Climate in the Facts about the Region chapter.)

Much also depends on your reason for visiting. If you've come for wildlife viewing then May to June is OK, but July and August are better, as the bush is sparse and animals congregate around watering holes, making sightings easier.

In September and October the wildlife viewing is excellent, but heat or humidity can be tiring. During the rainy season from October to February, some parks and reserves close completely.

Beach bums should come in winter, when it's warm and dry on the coast. Summer is often too hot or wet. Surfing on the east coast is reckoned to be best in April and May, and still very good up to July.

Diving and snorkelling are best in June and July on the east coast and in Lake Malawi, and in January and February on the south coast.

Winter is also best for hiking, again because it's dry, as well as cool in the highlands and warm (not hot) in lower areas. However, some aficionados prefer to hike in the summer as there's plenty of water (so no need to carry it), it's never *too* hot in the highlands, and the rain usually only lasts for a few hours per day at the most.

If flowers are your thing, come at the start of the rains as they burst into bloom then: August and September in the Cape and Namaqualand, and around October and November everywhere else.

There are several specific factors to consider in individual countries; all covered in more detail in each of the individual country chapters.

One final point to consider is the South African school holidays, when vast numbers of people head for the coast and national parks of South Africa, and to the parks in neighbouring countries. Hotels and camp sites can fill completely, and prices skyrocket.

For details, see Public Holidays in the Facts for the Visitor section of the South Africa chapter.

What Kind of Trip?

In Southern Africa *any* kind of trip is possible. If time is limited, you can visit for just a few weeks and get a lot out of it. If time is of no consequence, there's enough to do to keep you going for several months at least. If money is no problem, you can live like royalty and enjoy top-end hotels, exclusive island lodges, personally tailored safaris, hunting, game fishing, or fine food and wine. If money is a concern, you can still have a good trip in Southern Africa with the minimum of expenditure.

Generally speaking, the cost of travel here is a bit higher than in East Africa, and noticeably more than most parts of Asia. It's cheaper than Europe, though, and what you get for your money is normally good value.

More ideas are provided in the Suggested Itineraries section earlier.

Maps

Maps of individual countries are listed in the country chapters. The best regional map, without doubt, is Michelin's *Africa Central & South* (Sheet 955). The detail is incredible, given the limitations of scale (1:4,000,000), and the map is regularly updated. It's the kind of map that lingers in bookshops for ages though, so check that you buy a recent version. Even so, you should expect a few discrepancies between the map and reality, particularly with regard to roads, as old tracks get upgraded and once-smooth highways become potholed disasters. In South Africa, Struik publishes *Central & Southern Africa*, which covers a similar area.

For more detailed coverage of specific areas, Lonely Planet has a travel atlas to *Southern Africa*. The Automobile Association (AA) of South Africa also produces a useful sheet of South Africa, plus others covering Botswana and Namibia, available from any AA shop in South Africa.

What to Bring

Clothes With such a variety of things to do in the region, it's hard to generalise about what to bring although, particularly with clothes, you shouldn't carry too much.

Second-hand Clothes

In the last few years, second-hand clothes have become widely available all over Southern Africa, mostly collected by charities in Europe. You can also find factory overruns and items off-loaded by stores because they're out of fashion in the west. The clothes are sold at shops and market stalls or simply laid out on the ground in the street, where they're sometimes called 'bend-over boutiques'. The clothes are good quality and cost a fraction of what they'd be new, so local people can avoid having to pay hard-earned money for fancy gear. But there's a downside: the second-hand imports have wiped out any chance of the poorer countries of Southern Africa (especially Zambia, Malawi and Mozambique) having their own clothing industry. All over the region, market and street tailors who used to run up shirts and trousers from local material are going out of business.

Anything you find yourself without can easily be bought along the way. In cities or large towns, new clothes are comparably priced or cheaper than those in Europe, and in many markets you can find decent second -hand clothes (many originating from European charity stores – see the boxed text 'Second-hand Clothes'). Note that in most places, especially in cities, people dress smartly if they can afford to do so, so it might be worth taking some respectable clothes to avoid being seen as a TWOG (see Glossary). Generally, military-style clothing or baggage isn't recommended, as you may be taken for a soldier – leading to extra questions at border crossings or checkpoints, or being met with a certain reserve by local people.

Equipment To save money, or just to keep out of towns and cities, a tent and camping gear will be useful, and essential if you plan any hiking. Southern Africa has some marvellous camping grounds, although sometimes the price is often only slightly less than a backpackers hostel. Even if you're not into camping, a sleeping bag and sheet liner will be useful in budget hotels, cabins or overnight trains where bedding may be optional.

Absolute essentials include: basic medical kit, mosquito net, water bottle, purifying solution and water filter (all covered in the Health section later in this chapter); torch and batteries; and several passport-sized photos (two or three for each visa application).

Optional items include: camera and film (for more details see Photography & Video later in this chapter); binoculars (for viewing wildlife and birds); small padlock (to secure your pack against opportunistic rifflers); universal drain plug; travel alarm clock; Swiss Army-style knife; clothesline; and sewing kit.

Don't forget a wash kit and towel, although some travellers class these as optional.

Hiking Extras Even in warm months, highland areas get cold at night, so a jacket, a pullover or good sweatshirt, a hat, a pair of gloves and some warm socks are required. A thermal vest (with good warmth-retaining capacity for its size and weight) is also worth considering. A pair of gaiters may prove useful – to fend off thorns and dust, and to offer a thin line of protection against snakes.

A camping stove is essential, as fires are not allowed in many areas. One that runs on petrol will be the least hassle (don't rely on finding refined 'white gas' such as Shellite or Colemanfuel), but methylated spirits for Trangia-type stoves can usually be found in supermarkets, hardware shops or pharmacies. Butane 'gaz' cartridges can be bought in South Africa, but supply is unreliable elsewhere in the region.

Backpack To carry all your gear a backpack (rucksack) is most practical. Carry the sturdiest and best-made pack you can afford, paying special attention to the strength of the zips and straps. Internal-frame packs are easier to handle, but some hikers prefer external-framed packs as they're cooler in hot conditions. Many travellers favour the

Binoculars

If you've got even the slightest interest in watching wild animals (and that's why most visitors come to Southern Africa) you simply *must* bring a pair of binoculars. Some good inexpensive compact models are available, but if you can afford something larger and better you won't regret it. Many people say they don't need binoculars because they only want to look at elephants or lions, and aren't interested in smaller animals or birds – but that's because they never see them properly in the first place. And even watching big animals is better through binoculars. Looking with your bare eyes or down a camera zoom lens just isn't the same. With binoculars you can observe behaviour or pick out markings, and simply get closer to the animals you've come so far to see. It's so much more rewarding than squinting at some vague brown beast in the distance.

Once you become hooked, you may want to invest in a pair of quality optics. For serious birdwatching, consider a spotting scope. With a magnification usually at least twice that of binoculars, they can give stunning views but the drawback is their size – they must be mounted on a tripod for best results.

type of travel-backpack that neatly turns into a 'normal'-looking holdall. This is handy if you don't want to look like a backpacker, and is particularly useful for keeping straps out of the way when your bag is loaded onto planes or bus roof-racks. It's also wise to use plastic bags to protect the contents from moisture and dust.

RESPONSIBLE TOURISM

Tourism is one of the largest industries in the world, and the effects of tourists on destinations can be substantial. These effects can be positive – for example, throughout Southern Africa tourists pay to visit areas with attractive landscape or interesting wildlife, and some of this money reaches local people who then have an incentive to conserve the areas and the animals.

However, tourism can also have a very negative effect. Across East and Southern Africa there are many instances of indigenous people being excluded from their traditional lands to make way for wildlife reserves. As recently as 1997, groups of San have been moved against their will from their traditional homeland in Botswana's Central Kalahari Game Reserve. As always, the authorities' reasons for such moves – to 'protect' the animals or to make the areas more 'suitable' for tourists – conveniently overlook the fact that indigenous people and wildlife have coexisted for thousands of years. They also forget that tourist expectations of 'untouched' wilderness, with people excluded (local people that is – visitors are of course OK), are initially created by false pictures peddled by holiday companies and TV nature shows.

In popular tourist areas, the sheer numbers of visitors can sometimes put a strain on the local environment. It's ironic that although tourism frequently relies on natural resources such as healthy wildlife populations, pristine landscapes or rich cultural traditions, tourists and tour companies quite often do little to sustain them.

On your own trip through Southern Africa, you can make a difference by deciding where you want to spend your money. If you want to support tour companies with a good environmental record, you have to look beyond vague 'ecofriendly' claims and ask what they are really doing to protect or support the environment (and that includes local people too).

But the effects of tourism are not just financial. It is also important for visitors to behave in a manner that limits their impact on the natural environment and the local inhabitants. To be a responsible tourist you have to question some of your own actions and those of your tour companies. You also have to look pretty closely at the actions of governments, both local and around the world. Being a responsible tourist doesn't mean you have to get depressed and spoil your holiday. In fact, by asking a few questions and getting a deeper insight, it can make your trip even more rewarding.

Ivory Souvenirs

Ivory carvings sold in tourist shops in Zimbabwe and South Africa will come with a certificate, which may or may not be genuine, stating that they came from a legally killed elephant. It is not illegal to buy these souvenirs, but it *is* currently illegal to carry ivory products into countries that are signatories to the CITES agreement – virtually all western countries. In other words you won't be allowed to take your ivory souvenir back home. Also consider the environmental impact of a purchase. By buying ivory and other wildlife products – even certified items – you bolster the market and this may indirectly support the illicit trade in endangered animals.

For further information on responsible tourism, see under Ecology & Environment in the Facts about the Region chapter.

Guidelines for Responsible Tourism

Here are some guidelines for travellers who wish to minimise negative impacts on the countries they visit:

- Save precious natural resources. Try not to waste water. Switch off lights and air-con when you go out. Avoid establishments that clearly consume limited resources such as water and electricity at the expense of local residents.
- Support local enterprise. Use locally owned hotels and restaurants. Employ local guides. Support craft workers by buying locally made souvenirs, but avoid items made from natural material – wood, skin, ivory etc – unless they come from a sustainable source (although this is difficult to check).
- Recognise land rights. Indigenous peoples' ownership of land is recognised by international law and this should be acknowledged irrespective of whether the national government applies the law or not. (Governments are among the principle violators of tribal rights.) When in tribal lands, tourists should behave as they would on private lands at home.
- Ask before taking close-up photographs of people. Don't worry if you don't speak the language. A smile and gesture will be understood and appreciated.
- Please don't give money, sweets and pens to children, as it encourages begging and demeans the child. A donation to a recognised project – a health centre or school – is a more constructive and meaningful way to help.
- Respect for local etiquette earns you respect. Politeness is a virtue in all parts of the world, but remember that different people have different ideas about what's polite. In many places, tight-fitting, revealing shorts or skimpy tops is insensitive to local feelings. Loose lightweight clothing is preferable. Similarly, public displays of affection are often culturally inappropriate.
- Learn something about the history and current affairs of a country which will help you understand the idiosyncrasies of its people, and help prevent misunderstanding and frustration.
- Be patient, friendly and sensitive. Remember that you are a guest.

These guidelines are based on those issued by the British organisation Tourism Concern (☎ 020-7753 3330, ⓔ tourconcern@gn.apc.org), Stapleton House, 277-281 Holloway Rd, London N7 8HN. You can support its work by becoming a member – for more information see its Web site: www.tourismconcern.org.uk

Another UK-based body is Action for Southern Africa (☎ 020-7833 3133, ⓔ actsa@geo2.poptel.org.uk), which campaigns for (among other things) sustainable 'people-first' tourism throughout the region.

In the USA, the Rethinking Tourism Project (☎/fax 651-644-9984, ⓔ RTProject@aol.com), PO Box 581938, Minneapolis, MN 55458, is a similar organisation which aims to preserve and protect local cultures and lands.

VISAS & DOCUMENTS

Passport

You need a valid passport to enter every country covered in this book. To fit in visas and border stamps, your passport should have at least one empty page per country you intend to visit, although two per country would be better. If your passport is close to filling, get a new one – but apply for it long in advance. You should also change your passport if it's near the end of its life (some officials prefer passports that expire at least three months after your trip ends),

Who Needs a Visa?

Citizens of the following countries need visas (indicated by ✓) to enter these countries in Southern Africa:

	UK	Ireland	Australia	New Zealand	USA	Canada	France	Germany
Botswana	-	-	-	-	-	-	-	-
Lesotho	-	-	-	-	-	-	-	-
Malawi	-	-	-	-	-	-	✓	-
Mozambique	✓	✓	✓	✓	✓	✓	✓	✓
Namibia	-	-	-	-	-	-	-	-
South Africa	-	-	-	-	-	-	-	-
Swaziland	-	-	-	-	-	-	-	-
Zambia	✓	-	✓	✓	✓	✓	✓	✓
Zimbabwe	-	-	✓	✓	✓	✓	-	✓

or if it has stamps that might be considered suspect (eg, Libya).

Visas

Visa requirements change according to your nationality. More details about who needs what are given in the individual country chapters, and on Lonely Planet's Web site (www.lonelyplanet.com) – which also has links to other visa sites – but the table 'Who Needs a Visa?' will give you the basics.

Visas are normally available from embassies, high commissions or consulates, and should be obtained before arrival in a country, as they are rarely issued at land border crossings. Visas are sometimes available at airports, but if you're flying from outside Africa, airlines won't let you board without a visa anyway.

If you are only visiting one or two countries, you might choose to get your visas in your home country before you leave. If you're on a longer trip, you can get them as you go along – this gives you more flexibility, but does require careful planning as not all countries of the region have embassies in neighbouring countries. If you need to get visas for several countries before you leave home, or if there's no embassy in your home country, consider using a visa agency (a good travel agency can recommend one) – price and quality varies, so shop around.

Some visas are valid for a certain period from when they are issued, so you must enter the country pretty soon after getting the visa. For other visas you have to say when you plan to enter the country and get there within a month of that date. Usually a fee is payable, from a few dollars up to US$50 or more. Prices may also vary according to *where* you buy the visa. Some embassies issue multiple-entry visas, usually for an extra cost.

When applying for a visa you may have to show proof that you intend to leave the country (eg, an air ticket) or that you have enough funds to support yourself during your visit. Generally speaking, embassies in Europe or North America are more strict about this than those in African countries.

For nearly every visa application, you will need two or three passport photos. If you plan on getting several visas during your trip, take a good supply of photos.

A particular anomaly in many Southern African countries is that Commonwealth

International Driving Permit

An International Driving Permit (IDP) is easily and cheaply issued by your national motoring association, and is very useful if you're driving in countries where your own licence might not be recognised (officially or unofficially). It has the added advantage of being written in several languages, with a photo and lots of stamps, so it looks more impressive when presented to car rental clerks or police officers at roadblocks.

citizens of Asian descent sometimes need visas that are not required by their black or white compatriots.

Regulations are always liable to change, so it's best to check at the relevant embassy in your home country before you leave (or in a neighbouring country as you're travelling) otherwise you might arrive at the airport or border without a visa only to find that you now need one.

Travel Insurance

A travel insurance policy to cover theft, loss and medical problems is a good idea. There is a wide variety of policies available, so shop around carefully and always read the small print. Some policies specifically exclude 'dangerous activities', which can include scuba diving, motorcycling, even trekking.

Most hospitals in Africa are not free, and the good ones are not cheap. You may prefer a policy that pays doctors or hospitals directly rather than you having to pay on the spot and claim later. If you do have to claim later, ensure you keep all documentation. Some policies ask you to call (reverse charges) a centre in your home country where an immediate assessment of your problem is made.

It is important to ensure that the policy covers ambulances (including air ambulance) and emergency flights home.

Other Documents

Other vital documents include: a vaccination certificate to show you've been jabbed for yellow fever, and possibly some other diseases (for details see the Health section later in this chapter); driving licence and International Driving Permit (if you intend hiring a car, see the boxed text 'International Driving Permit' earlier); and a membership card for a youth hostels association (which gets you cheap accommodation in similarly affiliated hostels). A student or youth identity card (eg, the new credit card-style ISIC) is sometimes good for discounts on flights and other services.

Copies

Photocopies of all your important documents, plus air tickets and credit cards, will help speed up replacement if they are lost or stolen. Keep these and a list of travellers cheque numbers separate from other valuables, or leave copies with someone at home so they can be faxed to you in a dire emergency.

EMBASSIES & CONSULATES

If you're on a long trip or have a flexible itinerary, you can get your visas from embassies as you go along. Most of the Southern African countries covered in this book have embassies in neighbouring countries, and these are listed in the country chapters.

Embassies of most travellers' 'home' countries (Australia, UK, USA etc) in Southern Africa, are listed in the individual country chapters. Where 'home' countries have no embassy, often a consul is appointed, who is not a full time diplomat but has certain diplomatic responsibilities. There are not many embassies of Australia, Canada and New Zealand in Southern Africa, but in a genuine emergency travellers from these countries can contact the Consular Assistant at the nearest British High Commission for contact details of their own consul.

Also listed in country chapters are embassies of Southern African countries in 'home' countries. Readers from countries not listed should use the phone directory of their own capital city to check which Southern African countries are represented. (The term 'embassy' includes consulates and high commissions.)

MONEY

Details on specific currencies and places to exchange money are given in the individual country chapters.

Throughout most of the regional chapters and in countries where inflation is high, we have quoted prices in US dollars (US$) as these are more likely to remain stable; the South African rand (R) is also used in the chapters on South Africa and some of its neighbouring countries.

Exchanging Money

You can exchange money into local currency at banks and foreign exchange (forex)

Your Own Embassy

It's important to realise what your own embassy – the embassy of the country of which you are a citizen – can and can't do to help you if you get into trouble while travelling.

Generally speaking, it won't be much help in emergencies if the trouble is remotely your own fault. Remember that you are bound by the laws of the country you are in. Your embassy will not be sympathetic if you end up in jail after committing a crime locally, even if such actions are legal in your own country.

In genuine emergencies you might get some assistance, but only if other channels have been exhausted. For example, if you need to get home urgently, a free ticket is exceedingly unlikely – the embassy would expect you to have travel insurance. If you have all your money and documents stolen, it might assist with getting a new passport, but a loan for onward travel is out of the question.

Some embassies used to keep letters for travellers or have a small reading room with home newspapers, but these days the mail-holding service has usually been stopped and even the newspapers are out of date.

bureaus – normally in capital cities and tourist areas, but in some countries in provincial towns as well. The most readily recognised international currency, accepted all over Southern Africa, is the US dollar, and it is well worth carrying at least half of your money in this currency. Other currencies that are also usually accepted include UK pounds and German marks. In capital cities of some countries you can change other major currencies (eg, Australian or Canadian dollars), but anywhere else they are not accepted or you get a poor rate. The South African rand is also widely recognised and easy to deal with all over the region, but unless you're from South Africa it's not worth changing your own currency into rand to then change again into kwacha, pula or whatever.

Cash & Travellers Cheques Most travellers carry their money as a mix of cash and travellers cheques. Cash is quicker to deal with and gets better rates, but cannot be replaced; however, if your travellers cheques are lost or stolen you get a refund. When you buy your travellers cheques make sure you know what to do if the worse happens – most companies give you a 24-hour international phone number to contact.

It's worth carrying a mix of high and low denomination notes/bills and travellers cheques.

So, if you're about to leave a country, you can change for just a few days without having loads of spare cash to get rid of. Note that due to counterfeiting, old US$100 bills are not accepted at places that don't have a light machine for checking watermarks.

When exchanging travellers cheques, most banks also check the original purchase receipt (the papers you're normally supposed to keep separate, not the simple till receipt), so make sure you have this too.

ATMs Most credit and debit cards can be used in automatic teller machines (ATMs). These machines are found in all cities, large towns and main airports in South Africa and Namibia.

In countries such as Botswana and Zimbabwe there are ATMs in cities and major towns. In poorer countries such as Zambia and Malawi, ATMs are located in capital cities only, and even then are often not reliable.

Bank Charges & Commissions

When you're exchanging money, charges and commissions vary between banks and bureaus. The charge may be a flat fee (around US$2) or a commission (usually between 1 and 2%), and sometimes you have to pay a charge *and* a commission. At the other end of the scale there may be no charge or commission at all. But exchange rates can differ between banks, so it's important to check these too. The bureau without charges may offer a poor rate, while the bank with the higher commission may also offer a higher rate so you could still be better off. The moral of the tale is – shop around.

Some card companies don't charge a fee for using your card to get local cash from an ATM, wherever you are on the globe, and also use very fair exchange rates, which can make them cheaper than travellers cheques. Check this out with your bank.

Credit & Debit Cards You can use a credit card to pay for goods in various parts of Southern Africa. You can also use it to draw cash – either from an ATM (although in some countries this is not reliable) or from a bank (more reliable, although the process can take several hours). Contact your own card company to see which banks in which countries accept your card. You'll also need to ask your bank or card company about the charges, and arrange a way to pay off your card bills if you're travelling for more than a month or so.

Debit cards can be used to pay for goods or to draw cash with increasing ease around Southern Africa. The advantage of these is there's no bill to pay off (if you have the money in your account of course), so they are more suited for longer travels. Again, see your bank about where the card can be used.

Whatever card you use, it's not wise to rely totally on plastic, as computer or telephone breakdowns can leave you stranded. Always have some cash or travellers cheques as back-up.

International Transfers If you think your finances may need topping up while you're travelling in Southern Africa, ask your bank about international bank-to-bank transfers. This is usually a time-consuming, complicated and expensive business, especially outside the major capitals, although if you're

The Fine Art of Bargaining

In some African countries, bargaining over prices – often for market goods – is a way of life. Visitors often have difficulty with this idea, and are used to things having a fixed value, whereas in Africa commodities are considered worth whatever their seller can get for them. It really is no different to the concept of an auction and should be treated as one more aspect of travel in Southern Africa.

Basics In markets selling basic items such as fruit and vegetables *some* sellers will invariably put their asking price high when they see you as a wealthy foreigner. If you pay this – whether out of ignorance or guilt about how much you have compared to locals – you may be considered foolish, but you'll also be doing fellow travellers a disservice by creating the impression that all foreigners are willing to pay any price named! You may also harm the local economy: by paying high prices you put some items out of the locals' reach. And who can blame the sellers – why sell something to a local when foreigners will pay twice as much? So in cases like this you may need to bargain over the price.

Having said that, many sellers will quote you the same price that locals pay, particularly away from cities or tourist areas. It is very important not to go around expecting *everybody* to charge high. It helps of course to know the price of things. After the first few days in a country (when you'll inevitably pay over the odds a few times) you'll soon get to learn the standard prices for basic items. Remember, though, that prices can change depending on where you buy. For example, a soft drink in a city may be one third of the price you'll pay in a remote rural area, where transport costs have to be paid for. Conversely, fruit and vegetables are cheaper in the areas where they're actually grown.

Souvenirs At craft and curio stalls, where items are specifically for tourists, it's a very different story: bargaining is very much expected. The vendor's aim is to identify the highest price you're willing to pay. Your aim is to find the price below which the vendor will not sell. People have all sorts of formulae for working out what this should be, but there are no hard and fast rules. Some vendors may initially ask a price four (or more) times higher than what they're prepared to accept, al-

travelling for a long time it can save the worry (and sheer bulk) of carrying large wads of notes and cheques. It's probably better to consider the Western Union Money Transfer system, available in most countries worldwide, and set up for quick long-distance transfers.

Black Market In various parts of the world, artificially fixed exchange rates in the bank mean you can get more local money for your hard currency by changing outside, on the so-called black market. This is illegal, morally questionable and sometimes dangerous. However, in Southern Africa, it's hardly an issue: due to currency deregulation all over the region, exchange rates are not fixed. Thus, banks and foreign exchange bureaus can offer genuine rates, and the black market has virtually disappeared. You may be offered 5 or 10% more than bank or bureau rates by shady-looking characters on the street but it's very likely to be a set-up. If they offer more than 10% you *know* it's a set-up.

Moneychangers If the banks and foreign exchange bureaus are closed, you may be able to exchange money at top-end hotels or tour companies, but rates can be lousy. Another option is to ask discreetly at a shop selling imported items – saying 'The banks are closed, do you know anyone who can help me...?' is better than 'Do you want to change money?'.

At most border crossings where there is no bank, unofficial moneychangers are tolerated by the authorities. It's always important to be alert though, as these guys can pull all sorts of stunts with bad exchange rates or folded notes.

The Fine Art of Bargaining

though it's usually lower than this. Decide what you want to pay or what others have told you they've paid; your first offer should be about half this. At this stage, the vendor may laugh or feign outrage, while you plead abject poverty. The vendor's price then starts to drop from the original quote to a more realistic level. When it does, you begin making better offers until you arrive at a mutually agreeable price.

And that's the crux – *mutually agreeable*. You hear travellers all the time moaning about how they got 'overcharged' by souvenir sellers. When things have no fixed price, nobody really gets overcharged. If you don't like the price, it's simple: don't pay it.

Some people prefer to conduct their bargaining in a stern manner, but the best results seem to come from a friendly and spirited exchange. There's no reason to lose your temper when bargaining. If the effort seems a waste of time, politely take your leave. Sometimes sellers will call you back. Very few will pass up the chance of making a sale, however thin the profit.

If sellers won't come down to a price you feel is fair (or you simply can't afford), it either means he really isn't making any profit, or that if you don't pay his prices, he knows somebody else will. Remember the sellers are under no more obligation to sell to you than you are to buy from them. You can go elsewhere, or (if you really want the item) accept the price. This is the raw edge of capitalism!

Security

To keep your money and other valuables (such as passport and air ticket) safe from pickpockets, the best place is out of sight under a shirt or skirt, or inside your trousers. You can make or buy a pouch that goes around your neck or waist. Some travellers go for 'invisible pockets', moneybelts and other imaginative devices.

Costs

Very generally speaking, prices of things in Southern Africa are around 50 to 75% of what they are in Europe, Australasia or North America, especially when you get outside South Africa. Obviously there are exceptions: locally produced items (including food and beer) may be much cheaper, while imported items may be twice what they cost in the west.

Accommodation costs range from less than US$1 per night for basic local resthouses, US$3 to US$10 for camping, US$5 for hostel dorms, US$25 to US$50 for mid-range hotels, and up to US$100 or US$200 for top-end establishments. Couples can save on accommodation costs, as double rooms are cheaper than two singles. Often couples can share a single.

Transport options are equally varied: you can hitch for free or go by chartered plane at something like US$10 per minute. Most people, however, go by bus or train and these are relatively cheap compared to western prices.

Taking all these aspects into account, hardened shoestring travellers could get by on US$10 per day (or even less) for accommodation, food and transport, although US$15 gives you more options. For a bit more comfort, US$20 to US$25 per day is a reasonable budget for day-to-day living expenses. If you plan to stay in mid-range hotels, eat well and travel in comfort wherever possible, you're looking at around US$50 per day or more.

On top of these basic costs, you should also take into account extra items such as visa fees and national park entrance charges, plus of course the cost of any tours or activities (such as a wildlife safari or white-water rafting). Park fees can be relatively high in some countries, and very low in others, and are a particularly important aspect to consider if you are travelling on a tight budget.

More details of costs in individual countries are given in the relevant chapters.

Tipping

Tipping can a problem in Southern Africa because there are few clear rules applicable to all people. Anyone staying in a fancy hotel would be expected to tip porters and other staff, but there would not be the same expectation from a backpacker in a cheap hotel.

If service has been good, a tip is usually expected from diners (both locals and foreigners) at the better restaurants; around 10% is normal. But check the bill closely to see if service is included. It frequently is – although you're not obliged to pay it if service has been bad. At the more basic restaurants and eating houses no tipping is expected from anyone. There is a grey area between these two classes of restaurants, where tipping is rarely expected from locals but may be expected of foreigners. Even the wealthier Africans will sometimes tip at the smaller restaurants, not so much because it's expected but because it's a show of status.

In privately hired taxis, tipping is not the rule among locals, but drivers expect well-heeled travellers to tip about 10%. In bigger cities where there are numerous foreigners, taxi drivers may still hope for a small tip, even from backpackers.

POST & COMMUNICATIONS

Post & Telephone

Post and telephone/fax services are good in most parts of South Africa and Namibia, pretty good in Botswana and Swaziland, and range from OK to bad in Zimbabwe, Mozambique, Malawi, Lesotho and Zambia. In all these countries the service to/from towns and cities tends to be more reliable. In rural areas the service can range from slow to nonexistent. It definitely pays to plan where you make your calls or send

Telephone Country Codes

To dial a number in another country, you need to precede it with the relevant country code. Each country code has to be preceded by the international access code – 00, 09, 010 or something similar.

After dialling the access code and the country code, drop the first zero of the city code of the place you're calling.

Country	Code	Country	Code	Country	Code
Angola	☎ 244	Italy	☎ 39	South Africa	☎ 27
Australia	☎ 61	Japan	☎ 81	Spain	☎ 34
Belgium	☎ 32	Kenya	☎ 254	Swaziland	☎ 268
Botswana	☎ 267	Lesotho	☎ 266	Sweden	☎ 46
Canada	☎ 1	Malawi	☎ 265	Tanzania	☎ 255
Denmark	☎ 45	Mozambique	☎ 258	UK	☎ 44
France	☎ 33	Namibia	☎ 264	USA	☎ 1
Germany	☎ 49	Netherlands	☎ 31	Zambia	☎ 260
Ireland	☎ 353	New Zealand	☎ 64	Zimbabwe	☎ 263

your mail. For more specific details, see the individual country chapters.

If you need to receive mail, the poste restante service has letters sent to a main post office, usually in a capital city, where they are held for you to collect. Letters should be addressed clearly with your family name in capitals, to Poste Restante, General Post Office, Lusaka, Zambia (or wherever). To collect your mail, you need your passport, and may have to pay a small fee. Letters sometimes take a few weeks to work through the system, so have them sent to a place where you're going to be for a while.

Some hotels and tour companies operate a mail-holding service, and American Express customers can have mail sent to AmEx offices.

eKno Communication Card

Lonely Planet's eKno Communication Card is aimed specifically at travellers and provides cheap international calls, a range of messaging services and free email – for local calls, you're usually better off with a local card. The eKno card does not yet cover all the countries in this book, though new countries are being added all the time; check the Web site for updates. As we go to print, the only Southern African country from which you can access the eKno service is South Africa (see that chapter for details on how to join).

Email & Internet Access

Most capital cities (and some large towns) in the region have at least one Internet outlet. Several hotels and backpackers hostels also offer this service. You can send and receive email using their address, or check your own Web-based email. Hourly rates vary from a few cents to several dollars per hour, so it pays to shop around. Note that in some countries telephone technology has not kept up with computer technology, and simply getting your mail can sometimes be frustratingly slow.

INTERNET RESOURCES

The World Wide Web is a rich resource for travellers. You can research your trip, hunt down bargain air fares, book hotels, check on weather conditions or chat with locals and other travellers about the best places to visit (or avoid!).

There's no better place to start your Web explorations than the Lonely Planet Web site (www.lonelyplanet.com). Here you'll find succinct summaries on travelling to most places on earth, postcards from other travellers and the Thorn Tree notice board, where you can ask questions before you go or dispense advice when you get back. You can also find travel news and updates to many of our most popular guidebooks, and the subWWWay section links you to useful travel resources elsewhere on the Web.

Other useful Web sites include:

Africa Insites A very good brochure-style site, concentrating on tourism in Southern Africa, with good links to other relevant sites.
www.africa-insites.com

AfricaNet A wide-ranging site on many different aspects of Africa, including tourism.
www.africanet.com

African Travel & Tourism Association This site lists destinations, hotels and tour operators, with links to members' individual sites.
www.goafrica.org

Backpacker Africa A site for backpackers, with a Southern Africa bias and a list of around 400 travel-related companies, a live booking system and useful links to other sites.
www.backpackafrica.com

Getaway Today The site of *Getaway* magazine; includes a Travellers Talk forum for up-to-date advice on hotels, road conditions etc, as well as ads for destinations and tour companies.
www.getawaytoday.com

iafrica A South African-dominated site, which includes travel, news and lifestyle sections, plus links to sites on other Southern African countries.
www.iafrica.com

Just Backpacking Aimed at budget travellers in East and Southern Africa, although South Africa-biased; includes hostel lists, Internet cafe details, news, forums and links to other relevant sites.
www.backpacking.co.za

BOOKS

This section lists publications covering most of Southern Africa. Books on individual countries are listed in the relevant country chapters. Many books with 'Southern Africa' in their title are in fact heavily biased towards South Africa; these are listed in that chapter.

Note that due to the fact that books may have different publishers in different countries, and that a hardcover rarity in one country may be a readily available paperback in another, we have not included publishers in this list (unless relevant). In any case, bookshops and libraries search by title or author.

Lonely Planet

If you're looking for more in-depth coverage, Lonely Planet also publishes *South Africa, Lesotho & Swaziland* (4th edition), *Zimbabwe, Botswana & Namibia* (3rd edition) and *Mozambique* (1st edition). A new guide to Malawi will be published in early 2001. Lonely Planet also publishes a companion travel atlas to Southern Africa. Other titles include:

East Africa This is a good guide for onward travel and includes Tanzania, Uganda, Rwanda, Burundi and Kenya.

Trekking in East Africa This trekking guide covers a wide range of routes and also has a good section on hikes and long-distance walks in Malawi.

Guidebooks

Adventure Motorbiking Handbook by Chris Scott. Pan-continental motorcyclists should grip this book, which contains lots of information on riding through Africa.

Africa by Road by Bob Swain & Paula Snyder. A useful book if you're coming to Southern Africa overland in your own vehicle. The authors have done their ground work; half the book is no-nonsense advice on everything from paperwork and supplies to driving techniques, while the other half is a complete country-by-country rundown.

Complete Guide to Hiking Trails in Southern Africa by Jaynee Levy. If walking is more your game, this mammoth book has excellent coverage of the region. It describes more than 350 trails in South Africa, plus another 50 or so in Namibia, Botswana, Swaziland, Lesotho, Zimbabwe and Malawi, from short nature strolls to major expeditions in wild areas. The book provides all the practical details you need (where to book, what gear is required etc), plus wildlife and climate information and a list of detailed publications. There are colour maps and photos throughout, and major hikes get a route description too.

Illustrated Guide to Southern Africa (Readers Digest) and ***Secret Southern Africa*** (AA of South Africa) are large-format books full of photos, maps and descriptions for touring the region. Both books are recommended if you plan to drive in Southern Africa.

Sahara Overland by Chris Scott. Covers the northern part of the route travelling overland into Southern Africa (see *Africa by Road* earlier), and contains 600 pages of information, including when and where to go, vehicles, routes, history, people and culture.

Travel

Southern Africa has been fairly well covered by travel writers. Titles covering a single country are listed under Books in the individual country chapters, but those with a regional preference include the following:

The Electronic Elephant by Dan Jacobson. This book describes a journey through South Africa, Botswana and Zimbabwe. It combines frequently depressing contemporary encounters with fascinating historical flashbacks.

In Quest of Livingstone by Colum Wilson & Aisling Irwin. This is a new book worth looking out for about two British travellers who followed the footsteps of the great explorer through Tanzania and Zambia on mountain bikes. It combines contemporary observations with flashbacks to Livingstone's own journals. Their choice of transport may not have been ideal, and it was an incredibly difficult trip, but it was only through their discomfort that the authors got close to understanding Livingstone's own levels of suffering and doggedness.

South from the Limpopo by Dervla Murphy. In this sequel to *The Ukimwi Road* (described below), the author's journey continues through South Africa.

The Ukimwi Road by Dervla Murphy. In this book the famously eccentric 60-year-old Irish cyclist goes from Kenya to Malawi, Zambia and Zimbabwe, along the way downing numerous beers and observing life at a human scale – most notably the harrowing affects of AIDS.

History & Politics

Africa by Phyllis Martin and Patrick O'Meara. This is the nearest you'll get to a pocket library, with scholarly but accessible essays on a wide range of subjects including history, religion, colonialism, sociology, art, popular culture, law, literature, politics, economics and the development crisis.

Africa: Dispatches from a Fragile Continent by Blaine Harden. Provocative and pessimistic reading on several topics such as the failure of African political leadership (the 'Big Man' syndrome), although the author believes that positive African values still endure and make the continent a joy.

An Atlas of World Affairs by Andrew Boyd. Provides a concise rundown of contemporary history, with a good section on Southern Africa.

Banana Sunday – Datelines from Africa by Chris Munion. Contains humorous accounts of this journalist's coverage of various African wars.

Beggar Your Neighbours by Joseph Hanlon. Informative and accessible, this book discusses South Africa's policies towards other states in the region in the 1980s, which normally boiled down to encouraging economic dependence or promoting destabilisation.

Blood on the Tracks by Miles Bredin. The book chronicles an essentially hopeless journey between Angola and Mozambique. It's a tale of war, bureaucracy, corruption and inefficiency neatly outlining the problems faced by modern Africa.

Books on Birds

The classic field-guides to the region are *Roberts' Birds of South Africa* by GR McLachlan & GR Liversidge, and KB Newman's *Birds of Southern Africa* (popularly known simply as *Roberts'* and *Newman's*). Note, though, that these bird guides, and most other Southern African natural history field-guides, cover only the region south of the River Zambezi – with a few notable exceptions.

A Fieldguide to Zambian Birds not found in Southern Africa by Dylan Aspinwall & Carl Beel. This book describes all the birds of Zambia that are not already listed in the main *Roberts'* guide.

The Illustrated Guide to the Birds of Southern Africa by Ian Sinclar, Phil Hockey & Warwick Tarboton. An exhaustive, superbly illustrated book covering all species found in the region; indispensable for any serious birder and one of the finest field guides you're likely to find anywhere.

Newman's Birds of Malawi by KB Newman. This book covers all the species found in Malawi which are not already listed in the larger *Newman's* book, and is an invaluable supplement to the main guide.

Top Birding Spots in Southern Africa by Hugh Chittenden. This book provides a good introduction to birdwatching sites across the region and the species likely to be seen.

Where to Watch Birds in Southern Africa by A Berruti & JC Sinclair. An excellent introduction for keen birders.

The Exploration of Africa by Anne Hugon. A fascinating and beautifully illustrated little book, with good coverage on the journeys of Livingstone et al in Southern Africa.

Fishing in Africa by Andrew Buckoke. A depressing exposé of chaos, corruption and violence across the continent, enlightened only when the author seeks out secret angling spots – and real people – off the beaten track.

History of Southern Africa by JD Omer-Cooper (published by James Currey). Covers mainly South Africa, but mentions other countries in the region, from earliest human times to the present.

The History of Southern Africa by Kevin Shillington. This book objectively and sensitively discusses Botswana, Namibia, South Africa, Lesotho and Swaziland in textbook form, covering prehistory plus African and colonial history.

Introduction to the History of Central Africa – Zambia, Malawi, and Zimbabwe by AJ Wills (Oxford University Press). The title is misleading – this 500-page work is comprehensive and generally considered the best on the region.

Masters of Illusion – The World Bank and the Poverty of Nations by Catherine Caufield. This book discusses the influence that the global development lending agency has had on poor countries around the world. The book's observations – that the social and environmental effects of projects are inadequately analysed – are shocking, while the conclusions – that despite loans totalling billions of US dollars the people of the Third Word are worse off now than before – calls the whole institution seriously into question.

Field Guides

Many field guides regard Southern Africa's northern limits as the Kunene, Okavango and Zambezi Rivers and do not cover Zambia, Malawi or northern Mozambique, even though many of the species found south of the Zambezi also occur to the north. Which book you get depends on where you travel and how serious a naturalist you are.

Field Guide to Mammals of Africa by Haltenorth & Diller. Has wide coverage of the topic.

Field Guide to the Mammals of Southern Africa by Chris & Tilde Stuart. This is a comprehensive and well-illustrated book. The Stuarts have also written *Southern, Central & East African Mammals*, a handy pocket guide, and *Tracks & Signs of Southern & East African Wildlife*.

Flowers of Southern Africa by Auriol Batten is highly recommended if you're keen on vegetation – it's a large-format book, more celebration than field guide, illustrated with superb and colourful paintings.

The Kingdom Field Guide to African Mammals by Jonathan Kingdon. Covers more than 1000 species (with colour pictures and maps throughout), discussing ecology, evolutionary relationships and conservation status as well as the more usual notes on identification and distribution.

Land Mammals of Southern Africa by R Smithers. This book gives a rundown of 200 frequently observed species.

The Safari Companion by Richard Estes. A marvellous book for understanding animals – their courtship rituals, territorial displays etc.

Southern African Trees – A Photographic Guide by Piet van Wyk. A more portable work than *Trees of Southern Africa* (following) and perfectly adequate for amateurs.

Trees of Southern Africa by Keith Coates Palgrave. A classic volume, providing the most thorough coverage of the region's arboreal richness, with colour illustrations.

To learn more about the region's less fashionable wildlife, try *Complete Guide to Freshwater Fishes of Southern Africa* by Paul Skelton, *Snakes and Other Reptiles of Southern Africa* by Bill Branch and *Butterflies of Southern Africa* by Ivor Migdoll.

Literature

Specific works of literature by local authors are listed under Arts. Novels by other authors with local settings are listed under Books in the individual country chapters.

Being There, edited by Robin Malan. A good introductory collection of short stories from Southern African authors written since 1960.

The Heinemann Book of African Poetry in English, edited by A Maja-Pearce. Includes poetry by writers from several African countries including Zimbabwe and South Africa.

The Penguin Book of Modern African Poetry, edited by Moore & Beier. Another recommended poetry anthology.

The Penguin Book of Southern African Stories, edited by Stephen Gray. This literary anthology collates stories (some of which are thousands of years old) from around the region, deliberately not classified by original language to show the

Coffee-table Books

Southern Africa has inspired the production of numerous large-format 'coffee-table' books. Some contain nearly all colour pictures with brief captions, while others combine photos with informative text. Whatever their format, they make good introductory reading before you go, or splendid souvenirs after your visit. Most are available in good bookshops all over Southern Africa.

African Wildlife in Art, published by Clive Holloway Books. A collection of paintings and drawings celebrating the region's fauna.

Southern Africa's Spectacular World of Wildlife, published by Reader's Digest. Another celebration of wildlife, full of top-quality photos.

Spirit of the Zambezi by Jeff & Veronica Sutchbury. A very personalised account of the Sutchburys' pioneering work in tourism and wildlife conservation. Jeff died before the book was completed, and his stunning photos are a fitting memorial to him.

Zambezi – River of Africa by Mike Coppinger & Jumbo Williams. A great book with skilful photography and intelligent text.

Zambezi – River of the Gods by Jan & Fiona Teede. Combining text, drawings and photographs, this is an interesting and attractive book.

similarities and common threads in various literary traditions.

Traveller's Literary Companion – Africa, edited by Oona Strathern (published by In-Print). A truly excellent book, containing more than 250 prose and poetry extracts from all over Africa, with an introduction to the writing of each country, plus a list of 'literary landmarks' – real features that appear in novels written about the country.

General

Images of Power by D Lewis-Williams & T Dowson. A fascinating and deep study of the art of the San people, utilising modern scientific techniques and rediscovered records of discussions between the San and early European settlers.

At the Hand of Man by Raymond Bonner. This book discusses conservation issues and the destruction of African wildlife, holding that conservation will only work if African people see real benefits themselves.

Kakuli by Norman Carr. This book covers the now popular theme of the link between wildlife conservation and the benefits to local people, which the author first raised more than 30 years ago. It is also a personal account of life in the bush, working with animals, Africans and tourists.

The Last Elephant by Jeremy Gavron. The conservation of elephants has come to symbolise wider issues, and this book covers this very well, in particular outlining current debates on the ivory trade.

To Save an Elephant by Allan Thornton & Dave Currey. A gripping tale of undercover work for the Environmental Investigation Agency.

Zambezi – Journey of a River by Michael Main. A marvellous and immensely readable combination of history, geography, geology, anthropology, careful observation, humour, rumour and myth, following the River Zambezi through Zambia, Angola, Zimbabwe and Mozambique, with side-tracks into Malawi.

NEWSPAPERS & MAGAZINES

There is no newspaper covering the entire Southern African region, although several newspapers are available in each country (listed in the relevant country chapters), and some of these have good coverage of events in neighbouring states. News magazines that cover the continent include *Africa Now*, *Africa Today*, *Business Africa* and the BBC's *Focus on Africa*. These are available from newsagents in South Africa, and from bookshops in capital cities in other countries.

Getaway magazine covers travel in Southern Africa, with articles ranging from epic 4WD trips in Namibia or Zambia through active and not-so-active package tours of Zimbabwe or Malawi, to reviews of hotels and timeshare developments in South Africa. The advertisement section is a very useful source of ideas for places to go and things to do. Outdoor adventure buffs will like *Out There* with articles on the African wilds and from around the world. *Africa*

Environment & Wildlife is published six times a year and covers a wide range of environmental and conservation issues, mostly on Southern Africa, with quality and even-handedness, plus excellent photography.

Also look out for *Jungle*, which is a backpackers' freebie mag, full of information about fun places to visit, new hostels, special events, tours and cheap transport deals all over Southern Africa. You can find it at hostels, information centres and other places where budget travellers lurk.

PHOTOGRAPHY & VIDEO

Film & Equipment

In South Africa the availability of film/tapes, spares and equipment is good and prices are roughly on a par with Europe for standard items. In all other countries in the region, availability is restricted to cities and tourist centres, and prices are higher. If you have requirements that are remotely specialist (such as slide film), it's best to carry all you need with you.

The sunlight in Africa is intense, so most people find 100ASA perfectly adequate, with possibly 200ASA or 400ASA for long-lens shots.

Useful photographic accessories might include a small flash, a cable or remote shutter release, filters and cleaning kit. Also, remember to take spare batteries.

A few airports have fairly old X-ray machines for checking baggage and these may not be safe for film. Even newer film-safe models can affect high-speed film (1000ASA and higher), especially if the film goes through several checks during your trip. If pos sible, carry your film in your pocket, and have it checked manually by custom officials.

For video cameras, you may find tapes in capital cities and large towns, but qualities and formats vary. While travelling, you can recharge batteries in hotels as you go along, so take the necessary charger, plugs and transformer for the country you are visiting.

TIME

During the summer months (November to March), the countries of Southern Africa are two hours ahead of Greenwich Mean Time (GMT), which is now generally called UTC.

Photography Tips

Timing The best times to take photos on sunny days are the first two hours after sunrise and the last two before sunset, both of which take advantage of the low sun's colour-enhancing rays. Filters (eg, ultraviolet, polarising or 'skylight') can also produce good results; ask for advice in a good camera shop.

Exposure When photographing animals or people, take light readings on the subject and not the brilliant African background or your shots will turn out underexposed.

Camera Care Factors that can spoil your camera or film include heat, humidity, very fine sand, salt water and sunlight. Take appropriate precautions.

Wildlife Photography If you want to score some excellent wildlife shots, a good lightweight 35mm SLR automatic camera with a lens between 210 and 300mm should do the trick. Video cameras with zoom facility may be able to get closer. If your subject is nothing but a speck in the distance, try to resist wasting film but keep the camera ready. An early start is advisable because most wildlife is active during the cooler hours. Birds in particular are not usually too concerned about people in a vehicle and will go about their business if you approach slowly.

Restrictions Generally, you should avoid taking pictures of bridges, dams, airports, military equipment, government buildings and *anything* that could be considered strategic. You may be arrested or have your film and camera confiscated. Some countries – usually those with precarious military governments – are particularly hot on this. Others are more relaxed. If in doubt, ask first.

Most visitors come to Southern Africa between April and October, which roughly coincides with British Summer Time (daylight saving), which is one hour ahead of GMT/UTC. The only Southern African country to have daylight saving (April to October) is Namibia. From April to October, Namibia turns its clocks back an hour, making it, like the UK, one hour ahead of GMT/UTC. Confused? See the boxed text 'Time Zones' on the following page, which will hopefully help you avoid phoning the folks back home in the middle of the night.

ELECTRICITY

Electricity in Southern Africa is generated at 220V to 240V AC. The exceptions are Pretoria (250V) and Port Elizabeth (220/250V) in South Africa. Most plugs have three prongs (or pins), either round or rectangular ('square') in section. In South Africa, round-pin plugs are used. Outside South Africa, British-style square three-pin plugs are common. Few continental European or North American plug adaptors will cope, and you may have to buy a plug locally (eg, at a hardware store or travel agency) and connect it yourself if you plan to use your own electrical equipment. A voltage adaptor is also needed for US appliances.

Botswana	2-pin (round) SA-type
Lesotho	3-pin (round) SA-type
Malawi	3-pin (square) UK-type
Mozambique	3-pin (square) UK-type; 2 & 3-pin (round) SA-type
Namibia	2 & 3-pin (round) SA-type
South Africa	3-pin (round)
Swaziland	3-pin (round) SA-type
Zambia	3-pin (square) UK-type
Zimbabwe	3-pin (square) UK-type; 3-pin (round) SA-type

WEIGHTS & MEASURES

All the countries covered in this book use the metric system. To convert between metric and imperial units, refer to the conversion chart at the back of the book.

LAUNDRY

Throughout Southern Africa, laundrettes (laundromats) are very rare, although some camping grounds in South Africa and

Photography Tips

Photographing People Like people everywhere, some Africans may enjoy being photographed, but others do not. They may be superstitious about your camera, suspicious of your motives, or simply interested in whatever economic advantage they can gain from your desire to photograph them. To some people in poor areas, a foreigner with a camera is – understandably – seen as simply a chance to make money. If you want a picture, you have to pay, although doing this is a controversial issue. Other locals maintain their pride and never want to be photographed, money or not.

Some tourists go for discreet shots with long lenses, which is probably fine if you can get away with it, but smacks a bit of voyeurism. Ideally, you should always ask permission first. If you get 'no' for an answer, accept it. Just snapping away is rude and unbelievably arrogant.

Local people may agree to be photographed if you give them a picture for themselves. If you don't carry a Polaroid camera, take their address and make it clear that you'll post the photo. Your promise will be taken seriously. Never say you'll send a photo, and then don't. Alternatively, just be honest and say that so many people ask you for photos that it's impossible to send them to everyone.

Video photographers should follow the same rules, as most locals find these cameras even more annoying and offensive than still cameras.

Sacred Sites Some local people are unhappy if you take pictures of their place of worship or a natural feature with traditional religious significance. In some instances, dress may be important. In mosques, for instance, wearing long trousers and removing your shoes may make it more likely that your hosts won't object.

Time Zones

From April to October, when it's noon in Southern Africa (except Namibia), the time elsewhere is:

New York	6 am *
Los Angeles	3 am *
London	11 am *
Paris	noon *
Hong Kong	6 pm
Sydney	8 pm
Auckland	11 pm

From April to October, when it's noon in Namibia, the time elsewhere is:

New York	7 am *
Los Angeles	4 am *
London	noon *
Paris	1 pm *
Hong Kong	7 pm
Sydney	9 pm
Auckland	11 pm

From October to April, when it's noon in all of Southern Africa the time elsewhere is:

New York	5 am
Los Angeles	2 am
London	10 am
Paris	11 pm
Hong Kong	6 pm
Sydney	9 pm *
Auckland	11 pm *

(* Indicates that daylight saving time has been taken into account)

Namibia have washing machines. Otherwise, finding someone to wash your clothes is fairly simple. The top-end and mid-range hotels charge per item (normally less than US$1 per item), and in those national parks often simply include it in the overnight cost. At cheaper hotels, a staff member will do the job, or find somebody else who can – the charge is also usually per item, and often negotiable.

TOILETS

There are two main types of toilet in Africa: the western style, with a toilet bowl and seat; and the African style, which is a hole in the floor, over which you squat. Standards of both toilets can vary tremendously, from pristine to nauseating. Some travellers complain that African toilets are difficult to use, but it only takes a little practice to accomplish a comfortable squatting technique.

In rural areas, squat toilets are built over a deep hole in the ground. These are called 'long-drops', and the waste matter just fades away naturally, as long as the hole isn't filled with too much other rubbish (such as paper or synthetic materials, including tampons – these should be disposed of separately).

Some western toilets are not plumbed in, but just balanced over a long-drop, and sometimes seats are constructed to assist people who can't do the business unsupported. The lack of running water usually makes such cross-cultural mechanisms a disaster. Therefore a noncontact hole in the ground is much better to hover over than a filthy toilet bowl.

HEALTH

Travel health depends on your predeparture preparations, your daily health care while travelling and how you handle any medical problem that does develop. While the potential dangers can seem quite frightening, in reality few travellers in Southern Africa experience anything more than an upset stomach.

Everyday Health

Normal body temperature is up to 37°C (98.6°F); more than 2°C (4°F) higher indicates a high fever. The normal adult pulse rate is 60 to 100 per minute (children 80 to 100, babies 100 to 140). As a general rule the pulse increases about 20 beats per minute for each 1°C (2°F) rise in fever.

Respiration (breathing) rate is also an indicator of illness. Count the number of breaths per minute: between 12 and 20 is normal for adults and older children (up to 30 for younger children, 40 for babies). People with a high fever or serious respiratory illness breathe more quickly than normal. More than 40 shallow breaths a minute may indicate pneumonia.

Predeparture Planning

Immunisations You should seek medical advice at least six weeks before travel, and plan ahead for getting your vaccinations: some of them require more than one injection, while some vaccinations should not be given together. Note that some vaccinations should not be given during pregnancy or to people with allergies – discuss with your doctor.

It is recommended that you seek medical advice at least six weeks before travel. Be aware that children and pregnant women are often more prone to disease, and the effects can be more serious.

Discuss your requirements with your doctor, but vaccinations you should consider for a trip to Southern Africa include those listed below (for more details about the diseases themselves, see the individual entries later in this section). Carry proof of your vaccinations, especially yellow fever, as this is obligatory for entry into some countries.

Cholera Certificates showing proof of cholera vaccination are no longer required, as all countries and the World Health Organisation (WHO) have dropped cholera immunisation as a health requirement for entry.

Diphtheria & Tetanus Vaccinations for these two diseases are usually combined and are recommended for everyone. After an initial course of three injections (usually given in childhood), boosters are necessary every 10 years.

Hepatitis A Vaccinations provide long-term immunity (possibly more than 10 years) after an initial injection and a booster at six to 12 months.

Alternatively, an injection of gamma globulin can provide short-term protection against hepatitis A – two to six months, depending on the dose given. It is not a vaccine, but a ready-made antibody collected from blood donations. It is reasonably effective and, unlike the vaccine, it is protective immediately, but because it is a blood product, there are current concerns about its long-term safety.

A combined vaccine for hepatitis A and hepatitis B vaccine is also available. Three injections over a six-month period are required, the first two providing substantial protection against hepatitis A.

Hepatitis B Travellers who should consider vaccination against hepatitis B include those on a long trip, as well as those visiting countries where there are high levels of hepatitis B infection, where blood transfusions may not be adequately

Medical Kit Check List

Following is a list of items you should consider including in your medical kit – consult your pharmacist for brands available in your country.

- ☐ **Aspirin or paracetamol (acetaminophen in the USA)** – for pain or fever
- ☐ **Antihistamine** – for allergies, eg, hay fever; to ease the itch from insect bites or stings; and to prevent motion sickness
- ☐ **Cold and flu tablets, throat lozenges and nasal decongestant**
- ☐ **Multivitamins** – consider for long trips, when dietary vitamin intake may be inadequate
- ☐ **Antibiotics** – consider including these if you're travelling well off the beaten track; see your doctor, as they must be prescribed, and carry the prescription with you
- ☐ **Loperamide or diphenoxylate** –'blockers' for diarrhoea
- ☐ **Prochlorperazine or metaclopramide** – for nausea and vomiting
- ☐ **Rehydration mixture** – to prevent dehydration, which may occur, for example, during bouts of diarrhoea; particularly important when travelling with children
- ☐ **Insect repellent, sunscreen, lip balm and eye drops**
- ☐ **Calamine lotion, sting relief spray or aloe vera** – to ease irritation from sunburn and insect bites or stings
- ☐ **Antifungal cream or powder** – for fungal skin infections and thrush
- ☐ **Antiseptic (such as povidone-iodine)** – for cuts and grazes
- ☐ **Bandages, Band-Aids (plasters) and other wound dressings**
- ☐ **Water purification tablets or iodine**
- ☐ **Scissors, tweezers and a thermometer** – note that mercury thermometers are prohibited by airlines
- ☐ **Sterile kit** – in case you need injections in a country with medical hygiene problems; discuss with your doctor

screened or where sexual contact or needle sharing is a possibility. Vaccination involves three injections, with a booster at 12 months. More rapid courses are available if necessary.

Meningococcal Meningitis Vaccination is recommended for travellers to certain parts of Africa. A single injection gives good protection against the major epidemic forms of the disease for three years. Protection may be less effective in children under two years.

Polio Everyone should keep up to date with this vaccination, which is normally given in childhood. A booster every 10 years maintains immunity.

Rabies Vaccination should be considered if you will spend a month or longer in Southern Africa where rabies is common, especially if cycling, handling animals, caving or travelling to remote areas. It is also recommended for children (who may not report a bite). Pretravel rabies vaccination involves having three injections over 21 to 28 days. If someone who has been vaccinated is bitten or scratched by an animal, they will require two booster injections of vaccine; those not vaccinated require more.

Tuberculosis The risk of TB to travellers is usually very low, unless you will be living with or closely associated with local people in high risk areas – which includes some parts of Southern Africa. Vaccination against TB (called a BCG) is recommended for children and young adults living in these areas for three months or more.

Typhoid Vaccination against typhoid may be required if you are travelling for more than a couple of weeks. It is now available either as an injection or as capsules to be taken orally.

Yellow Fever A yellow fever vaccine is now the only vaccine that is a legal requirement for entry into certain countries, usually only enforced when coming from an infected area. Vaccination is recommended for travel in areas where the disease is endemic (including parts of Africa). To get the vaccination you may have to go to a special health centre.

Malaria Medication Antimalarial drugs do not prevent you from being infected but kill the malaria parasites during a stage in their development and significantly reduce the risk of becoming very ill or dying. Expert advice on medication should be sought, as there are many factors to consider, including the area to be visited, the risk of exposure to malaria-carrying mosquitoes, the side effects of medication, your medical history and whether you are a child or an adult or pregnant. Travellers to isolated areas in high risk countries may like to carry a treatment dose of medication for use if symptoms occur.

Health Insurance Make sure that you have adequate health insurance. See Travel Insurance under Visas & Documents earlier in this chapter for details.

Travel Health Guides If you are planning to be away or travelling in remote areas for a long period of time, you may like to consider taking a more detailed health guide.

CDC's Complete Guide to Healthy Travel Open Road Publishing, 1997. The US Centers for Disease Control & Prevention recommendations for international travel.

Staying Healthy in Asia, Africa & Latin America by Dirk Schroeder, Moon Publications, 1994. Probably the best all-round guide to carry; it's detailed and well organised.

Travellers' Health by Dr Richard Dawood, Oxford University Press, 1995. Comprehensive, easy to read, authoritative and highly recommended, although it's rather large to lug around.

Where There Is No Doctor by David Werner, Macmillan, 1994. A very detailed guide intended for someone, such as a Peace Corps worker, going to work in an underdeveloped country.

Healthy Travel Africa by Isabelle Young, Lonely Planet Publications, 2000. A handy pocket-size guide packed with useful information including pretrip planning, emergency first aid, immunisation and disease information and what to do if you get sick on the road.

Travel with Children by Maureen Wheeler, Lonely Planet Publications, 1995. Includes advice on travel health for younger children.

Before you go...

If you intend going on a wildlife safari while in Southern Africa, remember to alert the operator to any medical condition you may have that could present problems – such as diabetes, epilepsy, a heart condition or bee-sting allergy. It probably won't stop you going, but it could make matters easier if the guide knows of your condition before (and if) you do run into problems.

There are also a number of excellent travel health sites on the Internet. From the Lonely Planet home page there are links at www.lonelyplanet.com/weblinks/wlheal.htm to the World Health Organization and the US Centers for Disease Control & Prevention.

Other Preparations Make sure you're healthy before you start travelling. If you are going on a long trip make sure your teeth are OK. If you wear glasses take a spare pair and your prescription.

If you require a particular medication take an adequate supply, as it may not be available locally. Take part of the packaging showing the generic name rather than the brand, which will make getting replacements easier. It's a good idea to have a legible prescription or letter from your doctor to show that you legally use the medication.

Basic Rules

Food There is an old adage that says: 'If you can cook it, boil it or peel it you can eat it...otherwise forget it'. Vegetables and fruit should be washed with purified water or peeled where possible. Beware of ice cream that is sold in the street or anywhere it might have been melted and refrozen; if there's any doubt (eg, a power cut in the last day or two), steer well clear. Undercooked meat, particularly in the form of mince, and shellfish such as mussels, oysters and clams should be avoided. Steaming does not make shellfish safe for eating.

If a restaurant or food stall looks clean and well run and the vendor also looks clean and healthy, then the food is probably safe. In general, places that are packed with travellers or locals will be fine, while empty restaurants are questionable. The food in busy restaurants is cooked and eaten quite quickly with little standing around and is probably not reheated.

Water The number one rule is *be careful of the water* and especially ice. If you don't know for certain that the water is safe, assume the worst. Reputable brands of bottled water or soft drinks are generally fine, although in some places bottles may be refilled with tap water. Only use water from containers with a seal. Take care with fruit juice, particularly if water may have been added. Milk should be treated with suspicion as it is often unpasteurised, though boiled milk is fine if it is kept hygienically. Tea or coffee should also be OK, since the water should have been boiled.

Water Purification The simplest way of purifying water is to boil it thoroughly. Vigorous boiling should be satisfactory; however, at high altitude water boils at a lower temperature, so germs are less likely to be killed. You must boil it for longer in these environments.

Consider purchasing a water filter for a long trip. There are two main kinds of filter. Total filters take out all parasites, bacteria and viruses and make water safe to drink.

Nutrition

If your food is poor or limited in availability, if you're travelling hard and fast and therefore missing meals or if you simply lose your appetite, you can soon start to lose weight and place your health at risk.

Make sure your diet is well balanced. If you don't eat meat or eggs, then beans, lentils and nuts are all safe ways to get protein. Fruit you can peel (bananas, oranges or *nartjies* for example) is usually safe and a good source of vitamins. Try to eat plenty of grains (including rice) and bread. Remember that although food is generally safer if it is cooked well, overcooked food loses much of its nutritional value. If your diet isn't well balanced or if your food intake is insufficient, it's a good idea to take vitamin and iron pills.

In hot climates make sure you drink enough – don't rely on feeling thirsty to indicate when you should drink. Not needing to urinate or small amounts of very dark yellow urine is a danger sign. Always carry a water bottle with you on long trips. Excessive sweating can lead to loss of salt and therefore muscle cramping. Salt tablets are not a good idea as a preventative, but in places where salt is not used much, adding salt to food can help.

They are often expensive, but they can be more cost-effective than buying bottled water. Simple filters (which can even be a nylon mesh bag) take out dirt and larger foreign bodies from the water so that chemical solutions work much more effectively; if water is dirty, chemical solutions may not work at all. It's very important when buying a filter to read the specifications so that you know exactly what it removes from the water and what it doesn't. Remember also that to operate effectively a water filter must be properly maintained; a poorly maintained filter can be a breeding ground for germs.

Simple filtering will not remove all dangerous organisms, so if you cannot boil water it should be treated chemically. Chlorine tablets will kill many pathogens, but not certain parasites such as giardia and amoebic cysts.

Iodine is more effective in purifying water and is available in tablet form. Follow the directions carefully and remember that too much iodine can be harmful.

Medical Problems & Treatment

Self-diagnosis and treatment can be risky, so you should always seek medical help. An embassy, consulate or top-end hotel can usually recommend a good local doctor or clinic. Although we do give drug dosages in this section, they are for emergency use only. Correct diagnosis is vital. In this section we have used generic names (not the trade names) for medications – you can check with a pharmacist for brands available locally.

Note that antibiotics should ideally be administered only under medical supervision. Take only the recommended dose at the prescribed intervals and use the entire course, even if the illness seems to be cured earlier. Stop immediately if there are any serious reactions and don't use the antibiotic at all if you are unsure that you have the correct one.

Some people are allergic to commonly prescribed antibiotics such as penicillin; carry this information (eg, on a bracelet) when travelling.

Environmental Hazards

Heat Exhaustion Dehydration and salt deficiency can cause heat exhaustion.

Take time to acclimatise to high temperatures and make sure you drink sufficient liquids – don't rely on feeling thirsty to indicate when you should drink something. Dark yellow urine or not needing to urinate are both a danger sign. Remember to always carry a water bottle with you on long trips.

Salt deficiency is characterised by fatigue, lethargy, headaches, giddiness and muscle cramps; salt tablets may help, but adding extra salt to your food is better (and safer).

Heatstroke This serious, occasionally fatal, condition can occur if the body's heat-regulating mechanism breaks down and the body temperature rises to dangerous levels. Long, continuous periods of exposure to high temperatures and insufficient fluids can leave you vulnerable to heatstroke. The symptoms are feeling unwell, not sweating very much (or at all) and a high body temperature (39° to 41°C or 102° to 106°F). Where sweating has ceased, the skin becomes flushed and red. Severe, throbbing headaches and lack of coordination will also occur, and the sufferer may be confused or aggressive, eventually becoming delirious or convulsive. Hospitalisation is essential, but in the interim get the sufferer out of the sun, remove their clothing, cover them with a wet sheet or towel and then fan continually. Give fluids if they are conscious.

Hypothermia Too much cold can be just as dangerous as too much heat and hypothermia is a possibility in Southern Africa if you are hiking in any of the mountain areas. Hypothermia occurs when the body loses heat faster than it can produce it and the core temperature of the body falls. It is surprisingly easy to progress from very cold to dangerously cold due to a combination of wind, wet clothing, fatigue and hunger, even if the air temperature is above freezing.

To avoid hypothermia it is best to dress in layers; silk, wool and some 'thermal' artificial fibres are all good insulating materials.

A hat is important, as a lot of heat is lost through the head. A strong, waterproof outer layer (and a 'space' blanket for emergencies) is essential. Carry basic supplies, including food containing simple sugars to generate heat quickly and fluid to drink.

Symptoms of hypothermia are exhaustion, numb skin (particularly toes and fingers), shivering, slurred speech, irrational or violent behaviour, lethargy, stumbling, dizzy spells, muscle cramps and violent bursts of energy. Irrationality may take the form of sufferers claiming they are warm and trying to take off their clothes.

To treat mild hypothermia, first get the sufferer out of the wind and rain, remove their clothing if it's wet and replace it with dry, warm clothes. Give them hot liquids – not alcohol – and some high-energy, easily digestible food. Do not rub sufferers: instead, allow them to slowly warm themselves. This should be enough to treat the early stages of hypothermia. The early recognition and treatment of mild hypothermia is the only way to prevent severe hypothermia, which is a critical condition.

Jet Lag

Jet lag is experienced when a person travels by air across more than three time zones (each time zone usually represents a one-hour time difference). It occurs because many of the functions of the human body (such as temperature, pulse rate and emptying of the bladder and bowels) are regulated by internal 24-hour cycles. When you travel long distances rapidly, your body takes time to adjust to the 'new time' of the destination, and you may experience fatigue, disorientation, insomnia, anxiety, impaired concentration and loss of appetite. These effects will usually be gone within three days of arrival, but to minimise the impact of jet lag:

- Rest for a couple of days prior to departure.
- Try to select flight schedules that minimise sleep deprivation; arriving late in the day means you can go to sleep soon after you arrive. For very long flights, try to organise a stopover.
- Avoid excessive eating (which bloats the stomach) and alcohol (which causes dehydration) during the flight. Instead, drink plenty of non-carbonated, nonalcoholic drinks – or simply water.
- Avoid smoking.
- Make yourself comfortable by wearing loose-fitting clothes and perhaps bringing an eye mask and ear plugs to help you sleep.
- Try to sleep at the appropriate time for the time zone you are travelling to.

Motion Sickness Eating lightly before and during a trip will reduce the chances of motion sickness. If you are prone to motion sickness, try to find a place that minimises movement – near the wing on aircrafts, close to midships on boats, near the centre on buses. Fresh air usually helps; reading and cigarette smoke don't. Antisickness preparations, which can cause drowsiness, have to be taken before the trip commences. Ginger (available in capsule form) and peppermint (including mint-flavoured sweets) are natural preventatives.

Prickly Heat Prickly heat is an itchy rash caused by excessive perspiration trapped under the skin. It usually strikes people who have just arrived in a hot climate. Keeping cool, bathing often, drying the skin and using a mild talcum or prickly heat powder or resorting to air-conditioning may help.

Sunburn You can get sunburnt surprisingly quickly, even through cloud. Use a sunscreen, a hat, and a barrier cream for your nose and lips. Protect your eyes with good quality sunglasses, particularly if you will be near water, sand or snow. Calamine lotion or an after sun preparation are good for relieving mild sunburn.

Infectious Diseases

Diarrhoea Simple things such as a change of water, food or climate can all cause a mild bout of diarrhoea, but a few rushed toilet trips with no other symptoms is not indicative of a major problem.

Dehydration is the main danger with any diarrhoea, particularly for children or the elderly as dehydration can occur quite quickly. Under all circumstances *fluid replacement* (at least equal to the volume being lost) is the most important thing to remember – keep drinking small amounts often. Weak black tea with a little sugar, soda water, or soft drinks allowed to go flat and diluted 50% with clean water are all good. If you have severe diarrhoea a rehydrating solution will replace lost minerals and salts. Commercially available oral rehydration solution (ORS) are very useful; add them to boiled or bottled water. In an emergency, make up a solution of six teaspoons of sugar, a half teaspoon of salt and 1L of clean water. You need to drink at least the same volume of fluid that you are losing in bowel movements and vomiting. Urine is the best guide to the adequacy of replacement – if you have small amounts of concentrated urine, you need to drink more. Stick to a bland diet as you recover.

Gut-paralysing drugs such as loperamide or diphenoxylate can be used to bring relief from the symptoms, although they do not actually cure the problem. Only use these drugs if you do not have access to toilets (eg, if you *must* travel). Note that these drugs are not recommended for children under 12 years.

Diarrhoea with blood or mucus (dysentery), any diarrhoea with fever, profuse watery diarrhoea, persistent diarrhoea or severe diarrhoea not improving after 48 hours all suggest a more serious underlying cause. In these situations, a stool test may be necessary to diagnose what bug is causing your diarrhoea and antibiotics may be required, so you should seek medical help urgently (and avoid gut-paralysing drugs).

Where this is not possible the recommended drugs for bacterial diarrhoea (the most likely cause of severe diarrhoea in travellers) are norfloxacin 400mg twice daily for three days or ciprofloxacin 500mg twice daily for three days. These are not recommended for children or pregnant women. The drug of choice for children would be co-trimoxazole with dosage dependent on weight. A five-day course is given. Ampicillin or amoxycillin may be given in pregnancy, but medical care is necessary.

Two other causes of persistent diarrhoea are giardiasis and amoebic dysentery. **Giardiasis** is caused by a common parasite, *Giardia lamblia*. Symptoms include stomach cramps, nausea, a bloated stomach, watery, foul-smelling diarrhoea and frequent gas. Giardiasis can appear several weeks after you have been exposed to the parasite. The symptoms may disappear for a few days and then return; this can go on for several weeks. **Amoebic dysentery**, caused by the protozoan *Entamoeba histolytica*, is characterised by a gradual onset of low-grade diarrhoea, often with blood and mucus. Cramping abdominal pain and vomiting are less likely than in other types of diarrhoea, and fever may not be present. It will persist until treated and can recur and cause other health problems. You should seek medical advice if you think you have giardiasis or amoebic dysentery, but where this is not possible, the recommended treatment is a 2g single dose of tinidazole or 250mg of metronidazole three times daily for five to 10 days.

Hepatitis Hepatitis is a general term for inflammation of the liver. It is a common disease worldwide. There are several different viruses that cause hepatitis, and they differ in the way that they are transmitted. The symptoms are similar in all forms of the illness, and include fever, chills, headache, fatigue, feelings of weakness and aches and pains, followed by loss of appetite, nausea, vomiting, abdominal pain, dark urine, light-coloured faeces, jaundiced (yellow) skin and yellowing of the whites of the eyes.

Hepatitis A is transmitted by contaminated food and drinking water. If you get it, seek medical advice, but there is not much you can do apart from resting, drinking lots of fluids, eating lightly and avoiding fatty foods. Hepatitis E is transmitted in the same way as hepatitis A; it can be particularly serious in pregnant women.

Hepatitis B is spread through contact with infected blood, blood products or body fluids, for example through sexual contact, unsterilised needles and blood transfusions, or contact with blood via small breaks in the skin. Other risk situations include shaving and tattoo or body piercing with contaminated equipment. Early symptoms of hepatitis B may be more severe than those associated with type A and the disease can lead to long-term problems such as chronic liver damage, liver cancer or a long-term carrier state. Hepatitis C and D are spread in the same way as hepatitis B and can also lead to long-term complications.

There are vaccines against hepatitis A and B, but there are currently no vaccines against the other types of hepatitis. Following the basic rules about food and water (hepatitis A and E) and avoiding risk situations (hepatitis B, C and D) are important preventative measures. People who have had hepatitis should avoid alcohol for some time after the illness, as the liver needs time to recover.

HIV & AIDS Infection with the human immunodeficiency virus (HIV) may lead to acquired immune deficiency syndrome (AIDS), which is a fatal disease. Exposure to blood, blood products or body fluids puts you at risk. The disease is often transmitted through sexual contact – and Southern Africa has one of the highest populations of HIV/AIDS sufferers in the world (see the boxed text 'AIDS in Southern Africa' below) – so you should be careful in your choice of sexual partner, and particularly careful about protection. In new and short-term relationships, always use a condom. The disease can also be spread via dirty needles – vaccinations, acupuncture, tattooing and body piercing can be potentially as dangerous as intravenous drug use. Always make sure any needle you use is sterile. If you need an injection or blood test, make sure the needle and syringe is unwrapped in front of you, or carry a sterile kit (needle and syringe pack) in your medical kit for such emergencies.

HIV/AIDS can also be spread through infected blood transfusions, and unfortunately

AIDS in Southern Africa

The 11th World AIDS Conference was held in Zambia in September 1999, but despite the delegates' earnest discussions, AIDS continues to become an increasingly pertinent issue across Africa. For a continent not unused to wars, famines and natural disasters, AIDS is possibly the greatest problem that Africa has ever faced.

The following statistics make shocking reading: Since the mid-1990s AIDS has been the leading cause of death in Africa, and across the continent over 30 million people will die of AIDS by 2020. Around 90% of the world's AIDS sufferers live in Africa. In Zimbabwe around 25% of the population and up to 40% of pregnant women are HIV+; in Malawi and Zambia these figures are even higher. Over the next few years around 60% of children in Botswana will die from AIDS. In South Africa 1500 people become infected every day.

AIDS is acquired more quickly and is more easily transmitted in Africa than it is in the west due to a lack of nutrition and general poor health, the high incidence of venereal disease, limited awareness and limited precautions. In many Southern African countries there is still complete denial that a problem exists, particularly on the part of governments and some churches. This does little to alter the attitudes of local people who consider AIDS (and, in many cases, sex) a taboo subject.

Some commentators have proposed that AIDS is a 'solution' to Africa's problems of high birthrates and overpopulation, but this shows a total lack of comprehension (not to mention a lack of compassion). Unlike many diseases that have more effect on the very young and very old, AIDS tends to be a disease suffered by adults, and in Southern Africa particularly by those who are educated and have relatively high earnings or mobility. Thus, in some Southern African countries one in three teachers are HIV+, and similar figures are estimated for civil service employees. This creates problems for the running of the country, for the economy, and eventually for democracy and peace. Treating sufferers is a great burden for already underfunded health services, while the increasing number of orphans whose parents die from AIDS puts even more strain on the state or on extended families. Added to this, in many Southern African nations, the general morale of the people takes a plunge as the funerals of friends and family members become almost daily events.

some developing countries cannot afford to screen blood used for transfusions. If possible, you should avoid blood transfusions, but if medical conditions are serious enough that you need one, the fear of HIV infection should never preclude treatment.

Intestinal Worms These parasites are most common in rural, tropical areas. The different worms have different ways of infecting people. Some (eg, tapeworms) may be ingested in food such as undercooked meat, and some (eg, hookworms) enter through your skin. Infestations may not show up for some time, and although they are generally not serious, if left untreated some can cause severe health problems later. Consider having a stool test when you return home to check for these and determine the appropriate treatment.

Meningococcal Meningitis This serious disease can be fatal and there are recurring epidemics in sub-Saharan Africa. The first symptoms are fever, severe headache, sensitivity to light and neck stiffness which prevents forward bending of the head. There may also be purple patches on the skin. Death can occur within a few hours, so urgent medical treatment is required. Treatment is large doses of penicillin given intravenously, or chloramphenicol injections.

Bilharzia Also known as schistosomiasis, this disease is transmitted by minute worms found in rivers, freshwater lakes and particularly behind dams. The worms enter through your skin and infect your intestines or bladder. Symptoms sometimes show immediately after infection – you may experience a general feeling of being unwell, fever, or a tingling and sometimes a light rash where a worm entered. Often the disease has to become well established (several months to years after exposure) before symptoms show. These include abdominal pain and blood in the urine. It's the long-term damage that is potentially more harmful, as damage to internal organs is irreversible.

You can avoid this disease by staying away from water where bilharzia may be present. Highest risks are shallow or stagnant areas, near villages, and especially where reeds grow. The first move if you get unavoidably wet (eg, forced to wade a river) is to dry off quickly with brisk towelling and change wet clothes. If you swim in a lake (such as Lake Malawi, where swimming and watersports are very popular) it is *absolutely essential* to get a blood test (maybe combined with a stool or urine test) when you get home. You should get tested even for minor exposure.

You should note that many doctors and health centres have not heard of this disease, and may not be aware of appropriate tests and treatments, which may vary according to the strain of the disease. Note also that a blood test may not show positive until three months after exposure, and may occasionally show negative even if you are carrying the disease. Stool and urine tests may be intermittently positive. If you're in any doubt after the first test, take another test a few weeks later. If you have contracted bilharzia, the cure is a simple single dose of tablets. But don't let this easy treatment make you lower your guard. Bilharzia can be very serious indeed if not diagnosed early.

Sexually Transmitted Infections HIV/AIDS and hepatitis B can be transmitted through sexual contact (for more details see the relevant sections earlier). Other STIs include gonorrhoea, herpes and syphilis. Common symptoms are sores, blisters or rashes around the genitals and discharges or pain when urinating. In some STIs, such as wart virus or chlamydia, symptoms may be less marked or not observed at all, especially in women. Chlamydia infection can cause infertility in men and women before any symptoms have been noticed. Syphilis symptoms eventually disappear completely but the disease continues and can cause severe problems in later years. While abstinence from sexual contact is the only 100% effective prevention, using condoms is also effective. The different sexually transmitted infections each require specific antibiotics for treatment. There is no known cure for HIV or herpes. If you do have a sexual relationship while in Southern Africa there is a good case for having a full screen for sexual infections on your return home, even if you have no symptoms.

Typhoid Typhoid fever is a dangerous gut infection caused by contaminated water and food. In its early stages sufferers may feel they have a bad cold or flu, as early symptoms are a headache, body aches and a fever that rises a little each day until it is around 40°C (104°F) or more. The pulse is often slow relative to the degree of fever present – unlike a normal fever where the pulse increases. There may also be vomiting, abdominal pain, diarrhoea or constipation. In the second week the high fever and slow pulse continue and a few pink spots may appear on the body; trembling, delirium, weakness, weight loss and dehydration may occur. Complications such as pneumonia, perforated bowel or meningitis may occur. If you contract this disease, medical help is essential.

Fungal Infections Fungal infections occur more commonly in hot weather and are usually found on the scalp, between the toes (athlete's foot) or fingers, in the groin and on the body (ringworm). You get ringworm (which is a fungal infection, not a worm) from infected animals or other people. Moisture encourages these infections.

To prevent fungal infections wear loose, comfortable clothes, avoid artificial fibres, wash frequently and dry yourself carefully. If you do get an infection, wash the infected area at least daily with a disinfectant or medicated soap and water, and rinse and dry well. Apply an antifungal cream or powder such as tolnaftate. Try to expose the infected area to air or sunlight as much as possible and wash all towels and underwear in hot water, change them often and let them dry in the sun.

Insect-Borne Diseases

Malaria This serious and potentially fatal disease is spread by mosquito bites. If you are travelling in endemic areas, it is extremely important to avoid mosquito bites and to take tablets to prevent this disease. Symptoms range from fever, chills and sweating, headache, diarrhoea and abdominal pains and joint pains to a vague feeling of ill-health. Seek medical help immediately if malaria is suspected. Without treatment malaria can rapidly become more serious and can be fatal.

If medical care is not available, malaria tablets can be used for treatment. You need to use a malaria tablet that is different from the one you were taking when you contracted the disease in the first place. The standard treatment dose of mefloquine is two 250mg tablets and a further two tablets six hours later. For Fansidar, it's a single dose of three tablets. If you were previously taking mefloquine and cannot obtain Fansidar, then other alternatives are Malarone (atovaquone-proguanil; four tablets once daily for three days), halofantrine (three doses of two 250mg tablets every six hours) or quinine sulphate (600mg every six hours). There is a greater risk of side effects with these dosages than in normal use if used with mefloquine, so medical advice is preferable. Be aware also that halofantrine is no longer recommended by the WHO as emergency standby treatment because of side effects, and should only be used if no other drugs are available.

Malaria is a serious disease and travellers are strongly advised to avoid the disease by preventing mosquito bites at all times. The main messages are:

- Wear long trousers and long-sleeved shirts, ideally light-coloured and treated with a repellent such as permethrin.
- Use mosquito repellents containing the compound DEET on exposed areas of skin (prolonged overuse of DEET may be harmful, especially to children, but its use is considered preferable to being bitten by disease-transmitting mosquitoes).
- Avoid perfumes or aftershave, which may attract mosquitoes.
- Sleep under a mosquito net – ideally impregnated with repellent (such as permethrin); it is well worth carrying your own.

Dengue Fever This viral disease is transmitted by mosquitoes and is fast becoming one of the top public health problems in the tropical world. Unlike the malaria mosquito, the mosquito that transmits the dengue virus *(Aedes aegypti)* is most active during the day, and is found mainly in urban areas in and around human dwellings.

Signs and symptoms of dengue fever include a sudden onset of high fever, headache, joint and muscle pains (hence its old name, 'breakbone fever') and nausea and vomiting. A rash of small red spots sometimes appears three to four days after the onset of fever. In the early phase of illness, dengue may be mistaken for other infectious diseases, including malaria and influenza. Minor bleeding such as nose bleeds may occur in the course of the illness. Recovery even from simple dengue fever may be prolonged, with tiredness lasting for several weeks.

The illness can progress to the potentially fatal dengue haemorrhagic fever (DHF), characterised by heavy bleeding, which is thought to be a result of second infection due to a different strain (there are four major strains) and usually affects residents of the country rather than travellers. Recovery even from simple dengue fever may be prolonged, with tiredness lasting for several weeks.

You should seek medical attention as soon as possible if you think you may be infected. A blood test can exclude malaria and indicate the possibility of dengue fever. There is no vaccine and no specific treatment for dengue. Aspirin should be avoided, as it increases the risk of haemorrhaging. The best prevention is to avoid mosquito bites at all times by covering up and by using insect repellents containing the compound DEET and mosquito nets (for more advice, see the Malaria section earlier).

Cuts, Stings & Bites

Cuts Wash well and treat any cut with an antiseptic such as povidone-iodine. Where possible avoid bandages and sticking plasters, which can keep wounds wet. Note if you're diving that coral cuts are notoriously slow to heal. Small pieces of coral can become embedded in the wound if it is not adequately cleaned.

Stings Bee and wasp stings are usually painful rather than dangerous. Calamine lotion or a sting relief spray will give relief, and ice packs will reduce the pain and swelling. However, in people who are allergic to them severe breathing difficulties may occur and require urgent medical care. If you have a known allergy to bee or wasp stings, discuss your travel plans with your doctor. They may suggest you carry medication that can be self-administered in the event of a sting.

Scorpions often shelter in shoes or clothing and their stings are notoriously painful, so take care when camping.

If diving, avoid contact with jellyfish, which may have stinging tentacles – although most are simply painful rather than life-threatening. Dousing in vinegar will deactivate any stingers that have not 'fired'. Calamine lotion, antihistamines and analgesics may reduce the reaction and relieve the pain. There are various other sea creatures that can sting or bite dangerously – seek local advice.

Bedbugs & Lice You may be bitten by bedbugs if you're using budget hotels, as they tend to lurk in dirty mattresses and bedding, evidenced by spots of blood. Bedbugs leave itchy bites in neat rows. Calamine lotion or a sting relief spray may help.

Lice cause itching and discomfort. They make themselves at home in your hair (head lice), your clothing (body lice) or in your pubic hair ('crabs'). You catch lice through direct contact with infected people or by sharing combs, clothing etc.

Powder or shampoo treatment will kill the lice, and infected clothing should be washed in very hot, soapy water and left in the sun to dry.

Ticks Bites from ticks can cause skin infections and other more serious diseases. You will recognise a tick by the way it has firmly attached itself to your skin. You should always check all over your body if you have been walking through a potentially tick-infested area – especially long grass where cattle or other animals graze. If a tick is found attached, press down around the tick's head with tweezers, grab the head and gently pull upwards. Avoid pulling the rear of the body as this may squeeze the tick's gut contents through the attached mouth parts into the skin, increasing the risk of infection and disease. Smearing chemicals on the tick will not make it let go and is not recommended.

Snake Bites To minimise your chances of being bitten, always wear boots, socks and long trousers when walking through undergrowth where snakes may be present. Don't put your hands into holes and crevices, and be careful when collecting firewood.

Snake bites do not cause instantaneous death, and antivenins are often available. Immediately wrap the bitten limb tightly, as you would for a sprained ankle, and then attach a splint to immobilise it.

Keep the victim still and immediately seek medical help. Tourniquets and sucking out the poison are now comprehensively discredited.

Less Common Diseases

The following diseases pose a small risk to travellers, and so are only mentioned in passing. Seek medical advice if you think you may have any of these diseases.

Cholera This is the worst of the watery diarrhoeas and medical help should be sought. Cholera outbreaks are generally widely reported, so you can avoid problem areas. *Fluid replacement is the most vital treatment* – the risk of dehydration is severe as you may lose up to 20L of fluids a day. If there's a delay in getting to hospital, then begin taking tetracycline. The adult dose is 250mg four times daily. It is not recommended for children under nine years or for pregnant women.

Tetracycline may help shorten the illness, but adequate fluids are required to save lives.

Filariasis This is a mosquito-transmitted parasitic infection found in many parts of Africa, Asia, Central and South America and the Pacific. Possible symptoms include fever, pain and swelling of the lymph glands; inflammation of lymph drainage areas; swelling of a limb or the scrotum; skin rashes; and blindness. Treatment is available to eliminate the parasites from the body, but some of the damage already caused may not be reversible. Medical advice should be obtained promptly if the infection is suspected.

Leishmaniasis This is a group of parasitic diseases transmitted by sandflies, which are found in many parts of the Middle East, Africa, India, Central and South America and the Mediterranean. Cutaneous leishmaniasis affects the skin tissue, causing ulceration and disfigurement, and visceral leishmaniasis affects the internal organs. Seek medical advice, as laboratory testing is required for diagnosis and correct treatment. Avoiding sandfly bites is the best precaution. Bites are usually painless, though itchy, and are yet another reason to cover up and apply repellent.

Rabies This fatal viral infection is found in many countries, including those of Southern Africa. Many animals can be infected (such as dogs, cats, bats and monkeys) and it is their saliva that is infectious. Any bite, scratch or even lick from an animal should be cleaned immediately and thoroughly. Scrub with soap and running water, and then apply alcohol or iodine solution. Medical help should be sought promptly to receive a course of injections to prevent the onset of symptoms and death.

Sleeping Sickness In parts of tropical Africa, tsetse flies can carry trypanosomiasis, or sleeping sickness. The tsetse fly is about twice the size of a housefly and is recognisable by the scissor-like way it folds its wings when at rest. Only a small proportion of tsetse flies carry the disease, but it is a serious disease which can be fatal without treatment. The only protection available is avoiding the tsetse fly bites. The flies are attracted to large moving objects such as safari buses, to perfume and aftershave and to colours such as dark blue. Swelling at the site of the bite, five or more days later, is the first sign of infection; this is followed within two to three weeks by fever.

Tetanus This disease is caused by a germ that lives in soil and in the faeces of horses and other animals. It enters the body via breaks in the skin. The first symptom may be discomfort in swallowing, or stiffening of the jaw and neck; this is followed by painful convulsions of the jaw and whole body. The disease can be fatal. It is prevented by vaccination.

Tuberculosis (TB) TB is a bacterial infection usually transmitted from person to person by coughing, but which may be transmitted through consumption of unpasteurised milk. Milk that has been boiled is safe to drink, and the souring of milk to make yoghurt or cheese also kills the bacilli. Travellers are usually not at great risk, as close household contact with the infected person is usually required before the disease is passed on. You may need to have a TB test before you travel as this can help diagnose the disease later if you become ill.

Typhus This disease is spread by ticks, mites or lice. It begins with fever, chills, headache and muscle pains followed a few days later by a body rash. There's often a large painful sore at the site of the bite and nearby lymph nodes are swollen and painful. Typhus can be treated under medical supervision. Seek local advice on areas where ticks pose a danger and always check your skin carefully for ticks after walking in a danger area (eg, a tropical forest). An insect repellent can help, and walkers in tick-infested areas should consider having their boots and trousers impregnated with benzyl benzoate and dibutylphthalate.

Yellow Fever This viral disease is endemic in many African countries and is transmitted by mosquitoes. The initial symptoms are fever, headache, abdominal pain and vomiting. The possibility of contracting yellow fever is another good reason to protect yourself against mosquito bites. If you think you have contracted the disease, seek medical care urgently and drink lots of fluids.

Women's Health

Gynaecological Problems Antibiotic use, synthetic underwear, sweating and contraceptive pills can lead to fungal vaginal infections, especially when travelling in hot climates. Fungal infections are characterised by a rash, itch and discharge – Nystatin, miconazole or clotrimazole pessaries or vaginal cream are the usual treatment. They can also be treated with a vinegar or lemon-juice douche, or with yoghurt. Maintaining good personal hygiene and wearing loose-fitting clothes and cotton underwear may help prevent these infections.

Sexually transmitted infections are a major cause of vaginal problems. Symptoms include a smelly discharge, painful intercourse and sometimes a burning sensation when urinating. Medical attention should be sought and sexual partners must also be treated. For more details, see the section on Sexually Transmitted Infections earlier. Besides abstinence, the best preventative is to practise safer sex using condoms.

Pregnancy Consult your doctor if you're planning to travel while pregnant, as some vaccinations that are normally used to prevent serious diseases are not advisable during pregnancy (eg, yellow fever). Also, some diseases (eg, malaria) are much more serious during pregnancy, and may increase the risk of a stillborn child.

Miscarriage is not uncommon and can occasionally lead to severe bleeding. Most miscarriages occur during the first three months of pregnancy. The last three months should also be spent within reasonable distance of good medical care. A baby born as early as 24 weeks stands a chance of survival, but only in a good modern hospital.

Pregnant women should avoid all unnecessary medication, although vaccinations and malarial prophylactics should still be taken where needed – talk to your doctor about what vaccinations are safe during pregnancy. Additional care should be taken to prevent illness and particular attention should be paid to diet and nutrition. Alcohol and nicotine, for example, should be avoided. Airlines will usually allow pregnant women to fly up to the 36th week of pregnancy, but the policies of individual airlines should be checked.

Tampons & Sanitary Towels Tampons and towels imported from Europe or South Africa are available from pharmacies or big supermarkets in capitals (and less reliably in large towns) throughout the region. In tourist areas they are also available from shops at hotels.

WOMEN TRAVELLERS

Attitudes Towards Women

Generally speaking, women travellers in Southern Africa will not encounter specifically gender-related problems on a daily basis any more than they might in other parts of the world. In fact, many women travellers report that, compared with North Africa (including Morocco and Egypt), South America and many western countries, the region is relatively safe and unthreatening, and that friendliness and generosity are encountered far more often than hostility.

Southern Africa is one of the few places in the developing world where it is possible for women travellers to meet and communicate with local men – of any race – without their actions automatically being misconstrued. That's not to say that sexual harassment never happens (see later in this section), but local white women (mostly South Africans, Namibians, Zambians and Zimbabweans) have done much to refute the image that women of European descent are willing to hop into bed with the first taker.

Danger from muggers is another matter, though, and there are some areas of Southern Africa where this is a possibility (these are listed under Dangers & Annoyances in the individual country chapters). As anywhere, women, particularly lone women, are seen as easy targets, so it pays to keep away from these areas, especially at night.

When it comes to evening entertainment, Southern Africa is very much a conservative, traditional male-dominated society (among all races) and women travellers may come up against a few glass walls and ceilings. Many bars are completely male only (by law of the establishment, or by the law of tradition), and even where women are 'allowed', cultural conventions often dictate that you don't go in without a male companion. Even if you do, it's worth being aware that accepting a drink from a local man is usually construed as a come-on. That's the situation, however distasteful it may be to liberated westerners – and trying to buck the system will quite possibly lead to trouble. So, as an outsider, it's much better to go with the flow and only visit the places where women can go without attracting unwanted attention. Always try to get some local female advice first.

Because of these prevailing attitudes, it can be hard to specifically meet and talk with local women in the countries you're travelling through. It may require being invited into a home, although because many women (mostly nonwhite) have received little or no education, sometimes language barriers can be a problem. This is changing to some extent because more recently a surprising number of girls have had the opportunity to stay at school while the boys are sent away to work. This means that in some countries, many of the staff in tourist offices, government departments and so on are educated, young to middle-aged black women, and this can be as good a place as any to try striking up a conversation. In rural areas, a good starting point might be women teachers at a local school or staff at a health centre. In some cities there may be women's groups who specifically welcome visitors.

When you're actually travelling, the best advice on what can and can't be undertaken safely will come from local women. Unfortunately, many white women are likely to be appalled at the idea of lone travel and will do their best to discourage you with horrendous stories, often of dubious accuracy. Having said that, although the countries in this region are considerably safer than some other parts of the world, hitching alone is not recommended. If you decide to thumb it, you should refuse a lift if the driver is drunk (a sadly common condition) or the car is chock-a-block with men (eg, a military vehicle). Use common sense and things should go well.

Female travellers may like to join a global organisation called Women Welcome Women World Wide, which fosters international friendship by enabling women of different countries to visit one another. For details, contact the international headquarters (☎/fax 01494-465441) at 88 Easton St, High Wycombe HP11, UK, or check its Web site: www.womenwelcomewomen.org.uk

Sexual Harassment

Despite sexual harassment being less of a problem for women travellers in Southern Africa than it is in some other parts of the world, it is something that women (particularly lone women) have to occasionally deal with. Although unwanted interest is always unpleasant, it's worth remembering that although you may encounter a lewd border official, or an admirer who won't go away, real harm or rape is actually very unlikely.

Part of the reason for the interest shown in you arises from the fact that local women rarely travel long distances alone, and a single foreign female is a very unusual sight. Another reason is that, thanks to imported TV and Hollywood films, western women are sometimes viewed as being 'loose'.

What you wear may greatly influence how you're treated. African women dress conservatively, in traditional or western clothes, so when a visitor wears something significantly different from the norm, she will draw attention. In the minds of some men this peculiar dressing will be seen as provocative. In general, look at what other women are wearing and follow suit. Keep most of your legs covered, at least below the knee, with trousers or a skirt (see also the boxed text 'Dress Codes' in the Facts about the Region chapter).

If you're alone in an uneasy situation, act prudish. Stick your nose in a book. Or invent an imaginary husband who will be arriving shortly – either in the country or at that particular spot. If you are travelling with a male companion, one of the best ways to avoid unwanted interest is to introduce him as your husband.

GAY & LESBIAN TRAVELLERS

All the countries covered in this book are conservative in their attitudes towards gays and lesbians, and homosexuality as an issue is rarely discussed sensibly in public. In traditional African societies, gay sexual relationships are a cultural taboo, although some homosexual activity – especially among younger men – does occur. In the last few years, the presidents of Zimbabwe and Namibia have both spoken out publicly (see the Zimbabwe Facts for the Visitor section) and venomously against homosexuals, although observers see this as just another way of deflecting attention from government problems.

Male homosexual activity is illegal in all the countries in this book, except South Africa (where there is a small gay scene in the main cities – see that chapter for more information) and Lesotho. Lesbian activities are illegal in Malawi, Namibia, Swaziland and Zimbabwe, and only not illegal in the other countries due more to oversight than anything else.

In most places open displays of affection are generally frowned upon, whatever your orientation, and show insensitivity to local feelings.

DISABLED TRAVELLERS

People who cannot walk will not have an easy time in Southern Africa. Even though there are more disabled people per head of population here than in the west, there are very few facilities. In South Africa and the capitals of some other countries, some official buildings have ramps and lifts – but not many, and probably not the ones you want to visit.

Most wheelchair users find travel easier with an able-bodied companion. And travel in Southern Africa can have some advantages compared with other parts of the developing world: footpaths and public areas are often surfaced with tar or concrete, rather than with sand, mud or gravel; many buildings (including safari lodges and national park cabins) are single storey; car hire is easy in South Africa, and cars can be taken to neighbouring countries; and assistance is usually available on internal and regional flights.

Some companies specialising in tours for disabled travellers are listed under Disabled Travellers in the Facts for the Visitor section of the South Africa chapter.

SENIOR TRAVELLERS

Southern Africa is generally good for senior travellers (on the assumption that they want to rough it less than the younger folk) as facilities such as hotels and restaurants of a high standard are generally available. Many senior South Africans (mostly whites) tour their own country – there is a thriving caravan scene – and visit many of the neighbouring countries independently or with organised package tours. As an example of what is possible, we heard from a 52-year-old American who took his 73-year-old mother on a tour of South Africa. They stayed mostly in mid-range hotels and hired an Avis car, which could all be arranged in the USA. The three-week trip cost US$3000 for two, plus airfares.

Unfortunately, very few hotels or tour companies give specific discounts to holders of senior cards, and they are little to no use on public transport too.

TRAVEL WITH CHILDREN

In South Africa there is a very healthy domestic tourism industry, particularly on the coast, and much is aimed at families, although it's unlikely you'll come all the way here for the kind of beach holiday you could have at home. Away from the coast, many resorts, hotels and national park lodges or camping grounds have facilities for children, ranging from play-leaders and baby-sitting services to swings and roundabouts. Horses, boats and bicycles can also be hired. Many families hire camper vans in South Africa – see that country's Getting Around section for more details – and use these to tour the region. There are fewer child-orientated facilities in the other countries, but here the attractions usually provide entertainment enough: large wild animals in the national parks are a major draw, and even bored teenagers have been known to get a bit excited at Victoria Falls.

All over the region, in tourist hotels, family rooms and chalets are available for only slightly more than the price of a double. Arranging an extra bed or two so that children can share a standard adult double is generally not a problem. However, in some cheaper nontouristy hotels there are no discounts for children – a bed's a bed, whoever sleeps in it. Likewise on public transport – if you want a seat it has to be paid for. Most local kids go for free on buses but spend the whole journey on their parent's lap.

On the health front, compared with some other parts of the world, there's less in the way of nasty diseases, and good (if expensive) medical services can generally be reached fairly quickly. On the down side, some distances between 'sights' can be long, especially on public transport, so parents need to have a good supply of distractions to hand. ('Let's count how many black goats we can see...')

Lonely Planet's *Travel with Children* by Maureen Wheeler provides more sound advice, as well as several ideas for games on the bus.

DANGERS & ANNOYANCES

It is very important not to make sweeping statements about personal safety in Southern Africa. While there may be large risks in some areas, other places are completely safe. Essentially, robbery with violence is much more prevalent in cities and towns than in rural or wilderness areas. But even towns can differ; there's more of a danger in those frequented by wealthy foreigners than in places off the usual tourist track. Details are given in the individual country chapters.

Safety Tips

Some simple precautions will hopefully ensure that you have a trouble-free journey. Remember: Most travellers have no problems precisely because they were careful when required. The precautions suggested in this section are particularly relevant to cities, although some might apply to other places too.

Scams & Con-tricks

The main annoyances you'll come across in Southern Africa are the various hustlers, touts, con-men and scam-merchants who always see tourists as easy prey. Although these guys are not necessarily dangerous, they always want to get at your money. Some awareness and suitable precautions are advisable, and should help you deal with them effortlessly.

Remember Me? A popular trick in the tourist areas is for local lads to approach you in the street and say, 'Hello, it's me, from the hotel, don't you recognise me?'. You're not sure. You don't really remember him, but then you don't want to seem rude either. So you stop for a chat. Can he walk with you for a while? Sure. Nice day. A few more pleasantries. Then comes the crunch: How about a visit to his brother's souvenir shop? Or do you wanna buy some grass? Need a taxi? A tour? By this time you're hooked, and you probably end up buying or arranging something.

The way to avoid the trap is to be polite but firm: You don't remember anyone, and you'd like to be alone. You could ask 'which hotel' after the first greeting, but the guy may *really* work there, or at least have noticed you coming out, and then perfectly calls your bluff.

Dud Sounds You buy some cassettes from a booth in the market, or from the young guys who walk the streets selling from a box. When you get back to your hotel and open the box it's got a blank tape inside, or the music is by a completely different artist. Although often this is simply due

- On the streets, don't make yourself a target. Carry as little as possible. Consider leaving your day-pack and camera in your hotel room if the room is safe. Even passports, travellers cheques and credit cards are sometimes safer left behind – particularly if the hotel has a reliable security box.
- Don't wear jewellery or watches, however cheap they actually are. Use a separate wallet for day-to-day purchases, and keep the bulk of your cash out of sight, hidden in a pouch under loose-fitting clothing.
- Walk purposefully and confidently, and never look like you're lost (even if you are!). Don't obviously refer to this guidebook. Tear out the pages you need, or duck into a shop to have a look at the map and get your bearings.
- At night, don't walk in the back streets, or even some main streets; take a taxi – a dollar or two for the fare might save you a lot of pain and trouble.
- Don't fall into the trap of thinking all robbers are on the street. Although most hotels are reputable, some travellers have left money in a safe, only to find that less reputable members of staff with a spare key have helped themselves. Often this trick involves taking just a few notes, in the hope that you won't notice. To avoid this, store your valuables in a safe inside a pouch with a lockable zip, or in an envelope you can seal with tape.

Some travellers also report stuff occasionally going missing from hotel rooms, and especially from shared hostel dorms. It might be the hostel staff, but sometimes you can hardly blame them when travellers leave their gear, including handy little items like pocketknives, film and jewellery, scattered all over

Something to Consider

Lest we get too paranoid, remember this: Considering the wealth of most tourists, and the unimaginable levels of poverty suffered by most locals, the incidence of robbery or theft in most of Southern Africa is incredibly low. Even a shoestring traveller's budget of US$10 a day is more than the average local labourer makes in a month. When you sit in a bus station sipping a couple of soft drinks that cost a dollar and you see an old woman selling cakes for a tenth of this price, or a teenage youth trying to earn the same amount by cleaning your shoes, it reminds you with a jolt that the vast majority of local people are decent and hard-working, and want from you only respect and the chance to make an honest living.

Scams & Con-tricks

to faulty technology than a deliberate trick, it's still annoying. Wherever you buy tapes, always try to listen to them first.

Phone Home You give your address to a local kid who says he wants to write you letters. He asks for your phone number too, and you think 'no harm in that'. Until the folks back home start getting collect calls in the middle of the night.

A Nice Welcome You may be invited to stay for free in someone's house on the understanding that you are happy to buy them meals and drinks for a few days, but your new friend's appetite for food and beer may make this deal more expensive than staying at a hotel. More seriously, while you are entertaining, someone else will be back at the house of your 'friend' going through your bag. This scam is only likely to be tried in tourist areas – in remote or rural areas you'll quite often come across genuine hospitality.

Police & Thieves If you're unwise enough to sample local narcotics, don't be surprised if dealers are in cahoots with the local police who then come to your hotel room and find you 'in possession'. Large bribes will be required to avoid arrest or imprisonment. The solution is easy – don't buy drugs from strangers.

the bed or floor. There are travellers around who are not averse to 'liberating' other people's possessions. The moral – keep your gear in your bag. Out of sight, out of mind.

ACTIVITIES

The climate and landscape of Southern Africa lends itself to several types of outdoor activity – peaceful, relaxing, energetic or downright terrifying.

Wildlife viewing and **birdwatching** are probably two of the main activities that attract visitors to Southern Africa. Some details on the region's fascinating wildlife and national parks are provided in the Facts about the Region chapter, and the Wildlife Guide and 'Birds of Southern Africa' section, and are also given in the individual country chapters. Further information on wildlife-viewing trips is provided in the Organised Tours sections of the individual country Getting Around sections or the capital city sections. See also Safaris at the end of this section, and the boxed text 'Close Encounters' later in this chapter.

Many other activities are also available for visitors (ie, you can hire gear, arrange tuition, get permits etc) and all are covered in more detail in the relevant country chapters. The following list is not exclusive, but it will give you a good idea:

Air Sports – South Africa, Zambia
Beaches (if you count that as an 'activity') – South Africa, Mozambique, Namibia, Malawi
Bungee Jumping – Zambia, Zimbabwe
Canoeing/Kayaking – Zimbabwe, Zambia, Namibia, South Africa, Malawi
Diving & Snorkelling – South Africa, Mozambique, Malawi (Lake)
Fishing (deep-sea & surf) – South Africa, Namibia, Mozambique
Fishing (river) – South Africa, Zimbabwe, Malawi, Zambia
Horse Riding – South Africa, Zimbabwe, Lesotho, Zambia, Malawi
Rock Climbing – South Africa, Malawi, Zimbabwe, Namibia
Surfing – South Africa
White-water Rafting – South Africa, Zimbabwe, Zambia, Namibia
Windsurfing – South Africa, Mozambique, Malawi (Lake)

Cycling

Bicycles can be hired from hotels or tour companies in several tourist areas around Southern Africa. Mostly these are mountain bikes (usually the basic models), but you can also hire local-style sit-up-and-beg steel roadsters. You can use them to get around town for an hour or two, or explore a rural area for a week or more. For information on bringing your own bike to Southern Africa, see the Regional Getting Around chapter.

Diving & Snorkelling

The best area in Southern Africa for diving and snorkelling is along the coast of Mozambique. These activities are also excellent along the east coast of South Africa, especially in the far north, near the border with Mozambique, where you find coral reefs. Lake Malawi is one of the best freshwater diving areas in the world, and a particularly popular (and inexpensive) place to learn.

Football (Soccer)

Soccer is Africa's most popular participation and spectator sport. If you want to play, the universities and municipal stadiums are by far the best places to find a good-quality game, but outside every town in Africa is a patch of ground where informal matches are played most evenings (in coastal areas, the beach is used). The ball may be more suitable for tennis, or just a round bundle of rags, and each goal a couple of sticks, not necessarily opposite each other. You may have to deal with puddles, ditches and the odd goat or donkey wandering across the pitch, but the game itself is taken very seriously. Play is fast and furious, with the ball played low, but foreigners are usually warmly welcomed and joining in a game is one of the best ways to meet the locals. If you brought along your own ball (which could be deflated for travelling), you'll be the hit of the day.

Hiking

Across Southern Africa there are many excellent opportunities for hiking, and this is

Considerations for Responsible Diving

The popularity of diving places immense pressure on many sites. Please consider the following tips to help preserve the ecology and beauty of reefs and other underwater areas:

- Do not use anchors on the reef, and take care not to ground boats on coral. Encourage dive operators and regulatory bodies to establish permanent moorings at popular dive sites.
- Avoid touching living marine organisms with your body or dragging equipment across the reef. Polyps can be damaged by even the gentlest contact. Never stand on corals, even if they look solid and robust. If you must hold on to the reef, only touch exposed rock or dead coral.
- Be conscious of your fins. Even without contact the surge from heavy fin strokes near the reef can damage delicate organisms. When treading water in shallow reef areas, take care not to kick up clouds of sand. Settling sand can easily smother the delicate organisms of the reef.
- Practise and maintain proper buoyancy control. Major damage can be done by divers descending too fast and colliding with the reef. Make sure you are correctly weighted and that your weight belt is positioned so that you stay horizontal. If you have not dived for a while, have a practice dive in a pool before taking to the reef. Be aware that buoyancy can change over the period of an extended trip: initially you may breathe harder and need more weight; a few days later you may breathe more easily and need less weight.
- Ensure that you carry out all your rubbish and any litter you may find as well. Plastics in particular are a serious threat to marine life. Turtles can mistake plastic for jellyfish and eat it.
- Resist the temptation to feed fish. You may disturb their normal eating habits, encourage aggressive behaviour or feed them food that is detrimental to their health.

one of the most popular activities in the region. Some hiking guidebooks are listed in the Books section earlier in this chapter.

Hiking Trails 'Hiking' is a general term to cover all forms of walking for pleasure, but in South Africa particularly (and in some other countries in the region) it has a more precise usage, and nearly always refers to a walk along a prescribed route, or 'trail', normally of two days or more.

Hiking trails are normally established by national park authorities, conservation bodies and private landowners. In South Africa, Namibia and some other countries you must pay a fee to use the trail, and this covers the use of camp sites (which may have toilets or other facilities) or accommodation (ranging from simple shelters to comfortable cabins) along the route. These trails are sometimes called 'overnight hikes', but this doesn't mean you have to walk in the dark, just that you stay out for longer than one day. You can only do the trail in one direction (some are linear, some are circular) and, to preserve the condition of the trail, only a limited number of people are allowed to hike on any one day. In fragile areas, departures are only permitted once or twice per week – on a specific day – and even time of departure is sometimes stipulated. You must complete the trail in the set number of days; you are not allowed to link two days together (except perhaps the last two) or to stay extra nights at any camp site or hut, so they never become overcrowded.

Some trails have their own regulations, for example: no fires allowed – all hikers must carry stoves; no parties of less than four or more than 10 allowed. Anyone doing some of Namibia's tougher hiking trails must provide a doctor's certificate of health.

In South Africa and Namibia, it is usually necessary to make a reservation to do an overnight (multi-day) hiking trail. You have to contact the national park or other authority which administers the trail to see when there's space. Although it sounds like a hassle, it's usually just a formality, especially outside weekends. Only the popular 'classics' such as the Otter Trail and Fish River Canyon are likely to be fully booked. And even here you can sometimes find a slot when someone else has cancelled. (Although in Namibia this is not possible, making it even harder for individuals to do long routes.)

Once space has been confirmed, you are issued with a permit. This is posted to you if you have a local address, or is ready for your collection (eg, at the national parks' headquarters). You can either pay in advance over the phone with a credit card, or on arrival. Included in the price may be an information sheet or map of the route. You must turn up at the start of the trail on the arranged date (or usually the day before, and stay near the start) and report to the 'officer-in-charge'. You may have to fill in some kind of register (with

Recommended Hiking Trails & Areas

Some countries in Southern Africa offer specific hiking trails (South Africa in particular has a huge selection), while other countries have good hiking areas, but no specific trails that you *must* follow, giving you more scope to plan your own route. Below is a short list of some of the best-known hiking trails and hiking areas in the region; for more details see the specific country chapters.

Lesotho	Malealea Area
Malawi	Nyika Plateau; Mt Mulanje
Namibia	Fish River Canyon Trail; Naukluft Mountains
South Africa	Wild Coast Hiking Trail (Eastern Cape); Otter Trail (Eastern Cape); Drakensberg Range (KwaZulu-Natal); Cederberg Wilderness Area (Western Cape)
Swaziland	Malolotja Nature Reserve
Zimbabwe	Chimanimani Range

details like the number of people in your party, experience, equipment, colour of backpacks) in case of an emergency, then all you have to do is head off into the wilderness.

Although this sounds like an incredibly complicated way to go for a walk, many travellers 'do' long-distance hiking trails, especially in South Africa, and recommend them highly.

Backpacking Trails In South Africa and Namibia, 'backpacking trails' tend to be more serious than hiking trails: there are no signposts, and no facilities. You choose your own route, either following paths which may exist, or just moving across open country. You have to be completely self-contained, and competent in wilderness situations. You sleep in your tent (which you carry along with the rest of your gear and food). Alternatively, you can sleep under the stars, or in caves in some areas, but even these often have to be reserved to avoid overcrowding, and a fee is normally payable.

Wilderness Trails These are another very popular and highly rated option for walkers in Southern Africa. They do not follow set routes and are usually led by a guide (eg, in national parks this is a ranger or conservationist). 'Trail' in this sense simply means a 'guided walk', and so the term 'guided wilderness trail' is often used for clarification (although there are a few 'self-guided wilderness trails' and even 'unguided wilderness trails', just in case you thought you'd got the hang of all these definitions). In other parts of Africa these are often called walking safaris – the object is not always to see wildlife (which can normally be better observed from a vehicle) but to simply experience the wilderness and learn something about it.

Other Types of Trail 'Day-hiking trails' can range from 3km rambles to 20km marathons. In many parks and reserves throughout the region, an entire set of day-hiking trails are available from a single point (usually the park headquarters or main camp), following a set route, with arrows, markers and distance indicators. Maps are often available, but these vary in quality from the good to the dangerously confusing. For many visitors, day-hiking trails are the most convenient way to explore the region on foot. Although you won't get right out in the wilderness, you don't have to worry about making reservations, committing yourself to dates or carrying loads of gear.

One last point – in South Africa and Namibia the Afrikaans word *wandelpad* seems to refer to any kind of trail. Therefore, it's best to check the English translation, just to make sure your planned day-walk doesn't turn into a week's expedition.

Safaris

Throughout Southern Africa, most large animals are in national parks (or similar conservation areas), and usually the only way into the parks is by car. This is by law, and also by default, as there's usually no public transport. Therefore, if you don't have a vehicle (motorcycles and bicycles don't count), your usual option is to join an organised safari.

The word 'safari' may conjure up colonial images of white men with big guns and long lines of Africans with boxes on their heads, but these days it seems to refer to any organised trip in the region. Walking safaris or horseback safaris are quite common – even golf safaris or train safaris are possible. But most safaris are the wildlife-viewing sort, and involve travel in a vehicle with large windows, open sides or a pop-up roof to allow clear views (and endless photo opportunities) of the animals you've come all this way to see. A driver (who doubles as guide) comes with the car.

Depending on where you are, and on your time limitations, the range of wildlife-viewing safaris available in Southern Africa is enormous: you could go for a day or a month; you could camp and cook simple meals over a fire, or stay in a luxury lodge and be served a la carte; you could go on your own or join a group; you could drive great distances to bag the 'big five', or spend all day by a watering hole watching out for local specialities.

And of course, there's a range of prices too. These can start at several hundred dollars a day for those who want exclusivity and top-quality guides, plus all the comforts of home and more. At the other end of the scale are low-budget trips for those with less flexible wallets. If you don't need frills, and don't mind company, these are often very good value. And there's just about every other type of option in between.

Many safaris can be arranged in your home country before you arrive in Southern Africa (see the regional Getting There & Away chapter), and it's also possible to arrange things on the spot in main cities such as Cape Town, Windhoek and Harare, and the tourist towns of Livingstone and Victoria Falls. More details are given under Organised Tours in the individual country Getting Around sections, and (where relevant) under the places themselves.

Close Encounters

Although you'll hear lots of horror stories, the threat of attack by wild animals in Africa is largely exaggerated and problems are extremely rare. However, it is important to remember that most animals in Africa are *wild* and that wherever you go on safari, particularly on foot, there is always an element of danger. The tips below will further diminish your chances of a close encounter of the unpleasant kind, and on organised safaris you should always get advice from your guide.

Buffaloes are usually docile in a herd, but lone individuals can be unpredictable, making them particularly dangerous. If you encounter a buffalo while walking in the bush, back away quietly and slowly. If it charges, climb the nearest tree or dive into the bush and 'run like a rat'.

Elephants certainly aren't bloodthirsty creatures, but those who have had trouble from humans previously may feel the need to take revenge. If an elephant holds its trunk erect and sniffs the air, it probably detects your presence and may charge rather than retreat. In which case you should be the one who retreats – but move away slowly. When camping, don't keep fresh fruit in your tent, as it's not unknown for elephants to shake tents like a bag trying to reach the tasty morsels.

Hippos aren't normally vicious, but they may attack if you get too close or come between them and the water, or between adults and young. In fact, hippos kill more humans in Africa than any other animal. When boating or canoeing, steer well away from them, and never pitch a tent in an open area along vegetated riverbanks, as this will probably be a hippo run. Also near water, watch out for **crocodiles**. Never swim, paddle or even collect water unless you're absolutely sure it's safe. If local advice is not available, assume the worst.

Hyaenas are potentially dangerous, although they're normally just after your food. They aren't particularly fussy either: they'll eat boots and equipment left outside a tent, and have been known to gnaw right through vehicle tyres! However, there are plenty of frightening tales of hyaenas attacking people sleeping in an open tent – although this is rare, it's still wise to zip up.

Leopards are normally active only at night, so you're unlikely to encounter one on foot, although some have become accustomed to humans and may come close to lodges and camp sites after dark.

Lions have also been known to investigate lodges and camp sites. If you're camping out in the bush, zip your tent up completely. If you hear a large animal outside, lie still and don't try to leave your tent. While walking in the bush, if you encounter a lion try to avoid an adrenalin rush (easier said than done) and don't turn and run. If you act like prey, the lion could respond accordingly.

Rhinos tend to be wary of humans, although they may charge vehicles that get too close. If you are caught out on foot, face the charge and step to one side at the last moment in bullfight style (again, easier said than done).

If you're on a real shoestring budget and can't afford even the cheapest of safaris, you'll be frustrated by the rules and regulations that appear to be designed specifically to keep you out of the parks. There is no public transport, and hitching is forbidden. Even in parks where you are allowed to walk, you usually have to start from the park headquarters, which is deep in the park and only accessible by vehicle. Persistence, however, will normally pay off and anyone who really wants to see the parks rarely fails. Hitching may be prohibited *inside* the parks, but hours spent waving your thumb at the entrance gate may result in a lift that takes you precisely where you want to go. Most of the writers of this guide have at some stage hitched into parks, although sometimes the hours at the gate turned into very long days.

Avoiding the Animal Hype

In several of the region's national parks and wildlife reserves you can see the 'big five' – buffalo, elephant, leopard, lion and rhino. Along with giraffe, hippo and zebra, these ani-mals are undeniably attractive (and keep Fuji and Kodak in business) – but the way some safari companies and tourist brochures rant on about this group you'd think there was nothing else worth looking at. In Botswana's Moremi Wildlife Reserve we once spent a wonderful day watching several types of smaller mammals and birds, only to meet some travellers who complained that the place was 'empty', because they hadn't seen the 'big five' on the first morning. Another time we met a disgruntled group leaving Malawi's Nyika National Park because they hadn't seen a leopard, even though this beautiful area is inhabited by several other species, including the rare roan antelope and the zebra, whose speciality seems to be posing for pics on the skyline.

By all means aim for the 'big five', and relish your sightings, but don't let *not* seeing them spoil your day. This is Africa, not a zoo. Enjoy whatever you see – including the smaller, less hyped members of the animal kingdom. A group of social weavers, a dancing sand lizard or even a humble dung-beetle can be fascinating, and by appreciating the 'small stuff' as well as the 'big stuff', you'll get so much more out of your visit.

ACCOMMODATION

In all the countries covered in this book, you'll find a wide range of places to stay. Standards vary but quality generally reflects price.

In towns and cities, hotels at the top of the range have clean, air-con rooms with a private bathroom. In the mid-range, rooms probably have fans instead of air-con, and usually have a private bathroom, but there may not always be hot water. Near the budget end of the range, rooms are not always clean (they are sometimes downright filthy), bathrooms are usually shared and are often in an appalling state, and your only source of fresh air may be a hole in the window.

Many hotels – particularly the cheaper ones – double as brothels, so if this is your budget level don't be surprised if there's a lot of coming and going during the night.

In towns and cities frequented by budget travellers, there's usually at least one backpackers hostel; in places such as Harare and Cape Town there may be 10 or more. These are usually straightforward, no-frills places, with space for camping, beds in dorms, plus a few more private double or triple rooms, all at affordable prices. Having said that, some backpackers hostels offer remarkably good facilities and very comfortable rooms, which will appeal to travellers with a less spartan approach to travel. Many also have a TV room, swimming pool, bar, restaurant and email and phone service, as well as a travel desk where you can book tours and safaris. Several of the smarter backpackers hostels also take credit cards. How budget travel has changed!

Another option for the budget conscious are the resthouses run by local governments or district councils. These are found all over the region, and many date from colonial times. Some are very cheap and less than appealing; others are well-kept and good value. In resthouses and other cheap hotels, definitions of single and double rooms are not always consistent. It may be determined by the number of beds rather than the number of people. Therefore it is not unusual for two people to share a single room (which may have a large bed), paying either the single rate or something just a bit higher. If you want to save money, it's always worth asking about this.

Camping is a popular option for many visitors to Southern Africa, especially in national parks or at coastal and lakeshore areas. Some camping grounds are pretty basic, while others have good facilities such as hot showers and security fences. Wild camping (ie, not on an official site) is another option, although for security reasons – remembering the potential danger from people or animals – you should always choose your spot in the bush with great care. (For more details see the boxed text 'Minimum Impact Camping' below.)

Many places offer 'self-catering', but what this actually means varies from place to place. Sometimes all that's provided is a kitchen and stove, while you bring food, utensils – maybe even water and firewood. In other self-catering places, everything is provided, including a fully equipped kitchen staffed by cooks and helpers; you just bring your own food and they prepare it to your instructions (and wash up afterwards). The accommodation fee you pay covers their service, although tips are of course always appreciated.

In the national parks and wildlife reserves of Southern Africa, there's a wide choice of accommodation, ranging from

Minimum Impact Camping

The following guidelines are recommended for hiking or camping in the wilderness or other fragile areas of Southern Africa:

- The number one rule should always be to carry out your rubbish, unless it can be burnt completely. Do not leave cans or silver foil (including the inner lining from drinks and soup packets) in the fireplace. Some hikers bury rubbish, but this is generally a no-no, as animals may smell the food and dig it up, or it may be exposed by soil erosion during rain. Carrying out a few empty tins and packets should be no problem – it's got to be much lighter than when you carried it in.
- Select a well-drained camp site and, especially if it's raining, use a plastic or other waterproof groundsheet to prevent having to dig trenches, which just leads to more erosion.
- In some areas you have to camp at designated areas. In others you can camp where you like, but along popular trails it's still better to set up camp in established sites.
- Use toilet facilities if they are available. Otherwise, select a site at least 50m from water sources and bury wastes at least several inches deep. If possible, burn the used toilet paper or carry it in a couple of strong plastic bags until it can be burnt properly.
- Use only biodegradable soap products (you'll probably have to carry them from home) and use natural temperature water where possible. When washing up dishes with hot water, avoid pollution and damage to vegetation either by letting the water cool to outdoor temperature before pouring it out or dumping it in a gravelly place away from natural water sources and vegetation.
- Wash dishes and brush your teeth well away from watercourses.
- When building a fire, try to select an established site and keep fires as small as possible. Use only fallen dead wood and when you're finished, make sure ashes are cool and buried before leaving.

simple camping grounds, through to cabins, chalets and bungalows and luxurious, highly exclusive camps and lodges. It's important to note that the word 'camp' in this context is *not* the same as a camping ground or camp site. In some countries, the national park accommodation is run by the park authorities, while in other countries lodges and camps are managed by private hotel companies. Also note that many of the contact details for the accommodation in national parks refer to the offices in capital cities or major towns. These numbers are for bookings and inquiries, not direct contact with the lodge or camp.

In cities and towns, some hotels charge for a bed only, with all meals extra. If breakfast is included, it's usually on a par with the standard of accommodation: a full buffet in more expensive places; tea and bread further down the scale (still quaintly called a 'continental breakfast' in some countries). In the smaller and more exclusive national park lodges and camps, the price you pay normally includes accommodation, food, transfers, activities (such as boat rides or wildlife-viewing), laundry, even drinks at the bar.

Many hotels and lodges at the mid- and top end of the range charge in 'tiers'. Generally, visitors from overseas pay 'international' rates (ie, the full price); visitors from other Southern African countries pay 'regional rate' (about 25% less); and locals get 'resident rates' (around half price). Some places also give discounts in the low season. Where possible we have quoted international high season rates throughout this book. Whatever rate you pay, unfortunately you can't avoid the government tax which is normally added. This can be anything from 10% to a whopping 30%. We have usually included these taxes in the prices quoted in this book.

If you intend staying at mostly top-end hotels and lodges during your time in Southern Africa, it's always worth contacting a travel agent in the capital of the country you're in, or in your own country, to see if they can arrange hotel prices cheaper than the standard 'rack rates'.

FOOD

Local Food

You won't go hungry in Southern Africa. Whatever your budget, there's always something available, although it has to be said that the region's food can sometimes be bland and boring, and will never rate against the cuisine of, say, India or South-East Asia.

For shoestring travellers, or anyone on the move, takeaway snacks ('street food') of various sorts can be bought at roadsides, bus stations or in markets. These snacks include pieces of grilled meat, deep-fried potato or cassava chips, roasted corn cobs, boiled eggs, peanuts, biscuits, cakes and fried balls of flour-paste, which sometimes come close to tasting like doughnuts. Prices are always dirt cheap.

If you want something more substantial but still inexpensive, go to a food stall (sometimes called a 'tea stall'). These shacks, huts and other basic eating houses are usually found in markets, bus stations, or in any part of town that has low rent and a good passing trade (such as near factories – although tourists won't often visit such areas). The most common food you'll find at these places is the regional staple – a thick dough-like substance made from maize flour called *mealie meal* or *pap* in South Africa, and *nshima* or *nsima* in the countries further north. When fresh and cooked well, this is tasty and filling. It's usually eaten with a *relish*, which is either something very simple (just a few boiled vegetable leaves) or maybe something more grand such as a stew of beef, fish, beans or chicken. Sometimes rice is served instead of maize.

Meals at food stalls are served in a bowl, and although some locals prefer to eat with their hands, spoons are normally available. You may eat standing up, or a few rough chairs and a table might be provided. The time for the main meal is noon, and most of the very cheap places are closed in the evening. In the morning you can buy tea (with or without milk – the latter is cheaper) and bread, sometimes with margarine, or maybe a slightly sweetened bread-cake.

A grade above the food stalls are the cheap restaurants that exist in cities and large towns, or areas more used to tourists. These tend to be slightly larger, cleaner and with better facilities. You can buy traditional meals of rice/maize and sauce, or food that is less unusual to western tastes such as beef or chicken served with rice or chips (fries). In places along the coast or near lakes and rivers, fish is also available.

Up another level are cheap to mid-range restaurants, where meals cost from about US$3 to US$5. These places have facilities such as tablecloths, waiters and menus. They serve traditional food, and straightforward chicken-and-chips-type meals, as well as more elaborate options (steaks, pies and fish in sauce). Many of these places also serve meat or vegetable curries – in reality not very Indian, but often a good spicy stew that goes well with rice. *Samosas* (parcels of meat or vegetables wrapped in pastry) are another option often on the menu, as are burgers, pizzas and other western-style foods. Towns that receive a lot of visitors, such as Victoria Falls in Zimbabwe, Livingstone in Zambia or Nkhata Bay in Malawi, have restaurants specifically catering for the tourist trade, where you can get all the goodies you miss from home, such as a bacon sandwich or banana pancake.

As you go further up the quality scale to the mid-range restaurants where meals cost US$5 to US$10, you'll find the same kind of choices as you would in cheaper places but the price is usually determined by finer cooking, presentation, service and often the location. Here you will also find meals influenced by each country's former colonial power. Fish and chips may be a British leftover, while in Namibia you'll find German dishes on some menus, and Dutch or Malaysian influence in some South African meals. In Mozambique, there's a strong Portuguese flavour, and the seafood is especially good.

At top-end hotels and restaurants in cities and tourist areas, you can find straightforward international standards, often also influenced by colonial tradition, plus more elaborate French, British or Italian 'high' cuisine. In large cities you'll also find speciality restaurants, usually in the mid-range or top-end price bracket, serving genuine (or at least pretty close) Indian, Thai, Chinese, Lebanese, Italian or South American meals, or food from places in Africa such as Ethiopia.

For further information on local specialities, see the individual country chapters.

Game Meat

At top-end hotels and restaurants, and especially at lodges in or near national parks, you may find 'game meat' on the menu – sometimes quaintly termed 'local venison' in case the idea of eating a wild animal is less acceptable than eating a domesticated one. Although eating wildlife may at first seem distasteful, in reality, if you're going to eat meat, it's much better to eat from a local source, rather than from an animal that has been introduced to much of the region.

Having evolved over many centuries, indigenous animals, such as oryx, impala and buck, are adapted to their environment, more able to cope with extreme conditions and less prone to disease. In contrast, to breed good cattle requires constant attention from farmers, as well as reliable sources of water and grass. Thus, especially in places like Namibia and Zambia, the same area of land can support more 'game' animals than cows and potentially produce more food.

Despite these advantages, the farming of indigenous animals and the eating of game meat is only slowly catching on across the region, and there's a *very* long way to go before cows are replaced as the main protein source in Southern Africa.

Vegetarian

Although vegetarianism is rarely understood in Africa, and many locals think a meal is incomplete unless at least half of it once lived and breathed, you'll have a better chance in Southern Africa than many other parts of the continent of finding a meal without meat. Many cheap restaurants serve vegetarian meals because it's all the locals can afford – although even the simplest (and seemingly innocuous) vegetable sauce may sometimes have a small bit of meat or animal fat added. Fish is quite easy to find. You should note that in many places chicken is usually not regarded as 'real' meat, and might be served in a 'vegetarian' dish. In the more straightforward, upmarket establishments, vegetarian options do exist but are nearly always limited to omelettes or boiled vegetables. In cities and large towns, you're much better off seeking out a Lebanese, Indian or Italian restaurant, which will offer you more interesting meat-free choices.

Self-Catering

All over Southern Africa you'll find fresh fruit and vegetables for sale at shops, markets and roadside stalls. This is useful if you're self-catering with your own stove, and of course you can eat a lot of things raw (but see the advice on washing and peeling in the Health section earlier in this chapter).

Depending on the season, your diet can include bananas, pineapples, paw-paw (papaya), mangoes, avocados, tomatoes, carrots, onions and potatoes. Other foods in tins and packets can be bought from shops in small towns and villages, or from supermarkets in the cities.

DRINKS

Nonalcoholic Drinks

You can buy tea and coffee in many places, from top-end hotels and restaurants to the humble local eating house. International fizzy drinks such as Coke and Pepsi are widely available. As always, price reflects the standard of the establishment rather than the taste in your cup.

Alcoholic Drinks

In bars, hotels and bottle stores you can also buy beer and spirits – either imported international brands or locally brewed drinks. South African beers are available throughout the region, and in many areas they're pushing the local brands out of the market place.

Traditional beer of the region is made from maize, brewed in the villages and drunk from communal pots with great ceremony on special occasions, and with less ado in everyday situations. This product is also commercially brewed in many countries, and sold in large paper blue cartons, or by the bucket-full. For most Europeans, the thick texture and bitter-sweet taste is not appealing.

Other facts for the visitor in Southern Africa such as Legal Matters, Entertainment and Shopping are covered in the individual country chapters.

Getting There & Away

This chapter tells you how to reach Southern Africa from other parts of the world. An overview of travel within the region is given in the Getting Around the Region chapter. Details on travel between and around the individual countries are provided in the country chapters.

AIR

Airports & Airlines

You can fly to any major city in Southern Africa from anywhere in the world, but some routes are more popular (and therefore usually cheaper) than others. The main airports in Southern Africa that are of most use to tourists, with frequent flights to/from other parts of the world, are Johannesburg (Jo'burg), Durban, Cape Town, Windhoek, Harare, Lusaka and Lilongwe. There are also flights to other places covered in this book, but these are less convenient, or considerably more expensive, or both.

Where you fly to in the region depends on where you want to visit, but don't automatically aim to arrive at the airport nearest your intended start point. Even if you want to start your travels in, say, Zimbabwe or Namibia you might find it cheaper and easier to fly to South Africa first, from where you can easily travel overland or take a short regional flight to Harare or Windhoek. Having said that, even if you want to go first to South Africa, sometimes the cheapest deals are on flights via another country – such as Zimbabwe or Namibia!

> **Warning**
>
> The information in this chapter is particularly vulnerable to change: international air fares are volatile, routes are introduced and cancelled, schedules change, special deals come and go, and rules are amended. Airlines and governments seem to take a perverse pleasure in making price structures and regulations as complicated as possible. In addition, the travel industry is highly competitive and there are many lurks and perks.
>
> The upshot of this is that you should get opinions, quotes and advice from as many airlines and travel agencies as possible before you part with your hard-earned cash. The details given in this chapter should be regarded as pointers and are not a substitute for your own careful, up-to-date research.

Most major European airlines serve cities in Southern Africa. These include British Airways, KLM-Royal Dutch Airlines, Lufthansa, Air France and TAP Air Portugal. More airlines are listed in the Getting There & Away sections of the individual country chapters. Additionally, some Southern African airlines fly between Europe and Southern Africa. These include South African Airways and Air Namibia. South Africa is also linked to some other countries in West, North and East Africa.

Don't be put off by unlikely sounding carriers. For example, Ethiopian Airlines offers a very good-value international service between Europe and many parts of Africa. Also worth asking about is Alliance Air between London and Jo'burg, via Entebbe (Uganda) and Dar es Salaam (Tanzania).

Although there are a few airlines serving routes between the USA and Southern Africa (including American Airlines), many visitors find it cheaper to fly via Europe. Airlines flying between Australia and Southern Africa include Qantas.

Whichever airline you decide to take, when buying your air ticket, check out the possibility of 'open-jaw' deals – ie, flying into one country and out of another. Sometimes though, even if you want to do a linear trip (starting in Cape Town and finishing in Harare for example), it might be easier and cheaper to get a standard return (in and out of Cape Town) and a one-way regional flight (Harare to Cape Town) at the end of your trip.

Buying Tickets

To buy an air ticket you can deal direct with some airlines; sometimes they offer tremendous bargains, but they don't *always* supply the cheapest fares. Travel agencies usually offer a wider choice and are aware of special deals. But wherever you go, buying a plane ticket can be an intimidating business, so it's always worth taking time to do it properly. Start as soon as you can: some cheap tickets must be bought months in advance, and popular flights sell out early.

To find a suitable travel agency, look at the advertisements in weekend newspapers, travel magazines or on the Internet. Once you've got a list of five or six, start phoning around. Tell the agents which place/s you want to fly to, and they will offer you a choice of airline, route and fare. The fare is normally determined by the quality of the airline, the popularity of the route, the duration of the journey, the time of year, the length of any stopovers, the departure and arrival times, and any restrictions on the ticket (for definitions, see the boxed text 'Air Travel Glossary' later in this chapter). Also, the 'season' can greatly increase or reduce fares. The low season for flights to Southern Africa is usually April to June, while the high season is July to September and several weeks around Christmas. The rest of the year falls into the shoulder-season category.

When comparing agents' costs, you'll usually find that the cheapest flights are advertised by obscure 'bucket shops'. Many such firms are honest, but there are a few rogues who will take your money and disappear. If you feel suspicious, pay only a small deposit. Once you have the ticket, ring the airline to confirm that you are actually booked onto the flight before paying the balance. If the agent insists on cash in advance, go somewhere else.

Some agents may tell you that the cheap flights in the advertisement are fully booked, 'but we have another one that costs a bit more...'. Or the agent may claim to have the last two seats available for the whole month, which they will hold for two hours only. These are all old tricks. Don't panic – keep ringing around.

You may decide to opt for a more reliable service by paying more than a rock-bottom fare. You can go to a better-known travel agency chain (such as STA Travel, which has offices worldwide, Campus Travel in the UK, Council Travel in the USA or Travel CUTS in Canada) or to a small independent agency.

Once you have your ticket, keep a note of the number, flight numbers, dates and times and other details, and keep the information somewhere separate. The easiest thing to do is take a few photocopies – carry one with you and leave another at home. If the ticket is lost or stolen, this will help you get a replacement.

It's sensible to buy travel insurance as early as possible. That way you're normally covered for loss if an airport is closed by strike-action, or if you can't fly due to illness (see Travel Insurance under Visas & Documents in the Regional Facts for the Visitor chapter).

Some sample one-way and return fares are given in the following sections.

Travellers with Special Needs

If you have special needs of any sort – you're on crutches, vegetarian, in a wheelchair, taking the baby, terrified of flying – you should let the airline know as soon as possible so it can make arrangements. You should remind it when you reconfirm your booking (at least 72 hours before departure) and again when you check in at the airport. It may also be worth ringing the airlines before you make your booking to find out how they can handle your particular needs.

Getting Home

If you're already in Southern Africa and are looking for a flight home, Cape Town or Jo'burg offer the most options. Travel agencies are listed under the capital city sections in the individual country chapters.

Remember when buying tickets that standard one-way fares can often be more expensive than an excursion return fare – so you might be better off buying a cheap return and simply not coming back. (Or with a ticket in your pocket, maybe you will come back...!)

Airports and airlines can be surprisingly helpful, but they do need advance warning. If you're disabled, most international airports in Europe (although not all in Southern Africa) will provide escorts where needed, and there should be ramps, lifts and accessible toilets. Aircraft toilets are likely to present a problem; travellers should discuss this with the airline at an early stage and, if necessary, with their doctor.

Deaf travellers can ask for airport and inflight announcements to be written down for them. Outside South Africa, airports in Africa probably won't have these facilities. Blind travellers may have to travel separately from their guide dogs (the dog would be in a separate container) although smaller guide dogs may be admitted to the cabin. All guide dogs will be subject to the same quarantine laws (eg, six months in isolation) as any other animal when entering or returning to countries currently free of rabies, such as Britain or Australia.

Children aged under two travel for 10% of the standard fare (or free, on some airlines), as long as they don't occupy a seat. They don't get a baggage allowance either. 'Skycots' should be provided by the airline if requested in advance; these will take a child weighing up to about 10kg. Children between two and 12 years can usually occupy a seat for half to two-thirds of the full fare, and do get a baggage allowance. Push chairs can often be taken as hand luggage.

The UK

There are numerous airlines flying from Britain to Southern Africa. Some amazing bargains are sometimes available (or at least advertised), but most high-season return tickets from London to Jo'burg start at about UK£400, rising to UK£600 for a better-quality airline or a more direct route. Other return air fares from London include; Harare (around UK£450 to UK£650), Windhoek (UK£500 to UK£600), Lilongwe (UK£520 to UK£730) and Maputo (around UK£750). You can reach most of the Southern Africa capitals on flights via Jo'burg, which take longer but often work out cheaper than direct flights.

There are many travel agencies competing for your business. London is normally the best place to buy a ticket, and the following list of main players is a good starting point – although these days specialist travel agencies outside London can be just as cheap and easier to deal with. You should also check the ads in the weekend newspapers and travel magazines. In London, the freebie listings magazines (often found outside train stations) all contain travel ads.

Some of the companies listed under Organised Tours later in this chapter also sell flights, and some of the agents listed here also sell tours and safaris.

Africa Travel Centre (☎ 020-7383 4766) 21 Leigh St, London WC1H 9QX

Bridge the World (☎ 020-7911 0900) 52 Chalk Farm Rd, London NW1 8AN

STA Travel (☎ 020-7361 6262); nationwide telephone sales; plus branches in London, Manchester, Bristol and most large university towns.
Web site:www.statravel.co.uk

Trailfinders (☎ 020-7938 3366) 42-50 Earls Court Rd, London W8 6FT; also has offices elsewhere in London, plus Manchester, Bristol and several other cities.

usit CAMPUS (☎ 0870 240 1010, worldwide reservations) 52 Grosvenor Gardens, London SW1W OAG; offices also in YHA Adventure Shops and universities and colleges around the country.
Web site: www.usitcampus.co.uk

Also worth checking is North-South Travel (☎ 01245-492882), Moulsham Mill Centre, Chelmsford CM2 7PX, an experienced agency where profits support development projects overseas.

Getting back to the UK (or anywhere in Europe) from Southern Africa, the cheapest one-way fares from Jo'burg start at about UK£500, and about 10% more from Cape Town. From Harare, you can find tickets to Europe for about UK£500, while from Lusaka, Lilongwe and Maputo they cost around UK£600.

Continental Europe

You can fly to Southern Africa from any European capital, but the main hubs are

Paris, Amsterdam and Frankfurt. Some routes are more popular and frequent (and usually cheaper) than others. Specialist travel agencies advertise in newspapers and travel magazines, so check there for advertisements then start ringing around.

The USA & Canada

Although North Americans won't get the great deals that are available in London, there are a few discount agencies that keep tabs on the best air fare bargains. To give an idea, flights to Southern Africa (usually Jo'burg) from New York start at US$1050 and from San Francisco at US$1300. To reach one of the other capitals of Southern Africa, such as Harare, Lilongwe or Maputo, you can get a connection from Jo'burg for around US$200 more. It may be cheaper to fly on an economy hop from the USA to London, and then buy a discount ticket from there to Southern Africa. Canadians also will probably find the best deals travelling via London.

For more information, look in weekend newspapers or travel magazines for agencies' ads. Also worth checking are the student travel agencies, although in the USA you must be a student or be aged under 26 to qualify for discounted fares. STA specialises in student travel, but also sells to nonstudents.

The following list of agents will get you started – some also sell tours and safaris. Likewise, some of the companies listed under Organised Tours, following, also sell flights.

Council Travel (☎ 800-226 8624); offices nationwide.
Web site: www.counciltravel.com

Falcon Wings Travel (☎ 310-417 3590) 9841 Airport Blvd, Suite 822, Los Angeles, CA 90045

Magical Holidays to Africa (☎ 800-223 7452) 501 Madison Ave, New York, NY 10022

Pan Express Travel (☎ 212-719 9292) 55 W 39th St, Suite 310, New York, NY 10018

STA Travel (☎ 800-781 4040 or 800-925 4777); offices nationwide.
Web site: www.statravel.com

Travel CUTS Offices nationwide throughout Canada. Check www.travelcuts.com for details of your nearest office.

Uni Travel (☎ 314-569 2501) 11737 Administration Drive, Suite 120, St Louis, MO 63146

Travelling on the Internet

A few hours surfing the Web can help give you an idea of what you can expect in the way of good fares as well as be a useful source of information on routes and timetables.

Many airlines, full-service and no-frills, offer some excellent fares to Web surfers. They may sell seats by auction or simply cut prices to reflect the reduced cost of electronic selling. Many travel agencies around the world have Web sites and online ticket sellers will have an airfare for most destinations worldwide. Online ticket sales work well if you are doing a simple one-way or return trip on specified dates. However, online ticket sellers are no substitute for a travel agent who can sort complicated itineraries, has strategies for avoiding 10-hour layovers and can offer advice on everything from which airline has the best vegetarian food to the best travel insurance to bundle with your ticket.

Online Ticket Sellers

Bargain Holidays
www.bargainholidays.com – cheap flights, packages and last-minute deals from the UK.

Cheap Flights
www.cheap-flights.co.uk – connects you to hundreds of online travel agents in the UK.

Microsoft Expedia
expedia.msn.com – as well as the USA, Expedia has sites in Australia, Germany, Canada and the UK, with fares in the local currency.

Travel.com.au
www.travel.com.au – handles bookings for travel out of and around Australia.

Travelocity
www.travelocity.com – one of the best-known sites, it's well used but don't expect too many bargains.

If you're flying back home from Southern Africa, your best choice of one-way flights is from Jo'burg, where flights to New York cost from US$800. To Los Angeles the fare is about US$1400 and to Toronto it's about US$900. From Cape Town it's usually a bit more. From places like Lusaka or Lilongwe the cheapest fares to North America are around US$1100, via Europe or South Africa.

Air Travel Glossary

Cancellation Penalties If you have to cancel or change a discounted ticket, there are often heavy penalties involved; insurance can sometimes be taken out against these penalties. Some airlines impose penalties on regular tickets as well, particularly against 'no-show' passengers.

Courier Fares Businesses often need to send urgent documents or freight securely and quickly. Courier companies hire people to accompany the package through customs and, in return, offer a discount ticket which is sometimes a phenomenal bargain. However, you may have to surrender all your baggage allowance and take only carry-on luggage.

Full Fares Airlines traditionally offer 1st class (coded F), business class (coded J) and economy class (coded Y) tickets. These days there are so many promotional and discounted fares available that few passengers pay full economy fare.

Lost Tickets If you lose your airline ticket an airline will usually treat it like a travellers cheque and, after inquiries, issue you with another one. Legally, however, an airline is entitled to treat it like cash and if you lose it then it's gone forever. Take good care of your tickets.

Onward Tickets An entry requirement for many countries is that you have a ticket out of the country. If you're unsure of your next move, the easiest solution is to buy the cheapest onward ticket to a neighbouring country or a ticket from a reliable airline which can later be refunded if you do not use it.

Open-Jaw Tickets These are return tickets where you fly out to one place but return from another. If available, this can save you backtracking to your arrival point.

Overbooking Since every flight has some passengers who fail to show up, airlines often book more passengers than they have seats. Usually excess passengers make up for the no-shows, but occasionally somebody gets 'bumped' onto the next available flight. Guess who it is most likely to be? The passengers who check in late.

Promotional Fares These are officially discounted fares, available from travel agencies or direct from the airline.

Reconfirmation If you don't reconfirm your flight at least 72 hours prior to departure, the airline may delete your name from the passenger list. Ring to find out if your airline requires reconfirmation.

Restrictions Discounted tickets often have various restrictions on them – such as needing to be paid for in advance and incurring a penalty to be altered. Others are restrictions on the minimum and maximum period you must be away.

Round-the-World Tickets RTW tickets give you a limited period (usually a year) in which to circumnavigate the globe. You can go anywhere the carrying airlines go, as long as you don't backtrack. The number of stopovers or total number of separate flights is decided before you set off and they usually cost a bit more than a basic return flight.

Transferred Tickets Airline tickets cannot be transferred from one person to another. Travellers sometimes try to sell the return half of their ticket, but officials can ask you to prove that you are the person named on the ticket. On an international flight tickets are compared with passports.

Travel Periods Ticket prices vary with the time of year. There is a low (off-peak) season and a high (peak) season, and often a low-shoulder season and a high-shoulder season as well. Usually the fare depends on your outward flight – if you depart in the high season and return in the low season, you pay the high-season fare.

Australia & New Zealand

Airlines flying from Australia to Southern Africa include Qantas, Air Zimbabwe and South Africa Airways. If flying between New Zealand and Southern Africa you must go via Australia. The best place to start looking for cheap deals are the ads in major weekend newspapers. Standard return flights between Australia and Southern Africa (usually Jo'burg, Cape Town or Harare) start at around A$1750. For those not pressed for time, RTW tickets that include a stop in Southern Africa can be found for around A$2600. Another option is a RTW ticket or a return ticket to Europe with a stopover in Nairobi, from where Southern Africa can be reached by a regional flight or overland. Whichever way you get to Southern Africa, discuss your options with several travel agents before buying. Few have had much experience with cheap routes to Africa.

In Australia and New Zealand, inexpensive deals are available mainly from STA Travel, with branches in all capital cities and on most university campuses. In Australia, call ☎ 1300 360 960 for the latest fares and ☎ 131 776 for details of your nearest STA office (or check the Web site: www.statravel.com.au). In New Zealand, contact STA on ☎ 0800 874 773. Some of the companies listed under Organised Tours later in this chapter also sell flights.

One-way flights home are best bought in Jo'burg or Harare (Jo'burg to Perth is around A$1050, Jo'burg to Sydney about A$1200), and if you're elsewhere in the region it's normally best to go via Jo'burg or Harare anyway.

Africa

Many travellers on trans-Africa trips fly some sections, either because time is short or simply because the routes are virtually impassable. Some sample fares are given in the relevant country chapters.

The overland route between East Africa and Southern Africa is one of the most travelled in Africa, but if you do want to fly there are several options to choose from. In East Africa, by far the busiest hub is Nairobi. In Southern Africa the main hubs are Jo'burg, Cape Town and Harare. Many travellers fly the short hop between Dar es Salaam (Tanzania) and Lilongwe (Malawi) because doing this section overland is quite a grind. If you're heading from North Africa or north-east Africa (eg, Morocco, Egypt or Ethiopia), almost every flight to Southern Africa goes via Nairobi.

If you're travelling from West Africa, you have to fly as the overland route is blocked by war in Congo (Zaïre). Travellers also tend to avoid Congo-Brazzaville, Gabon, Cameroon and Nigeria. The most popular flight is from Abidjan (Côte d'Ivoire) to Jo'burg. You can also fly from Abidjan to Nairobi (Ethiopian Airways have one-way flights for around US$600) and then reach Southern Africa from there.

Asia

The main routes to/from Asia link South Africa to India; there are regular flights between Durban and Mumbai (Bombay) or Delhi. Alternatively, from other cities in Southern Africa, you can go via Nairobi, which also has regular flights to India. If you're coming from further east, Hong Kong is the discount-plane-ticket capital of the region. Its bucket shops are at least as unreliable as those of other cities, so seek advice from other travellers before buying a ticket. STA Travel, which is reliable, has branches in Hong Kong, Tokyo, Singapore, Bangkok and Kuala Lumpur.

LAND

Border Crossings

The most frequented routes into Southern Africa are from Tanzania into Malawi at Songwe (see Land in the Getting There & Away section in the Malawi chapter) and from Tanzania into Zambia at Nakonde (see Land in the Getting There & Away section in the Zambia chapter). The crossing point from Tanzania into Mozambique is rarely used, but described for intrepid travellers in the Mozambique chapter.

Other countries bordering the Southern African region are Angola and Congo (Zaïre). Both of these countries are embroiled in civil wars, although the far south of Angola (along the Kunene River) and the far south-east of the Congo (Zaïre) (around Lubumbashi) remain relatively unaffected. Nevertheless, even though the main border crossings at Ruacana and Oshikango (Namibia-Angola) and at Chilabombwe (Congo (Zaïre)-Zambia) *may* be open, tourists are very unlikely to go this way, firstly because it may not be safe or because security may decline further in the future, and secondly because once you've crossed the border you can't go very much further anyway.

Overland to Southern Africa

However you travel (by car, bike or public transport), if you're planning to reach Southern Africa overland, your first decision should be which of the two main routes through Africa you want to take.

From North & West Africa If you take the Sahara Route through North and West Africa, your options are currently limited to starting in Morocco and Mauritania, then into Senegal and the rest of West Africa, as the routes through Algeria into Mali and Niger were blocked in late 1999 due to political unrest. Once through West Africa, your route to Southern Africa will next be blocked by more unrest in Congo (Zaïre). This means a flight – probably from Accra (Ghana) or Lagos (Nigeria) to Nairobi, from where you can follow the route outlined under East Africa.

From North-East Africa The Nile Route through north-east Africa starts in Egypt, and goes into Sudan (either via Lake Nasser or via the Red Sea from Suez to Port Sudan). Southern Sudan is blocked to overland travellers due to civil war, so most people fly from Khartoum (Sudan) to Kampala (Uganda) or Nairobi, or go overland from northern Sudan through Eritrea and Ethiopia to Nairobi, where again you can follow the route outlined under East Africa.

From East Africa From Nairobi onwards, there are several options for reaching Southern Africa. The most popular route goes via Mombasa or Arusha to Dar es Salaam, capital of Tanzania. From here, drivers follow the Great North Road, and those without wheels take the Tanzania–Zambia Railway (TAZARA); both lead to Kapiri Mposhi in Zambia, from where Lusaka and Victoria Falls are easily reached. Alternatively, you can leave the road or train at Mbeya (in southern Tanzania) and go into northern Malawi at Songwe. Another option from Dar es Salaam takes you across the country to Kigoma on Lake Tanganyika, then by steamer to Mpulungu in Zambia, from where you can continue overland to Lusaka.

Other, more esoteric, possibilities from Nairobi include travelling through Uganda, Rwanda and Burundi, catching the Lake Tanganyika steamer from Bujumbura (if it's running), and connecting up with the previously outlined route at Mpulungu. However, as this book went to press, Rwanda, Burundi and Congo (Zaïre) were experiencing horrific civil wars. When the troubles are finally over, if you do reach Southern Africa by this route (especially if you also come through West Africa), arriving will be an absolute pleasure. Trouble is, once you've got this far, you may not feel like travelling any further!

Car & Motorcycle

Explaining how to drive your own vehicle through Africa to Southern Africa is beyond the scope of this book, although the overland routes outlined under 'Overland to Southern Africa' earlier in this chapter may be useful. Some manuals for trans-African drivers are listed under Books in the Regional Facts for the Visitor chapter. You might also want to check the Web site www.sahara-overland.com for information about crossing the Sahara.

The main points to emphasise include the incredibly long distances, the appalling nature of many roads, and the constant challenge of dealing with police or border officials. You should also be mechanically competent and carry a good collection of spares. You will need vehicle registration papers, liability insurance, a driving licence and international drivers' permit. You may also need a *carnet de passage*, effectively a passport for the vehicle and temporary waiver of import duty, designed to prevent car import rackets. Your local automobile association can provide details.

Liability insurance is not available in advance for some countries, but has to be bought when crossing the border. The cost and quality of such local insurance varies wildly, and you will find in some countries that you are effectively travelling uninsured.

Bicycle

Cycling is a cheap, convenient, healthy, environmentally sound and, above all, fun way to travel. It can also be addictive (see the boxed text 'Keep on Biking'). Not many people ride all the way to Southern Africa, but it's quite straightforward to take your bike with you on the plane and cycle around when you get there. For this, you can dismantle the bike and put the pieces in a bag or box, but it's much easier simply to wheel your bike to the check-in desk. Also, if it's not dismantled, the baggage handlers know it's a bike and are unlikely to pile suitcases on top of it. (Although some travellers say that if your bike doesn't stand up to baggage handlers it won't last long in Africa anyway!)

If you do decide not to dismantle the bike, you'll probably still have to remove the pedals, deflate the tyres and turn the handlebars sideways so the bike takes up less space in the hold. Check this with the airline well in advance, preferably before you pay for your ticket. Some airlines don't charge to carry a bike, and don't even include it in the weight allowance. Others charge an extra handling fee of around US$50.

Bikes in Africa are generally straightforward machines. Outside of South Africa, you'll have difficulty buying hi-tech European or American spares, so bring sufficient with you, and have a good idea of how to fit them. In particular, punctures will be frequent, so take at least four spare inner tubes. Consider the number of tube patches you might need, square it, and pack those too (plus tyre repair material and plenty of glue). A spare tyre is also worth carrying.

For more advice on cycling in Southern Africa, see the Getting Around the Region chapter.

Keep on Biking

We heard about a British traveller who had started out backpacking through Africa the 'normal' way. The first few weeks out of Cairo were fine, but by the time he got to Nairobi he was really fed up with long waits and interminable journeys on trucks and buses. So for less than US$80 he bought a local-style, all-steel 'black mamba' bicycle, fitted a few extras (such as water carriers) and started riding southwards through Tanzania, Malawi and Zimbabwe. The bike was a slower way of travelling, and his intended half-year away from home was soon used up. But he was having such a good time that he tore up his return air ticket and carried on for several more months, through Namibia and South Africa – all the way to Cape Town. By the end of his trip the 'white man on the black mamba' had become quite a famous figure among travellers on the Cape to Cairo route.

SEA

For most people, reaching Southern Africa by sea is not a viable option. The days of working your passage on commercial boats have vanished, although a few travellers do manage to hitch rides on private yachts going down the east coast of Africa from Mombasa to Mozambique or South Africa.

Alternatively, several cargo shipping companies sail between Europe and South Africa, with comfortable cabins for public passengers. The voyage between London and Cape Town takes about 16 days and costs from US$1500, all inclusive, one way. More details are available from Strand Voyages (☎ 020-7836 6363, fax 7497 0078, e voyages@strandtravel.co.uk), Charing Cross Shopping Concourse, Strand, London WC2N 4HZ. Web site: www.strandtravel.co.uk

ORGANISED TOURS

For people who are short on time or are new to travel in the region, an organised tour can be a very good way of reaching Southern Africa. You normally arrange and pay for your tour in your home country, either direct with the operating company, or through an agent. The tour may include flights from your home country, or you may have to arrange these separately. The tour can be anything from a few days (one company in London offers long weekends at Victoria Falls) to a few months.

Organised tours can be low-budget affairs, where you travel in an 'overland truck' with 15 to 30 other people and a couple of drivers and leaders, carrying tents and other equipment, buying food along the way, and cooking and eating together as a group.

At the other end of the spectrum are the 'tailor-made' or fully inclusive tours (FITs), arranged personally to your exact specifications. This is an increasingly popular option for visitors to Southern Africa, and although some companies offer highly exclusive and very expensive itineraries, others are reasonably priced and particularly attractive for individuals, families or groups of friends with specialist interests (such as watching birds, fishing or enjoying desert landscapes) who want to get away from larger organised groups.

In between the two extremes are the mid-range tours, leaving on set dates and keeping to a set itinerary, where you travel in a small group, probably in a minibus, staying at small hotels or maybe camping. The price would include transport, accommodation and the services of a tour leader, but you may be free to arrange (and pay for) some meals or extra activities.

Some companies offer a 'halfway house' between all-inclusive tours and going completely independently. They provide you with self-guided itineraries, including pre-booked flights, vehicle hire and accommodation where required, but let you decide on exactly where and when you want to go.

Around the world there are hundreds of tour companies and agencies featuring Southern Africa. The best place to begin looking for ideas are the advertisements in the weekend newspapers and travel magazines. If you have specialist interests, look in specialist magazines. For example, companies organising wildlife tours advertise in nature magazines, hiking tours in outdoor magazines, railway tours in train magazines and so on.

The following lists include just a few of the Southern Africa specialists, and will provide a few pointers. Some of the companies listed here also sell flights. Contact them directly, ask for a brochure or Web site address, see what appeals, then take it from there.

The UK

Acacia Expeditions (☎ 020-7706 4700, ⓔ acacia@afrika.demon.co.uk) 23a Craven Terrace, Lancaster Gate, London W2 3QH. Wide range of safaris, overland tours, diving, trekking and camping trips for travellers on less flexible budgets.
Web site: www.acacia-africa.com

Dragoman (☎ 01728-861133, fax 861127, ⓔ info@dragoman.co.uk) Camp Green, Kenton Rd, Debenham, Stowmarket, Suffolk IP14 6LA. Smart end of the overland tour market, with short and long trips throughout Southern Africa and the world.
Web site: www.dragoman.co.uk

Guerba (☎ 01373-858956, fax 838351, ⓔ info@guerba.co.uk) Wessex House, 40 Station Rd, Westbury, Wiltshire BA13 3JN. Short and long safaris on a budget by truck throughout Africa.
Web site: www.guerba.co.uk

Hartley's Safaris (☎ 01673-861600, fax 861666, ⓔ info@hartleys-safaris.co.uk) The Old Chapel, Chapel Lane, Hackthorn LN2 3PN. Tailor-made safaris for mid and upper-range clients.
Web site: www.hartleys-safaris.co.uk

Okavango Tours & Safaris (☎ 020-8343 3283, fax 8343 3287, ⓔ info@okavango.com) Marlborough House, 298 Regents Park Rd, London N3 2TJ. Small specialist outfit with top-class, good-value tours all over Southern Africa.
Web site: www.okavango.com

Safari Drive (☎ 01488-681611, fax 685055, ⓔ safari_drive@compuserve.com) Wessex House, 127 High St, Hungerford RG17 0DL. Experienced and specialised, providing self-drive 4WDs, with self-guided itineraries, plus tailor-made nondriving tours and safaris, all over Southern Africa.
Web site: www.safaridrive.com

Sunvil Discovery (☎ 020-8232 9777, fax 8568 8330, ⓔ africa@sunvil.co.uk) Sunvil House, Upper Square, Old Isleworth TW7 7BJ. Imaginative, flexible and good-value tours and fly-drives in Namibia, Zimbabwe and South Africa, plus tailor-made and scheduled safaris in Zambia and Botswana.
Web site: www.sunvil.co.uk

Tana Travel (☎ 01789-414200, fax 414420, ⓔ info@tanatravel.com) 2 Ely St, Stratford-upon-Avon CV37 6LW. Tailor-made tours and

safaris throughout Southern Africa for mid-range to top-end clients.
Web site: www.tanatravel.co.uk

France

Makila Voyages (☎ 01 42 96 80 00, fax 01 42 96 18 05) 4 Place de Valois, 75001 Paris. Upmarket company with tours and safaris all over East and Southern Africa.
Web site: www.makila.fr

The USA & Canada

Africa Travel Centre, Explorers Travel Group (☎ 800-631 5650, 732-542 9006, fax 542 9420, e explorers@monmouth.com) One Main St, Suite 304, Eatontown, NJ 07724. Flights, hotels, overland tours, safaris, tailor-made trips, plus visas and insurance.

Africa Adventure Company (☎ 954-491 8877, 800 882 9453, fax 954-491-9060, e noltingaac@aol.com) 5353 N Federal Hwy, Suite 300, Fort Lauderdale, FL 33308. Top safari specialists.
Web site: www.africa-adventure.com

Born Free Safaris (☎ 800-372 3274, fax 818-753 1460, e bornfreesafaris@att.net) 12504 Riverside Dr, North Hollywood, CA 91607. Safaris, trekking, cultural tours and flights.
Web site: www.bornfreesafaris.com

Bushtracks (☎ 800-995-8689, fax 650-463 0925, e info@bushtracks.com) 845 Oak Grove Ave, Suite 204, Menlo Park, CA 94025. Expeditions, tours and safaris.
Web site: www.bushtracks.com

Global Exchange (☎ 415-255 7269, fax 255 7498, e info@globalexchange.org) 2017 Mission St, No. 303, San Francisco, CA 94110. Offers 'reality tours' such as 'Redefining Development and Democracy' in South Africa.
Web site: www.globalexchange.org

Reservations Africa (☎ 250-386 1335, 888-891 5111, fax 250-386 3266, e info@reservationsafrica.com) 550-1070 Douglas St, Victoria BC V8W 2C4. Southern Africa specialists, offering tailor-made tours and safaris, plus flights.
Web site: www.reservationsafrica.com

Safaricentre (☎ 800-223 6046, e info@safaricentre.com) 3201 N Sepulveda Blvd, Manhattan Beach, CA 90266. Huge range of flights, camps, hotels, budget tours and luxury safaris.
Web site: www.safaricentre.com

Spector Travel (☎ 800-879 2374, fax 338 0110, e africa@spectortravel.com) 31 St James Ave, Boston, MA 02116. Budget tours all over Africa, plus discounted airfares.
Web site: www.spectatortravel.com

Voyagers (☎ 800-633 0299, e explore@voyagers.com) PO Box 915, Ithaca, NY. Photographic and wildlife viewing safaris.
Web site: www.voyagers.com

Australia & New Zealand

Adventure World (☎ 02-9956 7766, fax 9956 7707, e info@adventureworld.com.au) 73 Walker St, North Sydney, NSW 2060. Overland tours, safaris, car hire and hotel packages.
Web site: www.adventureworld.com.au

Africa Travel Centre (☎ 02-9267 3048, fax 9267 3047, e africa@travel.com.au) Level 11, 456 Kent St, Sydney, NSW 2000. Overland tours, hotels, custom safaris, plus flights.

Africa Travel Centre (☎ 09-520 2000, fax 520 2001) 21 Remuera Rd, Newmarket, Auckland 3. Diving, overland tours, tailor-made safaris and trekking.

African Wildlife Safaris (☎ 03-9696 2899, fax 9696 4937, e office@africansafaris.com.au) Level 1, 259 Coventry St, South Melbourne, Victoria 3205. Specialists mainly in safaris to Southern Africa.

Peregrine Travel (☎ 03-9663 8611, fax 9663 8618, e travelcentre@peregrine.net.au) Level 2, 258 Lonsdale St, Melbourne, Victoria 3000. Africa specialists, catering for all budgets.
Web site: www.peregrine.net.au

There are also many local tour companies (based mainly in South Africa, Zimbabwe and Namibia) that organise tours all over the region. These are listed under Organised Tours in the individual country chapters.

Wildlife Guide

PRIMATES

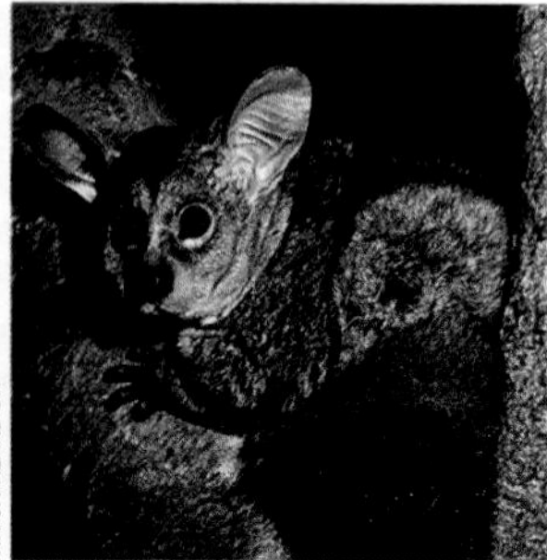

MITCH REARDON

Bushbabies Greater (or thick-tailed) bushbaby *Otolemur crassicaudatus* (pictured); lesser bushbaby *Gulag moholi*

Named for their plaintive wailing call, bushbabies are actually primitive primates. Both species have small heads, large rounded ears, thick bushy tails and the enormous eyes that are typical of nocturnal primates. The greater bushbaby has dark brown fur, while the tiny lesser bushbaby is very light grey with yellowish colouring on its legs. Tree sap and fruit are the mainstay of their diet, supplemented by insects as well as, in the case of the greater bushbaby, lizards, nestlings and eggs.

Size: *Greater bushbaby* length 80cm, including a 45cm tail; weight up to 1.5kg. *Lesser bushbaby* length 40cm; weight 150 to 200g. **Distribution:** the greater bushbaby is restricted to the region's east, the lesser bushbaby to South Africa, Mozambique and Namibia. **Status:** common but strictly nocturnal.

RICHARD I'ANSON

Vervet monkey *Cercopithecus aethiops*

The most common monkey of the woodland-savanna, the vervet is easily recognisable by its grizzled grey hair and black face fringed with white. The male has a distinctive bright blue scrotum, an important signal of status in the troop. Troops may number up to 30. The vervet monkey is diurnal and forages for fruits, seeds, leaves, flowers, invertebrates and the occasional lizard or nestling. It rapidly learns where easy pickings can be found around lodges and camp sites, but becomes a pest when it gets habituated to being fed. Most park authorities destroy such individuals, so one should avoid feeding them.

Size: up to 130cm long, including a 60cm tail; weight 3.5 to 8kg. **Distribution:** widespread in woodland-savanna throughout the region; absent only from deserts. **Status:** very common and easy to see.

RICHARD I'ANSON

Chacma baboon *Papio ursinus*

The dog-like snout of the chacma baboon gives it a more aggressive appearance than most other primates, which have much more human-like facial features. However, when you see the interactions within a troop, it's difficult not to make anthropomorphic comparisons. The chacma baboon lives in troops of up to 150 animals, and there is no single dominant male. It is strictly diurnal and forages for grasses, fruits, insects and (occasionally) small vertebrates. The baboon is a notorious opportunist and may become a pest in camp sites, which it visits for hand-outs. Such individuals can be very dangerous and are destroyed by park officials, so don't feed them.

Size: shoulder height 75cm; weight 25 to 45kg. **Distribution:** throughout the region. **Status:** common in many areas, and active during the day.

RODENTS

Springhare *Pedetes capensis*

In spite of its name and large ears, the springhare is not a hare, but a rodent. With its powerful, outsized hind feet and small forelegs, it most resembles a small kangaroo and shares a similar hopping motion. The springhare digs extensive burrows, from which it emerges at night to feed on grass and grass roots. Reflections of spotlights in its large, bright eyes often give it away on night safaris. Although swift, it is preyed upon by everything from jackals to lions.

ANTHONY BANNISTER/ABPL

Size: length 75 to 85cm; weight 2.5 to 3.8kg. **Distribution:** widespread throughout most of the region; favours grassland habitats with sandy soils. **Status:** common, but strictly nocturnal.

Cape porcupine *Hystrix africaeaustralis*

The prickly Cape porcupine is the largest rodent native to Southern Africa. Its spread of long black-and-white banded quills from the shoulders to the tail makes it unmistakable. For shelter, it either occupies caves or excavates its own burrows. The porcupine's diet consists mainly of bark, tubers, seeds and a variety of plant and ground-level foliage. The young are born during the hot summer months, in litters of between one and four.

DEANNA SWANEY

Size: length 75 to 100cm; weight 10 to 24kg. **Distribution:** throughout the region. **Status:** nocturnal, but occasionally active on cooler days; difficult to see.

Cape ground squirrel *Xerus inauris*

The ground squirrel is a sociable rodent living in colonial burrows, which it often shares with meerkats. It feeds on grass, roots, seeds and insects, but readily takes hand-outs from people in tourist camps. The ground squirrel is well adapted to its dry surroundings; it does not need to drink, and extracts all the moisture it requires from its food. It has an elegant fan-like tail, which it erects when alarmed and also uses as a sunshade.

MITCH REARDON

Size: length 45cm; weight up to 1kg. **Distribution:** Namibia, northern South Africa and south-central Botswana. **Status:** common; active throughout the day.

CARNIVORES

LUKE HUNTER

Genets Small-spotted (or common) genet *Genetta genetta;* large-spotted (or rusty-spotted) genet *Genetta tigrina* (pictured)

Relatives of the mongoose, genets resemble long, slender domestic cats and have a pointed fox-like face. The two species in the region are very similar, but can be differentiated by the tail tips (white in the small-spotted genet and black in the large-spotted). They are solitary animals, sleeping by day in abandoned burrows, rock crevices or hollow trees and emerging at night to forage. Very agile, they hunt equally well on land or in trees, feeding on small rodents, birds, reptiles, nestlings, eggs, insects and fruits.

Size: length 85 to 110cm; weight 1.5 to 3.2kg. **Distribution:** the small-spotted genet is widespread in Namibia, Botswana, south-western Zimbabwe and most of South Africa; the large-spotted genet is common in the rest of the region, with a slight overlap. **Status:** very common, but strictly nocturnal.

RICHARD I'ANSON

Mongooses

Though common, most mongooses are solitary and are usually seen fleetingly. The slender mongoose *(Galerella sanguinea)* is recognisable by its black-tipped tail, which it holds aloft like a flag when running. A few species, such as the dwarf mongoose *(Helogale parvula)*, the banded mongoose *(Mungos mungo*; pictured) and the meerkat *(Suricata suricatta),* are intensely sociable. Family groups are better than loners at spotting danger and raising kittens. Social behaviour also helps when confronting a threat: collectively, they can intimidate much larger enemies. Insects and other invertebrates are their most important prey.

Size: ranging in size from the dwarf mongoose at length 40cm/weight up to 400g, to the white-tailed mongoose *(Ichneumia albicauda)* at length 120cm/weight up to 5.5kg. **Distribution:** throughout the region. **Status:** common where they occur; sociable species are diurnal, solitary species are nocturnal.

MITCH REARDON

Aardwolf *Proteles cristatus*

Smallest of the hyaena family, the aardwolf subsists almost entirely on harvester termites and almost never consumes meat. Unlike other hyaena species, it does not form clans or den communally; rather, it forms loose associations between pairs and forages alone. The male assists the female in raising the cubs, mostly by babysitting at the den while the mother forages. The aardwolf is persecuted in the mistaken belief that it kills stock, and may suffer huge population crashes following spraying for locusts (this spraying also wipes out the termites, their major prey).

Size: shoulder height 40 to 50cm; length 80 to 100cm; weight 8 to 12kg. **Distribution:** throughout the region as far north as southern Zambia, but absent from Mozambique and Malawi. **Status:** uncommon; nocturnal, but occasionally seen at dawn and dusk.

Brown hyaena *Hyaena brunnea*

ANDREW MacCOLL

Once considered endangered, the brown hyaena is relatively numerous throughout the arid south-west of the region. It is a poor hunter and subsists largely by scavenging, visiting kill remains left by other animals and carrying off large parts to cache for later. It occasionally kills small animals and is partial to ostrich eggs and fruit. The brown hyaena forages alone, although groups numbering as many as 12 cooperate to raise young and defend territories. It is primarily nocturnal and generally difficult to see, though excellent viewing is possible in the Kgalagadi Transfrontier Park (South Africa–Botswana).

Size: shoulder height 80cm; length 120 to 160cm; weight 28 to 43kg. **Distribution:** throughout Botswana, Namibia except the south-east, the extreme south-west of Zimbabwe and northern South Africa. **Status:** widespread in semi-arid areas but uncommon elsewhere.

Spotted hyaena *Crocuta crocuta*

JASON EDWARDS

Widely reviled as a cowardly scavenger, the spotted hyaena is actually a highly efficient predator with a fascinating social system. Females are larger and dominant to males and even have male physical characteristics, the most remarkable of which is an erectile clitoris rendering the sexes virtually indistinguishable at a distance. The spotted hyaena is massively built and appears distinctly canine, but is more closely related to a cat than to a dog. It can reach speeds of up to 60km/h and a pack can easily dispatch adult wildebeests and zebras. The lion is its main natural enemy.

Size: shoulder height 85cm; length 120 to 180cm; weight up to 80kg. **Distribution:** occurs throughout the region, but is only common in protected areas; absent or rare in most of South Africa and Namibia. **Status:** common where there is suitable food; mainly nocturnal, but also seen during the day.

Cheetah *Acinonyx jubatus*

ALEX DISSANAYAKE

The world's fastest land mammal, the cheetah can reach speeds of at least 105km/h but becomes exhausted after a few hundred metres and therefore usually stalks prey to within 60m before unleashing its tremendous acceleration. The cheetah preys on antelopes weighing up to 60kg as well as hares and young wildebeests and zebras. Litters may be as large as nine but in open savanna habitats, most cubs are killed by other predators, particularly lions. Young cheetahs disperse from the mother when aged around 18 months. The males form coalitions, while females remain solitary for life.

Size: shoulder height 85cm; length 180 to 220cm; weight up to 65kg. **Distribution:** widespread (but at low densities) throughout the region; absent from most of South Africa and increasingly restricted to protected areas elsewhere. **Status:** uncommon, with individuals moving over large areas; active by day.

ALEX DISSANAYAKE

Leopard *Panthera pardus*

The leopard is the supreme ambush hunter, using infinite patience to stalk within metres of its prey before attacking in an explosive rush. It eats everything from insects to zebras, but antelopes are its primary prey. The leopard is highly agile and hoists its kills into trees to avoid losing them to lions and hyaenas. It is a solitary animal, except during the mating season, when the male and female stay in close association for the female's week-long oestrus. A litter of up to three cubs is born after a gestation of three months and the females raise them without any assistance from the males.

Size: shoulder height 70 to 80cm; length 160 to 210cm; weight up to 90kg. **Distribution:** widespread throughout the region except for central South Africa. **Status:** common but being mainly nocturnal, they are the most difficult of the large cats to see.

ALEX DISSANAYAKE

Lion *Panthera leo*

The lion spends much of the night hunting, patrolling territories and playing. It lives in prides of up to about 30, the core comprising between four to 12 related females, which remain in the pride for life. Males form coalitions and defend the female groups from foreign males. The lion is strictly territorial, defending ranges of between 50 to 400 sq km. Young males are ousted from the pride at the age of two or three, entering a period of nomadism that ends at around five years old, when they are able to take over their own pride. The lion hunts virtually anything, but wildebeests, zebras and buffaloes are the mainstay of their diet.

Size: shoulder height 120cm; length 250 to 300cm; weight up to 240kg (male), 160kg (female). **Distribution:** occurs in all major parks in the region but is rare outside them. **Status:** common in parks; mainly nocturnal, but easy to see during the day.

RICHARD I'ANSON

Caracal *Felis caracal*

Sometimes also called the African lynx due to its long tufted ears, the caracal is a robust, powerful cat that preys predominantly on small antelopes, birds and rodents but is capable of taking down animals many times larger than itself. Like most cats, it is largely solitary. Females give birth to one to three kittens after a 79- or 80-day gestation and raise the kittens alone. It is territorial, marking its home-range with urine sprays and faeces. The caracal has a wide tolerance for habitat but prefers semi-arid regions, dry savannas and hilly country; it is absent from dense forest.

Size: shoulder height 60cm; length 95 to 120cm; weight up to 13kg. **Distribution:** throughout the region. **Status:** fairly common, but largely nocturnal and difficult to see.

Serval *Felis serval*

MITCH REARDON

A tall, slender and long-legged cat, the serval resembles a miniature cheetah. Its tawny to russet-yellow coat is dotted with large black spots, forming long bars and blotches on the neck and shoulders. Other distinguishing features include very large upright ears, a long neck and a relatively short tail. The serval generally eats vegetation near water and is most common on floodplain savannas, wetlands and woodlands near streams. It feeds primarily on rodents, including mice, vlei rats, cane rats and hares, as well as birds, small reptiles and sometimes the young of small antelopes.

Size: shoulder height 60cm; length 95 to 120cm; weight up to 13kg. **Distribution:** northern Namibia, northern Botswana, eastern South Africa and widespread in other areas. **Status:** relatively common, but mainly nocturnal; sometimes seen in the early morning and late afternoon.

African wild cat *Felis lybica*

LUKE HUNTER

The progenitor of the household tabby, the African wild cat was originally domesticated by the Egyptians. African wild cats differ from domestic cats in having reddish backs to their ears, proportionally longer legs and a generally leaner appearance. They crossbreed freely with domestic cats close to human habitation and this is probably the greatest threat to the wild species. Wild cats subsist mainly on small rodents, but also prey on birds and insects and species up to the size of hares. They are solitary except when mating and when females have kittens.

Size: shoulder height 35cm; length 85 to 100cm; weight up to 6kg. **Distribution:** throughout the region. **Status:** common; nocturnal, although sometimes spotted at dawn and dusk.

Bat-eared fox *Otocyon megalotis*

JASON EDWARDS

The huge ears of this little fox detect the faint sounds of invertebrates below ground, before it unearths them in a burst of frantic digging. The bat-eared fox eats mainly insects, especially termites, but also wild fruit and small vertebrates. It is monogamous and is often seen in groups comprising a mated pair and offspring. Natural enemies include large birds of prey, spotted hyaenas, caracals and larger cats. It will bravely attempt to rescue a family member caught by a predator by using distraction techniques and harassment, which extends to nipping larger enemies on the ankles.

Size: shoulder height 35cm; length 75 to 90cm; weight up to 5kg. **Distribution:** widespread in Namibia, Botswana, western Zimbabwe and throughout South Africa except for the east. **Status:** common, especially in national parks; mainly nocturnal, but often seen in the late afternoon and early morning.

DENNIS JONES

Cape fox *Vulpes chama*

Southern Africa's smallest canid, the dainty Cape fox forms monogamous pairs but usually forages alone. It feeds on insects, small mammals and reptiles. In some parks, individuals visit tourist barbecues to scrounge for food and eventually become very tame. In farming areas the Cape fox is wrongly blamed for losses of lambs and goat kids and is heavily persecuted as a result.

Size: shoulder height 30 to 33cm; length 75 to 90cm; weight up to 4kg. **Distribution:** drier parts of Namibia, western South Africa and southern Botswana. **Status:** common; mostly seen at night or in the early morning, especially in the summer months, when they are often seen close to their breeding burrows.

ANDREW MacCOLL

Black-backed jackal *Canis mesomelas*

This jackal relies heavily on scavenging but is also an efficient hunter, taking insects, birds, rodents and even the occasional small antelope. It also frequents human settlements and takes domestic stock. As a result, it is persecuted by farmers but is very resilient and can be seen widely on farms. The black-backed jackal forms long-term pair bonds, and each pair occupies a home range varying from 3 to 21.5 sq km. Pups are born in litters of one to six, and are often looked after by their siblings from an older litter as well as their parents.

Size: shoulder height 35 to 50cm; length 95 to 120cm; weight up to 12kg. **Distribution:** throughout the region. **Status:** very common and easily seen; active both night and day.

CLEM HAAGNER/ABPL

Side-striped jackal *Canis adustus*

Resembling the black-backed jackal but with a distinctive white-tipped tail, the side-striped jackal is the most omnivorous of all jackals, commonly eating wild fruit, maize, eggs and invertebrates, as well as meat. It forages alone or in pairs, in a territory that it defends from other pairs. It has a varied vocal repertoire, including an explosive yap and an owl-like hoot.

Size: shoulder height 35 to 50cm; length 95 to 120cm; weight up to 12kg. **Distribution:** extreme northern Namibia, northern Botswana, throughout Zimbabwe, Zambia and Malawi, extreme eastern and northeastern South Africa. **Status:** widespread but not abundant; active at night and in the early morning.

Wild dog *Lycaon pictus*

RICHARD I'ANSON

The wild dog's blotched black, yellow and white coat, and its large, round ears, make it unmistakable. It is highly sociable, living in packs of up to 40, though 12 to 20 is typical. Marvellous endurance hunters, the pack chases prey relentlessly to the point of exhaustion, then cooperates to pull down the quarry. The wild dog is widely reviled for killing prey by eating it alive, but this is in fact probably as fast as any of the 'cleaner' methods used by carnivores. Mid-sized antelopes are its preferred prey, but it can kill animals as large as a buffalo. The wild dog requires enormous areas and is one of the most endangered large carnivores in Africa.

Size: shoulder height 65 to 80cm; length 105 to 150cm; weight up to 30kg. **Distribution:** fairly widespread in Botswana, but restricted to major parks elsewhere. **Status:** highly threatened, with numbers declining severely from a naturally low density.

Cape clawless otter *Aonyx capensis*

ROGER de la HARPE/ABPL

Very similar to European otters but much larger, the Cape clawless otter has a glossy chocolate-brown coat and a white or cream-coloured lower face, throat and neck. Unlike most otters, only its hind feet are webbed, and the front feet end in dexterous, human-like 'fingers' with rudimentary nails. The otter is normally active during early morning and evening, though it becomes nocturnal in areas where it is hunted by humans. Its main foods include fish, crabs and frogs as well as marine molluscs in seashore habitats. Its only known natural enemy is the crocodile.

Size: length 105 to160cm, including a 50cm tail; weight up to 28kg. **Distribution:** all large freshwater bodies and rivers in the region, as well as eastern and southern coastlines. **Status:** uncommon throughout its distribution, and very shy; usually seen in the early morning and late afternoon.

Honey badger (or ratel) *Mellivora capensis*

LORNA STANTON/ABPL

Africa's equivalent of the European badger, the honey badger has a reputation for a vile temper and ferocity. While stories of it attacking animals the size of buffaloes are probably folklore, it is pugnacious and astonishingly powerful for its size. Normally active between dusk and dawn, it is highly omnivorous, feeding on meat, fish, frogs, scorpions, spiders, reptiles, small mammals, roots, honey, berries and eggs. In some parks, the honey badger becomes used to scavenging from bins, presenting the best opportunity for viewing this normally elusive animal.

Size: length 90 to 100cm; weight up to 15kg. **Distribution:** widespread, although absent from central South Africa and from Lesotho. **Status:** generally occurs in low densities; mainly nocturnal.

UNGULATES (HOOFED ANIMALS)

ALEX DISSANAYAKE

African elephant *Loxodonta africana*

The African elephant usually lives in small family groups of between 10 and 20, which frequently congregate in much larger herds at a common water hole or food resource. Its society is matriarchal and herds are dominated by old females. Bulls live alone or in bachelor groups, joining the herds when females are in season. A cow may mate with many bulls during her oestrus. An adult's average daily food intake is about 250kg of grass, leaves, bark and other vegetation. An elephant's life span is about 60 to 70 years, though some individuals may reach 100 or more.

Size: shoulder height up to 4m (male); weight 5 to 6.5 tonnes. **Distribution:** mostly restricted to parks in northern Namibia, northern Botswana, northern Zimbabwe, northern South Africa, southern and central Zambia and southern Mozambique. **Status:** very common in some parks but very rare elsewhere.

LUKE HUNTER

Rock dassie *Procavia capensis*

The rock dassie (also known as the hyrax) occurs practically everywhere there are mountains or rocky outcrops. It is a sociable animal and lives in colonies of up to 60 individuals. Despite its resemblance to a large, robust guinea pig, the dassie is actually related to the elephant. It feeds on vegetation, but spends much of the day sunning itself on rocks or chasing other rock dassies in play. Where it's habituated to humans it is often quite tame, but otherwise it dashes into rock crevices when alarmed, uttering shrill screams.

Size: length 60cm; weight up to 5.5kg. **Distribution:** throughout the region, but absent from dense forest. **Status:** common and easy to see, especially where they have become habituated to humans.

RICHARD I'ANSON

Rhinoceroses White rhinoceros *Ceratotherium simum* (pictured); black rhinoceros *Diceros bicornis*

Aggressive poaching for rhino horn has made the rhino Africa's most endangered large mammal. The white rhino is a grazer and prefers open plains, while the black rhino is a browser, living in scrubby country. While the white rhino is generally docile, the black rhino is prone to charging when alarmed. Its eyesight is extremely poor and it has even been known to charge trains or elephant carcasses. The white rhino is the more sociable species, forming cow-calf groups numbering up to 10. The black rhino is solitary and territorial, only socialising during the mating season.

Size: (white rhino) shoulder height 180cm/weight 1200 to 2000kg; (black rhino) shoulder height 160cm/weight 800 to 1200kg. **Distribution:** restricted to protected areas, mainly in the parks of South Africa and Namibia. **Status:** black rhinos are endangered; white rhinos are threatened but well protected in South Africa.

Zebra Burchell's zebra *Equus burchelli* (pictured); mountain zebra *Equus zebra*

RICHARD I'ANSON

The Burchell's zebra has shadow lines between its black stripes whereas the mountain zebra lacks shadows and has a gridiron pattern of black stripes just above its tail. Both species are grazers but occasionally browse on leaves and scrub. The social system centres around small groups of related mares over which stallions fight fiercely. Stallions may hold a harem for as long as 15 years but single mares are often lost to younger males, which gradually build up their own harem. Both zebras are preyed upon by all the large carnivores, with lions being their main predators.

Size: shoulder height 140 to 160cm; weight up to 390kg. **Distribution:** Burchell's zebras are found throughout the region; mountain zebras are found in southern South Africa and scattered throughout Namibia. **Status:** Burchell's zebra is common; mountain zebra is far less numerous.

Warthog *Phacochoerus aethiopicus*

TONY WHEELER

The warthog's social organisation is variable, and groups usually consist of one to three sows with their young. Males form bachelor groups or are solitary, only associating with the female groups when a female is in season. The distinctive facial warts can be used to determine sex – females have a single pair of warts under the eyes whereas the males have a second set further down the snout. The warthog feeds mainly on grass, but also eats fruit and bark. In hard times, it will burrow with its snout for roots and bulbs. It rests and gives birth in abandoned burrows or in excavated cavities in abandoned termite mounds.

Size: shoulder height 70cm; weight up to 105kg, but averages 50 to 60kg. **Distribution:** widespread in the region; absent in deserts and in South Africa restricted to the north-east. **Status:** common and easy to see.

Hippopotamus *Hippopotamus amphibius*

RICHARD I'ANSON

The hippo is found close to fresh water, spending most of the day submerged and emerging at night to graze on land. It can consume about 40kg of vegetable matter each evening. It lives in large herds, tolerating close contact in the water, but forages alone when on land. Adult bulls defend territories against each other aggressively and most males bear the scars of conflicts, often a convenient method of sexing hippos. Cows with babies are aggressive towards other individuals. The hippo is extremely dangerous on land and kills many people each year, usually when someone inadvertently blocks the animal's retreat to the water.

Size: shoulder height 150cm; weight up to 2000kg (males are larger than females). **Distribution:** Zambia, Malawi, Mozambique and extreme eastern South Africa. Also along the Zambezi, Chobe and Cunene River system. **Status:** common in major water courses.

RICHARD I'ANSON

Giraffe *Giraffa camelopardalis*
The name 'giraffe' is derived from the Arabic word *zarafah* ('the one who walks quickly'). Both sexes have 'horns', short projections of skin-covered bone. Despite the giraffe's incredibly long neck, it still has only seven cervical vertebrae – the same number as all mammals, including humans. The giraffe browses on trees, exploiting a zone of foliage inaccessible to all other herbivores except elephant. Juveniles are prone to predation and a lion will even take down fully grown adults. The giraffe is at its most vulnerable at water holes and always appears hesitant when drinking.

Size: height 4.5m (female), up to 5.2m (male); weight 900 to 1400kg. **Distribution:** north-eastern South Africa, southern Zimbabwe, southern Mozambique, southern Zambia, northern Botswana and northern Namibia. **Status:** common where it occurs and easy to see.

ROB DRUMMOND

Common (or grey) duiker *Sylvicapra grimmia*
One of the most common small antelopes, the duiker is usually solitary, but is sometimes seen in pairs. The common duiker is greyish light-brown in colour, with a white belly and a dark brown stripe down its face. Only males have horns, which are straight and pointed, and rarely grow longer than 15cm. This duiker is predominantly a browser, often feeding on agricultural crops. This habit leads to it being persecuted outside conservation areas, though it is resilient to hunting. The duiker is capable of going without water for long periods but will drink whenever water is available.

Size: shoulder height 50cm; weight up to 21kg. **Distribution:** very widespread throughout the region except on Namibia's Skeleton Coast. **Status:** common; active throughout the day, except where disturbance is common.

RICHARD I'ANSON

Klipspringer *Oreotragus oreotragus*
A small, sturdy antelope, the klipspringer is easily recognised by its curious tip-toe stance – its hooves are adapted for balance and grip on rocky surfaces. The widely spaced 10cm-long horns are present only on the male. The klipspringer normally inhabits rocky outcrops; it also sometimes ventures into adjacent grasslands, but always retreats to the rocks when alarmed. This amazingly agile and sure-footed creature is capable of bounding up impossibly rough rock faces. Male and female klipspringers form long-lasting pair bonds and occupy a territory together.

Size: shoulder height 60cm; weight up to 13kg. **Distribution:** on rocky outcrops and mountainous areas throughout the region; absent from dense forests. **Status:** common.

MITCH REARDON

Steenbok *Raphicerus campestris*
The steenbok is a very pretty and slender small antelope; its back and hindquarters range from light reddish-brown to dark brown with pale underparts markings. The upper surface of its nose bears a black, wedge-shaped 'blaze' useful for identification. Males have small, straight and widely separated horns. It is a solitary animal and only has contact with others during the mating season. The steenbok is active in the morning and evening.

Size: shoulder height 50cm; weight up to 11kg. **Distribution:** widely distributed throughout the region in all habitats, except desert areas. **Status:** common where it occurs.

RICHARD I'ANSON

Impala *Aepyceros melampus*
Often dismissed by tourists because it is so abundant, the impala is a unique antelope with no close relatives. Males have long, lyre-shaped horns averaging 75cm in length. It is a gregarious animal. Though males defend female herds during the oestrus, outside the breeding season males congregate in bachelor groups. The impala is known for its speed and ability to leap; it can spring as far as 10m in one bound, or 3m into the air. It is common prey of lions, leopards, cheetahs, wild dogs and spotted hyaenas.

Size: shoulder height 90cm; weight up to 70kg. **Distribution:** widespread in the north-east of the region, with an isolated population in northern Namibia. **Status:** very common and easy to see.

LUKE HUNTER

Springbok *Antidorcas marsupialis*
Southern Africa's only gazelle, the springbok is extremely common in the arid areas of the subregion. It can survive without being near a water source (it gets enough water in its food), but may move large distances to find new grazing. It one of the fastest antelopes and has a distinctive bounding gait called 'pronking', which it displays when it sees predators. Both sexes have ridged, lyre-shaped horns. Cheetahs are its main predators, though lions prefer it in some areas of Namibia.

Size: shoulder height 75cm; weight up to 50kg. **Distribution:** Namibia, southern Botswana and north-western South Africa. **Status:** very common and easy to see.

LUKE HUNTER

Black wildebeest (Gnu) *Connochaetes gnou*
Black wildebeest once migrated across Southern Africa in enormous herds, but hunting decimated their populations and they are now restricted to a few parks in South Africa. The loud 'ge-nu' sound the black wildebeest makes when alarmed is the source of its other name 'gnu'. Young males form bachelor groups, while older males defend territories onto which they herd passing groups of females. Herds are prone to dissolve into cavorting madness if surprised or threatened.

Size: shoulder height 140cm; weight 230kg. **Distribution:** confined to a few ranches and reserves in central South Africa. **Status:** endangered but easy to see wherever it occurs.

RICHARD I'ANSON

Blue wildebeest *Connochaetes taurinus*
The blue wildebeest is gregarious, forming herds up to tens of thousands strong, often in association with zebras and other herbivores. In Southern Africa, numbers are much reduced and huge herds are a rarity. Males are territorial and attempt to herd groups of females into their territory. The wildebeest is a grazer, and moves constantly in search of good pasture and water. Because it prefers to drink daily and can survive only five days without water, the wildebeest will migrate large distances to find it. During the rainy season it grazes haphazardly, but in the dry season it congregates around water holes.

Size: shoulder height 150cm; weight 250kg. **Distribution:** occurs in all major parks in the region. **Status:** very common but mostly restricted to protected areas.

ANDREW MacCOLL

Hartebeest Red hartebeest *Alcelaphus buselaphus* (pictured); Lichtenstein's hartebeest *Sigmoceros lichtensteinii*
The hartebeest is a red-to-tan-coloured, medium-sized antelope easily recognised by its long, narrow face and short, stout horns, present in both sexes. The distinctly angular and heavily ridged horns form a heart shape, hence the name, which comes from 'heart beast' in Afrikaans. The hartebeest feeds exclusively on grass and prefers open plains for grazing, but is also found in sparsely forested woodlands. It is a social animal and often associates with other herbivores such as zebras and wildebeests. Its major predators include big cats, hyaenas and wild dogs.

Size: shoulder height 125cm; weight 120 to 150kg. **Distribution:** (red hartebeest) north-western South Africa, central Botswana, and Namibia; (Lichtenstein's hartebeest) some parks in Zambia, Malawi, Zimbabwe and South Africa. **Status:** (red hartebeest) common where they occur; (Lichtenstein's hartebeest) very rare.

Tsessebe *Damaliscus lunatus*

The tsessebe is similar to the hartebeest but darker, with glossy violet-brown patches on the rear thighs, front legs and face. The horns, carried by both sexes, curve gently up, out and back. A highly gregarious antelope, it lives in herds and frequently mingles with other grazers. During the mating season, bulls select a well-defined patch, which they defend against rivals, while females wander from one patch to another. The tsessebe is a grazer, and although it can live on dry grasses, it prefers flood plains and moist areas that support lush pasture. It is capable of surviving long periods without water as long as sufficient grass is available.

LUKE HUNTER

Size: height at shoulder 120cm; weight 120 to 150kg. **Distribution:** north-eastern South Africa, south-western Zimbabwe, northern Botswana and south-western Zambia. **Status:** common where they occur.

Bontebok & blesbok *Damaliscus dorcas*

Closely related subspecies, the bontebok and the blesbok are close relatives of the tsessebe. The best way to tell them apart is to look at their colour: the blesbok has an overall dullish appearance and lacks the rich, deep brown-purple tinge of the bontebok. Both species graze on short grass, and as with many antelope, males are territorial, while females form small herds. Both sexes have horns.

LUKE HUNTER

Size: shoulder height 90cm; weight up to 80kg. **Distribution:** both subspecies are endemic to South Africa; bonteboks are confined to the extreme south-west, while blesboks are widespread in the central region. **Status:** bonteboks are rare, but are easy to see where they occur; blesboks are common.

Gemsbok (oryx) *Oryx gazella*

Adapted for arid zones, the gemsbok can tolerate areas uninhabitable to most antelopes. It can survive without being near a water source (it gets enough water in its food) and can tolerate extreme heat. A solid powerful animal with long, straight horns present in both sexes, it is well equipped to defend itself and has been known to occasionally kill attacking lions. Herds vary from five to 40 individuals. The gemsbok is principally a grazer, but also browses on thorny shrubs unpalatable to many species.

MATT FLETCHER

Size: shoulder height 120cm; weight up to 240kg. **Distribution:** most of Namibia, Botswana and northern South Africa. **Status:** common where it occurs, but often shy, fleeing from humans.

LUKE HUNTER

Greater kudu *Tragelaphus strepsiceros*

The greater kudu is Africa's second tallest antelope and the males carry massive spiralling horns much sought after by trophy hunters. It is light grey in colour with between six and 10 white stripes down the sides and a white chevron between the eyes. The kudu lives in small herds comprising females and their young, periodically joined by the normally solitary males during the breeding season. It is primarily a browser and can eat a variety of leaves, but it finds its preferred diet in woodland-savanna with fairly dense bush cover.

Size: shoulder height 150cm; weight up to 250kg. **Distribution:** throughout the region, but absent from most of central South Africa. **Status:** common.

DAVID WALL

Eland *Taurotragus oryx*

Africa's largest antelope, the eland is a massive animal. Both sexes have horns about 65cm long, which spiral at the base and sweep straight back. The male has a distinctive hairy tuft on the head, and stouter horns than the female. The eland prefers savanna scrub, feeding on grass and tree foliage in the early morning and late afternoon into the night. It drinks daily, but can go for a month or more without water. It usually lives in groups of around six to 12, normally comprising several females and one male. Larger aggregations (up to a thousand) sometimes form at localised 'flushes' of new grass growth.

Size: shoulder height 170cm; weight up to 900kg (male). **Distribution:** distributed mostly in woodlands and semidesert. **Status:** naturally low density but relatively common in their habitat and easy to see.

RICHARD I'ANSON

African buffalo *Syncerus caffer*

The African buffalo is the only native wild cow of Africa. Both sexes have distinctive curving horns that broaden at the base and meet over the forehead in a massive 'boss': those of the female are usually smaller. It has a fairly wide habitat tolerance but requires areas with abundant grass, water and cover. The African buffalo is gregarious and may form herds numbering thousands. Group composition is fluid and smaller herds often break away, sometimes rejoining the original herd later. Although it is generally docile, the buffalo can be very dangerous and should be treated with caution.

Size: shoulder height 1.4m; weight up to 820kg (male). **Distribution:** widespread but now large populations only occur in parks. **Status:** common and can be approachable where they are protected.

Getting Around the Region

This chapter briefly outlines the various ways of travelling around Southern Africa. For specific detail, see the Getting There & Away and Getting Around sections of individual country chapters.

AIR

Distances are great in Africa, and if time is short a few flights around the region can considerably widen your options. For example, after touring South Africa for a while you could fly from Cape Town to Victoria Falls and then tour Zimbabwe or southern Zambia. Alternatively, after South Africa, you could fly to Lilongwe – a good starting point for travels in Malawi or eastern Zambia.

Even within a country, flying can save vital days for those on tight schedules (eg, Cape Town to Johannesburg in South Africa, Harare to Victoria Falls in Zimbabwe, Lilongwe to Nyika in Malawi, and Maputo to Pemba in Mozambique). Domestic flights (ie, those within a country) and regional flights (ie, those within Southern Africa) are usually operated by state airlines, although some private companies have entered the fray, and the competition generally keeps prices down to reasonable levels.

Sometimes the only practical way into the more remote parks and reserves is by air, and many national-park lodges have airstrips served by chartered flights. Although these are normally for travellers on less restrictive budgets, even shoestringers take flights occasionally, such as into the Okavango Delta.

Most flights in Southern Africa are reliable. Delays do occur, but they are rarely the 'sorry your plane has been commandeered by the president so you're stuck here for a week' variety.

BUS

International Bus

Long-distance buses (coaches) operate regularly between most of the countries of Southern Africa. International routes include those from Cape Town and Jo'burg (South Africa) to Maseru (Lesotho), Mbabane (Swaziland), Maputo (Mozambique), Gaborone (Botswana), Harare (Zimbabwe) and Windhoek (Namibia). Buses also run between Harare, Lilongwe (Malawi) and Lusaka (Zambia). Most routes are covered by fairly basic, cheap and annoyingly slow services, and also by more expensive luxurious express services. The latter includes Intercape Mainliner; see its Web site (www.intercape.co.za) for more details.

If you can't afford the luxury express services, but want to avoid the slow local-style buses, look out for minibuses running country-to-country routes. These are generally faster than a big bus – sometimes frighteningly so.

For bus travellers, border crossings can get extremely busy as customs officials search through huge amounts of luggage. It's particularly slow if you are crossing from a wealthier country to a poorer one (eg, South Africa to Zimbabwe, or Zimbabwe to Malawi), but this is not necessarily so if you're going the other way. It is sometimes worth choosing minibus services for cross-border travel, as fewer passengers mean less time at the border.

There are several international bus services specially designed for backpackers and other tourists. These normally use comfortable 16-seat buses, with helpful drivers, on-board music and pick-ups/drop-offs at main tourist centres and backpackers' hostels. Baz Bus (☎ 021-439 2323 in South Africa, ☎ 011-704242 in Zimbabwe, ⓔ info@bazbus.com) runs a service most days between Cape Town and Victoria Falls, making about 40 stops along a route that includes the Garden Route, Durban, Swaziland or the Drakensburg, Jo'burg and Bulawayo; you can buy a ticket and hop on or off as much as you like. Web site: www.bazbus.com.

Route 49 (☎ 021-788 7904 in South Africa, ⓔ zimcaper@dockside.co.za) runs twice-weekly direct services between Cape Town and Victoria Falls via Bulawayo, and between Jo'burg and Victoria Falls via Maun (Botswana). Web site: www.route49.liveshop.com.

Another international transfer bus service includes the Okavango Mama, which links Victoria Falls to Windhoek every week, via the Okavango Delta, and includes an overnight canoe safari in the delta. Several companies based in Cape Town run tours to Victoria Falls or Livingstone (Zambia) that include stops for sightseeing or activities on the way. These are more like tours than simple bus services, and you pay accordingly, but prices are often reasonable and this can be a good way to get from one side of the region to the other. More details are given in the Getting There & Away sections of the individual country chapters, and you can get details from backpackers hostels and budget travel agents throughout Southern Africa.

Overland Trucks

Several companies run budget overland camping tours around the region in trucks converted to carry passengers (these are listed under Organised Tours in the Getting Around sections in the individual country chapters). Sometimes the trucks finish one tour, then run straight back to base to start the next one, carrying 'transit' passengers. This is not a tour, but it can be a very comfortable way of getting quickly from, say, Victoria Falls back to Jo'burg for about $10 per day. Most operate out of tourist centres like Cape Town, Jo'burg, Harare, Victoria Falls, Windhoek and Lilongwe. If you're looking for such a ride, ask the drivers of trucks parked at camp sites and hostels.

National & Local Bus/Minibus

Within individual countries, public bus services also range from luxurious to basic. As well as big buses, in many countries routes are also served by minibuses. These are faster, and go more often, but can be more dangerous due to a combination of speed and the poor quality of many vehicles. More details are given in the country chapters.

A notable feature of Southern Africa is the complete lack of long-distance shared service taxis (such as the seven-seat Peugeots that you find in other parts of Africa). Some travellers occasionally get a group together and hire a city taxi for a long trip, but this is unusual.

In rural areas, the frequency of buses and minibuses drops dramatically – sometimes to nothing. In cases like this, the 'bus' is often a truck or pick-up, with people just piled in the back. Everyone pays a fare to the driver – normally a bit more than a bus would cost for the same distance. Riding in trucks can be great fun or very uncomfortable – but if it's the only way to get around you've got no choice anyway.

TRAIN

Train travel around Southern Africa is based largely on the South African network and its extensions into neighbouring countries: Botswana, Mozambique, Namibia, Swaziland, Zimbabwe and Zambia. Railway lines also run between Zambia and Tanzania, and between Malawi and Mozambique. Standards vary enormously – more details are given in the individual country chapters.

Most of the international train routes are very useful for independent travellers – they are often safer, quicker and more comfort-

Luggage Fees

On buses, you are not normally charged fees for luggage (including a backpack). On some minibuses, trucks and pick-ups you may well be charged for luggage. This is because luggage takes up space that could otherwise be filled by a paying passenger. Local people accept this, so travellers should too, unless of course the amount is beyond reason. The fee for a medium-sized rucksack is usually around 10% of the fare. Small bags will be less – a good reason for travelling light. Some travellers carry bags the size of a fridge and they're often the ones complaining the loudest when asked to pay. If you think you're being overcharged, ask other passengers – out of earshot of the driver. When you know the proper rate, stand your ground politely and the price will soon fall.

able than the bus, but cheaper than flying. The main exception to this rule is the train service between Malawi and Mozambique, which can be very slow indeed (for more details see the Getting There & Away section in the Malawi chapter).

Travelling by train *within* a country can be a different story. In some countries (eg, Zimbabwe) it's still a good option, but in other countries (eg, Zambia) it's much slower than buses and hardly any cheaper. In other countries (eg, Malawi) getting around by train is not recommended at all. More details are given under Train in the Getting Around sections of individual country chapters.

CAR & MOTORCYCLE

Some brief details on bringing your own wheels to Southern Africa are given in the regional Getting There & Away chapter. Details on getting around and other specific matters are given in the individual country chapters.

Rental

Car rental is never cheap, but it can be a convenient way to travel around, especially if you're short of time or want to visit out-of-the-way places, and costs can be reduced if you get a group together. In all countries covered by this book, you need to be at least 21 years old (or even 25) to hire a car.

A list of local car-rental firms is included in every country chapter. You can contact them direct, or if they are part of an international group (eg, Hertz or Avis) you can make bookings in your own country. If you plan to visit more than one country, check the deal on crossing borders. Some companies allow it, but some don't. As well as the more obvious per-day and per-kilometre costs, always check other items such as tax, damage and insurance – these can add considerably to your bill.

In South Africa and Namibia you can also hire campervans; small or large (two to six people). You can hire just the vehicle or

DISTANCE CHART

	Beira	Blantyre	Bloemfontein	Bulawayo	Cape Town	Durban	Gaborone	Harare	Johannesburg	Lilongwe	Lusaka	Maputo	Maseru	Maun	Mbabane	Swakopmund	Victoria Falls	Windhoek
Beira	---																	
Blantyre	779	---																
Bloemfontein	1806	2132	---															
Bulawayo	726	1051	1264	---														
Cape Town	2810	3136	1004	2268	---													
Durban	1734	2323	634	1456	1753	---												
Gaborone	1434	1759	622	708	1501	979	---											
Harare	559	612	1521	439	2525	1711	1147	---										
Johannesburg	1408	1735	398	866	1402	557	358	1123	---									
Lilongwe	1194	364	2488	1406	3493	2678	2115	968	2099	---								
Lusaka	1054	1113	2010	927	3014	2381	1636	481	1611	709	---							
Maputo	1101	1675	900	1061	1903	620	957	1648	593	2615	2211	---						
Maseru	1850	2290	157	1410	1160	590	702	1561	438	2537	2167	853	---					
Maun	1312	1637	1549	586	2257	1795	927	1025	1174	1992	1166	1773	1629	---				
Mbabane	1734	2005	677	1421	1680	562	719	1401	361	2460	1972	223	633	1535	---			
Swakopmund	3067	3126	1922	1988	1818	2287	1519	2392	1730	2758	2013	2323	2079	1165	2091	---		
Victoria Falls	1269	1594	1807	543	2898	1999	1251	982	1409	1200	491	1604	1953	675	1964	1569	---	
Windhoek	2704	2763	1559	1625	1455	1924	1156	2029	1367	2395	1650	1960	1716	802	1728	363	1443	---

one that is fully equipped with everything you'll need for the most demanding safari.

Also worth checking is a British company called Safari Drive, which specialises in self-drive Landrover rental in Southern Africa, fully equipped with spares and camping equipment, plus maps, route sheets, the lot – even a radio and GPS (global positioning system) so you're never out of touch. The company has bases in Botswana, Zimbabwe, Namibia and South Africa, so you can tour several countries or do a one-way drive.

For something more straightforward, another British company, Sunvil Discovery, has reasonably priced rental cars or 4WDs in Namibia, Zimbabwe and South Africa. What's unusual, is that it includes 100% collision-damage insurance in the cost. Contact addresses for Safari Drive and Sunvil Discovery are listed in the regional Getting There & Away chapter, or you can check its Web sites (www.safaridrive.com and www.sunvil.co.uk) for more details.

Purchase

An increasing number of people travelling in Southern Africa buy a car in South Africa, tour the region, then sell the car at the end of their trip. Although you need a relatively large amount of money up front, you can expect to get at least some of it back, and travelling this way can work out a lot cheaper than car rental – especially if split between a group. A car of your own is particularly ideal if you plan to visit countries like Namibia, Botswana or Zambia where major 'highlights' cannot always be reached easily by public transport.

For tourists, South Africa is the best country in the region to buy a car. (Other countries place restrictions on foreign ownership, have stiff tax laws, or simply don't have the choice of vehicles.) Also, South African registered vehicles don't need a *carnet de passage* to visit any of the countries covered by this book. Going through Botswana, Lesotho, Namibia, and Swaziland is very easy, while for Malawi, Mozambique, Zimbabwe and Zambia you can easily get temporary import permits at the border.

Jo'burg is the cheapest place to buy a car, but Cape Town is a far nicer place to spend time securing a deal. At backpackers' hostels you may even be lucky and find someone just back from a trip; otherwise the staff can advise on the buying and selling process. To get an idea of what's around and prices, check the newspapers: the *Cape Times* has ads every day – most on Thursday – and the weekend *Argus* also has a good selection.

It's usually cheaper to buy privately, but for tourists it is often more convenient to go to a dealer. The main congregation of used-car dealers is on Voortrekker Rd between Maitland and Bellville Sts in Cape Town. Some might agree to a buy-back arrangement – if you don't trash your car, you can reasonably expect to get about 60% of your purchase price back after a three-month trip, more for a shorter trip – but you need to check all aspects of the contract to be sure this deal will stick. Wayne Motors (☎ 021 465 2222), at 21 Roeland St, will guarantee a buy-back price in advance. We've also heard from readers who have used Drive Africa (☎ 021-447 1144, fax 4388262, ⓔ b-talbot@driveafrica.co.za), which specialises in buy-back sales for tourists. The company has saloon cars, 4WDs, campervans, motorbikes, and can help you with insurance and all the paperwork. It can also rent you camping and safari equipment, and even deliver or collect the car at Jo'burg, Durban or Windhoek.

Whoever you're buying from, make sure that the car details correspond with the ownership papers. Also check the owner's name against their identity document. Before buying, consider getting the car independently tested – the Automobile Association (AA) has a test station in Cape Town and charges about R300 for a full test (you don't need to be a member).

A roadworthy certificate is required when you register the change of ownership and pay for a road-licence disk. A reputable dealer will sell cars already carrying a roadworthy. Cheap cars will often be sold without – you'll have to get it yourself from a garage that is licensed to test cars – and maybe get some work done to bring it up to standard. (Note that there are a lot of unscrupulous testers around – a roadworthy certificate doesn't necessarily mean your car is safe.)

For a very rough idea of prices, you'll be lucky to find a decent vehicle for much less than US$2500. More realistically, in a private sale you should expect to pay about US$3500 for a 10-year-old Toyota Corolla or VW Golf in reasonable condition. If you want to go off-road, a five- to seven-year-old Landrover will cost anything from US$5000 to US$10,000. A good option if you're not doing serious off-roading is a pick-up ('bakkie'); a good five-year-old 2WD Toyota Hi-Lux should cost about $8000, an Isuzu DT about 25% more, and more again for 4WD or a double cab. Of course, dealer prices are higher than private prices. As an example, a dealer would sell a Toyota Hi-Lux with 4WD, double cab and canopy for about US$14,000, with a US$10,000 buy-back after two months.

Before you finalise purchase, you should get a certificate issued by the police to prove the vehicle isn't stolen.

To register your newly purchased car, go to the Motor Vehicle Registration Division (☎ 021-210 2385/6) in the Civic Centre, Cash Hall, on the foreshore in Cape Town. It's open from 8 am to 2 pm weekdays. You can collect a change-of-ownership form to complete, and also inquire about other documents required. The charge to re-register is about US$20. When registration is complete, you'll be issued with a new vehicle number, and you'll have to get a new set of number plates made.

Indicators – To Go or Not To Go?

One of Southern Africa's most potentially dangerous traffic quirks concerns the use of indicator lights. In some countries if the truck in front uses its right-side indicators it means it's OK for you to overtake. In other countries it means the exact opposite – something is coming the other way. The moral of the tale is never overtake unless you can see that the road ahead is completely clear.

Insurance against theft or damage is highly recommended. Again the AA will be able to advise. If you can't get (or can't afford) insurance to cover the whole region, you can normally get third-party insurance at borders. The cost and quality of such local insurance varies wildly, and in some countries is pretty worthless, but the certificate is always vital to show at police checkpoints.

Driving in Southern Africa

Whatever car you drive in Southern Africa, you should be prepared for local attitudes that may differ markedly from what you're used to at home. Driving standards all over the region are generally bad and drivers unpredictable. South Africa is especially dangerous as there's a greater proportion of good roads, fast cars and arrogant drivers. In all the countries covered in this book, traffic officially drives on the left – although you wouldn't always know it. Be especially prepared on blind corners and hills.

Road standards vary considerably, from smooth highways to dirt tracks (for more details, see the boxed text 'Driving off the Tar' later in this chapter). The most difficult to drive on are tar roads full of bone-crunching potholes – and in countries like Malawi, Zambia and Mozambique there are plenty of these.

Tree branches on the road are the local version of warning triangles; there's probably a broken-down vehicle ahead. Other things to be prepared for, even on busy highways, are children playing, people selling goods or drying seeds, and cyclists on the wrong side of the road.

If you come up behind someone on a bicycle, give a short hoot of the horn as a warning. This is not regarded as offensive (as it might be in the west), especially if followed by a friendly wave.

In rural areas, watch out for wildlife. Hitting even a small mammal can damage a car considerably, and hitting something large, like a kudu, can be fatal (for the driver). Everywhere, watch out for livestock; goats in particular run fast, but often go the wrong way *into* your path; cows have a better

Driving off the Tar

If you have your own car, or hire one, for touring Southern Africa only some of your driving will be on tar roads. Driving off the tar requires special techniques and appropriate vehicle preparation.

Gravel Roads

Many roads – even some main highways – in Southern Africa are surfaced with gravel instead of tar. Some are well maintained – others aren't. Even on the good gravel roads (deceivingly easy to drive on), keep your speed below 100km/h. For long drives, lower your tyre pressure by about 25%. If the road is corrugated, gradually increase your speed until the vibrations stop – usually at about 65km/h.

Avoid swerving sharply or braking suddenly, and keep out of soft gravel on the verge – you may lose control. Try to follow ruts made by other vehicles.

Some roads are crossed by patches of sand. If you hit these at high speed, you can also lose control. Likewise, if you enter a sudden corner too quickly, you'll carry straight on and end up in the ditch.

When a vehicle approaches from the opposite direction, reduce your speed and keep as far left as possible. Switch on your headlights so you can be seen in dusty conditions. (On remote roads, it's customary to wave at the other driver as you pass.)

Overtaking is extremely dangerous because your view ahead is obscured by dust from the car ahead. Flashing your headlights will indicate that you want to overtake. If someone behind you flashes their lights, move as far to the left as possible.

Be careful in rainy weather – gravel roads can turn to quagmires and dips may fill with water. If you're uncertain about the depth of the water, don't cross until it drains off.

Off-Road Driving

If you want to get right off the major roads, the following information will help to keep you, and your vehicle, out of trouble. You should also refer to an off-road driving manual. For more information, see under Car & Motorcycle in the main Getting Around section of the South Africa chapter.

For road conditions that are rough, your vehicle must be robust, but a 4WD is not essential. However, high ground-clearance is very important – and you don't often get the latter without the former. A vehicle with 4WD *is* usually essential if you're dealing with sand or mud – which in Southern Africa is likely.

Make sure your vehicle is in good running order before you start. Carry tools, spares and equipment, including towrope, torch, shovel, fan belts, vehicle fluids, spark plugs, wire, jump leads, fuses, hoses, a good jack and a wooden plank to act as a base in sand. A second spare tyre is highly advised, and even a third if you've got room. You could also carry tyre levers, spare tubes and repair kit, but mending punctures in the bush is much harder than the manuals imply, and to be avoided if at all possible. A pump *is* useful though, and a winch would also be an asset.

Wrap tools and heavy objects in blankets or padding. Strap everything down tightly on the roof or in the back. Keep breakable items with you in the cab. Once you're off the tar, dust permeates everything – so tightly wrap food, clothing and camera equipment in strong dust-proof containers.

sense of direction, but are slower, and make one hell of a dent. If you see kids with red flags on the road, it means they're leading a herd of cows. Slow down, even if you can't see any cows (especially if you can't see any cows).

All of these things become much harder to deal with in the dark. Additionally, many vehicles have faulty lights – or none at all. It is very strongly recommended not to drive at night.

BICYCLE

Cycling is one of the best ways to learn about the countries you travel through. You meet local people on an equal footing, you

Driving off the Tar

When calculating fuel requirements, estimate your intended distance and then double it to allow for getting lost and emergencies. For serious off-roading, remember to allow for petrol consumption up to four times higher than in normal conditions – it will probably be less than this, but can be frighteningly high on sandy tracks.

Carry at least 5L of water per person per day (and allow for delays and breakdowns). Carry fuel and water in indestructible containers. Bring water-purifying tablets.

Take the best maps you can find, plus a GPS or compass that you know how to use. Take readings periodically to make sure you're still travelling in the right direction. To get an accurate compass reading, stand at least 3m from the vehicle.

Bush Tracks

Bush tracks rarely appear on maps and their ever-changing routes can utterly confound drivers. Some provide access to remote cattle posts or small villages and then disappear, often to re-emerge somewhere else. Some never re-emerge, leaving you stranded.

Take care driving through high grass – seeds can block radiators and cause overheating. Dry grass next to the exhaust pipe can also catch fire. Stop and remove plant material from the grille or exhaust regularly.

Sand

In sandy conditions you may be following a faint track – often just the wheel marks of previous vehicles – or driving across completely bare wilderness. Either way, driving is easier if the air is cool (usually mornings), as the sand is more compact at these times.

Tyre pressure should be low – around half that for normal road conditions. To prevent bogging or stalling, move as quickly as possible and keep the revs up, but avoid sudden acceleration. Shift down a gear before you reach deep sandy patches, not when you're in them.

Allow the vehicle to wander along the path of least resistance when negotiating a straight course through rutted sand. Anticipate corners and turn the wheel slightly earlier than you would on a solid surface – this will allow the vehicle to slide smoothly around.

Pans

Many of the rules for bush-track or sand driving apply here, but some extra points are worth making. Firstly, never drive on a pan, unless you know exactly what you're doing. If you do venture onto a pan, stick to the edges until you're sure it's dry.

Even if the pan *seems* dry, it can still be wet underneath – vehicles can break through the crust and become irretrievably bogged. Foul-smelling salt can mean the pan is wet and potentially dangerous. If in doubt, follow the tracks of other drivers (unless, of course, you see bits of vehicles poking above the surface).

often stay in small towns and villages and you eat a lot of African food. In general, the remoter the areas you visit, the better the experience – if you are fully prepared. Some pointers on cycling *to* Southern Africa (or, more likely, bringing a bike on the plane) are given in the regional Getting There & Away chapter.

For getting around, traditional touring bikes will cope with most tar roads (and some good dirt roads) without too much trouble, although narrow tyres are unsuitable. If you want to get off the main routes, you'll find most secondary roads are rough dirt or gravel, and for this a fat-tyred mountain bike is recommended.

Hybrid bikes (a cross between a traditional tourer and a mountain bike) are ideal but should still have fat tyres fitted. Keep your tyre pressures low on rough roads to spread the load and soften the ride. In many parts of southern Africa minor roads can be very sandy, and even with the fattest softest tyres you'll still end up pushing!

Remember though, that motorists are more cause for alarm than any road surface. Cyclists are regarded as second-class citizens in Africa even more than they are in western countries, so make sure you know what's coming up behind you and be prepared to make an evasive swerve onto the verge, as local cyclists are expected to do. A rearview-mirror (handlebar or helmet mounted) is invaluable.

Other factors to consider are the heat, the long distances, and finding places to stay. Aim for the cool, dry period (see the When to Go section in the Regional Facts for the Visitor chapter). Even so, you'll need to work out a way to carry at least 4L of water. If you get tired, or simply want to cut out the boring bits, bikes can easily be carried on buses or trucks – although you'll need to pay an extra luggage fee, and be prepared for some rough handling as your beloved machine is loaded onto the roofrack. If you're camping near settlements in rural areas, for manners and security ask the village headman where you can pitch. Even if you don't have a tent, he'll find you a place to stay.

You might get more advice on African cycle-touring from a reputable bike shop, and there are several specialist manuals available.

Another good source of information may be your national cycling organisation. For example, in Britain the Cyclists' Touring Club (☎ 01483-417217, fax 426994, ⓔ cycling@ctc.org.uk) provides members with details on many parts of the world, and also organises a wide range of tours. Web site: www.ctc.org.uk

In the USA, the International Bicycle Fund (☎/fax 206-767 0848, ⓔ ibike@ibike.org) organises socially conscious tours and provides information. Web site: www.ibike.org

If you haven't got a bike of your own, but fancy a few days cycling, there are usually a couple of places in tourist areas where they can be rented. Otherwise, local people in villages and towns are often willing to rent their bikes for the day to travellers; ask at your hotel or track down a bicycle repair man (every town market has one).

HITCHING

All over Southern Africa, if local people hitch a ride in a car or truck, they usually offer some money to the driver. Often the driver expects this, and the price of the lift is agreed at the outset. You should play by these rules, too.

Hitching in the western sense (ie, because you don't want to get the bus, or because you don't want to pay) is also possible in all of the countries covered in this book, and can be a cheap and very interesting way to get around. However, as in any other part of the world, hitching is never entirely safe, and we therefore don't recommend it. Travellers who hitch should understand that they are taking a small but potentially serious risk. However, many people do hitch around Southern Africa (using buses to avoid potential hot spots), and have no difficulties. If you're planning to hitch, take advice from other hitchhikers (locals or travellers) first. Use common sense: hitching in pairs is obviously safer, while hitching through less salubrious suburbs and townships, especially at night, is asking for trouble.

ORGANISED TOURS

In several of the countries listed in this book, you can arrange a tour visiting a selection of Southern African countries. For example, in Cape Town, Jo'burg, Victoria Falls or Livingstone you can arrange tours of Zimbabwe, Botswana and Namibia. With all tours, the range of options is enormous: they can last from a week to a month or longer; involve staying in camp sites or five-star lodges; be priced from budget to high-class luxury; require travel by no-frills truck or by comfortable car with air-con and chilled wine in the fridge.

In countries that have a large choice of locally based tour companies, such as Botswana, Namibia, South Africa and Zimbabwe, a selection is listed in the Getting Around sections of those chapters, or under Organised Tours. In some countries, particularly Malawi and Zambia, only a few local tour companies exist, and these are often part of a travel agency (selling flights) or a budget hotel.

In the Malawi and Zambia chapters, some tour companies are listed under Travel Agencies & Tour Operators in the Lilongwe, Blanytre and Lusaka sections.

BOTSWANA MAP INDEX

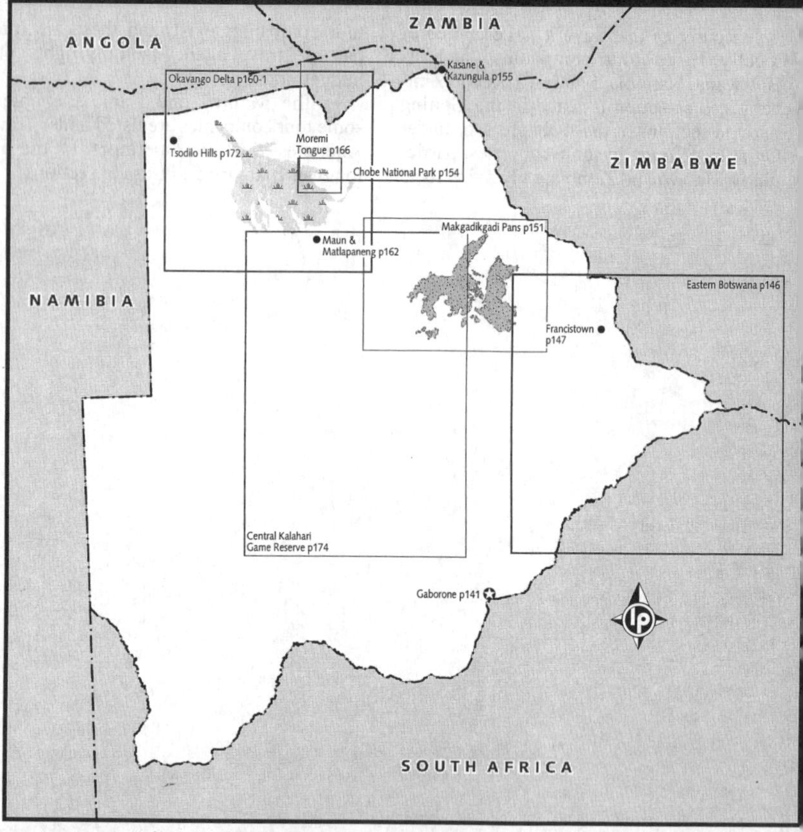

ZAMBIA
ANGOLA
Okavango Delta p160-1
Kasane & Kazungula p155
Tsodilo Hills p172
Moremi Tongue p166
Chobe National Park p154
ZIMBABWE
Makgadikgadi Pans p151
Maun & Matlapaneng p162
Eastern Botswana p146
NAMIBIA
Francistown p147
Central Kalahari Game Reserve p174
Gaborone p141
SOUTH AFRICA

RICHARD I'ANSON

Horse and cart, Maun

Botswana

Botswana, formerly Bechuanaland, is an African success story. A long-neglected British protectorate, Botswana achieved its timely independence under democratic rule in 1966 and soon after discovered three of the world's richest diamond-bearing formations. It enjoys politically and ideologically enlightened nonracial policies along with high health, educational and economic standards which, with the exception of South Africa, are unequalled elsewhere in sub-Saharan Africa.

Its modern veneer, however, belies the fact that much of Botswana remains a country for the intrepid, not to mention relatively wealthy, traveller. This largely roadless wilderness of vast spaces – savanna, desert, wetlands and salt pans – and myriad traditional villages requires time, effort and money to enjoy to its fullest.

Facts about Botswana

HISTORY

For a detailed account of the early history of the whole Southern African region, including Botswana's precolonial history, see History in the Facts about the Region chapter.

Early History

Botswana's first people were the San (also known as Bushmen), who have inhabited the Kalahari region for at least 30,000 years. They were followed by the Khoikhoi (Hottentots) who are thought to have originated from a breakaway San group. The language group of these two peoples is known collectively as Khoisan.

During the 1st or 2nd century AD, the Bantu people migrated from the north (see the boxed text 'The Bantu Migrations' in the Facts about the Region chapter). Relations between the Khoisan and Bantu societies appear to have been peaceful and

BOTSWANA AT A GLANCE

Area: 582,000 sq km

Population: 1.47 million

Capital: Gaborone

Head of State: President Festus Mogae

Official Languages: English, Tswana

Currency: pula (P)

Exchange Rate: US$1 = P4.8

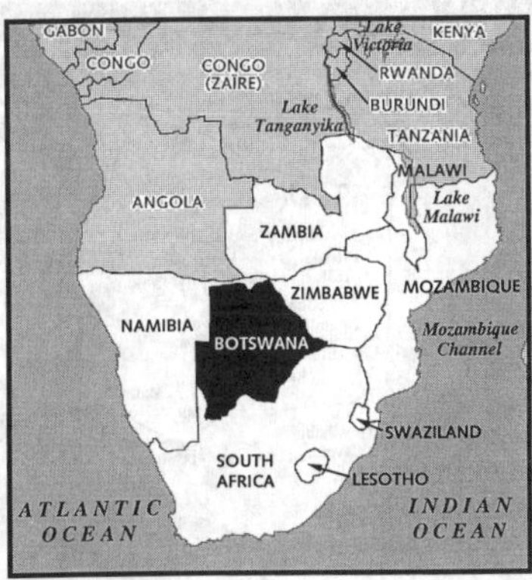

Highlights

- Okavango Delta and Moremi Wildlife Reserve – explore these wildlife-packed wonderlands
- Wild Kalahari – marvel at its vast spaces and incredible night skies
- Tsodilo Hills – see the 'Wilderness Louvre' of ancient San paintings in the country's most impressive range of hills
- Chobe National Park – don't miss this huge wildlife-rich reserve, with its magnificent riverfront, inland marsh and savanna zones
- Makgadikgadi & Nxai Pan National Park – experience the grassland wilderness of Makgadikgadi and Botswana's best wet season wildlife viewing at Nxai Pan

amicable, and the two groups probably traded, intermarried and mixed freely. The Bantu group known as the Tswana migrated from present-day South Africa sometime during the 14th century to colonise the country's south-eastern strip, and today forms Botswana's largest population group.

In 1818, the confederation of Zulu tribes in South Africa set out to conquer or destroy all tribes and settlements in its path, causing waves of disruption throughout Southern Africa. Tswana villages were scattered and some were pushed into the dead heart of the Kalahari. In response to this aggression, the Tswana regrouped and developed a highly structured society. Each Tswana nation was ruled by a hereditary monarch, and the king's subjects lived in the central town or satellite villages. Each clan was allocated its own settlement, which was under the control of village leaders. By the second half of the 19th century, some of these towns had grown to a considerable size.

The Early Colonial Era

The orderliness and structure of this town-based society impressed the early Christian missionaries, who arrived in 1817. None of

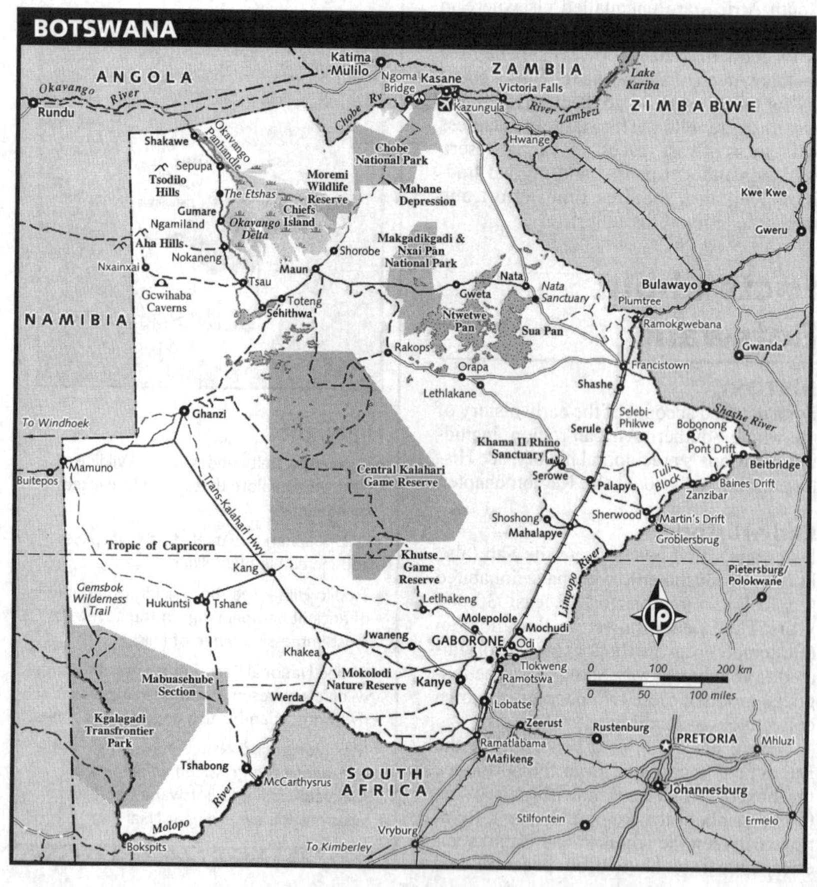

them managed to convert great numbers of Batswana (people of Tswana nationality) but they advised the Tswana, sometimes wrongly, in their dealings with the Europeans who followed – explorers, naturalists, traders, miners and itinerant opportunists.

From the late 1820s the Boers, dissatisfied with British rule in the Cape Colony, began their Great Trek across the Vaal River (the Cape Colony's frontier). Confident that they had heaven-sanctioned rights to any land they might choose to occupy in Southern Africa, 20,000 Boers crossed the Vaal River into Tswana and Zulu territory and established themselves as though the lands were unclaimed and uninhabited (indeed many were, having been cleaned out earlier by Zulu factions or tsetse fly). At the Sand River Convention of 1852, Britain recognised the Transvaal's independence and the Boers informed the Batswana that they were now subjects of the South African Republic. The Boer leader MW Pretorius notified the British that the Tswana were acquiring weapons from white traders and missionaries and preparing for war with the Boers.

The British Protectorate

Prominent Tswana leaders Sechele I and Mosielele refused to accept white rule and incurred the wrath of the Boers. After heavy losses of life and land, the Tswana sent their leaders to petition the British for protection. Britain, however, was in no hurry to support lands of dubious profitability and offered only to act as arbitrator in the dispute. By 1877, however, the worsening situation provoked the British annexation of the Transvaal and launched the first Anglo-Boer War.

Violence continued until the Pretoria Convention of 1881 when the British withdrew from the Transvaal in exchange for Boer allegiance to the Crown. In 1882, Boers again moved into Tswana lands and subdued Mafeking (now Mafikeng), threatening the British route between the Cape and possible mineral wealth in what is present-day Zimbabwe.

Again, the Tswana lobbied for British protection and in 1885, thanks to petitions from John Mackenzie (a friend of the Christian Chief Khama III of Shoshong), Britain resigned itself to the inevitable. Lands south of the Molopo River became the British Crown Colony of Bechuanaland and were attached to the Cape Colony while the area north became the British Protectorate of Bechuanaland.

A new threat to the Tswana chiefs' power base came in the form of Cecil Rhodes and his British South Africa Company (BSAC). By 1894, the British had all but agreed to allow him to control the country. An unhappy delegation of Tswana chiefs, Bathoen, Khama III and Sebele, accompanied by a sympathetic missionary, WC Willoughby, sailed to England to appeal directly to Colonial Minister Joseph Chamberlain for continued government control but their pleas were ignored. As a last resort, they turned to the London Missionary Society (LMS) who in turn took the matter to the British public. Fearing the BSAC would allow alcohol in Bechuanaland, the LMS and other Christian groups backed the Christian Khama. Public pressure mounted and the British government was forced to concede.

At this stage, the chiefs grudgingly accepted that their rites and traditions would be affected by Christianity and western technology. The cash economy was by now firmly in place and the Tswana were actively participating in it. The capital of the protectorate was established at Mafeking (now Mafikeng, in present-day South Africa) and a system of taxes was introduced. Each chief was granted a tribal 'reserve' in which he was given jurisdiction over all black residents and the authority to collect taxes; the chiefs would retain a 10% commission on all money collected. The sale of cattle, oxen and grain to the Europeans streaming north in search of farming land and minerals provided the basis of the protectorate's economy.

This system didn't last long, however. The construction of the railway through Bechuanaland to Rhodesia (Zimbabwe) and an outbreak of foot-and-mouth disease in the 1890s destroyed the transit trade. By 1920, maize farmers in South Africa and Rhodesia were producing so much grain that Bechuanaland no longer had a market.

Sir Seretse Khama

When Ngwato chief Khama III died in 1923, he was succeeded by his son Sekgoma, who died two years later. Because the heir to the throne, Seretse Khama, was only four years old, the job of regent went to his 21-year-old uncle, Tshekedi Khama, who left his studies in South Africa to return to Serowe – the capital of the Ngwato people.

As a royal, Seretse was expected – and required – to take a wife from a Tswana royal family; uproar occurred in 1948 when the heir to the Ngwato throne met and married an Englishwoman, Ruth Williams, while studying law in London. The indignant Tshekedi Khama had his nephew stripped of his inheritance, and he was exiled from Serowe by the Ngwato government and from the protectorate by the British, who assured him that he'd be better off in London than Bechuanaland.

However, a majority of the Ngwato people backed Seretse over his uncle, forcing Tshekedi Khama to gather his followers and settle elsewhere. Subsequent breakdowns in the Ngwato tribal structure prompted Seretse Khama to return in 1952 with a change of heart. He was still being detained in the UK, however, and it wasn't until 1956, when he renounced his claim to the Ngwato throne, that he was permitted to return to Serowe with Ruth and take up residence. There, they began campaigning for Botswana's independence, which came 10 years later. As a result, Seretse Khama was knighted and became the country's first president, a post that he held until his death in 1980.

In a final act of reconciliation, Sir Seretse Khama was buried in the royal cemetery in Serowe. Seretse's son, Ian Khama, was given the title of Kgosi (Chief) of the Ngwato and Ian's mother, Lady Ruth Khama, holds the title of Mohumagadi Mma Kgosi (Honoured Wife of the King and Mother of the Chief). For a thorough treatment of this amazing saga, see *A Marriage of Inconvenience – the Persecution of Seretse & Ruth Khama* by Michael Dutfield.

In 1924 South Africa began pressing for Bechuanaland's amalgamation into the Union of South Africa. When the Tswana chiefs refused, economic sanctions destroyed what remained of their beef market.

In 1923, Chief Khama III died and was succeeded by his son Sekgoma, who died after serving only two years. The heir to the throne was four-year-old Seretse Khama, and the job of regent went to his 21-year-old uncle, Tshekedi Khama, who was later criticised by colonial authorities for his handling of several local disputes according to tribal law.

Resident commissioner of the protectorate Sir Charles Rey determined that no progress would be forthcoming as long as the people were governed by Tswana chiefs and proclaimed them all local government officials and answerable to colonial magistrates. So great was the popular opposition to the move – people feared that it would lead to their incorporation into South Africa – Rey was ousted from his job and his proclamation annulled.

During WWII, 10,000 Tswana volunteered for the African Pioneer Corps to defend the British Empire. After the war Seretse Khama went to study in England where he met and married Ruth Williams, an Englishwoman. This breach of tribal custom infuriated not only Tshekedi Khama but also the entire tribe, the South African authorities and the British, and Seretse Khama was exiled in Britain. In 1956, after renouncing his right to power, he was permitted to return to Botswana with his wife and set up residence (see the boxed text 'Sir Seretse Khama').

Nationalism & Independence

The first signs of nationalist thinking among the Batswana occurred in the late 1940s; during the 1950s and early 1960s all Africa experienced political change as many former colonies gained their independence. By 1955 it had become apparent that Britain was preparing to release its grip on Bechuanaland. University graduates returned from South Africa with political ideas, and although the country had no real economic base, the first Batswana political parties surfaced and began thinking about independence.

Following the Sharpeville Massacre in 1960, South African refugees Motsamai Mpho of the African National Congress (ANC) and Philip Matante, a Johannesburg preacher affiliated with the Pan-Africanist Congress (PAC), together with KT Motsete, a teacher from Malawi, formed the Bechuanaland People's Party (BPP). Its immediate goal was independence for the protectorate.

In 1962, Seretse Khama and Ketumile 'Quett' Masire formed the more moderate Bechuanaland Democratic Party (BDP), and were later joined by Chief Bathoen II of the Ngwaketse. The BDP formulated a schedule for independence, drawing on support from local chiefs and traditional Batswana.

They promoted the transfer of the capital into the country (from Mafikeng to Gaborone), drafted up a new nonracial constitution and set up a countdown to independence, to allow a peaceful transfer of power. General elections were held in 1965 and Seretse Khama was elected president. On 30 September 1966 the country, now called the Republic of Botswana, gained independence.

Seretse Khama, who was knighted shortly after independence, was no revolutionary; because of Botswana's economic dependence on its neighbours, he adopted a neutral stance (at least until near the end of his presidency) towards South Africa and Rhodesia. Nevertheless, Khama refused to exchange ambassadors with South Africa and officially disapproved of apartheid in international circles.

Botswana was economically transformed by the discovery of diamonds near Orapa in 1967. The mining concession was given to South Africa's De Beers, with Botswana taking 75% of the profits. Although most of the population remains in the low income bracket, thanks to this mineral wealth, Botswana now possesses enormous foreign currency reserves. Its economic dependence upon its southern neighbour is waning, and South Africa remains an active trading partner.

Although Sir Seretse Khama died in 1980, his Botswana Democratic Party still commands a substantial majority in parliament. Dr Ketumile 'Quett' Masire, who served as president for 18 years, and Festus Mogae, who took the helm in March 1998, have continued in their predecessor's path (while the government cautiously follows pro-western policies). There is, however, growing urban support for the BDP's rival party, the Botswana National Front, which supports redistribution of wealth and a centrally regulated economy.

Botswana now has one of the world's highest rates of economic growth. Its biggest problems are unemployment, urban drift and a high birth rate – currently the third highest in the world. Still, Botswana remains a peaceful country that continues to be a bright and hopeful spot on the African continent.

GEOGRAPHY

With an area of 582,000 sq km, landlocked Botswana extends 1100km from north to south and 960km from east to west, making it about the same size as Kenya or France and somewhat smaller than Texas.

Most of the country lies at an average elevation of 1000m and consists of a vast and nearly level sand-filled basin characterised by scrub-covered savanna. The Kalahari (Kgalagadi), a semi-arid expanse of windblown sand deposits and long, sandy valleys covers nearly 85% of Botswana, including the entire central and south-western regions. In the north-west, the Okavango River flows in from Namibia and soaks into the sands, forming the Okavango Delta, which covers an area of 15,000 sq km. In the north-east are the great salty clay deserts of the Makgadikgadi Pans.

CLIMATE

Although it straddles the Tropic of Capricorn, Botswana experiences extremes in both temperature and weather. It's mainly a dry country, but it does have a summer rainy season, which runs roughly from November through March. (In January and February 2000, record rainfalls and subsequent flooding paralysed much of the country.)

From late May through August, rain is rare anywhere in the country. Days are normally

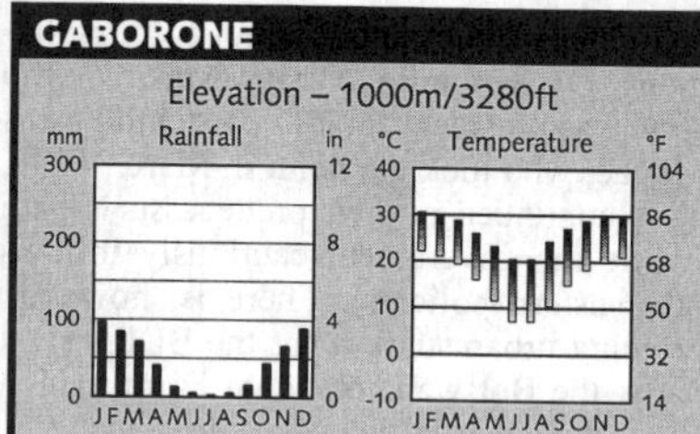

clear, warm and sunny, and nights are cool to bitterly cold. In the Kalahari, below freezing temperatures at night are normal in June and July and, where there's enough humidity, frosts are common.

ECOLOGY & ENVIRONMENT

Neighbouring Namibia is promoting a project that will tap the Okavango River to provide water for the dry central part of the country; if that happens, the decreased flow will affect the hydrology of the Okavango Delta. In the hope of preserving the precious ecosystems of the Delta area, Botswana has encouraged the Namibian government to examine other possibilities, such as desalination or use of the Kunene or Zambezi Rivers.

Another issue is Botswana's 3000km of 1.5m-high 'buffalo fence', officially called the 'veterinary cordon fence' – a series of high-tensile steel wire barriers that cross some of Botswana's wildest terrain. The fences were first erected in 1954 to segregate wild buffalo herds from domestic free-range cattle and thwart the spread of foot-and-mouth disease. However, it hasn't been proven that the disease is passed from species to species. What the fences do is not only prevent contact between wild and domestic bovine species, but also prevent other wild animals from migrating to water sources along age-old seasonal routes. While Botswana has set aside large areas for wildlife protection, they don't constitute independent ecosystems, and migratory wildlife numbers (particularly wildebeest, giraffe and zebra) continue to decline.

Cattle ranching is a source of wealth and a major export industry, but all exported beef must be disease-free, so understandably ranchers have reacted positively to the fences, and the government tends to side with the ranchers. Because much of Botswana's cattle ranching industry is subsidised by the EU and the World Bank, and international guidelines require strict separation of domestic cattle and wild buffalo, it's unlikely that the fences – or the issues they raise – will go away any time soon.

FLORA & FAUNA

If you are looking for the Africa of your wildest dreams – vast open savannas with

Elephant & Rhino

The happy news for the African elephant is that Botswana's herds are far from endangered; in fact, an estimated 60,000 to 75,000 elephant inhabit Chobe National Park alone. Herds of up to 500 elephants wreak havoc along the riverfront, as evidenced by the trampled bush and the numbers of rammed, flattened, uprooted, toppled and dismembered trees that litter the landscape.

Until recently, the Botswana government maintained that the best course would be to let nature handle the problem. Hunting bans were imposed in the hope that the pressure on riverfront vegetation would decrease once elephants felt safe to migrate elsewhere. Unfortunately, the elephants continued to multiply and elephants migrated from Namibia to this safe haven. In 1990, the government decided culling would begin the following year; as in Zimbabwe, entire herds rather than individual elephants were to be shot. These plans didn't go ahead and the elephant population continued to boom. In 1996 the government sanctioned a hunting of 80 elephants, and populations continue to be monitored.

As for rhino, poachers have caused the disappearance of both black and white rhino in Chobe, Moremi and other national parks and reserves. Currently, rhino may be observed only in the Gaborone Game Reserve, the Mokolodi Nature Reserve (near Gaborone) and the Khama II Rhino Sanctuary near Serowe. (For more on the region's wildlife, see the colour Wildlife Guide.)

free-ranging wildlife – Botswana may well be the best destination for you. Most of the country is covered with scrub brush and savanna grassland, although small areas of deciduous forest (mainly mopane, msasa and Zambezi teak) thrive along the Zimbabwean border. The Okavango and Linyanti wetlands of the north-west are characterised by riverbank and swamp vegetation, which includes reeds, papyrus and water lilies as well as larger trees such as acacia, jackalberry, leadwood and sausage trees.

Because the Okavango Delta and the Chobe River provide an incongruous water supply, nearly all Southern African species, including such rarities as puku, red lechwe, sitatunga and wild dog are present in Moremi Wildlife Reserve, parts of Chobe National Park and the Linyanti Marshes. In the Makgadikgadi & Nxai Pan National Park, herds of wildebeest, zebra and other hoofed mammals migrate between their winter range on the Makgadikgadi plains and the summer lushness of the Nxai Pan region.

National Parks & Wildlife Reserves

Botswana's national parks are among Africa's wildest, characterised by open spaces where nature still reigns supreme, and even the most popular parks – Chobe and Moremi – are dominated by wilderness. Although they do support a few private safari concessions, there's next to no infrastructure and few amenities.

The major parks include the Central Kalahari Game Reserve, Chobe National Park, Khutse Game Reserve, Kgalagadi Transfrontier Park (an amalgamation of Botswana's former Mabuasehube-Gemsbok National Park and South Africa's Kalahari-Gemsbok National Park), Makgadikgadi & Nxai Pan National Park and Moremi Wildlife Reserve. The North-East Tuli Game Reserve is cobbled together from several private Tuli Block game reserves.

Entry to the parks for nonresidents costs US$13 (P62) per person per day in park fees, plus US$5 (P24) per person for camping; foreign-registered vehicles pay US$2.50 per day (note that these rates are scheduled to increase substantially in the near future). While these rates may be high compared with those in travellers home countries, Botswana's parks are undeniably spectacular, and if you have the cash, you won't regret spending it to visit these unspoilt jewels. Children and Botswana residents and citizens get substantial discounts (residents of Botswana pay US$2.50/2.50/0.50 per day to enter/camp/bring in a vehicle and citizens pay US$0.25/0.25 per day to enter/camp). There are also discounts in park fees for those on organised safaris.

You can book accommodation in the national parks by post, phone, fax, email or in person up to one year prior to your intended visit. The Department of Wildlife & National Parks office (☎ 580774, fax 580775, ⓔ dwnpbots@global.bw) PO Box 131, Government Enclave on Khama Cres, Gaborone, is open from 9 am to 5 pm (closed for lunch between 12.30 and 1 pm) Monday to Saturday, and from 9 am to noon on Sunday. You can also book through their office in Maun (☎ 661265, fax 661264) PO Box 20364, Boseja, Maun (beside the police station). For Chobe National Park, you can also book at the Kasane Wildlife Office (☎ 650235), near Kasane.

When booking, include the name of the park, the camping ground, the dates of arrival and departure, the total number of campers and whether they are citizens, residents or nonresidents of Botswana. Payment (in Botswana pula) must be received within one month or you forfeit the booking.

GOVERNMENT & POLITICS

Botswana is one of Africa's success stories, with a stable multiparty democracy that oversees the affairs of a peaceful and neutral state. Freedom of speech, press and religion are constitutionally guaranteed.

The government has three divisions: the executive branch, headed by the president, 11 cabinet ministers and three assistant ministers; the legislative branch, made up of the parliament (which comprises the president and the assembly, in turn made up of the speaker, the attorney general, 40 elected MPs and four special members appointed by the rest of the assembly); and the judicial branch. A 15-member house of chiefs, comprising tribal representatives from around the country, advises on local tribal matters. Elections are held every five years.

ECONOMY

Since independence, Botswana has experienced one of the world's fastest-growing economic rates (between 11% and 13% annually), aided by a stable political climate and vast natural resources. Most of the natural wealth is based on mineral resources, specifically diamonds. Copper and nickel are mined in large quantities at two major deposits near Selebi-Phikwe, gold is still mined around Francistown and limited amounts of coal are taken from eastern Botswana. The most recent large-scale project is the soda ash (sodium carbonate) and salt extraction plant on Sua Pan.

Because Botswana is mostly arid, cattle ranching is the only significant agricultural enterprise. Subsistence farmers depend mostly on cattle, sheep and goats, and maize, sorghum, beans, peanuts, cottonseed and other dry-land crops.

POPULATION & PEOPLE

Of Botswana's 1.47 million people, about 60% claim Tswana heritage. It also has one of the world's most predominantly urban societies, with the bulk of the population concentrated in the south-eastern strip of the country between Lobatse and Francistown. The small number of Europeans and Asians live mainly in Gaborone, Maun and Francistown. Other groups in Botswana include the Herero, Mbukushu, Yei, San (see the special section 'The San' later in this chapter), Kalanga and Kgalagadi, who are mainly in the west and north-west.

ARTS

Material Arts

The original Batswana artists managed to convey individuality, aesthetics and aspects of Batswana life in their utilitarian implements. Baskets (see the boxed text), pottery, fabrics and tools were decorated with meaningful designs derived from tradition. Europeans introduced a new form of art, some of which was integrated and adapted to local interpretation, particularly in weavings and tapestries. The result is some of the finest and most meticulously executed work in Southern Africa.

Contemporary weavings, including tapestries, rugs and bed covers, are made from *karakul* (a variety of Central Asian sheep bred in Botswana) wool, and combine African themes with formats adopted from European art to produce work that appeals to both cultures.

Tools, spoons, bowls and containers have traditionally been carved from the densely grained wood of the mopane tree.

Early Batswana pottery was constructed from smoothed coils of clay and fired slowly, leaving it porous. Evaporation through the pot worked as a sort of refrigeration system, keeping the liquid inside cool and drinkable on even the hottest days. There are pottery workshops in the villages near Gaborone.

Literature

Since the indigenous languages have only been written since the coming of the Christian missionaries, Botswana lacks an extensive literary tradition. What survives of the ancient myths and praise poetry of the San, Tswana, Herero and other groups has been handed down orally and only recently written down.

Botswana's most famous modern literary figure, South African-born Bessie Head (who died in 1988), who settled in Sir Seretse Khama's village of Serowe and wrote works that reflected the harshness and beauty of African village life and the Botswana landscape. Her most widely read works include *Serowe – Village of the Rain Wind*, *When Rain Clouds Gather*, *Maru*, *A Question of Power*, *The Cardinals*, *A Bewitched Crossroad* and *The Collector of Treasures*; the last is an anthology of short stories. Welcome recent additions to Botswana's national literature are the works of Norman Rush, which include the novel *Mating*, set in a remote village, and *Whites*, which deals with the country's growing number of expatriates and apologists from South Africa and elsewhere.

Botswana Baskets

Botswana baskets are the most lauded of the country's material arts. Interestingly, some of the most beautiful designs aren't indigenous, but were brought to north-western Botswana by Angolan Mbukushu refugees in the 19th century.

Although the baskets are still used practically – for storage of seeds, grains and bojalwa mash for sorghum beer – the art has been fine-tuned and some of the work is incredibly exquisite, employing swirls and designs with such evocative names as Flight of the Swallow, Tears of the Giraffe, Urine Trail of the Bull, Knees of the Tortoise, Roof of the Rondavel, Forehead of the Zebra, Back of the Python and The Running Ostrich.

RICHARD I'ANSON

The baskets are made from fibrous shoots from the heart of the mokolane palm *(Hyphaene petersiana)*, which are cut and boiled in natural earth-tone dyes. Dark brown comes from motsentsila roots and tree bark, and pink and red are derived from a fungus that grows in sorghum husks; blood, ochre, clay and cow dung are also used as dyes. The mokolane strips are wound around a base of coils made from vines or grass. A medium-sized basket may require two to three weeks to make.

Generally, the finest and most expensive work comes from Ngamiland; more loosely woven but still beautiful Shashe baskets are produced mainly around Francistown.

LANGUAGE

English is the official language of Botswana and the medium of instruction from the fifth year of primary school. The most widely spoken language, however, is Tswana which is the first language of over 90% of people. See the Language chapter at the back of this book for some useful words and phrases in Tswana.

A good resource for students of Tswana is *First Steps in Spoken Setswana*, available at bookshops in major towns.

Facts for the Visitor

SUGGESTED ITINERARIES

Most tourist activity in Botswana focuses on the Okavango Delta, and if you have only a week, this is where you'll want to focus. Choose Maun or the Okavango Panhandle (the north-western extension of the Okavango Delta) as your base and organise a *mokoro* (dugout canoe) trip through the wetlands, followed by a wildlife-viewing trip through Moremi Wildlife Reserve.

With a month (and lots of money), Botswana will become the Africa of your dreams. Hire a 4WD or use a reputable safari company and see the best of the country: do a *mokoro* trip in the Okavango Delta; visit the main wildlife parks of Moremi and Chobe; camp and hike in the Tsodilo Hills; cruise on the Okavango Panhandle; and explore the furthest reaches of the Kalahari.

PLANNING

When to Go

If you want to hit the back roads, enjoy wildlife viewing or explore the Okavango Delta, summer (October through April) is not the best time to visit. In summer wildlife is harder to spot and rains can render sandy roads impassable and rivers uncrossable, and may even close off Chobe National Park and Moremi Wildlife Reserve. This is

[Continued on page 126]

THE SAN

The San people have probably inhabited Southern Africa for at least 30,000 years but unfortunately, their tenure hasn't yielded commensurate benefits. Although they're currently being catapulted into the modern world, most San are still regarded as second-class citizens in both Botswana and neighbouring Namibia.

Historically, the San had no collective name for themselves, but there's evidence that some referred to themselves as 'the harmless people' or in similarly self-depreciating terms. The early Europeans in Southern Africa knew them as Bushmen and that name stuck for several centuries. The Tswana generally refer to them by the rather derogatory name Basarwa, which essentially means 'people from the sticks'. The word 'San' originally referred to the language of one group of indigenous people in Southern Africa (the entire language group was known as Khoisan), but when the term Bushmen fell from grace as both racist and sexist, San was adopted by Europeans to refer to several groups of non-Negroid peoples of Southern Africa.

Some researchers have suggested that the San lived in a state of 'primitive affluence'. That is, they had to work only a short time each day to satisfy all their basic needs. At certain times and locations this might have been true, but during some seasons and in some conditions

ERIC WHEATER

Left: San of the Kalahari, Botswana

life could be harsh, for their sandy dry environment was above all very unpredictable.

Traditionally, this nomadic hunting and gathering society travelled in small family bands, following water, wildlife and edible plants. They had no chiefs or system of leadership, possessed no land, animals, crops or personal effects, and respected the individualism of its members. Women spent much of their time caring for children and gathering edible or water-yielding plants, while the men either hunted or helped with the food gathering.

One of the most unique peoples on earth, the San are now sadly resigned to the changes that have ended forever their traditional existence, in which they enjoyed complete integration and harmony with their environment, including the hardships it presented.

Of the remaining 55,000 or so San, approximately 60% live in Botswana, 35% in Namibia and the remainder are scattered through South Africa, Angola, Zimbabwe and Zambia. Tragically, most modern San work on farms and cattle posts or languish in squalid alcohol-plagued settlements centred on bore holes in western Botswana and north-eastern Namibia.

One contentious recent political issue in Botswana has been the forced relocation in March 1998 of the San from the Central Kalahari Game Reserve, which was set aside as a traditional hunting and gathering ground for them in 1961. In spite of vocal protests from the San, who realised that removal from their traditional lands would likely result in what would amount to indentured servitude on private ranches or cattle posts, they were shifted from the village of Xade to a settlement called New Xade – which has neither water nor permanent buildings – outside the reserve. They were advised that failure to move would result in less government money for health and educational facilities.

Officially, this action was justified due to the need to support wildlife preservation, tourism development and the need to 'rescue the Bushmen from their way of life and integrate them into mainstream Botswana society'. Cynics might also suggest that vast expanses of potential cattle grazing land and suspected diamond deposits within the reserve might also have played a role.

Through such grass-roots organisations as The First People of the Kalahari in Botswana and the Nyae Nyae Farmers' Cooperative in Namibia, some hopes for the future have emerged, and at the Namibian National Land Conference of 1991, the minister for land stated that the San system of land-holding would be recognised by the government. For more information on the San and their current situation in Southern Africa contact Survival International (☎ 020-7242 1441) 11-15 Emerald St, London WC1N 3QL UK, which is active on this issue. Web site: www.survival-international.org

[Continued from page 123]

also the time of the highest humidity and the most stifling heat; daytime temperatures of over 40°C are common.

In winter (late May through August) days are normally clear, warm and sunny, and nights are cool to cold. Wildlife never wanders far from water sources so sightings are more predictable. This is also the time of European, North American and – most importantly – South African school holidays, so some areas can be busy especially between mid-July and mid-September.

Maps

The most accurate country map is the *Shell Tourist Map of Botswana*, which shows major roads and includes insets of tourist areas and central Gaborone. It's sold in a packet with a small tourist guide in bookshops all over the region. Almost as good are the South African Automobile Association's 1:2,500,000 *Motoring in Botswana* and Rainbird Publishers 1:2,500,000 *Explorer Map Botswana*. The 1:1,750,000 *Republic of Botswana*, published by Macmillan, also contains insets of Gaborone and the tourist areas.

The Department of Surveys & Mapping, Private Bag 0037, Gaborone, publishes topographic sheets, city and town plans, aerial photographs, geological maps and Landsat images for US$2 to US$4 per sheet. For geological mapping, contact the Director, Department of Geological Survey, Private Bag 0014, Lobatse.

TOURIST OFFICES

The National Tourism office in Gaborone (☎ 353024, fax 308675) is conveniently located on The Mall, the heart of all activity in the capital. It has maps, pamphlets and brochures and the staff are quite helpful. Less worthwhile are the offices in Kasane (☎ 250327) and Maun (☎ 660492).

VISAS & DOCUMENTS

Visas

Visas are not required by travellers from most Commonwealth countries most European countries, and the USA. On entry, you'll be granted a 30-day visa.

Visas for Onward Travel

If you need visas for neighbouring countries, the embassies and high commissions are generally open for applications from 7.30 am to 12.30 pm and 1.45 to 4.30 pm weekdays. However, visas are easily available at the Botswana-Zambia and Botswana-Zimbabwe border crossings.

Visa Extensions Extensions are available for up to three months (for contact details of the immigration office, see under Information in the Gaborone section). You may be asked to show an onward air ticket or proof of sufficient funds for your intended stay. For more than a three-month extension, apply to the Immigration & Passport Control Officer (☎ 374545), PO Box 942, Gaborone before your trip. (Working visas are also available for nonresidents – see Work later in this section.)

Driving Licences & Other Documents

Travellers may drive using their home driving licence for up to six months (non-English language licences must be accompanied by a certified English translation). Those entering by vehicle need current vehicle registration papers and third-party insurance valid in the Southern African Customs Union. Otherwise, you must purchase insurance at the border for a nominal fee. At all border crossings, foreign-registered vehicles are subject to a road safety levy of US$1.25 (P6) upon entry.

EMBASSIES & CONSULATES

Botswana Embassies & High Commissions

Botswana has embassies and high commissions in Namibia, South Africa, Zambia and Zimbabwe (for details see the Facts for the Visitor sections in the individual country chapters), as well as in the following listed countries. Where Botswana has no diplomatic representation, information and visas are available through the British high commission.

UK
High Commission: (☎ 020-7499 0031, fax 7495 8595) 6 Stratford Place, London W1N 9AE
USA
Embassy: (☎ 202-244 4990, fax 244 4164) 3400 International Dr NW, Washington, DC 20008

Embassies & High Commissions in Botswana

All of the following are in Gaborone:

Angola
Embassy: (☎ 300204, fax 375089) 5131 Nelson Mandela Rd, Broadhurst (Private Bag 111)
France
Embassy: (☎ 353683, fax 356114) 761 Robinson Rd (PO Box 1424)
Germany
Embassy: (☎ 353143, fax 353038) 3rd floor, Professional House, Broadhurst (PO Box 315)
Namibia
Embassy: (☎ 372685) BCC Bldg, 1278 Lobatse Rd (PO Box 1586)
UK
High Commission: (☎ 352841, fax 356105) Queensway, The Mall (Private Bag 0023)
USA
Embassy: (☎ 353982, fax 356947) Government Enclave, Embassy Dr (PO Box 90)
Zambia
High Commission: (☎ 351951, fax 353952) Zambia House, The Mall (PO Box 362)
Zimbabwe
High Commission: (☎ 314495, fax 305863) Orapa Close (PO Box 1232)

CUSTOMS

Botswana is a member of the Southern African Customs Union, which allows unrestricted and uncontrolled carriage of certain items between member countries duty free. However, extra petrol and South African alcohol (more than 2L of wine and 1L of beer or spirits) are subject to duty. Goods from outside the union are subject to duty unless they are to be re-exported, but you can import up to 400 cigarettes, 50 cigars and 250g of tobacco duty free. Edible animal products such as untinned meat, milk and eggs are confiscated at the border (and also at veterinary cordon fences between the north-western province of Ngamiland and the rest of the country).

Officially, foreigners may export up to P10,000 (US$2083) in pula or foreign currency (or any amount of foreign currency that is declared upon entry). Note that currency checks at the border are very rare.

MONEY

Currency

Botswana's unit of currency is the pula (meaning 'rain'), which is divided into 100 thebe. Bank notes come in denominations of P5, P10, P20, P50 and P100, and coins in denominations of 5t, 10t, 25t, 50t, P1 and P2.

Exchange Rates

At the time of going to print, exchange rates for the pula were as follows:

country	unit		pula
Australia	A$1	=	P2.9
Canada	C$1	=	P3.3
euro	€1	=	P4.6
France	10FF	=	P7.0
Germany	DM1	=	P2.4
Japan	¥100	=	P4.5
New Zealand	NZ$1	=	P2.4
South Africa	R10	=	P7.4
UK	UK£1	=	P7.6
USA	US$1	=	P4.8

Exchanging Money

Full banking services are available in all main towns, but avoid the banks around the middle or end of the month, when the queues are formidable. Fortunately, there is a growing number of foreign exchange bureaus, which are typically much more efficient and change both cash and travellers cheques.

Credit Cards Most major credit cards (especially Visa and MasterCard) are accepted at tourist hotels and restaurants in the larger cities and towns, although you can't use them to buy petrol. At Barclays and Standard Chartered banks in Gaborone, Lobatse, Maun, Francistown and Kasane, you can use Visa or MasterCard to purchase pula (but very slowly!). Note that ATM machines don't yet accept credit cards or bank cards issued by other banks, and that in most hotels and restaurants, payment by credit card adds 10% to 12% to the bill (and don't bother arguing that credit card companies forbid such practices – no one wants to hear about it).

Costs

Travelling cheaply in Botswana isn't impossible, but if you can't afford a flight into the Okavango, a day or two at Moremi Wildlife Reserve or Chobe National Park, or a 4WD trip through the Kalahari, you may want to think twice before visiting this country. Meals and self-catering prices are comparable to those in Europe, North America and Australasia and although buses and trains aren't too expensive, they won't take you to the most interesting parts of the country.

Tipping

While tipping isn't exactly required, it's now expected in many tourist hotels and restaurants. However, in most places, a service charge is added as a matter of course, and further tipping is recommended only for exceptional service. At remote safari lodges, it's wise to leave a blanket tip with the management to be divided among the staff (say US$20 to US$25 for a stay of three days). Mokoro polers in the Okavango Delta always expect to be tipped – about US$2.50 (P12) per day is a good standard tip – and clients may well be reminded of that fact several times. Taxi drivers generally aren't tipped.

POST & COMMUNICATIONS

Post

Post is reliable but can be painfully slow. Allow two weeks to a month for delivery to/from overseas. Aerograms or postcards are the least expensive to send, followed by 2nd-class airmail letters, which are designated by clipping the corners off the envelope. For letters/postcards weighing up to 10 grams, postal rates are 55t within Botswana and to South Africa; 80t to Namibia or Zimbabwe; P1 to the rest of Africa; and P1.75 to other places. Items weighing from 10g to 20g go for P1 within Southern Africa; P1.40 to elsewhere in Africa; P2 to Europe and P2.50 to other places.

To post or receive a parcel in Gaborone, go to the parcel office around the side of the post office and fill out the customs forms. Parcels may be plastered with all the sticky tape you like, but in the end they must be tied up with string, so bring matches to seal knots with the red wax provided.

The best poste restante address is the main post office in The Mall in Gaborone, but it's not 100% efficient. To pick up mail, you must present your passport or photo ID.

Telephone

Botswana's country code is ☎ 267, and there are no regional area codes. When phoning from outside the country, dial the international access code (☎ 00 in most countries, ☎ 011 in the USA), then ☎ 267 followed by the telephone number. From Botswana, the international access code is ☎ 00.

Reliable phone boxes are found at post offices in all major towns, and direct dialling is available to most locations. Gaborone and Francistown have telephone offices for international calling, but they're only open during normal business hours. Phonecards are now appearing in larger towns, and cards are sold at post offices, Botswana Telecom offices and some petrol stations and shops.

Email & Internet Access

The good news is that public email and Internet access is now available in Gaborone and Maun (see those sections for details), and should soon emerge in other places.

INTERNET RESOURCES

Some useful Web sites include:

African Travel Getaway/Botswana Focus An online version of the magazine of the same name.
www.africantravel.com/stbrob.html

OnSafari.com Information on lodges and camps in Botswana's game parks.
www.onsafari.com

University of Botswana This Web site covers history, archaeology, politics, society and tourism in the country.
humanities.ub.bw/history/hist.htm

See also Internet Resources in the Regional Facts for the Visitor chapter for a listing of sites specific to Southern African.

BOOKS

This section covers books specific to Botswana. For information on books about the Southern Africa region as a whole, see Books in the Regional Facts for the Visitor chapter.

Lonely Planet

If your travels are concentrated on Botswana, check out Lonely Planet's *Zimbabwe, Botswana & Namibia*. If you're doing a grand tour of the African continent, *Africa on a Shoestring* covers 55 African countries.

Guidebooks

Visitors Guide to Botswana by Mike Main, John and Sandra Fowkes. This guide contains good off-road information for travellers venturing into the great unknown with their own vehicles.

History & Culture

Ditswammung – The Archaeology of Botswana compiled by the Botswana Society. Sold at Botswana Book Centre shops around the country, this is a compendium that archaeology buffs will appreciate.

History of Botswana by T Tlou & Alec Campbell. This book contains the best historical treatment of Botswana.

Lost World of the Kalahari by Laurens van der Post. A classic, which deals with the San people and contains some wonderful background on the Tsodilo Hills. The author's quest for an understanding of San religion and folklore is continued in ***Heart of the Hunter***.

A Marriage of Inconvenience: The Persecution of Seretse and Ruth Khama by Michael Dutfield. Details the negative responses to the marriage of Ngwato heir Seretse Khama and Englishwoman Ruth Williams in the 1950s.

Starlings Laughing by June Vendall-Clark. A memoir that describes the end of the colonial era in Southern Africa. (The author spent many years in the Maun area.)

General

Cry of the Kalahari by Mark & Delia Owens. An entertaining and readable account of an American couple's seven years studying brown hyaenas in the Central Kalahari.

Kalahari – Life's Variety in Dune and Delta by Michael Main. This book studies the faces of the Kalahari from its vegetation and wildlife to its geological and cultural history. It's full of personality and good colour photos.

Okavango – Jewel of the Kalahari by Karen Ross. This is similar to the Kalahari book by Michael Main listed earlier.

A Story Like the Wind by Laurens van der Post. An entertaining, fictional treatment of a meeting between European and San cultures, and its sequel ***A Far Off Place***.

The Sunbird by Wilbur Smith. A light read – two fanciful tales about the mythical 'lost city of the Kalahari'.

With My Soul Amongst Lions and ***Last of the Free*** by Gareth Patterson. The author carries Joy and George Adamson's 'Born Free' legacy from Kenya to Mashatu, in Botswana's Tuli Block. These rather tragic tales will probably make depressing reading for anyone inspired by Adamson's early efforts and visions.

NEWSPAPERS & MAGAZINES

The government-owned *Daily News*, published by the Ministry of Information and Broadcasting, is distributed free in Gaborone and includes government news, plus major national and international news. The *Midweek Sun* (Wednesday), the *Gazette* (Thursday) and the *Botswana Guardian* (Friday) take a middle-of-the-road political stance and are good for national news. For something more political, see the left-leaning *Mmegi* (*Reporter*), published on Wednesday.

Air Botswana's in-flight magazine, *Marung* (the name means 'in the clouds') includes articles on travel, local arts and culture. It's available by subscription from Marung (☎ 011-315 1771, fax 315 2072 in South Africa, ⓔ tapubs@iafrica.com) PO Box 30177, Kyalami 1684, South Africa.

RADIO & TV

Nationwide programming is provided by Radio Botswana, broadcasting in both English and Tswana. Botswana has one television station, the Gaborone Broadcasting Corporation (GBC), which transmits nightly for a few hours beginning at 7 pm and provides an interesting blend of foreign programming (mostly British and American) and occasional local productions.

HEALTH

As a relatively wealthy country, Botswana enjoys high standards of healthcare; the large hospitals in Gaborone and Francistown are comparable to those in Western Europe. Dental services are available in Gaborone and Francistown, and all the main towns have reasonably well-stocked pharmacies. For more general information on health issues, see the Health section in the Regional Facts for the Visitor chapter.

DANGERS & ANNOYANCES

The greatest dangers in Botswana are posed by natural elements, combined with a lack of preparedness. See the boxed text 'Driving off the Tar' in the Getting Around the Region chapter for some tips on remote travel.

While police and veterinary roadblocks, bureaucracy and bored officials may become tiresome, they're mostly just a harmless inconvenience. The officers are normally looking for stolen vehicles or meat products. Although theft occurs, Botswana enjoys a very low crime rate compared with other African (and many western) countries. However, don't leave valuables in sight in your vehicle, especially in Gaborone.

The State House, on State House Dr, in Gaborone should be avoided at all times – after dark don't even walk or drive past it.

The Botswana Defence Force (BDF) takes its duties seriously and is best not crossed. The most sensitive military base, which is operated jointly with the US government, lies in a remote area south of Gaborone and west of the Lobatse road. Don't stumble upon it accidentally!

BUSINESS HOURS

Normal business hours are from 8 am to 5 pm (often with a one- or two-hour closure for lunch). On Saturday, shops open early and close at noon or 1 pm, while on Sunday there's scarcely a whisper of activity anywhere.

In larger towns, banking hours are from 9 am to 3.30 pm weekdays and 8.30 to 11 am Saturday. Post offices are open from 8.15 am to 4 pm (closing for lunch between 12.45 and 2 pm). Government offices are open from 7.30 am to 12.30 pm and 1.45 to 4.30 pm weekdays.

PUBLIC HOLIDAYS & SPECIAL EVENTS

Public holidays in Botswana are:

New Year's Day 1 January
Day after New Year's Day 2 January
Easter March/April – Good Friday, Holy Saturday and Easter Monday
Ascension Day April/May
President's Day July
Day after President's Day July
Botswana Day 30 September
Day after Botswana Day 1 October
Christmas Day 25 December
Boxing Day 26 December
Day after Boxing Day 27 December

ACTIVITIES

Since Botswana is largely a high-budget, low-volume tourist destination, activity tourism focuses on the softer or more expensive options: wildlife viewing, 4WD safaris, mokoro trips and the like. If you're really flush with cash, the sky is the limit, and you can choose between elephant safaris in the Okavango, learning to fly in Maun, or hiring a 4WD and heading out into the Kalahari. Hiking opportunities are limited to the Tsodilo Hills in the northwest and several small ranges in the eastern and south-eastern parts of the country.

WORK

Botswana is developing rapidly and the education system cannot keep up with the demand. Nonresidents with a background, training and experience in a variety of professions (medical doctors, secondary school teachers, professors, engineers, computer professionals and so on) will have the best chances of finding a job.

As most nonresident workers want to remain around Gaborone or Francistown, a willingness to work in the bush improves your chances of finding work and being granted a three-year renewable residency permit. Applications are available from the Immigration & Passport Control Officer (see under Visas & Documents earlier in this section for contact details). Applications must be submitted from outside the country.

Numerous international volunteer organisations – including VSO and the Peace Corps – are active in Botswana.

ACCOMMODATION

Accommodation (with the exception of camp sites) is subject to a 10% accommodation bed tax. (See also the boxed text 'Rates for Safari Camps & Lodges' in the Okavango Delta section later in this chapter.) Payment by credit card normally requires an additional charge of 10% to 12%. Rates given in this chapter are for cash payments only.

Camping

Some hotels and lodges provide camp sites with varying amenities, but most of these are on the edge of town or deep in the bush. Camp sites average around US$7 per person per night.

Wild camping is permitted only outside national parks and away from government freehold lands. If you can't escape local scrutiny, visit the local chief or the police station to request permission to camp and get directions to a suitable site (see also the boxed text 'Minimum Impact Camping' in the Regional Facts for the Visitor chapter).

In national parks, camps are normally rudimentary and only a few have braai pits or flush toilets. Most are simply cleared spots in the dust, and are often good places to see wildlife activity. Bookings for park entry and camp sites (maximum six people per site) are now required for all parks in Botswana (with the exception of the privately owned Mashatu Game Reserve and the Kgalagadi Transfrontier Park, which is administered from South Africa). Bookings aren't available at the park gates, and without a booking you'll be denied entry to these parks; for more information, see National Parks & Wildlife Reserves in the Facts about Botswana section earlier in this chapter.

Safari Camps & Lodges

Most safari camps and lodges are found around Chobe National Park, the Tuli Block, and the Moremi Wildlife Reserve and Okavango Delta areas. They range from tent sites to established tented camps, brick or reed chalets and luxury lodges – or any combination of these. Prices range from around US$10 for simple huts, to around 150 times that for a luxurious chalet at Abu's Camp in the Okavango Delta (featuring circus elephant rides).

You need to prebook to stay at most upmarket camps, either before you arrive, in conjunction with an organised tour, or through a local travel agency or company representative. The main exceptions are some less expensive camps around Maun and Kasane, where you can just turn up.

Many lodges and camps, especially in the Okavango Delta, are in remote areas. Access is normally arranged by the booking agency or tour organiser, and is included in the package price (but not in most of the rack rates listed in this book). Other camps are readily accessible from the road system and are open to anyone with a suitable vehicle.

Hotels

Hotels in Botswana are much like hotels anywhere; every town has at least one and the larger centres offer several price ranges. However, you won't find anything as cheap as in other African countries, and the less expensive hotels in Botswana sometimes double as brothels. Mid-range and top-end hotels are available in Gaborone, Francistown, Maun and Kasane.

FOOD

Both takeaway and fastfood are popular in cities and towns, and cheap eating in larger towns revolves around quick chicken and burger fixes. Vegetarian cuisine hasn't really caught on, but places in Gaborone, Francistown and Maun do offer vegetarian options. International cuisine is available mainly in Gaborone, Maun and to a lesser extent, Francistown, where Chinese, Indian, French, Italian and other cuisines are represented. In smaller towns, expect little menu variation: chicken, chips, beef and greasy fried snacks are the norm.

Phaletshe (also called *mielie pap*), *mabele* and *bogobe* (maize, millet and sorghum porridge, respectively) form the basis of most Batswana meals and are normally served with some sort of meat relish. You may also want to try *vetkoek* (an Afrikaans word that is pronounced – and means – 'fat cake'), a type of doughnut.

To self-caterers entering Botswana from the north, the quantity and variety of food available in supermarkets may seem overwhelming. Open markets aren't as prevalent as in Zimbabwe and other countries, but Gaborone, Francistown and Maun do have growing informal markets.

Traditional Foods in Botswana

Traditionally, the Tswana staple was beef; the Yei depended on fish; and the Kalanga ate mainly sorghum, millet and maize; while the Herero subsisted on thickened, soured milk. Nowadays, most people get their food from agriculture or the supermarket, but before South African imports arrived, people herded animals and looked to the desert, which dished up a diverse array of wild edibles to augment their staple foods.

Historically, Batswana men were responsible for fishing or tending the herds – and lived mainly on meat and milk – while women were left to gather and eat wild fruits and vegetables. In remote areas, people still supplement their diets with these items. A useful desert plant is the *morama*, an immense underground tuber that contains liquid and is a source of water. Above ground, the morama grows leguminous pods that contain edible beans. Other desert delectables include marula fruit, plums, berries, tubers and roots, tsama melons, wild cucumbers and honey.

A fungus that grows on the *Grewia flavia* bush is related to the European truffle. In San mythology, these so-called Kalahari truffles are thought to be the eggs of the lightning bird because their presence is revealed by rings of cracked soil around the bush after electrical storms. The bush itself produces a small shrivelled berry, used locally to make *kgadi* wine. The nutritious and protein-rich mongongo nut, similar to the cashew, is eaten raw or roasted, and has historically been a staple for some San groups.

People also gather wild animal products, such as birds and their eggs, small mammals and reptiles and even ant eggs. Mopane worms, caterpillar-like inhabitants of mopane trees, are normally gutted and cooked in hot ash for about 15 minutes. Alternatively, they're boiled in salt water or dried in the sun to be later deep-fried in fat, roasted or eaten raw.

DRINKS

A range of 100% natural fruit juices from South Africa are sold in casks in supermarkets in the major cities and towns. You'll also find a variety of tea, coffee and sugary soft drinks.

Botswana's alcohol production is limited to beer; the three domestic beers are Castle, Lion and Black Label. Some of the more popular traditional alcoholic drinks are less than legal, including *mokolane*, or palm wine, a potent swill made from distilled palm sap. Another is *kgadi*, made from a distilled brew of brown sugar and berries or fungus. Home-brews include the common *bojalwa*, an inexpensive, sprouted sorghum beer that is also brewed commercially; a wine made from fermented marula fruit; light and non-intoxicating *mageu*, made from mielies or sorghum mash; and *madila*, a thickened sour milk.

SHOPPING

The standard of Botswana handicrafts is generally very high, particularly the beautifully decorative Botswana baskets that were originally produced in Ngamiland, in northwestern Botswana. In Gaborone, they're sold at Botswanacraft on The Mall and at other cooperatives. A range of basketware is available in Maun curio shops; alternatively, in Okavango Panhandle villages such as Gumare, the Etshas, Shorobe or Shakawe you can buy directly from the artists and craftspeople – you'll pay less and also contribute directly to the local economy.

In the western regions, beaded San jewellery and leatherwork are normally of excellent quality and you'll be deluged with offers. You'll find the famous leather aprons, ostrich eggshell beads (which cannot be imported into some countries) and strands of seeds, nuts, beads and bits of carved wood.

Beautiful weavings and textiles are also available. Some of the best and most reasonably priced work is available from weaving cooperatives around Gaborone and Francistown.

Note that in theory, an export permit is required for any item made from animal products, including ostrich eggshells, animal skins and feathers. If you purchase the item from a handicraft outlet, the items will have been registered upon acquisition but anything bought directly from locals must technically be registered with the local veterinary office.

For more details about traditional handicrafts in Botswana, see Arts under Facts about Botswana earlier in this chapter .

Getting There & Away

This section covers travel between Botswana and its neighbouring countries only. Information about reaching Southern Africa from elsewhere on the African continent and from other continents is outlined in the regional Getting There & Away chapter.

AIR

Botswana is served by Air Botswana, Air Malawi, Air Tanzania, Air Zimbabwe, British Airways, South African Airways and UTA.

Air Botswana and Air Zimbabwe fly nonstop between Gaborone and Harare (Zimbabwe) twice weekly. Air Botswana flies nonstop between Gaborone and Lusaka (Zambia) twice weekly and Air Namibia links both Gaborone and Maun with Windhoek (Namibia) and other parts of Southern Africa.

Between them, Air Botswana and South African Airways connect Gaborone and Johannesburg (South Africa) twice daily with connections to/from Durban and Cape Town.

The international air departure tax is US$6.25 (P30).

LAND

Border Crossings

Overland travel to or from Botswana is usually straightforward. Arriving travellers are often requested to clean all their shoes, even those packed away in their luggage, in a disinfectant dip to prevent them carrying foot-and-mouth disease into the country. Often vehicles must also pass through a pit filled with the same disinfectant.

Border opening hours change all the time, but in general, the major crossings open between 6 and 8 am and close between 6 and 10 pm. Minor crossings, such as the many across the Limpopo and Molopo Rivers between Botswana and South Africa, are normally open between 8 am and 4 pm, but close in periods of high water. The main crossings between Botswana and Zimbabwe or Zambia are open from 6 am to 6 pm. Some minor crossings close for lunch.

Note that during the winter months (late May to August), Namibia is one hour behind Botswana.

Namibia

The border crossings at Ngoma Bridge, Mahango-Mohembo and Mamuno-Buitepos are open to all vehicles, but between Ghanzi and Maun, several stretches remain quite rough and aren't suitable for small non-4WD vehicles.

On the Botswana side, petrol is available at Kasane, Ghanzi, Etsha 6 and Maun. In Shakawe, it's sold by the Brigades from steel drums and is quite expensive; ask at the Brigades camp about 5km upstream from the village.

Bus There is a bus from Ghanzi to the Mamuno-Buitepos border crossing, and on Fridays it connects with Namibia's Star Line (Trans-Namib Railways) bus, which runs between the border and Gobabis.

Hitching The easiest border crossing to use when hitching from Botswana to Namibia is Ngoma Bridge. The tarred 54km transit route from Kasane through Chobe National Park to Ngoma Bridge is relatively well travelled, and doesn't require payment of park fees. Since nearly everyone stops to refuel at Kasane, the petrol station is a good place to wait for lifts.

To hitch the new high-speed route between Ghanzi and Gobabis (Namibia), inquire about lifts at the petrol station next to the Kalahari Arms or Thakadu camp, both in Ghanzi. Most people head out in the morning.

South Africa

Most traffic between Botswana and South Africa passes through the Ramatlabama-Mmabatho border crossing, the Tlokweng Gate-Kopfontein border crossing near Gaborone or between Lobatse and Pioneer Gate/Skilpadshek-Zeerust, further south. Many other border crossings service back roads across the Limpopo River in the Tuli Block or across the Molopo River in southern Botswana.

Bus & Minibus An easy way to reach Johannesburg is by minibus; these leave when full from the main long-distance bus terminal in Gaborone and cost around US$15. To be assured of a place, get to the terminal as early as possible. Similarly, minibus services leave Lobatse for Mafikeng at around 10 am and cost US$4.

Indaba Services (☎ 660351, fax 660978) in Maun has comfortable weekly minibus services from Maun to the Sandton Holiday Inn in Johannesburg for US$113.

The Route 49 bus line (☎ 021-788 7904 in South Africa, ⓔ zimcaper@dockside.co.za) offers scheduled services from Victoria Falls (Zimbabwe) to Cape Town (South Africa) via Bulawayo, Francistown and Gaborone (Tuesday and Friday), or to Johannesburg via Kazungula (Zambia), Nata and Francistown (Saturday).

Train The *Bulawayo* runs once a week from Pretoria to Gaborone (and on to Bulawayo). It costs R225 in 1st class.

Hitching Hitching between Botswana and South Africa is straightforward, especially at the main border crossings. Fortunately, South African officials are no longer fussy about admitting hitchers.

Zambia

Direct travel between Botswana and Zambia is limited to the ferry across the River Zambezi at Kazangula. It has now been renovated but is still an interesting cultural experience. The crossing is free for foot passengers, travellers on public transport, and vehicles registered in Botswana. Foreign-registered motorcycles pay US$8, cars pay US$15 and large 4WDs pay US$25. Normally, it operates from 6 am to 6 pm daily.

If you're hitching from Kasane-Kazangula or the Zambian shore of the Zambezi, ask truck drivers about lifts to Livingstone.

The Botswana Bus (based in Livingstone, Zambia) runs basic seven-day bus tours between Botswana and Zambia, via northern Namibia, the Okavango Delta and the national parks. (For contact details see Organised Tours under Getting There & Away in the Livingstone section of the Zambia chapter.)

Zimbabwe

There are two well-used border crossings between Botswana and Zimbabwe: the road and rail link between Ramokgwebana and Plumtree; and the border between Kazungula and Kasane west of Victoria Falls. If you're driving, fuel is considerably cheaper on the Zimbabwe side.

Bus Express Motorways (☎ 304470) runs from the African Mall and the Gaborone Sun Hotel & Casino (both in Gaborone) to Bulaawayo and Harare via Francistown at least twice weekly. Several local companies offer daily services between Francistown and Bulawayo; the trip normally takes between three and six hours, depending on how much time is spent at the border.

Between Kasane and Victoria Falls, United Touring Company operates a transfer service for US$35. Note that although the Intercape Mainliner bus service between Victoria Falls and Windhoek passes through Kasane, passengers cannot embark or disembark in Botswana.

The Route 49 bus (☎ 021-788 7904 in South Africa, ⓔ zimcaper@dockside.co.za) travels from Johannesburg to Victoria Falls via Francistown, Nata and Kazungula on Tuesday and Friday, and from Cape Town to Victoria Falls via Gaborone, Francistown and Bulawayo on Saturday.

Train Trains run daily from Gaborone to Bulawayo, departing Gaborone at 9 pm and arriving in Bulawayo at 12.15 pm the following day. You can choose between 1st- and 2nd-class sleepers or economy-class seats. These trains usually have a buffet car. Fares are US$32/27/9 in 1st/2nd/economy. Customs and immigration formalities are handled on the train.

Sexes are separated in 1st- and 2nd-class sleepers unless you book a whole compartment or pay a surcharge for a two-person coupé (compartment). In the buffet car, you must pay for everything in pula or South African rand; Zimbabwe dollars aren't accepted on the train in Botswana. Never leave your luggage unattended.

Hitching Hitching between Francistown and Bulawayo via the Ramokgwebana-Plumtree border crossing is fairly easy. Mornings are best for hitching into Botswana, while in the afternoon, more traffic is headed towards Bulawayo. To hitch from Victoria Falls to Kazungula or Kasane, wait at the Kazungula road turn-off, about 1km south-east of Victoria Falls. From Kasane, the direct route to Maun across Chobe National Park is essentially unhitchable. The route from Kasane to Maun via Nata will prove far quicker even though it's laboriously roundabout.

Getting Around

Botswana's public transport network is quite limited, and the country's small population means that only a few locations are regularly served. Botswana's single railway line offers a limited but reliable service, and bus services are largely restricted to the main highway system. Air services are fairly good, although pricey for budget travellers.

AIR

The national carrier, Air Botswana, operates scheduled domestic flights between Gaborone, Francistown, Maun and Kasane; the best fares are available with a 14-day advance purchase (Apex) tickets. Botswana's domestic departure tax is US$2.50 (P12).

Under normal conditions (see the boxed text 'Air Botswana' below), Air Botswana has five flights weekly between Gaborone and Francistown (US$100), and daily flights between Gaborone and Maun (US$156). On Monday, Wednesday and Friday, you can fly between Francistown and Maun via Gaborone (US$130). There are flights from Kasane to Gaborone (US$230) and Maun (US$143) three times weekly. Air Botswana also offers discounted rates for flights booked and paid for at the same time and runs special weekend fares, such as the popular US$70 return ticket between Gaborone and Francistown, which is valid on Friday and Sunday. Air Botswana offices include:

Gaborone (☎ 351921, fax 374802) IGI Bldg, The Mall
Francistown (☎ 212393, fax 213834) Blue Jacket Mall
Kasane (☎ 650161) PO Box 92
Maun (☎ 660391, fax 660598) Airport Rd

Air Charter

Air charter provides the best access to remote villages and tourist lodges. Travel agencies and safari companies will make arrangements for a set fare, but individual charters are charged per kilometre for a *return*

Air Botswana

On 12 October 1999, a dismissed pilot hijacked an Air Botswana ATR-42 in Gaborone. Unable to get an audience with the national president, Festus Mogae, he circled in the air for two hours before running out of fuel, and dive-bombing the two remaining ATRs on the airport tarmac to destroy all three planes in a flaming inferno. As a result, Air Botswana's fleet was pared down from four planes to one. The airline has stated that normal schedules would resume shortly.

trip to the destination (charter companies charge for their return to home base once they've dropped you off). Individually arranged charters in a five-seater plane cost around US$225 per hour, plus US$0.85 per kilometre. Between Maun and Kasane, for example, a charter flight may average around US$600 (US$120 per person, with a minimum of five people). Major charter companies include:

Bush Free Air Charters (☎ 663599, @ bushfree@yahoo.com) PO Box 550, Maun
Delta Air (☎ 660044, fax 660589) PO Box 39, Maun
Ngami Air (☎ 660530, fax 660593) PO Box 119, Maun
Northern Air (☎ 660385, fax 660379) PO Box 40, Maun
Quicksilver Enterprises (Chobe Air) (☎ 650532, fax 650223) PO Box 280, Kasane
Swamp Air (☎ 660569, fax 660571) Private Bag 13, Maun

BUS

On the most popular runs along the highway corridor between Lobatse and Francistown, bus and minibus services generally operate according to demand and depart when full. Buses may connect Gaborone and Mahalapye 10 times daily, for example, but perhaps only six of these will go through to Francistown.

There are also services between Gaborone and Ghanzi; Francistown and Bulawayo (Zimbabwe); Serule and Selebi-Phikwe; Palapye, Serowe and Orapa; Francistown, Nata and Kasane; Francistown, Nata and Maun; Maun, Ghanzi and Mamuno; and Maun and Shakawe. There's no bus service through Chobe National Park between Kasane and Maun but safari companies offer three-day 4WD safaris via Moremi Wildlife Reserve (see Organised Tours later in this section).

TRAIN

Although it's slow, rail travel is a relaxing and effortless way to pass through the vast and dusty Botswana scrub. The domestic railway line runs between Ramatlabama on the South African border and Ramokgwebana on the Zimbabwe border, but currently, passenger services only extend as far south as Lobatse. The main stops are Gaborone, Mahalapye, Palapye, Serule and Francistown. There are also single-class commuter services from Gaborone to Pilane and Lobatse (US$1.50).

The train is an inexpensive way to go, but note that economy class is rather crowded and uncomfortable. Gaborone to Francistown takes about nine hours and costs US$27/22/7 in 1st/2nd/economy. Second-class sleepers accommodate six passengers, 1st-class sleepers accommodate four passengers, and bedding costs an additional US$2 per night. Other fares from Gaborone include Mahalapye (US$16/12/4, four hours) and Palapye (US$19/16/5, five hours).

Information, reservations and tickets are available at the Gaborone station from 7 am to 1 pm and 1.45 to 4.30 pm weekdays. In Francistown, the ticket windows are open from 8 am to noon and 1 to 4 pm weekdays. For 1st- and 2nd-class sleepers, advance bookings are essential.

CAR & MOTORCYCLE

To get the most out of Botswana, you'll need a vehicle. Road journeys normally fall into one of three categories: a high-speed rush along the excellent tarred road system; an uncertain rumble over a rapidly decreasing number of dusty secondary roads; or a wilderness expedition in a very sturdy, high-clearance 4WD vehicle. Conventional motorcycles perform excellently on the tarred roads and high-powered dirt bikes can be great fun on desert tracks; however, roads with clouds of dust and sand kicked up by high-speed vehicles are miserable. Motorcycles aren't permitted in national parks or reserves.

Driving is on the left. The national speed limit on tarred roads is 120km/h, while through towns and villages it normally drops to 80km/h. When driving through open areas, especially at night, be especially wary of animals wandering onto the road.

Rental

Hiring a vehicle – especially a 4WD – requires a lot of cash and given the great distances involved, the per kilometre charges rack up very quickly. However, in your own car or rented vehicle you'll have access to the best of Botswana. To hire a vehicle, you must be at least 25 years of age and have a valid driving licence from your home country. With all car hire, however, be wary of add-on charges and check the paperwork carefully. Also, check the vehicle before accepting it; make sure the 4WD engages properly and that you understand how it works. The wildest Kalahari is a harsh place to find out that the rental agency has overlooked something important.

Holiday Car Hire offers good value. A compact car such as a Hyundai Accent costs US$25 per day plus US$0.25 per kilometre or, with a minimum seven-day rental period, US$45 per day with 200 free km per day. A single/double-cab Toyota Hilux 4WD with a 150L reserve fuel tank, costs US$55/63 per day plus US$0.75 per kilometre or, with a minimum seven-day rental period, US$89/122 per day with 200 free km per day. For longer rental periods, you'll get even better deals and for an additional charge, they'll provide camping gear and safari outfitting.

If you want to rent a motorhome or 4WD, the agent for Maui Campers in Gaborone is Colin at Citi-Camp (☎/fax 311912, ⓔ citi camp@info.bw), or in Maun contact Donna Mackrill (☎ 661286, cell ☎ 7130 4868, ⓔ donyale@info.bw). Agencies include:

Avis
Gaborone: (☎ 375469, fax 312205 Central Reservations); (☎ 313093, fax 300445) Sir Seretse Khama international airport, PO Box 790; (☎ 304282) Grand Palm Hotel
Francistown: (☎ 213901, fax 212867) airport, PO Box 222
Kasane: (☎ 650144, fax 650145) Mowana Lodge, PO Box 339, Kasane
Maun: (☎ 660039, fax 661596) airport

Budget
(☎ 302030, fax 302028) Sir Seretse Khama international airport, Gaborone

Economic Car Hire
(☎ 375491) PO Box 1999, Gaborone

Holiday Car Hire
Gaborone: (☎ 312280, fax 357996, ⓔ van&truckhire@mega.bw) Broadhurst Industrial Area
Francistown: (☎ 214395, fax 216848, ⓔ lark@info.bw)
Kasane: (☎/fax 651263, ⓔ holidayhire@info.bw) Chobe Safari Lodge, PO Box 197
Maun: (☎/fax 662429, ⓔ holidayhire@info.bw)

Imperial Car Rental
Gaborone: (☎ 308609, fax 304460, ⓔ info@imperial.ih.co.za) Sir Seretse Khama international airport
Francistown: (☎ 204771)

Smart Car Rental
(☎ 561116, cell ☎ 7130 3561) Broadhurst, Gaborone

BICYCLE

Botswana is largely flat but that's the only concession it makes to cyclists. Unless you're an experienced cyclist and are equipped for extreme conditions, abandon any ideas you may have about a Botswana bicycle adventure. Distances are great, the sun can be intense, water is scarce and villages sparse. On tarred roads, which are mostly flat and straight, vehicles tend to crank up the speed and when a semitrailer passes at 150km/h, cyclists may unwittingly be blown off the road.

Off the beaten track, bicycles are also unsuitable and even die-hard cyclists have pronounced most of Botswana's back roads and tracks uncyclable. On good gravel, vehicles howl past in billowing clouds of sand and dust, and lesser-used routes are almost invariably just parallel ruts in deep sand. Also, bicycles aren't permitted in wildlife reserves.

HITCHING

Because public transport is somewhat erratic, many locals and travellers rely on hitching as their main means of getting around. On main routes, there should be no major problems. Before climbing aboard, ascertain a price or negotiate a fare. If you're riding inside, drivers may expect the equivalent of the bus fare. Otherwise, plan on one or two thebe per person per kilometre.

Hitching the back roads isn't as straightforward, and you'll probably need to be self-sufficient for as long as it takes to get a lift. For wilderness trips, such as to the Makgadikgadi Pans or Gcwihaba Caverns, lifts must be arranged in advance; inquire around the lodges at Maun, Nata, Gweta, Shakawe or Ghanzi. (For warnings on the potential dangers of hitching, see the Hitching section in the Getting Around the Region chapter).

LOCAL TRANSPORT

Gaborone has a local public transport system, but it's hardly adequate for the city's growing population; Francistown also has local bus services. Taxis are recognisable by their blue numberplates. Although the public transport minibuses in Gaborone are known collectively as 'taxis', conventional taxis (called 'special taxis') are thin on the ground (even in Gaborone) and it's difficult to flag one down. It's easiest to just phone for a taxi.

ORGANISED TOURS

The Botswana government promotes organised tours and offers tour discounts on national park entry fees. Most tours are more economically arranged through Botswana companies than through overseas agents. New Moon Safaris, Phakawe Safaris and Uncharted Africa Safaris offer the best deals for those on a tight budget. The following list includes major tour operators:

Audi Camp Safaris (☎ 660599, fax 660581, ⓔ audicamp@info.bw) Private Bag 28, Maun. Audi Camp offers budget mokoro trips around the Jao region of the Inner Delta; rates for a three-day/three-night trip are US$220 per person, including guides and polers, but not food or camping equipment. Trips in the Eastern Delta cost US$60/90/120 per person with two people, for one/two/three days (30% more for one person alone). They also do three-day safaris through Moremi (US$265 per person, with a minimum of four people), five-day safaris between Maun and Kasane (US$505 per person, with a minimum of four people), and five-day safaris in the Central Kalahari Game Reserve (US$635 per person, with a minimum of four people). Note that prices drop in the low season (1 November to 31 March). Audi Camp is affiliated with Ngepi Camp in Namibia's Caprivi Strip and for US$345 you can travel between Windhoek (Namibia) and Livingstone (Zambia) via the Okavango Panhandle and other sites of interest en route.

Crocodile Camp Safaris (☎ 660796, fax 660793, ⓔ sales@botswana.com) PO Box 46, Maun. This company does custom safaris around the Okavango Delta, Moremi, Chobe, the Central Kalahari, Makgadikgadi & Nxai Pan, Mabuasehube etc. Participation safaris start at around US$150 per person per day.
Web site: www.botswana.com

Desert & Delta Safaris (☎ 660022, fax 660037, ⓔ jng@afroventures.com) Private Bag 198, Maun. This company runs the plush Camp Moremi and Camp Okavango, both in the Moremi area, as well as Nxabega (Okavango Delta) and Camp Savuti (Chobe National Park).
Web site: www.afroventures.com

Elephant Back Safaris (☎ 661260, fax 661005, ⓔ ebs@info.bw) Ngami Data Bldg, Private Bag 332, Maun. This company runs Abu's Camp in the Okavango Delta. However, it's horrendously expensive (for rates, see Inner Delta/Places to Stay – Top End later in this chapter).

Gametrackers (☎ 660302, fax 660153, ⓔ pr@info.bw) PO Box 100, Maun. Gametrackers operates several Okavango Delta and Chobe lodges, including Makwena Lodge, Khwai River Lodge, San-ta-Wani, Eagle Island (Xaxaba) and Savuti Elephant Camp.
Web site: www.orient-expresshotels.com

Go Wild Safaris (☎ 650468, fax 650223, ⓔ go.wild@info.bw) PO Box 56, Kasane. This company offers Chobe wildlife drives and cruises, and runs custom safaris in Chobe, Moremi and the Okavango Delta. Participation safaris cost US$700 per day for up to 12 people, while basic/luxury safaris cost US$230/320 per person per day.
Web site: www.info.bw/~go.wild

Gunns Camp Safaris (☎ 660023, fax 660040, ⓔ gunnscamp@info.bw) This company runs budget safaris in the Okavango Delta, including relatively inexpensive Inner Delta mokoro trips from their base camp near Chiefs Island.

Gweta Rest Camp (☎/fax 612220, ⓔ gweta@info.bw) PO Box 124, Gweta. This company also run Makgadikgadi Camp and organises customised safaris around central Botswana. For rates, see under Gweta in The Makagadikgadi Pans section.

Hartley's Safaris (☎ 661806, fax 660528, ⓔ hartleys@info.bw) Private Bag 48, Maun. This friendly operation runs the luxury-class Xugana and Tsar camps in Moremi. From Xugana it offers mokoro trips and from Tsaro a unique two-night walking safari along the beautiful Khwai River.
Web site: www.hartleyssafaris.co.za

Island Safaris (☎ 660300, fax 662932, ⓔ island@info.bw) PO Box 116, Maun. This company runs

Island Safari Lodge and it operates tailor-made mobile safaris to Botswana's national parks and reserves, as well as mokoro and motorboat trips in the Okavango Delta. A standard three-day mokoro trip in the Eastern Delta costs US$165/280 for one/two people.

Janala Tours (☎ 650234/576, fax 650223, ⓔ chobe@info.bw) PO Box 55, Kasane. This company runs short safaris in Chobe for US$130/190 per day for one/two people, including park fees, wildlife drives, camping, meals and drinks. Day safaris to Chobe cost US$50 and transfers between Kasane and Victoria Falls are US$30/50 one way/return.

Ker & Downey (☎ 660375, fax 661282, ⓔ kerdowny@global.bw) PO Box 27, Maun. This company is Botswana's most exclusive luxury operator; it runs numerous very upmarket camps around the Okavango Delta.
Web site: www.kerdowney.com

Kwando Wildlife Experience (☎ 661449, ☎ 11-880 6138, fax 880 1393 both in Johannesburg, South Africa, ⓔ kwandojnb@global.co.za) PO Box 1264, Parklands 2121, South Africa. This company runs the Kwando Lagoon and Kwando Lebala camps in the Linyanti region, as well as Kwara Lodge, near Moremi.
Web site: www.kwando.com

Linyanti Explorations (☎ 650505, fax 650352, ⓔ selinda@info.bw) PO Box 22, Kasane. This upmarket operation runs several remote luxury lodges in Chobe, Moremi and the Linyanti region.
Web site: www.linyanti.com

Merlin Services (☎ 660635, fax 660036) Private Bag 13, Maun. This company isn't an operator, but acts as a booking agent for most Okavango Delta activities. It can also cobble together excursion programs around Botswana.

New Moon Safaris (☎/fax 661665, ⓔ newmoon@info.bw) Private Bag 210, Maun. This company is expertly and ethically run by Tiaan Theron and his wife, Sabine. They want to be known as the 'US$100 per day safari company', and are happy to take you just about anywhere in Botswana for that bargain rate. In addition to Eastern Delta mokoro trips, they can arrange tours through Moremi, the Central Kalahari and Tsodilo Hills; visits to their Sepupa Swamp Stop camp in the Okavango Panhandle; and stays in traditional San areas.

Okavango River Lodge (☎ 663707, cell ☎ 716 037 543) Private Bag 28, Maun. These very friendly folks run good-value day tours from Maun to Moremi for just US$100 per person.

Okavango Tours & Safaris (☎ 660220, fax 660589, ⓔ okavango@info.bw) PO Box 39, Maun. This company's speciality is lodge-based tours in the delta. It is also the agent for the popular budget camp Oddball's, as well as Delta Camp and Xakanaxa Camp.

Okavango Wilderness (☎ 660086, fax 660632, ⓔ info@sdn.wilderness.co.za) Private Bag 14, Maun. This subsidiary of South Africa's Wilderness Safaris arranges upmarket packages to Chitabe, Mombo, Duba Plains, Xigera and Vumbura camps in the Okavango Delta, and also runs safaris in Chobe, the Linyanti region, other parts of Botswana and neighbouring countries.

Phakawe Safaris (☎ 664377, cell ☎ 7160 6984, ⓔ phakawe@info.bw) Private Bag 0385, Maun. This recommended company offers excellent value. Delightfully informal participation safaris through Botswana's wildest regions cost US$100 per person per day (US$80 for transfers between Maun and Kasane, via Moremi and Chobe) and will take you beyond even the unbeaten track for a rare experience of Botswana at its best. Their Botswana Classic tour, which combines natural and cultural highlights, includes Moremi, a mokoro trip on the Okavango Panhandle, the Etshas, and the Tsodilo Hills. Other possible destinations include the Makgadikgadi Pans and the remotest corners of the Central Kalahari. Ask about elephant dung mokoro construction.
Web site: www.phakawe.demon.co.uk

Quadrum/Sedia Wildlife Safaris (☎/fax 662574, ⓔ sedia@info.bw) Private Bag 058, Maun. Birding safaris on the Thamalakane River (near Moremi) start at US$15 per person for 2½ hours; basic one-day/three-day mokoro trips in the Eastern Delta cost US$95/135.
Web site: www.info.bw/~sedia

Rann Safaris (☎ 660211, fax 660379, ⓔ rannsafaris@yahoo.com) Private Bag 248, Maun. This company runs Xudum Camp and does fully catered, luxury safaris in the Okavango Delta area. Camping costs US$440 per person per day; four-day walks with one/two people cost US$1050/1600; and horseback excursions for one/two people cost US$350/540 per day.
Web site: www.landela.co.zw

Travel Wild (☎ 660822, fax 660493, ⓔ t.wild@info.bw) PO Box 236, Maun. This friendly agency can make recommendations and help you organise trips in the Okavango Delta.

Uncharted Africa Safaris (☎ 212277, fax 213458, ⓔ unchart@info.bw) PO Box 173, Francistown. This company operates two incredible safari camps: Jack's Camp and San Camp in the Makgadikgadi Pans area, as well as the budget-oriented Planet Baobab and Kalahari Surf Club, near Gweta.

Gaborone

The Botswana capital, Gaborone, may be best described as a sprawling village suffering from the growing pains, the drabness and the lack of definition that accompany an abrupt transition from rural settlement to modern city. It has some sites of interest for visitors, but it is one of Southern Africa's most expensive cities and isn't worth going out of your way for.

History

In 1964, when the village of Gaborones (named after an early Tlokwa chief) was designated as the future capital of an independent Botswana, the task of designing the new city was assigned to the Department of Public Works, which never envisaged a population of more than 20,000. By 1990, however, the population was six times that, and Gaborone is now among the world's fastest-growing cities, with nearly 250,000 people.

Orientation

Although it's now developing a definite skyline, Gaborone (normally affectionately shortened to Gabs), lacks any real central business district, and the action focuses on its shopping malls. The main one, The Mall, is between the town hall and the government complex of ministries and offices on Khama Crescent.

Maps B&T Directories (☎ 371444, fax 373462), PO Box 1549, Gaborone, publishes a good town plan, complete with insets of main shopping centres. It comes in the US$3 Botswana Map Pack, which includes a Botswana map and street plans of urban centres. The Department of Surveys & Mapping (☎ 372390) publishes a large-scale city plan in several sheets, costing US$4 each.

Information

Tourist Office The Mall tourist office (☎ 353024, fax 308675), upstairs in the Koh-Hi-Noor House on The Mall, is the most useful one in the country. It's open from 7.30 am to 12.30 pm and 1.45 to 4.30 pm weekdays.

Immigration Office The Department of Immigration (☎ 374545), near the corner of State House Dr and Khama Crescent, handles inquiries, but visa extensions are available only at the small office on Nelson Mandela Dr, immediately north of the Molepolole flyover.

Money All major banks have branches on The Mall, but the quickest place to change cash or travellers cheques is the Barclays Bank at the Gaborone Sun Hotel. This branch is open from 8.30 am to 3.30 pm weekdays and 8.30 to 10.45 am Saturday. The Barclays Bank at Sir Seretse Khama international airport is open for currency exchange from 6 am to 8.15 pm, seven days a week.

Post & Communications The GPO on The Mall is open from 8.15 am to 1 pm and 2 to 4 pm weekdays, and 8.30 to 11.30 am Saturday. There are pay phones and cardphones outside the post office and the National Museum. Phonecards are sold at the post office, Botswana Telecom, the chemist on The Mall, and at Shell petrol station shops. At Botswana Telecom, on Khama Cres, international calls cost an average of US$3.70 per minute. It's open from 9.15 am to 1 pm and 2.15 to 4.30 pm weekdays and 8.15 to 11.30 am Saturday.

For fax services, go to the Copy Shop (fax 359922), north of Queensway. For email and Internet access, search out the Internet Cafe, behind the President Hotel, immediately south of The Mall.

Bookshops The Botswana Book Centre, on The Mall, is one of the region's best-stocked bookshops, with international literature as well as novels, reference books, school texts and souvenir publications. CNA in the Kagiso Centre, Broadhurst North Mall (north of the city), has a few popular novels, but focuses mainly on magazines and stationery. For book exchange, see J&B Books upstairs at Broadhurst North Mall.

Camping Equipment You'll find basic outdoor equipment, including butane cartridges, at Explosions, a gun shop in the African Mall, and at Gaborone Hardware, on The Mall.

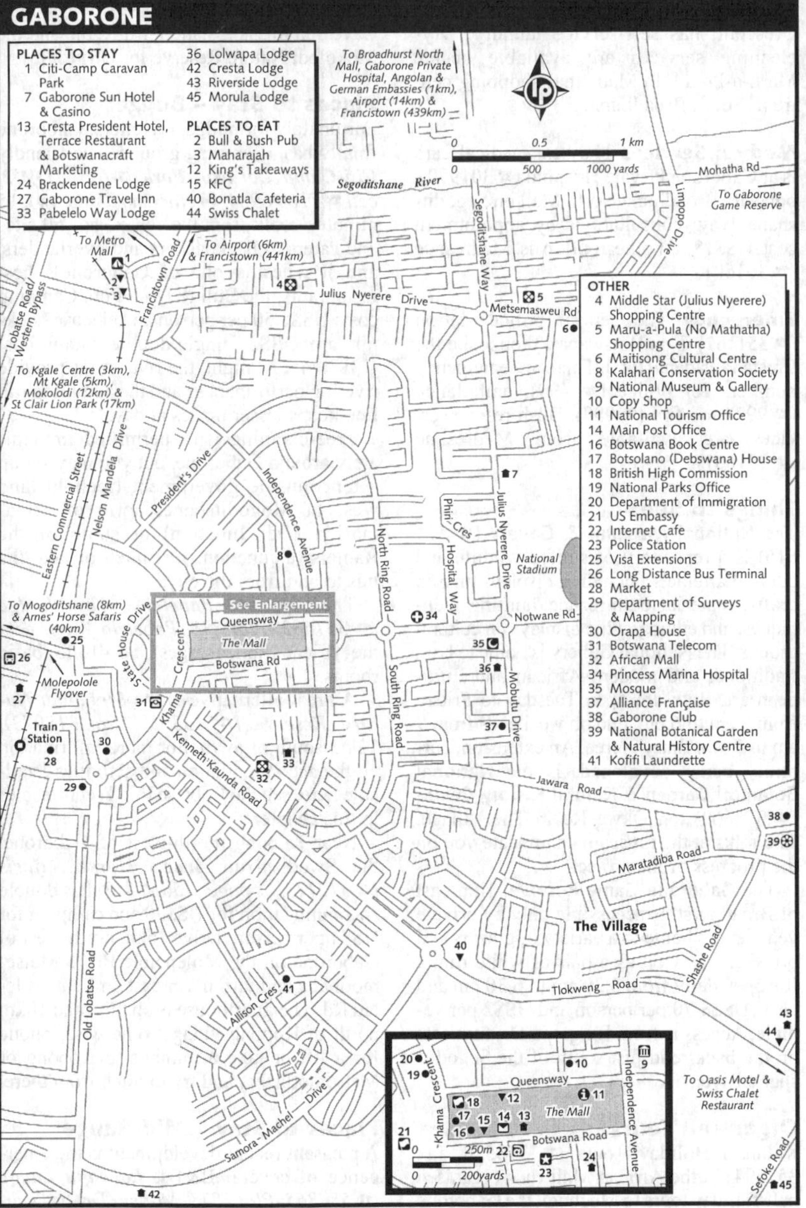
GABORONE
PLACES TO STAY
1 Citi-Camp Caravan Park
7 Gaborone Sun Hotel & Casino
13 Cresta President Hotel, Terrace Restaurant & Botswanacraft Marketing
24 Brackendene Lodge
27 Gaborone Travel Inn
33 Pabelelo Way Lodge
36 Lolwapa Lodge
42 Cresta Lodge
43 Riverside Lodge
45 Morula Lodge
PLACES TO EAT
2 Bull & Bush Pub
3 Maharajah
12 King's Takeaways
15 KFC
40 Bonatla Cafeteria
44 Swiss Chalet
OTHER
4 Middle Star (Julius Nyerere) Shopping Centre
5 Maru-a-Pula (No Mathatha) Shopping Centre
6 Maitisong Cultural Centre
8 Kalahari Conservation Society
9 National Museum & Gallery
10 Copy Shop
11 National Tourism Office
14 Main Post Office
16 Botswana Book Centre
17 Botsolano (Debswana) House
18 British High Commission
19 National Parks Office
20 Department of Immigration
21 US Embassy
22 Internet Cafe
23 Police Station
25 Visa Extensions
26 Long Distance Bus Terminal
28 Market
29 Department of Surveys & Mapping
30 Orapa House
31 Botswana Telecom
32 African Mall
34 Princess Marina Hospital
35 Mosque
37 Alliance Française
38 Gaborone Club
39 National Botanical Garden & Natural History Centre
41 Kofifi Laundrette
To Broadhurst North Mall, Gaborone Private Hospital, Angolan & German Embassies (1km), Airport (14km) & Francistown (439km)
0 0.5 1 km
0 500 1000 yards
Segoditshane River
Mohatha Rd
To Gaborone Game Reserve
Limpopo Drive
Segoditshane Way
To Metro Mall
To Airport (6km) & Francistown (441km)
Francistown Road
Lobatse Road/ Western Bypass
Julius Nyerere Drive
Metsemasweu Rd
To Kgale Centre (3km), Mt Kgale (5km), Mokolodi (12km) & St Clair Lion Park (17km)
Nelson Mandela Drive
Eastern Commercial Street
President's Drive
Independence Avenue
North Ring Road
Phiri Cres
Hospital Way
Julius Nyerere Drive
National Stadium
To Mogoditshane (8km) & Arnes' Horse Safaris (40km)
See Enlargement
Queensway
The Mall
Botswana Rd
State House Drive
Crescent
Khama
Notwane Rd
South Ring Road
Mobutu Drive
Molepolole Flyover
Train Station
Kenneth Kaunda Road
Jawara Road
Maratadiba Road
The Village
Shashe Road
Tlokweng Road
Old Lobatse Road
Allison Cres
Samora Machel Drive
To Oasis Motel & Swiss Chalet Restaurant
Sefoke Road
Khama Crescent
Queensway
The Mall
Botswana Road
Independence Avenue
0 250m
0 200yards

Laundry Kofifi Laundrette, on Allison Crescent, has self-service laundry. Dry-cleaning services are available beside Maru-a-Pula (No Mathatha) shopping centre in South Broadhurst.

Medical Services The best medical care is at Gaborone Private Hospital (☎ 301999), opposite Broadhurst North Mall on Segoditshane Way; consultations by appointment cost US$18. Another option is Medrescue (☎ 301601).

Emergency The central police station (☎ 351161) is on Botswana Rd opposite the Cresta President Hotel. There are emergency numbers for police (☎ 499), ambulance (☎ 997) and fire (☎ 998). Bush rescue services are available from Medrescue (☎ 301601).

Things to See

The **National Museum & Gallery** (☎ 374 616) is a repository of stuffed wildlife and cultural artefacts, including displays on San crafts, material culture and hunting techniques, and ethnographic displays on cultural groups. The National Gallery is home to both traditional and modern African and European art. Both are open Tuesday to Friday from 9 am to 6 pm, and on weekends from 9 am to 5 pm. Entry is free. An extension, currently being developed, is the **National Botanical Garden & Natural History Centre** (☎ 373860), on Okwa Rd in The Village. The folks at the museum can update you on the progress of the project.

The **Gaborone Game Reserve**, 1km east of Broadhurst, is accessible only by private vehicle. It's home to a variety of grazers and browsers, as well as a pair of white rhino. It's open daily from 6.30 am to 6.30 pm and costs US$3.70 per person and US$2 per vehicle. Access is from Limpopo Dr; turn east on the back road just south of the Segoditshane River.

Organised Tours

Kalahari Holiday Tours (☎ 313528, fax 357594) in the African Mall runs organised half/full-day tours to Mochudi, the Gaborone Game Reserve, Molepolole, Livingstone's Cave and mission station, Mt Kgale and the Mokolodi Nature Reserve for US$15/33.

Places to Stay – Budget

Fortunately for budget travellers, Gaborone finally has a camping ground. The friendly ***Citi-Camp Caravan Park*** *(☎/fax 311912, cell ☎ 7160 6924, ⓔ citicamp@info.bw)*, 15 minutes' walk from the centre, has 50 sites and caters to backpackers and overlanders, and it's beside one of Gaborone's best restaurants, the Bull & Bush Pub. Camping costs US$6.50 per person and electric hook-ups are US$2; single/double rooms cost US$30/45. At night, the river frogs provide riveting performances and the adjoining rail line keeps lesser noises at bay.

Free-camping isn't permitted immediately around Gaborone, but you may set up a tent outside government freehold land west of Mogoditshane, north of Mmamashia (Odi Junction) or south of the Ramotswa Junction. Just hitch or take the bus to and from the city.

The spartan ***Pabelelo Way Lodge*** *(☎ 351682, Plot 838, Pabelelo Way)*, near the African Mall, charges US$9/16 for basic rooms.

A great alternative is the ***Mokolodi Nature Reserve*** *(☎ 353959, fax 313973)*, 12km south of town. For more information on the accommodation and activities available here, see the Lobatse Road section later in this chapter.

Near Kopong, north-west of Gaborone, the Swedish-run ***Arne's Horse Safaris*** *(☎ 312173, or pager 1501 0018)* has double accommodation for US$30 and camping for US$4 per person. Drive 16km north-west of Gaborone on the Molepolole Rd to Metsemotlhaba and turn north-east on Lentsweletau Rd. The guesthouse is on this road 10km north of Kopong village; otherwise, phone for a lift or take a minibus to Kopong or Metsemotlhaba, and try to hitch from there.

Places to Stay – Mid-Range

A pleasant recent development is the emergence of several B&Bs. ***Lolwapa Lodge*** *(☎ 584865, Plot 2873, Mobutu Dr)* has simple rooms, with use of cooking facilities, starting at US$25/41 for singles/doubles, including breakfast and a private bath. Rooms with shared baths are US$22/36.

The acceptable ***Brackendene Lodge*** *(☎ 312886, fax 306246, PO Box 621, Gaborone)*, three minutes' walk from The Mall, has singles/doubles with shared bath starting at US$25/31, with breakfast. Rooms with private bath are US$28/33 and family rooms cost US$70. Meals are available on request.

The basic ***Riverside Lodge*** *(☎ 328805, PO Box 1771, Tlokweng)* has single and double rooms for US$42.

Morula Lodge *(☎ 328500, fax 353861, PO Box 1241, 329 Sefoke Rd)* charges US$30/35 for rooms without/with air-con; breakfast costs US$2.50.

The much improved ***Oasis Motel*** *(☎ 328396, fax 328568)* in Tlokweng has rooms for US$50/63 and chalets for US$43/55. However, there's no public transport. Much nicer is the ***Gaborone Travel Inn*** *(☎ 322777, fax 322727)*, north of the train station and opposite the bus terminal. Rooms with bath and TV cost US$50/61. It also has a great bar, a takeaway and live (loud) music at weekends.

Places to Stay – Top End

The ***Cresta Lodge*** *(☎ 375375, fax 300635, **e** crestalodge@info.bw)*, on the southern side of Samora Machel Dr near the old Lobatse road, has singles/doubles for US$88/103. English/continental breakfast costs US$7/5. Walking tracks lead from the hotel to scenic Gaborone Dam.

The once highbrow ***Gaborone Sun Hotel & Casino*** *(☎ 351111, fax 302555)* on Julius Nyerere Dr has now been humbled by competition. Standard rooms cost US$91/102; an English/continental breakfast is US$10/7 and the Indian-oriented Goombay Grill offers fine dining. An annual membership fee of US$30 allows access to the swimming pool and squash and tennis courts.

The ***Cresta President Hotel*** *(☎ 353631, fax 351840, **e** crestabs@iafrica.com)* on The Mall offers friendly, central accommodation. Standard rooms cost US$72/88 and a buffet English/continental breakfast is US$8.50/6.50. The attached Terrace Restaurant overlooking The Mall serves up healthy European cuisine, including vegetable-rich lunches, as well as coffee and pastries.

Places to Eat

Burgers, chips and snacks are found at ***King's Takeaways***, on The Mall. It's a favourite lunch spot for office workers. ***KFC*** has outlets on The Mall and in the African Mall; for something livelier, opt for ***Nando's***, in the African Mall, which does delicious Portuguese-style *piri-piri* chicken (chilli chicken). A similar choice is ***Max Frango***, in the Middle Star shopping centre.

For lunch, the ***Terrace Restaurant***, on the terrace of the Cresta President Hotel, serves spinach quiche, cream of asparagus soup and vegetable curries. Afterwards, you can linger over a rich and frothy cappuccino and eclairs while surveying the passing Mall scene below. In the evening it does grill specials.

For an exhaustive menu of sweets, salads, desserts, vegetarian options and coffee specialities, try the ***Kgotla*** *(☎ 356091)* in the Broadhurst North Mall. It's open from 9 am to 9 pm daily. Coffee addicts will love the ***Brazilian Cafe*** in the Kagiso Centre, Broadhurst North Mall, which serves coffee specialities and light lunches and dinners (US$3 to US$7) seven days a week.

The ***Taj*** *(☎ 313569)*, in the African Mall, dishes up Indian, Mauritian and continental cuisine and excellent salads, and does a buffet lunch for US$8 seven days a week. The ***Shebeen***, also in the African Mall, is a pleasant African bar serving traditional local specialities.

Da Alfredo *(☎ 313604)* at Broadhurst North Mall specialises in seafood and Italian cuisine. It's open daily for lunch, dinner, and takeaways. The ***Moghul*** *(☎ 375246)*, in the Middle Star shopping centre, serves Indian and Pakistani fare; its popular Indian buffet lunch costs US$8. In the Maru-a-Pula (No Mathatha) shopping centre is the popular ***China Restaurant*** *(☎ 357254)*, open for lunch and dinner.

A good choice for breakfast, lunch or dinner is the ***Bonatla Cafeteria*** *(☎ 352488)* in the Botswana National Productivity Centre (BNPC), which offers traditional Botswana meals for a set price and serves a range of salads, grills, pasta and game dishes. It's open daily from 6.30 am until late.

Mike's Kitchen, in the Kgale Centre on the Lobatse road, belongs to a family-oriented South African chain dishing up standard chicken, beef and seafood dishes. Another popular South African chain is represented by the ***Diamond Creek Spur*** steak house in the Kagiso Centre, Broadhurst North Mall.

If you prefer a British twist or a nice patio meal, try the ***Bull & Bush Pub*** *(☎ 375070)*; from Nelson Mandela Rd, look for the west-pointing sign reading 'Police Housing Bull & Bush'. The extensive menu offers everything from beef, pizza and pasta to elaborate vegetarian starters and main dishes; plan on US$7 to US$10 for a memorable meal. The ***Maharajah Restaurant***, next door, features Indian cuisine. An alternative European option is the ***Swiss Chalet*** *(☎ 312247)*, on Tlokweng Rd, which serves both Swiss and Italian dishes.

The atmospheric outdoor restaurant and bar at the ***Mokolodi Nature Reserve*** *(☎ 328692)* serves up creative meals, including seafood and game meat.

Entertainment

The 450-seat theatre in the ***Maitisong Cultural Centre*** *(☎ 371809)*, at Maru-a-Pula Secondary School, is a venue for cultural events, and the ***Alliance Française*** *(☎ 351650)* frequently screens classic films.

A favourite night spot with Gaborone youth is ***Night Shift*** in the Broadhurst North Mall, but it's not a classy establishment. The very popular ***Legends***, an R&B-oriented club in the Maru-a-Pula shopping centre, is the place to go on Friday night; on Thursday, it features local *kwasa kwasa* music of Congo (Zaïre). On Sunday, the ***Swiss Chalet*** hosts jazz performances. On weekends, the ***Take Five*** in Mogoditshane also plays jazz, but on weekends, it does '70s and South African pop music. For African disco, try the ***Platform*** in the Gaborone Sun Hotel.

Brits and pub fans will appreciate the ***Bull & Bush Pub*** (see Places to Eat), which is *the* expatriate hangout and sports bar. ***Harley's*** bar, upstairs from ***The Shebeen*** bar in the African Mall, imitates rebel watering holes in the USA; it's open in the evening only. The ***Gaborone Club***, on Okwa Rd in The Village, stages folk music; performances are held at 7.30 pm on the first Saturday of the month. The ***Waterfront***, at Gaborone Dam, south of the city, sometimes hosts live performances.

Shopping

The Botswanacraft Marketing Company (☎ 312471, fax 313189), on The Mall, deals in a selection of material arts and crafts from around Botswana. Several nearby villages – Mokolodi, Gabane, Mochudi, Odi and Thamaga – have worthwhile speciality craft centres.

Getting There & Away

Air The Sir Seretse Khama international airport is 14km from the centre.

Air Botswana operates scheduled domestic flights between Gaborone and Francistown (US$100), Maun (US$156) and Kasane (US$230).

In Gaborone, the Air Botswana office is in the IGI building on The Mall; it also serves as the agent for most other airlines flying to/from Botswana.

Bus Intercity buses to Lobatse, Mahalapye, Palapye, Serowe and Francistown (US$10, five hours), as well as minibuses to nearby villages and minibus services to Johannesburg, use the main bus terminal, over the Molepolole flyover near the town centre. Most departures are early in the morning and buses leave when full. From Gaborone to Ghanzi (US$12, six to seven hours), buses depart daily at 7 am and 10 am.

Train Gaborone has daily rail connections to and from Bulawayo (Zimbabwe), Francistown and Lobatse. The northbound train to Bulawayo (US$32/27/9 in 1st/2nd/economy), via Francistown, departs at 9 pm. There's also a daytime train between Gaborone and Francistown (US$5.50/8.25 in economy/club class), which departs from Gabs at 10 am. Commuter trains to Lobatse and Pilane offer only economy-class seats

(US$1.50). For current information, call Botswana Railways (☎ 351401).

Hitching To hitch north, catch the Broadhurst 4 minibus from any shopping centre along the main city loop and get off at the standard hitching spot at the northern end of town. There's no need to wave down a vehicle – anyone with space will stop for passengers. Plan on around US$6 to Francistown, where you can look for onward lifts to Nata, Maun and Kasane.

Getting Around

To/From the Airport The only reliable transport between the airport and town is the courtesy minibuses operated by the top-end hotels for their guests. If there's space, nonguests may talk the driver into a lift, but you'll have to tip a few pula. Taxis rarely turn up at the airport; if you do find one, you'll pay anywhere from US$3 to US$12 per person to the centre.

Minibus Packed white minibuses, recognisable by their blue number plates, circulate according to set routes and cost US$0.25 (P1). The main city loop passes all the shopping centres.

Taxi Public transport minibuses may be called 'taxis', but conventional private hire taxis (called 'special taxis') are operated by City Cab (☎ 324277) and Town Cab (☎ 580380).

AROUND GABORONE

Mochudi

Mochudi is probably the most interesting village in south-eastern Botswana. It was first settled by the Kwena in the mid-1500s, as evidenced by ruined stone walls in the hills. In 1871 it was settled by the Kgatla people, who had been forced from their lands by northward-trekking Boers. The Cape Dutch-style **Phuthadikobo Museum**, established in 1976, is one of Botswana's best, and reveals the history of Mochudi and the Kgatla people. It's open from 8 am to 5 pm weekdays and 2 to 5 pm on weekends. Entry is free but donations are gratefully accepted. After visiting the museum, it's worth spending an hour appreciating the variety of designs in the town's mud-walled architecture.

Buses to Mochudi depart from Gaborone when full. By car, go 35km north to Pilane and turn east; after 6km, turn left at the T-junction and then right just before the hospital, into the historic village centre.

The Lobatse Road

The 'sleeping giant', **Mt Kgale**, overlooks Gaborone, and you can easily hike to the top from where there's a good view of the capital. Take any Lobatse bus or hitch out along the new Lobatse road 5km from town to the satellite dish. A couple of hundred metres towards town, opposite the dish, cross the concrete stile, turn left, and follow the fence until it enters a shallow gully. From there a set of whitewashed stones leads to the summit. Because of recent robberies on this hike, it's wise not to walk alone or carry anything of value.

The 3000-hectare **Mokolodi Nature Reserve** (☎ 353959 or 561955, fax 313973), 12km south of Gaborone, concentrates on wildlife education for schoolchildren, but this scenic reserve also protects a full complement of Botswana's wildlife, including white rhino reintroduced from South Africa. Guided two-hour wildlife walks cost US$12 and day/evening wildlife drives, US$14/16.50. Entry to the reserve costs US$4 per vehicle, plus US$2.50 per person. There are also comfortable four/six-bed chalets (US$50/75 on weekdays and US$69/100 on weekends), dorms (US$15) and a super restaurant. Transport from town costs US$9 per person, with a minimum of three people. Otherwise take a Lobatse minibus 12km south of Gaborone and get off at the turning 2km south of the turning for Mokolodi village. From there, it's 1.5km west to the reserve entrance.

Lobatse

Despite its nice setting 68km south of Gaborone, Lobatse is one of Botswana's dullest places, and is known mainly as the site of the national mental hospital and the country's largest abattoir. The town's most beautiful structure is the thatch-roofed St Mark's Anglican Church.

ful structure is the thatch-roofed St Mark's Anglican Church.

The only accommodation is the quite decent ***Cumberland Hotel*** (☎ *330281, fax 332106,* ⓔ *cumberland@global.bw)*, which charges US$45/55, including breakfast. You'll find inexpensive meals at ***Chicken Licken*** and the ***You & I Takeaway***, on the street parallel to the railway line.

There are frequent minibuses between Gaborone and Lobatse, departing from the main bus terminal, and the trains run to and from Gaborone during commute hours, roughly from 6 to 8 am and 4 to 6 pm.

Eastern Botswana

Although in the winter months it bears a strong resemblance to a desert zone, the scrubland strip along the South African and Zimbabwean borders is the part of Botswana that is most amenable to agriculture and that therefore most suits human habitation. Though it can't by any means be called lush, it still receives most of the country's rainfall and as a result it takes on a pleasantly green cloak in the summer months.

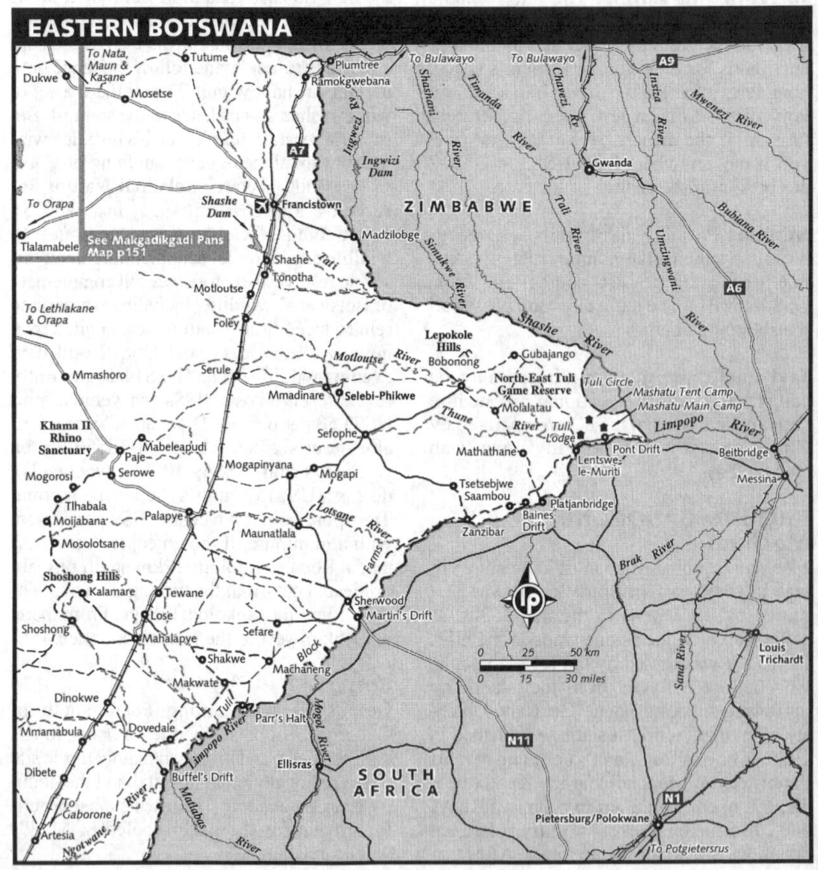

FRANCISTOWN

Francistown was originally a gold-mining centre, but industry and commerce have now taken over and the town has become an expanding retail and wholesale shopping mecca. Shopping malls are mushrooming, but beyond the centre, Francistown is a dusty, desultory place, and its perimeter contains Botswana's most squalid shantytowns. This is one of the few places in this prosperous country where you'll see real poverty.

The only real tourist attraction is the very basic Supa-Ngwao cultural and historical museum, about 500m along the Maun Rd, but the excellent booklet *Exploring Tati*, by Catrien van Waarden, provides enough information on historic sites for Francistown to become a fascinating place. It's available at the Supa-Ngwao Museum or through Marope Research, PO Box 910, Francistown.

Information

You'll find banks along Blue Jacket St and opposite the train station. The post office is on Blue Jacket St, and you can make phone calls from the Teletswana Office on Lobengula Ave near Blue Jacket St. Laundry

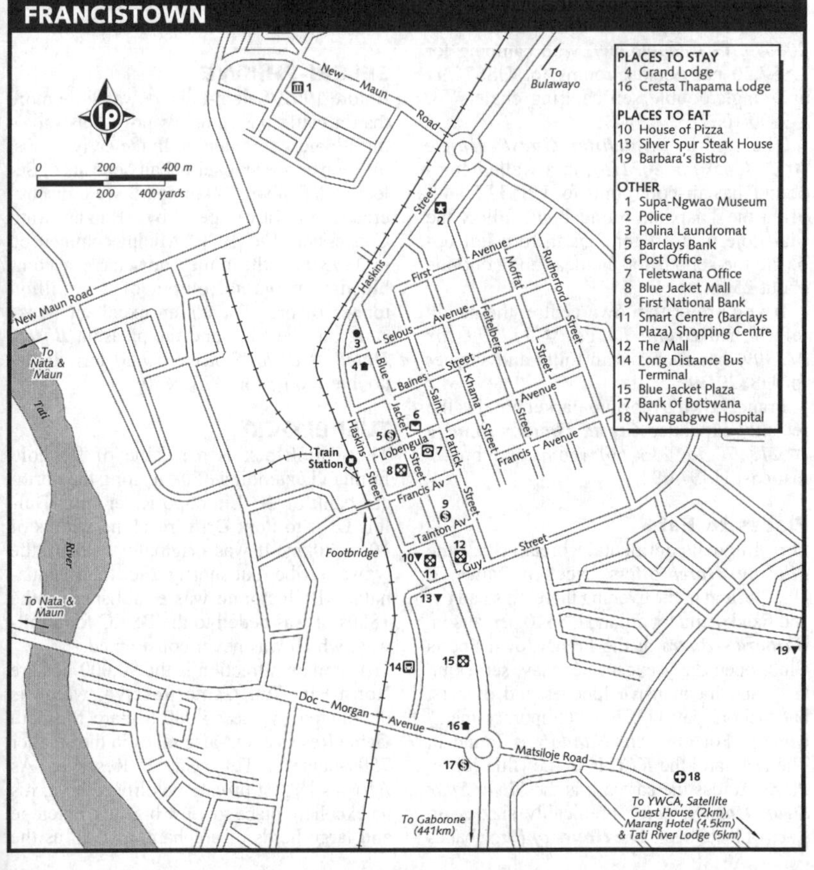

service is available at the Polina Laundromat at the eastern end of Blue Jacket St.

The Nyangabgwe Hospital lies just east of the Thapama roundabout. For emergency medical services dial ☎ 997. The Hana Pharmacy in Blue Jacket Plaza is the best stocked. The police station (emergency ☎ 999) is on Haskins St, east of the central area.

Places to Stay

The best deal is the friendly ***Marang Hotel*** *(☎/fax 213991)*, 5km from the centre on the old Gaborone road. Camping on the beautiful grassy lawns near the Tati River costs US$5.50 per person and single/double rooms or rondavels are US$87/98. Just over the river lies the new ***Tati River Lodge*** *(☎ 206000, fax 206080, ⓔ trl@info.bw)*, with camping for US$7.50 per person, rooms for US$74/97 and single/double self-catering chalets for US$90/106.

The quirky ***Satellite Guest House*** *(☎ 214665, fax 202115)*, in a walled compound, has air-con rooms for US$32.50/44. From the Thapama roundabout, follow the Matsiloje turn-off for 2.5km, turn left opposite the school for the deaf and continue about 250m.

If you prefer the town centre, the newly refurbished ***Grand Lodge*** *(☎ 212300, fax 212309)* has rooms with toilet and shower for US$29/39.

Francistown's most upmarket hotel is the recently expanded ***Cresta Thapama Lodge*** *(☎ 213872, fax 213766)*; rooms with breakfast cost US$74/92.

Places to Eat

For English/continental breakfasts, the ***Marang Hotel*** offers excellent value at US$7/5, and in the evening there's a salad bar and fixed menu for around US$10 per person. ***Barbara's Bistro*** at the Francistown Sports Club, open daily except Monday, serves up tasty and inexpensive lunches and dinners, but visitors pay US$2 for temporary membership. For chicken, ***Nando's*** is found in The Mall and the ***KFC*** is in the Blue Jacket Plaza. Across the car park is the ***Silver Spur Steak House***, which predicably sizzles up slabs of local beef. The ***House of Pizza*** bakes its pizzas in a wood-fired oven and also does chicken, kebabs and pasta dishes; you'll also find tasty pizzas at ***Milano Pizza & Chicken***, off the Blue Jacket Plaza car park.

Getting There & Away

As a transport hub of sorts, Francistown enjoys several daily services to Nata (US$3), Maun (US$8.50) and Gaborone (US$10). The bus terminal is wedged between the train line and the frontage road connecting Haskins St to Doc Morgan Ave. The overnight train between Bulawayo and Gaborone passes through Francistown at around 10 pm southbound and 6.45 am northbound, and the daytime train to Gaborone departs at 10 am (US$5.50/8.25 in economy/club class).

SELEBI-PHIKWE

Before 1967, Selebi-Phikwe was little more than a cattle post, but it's now Botswana's third-largest community. In the early 1960s, the twin copper-nickel-cobalt deposits of Selebi and Phikwe, 14km apart, were discovered and developed by Bamangwato Concessions Ltd (BCL). Mining commenced in 1973 and the mines now have a combined annual total output of 2.5 million tonnes of ore. There's an excellent bookstore on The Mall and the pleasant ***Bosele Hotel*** *(☎ 810675, fax 811083)* has single/double rooms for US$75/90.

TULI BLOCK

The Tuli Block is a swathe of freehold farmland extending 350km along the northern bank of the Limpopo River from Buffels Drift to Pont Drift, reaching widths of 10 to 20km. It was originally held by the Ngwato tribe, but shortly after the Bechuanaland Protectorate was established in the 1880s, it was ceded to the BSAC for a railway, which was never constructed.

The main attraction is the 90,000-hectare **North-East Tuli Game Reserve**, which is dominated by the 45,000-hectare Mashatu Game Reserve, but also takes in the smaller 7500-hectare Tuli Game Reserve. As Africa's largest private wildlife reserve, it's an excellent place to view big cats, antelope and large herds of elephant, as well as the stately mashatu tree *(Xanthocercis zambeziaca)* after which Mashatu Game Reserve is named. It also offers a sample of Botswana's wildlife and access to some of the country's best landscapes: savanna, rock kopjes, river bluffs, riverine forests and tidy villages.

Botswana's easternmost village, **Pont Drift**, is also a border crossing. There's no bridge, however, so when the Limpopo is too deep to be forded, passengers are ferried across on the rustic Pont Drift cableway for US$4 per person. Immediately beyond the immigration post is the Mashatu reception centre. Except for the small exclave east of the Motloutse crossing, Mashatu is open only to guests of the Mashatu lodges (see Places to Stay).

The sandy Motloutse (Large Elephant) River, 27km west of Pont Drift, rarely flows; as you plough through the riverbed, notice the bizarre dolerite dike known as **Solomon's Wall** that flanks the river.

Places to Stay

The luxury-class ***Mashatu Main Camp*** *(☎ 27-011-789 2677, fax 8864382, ⓔ jhb@malamala.com or mashatures@malamala.com, PO Box 2575, Randburg 2125, South Africa)* charges US$198/264 for single/double chalets. Its bush alternative, ***Mashatu Tent Camp***, costs US$165/220. Rates include accommodation, meals, wildlife drives and transfers from the Tuli Lodge airstrip or the Pont Drift cableway. Web site: www.bookorbuy.com/mashatu/home.htm

The more down-to-earth ***Tuli Lodge*** *(☎/fax 845303, ⓔ tuli@tulilodge.co.za, PO Box 83, Lentswe-le-Muriti, Botswana)* occupies a green riverine oasis beside the Limpopo, and is approached through lovely red-rock country. Rooms at the shady main lodge cost US$185 per person, including meals, two wildlife drives and a wildlife walk. The self-catering chalets, 2km upriver, cost US$500 per night for up to eight people, including two wildlife drives and a walk.

Getting There & Away

Most Tuli Block roads are well-graded gravel or dirt and negotiable by 2WD, but the Motloutse River crossing west of Pont Drift normally requires 4WD. The Mashatu and Tuli Game Lodges can arrange air transfers from Gaborone for around US$180 per person, return.

PALAPYE

The original name of this town was Phalatswe, meaning 'Many Impalas' in Sekgalagadi or 'Large Impalas' in Tswana. The commercial heart of town is the Engen shopping centre on the main highway.

The friendly ***Palapye Hotel*** *(☎ 420277)*, opposite the train station 5km off the highway, looks tatty but is good value at US$34/43 for single/double rooms, with breakfast. The more upmarket ***Cresta Botsalo*** *(☎ 420245)*, on the highway, charges US$59/67, with breakfast. The dining room is the finest restaurant in town. For just a quick bite, try ***Chicken Licken*** or ***Tla Pitseng Takeaways***, both in the Engen shopping centre.

SEROWE

With a population of 90,000, sprawling Serowe, the Ngwato capital, is the largest village in Botswana and has served as the Ngwato capital since King Khama III moved it from Phalatswe (Palapye) in 1902.

The **Khama III Memorial Museum** (☎ 430519) outlines the history of the Khama family. Displays include the personal effects of King Khama III and his descendants, as well as artefacts depicting the history of Serowe.

There is also a growing natural history exhibition, featuring a large collection of African insects and a display on snakes of the area. It's open from 8.30 am to 12.30 pm and 2 to 4.30 pm weekdays, and 11 am to 4 pm Saturday. Entry is free.

The 12,000-hectare **Khama II Rhino Sanctuary** (☎/fax 430713, ⓔ krst@mopane.bw), 28km north-west of Serowe, serves as a safe haven for most of Botswana's remaining rhino. Entry to the reserve costs US$2.50 per vehicle plus US$1.25 per person and day/evening wildlife drives are US$30/40 for up to four people, plus US$7.50 for each extra person. Minibuses between Serowe and Rakops will drop you at the entrance (US$0.75); from there, reserve officials provide transport to the camping ground or chalets. Access will become even more convenient with the completion of the tarred road through to Maun.

Places to Stay & Eat

The ***Serowe Hotel*** *(☎ 430234)* on the Palapye side of town has rooms with shared facilities starting at US$45/52 for singles/doubles. An alternative is the recommended ***Ilanga Lodge*** *(☎ 430520)* on the hill just over the road, which charges US$20 per person. Camping at the ***Khama II Rhino Sanctuary*** *(☎ 430713, @ krst@mopane.bw)* costs US$5 per person and small/large chalets are US$50/75.

The best option for meals is either the Serowe Hotel or ***Tshukudu (Rhino) Takeaways***, at the Engen petrol station. You'll find Indian and Chinese takeaway meals at the ***Central Supermarket***, in The Mall.

Getting There & Away

Buses run frequently between Serowe and Palapye, 46km away, but there are also direct services between Serowe and Gaborone.

MAHALAPYE

Mahalapye has little to offer but spacious skies, distant horizons and a welcome break from the highway between Gaborone and Francistown. Since it's mainly a refuelling stop for both vehicles and travellers, there are lots of petrol stations, shops and takeaway places.

The ***Mahalapye Hotel*** *(☎ 410200)*, 1.5km off the main road, has single/double rooms for US$49/55. Camping costs US$6 per person and a set English-style breakfast is US$6. The dining room is also good for other meals and isn't too expensive.

For meals, most travellers stop at ***Kaytee's***, 'the pride of Botswana', at the southern end of town, where you can choose between takeaway and a la carte meals.

The Makgadikgadi Pans

Botswana's great salt pans, Sua and Ntwetwe Pans, collectively comprise the 12,000-sq-km Makgadikgadi Pans and are like no other landscape on earth. Especially during the sizzling heat of late-winter days, the stark pans take on a disorienting and ethereal austerity. Heat mirages destroy all sense of space or direction, and imaginary lakes shimmer and disappear, ostriches fly and stones turn to mountains and float in mid-air. In September, herds of wildebeest, antelope and zebra begin moving into the thirsty grasslands west of the pans to await the first rains. Although the water is short-lived, animals gravitate towards depressions, which retain stores of water. Then around December, the deluge begins. The fringing grasses turn green and the herds of wildlife migrate in to partake of the bounty. As if from nowhere, millions of flamingoes, pelicans, ducks, geese and other water birds arrive at the mouth of the Nata River in Sua Pan to build their nests along the shoreline, feeding on the algae and tiny crustaceans, which have lain dormant in the salt awaiting the rains.

NATA

Nata, the main refuelling stop for cars and buses between Kasane, Francistown and Maun, is little more than a dust hole with a petrol station and a couple of lodges. The newly created **Nata Sanctuary**, a 230-sq-km refuge for wildlife near Sua Pan, lies about 20km south-east of Nata on the Francistown road. It has a broad range of birdlife, as well as antelope and other grassland wildlife. In the dry season, you won't need 4WD, but high clearance is advisable. The sanctuary is open from 7 am to 7 pm daily and entry for foreigners costs US$4 per person, including one night's camping and use of braai facilities.

In Nata, the action centres on ***Sua Pan Lodge*** *(☎/fax 611220)* with its fuel pumps, water tap, bottle store, bar, restaurant, hotel, swimming pool and camping ground. Single or double rondavels with bath cost US$33 while camping is US$4.50 per person.

Nata Lodge *(☎ 611260, fax 611265, @ natalodge@info.bw)*, 10km east of Nata on the Francistown road, is set in an oasis of monkey thorn, marula and mokolane palm. Three/four-bed chalets cost US$68/78, while

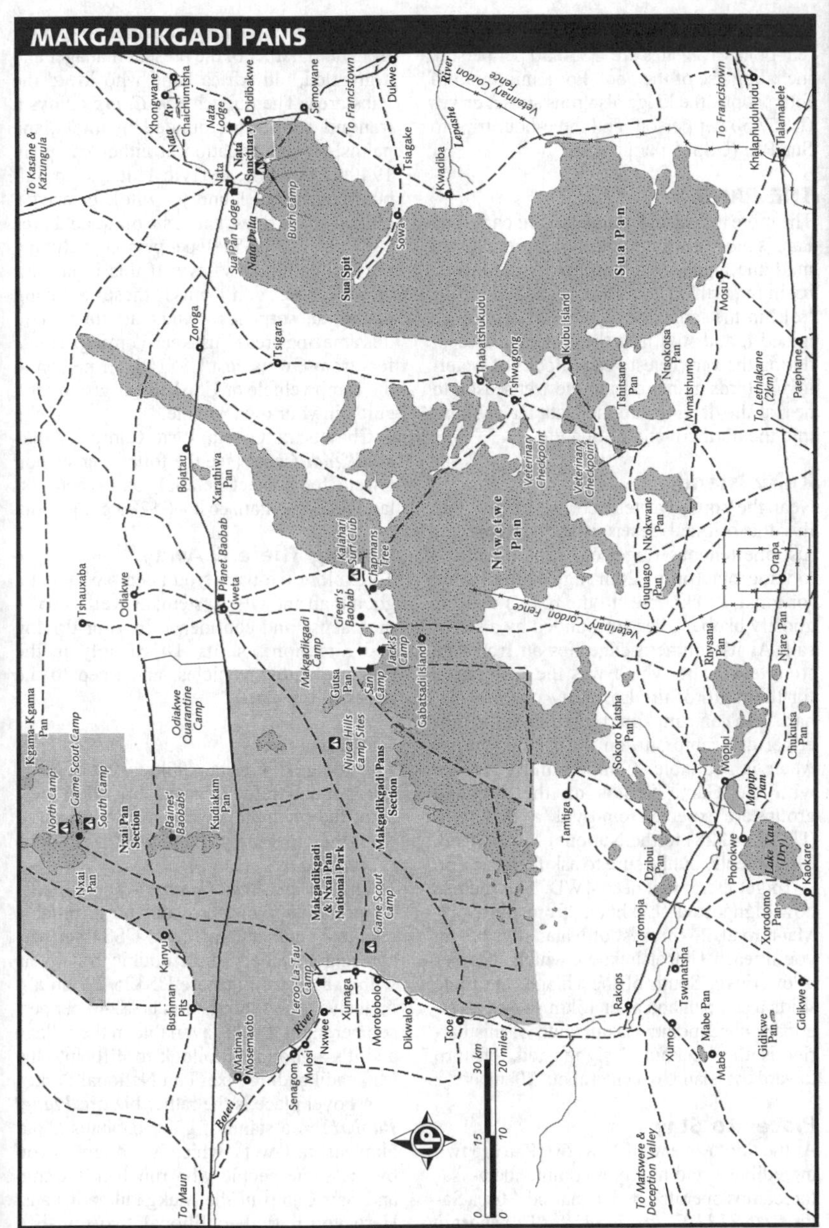
MAKGADIKGADI PANS
To Kasane & Kazungula
Xhongwane
Nata Rv
Chaichumtsha
Nata Lodge
Nata
Nata Sanctuary
Didibakwe
Semowane
To Francistown
Dukwe
Sua Pan Lodge
Nata Delta
Bush Camp
Sua Spit
Sowa
Tsiagake
Kwadiba
Lepashe
River
Veterinary Cordon Fence
To Francistown
Khalaphuduhudu
Tlalamabele
Sua Pan
Mosu
Zoroga
Tsigara
Thabatshukudu
Kubu Island
Tshwagong
Veterinary Checkpoint
Veterinary Checkpoint
Tshitsane Pan
Nsokotsa Pan
Mmatshumo
To Lethlakane (2km)
Paephane
Bojatau
Xarathiwa Pan
Ntwetwe Pan
Nkokwane Pan
Guguago Pan
Orapa
Tshauxaba
Odiakwe
Planet Baobab
Gweta
Kalahari Surf Club
Chapmans Tree
Green's Baobab
Makgadikgadi Camp
Jack's Camp
San Camp
Gabatsadi Island
Veterinary Cordon Fence
Rhysana Pan
Njare Pan
Kgama-Kgama Pan
Odiakwe Quarantine Camp
Gutsa Pan
Njuca Hills Camp Sites
Makgadikgadi Pans Section
Sokoro Katsha Pan
Mopipi
Chukutsa Pan
North Camp
Game Scout Camp
South Camp
Nxai Pan Section
Baines' Baobabs
Kudiakam Pan
Nxai Pan
Makgadikgadi & Nxai Pan National Park
Tamtiga
Mopipi Dam
Phorokwe
Lake Xau (Dry)
Kaokare
Dzibui Pan
Xorodomo Pan
Kanyu
Game Scout Camp
Toromoja
Tswanatsha
Leroo-La-Tau Camp
Xumaga
Morotobolo
Bushman Pits
Nxwee
Dikwalo
Rakops
Gidikwe
Matima
Mosemaoto
River
Senagom
Molosi
Tsoe
Xumo
Mabe Pan
Gidikwe Pan
Boteti
Mabe
0 15 30 km
0 10 20 miles
To Maun
To Matswere & Deception Valley

four-bed tents with bedding are US$55 and tent or caravan sites are US$6.50 per person, including use of the pool. For a minimum of four people, the lodge also runs sunset drives (US$7.50 per person) and three-hour trips to Sua Pan (US$15 per person).

THE PANS

The more accessible of the two big pans, Sua Pan, is mostly a single sheet of salt-encrusted mud and algae stretching across the lowest basin in north-eastern Botswana. *Sua* means 'salt' in the language of the San, who once mined it and sold it to the Kalanga. Except during the very driest years, flocks of water-loving birds gather during the wet season to nest at the delta where the Nata River flows into the northern end of Sua Pan.

Kubu Island

Near the south-western corner of Sua Pan lies the original desert island. Except for just one tenuous finger of grass, the alien-looking outcrop of 20m-high Kubu Island (originally Lekhubu, 'to the rock') with its ghostly baobabs lies surrounded by a sea of salt. At its southern edge lies an Iron Age stone enclosure which was the inspiration for the myth of the Lost City of the Kalahari. You can camp on the salt or at the otherworldly camp site on the island, but no water is available. Campers must register with the Game Scouts on the site and groups are expected to provide a 'donation' (US$6 or P28) to the National Museums & Monuments, but be sure to ask for a receipt.

To get there, you need 4WD. The route is now signposted 'Lekhubu' from the Nata-Maun road, 24km west of Nata; after 65km, you'll reach Thabatshukudu, which occupies a low ridge. South of the village, the route skirts a salt pan and after 15km passes a veterinary checkpoint; 1.5km south of this barrier is the 'Lekhubu' signposted left-turn toward the island, which is about 20km away.

Places to Stay

At the northern end of Ntwetwe Pan are two incredible – and highly recommended – safari camps operated by Uncharted Africa Safaris *(☎ 212277, fax 213458, ⓔ unchart@info.bw)*. ***Jack's Camp*** is named after Jack Bousfield, father of the present manager and a grizzled, old Africa hand who loved the Pans area. The quieter ***San Camp*** enjoys a tranquil setting surrounded by mokolane palms. Accommodation at either camp, in 1940s East African-style tents, with full board, drinks, laundry, wildlife drives, guides, park fees and use of quad bikes (ATVs), costs US$410 per person, including tax and community levy. If this is in your price range, don't miss these amazing places; the surprises – which are inherent in this amazing area – just keep coming! Transfers from Gweta cost US$100 per person in the camp vehicle or US$150 per group for a guide in your own vehicle.

Chalets at Gweta Rest Camp's ***Makgadikgadi Camp*** (see the following section Gweta for contact details), on Hyaena Island near Sua Pan, cost US$280 per person.

Getting There & Away

To explore the pans, you need 4WD and a good map and GPS system, as well as common sense and confidence in your driving and directional skills. Drive only in the tracks of other vehicles, and keep to the edges of the pan.

GWETA

The village of Gweta, 100km west of Nata, is a popular refuelling and travellers' rest stop; the onomatopoeic name was derived from the croaking of large bullfrogs *(Pyxicephalus adspersus)*.

The ***Gweta Rest Camp*** *(☎/fax 612220, ⓔ gweta@info.bw)* provides an affordable respite where camping costs US$4 per person and thatched single/double rondavels with shared facilities are US$25/29; an all-inclusive desert safari costs US$240 per person per night. Fuel is available in the village and it's a good spot to look for lifts into the Makgadikgadi & Nxai Pan National Park.

A novel place is the rather bizarre ***Planet Baobab***, in a stand of giant baobabs about 5km east of Gweta, which is brought to you by the same people who run Jack's Camp and San Camp in the Makgadikgadi Pans. Here you'll find traditional two/four-bed rondavels for US$120/200, two-bed beehive huts for US$50, and camping for US$5 per person. Camping and quad-biking trips to the pans are available for US$150, including transport, tents, a barbecue and breakfast.

All buses between Nata and Maun call in at Gweta.

MAKGADIKGADI & NXAI PAN NATIONAL PARK

West of Gweta, the main road between Nata and Maun slices through Makgadikgadi & Nxai Pan National Park. Because they complement each other in enabling wildlife migrations, Makgadikgadi Pans Game Reserve and Nxai Pan National Park were established concurrently in the early 1970s, in the hope of protecting the entire ecosystem.

Makgadikgadi Pans Section

The 3900-sq-km Makgadikgadi Pans Game Reserve section of the park takes in grasslands and beautiful savanna country. During the winter dry season, animals concentrate around the Boteti River, but between February and April huge herds of zebra and wildebeest migrate north to Nxai Pan, only returning to the Boteti when the rains cease in early May.

Nxai Pan Section

The Nxai Pan National Park section takes in over 4000 sq km. The grassy expanse of Nxai Pan is at its most interesting during the rains, when large animal herds migrate from the south and predators arrive to take advantage of the bounty. In the southern part of the park is the stand of hardy trees known as Baines' Baobabs, which were immortalised by artist and adventurer Thomas Baines on 22 May 1862, when he painted them for posterity.

Places to Stay

Makgadikgadi's main public camping ground is at ***Game Scout Camp***, near Xumaga. There are also two sites for free-camping atop the Njuca Hills, 20km from the Game Scout Camp; there's a pit toilet but no water. The nearest supplies are at the bush shops in Gweta and Xumaga village. From the Nxai Pan Game Scout Camp, North Camp lies 8km north across the Pan (it may be inaccessible during the wet). South Camp is 8km east of the Game Scout Camp. Camping is possible at Baines' Baobabs with a permit, but there are no facilities. (For information on booking camp sites throughout the park, see National Parks & Wildlife Reserves in the Facts about Botswana section earlier in this chapter.)

The tented camp ***Leroo-La-Tau*** *(☎ 434556, fax 434557, ⓔ wild-attract@info.bw)* occupies the banks of the Boteti, west of the reserve. In the summer, it becomes a lush oasis, rich in birdlife, while in the dry winter season it attracts thirsty wildlife. In the winter high season, singles/doubles cost US$400/600, including meals, wildlife drives and walking tours; off-season, you'll pay only US$117/175.

Getting There & Away

Access to either the Makgadikgadi Pans section or the Nxai Pan section is by 4WD only, but several Maun safari companies offer safaris (see Organised Tours in the Getting Around section earlier in this chapter).

Chobe National Park

Chobe National Park, which encompasses 11,000 sq km, is home to Botswana's most varied wildlife. The riverfront strip along the northern tier, with its perennial water supply, supports the greatest wildlife concentrations, but when they contain water, the lovely Savuti Marshes of the Mababe Depression in western Chobe also provide prime wildlife habitat and attract myriad water birds. Little-visited Ngwezumba, with its pans and mopane forests, is the park's third major region, and Chobe's north-western corner just touches another magnificent ecosystem, the vast Linyanti Marshes.

The northern park entrance lies 8km west of Kasane and is accessible to conventional vehicles. However, to proceed through the park or approach from Maun, you need high-clearance 4WD. Because of mud and flooding, Savuti is normally inaccessible (and closed) from January to March.

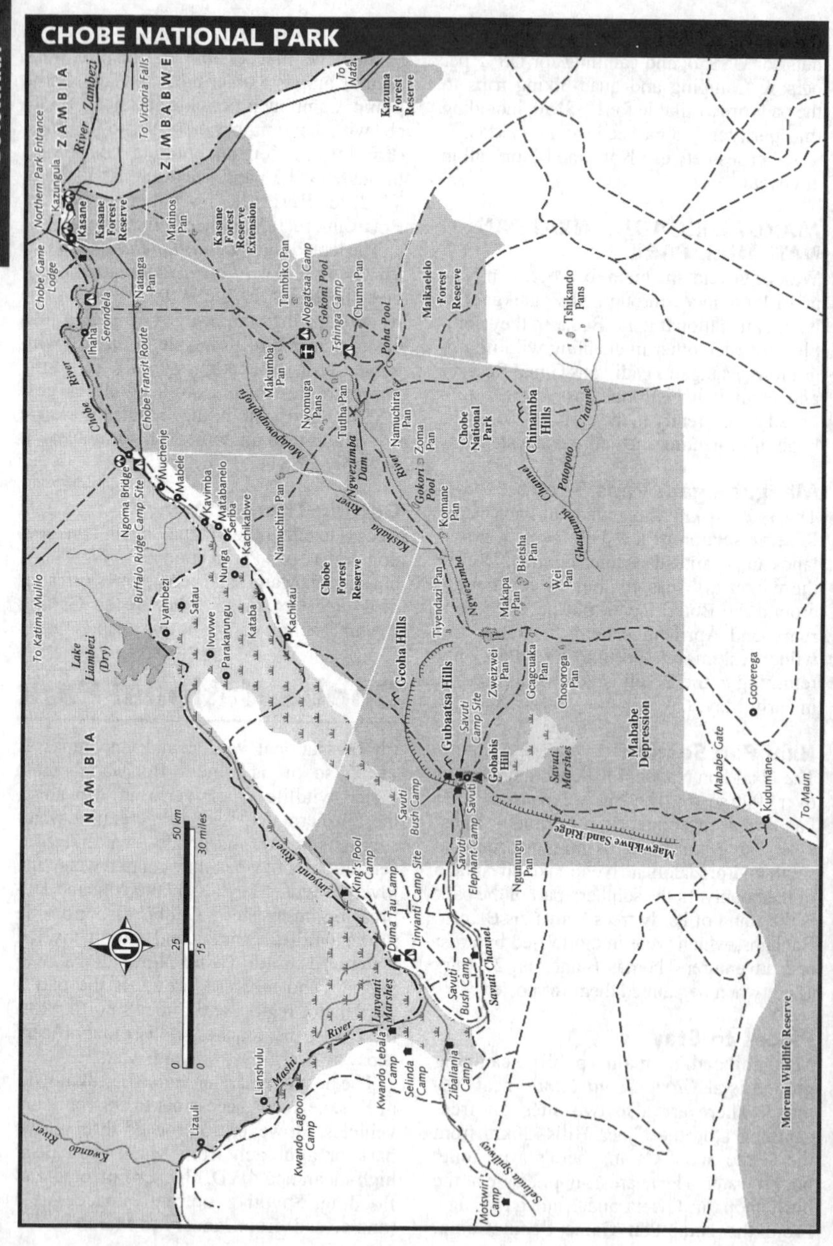
CHOBE NATIONAL PARK
ZAMBIA
ZIMBABWE
NAMIBIA
Zambezi River
To Victoria Falls
Northern Park Entrance
Kazungula
Kasane
Kasane Forest Reserve
Kasane Forest Reserve Extension
Kazuma Forest Reserve
To Nata
Matinos Pan
Chobe Game Lodge
Natanga Pan
Serondela
Ihaha
Chobe Transit Route
Chobe River
Tambiko Pan
Nogatsaa Camp
Gokoni Pool
Tshinga Camp
Chuma Pan
Poha Pool
Maikaelelo Forest Reserve
Tshikando Pans
Makumba Pan
Nyomuga Pans
Tutha Pan
Molapowojaphoja
Ngwezumba Dam
Namuchira Pan
Zoma Pan
Chobe National Park
Chinamba Hills
Potopoto Channel
Ghautumbi Channel
Muchenje
Ngoma Bridge
Buffalo Ridge Camp Site
Mabele
Kavimba
Matabanelo
Seriba
Kachikabwe
Nunga
Namuchira Pan
Kashaba River
Gokori Pool
Komane Pan
Ngwezumba River
Bietsha Pan
Wei Pan
Makapa Pan
Tiyendazi Pan
To Katima Mulilo
Lyambezi
Satau
Lake Liambezi (Dry)
Ivuvwe
Parakarungu
Kataba
Kachikau
Chobe Forest Reserve
Gcoha Hills
Gubaatsa Hills
Zweizwei Pan
Gcagcuaka Pan
Chosoroga Pan
Gcoverega
Savuti Camp Site
Gobabis Hill
Savuti Marshes
Mababe Depression
Mababe Gate
Kudumane
To Maun
Savuti Bush Camp
Savuti
Savuti Elephant Camp
Magwikhwe Sand Ridge
Ngumungu Pan
Linyanti River
King's Pool Camp
Duma Tau Camp
Linyanti Camp Site
Savuti Bush Camp
Savuti Channel
Linyanti Marshes
Mashi River
Lianshulu
Kwando Lebala Camp
Selinda Camp
Zibalianja Camp
Kwando Lagoon Camp
Lizauli
Kwando River
Selinda Spillway
Motswiri Camp
Moremi Wildlife Reserve
0 25 50 km
0 15 30 miles

For park information and bookings, contact the Kasane Wildlife office (☎ 650235).

KASANE & KAZUNGULA

Kasane sits at the meeting point of four countries – Botswana, Zambia, Namibia and Zimbabwe – and the confluence of the Chobe and Zambezi Rivers. It's also the gateway to Chobe National Park and, as such, this town of just a few thousand people is a focus of activity in northern Botswana. About 9km east of Kasane is the tiny settlement of Kazungula, which serves as the border crossing between Botswana and Zimbabwe, and the landing for the Kazungula ferry, which connects Botswana with Zambia.

Information

Kasane's friendly but less-than-helpful tourist office (☎ 250327) occupies a cluster of caravans east of the riverbank. The main branch of Barclays Bank changes money and travellers cheques, but to avoid the stagnant queues, pop over to the tiny Bureau de Change outside the Travel Shop (Audi Centre).

The post office lies about 300m north of Chobe Safari Lodge; you'll find public phones here, at the airport and in Kazungula village. The Stationery Box at the Audi Centre sells paperback novels and other books, while the Chobe Travel Shop (☎/fax 650828, after hours ☎ 650259, ⓔ travel@info.bw), next door, sells a range of Botswana theme books and also books accommodation and safari packages.

Places to Stay

The most popular budget choice is the camping ground at the ***Chobe Safari Lodge*** *(☎ 650336, fax 650437, ⓔ chobelodge@info.bw)*, where you'll pay US$7 per person to carve out a space on the riverbank. The lodge also offers basic double rondavels for US$48; chalets with private bathrooms for US$73; and riverview suites for US$88.

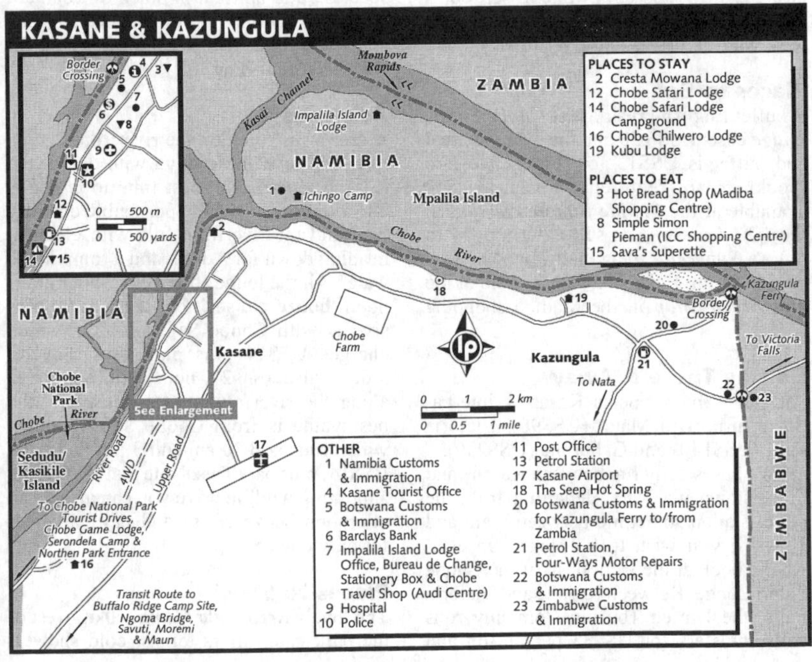

Kubu Lodge *(☎ 650312, fax 650412, @ kubu@info.bw)* in Kazungula lies about 1km north of the Kasane-Kazungula road. Thatched chalets cost US$100/140 for singles/doubles and riverside camp sites are US$9.50 per person.

Alternatively, splash out at the architecturally inspired ***Cresta Mowana Lodge*** *(☎ 650300, fax 650301, @ mowana@info.bw)*, which makes the most of the open air and superb views. For rooms with breakfast, you'll pay US$251/415, or US$369/650 with full board and activities.

Chobe Chilwero Lodge *(☎ 650505, fax 650352, @ chilwero@res-centre.co.za)* occupies a hill 3km from the Chobe entrance gate. High-season rooms cost US$405/610, including meals and activities. ***Chobe Game Lodge*** *(☎ 650340, fax 650223, @ chobe@fast.co.za)* in the national park managed to attract the likes of Richard Burton and Elizabeth Taylor on one of their honeymoons. Its suite, with a private pool, now costs US$530/860, while lesser rooms are US$380/660, including meals, park fees, wildlife drives and river trips.

Places to Eat

A buffet English breakfast at ***Chobe Safari Lodge*** costs US$6.50 and the evening braai and buffet is US$13 for respectable fare (bookings are required). Takeaways are available at the ***Simple Simon Pieman***, in the ICC Centre. For self-catering, go to ***Sava's Superette***, diagonally opposite the petrol station. Bakery goods are sold at the ***Hot Bread Shop*** in the Madiba shopping centre.

Getting There & Away

Air Botswana connects Kasane's international airport to Maun (US$90), Victoria Falls (US$140) and Gaborone (US$230).

Two buses daily run between Kasane and Francistown via Nata, departing from the petrol station sometime between 9 am and 1 pm; if you wish to be picked up elsewhere, book at the front desk of the Chobe Safari Lodge. Between Kasane and Victoria Falls, the United Touring Company runs daily transfers for US$35 per person and Janala Tours (☎ 650234, fax 650223) charges US$40. They pick up at hotels in Kasane between 9.30 and 10 am.

Hitching may prove more convenient than the bus for reaching Nata, Francistown or Namibia; wait at either the petrol station near the Chobe Safari Lodge or at the Kazungula road junction. For information on safaris between Kasane and Maun via Chobe National Park, see Organised Tours in the Getting Around section of this chapter.

CHOBE RIVERFRONT

The Chobe Riverfront is packed with wildlife, and for most visitors, appreciation of this natural wonderland will entail a river cruise or a wildlife drive. The most obvious feature of the landscape is the damage done by the area's massive elephant herds, but virtually every Southern African mammal species, except the rhino, is represented here. You can also see puku – an antelope species quite unusual in much of Southern Africa. In addition, the abundance and variety of birdlife in this zone of permanent water is astonishing.

Activities

A great way to enjoy the riverfront is on a **river trip** or **wildlife drive** with one of the Kasane lodges. The best time to cruise is late afternoon, when hippos amble onto dry land and the riverfront fills with elephant heading down for a drink and a romp in the water. All the lodges offer three-hour afternoon **'booze cruises'**, but the least expensive is with Chobe Safari Lodge, which charges US$14 plus park fees. Several lodges also run 2½-hour wildlife drives along the riverfront routes but again, the best value is from Chobe Safari Lodge, which runs at 6.30 am and 3 pm and costs US$14, plus park fees. Note that if you take a morning wildlife drive you can also do an afternoon booze cruise and pay park fees for only one day.

Places to Stay

The lovely ***Serondela Camp***, 10km west of the park gate, offers toilets, cold showers and lots of wildlife; however, it's soon to be replaced by Ihaha, further west, which is just as wild but less congested. When Ihaha opens, Serondela will be converted into a picnic site.

West of the Chobe transit route, just uphill from the Ngoma Bridge border crossing, is the ***Buffalo Ridge Camp Site*** *(☎ 650430, cell ☎ 082-659 1232, fax 650223)*, where you can camp for US$4 per person.

Getting There & Away

The northern park entrance lies 8km west of Kasane and is accessible by conventional vehicle, but to reach Savuti or other places in the interior of the park requires 4WD and high clearance. The transit route across Chobe to the Namibian border is free.

SAVUTI

The intensely flat expanses of Savuti are an obligatory stop for safaris and overland trips between Kasane and Maun. Gobabis Hill, south of the Savuti gate near the Savuti Channel, bears several sets of 4000-year-old rock art, which are probably of San origin.

Savuti's wildlife populations, particularly elephant and antelope, can seem overwhelming, especially in the aftermath of heavy rains, which bring copious quantities of fresh water to the area. Because of high water, Savuti is normally closed (and inaccessible anyway) between January and March.

Places to Stay

The Savuti camping ground is what park rangers like to call a 'rough camp', meaning

The Savuti Channel

Northern Botswana contains a bounty of odd hydrographic phenomena – a land of mysterious channels linking the otherwise unconnected Okavango and Linyanti-Chobe river systems. For instance, the Selinda Spillway passes water back and forth between the Okavango Delta and the Linyanti Marshes. Just as odd, when the River Zambezi is particularly high, the Chobe River actually reverses its direction of flow, causing spillage into the Liambezi area. Historically, there was also a channel between the Khwai river system in the Okavango and the Savuti Marshes.

But the strangest of all is probably the Savuti Channel, which links the Savuti Marshes with the Linyanti Marshes and – via the Selinda Spillway – with the Okavango Delta itself. This mysterious channel, which lies within the Mababe Depression, is a 100km-long river that meanders across level ground from the Linyanti Marshes, where the Linyanti-Chobe system makes a sharp bend. Instead of carrying water to the main river, as all good tributaries should, the Savuti channels it away and dumps it in the desert. At its finish, where in good years it seeps and disappears into the sand, it waters the lovely Savuti Marshes.

Most confounding about the Savuti Channel, however, is the lack of rhyme or reason to its flow. At times it stops flowing for years at a stretch, as it did from 1888 to 1957, from 1966 to 1967 and from 1979 through to the 1990s. When it's flowing, it creates an oasis that provides water for thirsty wildlife herds and acts as a magnet for a profusion of water birds. Between flows, the end of the channel recedes from the marshes back towards the Chobe River while at other times, the Savuti Marshes flood and expand. The dead trees now standing along its bed optimistically took root during the dry years, only to be drowned when the channel reawakened.

What's more, the flow of the channel appears to be unrelated to the water level of the Linyanti-Chobe river system itself. In 1925, when the river experienced record flooding, the Savuti Channel remained dry.

According to the only feasible explanation thus far put forward, the phenomenon may be attributed to tectonics. The ongoing northward shift of the River Zambezi and the frequent low-intensity earthquakes in the region reveal that the underlying geology is tectonically unstable. The flow of the Savuti Channel must be governed by an imperceptible flexing of the surface crust. The minimum change required to open or close the channel would be at least 9m, and there's evidence that it has happened at least five times in the past century!

it's prone to nocturnal invasion by wildlife, especially elephant and hyaena. The ***Savuti Elephant Camp***, run by Gametrackers from Maun, offers tented accommodation and overlooks the Savuti Channel. Single/double high-season rates are US$567/914; low-season rates are US$457/714. The adjacent ***Savuti Bush Camp***, formerly Lloyd's Camp, has all-inclusive high-season rates of US$525/750 (for contact details, see Desert & Delta Safaris under Organised Tours in Getting Around earlier in this chapter).

Getting There & Away

Under optimum conditions, it's a four- to six-hour drive from the northern park entrance to Savuti. As far as Kachikau the road is rough but still passable to 2WD vehicles. There, however, it turns south into the Chobe Forest Reserve and deteriorates into parallel sand ruts requiring 4WD and high clearance.

You can also approach from Maun and the Moremi Wildlife Reserve. Except for the first 100km, the route is sand, and in some sections, especially in the southern end of Chobe National Park, the going is terribly slow. There's no fuel anywhere along the route.

KWANDO & LINYANTI MARSHES

West of Chobe, on the Botswana-Namibia border, lies the Kwando area, which is dominated by the 900-sq-km Linyanti Marshes. The area may be reminiscent of the Okavango Delta, but it's actually just a broad, flooded plain along the Linyanti River, which is home to large herds of elephant and buffalo. As yet, there's no easy access, but several concessionaires run luxury camps.

Places to Stay

Kings Pool, Savuti Bush Camp and ***Duma Tau*** are three lodges run by Okavango Wilderness *(☎ 660086, fax 660632, ⓔ info@sdn.wilderness.co.za)*. Single/double accommodation costs US$515/830, including meals, wildlife drives, boat trips, guided walks and laundry.

Kwando Wildlife Experience *(☎ 27-011-8806138, fax 8801393, ⓔ kwandojnb@global.co.za)* operates ***Kwando Lebala*** and ***Kwando Lagoon*** camps, which occupy outstanding watery settings on the riverbanks. Single/double rates are US$550/850 in the high season, and US$405/580 in November and December and from March to June.

Linyanti Explorations *(☎ 650505, fax 650352, ⓔ selinda@info.bw)*, in the Selinda private concession, runs ***Selinda Camp, Zibalianja Camp*** and ***Motswiri Camp***. Single/double accommodation, including meals and wildlife-viewing activities, costs US$440/650. It also operates walking and canoeing safaris.

Getting There & Away

With a 4WD vehicle, you can reach the area either from Kasane along the river, or from Savuti, via the track along the Savuti Channel to the turn-off on the road along the Selinda Spillway. Otherwise, air transfers (with the various concessionaires) from Maun or Kasane cost from US$200 to US$300.

The Okavango Delta

The 1300km-long Okavango River rises in central Angola, then flows south-east across Namibia's Caprivi Strip, where it tumbles through Popa Falls before entering Botswana near Shakawe. There the river's waters begin to spread and sprawl as they're consumed by the thirsty air and swallowed up by the Kalahari sands, and eventually lose themselves in a vast 15,000-sq-km maze of lagoons, channels and islands. These waters attract myriad birds and other wildlife, as well as most of Botswana's tourists.

The best months to visit are July to September when water levels are high and the weather dry. During parts of the rainy season, particularly from January to March, some lodges may close. For information on the Okavango Panhandle (a thin strip of wetlands north-west of the main delta) see the North-Western Botswana section later in this chapter.

MAUN

In Maun, construction has recently run amok: office buildings are now sprouting

Travelling by Mokoro

Most visitors to the Okavango spend at least some time travelling by *mokoro* (plural, mekoro), a shallow-draft dugout canoe hewn from ebony or sausage tree log (or, more recently, moulded from fibreglass). The mekoro are poled from a standing position and their precarious appearance belies their amazing stability. A mokoro normally accommodates the poler, two passengers and their food and camping equipment.

On most mokoro trips, travellers ride for several days with the same poler, breaking their journey with walks on palm islands and moving between established camps or wild camping along the way. The quality of the experience depends largely upon the skill of the poler, the meshing of personalities and the passengers' enthusiasm. Because the polers are being booted into the Western economic system with little idea of how it works, the client satisfaction rate hasn't been 100%. Hopefully the new government licensing requirements for polers will change that.

The importance of finding a competent poler cannot be overstated, especially when you're expecting them to negotiate labyrinthine waterways or lead you on bushwalks through wildlife country. The keenest polers can speak at least some English; recognise and identify plants, birds and animals along the way; explain the delta cultures; and perhaps even teach clients how to fish using traditional methods.

If you're organising a budget mokoro trip, inquire in advance whether you're expected to provide food for your poler. Even if they do bring their own supplies, many travellers prefer to share meals. The polers may, for example, provide a sack of *mealie meal* (ground maize) and cooking implements while travellers supply the relishes: tins of curries, stews and vegetables. If you have arranged to provide your poler's meals, the standard daily rations are 500g of mealie meal, 250g of white sugar, six tea bags and sufficient salt and powdered milk.

For information on organising mokoro trips, see Organised Tours under Getting Around earlier in this chapter. You can also arrange trips through the various Delta lodges (see the boxed text 'Rates for Safari Camps & Lodges' later in this section) or through the Okavango Poler's Trust in Seronga (see under the Okavango Panhandle in the North-Western Botswana section later in this chapter).

alongside mud huts, the ubiquitous Toyota Hilux 4WDs share the roads with sedan touring cars from South Africa, and outsiders are pouring in to join the boom. It's a safe bet that the dusty old town that preceded the tarred road from Nata is gone forever and that Maun's future lies in the burgeoning international appreciation of the adjacent Okavango Delta.

Orientation

Maun proper contains most of the restaurants, shops and travel agencies, while the village of Matlapaneng, 10km north-east of the centre, has most of the budget lodges and camp sites. The exception is the Sedia Hotel, midway between these two zones of activity.

Information

Tourist Offices The official tourist office (☎ 660492) is of little use, but good advice and information are available from the lodges in Matlapaneng (see Places to Stay following) or the many tour companies in Maun (see Organised Tours in the Getting Around section earlier in this chapter).

Money The Mall has branches of both Barclays Bank and Standard Chartered Bank, but changing travellers cheques normally entails long waits and commissions of US$4 to US$7. Faster exchange services are available from the Sunny Bureau de Change (☎ 662786), above the First National Bank in the Ngami Centre; it's open from 7 am to 6 pm daily.

Post & Communications The post office, near The Mall, is open from 8.15 am to 1 pm and 2.15 to 4 pm weekdays and 8.30 to 11.30 am Saturday. Email and Internet access are available for US$7.50 per hour at

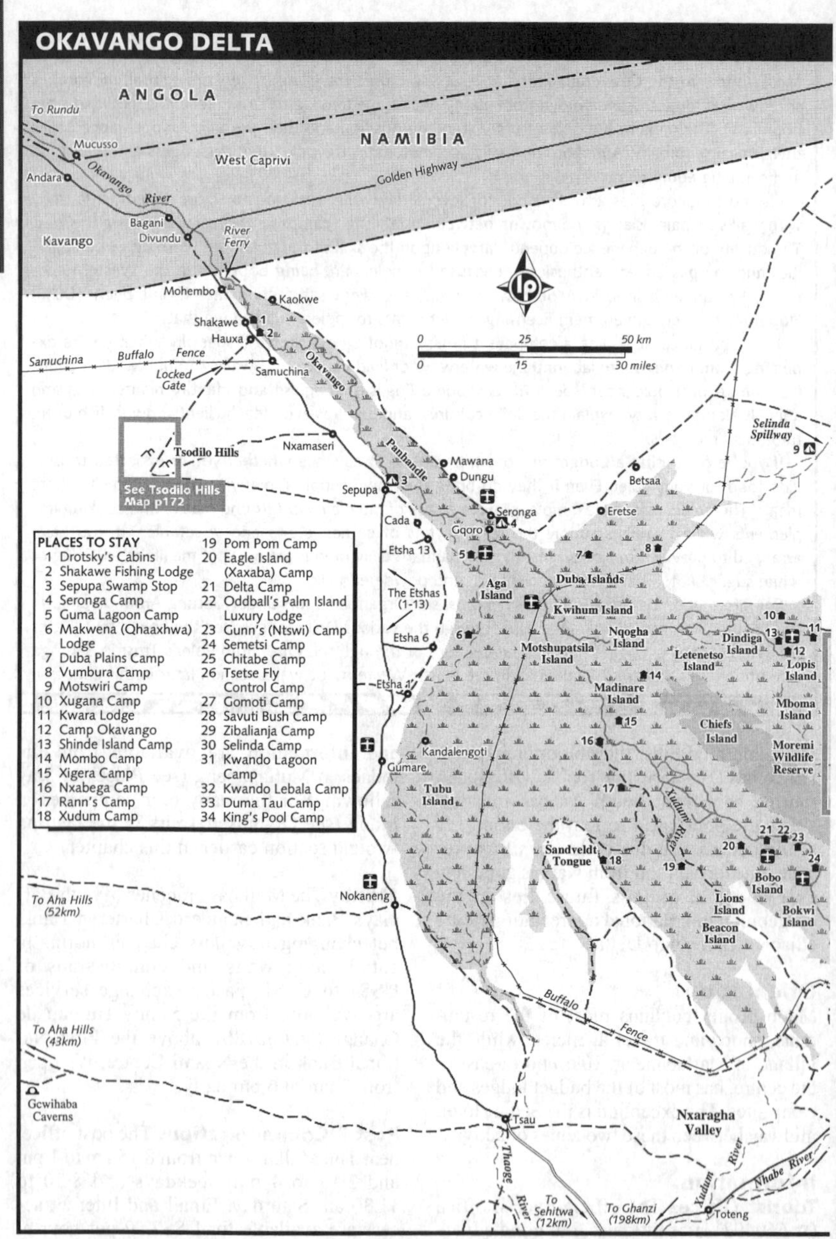
OKAVANGO DELTA
ANGOLA
NAMIBIA
To Rundu
Mucusso
West Caprivi
Andara
Okavango
River
Golden Highway
Bagani
Divundu
River Ferry
Kavango
Mohembo
Kaokwe
Shakawe
Hauxa
Samuchina
Buffalo
Fence
Samuchina
Locked Gate
Okavango
0 25 50 km
0 15 30 miles
Tsodilo Hills
See Tsodilo Hills Map p172
Nxamaseri
Panhandle
Selinda Spillway
Mawana
Dungu
Betsaa
Sepupa
Seronga
Eretse
Cada
Gqoro
Etsha 13
The Etshas (1-13)
Etsha 6
Etsha 1
Aga Island
Duba Islands
Kwihum Island
Nqogha Island
Motshupatsila Island
Dindiga Island
Letenetso Island
Lopis Island
Madinare Island
Mboma Island
Chiefs Island
Moremi Wildlife Reserve
Kandalengoti
Gumare
Tubu Island
Xudum
River
Sandveldt Tongue
Bobo Island
Lions Island
Bokwi Island
Beacon Island
To Aha Hills (52km)
Nokaneng
Buffalo
Fence
To Aha Hills (43km)
Gcwihaba Caverns
Tsau
Nxaragha Valley
Thaoge River
To Sehitwa (12km)
To Ghanzi (198km)
Xudum River
Nhabe River
Toteng
PLACES TO STAY
1 Drotsky's Cabins
2 Shakawe Fishing Lodge
3 Sepupa Swamp Stop
4 Seronga Camp
5 Guma Lagoon Camp
6 Makwena (Qhaaxhwa) Lodge
7 Duba Plains Camp
8 Vumbura Camp
9 Motswiri Camp
10 Xugana Camp
11 Kwara Lodge
12 Camp Okavango
13 Shinde Island Camp
14 Mombo Camp
15 Xigera Camp
16 Nxabega Camp
17 Rann's Camp
18 Xudum Camp
19 Pom Pom Camp
20 Eagle Island (Xaxaba) Camp
21 Delta Camp
22 Oddball's Palm Island Luxury Lodge
23 Gunn's (Ntswi) Camp
24 Semetsi Camp
25 Chitabe Camp
26 Tsetse Fly Control Camp
27 Gomoti Camp
28 Savuti Bush Camp
29 Zibalianja Camp
30 Selinda Camp
31 Kwando Lagoon Camp
32 Kwando Lebala Camp
33 Duma Tau Camp
34 King's Pool Camp

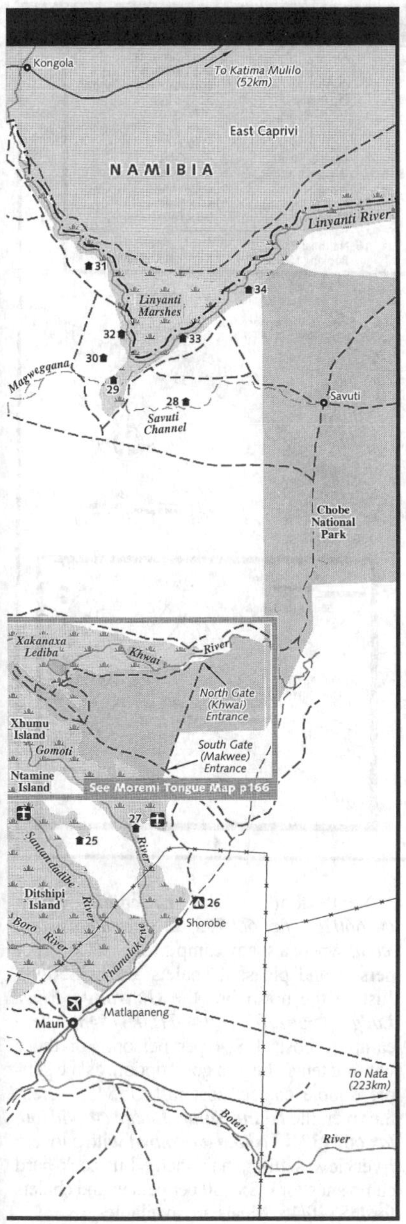

the Sedia Hotel's Internet Cafe & Computer Centre (cell ☎ 7161 6812, fax 662574, ✉ icafe.maun@info.bw).

Tour Companies Most agencies have affiliations with specific delta camps, so it's wise to visit several and get the full picture (see Organised Tours in the Getting Around section earlier in this chapter). You can outfit private safaris at Kalahari Kanvas (☎ 660568, fax 660035, ✉ kal.kanvas@info.bw), opposite the airport.

Medical Services For minor medical complaints, the pharmacist at the Okavango Pharmacy does brief consultations for US$1.25; malaria blood tests cost US$7.25. For other problems, see Dr Patrick Akhiwu (☎ 661411) beside the Shop-Rite supermarket.

Things to See

The **Maun Environmental Education Centre**, on 2.5 sq km of the eastern bank of the Thamalakane River, aims to provide schoolchildren with an appreciation of nature. It's open on weekdays and foreigners pay US$4 entry.

The **Nhabe Museum** (☎ 661346), housed in a historic building, outlines the natural history and culture of the Okavango area. Peripheral activities include local theatre presentations and sales of locally produced curios and artwork. It's open from 8 am to 5 pm weekdays and 9 am to 4 pm Saturday (closed for lunch from 12.30 to 2 pm). Entry is free but donations are welcome.

Organised Tours

For information on tour companies offering 4WD safaris through the national parks and mokoro trips in the Okavango Delta see Organised Tours in the Getting Around section earlier in this chapter.

Places to Stay

The friendly ***Sedia Hotel*** *(☎/fax 660177, ✉ sedia@info.bw)* 7km north of Maun on the road towards Matlapaneng charges US$58/67 for air-con singles/doubles, including breakfast. Camping costs US$5 per person and single/double pre-erected tents

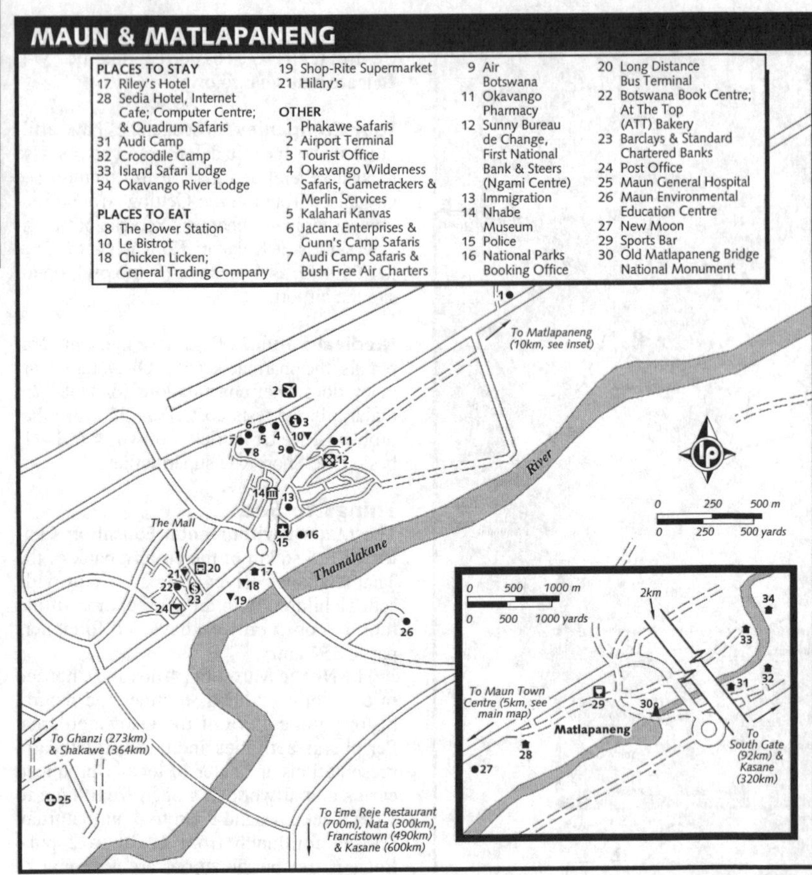

are US$12.50/19. There is also a recommended restaurant attached (see Places to Eat following).

In Matlapaneng, about 10km north-east of Maun, you'll find the most popular budget accommodation. A very good and friendly place is ***Audi Camp*** *(☎ 660599, fax 660581, ⓔ audicamp@info.bw)* where camping costs US$4 per person and pre-erected tents with bedding are US$19/26. There's a swimming pool, bar and restaurant serving snacks and three meals a day. Although it's normally very pleasant, it is frequented by overland trucks and can get quite raucous.

Next door is the ***Crocodile Camp*** *(☎ 660265, fax 660793, ⓔ sales@botswana.com)* where a shady camp site costs US$5 per person and pleasant chalets are US$50/90. Just to the north lies the ***Okavango River Lodge*** *(☎ 663707, cell ☎ 7160 37543)* where camping costs US$4 per person. For those without tents, this is a good option, as the simple double chalets cost just US$43. Across the river, the ***Island Safari Lodge*** *(☎ 660300, fax 662932, ⓔ island@info.bw)* with a lovely riverview setting, has shady but rock-hard camp sites for US$3.50 per person and chalets for US$40/45. Meals are available.

Rates for Safari Camps & Lodges

All Okavango Delta lodges and camps are superbly situated in scenic bush or on palm islands in lovely watery settings. Unless otherwise noted, the rates listed in this chapter include accommodation, meals and activities; most rates given are for the high season (July to October). In the low season (December to February), rates average 25 to 50% less, but some lodges close during this period. Some also have shoulder season (early March to mid-June and mid-October to the end of November) prices.

Note that the prices listed here are for overseas travellers. However, most lodges offer 'discounts' for regional travellers (ie, from within Southern Africa), which may also be available to walk-in clients. For travellers on organised tours that include several lodges, lower rates will be negotiated on their behalf by the travel agent.

To the published rates, you must also add 10% government accommodation (bed) tax, (which is normally US$7 per person per night as most lodges use US$70 as a standard accommodation cost, without meals, activities or frills), as well as park fees and air transfers (if applicable). Payment by credit card will also add to your bill; see the Facts for the Visitor section earlier in this chapter.

All these places offer transfers to/from Maun for around US$10 per person.

Riley's Hotel *(☎ 660320, fax 660580)* is the most upmarket accommodation in Maun, with rooms for US$82/103.

Places to Eat

Le Bistrot *(☎ 660718)* is a popular local hang-out that does excellent meals, including mean satays and a wide range of well-conceived dishes from pasta, fish and prawns to lamb, burgers and steaks. ***Steers*** in the Ngami centre across from Le Bistrot is a South African fastfood chain serving burgers, chicken, steak and ice cream.

Hilary's *(☎ 661610)* in The Mall is more low-key than Le Bistrot but an equally good option. Wonderfully earthy meals and daily specials, including vegetarian fare, baked potatoes, soups, sandwiches, cream teas and very nice sweets are available. It's open from 8 am to 4 pm weekdays and 8 am to 2 pm Saturday. Also in The Mall, a good snack choice is the ***ATT*** (At the Top) bakery.

The ***Power Station*** *(☎ 663391)* restaurant serves a menu of burgers, steak, chicken, pasta, Indian dishes and other standards (see also under Entertainment following).

In Matlapaneng the ***Sedia Hotel*** has an attached restaurant that offers excellent choices, including chicken dishes, sandwiches, pizzas, burgers and more sophisticated fare. Pub grub is also available from the ***Sports Bar*** nearby (see Entertainment following).

Entertainment

The ***Power Station***, housed in the ruins of the old power station, carries the industrial power-generation theme to its limit and features a bar, restaurant, crafts centre and cinema; films are screened nightly.

The renowned ***Sports Bar*** lies about 1km east of the Sedia Hotel in Matlapaneng. This dancing, drinking, pool-playing and raging spot is popular with expats, pilots and safari operators; light pub meals are available.

The latest happenings in Maun are revealed in the newspaper *Ngami Times* (☎ 662236), which is published on Fridays.

Getting There & Away

Air Air Botswana has daily flights between Maun and Gaborone (US$140). You can also fly to Francistown (US$229), Victoria Falls, Harare, Johannesburg and Windhoek. Travel into the delta is handled by various air charter companies (see under Air in the Getting Around section earlier in this chapter).

Bus At the long-distance bus terminal in the north-eastern corner of The Mall you'll find buses to Nata (US$6, four hours), Shakawe (US$10, six hours) and Francistown (US$8, six hours). Get to the terminal as early in the morning as possible, especially if you want to travel to Nata and connect with a bus to Kasane.

Hitching Heading east, a good hitching spot is the Ema Reje Restaurant on the Nata road.

If you're hitching north-east to/from Kasane on the Botswana/Zambia/Namibia/Zimbabwe border, the cheapest and easiest way is the long route via Nata (see Hitching under Zimbabwe in the Getting There & Away section earlier in this chapter).

EASTERN DELTA

The area normally defined as the Eastern Delta takes in the wetlands between the southern boundary of Moremi Wildlife Reserve and the buffalo fence along the Boro and Santandadibe Rivers, north of Matlapaneng. If you can't manage the air fare into the Inner Delta, the Eastern Delta provides an accessible alternative.

Mokoro Trips

Mokoro trips in the Eastern Delta are mainly organised by Maun lodges and tour companies, and while they're handy, it's extremely important to ensure that you use a reputable company and insist on a good experienced poler, who knows the area and understands what interests clients (see the boxed text 'Travelling by Mokoro' earlier in this section).

Several companies including Audi Camp Safaris, New Moon Safaris, Island Safaris and Quadrum operate mokoro trips in the Eastern Delta. Currently, three-day mokoro camping packages range from US$120/240 to around US$185/270 for one/two people, plus a tip for the poler (say P5 to P10 per day). For around US$180 more, they'll also provide food and camping gear, and most trips can be combined with three-day safaris in Moremi for an additional US$300 to US$400 (for more details, see Organised Tours in the Getting Around section earlier in this chapter and Moremi Wildlife Reserve later in this section).

The more adventurous can organise their own expedition by asking around in Matlapaneng village or at the buffalo fence or in Maun by making arrangements directly with mokoro owners, but given the current political situation (Botswana officially discourages independent travellers), this is sure to cause headaches and your chances of getting a satisfactory trip are very slim.

INNER DELTA

Roughly defined, the Inner Delta takes in the areas west of Chiefs Island and between Chiefs Island and the base of the Okavango Panhandle. It has lodges and camps catering to several budget ranges and offers some magnificent delta scenery and experiences.

Mokoro Trips

Mokoro trips through the Inner Delta are almost invariably arranged through the camps, each of which has its own pool of licensed (or trainee) polers. They operate roughly between June and December, depending on the water level. You must pay park fees to land on Chiefs Island, which is part of Moremi, but you'll normally see more wildlife than if you remain outside the reserve. Make sure you advise the poler if you'd like to break the trip with bushwalks around the palm islands.

Relatively inexpensive mokoro trips are available from Oddball's and Gunn's Camp (see their listings following). More upmarket lodges run mokoro trips between established permanent camps and offer some degree of luxury; you won't need to carry your own equipment but prices are considerably higher.

Places to Stay – Budget & Mid-Range

There are three relatively inexpensive lodges in the Inner Delta just across the Boro River channel from Moremi Wildlife Reserve, near the southern tip of Chiefs Island. In theory, campers may carry food and other supplies from Maun (about 70km away), but charter airlines limit passengers to 10kg of baggage and most people end up relying on camp meals and hire equipment from the camp shops. See Organised Tours in the Getting Around section earlier in this chapter for contact details and see the boxed text 'Rates in Safari Camps & Lodges' earlier in this section. Unless otherwise stated all of the following rates are for the high season.

Oddball's Palm Island Luxury Lodge (Okavango Tours & Safaris) on Noga Island is the delta's only real backpackers concession (the 'Luxury Lodge' bit is a facetious dig at its frightfully expensive neighbours).

Camping costs US$25 per person and chalets are US$55 per person; both rates include meals. There's a rustic bar, showers, Molly's Quickserv food shop and camping equipment rental. Camping packages, including air transfers from Maun, equipment, park fees, two nights at Oddball's and two/three/four nights on a mokoro trip, cost US$465/540/615 per person.

Beside the Boro River on palm-studded Ntswi Island is ***Gunn's Camp/Ntswi Camp*** (Gunn's Camp Safaris). It's a bit more upmarket than Oddball's. The camping ground has hot showers, flush toilets, braais, a basic shop and bar and costs US$15 per person. Single/double 'luxury tents' cost US$395/590, with meals, drinks and wildlife-viewing. No-frills one-day mokoro trips are US$60 for two people and overnight trips cost US$159/198 for one/ two people, with camping and food only. Four/five/six-day mokoro trips cost US$255/285/315 per person, with a minimum of two people (for one person, add 30%), including return flights from Maun.

Semetsi Camp (Crocodile Camp Safaris) is a luxury tented camp (the name means 'place of water') that sits on a palm island opposite Chiefs Island. It charges US$207/268 in dome tents, including meals, mokoro trips and wildlife-viewing activities.

Places to Stay – Top End

Duba Plains Camp (Okavango Wilderness) is a tented camp situated in a remote savanna and wetland region north of the main delta. All-inclusive single/double rates are US$495/790 per day, including wildlife drives, mokoro trips and walks while air transfers are extra.

Vumbura Camp (Okavango Wilderness) is a twin camp to Duba Plains and it sits at the transition zone between the savannas and swamps north of the delta and northwest of Moremi. It's one of the most remote delta camps and the region is known for large buffalo herds. Rates are US$495/790.

Near the southern end of Chiefs Island is ***Delta Camp*** (Okavango Tours & Safaris) sitting in a scenic, shady spot at the end of its airstrip. Motorboats are prohibited and the silence is inspiring. All-inclusive catered mokoro trips and guided walks around the island are available. Accommodation in thatched chalets, three meals, drinks and laundry costs US$450/720 per day. Transfers from Maun cost US$120 per person.

Eagle Island/Xaxaba Camp (Gametrackers) is a luxury camp (Xaxaba means 'Island of Tall Trees') beside a beautiful lagoon offering gourmet food, a swimming pool and bar. Mokoro trips are available as well as booze cruises, guided walks and birdwatching. Reed chalets cost US$567/914. Air transfers from Maun start at US$150 per person.

Xigera Camp (Okavango Wilderness), in a remote permanent wetland region of the Inner Delta, is known for its birdlife and the sitatunga antelope, as well as other wildlife. Tented accommodation, meals and activities costs US$495/790 per day.

Under new management at the former site of Abu's Camp, ***Nxabega Camp*** (Desert & Delta Safaris) offers tented accommodation, with sundecks overlooking the Okavango Delta floodplains for US$525/750 per day.

The remote, tented ***Pom Pom Camp*** (Ker & Downey) is accessible via air or bush track from the south-western end of the delta. It's a particularly good area for birdwatching; other activities include wildlife drives and short mokoro excursions. Rates with meals and activities cost US$630/860 per day; air transfers are extra.

As with its sister camp Xudum, ***Rann's Camp*** (Rann Safaris) sits in a remote area in the western end of the delta. All-inclusive rates are US$621/932 per day.

Xudum Camp (Rann Safaris) is a lovely wilderness camp in the remote southern end of the delta offering tented accommodation for US$621/932 per day.

Abu's Camp (Elephant Back Safaris) is without doubt the most unique and expensive camp in the delta. It was the brainchild of operator Randall Moore, who's responsible for the return of three African-born, circus-trained elephants from North America to Botswana to ferry visitors around on their backs. Experiencing this novelty doesn't come cheap, however, and the rate for a five-night stay, with meals and elephant rides, is

US$9000/13,000;that's US$1800/2600 per day or US$1.25/1.81 per minute. Think about that when you're wasting time relaxing!

MOREMI WILDLIFE RESERVE

Moremi Wildlife Reserve, encompassing more than 3000 sq km, is part of the Okavango Delta but is officially cordoned off for the preservation of wildlife. It was set aside as a reserve in the 1960s when it became apparent that overhunting was decimating wildlife. The park has a distinctly dual personality, with large areas of dry land rising between vast wetlands. The two most prominent dry features are Chiefs Island, deep in the Inner Delta (see earlier in this chapter), and the Moremi Tongue/Peninsula, comprising the north-eastern end of the reserve. Habitats range from mopane woodland and thorn scrub to dry savanna, riverbank woodlands, grasslands, floodplains, marshes, permanent waterways, lagoons and islands.

The park entry gates (see South Gate and North Gate following) are open from 6 am to 6.30 pm March to September and 5.30 am to 5.30 pm at other times. For fees and booking information see National Parks & Wildlife Reserves in the Facts about Botswana section earlier in this chapter.

For camping away from the park gates, you'll have to join a 4WD safari (see Organised Tours in the Getting Around section earlier in this chapter) or have access to a 4WD vehicle. Individuals are limited to Third Bridge or Xakanaxa Lediba. Safari operators are given a bit more latitude and are allowed to use exclusive Hotels & Tourism Association of Botswana (HATAB) sites scattered around the park.

South Gate

The more southerly of Moremi's two road entrances is aptly known as South Gate, 84km north-east of Maun. Here visitors pay park fees; just inside the entry gate is a large

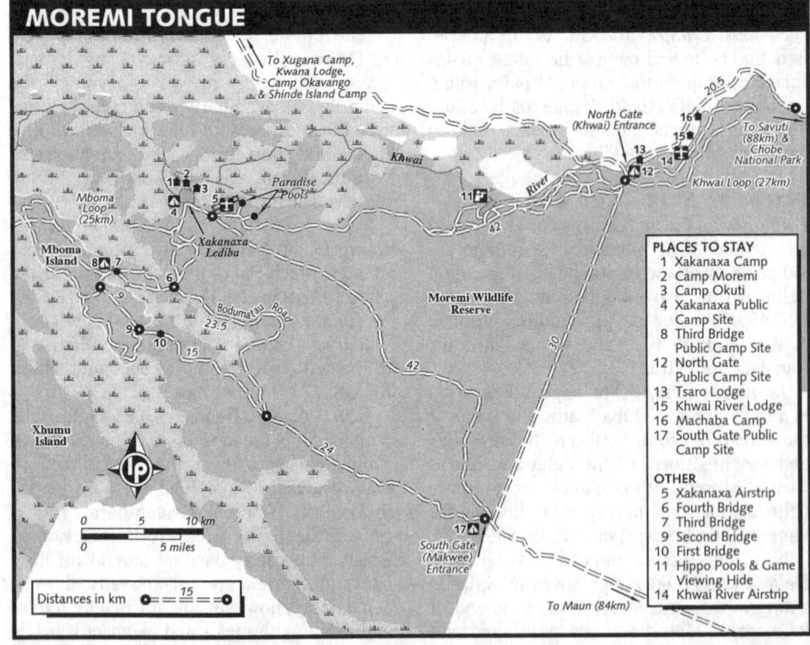

developed camping ground with showers and a shady picnic area (for an idea of rates, see under National Parks & Wildlife Reserves in the Facts about Botswana section).

Third Bridge

Third Bridge is literally the third log bridge after entering the reserve at South Gate, 48km away. The bridge, which crosses a very sandy-bottomed pool on the Sekiri River, is rustically beautiful and is used by wildlife (particularly lions) as well as vehicles. Contrary to official advice, nearly everyone swims, but we don't recommend it as there are crocodiles. If you can't be swayed, swim only in broad daylight and keep a close watch on the reeds. Also don't camp on the bridge or sleep in the open as lions are common.

Camp sites are strung out on either end of the bridge. However, there are no facilities, so use common sense when cooking and performing ablutions. Burn your rubbish, bury solid waste well away from the water, use a basin when washing up and pour waste water into the sand.

Mboma Island

The grassy savanna of Mboma Island – actually just a long extension of the Moremi Tongue – covers 100 sq km and contrasts sharply with surrounding landscapes. The sandy Mboma Loop route turns off 2km or so west of Third Bridge and makes a pleasant side trip off the standard Moremi Loop route.

Xakanaxa Lediba

Around Xakanaxa Lediba are many of the private camps within Moremi Wildlife Reserve. There's also a public camping ground, which occupies a narrow strip of land surrounded by marsh and lagoon. With one of the largest heronries in Africa, it's known as a birdwatchers' paradise. Potential sightings include marabou and saddlebill storks; egrets; wood, sacred and glossy ibis; and seven species of heron. The area also supports large wildlife populations.

North Gate

North Gate, with a developed camping ground, is the road entrance for southbound traffic coming from Chobe. Vehicles enter the park on a long and clattery log bridge over the Khwai River (it's tempting to suggest the obvious name for this bridge, but I'll resist). The drive between North Gate and Xakanaxa Lediba follows one of the most scenic routes in Botswana. Worthwhile stops along this route include the viewing hide at Hippo Pools, where hippos crowd along the shore, and Paradise Pools, two watering holes that are as lovely as their name would suggest.

Places to Stay

Safari Camps & Lodges The following list includes camps and lodges both inside and nearby the Moremi Tongue section of Moremi Wildlife Reserve (see both the Okavango Delta and Moremi Tongue maps). All of the rates are for the high season and do not include air transfers or park fees. For the contact details of tour companies, see Organised Tours in the Getting Around section earlier in this chapter as well as the boxed text 'Rates for Safari Camps & Lodges'.

Gomoti Camp (Crocodile Camp Safaris) is an affordable tented camp on the Gomoti River, midway between Maun and Moremi Reserve. It charges US$237/298 for accommodation and is readily accessible from the Maun-Moremi road.

In the heart of Moremi, ***Xakanaxa Camp*** (Okavango Tours & Safaris) is excellent for wildlife viewing and birdwatching. It also contains three of the delta's largest heronries: Xakanaxa, Gadikwe and Xobega Madiba lagoons. Singles/doubles in luxury tents cost US$475/720 per day (US$390/550 in low season), including meals, wildlife drives, boat trips, fishing and birdwatching; park fees are extra. Air transfers from Maun are US$155 per person, but the camp is also accessible by 4WD.

Camp Moremi (Desert & Delta), beside Xakanaxa Lediba and amid giant ebony trees, enjoys more of a savanna than a wetland environment. Activities include wildlife drives, birdwatching trips and sundowner cruises. Rates are US$525/750, including meals in a lovely elevated dining room, transfers and activities. Access is via Xakanaxa airstrip and 4WD.

Camp Okuti (Ker & Downey) on Xakanaxa Lediba, accommodates 14 guests in thatch-roofed brick bungalows. High season rates of US$435/630 per day (US$350/520 in low season) include meals, wildlife drives, motorboat trips and guided walks. Park fees and air transfers (US$150 per person) cost extra.

Camp Okavango (Desert & Delta) is a lovely camp, set amid sausage and jackalberry trees on Nxaragha Island. It was started by a Californian with elegant taste. If you want the Okavango served up with silver tea service, candelabras and fine china, this is the place to go. Rates of US$525/750 per day (with a minimum stay of two nights) include tented accommodation, air transfers, gourmet meals, wildlife-viewing canoe trips and meticulous attention to detail. Suites cost up to US$900.

The area of ***Xugana Camp*** (Hartley's Safaris) was originally frequented by San hunters; the name Xugana means 'Kneel Down to Drink', in reference to the welcome sight of perennial water after a long hunt. Accommodation in luxury tents under big shady trees costs US$435/630 per day in the low season and about 25% more in the high season; air transfers cost extra. For a mokoro/camping trip, you'll pay the same, plus park fees.

The name of the solar-powered ***Kwara Lodge*** (Kwando Wildlife Experience) means 'Where the Pelicans Feed', and in fact, pools fed by subterranean springs support enough fish to attract flocks of pelicans. Tented accommodation beside a lagoon costs US$550/840 per day.

Shinde Island Camp (Ker & Downey), beside a lagoon in a remote area of Moremi, lies at the division between the savannas and wetlands, and offers both 4WD wildlife drives and mokoro trips to the heronries and the nesting sites of water birds. Rates of US$685/920 per day include meals and activities; air transfers cost extra.

Chitabe Camp (Okavango Wilderness), situated on the Santandadibe River near the southern borders of Moremi, tented Chitabe Camp is technically in the Eastern Delta. The camp supports the Wild Dog Conservation Fund and there's a good chance of seeing wild dogs here. Rates are US$495/790 per day.

Although ***Khwai River Lodge*** (Gametrackers) sits at the edge of the Okavango (just outside of Moremi's North Gate) and allies itself more with dryland Moremi than the water world of the Okavango, both elephant and hippo abound. Rates are US$457/714 per day, and include wildlife drives, walking safaris and guided birdwatching trips. Air transfers from Maun start at US$150 per person.

Tsaro Lodge (Hartley's Safaris) overlooks the biologically diverse Moremi floodplains near the Khwai River, at the reserve's North Gate. A real plus is the exclusive two-night Tsaro Walking Trail, a wilderness camping and hiking trip that reveals the profuse birdlife and wildlife along the Khwai River. Low season rates start at US$435/630 per day.

Machaba Camp (Ker & Downey) sits along the Khwai River, just outside Moremi's North Gate. The name comes from the local word for the sycamore fig trees that shelter the tents. The surrounding waters are an evening drinking venue for hundreds of animals, including elephant, antelope and zebra. Rates of US$630/860 per day include wildlife drives and photo safaris in Moremi.

Mombo Camp (Okavango Wilderness), off the north-western corner of Chiefs Island, is excellent for wildlife viewing; the area is known for its population of Cape hunting dogs. The camp accommodates 12 guests and offers mokoro trips, 4WD safaris and guided bushwalks. Rates are US$650/1100 per day.

Getting There & Away

From Maun, head north-east past Shorobe village, where the road becomes good gravel. At the tsetse fly control post, 10km north of Shorobe, it deteriorates into sand. A further 17km drive brings you to the signposted Moremi turn-off.

If you're booked into one of the delta camps, air, road or boat transport is normally arranged by the camp, but prices do vary.

Traditional dancing in The Mall, Gaborone

Weaver's loom in Odi village, near Gaborone

Modern buildings in the capital, Gaborone

ALL PHOTOGRAPHS BY RICHARD I'ANSON

RICHARD I'ANSON

DENNIS JOHNSON

ANDREW VAN SMEERDIJK

RICHARD I'ANSON

Botswana **Top:** A view of the Okavango Delta from a *mokoro* (dugout canoe) **Middle Right:** Playful cheetahs in Moremi Game Reserve **Middle Left:** River view in Chobe National Park **Bottom:** You'll need a 4WD and a good compass to explore the Sua Pan of north-eastern Botswana.

North-Western Botswana

In north-western Botswana, the Kalahari sands meet the Okavango Delta. Here, the Okavango Panhandle, which is distinct from the main body of the delta, is characterised by clusters of fishing villages where a cosmopolitan mix of people (Mbukushu, Yei, Tswana, Herero, European, San and refugee Angolans) extract their livelihoods from the rich waters and growing tourist industry. Beyond the Panhandle green belt, the Kalahari country sprawls west towards the Namibian border, where access is difficult and distances seem great on the sandy roads.

Technically, access to the San areas of the western Kalahari, including Gcwihaba Caverns and the Aha Hills, is subject to a community levy of US$12.50/4 for non-residents/residents of Botswana and US$2.50 per person per night for camping at the five community camping grounds. The Dutch trust that organises these communities also offers tours of both sites, as well as excursions to the remote Nqumtsa Cave and 'traditional' hunting and gathering tours. For details, contact Cgaecgae Tlhabololo Trust (CTT) Xaixai (☎ 352413, fax 314123) Private Bag 235, Maun.

GCWIHABA CAVERNS (DROTSKY'S CAVE)

In the !Kung language, the name of this decorated cavern system in the Gcwihaba Hills means 'hyaena's hole'. They weren't brought to European attention until the mid-1930s when the !Kung showed them to a Ghanzi farmer, Martinus Drotsky, and for years they were known as Drotsky's Cave. The two entrances are 300m apart, but the route through the cave is about 800m. There are no guides, no lights and no indication of which route to take, so you must carry several powerful torches as well as emergency lights, such as matches and cigarette lighters. The hardest part is a short, vertical climb down into a pit and then up the other side to a shelf, where there's a tight squeeze before you emerge in a large room. Note that the nearest water is the borehole at Nxainxai village.

Getting There & Away

Self-drivers need a 4WD with high clearance, long-range petrol tanks, water reserves and camping equipment. The road is good tar from Maun to the unsignposted caverns turn-off, 2km north-west of Tsau. After 86km you'll reach the turn-off to Xhaba bore hole (which lies 27km to the south-west). This turn-off leads 55km down the Gcwihabadum fossil valley to the caverns. Alternatively, you can continue 144km (from Tsau), take the left turn-off down the Nxainxaidum fossil valley and follow this track 27km to the caverns.

AHA HILLS

Straddling the Botswana-Namibia border, the 700-million year old limestone and dolomite Aha Hills rise 300m from the flat, thorny Kalahari scrub. They're scenic enough, but the foremost attraction is their end-of-the-world remoteness and utter silence, due mainly to the almost total absence of water. There are no facilities, but you can camp anywhere and basic supplies and water are available at Nxainxai.

Two taxing 4WD routes lead to the Aha Hills. One follows the track that passes the Gcwihaba Caverns turn-off (see Getting There & Away under Gcwihaba Caverns earlier), and the other turns west from the Maun-Shakawe road, north of a small bridge near Nokaneng. From there, it's 190km west to the Aha Hills.

THE ETSHAS

The Etshas, a refugee settlement constructed for Mbukushu refugees from the war in Angola, was divided into 13 parts based on clan and social structure carried over from Angola. In Etsha 6 it's worth visiting the House of the River People, a museum and cultural centre featuring the traditions and artistry of the Bayei, Mbukushu and San people of the Okavango region; entry is US$1.50. The adjacent Okavango Basket Shop is an excellent place to buy Ngamiland baskets, pottery and carvings.

Etsha Guesthouse & Camping, in Etsha 6, has four thatched guest lodges, each with two single beds, a braai stand and communal facilities. Camping costs US$3 per person and a single bed costs US$9. Tea, coffee, potato soup, sausages and the best hot chips in rural Botswana are available at ***Ellen's Cafe***, beside the Shell petrol station, also in Etsha 6.

Getting There & Away

From the main highway, tarred spur routes turn off to Etsha 6 and Etsha 13. Motorists normally drop by Etsha 6 to buy fuel or pick up supplies at the Etsha 6 Cooperative. Mahube Express buses between Maun and Shakawe call in at Etsha 6 and Makwena village.

SHAKAWE

When the tarred road came through in 1995, the formerly sleepy outpost of Shakawe awoke to tourism. Travellers come here for a Botswana entry or exit stamp or use it as a base to visit the Tsodilo Hills, 40km away. For Southern African holiday-makers, it's most often the start of a fishing trip in the Okavango Panhandle. You can exchange pula for Namibian dollars or South African rand at either Shakawe Fishing Camp or Wright's Trading Store.

Places to Stay & Eat

For those with transport, accommodation and meals are available at ***Drotsky's Cabins*** and ***Shakawe Fishing Lodge***, 5km and 8km south of town respectively (see their listings under Places to Stay in the Okavango Panhandle section, following).

The heart of Shakawe is Wright's Trading Store, with a self-service supermarket and bottle shop. In the compound opposite Wright's is ***Mma Haidongo's Nice Bread Bakery***, where you can buy excellent home-made bread for US$1 per loaf.

Getting There & Away

There are now several daily Mahube Express buses between Wright's Trading Store in Shakawe and Maun (US$10, six hours). Although Shakawe has been granted a petrol station permit, at the time of research petrol was only available out of drums in military-looking Brigades compound, north along the river beyond the secondary school.

OKAVANGO PANHANDLE

Distinct from the main body of the Okavango, the Panhandle ushers the Okavango waters from the Namibian border into the spreading wetlands. Excess waters spread across the valley on either side to form vast reed beds and papyrus-choked lagoons. The locals, whose livelihoods are largely dependent upon fishing with nets, lines and baskets, have built their villages in those places where the river meanders past dry land and forms proper riverbanks. Travellers are flocking to the Panhandle as mokoro trips and accommodation are much more affordable here than they are in other parts of the delta.

Mokoro Trips

As the Eastern Delta declines in popularity and quality, the Okavango Panhandle booms. This is thanks largely to the Okavango Polers Trust (☎ 676861) Private Bag 109, Maun, capably managed by Susan Sainsbury in the Panhandle village of Seronga (see also the boxed text 'Travelling by Mokoro' earlier in this section for more information on mokoro trips). The idea behind this trust is to join polers into a cooperative system with which clients can deal directly, without having to pay agency commissions. Despite the lower prices, the polers themselves receive a larger percentage of the earnings than those who work through agencies or lodges. The trust also looks after quality control issues.

From Seronga, mokoro trips cost US$30 per day for two people, including luggage (see Places to Stay following for more details).

Audi Camp Safaris, in Maun, has also shifted its emphasis to this area and now focuses on the Jao area, at the base of the Panhandle, for its mokoro trips. New Moon Safaris and Phakawe Safaris also organise tours on the Panhandle (for contact details, see Organised Tours in the Getting Around section earlier in this chapter).

Places to Stay

Panhandle camps are mostly mid-range and have until recently catered for the sport-fishing crowd; the increase in travellers to the area looking for affordable delta trips is changing that.

The lovely and welcoming ***Drotsky's Cabins*** *(☎ 675035, fax 675043)*, owned by Jan and Eileen Drotsky, is situated beside a channel of the Okavango River about 5km south of Shakawe. It's set amid a thick riverine forest with fabulous birdwatching and fine views across the reeds and papyrus. Camping costs US$7 per person, single/double A-frames cost US$42/75, four-person chalets cost US$84 and all-inclusive packages cost US$135. They also rent boats and run tours to Mahango, the Tsodilo Hills and the affiliated Makwena/Qhaaxhwa Lodge (see listing at the end of this section for contact details).

The quirky ***Shakawe Fishing Lodge*** (Travel Wild; *☎ 660822, fax 660493, @ t.wild@info.bw)* is situated on the Okavango River 8km south of Shakawe. Camping in the riverside camping ground costs US$7 per person and single/double chalets cost US$75/110.

A very friendly spot is ***Sepupa Swamp Stop*** (New Moon Safaris; *☎/fax 661665, @ newmoon@info.bw)* in Sepupa village. It offers riverside camping for US$4 per person. All-inclusive three-day mokoro trips around Seronga cost US$120, Panhandle motorboat trips cost US$15 per hour, and leisurely 'Lazy S' houseboat tours on the Okavango Panhandle cost US$40 per person per day (minimum five people). Transfers to the Tsodilo Hills cost US$40 per person (minimum four people) and return transfers from Maun cost US$100 per person.

Okavango Polers Trust (see the earlier Mokoro Trips section for contact details) offers wild camping while on a mokoro trip or camping at the trust's Seronga camping ground costs US$4 per person.

Guma Lagoon Camp (Ensign Agencies; *☎ 660351, fax 660571)* is a good-value camp situated east of Etsha 13, on the Thaoge River. The focus is tiger-fish and bream fishing, and Guma profiles itself as a family resort. Simple half board costs US$49 per person per day and all-inclusive accommodation, with meals, drinks, boat trips and fuel, fishing tackle and mokoro trips costs US$110. Camping costs US$5 and pre-erected tents cost US$12 per person. The final 11km from Etsha 13 requires a 4WD, but the lodge provides safe parking facilities and transfers from Etsha 13 for US$42 per trip.

Makwena/Qhaaxhwa Lodge (Drotsky's Cabins; *☎ 674299, fax 674302)* on Qhaaxhwa (Birthplace of the Hippo) Lagoon, at the base of the Panhandle, offers accommodation in reed chalets for US$28/100, without/with meals and activities. Camping costs US$6 and backpackers' accommodation is US$30/45. Inexpensive mokoro trips can be arranged, and transfers from Etsha 6 cost US$10 per person.

Getting Around

You can reach Seronga on the daily bus from Mohembo (US$3.75, 2½ hours); cross the river via the free Okavango ferry. If you hitch, you'll pay P3 or so for a lift from Shakawe to Mohembo. The bus leaves the eastern bank of the river after noon and departs from Seronga in the morning.

Boat transfers between Sepupa Swamp Site and Seronga, down the Okavango River, cost US$63 per boat for up to 12 or so people, while local boats charge US$6 per person.

Land transfers between Seronga and the low-water (low season from July to March) poling area near Xau, about 30km east of Seronga, cost US$13 per person.

TSODILO HILLS

The four Tsodilo Hills (Male, Female, Child and North Hill) rise abruptly from a rippled, ocean-like expanse of desert and are threaded with myth, legend and spiritual significance for the San people. More than 2750 ancient rock paintings have been discovered at well over 200 sites. And as in most of Southern Africa, the majority of these are attributed to ancestors of today's San people.

Local San will guide you around the major rock paintings for around US$10 per group.

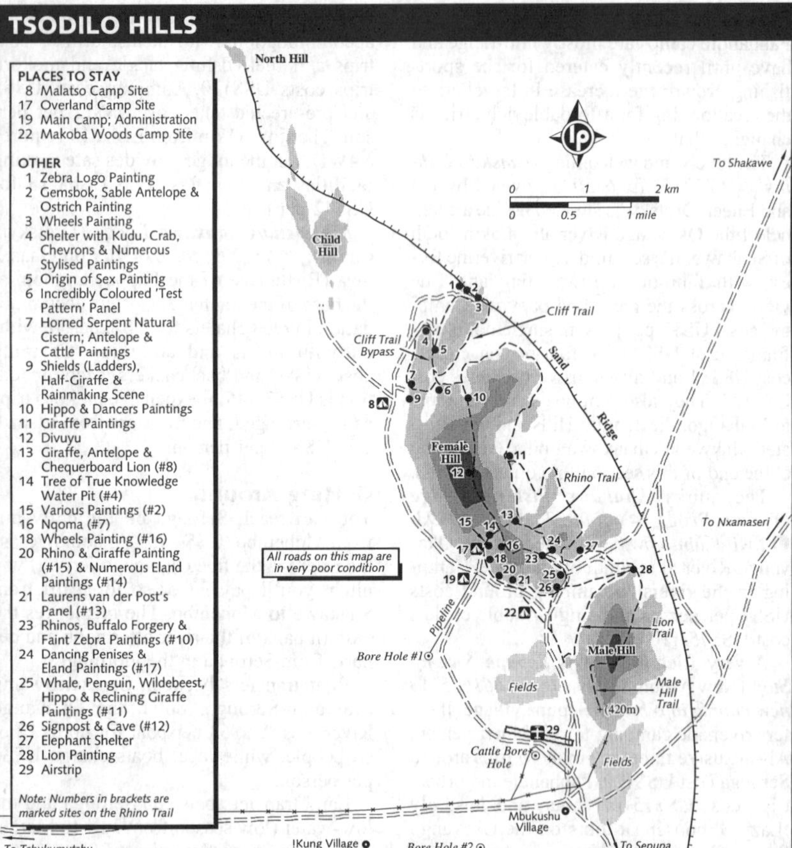

Places to Stay

Visitors can camp at the Main, Malatso or Makoba Woods ***camping grounds***, or at wild ***camp sites*** around the base of the hills. There are no shops or services in the San (!Kung) or Mbukushu villages. Water is available at the Game Scouts Camp and at the bore hole several hundred metres from the airstrip (this water is intended for cattle and has a number of interesting flavours, so it's wise to purify it).

Getting There & Away

Several Maun travel agencies organise one-day air tours and charters starting at US$185, but they allow only three hours of sightseeing, with no time to climb and explore. The cheapest (and best) ways to visit the Tsodilo Hills are with Phakawe Safaris in Maun, which charges US$100 per person per day, or with New Moon Safaris from their camp Sepupa Swamp Stop in Sepupa, where you'll pay US$40 per person for transfers, with a minimum of four people. Drotsky's Cabins in Shakawe also offers tours.

Visitors who fly to the Tsodilo Hills miss an excruciating but unforgettable drive. There are three main 4WD routes: one from the east that is signposted and turns off 7km south of Sepupa, one from Nxamaseri (also from the east) and another that turns off just south of the Samuchina buffalo fence; follow the fence from Samuchina for 7.6km and turn left at the blue sign reading 'I-3', which will take you to the hills.

The Kalahari

The Kalahari offers a solitude all its own. A small portion of the area is classic desert, but much of the Kalahari is a vast deposit of sandy sediments that receive too much rainfall to be classed officially as an arid zone. The Kalahari sands stretch across parts of seven countries: Congo (Zaïre), Angola, Zambia, Namibia, Botswana, Zimbabwe and South Africa, and form one of Africa's most prominent geographical features.

In Botswana's part of the Kalahari, distances are vast, roads are rudimentary, transport is rare to nonexistent, facilities are few and the scant villages huddle around feeble bore holes. The most notable human inhabitants of the Kalahari are the San people (also called Bushmen). For more details see the special section 'The San' earlier in this chapter.

KHUTSE GAME RESERVE

The Khutse Game Reserve covers 2600 sq km and is a popular weekend excursion for Gaborone dwellers. Expect to see a variety of antelope, as well as such predators as lion, leopard, brown and spotted hyaena, jackal, caracal (which the San people believe to be the incarnation of the morning star) and even hunting dogs.

Khutse has three ***camping grounds*** but only Golalabodimo Pan, near the entry gate, and the Game Scout Camp, have running water and showers. Khutse II Pan, with a rudimentary camping ground, is 14km west from the entry gate. Much nicer is Moreswa Pan, which is situated 67km from the gate.

A 4WD is strongly recommended in this area. Hitching is best on Friday night and Saturday morning, especially if you wait just outside Lethlakeng on the Gaborone-Khutse road.

CENTRAL KALAHARI GAME RESERVE

The Central Kalahari Game Reserve covers 52,000 sq km and is Africa's largest protected area, sprawling across the nearly featureless heart of Botswana. It's perhaps best known for Deception (or Letiahau) Valley, the site of Mark and Delia Owens' 1974 to 1981 brown hyaena study, which is described in their book *Cry of the Kalahari*. At Deception Pan, brown hyaenas emerge just after dark and you may also see lions. Three similar fossil valleys: the Okwa, the Quoxo (or Meratswe) and the Passarge also bring topographical relief to the virtually featureless expanses, although the rivers ceased flowing more than 16,000 years ago. Other pans in the northern area of the reserve: Letiahau, Piper's, Sunday and Passarge, are artificially pumped to provide water for wildlife.

The only reasonably convenient public access is via the Matswere gate in the north-eastern corner of the reserve. For fees and booking information, see National Parks & Reserves in the Facts about Botswana section earlier in this chapter.

Places to Stay

There are basic ***camping grounds*** at Deception Pan, Sunday Pan and Piper's Pan, but they lack facilities. Deception Pan is the nicest, with some inviting acacia trees, while Piper's Pan is known for its bizarre ghost trees *(Commiphora pyracanthoides)*. Other remote camping grounds include ***Okwa*** (also known as Xaka) and ***Xade***, in the southern part of the reserve. Drinkable water is available only at the ***Matswere Game Scout Camp***, near the north-eastern gates of the reserve. Bring all your firewood from outside.

Getting There & Away

Plenty of Maun-based operators offer tours; independent access requires a high-clearance 4WD vehicle, a compass or GPS, and reserve petrol (the nearest supply is at Rakops, 40km north-east of Matswere Gate). You can pick up an entry permit and fill up with water at Matswere Game Scout Camp. From Matswere, it's 70km to Deception Pan. The alternative approach, from Makalamabedi

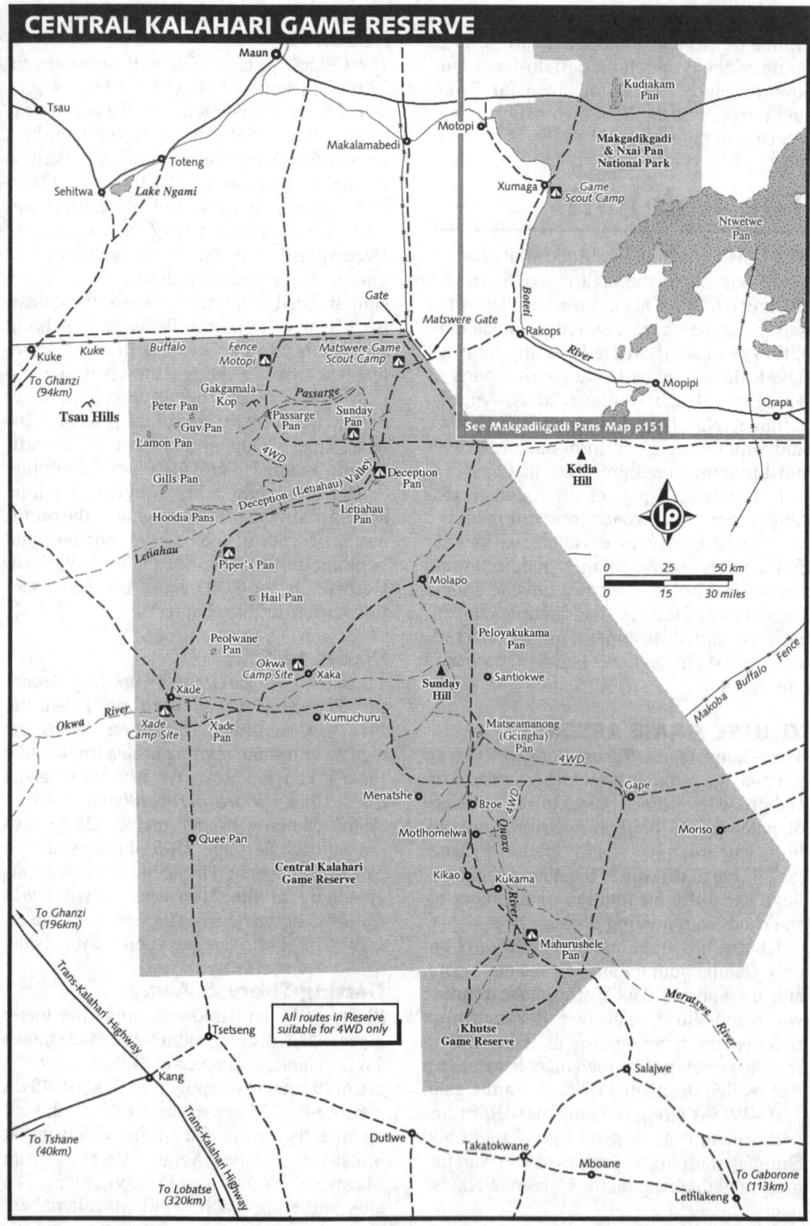
CENTRAL KALAHARI GAME RESERVE
Maun
Tsau
Toteng
Sehitwa
Lake Ngami
Makalamabedi
Motopi
Kudiakam Pan
Makgadikgadi & Nxai Pan National Park
Xumaga
Game Scout Camp
Ntwetwe Pan
Boteti
Gate
Matswere Gate
Rakops
River
Kuke
Kuke
Buffalo
Fence
Motopi
Matswere Game Scout Camp
Mopipi
Orapa
To Ghanzi (94km)
Gakgamala Kop
Passarge
Peter Pan
Tsau Hills
Passarge Pan
Sunday Pan
Guv Pan
Lamon Pan
See Makgadikgadi Pans Map p151
Kedia Hill
4WD
Deception Pan
Gills Pan
Deception (Letiahau) Valley
Hoodia Pans
Letiahau Pan
Letiahau
Piper's Pan
Molapo
0 25 50 km
0 15 30 miles
Hail Pan
Peloyakukama Pan
Peolwane Pan
Okwa Camp Site
Xaka
Sunday Hill
Santiokwe
Makoba Buffalo Fence
Xade
Okwa
River
Xade Camp Site
Xade Pan
Kumuchuru
Matseamanong (Gcingha) Pan
4WD
Gape
Menatshe
Bzoe
4WD
Okwa
Moriso
Motlhomelwa
Quee Pan
Central Kalahari Game Reserve
Kikao
Kukama
River
To Ghanzi (196km)
Mahurushele Pan
Trans-Kalahari Highway
Meratswe River
All routes in Reserve suitable for 4WD only
Tsetseng
Khutse Game Reserve
Kang
Salajwe
Trans-Kalahari Highway
To Tshane (40km)
Dutlwe
Takatokwane
Mboane
To Lobatse (320km)
To Gaborone (113km)
Lethlakeng

near the Maun-Nata road, heads south for about 105km along the eastern side of the buffalo fence to the Matswere Gate.

THE TRANS-KALAHARI HIGHWAY

The Trans-Kalahari Highway between Gaborone and Windhoek (Namibia) has opened up the once-wild reaches of the Kalahari to all and sundry. The new tar road follows the cattle route between the BMC abattoir in Lobatse and the Ghanzi freehold ranches (near the border with Namibia) via Jwaneng – the centre of Botswana's diamond industry.

Jwaneng

The world's largest diamond deposit was discovered at Jwaneng in 1978 and now produces nearly nine million carats annually. Mine tours may be arranged by appointment through Debswana (☎ 351131, fax 352941) Botsalano House, PO Box 329, Gaborone. The ***Mokala Lodge*** *(☎ 380835)* is a cosy little place with pleasant gardens; singles/doubles cost US$55/72, including breakfast. It also has an a la carte restaurant.

Ghanzi

Ghanzi's main attraction is the Ghanzicraft Cooperative, which markets well-made **San crafts**. If you're visiting in June, be sure to check out the **Agricultural Show**, which is an unforgettable experience. The Ncoakhue San people at Dqãe Qare (☎ 596285), in D'kar, north of Ghanzi, offer guided **hunting** and gathering **bushwalks**, and insight into the lifestyles of the traditional Kalahari San.

The well-appointed and recommended ***Thakadu Camp*** *(cell ☎ 7212 0695, fax 569169, ⓔ thakadu@global.bw)*, 4km from Ghanzi on the Namibia road, charges US$4 per person for camping.

Life in town revolves around the ***Kalahari Arms Hotel*** *(☎ 596311)*, which has a pub and basic restaurant; camping costs US$4 per person and singles/doubles cost US$41/49.

Travelling the Trans-Kalahari

There's a daily bus along the Trans-Kalahari Highway between Gaborone and Ghanzi (US$17, eight hours). Those heading from Ghanzi to Namibia should remember that the Mamuno-Buitepos border crossings close at 5 pm (that's 4 pm Namibian time in the winter). On Fridays, a bus from Ghanzi to Mamuno connects with Namibia's Star Line bus to Gobabis.

Hitching isn't too difficult, but you may get stuck at the border; on the Namibian side, you can stay at the ***East Gate Service Station & Rest Camp***. See Buitepos under Around Windhoek in the Namibia chapter for details.

KGALAGADI TRANSFRONTIER PARK

The former Mabuasehube-Gemsbok National Park has now been combined with South Africa's former Kalahari-Gemsbok National Park into the new Kgalagadi Transfrontier Park. The result is one of the world's largest (28,400 sq km) and most pristine wilderness areas. See Kgalagadi Transfrontier Park in the Northern Cape section of the South Africa chapter for a map and information on the South African side.

Direct road access to Botswana's portion of the park is limited to the Mabuasehube section. The Nossob River and the Gemsbok Wilderness Trail 4WD track may be reached only through South Africa, as there's no road access between the Mabuasehube and Nossob regions. See Getting There & Away following for details.

The Mabuasehube Section

The Mabuasehube section of the park covers 1800 sq km and focuses on three major pans and several minor ones. The largest pan is Mabuasehube in the north, which is used as a salt lick by herds of eland and gemsbok. Further south is the grassy Bosobogolo Pan, which attracts springbok as well as lion, cheetah, brown hyaena and hunting dog. There are also four other large pans: Lesholoago, Monamodi, Khiding and Mpaathutlwa, and a number of smaller ones.

Mabuasehube is best visited in late winter and early spring when herds of eland and gemsbok migrate from the rest of the park. It's open to day visitors from 6.30 am to

6.30 pm March to September and 5.30 am to 7.30 pm October to February. You can pay park fees at the Game Scout Camp at Mpaathutlwa Pan. For fees and booking information, see National Parks & Wildlife Reserves in the Facts about Botswana section earlier in this chapter.

The Mabuasehube region has rudimentary ***camping grounds***, for up to two groups of up to about 12 people each, at Lesholoago Pan, Mpaathutlwa Pan (the Game Scout Camp) and Khiding Pan, as well as two sites at Mabuasehube Pan. Water is available at the Game Scout Camp, but you should still carry plenty of water into the park.

The Gemsbok Section

In the Gemsbok portion of the park is the recently opened Gemsbok Wilderness Trail, a three-day, 285km 4WD route through the park's northern extreme, which must be booked through Botswana Department of Wildlife & National Parks; the usual park fees apply. It's accessed from Polentswe camping ground via Grootbrak, on the Nossob River in South Africa. There are two obligatory camping grounds along the Gemsbok Wilderness Trail.

The ***Game Scout Camp***, on the Botswana side of the Nossob River opposite South Africa's Twee Rivieren Camp, has cold showers and toilets. There are also three undeveloped sites on the Botswana side of the Nossob: Rooiputs, 30km north-east of Twee Rivieren; Polentswe Pan, 60km north of Nossob Camp; and Swart Pan, 30km south-east of Unions End (near the Namibian border). All are accessed from South Africa.

Getting There & Away

Tracks into Mabuasehube are very poor and require a 4WD vehicle. The shortest route is the little-used track from the Khakea-Werda road; turn west 2km north of the Moselebe River, about 50km south of Khakea and 20km north of Werda. You can also enter from Tshabong in the south-east. The nearest reliable petrol pumps are at Kang, Ghanzi and Jwaneng (and sometimes Tshabong).

From south-western Botswana, the easiest access into South Africa is at McCarthysrus, but it's a rather roundabout route from there to the South African section of the park (the former Kalahari-Gemsbok National Park). For the fee structure on the South African side, see the South Africa chapter.

Lesotho

Lesotho (le-**soo**-too) is a mountainous kingdom about the size of Belgium, which is surrounded by South Africa. Its forbidding terrain and the defensive walls of the Drakensberg and Maluti Ranges gave both sanctuary and strategic advantage to the Basotho (the people of Lesotho), who forged a nation while playing a key role in the manoeuvres of the white invaders on the plains below.

LESOTHO AT A GLANCE

Area: 30,350 sq km

Population: 1,992,960

Capital: Maseru

Head of State: King Letsie David Mohato III

Official Languages: South Sotho, English

Currency: maloti (M); fixed at a value equal to the South African rand

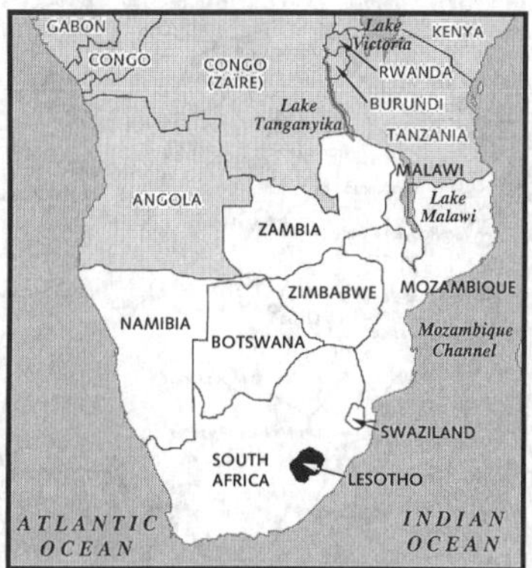

Highlights

- Malealea – pony trek through the rugged interior with its breathtaking scenery, and stay in traditional Basotho villages
- Teyateyaneng – shop for gorgeous tapestries at the craft centre of Lesotho
- Thabana-Ntlenyana – hike to Southern Africa's tallest mountain

Facts about Lesotho

HISTORY

Lesotho was settled by Sotho peoples comparatively recently, possibly as late as the 16th century. Already here were the Khoisan, with whom there was some intermarriage and mingling of language. There might also have been some Nguni people.

The early society was made up of small chiefdoms. Cattle and cultivation were the mainstays of the economy. Grain and hides were exported in exchange for iron from the area in the north-east of today's South Africa.

By the early 19th century white traders were on the scene, exchanging beads for cattle. They were soon followed by the Voortrekkers (Boer pioneers) and pressure on Sotho grazing lands grew. Even without white encroachment, Sotho society had to face that it had expanded as far as it could and would have to adapt to living in a finite territory. On top of this came the disaster of the *difaqane* (forced migration).

The rapid consolidation and expansion of the Zulu state under the leadership of Shaka, and later Dingaan, resulted in a chain reaction of turmoil throughout the whole of Southern Africa. Huge numbers of people were displaced, their tribes shattered and their lands lost, and they, in turn, attacked other tribes. That the loosely organised southern Sotho society survived this period was largely due to the abilities of Moshoeshoe the Great (pronounced as mo-shesh).

Moshoeshoe the Great

Moshoeshoe began as a leader of a small village and in about 1820 he led his villagers to Butha-Buthe. From this mountain stronghold his people survived the first battles of the difaqane and in 1824 Moshoeshoe began his policy of assisting refugees who helped in his defence. Later in the same year he moved

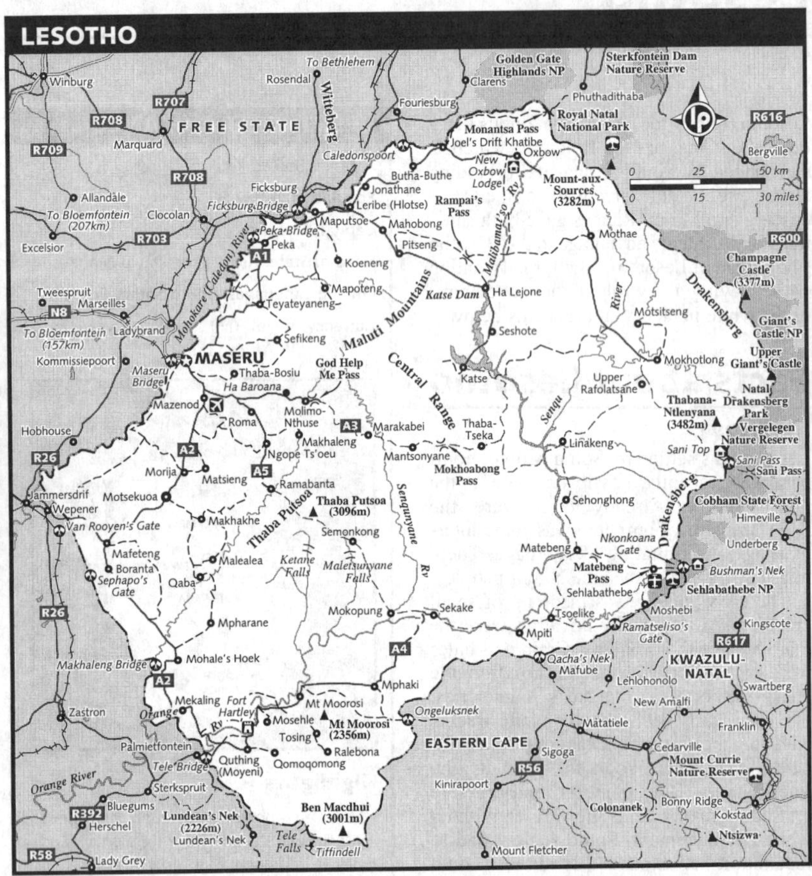

his people to Thaba-Bosiu, a mountain top that was even easier to defend.

From Thaba-Bosiu, Moshoeshoe played a patient game of placating the stronger local rulers and granting protection – as well as land and cattle – to refugees. These people and others like them were to form Basutholand which, by the time of Moshoeshoe's death in 1870, had a population of more than 150,000.

Another factor in Basutholand's emergence and survival was Moshoeshoe's welcoming of missionaries, and his ability to take their advice without being dominated by them. The first missionaries to arrive in the area in 1833 were from the Paris Evangelical Missionary Society. In return for some Christianisation of Sotho customs, the missionaries were disposed to defend the rights of 'their' Basotho against the new threat – British and Boer expansion.

The Boers had crossed the Orange River in the 1830s, and by 1843 Moshoeshoe was sufficiently concerned by their numbers to ally himself with the British Cape government. The British Resident, installed in Basutholand as a condition of the treaties, decided that Moshoeshoe was too powerful and engineered an unsuccessful attack on his kingdom.

In 1854 the British withdrew from the area, having fixed the boundaries of Basutholand. The Boers pressed their claims on the land and increasing tension led to the 1858 Free State-Basutho War. Moshoeshoe won yet another major battle, and the situation simmered along until 1865 when another Free State-Basutho war erupted. This time Moshoeshoe suffered setbacks and, as a consequence, was forced to sign away much of his western lowlands.

In 1868 Moshoeshoe again called on British assistance, this time on the imperial government in London. A high commission was formed to adjudicate the dispute and the result was the loss of more Basotho land. It was obvious that no treaty between Boers and Basotho would hold for long, and continual war between the Free State and Basutholand was not good for British interests. The British solution was to simply annex Basutholand.

After Moshoeshoe the Great

The British gave control of Basutholand to the Cape Colony in 1871. Moshoeshoe the Great had died the year before and squabbles over succession were dividing the country. The Cape government exploited this and reduced the powers of chiefs and limited them to their individual areas.

The Gun War of 1880 began as a protest against the Cape government's refusal to allow the Basotho to own firearms, but it quickly became a battle between the rebel chiefs on one side and the government and collaborating chiefs on the other. The war ended in a stalemate with the Cape government being discredited.

A shaky peace followed until another war appeared imminent, and in 1884 the British government again took direct control of Basutholand. The imperial government decided to back strong local leaders rather than rule through its own officers, and this helped to stabilise the country. One unexpected benefit of direct British rule was that when the Union of South Africa was created, Basutholand was a British Protectorate and was not included in the Union.

Home Rule & Independence

In 1910 the advisory Basutholand National Council was formed from members nominated by the chiefs. After decades of allegations of corruption and favouritism, reforms were made in the 1940s that introduced some democracy into appointments to the council.

In the mid-1950s the council requested internal self-government from the British and in 1960 a new constitution was in place and elections were held for a Legislative Council.

Meanwhile, political parties had formed. The main contenders for elections were the Basutholand Congress Party (BCP), similar to South Africa's African National Congress (ANC), and the Basutholand National Party (BNP), a conservative party headed by Chief Leabua Jonathan.

The BCP won the 1960 elections and demanded full independence from Britain. This was eventually agreed to and a new constitution was drawn up, with independence to come into effect in 1966. However, at the elections in 1965 the BCP lost power to the BNP and Chief Jonathan became the first prime minister of the new Kingdom of Lesotho. During the election campaign the BNP promised cooperation with the South African apartheid regime and in turn received massive support from it.

As most of the civil service was still loyal to the BCP, Jonathan did not have an easy time. Stripping King Moshoeshoe II of the few powers that the new constitution had left him did not endear Jonathan's government to the people and, in the 1970 election, the BCP won government.

Jonathan responded by suspending the constitution, arresting and expelling the king, and banning opposition parties. The king, after an exile in Holland, was allowed to return, and Jonathan attempted to form a government of national reconciliation. This ploy was partly successful, but some BCP members, including the leader Ntsu Mokhehle, resisted and attempted to stage a coup in 1974. The coup failed miserably and resulted in the death of many BCP supporters and the jailing or exile of the BCP leadership.

Trouble continued and repressive measures were applied. Jonathan changed tack in his attitude to South Africa, calling for the return of land in the Orange Free State that had been stolen from the original Basutholand, and, more seriously from the South African point of view, began criticising apartheid, allegedly offering refuge to ANC guerrillas and flirting with Cuba. Relations soured to the point where South Africa closed Lesotho's borders, strangling the country.

The Lesotho military took action. Jonathan was deposed in 1986 and the king was restored as head of state. This was a popular move, but eventually agitation for democratic reform rose again. In 1990 King Moshoeshoe II was deposed by the army in favour of his son, Prince Mohato Bereng Seeisa (Letsie III). Elections in 1993 resulted in the return of the BCP.

In 1995 Letsie III abdicated in favour of his father and, five years after being deposed, Moshoeshoe II was reinstated. He restored calm to Lesotho after a year of unrest. Tragically, less than a year later he was killed when his 4WD plunged over a cliff in the Maluti Mountains. Letsie III was again made the king.

The BCP was split between those who wanted Prime Minister Ntsu Mokhehle to remain as leader and those who didn't. Mokhehle formed the breakaway Lesotho Congress for Democracy (LCD) party and continued to govern.

Elections & Invasion

Elections were held in 1998 and many people protested that there had been widespread cheating by the LCD, which won in a landslide. Tensions between the public service and the government became acute, and the military was also split.

Following months of protests, the government was losing control. In late September 1998 it called on the Southern African Development Community (SADC) treaty partners, Botswana, South Africa and Zimbabwe, to help restore order. Troops, mainly South African, invaded the kingdom.

Rebel elements of the Lesotho army put up strong resistance and there was heavy fighting in Maseru. The fighting was soon over but order had broken down and many shops and other businesses in Maseru were looted and torched.

The government agreed to call new elections sometime in 2000, but the political situation remained tense.

GEOGRAPHY

From Lesotho's northern tip to its western side where it juts out almost to the town of Wepener in South Africa, the border is formed by the Mohokare (Caledon) River. The eastern border is defined by the rugged escarpment of the Drakensberg, and high country forms much of the southern border.

All of Lesotho exceeds 1000m in altitude, with peaks in the central ranges and near the escarpment reaching to more than 3000m. Lesotho has the highest lowest point of any country. The highest mountain in Southern Africa (the highest point south of Mt Kilimanjaro) is the 3482m Thabana-Ntlenyana, near Sani Pass in eastern Lesotho.

CLIMATE

Lesotho winters are cold and clear. Frosts are common and there are snowfalls in the high country and sometimes at lower altitudes. At other times of the year, snow has been known to fall (especially on the high peaks where the weather is dangerously changeable) but rain and mist are more common bugbears for drivers and hikers. Nearly all of Lesotho's rain falls between October and April, with spectacular thunderstorms in summer – quite a few people are killed by lightning every year. Down in the valleys, summer days can be hot with temperatures exceeding 30°C.

Never go out into the mountains, even for an afternoon, without a sleeping bag, tent

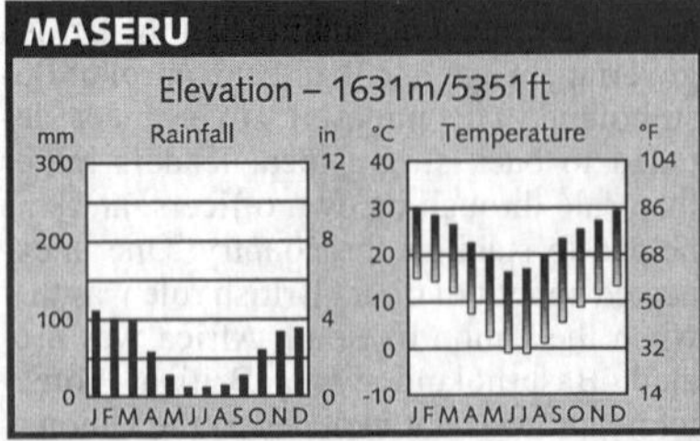

and sufficient food for a couple of days in case you get fogged in. Even in summer it can be freezing.

ECOLOGY & ENVIRONMENT

There are serious environmental concerns about the controversial Highlands Water Project, which will provide water and electricity to South Africa.

Traditional Basotho communities have been disrupted (though compensation is promised) and with only around 10% of Lesotho's land suitable for agriculture, the proposed Mohale Dam (about 35km from Katse Dam) will flood some of the most fertile land in the country. There is also the effect on the ecology of the Senqu and Orange Rivers and the impact on Namibia, a downstream user with its own water shortage problems; these are troubling unknowns.

Other key environmental issues include animal population pressure (which results in overgrazing) and soil erosion. About 18 to 20 tonnes of topsoil per hectare are lost each year and it has been estimated that there will be no cultivatable land left in Lesotho by 2040.

On a brighter note Lesotho and South Africa have recently combined in a multimillion dollar conservation project. Beginning in 2000, the Maluti-Drakensberg Transfrontier Conservation and Development Project will aim to protect and develop the eastern-alpine ecosystem of the Maluti-Drakensberg Mountains, which includes the spiral aloe flower and the rare bearded vulture.

FLORA & FAUNA

The high plains and mountains are home to Cape alpine flowers. The national flower, spiral aloe *(Aloe polyphylla)*, is a strange plant unique to Lesotho. Its leaves form rows of striking, spiral patterns and you'll see it in left- and right- handed (clockwise and anti-clockwise) varieties on the slopes of the Maluti Mountains.

Due mainly to its altitude, Lesotho is home to fewer animals than many southern African countries. You may come across rhebok and reedbuck, and in the Drakensberg eland are still represented. Baboon and jackal are reasonably common and there are also mongoose and meerkat.

The birdlife is rich, with just under 300 species recorded. The Drakensberg is an excellent place for birdwatching and bearded vultures and black eagles are both found here. Lesotho is one of the few places you may spot the extremely rare bald ibis.

GOVERNMENT & POLITICS

The head of state is King Letsie III, and the prime minister is Ntsu Mokhehle of the Lesotho Congress for Democracy party. Under traditional law, the king can be deposed by a majority vote of the College of Chiefs.

ECONOMY

Lesotho is one of the world's poorest countries. Much of the country's food is imported, although in the 19th century Lesotho exported grain. The main export is now labour; many Basotho work in South Africa.

The Highlands Water Project is creating a series of dams on the Orange River (Lesotho), and sales of water and hydroelectricity to South Africa might make Lesotho more economically independent. Very little manufacturing occurs in the kingdom and most goods are imported from South Africa.

POPULATION & PEOPLE

The 1,992,960 citizens of Lesotho are known as the Basotho people. Culturally, most are southern Sotho and most speak South Sotho. The melding of the Basotho nation was largely the result of Moshoeshoe the Great's 19th-century military and diplomatic triumphs and many diverse subgroups and peoples have somehow merged into a homogeneous society. Maseru, with 110,000 people, is the only large town.

Traditional culture, which is still strong, consists largely of the customs, rites and superstitions with which the Basotho explain and enrich their lives.

Music and dance play their part, mainly as important components of ceremony and everyday life. There are various musical instruments, from the *lekolulo* (a flute-like instrument played by herd boys), to the

The Basotho Hat

A distinctive feature of Basotho dress is the conical hat with its curious top adornment, known to the Basotho as *mokorotlo*, or *molianyeoe*.

The style of this hat is taken directly from the shape of a hill, Qiloane, near Moshoeshoe the Great's Thaba-Bosiu fortress.

These hats can be purchased in Maseru from vendors in front of the tourist office and at the border posts. A large adult-sized hat is about M20. You'll pay M5 for one that could hang from your rear-view mirror next to those cute FIFA soccer boots. The large hats are highly prized in South Africa; I lost mine to a local angler in an eel-fishing competition in Eastern Cape Province.

Jeff Williams

thomo (a stringed instrument played by women) and the *setolo-tolo* (a stringed instrument played with the mouth, by men).

Traditional medicine mixes rites and customs with a *sangoma* (witchdoctor), developing their own charms and rituals. The Basotho are traditionally buried in a sitting position, facing the rising sun – ready to leap up when called.

LANGUAGE

The official languages are South Sotho and English. For some useful words and phrases in South Sotho, see the Language chapter at the back of this book.

Facts for the Visitor

SUGGESTED ITINERARIES

If you're here for a week, there's no need to stop long in Maseru – head south toward Morija where you'll find a great museum with displays of Basotho culture. Then continue to Malealea – the 'gem' of Lesotho. Malealea Lodge is the best place in the country to go pony trekking. Depending on time, you could then pop down to Quthing (Moyeni) and check out the 180 million-year-old dinosaur footprints.

With two weeks you could add on a visit to Teyateyaneng, north of Maseru, the craft centre of Lesotho. Then after Morija, Malealea and Quthing (Moyeni) you could head to Lesotho's only national park, the remote Sehlabathebe National Park, where you can really get away from it all for a few days, before returning to the tension of South Africa.

PLANNING

Lesotho is worth visiting year-round but the weather can determine what you do. In winter be prepared for cold conditions and snow. In summer rain and mist should be taken into account. In remote areas (which make up a large proportion of the country) roads are often overrun by flooding rivers in summer.

The Department of Land Surveys & Physical Planning in Maseru sells some excellent maps of Lesotho. The 1:250,000 scale map (1994), which covers the entire country, is best for driving and costs M30. For trekking or driving in very rugged areas you might want the 1:50,000 series, at about M10 each.

TOURIST OFFICES

The only tourist office (☎ 313760, 312896, fax 310108) in Lesotho is on Kingsway in Maseru.

VISAS & DOCUMENTS

Citizens of most Western European countries, the USA and most Commonwealth countries are granted an entry permit (free) at the border. The standard stay permitted is two weeks, although if you ask for longer you might get it. For citizens of other countries, if you arrive at the Maseru Bridge border without a visa you might be given a temporary entry permit which allows you to go into Maseru and apply for a visa at the Department of Immigration (☎ 317339) office on Kingsway. Don't count on this, as it depends on the whim of the border officials.

A single-entry visa costs M20 and a multiple-entry visa is M40. At most border posts you get two weeks' stay renewable by either leaving the country and re-entering, or by application at the Department of Immigration in Maseru. For a longer stay, apply in advance to the Director of Immigration & Passport Services, PO Box 363, Maseru 100, Lesotho.

No vaccination certificates are necessary unless you have recently been in a yellow fever area.

EMBASSIES & CONSULATES

Lesotho Embassies

Lesotho has an embassy in South Africa (see Embassies & Consulates in the South Africa chapter). Elsewhere in the world, countries with a Lesotho embassy include:

Belgium (☎ 02-705 3976) Boulevard General Wahis 45, 1030 Brussels
Germany (☎ 228-308 430) Godesberger Alle 50 53175, Bonn
UK (☎ 020-7235 5686) 7 Chesam Place, Belgravia, London SW1 8HN
USA (☎ 202-797 5533/4) 2511 Massachusetts Ave NW, Washington DC 20008

Embassies & Consulates in Lesotho

A number of countries have representation in Maseru, including:

Canada
Consulate: (☎ 316435) 1st floor, Maseru Book Centre Bldg, Kingsway, Maseru
France
Consulate: (☎ 327522) Inquiries handled by Alliance Française, but all visas issued in Johannesburg.
Germany
Consulate: (☎ 314426) 70C Maluti Rd, Maseru West. All visa applications sent to Pretoria.
Ireland
Consulate: (☎ 314068) Christie House, Tonakholo Rd, Maseru West. Open from 8 am to 12.45 pm and 2 to 4.30 pm weekdays.
The Netherlands
Consulate: (☎ 312114) Lancer's Inn, Maseru
South Africa
High Commission: (☎ 315758) 10th floor, Lesotho Bank Towers, Kingsway, Maseru. Open from 8.30 am to 12.30 pm weekdays.
UK
High Commission: (☎ 313961) Linare Rd (opposite police headquarters), Maseru. Open from 8 am to 1 pm weekdays.
USA
Embassy: (☎ 312666) 254 Kingsway, Maseru. Open from 9 am to noon and 2 to 4 pm Monday and Wednesday.

CUSTOMS

Customs regulations are broadly the same as those for South Africa, but you can't bring in alcohol unless you're arriving from a country other than Botswana, Swaziland and South Africa – and that isn't likely.

MONEY

Currency

The unit of currency is the maloti (M), which is divided into 100 liesente.

Exchange Rates

The maloti is fixed at a value equal to the South African rand, and rands are accepted everywhere – there is no real need to convert your money into maloti. When changing travellers cheques you can usually get rand notes and this saves having to convert unused maloti. (For exchange rates, see Facts for the Visitor section in the South Africa chapter.)

Exchanging Money

The only banks where you can change foreign currency, including travellers cheques, are in Maseru. The banks are the Lesotho Development Bank, Standard Bank and Nedbank. Banks are open from 8.30 am to 3 pm weekdays (until 1 pm on Thursday) and 8.30 to 11 am Saturday.

Costs

Lesotho is a cheaper country to travel in than South Africa if you take advantage of the opportunities to stay with local people and to camp in remote areas. Otherwise, hotel prices are about the same as South Africa. A goods and services tax (GST) of 10% is added to most transactions. Note that hotels don't usually include the GST when quoting rates.

POST & COMMUNICATIONS

Post offices are open from 8 am to 4.30 pm weekdays and 8 am to noon Saturday.

The telephone system works reasonably well. There are no area codes within Lesotho. Lesotho's country code is 266; to call Lesotho from South Africa dial the prefix 09-266. To call South Africa from anywhere in Lesotho, dial 00-27 and then the South African area code and phone number.

INTERNET RESOURCES

Web sites that are worth a look before you go to Lesotho are:

African Studies – Lesotho Page A good place to start surfing: heaps of links to sites about Lesotho on the Internet.
www.sas.upenn.edu/African_Studies/Country_Specific/Lesotho.html

Kingdom in the Sky An excellent resource with all kinds of tourist information for planning a trip to Lesotho.
www.africa-insites.com/lesotho/

BOOKS

If you're keen on walking or hiking, there are some helpful books available:

A Backpackers Guide to Lesotho by Russell Suchet. Outlines several walks in the country; it costs M18.

Guide to Lesotho by David Ambrose. A good guide for hiking.

Hill Walks In & Around Maseru. This is worth buying (M3.75) at the local craft shops; note, however, that some walks in the book have been overwhelmed by urban sprawl and are no longer possible.

NEWSPAPERS

Several thin newspapers such as *Southern Star* are available in the morning in Maseru and later elsewhere. Day-old South African newspapers are available in Maseru.

RADIO

If you're a fan of the BBC World Service, Lesotho is a mecca as there's a transmitter here and you can pick up the Beeb on short wave, medium wave (1197 kHz) and FM.

PHOTOGRAPHY & VIDEO

You're better off bringing film into Lesotho and waiting until you're back home before getting it developed.

HEALTH

There is neither malaria nor bilharzia in Lesotho, but avoid drinking untreated water taken downstream from a village. The cold and changeable weather is the greatest threat to your health, and the consequences could be a lot more serious than catching a cold if you're trapped on a mountain without proper clothing. For more information, see Health in the Regional Facts for the Visitor chapter.

DANGERS & ANNOYANCES

The last Friday of the month is when many people are paid, and by mid-afternoon some towns become like street parties. These can be fun but as the day wears on some of the drunks become over-friendly, boisterous and ultimately aggressive.

If you're not South African then it doesn't hurt to let people know where you are from, especially if you drive into town in a rental car that has South African number plates.

If you're hiking without a guide, you might be hassled for money or 'gifts' by shepherds in remote areas. There's a very slight risk of robbery.

Several lives are lost each year from lightning strikes; remember to keep off the high ground during an electrical storm and avoid

ALL PHOTOGRAPHS BY DI JONES

Lesotho Clockwise from Top: Basotho kids having fun, Qachas Nek; pony trekkers passing the beautiful Makhaleng Gorge; a spectacular mountain view of the Ribaneng Valley; a rugged-up *sangoma* (witchdoctor) in snowy Malealea

ALL PHOTOGRAPHS BY DENNIS JOHNSON

Malawi **Clockwise from Top:** View of Lake Malawi, near Livingstonia; one of the many minibuses on the Mzuzu–Chtimba road; Lake Malawi at sunset; a shop at Mwanza, the Mozambique border crossing camping in the open. The sheer ferocity of an electrical storm in Lesotho has to be seen to be believed.

EMERGENCIES

The contact numbers for emergency services are: police ☎ 123; ambulance ☎ 121 (available in Maseru and a few other areas only).

BUSINESS HOURS

Most businesses are open from 8 am to 5 pm weekdays and 8 am to noon Saturday. The civil service works between 8 am and 4.30 pm weekdays with a break for lunch from 12.45 to 2 pm.

PUBLIC HOLIDAYS

Public holidays include Christmas, Boxing and New Year's days, Good Friday and Easter Monday, plus Independence Day (4 October), and Moshoeshoe Day (11 March).

ACTIVITIES

Hiking

Lesotho offers great remote-area trekking in a landscape that is reminiscent of the Tibetan plateau. You can walk just about anywhere in Lesotho as there are no organised hiking trails, just footpaths. Know how to use a map and compass and get the relevant 1:50,000 maps from the map office at the Department of Land, Surveys & Physical Planning in Lerotholi Rd, Maseru.

In all areas, but especially the remote eastern highlands, walking is dangerous if you aren't prepared. Temperatures can plummet to near zero even in summer, and thunderstorms are common. Waterproof gear and plenty of warm clothes are absolutely essential. In summer many of the rivers flood, and fords can become dangerous. Be prepared to change your route or wait until the river subsides. Thick fog can also cause delays. By the end of the dry season, especially in the higher areas, clean water can be scarce.

There are stores in the towns but these stock only very basic foodstuff. Bring all you need from Maseru, or from South Africa if you want specialist hiking supplies. There are trout streams in the east – if you don't catch your own, buy some from locals.

Hikers should respect the mounds of stones (cairns) that mark graves. However, a mound of stones near a trail, especially between two hills, should be added to by passing travellers, who ensure their good luck by spitting on a stone and throwing it onto the pile. Note that a white flag waving from a village means that *joala* (sorghum beer) has just been brewed; a yellow flag indicates maize beer, red is for meat and green for vegetables.

The entire country is good for trekking, but the eastern highlands and the Drakensberg's crown attract serious hikers, with the walk between Qacha's Nek and Butha-Buthe offering the best challenge.

Pony Trekking

This is an excellent and popular way of seeing the Lesotho highlands. The main centres are the Basotho Pony Trekking Centre, isolated Semonkong Lodge and Malealea Lodge (see the relevant entries later in this chapter for details).

There are basic stores near all these centres but it's better to bring food from Maseru. Waterproof gear is a must, as is sun protection. Visitors do not need prior riding experience to go pony trekking into the interior.

Birdwatching

About 280 species of bird have been recorded in Lesotho – surprising for a landlocked

> **The Basotho Pony**
>
> The Basotho pony is strong and sure-footed and generally docile. Its size and physique is the result of crossbreeding between short Javanese horses and European full mounts.
>
> A few horses were captured from invading Griqua forces by Basotho warriors in the early 1800s and Moshoeshoe the Great is recorded as having ridden a horse in 1830. Since that date the pony has become an integral part of life in the highlands and the preferred mode of transport for many villagers. In 1983 the Basotho Pony Trekking Centre was set up near Molimo-Nthuse (God Help Me) Pass in an attempt to prevent dilution of the ponies' gene pool.

country. The mountainous terrain provides habitats for many species of raptor (birds of prey). You might see the Cape vulture *(Gyps coprotheres)* or the rare bearded vulture or lammergeyer *(Gypaetus barbatus)*.

Good birdwatching places include eyries in the Maluti Mountains and near the eastern Drakensberg escarpment.

Fishing

Trout fishing is very popular. The trout season runs from September to the end of May. There is a minimal licence fee, a bag limit of 12 fish and a size limit; only rod and line and artificial nonspinning flies may be used. For more information contact the Livestock Division of the Ministry of Agriculture (☎ 323986), Private Bag A82, Maseru 100.

The nearest fishing area to Maseru is the Makhalaneng River, 2km downstream from the Molimo-Nthuse Hotel (a two-hour drive from Maseru). Other places where you can cast a line are in the Malibamat'so near Butha-Buthe, 2km below the New Oxbow Lodge; in the De Beers' Dam, Khubelu and Mokhotlong Rivers near Mokhotlong; the Tsoelikana River, Park Ponds and Leqooa River near Qacha's Nek; and the Thaba-Tseka main dam.

Indigenous fish include barbel in lowland rivers, yellowfish in the mountains and the Maloti minnow in the upper Tsoelikana.

ACCOMMODATION

Camping isn't really feasible close to towns, but away from population centres you can camp anywhere as long as you have the permission of the local landowners. As well as being an essential courtesy, you might be offered a hut for the night; pay about M20 per person for this.

There are a couple of hostels in Maseru and one near Butha-Buthe.

There are missions scattered around the country (the 1:250,000 Lesotho map shows them) and you can often get a bed. There are also Agricultural Training Centres in several places that provide a bed for a small fee.

Maseru has a reasonable range of hotel accommodation. Most towns have small hotels that have survived from protectorate days. These are usually now just run-down bars and liquor stores but with some persuasion you might get a room.

SHOPPING

Unfortunately, Lesotho's all-purpose garment, the blanket, is usually made elsewhere. There are plenty of other handicrafts to buy, including mohair tapestry, mohair ponchos and woven grass products such as mats, baskets and, of course, the Basotho hat. If you're going trekking you might want a sturdy stick. They come plain or decorated and can be found everywhere from craft shops to bus parks, where prices start at about M40 but bargaining is essential.

In and around the town of Teyateyaneng there are many craft shops and cottage industries.

Getting There & Away

This section covers access into Lesotho from neighbouring countries only. Information about reaching Southern Africa from elsewhere on the African continent and from other continents is outlined in the regional Getting There & Away chapter.

AIR

At the time of writing, Lesotho Airways was no longer operating, but this situation may change by the time you read this.

Airports & Airlines

Lesotho's Moshoeshoe International Airport is 18km from Maseru.

South African Airways (SAA) flies daily between Moshoeshoe International Airport and Johannesburg (Jo'burg) in South Africa for M450, one way. There is an airport departure tax of about M20.

LAND

All the land borders are with South Africa. Most people enter via Maseru Bridge. The border crossings are shown in the table on the next page.

Lesotho/South Africa Border Crossings

border crossing	opening hours	nearest Lesotho/South African towns
Caledonspoort	6 am to 10 pm	Butha-Buthe/Fouriesburg
Ficksburg Bridge	24 hours	Maputsoe/Ficksburg
Makhaleng Bridge	8 am to 6 pm (weekdays)/ 8 am to 4 pm (weekends)	Mohale's Hoek/Zastron
Maseru Bridge	6 am to 10 pm	Maseru/Ladybrand
Nkonkoana Gate	8 am to 4 pm	Sehlabathebe/Bushman's Nek
Qacha's Nek	7 am to 8 pm	Mpiti/Mafube
Ramatseliso's Gate	7 am to 5 pm	Tsoelike/north-east of Matatiele
Sani Pass	8 am to 4 pm	Mokhotlong/Himeville
Sephapho's Gate	8 am to 4 pm	south of Mafeteng/Boesmanskop
Van Rooyen's Gate	6 am to 10 pm	north of Mafeteng/Wepener

Bus & Minibus Taxi

There are no longer any direct buses between major South African cities and Maseru. Take a bus to Bloemfontein or Ladybrand and catch a minibus taxi into Lesotho from there.

Minibus taxis run between Jo'burg and Maseru for about R70. Buses from Maseru for places in South Africa leave from the bridge on the South African side of the border.

Car & Motorcycle

You can't enter Lesotho via Sani Pass unless your vehicle is 4WD, but you can leave that way in a conventional vehicle, although most 2WDs won't have the necessary ground clearance. Most of the other entry points in the south and the east of the country also involve very rough roads. The easiest entry points are on the north and west sides.

Hertz (☎ 314460), Avis (☎ 314325) and Budget (☎ 316344) have offices in Maseru (see Getting There & Away under Maseru later in this chapter). In Lesotho it is far more economical to use a car hired in South Africa; just ensure that you have the written agreement of the hirer. There is a road tax of M2, payable on leaving Lesotho.

Getting Around

AIR

Now that Lesotho Airways no longer operates, it's difficult to get around the country by air. Try Mission Aviation (☎ 325699) to arrange charter flights out of Maseru to various destinations in Lesotho.

BUS & MINIBUS TAXI

There is a good network of slow buses running to many towns. Minibus taxis are quicker but tend not to run long distances. In more remote areas you might have to arrange a ride with a truck, for which you'll have to negotiate a fare. Be prepared for long delays once you're off the main routes.

You'll be quoted long-distance fares on the buses but it's better to just buy a ticket to the next major town, as most of the passengers will get off there and you'll be stuck waiting for the bus to fill up again, and other buses might leave before yours. Buying tickets in stages is only slightly more expensive than buying a direct ticket.

Some examples of fares are: Maseru to Teyateyaneng, M5; Maseru to Maputsoe, M13; and Maseru to Thaba-Tseka, M26.

CAR & MOTORCYCLE

Driving in Lesotho is getting easier as new roads are built in conjunction with the massive Highlands Water Project, but once you get off the tar there are still plenty of places where even a 4WD will get into trouble. Apart from rough roads, rivers flooding after summer storms present the biggest problems, and you can be stuck for days. People and animals on the roads are another hazard.

There are sometimes army roadblocks, usually searching for stolen cars. If you're driving a car hired in South Africa, make sure that you have a letter from the rental agency giving you permission to take it into Lesotho.

The national speed limit is 80km/h and the speed limit in villages is 50km/h. Petrol is about the same price as it is in South Africa.

Before attempting a difficult drive, try to get some local knowledge of current conditions; ask at a police station. You might also ask at the bar in the Maseru Club where there is a good cross section of people who know all areas of Lesotho. There's a M50 fine for not wearing a seat belt.

ORGANISED TOURS

The tourist office in Maseru sporadically organises tours to places of scenic and cultural interest for locals. Day tours cost around M75 and there are sometimes weekend trips as well.

Malealea Lodge, near Mohale's Hoek, organises vehicle safaris and several tours are run from South Africa – ask around the hostels.

Several South African operators run tours up Sani Pass and a little way into Lesotho (see Places to Stay under Sani Pass later in this chapter and Sani Pass in the KwaZulu-Natal section in the South Africa chapter).

Maseru

Maseru has been a quiet backwater for much of its history. Kingsway was paved for the 1947 visit by the British royal family and remained the capital's only tarred road for some time. Most of Maseru's 110,000 people have arrived since the 1970s, yet despite its rapid expansion, and its status as a capital city, it remains a fairly easy-going place.

The 1998 invasion left many buildings scarred by torching and rampant looting. The city is now undergoing a major rebuilding program.

Orientation

Most places to stay, eat and shop are on or near Maseru's main street, Kingsway. It runs from the border post at Maseru Bridge right through town to the Circle, a traffic roundabout and landmark. At the Circle the street splits to become two important highways: Main North Rd and Main South Rd.

Information

The tourist office (☎ 313760, 312896, fax 310108) is on Kingsway, next to the Hotel Victoria. The staff are friendly and helpful, although they don't have much in the way of resources. The price guide for accommodation around the country and the cheap map of Maseru are handy.

The Department of Land Surveys & Physical Planning sells good topographic maps of the country. The office is open between 8 am and 12.45 pm, and 2 and 4.30 pm weekdays. It's on Lerotholi Rd, near the corner of Constitution Rd.

For bookings at Sehlabathebe National Park, contact the Conservation Division (☎ 323600, ext 30), in the Ministry of Agriculture (the sign says Bosiu Rural Development Project) on Raboshabane Rd, which is off Moshoeshoe Rd, near the train station.

Money Changing money is no hassle except for the short banking hours: 8.30 am to 3 pm weekdays (1 pm on Thursday) and 8.30 to 11 am Saturday. The last Friday of the month is pay day and there are huge, slow-moving queues.

Three banks – Lesotho, Nedbank and Standard – are all on Kingsway and the Standard has an unreliable ATM. These are the only places in the country where you can change money.

Post & Communications If you can help it don't use Maseru as a poste restante address, or you'll join the permanent group of people waiting to complain about missing mail. There was a public call centre where you could make international phone calls, but at the time of research it was closed.

Cultural Centres In Maseru there's a British Council, an Alliance Française on Kingsway and an American Cultural Center in the US embassy.

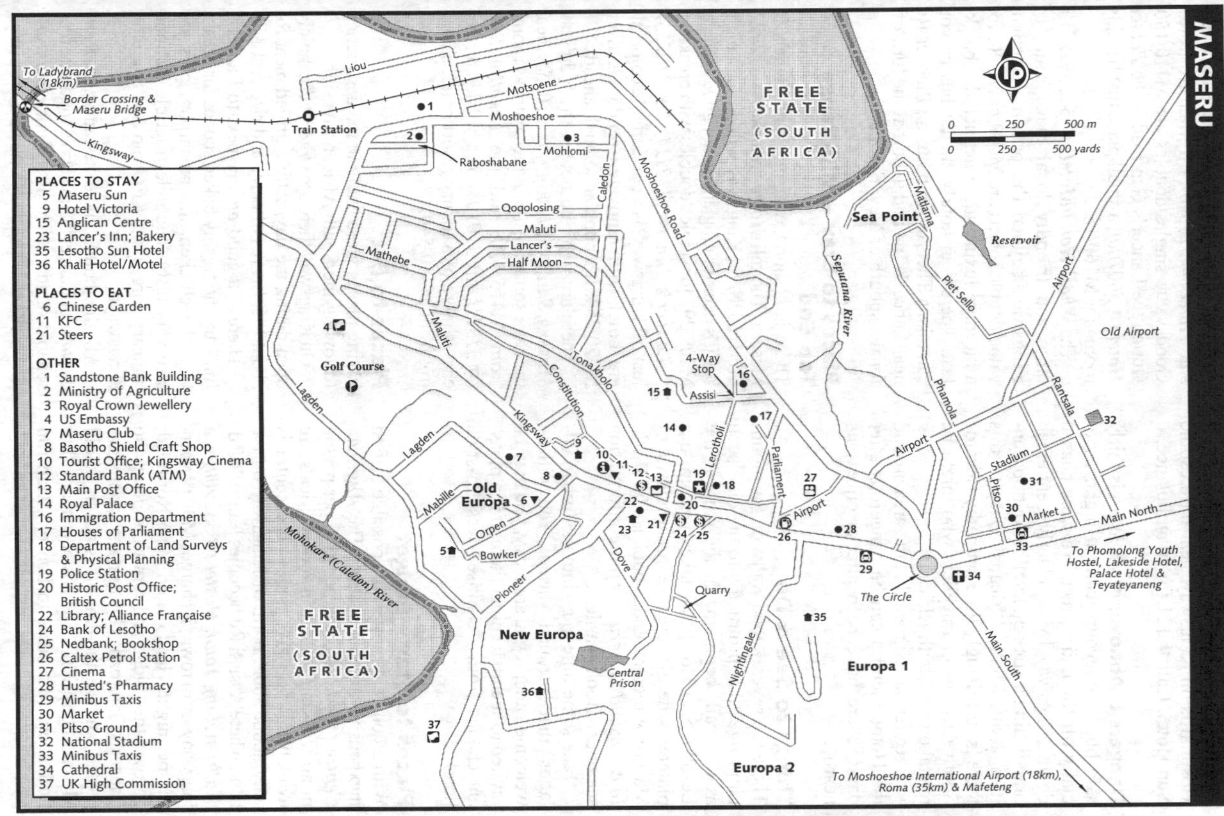
MASERU
PLACES TO STAY
5 Maseru Sun
9 Hotel Victoria
15 Anglican Centre
23 Lancer's Inn; Bakery
35 Lesotho Sun Hotel
36 Khali Hotel/Motel
PLACES TO EAT
6 Chinese Garden
11 KFC
21 Steers
OTHER
1 Sandstone Bank Building
2 Ministry of Agriculture
3 Royal Crown Jewellery
4 US Embassy
7 Maseru Club
8 Basotho Shield Craft Shop
10 Tourist Office; Kingsway Cinema
12 Standard Bank (ATM)
13 Main Post Office
14 Royal Palace
16 Immigration Department
17 Houses of Parliament
18 Department of Land Surveys & Physical Planning
19 Police Station
20 Historic Post Office; British Council
22 Library; Alliance Française
24 Bank of Lesotho
25 Nedbank; Bookshop
26 Caltex Petrol Station
27 Cinema
28 Husted's Pharmacy
29 Minibus Taxis
30 Market
31 Pitso Ground
32 National Stadium
33 Minibus Taxis
34 Cathedral
37 UK High Commission
0 250 500 m
0 250 500 yards
FREE STATE (SOUTH AFRICA)
FREE STATE (SOUTH AFRICA)
Mohokare (Caledon) River
Seputana River
Reservoir
Sea Point
Old Europa
New Europa
Europa 1
Europa 2
Central Prison
The Circle
Golf Course
Train Station
Old Airport
4-Way Stop
To Ladybrand (18km)
Border Crossing & Maseru Bridge
To Phomolong Youth Hostel, Lakeside Hotel, Palace Hotel & Teyateyaneng
To Moshoeshoe International Airport (18km), Roma (35km) & Mafeteng
Kingsway
Liou
Motsoene
Moshoeshoe
Raboshabane
Mohlomi
Caledon
Qoqolosing
Maluti
Lancer's
Half Moon
Mathebe
Lagden
Tonakholo
Constitution
Assisi
Moshoeshoe Road
Matlama
Piet Sello
Phamola
Rantsala
Airport
Stadium
Pitso
Market
Main North
Main South
Parliament
Lerotholi
Quarry
Nightingale
Dove
Pioneer
Bowker
Orpen
Mabille

LESOTHO

Medical Services The Queen Elizabeth II Hospital is on Kingsway, near the Lesotho Sun Hotel. Call ☎ 121 for an ambulance.

Dangers & Annoyances Maseru is fairly safe but be on your guard at night, especially off the main street. We were chased down Kingsway by an elderly gentleman brandishing a stick and yelling out obscenities about South Africans! Despite this there is surprisingly little antipathy towards South Africans or travellers who might be mistaken for South Africans.

A reader has warned that the area around the Hotel Victoria can be dangerous after dark. There have been attacks on expats nearby.

Things to See & Do

There are several good **walks** on the mountain ridges that protrude into the city, such as the walk beginning at the gate of the Lesotho Sun Hotel that takes you up to a plateau where there are great views of Maseru. A recommended book is *Hill Walks In & Around Maseru* (for more information see under Books earlier).

Take some time to go into the **'urban villages'** that surround Maseru. You will be welcomed and, if you are lucky, you may be invited to spend the night there. It is a pleasant change from a sanitised western-style hotel.

Places to Stay – Budget

With a couple of hostels it's possible to find inexpensive accommodation. The ***Anglican Centre*** *(☎ 322046)* charges M35 per person in austere dorms or twin rooms. Meals are available if you give notice. The centre is only about 500m north of Kingsway on the bend where Assissi Rd becomes Lancer's Rd.

Phomolong Youth Hostel *(☎ 332900)* is a long way from town; it charges M30 per person per night. Head out on Main North Rd, go over the bridge and turn right down the Lancer's Gap road. This turn-off is not signposted but near the turn-off is a sign, 'Gold Medal Enterprises'. The hostel is about 2km further on. Minibuses to Lancer's Gap run past it.

About 5km east of the centre is the ***Lakeside Hotel*** *(☎ 313646)*, off Main North Rd. Good value singles/doubles are M110/150. Out on the Lancer's Gap road is the ***Palace Hotel*** *(☎ 500700)*, a small place that has tidy rooms for M160/180.

The ***Khali Hotel/Motel*** *(☎ 322822)* is a large and friendly local place south of Kingsway, beyond the prison. Excellent value double rooms are M150 or M200, for a bit more luxury; the rate includes breakfast. There's an hourly shuttle bus or you can take a Thetsane minibus on Pioneer Rd near Lancer's Inn and get off at the turn-off for the suburb of New Europa.

Places to Stay – Mid-Range & Top End

There is a shortage of mid-range hotels in Maseru. The tall ***Hotel Victoria*** *(☎ 312922, fax 310318)* on Kingsway will do for a night but it's deteriorating and is not good value at M209/297 for singles/doubles with breakfast.

Lancer's Inn *(☎ 312114, fax 310223)*, just off Kingsway, is a comfortable colonial-era hotel with renovated rondavels from M220/254. It's popular so book ahead.

There are two Sun hotels: the indulgent ***Maseru Sun*** *(☎ 312434, fax 310158)* near the river south-west of Kingsway has rooms from M415/520; and the ***Lesotho Sun*** *(☎ 313111, fax 310104)* on a hillside further east is more of a luxury resort hotel, charging from M430/540.

Places to Eat

Eating places fared badly in the destruction following the South African invasion.

On Kingsway there are ***street stalls***, mainly open during the day, selling grilled meat for about M5. Serves of curry and rice cost M4.

There is a good ***bakery*** next to Lancer's Inn – try the freshly baked scones for breakfast; the chicken and mushroom pies are also very tasty. The indestructible fastfood industry forges on; ***KFC*** and ***Steers*** are on Kingsway.

All the hotels have restaurants. ***Rendezvous*** at Lancer's Inn serves food of a reasonable standard. The first-floor ***restaurant*** at the Hotel Victoria has pretty good food, but awful service at lunchtime. Burgers are M15 and appetising wood-fire-cooked pizzas are around M26.

Chinese Garden is a big place on Orpen Rd off Kingsway; the food is OK.

Entertainment

The *Maseru Club* is on Lagden Rd. It's a fine old colonial club and a meeting place for expats and aid workers. There's a bar and restaurant. It's easy to be signed in as a guest.

On top of the Hotel Victoria, *The Penthouse* has good jazz on weekends, with an entry charge of M15. The hotel's disco *Cross Roads* is in the building to the west of the tower. It is really worth a visit as many locals come here to dance into the wee hours.

Both Sun hotels have *bars* in which there are slot machines.

You can take in a movie at the *cinema*. Coming from the border end of town, turn left off Kingsway onto Parliament St and take the first street to the right (Airport Rd); the cinema is on the left, just a little way down the road.

Shopping

The Basotho Shield on Kingsway is a government-run craft shop. It's well worth a look but the prices are generally higher than you'll find in rural areas. If you plan on pony trekking or walking it's a good idea to buy a horsehair fly-whisk.

Thorkelds Weavers (☎ 316858) at 226 Moshoeshoe Rd, just before Caledon Rd, has been recommended by a reader. Apparently the tapestries are quite expensive, but you can see the weavers at work.

Getting There & Away

Bus & Minibus Taxi Buses and long-distance minibus taxis now congregate, haphazardly, in the streets north of the Circle. The destination of minibus taxis is displayed on the left side of the front window.

Fares from Maseru include: Mafeteng M10 (Mafeteng to Quthing M14); Pony Trekking Centre (God Help Me Pass) M12; and Mohale's Hoek M16.

Car Hertz (☎ 314460) is based in the Lesotho Sun Hotel; Avis (☎ 314325), slightly cheaper, is on Kingsway in the block east of the Bank of Lesotho and at the airport; and Budget (☎ 316344) is at 12 Orpen Rd, Old Europa.

Getting Around

To/From the Airport Moshoeshoe International Airport is 18km from town, off Main South Rd. The Khali Hotel/Motel's shuttle bus runs to the airport.

Local Transport The standard minibus taxi fare around town is M1.40. There are a few conventional taxi services – try Moonlite Telephone Taxis (☎ 312695).

Around Maseru

Most towns have risen around trading posts or protectorate-era administration centres and none approach Maseru in size or facilities.

THABA-BOSIU

Moshoeshoe the Great's mountain stronghold, first occupied in July 1824, is east of Maseru. Thaba-Bosiu (Mountain at Night), played a pivotal role in the consolidation of the Basotho nation. The name may be due to the site being first occupied at night, but another legend suggests that Thaba-Bosiu, a hill in daylight, grows into a mountain at night.

There's an information centre at the base of Thaba-Bosiu where you pay an M4 entry fee; an official guide will take you to the top of the mountain. There are good views from here including the Qiloane pinnacle, inspiration for the Basotho hat. On the summit are the remains of fortifications, Moshoeshoe's grave, and parts of the original settlement.

Places to Stay & Eat

About 2km before the Thaba-Bosiu visitors centre is the *Melesi Lodge (☎ 852116)* with singles/doubles for M150/250. The lodge has a terrific restaurant.

Getting There & Away

To get here from Maseru, look for a minibus taxi near the Circle; these go as far as the visitor centre (M5). If you're driving, head out on Main South Rd, take the turn-off to Roma and after about 6km (near Mazenod) turn off to the left. Thaba-Bosiu is about 10km further along.

BASOTHO PONY TREKKING CENTRE

The pony trekking centre is on the road between Maseru and Thaba-Tseka on the top of God Help Me Pass.

Treks range from a two-hour ride (about M35) to a week-long ride (about M400). There are minimum numbers required for some of the longer rides, but they are only two or four, so it's easy to get a group together. There are discounts for larger groups. Contact the tourist office in Maseru for details and bookings.

Accommodation on overnight treks is in villages along the way, and costs about M10 per person a night or M5 if you have a tent. This is not included in the trekking fees, so bring enough money to cover costs. You can't stay at the centre (although travellers have wangled floor space) so if your trek departs early in the morning you'll have to camp out or stay at the ***Molimo-Nthuse Lodge*** *(☎ 312922, 370211)*, 3km back down the pass. This means a steep walk the next morning. The lodge charges from M150/190 for singles/doubles (good value).

Pony treks are also available from Malealea Lodge (see Malealea later in this chapter) and from Semonkong Lodge (see Semonkong later in this chapter).

The bus trip to the centre from Maseru costs M10 and takes about two hours.

ROMA

Roma, only 35km from Maseru, is a university town and a good place to meet students. There are some attractive sandstone buildings dotted around the town and the entry to town by the southern gorge is spectacular.

North of Roma is the important **Ha Baroana** rock painting site. Although suffering from neglect and vandalism (including damage done by tourists who spray water on the paintings to produce brighter photos) this site is worth seeing.

To get to the paintings from Roma head back to the Maseru road and turn right onto the road heading west to Thaba-Tseka and the pony trekking centre. After about 12km turn off to the left, just after the Ha Ntsi settlement on the Mohlsks-oa-Tuka River. To get to the site by minibus taxi from Maseru, head for Nazareth and get off about 1.5km before Nazareth. A signpost indicates the way to the paintings off to the left. Follow the gravel track 3km to the village of Ha Khotso then turn right at a football field. Follow this track a further 2.5km to a hilltop overlooking a gorge. A footpath zigzags down the hillside to the rock shelter where the paintings can be found.

Places to Stay & Eat

The ***Trading Post Guest House*** *(☎ 340267)* is 2km west of Roma off the Maseru road. The trading post has been here since 1903, as has the Thorn family, who own the store and guesthouse. There are walks and horse riding in the area, including a 20-minute walk to dinosaur footprints. The accommodation is good value at M55 per person; camping costs M15 per person. There is no restaurant but you can use the kitchen. Everything is provided except towels.

In Roma, try the ***Speakeasy Restaurant***.

Getting There & Away

A minibus taxi from Maseru to Roma costs M4.30.

Northern Lesotho

TEYATEYANENG

Teyateyaneng (Place of Quick Sands) is usually known as TY. The town has been developed as the craft centre of Lesotho and there are several places worth visiting.

Some of the best tapestries come from Helang Basali Crafts in the St Agnes Mission, 2km before TY on the Maseru road. More tapestries are available from Hatooa-Mose-Mosali and wool products from Setsoto Design, Tebetebeng, and Letlotlo Handcrafts. About 10km north of town beyond the Phutiatsana River, in **Kolonyama**, is the largest pottery in Lesotho. Here beautiful stoneware products are fashioned from fine clay and minerals.

The ***Blue Mountain Inn*** *(☎ 500362)* has singles/doubles for M120/160 or you can camp (make sure you get permission from the local chief).

A reader recommends the drive on a good gravel road between Teyateyaneng and Mapoteng. He says that the villages along the road are unusually traditional for the lowlands.

MAPUTSOE

This border town, 86km north of Maseru, is across the Mohokare (Caledon) River from Ficksburg in South Africa. It has a shopping centre and a few other civic amenities, but its status as a black dormitory suburb of Ficksburg is still apparent – it is very rundown and impoverished. When it rains the streets turn to mud. Still, it is close to a border crossing with good transport connections, especially now that it is a gateway to the Highlands Water Project.

The run-down ***Sekekete Hotel*** *(☎ 430621)* charges R120/180 for singles/doubles, but you're better off staying across the border in Ficksburg (see Free State in the South Africa chapter).

LERIBE (HLOTSE)

A large town by Lesotho's standards, Leribe is a quiet village serving as a regional shopping and market centre. It was an administrative centre under the British and there are some old buildings slowly decaying in the leafy streets. **Major Bell's Tower**, on the main street near the market, was built in 1879.

There is a set of **dinosaur footprints** a few kilometres south of Leribe at Tsikoane village. Going north towards Leribe, take the small dirt road going off to the right towards some rocky outcrops. Follow it up to the church and ask someone to direct you to the *minwane*. It's a 15 to 20 minute slog up the mountainside to a series of caves. The prints are clearly visible on the ceiling of the rock.

About 10km north of Leribe are the **Subeng River dinosaur footprints**. There is a signpost indicating the river but not the footprints. Walk down to the river from the road to a concrete causeway (about 250m). The footprints of at least three species of dinosaur are about 15m downstream on the right bank.

Places to Stay & Eat

The ***Agricultural Training Centre*** is just outside town, or try the ***Catholic Mission*** about 10km past Leribe towards Butha-Buthe. The old-style ***Leribe Hotel*** *(☎ 400559)* on Main St has singles/doubles for M130/180. There is also a tea garden surrounded by well-established trees.

KATSE & THE HIGHLANDS WATER PROJECT

One of the benefits of the Lesotho Highlands Water Project is better accessibility for travellers into this remote part of Lesotho.

From Leribe (Hlotse) you can now take a tar road all the way to the project headquarters at Katse. When you near the dam, ignore the two turn-offs signposted 'Katse Dam' and keep going until you see signs directing you to Katse village. Here you'll find the information centre in some blue buildings by the workers' compound, and a viewpoint overlooking the dam wall. You need a permit from the information centre (which you might not get) to visit the project's headquarters (in the nearby large yellow building with a blue roof) and to get closer to the dam wall. Continue further along to get to Katse village, which is a rather dreary, modern development housing the project's management.

The ***Katse Lodge*** *(☎ 910202)* is modern and a reasonable standard but it can fill up with sightseers on weekends. Singles/doubles cost M121/196.

The spectacular road from Leribe to Katse passes the lowland village of Pitseng and climbs over the Maluti Mountains to drop to Ha Lejone, which one day will be at the edge of the dam's lake. It continues south past Mamohau Mission, crosses the impressive Malibamat'so Bridge, climbs over another series of hills to the Matsoku Valley, recrosses the Malibamat'so River and ends in Katse. From Katse, you can continue on an improved dirt road to Thaba-Tseka, 45km to the south.

There are taxis from Leribe to Katse (M30), and plenty of traffic if you want to hitch.

BUTHA-BUTHE

Moshoeshoe the Great named this town Butha-Buthe (Place of Lying Down) because it was here that his people first retreated during the difaqane. The small town is built alongside the Hlotse River and has the beautiful Maluti Mountains as a backdrop.

There are signs on the road to ***Ha Thabo Ramakatane Youth Hostel,*** though you may have to ask directions. It's about 4km from the village. There are no supplies so buy food in the village before arriving. There's no electricity; you cook using gas and you fetch your own water just as the villagers do. Basic accommodation costs about M30 per night.

The simple, clean ***Crocodile Inn*** *(☎ 460223)*, Reserve Rd, has singles/doubles from M96.50/126.50. The ***restaurant*** here is OK – it's probably the only adequate place to eat in town.

OXBOW

South African skiers used to come to Oxbow in winter but the place has slowly died as a ski resort. The large ***New Oxbow Lodge*** *(☎ 051-933 2247 in Ficksburg, South Africa, for bookings)* on the banks of the Malibamat'so River has a cosy bar and charges M215/390 for singles/doubles. A few kilometres further north is a ***private chalet*** belonging jointly to the Maloti and Witwatersrand University ski clubs. It's possible to sleep here for M25 although winter weekends are crowded. See the caretaker or write to Club Maluti, PO Box 783308, Sandton 2146, South Africa.

Eastern Lesotho

THABA-TSEKA

This remote town is on the eastern edge of the Central Range, over the sometimes tricky Mokhoabong Pass. It was established in 1980 as a centre for the mountain district.

You can usually get a bed at the ***Farmer Training Centre*** for about M20, and there's also a guesthouse.

About four buses a day run from Maseru to Thaba-Tseka (M25), but heading south from Thaba-Tseka to Sehonghong and Qacha's Nek is more difficult – you'll probably have to negotiate with a truck driver.

MOKHOTLONG

The first major town north of Sani Pass and Sehlabathebe National Park, Mokhotlong has basic shops and transport to Oxbow and Butha-Buthe. The town, about 270km from Maseru and 200km from Butha-Buthe, has the reputation as being the coldest, driest and most remote place in Lesotho. The horses 'parked' outside the shops give the town a wild west feel.

At the ***Farmer Training Centre*** a bed costs about M25 per night; there are cold-water washing facilities and a kitchen. The ***Lefu Senqu Hotel*** *(☎ 920330)*, 5km from the airport, has singles/doubles for M120/160.

About 15km south-west of Mokhotlong in Upper Rafalotsane village is the ***Molumong Lodge***; it costs M65 per person but you need to bring your own sleeping bag. There are three buses a day to the lodge from Mokhotlong.

SANI PASS

This steep pass is the only dependable road between Lesotho and KwaZulu-Natal. On the South African side the nearest towns are Underberg and Himeville.

From the chalet at the top of the pass there are several day walks, including a long and strenuous one to **Thabana-Ntlenyana** (3482m), the highest peak in Southern Africa. There is a path but a guide would come in handy. Horses can do the trip so consider hiring one.

Another walk leads to **Hodgson's Peaks**, 6km south, from where you get the benefit of views to Sehlabathebe National Park and to KwaZulu-Natal.

One three-day walk in this area that you could try before attempting something more ambitious is from the Sani Top chalet (at the top of Sani Pass), south along the edge of the escarpment, to the Sehlabathebe National Park. From here there's a track leading down to Bushman's Nek in South Africa. As the crow flies, the distance from Sani Top to Nkonkoana Gate is about 45km but the walk is longer than that. Much of this area is more than 3000m and it's remote even by Lesotho's standards – there isn't a horse trail much less a road or a settlement. Don't try this unless you are well prepared, experienced and in a party of at least three people.

Places to Stay

Sani Top, at the top of the pass, charges M150 per person including meals, or M40 for backpackers. There's a bar and self-catering facilities. (Travellers coming from South Africa should note that alcohol is likely to be confiscated at the Lesotho border.) In winter the snow is often deep enough to ski (there are a few pieces of antique equipment available at the chalet) and horse trekking is available with prior arrangement. Book accommodation and tours through Southern Drakensberg Tours (☎ 033-702 1158, e drakensberg.info@futurenet.org.za) in South Africa.

The other places to stay are the hostels on the South African side of the pass (see Natal-Drakensberg in the KwaZulu-Natal section in the South Africa chapter).

Getting There & Away

The South African border guards won't let you drive up the pass unless you have a 4WD, although you can come down from Lesotho without one (though it's not recommended). The South African border is open from 8 am to 4 pm daily; the Lesotho border stays open an hour later to let the last vehicles through. Hitching up or down the pass is best on weekends when there is a fair amount of traffic to and from the lodge.

South African hostels at the bottom of the pass arrange transport up the pass, and some agencies in Himeville and Underberg arrange tours. A minibus taxi from Underberg to Sani Top is about M20. There are a few minibus taxis running Basotho into South Africa for shopping, which cost much less. You might have to wait a day or so for one of these.

Public transport between Sani Top and the rest of Lesotho is sparse, but with patience you'll find something.

SEHLABATHEBE NATIONAL PARK

Lesotho's only national park, proclaimed in 1970, is remote and rugged and always an adventure to get to. The park's main attraction is its sense of separation from the rest of the world. Other than a rare Maloti minnow, thought to be extinct but rediscovered in the Tsoelikana River, rare birds such as the bearded vulture, and the odd rhebok or baboon, there are relatively few animals. As well as hikes and climbs, the park has horse riding (or 'equine rental'); guided horseback tours are M50.

This is a summer rain area and thick mist that's potentially hazardous to hikers is common. Winters are clear but cold at night and there are sometimes light falls of snow.

Near the village of Sehonghong, to the north-west of the park, is **Soai's Cave**. Soai, the last chief of the Maloti San people, was attacked and defeated here by Cape and Basotho forces in 1871.

For bookings at the park, contact the Conservation Division of the Ministry of Agriculture (☎ 323600, ext 30), PO Box 92, Maseru 100, Lesotho. Its building is on Raboshabane Rd, near the train station in Maseru (the sign says Bosiu Rural Development Project).

Places to Stay & Eat

You can camp in the park but there are no facilities (other than plenty of water) except at the ***Sehlabathebe Lodge***, where camping costs M10 per person. The lodge has singles/doubles for M30/50 and four-bed family rooms for M90. The entire lodge costs M240 per night. You can buy firewood and coal here, but for food (very limited) and petrol or diesel you'll have to rely on a small store about 4km west of the park entrance and quite a way from the lodge and hostel. You have to book the lodge in Maseru at the Conservation Division of the Ministry of Agriculture (see earlier for contact details).

In Sehlabathebe village, 1.5km down the road to Sehonghong, the ***Range Management Education Centre*** has dorms for M20 per person. A reader has recommended the ***Green Hotel***, which charges R35 for large rondavels with bathroom. It's about 18km from here to Sehlabathebe Lodge in the park.

Getting There & Away

Sometimes there are charter flights (see Getting Around earlier for details on Mission Aviation) from Maseru to Ha Paulus, a village near the park entrance, and you can arrange to be picked up from there for M40.

Driving into the park can be a problem in spring and summer, as the roads are 4WD tracks that become impassable after the heavy rains. Bear in mind that at the park you could be stuck waiting for a river to go down. Still, people usually do make it in and out without too many problems and most agree that the journey was worth it. The road-building accompanying the hydroelectric scheme should improve at least some of the routes. Check with the Conservation Division of the Ministry of Agriculture in Maseru when you book accommodation.

There are several routes into the park, all of which currently require a 4WD. The longest is the southern route via Quthing (Moyeni) and Qacha's Nek. There's also a route via Thaba-Tseka then down the Senqu River Valley past the hamlet of Sehonghong and over the difficult Matebeng Pass. The park can also be reached from Matatiele in the extreme west of KwaZulu-Natal. This route doesn't have as many difficult sections as the other routes but it is not well maintained so it is sometimes closed; check in Matatiele before trying it.

There is a daily bus between Qacha's Nek and Sehlabathebe village. This relatively short distance takes 5½ hours and costs M19; the bus departs from Sehlabathebe at 5.30 am and returns from Qacha's Nek at noon.

Probably the simplest way in is to hike the 10km up the escarpment from Bushman's Nek (South Africa). From Bushman's Nek to Nkonkoana Gate, the Lesotho border crossing, takes about six hours. You can also take a horse up or down for M40.

QACHA'S NEK

This pleasant town, with a number of sandstone buildings, was founded in 1888 near the pass (1980m) of the same name. There are Californian redwood trees nearby, some more than 25m high.

The ***Nthatuoa Hotel*** (☎ *950260)* offers adequate accommodation starting at M120/150 for singles/doubles. It is within easy walking distance of the airstrip.

There are cafes in town including the ***Vuka Afrika*** and you can get meals at the hotel.

Weather permitting (this area can get snowed in during winter), a bus to Sehlabathebe leaves daily at around noon (M20). There is more transport between here and Quthing (Moyeni). A bus leaves from both towns at 9 am, takes about six hours and costs M32. It is a spectacular drive.

Southern Lesotho

SEMONKONG

The **Maletsunyane Falls**, also known as Lebihan Falls after the French missionary who reported them in 1881, are about a 1½-hour walk from Semonkong (Place of Smoke). The 192m falls are at their most spectacular in summer and are best appreciated from the bottom of the gorge (where there are ***camp sites***).

The remote 122m **Ketane Falls** are also worth seeing. These are a solid day's ride (30km) from Semonkong or a four-day return horse ride from Malealea Lodge.

You can usually find a bed at the ***Roman Catholic Mission*** in Semonkong for a small contribution.

The ***Semonkong Lodge*** (☎ *051-933 3106 in Ficksburg, South Africa, for bookings)* charges M15 for a camp site, M35 for a dorm and M198 for a double/family room. The lodge offers hiking and pony trekking, with rates and options similar to those at the Malealea Lodge (see Malealea later in this section).

Buses between Maseru and Semonkong (M15) leave from both places in the morning and arrive late in the afternoon.

MORIJA

This small village, about 40km south of Maseru on the Main South Rd, is where you will find the **Morija Museum & Archives**

(☎ 360308). The collection includes archives from the first mission to Basutholand, and as the missionary was associated with Moshoeshoe the Great, the collection is of great importance. Part of the tea set given to the king by the mission society is on display at the museum, together with displays of Basotho culture, some finds from the Stone and Iron Ages, and dinosaur relics. The museum is open from 8 am to 5 pm Monday to Saturday and 2 to 5 pm Sunday; entry is M5.

Near the museum is the ***Mophato Oa Morija*** *(☎ 360308)*, an ecumenical centre with beds for M45 and camping for M20 per person. There's also ***Ha Matela Guest Cottages***, a pleasant self-catering cottage that costs M60 to M75 per person (no minimum number required). For bookings, call the museum and ask for Stephen Gill.

MALEALEA

This is one of the gems of Lesotho and is appropriately advertised as 'Lesotho in a nutshell'. You can go on a well-organised pony trek from here or wander on foot freely through the hills and villages.

The valleys around Malealea have been occupied for a very long time, as evidenced by the many **San paintings** in rock shelters.

Pony Trekking

Malealea Lodge is the best place in Lesotho to arrange pony trekking. These treks offer a good chance to come face to face with Basotho villagers as well as to experience the awesome scenery of the mountains and deep valleys. The treks are conducted with the full cooperation of the villagers. In fact, they act as guides and provide the ponies so if you undertake a trek you are contributing to the local village economy.

You need to bring food, a sleeping bag, rainwear, sunscreen, warm clothing, a torch (flashlight) and water purification tablets. A long ride can be hard on the legs and backside if you're not used to it, but if you're fit enough to mix it with some walking, you don't *have* to ride all day.

The pony treks are priced on a per-day basis. If there are two/three people, the cost for day rides is M110/100. Overnight rides cost M135 per person. There is an additional cost of M30 for each night spent in one of the Basotho village huts.

Walks

If you don't want to ride a pony, the owners of Malealea Lodge have put together a number of walking and hiking options, and also provide a map. They will arrange for your packs to be carried on ponies if you wish to go for longer than one day.

The walks include a two-hour return walk to the Botso'ela Waterfall; a six-hour return walk to the Pitseng Gorge (take your swimwear); a short, easy one-hour walk along the Pitseng Plateau; a walk along the Makhaleng River; and a hike from the Gates of Paradise back to Malealea. The scenery along these walks is nothing short of stunning and all include the local villages which dot the landscape.

Drives

Although it is slow-going on the dirt roads in this area, there are some very scenic drives. Perhaps the best is the road that forms part of the Roof of Africa Rally. Take a right turn at the first junction you come to when leaving Malealea, heading north. The road passes through some picturesque villages before crossing the top of the **Botso'ela Waterfall**. After a few kilometres it reaches an impressive lookout over the Makhaleng and Ribaneng Valleys. In a conventional car it takes one hour to reach the viewpoint from Malealea; rally drivers take 20 minutes to cover this distance!

If you continue north from the lookout to Sebelekoane, you can return to Maseru via Roma. This scenic road leads to Basotho villages and missions tucked away in the valleys. Be warned that it is rough in places and the going can be slow; allow three hours from Sebelekoane to Maseru.

Places to Stay

The ***Malealea Lodge*** *(☎ 051-447 3200 in Wepener, South Africa, for bookings, @ malealea@pixie.co.za)* is part of the original Malealea Trading Store established in 1905 by Mervyn Smith, a teacher, diamond miner and soldier. It is now run by the exceedingly friendly Mick and Di Jones. There is a variety of accommodation, including a dorm where beds are M40 per person, and rondavels are M70 per person. Rooms with bathrooms cost M100 to M150 per person and camping costs M20 per person. Meals are served if you give prior notice; there are self-catering facilities and the nearby shop is fully stocked.

About 6km from the Malealea Lodge turn-off is the ***Qaba Lodge*** *(☎ 051-922 370 in Ficksburg, South Africa, for bookings)*, which has accommodation in run-down surroundings for M50 per person; it also has a fully equipped kitchen, bar and store where you can buy supplies.

Getting There & Away

Travellers advise that from Maseru, a minibus to Motsekuoa, and from there another to Malealea, is the fastest public transport option (M13).

Maseru to Malealea is 83km. From Maseru, head south on the well-signposted Mafeteng road for 52km to the town of Motsekuoa. Look out for the Golden Rose restaurant, the proliferation of taxis and the huddles of potential passengers. Opposite the restaurant turn left (east) onto the dirt road and follow it for 24km. When you reach the signposted turn-off to Malealea, it is another 7km to the lodge. You know that you are on the right track when you pass through the Gates of Paradise and are rewarded with a stunning view of your destination. The plaque here reads 'Wayfarer – Pause and look upon a gateway of paradise'. Romantic stuff.

The road to Malealea from the south, via Mpharane and Masemouse, is much rougher. Most drivers take the Motsekuoa road.

The lodge can sometimes arrange transfers from Bloemfontein (if you're there, ask at Taffy's Backpackers – see Bloemfontein in the Free State section in the South Africa chapter).

MAFETENG

The name Mafeteng derives from 'place of Lefeta's people'. An early magistrate, Emile Rolland, was called Lefeta (or the 'one who passes by') by local Basotho. To the east is the 3096m Thaba Putsoa (Blue Mountain), the highest feature in this part of Lesotho.

There is not much of interest in town, although it is important as a bus and minibus taxi interchange.

The ***Mafeteng Hotel*** *(☎ 700236)* has singles/doubles for M180/230, and a restaurant.

MOHALE'S HOEK

This comfortable town is 125km from Maseru by tar road. The younger brother of Moshoeshoe the Great, Mohale, gave this land to the British for administrative purposes in 1884. It is a much nicer little place than nearby Mafeteng.

Mohale's Hoek has the ***Hotel Mount Maluti*** *(☎ 785224)* with singles/doubles from M140/170. There's a large garden with a pool and tennis court.

For desperadoes there is possibly a bed at the ***Farmer Training Centre*** for M20 per night.

QUTHING (MOYENI)

Quthing, the southernmost town in Lesotho, is often known as Moyeni (a Sephuthi word meaning 'place of the wind'). The town was established in 1877, abandoned three years later during the 1880 Gun War and then rebuilt at the present site.

Most of the town is in Lower Quthing. Up on the hill overlooking the dramatic Orange River Gorge is Upper Quthing, where there is a good hotel, a mission and sundry colonial-era structures. A minibus taxi between the two costs M1.50 – you can hitch but you should still pay.

Off the highway, about 5km west of Quthing, is the five-roomed **Masitise Cave House**. This mission building was built into a San rock shelter in 1866 by one Rev Ellenberger. His son Edmund, a latter day troglodyte, was born in the cave in 1867. Edmund later became the mayor of Bethlehem in the Orange Free State. Inquire at the school about access to the cave house and someone will unlock it for you. There are San paintings nearby.

Probably the most easily located of the **dinosaur footprints** in Lesotho are close to

Quthing. To get to them, go up the Mt Moorosi road from Quthing until you reach a thatch-roofed orange building. There is a short walk to the footprints, which are believed to be 180 million years old.

Between Quthing and Masitise there is a striking twin-spired **sandstone church**, part of the Villa Maria Mission.

At Qomoqomong, 10km from Quthing, there's a good gallery of **San paintings**; ask at the General Dealers store about a guide for the 20-minute walk to the paintings.

Places to Stay & Eat

The cheapest place is the ***Merino Stud Farm***, which has clean double rooms with bath for M35 per person; breakfast and dinner are about M10 each.

The ***Orange River Hotel*** *(☎ 750252)* in Upper Quthing is a pleasant place with stunning views across the gorge to the bleak hills beyond. Single/double rooms cost M77/115. There's a restaurant and a bar, but for a better place to drink, head up the driveway to the old thatched pub and sit with the locals on the lawn under an oak tree.

In Lower Quthing, the ***Mountain Side Hotel*** *(☎ 750257)* is a basic pub with a restaurant that might have rooms, depending on who's behind the bar when you ask. If you do get in, expect to pay M97/124.

Getting There & Away

Minibus taxis run daily between Maseru and Quthing (Moyeni).

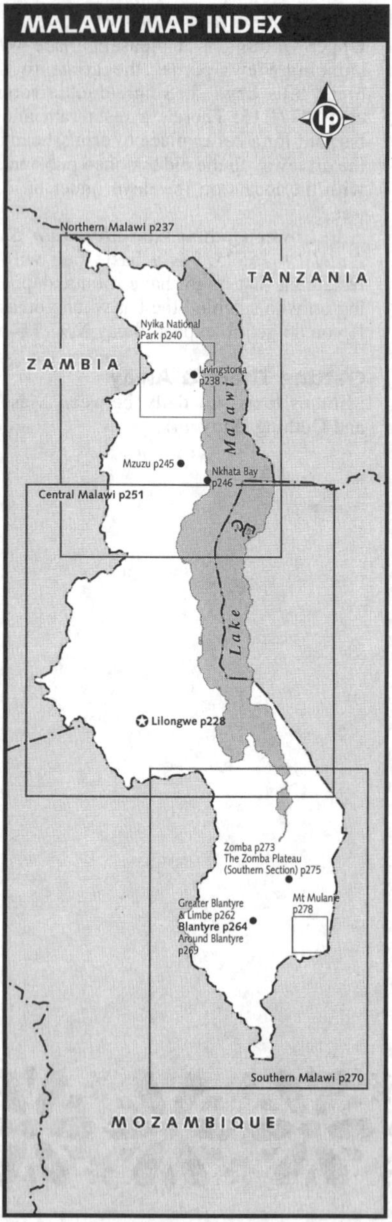

MALAWI MAP INDEX

Northern Malawi p237
TANZANIA
Nyika National Park p240
ZAMBIA
Livingstonia p238
Lake Malawi
Mzuzu p245
Nkhata Bay p246
Central Malawi p251
Lilongwe p228
Zomba p273
The Zomba Plateau (Southern Section) p275
Greater Blantyre & Limbe p262
Blantyre p264
Around Blantyre p269
Mt Mulanje p278
Southern Malawi p270
MOZAMBIQUE

DENNIS JOHNSON

Lake Malawi sunset

DAVID ELSE

Pounding maize, Livingstonia

Malawi

The tourist brochures bill Malawi as 'the warm heart of Africa' and, for once, the hype is true: Malawi's scenery is beautiful and (although we hate to generalise) Malawians really do seem to be among the friendliest people you could meet anywhere.

For most travellers, the country's main attraction is Lake Malawi, stretching some 500km along the eastern border. The high-profile Liwonde National Park is at the southern end of the lake, and there's an ever-increasing number of hotels, lodges and camping grounds being built along the western shore. The freshwater diving and snorkelling here are very highly rated.

Away from the lake are several more parks and reserves, and the highland wilderness areas of Mt Mulanje and the Nyika Plateau, where you find sheer escarpments, dramatic peaks, endless rolling grassland and some of the most enjoyable hiking routes in the whole of Africa.

MALAWI AT A GLANCE

Area: 118,484 sq km (land area 94,080 sq km)

Population: 11 million

Capital: Lilongwe

Head of State: President Bakili Muluzi

Official Languages: English, Chichewa

Currency: Malawi kwacha (MK)

Exchange Rate: US$1 = MK47

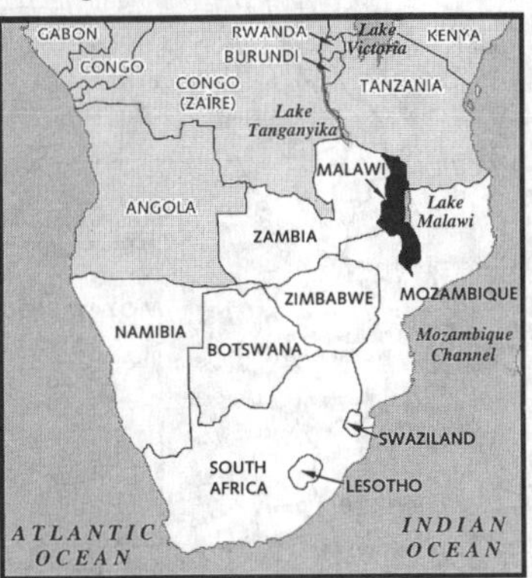

Highlights

- Lake Malawi – relax in budget beach-huts or high-class hotels, then go diving, snorkelling, birding and boating
- The *Ilala* – a trip on this historic steamboat is the best way to see the lake
- Liwonde National Park – see elephant, hippo and numerous birds in Malawi's flagship wildlife area
- Mt Mulanje – hike in awesome highlands, with easy access and wonderful views
- Vwaza Marsh & the Nyika Plateau – walk or horse ride in these fascinating and sharply contrasting wildlife areas
- Malawi's colonial heritage – marvel at the magnificent cathedrals of Blantyre and Likoma Island, or the missionary centre of Livingstonia

Facts about Malawi

HISTORY

The pre-colonial history of Malawi is linked to the history of Southern Africa as a whole. For more detail see the History section of the Facts about the Region chapter.

Bantu Migrations

The Bantu people had been migrating from Central Africa into the area now called Malawi since the first millennium, but significant groups called Tumbuka and Phoka first settled around the highlands of Nyika and Viphya sometime during the 17th century. Meanwhile, in the south, the Maravi people (of whom the Chewa became the dominant group) established a large and powerful kingdom that spread all over southern Malawi and parts of present-day Mozambique and Zambia.

The early 19th century brought two more significant migrations. The Yao invaded

southern Malawi from western Mozambique, displacing the Maravi, while groups of Zulu migrated northward to settle in central and northern Malawi (where they became known as the Ngoni).

The Rise of Slavery

Slavery, and a slave trade, had existed in Africa for many centuries, but in the early 19th century demand from outside Africa increased considerably. Swahili-Arabs, who dominated the trade on the east coast of Africa, pushed into the interior, often using the services of powerful local tribes such as the Yao to raid and capture their unfortunate neighbours. Several trading centres were established in Malawi, including Karonga and Nkhotakota – towns that still bear a strong Swahili-Arab influence today. (For more details on the slave trade, see the boxed text 'The Horrors of Slavery' in the History section of the Facts about the Region chapter.)

Early Europeans

The first Europeans to arrive in Malawi were Portuguese explorers who reached the interior from Mozambique. One of these was Gaspar Bocarro who, in 1616, journeyed from Tete (on the River Zambezi) through the Shire Valley to Lake Chilwa (to the south of Lake Malawi), then through the south of what is now Tanzania and back into Mozambique.

The most famous explorer to reach this area was David Livingstone from Scotland, even though his claim to have been the first European to see Lake Malawi is refuted by the records of another Portuguese called Candido da Costa Cardoso, who came here in 1846. However, Livingstone's exploration heralded the arrival of Europeans in a way that was to change the nature of the region for ever.

Livingstone & the First Missionaries

Between 1842 and 1856, Livingstone had been busy further south exploring the Kalahari Desert and the upper Zambezi. On his return to Britain, a speech in 1857 led to the founding of the Universities Mission in Central Africa (UMCA), which hoped to combat the slave trade by encouraging alternative commerce, and by establishing missions to promote Christianity.

Livingstone returned to Africa in 1858. His route up the Zambezi was blocked by the gorge and rapids at Cahora Bassa, so he followed a major Zambezi tributary called the Shire into southern Malawi. Blocked by more rapids at Kapichira, he continued on foot and in September 1859 finally reached Lake Malawi, which he named Lake Nyassa. He returned in 1861 with seven UMCA missionaries. They established a mission in the Shire Highlands, and later on the Lower Shire, but suffered terribly from malaria and other illnesses, and were in conflict with slave-traders and local people. In 1864 the surviving missionaries withdrew to Zanzibar.

In 1866 Livingstone returned to Malawi again, on his quest to find the source of the Nile. In July 1869 he pushed north, to be eventually found by Henry Stanley at Lake Tanganyika in 1871, when Stanley uttered the immortal phrase 'Dr Livingstone, I presume'. Refusing to return with Stanley, Livingstone doggedly continued on his quest, finally dying near the village of Chief Chitambo, south-east of Lake Bangweulu in Zambia, in 1873.

Livingstone's death rekindled missionary zeal; in 1875, a group from the Free Church of Scotland built a new mission at Cape Maclear, which they named Livingstonia. In 1876, the Established Church of Scotland built a mission in the Shire Highlands, which they called Blantyre. Cape Maclear proved to be malarial, so the mission moved to Bandawe, then finally in 1894 to the high ground of the eastern escarpment. This site was successful; the Livingstonia mission flourished and is still there today (see Livingstonia in the Northern Malawi section later in this chapter).

The Colonial Period

The early missionaries blazed the way for various adventurers and pioneer traders. In 1878 the Livingstonia Central African Mission Company (later renamed the African Lakes Corporation) was formed and built a trading centre in Blantyre. The company then established a commercial network along the Shire River and the shores of Lake Nyassa. As intended, this had a serious effect on the slave trade in the area, and after several clashes (the most notable being at Karonga) many slave-traders were forced to leave the area.

By the 1880s the competition among European powers in the area (known as the 'Scramble for Africa') was fierce. In 1889, Britain allowed Cecil Rhodes' British South Africa Company to administer the Shire Highlands, and in 1891 the British Central Africa (BCA) Protectorate was extended to include land along the western side of the lake. Sir Harry Johnston was appointed first commissioner. In 1907 the BCA Protectorate became the colony of Nyasaland, and the number of settlers increased further from then on.

Initially colonial rule had some positive effects on the Africans in the region. Firstly, the colonialists got rid of the slave-traders. The intertribal conflicts that had plagued the area for so long also ceased, and other spin-offs included improvements in health care. However, as more European settlers arrived, the demand for land grew, and vast areas were bought from local chiefs. The hapless local inhabitants of the land found themselves labelled 'squatters' or tenants of a new landlord. A 'hut tax' was introduced and traditional methods of agriculture were discouraged. Hence, increasing numbers of Africans were forced to seek work on the white-settler plantations or to become migrant workers in Northern and Southern Rhodesia (present-day Zambia and Zimbabwe) and South Africa. By the turn of the 18th and 19th centuries some 6000 Africans were leaving the country every year. (The trend continued through the colonial period: by the 1950s this number had grown to 150,000.)

Early Protest

The first serious effort to oppose the Nyasaland colonial government was led by Reverend John Chilembwe, who protested in his preaching about white domination, and later about the forced conscription of African men into the British army at the outbreak of WWI.

In January 1915, Chilembwe and his followers attacked and killed the manager of a large estate. His plan had been to trigger a mass of uprisings, but these failed or didn't materialise, and the rebellion was swiftly crushed by the colonial authorities. Chilembwe was executed, his church was destroyed, and many supporters were imprisoned. Today Chilembwe is remembered as a national hero, with many streets named in his honour.

Transition & Independence

After WWI, the British began allowing the African population a part in administrating the country. Things happened slowly, however, and it wasn't until the 1950s that Africans were actually allowed to enter the government. The economic front was similarly sluggish; Nyasaland proved to be a relatively unproductive colony with no mineral wealth and only limited plantations.

In 1953, in an attempt to boost development, Nyasaland was linked with Northern and Southern Rhodesia in the Federation of Rhodesia and Nyasaland. But African disenchantment with colonial rule continued, and the federation was opposed by the pro-independence Nyasaland African Congress (NAC) party, led by Dr Hastings Banda. The colonial authorities declared a state of emergency and Banda was jailed.

By mid-1960, Britain was loosing interest in its African colonies. Banda was released, and returned to head the now renamed Malawi Congress Party (MCP), which won elections held in 1962. The federation was dissolved, and Nyasaland became the independent country of Malawi in 1964. Two years later, Malawi became a republic and Banda was made president.

The Banda Years

President Banda began consolidating his position and demanded that several ministers declare their allegiance to him. Rather than do this, many resigned and took to opposition. Banda forced them into exile and banned other political parties. He continued to increase his power by becoming 'President for Life' in 1971, banning the foreign press, and waging vendettas against any group regarded as a threat. He established Press Holdings, effectively his personal conglomerate, and the Agricultural Development and Marketing Corporation, to which all agricultural produce was sold at fixed rates, and thus gained total economic control.

Alongside this move towards dictatorship, Banda remained politically conservative. South Africa, concerned about the regional rise of African-governed socialist states elsewhere in the region, was delighted to have an ally, and rewarded Malawi with aid and trade. The Organisation of African Unity (OAU) was furious at Banda's refusal to ostracise the South African apartheid

The Naming of Malawi

The derivation of the name Malawi is disputed. When the explorer David Livingstone first reached Lake Malawi he called it Lake Nyassa (derived from the word *nyanja*, which simply means 'lake' in the language of the indigenous Chewa people) and recorded in his journal that Maravi people inhabited the area. Chewa and Nyanja may be two names for the same people, although some authorities refer to them as separate but part of the larger Maravi group. During colonial times, when the country was known as Nyasaland, the language of the Chewa was called Chi-Nyanja (or Chinyanja). (It was renamed Chichewa in 1968 and became the national language.)

At independence in 1964 a commission was established to find a new name for the new country. Malaŵi was chosen – inspired by the word *malavi*, which means 'reflected light', 'haze', 'flames' or 'rays' in Chichewa. (The word is also spelt *maravi* – 'l' and 'r' seem interchangeable in Chichewa.) This new name was seen as a reference to the sun rising over the lake, bringing a fresh light to the country. It may also be connected to the Maravi people.

The 'ŵ' in Malawi was originally pronounced as a soft 'v'; English speakers should pronounce a sound somewhere between 'w', 'v' and 'f'. Nowadays the name of the country is generally pronounced with the 'w' sound, and the circumflex is often dropped.

regime, although some commentators argued that at least his approach was honest and avoided the hypocrisy of countries that outwardly condemned South Africa while secretly maintaining links.

In 1978, in the first general election since independence, Banda personally vetted every candidate, and demanded that each pass an English examination (thereby precluding 90% of the population). Even with these advantages, one Banda supporter lost his seat. He was simply reinstated.

Banda retained his grip on the country through the 1980s. The distinctions between the president, the MCP, the country, the government and Press Holdings became increasingly blurred. Quite simply, Banda *was* Malawi.

The end of the East-West 'cold war' in the 1990s meant South Africa and the west no longer needed to support Banda, and inside the country there was increasing opposition to him. In 1992, the Catholic bishops of Malawi condemned the regime and called for change. This was a brave action, for even bishops were not immune from Banda's iron grip. Demonstrations, both peaceful and violent, added their weight to the bishops' move. As a final blow, donor countries restricted aid until Banda agreed to relinquish total control.

In June 1993 a referendum was held for the people to choose between a multiparty political system and Banda's autocratic rule. Over 80% of eligible voters took part; those voting for a new system won easily, and Banda accepted the result.

Multiparty Democracy

Malawi's first full multiparty election (in May 1994) was a three-horse race between the United Democratic Front (UDF), led by Bakili Muluzi; the Alliance for Democracy (AFORD), led by trade unionist Chakufwa Chihana; and the MCP. Voting was largely along ethnic and regional lines: the MCP held the centre of the country, and AFORD dominated the north, but support in the more heavily populated south gave the UDF victory, although not an overall majority.

Once again, Banda accepted the result and Bakili Muluzi became Malawi's second president. He moved quickly – the political prisons were closed, freedom of speech and print was permitted, and free primary school education was to be provided. The unofficial night curfew that had existed during Banda's time was lifted. For travellers, the most tangible change was the repeal of Banda's notorious dress code that forbade women to wear trousers and men to have long hair.

The Muluzi government also made several economic reforms with the help of the World Bank and the IMF; these included the withdrawal of state subsidies and the liberalisation of foreign exchange laws. Further measures led to the closure of many state-owned businesses. The downside of this was a rise in unemployment. A rationalisation of the civil service was also planned, which would add to the job losses.

In April 1995, former president Banda was brought to trial (with five others, including his 'official hostess' Cecelia Kadzamira and her uncle John Tembo, former second-in-command of the MCP). They were accused of ordering the murder of three government ministers who died in a mysterious car accident in 1983. All were acquitted and the result was greeted with general approval, especially when Banda went on to apologise publicly. As the population warmed once more to Banda, it became clear that the UDF's honeymoon period was well and truly over. Running the country was proving a tough job. Civil servants had gone on strike in mid-1995, following pay and job cuts. A scandal involving ministerial funds surfaced briefly, but was weathered.

By 1996 the economic reforms were hitting the average Malawian citizen very hard. Food prices soared as subsidies were reduced or withdrawn. The price of bread doubled, and the price of maize flour (the country's staple) rose eight-fold between mid-1994 and mid-1996. Unemployment was officially recorded at 50%, but may have been higher. There were reports of increased malnutrition, especially among the young. Crime, particularly robbery, increased in urban areas. Matters were made worse by a slow resumption of international aid, after it had been frozen in the final years of Banda's rule.

Modern Times

In November 1997 Dr Banda finally died. His age was unknown, but he was certainly over 90. His death revived support for the MCP (now led by John Tembo), which was also helped by the continued poor performance of the UDF government. Unemployment and inflation remained high, while opposition politicians complained of corruption and mismanagement at the highest government levels. A UN report concluded that at least 70% of the population is nutritionally at risk.

Elections for the presidential and parliamentary elections were held in May 1999. President Muluzi won the race for president, and his party, the UDF, retained its majority in parliament, despite the two main opposition parties (MPC and AFORD) forming an alliance. Before and during the election the opposition accused the UDF of vote-rigging, and afterwards took their complaints to an electoral commission and then to the high court, claiming that Muluzi holding the position of president was unconstitutional.

While the MPs' claims and counter-claims are bandied back and forth, the ordinary people of Malawi have become increasingly cynical and mistrustful of their politicians, and apathetic about the entire democratic process. Many Malawians we spoke to during our research for this book ruefully admitted that the new freedom of speech is marvellous, but then politely pointed out that they now have no money and no food. When well-fed politicians are frequently seen in large cars, or reported to be voting themselves increased salaries, they do little to alleviate resentment. Claims in the press of massive corruption and mismanagement of funds only adds fuel to the fire.

The next elections are due in 2004. President Muluzi and the UDF have until then to make a significant change to the country they govern, and to satisfy the heightened expectations of the Malawian people.

GEOGRAPHY

Malawi is wedged between Zambia, Tanzania and Mozambique, measuring roughly 900km long and between 80km and 150km wide, with an area of 118,484 sq km.

Lake Malawi covers almost a fifth of Malawi's total area. A strip of low ground runs along the western lakeshore, sometimes 10km wide, sometimes so narrow there's only room for a precipitous footpath between the lake and the steep wall of the valley. Beyond the lake, escarpments rise to high rolling plateaus covering much of the country. Malawi's main highland areas are Nyika and Viphya in the north, and Mt Mulanje in the south.

Malawi's main river is the Shire (**shir**-ee); it flows out of the southern end of Lake Malawi, through Lake Malombe and then southward as the plateau gives way to low ground, to flow into the River Zambezi in Mozambique. In this area, the lowest point is a mere 37m above sea level.

CLIMATE

Malawi has a single wet season, from mid-October or early November to mid-April, when daytime temperatures are warm and conditions humid. May to August is dry and cool. In September and October, it can become hot and humid, especially in low areas.

Average daytime maximums in the lower areas are about 21°C in July and 26°C in January. In highland areas, average daytime temperatures in July are between 10°C and 15°C, while in September they reach 20°C and above. Average night-time temperatures in the highlands are low, sometimes dropping below freezing on clear nights in July.

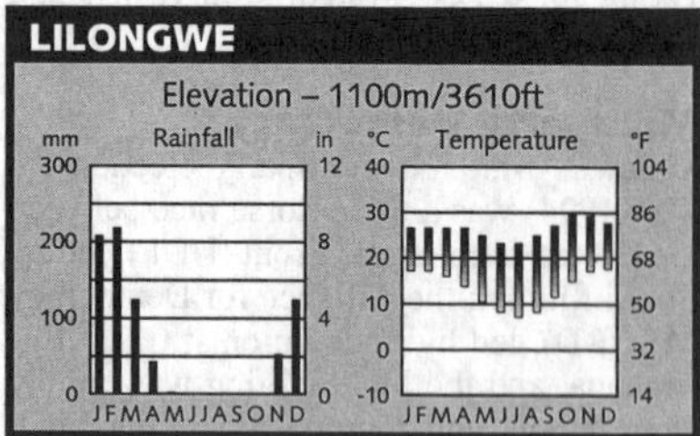

ECOLOGY & ENVIRONMENT

The main environmental challenges facing Malawi are deforestation and soil erosion, which result from a rapidly growing population and increasingly massive pressures on the land. Malawi has more people than Zambia, Namibia and Botswana combined, and is far smaller than any one of them. Put even more starkly, Malawi's population is about the same as Mozambique's, but Malawi is one tenth of the size, giving it one of the highest population densities in Africa.

Deforestation

In the mid-1970s Malawi's forest cover was 4.4 million hectares. It's now under two million, with 50,000 hectares being cleared each year, mostly for fuel. Although some replanting is taking place, at this current unsustainable rate the woodlands and forests will eventually disappear.

Areas of grassland and scrubland (low bush) throughout Malawi are also being cleared and the land used to cultivate crops. Much of this is marginal land (ie, with poor soil or on steep hillsides), which would previously have been ignored by farmers. Because the soil is exposed for part of the year it is often washed away by rain, and the problem is compounded by unreliable rainfall; some years there's no rain, so the crops fail and the bare soil is blown away by the wind. Even if the crops do grow, on the poor ground they tend to be stunted and low in nutrition. It's a grim scenario, and the end result is an increasing number of people living at starvation levels.

Overfishing

On Lake Malawi, things are also at a difficult stage. Traditionally, people living by the lake have enjoyed a better standard of living than their cousins in the highlands. Fish supplies were plentiful and a good source of protein. But once again the population growth means things have changed. The demand for fish has grown, so more fish are caught every year, to an extent that stocks are now taken from the lake at an unsustainable level. As demand increases, fishermen are using nets with smaller holes, so even the youngest fish are taken, which reduces next year's catch even further. The amount of fish eaten by the average Malawian has fallen to half its mid-1970s level, a fall that means more people are living nearer starvation levels.

There is a glimmer of hope on the fishing front. Whereas fishing on Lake Malawi used to be controlled by an inefficient government department, in some areas decisions regarding net sizes and closed seasons are now being made by local communities. It's hoped that local people now have more incentive to protect their fish stocks and harvest them at sustainable rates.

Poaching

Poaching of wildlife from national parks was a major environmental problem in the 1980s and early 1990s (despite lip service paid to conservation by the former government), and wildlife was severely depleted. This hit tourism – a major money-earner – in many parts of Malawi. The new government promised to combat poaching, but a lack of resources and commitment meant little changed. However, since the mid-1990s several parks and reserves have received funds from donor countries or organisations that should result in better anti-poaching measures, plus improved access roads, management and staff morale. Part of the deal in most cases is that accommodation is leased out to private companies instead of being run by the Department of National Parks and Wildlife. This attracts tourists back, and is better for Malawi in the long run. Ideally, in the future, park management will also be leased to private companies, and operated with the backing of (and for the benefit of) local communities, but this is still a long way off.

FLORA

For an overview of Southern Africa's vegetation zones, see the Vegetation section of the Facts about the Region chapter.

Malawi's vegetation zones include: miombo woodland in reliable rainfall areas (eg, Kasungu National Park); mopane woodland in hot lowland areas (eg, Shire Valley, lakeshore plains, Liwonde National Park); montane evergreen forest in highland areas (eg, Mulanje); semi-evergreen forest along river courses and on escarpment sides (eg, Zomba); montane grassland between 1800m and 2000m (eg, the Nyika Plateau); dense riverine woodland (eg, along the shores of

The sausage tree is named after the shape of its fruit, each of which weighs up to 10kg.

Lake Malawi and along riverbanks); and wetland areas of reeds and grasses (all over the country – known locally as *dambos*).

FAUNA

For detailed information on Southern Africa's indigenous animals, see the colour Wildlife Guide earlier in this book.

Because Malawi lacks vast herds of easy-to-recognise animals such as rhino and lion, it is not considered a major wildlife-viewing country. However, for those less concerned with simply ticking off the 'big five', the country has plenty to offer. The country's main park is Liwonde, noted for its herds of elephant, plus hippo and plenty of antelope (including impala, bushbuck and kudu). Elephant also inhabit Kasungu National Park, as do buffalo, zebra, several antelope species and hippo. Nyika National Park is renowned for roan antelope and reedbuck, plus zebra, warthog, eland, klipspringer, jackal, duiker and hartebeest. There's also a chance of seeing hyaena and leopard. Nearby Vwaza Marsh is renowned for its hippo, and elephant, buffalo, waterbuck, eland, roan, sable, hartebeest, zebra, impala and puku are also present. In southern Malawi, Lengwe National Park supports a population of nyala – at the northern limit of its distribution in Africa.

Birds common to the Southern African region are covered in the special section 'Birds of Southern Africa'. Malawi is a bird-watcher's dream because there's a good range of habitats in a relatively small area; over 600 species have been recorded, with several from the Central and East African regions.

Lake Malawi has more fish species than any other inland body of water in the world, with a total of over 500, of which more than 350 are endemic. (For more information see the boxed text 'Cichlid Fish' in the Central Malawi section later in this chapter.)

NATIONAL PARKS & WILDLIFE RESERVES

Malawi has five national parks: Liwonde, Lengwe, Kasungu, Nyika and Lake Malawi (around Cape Maclear). There are also four wildlife reserves: Vwaza Marsh, Nkhotakota, Mwabvi and Majete, which are less developed than the national parks, with fewer accommodation options and a more limited network of roads and tracks (if they exist at all). For more information on the facilities at each park and reserve see their individual listings later in this chapter.

Malawi also has many forest reserves including Mt Mulanje and the Zomba Plateau. Some forest reserves have resthouses, and there's a series of huts on Mulanje for hikers.

Fees

All parks and reserves (except Lake Malawi) cost US$5 per person per day (each 24-hour period), plus US$2 per car per day. Citizens and residents pay less. Other costs are for optional services: a fishing licence costs US$4; hire of a game scout guide to ride with you costs US$2. All fees are payable in kwacha. (Guiding fees are paid to the park, so it is usual to tip the scouts an extra US$2 or so.)

On top of these fees you pay for your accommodation; camping grounds and lodges are run by private safari companies in the most popular parks and reserves, but oper-

National Park Maps

The maps of national parks in this Malawi chapter show main routes only. It is not possible to show all roads: many original tracks have become overgrown or simply disappeared; some tracks are lost after heavy rains and rebuilt in other positions; and several new routes will be built as part of planned rehabilitation schemes.

ated by the government national parks department elsewhere.

Details of accommodation options in each park and reserve are given in the relevant sections.

GOVERNMENT & POLITICS

Malawi has a parliamentary system of government, with elections every five years. Separate presidential elections are held at the same time. The main parties are the Malawi Congress Party (MCP), the Alliance for Democracy (AFORD), and the United Democratic Front (UDF).

There are no major ideological differences between the various parties, except that the MCP is considered more 'traditional' or 'conservative'. Party following is based largely on regional or ethnic allegiances, and although various matters are hotly debated in parliament, there is very little genuine discussion on issues or policies. See the History section at the beginning of this chapter for more on government and politics.

ECONOMY

Malawi's economy is dominated by agriculture. Tobacco accounts for more than 60% of the country's export earnings. It is grown on large commercial plantations and on smaller farms cultivated by single families. Tea and sugar make up another 20% of export earnings. Tourism is seen as a great potential foreign currency generator, but has yet to be exploited fully.

For the average Malawian, economic conditions are not good. Malawi remains one of the world's 10 poorest countries, with a per capita gross national product (GNP) of US$180. Other socio-economic indicators paint a grim picture: the population growth rate is around 4% per year; infant mortality is around 20%; and Malawi has the second-highest disparity between rich and poor in the world.

In 1998 the Malawi kwacha was devalued by around 50%. This meant prices for some items, including staple foods such as maize flour, went up by over 80%. This had a devastating effect on local people, but because exchange rates also increased it had little effect on foreign visitors. Inflation ran at about 50% through 1998, but levelled out in 1999, although economic mismanagement and political uncertainty have hindered domestic investment. Meanwhile, the national debt is reported to be around US$2 billion, with very little prospect of it being reduced. Unemployment is also alarmingly high. In January 1999 *Africa Today* magazine reported that of every 250,000 young Malawians entering the job market each year, only 16,000 to 20,000 will get jobs – far less than 10%.

Press Holdings, the giant business group that was owned by former president Banda and controlled or had interests in virtually all of Malawi's economic activity, was confiscated from Banda in 1995 and became a nominally independent trust. Despite these reforms, since the 1999 election, political opponents of the UDF have said that the ruling party still has an unwarranted degree of control and influence in the Press Holdings group of companies.

POPULATION & PEOPLE

Estimates put Malawi's total population between 11 and 12 million. About 85% of the people live in rural areas and are engaged in subsistence farming or fishing, or working on commercial farms and plantations.

The main ethnic groups are: Chewa, dominant in the central and southern parts of the country; Yao in the south; and Tumbuka in the north. Other groups are: Nguni, in parts of the central and northern provinces; Chipoka, also in the central area; and Tonga, mostly along the lakeshore. There are small populations of Asians and Europeans involved in commerce, plantations, aid or the diplomatic service. They are found mainly in the cities.

ARTS

Dance & Music

The most notable traditional dance in Malawi is the 'Gule Wamkulu' of the Chewa people, which reflects their beliefs in spirits and is connected to activities of their secret societies. Leading dancers dress in ragged costumes of cloth and animal skins, usually wearing a mask and occasionally on stilts.

Home-grown contemporary music is not a major force in Malawi as it is in, say, Zimbabwe. Among local musicians, the most influential and popular is Lucius Banda, who plays soft 'Malawian-style' reggae with his band Zembani. Other reggae names to look out for are Billy Kaunda, Paul Banda and the Aleluya Band. Bubulezis play a Jamaican-style reggae, while the Sapitwa Band tends towards Congo-style rhumba. Also popular is Ethel Kamwendo, one of Malawi's leading female singers.

Visual Arts & Crafts

You'll see woodcarvings and stone carvings in craft shops and markets all over the country, but you won't find anything there by Kay Chirombo, Lemon Moses, Willie Nampeya, Berling Kaunda, Charley Bakari or Louis Dimpwa. These are some of Malawi's leading artists, producing sculpture, batiks and paintings, and many have exhibited outside Malawi. Possibly the best-known artist is Cuthy Mede – he is also actively involved in the development and promotion of Malawian art within the country and around the world. (See also Shopping in the Facts for the Visitor section later in this chapter.)

MALAWI

Literature

Like most countries in Africa, Malawi has a very rich tradition of oral literature. Since independence, a new school of writers has emerged, although thanks to the despotic President Banda's insensitivity to criticism, many were under threat of imprisonment and lived abroad until the mid-1990s. Not surprisingly, oppression, corruption, deceit and the abuse of power are common themes in their writing.

If you want a taste of current literature by well-known or new writers, try any of the short novels or poetry collections under the Malawi Writers Series imprint, available in good bookstores in Blantyre and Lilongwe. Most cost less than US$1.

Poetry is very popular: Steve Chimombo is a leading poet whose collections include *Napolo Poems*. His most highly acclaimed work is a complex poetic drama, *The Rainmaker*. To many Malawians he is better known for his popular short stories in newspapers and magazines, which touch on a strange but vivid combination of traditional themes and harsh urban settings.

Jack Mapanje's first poetry collection *Of Chameleons and Gods* (published in 1981), with much of its symbolism (chameleons play an important role in traditional Malawian beliefs) obscure for outsiders. Not too obscure for President Banda though – in 1987 Mapanje was arrested and imprisoned without charge. He was released in 1991, and two years later published *The Chattering Wagtails of Mikuyu Prison* – a reference to Malawi's notoriously harsh political jail.

Another significant literary figure is David Rubadi, who has compiled an anthology called *Poetry from East Africa* (which includes a section on Malawi) and also writes poetry himself. His novels include *No Bride Price*, which discusses the familiar themes of corruption and oppression.

Most critics agree that Malawi's leading novelist is Legson Kayira, whose semi-autobiographical *I Will Try* and *The Looming Shadow* earned him acclaim in the 1970s. A later work is *The Detainee*. Another novelist is Sam Mpasu. His *Nobody's Friend* was a comment on the secrecy of Malawian politics – it earned him a 2½-year prison sentence. After his release he wrote *Prisoner 3/75*, and later became minister for education in the new UDF government. His comments on the time of Banda's rule sum up the situation for all Malawian writers, and the people of Malawi too: 'We had peace, but it was the peace of a cemetery. Our lips were sealed by fear'.

LANGUAGE

English is the official language and very widely spoken. All the different ethnic

Banning the Press

It's worth noting that it wasn't only works of literature that incurred the wrath of President Banda. Several books on contemporary history were also banned, including, perhaps not surprisingly, *Malawi – the Politics of Despair*. Newspapers from other countries and from within Malawi were also frequently barred from circulation, especially if they were seen to be critical, but sometimes even if they weren't. Any form of pornography was also prohibited, but this included several medical textbooks, on the grounds that the diagrams were indecent. Even guidebooks didn't escape; an early Lonely Planet book called *Africa on the Cheap* (forerunner of *Africa on a shoestring*) was critical of the regime in the Malawi chapter, and was promptly banned as well. This meant travellers with a low-budget look were often searched for the scurrilous tome, and when I first visited Malawi in the early 1980s, getting across the Songwe border with the book intact was notoriously difficult.

David Else

groups in Malawi also have their own language or dialect.

The Chewa are the dominant group and Chichewa is the national language, widely used throughout the country as a common tongue. (The 'Chi' prefix simply signifies 'language of'.) Of the other languages Tumbuka is dominant in the north, and Yao in the south. See the Language chapter for some useful words and phrases in Chichewa, Tumbuka and Yao.

Facts for the Visitor

SUGGESTED ITINERARIES

Malawi is the smallest country in the region and most of its attractions are relatively easy to reach. If you've come mainly to see wildlife, then a visit to Liwonde National Park is highly recommended. Nyika National Park and Vwaza Marsh Wildlife Reserve are also rewarding.

If you simply enjoy wilderness, then Malawi's parks can provide the required atmosphere, as can the reserves of Majete and Nkhotakota. Lake Malawi National Park is not really wilderness, but this patch of lakeshore and nearby islands is a major highlight for most travellers.

If you're a keen birdwatcher, then any park or reserve will keep you busy for days, as will, of course, the lakeshore. More obscure places, such as the Elephant Marsh or Dzalanyama Forest, are also worth a visit.

If you're into water sports, particularly diving or snorkelling, then Lake Malawi will feature largely in your plans. But beware of bilharzia (see the boxed text 'The Great Bilharzia Story' later in this section).

For hiking and trekking, the main highland areas are Mt Mulanje and the Nyika and Zomba Plateaus. Nyika is also particularly well known for its wildflowers.

Two Weeks

A two-week tour might go as follows: from Lilongwe, head for the lakeshore (eg, Senga Bay, Cape Maclear or Club Makokola), continue to the pleasant town of Mangochi, then visit Liwonde National Park. Go on to Zomba, famous for its huge market and the nearby Zomba Plateau, with good hiking, excellent views and several good places to stay. Continue south to Blantyre, from where you can head east through the tea plantations to Mt Mulanje (then go walking for a day or trekking for a week according to your inclin- ation), or south, down the escarpment to the Lower Shire area, taking in Lengwe National Park or Majete Game Reserve and possibly the Elephant Marsh. From there, return to Blantyre and go back to Lilongwe via Dedza.

Alternatively, in two weeks you could go north from Lilongwe via Kasungu National Park or the Viphya Plateau to Mzuzu, from where you can reach Vwaza Marsh, Nyika Plateau and Livingstonia's historic sites, plus the beaches and quiet villages of the northern lakeshore. Return to Lilongwe on the road via Nkhata Bay, Nkhotakota or Salima.

One Month

With a month or longer at your disposal you could visit both the north and south as described earlier, and divert to more-out-of-the-way places such as Likoma Island. Or maybe you'd prefer to spend the time learning to dive, or simply lazing on the beach.

Another loop from Lilongwe that is becoming increasingly popular is a visit to South Luangwa National Park in neighbouring Zambia, to see large-scale wilderness and sheer quantities of wildlife that Malawi cannot offer (see the Eastern Zambia section of the Zambia chapter). Tours are organised in Lilongwe (see Travel Agencies & Tour Companies in the Lilongwe section later in this chapter).

PLANNING

When to Go

The best time to visit Malawi is during the dry season from April/May to October. From May to July the landscape is attractive because the vegetation is green and lush. Malawi is coolest in July, increasingly warm towards September and when the landscape starts to dry out, positively hot in early October before the rains break. Late in the dry season is the best time for wildlife viewing, but conditions can be very hot.

Maps

Useful maps, available in local bookstores, include the government-produced *Malawi* (1:1,000,000), showing shaded relief features and most roads, and *Malawi Road & Tourist Map* (same scale), showing all main roads, some minor roads and national parks (but no relief) plus street maps of the main towns.

For more detail, government survey maps (1:50,000 and 1:250,000) are available from the Department of Surveys public map sales offices in Blantyre and Lilongwe. Specific maps and guidebooks on national parks and hiking areas are detailed under the listings for these areas.

TOURIST OFFICES

There are tourist offices in Blantyre and Lilongwe, and there are Department of Wildlife & Tourism offices in Lilongwe (see that section for details). Outside Malawi, tourism promotion is handled by UK-based Malawi Tourism (☎ 0115-982 1903, fax 981 9418, e enquiries@malawitourism.com), which responds to inquiries from all over the world. Web site: www.malawitourism.com

VISAS & DOCUMENTS

Visas

Visas are not needed by citizens of Commonwealth countries, the USA and most European

Visas for Onward Travel

If you need visas for neighbouring countries while in Malawi, these are the conditions:

Mozambique

Visas are available in Lilongwe and Limbe; both offices are open from 8 am to noon weekdays. Transit visas cost US$5 (US$10 for double transit), and are issued within 24 hours. One-month single-entry visas cost US$10 and take a week to issue, although four-day service costs US$15, and next-day service costs US$20. A three-month multiple-entry visa is US$30. All fees are payable in kwacha.

South Africa

Visas are free and take two days to issue. The high commission in Lilongwe is open from 8 am to noon weekdays.

Tanzania

Be warned that there is no Tanzanian representation in Malawi, so if you need a visa it must be obtained elsewhere – Lusaka (Zambia) and Harare (Zimbabwe) are the closest places. If you're flying into Tanzania, you can get a visa at the airport on arrival.

Zambia

Visas are issued on the same day if you come early. The cost depends on your nationality: Brits pay US$60 for a single entry; all others pay US$25, except Norwegians (free). Payment in US dollars is preferred. The office in Lilongwe is open from 9 am to noon weekdays.

Zimbabwe

Single-entry visas for up to six months cost US$35 (payable in kwacha) and take a week to issue. The office in Lilongwe is open from 8 am to 12.30 pm weekdays. Visas are also available at the border and are probably cheaper there.

nations (except France). Visas are limited to 30 days, although extensions are easy to get.

Visa Extensions

You can get extensions at immigration offices in Blantyre or Lilongwe (see those sections for details) or at regional police stations. The process is straightforward and free.

EMBASSIES & CONSULATES

Malawi Embassies & High Commissions

Malawi has diplomatic missions in the following African countries: Kenya, Mozambique, South Africa, Tanzania, Zambia and Zimbabwe (embassies for countries in this book are listed in the relevant country chapters). Elsewhere around the world, Malawian embassies include:

Canada
High Commission: (☎ 613-263 8931) 7 Clemow Ave, Ottawa, Ontario KIS 2A9
France
Embassy: (☎ 01 47 20 20 27) 20 Rue Euler, 75008 Paris
UK
High Commission: (☎ 020-7491 4172) 33 Grosvenor St, London W1X 0DE
USA
Embassy: (☎ 202-797 1007) 2408 Massachusetts Ave, Washington DC 20008

Malawi has no high commission in Australia, but is represented by the Consular Office, Australian Department of Foreign Affairs and Trade (☎ 02-6261 3305), John McEwen Crescent, Barton, ACT 2600.

Embassies & Consulates in Malawi

The following countries have diplomatic representation in Malawi:

Germany
Embassy: (☎ 782555) Convention Dr, City Centre, Lilongwe
Mozambique
High Commission: (☎ 784100) Commercial Bank Bldg, African Unity Ave, City Centre, Lilongwe
Consulate: (☎ 643189) Chilembwe Hwy, Limbe
South Africa
High Commission: (☎ 783722) off Kenyatta Rd, City Centre, Lilongwe
UK
High Commission: (☎ 782400) off Kenyatta Rd, City Centre, Lilongwe
Consulate: Hanover Ave, Blantyre
USA
Embassy: (☎ 783166) off Kenyatta Rd, City Centre, Lilongwe
Zambia
High Commission: (☎ 782100, 782635) off Convention Dr, City Centre, Lilongwe
Zimbabwe
High Commission: (☎ 784988) off Independence Dr, City Centre, Lilongwe

CUSTOMS

There are no restrictions on the amount of foreign currency that travellers can bring into or take out of Malawi. Technically, import or export of more than MK200 is forbidden, but a bit more than this is unlikely to be a problem.

MONEY

Currency

Malawi's unit of currency is the Malawi kwacha (MK). This is divided into 100 tambala (t). Bank notes include MK200, MK100, MK50, MK20, MK10 and MK5. Coins include MK1, 50t, 20t, 10t, 5t and 1t, although the small tambala coins are virtually worthless.

Inflation is high in Malawi, so quoting costs in MK is not helpful, as prices may have changed significantly by the time you arrive. Therefore we have used US dollars (US$) throughout this chapter. Although the actual exchange rate will have changed by

'Sorry, No Change'

The lack of small coins and notes in shops and markets constantly frustrates travellers, who inevitably get large denomination notes when they change money in the banks and bureaus. Get and keep as much small change as you can, especially if you're going to Lake Malawi. Otherwise you'll end up with a pocket full of 'Cape Maclear currency' – little bits of cardboard saying 'I owe you 3 kwacha'.

the time you reach Malawi, the cost of things in US dollars (or any other hard currency) will not have altered much. At big hotels and other places that actually quote in US dollars you can pay in hard currency or kwacha at the prevailing exchange rate.

Exchange Rates

The following rates were correct at the time of print:

country	unit		Malawi kwacha
Australia	A$1	=	MK29
Canada	C$1	=	MK32
euro	€1	=	MK45
France	10FF	=	MK69
Germany	DM1	=	MK23
Japan	¥100	=	MK44
New Zealand	NZ$1	=	MK23
South Africa	R1	=	MK7
UK	UK£1	=	MK74
USA	US$1	=	MK47

Exchanging Money

You can exchange cash and travellers cheques at the National Bank of Malawi and the Commercial Bank of Malawi (for opening hours, see Business Hours later in this section). The charge is usually 1% of the transaction amount; for travellers cheques the bank also checks the original purchase receipt.

There are foreign exchange bureaus in the cities and large towns. These usually offer a slightly better rate than the banks, and have lower charges (or none at all), so are worth checking.

There's no real black market. You may get one or two kwacha more for your dollar on the street, but the chances of robberies or cons (or fake US$50 and US$100 bills) make this not worth the risk. Alternatively, shops that sell imported items sometimes need dollars and buy at around 5% to 10% more than bank or foreign exchange bureau rates.

Credit & Debit Cards You can get cash with a Visa card at branches of the Commercial Bank in Blantyre and Lilongwe. The charge is US$2; the process sometimes takes several hours, but if you go in the morning before 9 am it can be quicker. Otherwise, leave your card and details, and come back later to pick up your cash. No card transactions are started after 1 pm.

You can use Visa cards at some but not all of the large hotels and top-end restaurants (be warned that this may add a 5% to 10% surcharge to your bill). It seems even harder to use a MasterCard, although Diners Club card is accepted at a few places in Blantyre and Lilongwe that won't take Visa. If you usually rely on plastic, you're better off using it to draw cash and paying with that.

Costs

A general overview of day-to-day travel costs throughout Southern Africa is given in the Regional Facts for the Visitor chapter. Generally, costs in Malawi are low compared to costs in most other countries in the region, although some national park accommodation is relatively expensive. (More details on costs of accommodation and transport in Malawi are given in the Accommodation and Getting Around sections later in this chapter.)

Details of fees and accommodation costs in Malawi's national parks and wildlife reserves are given in the relevant sections. Malawi's national parks generally cannot be reached by public transport and so require most visitors to take relatively expensive transfers by boat or vehicle (details are given in the national park sections). Other activities such as hiking and various water sports are cheap compared to other countries in the region.

POST & COMMUNICATIONS

Post

Post in and out of Malawi is a bit of a lottery. Some letters get from Lilongwe to London in three days, while others take three weeks. Mail from Lilongwe or Blantyre to Cape Town often takes a month. In rural areas, the post can be very slow. The post offices in Blantyre and Lilongwe have poste restante services.

To African destinations, letters less then 10g cost US$0.10. To Europe, the Americas or Australasia postage is US$0.20. It's quicker (and probably more reliable) to use the EMS Speedpost service at post offices.

Letters up to 500g cost US$5 to Europe and US$7 to Australia and the USA.

Airmail parcel rates used to be famously cheap, allowing you to send home large woodcarvings at a very low price. It now costs about US$8 plus US$3 per kilogram to send items outside Africa. Surface mail is cheaper.

Telephone

International calls (to destinations outside Africa) from public phone offices cost around US$10 for a three-minute minimum. At hotels the service may be quicker, but charges are often US$25 for three minutes to anywhere outside Africa. To make an international call from Malawi, the code is 00. The international code for Malawi if you're dialling from abroad is 265.

Telephone calls within Malawi are inexpensive, and the network between main cities is reliable, although the lines to outlying areas are often not working. Public phones (called 'booths') take new MK1 coins only.

Malawi does not have area codes, so whatever number you dial within the country will have just six digits. Numbers starting with 7 are on the Lilongwe exchange; those starting with 6 are in Blantyre; 5 is around Zomba; 4 is the south; 3 is the north; and 2 is the Salima area. Numbers starting with 8 are for cell phones and are more expensive to call.

Email & Internet Access

There is Internet access in Lilongwe and Blantyre (see those sections later in this chapter for details). Elsewhere, some hotels and lodges will let guests send or receive email for a nominal fee.

INTERNET RESOURCES

The following Web sites are worth a look (see Internet Resources in the Regional Facts for the Visitor chapter for a more comprehensive listing).

Africa News Follow the links for Malawi News online.
www.africanews.org

Malawi/Cities.Com Glossy and informative site with some useful links.
www.malawi.com

Malawi.Net This has links to sites of local newspapers and political parties.
www.malawi.net

Omni Resources Topographic maps of Malawi can be ordered online.
www.omnimap.com

BOOKS

This section covers books specific to Malawi; titles on the whole Southern Africa region are covered under Books in the Regional Facts for the Visitor chapter. Literature by Malawian writers is covered under Arts in the Facts about Malawi section.

Lonely Planet

Malawi, Lonely Planet's specific guide, gives more in-depth coverage of Malawi.

Trekking in East Africa, which includes a good section on Malawi, is recommended for trekkers and hikers.

Guidebooks & Field Guides

Day Outings from Lilongwe and ***Day Outings from Blantyre***, both published by the Wildlife Society of Malawi. These guides are highly recommended. Both are well written and researched, and include suggestions on places to visit, things to see and local walks. They have an emphasis on wildlife and cover a surprisingly wide area. The only problem is that they're aimed mostly at people with cars – thereby precluding many travellers and about 99% of Malawi's population.

Malawi's National Parks & Game Reserves by John Hough. Covers all parks and reserves in the country, with full details of flora and fauna occurring in each.

Lake Malawi's Resorts by Ted Sneed. Covers in detail every place to stay (more than 70) on the lakeshore. It took so long to research that by the time Ted got to the southern end, some new places had opened in the north!

Birds of Malawi: A Supplement to Newman's Birds of Southern Africa by KB Newman. This book 'bridges the bird gap' between species covered in Southern Africa and East African guides. (For more titles on birdwatching, see the boxed text 'Books on Birds' under Books in the Regional Facts for the Visitor chapter.)

Cichlids & Other Fishes of Lake Malawi by A Koning. This book is encyclopaedic – in both size and coverage.

Guide to the Fishes of Lake Malawi by L Digby. In contrast to Koning's tome, this guide is small, portable and perfect for amateurs, although not easy to find as it was published in 1986. It is sometimes called the 'WWF guide' as this organisation was the publisher.

Trees of Malawi by JS Pullinger & AM Kitchen. A large-format book with detailed colour illustrations.

Travel

Venture to the Interior by Laurens van der Post. This book describes the author's 'exploration' of Mt Mulanje and the Nyika Plateau in the 1940s, although in reality this was hardly trail-blazing stuff.

History

A Lady's Letters from Central Africa by Jane Moir. This book was written in the 1890s by 'the first woman traveller in Central Africa'.

Livingstone's Lake by Oliver Ransford. This classic book on Lake Malawi and the surrounding countries was published in the 1960s and is now quite rare.

Nyasa – A Journal of Adventures by ED Young. A local history book written in the 1870s (reprinted in 1984); it's a missionary's account of the original Livingstonia mission at Cape Maclear.

A Short History of Malawi by BR Rafael. Hard to find, but the writing is quite accessible.

General

Between the Cape and Cairo by artist Tony Grogan. A splendid coffee-table book, with a collection of sketches and paintings from all parts of Malawi.

Jungle Lovers by Paul Theroux. A light humorous novel, set in a mythical country immediately recognisable as Banda-era Malawi, neatly capturing life in Africa for locals and foreigners.

Malawi – Lake of Stars by Frank Johnston. This book features a collection of beautiful photographs with evocative text by Vera Garland.

NEWSPAPERS

Malawi's main newspapers are *The Malawi Times* – a survivor from the old days, and still a supporter of the MCP – and *The Nation*, which is blatantly pro-UDF.

RADIO & TV

Malawi's national radio station, the Malawi Broadcasting Corporation, combines music, news and chat shows in English, Chichewa and some other local languages. International news is brief but wide-ranging. There are also commercial music stations in the large cities.

Until recently, Malawi was the only country in Southern Africa not to have a national TV station. In one of his wiser moves, Banda decreed it was not necessary. However, a fledgling service has recently been introduced, which broadcasts in the evening and on weekends, with imported programs, and local news in English. International satellite channels are available in most mid-range and top-end hotels.

PHOTOGRAPHY & VIDEO

General aspects of photography in the region are covered in the Regional Facts for the Visitor chapter. In Malawi, film and camera spares are generally only available in Blantyre and Lilongwe.

In the cities, Fuji or Konika 100 ASA 36-exposure print film costs about US$4; developing and printing costs about US$6 for 12 exposures or US$12 to US$15 for 36. A set of passport pictures will cost US$7.

HEALTH

General aspects are covered under Health in the Regional Facts for the Visitor chapter. The most important health concern specific to Malawi is the presence of bilharzia in Lake Malawi (see the boxed text 'The Great Bilharzia Story' opposite).

Most large towns have a hospital and pharmacy that are reasonably well stocked. Malawi's main hospitals are at Blantyre and Lilongwe (see Information in those sections for more details).

DANGERS & ANNOYANCES

This section is specific to Malawi. Some general warnings and safety tips are given under Dangers & Annoyances in the Regional Facts for the Visitor chapter.

Crime

Unfortunately, reports of travellers being robbed in Lilongwe and Blantyre have increased. However, incidents are still rare compared with other countries, and violence is not the norm. Some safety advice is given in the Lilongwe and Blantyre sections. There have also been robberies at popular lakeshore areas such as Cape Maclear and

Nkhata Bay, but here violence is very rare. While robbery can never be condoned, this problem shouldn't be blamed entirely on Malawians. It's also due partly to the increased number of tourists, some of whom are incredibly insensitive when it comes to displays of wealth and possessions, or downright irresponsible when it comes to walking in unlit areas late at night. Whatever the reason, the situation should be put into perspective: Malawi is still safer than many other parts of Southern Africa. A reader wrote to us saying 'everywhere in Africa there's always a bit of danger, but it can always be avoided. Malawi has just caught up, that's all'.

Scams to be aware of if you're buying curios are the eager young men who offer to wrap your purchase in paper and cardboard, then want more for this job than you paid for the carving. Also on the economic front, beware of locals asking you to break a US$100 bill into $10 bills and $20 bills. Naturally, the US$100 bill is a fake.

Wildlife

Potential dangers at Lake Malawi include encountering a hippo or crocodile, but for travellers the chances of being attacked are extremely remote. Crocodile tend to be very wary of humans and are generally only found in quiet vegetated areas around river mouths (although they may sometimes be washed into the lake by floodwater). Therefore you should be careful if you're walking along the lakeshore and have to wade a river. Popular tourist beaches are safe, although, just to be sure, you should seek local advice before diving in. The most dangerous animals in Malawi are the mosquitoes that transmit malaria (see the Health section in the Regional Facts for the Visitor chapter).

LEGAL MATTERS

Drugs

Cannabis (*chamba* or 'Malawi gold') can be easily bought in much of Malawi, especially in some lakeshore resorts. A 'cob' (sausage-shaped bundle of grass about the size of two fists) sells for anything between US$2 and US$20, depending on quality, scarcity of supply and the gullibility of the buyer. Whatever,

The Great Bilharzia Story

Bilharzia (or schistosomiasis) is a disease that occurs all over Africa. It is transmitted by minute worms carried by infected humans and water snails. Both 'hosts' need to be present for the worms to transmit the disease. Bilharzia can be contracted if you swim or paddle in lakes, ponds or any shallow water, especially near villages or where reeds grow.

For many years Malawi's health and tourism departments stated that Lake Malawi was bilharzia-free. Only since the mid-1990s has it emerged that this claim was simply untrue – bilharzia is definitely present. A lot of people fell for it, including, it has to be said, Lonely Planet. Early editions of our *Africa on a shoestring* duly reported that Lake Malawi was free of bilharzia. Local tour companies were hoodwinked also, or went along with the pretence. A hotel on the shore of Lake Malawi sent its staff out early every morning to clear surrounding reeds of snails, without warning guests that the worms might still be present.

Although parts of the lake may be very low risk, in other areas – including some popular tourist destinations – you undoubtedly have a high chance of contracting bilharzia. There's no need to panic, and absolutely no reason to avoid coming to Lake Malawi – and once there, who could resist swimming in those beautiful waters?! But you must be aware of the risk.

If you do decide to swim, and you do contract bilharzia, you might suffer from some symptoms almost immediately, in which case you should seek treatment fast. But usually symptoms do not show until the disease is well established – and this can be weeks or months after exposure. Long-term effects can be very harmful, so it is *absolutely essential* that you have a check-up for the disease when you get back home or reach a place with good medical services. Be sure your doctor is familiar with bilharzia, and be aware that the disease may have a long incubation period and may not be initially apparent, so you might need more than one test. For more information see the Health section in the Regional Facts for the Visitor chapter.

don't be fooled into thinking it is legal in Malawi. Buying, selling, possessing and using are all serious offences. The maximum penalty is life imprisonment or a fine of US$35,000. Travellers caught may be fined a lesser amount and then deported. Some dealers are police informers, and the police have been known to raid camp sites, arrest offenders and then let them go free on payment of a large unofficial 'fine'. Either way it can be scary and very expensive.

BUSINESS HOURS

Offices and shops in the main towns are usually open from 7.30 or 8 am to 5 pm weekdays, with an hour for lunch between noon and 1 pm. Many shops are also open Saturday morning. In smaller towns, shops and stalls are open most days, but keep informal hours. Bank hours are usually from 8 am to 1 or 2 pm weekdays. Post and telephone offices are usually open from 7.30 am to 4.30 pm weekdays. In Blantyre and Lilongwe, they also open Saturday morning.

PUBLIC HOLIDAYS & SPECIAL EVENTS

Public holidays in Malawi are:

New Year's Day 1 January
John Chilembwe Day 16 January
Martyrs' Day 3 March
Easter March/April – Good Friday, Holy Saturday and Easter Monday
Labour Day 1 May
Freedom Day 14 June
Republic Day 6 July
Mother's Day 2nd Monday in October
National Tree Planting Day 2nd Monday in December
Christmas Day 25 December
Boxing Day 26 December

When one of the above dates falls on a weekend, normally the following Monday is a public holiday. In northern Malawi and along the lake, many people are Muslim and observe Islamic celebrations.

ACTIVITIES

This section provides only a brief overview of what's available throughout Malawi; for more information see the relevant sections (eg, for hiking see the Mulanje section).

Water Sports

Lake Malawi's population of colourful fish attracts travellers to **scuba diving**. The lake is reckoned by experts to be among the best freshwater diving areas in the world – and one of the cheapest places to learn how to dive. Places where you can hire scuba gear and learn to dive include Nkhata Bay, Cape Maclear and Senga Bay, plus Club Makokola and some of the other hotels and camping grounds on the southern lakeshore. Most hotels and camps also rent **snorkelling** equipment. (See also the boxed text 'Cichlid Fish' in the Central Malawi section later in this chapter.)

Many of the more upmarket places along the lake have facilities for **water-skiing** or **windsurfing**. You can also go sailing, or join luxurious 'sail safaris' where everything is done for you. **Canoeing** is available at Cape Maclear and Nkhata Bay.

You can go **fishing** in Lake Malawi for *mpasa* (also called lake salmon), *ncheni* (lake tiger), *sungwa* (a type of perch), *kampango* or *vundu* (both catfish). There are trout in streams on Nyika, Zomba and Mulanje Plateaus, and tigerfish can be hooked in the Lower Shire.

Other Activities

The main areas for **hiking** are Nyika and Mulanje. Other areas include Zomba, and various smaller peaks around Blantyre. Mulanje is Malawi's main **rock climbing** area, with some spectacular routes (including the longest in Africa), although local climbers also visit smaller crags and outcrops around the country.

The main area for **horse riding** is the Nyika Plateau, which lends itself perfectly to travel on horseback. You can go on short rides or longer multiday safaris.

ACCOMMODATION

Malawi's range of places to stay has expanded rapidly in the last few years. Several smart new hotels and lodges have been built along the lake and in the national parks. Additionally, former government-run places have been privatised, with greatly improved facilities and services.

Budget

At the budget end of the price range, in almost every town there is a council or government resthouse. Prices vary from as little as US$1 up to around US$5 a double, but conditions are generally spartan to say the least and downright disgusting at worst. In national parks and along the lakeshore, many places offer camping and self-catering chalets or cabins. Some camping grounds are pretty basic, while others have good facilities.

The last few years have also seen a dramatic rise in the number of backpacker hostels for independent budget travellers. Most of these are along the lakeshore, but there are a few in the cities too. Prices range from US$1 for a dorm up to about US$5 per person for a double or triple. Camping is usually about US$1 to US$2.

Mid-Range & Top End

Mid-range hotels range from about US$30 to US$100 per double, including taxes, usually with private bathroom and breakfast. The quality of service at a smaller place can be just as good as or even better than at the pricey establishments, though.

Top-end hotels or lodges generally range from US$100 to US$200 for a double room, with facilities such as private bathroom, TV, air-con and telephone, and including taxes and breakfast. At the very top of the scale in Malawi you may pay US$230 per person per night, although in such places (eg, Mvuu Wilderness Lodge in Liwonde National Park) this includes all meals and activities such as wildlife drives.

In January 2000, the management of many mid-range and top-end hotels around Malawi was taken over by the international Le Meridien group. The Capital Hotel in Lilongwe and the Mount Soche Hotel in Blantyre will have the Meridien tag added in mid-2000, after refurbishment. The same will happen to the Livingstonia Beach Hotel (Senga Bay), the Ku Chawe Inn (Zomba) and the Lilongwe Hotel (Lilongwe) in 2001. If you're planning to stay in one of these hotels, be prepared for the name changes, but also be prepared for local people (eg, taxi drivers) continuing to use the old names for some time to come.

FOOD

Self-Catering

If you're self-catering, PTC supermarkets are found all over Malawi, stocking locally produced and imported goods, many of them from South Africa or Europe and sold at similar prices. Malawian specials include guava jam and 'Tambala' peanut butter.

Budget

There are simple restaurants or food stalls called 'tea rooms' – often at markets and bus stations – where in the morning you can get tea with milk for US$0.15 and a bread cake for US$0.03. At lunchtime, these may serve simple meals of beans and *nsima* (maize meal) for about US$0.50.

Up a grade from here are the local restaurants in small towns where the food is the same but the surroundings slightly better. Malawian meals cost around US$1 in these places.

In cities and larger towns, cheap restaurants serve traditional Malawian food for around US$1 to US$1.50, and other options such as chicken with rice or chips for around US$2. The most popular fish is *chambo*. Slightly fancier places do European- or American-style food such as burgers, fried chicken or simple curries. Prices are normally around US$3 to US$5, depending on the surroundings as much as the food itself, and if you eat in or takeaway. Most also serve cheaper snacks such as sandwiches or sausage rolls for US$1 to US$2.

Mid-Range & Top-End

Most mid-range hotels and restaurants serve European-style food: steak, chicken or fish, which is served with vegetables and chips or rice, usually for between US$5 and US$10.

At top-end hotels and restaurants in cities and along the lakeshore, you can find the straightforward international standards mentioned above, plus more elaborate French, British or Italian cuisine. Blantyre and Lilongwe also have places doing Ethiopian,

Food & Accommodation Taxes

All mid-range and top-end restaurants and hotels charge 10% service charge and 10% tourist tax. You should therefore add 20% to the costs shown on menus and tariff sheets. If in doubt, ask if the price is inclusive or not, as it can make quite a difference. Wherever possible in this book we have given prices inclusive of these taxes.

The 10% service charge officially means that tipping is not necessary, but this is not all it seems as hotels and restaurants who make the 10% service charge have to pass on 60% of this to the Ministry of Tourism, for use in a general marketing fund, so that the staff actually receive only 4% of the total you pay for your room and meal.

Indian, Korean and Portuguese food. Main courses range from around US$8 to US$15.

DRINKS

International fizzy drinks are widely available, and tea and coffee are available in many places, from top-end hotels and restaurants to the lowliest local eateries.

Traditional beer of the region is made from maize; in Malawi this is commercially brewed as Chibuku, and sold all over the country in large red-and-blue cartons. For most travellers, the thick texture and bittersweet taste are not appealing.

Most travellers (and many Malawians) prefer the beer produced by Carlsberg at its Blantyre brewery (the only one in Africa). There are three main types of beer: 'greens' (lager), 'browns' (like a British ale) and 'golds' (a stronger brew). If you're a beer fan, you can visit the brewery (see Things to See & Do in the Blantyre & Limbe section in this chapter).

SHOPPING

For intrepid shoppers, Malawi offers a wide range of curios and souvenirs, including animals and figures carved from wood; ornaments such as bowls and chess sets; and the very popular chief's chair, a two-piece three-legged stool with a high back decorated with pictures.

You can also find plenty of objects made from grass and palm leaves, such as baskets and boxes, or intricate models of cars and lorries, and even overland trucks! Contemporary soapstone carvings, paintings, pottery, clay figures and malachite jewellery are also available.

You can buy at roadside craft stalls or curio shops – in among the stuff that's hammered out in a hurry you will also find works in wood and stone (and occasionally paintings) that have been created by artists of better-than-average talent. Salesmen often seem to make no distinction between good and mediocre work, so it's always worth spending time to search the better pieces out. Prices are usually not fixed, so you have to bargain. However, if you prefer not to haggle, there are some shops in Blantyre and Lilongwe that use price-tags. (See also Arts in the Facts about Malawi section earlier in this chapter.)

In markets all over Malawi you can buy *chitenjas*, sheets of brightly coloured cloth

SARAH JOLLY

The *chitenja* is a multipurpose piece of bright cloth that is often used as a garment.

MALAWI

that local women use as wraps, cloaks, scarves and baby carriers. They're also available at several shops along Haile Selassie Rd in Blantyre. They make nice souvenirs and are practical items for women travellers, especially if you're heading for the beach or rural areas where shorts are frowned on.

Getting There & Away

This section covers access into Malawi from neighbouring countries only. Information about reaching Southern Africa from elsewhere on the African continent and from other continents is outlined in the regional Getting There & Away chapter.

AIR

Airports & Airlines

Malawi's main airport for international flights is at Lilongwe. It has a pharmacy, a post office, a bookstore, banks and car hire desks, plus a restaurant and bar overlooking the runway where you can use up the last of your kwacha before flying out (although beware of waiters overcharging).

There is also an airport at Blantyre, which is mostly served by regional and domestic flights. It has a small cafeteria, a bookstore and an Avis desk.

Departure Tax

For travellers flying out, the airport departure tax for international flights is US$20 – in US dollars in cash. No other currency is accepted.

Southern Africa

For details on flying to places beyond Southern Africa, see the regional Getting There & Away chapter. Most regional flights go to and from Lilongwe, but some flights serve Blantyre. All of the following fares are one way; returns are double, but 'excursion fares' can be cheaper.

Air Malawi has a pretty good regional network, with flights to Harare (US$160) and Lusaka (US$170), both three times per week, and to Johannesburg (Jo'burg) (US$400) once per week. The following regional airlines also serve Malawi, usually flying on the days Air Malawi doesn't (so you get a wider choice of flights), with fares mostly on a par: Air Zimbabwe flies three times per week to/from Harare (with connections to Victoria Falls and other parts of Southern Africa); South African Airways flies twice per week to/from Jo'burg (with connections to Durban, Cape Town etc); and Kenya Airways flies three times per week to/from Nairobi (US$360).

If you're heading for South Luangwa National Park in Zambia, Air Malawi flies to Mfuwe (near the park gate and main lodges) from Lilongwe twice weekly. (See South Luangwa National Park in the Eastern Zambia section of the Zambia chapter for details.)

LAND

Border Crossings

Malawi shares borders with Tanzania, Zambia and Mozambique. The only land crossing to/from Tanzania is at Songwe, north of Kaporo, where a bridge crosses the Songwe River. (A new bridge is planned further upstream). The main border crossing with Zambia is about 100km north-west of Lilongwe, on the main road to Lusaka. Malawi does not directly border Zimbabwe, but a lot of traffic between these two countries passes through a neck of Mozambican territory called the Tete Corridor.

All Malawi's border crossings are officially open from 6 am to 6 pm (possibly open later and shut earlier, but never the other way around).

If you're bringing a car into Malawi from any other country without a carnet, a temporary import permit costs US$3 (payable in kwacha) and compulsory third-party insurance is US$9 for one month. When you leave Malawi, a permit handling fee of US$3 is payable. Receipts are issued.

Mozambique

Road Travelling by road is a good idea because the train service between Malawi and Mozambique can be very slow.

South The most direct way to Mozambique south of the Zambezi is a bus between Blantyre and Harare, which can drop you at Tete, from where buses go to Beira and Maputo. You can also do the trip in stages by taking a local bus from Blantyre to the Malawi border crossing at Mwanza, then walking or hitching the 6km to the Mozambique border crossing at Zóbuè (**zob**-way).

Central If you are heading for central Mozambique, there are several buses per day from Blantyre to Nsanje, or all the way to the Malawi border at Marka (**ma**-ra-ka). It's a few kilometres between the border crossings – you can walk or take a bicycle taxi – and you can change money on the Mozambique side. From here minibuses and pick-ups go to Mutarara, Nhamilabue and Vila de Sena, from where you can reach Caia.

North If you are heading for northern Mozambique, you can take the route between Blantyre and Mocuba. There are regular buses from Blantyre, via Mulanje, to the Malawi border crossing at Muloza (US$3). From here, you walk 1km to the Mozambique border crossing at Milange, from where it's another few kilometres into Milange *vila* (town) itself. There are bicycle taxis for US$1, and a *pensão* (cheap hotel) and a bank here if you need them. From Milange there's usually a *chapa* (pick-up or converted minibus) or truck about every other day in the dry season to Mocuba (US$4), where you can find transport on to Quelimane or Nampula.

Your other option for northern Mozambique is the route between Mangochi and Cuamba. Minibuses run a few times per day between Mangochi and the Malawi town of Namwera (US$2), where there are resthouses if you need one, or all the way to the Malawi border crossing at Chiponde (10km from Namwera) for US$2.50. If there's no bus on this last bit, you can walk, or take a bicycle taxi between Namwera and Chiponde (US$3). It's 6km to the Mozambique border crossing at Mandimba. You might be able to hitch or take a bicycle taxi (US$2). Mandimba has a couple of pensãos, and there's usually a daily chapa between here and Cuamba (US$4).

Another option into northern Mozambique is to go by minibus from Liwonde to the border at Nayuchi, along the dirt track running parallel to the railway. From the border you can get a train to Cuamba, as described under Train following.

Train If you're heading to northern Mozambique, a passenger train departs daily at 5 am from Balaka, and goes via Liwonde to the border at Nayuchi (US$1.80). It arrives at the border at around 10 am (returning to Balaka in the afternoon). You can also get on in Liwonde but the train is crowded so there's less chance of getting a seat.

From Nayuchi (where there are moneychangers) you can walk to the Mozambique border post at Entre Lagos, where you can catch a Mozambique freight train to Cuamba (officially daily, but sometimes it's cancelled). The fare is US$1.50, payable in meticais. From Cuamba, you can continue to Nampula. (See Cuamba in the Northern Mozambique section of the Mozambique chapter for more information.)

South Africa

If you need to get to South Africa quickly and cheaply, Intercape and Translux run direct luxury coaches from Blantyre to Jo'burg, five times per week between them, for about US$60. The coaches depart mid-morning and arrive mid-afternoon the next day. Connections from Lilongwe leave at 6 am.

Tanzania

If you want to go the whole way between Lilongwe and Dar es Salaam, there are two companies running two buses per week. Each has a depot and ticket office on Devil St in Lilongwe. Fares are US$33, and if you're travelling from the south, your first sight of a Tanzanian bus – like something from the movie *Mad Max* or the worst carnival ride you've ever had – may be quite a shock. These buses also pick up and drop off in Mzuzu and Mbeya (Tanzania) and are handy for going between northern Malawi and southern Tanzania.

If you're going in stages, the Stagecoach bus runs twice per day between Mzuzu and Karonga for US$4, and minibuses run for US$5, but the journey takes a long time because the road is so bad. Minibuses and matolas run between Karonga and the Songwe border crossing for around US$1. It's 200m across the bridge to the Tanzanian border crossing.

Once you're on the Tanzanian side of the border crossing, buses go north-west to Mbeya (sometimes looping to Kyela – about 5km off the road between the border and Mbeya). If there's nothing, you'll have to walk, hitch or take a bicycle taxi (US$1) about 7km to the junction with the road between Kyela and Mbeya. You can change money with the bicycle taxi boys but beware of scams. From the junction you can find a bus or lift to Mbeya, where you can pick up a bus or train to Dar es Salaam.

Zambia

Direct buses run between Lilongwe and Lusaka three or four times a week, but they're slow, so you're better doing the trip in stages. Regular minibuses run between Lilongwe and the Malawi border crossing, 2km west of the town of Mchinji (US$2.50). From here, it's 12km to the Zambian border. Local shared taxis shuttle between them for US$1.20 per person, or US$7 for the whole car.

From the Zambian border crossing minibuses run to Chipata (about 30km west of the border) for US$1, from where you can reach Lusaka or South Luangwa National Park (for more details see the Eastern Zambia section of the Zambia chapter).

A new Malawian border post is being built only a few metres from the Zambian post. When this is completed, minibuses will probably run straight to here from Lilongwe.

Zimbabwe

Although Zimbabwe doesn't border Malawi, many travellers go directly between the two countries. Most popular with budget travellers is the daily Munorurama bus, which leaves Blantyre's Chileka Rd bus station at 6 am, and arrives in Harare by late afternoon. The service is good and costs US$16. Coming the other way costs the same, but is a much slower trip because local people bring in loads of Zimbabwean goods and there are big searches at the border. Some travellers have been on the northbound bus for over two days! If you do get interminably stuck at the Mwanza border crossing, you're better off abandoning the big bus, and getting a local minibus to Blantyre (US$2.50).

Luxury coaches operated by Trans-Zambezi Express and Translux go from Blantyre to Jo'burg via Harare a few times per week. You can get details from the Business Centre at the Mt Soche Hotel in Blanytre and the Stagecoach booking office next to the Mt Soche Hotel in Blantyre.

LAKE

Mozambique

The Lake Malawi steamboat *Ilala* stops at Likoma Island twice per week, and there's

Malawi to Mozambique by Dhow

From Cóbuè we caught a sailing dhow to Metangula as the motorboat was going later in the week. We left Cóbuè at 11 am and sailed until 4 pm when the wind dropped, after which the dhow complete with 30 passengers, crew, children, chickens, maize etc was rowed for another four hours. After this the crew pulled it along the shore, through reeds and everything, for another hour or two! We then camped on an idyllic sandy beach until dawn and with the aid of a little wind and lots of rowing arrived in Metangula by 9.30 am. It was a great experience especially as the sun set, with children singing and chickens running around. The crew, despite a few bottles of early morning Kachasu, were friendly and helpful. There is no shade on the boat so precautions need to be taken against the sun. From Metangula we got a lift to Lichinga and went on to Nampula. It is possible to get from Likoma to the coast in five days but it could take eight. The latter would be unlucky.

Louse Kerbiriou and Stephen O'Conner (UK)

an immigration post in Chipyela (the main village) where you must get your passport stamped. From here a local boat goes most days across to Cóbuè (**kob**-way) on the Mozambique mainland (US$2 by motorboat, US$0.50 under sail), where there's an immigration post (where you pay US$2.50 to enter) and a small friendly hotel in case you get stuck (which is likely).

There is a road to Lichinga but it's rough, virtually impassable when a bridge is down, and there's hardly any traffic. So it's more reliable to go by boat from Cóbuè down the shore to Metangula (often on the same boat that brought you over from Likoma). Boats usually leave on the morning after the *Ilala* arrives. By motorboat it costs around US$5 and takes six hours; a dhow costs US$2.50 and can take one to three days, so bring your own food and water. For detailed information on the Ilala, see the main Getting Around section following. For more information on the Mozambique side of Lake Malawi, see Lake Niassa in the Northern Mozambique section of the Mozambique chapter.

Getting Around

You can travel around Malawi by air, road, rail or boat. Compared to other countries in the region, distances between major centres are quite short, and generally roads and public transport systems are quite good, making independent travel fairly straightforward.

I found Malawi one of the friendliest, easy-to-travel, inexpensive places that I have ever been to. No problem travelling alone, and hitching is easy. But get out there – there is more to Malawi than Cape Maclear, although you'd hardly know it by the number of tourists you see elsewhere!

Joanna Rees, UK

AIR

Air Malawi has at least two flights daily between Lilongwe and Blantyre, and most days between Lilongwe and Mzuzu, both for US$51 one way. You can also fly from Lilongwe to Nyika National Park (US$72) or from Lilongwe/Blantyre to Lake Malawi's Club Makokola (US$45 – you don't have to be a guest), from where you can reach other points on the lake. Domestic flights can be paid for in kwacha. Air Malawi's booking system is not always reliable, so be prepared for lost reservations or double bookings.

The air charter company Sefofane Malawi links major towns and tourist centres around the country. Fares vary according to the number of people in your group, so contact a travel agent in Lilongwe or Blantyre for more details. For domestic flights, departure tax is $2.

BUS

Most buses around Malawi are operated by a private company called Stagecoach and come in several different types. Top of the range is Coachline, a daily luxury nonstop service between Blantyre and Lilongwe (US$18) with air-con, toilet, snacks, steward service and good drivers. Next comes Express or Speedlink service, fast buses between the main towns with limited stops and no standing passengers allowed. Intercity buses (often just called the 'ordinary' buses) cover long-distance routes but stop everywhere, so are very slow. As a rule of thumb, Express buses charge between US$2 and US$2.50 per 100km, and Intercity buses slightly less. Stagecoach also runs local services that cover the quieter rural routes and tend to be slow and crowded.

For Coachline and Express buses you can buy a ticket in advance and have a reserved seat. The day before is usually sufficient for Express, but on Coachline a week's notice is sometimes needed, particularly for Friday and Sunday services.

There are also many private buses and minibuses on the roads, either slotting in between Stagecoach services, or serving the routes Stagecoach won't. Fares are about the same as Stagecoach, or slightly more, depending on the severity of the route. There are also local minibus services around towns and to outlying villages, or along the roads that the big buses can't manage. (In Malawi vehicles with about 30 seats are called 'half-buses' to distinguish them from big buses and minibuses.)

In rural areas, the frequency of buses and minibuses drops dramatically – sometimes to nothing. In cases like this, the 'bus' is often a truck or pick-up, with people just piled in the back. In Malawi this is called a *matola*. Everyone pays a fare to the driver – normally a bit more than a bus would charge (ie, around US$3 per 100km).

If you get an overnight bus, when it arrives at its destination you're normally allowed to stay onboard until dawn.

TRAIN

Trains go daily on weekdays between Blantyre and Balaka (US$1.50), but passengers rarely use them as road transport on this route is quicker and cheaper. The twice-weekly train service between Limbe and Nsanje (US$2), in the far south of Malawi, is popular as the line reaches areas where road transport is limited. Since a bridge washed away in 1998, trains terminate at Makhanga. The service of most use to travellers runs between Balaka and Nayuchi (on the border with Mozambique) via Liwonde. For details, see Train under Mozambique in the Getting There & Away section earlier in this chapter.

CAR & MOTORCYCLE

The majority of main routes are mostly good-quality tar, but in recent years several stretches of road have not been repaired and potholes are opening up. In some areas these have made driving slow, difficult and dangerous. Secondary roads are usually graded dirt and also vary in condition. Some are well maintained and easy to drive on in a normal car; others are very bad, especially after the rains, and slow even with 4WD. Rural routes are not so good, and after heavy rain they are often impassable, sometimes for weeks.

The cost of fuel is fixed throughout the country: $0.55 per litre for petrol; $0.50 per litre for diesel. Supplies are usually reliable and distances between towns with filling stations are not long in Malawi, so you rarely need to worry about running dry.

Rental

Most car hire companies are based in Blantyre and Lilongwe. Those with offices in more than one city can arrange pick-up-drop-off deals. International names include Avis, and there are several independent outfits. You should shop around as companies often have special deals and some will negotiate. You can also hire a car through a travel agent – they may have access to special deals. Whoever you hire from, be prepared for a car that is not up to western standards. Check the tyres and as much else as you can. If anything is worn or broken, demand repairs or a discount.

Self-drive rates for a small car start at US$30 per day, plus around US$0.30 per kilometre. Unlimited mileage (minimum seven days) costs from US$50 per day. To this add 20% government tax, plus another US$3 to US$7 a day for insurance.

Rental companies in Malawi include the following:

Avis (☎ 723113, 723812) Lilongwe; (☎ 623792) Blantyre; plus offices at Lilongwe and Blantyre airports and at some large hotels

Ceciliana Car Hire (☎ 720188) Lilongwe; (☎ 641219, cell ☎ 822572) Blantyre

Sputnik Car Hire (☎ 723774, 781013) Lilongwe

SS Rent-a-car (☎ 721179) Lilongwe; (☎ 636836) Blantyre

HITCHING

On the main routes, especially between Mzuzu, Lilongwe, Zomba, Blantyre and Lake Malawi, hitching free lifts, in the western fashion, is fairly easy. At weekends well-off residents and expats living in Blantyre and Lilongwe head for Salima, Cape Maclear and the southern lakeshore, so it's easy to get a lift there on Friday (and Sunday in the opposite direction). Note, however, that just because we say hitching is possible doesn't necessarily mean we recommend it. See the general warning under Hitching in the Getting Around the Region chapter.

All over the country you will see Malawi government cars (with 'MG' numberplates). These are of course always on important official business, although drivers frequently assist stranded travellers and normally expect a payment.

BOAT

The large passenger steamboat the *Ilala* chugs up and down Lake Malawi, once per week in each direction, between Monkey Bay in the south and Chilumba in the north, stopping at about a dozen lakeside towns and villages. (You can get to the Mozambique mainland via Likoma Island on the *Ilala*; see Mozambique under Lake in the Getting There & Away section earlier in this chapter.) Many travellers rate this journey as a highlight of the country, although there are occasionally nasty storms, so you should be ready for some pitching and rolling.

The whole trip, from one end of the line to the other, takes about three days. Note, however, that this boat is notoriously prone to delays. It can sometimes be a day late, especially towards the end of the schedule. The official schedules, as well as the more likely schedules, are as follows (only main ports shown):

Northbound

port	arrival	departure
Monkey Bay	8 am (Fri)	
Chipoka	8 pm	10 pm (Fri)
Nkhotakota	5 am	6 am (Sat)
Likoma Island	11am	2 pm (Sat)
Nkhata Bay	7 pm (Sat)	5 am (Sun)
Chilumba	6 pm (Sun)	

Southbound (Official Schedule)

port	arrival	departure
Chilumba	3 am (Mon)	
Nkhata Bay	11 am	2 pm (Tues)
Likoma Island	6 pm	10 pm (Tues)
Nkhotakota	3 am	4 am (Wed)
Chipoka	11 am	1 pm (Wed)
Monkey Bay	6 am (Thurs)	

Southbound (More Likely Schedule)

port	arrival	departure
Chilumba	3 am (Mon)	
Nkhata Bay	4.30 pm	7 pm (Tues)
Likoma Island	8.30 am	11.30 am (Wed)
Nkhotakota	4.30 pm	5.30 pm (Wed)
Chipoka	1 am	3 am (Thurs)
Monkey Bay	3 pm (Thurs)	

The *Ilala* has three classes. Cabin Class was once luxurious and the cabins are still in reasonable condition. First Class Deck is generally quite spacious, with seats, a small shaded area and a bar. Economy covers the entire lower deck and is dark and crowded with engine fumes permeating from below.

Cabin and First Class Deck fares include food, which is served in the ship's restaurant. Economy fares don't include food. Food is served from a galley on the Economy deck; a meal of beans, rice and vegetables costs under US$1.

Reservations are usually required for Cabin class. For other classes, tickets are sold only when the boat is sighted, so queuing tends to start about a day before it's due to arrive. However, there's no question of anyone being refused – it just keeps filling up! If you travel Economy class, you'll probably be allowed onto the First Class Deck to buy a beer.

***Ilala* Sample Routes & Fares** All of the following sample fares are from Nkhata Bay.

destination	cabin ($US)	1st class ($US)	economy ($US)
Likoma Island	15	8	2
Nkhotakota	15	13	3
Mbamba Bay	17	9	2.50
Chilumba	17.50	11.50	2.50
Monkey Bay	41	26	5

When the *Ilala* stops at lakeside towns or villages, the water is too shallow for it to come close; the lifeboat is used to ferry passengers ashore. Local village boats also carry people to the shore, for which there is a small charge. At the same time, traders come out in canoes and sell fruit, dried fish and other food.

LOCAL TRANSPORT

In the cities and large towns, minibuses travel local routes. Private hire taxis also operate in cities and large towns, and can be found outside bus stations, airports or large hotels. There are no meters, so rates are negotiable, particularly on airport runs – check the price at the start of the journey. For more information, see the Getting Around information in the city and town listings.

ORGANISED TOURS

Several companies organise tours around the country, ranging from a few days to three weeks. Trips into Zambia or Mozambique are also available, although Malawi's safari scene is much smaller than, say, South Africa's or Zimbabwe's. Tours may be 'mobile' (ie, moving from camp to camp every few days) or based in one place, with excursions each day. Most are vehicle-based although some outfits also organise walking trips, horseback safaris, or boating on the lake. Tours normally include transport, accommodation and food, but prices vary considerably according to standards – from budget to luxury. There are only a few budget companies that can arrange tours on the spot – most prefer advance bookings, although sometimes a couple of days is enough. Budget tours usually cost between US$50 and US$70 per day. Most mid-range and top-end companies also need advance bookings, and charge from US$100 per person per day, easily going up to US$200 per day or more.

Most tour companies covering the whole country are based in Lilongwe, and are listed under Information in that section. More specialist companies covering smaller areas include: Red Zebra Tours, which offers specialist diving and fish-watching safaris (see Senga Bay in the Central Malawi section); Kayak Africa (see Activities in the Cape Maclear section) and Monkey Business (see Activities in the Nkhata Bay section), which both offer kayak expeditions on the lake; and The Nyika Safari Company, which offers horseback safaris on the Nyika Plateau (see Nyika National Park in the Northern Malawi section).

Lilongwe

Lilongwe is the political capital of Malawi, while Blantyre is the commercial capital. Originally a small village on the banks of the Lilongwe River, it became a British colonial administrative centre around the turn of the 20th century, after its chief requested protection from warlike neighbours. Lilongwe grew into a settler town, and its location on the main north-south route and the road to Northern Rhodesia (later Zambia) meant that by the 1960s it was the second-largest urban area in Malawi. In 1968 plans were announced to move the country's administration from Blantyre to Lilongwe, which was more central. The construction of the pleasantly landscaped but sprawling new city, including wide boulevards and grand ministerial buildings, was largely funded by South Africa, and the new capital was officially declared in 1975.

Orientation

Lilongwe has two centres: City Centre, which has ministries, embassies, some smart hotels, a shopping centre, airline offices and some travel agents; and Old Town, with a good range of places to stay, the bus station, the market and several restaurants. City Centre is a rather sterile place whereas Old Town has soul. The two centres are 3km apart and minibuses run between them.

Maps The Department of Surveys public map office is about 500m south of the roundabout where Glyn Jones Rd meets Kamuzu Procession Rd.

Information

Tourist Offices The tourist office is at the Department of Wildlife & Tourism (☎ 723566, 723676) on Murray Rd (PO Box 30131) in Old Town. At another office in the same building you can get information about national parks. The people are friendly but information is limited. For details on tours, flights and hotels you're better off at a travel agency; several are listed in the Travel Agencies & Tours Operators section later in this chapter.

Immigration Office Lilongwe's immigration office (☎ 722995) is on Murray Rd in Old Town, next to the Department of Wildlife & Tourism office.

Money There are branches of National Bank and Commercial Bank on Kamuzu Procession Rd in Old Town. In the same area – in the Nico shopping centre – and on

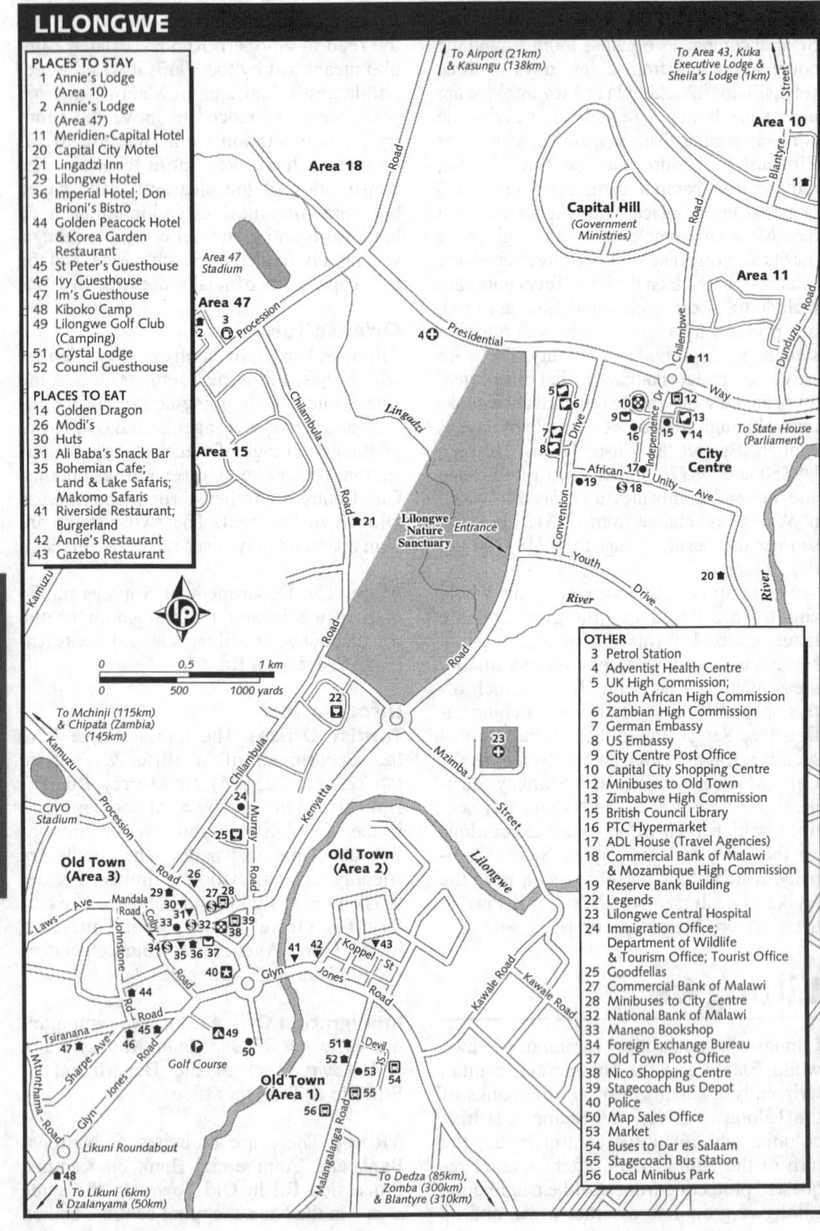
LILONGWE
PLACES TO STAY
1 Annie's Lodge (Area 10)
2 Annie's Lodge (Area 47)
11 Meridien-Capital Hotel
20 Capital City Motel
21 Lingadzi Inn
29 Lilongwe Hotel
36 Imperial Hotel; Don Brioni's Bistro
44 Golden Peacock Hotel & Korea Garden Restaurant
45 St Peter's Guesthouse
46 Ivy Guesthouse
47 Im's Guesthouse
48 Kiboko Camp
49 Lilongwe Golf Club (Camping)
51 Crystal Lodge
52 Council Guesthouse
PLACES TO EAT
14 Golden Dragon
26 Modi's
30 Huts
31 Ali Baba's Snack Bar
35 Bohemian Cafe; Land & Lake Safaris; Makomo Safaris
41 Riverside Restaurant; Burgerland
42 Annie's Restaurant
43 Gazebo Restaurant
OTHER
3 Petrol Station
4 Adventist Health Centre
5 UK High Commission; South African High Commission
6 Zambian High Commission
7 German Embassy
8 US Embassy
9 City Centre Post Office
10 Capital City Shopping Centre
12 Minibuses to Old Town
13 Zimbabwe High Commission
15 British Council Library
16 PTC Hypermarket
17 ADL House (Travel Agencies)
18 Commercial Bank of Malawi & Mozambique High Commission
19 Reserve Bank Building
22 Legends
23 Lilongwe Central Hospital
24 Immigration Office; Department of Wildlife & Tourism Office; Tourist Office
25 Goodfellas
27 Commercial Bank of Malawi
28 Minibuses to City Centre
32 National Bank of Malawi
33 Maneno Bookshop
34 Foreign Exchange Bureau
37 Old Town Post Office
38 Nico Shopping Centre
39 Stagecoach Bus Depot
40 Police
50 Map Sales Office
53 Market
54 Buses to Dar es Salaam
55 Stagecoach Bus Station
56 Local Minibus Park
To Airport (21km) & Kasungu (138km)
To Area 43, Kuka Executive Lodge & Sheila's Lodge (1km)
Area 10
Area 18
Area 11
Area 47
Area 15
Capital Hill
(Government Ministries)
City Centre
Area 47 Stadium
Lilongwe Nature Sanctuary
Entrance
To State House (Parliament)
Old Town (Area 3)
Old Town (Area 2)
Old Town (Area 1)
CIVO Stadium
Golf Course
Likuni Roundabout
To Mchinji (115km) & Chipata (Zambia) (145km)
To Likuni (6km) & Dzalanyama (50km)
To Dedza (85km), Zomba (300km) & Blantyre (310km)
Presidential Way
Procession Road
Chilambula Road
Kenyatta Road
Mzimba Street
Convention Drive
Independence Dr
African Unity Ave
Youth Drive
Chilembwe Road
Dunduzu Road
Blantyre Street
Kamuzu Procession Road
Murray Road
Mandala Road
Colby Road
Johnstone Rd
Laws Ave
Tsiranana Road
Sharpe Ave
Glyn Jones Road
Mtunthama Road
Malangalanga Road
Kawale Road
Koppel St
Devil St
Lingadzi
Lilongwe River
0 0.5 1 km
0 500 1000 yards
MALAWI

nearby Mandala Rd, are several foreign exchange bureaus, generally offering better rates and quicker service.

Post & Telephone Lilongwe has two main post offices: in Old Town on Kamuzu Procession Rd and in City Centre at City Centre shopping centre. For details of rates, see Post & Communications in the Facts for the Visitor section earlier in this chapter. If you're receiving post restante mail addressed to GPO Lilongwe, most goes to Old Town, but some mysteriously lands at City Centre, so the only way to avoid this is to have your letters addressed specifically Old Town or City Centre. The office for the American Express (AmEx) client mail service is at Manica Travel, ADL House, City Centre.

For telephone calls and faxes, Lilongwe's only public office is in City Centre shopping centre, in the depths of Centre House Arcade. Calls cost US$9 for three minutes anywhere outside Africa, any time.

Email & Internet Access Lilongwe's only Internet bureau is Epsilon & Omega (☎ 784444) at ADL House, City Centre, where computers are available from 9 to 11.30 am and 1.30 to 4.30 pm Monday to Thursday, plus all day Friday, and Saturday morning. Full Internet access costs US$3 for the first 10 minutes, then US$0.20 per minute. For email (sending only), 15-minutes' access costs US$2. You can also get Internet access at the British Council at US$1 for 15 minutes (but there's a long queue and only one terminal) and at the business centre at the Capital Hotel at US$10 for 20 minutes. Some travel agents in Old Town plan to offer Internet access soon, so check here too.

Travel Agencies & Tour Operators In Old Town, travel agencies selling flights include Midland Travel (☎ 741876, 744444) and Rainbow Travel (☎ 740963, 740306), both on Kamuzu Procession Rd.

In the Nico Centre, Ulendo Safaris (☎ 743501, fax 743492, ⓔ ulendo@malawi.net) sells air tickets and tours, and often has deals on trips to South Luangwa National Park (Zambia), including flights and accommodation. It represents the Nyika Safari Company (☎ 740579, fax 740848, ⓔ nyika-safaries@malawi.net), which runs accommodation and activities in Nyika National Park and Vwaza Marsh Wildlife Reserve.

Land & Lake Safaris (☎ 743213, fax 744408, ⓔ landlake@malawi.net) at the Bohemian Cafe on Mandala Rd, just west of the post office, offers budget and mid-range safaris to South Luangwa and various parts of Malawi. It also arranges car hire, sells hiking equipment and runs some of the forest resthouses. Next door is Makomo Safaris (☎ 743219, fax 743471, ⓔ Makomo@malawi.net), offering mid-range tours and budget camping trips.

Kiboko Safaris (☎ 740135), based at Kiboko Camp (see Places to Stay – Budget) specialises in budget tours; three weeks all round Malawi costs from US$1200 and four days to South Luangwa costs US$250. Web site: www.kiboko-safaris.com

In the City Centre shopping centre, flight agencies include Air Tour & Travel (☎ 781053, 781362) and Soche Tours & Travel (☎ 782377, fax 781409); both can also make hotel reservations. In ADL House are Manica Travel (☎ 760024), which sells flights, and Central African Wilderness Safaris (☎ 781393, 781153, fax 781397, ⓔ info@wilderness.malawi.net), a mid-range to top-end safari operator, travel agent and booking agency dealing with hotels, flights, air charters, tours, car hire and so on.

Barefoot Safaris (☎ 831847, fax 782657, ⓔ charlotte.smith@lilongwe.mail.fco.gov.uk) offers budget or mid-range tours, usually organised in advance, but you can also contact them for on-the-spot arrangements.

Bookshops In Old Town, TBS bookshop in the Nico Centre sells international and local newspapers and magazines, and some paperback novels. Maneno Bookshop on Mandala Rd has a better range. In City Centre shopping centre, Central Bookshop also sells magazines and paperbacks, plus a surprisingly good stock of African literature, local guidebooks and other books on Malawian subjects.

Photography Print film, developing, printing and instant passport photos are available at Central African Studio in the City Centre shopping centre and Lee Photographic at the Nico shopping centre in Old Town. Note that photos printed in Lilongwe sometimes come out overexposed. If you're particular, save them for Zimbabwe or South Africa.

Libraries & Cultural Centres The British Council library is just off Independence Dr in City Centre (open from 8.30 am to 4.30 pm Tuesday to Friday, plus Monday afternoon and Saturday morning). The US Information Service library is in the Old Mutual building in City Centre shopping centre (open from 8.30 am to 4.30 pm Tuesday to Friday, plus Monday afternoon; it's closed Wednesday afternoon). Nonmembers are allowed to read books and magazines in the library, but not to take them away. The USIS shows the previous day's CBS evening news at lunchtime. Both places also show films on some afternoons and evenings. Check their noticeboards for details.

Medical Services For malaria blood tests, Medicare (☎ 742390) next to Mobil station on Mandala Rd, Old Town charges US$2.50. On the same street, next to Bohemian Cafe, Dr Tayoub is recommended for private consultations. The Adventist Health Centre (☎ 731049, 731819) in City Centre is also good for consultations, plus eye and dental problems. Another dentist is Dr Mazloum (☎ 780853) in ADL House, City Centre.

At Lilongwe Central Hospital (☎ 721555) conditions and facilities are not good, but an 'expat bed' (a private ward) costs about US$50 per night. A better option is Likuni Mission Hospital (☎ 721400, 721282), 7km south-west of Old Town, with public wards, private rooms, and some expat European doctors on staff. Fees for those who can afford them start at US$100 per day.

The best place for minor or major matters is the MRS Clinic (☎ 730389, 823590) off Ufulu Rd in Area 43. Fees are US$70 per consultation, US$110 after hours, US$100 for an overnight stay. MRS also has ambulances with staff highly trained in emergency treatment. They will rescue you anywhere within 50km of Lilongwe for US$160, but need proof that you are insured or can pay. MRS is linked to Health International and MARS (Medical Air Rescue Service) and can arrange evacuation to Harare or Jo'burg if things get really serious.

There are MPL pharmacies at the Nico Centre in Old Town and in City Centre shopping centre.

Emergency The emergency number for police and ambulance is ☎ 199 (Lilongwe and Blantyre only), but there are never enough vehicles, so if you need assistance you'll probably have to go to the police station by taxi and bring an officer back to the scene of the crime. Once you've contacted the police, put aside several hours while they laboriously take a statement. If you are seriously injured, don't waste time phoning an ambulance – get a taxi straight to hospital.

Dangers & Annoyances We've had several reports from travellers who had pockets picked or bags slashed as they pushed through the busy crowds around the market and bus station. Be on your guard here. During the day, once you leave Malangalanga Rd, things are OK and you can walk to Area 3. At night, Malangalanga Rd can be dangerous, and walking to Area 3 is not recommended. The bridge between Area 2 and Area 3 is a favourite haunt for muggers. If you arrive on a bus after dark, take a minibus or taxi to your accommodation.

Travellers report a new con being played in Lilongwe. Some local youths around town pose as bus ticket sellers; they promise a charter minibus service to Blantyre or Cape Maclear, and even issue phoney receipts. But when you go to the bus station, of course no such bus exists. Some promise that the bus will come to pick you up from your hotel – it never comes. You should not buy tickets anywhere except at the bus station itself.

Things to See & Do

Despite rumours to the contrary, Lilongwe has enough to keep you occupied for a couple of days. The main **market** (see Shopping later in the Lilongwe section) is fun and frenetic, but for a total change of pace head for the **nature sanctuary** – an incredibly peaceful wilderness area by the Lingadzi River just off Kenyatta Rd. There is a signposted network of walking trails, and the information centre lists the birds and animals that may be seen. Less pleasing are the caged hyaena and leopard, but despite this the sanctuary is well worth a visit. It's open from 8.30 am to 4 pm weekdays, and Saturday morning. The open-air cafe by the entrance is a good place to relax after your stroll.

For a view of Malawi's economic heart, go to the public gallery overlooking the **tobacco auction floors** at the vast Auction Holdings warehouse about 7km north of the city centre, in the Kenango industrial area east of the main road towards Kasungu. This is best reached by taxi, but local minibuses serve the

Tobacco

Tobacco is Malawi's most important cash crop, accounting for more than 60% of the country's export earnings, and Lilongwe is the selling, buying and processing centre of this vital industry. Most activity takes place in the Kenango industrial area on the northern side of Lilongwe, the site of several tobacco processing factories and the huge and impressive tobacco auction rooms.

Tobacco was first grown in Malawi by a settler called John Buchanan, who planted the crop on his farm near Blantyre in the 1880s. Large-scale tobacco farming started in the area around Lilongwe in the 1920s and has grown steadily in importance ever since. Two types of tobacco are produced in Malawi: 'flue', which is a standard-quality leaf, and 'burley', which is a higher-quality leaf much in demand by cigarette manufacturers around the world. Malawi is the world's largest producer of burley.

Tobacco is grown on large plantations or by individual farmers on small farms. The leaves are harvested and dried, either naturally in the sun or in a heated drying room, and then brought to Lilongwe for sale. (In southern Malawi the crops go to auction in Limbe.)

In the auction room (called auction 'floors'), auctioneers sell tobacco on behalf of the growers. It is purchased by dealers who resell to the tobacco processors. The tobacco comes onto the auction floors (the size of several large aircraft hangars) in large bales weighing between 80kg and 100kg and is displayed in long lines. Moisture content determines the value of the leaves: if the tobacco is too dry, the flavour is impaired; if it's too wet, mould will set in and the bale is worthless.

Dealers will have inspected the tobacco leaves in advance – employing a skilled eye, nose and 'feel' – then move down the line in a small group with an auctioneer, pausing briefly at each bale to put in their bids, recorded by the auctioneer in a rapid-fire language completely unintelligible to outsiders. It takes an average of just six seconds to sell a bale, and the auctioneer and buyers hardly miss a step as they move swiftly down the line.

As soon as the dealers reach the end of the line, they move straight onto the next (there may be as many as 100 lines, each containing 100 bales) and the sale continues. Barrow boys whisk the sold tobacco off the floor, and within an hour a new line of bales is in place ready for the next group of auctioneers and dealers. The sold tobacco is taken to one of the nearby processing plants; some goes by truck but a few processors are so close to the auction floors that it simply goes on a conveyor belt.

A small proportion of tobacco is made into cigarettes for the local market, but more than 90% gets processed in Malawi (the leaves are stripped of their 'core' and shredded into small pieces) before being exported to be made into cigarettes abroad. Most processed tobacco goes by road to Durban in South Africa, to be shipped around the world, but an increasingly large amount goes by rail to the port of Nacala in Mozambique, and is shipped out from there.

The price for tobacco is around US$2 per kilogram. Every day during the six-month harvesting and selling season, the auctions shift somewhere between 13,000 and 15,000 bales of tobacco. This means a daily turnover of around US$2 million and explains the rather sardonic sign on the wall of the main auction hall. It says 'Thank you for smoking'.

industrial area. Alternatively, some companies listed under Travel Agencies & Tour Companies earlier in the Lilongwe section can arrange visits. The auction season is May to October. See the boxed text 'Tobacco' for more information on this vital commodity.

If you'd prefer a political view, tour companies can also arrange visits to the **Parliament Building**, which moved from Zomba in the mid-1990s to the palace of former president Banda on the outskirts of Lilongwe. At least this obscenely grandiose monstrosity is being used now – during Banda's rule he stayed here only one night.

If you're the sporting type, **Lilongwe Golf Club** offers daily membership for US$7. This allows you to enter the club, and use the bar or restaurant. To use the sports facilities there's a small extra charge: swimming pool, squash or tennis, about US$1; 18 holes of golf with hired clubs, US$7.

Places to Stay – Budget

All the budget places to stay are in Old Town.

The ***Council Resthouse*** near the bus station is hard to find with its entrance behind a row of shops. Basic doubles in the old wing are US$2.50; better ones in the new wing are US$4 (US$5.50 with bathroom). Three or four people can share a double for no extra charge. There's also a bar and restaurant. We have heard reports that theft of gear from empty rooms is a problem here.

Another cheapie is ***Annie's Restaurant*** in Area 2 of Old Town (see Places to Eat), which has a small dorm out the back for US$3 per person and camping for US$1.50. Again, travellers report that gear goes missing here. Another option for campers is ***Lilongwe Golf Club***, which though expensive at US$8 per person, offers a clean, safe site with hot showers and day-membership of the club, so you can use the bar, restaurant, swimming pool and some of the sporting facilities.

In the same part of town is ***St Peter's Guesthouse***. It's quiet, clean and safe at US$4 a bed in doubles or triples and US$7 for a private double, plus US$1 for breakfast. Unfortunately it's nearly always full.

The most popular place for backpackers is the friendly ***Kiboko Camp*** *(☎ 740135, 828384, @ kiboko@malawi.net)*, where camping costs US$2.50 per person, a dorm US$4 and a double room US$10. There's a good bar (it closes at 10.30 pm) and evening meals can be ordered. The people who run this place know Malawi well and can advise on buses, taxis, scams etc. To get here from the bus station, take any minibus heading for Likuni and get off at Likuni roundabout (the fare is US$0.25). Alternatively, a taxi (highly recommended at night) costs US$4 to US$5.

Top of this range, safe and good value is the ***Golden Peacock Hotel*** *(☎ 742638)* on Johnstone Rd, known affectionately as the Golden Cockroach, with standard doubles/triples for US$10/12, and doubles with bathroom for US$15.

Places to Stay – Mid-Range

All rooms in this category have private bathroom and include breakfast in the price.

The best in Old Town is ***Imperial Hotel*** *(☎ 743243, 831635, @ imperial@malawi.net)* on Mandala Rd, with very cool and airy singles/doubles from US$48/78. The bar serves snacks from US$2 and the restaurant has meals from US$5.

Lingadzi Inn *(☎ 720644)* on Chilambula Rd is clean and friendly but a little frayed around the edges (it's due for refurbishment), with a nice large garden, an incredibly small restaurant and rooms for US$72/94.

Most other mid-range places are converted villas in the suburbs. The cheapest is ***Annie's Lodge (Area 47)*** *(☎ 721590)*, just off Kamuzu Procession Rd in Area 47, where doubles are US$30 and smaller rooms with shared bathroom US$23. The eponymous proprietor also has ***Annie's Lodge (Area 10)*** *(☎ 780602)*, just off Blantyre St in – you've guessed it – Area 10. This quiet place with restaurant, garden and pool has doubles for US$48 (US$40 with shared bathroom).

Sheila's Lodge *(☎ 734258, fax 723806)* off Blantyre St in Area 43 is also quiet, with a pleasant garden and rooms for US$72/87. Meals in the restaurant cost US$4 to US$5.

Places to Stay – Top End

All rooms in this category have private bathroom and rates include breakfast.

MALAWI

In Old Town, the ***Lilongwe Hotel*** *(☎ 740488, 620071 for central reservations in Blantyre, fax 740505)* on Kamuzu Procession Rd is a low-rise building set around small areas of garden, but is poor value with singles/doubles at US$175/210 (although due for refurbishment in 2001). Facilities include a travel desk, business centre, swimming pool, restaurant and bar (see Entertainment later in this section).

The ***Meridien-Capital Hotel*** *(☎ 783388, fax 781273)* is the smartest place to stay in Lilongwe, and is used mainly by top-end tourists, business travellers and diplomats. Rooms cost from US$170/210, although as an international-class hotel the place lacks character. Facilities include a gift shop, bookshop, pharmacy, business centre, swimming pool, car hire and travel desk.

Places to Eat

Food Stalls & Cafes Around the market and in the back streets off Kamuzu Procession Rd in Area 3 are ***food stalls*** selling deep-fried cassava or potato chips and roasted meat at very cheap prices. The Peace Corps' favourite ***Chip Man*** is on the street that runs behind the Nico Centre; he has benches to sit on and also sells cold drinks.

For sit-down food, a perennial favourite is ***Annie's Restaurant*** in Area 2 of Old Town, where filling meals such as chicken and chips or curry and rice cost less than US$2. Also in this area is the clean, no-frills ***Gazebo Restaurant***, with good curries for around US$3 and snacks from US$1.

In Area 3, on Kamuzu Procession Rd ***Ali Baba's Snack Bar*** is open daily until 10 pm, serving pizzas from US$2.50 and kebabs and burgers for around US$1.50, plus ice cream and coffee. Behind here is ***The Summer Park***, a pleasant garden area where ice creams are US$0.60, snacks cost from US$1 and full meals US$3. The nearby ***Byee! Takeaway*** does cheap local meals for around US$1. On Mandala Rd, the popular European-style ***Bohemian Cafe*** (open from 8 am to 4 pm) serves breakfast, snacks and salads for US$1, big sandwiches for US$2, plus good coffee and cakes.

In City Centre, ***food stalls*** around the PTC Hypermarket serve cheap eats at lunchtime to local office workers. A plate of meat, veg and rice costs US$1. In City Centre shopping centre, ***Tasty Takeaway*** has seats outside and is also good for lunch, with Malawian meals from US$1, burgers US$1.50, curries US$2 and chicken US$2.50.

Restaurants Some restaurants are closed on Monday; call first to check.

In Old Town, ***Don Brioni's Bistro*** *(☎ 826756)*, under the Imperial Hotel, is open every night and always has a good lively atmosphere. Pizza and pasta start at US$4, and Zimbabwean T-bone steaks at US$8. Groups can negotiate a special eat-all-you-can salad and pasta deal for US$10 per person. ***Huts*** *(☎ 744756)*, near the Lilongwe Hotel, has good Indian food and swift service, with three-course meals at around US$10. Almost opposite is ***Modi's*** *(☎ 743965)*, which does curries, steak, chicken and fish dishes; it's usually acceptable, and sometimes marvellous, with prices about the same as Huts'. The ***Korea Garden***, next to the Golden Peacock Hotel, has a slightly rustic outdoor setting, with main courses from US$5 and a set menu of specialities for US$12.

In City Centre, the ***Golden Dragon*** *(☎ 780414)* serves large helpings of straightforward Chinese food; main dishes are US$2 to US$3, noodles US$1 to US$2 and specials US$7. Takeaways are the same price (but not taxed). The ***Restaurant Koreana*** *(☎ 781004)* in Gemini House, City Centre shopping centre, has very good east Asian food, with main dishes US$4 to US$7, and side orders US$1 to US$2 (closed Sunday). Nearby is the long-standing ***Causerie*** *(☎ 783828)*, where steaks, fish and curries start at US$5 but are of varying quality.

Hotel Restaurants Most of the mid-range and top-end hotels listed have restaurants open to nonresidents where standards and prices are on a par with the hotel. At the ***Imperial Hotel*** the terrace restaurant serves tasty kebabs and grills from US$2 to US$5. The restaurant at the ***Lilongwe Hotel*** has an open-air terrace – a popular lunch spot and meeting place for business travellers and well-heeled tourists; light meals start at US$3. At the Capital Hotel, the outdoor ***Patio Restaurant*** offers snacks from US$3 and meals for around US$6, while the indoors ***Greenery Restaurant*** has starters for around US$3, and main courses from US$6 for vegetarian dishes, US$7 for steaks and up to US$20 for prawns.

Entertainment

In Old Town, the streets near the market have several ***bottle stores*** which play music loud and late, but this area has a very hard edge, so go here only with a streetwise friend, enough money for an evening's supply of beer and nothing that you can't afford to lose. At the ***Lilongwe Hotel***, the residents' bar is smart and open to nonguests, while the nonresidents' bar is livelier; the predominance of male business travellers and well-off locals attracts flocks of good-time girls. There's a disco or live band on some evenings (cover charge US$2).

The bar at the ***Imperial Hotel*** is relaxed and extremely popular with expats (Friday evening happy hour can be busy). The music and the snacks are good, and you can watch the world go by from the upstairs veranda. Livelier is ***Goodfellas Pub***, in the area between Chilambula and Kenyatta Rds. It draws mainly an expat crowd, with pool tables and draught beer, open from noon (lunch available) to 11 pm.

Nearby is ***Legends***, a bar most evenings and a nightclub at weekends. It has a relaxed atmosphere and mixed crowd of young expats and well-to-do Malawians, as well as a fair blend of western and African music. For a more local feel, the ***Zebra Disco*** at the Lingadzi Inn plays mostly African music to a mostly Malawian clientele; it's open Friday and Saturday nights, with a cover charge of US$1.50.

Spectator Sports

Football matches are played at the CIVO stadium, off Kamuzu Procession Rd, and at the stadium in Area 47. There is no set program – look out for posters, or ask local fans for information.

Shopping

In Old Town, the Nico Centre has a PTC Hypermarket, bookshop, travel agency, pharmacy and several other shops. Opposite is a Kandodo supermarket where the stock is more limited though the prices are a bit cheaper. Tutla's supermarket on Mandala Rd and the 7-Eleven (which closes at 10 pm!) on Kamuzu Procession Rd, next to Ali Baba's, both have a good range of imported items, although they're more expensive than the PTC.

City Centre shopping centre, reached from Independence Dr, has shops, travel agents, restaurants, a bank and a post office. Nearby is a large PTC Hypermarket.

If you're looking for souvenirs, there are several craft stalls outside the post office in Old Town, where you can buy woodcarvings, basketware, jewellery, paintings and so on.

To see what Malawians buy, go to the city's main market on Malangalanga Rd. It's always lively and colourful, and is a great place to buy second-hand clothes, although photographs are not appreciated. Note also that pickpockets operate in the crowds and that some visitors with large bags have been violently robbed, so travel lightly here.

Getting There & Away

Air For details on flights, see the main Getting There & Away and Getting Around sections earlier in this chapter. If you're buying a ticket, it's worth trying an agent first (see Travel Agencies & Tour Operators earlier) as they offer a wider range of options, charge the same rates as the airlines and sometimes have special deals. Airlines with offices in Lilongwe include:

Air Malawi (☎ 720966, 782132) Lilongwe Hotel and Capital Hotel
Air Tanzania (☎ 783636) City Centre shopping centre
KLM & Kenya Airways (☎ 781330) Capital Hotel
South African Airways (☎ 782242) Capital Hotel

Bus For general information on the types of buses serving Lilongwe, see Bus in the main Getting Around section earlier in this chapter.

Coachline runs between Lilongwe and Blantyre (US$18, four daily, four hours). You can make reservations at the Capital

Hotel or at the Stagecoach depot (☎ 743927) near the Nico Centre in Old Town.

Express buses from Lilongwe run to: Blantyre (via Zalewa, US$5, two daily, five hours; or via Zomba, US$6, three daily, seven hours), Zomba (US$4.50), Mzuzu (US$6, two daily) and Kasungu (US$2.50, two daily). You can buy advance tickets for express buses at the Stagecoach bus station near the market in Old Town, where you can also make general timetable inquiries.

All other buses are ordinary (ie, slow). There are services from Lilongwe to Mchinji (US$1.50, hourly) and Nkhotakota (US$3, twice daily, via Salima). Getting to Monkey Bay can be a nightmare (see that section later in this chapter for more details).

Minibuses to nearby destinations such as Salima, Mchinji and Dedza (all around US$1.50) leave from the street outside the Stagecoach bus station.

Getting Around

To/From the Airport Lilongwe international airport is 24km north of the city. A taxi from the airport into town costs about US$10, but less in the other direction. The fare is negotiable but the driver will expect a tip of 10%.

At the airport look out for the Air Tours & Travel shuttle minibus which will drop you at any of the main hotels in town for US$4. Going the other way, ask at any main hotel.

Local buses and minibuses run between Old Town and the commercial part of the airport (about 200m from the passenger terminal) for just US$1, or you can catch any minibus running along the main road towards Kasungu and get off at the airport junction, from where it's 3km to the airport. Coming from the airport, you can hoof it to the main road, from where minibuses run to Lilongwe, or hitch.

Bus The most useful local minibus service for visitors is between Old Town and City Centre. Minibuses leave from the bus park opposite the market in Old Town and go southwards along Malangalanga Rd (a one-way street). They then go around the block to go west along Glyn Jones and Kamuzu Procession Rds, then turn right into Kenyatta Rd at the junction near the post office. There's a bus stop at the western end of Kenyatta Rd (opposite the Nico Centre). Buses then go north up Kenyatta Rd, via Youth and Convention Drs or via Independence Dr, to reach City Centre. From City Centre back to Old Town, the bus stop for the return journey is at the northern end of Independence Dr. Either way the fare is US$0.30.

Taxi The best places to find taxis are the main hotels. There's also a rank on Presidential Way, just north of City Centre shopping centre. The fare between Old Town and City Centre is about US$5. From the City Centre to any of the hotels fare is about US$4; from Old Town it's US$6.

AROUND LILONGWE

Dzalanyama

Dzalanyama is a beautiful forest reserve in a range of hills about 50km by road south-west of Lilongwe. The log-cabin-style ***Forest Resthouse*** (charging from $12 per person) is run by Land & Lake Safaris (listed under Information in the Lilongwe section earlier in this chapter) and offers walking trails, mountain biking, birdwatching – or simply relaxing. They also arrange lifts to the forest, as there's no public transport here.

DEDZA

Dedza is a small town 85km south-east of Lilongwe, just off the main road between Lilongwe and Blantyre. The many trees give the town a foresty feel, and there are some good walks and spectacular views in the nearby **Dedza Mountain Forest Reserve**; as described in *Day Outings from Lilongwe* (see Books in the Malawi Facts for the Visitor section earlier in this chapter).

You can camp at the dreary ***Golf Club*** for an high US$10 per tent, or try one of the cheapie resthouses on the main street. ***Rainbow Resthouse & Restaurant*** is clean and friendly; doubles with bathroom are US$2.50.

On the northern outskirts of town is Dedza Pottery, with ceramic products aimed squarely at the expat and tourist market, and a pleasant ***coffee shop***; try the fresh scones and jam at US$1.50. If you're a serious hiker, the ***Forest Resthouse***, 8km north of town in the forest reserve, makes a good base.

Northern Malawi

This section covers most parts of Northern Province, from the northern tip of the country down to the Mzuzu and Nkhata Bay areas. Places are described roughly north to south.

KARONGA

Karonga is the first and last town on the road between Malawi and Tanzania. Its facilities include the only bank north of Mzuzu (although it doesn't accept Tanzanian shillings).

The town is strung out for about 2km along the main street between a roundabout on the north-south road and the lakeshore. The ***Mukumbukeghe Resthouse*** near the roundabout has doubles for US$3; the ***Fukafuka Resthouse*** next door is cheaper. Down by the lake is ***Mufwa Lakeside Centre***, with clean rooms for US$2.50 per person, shady camping for US$1 and cold beer – well worth the long, hot walk from the roundabout. The nearby ***Club Marina*** has chalets with bathrooms for US$10 per person. Both places can advise on places to change money (including Tanzania shillings).

For transport details, see Tanzania under Land in the Getting There & Away section earlier in this chapter.

CHITIMBA

This is where you turn off the main north-south road to reach Livingstonia. The nearby long white beaches and clear waters of Lake Malawi make Chitimba a good place to chill out, especially if you've just travelled down from Tanzania.

There are three local places to stay at the junction – all much of a muchness, and all very reasonable. They can store your gear and arrange a guide if you want to walk up to Livingstonia. About 1km north of the Livingstonia turn-off, on the beach, ***Chitimba Campsite*** is very popular with overland trucks, with camping or a dorm for US$2, simple cabins US$3 and doubles with bathroom US$20. Food is available and the bar rocks until late if there's a couple of trucks in.

About 5km north of Chitimba is ***Mdokera's Beach Campsite***, close to the road and the beach, run by a friendly Malawian couple. Camping is US$1.50; huts are US$3 per person. Our favourite was the bed in the tree! Meals in the simple but clean local restaurant range from US$0.50 to US$2.50, and there's a visitors book of hints and comments. If you want something a bit smarter, about 5km south of Chitimba ***Namiashi Resort*** has camping for US$3, pleasant self-contained doubles US$10/15 with breakfast, and a good menu of European and Malawian dishes.

A minibus or *matola* (pick-up) between Chitimba and Mzuzu or Karonga is around US$2.50.

LIVINGSTONIA

The story of the founding of Livingstonia is covered under History in the Facts about Malawi section earlier in this chapter. The place is still fascinating today – like a small piece of Scotland in the heart of Africa – and it's quiet and restful, an ideal place to recover from hard travel in Tanzania or the rigours of beachlife on the lake.

Things to See & Do

The **museum** in the Stone House is open from 8 am to noon and 2 to 5 pm Monday to Saturday, and Sunday afternoon. Entry is US$0.30. The exhibits detail the early European exploration and missionary work in Malawi. Many original items that once belonged to Livingstone and the Livingstonia missionaries are still here (eg, a collection of magic lantern slides). Outside the Stone House you might notice some huge letters almost hidden by the grass, designed to be read by anyone who happens to be flying overhead in a small plane. They read *Ephesians 2-14*. Visit the museum for an explanation.

Nearby is the **church**, dating from 1894, with a beautiful stained-glass window featuring David Livingstone with his sextant, his medicine chest and his two companions, and Lake Malawi in the background.

Other places of interest include the **clock-tower**. The nearby **industrial block** was

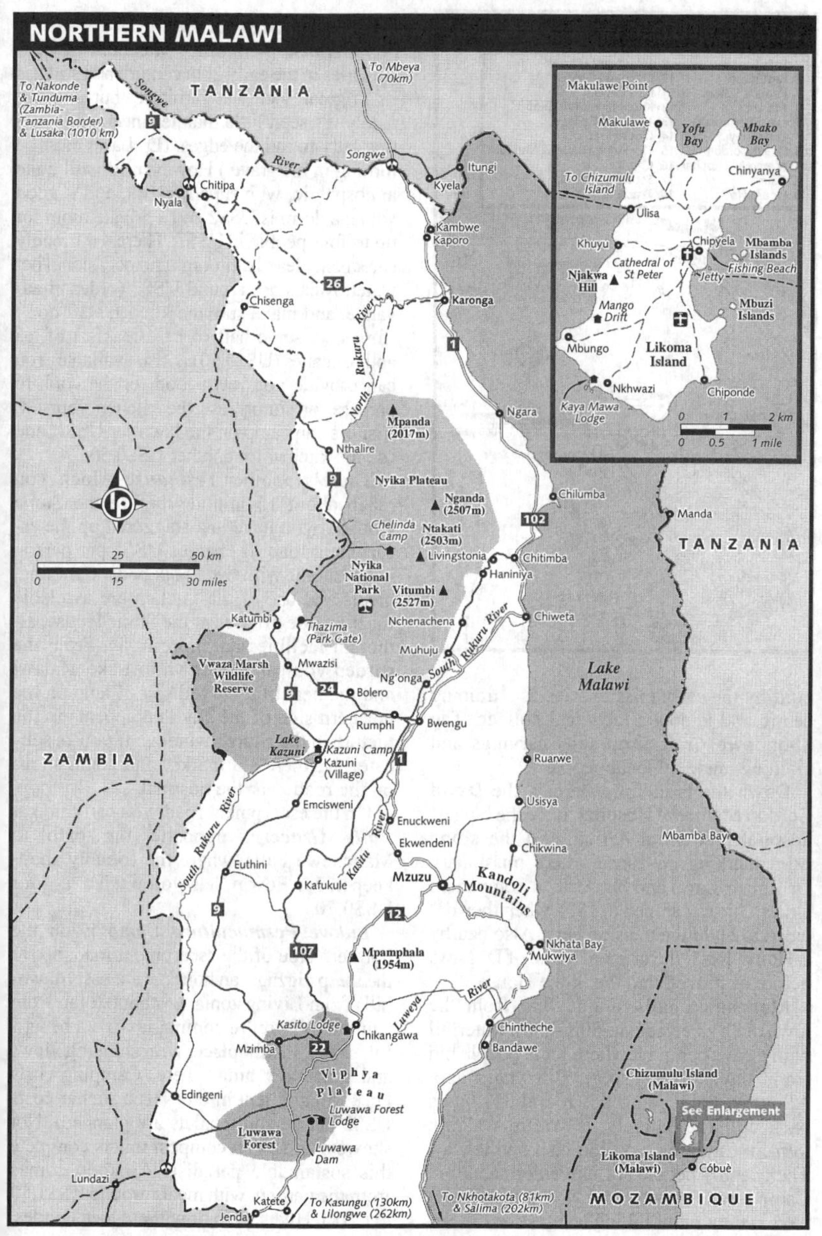
NORTHERN MALAWI
TANZANIA
ZAMBIA
MOZAMBIQUE
To Mbeya (70km)
To Nakonde & Tunduma (Zambia-Tanzania Border) & Lusaka (1010 km)
Songwe
River
Chitipa
Nyala
Itungi
Kyela
Kambwe
Kaporo
Chisenga
Karonga
North Rukuru River
Mpanda (2017m)
Ngara
Nthalire
Nyika Plateau
Nganda (2507m)
Chelinda Camp
Ntakati (2503m)
Livingstonia
Chitimba
Haniniya
Nyika National Park
Vitumbi (2527m)
Chilumba
Manda
Nchenachena
Chiweta
Katumbi
Thazima (Park Gate)
Muhuju
South Rukuru River
Vwaza Marsh Wildlife Reserve
Mwazisi
Ng'onga
Bolero
Rumphi
Bwengu
Lake Kazuni
Kazuni Camp
Kazuni (Village)
Lake Malawi
Ruarwe
Usisya
Emcisweni
Enuckweni
Kasitu River
Ekwendeni
Chikwina
Mbamba Bay
Euthini
Kafukule
Mzuzu
Kandoli Mountains
Mpamphala (1954m)
Nkhata Bay
Mukwiya
Luweya River
Kasito Lodge
Chikangawa
Chintheche
Bandawe
Mzimba
Viphya Plateau
Edingeni
Luwawa Forest Lodge
Luwawa Forest
Luwawa Dam
Lundazi
Katete
Jenda
To Kasungu (130km) & Lilongwe (262km)
To Nkhotakota (81km) & Salima (202km)
Chizumulu Island (Malawi)
Likoma Island (Malawi)
See Enlargement
Cóbuè
0 25 50 km
0 15 30 miles
Makulawe Point
Makulawe
Yofu Bay
Mbako Bay
Chinyanya
To Chizumulu Island
Ulisa
Khuyu
Chipyela
Mbamba Islands
Fishing Beach
Jetty
Cathedral of St Peter
Njakwa Hill
Mango Drift
Mbuzi Islands
Mbungo
Likoma Island
Nkhwazi
Chiponde
Kaya Mawa Lodge
0 1 2 km
0 0.5 1 mile
9
26
1
102
24
12
107
22

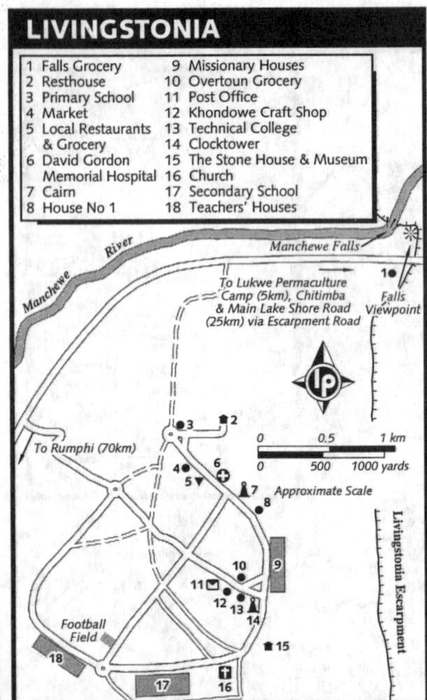

built by the early missionaries as a training centre and is now a technical college. The **Khondowe Craft Shop** sells carvings and clothing made by local people.

Down the road from here is the **David Gordon Memorial Hospital**, once the biggest hospital in Central Africa, and the **stone cairn** marking the place where missionary Dr Robert Laws and his African companion Uriah Chirwa camped in 1894 when they decided to build the mission here. Also nearby is **House No 1**, the original home of Dr Laws before he moved into the Stone House.

Manchewe Falls, about 4km from the town, is a spectacular 50m-high waterfall with a cave behind it where local people hid from slave-traders some 100 years ago. Allow an hour going down and 1½ hours back up. Alternatively, if you're walking to/from Chitimba, you can visit on the way. The friendly people at Lukwe Permaculture Camp (see Places to Stay & Eat following) have plenty more hiking suggestions.

Places to Stay & Eat

Stone House *(☎ 368223)* was built by missionaries in the early 20th century and still has its original Victorian furniture, but unfortunately it's seen little maintenance and is getting tatty round the edges. (Dr Laws must be turning in his grave.) However, it's still quite atmospheric, with superb views, and is good value: a dorm is US$2 and a private room for up to four people is US$7. There's a friendly caretaker, clean bathrooms and occasional hot water. Meals are around US$2 (order in advance, and make sure the kitchen staff don't 'forget' to serve half of it). Breakfast of tea and pancakes (US$0.50) is also available. You can provide your own food for the cook to prepare, or simply use the kitchen yourself. Visitors can camp on the lawn for US$1, and use the kitchen for another US$0.50.

There's another ***resthouse*** which you reach about 15 minutes before the Stone House if you have just staggered up the escarpment road. It charges US$1 per person in bedrooms with two to six beds. Camping, meals and use of the kitchen are available for the same price as at the Stone House, although facilities are more basic. From the garden you can see down to Lake Malawi and the beautiful curved spit of land on the northern side of the bay that appears in the picture in the church window. If you're self-catering, there's a market and some shops on the road near the hospital.

On the escarpment road, you can camp at ***Falls Grocery***, opposite the path to Manchewe Falls, where the friendly shopkeeper, Mr Edwin, lets you pitch a tent for US$0.70.

Lukwe Permaculture Camp is on the northern side of the escarpment road, above the steep zigzags, an hour's walk east (downhill) from Livingstonia, or about 20km from Chitimba if you're coming up. It's a beautiful, shady, restful place, with stunning views and a friendly atmosphere. Camping costs US$1.50 and tent hire or basic shelter costs US$2 per person (chalets are planned). Hot showers and clean compost toilets complete this sustainable paradise. All food comes from the garden, with meals around US$1.50 to US$3. Hikes, with or without local guides, can be arranged to surrounding hills and peaks, or down to Chitimba.

Getting There & Away

From the main north-south road between Karonga and Mzuzu, the road to Livingstonia turns off at Chitimba, forcing its way up the escarpment in a series of acute hairpin bends. If you're driving, it starts off well but the wide dirt road soon becomes a steep rutted track, only just passable even with 4WD. There's no bus, and you'll wait a very long time if you're hitching.

The alternative is to walk up – it's about 25km, and steep, so it takes five hours from Chitimba if you follow the road. There are short cuts that can cut it to three or four hours, but these are even steeper. Local children will offer to carry your pack for about US$2. Take care though – we heard from a traveller who unfortunately was mugged on this road. This may have been an isolated incident – probably hundreds of travellers walk up here every year – but it may be worth checking the latest situation before you set off, or taking a local guide.

The other way to reach Livingstonia, especially if you're coming from the south, is to go to Rumphi (see following), and catch a minibus or matola up the scenic 'old road' (west of the main north-south road) to Livingstonia. Sometimes these only go as far as Nchenachena (17km from Livingstonia) or Hananiya (7km from Livingstonia), from where you'll have to walk the remaining distance to Livingstonia. The fare is US$1 to US$3, depending on the state of the road.

A third option is to walk to Livingstonia from the Nyika Plateau. See the boxed text 'Hiking & Trekking on the Nyika Plateau' later in this section for details.

RUMPHI

Rumphi (**rum**-pee) is a small town west of the main road between Mzuzu and Karonga, which you'll probably visit if you're heading for Nyika National Park, Vwaza Marsh or Livingstonia. The ***Happy Landing Motel***, between the petrol station and the Stagecoach bus stop, has basic rooms for US$3, although you should try to get one with a bathroom, as the shared facilities are dirty. The ***Lunyina Guesthouse*** opposite is better, with simple rooms for US$1, and 'executive' singles/doubles for US$2/3.

Matolas to Nyika and Vwaza go from opposite the PTC supermarket. You can ask here about matolas to Nchenachena or Hananiya (for Livingstonia). A minibus between Mzuzu and Rumphi is US$1.

Mr Ngoma's House

South of Chitimba and about 20km north of the junction where the Rumphi road turns west off the main north-south road, you pass (on your right, if heading south) a remarkable two-storey building constructed of scrap metal, old car parts, brightly painted wood, ancient beds and disused road signs. This is the house of Mr SS Ngoma, one of Africa's great eccentrics, who spends most of his time sitting on his front porch watching the world go by. Mr Ngoma, in the nicest possible way, is obsessed with his forthcoming death, and has already built his coffin, grave and tombstone. He welcomes visitors, and will happily show you around his bizarre house. It was once a shop, and the sign still says 'Grocery', but the shelves have been empty for years. It has several bedrooms, which he seems to use in rotation, a 'mortuary', a 'hospital', a chapel (complete with ancient record player with a speaker wired to the veranda so that hymns can be played to the local inhabitants), an intriguing upstairs toilet, a couple of bells, plus hundreds of letters, cards and photos from admirers all over the world. Mr Ngoma used to have a red telephone by his graveside, which he said was linked directly to God and other friends who have already gone to heaven. But times change, and now he's got a portable phone hanging around his neck at all times. Mr Ngoma is weird but likeable and a visit to his house will never be forgotten. On leaving you should sign the visitors book (he's on his sixth) and make a small donation to his long-suffering daughter.

NYIKA NATIONAL PARK

Nyika National Park was established in 1965, making it Malawi's oldest; it has also been

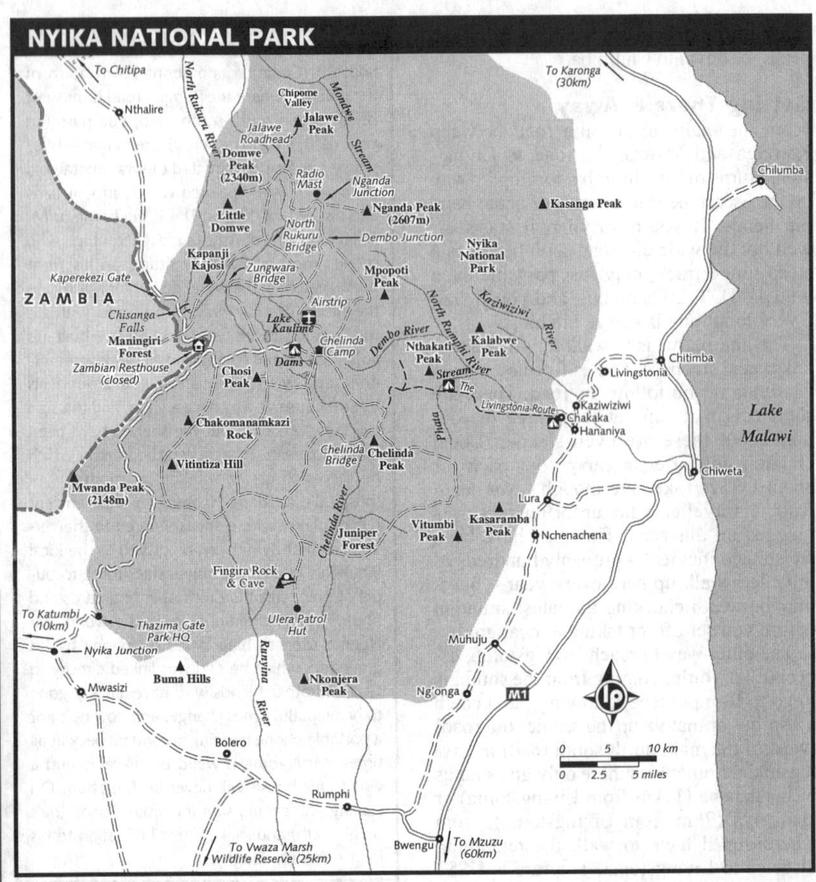

extended since then, so it is now the largest in the country, covering some 3000 sq km. The main feature of the park is the Nyika Plateau, with a landscape and climate unique in Malawi, and unusual in Africa: a vast range of high rolling hills, covered in montane grassland, where the air is cool and crisp, and the views (on clear days) are endless.

Much of the Nyika is above 1800m, with several peaks on the western, northern and eastern sides over 2000m, where the plateau drops in a series of escarpments to the plains below. The valleys and escarpment edges are covered in miombo woodland, while other areas consist of dense evergreen forest, and there are also small patches of bog. Common animals here include zebra and reedbuck, but you'll also see eland and roan antelope (rare elsewhere), warthog, klipspringer, jackal, duiker and possibly hyaena and leopard. In the grassland, spotting is easy – in fact the Nyika zebra seem to delight in posing for photos on the skyline. More than 400 species of bird have been recorded here.

Nyika is also famous for its wildflowers. The best time for viewing them is during and just after the wet season (September to April), when the grassland is covered in

> **Warning**
>
> It can get surprisingly cold on the Nyika Plateau, especially at night from June to August, when frost is not uncommon. Log fires are provided in the chalets and rooms, but bring a warm sleeping bag if you're camping.
>
> During dry periods, sectors of the park are burnt to prevent larger fires later in the season. Before setting off for drives or walks, inquire at the park headquarters and avoid areas that are being burnt.

colour and small outcrops turn into veritable rock gardens. Around 200 species of orchid alone grow on the plateau.

Entry fees are payable (see National Parks & Wildlife Reserves in the Facts about Malawi section). All accommodation and tourist activities are operated by The Nyika Safari Company, a small professional outfit which has made significant improvements here in the past few years. The company is based at Chelinda Camp (see Places to Stay for contact details), at the heart of the plateau, but also has a representative in Lilongwe (☎ 743501).

Activities

Wildlife Viewing To appreciate the animals and flowers of Nyika, you can tour the park tracks in your own car, or arrange a guided wildlife-viewing drive at Chelinda Camp. Most go in the morning or evening, but you can also go all day, or at night, where the guide uses a spotlight to pick out animals. Wildlife viewing is good all year, although in July and August the cold weather means the animals move to lower areas. Birdwatching is particularly good between October and April when migratory birds are on the move.

Day Hiking Although you can't enter the park on foot, once you are inside hiking is allowed. There are several spots where you can leave your car and walk for an hour or all day; staff can advise you on routes. One of the most popular options is to park at the Jalawe roadhead, north of Chelinda Camp, then follow the path for 5km to Jalawe Peak. Beyond the summit is a rocky outcrop overlooking the Chipome Valley, some 1000m below. You can sometimes spot elephant here.

For long walks, you can hire a scout (park ranger) to guide you. Various paths and tracks wind through the plantation woodland, or across the grassland to nearby dams. For longer walks of more than a day, see the boxed text 'Hiking & Trekking on the Nyika Plateau' later in this section.

Mountain Biking Mountain bike hire is planned at Chelinda, or you could bring your own bike; the park tracks are ideal for fat-tyred cycling.

Horse Riding The wide open Nyika landscape lends itself perfectly to horse riding, and this is by far the most enjoyable and exhilarating way to experience the plateau. The tussock grass and boggy valley bottoms that can tire hikers are crossed easily by horse, and the extra height means the views are excellent. You can also get much closer to animals such as zebra, eland and roan when on horseback. At Chelinda Camp you can hire good-quality horses that are suitable for beginners and experts. Rates are US$10 per hour or US$50 all day. Longer horse safaris are available, for two to 10 days, according to your itinerary, budget and hardiness. These can be mobile, staying in luxury tents and exploring the remote parts of the plateau, or based at Chelinda Lodge. The cost is US$200 per person per night all inclusive.

Fishing Some anglers reckon Nyika offers some of the best rainbow trout fishing in Malawi. The best time of year to fish is October and November. Fishing is allowed in the dams near Chelinda Camp and in nearby streams. A daily licence costs US$4. Rods can be hired. Only fly fishing is permitted.

Places to Stay

Chelinda Camp (☎ 740579, fax 740848 in Lilongwe, ⓔ nyika-safaries@malawi.net) is run by The Nyika Safari Company. Chalets with two bedrooms (each with two beds), bathroom, lounge and fully equipped kitchen cost US$100 per night for four people. You provide your own food and each

MALAWI

Hiking & Trekking on the Nyika Plateau

A good range of long-distance routes (sometimes called 'wilderness trails') are available on Nyika, and all hiking is now efficiently organised by The Nyika Safari Company at Chelinda Camp (see Places to Stay in this section). The company provides the obligatory guide and porters, who have their own sleeping bags, tents, cooking pots and food. You must provide all the equipment and food you need.

There is only one set route in the park; generally you either follow the park tracks, paths and wildlife trails or simply walk across the trackless grassland, but some paths are more popular than others – those to the peaks and viewpoints on the western and northern escarpments are especially popular. There are no set camp sites either. The wilderness trails are not designed so you can stalk wildlife to get better photos, but rather to show you the animals as part of the wider environment, and help you enjoy the splendid feeling of space that walking on Nyika provides. If you discuss your interests with the staff at Chelinda Camp, they can advise on a suitable route.

The only set route on Nyika – and by far the most popular – goes from Chelinda to Livingstonia, a spectacular and hugely rewarding walk, crossing east through the high grassland, then dropping steeply through the wooded escarpment and passing through villages and farmland to reach the old mission station at Livingstonia. This route takes three days. The third night is spent in Livingstonia, and you can walk down to the lakeshore at Chitimba on the fourth day. For more ideas, a chapter on trekking in Malawi is included in Lonely Planet's *Trekking in East Africa*.

Organised hikes can usually run with a day or two's notice, but advance warning (through The Nyika Safari Company's office in Lilongwe) is preferred. They are proving so popular that they may soon run on set days only – probably with departures from Chelinda twice per week.

Two-day (one-night) hikes cost US$30 per person for two hikers (US$50 for three days, US$90 for five days); add US$5 for each extra hiker. The Livingstonia Trail (three days, two nights) costs US$80 per person for two hikers; add US$10 for each extra hiker. Fees cover the guide and all his costs; porters are also available.

chalet has a cook who will prepare meals for you. (Chalet guests can also order meals in the restaurant.) Double rooms with private bathroom cost US$60 per person, including all meals, which are filling and wholesome. There's also a bar, an information room and a shop. This place became very run-down when it was operated by the national park, but since The Nyika Safari Company took over it's been nicely spruced up, without losing any of the friendly cosy atmosphere for which Chelinda was famous. A beer by the roaring fire after a long day's walk on the hills is one of Malawi's great pleasures.

About 2km from the main camp is a ***camping ground***, with clean toilets, hot showers, endless firewood and shelters for cooking and eating. Camping costs US$5 per person. If you don't have your own tent, you can hire one for US$10 (sleeps two people).

New on the scene is ***Chelinda Lodge***, about 1km from Chelinda Camp, where luxury log cabins perched on a hillside affording stunning views over the plateau cost US$200 per person, including all meals, wildlife drives and walks.

Getting There & Away

Despite most maps showing otherwise, there is *no road of any sort* between Chelinda and Livingstonia or any other town on the eastern side of the plateau.

Air The quickest way to reach Nyika is by the twice-weekly Air Malawi flight from Lilongwe (US$72) via Mzuzu (US$35) to Chelinda's airstrip; note that planes won't land in bad weather. Contact a Lilongwe travel agent or the Air Malawi office in Mzuzu.

Bus There are no public buses into the park; the nearest you can get to the park by bus is the service from Mzuzu to Rhumpi (US$1). From there, matolas and minibuses run once or twice per day to Katumbi via Nyika Junction (8km from Thazima gate). You can try hitching from the junction – it's what the staff who work at Chelinda do – but be prepared for a long wait. You may be lucky and find a matola in Rumphi heading for the Zambian Resthouse junction, about 12km west of Chelinda (the resthouse is now closed). From the Zambian Resthouse junction you'll have to hitch or walk to Chelinda.

Taxi You can hire a taxi (or a matola) in Mzuzu or Rumphi to take you all the way to Chelinda Camp. This costs around US$100 (less from Rumphi), which is not too bad if you get a few people together. Of course, if the taxi has to wait around for a few days to take you out again this will be more expensive, but we've heard from several travellers who used this method to reach Chelinda – even in standard 2WD taxis, although a high-clearance matola pick-up would be better – then hitched out a few days later, or walked off via the Livingstonia route. If you take the taxi option, it's essential to leave early in the morning so your driver has time to get back.

Car The main Thazima gate (pronounced and sometimes spelt Tazima) is in the southwest of the park, 54km from Rumphi; to Chelinda Camp it's another 55km. The road is dirt after Rumphi and in fair condition as far as Thazima gate. In the park the tracks are rough in a few places but easily passable in a vehicle with high clearance (4WD not required). Kaperekezi gate, in the west of the park, is rarely used by travellers. Fuel is available at Chelinda.

Bicycle Nyika's network of dirt roads is ideal for mountain biking. You can base yourself at Chelinda and go for day rides in various directions, or camp out overnight. We heard of a hardy Norwegian traveller who flew with his bike on Air Malawi to Chelinda, then rode eastwards, finally carrying his bike down the precipitous path to Livingstonia (an option only for the truly mad).

VWAZA MARSH WILDLIFE RESERVE

This pleasant and all-too-frequently overlooked reserve is well worth visiting. Access is easy by car, and pretty straightforward by public transport, making Vwaza an ideal destination for those without wheels. The best way to get around is on foot, and a lot of wildlife can be seen from the main camp. Entry fees are payable (see National Parks & Wildlife Reserves in the Facts about Malawi section earlier in this chapter). All tourist activities and places to stay are operated by The Nyika Safari Company (see Chelinda Camp under Places to Stay in the Nyika National Park section earlier for contact details) and have improved considerably.

There's a range of vegetation and habitats in the reserve. In the north is Vwaza Marsh itself and a large area of swamp surrounded by miombo woodland. There are also smaller areas of mopane and acacia woodland. The Luwewe River runs through the reserve (draining the marshland) and joins the South Rukuru River (the reserve's southern border), which flows into Lake Kazuni. The two places to stay are both at the lake, and the main gate is nearby.

Several hundred elephant inhabit the reserve, and can often be seen around Lake Kazuni. Other mammals include buffalo (rumoured to be particularly aggressive here), waterbuck, eland, roan, sable, zebra, hartebeest, impala and puku, all surprisingly easy to see from the area around the lake, which also supports a good population of hippo. The **birdwatching** is excellent – this is one of the best places in Malawi for seeing waders.

There are several driveable tracks in the reserve, but these are suitable only for high-clearance vehicles, and not really designed for wildlife viewing anyway. The best driving route is along the southern edge of the reserve, parallel to the river, heading to Zoro Pools.

Construction of proper wildlife-viewing tracks is planned, but meanwhile you're better off hiking – either around Lake Kazuni or on a longer wilderness trail. For either, you must be accompanied by a scout (park ranger) at all times (for information on the cost of this service, see National Parks & Wildlife Reserves in the Facts about Malawi section earlier in this chapter).

Places to Stay

Kazuni Camp has simple rustic chalets with beds, clean sheets, mosquito nets and shared bathrooms for US$10 per person. Camping is US$3. You must bring food, and the very friendly staff will cook for you if required. Basic supplies can be bought in Kazuni village, which is a few kilometres outside the park gate. The smarter ***Kazuni Safari Camp*** has stylish chalets overlooking the lake. Full board costs US$140 per person, which includes drives and walks, but if you don't want the whole package, cheaper rates may be available.

Getting There & Away

First get to Rumphi (reached from Mzuzu by minibus for US$1). From there fairly frequent matolas and minibuses run to Kazuni village (a few kilometres beyond the entrance to the reserve) for US$2. By car, head west from Rumphi. Turn left after 10km (Vwaza Marsh Wildlife Reserve is signposted), and continue for about 20km. Where the road swings left over a bridge, go straight on to reach the park gate and camp after 1km.

MZUZU

Mzuzu (known as 'the capital of the north') is a large town with banks, shops, a post office, supermarkets, pharmacies, petrol stations and other facilities, which are especially useful if you've come into Malawi from the north. Most travellers find themselves staying for at least one night, as a stopover on the north-south route, or as a jumping-off point for Vwaza, Viphya, Nyika or Nkhata Bay.

The **museum** on M'Mbelwa Rd, just off Orton Chewa Ave, has good displays on the history of African and European peoples in northern Malawi, and a section on indigenous plants and wildlife. It's open from 7 am to noon and 1 to 5 pm daily. Entry and guided tours are free, but a small donation to the curator (always around to answer questions) may be appropriate.

Places to Stay

If you're really short of cash, the ***Council Resthouse*** near the small market has basic rooms for US$1.50 per person. Most budget travellers head for ***CCAP Resthouse***, north-east of the bus station. It costs US$4 per person in rooms with two, three or four beds, but some travellers have reported items going missing while they were out. The nearby ***Chiwanja City Resthouse*** has straightforward singles/doubles with shared bathroom for US$3/5. Better still is the homely ***Flame Tree Guesthouse***, offering B&B for US$7/9. The nearby ***Katoto Guesthouse*** is simple, but friendly and clean, charging US$4 per person, including breakfast.

The ***Government Tourist Lodge***, east of the town centre on the Nkhata Bay road, offers (as its sign proudly states) 'accommodation, meals and an assortment of drinks and camping services'. Clean and comfortable rooms with a colonial feel and shared bathrooms cost from US$25/35 with breakfast. Camping on a fenced grassy site is US$4, or US$5 if you want hot showers. Evening meals cost around US$3.

The ***Mzuzu Hotel*** *(☎ 332622)* is the best in town, with doubles for US$130. In the restaurant, starters cost around US$3 and main courses from US$5 to US$10. There is a quiet bar for residents, while next to the hotel the Choma Bar provides loud evening entertainment with a local flavour.

Places to Eat

Most of the places to stay have restaurants. Also, there's street food around the market, a supermarket opposite the tourist office and several shops and a ***bakery*** by the bus station.

The ***Tropicana Restaurant*** has a bar, a shady terrace, snacks from US$1, Malawian meals for around US$1.50 and chicken and chips for around US$2. The clean and friendly ***At'Tayyiba Restaurant*** has a wider choice, with meals like beef and nsima for around US$1.50.

For more stylish surroundings, the restaurant at ***Mzuzu Club***, next to the Mzuzu Hotel, is usually open to nonmembers, with good-value Malawian and western-style food from about US$2.50.

Getting There & Away

Stagecoach express buses run to Lilongwe (US$6) via Kasungu (US$3.50), and ordinary

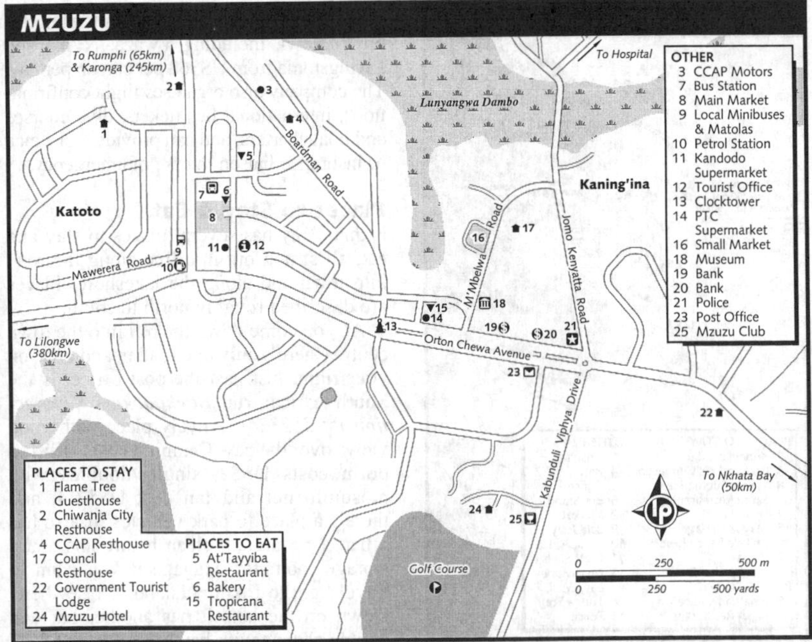

buses and minibuses go to Rumphi (US$1) and Nkhata Bay (US$0.75). Buses go to Chitimba (US$2.50), and buses/minibuses go to Karonga (US$4/5).

A bus goes via Mzuzu between Lilongwe and Dar es Salaam twice weekly for US$33. Heading north, it leaves Mzuzu around midnight, crosses the border at first light, goes through Mbeya in the morning and gets to Dar es Salaam late in the afternoon.

NKHATA BAY

Nkhata Bay lies on the lake about 50km south-east of Mzuzu. This is probably the most scenic of Malawi's lakeshore towns, and a few travellers have even described it as 'Caribbean'. That may be a touch too fanciful, although at sunrise and sunset it does become quite picturesque. It's busy too – the *Ilala* docks here on its voyage up and down the lake, and buses go regularly to/from Mzuzu and Salima. In the past few years, Nkhata Bay has started to rival Cape Maclear as a budget travellers destination, and it has several good places to stay. Despite the influx of foreigners, the town retains its strong Malawian feel, especially around the large and lively market.

Information

You can exchange cash or travellers cheques, buy US dollars, or get cash on Visa or MasterCard at the Easy Money foreign exchange bureau. Next door are the equally efficient Easy Mail Internet bureau and Tonga Tours.

Activities

Swimming On the southern side of Nkhata Bay, the fabulous **Chikale Beach** is a popular spot for swimming and lazing on the sand, especially at weekends.

Kayaking For something more active, **kayaks** can be hired from Monkey Business (☎ 352365, ⓔ njayalodge@malawi.net). You can go for a few hours, or take an organised

MALAWI

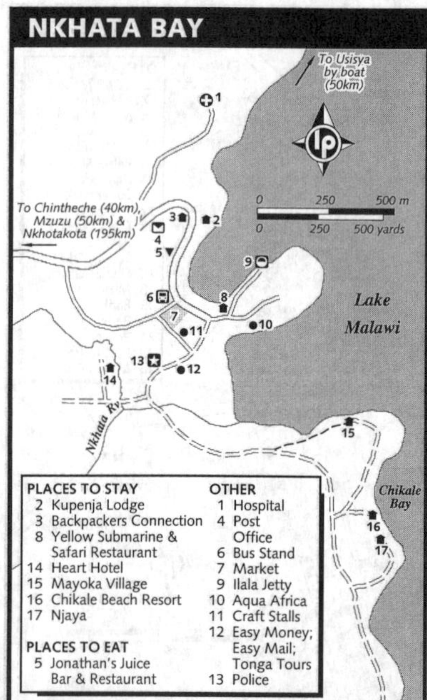

trip along the lakeshore for a few days or longer, staying at fishing villages or empty beaches along the way, for US$30 per day. These trips are highly rated by travellers. Spectacular trips to Likoma Island, sailing aboard the *Ilala*, then paddling around the island and the Mozambique shore, are also available.

Diving If you want to learn **scuba diving**, Aqua Africa (☎/fax 352284, ⓔ andy@aqua-africa.com) runs four-day courses for US$130, normally twice a week. Again, they come highly recommended, and people who have done the course comment particularly on the company's attention to safety. You should try to book in advance, but if they're full you only have to wait a few days for the next course to start.

Organised Tours

For trips further afield, Tonga Tours (☎ 352341, ⓔ tongatours@malawi.net) organises tours and **safaris** to all parts of northern Malawi, including Vwaza, Nyika and Livingstonia from US$60 per person per day. The company also organises flight confirmations, international bus tickets, dive courses and boat charters, and can provide assistance or insurance liaison in case of emergency.

Places to Stay & Eat

Nkhata Bay has several places to stay and eat, all strung out in a line along the road into town and along the lakeshore. Places are described roughly north to south.

As you come down the hill into the town centre (there's only one road in and out), on your right, just past the post office, is the South African-run ***Backpackers Connection*** *(☎ 352324)*, a lively place with good views over the bay. Camping costs US$1, a dorm costs US$2, singles/doubles with mosquito net and fan cost US$3/4, and there's a place to park vehicles. It also has a bar, a restaurant, clean bathrooms and a storage room for baggage if you want to travel light to Likoma Island or elsewhere. Down on the lake it has another bar and double chalets with bathroom for US$8.

Near Backpackers Connection, on the lakeshore, are some locally run places including ***Kupenja Lodge***, which has a much quieter feel. Rooms are US$1.50 per person, and 'floor squatting' costs US$0.50. Food is available only to order. Because all these places are open to the lake, security

Warning

Unfortunately, security has become a bit of a problem in Nkhata Bay. Travellers have been attacked and robbed when walking outside the town centre (especially to/from Chikale Bay), and a few people have had bags snatched near the bus station while looking for a place to stay (thieves love new arrivals). These have been isolated incidents, but to combat the problem, the hotels, lodges, restaurants and Aqua Africa have got together and will 'lend' their watchman free of charge to anyone walking outside the town centre. Use this service and you'll have no worries.

has occasionally been a problem, so don't leave valuables in the rooms.

A little further down the road is ***Jonathan's Juice Bar & Restaurant***, a mellow terrace under trees, with cool drinks from US$0.50, breakfasts and snacks from US$1, plus pizzas, pastas and stir-fries, including vegie options, from US$2.50.

At the bottom of the hill near the bus stand, market and shops, you'll find the ***Safari Restaurant***, a popular travellers haunt with another great view across the bay; omelettes and sandwiches cost US$1, pizzas and moussaka cost from US$2 and pepper steak and chips or honey garlic chicken costs US$3.

Next door is the ***Yellow Submarine***, near the ferry jetty, with rooms for US$2.50/3 and a small private garden.

Turn right onto a dirt road just after the market, go past Tonga Tours, then turn right again to reach the decidedly no-frills ***Heart Hotel*** – one of the few Malawian-run tourist places in town. Many budget travellers have recommended this place, although its village setting means a lot of people come and go, so you should be discreet with your valuables. You can sleep on the floor for US$0.60, or take the luxury option of a bed for US$1 (with breakfast); other meals are US$2. Mr Philip, the friendly proprietor, has opened a secluded budget camping ground on the lakeshore about 20km south of Nkhata Bay – ask at the hotel for details.

If you keep on the dirt road, you cross a bridge and head up hill and down dale (always seems harder with a backpack) to reach some other places to stay. ***Mayoka Village*** has small, simple, but clean and mozzie-proof chalets on a steep hillside overlooking the bay for US$2.50/3. Camping is US$1. There's a bar, a restaurant and free use of snorkel gear and dugout canoes.

Chikale Beach Resort, on Chikale Beach, has nice-looking double chalets with bathroom for US$16/25 (less in the low season), including breakfast; they're bare but functional inside. The bar and restaurant is bang on the fabulous beach, although this place is quiet in the evening.

Njaya *(☎/fax 352342, ⓔ njayalodge@compuserve.com)*, run by English couple Claire and Paul, is legendary on the travellers' grapevine. It offers Asian-style reed chalets on Chikale Beach and a range of cabins and bungalows on the hillside overlooking the lake, all with mosquito nets, from US$3 per person in a simple hut, up to US$20 for a cottage with private bathroom. Camping costs US$2. The breezy bar overlooks the lake, and tasty food ranges from US$1 to US$3. You can get your laundry done, send email, use the visa service if you're heading for Mozambique, and for all you city slickers, credit cards are accepted. A transfer van runs between Njaya and the town centre a few times each day, and also meets the *Ilala*.

Getting There & Away

All buses and minibuses go from the bus stand next to the market. The fare to Mzuzu or Chintheche is US$0.75; to Nkhotakota it's US$2. To reach Lilongwe, go to Mzuzu and transfer. Many travellers also come or go on the *Ilala* (for details, see the main Getting Around section earlier in this chapter).

AROUND NKHATA BAY

North of Nkhata Bay, the steep slopes of the Rift Valley escarpment plunge straight down to the lake and there's no room for a road alongside the shore. The villages here can only be reached on foot, by the *Ilala* or by local (and invariably overloaded) 'taxi boats', which chug along the shore north of Nkhata Bay. At **Usisya**, a new backpackers hostel is under construction. You can get more details from the places in Nkhata Bay.

THE CHINTHECHE STRIP

Chintheche is an unremarkable village about 40km south of Nkhata Bay. Nearby is a long and beautiful stretch of lakeshore known as the 'Chintheche Strip'. It's lined with hotels, lodges and camping grounds, each catering for different types of traveller. They all lie between 2km and 5km east of the main road that runs between Nkhata Bay and Nkhotakota, and usually involve a drive or walk along a dirt track through forest or farmland. If you're travelling by bus, the express services may not stop at every turn-off, but minibuses stop almost anywhere on request.

Places to Stay

About 3km north of Chintheche village is ***Kawiya Kottages*** *(e sosmalawi@malawi.net)*, two comfortable cabins, each with kitchen and bathroom, in a shady site on a private bit of beach, which are good value at US$7 per person. Camping is US$1.75.

Nearer Chintheche village, the ***Forest Resthouse*** has beds in clean wood cabins for US$2.50. Nearby, another dirt track leads to ***London Cottages***, where local-feel single/double chalets with bathroom cost US$3/4. Camping is US$0.75.

About 2km down the main road, and another 2km along a track, is the ***Flame Tree Lodge*** *(☎ 357276)*, run by a friendly English-Malawian couple, on a beautiful promontory jutting into the lake. Smart chalets are US$15/25 with bathroom and breakfast (no extra charge for children sharing). Camping is US$2, and the showers are hot. This is a suitable place for families or small groups. There's a bar, a library and a restaurant with meals from US$3. Breakfast (with home-made jam) costs US$1.50. If you call in advance, they'll pick you up from Chintheche village.

Another 3.5km south along the main road, a tar road leads to ***Chintheche Inn*** *(☎/fax 357211, e wildsaf@eomw.net or info@wilderness.malawi.net)*, a small and friendly place with stylish Mediterranean-style decor in the rooms, beautiful gardens, and thatched verandas overlooking the beach. Dinner, bed and full buffet breakfast costs US$90/150. The food is very good. Young children sharing with their parents pay for meals only. The inn also has a ***camping ground*** with grassy lawns, its own bar and restaurant, and hotel-quality bathrooms for US$5 per person. If you want to reserve a room and can't get through, call Central African Wilderness Safaris in Lilongwe – they have a radio link with the inn (see Travel Agencies & Tour Operators in the Lilongwe section earlier in this chapter).

Another 1km south down the main road is a signpost to the 'CCAP School' (also called New Bandawe); go through here to reach the South African-run ***Nkhwazi Lake Camp***, a good place overlooking a small sandy cove. Camping is US$1. There are basic but clean ablution blocks, and a 'pub' with home-cooked meals from US$3 to US$5. Scuba gear and motorboats for anglers can be hired.

Continuing south down the main road you reach the turn-off to Bandawe (also called Old Bandawe) and ***Makuzi Beach Retreat***, another 3.5km down the track. This quiet and relaxing place offers camping for US$3, simple chalets for US$5 and cool comfortable chalets with bathroom for US$30 per person. Breakfast and lunch range from US$1 to US$4, with a set evening meal for US$5, including lots of vegie options. Courses here include raiki, yoga, massage, herbalism and similar pursuits.

About 7km from the Makuzi turn-off (55km south of Nkhata Bay) is ***Kande Beach Camp***, a legendary stop for overland trucks, where beachlife, good times and late night partying is the name of the game. Trucks get special rates; individual drivers and backpackers looking to join in the fun pay US$1 for camping or US$10 for simple chalets. Also on site is a restaurant, a large bar, a games room and a fully set-up dive centre. Mountain bikes, canoes, kayaks and sailboards are available for hire.

Another 7km further south is the ***Mwaya Beach Lodge***, where the atmosphere is quiet and restful – the entrance track crosses weak bridges, a ploy to keep out the overland trucks! Camping is US$1.50 and simple chalets cost US$3.50 per person. There's a bar, and food includes banana bread, bean-burgers, pumpkin ravioli and meals with chicken and fish for US$2 to US$4. Clean drinking water is free. You can stay here and learn to dive at Kande Beach for US$200, which includes the course, all food and accommodation.

LIKOMA ISLAND

The islands of Likoma and Chizumulu are on Lake Malawi, within the waters of Mozambique but part of Malawi, and linked to the rest of the country by the *Ilala* steamboat. Likoma is something of an enigma: it's not a paradise isle in the usual sense, although it does have some excellent beaches. Instead it has a rather sparse beauty, which not all travellers will appreciate. Some love it and stay for weeks; others are disappointed and leave as soon as possible. Either way, you'll meet few other travellers here.

Likoma measures 17 sq km, with a population of about 6000. The south is fairly flat, dry and sandy, with baobab trees a common feature. The north is more hilly and quite densely vegetated. The main settlement is Chipyela, and there are several other fishing villages dotted around the coast.

Things to See & Do

Unless you charter a plane or boat, you're tied to the *Ilala* schedules, which means being here at least three days, so you'll have to relax whether you like it or not! Likoma Island has some lovely long stretches of **sandy beach**, mostly along the southern coast but also notably at Jofu in the north. Crocodiles have killed a couple of people here in recent years, so ask around locally before diving in.

For something more active, Likoma is small enough to explore on foot. Akuzike Guesthouse (see Places to Stay & Eat following) has produced a map of the island, showing the best beaches and areas of interest and suggesting a number of **walks**. If you walk around, remember this isn't the Costa del Sol – the people here live a very trad- itional way of life, so keep your clothing and behaviour suitably modest.

In Chipyela, the impressive Anglican **Cathedral of St Peter** should not be missed (see the boxed text 'Likoma Missionaries & The Cathedral of St Peter'). Nearby, the neat **market place** contains a few shops and stalls, and an old baobab overtaken by a strangler fig, now rotted away from underneath and used by the locals as a storeroom. Down on the lakeshore is a beach where local boats come and go, and the people wash and sell fish. Don't be surprised if some people greet you in Portuguese; traders come here from nearby Mozambique to sell firewood, vegetables and – bizarrely – fish. The *Ilala* stops at another beach about 1km to the south.

Places to Stay & Eat

In Chipyela, the ***Akuzike Guesthouse*** is justifiably popular, with clean rooms around a courtyard for US$3 per person. There's running water, mosquito nets and a small restaurant (with meals for US$2 to US$3) and a map of the island on the wall, which is good for getting your bearings and planning walks.

Mango Drift, on a beautiful sandy beach on the western side of the island, charges US$1 for camping, US$2 for a dorm, US$4 per person in a simple hut, and US$20 for comfortable double chalets. There are plans for a dive school here. You can get more information from the backpackers places in Nkhata Bay.

A luxury lodge called ***Kaya Mawa***, on the southern side of the island, is quite simply unique. Each chalet is different, designed with flair and wild imagination, and has private access to the lake (the honeymoon suite even has its own islet). The bar and restaurant is balanced on the top of a huge rock buttress, with splendid views of sunrise and sunset. Rates are US$150 per person, including full board and boat trips. Book at any travel agency in Lilongwe.

For cheap eats in Chipyela, try the ***Women's Restaurant*** near the market, or the nameless ***food shack*** on the fishing beach. Wherever you go, ordering meals in advance may prove rewarding, and don't expect a huge menu – the staples here are fish, nsima and rice; fruit and veg are more limited.

Getting There & Away

Most people come to Likoma Island by the *Ilala* steamboat (see the Getting Around section earlier in this chapter for details). The boat usually stops for three to four hours, so even if you're heading elsewhere, you might be able to nip ashore to have a quick look at the cathedral (see the boxed text 'Likoma Missionaries & the Cathedral of St Peter'). Check with the captain before you leave the boat.

The island is only about 10km off the coast of Mozambique, and dhows sail to the town of Cóbuè (**kob**-way) on the Mozambique mainland. For more details, see Mozambique under Lake in the main Getting There & Away section earlier in this chapter.

Likoma Missionaries & The Cathedral of St Peter

European involvement on Likoma Island began in 1882 when members of UMCA (Universities Mission to Central Africa) established a base here. The leaders of the party, Will Johnson and Chauncey Maples, chose the island as protection from attacks from the warlike Ngoni and Yao peoples.

Chauncey Maples became the first bishop of Likoma, but he died only a few months after being appointed, drowning in the lake off Monkey Bay. Despite the setback, missionary work on the island continued. Between 1903 and 1905 the huge cathedral was built and dedicated to St Peter – appropriately a fisherman. Today it remains one of Malawi's most remarkable buildings.

The cathedral measures over 100m long by 25m wide (for British travellers, that's the size of Winchester Cathedral), and has stained-glass windows and elaborate choir stalls carved from soapstone. The crucifix above the altar was carved from wood from the tree where Livingstone's heart was buried in Zambia.

It was built at a part of the island called Chipyela, meaning 'Place of Burning', because the early UMCA arrivals had witnessed suspected witches being burnt alive here. The island's main settlement grew up around the cathedral, and is still called Chipyela today.

The UMCA missionaries remained on Likoma until the 1940s. During that time they were hard at work – they claimed 100% literacy among the local population at one point. The cathedral fell into disrepair, but was restored in the 1970s and 1980s, and local people are understandably very proud of it.

CHIZUMULU ISLAND

Chizumulu Island is smaller than Likoma (and just a few kilometres away), and even more detached from the mainland – it's possibly the perfect lake hideaway. If you want to visit both islands, transport links make it best to go to Chizumulu first.

The main place to stay is ***Wakwenda Retreat***, near where the *Ilala* stops, by a good beach. The staff are very friendly and there's a pleasant bar built in a baobab tree. You can also hire snorkelling and diving gear. Camping costs US$1.50, simple huts cost US$2.50 and chalets cost US$3.50 per person. There are two other resthouses on the island where facilities are more basic and rates cheaper.

The *Ilala* stops here from Nkhata Bay, en route to Likoma Island, once per week. Or you can get the dhow ferry that runs every morning from Ulisa on the western coast of Likoma to Chizumulu (US$0.50), but it is an extremely choppy ride when the wind is blowing, and potentially dangerous if a storm comes up.

Central Malawi

This section covers most parts of Malawi's Central Province with the addition of the Viphya Plateau. Places are described north to south.

THE VIPHYA PLATEAU

The Viphya Plateau is a highland area, running like a broad backbone through north-central Malawi. Despite its name, this area is not flat but consists mostly of rolling hills, cut by river valleys and punctuated by occasional rocky peaks. Much of the Viphya Plateau is pine plantation or dense bush, but the journey along the main road between Kasungu and Mzuzu is beautiful, especially if the sun is shining (but don't be surprised if there's dense mist and rain). If you've got a few days to spare this is a good area to relax away from the hubbub of towns or cool down from the heat of the lakeshore.

Places to Stay

Luwawa Forest Lodge (*☎ 320897, 829725, ⓔ wardlow@malawi.net*) lies 10km east of the main road between Kasungu and Mzuzu. It used to belong to the forestry department, but it's managed now by the energetic George Wardlow. Comfortable accommodation in rooms sleeping up to four, with bathroom and kitchen, cost US$15 per person (half price for children). Breakfast and lunch cost US$4, and a big

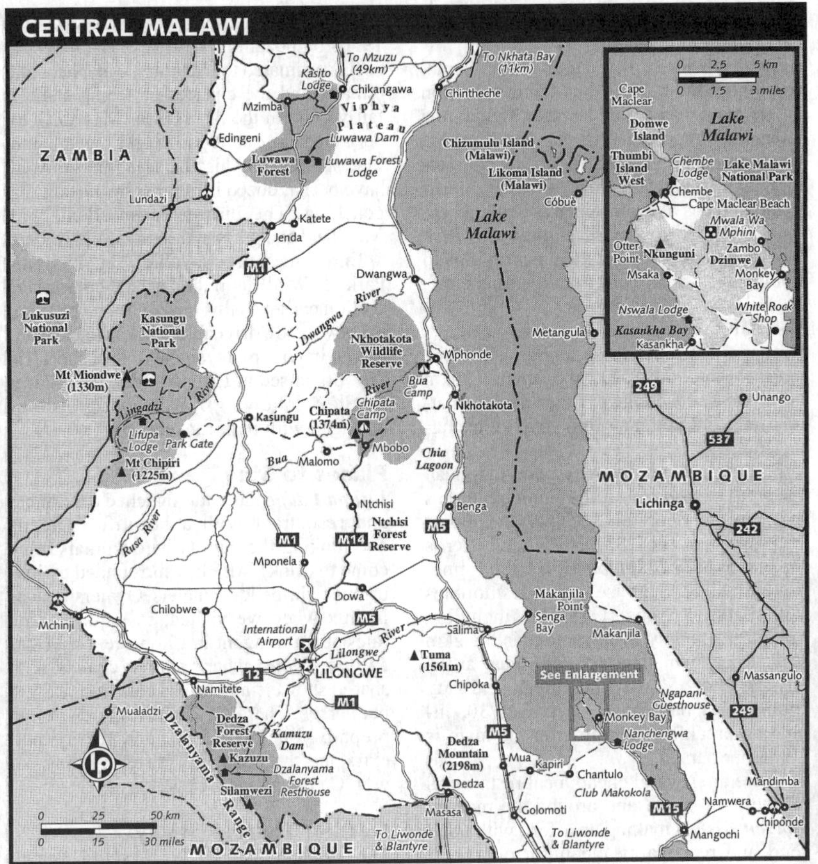

three-course dinner is US$12. But you'll soon wear off the calories with the activities on offer: walking trails, mountain biking (US$20 per day), long-distance wilderness walks and rides to Chintheche on the lakeshore, sailing, boating (US$5 per hour) and fishing are available. There's no public transport to Luwawa, so if you haven't got wheels you'll have to walk, although you may be lucky and get a ride from the main road on a logging truck.

Kasito Lodge (sometimes called Chikangawa Resthouse) is less than 1km west of the main road between Kasungu and Mzuzu. There are five rooms, with four beds in each. Sheets and blankets are provided, the communal showers are hot, the toilets are clean and the lounge has a roaring wood fire. It is an absolute bargain at US$3 per person. You must supply your own food, but there's a kitchen and the caretaker will cook (he's very good) and wash up, for which an extra tip is appropriate. Camping is US$1.50 per person, and the caretaker will probably allow you to use a bathroom inside. Bookings are recommended, but are not required for camping. If the lodge is full, nearby is ***Resthouse No 2***, cheaper but slightly less comfortable, and ***The Annex***, which is more basic again.

To reach Kasito by car from the south, continue 27km beyond the Mzimba junction on the main tarred road towards Mzuzu; the lodge is signposted on your left. Coming from the north, you pass a large wood factory at Chikangawa village, and the turn-off to the lodge is a few kilometres beyond here on the right. If you're travelling by bus, ask the driver to drop you at the junction. Kasito Lodge is less than 1km from the junction.

KASUNGU

Kasungu is a fairly large town, just off the main north-south road, and about 130km north-west of Lilongwe. It has no major attractions, but you may find yourself changing transport here.

For a place to stay, the none-too-clean ***Council Resthouse*** on the main street has mats on the floor for US$0.20 and rooms with two beds for US$1.50. Much better is the quaint old ***Chikambe Motel*** (the former government resthouse); singles/doubles with bathroom cost US$7/11, including breakfast. Its only disadvantage is the 2km walk from town. The ***Kasungu Inn***, at the eastern end of town, has clean and tidy rooms with bathroom for US$20/30, including breakfast; camping on the lawn is US$3 per person.

There are several cheap local restaurants on the main street and around the market. ***Golden Dish*** is making an effort, with good food and reasonably clean surroundings. For a beer, try ***Gab Pub*** on the main street.

All buses and minibuses between Lilongwe and Mzuzu come through the town, and there are infrequent matolas along the road through Nkhotakota Wildlife Reserve to the lakeshore.

MALAWI

KASUNGU NATIONAL PARK

Kasungu National Park lies to the west of Kasungu town, and covers more than 2000 sq km. The gently rolling hills, with a few pointed rocky outcrops, are covered in miombo woodland, which is relatively dense because the park's population of elephant (who would naturally act as 'gardeners') has been seriously reduced since the 1970s by poaching.

It is estimated that about 300 elephant still remain, and the chances of seeing some is fairly good in the dry season (May to October). Buffalo, zebra, hippo and several antelope species may also be seen, but sadly, all have been reduced in number by the ongoing poaching. The birdlife is excellent, with woodland and grassland species, and waders.

Entry fees are payable (see National Parks & Wildlife in the Facts about Malawi section earlier in this chapter). The park has a network of driveable tracks that can be toured in your own vehicle or on a short 'safari' organised at Lifupa Lodge (see Places to Stay following). Walks can also be arranged with park rangers.

Places to Stay

Lifupa Lodge has a tall thatched central bar and restaurant with a beautiful veranda overlooking the dam (where animals often come to drink), which is surrounded by luxurious twin-bedded chalets. Ownership was in flux when we visited, so inquire about rates at a tour agent in Lilongwe. Nearby is ***Lifupa Camp,*** where simple chalets with shared showers and toilets cost from US$30 per person. There's a kitchen where you can prepare your own food, and for a small extra fee the cook will do everything for you. Camping costs US$2.

Getting There & Away

The park entrance is 35km west of Kasungu town. From the entrance, it's 17km by the shortest route to Lifupa Lodge. There's no public transport, so without a car you'd have to hitch from Kasungu – the best place to wait is the turn-off to the park (signposted) near the petrol station on the main road.

NKHOTAKOTA

This was once the centre of slave trading in this region and is reputedly one of the oldest market towns in Africa. Today, it's strung out over 4km between the main road and the lake. Things to see include the mission (with a large mango tree in the grounds) where Livingstone camped in the 19th century. In the part of town called Kombo is another 'Livingstone Tree', and one where an aspiring politician called Hastings Banda made political speeches in the 1960s. The trees are nothing special but the walk through the village-like outskirts of the town is very pleasant.

Places to Stay & Eat

On the main north-south road, the ***Nawo Guesthouse*** is clean and quiet, with safe parking; all the rooms are good value at US$3 (with bathroom). Nearby are the market and the ***Yamikani Restaurant & Bar***.

About 1.5km from the main road, as you go through the town towards the lake, is the ***Livingstone Resthouse*** (in the mission grounds) with basic singles/doubles for US$2/3, and a kitchen where you can cook your own food. Carry on down the road towards the lake for 500m to reach the friendly ***Pick & Pay Resthouse*** *(☎ 292459)*, where clean rooms with mosquito nets cost from US$1.50 to US$3, and camping costs US$1. The food is good, although ***Alekeni Anene Restaurant*** next door keeps the competition fierce.

Another 2km down the road, near the jetty, the terrace of the ***District Council Resthouse*** is worth visiting for a drink (although the rooms should be avoided). The balustrade is built from crankshafts, axles and other old vehicle parts, while the windows on the staircase are still attached to the doors of the car they came from. It's a fine place for an evening beer overlooking the lake.

Getting There & Away

Stagecoach buses running along the main road between Nkhata Bay and Salima swing in to the depot opposite the Pick & Pay Resthouse. Buses run hourly to Salima (US$1.50). For minibuses you have to go up to the main road. You can also go to/from Nkhotakota by steamboat (see details for the *Ilala* in the Getting Around section earlier in this chapter).

SOUTH OF NKHOTAKOTA

About 11km south of Nkhotakota is ***Sani Beach Resort***, on the lake a few kilometres off the main north-south road. Camping costs US$1.50, simple single/double huts cost US$13/25, and smart chalets cost US$25/31, including breakfast.

About 2km beyond here is the smarter and more organised ***Njobvu Safari Lodge*** *(☎ 292506)* on the lakeshore. Camping costs US$2, simple chalets cost US$15 per person, and nicely decorated chalets with bathroom cost US$30 per person, including breakfast. There's a bar and restaurant (snacks cost around US$1.50, lunch costs US$4, and a three-course dinner costs US$11), and the owners are extremely informative.
Web site: www.birdsafaris.co.uk

About 24km south of Nkhotakota is the entrance to **Chia Lagoon**, a large bay linked to the main lake by a narrow channel, which is crossed by a bridge near the main road. Local people fish here using large triangular nets on poles, and seem resigned to having their photos taken by tourists on the bridge. Njobvu Safari Lodge (see its listing) organises boat trips into this 'mini-Okavango' and to other points along the lake.

NKHOTAKOTA WILDLIFE RESERVE

Nkhotakota Wildlife Reserve lies west of the main lakeshore road, and covers a broad area of hills and escarpments. It's the largest reserve in Malawi, but was virtually abandoned during the 1980s and early 1990s. Today, it's being rehabilitated, and although big game (including elephant and lion) occurs here, it's difficult to see in the dense vegetation. Walking is an excellent way to experience the reserve and sample true Malawian wilderness. There's a mix of miombo woodland and patches of evergreen forest, and the reserve is crossed by several large rivers, so the birdlife is varied and rewarding.

Entry fees are payable (see National Parks & Wildlife Reserves in the Facts about Malawi section earlier in this chapter). You can hire a scout (ranger) here to be a guide. If you don't have your own car, you can hire one at the Pick & Pay Resthouse in Nkhotakota for US$25 per day. Alternatively, properly organised day safaris to the reserve can be arranged from Njobvu Safari Lodge (see its listing in the South of Nkhotakota section earlier), at US$50 per person, including transport, lunch, professional guide and entry fees. The lodge can also arrange birding trips, night-time safaris to look for lions and longer safaris of several days.

There are some dilapidated rondavels at ***Chipata Camp***, the reserve headquarters, about 5km north of the end of the dirt road from Lilongwe, about 35km from Nkhotakota town. The best place to aim for is ***Bua Camp***, a beautiful clearing on the banks of a rocky river, where camping costs US$1. The turn-off to Bua is 10km north of Nkhotakota town, then 15km on a dirt track; without your own wheels the only way to get here is on foot.

SALIMA

The town of Salima is about 20km from the lake, where the road from Lilongwe meets the main lakeshore road. The ***Mai Tsalani Motel*** near the PTC supermarket, about 10-minutes' walk from the bus station, has basic doubles with bathroom for US$3; singles are cheaper and the shared bathrooms not too bad. ***Mwambiya Lodge*** across the train line from the bus station has better single/double rooms for US$10/13 with breakfast.

To reach Salima from Lilongwe, it's easiest to take a minibus (US$1.50). There are also buses and minibuses to/from Mzuzu (via Nkhata Bay) and to/from Blantyre (via Mangochi) for US$4. Local minibuses and matolas run between Salima and Senga Bay for US$1.

SENGA BAY

Senga Bay is at the eastern end of a broad peninsula that juts into the lake from Salima. The water is remarkably clear here, and the beaches are also good. As a break from lazing on the beach, you can go windsurfing or snorkelling, take a boat ride or learn to dive. Alternatively, you can go hiking in the nearby **Senga Hills**. It's best to hire a local guide to show you the way (also because there have been isolated incidents of robbery and harassment here). Birdwatching in the area is excellent, with a good range of habitats in close proximity. If you prefer shopping, a few kilometres outside Senga Bay on the Salima road are craft stalls with the best range you'll find anywhere.

About 10km from Senga Bay is Stewart Grant's Tropical Fish Farm (☎/fax 263165 or 263407), which breeds and exports cichlids; visits can be arranged if you're genuinely interested. Red Zebra Tours (**e** redzebras@malawi.net) is also based at the fish farm, and offers day snorkelling trips, or multiday fish-watching safaris (snorkelling or diving) around the lake, with an experienced guide, from around US$75 per day. For more information, check its Web site: www.lakemalawi.com.

Dangers & Annoyances

Take great care when swimming near the large rocks at the end of the beach at Steps Campsite; you'll find there's a surprisingly strong undertow.

Many travellers have complained about persistent hassling from local youths, all wanting to sell souvenirs or arrange boat rides. Beware especially of the enthusiastic guys at the craft stalls who offer to wrap your purchase – they'll charge more for this than you paid for the carving, and swapping your souvenir for a lump of wood has been tried more than once. Be polite and firm in your dealings and you should be OK.

Places to Stay & Eat

There's a good choice of places to stay and eat in Senga Bay. The following places are described roughly from west to east, as you come into town from Salima.

At the western end of Senga Bay's main street a dirt road leads 4km to ***Carolina's Lakeside Resort*** *(☎ 263220,* **e** *shelagh@malawi.net, PO Box 441, Salima)*, where a dorm bed costs US$5 and chalets with bathroom are US$35 for one to three people. Plain rooms with shared bathroom in a small block are US$20 to US$30. Meals range from US$3 to US$5, and there's a bar and outside terrace. Shady gardens overlook the lake, even though Carolina (who planted them) has moved on to new pastures. You can hire boats for fishing, snorkelling or day-trips. The use of bikes, sailboards and kayaks is free for guests.

Nearby is ***Baobab Lodge***, a neat, low-key and friendly place with a shady bar overlooking the beach. Single or double rooms cost US$13, and triples are US$21. Snacks cost US$1 and meals cost about US$3. Next door, the smaller ***Chimphango's*** has camping for US$0.50 and rooms for US$8.

Back in town, off the main street towards the beach, the basic ***Hippo Hide Resthouse*** is run by a group of local youths, with single/double rooms for US$2.50/US$4. They can also arrange boat trips and hikes, and they sell souvenirs and anything else you might (or might not) want. Some travellers rave about this place, others complain about the hard-sell and harassment. You might want to get opinions from others before staying here.

The main street continues for 2km to the imposing gates of the ***Livingstonia Beach Hotel*** *(☎ 744022, fax 744483)*, which is set in lush gardens with picture-postcard views over the lake. Style and luxury don't come cheap though: rooms cost US$130/170 and chalets cost US$170/185, including breakfast. The hotel has a tennis court, and also organises guided walks or drives to various places of interest in the area, such as Mua Mission (see the Mua section following) and the nearby fish farm.

Next door is ***Steps Campsite***, a clean and safe place with flat pitches, electric hook-ups and spotless toilets and showers (but no hot water). Camping costs US$2.50. There's also a bar and a takeaway place serving fast-food (burgers US$3, chicken and chips US$6) and fresh bread. On the site is Scuba Do Dive School, offering dive courses, snorkel equipment hire and boat charter.

Just before the gates to the Livingstonia Beach Hotel, a dirt road runs for 1km to ***Safari Beach Lodge*** *(☎ 912238, ⓔ safwag@malawi.net)*. It's in a lovely spot with a private beach, excellent for spotting local wildlife. Rooms with bathroom cost US$35/55, including breakfast. Day safaris to Tuma Forest Reserve (where another small lodge is planned) can be arranged from here.

The best place to eat is ***Red Zebra Restaurant***, 500m from the Livingstonia Beach Hotel. It's open from 7 am to 10 pm, serving breakfast (from US$1.50 to US$3), snacks (from US$1 to US$2), burgers and omelettes (around US$3), and good main meals such as *kampengo* (lake fish) and nsima or chips (US$3.50). Or you can sit on the veranda and just have a beer, coffee or slice of chocolate cake (US$0.75).

Getting There & Away

First get to Salima (see the Salima section earlier). From here, local pick-ups run to Senga Bay for about US$1, dropping you in the main street. If you want a lift all the way to Steps Campsite, negotiate an extra fee with the driver. If you're travelling to/from Cape Maclear consider chartering a boat; it's not too expensive (US$100) if you get a group together, it's good fun and it saves one hell of a trip on the bus.

MUA

Mua is a small town between Salima and Balaka, and consists mostly of a large mission with a church, a school and a hospital, which has been here since the beginning of the 20th century. There is also a fabulous **craft shop**, full of paintings and wood sculptures by local people who have been encouraged in their work by one of the priests at the mission. Some is of very high quality, and quite unusual, covering religious and secular subjects. Prices are reasonable. Nearby is a workshop where you can see the carvers in action.

For a deeper understanding of the ideas behind the sculptures, a visit to the **museum** is an absolute must. It concentrates on the three main cultural groups of the region (Chewa, Ngoni and Yao) and their approach to traditional beliefs, with exhibits from rituals and rites of passage. This is no dusty exhibition, but a journey deep into the very soul of Malawi. A guided tour is essential; it takes three hours and costs US$5. The museum is open Monday to Saturday.

See Getting There & Away under Monkey Bay (following) for transport connections to/from Mua.

MONKEY BAY

Monkey Bay is a port at the southern end of Lake Malawi which most travellers pass through on the way to Cape Maclear. If you're here for a while, go to ***Gary's Cafe*** (☎ *587296*); the friendly people here offer snacks, meals and drinks at local rates, plus there is a shop, an art showroom, a beer garden and a camping ground (more accommodation is planned). They can also advise on transport, changing money and anything else in the area. Opposite is ***Ziwadi Resthouse*** with fairly clean singles/doubles for US$2/2.50. Camping is allowed in the yard, but the lack of a fence means security is questionable. Monkey Bay also has a market and a PTC supermarket.

Just outside Monkey Bay, ***Venice Beach*** backpackers hostel and camping ground was under construction when we passed through. The setting is beautiful. Ask for details at Gary's Cafe.

Getting There & Away

From Lilongwe, there's one Stagecoach express bus per day, which leaves around 8 am (but can be delayed until noon). It goes via Salima and the southern lakeshore between Mua and Monkey Bay (called the Matakataka road even though it doesn't actually go to Matakataka) and takes about seven hours. All other buses from Lilongwe to Monkey Bay go the long way round via Salima, Balaka, Liwonde and Mangochi, and take up to 12 hours. From Lilongwe you're probably better off going by minibus to Salima (US$1.50), from where you might find a minibus or matola going direct to Monkey Bay. If not, take a minibus towards Balaka, get off at the Matakataka road junction near Mua (look out for the craft stalls), then take a matola (US$2) along the Matakataka road to the main road between Monkey Bay and Mangochi. Another option if you're in a group is to charter your own matola. We heard from a group of travellers who hired a matola in Salima to take them all the way to Cape Maclear for US$100.

It's much easier to reach Monkey Bay from Blantyre: there's a daily Stagecoach bus, via Liwonde and Mangochi, for US$3.80. During the morning, minibuses also serve this route. The best option from Blantyre is the backpackers minibus that shuttles straight to/from Monkey Bay and Cape Maclear a few times each week. Ask for details at Doogles (see Places to Stay in the Blantyre & Limbe section later in this chapter).

To avoid the bus hassles, many travellers use the *Ilala* steamboat to travel up and down the country to or from Monkey Bay (see the main Getting Around section earlier in this chapter for details).

From Monkey Bay, a matola shuttles to Cape Maclear a few times each day for US$1 per person. It usually meets the buses from Lilongwe and Blantyre. Otherwise, the people at Gary's Cafe will tell you when it's due.

CAPE MACLEAR

Cape Maclear – the closest thing you'll find to an Indian Ocean beach in inland Africa – has become a travellers' byword for sun, sand, rest and recreation, and most people passing through Malawi stay here at one time or another. You may meet friends you last saw in Cape Town, Harare or wherever. It's the sort of place where you sit on the beautiful beach, have a few beers, and next thing you know your visa's run out. Despite an increased influx of travellers over the past few years, this place hasn't lost its village feel. Most local people are friendly because they know outsiders bring money and jobs to the area. Others are less happy when they see their children adopting unpleasant western ways, and when food prices for locals are double what they are in nontouristy places.

Things to See

Much of the area around Cape Maclear, including several offshore islands, is part of **Lake Malawi National Park**, one of the few freshwater aquatic parks in Africa. The park headquarters are at Golden Sands Holiday Resort (see Places to Stay & Eat later).

There's also a **museum** and **aquarium**, which are well worth a visit to learn about the formation of the lake and the evolution of the fish. The information is nontechnical and well presented.

Near the entrance gate to the Golden Sands, a path leads towards the hills overlooking the bay. A few hundred metres up here is a small group of **missionary graves**, marking the last resting place of the missionaries who attempted to establish the first Livingstonia Mission here in 1875 (see History in the Facts about Malawi section and also Livingstonia in the Northern Malawi section, both earlier in this chapter).

Activities

Snorkelling Local youths organise day trips to nearby islands for about US$10 to US$40 per boat, or around US$5 per person, including snorkelling and lunch (fish and rice cooked on an open fire). Before arranging anything, though, check with other travellers for recommendations; some of the lads are very good, but others can be sharks.

If you prefer to go snorkelling on your own, many places rent gear (rates start at about US$2 – but check the quality of your mask). Otter Point, less than 1km beyond Golden Sands, is a small rocky peninsula and nearby islet that is very popular with fish and snorkellers. You may even see otters here.

Diving For diving, go to Scuba Shack (near Stevens Resthouse), Lake Divers (see The Ritz under Places to Stay & Eat following), Chembe Lodge (see Places to Stay & Eat following) or Kayak Africa (see Kayaking following). The courses here are among the cheapest in the world, and there are plenty of options for experienced divers. All companies' course prices are similar (beginners from US$130 to US$150, advanced around US$120), but they all have other deals to attract clients. For example, Lake Divers' package includes accommodation; Chembe Lodge's packages involving diving from a catamaran; and Kayak Africa has a beautiful offshore island base. Talk to anybody who has done a dive course already and get personal recommendations. For those already qualified, shore dives are US$15, boat dives US$20 and night dives US$30.

Kayaking If you prefer to stay on top of the water, Kayak Africa (☎ 584456, @ kayakafrica@earthleak.co.za) has top-of-the-range kayaks (single and double) suitable for experts or beginners, which can be hired from around US$10 for a few hours. A day trip with lunch costs US$25. The best option, if you've got the money, is to take a guided two- or three-day island-hopping trip, using Kayak Africa's delightful camps on Domwe and Mumbo Islands. The charge is US$75 per person per night, and includes a roomy tent with mattress and duvet, good meals, hot showers, snorkel gear and park fees. Everyone who's done this trip raves about it.

Warning

Scams to watch out for at Cape Maclear include the boys who take money in advance for a boat ride or barbecue and then disappear, or who take you on a boat then go through your day-pack while you're snorkelling. Real robberies do occasionally happen on the beach or surrounding hills; violence is very unlikely, but don't carry anything valuable.

Boat Cruises Yet another option is sailing with an outfit called Hello Afrika, based at Chembe Lodge (see Places to Stay & Eat following). A sunset cruise on their 8m catamaran costs US$8 per person, a full-day cruise is US$20, and a stylish three-day cruise (including all meals) costs US$150. All trips can be combined with snorkelling or diving.

Hiking There's a good range of hikes and walks in the hills that form a horseshoe around the plain behind the village and the beach. You can go alone (see the boxed text 'Warning' earlier in this section) or arrange a guide, either from the village or at the national park headquarters at Golden Sands Holiday Resort; the park's rate for a guide is US$10 for a full-day trip. The main path starts by the missionary graves and leads up through woodland to a col below **Nkhunguni Peak**, the highest on the Nankumba Peninsula, with great views over Cape Maclear, the lake and surrounding islands. It's six hours return to the summit; plenty of water and a good sun hat are essential.

Another interesting place to visit on foot is **Mwala Wa Mphini** (Rock of the Tribal Face Scars), which is just off the main dirt road into Cape Maclear, about 5km from the park headquarters. This huge boulder is covered in lines and patterns that seem to have been gouged out by long-forgotten artists, but are simply a natural geological formation.

If you want a **longer walk**, a small lakeside path leads south-west from Otter Point, through woodland above the shore, for about 4km to a small fishing village called Msaka (which has a small bar/shop serving cold drinks). From here a track leads inland (west) to meet the main dirt road between Cape Maclear and Monkey Bay. Turn left and head back towards Cape Maclear, passing Mwala Wa Mphini on the way. The whole circuit is about 16km and takes four to five hours.

Places to Stay & Eat

Places to stay and eat in this section are described roughly from east to west.

The main dirt road from Monkey Bay leads all the way to ***Golden Sands Holiday Resort***, at the far western end of the beach. This is also Lake Malawi National Park headquarters, and as it's inside the park you have to pay fees: US$1.20 per person per day, plus US$0.30 per car per day. The beach is cleaner and the atmosphere is generally much quieter (one traveller said 'more sensible') than some other places in Cape Maclear. It's suitable for families, drivers and people who don't want to drink and smoke all night. Camping costs US$1 per person. Small rondavels with private bathroom cost US$2/3/4 for one/two/three people. There's a small bar, but no restaurant and there's a kitchen where staff will prepare your food, or you can cook yourself. If you camp, watch out for the monkeys – they'll run off with anything edible. If you're in a group it's worth renting a rondavel to store your gear – you also get your own bathroom, which will be in better condition than the communal ones. It's possible that Golden Sands will be leased to a private investor, so don't be surprised if there's a brand new hotel here by the time you arrive.

Next along the beach, about 1.5km from Golden Sands, is ***Emmanuel's Campsite***, charging US$0.75 for camping and US$1 per person in basic rooms. It's clean and quiet, with a bar but no food available. The same people also run ***Thumbi Island Camp*** on the island opposite Cape Maclear beach, where large walk-in tents cost US$5.50 per person, including boat transfers and park fees. Meals are available and you can hire snorkel gear and kayaks.

Next along is the ***Sakondwera Restaurant & Shop***, where you can buy meals from US$1 to US$2, plus cheap beer, bread, tinned foods and groceries. The owner can advise on places to change money. Next door is Kayak Africa, and near here is ***Chip's Bar***, which serves (naturally!) deep-fried potato pieces plus takeaway snacks at budget prices.

A bit further along, and set back slightly from the beach, is the relaxed and peaceful ***Top Quiet Resthouse***, with clean rooms around a sandy courtyard. Singles/doubles are good value at US$1.50/2.10, and it's US$5 for a double with private bathroom. Very close to here is the legendary ***Stevens Resthouse***, run by the Stevens family for as long as anyone can remember. This used to be one of *the* places to stay on the backpackers' Cape to Cairo route, but there's stiff competition these days and it's lost some of its friendliness and atmosphere. Clean rooms cost US$1.20/2.40; new doubles with bathroom and better beds cost US$5. Breakfast costs US$0.50 and other meals cost from US$1 to US$2, although you can wait several hours between ordering and eating. The bar on the beach is a popular meeting place, but it's amazing that anyone able to build in such a fabulous position could come up with something so ugly.

A bit further along the beach are two more places. ***The Ritz*** at Lake Divers is aimed mainly at people on dive courses, but anyone can stay; clean rooms with lights, mosquito nets, sheets and towels are good value at US$7.50. Dorms cost US$2.50 per person. Next door is ***The Gap***, which is constantly popular, with simple rooms at US$0.75 per person and camping for US$0.30. The beach bar serves breakfast and snacks from US$1, and meals for around US$3, and is the social epicentre most evenings.

Along from here are two very basic local places: the ***Bodzalakani Resthouse***, charging US$0.75 per person for very basic rooms; and the similar ***Mayi Tsalani Resthouse,*** charging US$2 per person. About 1km further on is ***Fat Monkeys***, a huge camping ground aimed primarily at overland trucks and car-campers, with good security, showers, bar and restaurant (cabins are planned).

At the far eastern end of Cape Maclear beach, a very long way from all the other places (in distance and quality), is ***Chembe Lodge*** *(☎/fax 584334, or ☎ 633489 in Blantyre, e hello-afrika@iafrica.com or tum buka@ malawi.net)* with large walk-in tents under thatch shelters, set in beautiful gardens and overlooking a very nice beach. Rooms cost US$29/33, including breakfast. Other meals cost US$3 to US$5, and there's a bar. The private camping ground is also good value at US$1.50 (tents are provided). Free sailboards are available for guests; water-skiing and sailing can be arranged.

Another place to consider if Cape Maclear sounds too frenetic is ***Nswala Lodge*** *(☎ 620629, e nswalasafaris@malawi.net)*, near Kasankha village, on a small hill overlooking the lake (high enough to catch the breeze, near enough to reach the beach) about 12km off the dirt road running between Monkey Bay and Cape Maclear. Camping is US$3 per person, a dorm costs US$10, and nice double chalets cost US$30 per person, with breakfast. Double luxury chalets with private bathroom are planned for 2000 and will cost US$65 per person, with breakfast. These rates include laundry and tea/coffee until 10 am – even for campers. If you don't have wheels it's a long walk, but boat transfers to/from Cape Maclear beach cost US$2.50. Water sports, diving, fishing, hiking and birdwatching are all available. Guests can get rides on the supply run that goes to/from Blantyre twice per week.

Getting There & Away

By public transport, first get to Monkey Bay (see Getting There & Away in the Monkey Bay section earlier). If you're driving from Mangochi, the dirt road to Cape Maclear (signposted) turns west off the main road, about 5km before Monkey Bay.

From Cape Maclear, if you're heading for Senga Bay, ask at the dive schools about chartering a boat. It will cost around US$100, but it's not bad when split between a group, and much better than the long hard bus ride.

Cichlid Fish

There are over 600 species of fish in Lake Malawi. Most of these are of the family Cichlidae – the largest family of fish in Africa – and 99% of these cichlids are endemic to the lake. Chambo, familiar to anyone who has eaten in a restaurant in Malawi, are one type of cichlid. Others include the small *utaka*, which move in big shoals and are caught by fishermen at night. But Lake Malawi is most famous for the small, brightly coloured cichlids known as *mbuna*, of which there are many species. As well as being attractive to snorkellers and divers, mbuna are popular with aquariums, and for scientists they provide a fascinating insight into the process of evolution. Mbuna identification and classification is an ongoing process, and it is thought that many species of mbuna remain undiscovered, particularly around the north-eastern shore of the lake.

Cichlids have evolved over the millennia from one common species into many hundreds, yet they have continued to coexist. This has been achieved by different species developing different ways of feeding. Chambo eat phytoplankton, which they filter out of the water through their mouths, but the different mbuna have developed a whole range of feeding mechanisms. Some mbuna have specialised teeth to scrape algae off the rocks; others specialise in scraping the algae off aquatic plants. There are also 'snail eaters', with strong flat teeth for crushing shells; 'sand diggers', which filter insects and small animals out of the sand; and 'zooplankton eaters', which have tube-like mouths for picking up minute creatures. Other species include plant-eaters and fish-eaters.

Equally fascinating is the cichlid breeding process. The male attracts the female with his bright colours, and if suitably impressed she lays eggs, which she immediately takes into her mouth for protection. The male has a pattern near his tail resembling the eggs, which the female tries to pick up, at which point the male releases sperm into the water which the female inevitably inhales. This process is repeated until all or most of the eggs are fertilised. The female keep the eggs in her mouth, and even when they become baby fish they stay there for protection. They emerge only to feed, but at the slightest sign of danger, the mother opens her mouth and the young swim straight back in.

MONKEY BAY TO MANGOCHI

From Monkey Bay the main road runs south to Mangochi. Along this stretch of lake are several places to stay, catering for all tastes and budgets. A selection is described here, arranged north to south.

Leaving Monkey Bay, you pass the junction for Cape Maclear, then the Matakataka road west to Mua. Continue for another 18km to the turn-off for ***Nanchengwa Lodge*** *(☎ 830062, fax 584417)*, reached by a dirt track through baobabs, 1.5km west of the main road. This is a firm favourite for overland trucks and backpackers. The camping ground is US$2.50 and a dorm costs US$3.50, but the tree-houses on stilts for US$8 are most popular. Chalets cost US$15 a double, or US$35 for four on the beach. There's a bar with food available (meals from US$2.50 to US$4), plus a range of activities such as horse riding, sailing, snorkelling and diving. The friendly family that runs this place, with the backing of local communities, has big plans to open a wildlife sanctuary in the wooded hills behind the lodge, where elephant, buffalo and other wild animals are often seen.

About 3km further south, and 1.5km off the main road, is the small and quiet ***OK Lake Shore Hotel***; very nice singles/doubles with private bathroom cost US$15/20. No meals are available but there's a kitchen and chef, so it's ideal for self-catering.

About 50km south of Monkey Bay, ***Club Makokola*** *(☎ 584244, fax 584417, @ clubmak@malawi.net)* is a full-on luxury holiday resort, with nicely decorated rooms and chalets, two swimming pools, restaurants, bars, water sports, floodlit football fields, squash, tennis and volleyball courts and a long strip of private beachfront. Comfortable rooms cost US$105/170, including full buffet breakfast. Three-course meals cost US$10, and lunches and snacks are also available. The club recently enjoyed a stylish million-dollar renovation, but some rooms have yet to be done, so make sure you ask for a new one. Club Mak (as it's known) has its own airport, which is served by daily Air Malawi flights to/from Blantyre and Lilongwe. Based at the club, Scuba Blue offers diving on Boadzulu Island from US$30, and dive courses from US$160. Paradise Watersports offers fishing, boat trips to the islands, and water-ski and wakeboard hire from US$10.

The ***Florence Motel***, on the beach next to (and overshadowed by) Club Makokola, has rooms for US$10/18, including breakfast.

Just 1km down the road from here is another top-end establishment. The ***Nkopola Lodge*** has cool and unfussy rooms in well-kept gardens overlooking a beach from US$104/149, including breakfast. The restaurant serves main meals for around US$5 to US$8, with special weekend buffets for US$12. Sailboards, canoes and small sailing boats are free for guests' use; motorboats cost about US$15 per hour. More-questionable attractions include a bird sanctuary, petting zoo and casino. Further along the beach the hotel also has no-frills chalets sleeping up to three people, which are good value at US$46. Large double walk-in tents which sleep one or two people cost US$18. There's also a camping ground that costs US$8 per tent, or US$26 per caravan. The ablution blocks are clean, and there's a small bar and restaurant overlooking the lake.

North of Mangochi, ***Palm Beach Leisure Resort*** was established some years ago as a smart resort on a beautiful beach surrounded by (not surprisingly) a grove of palm trees, and lawns. Chalets with private bathroom are now slightly dowdy, but fair value at US$16/30. Full breakfast is US$4, and other meals US$2 to US$4. Camping costs US$1 per person. This place is quiet during the week, but livelier at weekends when people come from Blantyre and Lilongwe for boating and fishing.

MANGOCHI

Mangochi lies near the southern end of Lake Malawi, strung out between the main lakeshore road and the Shire River. This place was once an important slave market, and then an administrative centre in colonial days, when it was known as Fort Johnston. Relics of these times include a large mosque and the Queen Victoria clock tower. Even today the town has a vaguely Swahili feel, with palm trees, Arab-looking people and coconuts for sale in the street.

The HMS *Guendolin*

The HMS *Guendolin* was a military boat, made in Britain and assembled in Mangochi in 1899. For many years it was the largest boat on the lake (340 tonnes), with a top speed of 12 knots. It was also equipped with two powerful guns. The colonial authorities regarded such a show of strength necessary firstly to deter slave-traders, who crossed the lake in dhows with their human cargo, and secondly because both rival colonial powers, Germany and Portugal, had territory facing Lake Malawi (then Lake Nyassa) and were believed to want to increase their influence in the region.

The Germans also had a gunboat, called *Herman von Wissemann*, but despite the territorial disputes of their governments the captains of the two ships were reported to be great friends and drinking partners, often meeting at various points around the lake for a chat and a few beers.

When WWI was declared in 1914, the *Guendolin* was ordered to destroy the German boat. The British captain knew where the *von Wissemann* would be, as he and the German captain had previously arranged one of their regular get-togethers.

But the German captain was unaware that war had broken out, and his ship was completely unprepared. The *Guendolin* steamed in close, then bombed the *von Wissemann* and rendered it unusable. The German captain and crew were then informed of the commencement of hostilities and taken prisoner. This rather unsporting event happened to be the first British naval victory of WWI, and Lake Malawi's only recorded battle at sea.

In 1940 the *Guendolin* was converted to a passenger ship, and one of the guns was set up as a memorial in Mangochi, near the clock tower. Some years later the ship was scrapped. All that remains today is the gun, while the compass and the ship's bell are on display at the museum.

The Shire Bridge is scenic, and the museum is well worth a visit. Facilities include several shops, supermarkets, a post office and banks.

Places to Stay & Eat

There are several cheap dives near the junction where the road through town branches off the main road. The ***Safari Resthouse*** has grimy rooms for US$2, though the attached restaurant gets good reports. The nearby ***Icecream Den & Restaurant*** is more inspiring, however, with snacks around US$1, Malawian food from US$1.20, fish and chips for US$2 and, of course, icecream. Near the clock tower is the small and friendly ***Mangochi Lodge*** with rooms for US$3/5. Nearby is the larger ***Holiday Motel***, with simple but clean rooms for US$2.50/3.50 and better rooms with bathroom for US$5/6, plus a cheap restaurant, big bar and good bakery.

Getting There & Away

All buses between Blantyre and Monkey Bay stop in Mangochi. There are minibuses to/from Liwonde (US$1.20), Zomba (US$1.50) and Blantyre (US$3). A matola to Ulongwe (for Liwonde National Park) is US$1. If you're heading for Mozambique, matolas to Chiponde (via Namwera) cost US$2 (for border crossing information see Mozambique under Land in the main Getting There & Away section earlier in this chapter).

Blantyre & Limbe

Blantyre is the commercial and industrial capital of Malawi. It stretches for about 20km, merging into Limbe – its 'sister city'. Many travellers find that Blantyre has a bit more of a buzz than Lilongwe (if any of Malawi's sleepy cities can be said to buzz at all), but most stop only for a few days to send or receive mail, buy maps and books or pick up a Mozambique visa. Blantyre is a pleasant place, with some interesting sights, several enjoyable restaurants and bars, and a fair selection of places to stay. (Unless

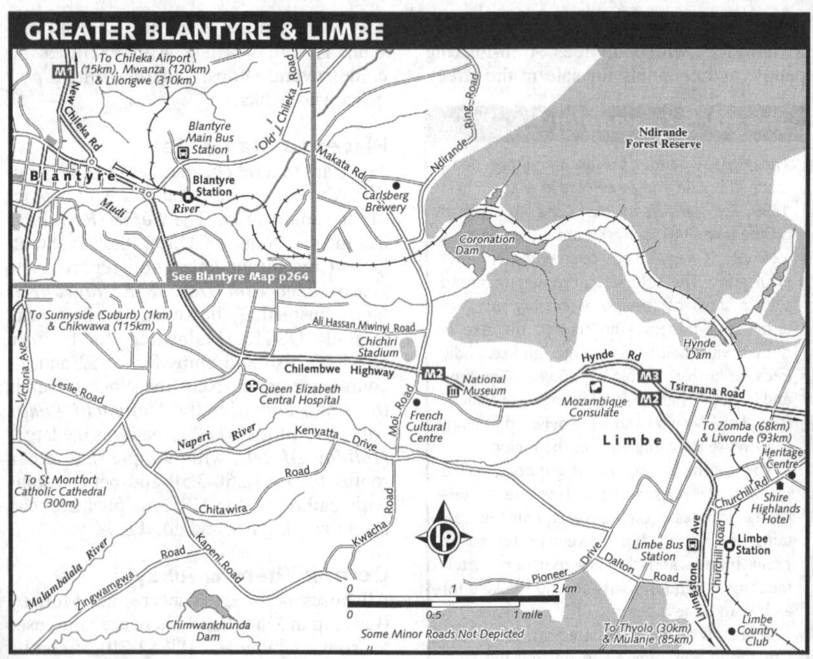

stated otherwise, every address in this section is in Blantyre, rather than Limbe.)

Orientation

Despite the sprawling suburbs and townships surrounding Blantyre, the city centre is very compact, with most of the places of importance to travellers well within easy walking distance. Central Blantyre's main street is Victoria Ave; along here are several large shops, the tourist office, the map sales office, banks, foreign exchange bureaus and travel agents. To the east is Haile Selassie Rd, which contains many smaller shops. At the northern end of Victoria Ave is the landmark Mount Soche Hotel.

East of the Mount Soche Hotel is a major traffic roundabout, from where the main road north leads to the airport, Mwanza and Lilongwe. This road has no official name but is known as New Chileka Rd. About 500m further east is another roundabout, with a small clock on a concrete pedestal in the middle: from here Chileka Rd leads north to the bus station and outer suburbs; and the main Chilembwe Highway leads east towards Limbe, where the main roads to Zomba and Mulanje branch.

Maps Survey maps of Blantyre and the surrounding area are available from the Department of Surveys public map sales office at the southern end of Victoria Ave. See also Maps under Planning in the Facts for the Visitor section earlier in this chapter.

Information

Tourist Office The tourist office on Victoria Ave has a few leaflets, and the people here make quite an effort to provide information and assistance. It's open from 7.30 am to noon and 1 to 5 pm.

Immigration Office The immigration office is in Building Society House on Victoria Ave. It's open from 7.30 am to noon and 1.30 to 4 pm weekdays, 7.30 am to noon Saturday.

Money There are branches of the National Bank and Commercial Bank on Victoria Ave. Banks are usually open from 8 am to 1 or 2 pm weekdays. At the southern end of Victoria Ave are the Manica Travel and Finance Bank foreign exchange bureaus, and there are two more private bureaus at the northern end, which often have competitive rates. If you've got the time, shop around, as rates and commissions can vary considerably.

Post Blantyre's main post office is on Glyn Jones Rd; it's open from 7.30 am to 4.30 pm weekdays, 8 to 10 am Saturday, and 9 to 10 am Sunday. There is poste restante here. If you're using the AmEx 'client mail' service, the office is at Manica Travel on Victoria Ave.

Telephone For international calls, the Executive Telephone & Fax Bureau on Henderson St is open from 7 am to 4 pm weekdays, 8 am to 2.30 pm Saturday and 9 am to 1.30 pm Sunday. Three minutes to anywhere outside Africa costs US$10. Reverse-charge calls are not possible.

Email & Internet Access Malawi.Net Internet Bureau on St George's St charges US$4 for 30 minutes. The best deal is at Tecktel Internet Bureau in Fatima Arcade on Haile Selassie Rd, charging US$1 for 45 minutes offline, and US$1 for 10 minutes online.

Travel Agencies & Tour Operators Most agencies are based on or just off Victoria Ave, including Airtour & Travel (☎ 622918), AMI Travel (☎ 624733) and Manica Travel (☎ 624533). The switched-on Galaxy Travel (☎ 633637) is on Glyn Jones Rd. Most of the above deal mainly in outbound flights.

Soche Tours & Travel (☎ 620777, fax 620440, @ sochetours@malawi.net) on Chilembwe Rd arranges flights, coach travel, tours, safaris, car hire and hotel reservations.

Nswala Safaris (☎ 620629, fax 620027, @ nswalasafaris@malawi.net) mainly handles incoming tour groups, but can also arrange customised itineraries.

Bookshops There's a TBS bookshop on Victoria Ave and a smaller one at the Mount Soche Hotel. For a much wider selection, visit the Central bookshop at the eastern end of Henderson St. It stocks stationery, books and guides about Malawi, local language dictionaries and a good range of novels by local writers. There's also a pleasant coffee shop. The Central Africana bookshop, next to the PTC supermarket on Victoria Ave, specialises in antiquarian and specialist African titles, plus old prints and maps.

The Wildlife Society of Malawi giftshop at the Heritage Centre in Limbe, next to the Shire Highlands Hotel, specialises in books about natural history and national parks; its prices are very reasonable.

Libraries & Cultural Centres Blantyre's main public library, the National Library, is off Glyn Jones Rd, near the Mount Soche Hotel. The British Council library, on Victoria Ave opposite the tourist office, is open from 8 am to 5 pm Tuesday to Friday, Monday afternoon and Saturday morning. Nonmembers may read books and magazines in the library. Films are shown some afternoons and evenings – check the notice boards for details. The French cultural centre is on Moi Rd, off Chilembwe Highway, towards Limbe.

Medical Services The Malaria Test Centre at the government-run Queen Elizabeth Central Hospital (☎ 630333) just south of Chilembwe Highway, charges US$1 for a malaria test. Ask for directions as the Test Centre is hard to find.

For private medical consultations or blood tests, Mwaiwathu Private Hospital (☎ 622999) on Chileka Rd, east of the city centre, is open 24 hours and is good. A consultation is US$15; all drugs and treatment are extra. An overnight stay in a private ward is US$80 – before any treatment, you must put down a US$220 deposit.

For medical or dental problems, the Seventh Day Adventist clinic (☎ 620488 or 620006) next to the Mount Soche Hotel charges US$6 for a doctor's consultation and US$10 for a malaria test.

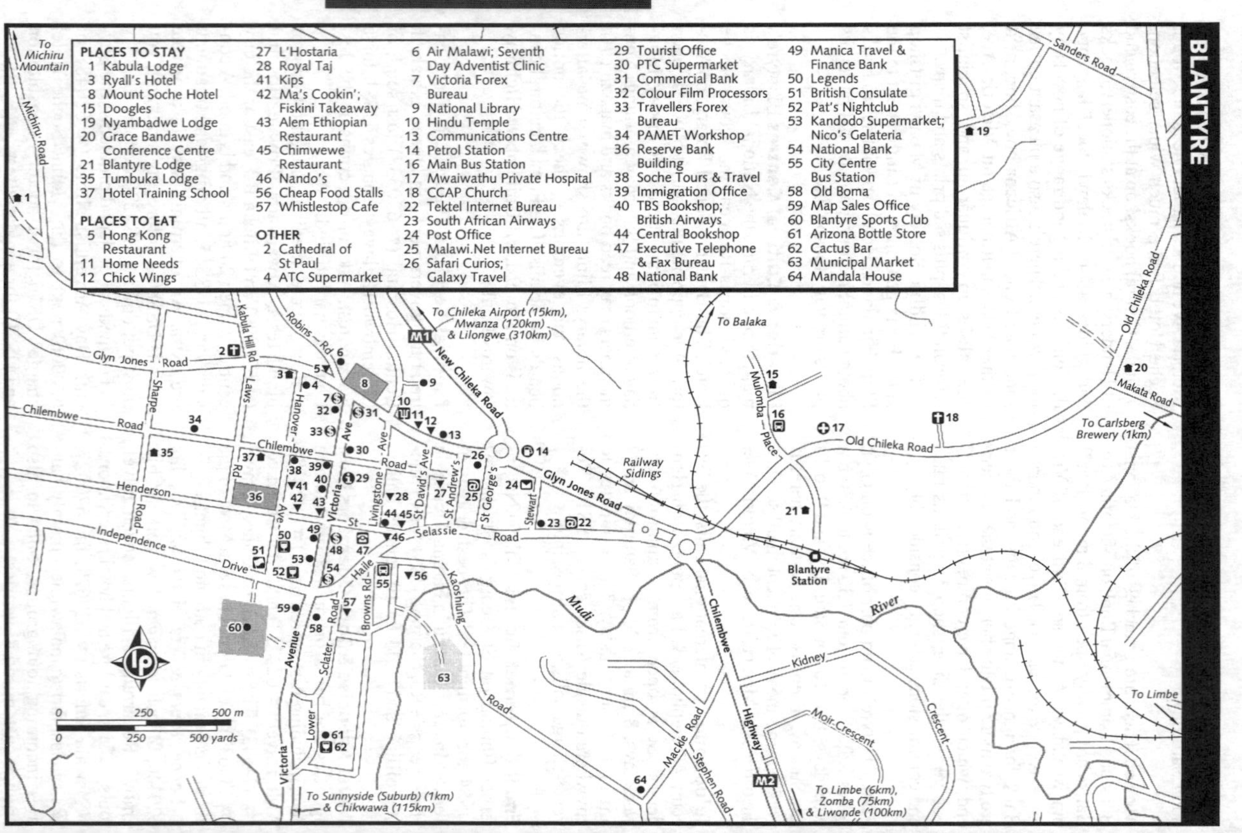
MALAWI
BLANTYRE
PLACES TO STAY
1 Kabula Lodge
3 Ryall's Hotel
8 Mount Soche Hotel
15 Doogles
19 Nyambadwe Lodge
20 Grace Bandawe Conference Centre
21 Blantyre Lodge
35 Tumbuka Lodge
37 Hotel Training School
PLACES TO EAT
5 Hong Kong Restaurant
11 Home Needs
12 Chick Wings
27 L'Hostaria
28 Royal Taj
41 Kips
42 Ma's Cookin'; Fiskini Takeaway
43 Alem Ethiopian Restaurant
45 Chimwewe Restaurant
46 Nando's
56 Cheap Food Stalls
57 Whistlestop Cafe
OTHER
2 Cathedral of St Paul
4 ATC Supermarket
6 Air Malawi; Seventh Day Adventist Clinic
7 Victoria Forex Bureau
9 National Library
10 Hindu Temple
13 Communications Centre
14 Petrol Station
16 Main Bus Station
17 Mwaiwathu Private Hospital
18 CCAP Church
22 Tektel Internet Bureau
23 South African Airways
24 Post Office
25 Malawi.Net Internet Bureau
26 Safari Curios; Galaxy Travel
29 Tourist Office
30 PTC Supermarket
31 Commercial Bank
32 Colour Film Processors
33 Travellers Forex Bureau
34 PAMET Workshop
36 Reserve Bank Building
38 Soche Tours & Travel
39 Immigration Office
40 TBS Bookshop; British Airways
44 Central Bookshop
47 Executive Telephone & Fax Bureau
48 National Bank
49 Manica Travel & Finance Bank
50 Legends
51 British Consulate
52 Pat's Nightclub
53 Kandodo Supermarket; Nico's Gelateria
54 National Bank
55 City Centre Bus Station
58 Old Boma
59 Map Sales Office
60 Blantyre Sports Club
61 Arizona Bottle Store
62 Cactus Bar
63 Municipal Market
64 Mandala House
To Michiru Mountain
Michiru Road
Sanders Road
Old Chileka Road
Makata Road
To Carlsberg Brewery (1km)
To Limbe
To Balaka
Mulomba Place
Blantyre Station
Railway Sidings
River
Mudi
Crescent
Moir Crescent
Kidney
To Limbe (6km), Zomba (75km) & Liwonde (100km)
Chilembwe Highway
Stephen Road
Mackie Road
Glyn Jones Road
New Chileka Road
To Chileka Airport (15km), Mwanza (120km) & Lilongwe (310km)
Kaoshiung Road
Haile Selassie Road
St George's
St Andrew's
St David's Ave
Livingstone Ave
Victoria Ave
Stewart
Browns Rd
Sclater Road
Lower
Victoria Avenue
To Sunnyside (Suburb) (1km) & Chikwawa (115km)
Robins Rd
Hanover Ave
Chilembwe Rd
Kabula Hill Rd
Laws
Sharpe Road
Henderson
Independence Drive
Chilembwe Road
0 250 500 m
0 250 500 yards

There's a large MPL pharmacy on Victoria Ave, and several smaller ones elsewhere around the city centre.

Emergency The advice in Blantyre is the same as for Lilongwe; see that section earlier in this chapter.

Dangers & Annoyances Don't walk around alone at night. Some travellers walking between the city centre and Doogles, east of the city (see Places to Stay), have been attacked at night under the railway bridge on Chileka Rd. During daylight this route is fine, but after dark a taxi is recommended (from the centre to Doogles is US$4). At night, taxi drivers will take you from the bus station to Doogles – all of 300m – but still charge US$1! As always, watch your back in busy bus stations. Limbe is particularly crowded, so stay alert there.

Photography Colour Film Processors at the top of Victoria Ave has print film, and can do passport pics on the spot. Developing and printing are also available. (See Photography & Video in the Malawi Facts for the Visitor section earlier in this chapter.)

Things to See & Do

The **Municipal Market** is on Kaoshiung Rd. The new buildings give it a more formal feel than the hectic market in Lilongwe; it's still worth a visit even if you don't want to buy anything.

Probably the most impressive building in Blantyre is the **CCAP Church**, officially called the Church of St Michael and All Angels, just off Chileka Rd. This magnificent church was built in 1891 by Scottish missionaries who had no construction training, using only local handmade bricks and wood. It has a basilica dome, towers, arches and bay windows. Although extensively renovated in the 1970s, what you see today is pretty much how it looked the day it was completed.

PAMET (Paper Making Education Trust) is an inspiring project that was set up to teach people how to recycle paper. This is an important issue in Malawi, where some people are too poor to buy school exercise books for their children. They also make beautiful paper from materials such as banana leaves and baobab bark (even elephant dung!), and they sell a lovely range of cards and other paper products. You can visit their workshop on Chilembwe Rd.

The **National Museum** is midway between Blantyre and Limbe, just off Chilembwe Highway. There's a collection of traditional weapons and artefacts, and exhibits relating to traditional dance, European exploration and slavery. Entry is free.

Blantyre Sports Club offers daily membership for US$5, which allows you to enter the club and use the bar and restaurant. To use the pool or to play squash or tennis costs another US$0.60. Nine holes of golf costs US$2.50; equipment can be hired.

If you're of a less active inclination, a visit to the **Carlsberg Brewery**, east of the centre, may appeal. Free tours go most afternoons for groups of four or more people (if you're alone, you can join a group); you must book with the public relations department (☎ 670022 or 670133). The tour ends with a free tasting session. Some places to stay in Blantyre arrange transport here. Alternatively, you can walk or get a taxi.

There are very good **craft stalls** outside the PTC supermarket on Victoria Ave, and smarter (fixed price) arts and crafts at Safari Curios on Glyn Jones Rd near the roundabout.

Places to Stay – Budget

Apart from the Limbe Country Club all of the following are in Blantyre:

Camping Backpackers can pitch their tents at ***Doogles*** (see later) for US$3; there's also room for a few trucks and cars with tents. For camping in a quieter locale see the listing for Nyambadwe Lodge following.

An alternative for those with wheels is ***Limbe Country Club,*** where you can park and camp on the edge of the playing fields for US$6 per person. Rates include club membership, so you can use the nice showers and restaurant inside.

Hostels & Guesthouses Backpackers rave about ***Doogles*** (*☎ 621128, fax 634981,*

MALAWI

doogles@malawi.net), close to the main bus station, where a bed in the dorm costs US$5, and doubles with private bathroom cost US$15. There's good security, and the friendly staff know a lot about travel in Malawi, transfer buses to Cape Maclear and Mulanje, and places to change money. They also provide a Mozambique visa service. The restaurant serves snacks from US$1, and lunch or dinner for US$4 to US$5. The lively bar is very popular at night with local volunteer workers, expats and well-to-do Malawians. Clean drinking water costs US$0.20. You can make international phone calls for US$3 per minute and send email. Some budget tour outfits run excursions from here.

If Doogles is full, you may be forced to take a room at the nearby ***Blantyre Lodge*** (the former council resthouse) near the train station. Rooms cost around US$2, although those in the new wing for US$6 are preferable. The shared toilets are filthy and the security may be questionable.

The ***Grace Bandawe Conference Centre*** *(☎ 634267)*, about 2km from the city centre along Chileka Rd, is a far better option, with quiet and clean singles/doubles for US$7/12 (two rooms share a bathroom). Breakfast is US$1 and dinner (always chicken and rice) is US$2.40. A bed in the spartan dorm annexe (over the road behind Phoenix School) costs US$3.

Kabula Lodge *(☎ 621216)* is another good budget option, off Michiru Rd, north-west of the city centre. Small simple rooms with shared bathroom cost US$5, while more comfortable rooms (some with private bathroom) cost around US$10. The friendly Malawian lady who runs this place can prepare meals to order, and you may be allowed to use the kitchen.

Nyambadwe Lodge *(☎ 633551)* 3km by road north of the main bus staion, has clean and tidy rooms for US$14/20 with shared bathroom (US$17/23 with private bathroom). Camping costs US$10 per tent.

Places to Stay – Mid-Range & Top End

Rooms at all of the following places include breakfast and a private bathroom:

The ***Hotel Training School*** *(☎ 621866)* on Chilembwe Rd, in the centre, has good singles for US$55. There's safe parking, and the restaurant does three-course meals for US$4.10.

Tumbuka Lodge *(☎ 633489, tumbuka@malawi.net)* is deservedly popular. It's in an old colonial bungalow in a shady garden with friendly staff. Tastefully decorated rooms cost US$72. Drinks are served on the terrace, there's a TV lounge, dinner is around US$5 and you can make international phone calls or send email. The ***Ryall's Hotel*** *(☎ 620955)* on Glyn Jones Rd has rooms from US$120/145 (Central African Wilderness Safaris have a branch here).

The ***Mount Soche Hotel*** *(☎ 620588)* is favoured by business travellers; rooms with air-con and TV cost from US$150/195. Both Ryall's Hotel and the Mount Soche Hotel have swimming pools and restaurants.

Places to Eat

Food Stalls & Cafes For cheap eats, there are ***food stalls*** around the main bus station near Doogles, and at the city centre bus station, selling chips from US$0.30, grilled meat for US$0.40 and bowls of nsima and sauce for around US$0.50. South of the centre on Lower Sclater Rd, ***Whistlestop Cafe*** does good local dishes from US$1.20. Next door, ***City Fish & Chips*** serves large portions for US$1. Two other cheapie restaurants are ***Ma's Cookin'*** and ***Fiskini Takeaway*** (open daily) on the corner of Henderson St and Hanover Ave. Nearby is ***Kips***: clean, friendly and open daily, with breakfast from US$1 and other meals around US$2.

Restaurants For some different African flavours, go to ***Alem Ethiopian Restaurant*** on Victoria Ave (open for lunch only), where *injera* (sour millet pancake) and *wot* (sauce) costs from US$4, and you can also get 'normal' meals like chicken and chips or curry for US$1.50.

Home Needs on Glyn Jones Rd is a South Indian snack bar and hardware shop. It's open for lunch and in the early evening, serving *masala dosas* (spicy pancakes) and other tasty snacks at cheap prices.

***The Royal Taj** (☎ 622376)* on Livingstone Ave is the best Indian restaurant in Blantyre, although it's not cheap.

Western-style takeaways include: ***Nando's*** on Haile Selassie Rd, with steak rolls and burgers for US$2.30 and spicy chicken and chips US$4; and the cheaper ***Chick Wings*** on Glyn Jones Rd.

Nico's Gelateria is popular for its Italian ice creams, cappuccinos (US$1.50) and pizzas (around US$3). Up from here in price is the Italian-flavoured ***L'Hostaria*** *(☎ 625052)* on Chilembwe Rd; it's popular and has a rustic terrace setting. Pizzas start at US$5, but at US$7 for small bowls of pasta it's not great value.

The ***Hong Kong Restaurant*** *(☎ 620859)* near the Mount Soche Hotel has all the usual Chinese dishes; a small selection goes for between US$5 and US$7, or you can splash out and spend up to US$10 or US$15. Quality is very varied though – care seems to go out the window on busy nights.

The Green House *(☎ 636375, 833518)* in the posh suburb of Sunnyside is open evenings only. The menu is European and the food is fine; starters cost from US$3, and main courses cost around US$6 to US$8.

The plush ***21 Restaurant*** at Ryall's Hotel is highly rated, with main meals from around US$7 and specialities such as seafood for US$17. At ***Moir's Coffee Shop*** in the same hotel, the food is more affordable and also recommended.

The smart ***Michiru Restaurant*** at the Mount Soche Hotel has a good view. Steak, fish and chicken dishes cost around US$12 and specials such as prawns are around US$17. In the same hotel, the less formal ***Gypsy's*** has main courses for around US$8.

Self-Catering The main ***PTC supermarket***, on the corner of Victoria Ave and Chilembwe Rd, sells food and other goods, much of it imported from South Africa or Europe and sold at similar prices. A bit further down Victoria Ave is a ***Kandodo supermarket,*** where the stock is similar, but slightly cheaper and more limited. The ***ATC supermarket*** on Glyn Jones Rd has a better selection, especially of imported goods, but is a bit more pricey. Traders sell fruit and vegetables outside all the supermarkets.

Entertainment

Pat's Nightclub (in a yard set back from the junction of Victoria Ave and Independence Dr) is a serious drinking den in the day and evening, and is popular with a young crowd of poseurs at night.

The ***Chimwemwe Restaurant***, on the corner of Henderson St and Haile Selassie Rd, is actually more like a bar, with snacks, music and gaming machines.

For more tranquil surroundings during the day, try the ***garden terrace bar*** at the Mount Soche Hotel, where snacks are also available for around US$3. Also at this hotel, the ***Sportsman's Bar*** is favoured by local businessmen and other movers and shakers.

The liveliest bar in town is at Doogles (see Places to Stay – Budget earlier), with a good blend of travellers, local expats and well-to-do Malawians. This bar closes at 10.30 pm, and people tend to move on to the ***Cactus Bar***, on Lower Sclater Rd, which gets very lively late in the evening, and has a very distinct expat feel about it. Next door, the ***Arizona Bar*** has a much more local flavour, and is not for the fainthearted.

Legends is a popular American-style bar and nightclub, which gets hot and busy after around 10 pm. Entry is US$2, unless there's live music when it's US$3.

Other occasional live music venues include the ***Mount Soche Hotel*** and the ***Ryall's Hotel***, where entry is also about US$3. There's live music at the ***Blantyre Sports Club*** on the last Friday of every month. To find out what else is going on in the live music scene just check out the fliers stuck to walls and lampposts all over town.

Spectator Sports

Blantyre's main sports venue is the Chichiri Stadium between the city centre and Limbe. This is also Malawi's national stadium; international football and other events are held here. There's no regular program, but matches are advertised in the newspaper and on billboards around town.

Getting There & Away

Air Blantyre's Chileka airport is about 15km north of the city centre. For details on the airport and flights to/from Blantyre see the main Getting Around and Getting There & Away sections earlier in this chapter.

Airline offices in Blantyre include: KLM & Kenya Airways (☎ 620106) at the Mount Soche Hotel; British Airways (☎ 624333) on Victoria Ave; and South African Airways (☎ 620629) on Haile Selassie Rd.

Bus & Minibus The luxury Coachline service goes four times per day between Blantyre and Lilongwe (US$18, four hours). It goes to/from the Mount Soche Hotel (the booking office is also there), not the bus station.

Blantyre's main bus station (for long-distance express and ordinary services run by the Stagecoach company) is east of the centre on Chileka Rd. There are five express buses each day between Blantyre and Lilongwe; two go direct via Zalewa (the junction with the Mwanza road) (US$5, five hours); and three go via Zomba (US$6, seven hours). Ordinary buses between Blantyre and Lilongwe via Zalewa go hourly (US$5). Blantyre to Zomba costs US$1.50 on the express bus, and US$1 by ordinary bus. Other ordinary buses go to Mulanje (US$2, hourly); Mwanza (US$2.50); and Monkey Bay (US$3.80, daily), via Liwonde (US$2) and Mangochi (US$3).

Other buses (ie, not Stagecoach) and long-distance minibuses go from the bus station in Limbe; most leave on a fill-up-and-go basis. Rather than wait for a Stagecoach service in Blantyre, it's often quicker to get a local minibus to Limbe bus station, and get a long-distance bus or 'half-bus' from there. Routes include: Zomba (US$1); Mulanje (US$1.50); and Mangochi (US$3).

For more details on Malawi's bus services, see the main Getting There & Away section earlier in this chapter.

Train For information on trains that stop at Blantyre and Limbe, see Train in the main Getting Around section earlier in this chapter.

Getting Around

To/From the Airport A taxi from the airport to the city costs around US$10, but agree on a price with the driver first. The price can be negotiated down a bit if you're going from the city to the airport. If your budget doesn't run to taxis, frequent local buses between the Blantyre city centre bus station and Chileka township pass the airport gate. The fare is US$0.35.

Bus Blantyre is a compact city, so it's unlikely you'll need to use public transport to get around, apart from the minibuses that shuttle along Chilembwe Highway between Blantyre city centre bus station and Limbe bus station. The one-way fare is US$0.25.

Taxi You can find private hire taxis at the Mount Soche Hotel or at the bus stations. A taxi across the city centre is around US$2; between the centre and the main bus station costs from US$3 to US$4; and a taxi from Blantyre to Limbe costs around US$5.

AROUND BLANTYRE

Blantyre is surrounded by three 'mountains', Michiru, Soche and Ndirande, all actually large hills that can all be hiked to the summit. Some hikers have been attacked on **Ndirande Mountain**, so you should only go here with a switched-on local (preferably several). The path up **Soche Mountain** starts at Soche Secondary School. Local schoolboys will act as guides for the one-hour hike to the summit.

The most rewarding is **Michiru Mountain**, 8km north-west of the city, a conservation area with nature trails. Animals here include monkey, klipspringer and even leopard, but you're unlikely to see much of them. Birdwatching is much more rewarding – over 400 species have been recorded here. To reach the visitor centre (where the trails start), take Kabula Hill Rd from the city and Michiru Rd through a select suburb and then a township. At the end of the tar (3km from Blantyre) a dirt road leads along the eastern foot of the mountain. Take the

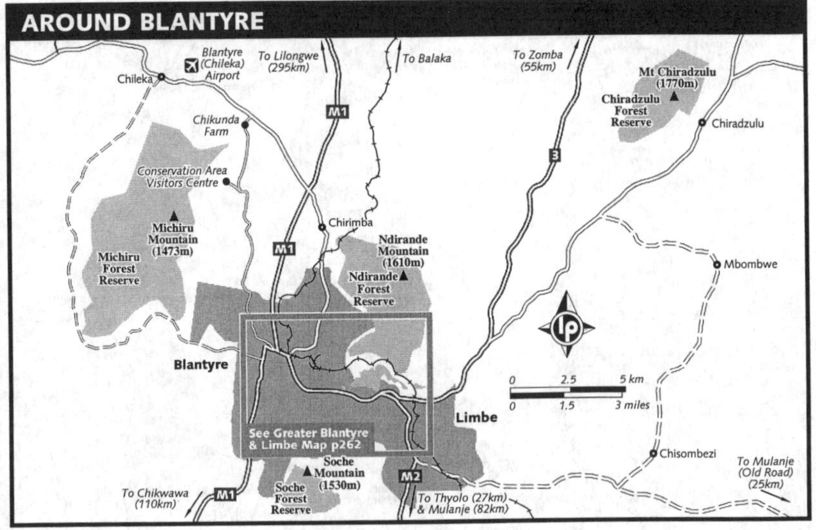

left turn signposted 'nature trails', which takes you to the visitor centre, where you can buy a map. There's no public transport, but you can get a taxi as far as the driver is prepared to go along the dirt road, and walk the rest of the way. You may be able to get a lift back with other visitors.

Southern Malawi

Malawi's Southern Province, with Blantyre roughly at its centre, lies between the southern end of Lake Malawi and the far southern tip of the country. Places are described roughly north to south.

LIWONDE

You may visit Liwonde town if you're heading for Liwonde National Park or for Mozambique by train. The town is divided by the Shire River; on the eastern side are the train station, the market, a supermarket and several shops.

Places to stay include the ***Market Square Motel***, with good singles/doubles with bathroom and breakfast for US$5/10. Down by the river is ***Manpower Shireside Lodge***, where simple but clean rondavels with bathroom, hot water, mosquito nets and fan, in a garden overlooking the river, are fair value at US$8.50/13. There's a bar and restaurant, and camping is allowed.

On the western side of the river, the best cheapie is ***Liwonde Holiday Resort***, just off the main road, with clean bathrooms, a friendly owner and basic rooms for US$1.50 per person. Another 1.5km off the main road is ***Kudya Discovery Lodge*** (☎ *532497)*, which is a bit run-down with tatty overpriced rooms from US$16/20, but it does have a pool and a restaurant overlooking the river where you can always see a big herd of hippo. Wildlife-viewing boat trips into Liwonde National Park are run from here.

LIWONDE NATIONAL PARK

Liwonde National Park is the best in Malawi: well managed and with increasing numbers of animals, especially in the northern half of the park and along the river. There is a very healthy elephant population, and the Shire River seems to be overflowing with crocodile and hippo. Antelope such as waterbuck are often seen near the water, and you may see the beautiful sable on the flood plains.

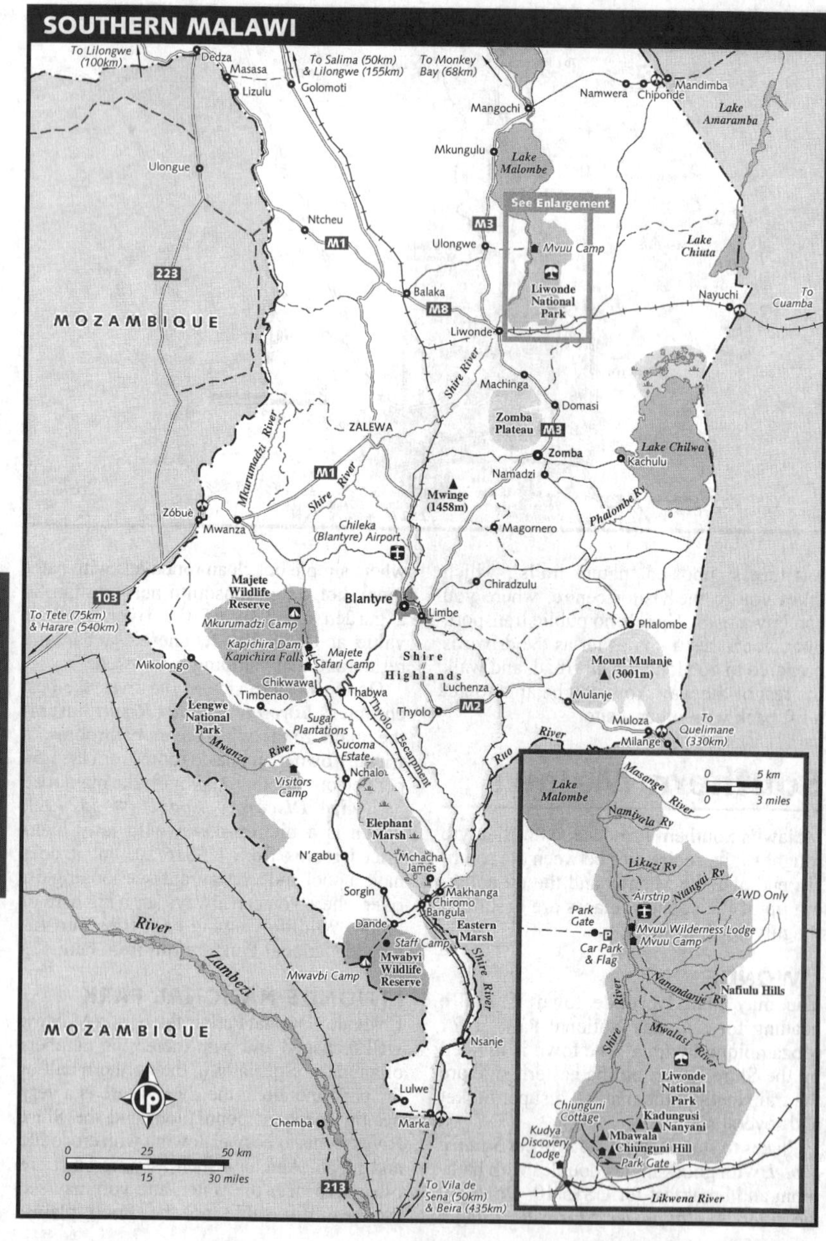
SOUTHERN MALAWI
To Lilongwe (100km)
Dedza
Masasa
Lizulu
To Salima (50km) & Lilongwe (155km)
Golomoti
To Monkey Bay (68km)
Mangochi
Namwera
Chiponde
Mandimba
Lake Amaramba
Mkungulu
Lake Malombe
Ulongue
See Enlargement
Ntcheu
M1
M3
Ulongwe
Mvuu Camp
Lake Chiuta
223
Balaka
M8
Liwonde National Park
Nayuchi
To Cuamba
MOZAMBIQUE
Liwonde
Shire River
Machinga
Domasi
Mkurumadzi River
ZALEWA
Zomba Plateau
M3
Zomba
Lake Chilwa
Kachulu
M1
Shire River
Namadzi
Mwinge (1458m)
Phalombe Rv
Zóbuè
Mwanza
Chileka (Blantyre) Airport
Magornero
Majete Wildlife Reserve
Chiradzulu
103
Blantyre
Limbe
To Tete (75km) & Harare (540km)
Mkurumadzi Camp
Phalombe
Kapichira Dam
Kapichira Falls
Majete Safari Camp
Shire Highlands
Mount Mulanje (3001m)
Mikolongo
Chikwawa
Thabwa
Luchenza
Timbenao
Mulanje
Lengwe National Park
Sugar Plantations
Thyolo Escarpment
Thyolo
M2
Muloza
To Quelimane (330km)
Mwanza River
Sucoma Estate
Ruo River
Milange
Visitors Camp
Nchalo
Elephant Marsh
N'gabu
Mchacha James
Sorgin
Makhanga
Chiromo
Bangula
Dande
Eastern Marsh
Staff Camp
River
Mwabvi Wildlife Reserve
Mwavbi Camp
Zambezi
Shire River
MOZAMBIQUE
Nsanje
Lulwe
Chemba
Marka
0 25 50 km
0 15 30 miles
213
To Vila de Sena (50km) & Beira (435km)
Lake Malombe
Masange River
0 5 km
0 3 miles
Namivala Rv
Likuzi Rv
Ntangai Rv
Airstrip
4WD Only
Park Gate
Mvuu Wilderness Lodge
Mvuu Camp
Car Park & Flag
Nanandanje Rv
Nafiulu Hills
Shire River
Mwalasi River
Liwonde National Park
Chiunguni Cottage
Kadungusi
Nanyani
Mbawala
Kudya Discovery Lodge
Chiunguni Hill
Park Gate
Likwena River
MALAWI

Tea Growing

South and east of Blantyre, on the rolling hills of the Shire Highlands, the climate is ideal for growing tea, and the area is covered with plantations (or 'estates'). The first tea bushes were imported from India during the early days of the Nyasaland colony, and tea production quickly became a major industry. Growing tea is a very labour intensive form of agriculture and only viable in countries where wages for manual workers are low. In Malawi, tea is a major export crop (along with tobacco and sugar) and provides thousands of people with jobs.

Travelling on the main road between Limbe and Mulanje you'll see the seemingly endless fields of tea, with vivid green bushes in neat lines covering the hillsides. The tea-pickers (men and women) work their way slowly down the lines, picking just a few leaves and a bud from the top of each bush and throwing them into large baskets they carry on their backs. At the end of each shift, the baskets of fresh tea leaves are taken to a collection area, where they are weighed and each worker's wages are calculated. The leaves are then transported to a tea factory, where they are trimmed and dried before being packed in bags and boxes ready for export. A small proportion of low quality tea stays within the country to be sold locally.

If you have a genuine interest in tea production it may be possible to arrange a tour of an estate and factory. There is no established set-up; you simply call an estate and ask a senior manager if it's possible to visit. You'll probably need your own vehicle, or have to take a taxi, as most estate offices are off the main road and difficult to reach by public transport.

ERIC WHEATER

The best place to start with is Satemwa Estate (☎ 472233), near the small town of Thyolo (**cho-low**) on the main road between Limbe and Mulanje. At the estate, ***Chawani Bungalow*** *(☎ 472356)* can be hired for US$65 per night. It sleeps up to eight in four double bedrooms and the price includes the services of a caretaker/cook. From the bungalow you can walk through the tea estates or go through the evergreen forest remnants on nearby Thyolo Mountain, which is a popular birdwatching spot.

Other tea estates that may allow visits include British African Estates (☎ 472266) and Namingomba Estates (☎ 472300). The tourist office in Blantyre may have more suggestions.

Liwonde also has a small herd of rhino, which is protected in a sanctuary within the park.

Some visitors are disappointed by the lack of variety of animals, but Liwonde is lovely, and as long as you are not desperate to tick off the 'big five' it would be hard not to enjoy it. Having said that, through 2000 and 2001, the park will be restocked with more animals, including buffalo, eland, Niassa wildebeest, reedbuck, zebra, roan and hartebeest, which may in turn attract lion, so travellers keen to spot a wider range may be rewarded.

The combination of rich riverine, mopane and grassland habitats also means birdlife is very varied: over 400 species of Malawi's 650 total have been recorded here. All in all, after a slump in the 1980s and early 1990s, the future of Liwonde looks bright and a visit is recommended.

Entry fees are payable (see National Parks & Wildlife Reserves in the Facts about Malawi section earlier in this chapter).

Tourism in the park revolves around Mvuu Camp. If you have your own vehicle you can tour the park's network of tracks (although they close in the wet season and vary from year to year, so check the situation with the camp). Alternatively, wildlife-viewing tours in an open-top 4WD (US$18 per person) or guided wildlife walks (US$10) can be arranged at Mvuu Camp. To enter the rhino sanctuary costs an extra $2 (the money goes directly to this project). Most rewarding and enjoyable are boat rides on the river (US$18), morning or evening, when you're virtually guaranteed to see elephant, hippo, crocodile and a whole host of birds.

If you can't stay in Liwonde National Park, there is a company called Waterline (☎/fax 532552), based at Kudya Discovery Lodge (see Liwonde earlier), that runs wildlife-viewing boat trips. Prices depend on the length of the trip and the number of people, but a two-hour tour for two or three people costs US$22 per person.

Places to Stay

Places to stay in Liwonde remain open all year – you can reach them by boat even if rain closes some of the park tracks.

Mvuu Camp, managed by Central African Wilderness Safaris (☎ 781393 or 781153, fax 781397 in Lilongwe, ⓔ info@wilderness.malawi.net) is deep in the northern part of the park on the banks of the river. There's a range of options: camp in your own tent for US$8, or stay in big walk-in tents for US$39 or comfortable chalets for US$42 (all charges per person). The shared showers and toilets are the cleanest we've seen north of the Limpopo, and there's a fully equipped kitchen (with staff on hand to help) if you want to self-cater. Or you can eat at the open-plan thatched restaurant that overlooks the river; breakfast is US$8.40, lunch is US$11 and dinner is US$15. There's also a bar-lounge area. Full board in a chalet (including meals, wildlife drives, boat rides etc) costs US$130 per person. Children between four and 12 are charged half price, but those under six are not allowed on wildlife-viewing trips.

A short distance upriver is ***Mvuu Wilderness Lodge*** (also managed by Central African Wilderness Safaris), with large luxury double tents with private balconies overlooking a water hole where wildlife and birds are active. There's a maximum of only ten guests, so this place is relaxed and intimate, with attentive staff and excellent food. There's also a small swimming pool. Luxury comes at a price though: US$230 per person, which includes full board, park fees and all wildlife drives, boat rides, bird walks etc.

At least two new places are planned to open in Liwonde by 2001.

Getting There & Away

The main park gate is 6km east of Liwonde town. There's no public transport beyond here, but hitching is possible. From the gate to Mvuu Camp is 28km along the park track (closed in the wet season).

Another way for vehicles is via the dirt road (open all year) from Ulongwe, a village between Liwonde town and Mangochi. This leads for 14km through local villages to the western boundary. There's a car park near the riverbank (with a watchman); you hoist a flag, and a boat from Mvuu Camp comes to pick you up. This service is free if you're staying at the camp.

Alternatively, if you make an advance booking for Mvuu Camp through its Lilongwe office (for details see Places to Stay), the camp can arrange a transfer from Liwonde town for US$20 per person (minimum four).

For those without wheels, the best option is to get any bus or minibus between Liwonde town and Mangochi and get off at Ulongwe (make sure you say this clearly, otherwise the driver will think you want to go to Lilongwe). In Ulongwe local boys wait by the bus stop and will take you by bicycle to the park gate or all the way to the boat jetty and flag. This costs US$2 to US$3, although if you've got a big pack there may be an extra charge or you may need two bikes.

> The hour-long cycle ride through the villages is superb, with a great commentary from your pedalist. However, do not leave it too late. At dusk elephants come much nearer to the track – and so the cyclists demand extra money. We had a very close encounter with three elephants and without the bikes we would have been flattened.
>
> **George Casley, UK**

Another option is the boat transfer service along the Shire River offered by Waterline (☎/fax 532552), based at Kudya Discovery Lodge (see its listing under Liwonde earlier). It will drop you at Mvuu Camp, and return to pick you up, for US$72 each way (the price is for the boat), or US$20 per person for groups of four or five.

Approaching Mvuu by river is very enjoyable; along the way you're likely to see elephant and certain to see hippo.

ZOMBA

Zomba was the capital of Malawi until the mid-1970s and it's still a large, busy place, with all the attractions of a town and none of the downsides of a city. At its heart is the vibrant market and shopping area (the largest market in the country), a great place to do your shopping, or simply to wander around and watch Africa at work.

Overshadowing the town is the Zomba Plateau, and a walk through the suburbs on the lush and peaceful foothills reveals faded but still impressive colonial and government buildings – a reminder of Zomba's historical importance.

Zomba is not a place for wild parties, and you won't see many other tourists, but it somehow encapsulates what Malawi is all about; a visit here is highly recommended.

Places to Stay & Eat

The ***Council Resthouse*** opposite the bus station has dorms for US$0.50 and singles/doubles for US$1.50/2 but the toilet block is disgusting. Much better is the nearby ***Ndindeya Motel***, where large rooms with clean shared bathrooms cost US$3/6, or US$7/10 with private bathroom. The restaurant is good, with breakfast from US$1 and other meals from US$2.

Up the hill and price scale from here is the ***Government Hostel***, the house of the first colonial governor. Rooms cost US$35/40 with bathroom and breakfast. Staff will assume you'll want one of the more modern rooms in the garden, but those in the old house have more atmosphere – try for the west tower! Main dishes in the

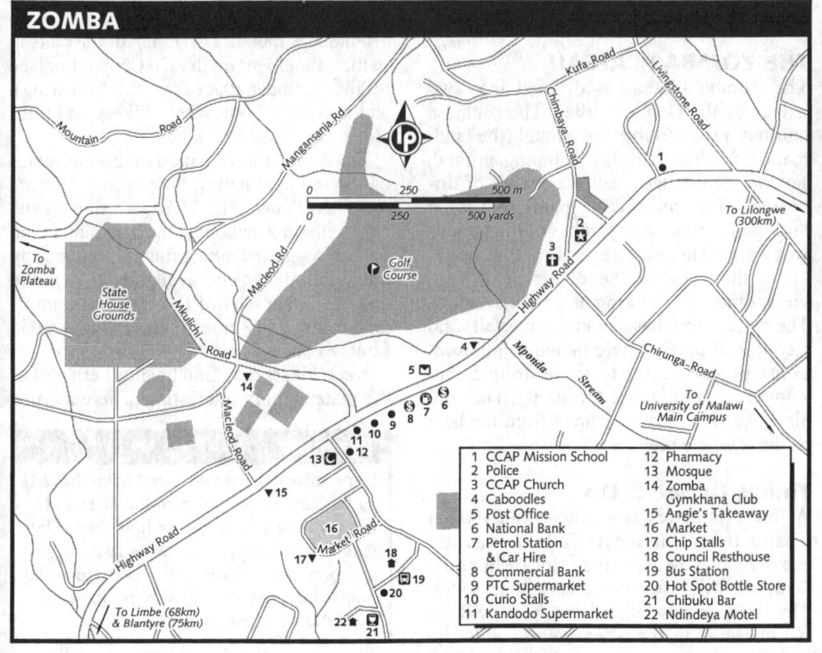

restaurant are US$3 to US$5, and the set menu is US$10.

There are two ***supermarkets*** in town, and plenty of cheap restaurants; we found ***Angie's Takeaway*** on the main street the best. Around the market area there are several chip stalls serving up deep-fried potato chips, and one or two offer grilled meat and other street food too.

For a splurge, ***Caboodles***, also on the main street, serves good coffee and sticky cakes (US$1.50), ham and salad or BLT rolls (US$2), and pizza and salad (US$3). At the ***Gymkhana Club***, another colonial relic, you can have meals and drinks in pleasant surroundings.

Getting There & Away

Zomba is on a main route between Lilongwe and Blantyre, and there are frequent Stagecoach buses. The express to/from Lilongwe is US$4.50; to/from Blantyre is US$1.50. Minibuses go every hour or so to Limbe for US$1. To Liwonde by bus or minibus is US$0.80.

THE ZOMBA PLATEAU

The Zomba Plateau is divided into two halves by the Domasi Valley. The southern half has a road to the top, a hotel (the landmark Ku Chawe Inn), a camping ground, several picnic places and a network of driveable tracks and hiking paths that wind through pine forest or patches of indigenous woodland. There are several narrow ridges along the edge of the escarpment, with viewpoints overlooking the plains below. The plateau also has streams, waterfalls and a couple of lakes, where fishing is allowed. Some people prefer to drive around, but Zomba is a good place for hiking. The cool air makes a welcome change from the heat of the lowland areas.

Things to See & Do

A few kilometres from the landmark Ku Chawe Inn are **Mandala Falls**, not as impressive as they used to be since **Mlunguzi Dam** was significantly enlarged in 1999. The area downstream from here will be worth avoiding for a few years while the landscape recovers from the construction. A nature trail leads upstream from Mandala Falls, through some beautiful indigenous forest and a trout farm, to **Williams Falls**, another fairly impressive cascade.

A popular place to visit is **Chingwe's Hole**, on the western side of the plateau, supposedly bottomless and the basis of various local legends, although now overgrown and not especially impressive. Nearby, however, is a splendid viewpoint, looking westward over the Shire Valley.

For even more impressive views, head for the eastern side of the plateau, where **Queen's View** (named after Queen Elizabeth, wife of King George VI, who visited Zomba in 1957) and **Emperor's View** (after Emperor Haile Selassie of Ethiopia, who visited in 1964) overlook Zomba town and out towards Mulanje.

Hiking

The southern half of the plateau is ideal for hiking. The network of tracks and paths can be confusing though, so for more help with orientation, there's a 3-D map of the plateau in the Model Hut by the Ku Chawe Inn (see its listing under Places to Stay following), and a visitors book where hikers and travellers have added comments.

For detailed information on hiking routes on the southern half of the plateau, *A Guide to Zomba Plateau* (US$1.50) is a single sheet map with information on the back, including several suggested hiking routes, produced by the Wildlife Society, available in Blantyre and at the Ku Chawe Inn. For more information still, the Zomba Plateau is covered in Lonely Planet's *Trekking in East Africa*.

Keen hikers may find the northern half of the plateau more interesting. There are few

Warning

Some travellers have reported being hassled by 'ruffians' when hiking on the plateau. Locals say these are not people from Zomba but outsiders working on the Mlunguzi Dam construction site. Whatever the case, to avoid trouble, arrange a guide with the forest officer stationed at the Model Hut.

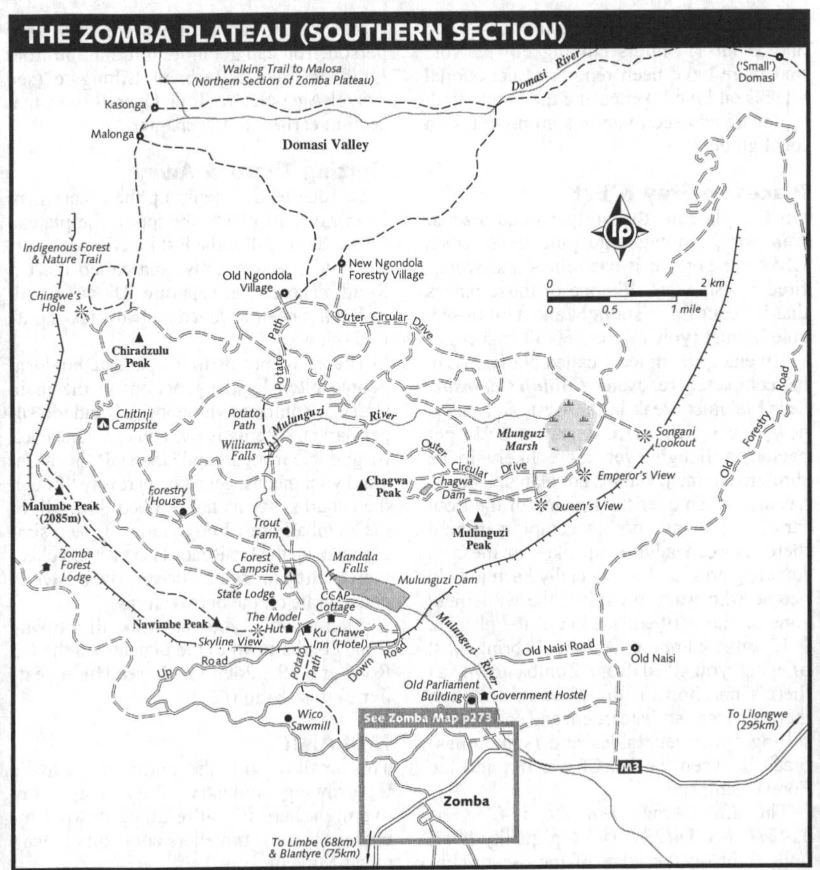

tracks here, and no pine plantation – the landscape is similar to that of Mt Mulanje and Nyika Plateau. For advice on hiking on the northern plateau, contact Chitinji Campsite (see Places to Stay & Eat following).

The Potato Path You can hike all the way from Zomba town to the plateau via a direct route called the Potato Path, signposted at a sharp bend on the road up to the plateau about 2km from Zomba town. The path climbs steeply through woodland to reach the part of the plateau near the Ku Chawe Inn.

From near the Ku Chawe Inn, the Potato Path then goes straight across the southern half of the plateau, sometimes using the park tracks, sometimes using narrow short cuts, and leads eventually to Old Ngondola Village, from where it descends quite steeply into the Domasi Valley.

The Domasi Valley is well known for its fertile soil, plentiful water and good farming conditions, so here the local people grow vegetables (especially potatoes) and take them along the Potato Path (hence the name) down to Zomba town to sell in the market.

Allow two to three hours for the ascent, and about 1½ hours coming down. Note that there have been reports of occasional attacks on lone hikers using the Potato Path – you are advised to go in a group or take a local guide.

Places to Stay & Eat

On the plateau, the aptly named ***Forest Campsite***, among large pine trees, costs US$1 per person; it has toilets and wood-fired hot showers. It's one of those places that is beautiful in sunlight and a bit miserable in mist (you've got a 50:50 chance).

An enterprising local called Nasiv Jussab has completely renovated ***Chitinji Campsite***, near Malumbe Peak in the west, and this is now an excellent place to stay at US$3 per person, although even more likely to be shrouded in mist. Cabins are planned. Nasiv has also taken over the running of the trout farm, and plans another camping ground there. He can advise on hikes in the surrounding area, and is especially keen to help people who want to explore the wilderness zone on the northern section of the plateau.

If you're camping, you should bring most of what you need from Zomba town, as there's no shop on the plateau, although there's a local-style tearoom and some stalls selling fruit, vegetables and (sometimes) bread between the Ku Chawe Inn and the Forest Campsite.

The ***Ku Chawe Inn*** *(☎ 514253 or 514211, fax 514230)* is a top-quality hotel built right on the edge of the escarpment with excellent views and very comfortable singles/doubles from US$100/154, including breakfast. Evening meals cost around US$9. There's a good restaurant and bar where they keep a fire going on cold nights, and the terraced gardens are particularly pleasant. Nonguests can drink in the bar or eat dinner here, or enjoy the buffet breakfast for US$6.50.

Another option is ***Zomba Forest Lodge*** on the western slopes of the plateau, 6km by winding dirt road off the Up Road. This is the former Kachere Forest Resthouse, which has now been nicely renovated with a kitchen for self-catering and comfortable rooms with private bathroom for US$18 per person. You can get more information from Land & Lake Safaris in Lilongwe (see Travel Agencies & Tour Operators in that section earlier in this chapter).

Getting There & Away

A tar road leads steeply up the escarpment from Zomba town to the top of the plateau (about 8km). After the last junction, it's narrow and one-way only, and called the Up Road. There's a separate Down Road, which has been widened and now takes traffic both ways.

There's no bus up to the plateau, but local people hitch by the junction on the main street in Zomba town opposite Kandodo supermarket. Alternatively, you can take a taxi (negotiable from around US$8). If this is beyond your means, get a taxi part way through the suburbs, say as far as Wico Sawmill, or the Zomba Forest Lodge turn-off, then simply walk up the Up Road. There are excellent views, often missed by drivers, who have to concentrate on the narrow turns!

Alternatively, you can walk all the way from Zomba town to the plateau via the Up Road or on the Potato Path (see Hiking earlier in this section).

MULANJE

This small town is the centre of Malawi's tea-growing industry. You may stay overnight here if you're going to Mozambique, but most travellers come on the way to Mt Mulanje.

Camping is possible at ***Mulanje Golf Club***, on the eastern side of town, for US$2.50, which includes membership, so you can use the showers and bar.

The ***Council Resthouse*** has doubles from US$1.50, but the ***Mulanje Motel***, down from the bus station, is better, with doubles for US$3. Next door is the smarter ***Mulanje View Motel***, with a wide choice: you can pitch a tent for US$1 or pay from US$3 for a simple single to US$7 for a double with bathroom and breakfast. There's a bar and there's good-value food in the restaurant.

Buses and minibuses go to/from Blantyre and Limbe throughout the day for around

MALAWI

US$2. If you're heading for the Mozambique border, a minibus or matola is US$0.60. (For more border crossing information, see Land in the main Getting There & Away section earlier in this chapter.)

MT MULANJE

Mt Mulanje (also called the Mulanje Plateau) rises steeply from the undulating plain of the highlands, surrounded by near-vertical cliffs of bare rock, many over 1000m high. The cliffs are dissected by vegetated valleys, where rivers drop in spectacular waterfalls. It is often misty here and Mulanje's high peaks sometimes jut above the cloud, giving rise to the local name 'Island in the Sky'. Some people come to the base of the mountain just for a day visit, but the stunning scenery, easy access, clear paths and well-maintained huts make Mulanje a fine hiking area and many travellers spend at least a few days here.

Mulanje measures about 30km from west to east and 25km from north to south, with an area of at least 600 sq km. On its north-eastern corner is the outlier Mchese Mountain, separated from the main massif by the Fort Lister Gap. The massif is composed of several bowl-shaped river basins, separated by rocky peaks and ridges. The highest peak is Sapitwa (3001m), the highest point in Malawi and in all Southern Africa north of the Drakensberg. There are other peaks on the massif above 2500m, and you can reach most of the summits without technical climbing.

Information

Hiking on Mt Mulanje is controlled by the Likabula Forest Station (☎ 465218, PO Box 50, Mulanje), at the small village of Likabula, about 15km from Mulanje town. It's open from 7 am to noon and 1 to 5 pm daily, including most holidays, and run by a very friendly lady called Dorothy. You must register here and make reservations for the mountain huts (you can also call or write in advance). This is the best place to arrange guides and porters.

Camping is permitted only near huts. Open fires are not allowed – this is especially important during the latter part of the dry season, when there is a serious fire risk. The collecting of plants and animals is forbidden.

There is nowhere to buy food on Mt Mulanje, so you must carry all you need. At Likabula there's a small market, but you're better off getting supplies at Chitikali (where the dirt road to Likabula turns off the main tarred Blantyre-Mulanje road), which has shops, stalls and a small supermarket, or in Blantyre.

Guidebooks & Maps

The *Guide to Mulanje Massif*, by Frank Eastwood, has information on ascent routes and main peaks plus a large section on rock climbing, but nothing on the routes between huts. There's more detail on Mulanje in Lonely Planet's *Trekking in East Africa*, which also covers Nyika and Zomba.

If you need detailed maps, Mulanje is covered by the government survey sheet number 1535 D3, at 1:50,000, which shows most paths and all the huts, except Minunu Hut, which is at approximate grid reference 826377. The 1:30,000 *Tourist Map of Mulanje* covers a similar area, overprinted with extra information for hikers. These maps are usually available from the public map sales offices in Blanytre and Lilongwe, but stocks occasionally run dry.

Guides & Porters

Porters are not obligatory, but they make the hiking easier, especially for the first day's steep hike from Likabula Forest Station; they can also guide you through the maze of paths. Most porters can act as guides on the routes between huts, but you need a porter with proper guiding experience if you plan to go up the peaks.

As you arrive in Likabula (or Mulanje town) you'll be besieged by hopeful locals looking for work, but you should arrange porters only at Likabula as the forest station keeps a list of registered porters who are known to be reliable. Some porters are not on the list but are 'cleared' by the office staff.

There is a standard charge of US$4 per day per porter, payable in kwacha (you should avoid hiring porters who undercut this price in their eagerness to get work). If your porter also guides you up peaks, an extra fee may be

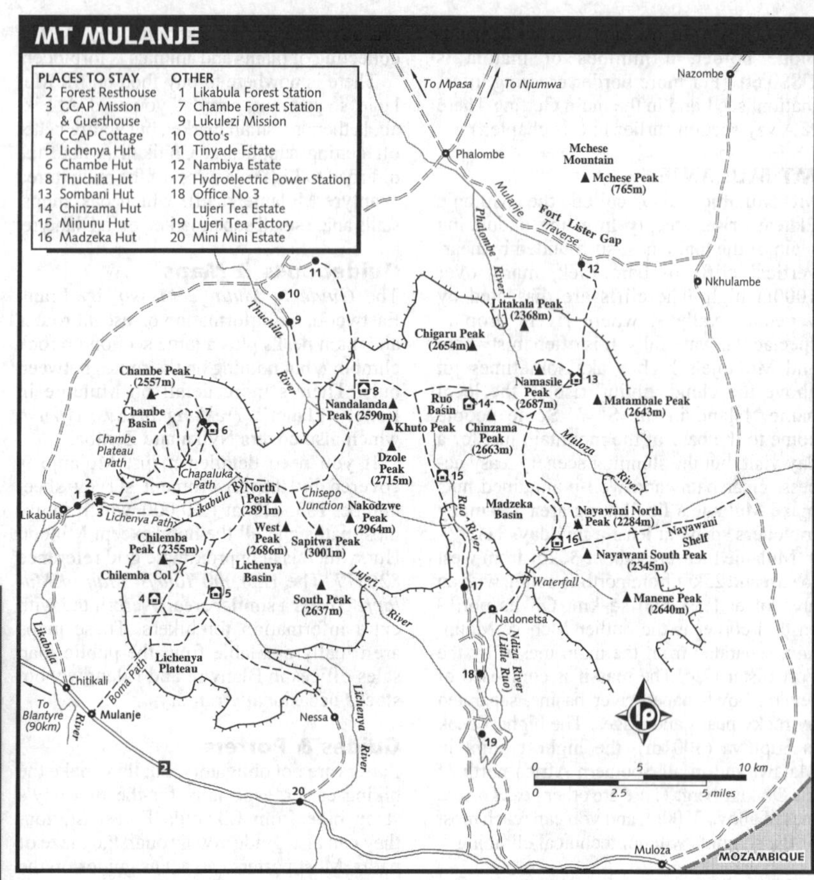

payable. Before agreeing to anything, check with the forest station that the porter is familiar with the routes. The total fee for the whole trip should be agreed before departure and put in writing. Fees are paid at the end of the trip but porters are expected to provide their own food, so about 25% may be required in advance. Make sure porters bring everything they need, and tell them no other food can be provided. Even if you do this, you'll still feel guilty when you stop for lunch and the porters sit and watch you, so take a few extra packets of biscuits for them. You may want to tip your porters if the service has been good; a rule of thumb is to pay something around an extra day's wage for every three to five days. The maximum weight each porter can carry is 18kg.

Places to Stay

Below the Mountain At Likabula, the ***Forest Resthouse*** is spotlessly clean, with a kitchen, comfortable lounge, several twin bedrooms and a clean shared bathroom, for US$3.50 per person. A cook will prepare your food and wash up. You can camp in the grounds for US$1. The nearby ***Mission Guesthouse*** at the CCAP Mission has rooms and self-catering chalets for US$2.50 per person; camping costs US$0.75 per tent. We've heard rumours that a luxury lodge may be built in the Likabula area, so if this is your style ask around for details when you arrive.

On the Mountain On Mulanje are seven *forestry huts*: Chambe, Lichenya, Thuchila (**chu**-chila), Chinzama, Minunu, Madzeka and Sombani. Each is equipped with benches, tables and open fires with plenty of wood. Some have sleeping platforms (no mattresses); in others you just sleep on the floor. You provide your own food, cooking gear, candles, sleeping bag and stove (although you can cook on the fire). A caretaker chops wood, lights fires and brings water, for which a small tip should be paid.

Payments must be made at Likabula Forest Station – show your receipt to the hut caretaker. The huts cost just over US$1 per person per night – an absolute bargain. Camping is permitted outside the huts for US$0.60 per person. Some huts may be full at weekends, but you can normally adjust your route around this. As the reservation system doesn't require a deposit, some local residents book and then don't turn up – it's worth checking to see if this has happened. Some hut improvements (such as mattresses and piped water supplies) may be introduced in the future, and a price rise is also likely.

The ***CCAP Cottage*** on the Lichenya Plateau is similar to the forestry huts, but there are utensils in the kitchen, plus mattresses and blankets. For this extra luxury you pay US$1.25 per night. You can make reservations at the CCAP Mission in Likabula.

Hiking Routes

There are about six main routes up and down Mulanje. The three main ascent routes go from Likabula: the Chambe Plateau Path (also called the Skyline Path), the Chapaluka Path and the Lichenya Path. Other routes, more often used for the descent, are: Thuchila Hut to Lukulezi Mission; Sombani Hut to Fort Lister Gap; and Minunu Hut to Lujeri tea estate.

Once you're on the massif, a network of paths links the huts and peaks, and many different permutations are possible; we outline some choices below. Be warned that some of the routes are impassable or otherwise dangerous. The route from Madzeka Hut to Lujeri is very steep, and the wooden ladders required to cross the steepest sections have rotted away, making it effectively impassable. On the south-western side of Mulanje, the Boma Path and the path from Lichenya to Nessa are both dangerously steep and very rarely used.

It normally takes about three to six hours to hike between one hut and the next, which means you can walk in the morning, dump your kit, then go out to explore a nearby peak or valley in the afternoon.

> **Warning**
>
> Mulanje is a big mountain with notoriously unpredictable weather. After periods of heavy rain, streams can become swollen and impassable – do not try to cross them! Wait until the flood subsides (sometimes after a few hours) or adjust your route to cross in safety further upstream. Even during the dry season, it's not uncommon to get rain, cold winds and thick mists, which make it easy to get lost. Between May and August, periods of low cloud and drizzle (called *chiperones)* can last for several days, and temperatures drop below freezing. None of this is a problem as long as you've got warm, waterproof gear and don't get lost. Otherwise, you risk suffering from severe exposure. In 1999 an unfortunate traveller died up here.

A Mulanje Traverse There are many ways to traverse the Mulanje massif. The route we describe briefly here, from Likabula to Fort Lister, is one of several options, although it seems to be the most popular. It can be done in four days, but there are several variations that can extend this period, and plenty of opportunities for sidetracking, to take in a few peaks and ridges or explore small valleys.

Stage 1: Likabula Forest Station to Chambe Hut There are two options: the Chambe Plateau Path, which is short and steep (two to four hours); and the Chapaluka Path (3½ to five hours), which is less steep and more scenic. From the hut veranda, there are good views of the south-eastern face of Chambe Peak (2557m), but if you fancy reaching the summit of this spectacular peak, from Chambe Hut it will take you five to seven hours to get to the top and back. The ascent is stiff and the paths are vague, so you may need a guide. About two to 2½ hours from the hut, you reach a large cairn on a broad level part of the ridge at the foot of the main face. You might be happy with reaching this point, which offers excellent views over the Chambe Basin to the escarpment edge and the plains far below.

Stage 2: Chambe Hut to Thuchila Hut (12km, four to five hours) About two hours from Chambe, you reach Chisepo Junction, where a path leads up to the summit of Sapitwa Peak (3001m). You can hike to the summit of Sapitwa, but it's a toughie, and the upper section involves some tricky scrambling among large boulders and dense vegetation. From Chisepo Junction you should allow three to five hours for the ascent, plus two to four for the descent, plus the time it takes you to get from and back to either Chambe or Thuchila Hut). Perhaps not surprisingly, Sapitwa means 'Don't Go There' in the local language. If you're short of time, you can do a shorter loop by descending from Thuchila Hut to Lukulezi Mission, then hiking or catching a matola back to Likabula.

Stage 3: Thuchila Hut to Sombani Hut (12km, four to five hours) This stage takes you across a small col and down into the Ruo Basin. About two hours from Thuchila Hut, you reach Chinzama Hut, where you can stop if you want an easy day. The large mountain directly opposite Sombani Hut is Namasile (2687m), which takes about three hours to ascend, plus two hours on the descent. The path is steep and strenuous in places, spiralling round the northern side of the mountain to approach the summit from the west. A guide is recommended unless you're competent on vague paths in bad weather.

Stage 4: Sombani Hut to Fort Lister Gap (5km, three hours) This is all downhill, with great views over the surrounding plains. There are a lot of forks, so a guide is useful to show you the way, but otherwise at every fork keep going down. For the last section you follow a dirt track, past Fort Lister Forest Station, from where it's another 8km along the dirt road to Phalombe village. There's little or no traffic, so you'll have to hike (about two hours), but it's pleasant enough. Most porters include this stretch in the fee you pay for the final day.

From Phalombe you can get a matola back to Likabula or Mulanje.

The Chambe-Lichenya Loop This short but beautiful route is not an officially named trail, but we give it this title and recommend it for a good taste of Mulanje if you haven't got time for a traverse of the whole massif. It starts and finishes at Likabula Forest Station, and takes three days and two nights, but could be shortened to two days.

Stage 1: Likabula Forest Station to Chambe Hut This stage is the same as stage 1 of the Mulanje traverse described earlier.

Pines on Mulanje

The pine plantations on Mulanje were first established by the colonial government in the early 1950s, mainly around Chambe. The sides of the massif are too steep for a road, so all the timber is cut by hand and then carried down on a cableway (called the 'skyline') or on the heads of forest labourers. As you're going up the Chambe Plateau Path you'll see these incredibly hardy guys walking downhill, sometimes running, with huge planks of wood balanced on their heads.

The plantations provide employment for local people and wood for the whole of southern Malawi. A bad side effect, apart from the ugliness of the plantations, is the tendency of pine trees to spread slowly across the natural grassland as seeds are blown by the wind. These introduced trees disturb the established vegetation balance – which is always precarious in highland areas.

Stage 2: Chambe Hut to Lichenya Basin (four to five hours) Heading east from Chambe Hut (towards Thuchila), turn right at a junction about 1½ hours from Chambe Hut to reach the Lichenya Basin, and either the CCAP Cottage or Lichenya Hut.

Stage 3: Lichenya Basin to Likabula Forest Station (four to five hours) Go across a col to the east of Chilemba Peak (you could sidetrack up here for fine views – allow two hours return) then descend through beautiful forest to eventually reach Likabula.

Getting There & Away

Buses between Blantyre and Mulanje town are detailed in those sections. The dirt road to Likabula turns off the main tarred Blantyre-Mulanje road at Chitikali, about 2km west of the centre of Mulanje town – follow the signpost to Phalombe. If you're coming from Blantyre on the bus, ask to be dropped at Chitikali. From here, irregular matolas run to Likabula for US$0.50. If you're in a group, you can hire the whole matola to Likabula for around US$10. Alternatively, you can walk (10km, two to three hours); it's a pleasant hike through tea estates, with good views of the south-western face of Mulanje on your right.

THE LOWER SHIRE

The main road south from Blantyre plunges down the Thyolo Escarpment in a series of hairpin bends to reach the Lower Shire: a thin spine of Malawian territory jutting into Mozambique. From the escarpment road, there are excellent views across the Shire River floodplains and out towards the Zambezi on the hazy horizon. Even when it's cool in the highlands, it can be blisteringly hot down here. The sharp change of temperature and landscape, in less than 30km, is most striking.

This is one of the least visited areas of Malawi, very different from the rest of the country, and contains Lengwe National Park, the reserves of Majete and Mwabvi, and the Elephant Marsh, a vast area of seasonally flooded swampland. Lengwe, Majete and Mwabvi are often overlooked, but plans are afoot to improve their infrastructure and facilities, so this may change in the future.

Majete Wildlife Reserve

Majete Wildlife Reserve lies west of the Shire; it's mainly miombo woodland, with dense patches of forest along the river. Animals recorded here include elephant, sable, kudu and hartebeest, but very few remain because of heavy poaching, so it's best to forget about mammals and appreciate the reserve simply as a beautiful wilderness area. You're almost certain to have the place to yourself. The birdwatching is good, and hiking is allowed (with a game scout), although the entry fees seem a little steep here (see National Parks & Wildlife Reserves in the Facts about Malawi section earlier in this chapter).

The only driveable track in the reserve runs parallel to the Shire River (although not near enough for you to see it from the track), to the Shire River's confluence with the Mkurumadzi River, where you can pitch a tent at the Mkurumadzi Camp ranger post (although there are no facilities). If you're in a car, this track crosses some steep gullies so high clearance is essential. If you're hiking you can go from the gate to Mkurumadzi in a day, stay the night and hike back. Just past the gate, a track leads east to the spectacular Kapichira Falls, although the view is tarnished slightly by the vast dam and power station under construction here.

Places to Stay The friendly ***Majete Safari Camp*** is outside the reserve, just a few kilometres from the gate, overlooking the Shire River and the Matitu Falls, the southernmost of the Shire cataracts. (This was one of the notorious barriers to Livingstone's exploration; he camped in this very spot in 1858 – for more detailssee History in the Facts about Malawi section earlier in this chapter.) The camp has seen better days but the chalets with bathrooms from US$7 per person are fair value, and camping costs US$3. The service is relaxed: there's a bar and a kitchen for self-catering, or you can buy meals (US$1.50 to US$3) if you order long in advance. Motorboat hire for fishing or birding costs US$1.50 per hour.

Getting There & Away Majete Safari Camp is 15km north of Chikwawa, on the road to Majete Wildlife Reserve. By bus, the nearest you can get is Chikwawa; there are several per day to/from Blantyre. From Chikwawa, matolas run to Kapichira village, which is on the eastern bank of the Mkurumadzi River (this place has recently grown to house staff from the dam and power station).

Lengwe National Park

Lengwe is Malawi's southernmost park. Much of the surrounding area has been turned into sugarcane plantations, but the natural vegetation – mixed woodlands and grassy *dambos* (wetlands) – is protected here. Mammals include nyala (at the northern limit of its distribution in Africa), bushbuck, impala, duiker and kudu, but sightings are harder than in some other parks because of dense vegetation, and because numbers have been reduced by poaching. You're better off admiring the large and varied bird population.

Standard entry fees must be paid at the gate (see National Parks & Wildlife Reserves in the Facts about Malawi section earlier in this chapter). There's a network of vehicle tracks for driving (some are impassable), but it's more rewarding to walk in the park or spend some time at the hides overlooking water holes; there's one within walking distance of the Visitors Camp.

Places to Stay The only place to stay inside the park is the ***Visitors Camp***, in a beautiful setting under big shady trees. Camping costs US$1 per person, and double chalets cost around US$7 (for one or two people). Shared bathrooms are basic and the kitchen for self-catering is virtually unusable. Some chalets have their own kitchen and bathroom and are better. You must bring all your own food.

If you've got a car and seek more comfortable accommodation, you can stay at ***Sucoma Sports Club*** (☎ *428200 ext 287*) 8km east of Nchalo, where comfortable chalets overlooking the river cost US$5.50 per person. This club is for senior staff at the sugar estate; meals and drinks are also available.

The Majete Chapel

An interesting feature of Majete Safari Camp is the small chapel, built by the owners in 'Afro-Saxon' style and dedicated to 'the wilderness', rather than to a saint. It deliberately has no door, so people (and birds, bats and frogs) can come and go as they like, and there's a large open window looking out across the river. When Livingstone camped just below Matitu Falls in 1858 he wrote that he wished to 'hear a church bell ring out across the Shire River'. He was probably speaking metaphorically – he wanted to bring Christianity to the whole area – but the chapel at Majete reminds us of his words.

Getting There & Away By car, take the main road from Blantyre, south towards Nsanje. By public transport, take a bus from Blantyre to Nchalo or Nsanje. About 20km from the Shire Bridge a signpost indicates Lengwe National Park to the right. The park entrance is another 10km to the west through sugarcane plantations. If you're without wheels you may be able to hitch this last bit on a tractor.

To reach Sucoma Sports Club, enter the sugar estate at the main gates in Nchalo, then follow the signs to the 'Sports Club' (not the Shire Club).

Mwabvi Game Reserve

In the southernmost tip of Malawi, Mwabvi is the country's smallest (under 350 sq km) and least-visited game reserve, with a genuine wilderness atmosphere. It consists of low hills covered by mixed woodland, with numerous streams in rocky gorges and spectacular views over the Shire and Zambezi Rivers. Mwabvi was virtually abandoned in the 1980s and early 1990s; rhino and lion were once recorded here, but apart from a few buffalo and nyala it's unlikely that any large wildlife remains today.

At the time of writing, access was posible only with a car or great determination. The reserve office is reached from the main road between Chikwawa and Nsanje, just east of the village of Sorgin, and about

10km west of Bangula. The Wildlife Society of Malawi is currently involved in projects to protect the reserve that encourage local people to benefit from its resources. These may also improve access for visitors, so it would be worth inquiring about the latest situation at the Wildlife Society giftshop in Limbe (see Bookshops in the Blantyre & Limbe section earlier in this chapter).

The Elephant Marsh

The Elephant Marsh is a large area of seasonally flooded plain on the Shire River about 30km downstream from Chikwawa, just south of the vast Sucoma sugar estates. Despite the name there are no elephants here any more, although vast herds inhabited the area less than 100 years ago. Some hippo and crocodile occur in quiet areas, but the main draw is the spectacular selection of birds – predominantly water species. This is one of the best **birdwatching** areas in Malawi, but it's well worth considering a visit here if you simply want to sample this peaceful and very unusual landscape.

As mornings and evenings are the best times to see birds (it's also not so hot), travellers without wheels may find it convenient to stay overnight in the village of Makhanga, about 10km north-east of Bangula. The ***Makhanga Leisure Centre*** has cheap rooms, and the ***New Makhanga Restaurant*** offers cheap food. If you have a car, you could stay at Sucoma Sports Club (see Lengwe National Park earlier in this section).

Getting There & Away The only way to see the marsh properly is by boat. The usual way of doing this is to hire a local boat from the Fisheries Depot at a place called Mchacha James on the east side of the marsh, north of Bangula, about 5km from Makhanga.

Reaching Makhanga is less straightforward than it used to be since the road and railway between Makhanga and Bangula got completely washed away. By car, your only option is to turn left (east) at Thabwa (the bottom of the escarpment), about 30km from Blantyre, and go along the northern bank of the river. Matolas run along this road too, so you can get off the bus running between Blantyre and Nchalo or Nsanje here and get a matola to Makhanga. Alternatively, by public transport you can get off this bus at Bangula, then walk 3km to the point where the road is washed away, get a canoe across, and then take a matola through Chiromo to Makhanga. A final option to consider might be the train from Limbe to Makhanga (see Train in the main Getting Around section earlier in this chapter).

Once in Makhanga, aim northward on the road towards the village of Muona. After 2.5km a dirt track leads west for 4.5km through villages and small fields to a small village called Mchacha James, where the Department of Fisheries has a jetty and a couple of boats. The route is not signposted, so you'll have to get directions – it may be worth arranging a local guide in Makhanga. If you don't have a car you can walk, take a bicycle taxi, rent a bike or charter a matola. Another option is to visit the Department of Fisheries office in Makhanga, on the Muona road, about 1km west of the train tracks – the staff here have motorcycles and may be able to help you with a lift to the jetty.

Once at Mchacha James, local boat owners may offer to take you in dugout canoes, but there's also a couple of more stable rowing boats for hire, owned by two brothers called Willis and Coaster Saidi. These friendly guys speak good English and can tell you a lot about the birds and human inhabitants of the marsh. Their rates are extremely fair at around US$10 for two people for a morning or afternoon trip.

BIRDS OF SOUTHERN AFRICA

Birds rate highly among the many attractions of Southern Africa. For sheer abundance and variety, few parts of the world offer as much for the birdwatcher, whether expert or beginner. Southern Africa is host to nearly 10% of the world's bird species – over 900 species have been recorded in the region. More than 130 are endemic to Southern Africa or are near-endemic, also being found only in adjoining territories to the north.

With the exception of nocturnal, cryptic (camouflaged) or rare species, birds can be easily seen – not just in national parks and game reserves, but at popular tourist destinations and even in the middle of large cities.

Birdwatching is a popular pastime for residents and visitors alike; birds and birdlore are not only intrinsic to ancient African customs, but have been assimilated into the lives of white settlers, and there is an English and an Afrikaans name for nearly every type. Visitors will find ample books and other publications on birds (see the boxed text 'Books on Birds' under Books in the Regional Facts for the Visitor chapter), and many hotels and lodges have a resident birder.

Bird Habitats

The astonishing variety of the region's birdlife can be attributed to the number of habitats. The climate ranges from cool temperate with winter rainfall in the south-west, to a hot tropical zone with summer rains in the north-east. The geographical features in the region are responsible for a variety of habitats that are unequalled anywhere else on the African continent.

These habitats are well defined and can be separated into eight main categories: forest; savanna-woodland; fynbos; grassland-semidesert; Karoo (South Africa's desert); the Namib Desert; freshwater areas (rivers, marshes, lakes, pans, and their adjoining shores); and seashore areas (including areas of brackish water where fresh water meets salt water in lagoons and estuaries). For more information on these habitats, see Vegetation under Flora & Fauna in the Facts about the Region chapter.

Many species of birds are wide-ranging, but the vast majority have feeding, breeding or other biological requirements that restrict them to a habitat or group of habitats. Therefore, to see a wide variety of birds you should try to take in as many different habitats as possible.

Where to See Birds in Southern Africa

All the national parks and game reserves are home to a great range of birdlife. Those particularly known for their rich birdlife include Mana Pools National Park, Victoria Falls, Hwange and Gonarezhou National Parks in Zimbabwe; Etosha National Park in Namibia; and virtually any part of the Okavango Delta in Botswana.

Inset: Natal francolin, Hluhluwe-Umfolozi Park, South Africa (Photo by Mitch Reardon)

In South Africa, birding is especially fruitful at Kruger and Pilanesberg National Parks in the north-east; Ndumo and Mkuzi Game Reserves, Lake St Lucia and Oribi Gorge in KwaZulu-Natal; and Karoo, West Coast and Bontebok National Parks in Western Cape.

In Malawi, the areas around Lake Malawi are rewarding, as are the various woodlands of Liwonde, Kasungu and Lengwe National Parks. Although not a reserve, the Elephant Marsh in Southern Malawi also has particularly rich birdlife.

In Zambia, top-class birding areas include the plains of Barotseland and the swamps of Lake Bangweulu, as well as Kafue, South Luangwa and Lochinvar National Parks.

Mozambique has over half of all bird species identified in Southern Africa; on Inhaca Island alone, about 300 bird species have been recorded. The Chimanimani Mountains, Mt Gorongosa, Mt Namúli and Bazaruto Archipelago are of particular note for birdwatching.

For tips on photographing birds, see the boxed text 'Photography Hints' under Photography & Video in the Regional Facts for the Visitor chapter.

The Birds

Following is a group-by-group description of some of the birds you'll see in Southern Africa. This is not a comprehensive list; the focus is on common, unusual and spectacular species. For more detailed descriptions, refer to one of the field guides mentioned under Books in the Regional Facts for the Visitor chapter.

Bee-Eaters, Rollers & Hoopoes 'What's that beautiful purple bird we see everywhere?' is a question travellers commonly ask. It's usually the lilac-breasted roller, a colourful relative of the kingfisher, and just one of five species that can be seen in the region. The various species of bee-eaters are equally, if not more, colourful; they are commonly seen perched on fences and branches – sometimes in mixed flocks – from where they pursue flying insects, particularly, as their name suggests, bees and wasps. The most stunning of all is the carmine bee-eater. Mention should also be made of the bizarre hoopoe, a salmon pink migrant from Europe and Asia that sports a dashing black-and-white crest.

Birds of Prey The hawks, eagles, vultures, falcons and the unique secretary bird fall under this broad heading and together number nearly 70 species in the region. Their presence is almost ubiquitous and you'll soon notice a few different species, from soaring flocks of scavenging vultures to the stately bateleur perched atop a *kopje* (hill), from where it surveys the surrounding plain for prey. Many have specialised prey or habitat requirements: the osprey and the striking fish eagle of large waterways feed almost exclusively on fish; and the pygmy falcon is so small it nests in the colonies of sociable weavers. In the wet season thousands of kestrels roost in the suburbs of Harare (Zimbabwe).

Bustards, Francolins & Korhaans These stately, long-legged birds of the grasslands are among the heaviest of flying birds. Some species are quite large, but all are well camouflaged. Some members of this group have bizarre courtship displays: the red-crested korhaan flies vertically to a height of 30m then tumbles to the ground as if shot; and the black-bellied korhaan glides back to earth while displaying its boldly marked wings in a dramatic 'V' position.

Cranes These graceful, long-legged birds superficially resemble storks and herons, but are typically grassland-dwelling birds. The crowned crane is eccentrically adorned with a colourful crest. The blue or Stanley crane is South Africa's national bird and a third species, the wattled crane, also may be seen in the region.

Finches, Weavers & Whydahs This large group includes many small but colourful species, readily seen in flocks at camping grounds, along roads and wherever there is long grass. All are seed eaters and while some, such as the various finches, are not spectacular, others develop showy courtship plumage and tail plumes of extraordinary size. The finches come typically in shades of brown and grey; whydahs are similar while not breeding, but males moult into black plumage with red or yellow highlights when courting. Whydahs are predominantly black with a lighter breast coloration and develop striking tail plumes during courtship. The three species of bishop weavers moult from drab coloration to brilliant reds and yellows – during courtship, a field can have a black and red dot every few metres as males perch on top of stems trying to attract a mate.

Honeyguide The honeyguide displays one of the most remarkable behaviours of any bird. It seeks out mammals such as the honey badger or even humans, then 'guides' them to a beehive. Once it has attracted the attention of a 'helper', the honeyguide flies a short way ahead then waits to see if it is being followed. In this way it leads its helper to the hive and while the obliging creature, which could also be a genet, mongoose or baboon, breaks open and robs the hive, the honeyguide feeds on wax and bees' larvae and eggs.

Hornbills Hornbills are medium-sized birds found in forests and woodland that all sport massive, down-curved bills. The yellow-billed and red-billed hornbills are common and readily seen by visitors; other species are more restricted in their range. The extraordinary ground hornbill moves about in groups along the ground and stands nearly a metre high.

Kingfishers Colourful and active, the 10 species found in Southern Africa can be divided into two groups: those that typically dive into water after fish and tadpoles (and as a consequence are found along waterways); and those that usually live away from water for much of their lives, preying on lizards and large insects. Of the former, the giant kingfisher reaches 46cm in height and the jewel-like malachite and pygmy kingfishers a mere 14cm. The less brightly coloured 'forest' kingfishers are inhabitants of woodland and forest.

Larks & Pipits Larks and pipits may not be the most spectacular group of birds, but in Southern Africa they are diverse and biologically significant to the grasslands they inhabit. Many are endemic to the region, and for the keen birdwatcher, their identification can pose some real challenges.

Long-Legged Wading Birds Virtually any waterway will have its complement of herons, egrets, storks, spoonbills and ibis. All species have long legs and necks, and bills adapted to specific feeding strategies: herons and egrets have dagger-like bills for spearing fish and frogs; storks have large powerful beaks to snap up small animals and fish; spoonbills have peculiar, flattened bills, which they swish from side to side to gather small water creatures; and ibis have long, downcurved bills to probe in soft earth or seize insects. Other rarities of the region are the endangered bald ibis of South Africa and the slaty egret, restricted to Botswana's Okavango Delta. Abdim's stork is particularly noteworthy because large migrating flocks are known to suddenly arrive in an area. An unusual member of this group is the hamerkop, a small heron-like bird that makes an enormous nest of twigs and grass.

Louries In Southern Africa, three beautifully coloured species of these medium-sized birds inhabit forests. They can be difficult to see because they hide in the canopy; often you will only catch a tantalising view as one flies across a clearing, showing its broad, rich-crimson wing patches. A fourth species, the grey lourie, is often seen in noisy parties in thornveld; its raucous call has earned it the alternative name 'Go-away Bird'.

Migratory Waders Every year millions of shorebirds arrive in Southern Africa after completing a journey of many thousands of kilometres from their breeding grounds in the northern hemisphere. A number of species are also resident: plovers, dikkops and their close relatives the gulls and terns. With few exceptions these birds are found near fresh and saline waterways, feeding along the shores on small creatures or probing the intertidal mud for worms. Migrants include the long-distance champions: the sandpipers and plovers. Residents include the boldly marked blacksmith plover, lapwings and the odd dikkops (a lanky, cryptic, nocturnal species with weird wailing cries).

Mousebirds This uniquely African group comprises a small group of common and rather plain birds. They are so named because they forage by crawling up tree trunks and along branches, dragging their long tails behind them and appearing, as their name suggests, like tree-dwelling rodents.

Nightjars Another nocturnal group, these small birds are not related to owls. Nightjars are common and you may be oblivious to their presence until one flies up near your feet. The identification of several species is difficult and often relies on call, but when flushed out during the day, nightjars typically fly to a nearby horizontal branch and perch there, allowing you a closer look. The incredible pennant-winged nightjar is probably the most spectacular example.

Ostrich The largest and heaviest of all birds, the ostrich is a wide-ranging inhabitant of grassland and savanna and the only member of this flightless group found on the continent.

Owls Many African tribes have deep superstitions about these nocturnal birds of prey. Owls have soft feathers (which make their flight inaudible to prey), exceptional hearing and can turn their heads in a 180° arc to locate their prey (which ranges from insects to small mammals). Southern Africa has some splendid examples, such as the Cape eagle owl and Pel's fishing owl, which hunts along rivers and feeds exclusively on fish.

Shrikes (Bushshrikes, Vangas & Boubous) Although most are rather plain and known for their predatory habits, among this group are some spectacular species, with names such as gorgeous bushshrike and crimson-breasted shrike.

Starlings At any of the game parks you'll sooner or later see fast-flying flocks of iridescent starlings. Intelligent, opportunistic and adaptable, starlings in Africa have reached the pinnacle of their evolution. Colourful, noisy and gregarious, there are many species, including the glossy and blue-eared starlings; the two species of oxpecker (often seen clinging to game, from which they prise parasitic ticks and insects); the bizarre wattled starling; and the red-winged starlings, which hang around the peak of Cape Town's Table Mountain.

Sunbirds & Sugarbirds Sunbirds are small, delicate nectar-feeders with sharp down-curved bills. The males of most species are brilliantly iridescent while the females are relatively drab. Sunbirds are commonly seen feeding on the flowers of proteas. The two species of sugarbirds are endemic to South Africa's Western Cape and while they are less colourful than their relatives the sunbirds, the males sport long, showy tail feathers.

Woodpeckers & Barbets There are a few species of woodpeckers in the region, but perhaps more conspicuous are their colourful, tropical cousins, the barbets. Rather than drilling into bark after grubs like woodpeckers, barbets have strong, broad bills adapted to eating fruit and a variety of insect prey.

ANDREW VAN SMEERDIJK

Carmine bee-eater

DAVID WALL

African fish eagle

ANDREW VAN SMEERDIJK

Lilac-breasted roller

DANIEL BIRKS

Yellow hornbill

RICHARD I'ANSON

Glossy starling

ANDREW VAN SMEERDIJK

Crowned crane

RICHARD I'ANSON

Ground hornbill

MITCH REARDON

Goliath heron

RICHARD I'ANSON

Great white egret in breeding plumage

ANDREW VAN SMEERDIJK

Hadeda ibis

RICHARD I'ANSON

Blacksmith plover

RICHARD I'ANSON

Ostrich

MITCH REARDON

Lesser striped kingfisher

Mozambique

Warning

Severe flooding in early 2000 inundated large areas of Maputo, Gaza and Inhambane; parts of southern Sofala and Manica provinces were also affected. In the worst hit areas, roads were cut, bridges washed away, crops damaged, homes and buildings destroyed. Many people lost their lives and countless others were left stranded. As this book went to print, the extent of the damage was not yet clear. While it is likely that main roads will soon be passable again, travellers should expect that secondary roads and bridges in many areas may not yet have been repaired, and that road conditions may differ from those described here. Many coastal resorts also suffered heavy damage, and some hotels and lodges listed in this chapter may not have re-opened. Get an update on conditions before setting your plans.

Although barely a decade has passed since peace accords were signed ending Mozambique's 17-year civil war, devastation and dark times have moved into the past. The atmosphere is upbeat, and reconstruction – particularly in the southern and central portions of the country – has proceeded at a remarkable pace. Even tourism – unthinkable in the early 1990s – has gotten off to an ambitious start, although it's much less developed than elsewhere in the region. Among Mozambique's attractions are beautiful beaches, vibrant and fascinating cultures, and artistic and musical traditions which are among the best on the continent.

Because of the country's vast size and a still-developing transport infrastructure, travel in Mozambique can be difficult and exhausting, although visitors in the south – where roads are decent and good lodging options abound – should have few difficulties. In the north, travel is very much an adventure, requiring plenty of time and a willingness to rough it. Yet no matter what part of the country you visit, the rewards make it well worth the time and effort.

MOZAMBIQUE AT A GLANCE

Area: 801,590 sq km

Population: 16 million

Capital: Maputo

Head of State: President Joaquim Chissano

Official Language: Portuguese

Currency: metical (Mtc)

Exchange Rate: US$1 = Mtc15,286

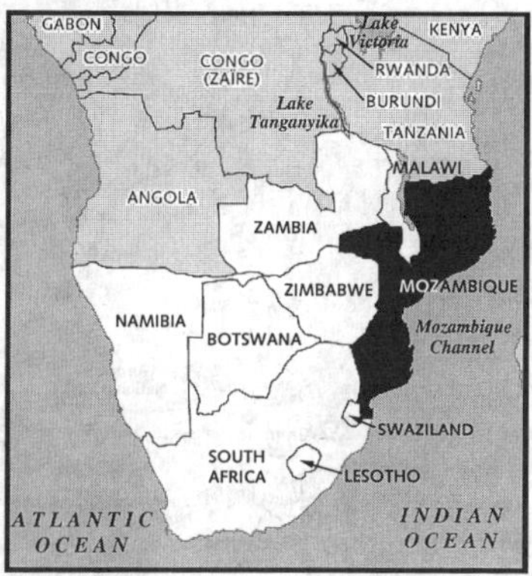

Highlights

- Maputo – relax by day at a sidewalk cafe; in the evenings, experience the energetic pace of the capital's nightlife
- Inhambane Province – visit historical Inhambane city and relax on Barra, Tofo or one of the province's other idyllic beaches
- Bazaruto Archipelago – snorkel in azure waters with colourful tropical fish, and explore pristine coral reefs
- Central and Western Hills – hike around Gurúè or in the mountains bordering Zimbabwe
- Mozambique Island – take a walk at sunset through an architectural and historical treasure trove

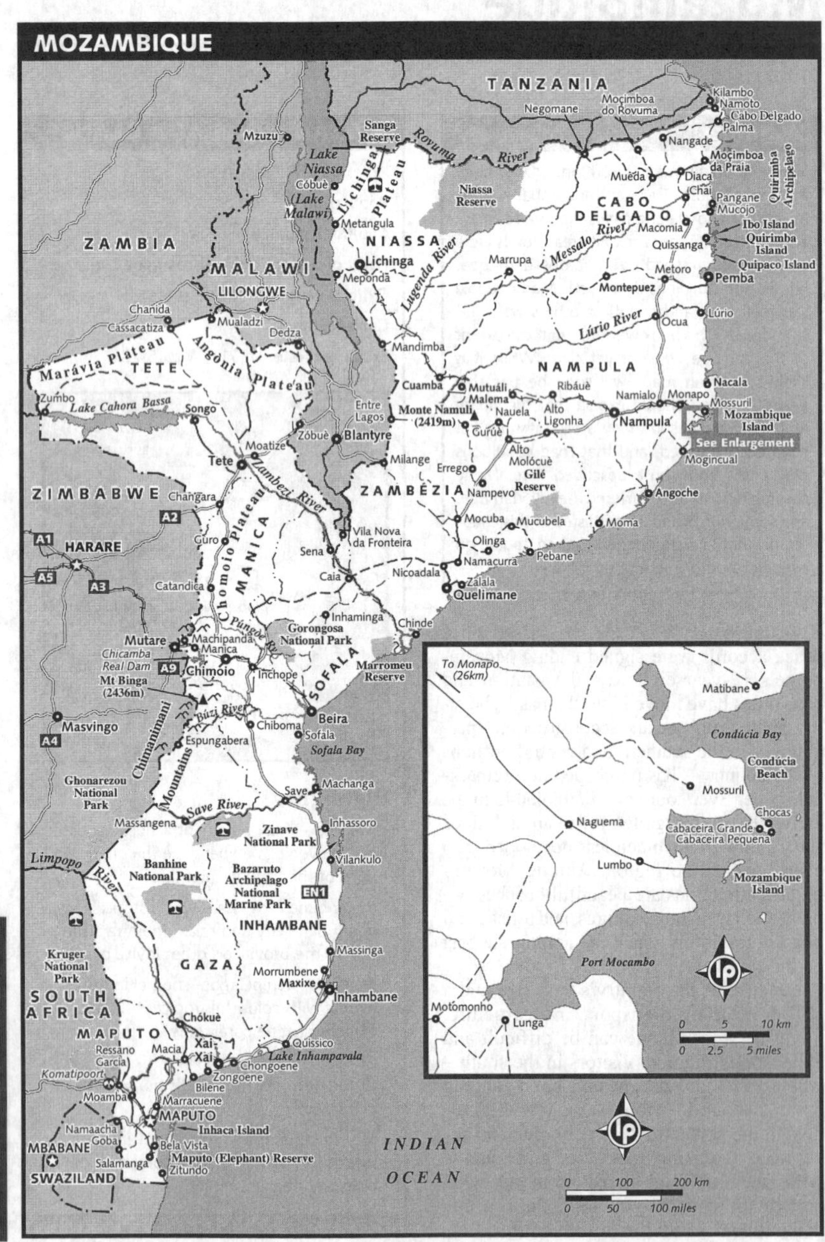
MOZAMBIQUE
TANZANIA
Negomane
Moçimboa do Rovuma
Kilambo
Namoto
Cabo Delgado
Palma
Nangade
Mocimboa da Praia
Quirimba Archipelago
Mueda
Diaca
Chai
Pangane
Mucojo
Ibo Island
Quirimba Island
Quipaco Island
CABO DELGADO
Messalo River
Macomia
Quissanga
Metoro
Pemba
Montepuez
Marrupa
Niassa Reserve
Sanga Reserve
Rovuma River
Mzuzu
Lake Niassa
(Lake Malawi)
Cóbuè
Lichinga Plateau
Metangula
NIASSA
Lichinga
Meponda
Lugenda River
ZAMBIA
MALAWI
LILONGWE
Chanida
Cassacatiza
Mualadzi
Dedza
Marávia Plateau
TETE
Angónia Plateau
Mandimba
Lúrio River
Ocua
Lúrio
NAMPULA
Cuamba
Mutuáli
Malema
Ribáuè
Nacala
Namialo
Monapo
Mossuril
Mozambique Island
See Enlargement
Zumbo
Lake Cahora Bassa
Songo
Entre Lagos
Monte Namuli (2419m)
Nauela
Alto Ligonha
Nampula
Gurúè
Zóbuè
Blantyre
Alto Molócuè
Mogincual
Tete
Moatize
Milange
Errego
Gilé Reserve
Zambezi River
ZIMBABWE
Changara
ZAMBÉZIA
Nampevo
Angoche
A2
MANICA
Mocuba
Mucubela
Moma
A1
HARARE
Guro
Chomoio Plateau
Vila Nova da Fronteira
Sena
Olinga
Pebane
Namacurra
A5
A3
Catandica
Caia
Nicoadala
Zalala
Quelimane
Inhaminga
Púngoè River
Gorongosa National Park
Chinde
Mutare
Machipanda
Manica
Chicamba Real Dam
A9
Chimoio
Inchope
Marromeu Reserve
Mt Binga (2436m)
SOFALA
Búzi River
Beira
Masvingo
Chiboma
Sofala
A4
Chimanimani Mountains
Espungabera
Sofala Bay
Ghonarezou National Park
Save
Machanga
Save River
Massangena
Inhassoro
Zinave National Park
Vilankulo
Limpopo River
Banhine National Park
Bazaruto Archipelago National Marine Park
EN1
INHAMBANE
Kruger National Park
Massinga
GAZA
Morrumbene
Maxixe
Inhambane
SOUTH AFRICA
Chókuè
MAPUTO
Ressano Garcia
Macia
Xai-Xai
Quissico
Lake Inhampavala
Komatipoort
Chongoene
Zongoene
Bilene
Moamba
Marracuene
MAPUTO
Namaacha
Goba
Inhaca Island
MBABANE
Bela Vista
Salamanga
Maputo (Elephant) Reserve
Zitundo
SWAZILAND
INDIAN OCEAN
0 100 200 km
0 50 100 miles
To Monapo (26km)
Matibane
Condúcia Bay
Condúcia Beach
Mossuril
Chocas
Naguema
Cabaceira Grande
Cabaceira Pequena
Lumbo
Mozambique Island
Port Mocambo
Motomonho
Lunga
0 5 10 km
0 2.5 5 miles

MOZAMBIQUE

Facts about Mozambique

HISTORY

The early history of Mozambique (*Moçambique* in Portuguese), along with the history of Southern Africa, is covered in the Facts about the Region chapter.

The Arrival of the Portuguese

European involvement in the area which is now Mozambique began in 1498 when Portuguese explorer Vasco da Gama landed at Mozambique Island en route to India. Portuguese interest in the area stemmed in part from the need for supply points on the sea route between Europe and the East, and in part from the desire to control the lucrative gold trade with the interior. Within a decade, the Portuguese had established a permanent settlement on the island. Over the next 200 years, they established numerous other trading enclaves and forts along the coast, and several settlements in the interior along the Zambezi River Valley. By mid-16th century, ivory had replaced gold as the main trading commodity. By late 18th century, slaves had been added to the list, with hundreds of thousands (some estimates say as high as one million) Africans sold into slavery through Mozambique's coastal ports. Despite this, there was little cohesion to the Portuguese ventures, and their influence in Mozambique remained weak and fragmented.

Beginning in the 17th century, the Portuguese attempted to strengthen their control in the region by establishing *prazos* (privately owned agricultural estates) on land granted by the Portuguese crown or obtained by conquest from African chiefs. This, however, served only to consolidate power in the hands of individual *prazeiros*, or holders of the land grants.

The Colonial Period

With the onset of the 'Scramble for Africa' in the 1880s, Portugal faced growing competition from the other colonial powers and was forced to strengthen its claims on its territories. In 1891, after considerable dispute, a British-Portuguese treaty was signed which gave the country its present shape and formalised Portuguese control. However, even after this, the Portuguese were only able to directly administer the southern part of the country. In the north, large areas of land were carved out and leased as concessions to private firms which operated as independent fiefdoms and soon became notorious for forced labour abuses.

Early 20th century Mozambique was characterised by a large-scale labour migration to South Africa and Rhodesia. Economic ties with South Africa were strengthened, a rail link was built between Beira and Mutare (Rhodesia), and the Portuguese transferred their capital from Mozambique Island to Lourenço Marques (as Maputo was then known).

In the late 1920s António Salazar came to power in Portugal. He sealed off the colonies from non-Portuguese investment to ensure that Portugal would profit from them directly; terminated the leases of the various concession companies in the north; and consolidated Portuguese control over Mozambique. Over the next decades, the numbers of Portuguese in Mozambique steadily increased, as did repression of the indigenous population. There was not even a pretence of social investment in the African population, and of the few schools and hospitals that did exist, most were in the cities and reserved for Portuguese, other whites and *asimilados* (Africans who assimilated to European ways). Forced cultivation of cash crops led to a dramatic decrease in food production, and famines became frequent.

The Independence War

In June 1960, at Mueda in northern Mozambique, an official meeting was held by villagers protesting peacefully about taxes. Portuguese troops opened fire on the crowd, killing large numbers of demonstrators. Resentment at the 'massacre of Mueda' was one of the sparks kindling the independence struggle. Resistance to colonial rule coalesced in 1962 with the formation of Frelimo, the Mozambique Liberation Front.

Led by the charismatic Eduardo Mondlane (who was assassinated in 1969), and operating from bases in Tanzania, Frelimo's aim was the complete liberation of Mozambique. By 1966 it had liberated two northern provinces, but progress was slow and the war dragged on into the 1970s. The Portuguese attempted to eliminate rural support for Frelimo with a scorched earth campaign and by resettling people in fenced villages. However, struggles within its colonial empire and increasing international criticism sapped the government's resources. The final blow for Portugal came in 1974 with the overthrow of the Salazar regime. On 25 June 1975, the independent People's Republic of Mozambique was proclaimed with the wartime commander Samora Machel as president.

Independence

The Portuguese pulled out virtually overnight and left the country in a state of chaos with few skilled professionals and virtually no infrastructure. Frelimo, which found itself suddenly faced with the task of running the country, threw itself headlong into a policy of radical social change. Ties were established with the former USSR and East Germany, and private land ownership was replaced with state farms and peasant cooperatives. Meanwhile, schools, banks, and insurance companies were nationalised, and private practice in medicine and law was abolished in an attempt to disperse skilled labour. Education assumed a high priority and literacy programs were launched with the aim of teaching 100,000 people to read and write each year. Much assistance was received from foreign volunteers, notably from Sweden. Maoist-style 'barefoot doctors' provided basic health services, such as vaccinations, and taught about hygiene and sanitation.

However, Frelimo's socialist program proved unrealistic, and by 1983 the country was almost bankrupt. Money was valueless and shops were empty. While collective agriculture had worked in some areas, in many others it was a complete disaster. The crisis was compounded by a disastrous three-year drought and by South African and Rhodesian moves to destabilise Mozambique because the ANC and ZAPU (both fighting for majority rule) had bases there.

Onto this scene came the Mozambique National Resistance (Renamo), which had been established in the mid-1970s by Rhodesia as part of its destabilisation policy, with later backing from the South African military and certain sectors in the west.

The Civil War

Renamo, created solely by external forces rather than by internal political motives, had no ideology of its own beyond the wholesale destruction of social and communications infrastructure within Mozambique and destabilisation of the government. Many commentators have pointed out that the war which went on to ravage the country for the next 17 years was thus not a 'civil' war, but one between Mozambique's Frelimo government and Renamo's external backers.

Recruitment was sometimes voluntary, but frequently by force. Roads, bridges, railways, schools and clinics were destroyed. Villagers were rounded up and anyone with skills – teachers, medical workers etc – was shot. Atrocities were committed on a massive and horrific scale.

Ironically, part of the problem stemmed indirectly from the Frelimo re-education camps, established after independence, where inmates included any political opponents as well as common criminals, and numerous human rights abuses took place. Rather than establishing respect for state authority, the result was to provide a fertile recruitment ground for Renamo.

The drought and famine of 1983 crippled the country. Faced with this dire situation, and with the reality of a failed socialist experiment, Frelimo opened Mozambique to the west in return for western aid.

On 16 March 1984, South Africa and Mozambique signed the Nkomati Accord, under which South Africa undertook to withdraw its support of Renamo and Mozambique agreed to expel the ANC and open the country to South African investment. While Mozambique abided by the agreement, South Africa exploited the situation to the full and Renamo activity did not diminish.

Samora Machel died in a plane crash in 1986 under questionable circumstances, and his place was taken by the more moderate Joaquim Chissano. While the war between the Frelimo government and the Renamo rebels continued, by the late 1980s, political change was sweeping through the region. The collapse of the USSR altered the political balance, and the new president of South Africa, FW de Klerk, made it more difficult for right-wing factions to supply Renamo.

By the early 1990s, Frelimo had disavowed its Marxist ideology, announcing that Mozambique would switch to a market economy, state enterprises would be privatised, and multiparty elections were to be scheduled. After protracted negotiations in Rome during 1990, a ceasefire was arranged, followed by a formal peace agreement in October 1992 and a successful UN-monitored disarmament and demobilisation campaign.

Modern Times

In October 1994, Mozambique held its first democratic elections, in which Renamo won a surprising 38% of the vote against 44% for Frelimo, and majorities in five provinces. The victory was attributable in part to ethnic considerations and in part to Frelimo's inability to overcome widespread grassroots antipathy. In the country's second national elections, held in December 1999, Renamo made an even stronger showing, winning in six out of 11 provinces and taking 48% of the votes against 52% for Frelimo. However, unlike the first elections, which were lauded for their fairness and transparency, and which earned Mozambique widespread acclaim as an African model of democracy and reconciliation, the 1999 balloting was marred by apparent irregularities in tabulating some of the votes. In protest, Renamo leader Afonso Dhlakama boycotted the presidential inauguration and moved some of Renamo's offices from Maputo to his traditional stronghold in Beira. It remains to be seen how Dhlakama will press his case.

Yet, despite concerns by some, most observers feel that Renamo's relatively measured response thus far is evidence that the party's transition from guerrilla organisation to viable political party is progressing, and that Mozambique still deserves to be counted among the continent's success stories.

GEOGRAPHY

Mozambique has an area of just more than 800,000 sq km, and a coastline of approximately 2500km. Its coastal plain, 100 to 200km wide in the south, narrower in the north, rises to mountains and plateaus on the borders with Zimbabwe, Zambia and Malawi. The highest peak is Mt Binga (2436m) in the Chimanimani Range on the Zimbabwe border.

Two of Southern Africa's largest rivers – the Zambezi and the Limpopo – flow through the country. Other major rivers are the Save (also written Savé) and the Rovuma (which forms the border with Tanzania).

CLIMATE

There are many regional variations, but generally the dry season runs from April/May to October/November, during which daytime maximums are around 24°C to 27°C on the coast, cooler inland. In the rainy season from November to March, average temperatures range from 27°C to 31°C, with high humidity.

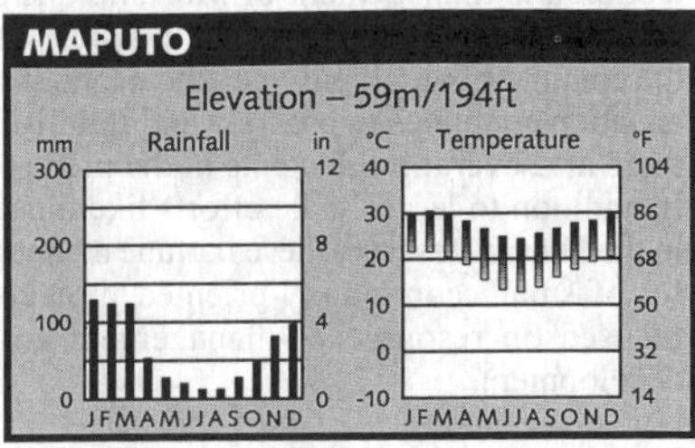

ECOLOGY & ENVIRONMENT

Mozambique is characterised by a diversity of ecosystems. Among the most notable are its extensive wetlands, including numerous coastal barrier lakes along the southern coast; rich offshore marine habitats; and montane habitats, including the Chimanimani Range to the west, and the Gorongosa massif in central Mozambique. While some of these areas are protected, and their flora and fauna relatively well documented, many are not. Even where official protection has been extended, there is a lack of financial and other resources to adequately enforce conservation measures and many of the country's natural resources are being ignored or squandered.

One example is seen in northern and central Mozambique, where rapid growth in the tropical hardwood timber trade is posing significant environmental issues as large trees are felled with little or no regulation. Although Mozambique has a department of Wildlife & Conservation, the inspectors who are supposed to patrol forest areas and control logging activity are poorly paid, with little incentive and inadequate resources to do their job. Reports indicate that even if companies get a logging permit they often operate outside the areas assigned to them, resulting in great damage to the natural environment. In addition to environmental damage, inappropriate logging practices mean that local communities receive little benefit from timber resources. There's often neither replanting, nor sustainable harvesting (ie, taking one tree in every 10 in a cyclical pattern). Farming on the cleared forest generally has only a limited life, as soils are unsuitable or too thin.

While lasting improvements in the protection and management of Mozambique's natural resources will only be possible as the country's overall political and economic situation continues to progress and stabilise, there are several bright spots in the picture. In addition to larger-scale efforts like those in the Niassa Reserve, these include a handful of small, community-oriented projects focused on resource co-management and development.

FLORA & FAUNA

Mozambique's diverse ecosystems support an abundance of flora, including numerous endemic species. Two notable areas are the Chimanimani Range, with at least 45 endemic plant species, and the Maputaland area south of Maputo.

The country has more than 200 mammal species, although most large mammal populations were decimated during the war. While recovery has started in some areas, numbers remain only a shadow of previous levels. In Gorongosa National Park, for example, 108 elephants were recorded in a 1994 aerial survey in comparison with an estimated 3000 prior to the war. The numbers are similar for buffalo (from 14,000 pre-war to zero in 1994), hippo and other large mammals. An exception to these otherwise bleak figures is the northern Niassa Reserve. Despite major losses over the past decades due to poaching, significant wildlife populations remain here, including more than 6000 elephant, 2000 buffalo and 2800 zebra.

SARAH JOLLY

Loggerhead turtles are among the many turtle species found along the Mozambican coast.

Notable marine species to be found include dolphins, whales and the endangered dugong. Loggerhead, leatherback, green, hawksbill and olive ridley turtles are found along the coast, although these populations have been exploited by the widespread use of turtles and their eggs as food; by sales of turtle shells as souvenirs; and, by medicinal use of turtle products.

About 580 bird species have been recorded in Mozambique, including several near endemics, and several rare or endangered species, such as the Cape vulture, the east coast akalat and the wattled crane.

National Parks

Mozambique has three national parks on the mainland – Gorongosa, Zinave and Banhine – and Bazaruto Archipelago National Marine Park offshore. Bazaruto is the only one which attracts significant numbers of visitors. Gorongosa recently re-opened and infrastructure is limited. Zinave and Banhine are closed. There are also five wildlife reserves – Niassa, Marromeu, Pomene, Maputo and Gilé – and numerous controlled hunting areas and forest reserves. Only the Niassa Reserve (see the Lichinga section later in this chapter) and the Maputo Elephant Reserve (see the Ponta d'Ouro section) are of interest to travellers.

In addition to these gazetted areas, the government has approved development of Transfrontier Conservation Areas (TFCAs) which emphasise multiple resource use and management by local communities. These include the Maputo TFCA, which would ultimately link the Maputo Elephant Reserve with South Africa's Tembe Elephant Park and Ndumo Game Reserve; the Chimanimani TFCA, contiguous with Chimanimani National Park in Zimbabwe; and the Gaza TFCA, encompassing Zinave and Banhine national parks as well as a controlled hunting area bordering on South Africa's Kruger National Park. Gaza TFCA would ultimately link with Kruger Park and Gonarezhou National Park in Zimbabwe.

GOVERNMENT & POLITICS

Representatives of political parties are elected to the National Assembly by universal suffrage using a system of proportional representation. The president is elected separately. Since the October 1994 elections, politics have been dominated by Frelimo and Renamo. There are about a dozen minor parties, some with a few seats in the National Assembly, others with none at all because of a 5% cut-off rule. Political allegiance tends to be on a regional basis, with Renamo enjoying considerable support in the centre while Frelimo is stronger in the north and south.

ECONOMY

During the past decade, Mozambique has pursued a very rigorous program of market-oriented reforms, including privatisation of more than 900 companies. As a result, it's one of sub-Saharan Africa's fastest growing economies. The inflation rate has been curbed, and is now one of the lowest of any African country, at less than 1% in 1999. Economic progress is particularly evident in the south, where proximity to South Africa and to the 'Maputo corridor' transport and development initiative (linking Maputo with Johannesburg) have pushed things along at a faster pace than in the more isolated north.

Agriculture accounts for the largest share of gross domestic product (GDP) and for about 80% of employment. Fishing is another important sector, constituting more than 40% of merchandise exports.

Despite the generally improved economic situation, statistics continue to place Mozambique as one of the world's poorest countries, with per capita GDP estimated at US$134 in 1998, and a legal minimum wage of about US$35 per month.

Mozambique's Provinces

Mozambique is divided administratively into 10 provinces, each with a governor and some autonomy. These provinces (and their capitals) are: Maputo (Maputo); Gaza (Xai-Xai); Inhambane (Inhambane); Sofala (Beira); Manica (Chimoio); Tete (Tete); Zambézia (Quelimane); Nampula (Nampula); Niassa (Lichinga); Cabo Delgado (Pemba). The city of Maputo is regarded as an 11th province.

POPULATION & PEOPLE

Mozambique's population is approximately 16 million, of which about 53% are concentrated in the north. There are 16 main tribes including: the Makua, the country's largest group, in the provinces of Cabo Delgado, Niassa, Nampula and parts of Zambézia; the Makonde, in Cabo Delgado; the Sena, in Sofala, Manica and Tete; and the Shangaan, who dominate the southern provinces of Gaza and Maputo.

Other groups include: Lomwe and Chuabo (in the north-centre areas); Yao and Nyanja (Niassa Province); Nyungwe (Tete Province);

Shona, (Manica Province); Tswa (Inhambane Province); and Ronga and Chopi (the south).

Native Portuguese comprise about 1% of the population. There are also small numbers of other European and Asian residents.

ARTS

Mozambique has a rich artistic tradition that continues to thrive after decades of colonial occupation and civil war.

Music

Traditional music is widely played in Mozambique. The Makonde in the north are noted for their *lupembe* (wind instruments). These are usually made from animal horn, less often with wood or gourds. In the south, Chope musicians play the *timbila*, a form of *marimba* or xylophone, and are famous for their timbila orchestras.

Modern music flourishes in the cities, and Maputo's live music scene is excellent. Marrabenta is perhaps the most typical Mozambican music, its light style inspired by traditional rural *majika* rhythms. One of its most well-known proponents was Orchestra Marrabenta, formed in the 1980s by members of another well-known band, Grupo RM with dancers from the National Company of Song and Dance. When Orchestra Marrabenta split in 1989, several members formed Ghorwane, who perform frequently in Maputo. Kapa Dêch is one of the best known of the new generation groups.

Other well-known musicians include: Chico António, who plays sophisticated, traditionally based melodies with congo drums, flute and bass, electric and acoustic guitars; Léman, a trumpeter and former member of Orchestra Marrabenta whose music combines traditional beats with contemporary inspiration; Roberto Chidsondso; José Mucavele; and Elvira Viegas.

Some good CDs to watch for include Léman's *Automy dzi Txintxile* (Changes of Life) and *Katchume* by Kapa Dêch.

Literature

During the colonial era, local literature – which was often repressed – generally focused on nationalist themes. Two of the most famous poets of this period were Rui de Noronha and Noémia de Sousa.

In the late 1940s José Craveirinha began to write poetry focusing on the social reality of the Mozambican people and calling for resistance and rebellion. This eventually led to his arrest. He is now recognised as one of Mozambique's most outstanding writers, and his work, including *Poem of the Future Citizen*, is recognised worldwide.

A contemporary of Craveirinha's was another nationalist called Luis Bernado Honwana, famous for short stories such as *We Killed Mangey Dog* and *Dina*.

As the armed struggle for independence gained strength, Frelimo freedom fighters began to write poems reflecting their life in the forest, their marches and the ambushes. One of the finest of these guerrilla poets was Marcelino dos Santos. Others included Sergio Vieira and Jorge Rebelo.

With Mozambique's independence in 1975, writers and poets felt able to produce literature free of interference. The new-found freedom was soon shattered by Frelimo's war against the Renamo rebels, but new writers emerged, including Mia Couto, whose works include *Voices Made Night* and *The Tale of the Two Who Returned from the Dead*. Other writers from this period include: Ungulani Ba Ka Khossa, Lina Magaia, Heliodoro Baptista and Eduardo White. A more recently published book is *A Shattering of Silence* by Farida Karodia, which describes a young girl's journey through Mozambique following the death of her family.

A significant development occurred in 1982 with the establishment of the Mozambique Writers' Association, which has been active both in publishing new material and in advancing the spread of indigenous literature throughout the country.

Other than the titles mentioned here, all of which have been translated into English, much Mozambican literature is only available in Portuguese. An exception to this is *Short Stories from Mozambique*, edited by Richard Bartlett, which is a good collection of translated short stories by a variety of Mozambican writers.

Visual Arts

Mozambique's most famous sculptor is the late Alberto Chissano, whose work has received wide international acclaim and inspired many younger artists.

In the north of the country, most woodwork is done by Makonde carvers. While some is traditional, many Makonde artists have developed contemporary styles. One of the leading members of the new generation of Makonde sculptors is Nkatunga, whose work portrays different aspects of rural life. Others include Miguel Valingue and Makamo.

Probably the most famous painter in the country is Malangatana, whose art is exhibited around the world. Other internationally famous artists include Bertina Lopes, whose work reflects her research into African images, colours, designs and themes, and Roberto Chichorro, known for his paintings which deal with childhood memories. Naguib, Victor Sousa and Idasse are among the best known artists in the newer generation. All of these painters and sculptors have exhibits in the National Art Museum in Maputo.

Mozambique's Murals

Murals – usually focused on revolutionary themes – are one of the most common forms of public art in Mozambique. The development of these occurred in three phases. The first, beginning immediately after independence, was marked by great spontaneity and is most evident in the many (now faded) political slogans adorning walls and buildings throughout the country. The second phase was characterised by colourful and more complex artwork, generally without text. In the third phase, murals (often of massive proportions) were commissioned in prominent places to commemorate the revolution. The 95m-long mural opposite Praça dos Heróis Moçambicanos in Maputo (on Avenida Acordos de Lusaka on the way to the airport) is an example of this last phase. Another notable mural in Maputo is that by Malangatana in the garden of the Natural History Museum.

LANGUAGE

Portuguese, the official language, is widely spoken in larger towns, less so in rural areas. African languages spoken in the country all belong to the Bantu language family and can be divided into three groups: Makua-Lomwe languages, spoken by more than one-third of the population, primarily in the north; Sena-Nyanja languages (of which Chichewa is a dialect) in the centre and near Lake Niassa (Lake Malawi); and Tsonga languages in the south. Outside southern resort areas and areas bordering Zimbabwe and Malawi, English is not widely spoken. Near the Tanzanian border, Swahili is often more useful than Portuguese.

See the Language chapter at the back of this book for a guide to Portuguese pronunciation and some useful words and phrases.

Facts for the Visitor

SUGGESTED ITINERARIES

If you want amenities, relaxation and the company of other tourists, or if your time is limited, stay in the south. If you don't mind roughing it, have plenty of time and want to delve into Mozambican history and culture away from the developed tourist industry, head north.

To combine itineraries in the south and north of the country, you'll need at least a month, ideally longer, unless you fly everywhere. The following suggestions are based on land travel. If you intend to fly, remember that flights frequently don't coordinate well and are often full, so you'll need to build extra days into your itinerary to account for delays.

Two Weeks

In southern Mozambique: after a few days in Maputo, head north to historical Inhambane town. Spend several days visiting Inhambane and enjoying Tofo, Barra or other nearby beaches. Wind up with a few days snorkelling around the Bazaruto Archipelago before flying back from Vilankulo to Maputo.

For travellers entering Mozambique from Zimbabwe via Machipanda: two weeks would be ideal to make your way to Beira (with a stop in Manica for some walking in the Penha Longa Mountains), before heading down the coast to Maputo, visiting the Bazaruto Archipelago and other beaches.

Two weeks in northern Mozambique could easily be spent entirely on the coast between Mozambique Island and the Quirimba Archipelago: after a day or two in Nampula head to Mozambique Island. From there, go by road to Pemba, from where you could visit an island or two in the southern Quirimbas before flying to Maputo or continuing north by road or air to Tanzania.

One Month

After a few days in Maputo, head north with stops at beaches along the way. Relax for several days at Vilankulo or Bazaruto before continuing to Beira. From Beira, continue west to Zimbabwe, stopping en route for some hiking around Manica. Alternatively (though this might run over one month), from Beira, travel via Tete and Malawi to Cuamba and then to Nampula and Mozambique Island, returning by plane from Nampula to Maputo.

Adventurous travellers coming in from Malawi via Cóbuè can head south to Metangula, then to Lichinga. Continue via Cuamba to Gurúè for some good hill walking. From Gurúè, head to Nampula and Mozambique Island. Return to Nampula and fly to Maputo or (time permitting) continue on to Pemba.

PLANNING

When to Go

The best time to visit is during the cooler, dry season from June to November. During the rainy season, many roads are impassable or difficult to negotiate.

Maps

The best is the Ravenstein (1:2,000,000), readily available outside Mozambique. Essentially the same map published by Cartographia is sometimes for sale in Maputo.

TOURIST OFFICES

The ENT (National Tourist Organisation) has an office in Maputo (see that section for details). In South Africa, ENT is represented by Mozambique National Tourist Co (☎ 011-339 7275, fax 339 7295), Braamfontein (PO Box 31991), Johannesburg 2017. The South African office can arrange visas, car hire, flights etc and advise on bus travel, accommodation and diving/fishing outfits in Mozambique.

VISAS & DOCUMENTS

Visas

Visas are required by all visitors and must be arranged in advance. Fees vary according to where you buy your visa. Outside Africa, it costs about US$20 for a one-month single-entry tourist visa, and about US$40 for a three-month multiple-entry visa. Within Southern Africa, one-month single-entry visas average about US$10 to US$15, although you'll often need to pay more than this for fast (ie, one-day) service. For more details, see under Visas & Documents in the individual country chapters.

The entry stamps given at some borders are not equivalent to a visa, and won't be accepted for travel beyond the immediate area where they are issued. Visas are not issued at airports.

Visas can be extended at immigration offices in all provincial capitals provided you haven't exceeded the three-month maximum stay. Processing takes one to three days.

Driving Licence & Permits

In addition to a passport, drivers in Mozambique need an international or South African driving licence, third-party insurance and vehicle registration papers. If bringing a vehicle into the country, you'll also need a temporary import permit (see Land in the Getting There & Away section later in this chapter for further information).

International Health Card

You need a health card with proof of yellow fever and cholera vaccinations, although you'll rarely be asked to show it.

EMBASSIES & CONSULATES

Mozambican Embassies & Consulates

Mozambique has diplomatic representation in the following African countries: Angola,

Ethiopia, Kenya, Malawi, South Africa, Swaziland, Tanzania, Zambia and Zimbabwe. Embassies for countries covered by this book are listed in the relevant country chapters. Mozambique embassies, high commissions and consulates elsewhere in the world include:

France
Embassy: (☎ 01 47 64 91 32) 82 Rue Laugier, Paris 75017

Germany
Consulate: (☎ 0228-224024/5) Adenauerallee 46A, 53113 Bonn

Portugal
Embassy: (☎ 021-797 1747, 797 1994) Avenida de Berna 7, 1000 Lisbon

Tanzania
Embassy: (☎ 051-33062) 25 Garden Ave, Dar es Salaam

UK
High Commission: (☎ 020-7383 3800) 21 Fitzroy Square, London W1P 5HJ

USA
Embassy: (☎ 202-293 7146) 1990 M St, NW, Suite 570, Washington, DC 20036

Embassies & High Commissions in Mozambique

The following countries have embassies or high commissions in Maputo. For a more complete listing, check *Time Out* (see Newspapers & Magazines later in this chapter) or the Maputo telephone directory.

Australia
High Commission: (☎ 01-422780) 1st floor, 33 Storey Bldg, corner Avenidas Zedequias Manganhela and Vladimir Lenin

Canada
High Commission: (☎ 01-492623) 1128 Avenida Julius Nyerere

France
Embassy: (☎ 01-491603) 2361 Avenida Julius Nyerere

Germany
Embassy: (☎ 01-492714) 506 Rua Damião de Gois

Malawi
High Commission: (☎ 01-492676) 75 Avenida Kenneth Kaunda

Portugal
Embassy: (☎ 01-490316) 720 Avenida Julius Nyerere

South Africa
High Commission: (☎ 01-490059) 41 Avenida Eduardo Mondlane

Swaziland
High Commission: (☎ 01-492451) Avenida Kwame Nkrumah

Tanzania
High Commission: (☎ 01-490110) 852 Avenida Mártires de Machava

UK
High Commission: (☎ 01-420111) 310 Avenida Vladimir Lenin

USA
Embassy: (☎ 01-492797) 193 Avenida Kenneth Kaunda

Zambia
High Commission: (☎ 01-492452) 1286 Avenida Kenneth Kaunda

Zimbabwe
High Commission: (☎ 01-490404) 1657 Avenida Mártires de Machava

Visas for Onward Travel

If you need visas for neighbouring countries, these are the conditions (all embassies and high commissions are in Maputo):

Malawi The high commission is open for applications from 8 am to noon. Visas cost US$15/40/55 for transit/single/multiple entry, require two photos, and are generally issued within 24 hours.

South Africa The high commission is open for applications from 8.30 am to noon. Visas cost R180 and are issued within 24 hours.

Swaziland The high commission is open for applications from 8 to 11 am. Visas cost R40, require one photo and are issued within 24 hours.

Tanzania The high commission is open for applications from 8 to 11 am. Visas cost from US$20 to US$50 depending on nationality, require two photos and are issued within 24 hours.

Zambia The high commission is open for applications from 8 am to noon. Visas cost US$25, require two photos and are generally issued within 24 hours.

Zimbabwe The high commission is open for applications from 8 to 11.30 am. Visas cost US$30/45/55 for single/double/multiple entry, require two photos and are generally issued within 24 hours.

MONEY

Currency

Mozambique's currency is the metical (plural meticais, pronounced *meticaish*), abbreviated Mtc. Note denominations include Mtc1000, 5000, 10,000, 20,000, 50,000 and 100,000. The most commonly used coins are Mtc1000 and 5000. A unit of Mtc1000 is called a *conto* – thus a price of Mtc5000 will usually be quoted as *'cinco contos'*. Because of the weakness of the metical and the absence of large denomination notes, you'll always be carrying around large bundles of cash. Especially upcountry, you'll need a lot of coins and small bills, as nobody ever has change.

Exchange Rates

Although the metical has stabilised, prices throughout this chapter are quoted in US dollars as they're likely to remain more constant. We've converted prices at the official bank rate; if you use exchange bureaus, you will generally get a better deal. Bank rates at the time of going to print were as follows:

country	unit		metical
Australia	A$1	=	Mtc9248
Canada	C$1	=	Mtc10,403
euro	€1	=	Mtc14,688
France	10FF	=	Mtc22,392
Germany	DM1	=	Mtc7510
Japan	¥100	=	Mtc14,291
New Zealand	NZ$1	=	Mtc7445
Portugal	Esc1	=	Mtc73
South Africa	R1	=	Mtc2369
UK	UK£1	=	Mtc24,132
USA	US$1	=	Mtc15,286

Exchanging Money

Cash US dollars are the best currency to carry, and are easily exchanged anywhere in the country. South African rand are also widely accepted in the south, and many places accept direct payment in rand (or dollars). Other major currencies can be changed in Maputo, but often not elsewhere.

Banks which change money include Banco Comercial de Moçambique (BCM), Banco Standard Totta and Banco Internacional de Moçambique (BIM), with branches in provincial capitals and some larger towns. Most banks do not charge commission for changing cash. In Maputo and occasionally upcountry there are private exchange bureaus which give a rate about 5% higher than the banks, with quick service and also without commission. Supermarkets and shops selling imported goods will often change cash dollars or rand into meticais at a rate about 5% higher than the bank, and can be helpful if you arrive after the banks are closed. Changing money on the street is not safe anywhere.

Travellers Cheques Travellers cheques can be changed with a minimum of hassle in Maputo and provincial capitals. You'll need to show the original purchase receipt. Most banks accept Thomas Cook and American Express (AmEx) cheques (Banco Standard Totta takes Thomas Cook only). BCM charges a flat US$15 fee for amounts up to US$1000, while Banco Standard Totta – probably the most expensive – charges US$30 for amounts up to US$300. BIM's head office in Maputo changes travellers cheques for a 2% commission, regardless of the amount, and their Nacala and Nampula branches charge US$5. It's worth inquiring at BIM's other upcountry branches to see whether these commission levels have been implemented countrywide.

Private exchange bureaus almost never change travellers cheques, with the notable exceptions in Maputo of Cotacambios and the exchange bureau at Hotel Polana (see the Maputo section). Travellers cheques are accepted as direct payment by only a few hotels around the country.

ATMs Maputo has ATMs, but most are useful only if you have a local bank account. Banco International de Moçambique announced it will open ATMs linked to the worldwide Cirrus network, but it isn't yet clear if these will function with foreign cards.

Credit Cards Credit cards are really only useful at top-end hotels in Maputo, at a few Maputo-based travel agencies, and at larger car rental agencies. The most accepted are

Visa and MasterCard, while AmEx is occasionally accepted. You can get cash advances with your Visa or MasterCard at several places in Maputo, including the head office of Banco Standard Totta (R160 fee, cash in meticais or rand), Banco de Fomento (R62 plus 3% of value, meticais only) and BIM (Visa only, 1.5% of value if you want your cash in dollars, no commission for meticais).

Costs

Mozambique is expensive compared to its neighbours. While locally produced goods are cheap, most tourist-related items are costly. Accommodation in particular is poor value for money. Budget travellers staying in basic lodging, and eating local food should plan on at least US$20 per day. Mid-range travel with some comforts will cost from US$35/40 per day. Where top-end standards are available, plan on at least US$100 per day – more including rental car or charter plane.

POST & COMMUNICATIONS

Post

International mail from Maputo takes about two weeks to Europe and costs about US$1 per letter. Domestic mail is more sporadic, with letters taking between two weeks and two months to reach their destination.

The main post offices in Maputo and provincial capitals have poste restante. Letters are held about one month, and cost US$0.15 to receive.

Telephone & Fax

Mozambique's telephone system is fairly efficient. For international calls, most towns have telecom offices open daily. For domestic calls, *cabines publicas* (public phonebooths) are found in most larger towns, generally near shops or hotels. In Maputo and larger towns there are also cardphones good for local and regional calls. Cards are sold at nearby shops in denominations of US$4 and US$8.

Domestic calls are charged at US$0.10 per impulse; most short calls will not use more than two or three impulses. International calls connect fairly quickly, although lines to neighbouring countries fail frequently. Calls to Europe, the USA and Australia cost US$6 for the first three minutes (minimum), plus US$2 for each additional minute. Regional calls cost about US$3 for the first three minutes. Rates are slightly cheaper on weekends and evenings.

Faxes can be sent and received from telecom offices in Maputo, Beira and a few larger towns. Rates are US$17 per page to send to Europe, Australia and the USA and US$0.50 per fax to receive.

Telephone Codes Telephone codes are listed under individual town entries in this chapter. Where a telephone code is not listed, you'll need to go through the operator. When calling Mozambique from abroad, dial the international access number (usually 09 or 00), then the international code 258, then omit the zero of the area code.

Email & Internet Access

There are public Internet services in Maputo, Beira and Pemba, with expansion to other provincial capitals likely in the near future. Rates are from US$5 per 30 minutes. Many businesses and organisations also have private Internet links.

INTERNET RESOURCES

Useful Web sites on Mozambique include:

Kanimambo In Portuguese, but with some pictures as well as information on other sites in English.
www.kanimambo.com

Mozambique Gateway A helpful site with information on Mozambique; also has some good links.
www.newafrica.com/gateways/mozambique.htm

Mozambique Home Page General information on Mozambique in Portuguese and English, with good links to other sites.
www.mozambique.mz

See also Internet Resources in the Regional Facts for the Visitor chapter for a more comprehensive listing.

BOOKS

Literature by Mozambican writers is covered under Arts in the Facts about Mozambique section.

Lonely Planet

Mozambique Lonely Planet's comprehensive guide, has in-depth coverage of Mozambique. ***Malawi, Mozambique & Zambia*** and ***Africa on a shoestring*** also have coverage of Mozambique.

Portuguese phrasebook A highly recommended language guide for travel around Mozambique.

Swahili phrasebook A useful supplement if you plan on spending an extended period in northern Cabo Delgado and Niassa Provinces.

Guidebooks

Maputo by David Martin. This book has good information about the history of Mozambique's capital (available in Maputo for about US$10).

Mozambique: Indian Ocean Treasure by Luis Palanque. An overview of the history and attractions of Mozambique's provinces. It's available in Maputo or through Pangolim (☎ 01-490674, fax 492493, e pangolim@zebra.uem.mz).

History & Politics

And Still They Dance by Stephanie Urdang. A study of women's roles in the wars and struggles for change in Mozambique.

Apartheid's Contras by William Minter. An inquiry into the roots of the civil wars in Angola and Mozambique and the role of South Africa in continuing the conflicts.

Assignments in Africa by Per Wästberg. Includes a section on Mozambique, where this Swedish journalist spent some time in the early years of independence, talking to poets and artists who had been given mundane jobs by the new government.

A Complicated War – The Harrowing of Mozambique by William Finnegan. Covers the same subject as William Minter's book (see *Apartheid's Contras* above).

A History of Mozambique by Malyn Newitt. An excellent book covering the country's history since about 1500.

Kalashnikovs and Zombie Cucumbers: Travels in Mozambique by Nick Middleton. Part travelogue, part historical overview, this entertaining book covers colonial times, the war, South African and superpower involvement, aid and development and more.

General

Who We Are: Voices from Mozambique by Lorraine Johnson. An excellent anthology of Mozambican poetry, proverbs and stories, and an ideal place to start for anyone seeking to get to know Mozambique and Mozambicans. It's available through Sensações in Maputo (see under Bookshops & Music Stores in the Maputo section).

Numerous books – mostly coffee-table books with text in English and Portuguese – dating from Mozambique's exhibition at Expo 92 in Spain are still available in Maputo, either at the Public Information Bureau (see Tourist Offices in the Maputo section) or in bookshops. They include: *Artistas de Moçambique*, an overview of the country's principal artists; *Mascaras*, a study of traditional masks; *Ilha de Moçambique*, about the former island capital; and a series of three books covering the south, centre and north of the country called *Olhar Moçambique*.

NEWSPAPERS & MAGAZINES

Mozambique's major national newspapers (in Portuguese) are *Notícias* and *Diário de Moçambique*.

Time Out, published by Austral, is a bilingual magazine with helpful general information on Mozambique as well as good overviews of attractions, hotels and restaurants in Maputo, Gaza, Inhambane, Sofala and Manica Provinces. It's widely available in Maputo for about US$5.

The monthly English edition of *MozambiqueFile*, put out by the official news agency, has good coverage of politics and current affairs.

Índico, LAM's bimonthly and bilingual inflight magazine, has articles on cultural and other aspects of Mozambique.

RADIO & TV

Radio Maputo has an English language service, broadcasting at 1 and 8 pm on 88 FM. The country has two TV channels: the state-run TVM and the commercial RTK. Portuguese TV is also available.

PHOTOGRAPHY & VIDEO

General photographic hints are given in the Regional Facts for the Visitor chapter. Print film is available in Maputo, Beira and larger towns (from US$5 for a roll of 100ASA 36-exposure film). Slide film is occasionally available in Maputo (about US$9 for 36-exposure 100ASA colour). There are several fairly reliable film processing shops in Maputo (see that section for details).

As elsewhere in the region, you should not photograph government buildings, ports, airports, or anything connected with the police or military, and ask permission before photographing people.

HEALTH

For general information see Health in the Regional Facts for the Visitor chapter.

Malaria is widespread in Mozambique, and precautions are essential. Although levels of bilharzia infestation on the Mozambican side of Lake Niassa (Lake Malawi) are not considered to be as bad as on the Malawi side, you should exercise caution.

Maputo has good emergency medical service. Upcountry, facilities are generally inferior, although all provincial capitals have hospitals that can test for malaria. If you become seriously ill, it's best to seek treatment in South Africa or return home.

DANGERS & ANNOYANCES

Mozambique has calmed down considerably from the war days when going anywhere by road meant a convoy and a high risk of attack. Today, it's as safe as anywhere in the region, and most travellers shouldn't have any difficulties. That said, there are a few areas where a bit of caution is warranted to prevent problems from arising.

Road Accidents

Drunken driving is common and speeds are often high. It's best to travel in the mornings, and (when there's a choice) by bus rather than *chapa* (pick-up or converted minivan). Night travel should be avoided.

Crime

Petty theft is the main risk: watch your pockets or bag in markets; don't leave personal belongings unguarded on the beach or elsewhere; and minimise trappings such as jewellery, watches, headsets and external money pouches. If you leave your vehicle unguarded, expect windscreen wipers and other accessories to be gone when you return. Don't leave anything inside a parked vehicle.

In Maputo and southern Mozambique, due to the proximity to South African organised crime rings, car jackings and more violent robberies do occur, though the situation is nowhere near as bad as in Johannesburg (Jo'burg), and most incidents can be avoided by taking the usual precautions: avoid driving at night, and don't wander around isolated or dark streets.

More likely are the simple hassles such as underpaid authorities in search of bribes, though this is not as common as it's made out to be. If you do get stopped you should not have any problem as long as your papers are in order, and you're friendly and respectful.

WARNING: Land Mines

! An unknown number of unexploded land mines – the legacy of Mozambique's long war – mean that it's unsafe to go wandering off into the bush anywhere without first seeking local advice. Even then, stick to well-used paths. Areas which should always be avoided include the base of bridges, old schools or abandoned buildings, and antennas, water tanks or other structures. Also take special care on road verges in rural areas – if you need to relieve yourself, stay on the road or seek out a trodden path.

BUSINESS HOURS

Banks are generally open from 8 am to 3 pm weekdays. Most shops and offices open from 8 am to noon and 2 to 6 or 6.30 pm weekdays, and on Saturday morning. In northern Cabo Delgado, many places open earlier – by 7 or 7.30 am, and close by about 5 or 5.30 pm.

PUBLIC HOLIDAYS & SPECIAL EVENTS

Mozambique's public holidays include:

New Year's Day 1 January
Mozambican Heroes' Day 3 February
Women's Day 7 April
International Workers' Day 1 May
Independence Day 25 June
Lusaka Agreement/Victory Day 7 September
Revolution Day 25 September
Christmas/Family Day 25 December

Each city/town also has a 'city/town day' when businesses are closed; Maputo's is 10 November.

ACTIVITIES

Naturally, the coast is popular for water sports. The main areas for **diving** are Ponta d'Ouro, Inhaca Island, Barra, Bazaruto and Pemba. Diving in Mozambique doesn't always offer exceptional visibility, and conditions tend to be quite variable, with a string of mediocre days punctuated by a few days of superb diving. However, most areas have good fish diversity, and reefs are in generally good condition. This, and the natural beauty of Mozambique's coast, the adventure of exploring relatively unknown sites, and the chance of spotting sharks, dugong and more can make for some very rewarding dives.

Mozambique has good **game fishing**, particularly in the south-east between Ponta d'Ouro and Inhassoro. If you're bringing your own boat, you'll need a licence.

The best areas for **surfing** are Ponta d'Ouro and Tofinho (just south of Tofo). In general, however, waves are not as good as they are elsewhere in the region (Durban, for example), though the setting's great.

Mozambique has diverse birdlife. Particularly good areas for **birdwatching** include the Bazaruto Archipelago and Gorongosa National Park.

Other possible activities include **hiking** and **rock climbing**, though for both, you'll need to inquire about the presence of land mines and be fully equipped, including with compasses or a good GPS (global positioning system). Large areas of Mozambique's interior are trackless bush and getting lost is a real concern.

ACCOMMODATION

Outside of southern resort areas, accommodation standards in Mozambique, particularly in the north, are generally inferior to those elsewhere in the region. The *pensões* (cheapest hotels) start at US$6 per room and usually offer only the most basic conditions. Even in mid-range places, luxuries such as electricity and running water are often in short supply.

When quoting prices, many places distinguish between a *duplo* (room with two twin beds) and a *casal* (double bed). Many places offer mid-week and low-season discounts, and resorts sometimes have reductions for children under 12.

FOOD

In Mozambique, the maize and cassava-based staples are *xima* and *upshwa*. Good seafood is widely available, notably excellent *camarões* (prawns) and *lagosta* (crayfish). A plate of king prawns starts at about US$9. (For general information, see Food in the Regional Facts for the Visitor chapter.)

SHOPPING

Maputo, Nampula and Pemba are good places to shop for Makonde woodcarvings, for the sandalwood carvings common in the south and the etched clay pots made by Makonde women (which make beautiful but heavy souvenirs).

Inhambane Province is good for baskets. In Cabo Delgado, you'll find attractive woven mats. Some of the best silver craftsmanship comes from Ibo Island in the far north, although the silver itself is often not of high quality. *Capulanas*, the colourful cloths worn by women around their waist, can be found at markets everywhere.

SARAH JOLLY

The markets of Mozambique offer many opportunities to bargain for souvenirs.

Getting There & Away

This section covers access into Mozambique only from neighbouring countries. Information about reaching Southern Africa from elsewhere on the African continent and from other continents is outlined in the regional Getting There & Away chapter.

AIR

Airports & Airlines

Mozambique's national carrier is Linhas Aéreas de Moçambique (LAM). Flights connect Maputo six times weekly with Jo'burg (US$140 one way) and three times weekly with Harare (US$225).

Regional airlines serving Mozambique include: South African Airways, with daily flights between Jo'burg and Maputo for about US$300 return; and SAAirlink, with flights five times weekly between Maputo and Durban (US$140). There's a weekly flight between Pemba and Mtwara (Tanzania) costing US$175/340 one way/return.

Departure Tax

Departure tax is US$20 for intercontinental flights and US$10 for regional flights, payable in US dollars or SA rand, cash.

LAND

Mozambique has land borders with Malawi, South Africa, Swaziland, Tanzania, Zambia and Zimbabwe. Foreigners entering Mozambique overland must pay an immigration tax of US$2.25 (Mtc28,800 or R12) at the border, for which you should get a receipt or a stamp in your passport. Drivers also need to pay between US$2 and US$12 (depending on vehicle size) for a temporary import permit plus US$15 (R86) for one-month compulsory third-party insurance.

Most land borders are open from 6 am to 6 pm (7 am to 7 pm at Namaacha; 8 am to 5 pm at Ponta d'Ouro).

Malawi

Road The busiest crossing is Zóbuè, on the road linking Blantyre and Harare (Zimbabwe). From Tete to the border there are daily chapas as well as buses from Beira, Chimoio and Harare. At the border, walk about 300m for transport to Mwanza and Blantyre.

The crossing at Dedza (north of Zóbuè) is more convenient to Lilongwe, and scenic, passing through cool and hilly Angónia; however, there's only sporadic public transport.

From central Mozambique, there's a crossing at Vila Nova da Fronteira on the southern tip of Malawi. The border can be reached by sporadic chapas from Mutarara and Sena (which are on opposite sides of a bridge over the River Zambezi). Sena is connected during the dry season by road with Caia, on the main north-south road; chapas run this route sporadically during the dry season. At the border, you can find transport to Nsanje and Blantyre.

Several vehicles run daily between Mocuba (north of Quelimane) and Milange, from where you walk 2km to the border, and another 1km for Malawian transport to Mulanje and Blantyre.

To get to Entre Lagos from Cuamba, most people take the train (see Train, following).

From both Lichinga and Cuamba, the most commonly used land route to Malawi is via Mandimba. Several vehicles run daily between Lichinga and Mandimba. From here it's 7km to the border (about US$1 on a bicycle-taxi), where you can find transport to Mangochi.

Train There's a daily train from Cuamba to the border crossing at Entre Lagos (see the Cuamba Getting There & Away section). It's a short walk to the Malawi border crossing at Nayuchi, from where you can catch the train to Liwonde (officially, daily, but sometimes it's cancelled). There are also minibuses along the rough road from Nayuchi to Liwonde.

South Africa

Road Daily minibuses (departing by 7 am) connect Maputo with Ressano Garcia on the border (US$3), Nelspruit (US$8) and Jo'burg (US$16), though most travellers use one of the large 'luxury' buses which do the route daily for about US$30 (student discounts available) and take about eight hours. The best option is Translux (☎ 011-774 3333 in Jo'burg), which departs Maputo daily from the South African Airways office (see under Getting There & Away in the Maputo section) at 8 am and from Jo'burg (on the corner of Walmarans and Rissik Sts) at 7 am. You can also embark/disembark in Pretoria.

Panthera Azul (☎ 01-498868 in Maputo) departs Maputo daily at 8 am (10 am Sunday) from the Panthera Azul office on Avenida Julius Nyerere. Departures from Jo'burg are at 7.30 am (8.30 am Sunday). The drop-off/pick-up point in Jo'burg is 105 Kerk St, on the corner of Polly Ave.

Intercape (☎ 01-431006, 425078 in Maputo) departs from Tropical Air Tours at 909 Avenida 24 de Julho at 8 am daily (10 am Sunday). Departures in Jo'burg (☎ 011-337 9169) are from 108 Kerk St near Panthera Azul at 7.30 am daily (10 am Sunday).

You can also travel in each direction on any of these bus lines between Maputo and Nelspruit (R130, three to four hours, drop-off/pick-up at Promenade Hotel in Nelspruit), but not between Nelspruit and Jo'burg.

Panthera Azul and Intercape also have twice weekly services between Maputo and Durban via Swaziland. Departures on Panthera Azul (R180) are 7.30 am Wednesday and Saturday from Maputo, arriving about 4 pm in Durban, and 7 am Thursday and Sunday from Durban. Intercape (R160) departs Maputo at 7 am Monday and Friday, and from Durban at 7 am Wednesday and Sunday.

To get to South Africa via Ponta d'Ouro you'll need your own 4WD.

Train A daily train connects Maputo with Jo'burg via Komatipoort, Nelspruit and Pretoria, departing Maputo daily at 11 am and arriving in Jo'burg the next day about 6.15 am. Departures from Jo'burg are at 6.10 pm, arriving Maputo the next day at about 11.30 am. In Maputo, you can purchase a ticket to Komatipoort, where you'll need to change trains and purchase a second ticket for the South African leg. The entire trip (Maputo to Jo'burg) costs R150/123/67 in 1st/2nd/3rd class. Bedding is included for 1st class.

A faster alternative is to take a minibus for the Maputo-Komatipoort leg (US$3), and the train between Komatipoort and Jo'burg (R120/100/55). Departures from Komatipoort to Jo'burg are at 6.07 pm; from Jo'burg, the train reaches Komatipoort at about 6.45 am.

A passenger train (known as *Trans Lubombo* in South Africa) runs between Maputo and Durban (R185 in a 2nd-class sleeper), departing Maputo Thursday and Sunday at 11.20 am, arriving early the next morning in Durban. Departures from Durban are Wednesday and Saturday at 7.35 pm, arriving in Maputo late afternoon. Recently there have been a few disruptions to this service, so check at the station for current details.

Swaziland

Road Direct minibuses depart Maputo about 6 am for Manzini (R25) and Mbabane. Otherwise, change vehicles at the border at Namaacha.

Train The train between Durban and Maputo (Mozambique) runs via Swaziland. From Mpaka in eastern Swaziland, the train to Maputo departs at about 11.30 am on Wednesday and Saturday and the train to Durban departs at about 5 pm Thursday and Sunday. All seats are 2nd-class sleepers. Recently there have been a few disruptions to this service, so check at the station for current details.

Tanzania

Daily chapas connect Moçimboa da Praia, Palma and Namoto (the Mozambican immigration post). During the dry season, these continue from Namoto another 2km to the Rovuma River, which you cross by dugout canoe (US$1), although a ferry equipped to carry vehicles is planned for the near future. When the river is low, you will need to walk and wade for between 25 and 45 minutes through the riverbed on the Tanzanian side, from where transport will take you to Kilambo (also called Mwambo, the Tanzanian border crossing), and on to Mtwara. During the rainy season the river crossing can take up to an hour, and can be dangerous because of fast-moving water.

We were told there are border crossings upriver near Nangade and Moçimboa do Rovuma. Both routes involve long walks (at least 10km on the Mozambican side and 30km in Tanzania) and crossing the river by dugout canoe. It's also questionable whether you'll be able to get your passport stamped at either of these crossings. There is usually one chapa daily from Mueda to Nangade and one or two weekly to Moçimboa do Rovuma.

Zambia

The main border crossing is between Cassacatiza and Chanida, north-west of Tete. The road is in decent shape, but infrequently used, with only sporadic public transport from Matema. Most travellers go through Malawi. Once at the border, there's occasional transport to Katete, and on to Lusaka or Chipata.

You can also cross into Zambia via Zumbo (at the western end of Lake Cahora Bassa), but this route is rarely used. The best way to Zumbo from Tete is via Zimbabwe.

Zimbabwe

The two main crossing points between Mozambique and Zimbabwe are: Nyamapanda on the Tete Corridor, linking Harare with Lilongwe; and Machipanda on the Beira to Harare road. Both are heavily travelled, including by buses. Hitching is not difficult. From Tete, there's frequent transport to Changara (US$2.50) and to the border, for onward transport to Harare.

From Chimoio, there's frequent transport to Machipanda and on to the border, from where you'll need to take a taxi (about US$5) or hitch the 12km to Mutare.

The other route via Espungabera further to the south is scenic, and a good option for those with a 4WD. Public transport on the Mozambique side is scarce.

SEA & LAKE

Malawi

From Metangula (accessed from Lichinga by road) you can take a boat up the lakeshore to Cóbuè (where you get stamped out by Mozambique border guards) and onwards to Likoma Island (Malawi territory – so you must also report to the immigration officials here). This journey can take three days, but you can sometimes hitch a ride on a private speedboat, which does the trip in eight hours. (In general, it's easier to get from Metangula to Cóbuè, than vice versa, especially if you have extra cash to charter your own boat.) From Likoma you can reach Nkhata Bay on the Malawi mainland. For more details on this interesting but slow route, see the Cóbuè section later in this chapter, and the Getting There & Away section in the Malawi chapter.

Local boats also travel frequently between Meponda and Senga Bay (Malawi), but the crossing can be risky as lake squalls blow up quickly. Leaving Mozambique, you'll need to get stamped out at immigration in Lichinga and show this to the police in Meponda. For entering Mozambique here, the procedure should be that you show your visa (which you'll need to arrange in advance) to the police in Meponda and then get it stamped in Lichinga, although we haven't met anyone who's actually done this.

South Africa

We've heard about a Unicorn Lines cargo ship sailing weekly between Durban and Nacala, with reasonably priced passenger accommodation. For details in South Africa, call ☎ 031-301 1476 in Durban, or ask at a backpackers lodge in Durban. For details in Mozambique, ask at Nacala port.

Tanzania

Some travellers go between Mozambique and Tanzania by local *dhow* (ancient Arabic sailing vessel). The best places to arrange this are Moçimboa da Praia and Palma. In Tanzania, dhow ports include Mikindani, Mtwara and Msimbati.

Getting Around

AIR

LAM flies between Maputo, Beira, Quelimane, Nampula, Tete, Lichinga and Pemba. Flights can be paid for in local currency, dollars or rand, and in Maputo by Visa or MasterCard. Sample one-way fares are: Maputo to Beira US$160 (daily); Beira to

Nampula US$158 (three times weekly); Beira to Quelimane US$105 (six times weekly); Maputo to Tete US$210; Maputo to Pemba US$300 (three times weekly). LAM offers special fares, including several less expensive night flights between Maputo and Beira (US$90), and a weekend return-trip between Maputo and Pemba (US$370).

LAM has improved markedly in recent years. While delays and cancellations occur, flights are generally reliable. More problematic are overbookings, particularly on flights from upcountry: always reconfirm your ticket and get to the airport well in advance. Buying a 1st class ticket (only slightly more expensive than economy) will usually ensure you a seat. Baggage handling has also improved, although you should carry with you anything of value.

Sabin Air, a private charter airline, has scheduled flights three times weekly between Maputo and Vilankulo via Bazaruto, and daily between Maputo and Inhaca Island.

Most larger towns have airstrips. Charter flights can be arranged with the following operators:

Sabin Air (☎ 01-465108, fax 465011) Maputo airport
SANAir (☎/fax 04-213085) Quelimane airport
STA (☎ 06-214653) Nampula airport
Unique Air Charter (☎ 01-465592, fax 465525) Maputo airport
Viatur (☎ 072-3431, fax 2249) Pemba airport

Domestic Departure Tax

Tax on domestic flights is US$5 (Mtc55,000).

BUS

Good bus *(machibombo)* services connect major towns at least once daily where road conditions permit. The main companies are: Transportes Oliveiras, with an extensive route network in southern and central Mozambique; Transportes Virginia, with a few routes in southern Mozambique; and TSL (tay-say-el), which operates on the southern routes and to Tete, Quelimane and Nampula. Other lines include Bengala and Panga Panga. Most lines run both express and stopping services; it's usually worth paying the small difference between the two, as express is generally significantly faster. Transportes Virginia (no overcrowding) and TSL (which operates with two drivers on longer routes) are considered to be the best; Oliveiras is often slightly cheaper. Sample fares include: Chimoio to Tete US$5; Maputo to Inhambane US$6; Nampula to Pemba US$8; Maputo to Beira US$20 (US$30 express); and Maputo to Nampula US$80.

Most places don't have central bus stations. Rather, transport usually leaves from the start of the road towards the destination, which all too frequently seems to involve a hike of 1 to 2km from the centre of town. Long-distance transport in general, and all transport in the north, usually leaves very early (between 3.30 and 7 am); outside of southern Mozambique and along the Beira corridor, it's often difficult to get a vehicle *anywhere* after mid-morning. And, unlike many countries, where you spend interminable periods waiting for vehicles to fill, Mozambican transport usually leaves quickly and close to the stated departure time. If a driver tells you he'll be departing at 4.30 am, get there between 4 and 4.15 am. Outside resort areas (where hitching will be possible with holidaymakers returning from the beach), Sundays generally aren't good travel days as there are fewer vehicles.

For information on chapas, see Local Transport later in this section.

Roads in Mozambique

Only a small percentage of Mozambique's roads are paved, and many become impassable during the rainy season. Even during the dry season, distances are long and road travel takes time, particularly in northern Mozambique. For example, the 500km from Beira to Vilankulo (a combination of good and bad roads) takes from eight to 10 hours by car and up to 15 hours by bus, while the 300km between Lichinga and Cuamba takes eight to 11 hours. Travelling by public transport between Maputo and Pemba along the north-south road can take up to a week. Always inquire locally about current conditions before setting off.

TRAIN

Passenger trains run between Nacula and Nampula, Nampula and Cuamba, and Cuamba and Entre Lagos (Malawi border). See the Cuamba and Nacala sections for details. The lines connecting Maputo with Ressano Garcia/Komatipoort and Jo'burg, and with Durban in South Africa are described in the Getting There & Away section.

CAR & MOTORCYCLE

For information of a general nature, see the Getting Around the Region chapter. In addition to full documentation (see Driving Licence & Permits under Visas & Documents earlier in this chapter), you're required to carry two red hazard triangles, and the driver and front seat passenger must wear seatbelts. If you get stopped in violation of these requirements, expect to pay a fine. In some areas, including the Beira corridor between Beira and Machipanda on the Zimbabwe border, police have radars and levy fines if you're exceeding 80km/h (50km/h in towns). It's best to avoid excessive speeds anyway, as axle-shattering potholes can appear out of nowhere. With a few exceptions, unless you plan to stay only on the Maputo to Vilankulo road, or along the Beira corridor, you'll need a 4WD and, more importantly, high clearance. Petrol is hard to find off the main roads, especially in the interior, but diesel supplies are more reliable. If you have a petrol vehicle, carry fuel with you. Even with a diesel vehicle, it's a good idea to carry an extra can or two and tank up whenever possible, as filling stations sometimes run out.

If you're travelling by motorcycle, remember that many beach access roads are very sandy – some with deep, soft sand – and you may wind up pushing your bike more than riding it.

Rental

Europcar, Avis, Hertz, Imperial and several smaller agencies have offices in Maputo (see that section for details). Avis and Imperial also have offices in Beira and Imperial has an office in Nampula. In Pemba, car rentals can be arranged through Viatur (see the Pemba section). In Maputo, rates average about US$35 per day for a small car, plus about US$0.35 per kilo-metre and about US$15 per day for collision and theft damage waiver. Prices at smaller outfits are often lower, and prices for upcountry and 4WD rentals are higher.

BICYCLE

Cycling is a good way to see Mozambique, but you'll need plenty of time as distances are long. You'll also need to plan the legs of your trip fairly carefully and to carry almost everything with you, as there are long stretches with little or nothing en route. Try to avoid main roads; there's often no shoulder, traffic moves fast, drivers have little respect for cyclists (assuming they see you at all) and it's not uncommon for trucks to be carrying long poles or similarly lethal objects *sideways* across their truck. Also, to avoid the heat and the worst of the traffic, try to plan your cycling between dawn and mid-morning. Because of land mines, wildlife and security, it's never a good idea to free camp (plus it's illegal in Mozambique). Plan your route around established camp sites, or arrange something with villagers in rural areas. Off the main roads, you'll need a mountain bike, especially for beach access.

TAXIS

Taxis are available in Maputo and Beira for getting around. Quelimane and Nampula each have one taxi which usually meets incoming scheduled flights at the airport. Apart from airport arrivals, taxis don't cruise for business anywhere in Mozambique, so you'll need to seek them out (see the Maputo and Beira sections for information on locations of taxi ranks). In Maputo, many taxis have meters; elsewhere, you'll need to negotiate a price. Depending on location, expect to pay at least US$3 for a trip within town.

HITCHING

Hitching in Mozambique isn't particularly difficult, though it can be slow off main routes. To/from beaches, it's easiest on weekends. For general information on safety considerations, see Hitching in the Getting Around the Region chapter.

BOAT

There's no regular passenger service between major coastal towns. On Lake Niassa, the only somewhat regular connections are between Metangula and Cóbuè (see those sections for details). If you want to travel by boat, inquire at ports and harbours as there's frequent cargo traffic along the coast and captains are sometimes willing to take passengers. Manica Shipping Lines at Beira port is a good place to start. Chances improve the further north you go; for example, small freighters and dhows go between Quelimane, Nacala and Pemba for negotiable fees of about US$10. In the far north, dhows can be arranged to most destinations; fees are negotiable, averaging US$15 per day. There are no luxuries on board, and journeys often take far longer than anticipated. Bring plenty of extra water, food and sun protection, and stay with the winds – south to north from April to September and north to south from November to February. We've heard several horror stories from readers who tried to sail against the winds, only to wind up stranded for days in the sun without adequate food and water.

LOCAL TRANSPORT

Where roads are bad and in rural areas, your only option will be chapas or *camião* (normal truck). Many have open backs, and on long journeys the sun and dust can be brutal.

ORGANISED TOURS

Most organised tours focus on southern Mozambique. They can be arranged by travel agencies (see Travel Agencies in the Maputo section), or by tour companies specialising in Mozambique. These companies, most of which are based outside the country, include:

Mozaic (☎/fax 04-301348 in Zimbabwe, ⓔ mozaic@icon.co.zw or traveller@primenetzw.com)
Mozambique Connection (☎ 011-8034185 in South Africa, fax 8033861, ⓔ mozcon@pixie.co.za)
Mozambique National Tourist Co (see under Tourist Offices in the Facts for the Visitor section earlier in this chapter)
The Mozambique Travel Centre (☎ 011-706 1959 in South Africa, 659 1766, fax 706 6445, ⓔ moztrav@mweb.co.za)

Another good source of information on package tours and cruises are the Mozambique pages that appear at the end of each edition of the South African travel magazine *Getaway*; check out its Web site: www.getawaytoday.com.

Maputo

☎ 01

Maputo (formerly Lourenço Marques), is one of Africa's most attractive capitals. It's set on a small cliff overlooking Maputo Bay, with wide avenues lined by jacaranda and flame trees, a plethora of pleasant sidewalk cafes and a relaxed atmosphere. For decades, the city's charms and its economic potential were overshadowed, first by colonialism, then by war, and it's only recently that the city has come into its own. Today Maputo is a bustling place with colourful markets, interesting architecture, a lively cultural scene and great nightlife. It's well worth spending some time here before heading north.

Orientation

Maputo can be likened to an inverted cup (ie, dome-shaped), with the long avenues of its upper-lying residential sections running down to the busy port and commercial area *(baixa)*. Its streets are set out in a grid pattern. Major north-south roads paralleling the seaside Avenida Marginal are Avenidas Julius Nyerere and Vladimir Lenine. Main east-west thoroughfares parallel to the port are Avenidas 25 de Setembro, 24 de Julho and Eduardo Mondlane.

Many businesses, the train station, banks, post and telephone offices and some budget accommodation are located in the baixa, on or near Avenida 25 de Setembro, while embassies and most of the mid-range to top-end hotels are in the city's upper section. The city's tallest building and a good landmark is the 33 Storey building (known locally as 'trinta e trés andares') in the baixa on the corner of Avenidas 25 de Setembro and Rua da Impresa. At the northernmost end of the Marginal and about 7km from the centre is Bairro Triunfo and the Costa do

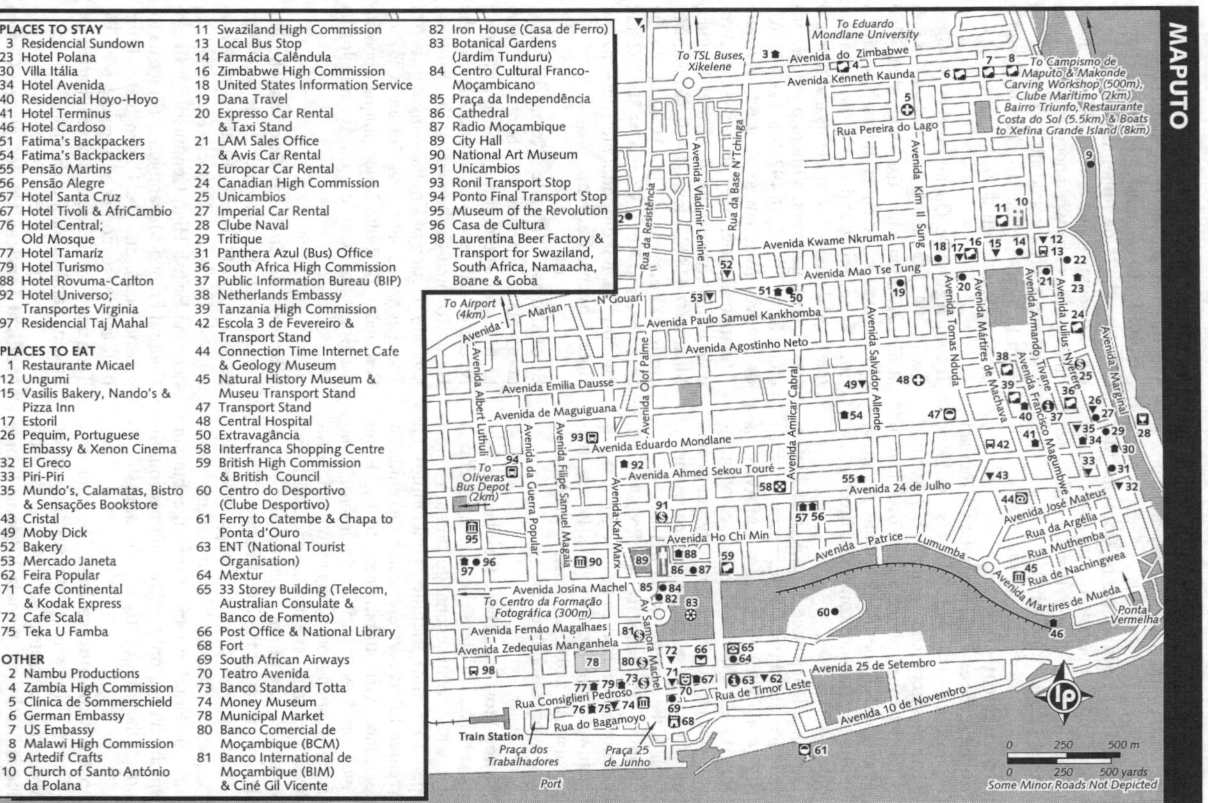
MAPUTO
PLACES TO STAY
3 Residencial Sundown
23 Hotel Polana
30 Villa Itália
34 Hotel Avenida
40 Residencial Hoyo-Hoyo
41 Hotel Terminus
46 Hotel Cardoso
51 Fatima's Backpackers
54 Fatima's Backpackers
55 Pensão Martins
56 Pensão Alegre
57 Hotel Santa Cruz
67 Hotel Tivoli & AfriCambio
76 Hotel Central; Old Mosque
77 Hotel Tamaríz
79 Hotel Turismo
88 Hotel Rovuma-Carlton
92 Hotel Universo; Transportes Virginia
97 Residencial Taj Mahal
PLACES TO EAT
1 Restaurante Micael
12 Ungumi
15 Vasilis Bakery, Nando's & Pizza Inn
17 Estoril
26 Pequim, Portuguese Embassy & Xenon Cinema
32 El Greco
33 Piri-Piri
35 Mundo's, Calamatas, Bistro & Sensações Bookstore
43 Cristal
49 Moby Dick
52 Bakery
53 Mercado Janeta
62 Feira Popular
71 Cafe Continental & Kodak Express
72 Cafe Scala
75 Teka U Famba
OTHER
2 Nambu Productions
4 Zambia High Commission
5 Clínica de Sommerschield
6 German Embassy
7 US Embassy
8 Malawi High Commission
9 Artedif Crafts
10 Church of Santo António da Polana
11 Swaziland High Commission
13 Local Bus Stop
14 Farmácia Calêndula
16 Zimbabwe High Commission
18 United States Information Service
19 Dana Travel
20 Expresso Car Rental & Taxi Stand
21 LAM Sales Office & Avis Car Rental
22 Europcar Car Rental
24 Canadian High Commission
25 Unicambios
27 Imperial Car Rental
28 Clube Naval
29 Tritique
31 Panthera Azul (Bus) Office
36 South Africa High Commission
37 Public Information Bureau (BIP)
38 Netherlands Embassy
39 Tanzania High Commission
42 Escola 3 de Fevereiro & Transport Stand
44 Connection Time Internet Cafe & Geology Museum
45 Natural History Museum & Museu Transport Stand
47 Transport Stand
48 Central Hospital
50 Extravagância
58 Interfranca Shopping Centre
59 British High Commission & British Council
60 Centro do Desportivo (Clube Desportivo)
61 Ferry to Catembe & Chapa to Ponta d'Ouro
63 ENT (National Tourist Organisation)
64 Mextur
65 33 Storey Building (Telecom, Australian Consulate & Banco de Fomento)
66 Post Office & National Library
68 Fort
69 South African Airways
70 Teatro Avenida
73 Banco Standard Totta
74 Money Museum
78 Municipal Market
80 Banco Comercial de Moçambique (BCM)
81 Banco International de Moçambique (BIM) & Ciné Gil Vicente
82 Iron House (Casa de Ferro)
83 Botanical Gardens (Jardim Tunduru)
84 Centro Cultural Franco-Moçambicano
85 Praça da Independência
86 Cathedral
87 Radio Moçambique
89 City Hall
90 National Art Museum
91 Unicambios
93 Ronil Transport Stop
94 Ponto Final Transport Stop
95 Museum of the Revolution
96 Casa de Cultura
98 Laurentina Beer Factory & Transport for Swaziland, South Africa, Namaacha, Boane & Goba
To Eduardo Mondlane University
To TSL Buses, Xikelene
To Campismo de Maputo & Makonde Carving Workshop (500m), Clube Marítimo (2km) Bairro Triunfo, Restaurante Costa do Sol (5.5km) & Boats to Xefina Grande Island (8km)
To Airport (4km)
To Oliveras Bus Depot (2km)
To Centro da Formação Fotográfica (300m)
Avenida do Zimbabwe
Avenida Kenneth Kaunda
Rua Pereira do Lago
Avenida Kim Il Sung
Avenida Vladimir Lenine
Rua da Base N'Tchinga
Rua da Resistência
Avenida Kwame Nkrumah
Avenida Mao Tse Tung
Avenida Marian N'Gouari
Avenida Paulo Samuel Kankhomba
Avenida Agostinho Neto
Avenida Emília Dausse
Avenida de Maguiguana
Avenida Eduardo Mondlane
Avenida Ahmed Sekou Touré
Avenida 24 de Julho
Avenida Ho Chi Min
Avenida Patrice Lumumba
Avenida Josina Machel
Avenida Fernão Magalhaes
Avenida Zedequias Manganhela
Av Samora Machel
Rua Consiglieri Pedroso
Rua do Bagamoyo
Rua de Timor Leste
Avenida 25 de Setembro
Avenida 10 de Novembro
Avenida Albert Luthuli
Avenida da Guerra Popular
Avenida Filipe Samuel Magaia
Avenida Karl Marx
Avenida Olof Palme
Avenida Amilcar Cabral
Avenida Salvador Allende
Avenida Tomas Nduda
Avenida Mártires de Machava
Avenida Armando Tivane
Avenida Julius Nyerere
Avenida Marginal
Avenida Francisco Magumbwe
Avenida José Mateus
Rua da Argélia
Rua Muthemba
Rua de Nachingwea
Avenida Martires de Mueda
Ponta Vermelha
Train Station
Praça dos Trabalhadores
Praça 25 de Junho
Port
0 250 500 m
0 250 500 yards
Some Minor Roads Not Depicted

Sol area with a small beach, a fishing village and several places to stay and eat.

Maps The best is put out by Conselho Municipal and Coopération Française, for sale at Public Information Bureau (BIP; see Tourist Offices following).

Information

Tourist Offices ENT, the National Tourism Organisation (☎ 421794, fax 421795, ⓔ entur@virconn.com), is at 1179 Avenida 25 de Setembro above Lusoglobo Travel. Although ENT doesn't have many resources for tourists, the staff can often direct you to someone who does.

An excellent source of background information is the Public Information Bureau (BIP; ☎ 490200) on the corner of Avenidas Eduardo Mondlane and Francisco Magumbwe, where you can buy city maps and books, or browse in the reference library. Much of the material is in English.

Nambu Productions (☎/fax 419150, ⓔ timbila@zebra.uem.mz) at 37 Rua Vilanamwali can organise visits to see traditional music and dance sessions in Maputo's bairros for reasonable fees.

Money Most banks have their head offices in the baixa, with branches in the upper part of town. Private exchange bureaus (most open to 5 pm) include: Unicambios on Avenida Julius Nyerere, and on Avenida 24 de Julho; AfriCambio, next to the Hotel Tivoli on Avenida 25 de Setembro; Cotacambios (open from 8.30 am to 9 pm weekdays, 8 am to noon Saturday and 2 to 10 pm Sunday) at the airport; and the foreign exchange bureau at the Hotel Polana.

The best places to change travellers cheques are Cotacambios (no commission), and the Hotel Polana exchange bureau, which charges only a 2% commission, although they frequently run out of cash.

Post & Communications The main post office (CTT) with poste restante is on Avenida 25 de Setembro. The telephone office is nearby on Avenida Vladimir Lenine on the ground floor of the 33 Storey building, open from 7.30 am to 10 pm daily. For email and Internet access, try Connection Time (☎ 499147, ⓔ webmaster@contime.com) at 355 Avenida 24 de Julho, next to the Geology Museum. Rates are US$4/7 for 30/60 minutes, lower between noon and 3 pm, and discounts apply for students. It's open from 9 am to 8 pm Monday to Thursday (until 6 pm Friday and Saturday).

Travel Agencies Dana Travel (☎ 494060, fax 494042, ⓔ dana@mail.tropical.co.mz) at 729 Avenida Mao Tse Tung, about five blocks west of Avenida Julius Nyerere is English speaking and can assist with domestic and international flights and tour and travel arrangements. Others agencies include Euro Travel (☎ 492 446, fax 494462, ⓔ eutravel@virconn.com) at 645 Avenida Armando Tivane, one block west of Avenida Julius Nyerere, behind Hotel Avenida; Mextur (☎ 428427, fax 428430, ⓔ mextur@emilmoz.com) at 1233 Avenida 25 de Setembro and Novo Mundo (☎ 306202, fax 306206, ⓔ novomundo@teledate.mz) at Hotel Rovuma-Carlton.

Bookshops & Music Stores BIP sells books about Mozambique. Sensações, with branches on the corner of Avenidas Julius Nyerere and Eduardo Mondlane, at the Hotel Rovuma-Carlton and at Shoprite, has a good selection of English-language books and magazines. For cassettes and CDs, try Sensações, or Radio Moçambique opposite the Botannical Gardens on Avenida Josina Machel.

Libraries & Cultural Centres The National Library is on Avenida 25 de Setembro, next to the post office. Most items are in Portuguese. The British Council (Rua John Issa, near the British High Commission); Centro Cultural Franco-Moçambicano (Praça da Independência); and the United States Information Service (corner of Avenidas Mao Tse Tung and Kim Il Sung) all have libraries, exhibitions and cultural offerings.

Medical Services The best place is Clínica de Sommerschield (☎ 493924), 52 Rua

Pereira do Lago, just off Avenida Kim Il Sung. It's open 24 hours and always has a doctor on call. Advance payment is required (credit cards accepted for amounts more than US$500). Malaria testing costs US$10.

There are many decent pharmacies. Farmácia Calêndula (☎ 497606) at 222 Avenida Mao Tse Tung, near Avenida Julius Nyerere is well stocked. It's open from 8 am to 8 pm Monday to Saturday, 9 am to 1 pm Sunday.

Photography Kodak Express on Avenida 25 de Setembro near Cafe Continental and Alpha Cooperativa de Fotografia at Inter-Franca shopping centre on Avenida 24 de Julho are usually reliable for film processing. Both places also sell a limited selection of print film. For slides, the only place is Centro de Formação Fotográfica (☎ 421545) at 1071 Avenida Josina Machel, which does black and white processing only. Slide film is sometimes available at Kodak Express, or at the Fuji film shop at the Hotel Rovuma-Carlton.

Dangers & Annoyances You'll need to carry your passport (or a copy) with you at all times in Maputo. If you get stopped and the police insist that something is wrong with your passport (assuming your visa is in order), it's likely they are just looking for bribes.

There are several restricted areas which are off-limits to pedestrians (no photos). These include the eastern footpath on Avenida Julius Nyerere in front of the president's residence and the Ponta Vermelha zone in the city's south-eastern corner.

Things to See & Do

The **fort** on Praça 25 do Junho was built by the Portuguese in the mid-19th century on the site of an earlier fort. It's presently closed to the public. Several blocks west is the impressive **train station** dating from 1910, with a dome designed by Gustav Eiffel of Eiffel Tower fame. Between the fort and the train station is the oldest part of town, centred around **Rua de Bagamoyo**, with some interesting architecture and the city's oldest **mosque** *(mesquita)*. Near the train station on Avenida 25 de Setembro is the **Municipal Market** (Mercado Municipal) with everything from fruit, vegetables, spices and basketware.

Several blocks north-east of the market on Praça da Independência is the modern **cathedral**. Nearby are the neo-classical **City Hall** building; the **Botanical Gardens** (Jardim Tunduru); and the **Iron House** (Casa de Ferro). This house was designed (also by Eiffel) in the late 19th century as the governor's residence, but its metal-plated exterior proved unsuitable for tropical conditions.

The **National Art Museum** (Museu Nacional de Arte) on Avenida Ho Chi Min (open from 3 to 7 pm Tuesday to Sunday) has an excellent collection of works by Mozambique's finest contemporary artists; entry is free. Also excellent is the **Chissano Museum** (☎ 780705), containing the work of renowned sculptor Alberto Chissano. It's outside Maputo in Matola on Rua Torre de Vale in Bairro Sial, and open from 9 am to noon and 3 to 5 pm Tuesday to Sunday; entry is US$1.

The **Museum of the Revolution** (Museu da Revolução) on Avenida 24 de Julho documents Mozambique's independence struggle. The displays are labelled in Portuguese, but have good photos, and is open from 9 am to noon and 2 to 6 pm daily (3 to 6 pm Sunday, closed Saturday morning); entry costs US$0.50. Also interesting is the **Money Museum** (Museu da Moeda) on Praça 25 do Junho in one of the city's oldest buildings, with exhibits of local currency from early barter-tokens to modern-day bills. It's open from 9 am to noon and 2 to 4.30 pm Tuesday to Saturday, and 2 to 5 pm Sunday.

The **Natural History Museum** (Museu da História Natural) near Hotel Cardoso is closed for renovations, but it's worth visiting to see its architecture and garden with a mural by Malangatana. The **Geology Museum** (Museu da Geologia) on Avenida 24 de Julho has mineral exhibits and a geological relief map of the country (open from 3 to 6 pm Tuesday to Saturday, and Saturday morning).

Places to Stay – Budget

Parque Campismo *(☎ 305247, 012-328 3481, fax 328 3484 in South Africa)* on the

Marginal north of the city centre has camping for R40 per tent (R75 per caravan) plus R6 per person. It's being renovated; running hot/cold water and power points will be installed.

The best budget option by far is ***Fatima's Backpackers*** *(fax 494462, @ fatima@virconn.com)*. Fatima has two pleasant houses in the suburbs, one at 1317 Avenida Mao Tse Tung, the other nearby at 82 Rua Carlos Albers. Singles/doubles cost US$12/20 and dorms US$6. There are self-catering facilities and shops nearby, or meals can be arranged. Fatima speaks English and is a wealth of information on Maputo and Mozambique. She also offers free airport pick-ups and transfers to the Oliveiras bus depot (US$4).

Pensão Alegre *(☎ 307742, 1371 Avenida 24 de Julho)* has rooms for US$12/20 and a bathroom on each floor; ***Hotel Santa Cruz*** *(☎ 303004, 304246, fax 303066)* next door has straightforward rooms from US$29/45.

Residencial Taj Mahal *(☎ 732122)* on Avenida Ho Chi Min near Casa de Cultura, has clean rooms from US$15/20, but the area isn't safe at night.

The ***Hotel Universo***, on the corner of Avenidas Eduardo Mondlane and Karl Marx, has gloomy rooms from US$25/30, but is convenient for Transportes Virginia buses.

The ***Hotel Central*** *(☎ 431652)* on Rua Consiglieri Pedroso, near the train station has basic rooms from US$15/20. Better is ***Hotel Tamaríz*** *(☎ 422596, fax 428609)* nearby on Rua Consiglieri Pedroso, with rooms from US$28/38 (US$45/56 with air-con).

About 5km north of the city centre are two options. The ***Burger Inn*** *(☎ 450211)* in Bairro Triunfo has rooms for US$25/35 and inexpensive meals.

A step up is the ***Restaurante Costa do Sol*** *(☎ 450038)* overlooking Costa do Sol beach at the northern end of the Marginal, with rooms for R130/220 and more expensive bungalows. There's a good restaurant downstairs which is popular on Saturday nights (jazz night) and Sunday afternoons.

Places to Stay – Mid-Range

The ***Hotel Terminus*** *(☎ 491333, fax 491284)* on the corner of Avenidas Francisco Magumbwe and Ahmed Sekou Touré has a restaurant, small pool and good rooms from US$60 (credit cards accepted). It's popular with business travellers and often fully booked.

Residencial Hoyo-Hoyo *(☎ 490701, fax 490724)* nearby on Avenida Francisco Magumbwe is also popular, with rooms from US$40/60 and a restaurant.

Pensão Martins *(☎ 424930, fax 429645, 1098 Avenida 24 de Julho)* has rooms from US$55/70 plus 17% tax (US$80 for a suite with bathroom), an outdoor restaurant and a small pool. Credit cards are accepted.

Residencial Sundown *(☎ 499282, fax 499281, 1726 Avenida do Zimbabwe)* in Sommerschield has rooms in a private house from US$50/55, including breakfast.

Villa Itália *(☎ 497298, fax 496190, @ vitalia@virconn.com, 635 Avenida Friedrich Engels)* is a converted house with good value rooms for US$65/75 (US$85 for a suite) and a popular restaurant.

Places to Stay – Top End

The ***Hotel Polana*** *(☎ 491001, fax 491480, @ res@polana-hotel.com, 1380 Avenida Julius Nyerere)* in a superb location overlooking the sea is Mozambique's best. Rooms in the elegant main building cost from US$175; those in the 'Polana Mar' from US$115. There's a beautiful pool, several restaurants, and good-value breakfast, lunch and dinner buffets.

The ***Hotel Cardoso*** *(☎ 491071, fax 491804, @ hcardoso@zebra.uem.mz, 707 Avenida Mártires de Mueda)* opposite the Natural History Museum has views over the bay, well-appointed rooms from US$115/145, including buffet breakfast, a pool and restaurant.

The ***Hotel Rovuma-Carlton*** *(☎ 305000, fax 305305)* opposite the cathedral has similar rooms from US$105/130, including buffet breakfast. There's a restaurant and many boutiques.

The ***Hotel Avenida*** *(☎ 492000, fax 499600, @ h.avenida@teledata.mz, 627 Avenida Julius Nyerere)* has rooms with all the amenities for US$105/125, including buffet breakfast.

The ***Hotel Tivoli*** *(☎ 307600, fax 307609, @ tivoli@teledata.mz, 1321 Avenida 25 de*

Setembro) has rooms for US$80/100, including breakfast.

Places to Eat

Restaurants Maputo has many good mid-range options with main dishes ranging from US$5 to US$12. *Time Out* has extensive listings.

Popular places include: ***Micael*** on Rua da Resistência (Brazilian); ***El Greco*** *(☎ 491898)* on Avenida Julius Nyerere (Italian); ***Calamatas*** *(☎ 494080)* on the corner of Avenidas Julius Nyerere and Eduardo Mondlane (Greek); ***Mundo's*** *(☎ 494080)* next to Calamatas (steaks and burritos); and ***Bistro*** *(☎ 497644)* near Calamatas (French).

The ***Pequim*** *(☎ 493899)* on Avenida Julius Nyerere is popular for seafood and steaks; it's closed on Sunday

Moby Dick *(☎ 308738, 313 Avenida Salvador Allende)* has good ambience and live music on weekends.

By the sea, in addition to the ***Restaurante Costa do Sol*** (see Places to Stay – Budget), try the ***Clube Marítimo***, which has a Sunday lunch buffet and a less-expensive snack bar in the yacht club next door (entry is US$1).

Ungumi near Hotel Polana in a restored colonial house with a small art gallery has Maputo's finest dining. Main courses start at about US$20, but plan on US$70 to US$100 per person for a full meal with wine. At lunchtime, there's a four-course menu for US$30.

The ***Piri Piri Restaurante*** at the eastern end of Avenida 24 de Julho has spicy chicken from US$4.

The Feira Popular complex, Avenida 25 de Setembro, has dozens of small bars and restaurants. ***O Escorpião*** and ***Coqueiro*** are two of the most popular. There's a US$0.40 entry fee to the fair grounds, and car parking is available.

Cafes On the corner of Avenidas Vladimir Lenine and Mao Tse Tung is ***Mercado Janeta*** which has plates of xima and sauce for US$0.40. Opposite is a ***bakery***.

Good cafes serving pastries and light meals include: ***Cafe Continental*** and ***Cafe Scala*** on Avenida 25 de Setembro; ***Estoril*** on Avenida Mao Tse Tung; and ***Cristal*** on Avenida Eduardo Mondlane.

Vasilis Bakery/Nando's/Pizza Inn together on Avenida Mao Tse Tung have pastries, chicken and pizza from US$2.50.

Teka U Famba *(☎ 429818)* off Praça 25 do Junho has good-value takeaway meals from US$1; it's closed Saturday evening and Sunday.

Entertainment

For movies, try ***Ciné Xenon*** on Avenida Julius Nyerere and ***Gil Vicente*** on Avenida Samora Machel. There are foreign-language films and concerts at the ***Centro Cultural Franco-Moçambicano*** (for more details, see under Information earlier in this section).

The best theatre is ***Teatro Avenida*** on Avenida 25 de Setembro, with good performances in Portuguese by local theatre groups. Mozambique's excellent National Company of Song and Dance is based at the ***Casa de Cultura*** (House of Culture) on the corner of Avenidas Albert Luthuli and Ho Chi Minh. Rehearsals are often open to the public.

Maputo has a thriving nightlife with many pubs, clubs, bars and discos. It gets going on Friday and Saturday, but never before 11 pm. There's a choice of bars at ***Feira Popular*** (see Places to Eat), and taxis wait by the main gate to take you home afterwards.

Other places include: ***Complexo Mini-Golf***, a disco on the Marginal, popular with Maputo's younger crowd; the pricey ***Complexo Sheik*** disco near the intersection of Avenidas Julius Nyerere and Mao Tse Tung; ***Kowhana***, near Xipamanine market (go here in a group and carry only enough money for the evening), with a bar and dancing; and ***Clube Matchedje***, a disco and music venue on Avenida 24 de Julho next to the parliament building. Cover charges at most places range from US$3 to US$7.

In addition to ***Costa do Sol*** and ***Moby Dick*** (see under Places to Eat – Restaurants), the cinema ***Gil Vicente*** has popular jazz evenings on Thursdays.

Shopping

For crafts, try the Saturday morning craft market on Praça 25 do Junho; the stalls outside the Piri Piri Restaurante and the Hotel Polana; and the Makonde carving workshop (Grupo Favana) behind Parque Campismo. North of the Hotel Polana is Artedif, with good crafts made by disabled people.

Extravagância (☎ 427653, 1247 Avenida Mao Tse Tung) near Mercado Janeta is a great place selling products made by students at Maputo's visual arts school. Quality is high, selection is good and prices are reasonable; it's also possible to have things made to order. It's open from 8.30 am to 12.30 pm and 2.30 to 6.30 pm Monday to Saturday.

Shanty Craft (☎ 450111) in Bairro Triunfo is also good, with a unique assortment of high-quality crafts from around the country. It's open from 10 am to 5 pm daily except Monday. Moçambique Arte at the Hotel Rovuma-Carlton has expensive woodcarvings. Tritique off Avenida Julius Nyerere is good for tie-dyed fabrics.

Getting There & Away

Air Details for domestic and international flights to/from Maputo are given in the main Getting There & Away and Getting Around sections earlier in this chapter.

Airlines with offices in Maputo include:

LAM (☎ 426001, 465810, central reservations) corner of Avenidas 25 de Setembro and Karl Marx; (☎ 490590, sales office) corner of Avenidas Julius Nyerere and Mao Tse Tung
SAAirlink (☎ 465487) Maputo airport
Sabin Air (☎ 465108) Maputo airport
South African Airways (☎ 420740/2) Avenida Samora Machel
TAP Air Portugal (☎ 431006/7) Hotel Rovuma-Carlton

Bus Long-distance transport depots are often well outside the city/town centre, so time your travels from upcountry to avoid arriving at night in Maputo. They include:

Transportes Oliveiras (☎ 405108) Avenida 24 de Julho, just beyond Praça 16 de Junho. A taxi from the centre is US$6. Otherwise, take any Matola or Boane *chapa* (pick-up or converted minivan) and ask them to drop you off. Coming into Maputo, some Oliveiras buses conveniently continue past the Oliveiros depot to the intersection of Avenidas 24 de Julho and Amilcar Cabral, near Pensão Alegre.
Transportes Virginia (☎ 421271) Hotel Universo, corner of Avenidas Eduardo Mondlane and Karl Marx. All chapas running along Avenida Eduardo Mondlane stop here.
TSL Praça dos Combatentes at the end of Avenida das FPLM. Taxis charge about US$10. To reach the TSL depot by public transport take any chapa heading to 'Xikelene'. These leave from Praça dos Trabalhadores, and from the corner of Avenidas Julius Nyerere and Mao Tse Tung. Coming into Maputo, some TSL buses continue to Ponto Final (see Getting Around, following).
Transport for Swaziland, South Africa, Namaacha, Boane and Goba Fábrica de cerveja Laurentina (Laurentina beer factory), corner of Avenidas 25 de Setembro and Albert Luthuli.
'junta' Avenida de Moçambique just past Lhanguene cemetery. All northbound transport stops here, although for a good seat it's better to go to the bus depots.

An Oliveiras express to Xai-Xai, Maxixe and Vilankulo departs at 6 am (7 am for an ordinary bus). Transportes Virginia to Maxixe and Inhambane departs at 6 am. Most TSL northbound buses depart between 6 and 8 am. TSL buses to Nampula and Quelimane via Tete and Malawi depart at 8 am Monday and Thursday. For international services, see the main Getting There & Away section earlier in this chapter.

Train There is no train service from Maputo to destinations within Mozambique. For international services to Durban (via Swaziland) and Komatipoort (including to the border at Ressano Garcia), see the Getting There & Away section earlier in this chapter.

Getting Around

To/From the Airport Mavalane international airport is 6km north-west of town. Bus No 18 runs from the Natural History Museum to the airport (US$0.10). Bus No 24 (from the Natural History Museum) and bus No 25 (from Praça dos Trabalhadores via Ponto Final) go nearby. A taxi to/from the city centre costs about US$10.

Bus & Chapa Buses (Transportes Publicas de Maputo or TPM) are numbered, and have nameboards with their destination. All city rides cost US$0.10.

Chapas (minibuses and converted trucks) go everywhere (US$0.15, extra for baggage). Some have nameboards, otherwise listen to the destination called out by the conductor. Major transport stands include:

Hospital Central/Escola 3 de Fevereiro Avenida Eduardo Mondlane four blocks down from Avenida Julius Nyerere; transport to Ronil and various city destinations
Museu Natural History Museum; transport to the airport and numerous city destinations
Ponto Final intersection of Avenidas Eduardo Mondlane and Guerra Popular; terminus for many bus and chapa routes; transport along Avenida Eduardo Mondlane
Praça dos Trabalhadores the train station; transport to Xikelene, Costa do Sol, Ronil and elsewhere
Ronil Intersection of Avenidas Eduardo Mondlane and Karl Marx; transport to 'junta', Benfica and Matola

For Costa do Sol and Bairro Triunfo, you can also take bus No 17 or a chapa from the intersection of Avenidas Mao Tse Tung and Julius Nyerere. Chapas to Matola also leave from in front of the Laurentina beer factory. For the Chissano Museum, take any Matola chapa and ask the driver to drop you as close as possible to Bairro Sial.

Car Car rental agencies in Maputo include:

Avis (☎ 465498, 494473, fax 465493) intersection of Avenidas Julius Nyerere and Mao Tse Tung; also at the airport
Europcar (☎ 497338, 082-300241, fax 497334, @ europcar@virconn.com) 1418 Avenida Julius Nyerere, next to the Hotel Polana; also at the Hotel Rovuma-Carlton
Expresso (☎ 493619, fax 493620) 541 Avenida Mao Tse Tung, several blocks down from Avenida Julius Nyerere
Hertz (☎ 494982, fax 426077) at the Hotel Polana and at the airport
Imperial (☎ 493545, fax 493540) corner of Avenidas Julius Nyerere and Eduardo Mondlane

Taxi Taxis do not cruise for business. Places to find them include the Hotel Polana, the Hotel Rovuma-Carlton and the Hotel Cardoso; on Avenida Mao Tse Tung, near Avenida Julius Nyerere; and sometimes near the train station and central market. Many have meters. Trips within town cost between US$4 and US$8.

AROUND MAPUTO

Across the bay from Maputo is the town of **Catembe**, which offers views of Maputo's skyline and a taste of upcountry atmosphere for those who won't have a chance to leave the capital. The ferry takes about 20 minutes, runs every two hours from 6.30 am and costs US$0.15 per person and US$8 per vehicle (US$0.25/12 on weekends). ***Restaurante Diogo*** near the jetty makes a good lunch stop.

Xefina Grande Island, offshore from Costa do Sol, has a very long history as a trading base, prison and war garrison. Now, there is nothing but old cannons, dilapidated buildings and beaches. You can arrange motorboat charters through Maputo travel agencies (about US$35 per person, minimum of four) or by asking around at Clube Naval. Less expensive local boats from the fishing village 3km beyond Restaurante Costa do Sol will take you there.

Pequenos Lebombos Dam (Barragem dos Pequenos Lebombos), about 45km south-west of Maputo, supplies the capital's water. The nearby Lebombo Mountains offer wide views and pleasant cycling. There's ***accommodation*** at the dam from US$30 a double (US$60 per four-person self-catering chalet), and a restaurant. Book through ARA-Sul (☎ 01-306729, 306730). Chapas travelling between Maputo and Goba will drop you off at the entrance to the dam (US$0.55). Alternatively, take a chapa from Maputo to Boane (US$0.30) and get transport from there.

Macenta Beach

☎ 01

About 35km north of Maputo is Marracuene and the turn-off for Macaneta Beach.

From there, it's 10km along a sandy road (usually negotiable in 2WD) to the beach and ***Complexo Turístico Macaneta*** *(☎ 650006, 309073)*, a popular restaurant with two and four-person chalets.

Jay's Beach Lodge *(☎ 082-300143 from 8 to 9 am and 5 to 6 pm, fax 330143)* has good camping for USS$20 per tent, comfortable self-catering chalets from US$75/120 for four/six people, and a restaurant. Each vehicle (you'll need 4WD) pays US$5 entry.

At the end of the peninsula on the river is ***Nkomati River Camp*** *(@ nkomati@mail.tropical.co.mz)* with accommodation for US$70. Access is via 4WD or boat transfer from Marracuene, arranged through Nkomati River Camp.

To reach Macaneta by public transport, take any northbound chapa from the 'junta' in Maputo (see the under Getting Around in the Maputo section) and get out at Marracuene. It's a 10-minute walk to the Nkomati River which you'll need to cross by ferry (US$1/7 per person/vehicle, five minutes). On the other side you'll need to hitch, which is easy on weekends.

Inhaca Island

☎ 01

Inhaca, about 40km east of Maputo, is an important marine research centre and a popular weekend getaway. Its offshore coral reefs are among the most southerly in the world, and parts of the island and surrounding waters have been designated a protected reserve. About 3km north-west of Inhaca is tiny Portuguese Island (Ilha dos Portuguêses), formerly a leper colony and now part of the Inhaca marine reserve system.

Things to See & Do There are good **beaches** on Inhaca's north-eastern edge, and on Portuguese Island. On Inhaca's south-western corner is a marine research station and a small **museum** (free entry) containing some specimens of the island's fauna. Transport to the research station (US$5) and the lighthouse at Inhaca's northern tip (US$10) can be arranged through Inhaca Island Lodge. Otherwise, it's a 50-minute walk from the lodge to the biology station, and about double that to the lighthouse. Dive Africa Watersports (see the following section) rents mountain bikes for US$10 per half day.

MOZAMBIQUE

Diving & Water Sports Dive Africa Watersports (☎ 760005/6/10, @ mozambique@diveafrica.com) operates out of Inhaca Island Lodge. In addition to **water-sports** equipment rental, it offers windsurfing, sea kayaking and snorkelling. The Web site has more information: www.diveafrica.com. **Dives** are tide dependent and conditions vary, though on good days you can expect to see a variety of sharks, manta rays, potato bass and more. The best months are November to April, and the worst are August and September, when it's often too windy.

Places to Stay & Eat At Ponta Torres, the south-eastern tip of Inhaca, and on Portuguese Island (US$2.50 per person), ***camping*** is permitted. There's a guard at both sites, and brackish water sources; you'll need to bring all supplies from the mainland.

Indigo Charters next to Inhaca Island Lodge has basic tented accommodation for R80, and no-frills huts for R100 per person. Book through Lucas Restaurant.

The ***Marine Biology Research Station*** *(☎ 760009, 490009, fax 492176)* offers basic rooms with shared facilities for US$15 per person. It's primarily for students and researchers, but open to the public on a space-available basis. There's a cook, but you'll need to bring your own food. Book rooms at least five days in advance.

The ***Inhaca Island Lodge*** *(☎ 305000, fax 305305)* on the island's western side has a pool and comfortable chalet-style accommodation for US$125/200, including full board (US$105/150 mid-week and discounts apply for children).

Apart from the ***restaurant*** at Inhaca Island Lodge (which alternates between buffets and set menus, both about US$18), the only dining option is the pleasant ***Lucas Restaurant*** *(☎ 431857)* just past the market. It's best to give advance notice, especially for groups. Meals cost from US$4.

Getting There & Away Sabin Air has daily flights to/from Maputo for US$33/50 one way/return.

Speedboat charters (arrange with any Maputo travel agency) cost US$50 return, minimum four, and take about an hour. All boats drop you off at Inhaca Island Lodge. The ferry to Inhaca is out of service; inquire at the Catembe ferry pier in Maputo for an update.

For Portuguese Island, arrange a boat from the beach in front of Inhaca Island Lodge or, at very low tide, walk.

Southern Mozambique

This section covers the area between Ponta d'Ouro and the Save River, encompassing Maputo, Gaza and Inhambane Provinces. It's by far the most developed part of the country for tourism, although this is almost completely concentrated along the coast, where the main attractions are seemingly endless stretches of white-sand beach and clear, blue water. Many resorts fill up during South African and Zimbabwean school holidays. Places are described roughly from south to north.

PONTA D'OURO

☎ 01

Ponta d'Ouro offers surfing, good beaches and waters with abundant sea life, including dolphins, whale sharks and more. Dolphin-sighting excursions can be organised with Dolphin Encounters (see Places to Stay). The area is popular with South Africans; on holiday weekends it can be easy to forget you're in Mozambique. About 5km north is the quieter **Ponta Malongane**, with attractive stretches of windswept coastline.

Diving

There's some good diving off Ponta d'Ouro, and numerous operators have set up shop here. Most are based at the Parque de Campismo. Rates average R110 for a single dive, R450 for a five-dive package, plus R25 per item per day for equipment. Four-day open-water certification courses (book in advance) cost from R1100. Diving is best from November to April/May.

Places to Stay

Ponta d'Ouro ***Parque de Campismo*** *(☎ 303177, 011-425 2866 in South Africa)* at the southern end of town has camping for US$8 per person and functional chalets from US$24 a double.

In the same complex are several dive operators offering tented accommodation and catered or self-catering facilities (all telephone numbers are in South Africa):

African Watersports (☎/fax 013-245 1691, ☎ 082-572 0671) R65 per person sharing (R75 for divers, R55 with your own tent); chalets from R175 per double

Blu International Dive Charters (☎ 011-463 4914, fax 463 4915, @ bluinter@global.co.za) R70 per person sharing

Dolphin Encounters (☎ 082-920 8952, 011-315 5510) R80 per person sharing; dolphin-sighting trips cost R70 per person (minimum seven)

Simply Scuba (☎ 031-502 5261, fax 502 5263) R80 per person in a two-person tent (R70 for divers)

The ***Motel do Mar*** *(☎/fax 650000, 012-362 1355 in South Africa)* beside the water has four-person self-catering chalets for R250/350 a single/double, including breakfast.

The ***Blues Beach House*** has three double rooms for US$65 per person sharing, including half board. Book through Prosol in Maputo (☎ 01-304098, fax 421908, @ prosol@mail.tropical.co.mz).

Ponta Malongane Based at Parque de Malongane, ***Malongane Dive Charters*** *(☎ 012-348 4262, fax 348 1252 in South Africa)*, has camping for R52 per person and a bunkhouse with self-catering facilities. There are no-frills two-bed chalets from R149 and self-catering four-bed chalets from R370. Packages include a midweek backpacker special for R600 with three nights tented accommodation and unlimited diving.

The quieter ***Thabundu*** on a small cliff overlooking the sea was scheduled to open after the time of writing with camping for US$5.50 and chalet accommodation.

Getting There & Away

Sabin Air has scheduled flights on Friday and Sunday to/from Maputo (R450 return, minimum five people), although these are usually cancelled due to lack of passengers.

Ponta d'Ouro is 120km south of Maputo (3½ hours by 4WD). A direct chapa departs from Maputo's Catembe ferry pier at 8 am on Tuesday and Friday (US$5.50). Departures from Ponta d'Ouro are Wednesday and Saturday at 8 am. Otherwise, take the ferry to Catembe, where you can find transport to Salamanga (US$2.50) or Zitundo (US$4). From Zitundo, there's sporadic transport to Ponta d'Ouro (US$1.60), 20km further south.

The border crossing is 10km south of Ponta d'Ouro (4WD only). Coming from South Africa, there's a guarded lot at the border where you can leave your vehicle (R10 per day). Pick-ups can be organised with Motel do Mar and Ponta d'Ouro/Ponta Malongane dive operators for R20 to R50 per person (minimum two).

Maputo travel agencies can arrange trips for about US$75 per person return, minimum four. For information on private shuttle service, check at Fatima's Backpackers (see Places to Stay – Budget earlier) in Maputo for an update.

MAPUTO ELEPHANT RESERVE

En route to Ponta d'Ouro and two hours from Maputo is the Maputo Elephant Reserve. The reserve and its camp site are temporarily closed, but it's possible to visit and – with some difficulty – to spot an elephant. Apart from its elusive elephants the reserve's other attraction is its birdlife, which includes fish eagle and many wetland species. To arrange a visit, try Kutlhanga Tours in Maputo (☎ 01-490845, 082-308031, ⓔ kutlhanga@hotmail.com). Some Maputo travel agencies (see listings under Travel Agencies in the Maputo chapter) may be willing to organise day excursions to the reserve, with overnight accommodation at Ponta d'Ouro. Expect to pay from about US$125 per person (minimum four people), not including lodging costs. If you head into the reserve on your own, you'll need a 4WD and all your own provisions, including a tent, food and water.

NAMAACHA

☎ 01

Namaacha, on the Swaziland border, has an ornate colonial-era church. East of town is a rusty sign marking the way down to a small but scenic **waterfall** *(cascata)* 3.6km north of the main road.

The ***Libombos Hotel*** *(☎ 960102, fax 960099)* on the main road has comfortable rooms from US$45/65 a single/double and an expensive ***restaurant***.

For cheap food, try ***Simão da Costa***, a local eatery at the border (on the right heading towards Swaziland).

Chapas run frequently to and from Maputo (US$1.60). You can catch chapas at the border for onward travel to destinations in Swaziland and South Africa.

BILENE

☎ 022

Praia do Bilene is a resort town on a lagoon separated from the ocean by a sandy spit. To get from the lagoon to the sea you'll need a boat or 4WD. It's 140km north of Maputo and 40km off the main road. The junction is at Macia, from where pick-ups run to/from Bilene (US$0.50).

At the northern end of town by the water is ***Complexo Palmeiras*** *(☎ 59019, 013-755 2257 in South Africa)* with camping for US$10 per site plus US$5 per person, no-frills four-person chalets (shared ablutions) from US$40, and a restaurant.

Complexo Lagoa Azul *(☎ 59006)* back from the water at the southern end of town has clean, self-catering four-person chalets for US$75 (US$85 on weekends).

Nearby are basic ***cottages*** belonging to the CFM (national railway); it's US$50/60 for three/five people. Book through CFM (☎ 01-426943) in Maputo.

Pousada de São Martinho, 200m inland from the beach past the market, has good-value doubles with spotless common bath for US$16 and four-person self-catering chalets for US$40. Renovations are underway, with prices set to rise once they're completed.

Next door is ***Pousada do Paraíso*** with basic rooms for US$12.

Praia do Sol, 4km south of town along the beach, has camping; or half board in comfortable tented accommodation for US$28 per person sharing or two-bed chalets from US$65.

Complexo Humula *(☎ 59020, 59009, 01-415766, fax 415769 in Maputo)* is set away from the water amid manicured

ALL PHOTOGRAPHS BY DAVID ELSE

Mozambique **Top:** The waterfront, near the fish market, Mozambique Island **Bottom Left:** Fishermen mending their multicoloured nets, Mozambique Island **Bottom Right:** The cathedral in Nampula

Namibia Clockwise from Top : The ghost town of Kolmanskop is a popular excursion from Lüderitz; a San child of the Kalahari; a traditional home in a Himba village; a sleeping Himba child

lawns, and it's signposted. Comfortable self-catering chalets for two/five/six persons cost US$64/133/150.

If eating out: ***Estrela do Mar*** on the beach road serves seafood and other dishes. ***Pavilhão Tamar*** beside the water and the nearby ***Tchin-Tchin*** have light meals from US$3.

There's a daily bus to Maputo from Pousada do Paraíso departing at 6 am. It's faster to take a chapa to Macia from the roundabout at the entrance to Bilene (2km from the beach), and get a north/southbound express bus from there.

XAI-XAI

☎ 022

Xai-Xai (shy-shy) is the capital of Gaza Province. Most visitors head for the beach at **Praia do Xai-Xai**, 8km off the main road and 10km from the town centre. BCM on the main road changes travellers cheques.

Places to Stay & Eat

Complexo Halley *(☎ 35003)* on the beach, just to the north of the main road, has doubles from US$36 (US$56 for an air-con suite), a restaurant and a disco.

Just north of Complexo Halley is ***Xai-Xai Camping & Caravan Park*** *(☎ 35022)*, which has camping for US$6 plus US$3 to park your caravan. There are no-frills bungalows from US$20/double, a three-bed house for US$40, and a four-bed self-catering house for US$56. Children under 12 pay half price. Meals are available with advance notice. The dive operator based here arranges diving and fishing charters. For details, contact Mozambique Connection (see Organised Tours in the Getting Around section at the beginning of this chapter).

Further north along the beach is the popular ***Terry's Backpackers*** with beds for US$6 and simple bungalows sleeping two (or more, if you like) for US$16. There's free snorkelling equipment and volleyball gear. Good-value meals are available through a special 'backpacker's arrangement' with Golfinho Azul restaurant.

Other options include a new, top-end hotel being built north of Terry's, or private house rental (inquire at Complexo Halley).

> **Warning**
>
> Xai-Xai suffered particularly heavy damage during the flooding in early 2000, and it is likely that many of the places listed here may not yet have re-opened. Get an update before making your plans.

Golfinho Azul on the beach south of Complexo Halley has moderately priced seafood dishes.

In Xai-Xai town, ***Pastelaria Chave d'Ouro*** on the main road is good for inexpensive meals.

Getting There & Away

Oliveiras runs twice daily express buses between Xai-Xai and Maputo, departing in each direction about 6 am and 1.30 pm (US$3). There are also frequent ordinary buses (US$2.50) from the Oliveiras depot on the main road in Xai-Xai diagonally opposite the Catholic church.

Otherwise, all north-south express buses (such as TSL) stop in Xai-Xai. Wait by Pôr do Sol Restaurant on the main road at the southern end of town next to the *praça* (transport stand).

Chapas from the praça run frequently to/from the Praia do Xai-Xai roundabout, which is about 700m uphill from the beach (US$0.40).

AROUND XAI-XAI

Along the coast are several resorts. The ***Zongoene Lodge*** *(☎ 01-499523, 012-346 1286, fax 012-346 1269 in South Africa, e zongoene@satis.co.za)* has luxury chalets on the mouth of the Limpopo River. Activities include fishing, riverboat cruises, birdwatching and more. The turn-off is about 15km south of Xai-Xai, from where it's 35km to the resort (4WD only). There's an airstrip for charter flights.

About 60km north-east of Xai-Xai and 5km off the main road is **Chidenguele** and **Lake Inhampavala**. ***Paraíso de Chidenguele*** *(☎ 011-782 1026 in South Africa)* has self-catering four-bed chalets in the dunes for US$65.

QUISSICO

Quissico, on the north-south road overlooking some beautiful lagoons, is the capital of Zavala district, which is famed for its Chope *timbila* (marimba) players. The most famous is Venâncio Mbande, whose internationally acclaimed orchestra rehearses most Sunday afternoons at his house about 20km north of Quissico in Helene. Nambu Productions (see Information in the Maputo section) can organise trips. There's also an annual Timbila Festival here on the last weekend in August.

Pousada de Zavala 'Quissico' on the main road has basic rooms for about US$8 and a restaurant.

About 55km north of Quissico and 17km off the main road (4WD only) is **Praia de Závora** and the ***Závora Lodge*** *(☎ 013-706 4926 in South Africa)* with camping for US$6 and simple but pleasant chalets. Meals and snorkelling gear are available.

Most transport between Maputo and Maxixe stops at Quissico. For Závora, you'll need your own vehicle.

MAXIXE

☎ 023

Maxixe (ma-sheesh), about 450km north-east of Maputo on the EN1, is a popular resting point for traffic up and down the coast. It's also the place to get off the bus if you want to visit Inhambane, which lies across the bay.

Places to Stay & Eat

Maxixe Camping *(☎ 30351)* near the jetty is a clean camping ground with good security, hot showers, and self-catering facilities. Camping costs US$4 per person plus US$1.60 per vehicle (US$12 for a caravan site with electric hook-up). There's also a self-contained, two-person cottage on the beach (US$30), a couple of simpler two-person chalets (US$27), and bungalows with shared shower and toilet (US$24). Advance bookings are recommended.

Across the road are the ***Hotel Golfinho Azul*** *(☎ 30071)* with adequate rooms for US$12/16, and ***Pousada de Maxixe*** *(☎ 30199)*, which charges US$13 a double.

Stop at the jetty has good views and good meals. ***Restaurante Dom Carlos*** near the bus park is also good, with main dishes from US$4.

Getting There & Away

Several buses daily run to/from Vilankulo (US$2.50) and Maputo (US$6). (For information on getting to Inhambane, see under Getting There & Away in the Inhambane section, following.)

INHAMBANE

☎ 023

Inhambane is one of Mozambique's oldest towns and one of its most charming. Well before the Portuguese arrived, it was a stop for Muslim *dhows* (ancient Arabic sailing vessels) trading along the coast. From the 18th century, Inhambane was an important trading port for ivory and slaves, with commerce controlled primarily by Indians. In 1834, the town was ravaged by the warriors of chief Soshangane, but soon recovered to again become one of the largest towns in the country. During the 20th century, focus shifted elsewhere and Inhambane declined. Today, you can see many old houses and buildings. Among the most interesting are the old **cathedral**, near the water, the nearby **mosque**, and some of the houses on the streets near the cathedral. Pensão Pachiça (see Places to Stay) has a leaflet with a walking tour.

BCM changes travellers cheques. International telephone calls can be made from the telecommunications building near the jetty. **Xiphefo** on the road to the train station, and the **Casa de Cultura** near the cinema, have information on cultural events.

Places to Stay

Pensão Pachiça *(☎ 20565, 011-622 2242 in South Africa, ⓔ inhambane@africamail.com)* on the waterfront near the cathedral is a great place for backpackers. Clean private rooms cost from US$10 per person while dorms cost from US$6 and camping is US$4. The owner is very helpful, and can assist with changing money, sightseeing, excursions etc.

The only other real option is the ***Escola Ferroviária de Moçambique*** *(☎ 20781)* by the train station at the eastern edge of town, which charges US$8 per bed in a reasonably clean four-bed room with bathroom. Unless they're full, you'll usually only be charged per occupied bed.

Places to Eat

Inhambane's best, and one of the best restaurants in upcountry Mozambique, is ***Á Maçaroca*** *(☎ 20489)* near BCM. Service is prompt, the atmosphere pleasant and the food delicious. Good value main dishes average US$7.

For cheap eats, try ***Restaurant Tic-Tic*** near the market; ***Ti Jamú*** near the pier, where a main dish with bread and salad costs US$4; and ***Ponto Final*** by the bus stand.

Getting There & Away

Bus Transport leaves from behind the market. For southbound travel: Transportes Virginia (US$7) and Oliveiras (US$6) run daily express buses to/from Maputo, departing at 6 am (six to seven hours). Virginia (the best) also runs a second bus on Friday and Sunday, departing in each direction about 1.30 pm. TSL has a daily bus between Tofo Beach and Maputo via Inhambane, departing Inhambane for Maputo about 6.30 am. Otherwise, you can go via Maxixe.

Boat An old and precipitously overloaded ferry runs throughout the day between Inhambane and Maxixe (US$0.20, 25 minutes). Dhows do the trip for US$0.15. Motorised boat hire costs US$4 for the boat and takes about 10 minutes. For Vilankulo and Beira, take the ferry or dhow to Maxixe and get onward transport from there.

AROUND INHAMBANE

There are many good beaches nearby. Tofo and Barra – the most popular – are covered later in this chapter. Other choices include: **Pandane**, about 30km south of Inhambane, with good snorkelling, a ***camping ground*** and ***chalets*** *(☎ 012-807 1464, fax 807 1461 in South Africa)*; **Guinjata Bay**, north of Pandane, with ***camping*** and ***chalets***, fishing charters, and diving for those with their own equipment *(☎ 083-283 6918, fax 013-741 3149 in South Africa)*; **Jangamo**, north of Guinjata Bay; and **Baía dos Cocos**, north of Jangamo and 17km off the main road, with basic ***camping***.

All places require a 4WD for access.

Linga Linga

Ponta Linga Linga, about 15km north of Inhambane, is accessible only by boat. ***Funky Monkeys***, a popular backpackers hostel, has camping for US$5, dorms from US$5 and breakfast/dinner for US$1.60/4. Drinking water is available.

Pensão Pachiça in Inhambane runs a dhow twice weekly to/from Funky Monkeys (US$3); motorboat hire costs US$30. Otherwise, take a chapa to Morrumbene (US$0.40 from Maxixe, US$2 from Vilankulo), then walk about 20 minutes to the water (ask for the 'ponta') for a dhow to Linga Linga (US$0.40). One usually departs at about 11 am daily except Sunday. Otherwise, hire your own (US$4, best arranged before 3 pm due to tides and winds).

Pousada do Litoral on the main road in Morrumbene has basic rooms for about US$8.

TOFO & BARRA

☎ 023

These beaches are popular holiday destinations. Tofo is more accessible and more developed. Barra is quieter, with a better setting amid surf, sand dunes and palm groves. Barra Lodge and Barra Reef (see Places to Stay & Eat) have dive shops. Dive operations at Tofo are based at Casa Azul (☎ 082-959 6975 or through Casa Azul, see Places to Stay). Just south of Tofo is **Tofinho**, known for its surfing; there are no tourist facilities, but it's easily accessed from Tofo.

Places to Stay & Eat

Tofo Going north to south: ***Nordin's Lodge*** *(☎ 29009)* has a beachfront location and comfortable four-person chalets with bathroom and fridge for US$64. At the time of research a 14-bed bunkhouse was planned for early 2000, with beds for US$7. Self-catering facilities are available for an extra US$1.60 or you can get cooked meals for US$4.

The recently renovated ***Hotel Marinhos*** *(☎ 29015, fax 29002)*, also on the beach, has good rooms overlooking the sea from US$40 per person sharing (US$30 with no sea view, less during the off season). All rates are negotiable and include breakfast, but exclude 17% tax. There's also a restaurant.

Further down is ***Casa Azul*** *(☎ 29021)*, a private house that you can rent in its entirety (US$160, sleeps 10) or per room (US$32 for a reasonable double). There's a kitchen, or meals can be arranged.

On the hill above Casa Azul is ***Casa Barry*** *(☎ 29007, ☎/fax 031-904 3524 in South Africa)*, with camping for US$5 and fully equipped reed chalets for US$75 (four people).

Just off the road into Tofo and convenient to Tofinho is ***Turtle Cove*** (book through Casa Azul), a backpackers place with camping for US$4, dorms for US$6 (including breakfast) and simple bungalows for US$10 per person. There's surfboard rental and a restaurant.

Restaurante Ferroviário *(☎ 29018)* in the town centre has good food; it's closed Monday.

Bar Babalaza, 15km from Inhambane on the turn-off to Barra, is a popular restaurant. Campers are welcome.

Barra The ***Barra Lodge*** *(☎ 011-314 3355, fax 314 3239 in South Africa, e barra@pixie.co.za)* has camping for US$6, dorms for US$7, and chalets for US$35 per person, including full board. There's diving (US$25 per dive, including equipment) and horse riding, as well as sailing, water-skiing and more.

Barra Reef *(☎/fax 011-867 3982 in South Africa, e execupol@mweb.co.za)*, which is 2km beyond Barra Lodge, has camping for US$7, two-person self-catering chalets with shared bathroom for US$47, as well as self-catering four-person houses for US$125. A bunkhouse is planned.

Both places have ***restaurants***, or you can buy fish from the local fishermen. There are no shops or other restaurants.

Getting There & Away

Air Barra Lodge offers fly-in packages from Jo'burg to Inhambane, with transfers to Barra.

Bus & Chapa Regular chapas connect Inhambane and Tofo (US$0.40). To Barra, take a chapa from Inhambane to Conguiana (US$0.40), which will deposit you at a car park. If you're lucky, you may see a vehicle from Barra Lodge here. Otherwise, you can walk (4km). Alternatively, take a chapa from Inhambane to Bar Babalaza, then hitch or arrange a lodge pick-up from there (R65, maximum seven people).

The daily TSL bus to/from Maputo via Inhambane departs Tofo at about 5.30 am.

Car A tar road connects Inhambane with Tofo (22km). After 15km a sand road splits off to Barra, which is 7km further (4WD only). If you don't have a 4WD, you can leave your car at Bar Babalaza and arrange a transfer.

MASSINGA

Massinga, a bustling district capital, has basic lodging at the ***pousada*** next to the bus stand, and good meals at ***Dalilo's*** on the main road.

North of town is the signposted turn-off for the ***Morrungulo Beach Resort*** *(☎ 011-783 7116 in South Africa, 04-303504 in Zimbabwe, e bookings@divetheworld.co.za)*, a relaxing place 13km from the main road set on a seemingly endless stretch of beach. Camping costs US$9 (US$15 for use of a thatched hut with plug points).

Self-catering four-person chalets are US$120. Fishing and diving can be arranged, and there's an eight-bed dive centre bungalow for US$170 per day. Access is usually possible with a 2WD.

VILANKULO

This town is one of southern Mozambique's most popular destinations. During South African holidays, it's overrun with 4WDs. Apart from good beaches, the main attraction is the nearby Bazaruto Archipelago.

BCM, just up from the Dona Ana Hotel, changes travellers cheques. There are no telephones in Vilankulo, though service is planned to start 'soon'.

Diving & Snorkelling

Vilankulo is close to the reefs of the Bazaruto Archipelago and offers good diving. Vilanculos Dive Charters (☎ 021-847 1160, fax 847 1169 in South Africa, ⓔ hotel@erinvale.co.za), based at the Aguia Negra Lodge (see Places to Stay) has many packages. A double dive including equipment and relaxation on Benguera Island costs US$80 per person; a five-dive package with gear is about US$200. They also arrange day snorkelling trips to Santa Carolina Island (US$40 per person, minimum five), and island transfers elsewhere in the archipelago. March to June, and November are the best months, and February (due to rain) is the worst.

If your budget is limited, the best contact is Sail Away, which offers relaxing two to four-day dhow safaris in the Bazaruto Archipelago from Vilankulo for US$40 per day all inclusive (minimum four people), with snorkelling, and overnights at Gabriel's Lodge on Benguera Island. Book through Mozaic (see Organised Tours in the Getting Around section), attention Kerry Butler, or stop by Sail Away's base in Vilankulo one road back from the beach between Campismo de Vilankulo and the Dona Ana Hotel (ask for Dave and Ema).

Places to Stay – Budget

The best place for backpackers is ***The 'New' Last Resort*** on the beach, about a 20-minute walk south from the bus stand/market. It's US$3 for camping, US$5 for a dorm, and US$14 for a two-person chalet. Every seventh night is free. There are cooking facilities, running water is planned, and meanwhile there are bucket showers. There's information on activities in the area, including walks and excursions to Bazaruto. To reach The 'New' Last Resort, head to John's Place and ask someone there to point the way.

The friendly ***Casa de Josef e Tina***, offers camping, and clean rooms in thatched cottages with bathroom for US$12 a double. ***Campismo de Vilankulo*** nearby has camping for US$5 per tent.

Na Sombra near the BCM has rooms for US$10/14. ***Cafe Edson***, further south on the same road, also has inexpensive rooms.

Sam's Backpackers at the entrance to town has basic rooms for US$8 (US$4/5 in one/two-person huts).

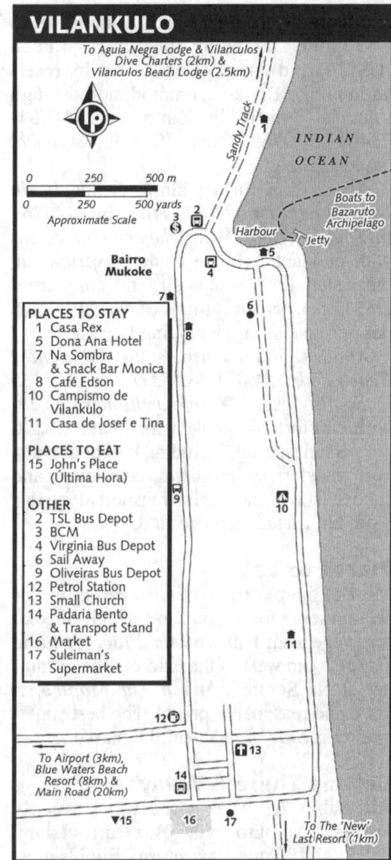

The once-grand ***Dona Ana Hotel***, with rooms overlooking the harbour from US$10, is usually deserted. It's slated for renovation in the near future.

About 8km out of town past the airport is the ***Blue Waters Beach Resort*** (ⓔ *backpack@harare.iafrica.com*), which has good camping for US$5 per person and a restaurant. You'll need your own transport.

Places to Stay – Mid-Range & Top End

About 500m north of the Dona Ana Hotel is ***Casa Rex***, a small, upmarket place with manicured grounds and rooms from US$70/90, including breakfast. Lunch (US$10) and dinner (US$15) are by reservation only. Book accommodation through Landela Safaris in Zimbabwe (☎ 04-734043, 707622, fax 708119, ⓔ res@landela.co.zw).

About 2km further along is the ***Aguia Negra Lodge*** *(☎ 021-847 1160, fax 847 1169 in South Africa, ⓔ hotel@erinvale.co.za)* with pleasant A-frame chalets overlooking the water. Each sleeps six and costs from US$33 per person (groups of six) to US$45 per person sharing, including breakfast.

Another 500m north is the ***Vilanculos Beach Lodge*** *(☎ 021-683 5337, fax 683 5336 in South Africa, ⓔ info@vilanclos.co.za)* with comfortable chalets for about US$90 per person sharing, including half board, airport transfers, windsurfing equipment and canoes. There's no public transport along this road, but lifts are easy to find.

Places to Eat

Most of the places mentioned earlier in this section serve food. You can eat well (including vegetarian) at ***John's Place (Última Hora)*** 200m west of the market. The restaurant at Na Sombre, ***Snack Bar Monica***, is good and reasonably priced. The best supermarket is ***Suleiman's*** near the market.

Getting There & Away

Air Sabin Air flies three times weekly to/from Maputo via Bazaruto Island (US$127/190 one way/return). Flights must be booked in Maputo; seats from Vilankulo, unless previously reserved, are on a standby basis.

Bus & Chapa Vilankulo lies 20km east of the main road. Some buses come into town, while others drop you off at the intersection. Chapas to the town centre cost US$0.40. To Maputo: Oliveiras (US$10) and TSL (US$12) depart daily at 5 am; Oliveiras also has a second bus departing about 8 am. For northbound travel, Oliveiras buses for both Chimoio (US$10) and Beira (US$10) depart about 5 am; otherwise, you'll need to go to the main road and catch transport from there.

Vilankulo's Name

Like many towns in Mozambique, Vilankulo takes its name from an early *régulo* (chief), Gamala Vilankulo Mukoke. The name was rendered as 'Vilanculos' during colonial times, but changed back to Vilankulo after independence. Mukoke (Mucoque) bairro, west of BCM, takes its name from Gamala Vilankulo's son.

The Oliveiras depot is about 1.5km north of the roundabout. The TSL and Virginia depots are further north, near the bank. Otherwise wait at Padaria Bento (bakery) near the market, as all buses stop here before leaving town. Chapas depart from near the market.

There's no regular public transport to the airport. If you'll be staying in one of the top-end lodges in Vilankulo or on the Bazaruto Archipelago, arrange transport with them in advance. Otherwise, it's usually easy to find lifts into town.

BAZARUTO ARCHIPELAGO

The Bazaruto Archipelago, 10 to 25km offshore between Vilankulo and Inhassoro, consists of five main islands – Magaruque (Santa Isabel), Benguera (Santo António), Santa Carolina ('Paradise Island'), Bazaruto and tiny Bangué. Much of the area is protected as a national park, with funding and management provided by various bodies, including the World Wildlife Fund (WWF). For the visitor, the archipelago offers azure waters, sandy beaches, diverse birdlife, pristine coral reefs, and abundant marine life such as the endangered dugong. Diving and birdwatching are the main activities. Entry is US$4.

Many visitors come on a fly-in package from South Africa, arranged through one of the top-end lodges, all of which also arrange diving and fishing charters.

Places to Stay & Eat

Gabriel's Lodge on Benguera Island has good camping for US$5 per day, with ablutions block and restaurant.

The other options (all top end) need advance bookings to their head office or through a tour operator, although if you turn up at Vilankulo or Inhassoro and talk to a boat owner with a radio link to the islands you can often arrange something on the spot. Rates are between US$150 and US$300 per person per night, including full board.

On Benguera Island, there's the ***Benguera Lodge*** *(☎ 011-483 2734, fax 728 3767 in South Africa, ⓔ benguela@icon.co.za)* and the ***Marlin Lodge*** *(☎ 012-543 2134, fax 543 2135 in South Africa, ⓔ marlinlodge@mweb.co.za)*.

Bazaruto Island has the ***Bazaruto Lodge*** *(☎ 01-305000, fax 305305)* and ***Indigo Bay*** *(☎ 04-745011 in Zimbabwe for information)*, currently being renovated.

The ***hotel*** on Magaruque Island is being renovated, while Santa Carolina's ***hotel*** is rundown but slated for renovation in the future.

Getting There & Away

Air For flights to Maputo, see under Getting There & Away in the Vilankulo section. Bazaruto Lodge operates a helicopter service between Vilankulo and Bazaruto (US$40 one way).

Boat The top end lodges provide speedboat transfers from the mainland for guests, often included in the price; otherwise it's about US$100 return. For day visitors, a speedboat from Vilankulo costs between US$80 and US$200 return, depending on the island. From Inhassoro to Bazaruto is about US$60.

Alternatively, you can go by dhow from Vilankulo or Inhassoro. Sail Away in Vilankulo can put you in touch with reliable dhow operators if you want to hire one for the day. Prices average US$16 per boat per day. For nonmotorised dhows, allow plenty of extra time to account for wind and water conditions; from Vilankulo to Benguera or Magaruque takes two to six hours.

INHASSORO

Inhassoro is a jumping-off point for Bazaruto and Santa Carolina islands, and a popular destination for South African anglers. The best place to stay is the pleasant ***Hotel Seta*** *(☎ 082-302099)*, with camping for US$5 and chalets for US$25. There's a restaurant and the hotel can assist with motorboat arrangements to the archipelago. For something cheaper, try the ***Complexo Salema Mfundisse Chibique*** near the bus station, with rooms for about US$12. Inhassoro suffered heavy flood damage during early 2000, so get an update on whether these places have re-opened before heading up here.

Inhassoro is about 15km east of the main road. Oliveiras has a daily bus to Vilankulo (US$1), and on to Maputo (US$11). There is also at least one bus daily northwards.

Central Mozambique

This section covers the provinces of Sofala, Manica, Tete and Zambézia. While the area doesn't have as many tourist destinations as southern Mozambique, it has much to offer, including interesting cultures and beautiful landscapes – particularly in western Manica and north-western Zambézia. It's also an important transit zone, encompassing both the Beira corridor (connecting Zimbabwe with Beira and the sea) and the Tete corridor (connecting Zimbabwe and Malawi); many travellers will at least pass through here. You'll encounter more English speakers in central Mozambique than elsewhere in the country. Places are described roughly south to north.

BEIRA

☎ 03

Beira, Mozambique's second-largest city, dates from the late 19th century. Its growth was fuelled by the development of its port (Mozambique's busiest) and the construction of the railway from Zimbabwe. Beira's compact central area, its numerous colonial-era buildings and its relaxed ambience make the city well worth visiting for a day or two.

About 40km south of Beira is the site of the ancient gold-trading port of **Sofala**, dating from at least the 9th century. In its heyday, Sofala was one of East Africa's most influential centres, with links to Kilwa (Tanzania), Madagascar, India and even Indonesia. San Caetano, the first Portuguese fort

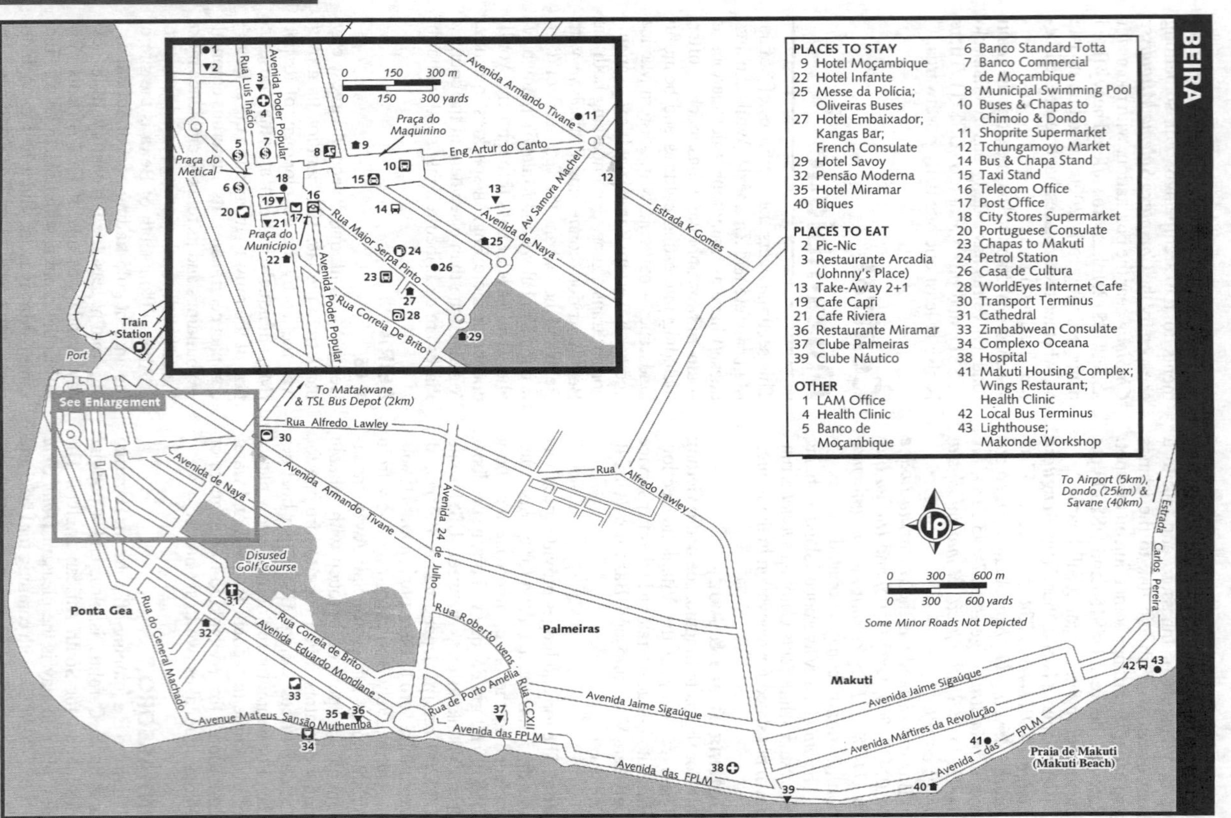
BEIRA
PLACES TO STAY
9 Hotel Moçambique
22 Hotel Infante
25 Messe da Polícia; Oliveiras Buses
27 Hotel Embaixador; Kangas Bar; French Consulate
29 Hotel Savoy
32 Pensão Moderna
35 Hotel Miramar
40 Biques
PLACES TO EAT
2 Pic-Nic
3 Restaurante Arcadia (Johnny's Place)
13 Take-Away 2+1
19 Cafe Capri
21 Cafe Riviera
36 Restaurante Miramar
37 Clube Palmeiras
39 Clube Náutico
OTHER
1 LAM Office
4 Health Clinic
5 Banco de Moçambique
6 Banco Standard Totta
7 Banco Commercial de Moçambique
8 Municipal Swimming Pool
10 Buses & Chapas to Chimoio & Dondo
11 Shoprite Supermarket
12 Tchungamoyo Market
14 Bus & Chapa Stand
15 Taxi Stand
16 Telecom Office
17 Post Office
18 City Stores Supermarket
20 Portuguese Consulate
23 Chapas to Makuti
24 Petrol Station
26 Casa de Cultura
28 WorldEyes Internet Cafe
30 Transport Terminus
31 Cathedral
33 Zimbabwean Consulate
34 Complexo Oceana
38 Hospital
41 Makuti Housing Complex; Wings Restaurant; Health Clinic
42 Local Bus Terminus
43 Lighthouse; Makonde Workshop
0 300 600 m
0 300 600 yards
Some Minor Roads Not Depicted
To Airport (5km), Dondo (25km) & Savane (40km)
Estrada Carlos Pereira
Estrada K Gomes
Rua Alfredo Lawley
Avenida 24 de Julho
Avenida Armando Tivane
Avenida de Naya
Rua Roberto Ivens
Rua CCXII
Rua de Porto Amélia
Rua Correia de Brito
Avenida Eduardo Mondlane
Avenue Mateus Sansão Muthemba
Rua do General Machado
Avenida Jaime Sigaúque
Avenida Mártires da Revolução
Avenida das FPLM
Palmeiras
Makuti
Ponta Gea
Praia de Makuti (Makuti Beach)
Disused Golf Course
Train Station
Port
See Enlargement
To Matakwane & TSL Bus Depot (2km)
0 150 300 m
0 150 300 yards
Praça do Maquinino
Eng Artur do Canto
Av Samora Machel
Rua Major Serpa Pinto
Rua Correia De Brito
Avenida Poder Popular
Rua Luís Inácio
Praça do Metical
Praça do Município

in Mozambique (1505), was built here with stones shipped from Portugal. Today, nothing remains of Sofala's former glory; the ruins of the fort have been taken over by the sea.

Orientation

The heart of Beira is Praça do Município, with shops, banks and telecom facilities nearby. The main street into town from the north is Avenida Samora Machel. Most public transport terminates at the square near the intersection of Avenida Samora Machel and Avenida Armando Tivane near Tchungamoyo Market, or at Praça do Maquinino. From Praça do Município, various streets lead through Ponta Gea to Avenida das FPLM, which runs along the ocean past the hospital, to Makuti Beach and the lighthouse.

Information

BCM off Praça do Metical changes travellers cheques. There's Internet access at WorldEyes on Rua Correia de Brito, near Hotel Embaixador (US$5 per hour, closed Sunday and on Monday morning).

For medical emergencies, try the new clinic near Restaurante Arcadia (see Places to Eat), or the clinic in the Makuti housing complex on Avenida das FPLM. Several countries have consulates in Beira, including Zimbabwe, France and Portugal.

Things to See & Do

The **cathedral**, south-east of the centre on Avenida Cahora Bassa, was built in the early 20th century with stones from the fort at San Caetano in Sofala. Near the **port** are many old colonial era buildings. East of the centre is **Praia de Makuti**, a good beach with fairly clean water and a few places to stay and eat.

There are two swimming pools; the municipal pool opposite Hotel Moçambique and the one at Clube Náutico. For **crafts**, try the market in front of Clube Náutico or the Makonde woodcarving workshop near the lighthouse. The lively **Tchungamoyo market** is full of imported goods, contraband and unsavoury characters, so travel lightly.

Places to Stay – Budget

Biques *(☎ 313051)* on Makuti Beach has good camping for US$5 per person and two-bed caravan trailers for US$10 (US$12 with three beds). Take any chapa heading to Makuti and ask them to drop you at Biques (US$0.15). A hire taxi costs about US$3.50. The bar also has food, and is a good place to meet other travellers.

Near the centre of the city, the ***Hotel Savoy*** near the Hotel Embaixador has rooms from US$8. ***Pensão Moderna*** *(☎ 324537)* two blocks south of the cathedral is better, with double/triple rooms for US$18/28, and a restaurant.

More popular is the ***Hotel Miramar*** *(☎ 322283)* near the beach. Clean rooms with bathroom cost US$13 (US$17 with air-con). ***Messe da Polícia*** near the bus stand has basic rooms for US$7/10, but is only worth considering if you need to catch early morning transport.

About 40km north of town on the Savane River is ***Savane*** *(☎ 04-495470 in Zimbabwe)*, a quiet resort with camping (US$6 per person), simple huts (no beds) for US$11, and one self-catering chalet (US$110). From town you'll need your own vehicle (4WD). Take the Dondo road past the airport to the right-hand turn-off for Savane. Continue 35km to the estuary, where there's secure parking and a boat to take you to the camp site.

Places to Stay – Mid-Range & Top End

The ***Hotel Infante*** *(☎ 326603)* south of Praça do Município has good-value doubles with bathroom and fan for US$23/24 (US$28/29 with air-con) and a rooftop restaurant.

Up a grade is the ***Hotel Moçambique*** *(☎ 329353)*, a blue high-rise building dominating the city centre, with singles/doubles from US$54/71.

The best in town is the ***Hotel Embaixador*** *(☎ 323121)* east of Praça do Município, where comfortable rooms are US$36/48 (US$54/66 with TV, air-con and hot water). Travellers cheques are accepted.

Places to Eat

Cafe Capri and ***Cafe Riviera***, both on Praça do Município, serve pastries and light meals and are great places to watch the passing scene.

The long-standing ***Pic-Nic*** *(☎ 326518)* north of Praça do Município has good meals from about US$6. Between the port and Praça do Metical is the less-expensive ***Restaurante Arcadia (Johnny's Place)*** *(☎ 322266)*, another Beira institution.

Take-Away 2 + 1 between Praça do Maquinino and Avenida Samora Machel has takeaway meals from around US$3 and a dining room upstairs.

Miramar Restaurante on the beach near the Hotel Miramar has standard fare from US$3. ***Clube Náutico*** *(☎ 313093)* also on the beach is a popular family place with main dishes from US$5.

Clube Palmeiras *(☎ 312947)* just off Avenida das FPLM has a good selection of local and Portuguese dishes from US$5.

For Chinese food, try ***Wings*** off Avenida das FPLM in the Makuti housing complex (open only in the evening from Tuesday to Friday, and from noon on Sunday).

The best two supermarkets are ***City Stores*** near Praça do Município, and the soon-to-open ***Shoprite***, off Avenida Armando Tivane.

Entertainment

Popular ***bars*** include Biques (see Places to Stay – Budget), Clube Náutico (see above) and the smarter ***Kangas*** at the Hotel Embaixador.

Inquire at the Casa de Cultura opposite Hotel Embaixador for information about music and dance performances. ***Complexo Oceana*** near the beach is a somewhat tawdry night-spot with live music and dancing.

Getting There & Away

Air LAM (☎ 324141) is at 85 Rua Costa Serrão, near Pic-Nic restaurant. It flies between Beira and Maputo (daily); Tete, Nampula and Quelimane (several flights weekly); and Pemba and Lichinga (weekly). There's a weekly flight direct to Jo'burg.

Bus & Chapa TSL and Oliveiras have daily buses between Beira and Maputo (US$28 express, 17 to 24 hours; US$20 ordinary, two days), and Oliveiras goes daily from Beira to Vilankulo (US$10, departing between 4 and 5 am). To Tete (US$6), there's a bus departing about 2 am from the Messe da Polícia. Otherwise, it's better to go to Chimoio and get transport there, as most traffic between Maputo and Tete does not enter Beira. This will mean overnighting in Chimoio since transport to Tete leaves there in the morning.

Chapas and minibuses run frequently to/from Chimoio (US$2.50) and Machipanda (US$3).

To Quelimane and Nampula, it's generally better to go via Tete and Malawi. Via Caia, you'll need to travel by truck and in stages; allow two days to Quelimane. At Caia there's a ferry which – as well as having frequent mechanical problems – can only run when the water levels are right. Backpackers can cross by dugout canoe, but drivers will need to inquire locally about whether the ferry is operating before heading this way. The road between Beira and Caia is in terrible shape (allow up to 10 to 12 hours), and often impassable in the rainy season.

Train Passenger trains to/from Zimbabwe have been indefinitely suspended.

Getting Around

To/From the Airport The airport is about 7km north-west of town (about US$8 in a hire taxi). Dondo chapas pass nearby, though you'll need to walk the last kilometre or so.

Bus & Chapa Chapas to Makuti (US$0.15) leave from Rua Major Serpa Pinto near Hotel Embaixador. Most other transport, including to Chimoio and Dondo, leaves from Praça do Maquinino near Hotel Moçambique. The TSL bus depot is in Matakwane, 2km north-east of town (reached by chapa from Praça do Maquinino). You can catch Oliveiras buses at the Messe da Polícia. Most long-distance buses stop at Tchungamoyo market to pick up passengers, though they're often full when they reach there.

Car Imperial (☎ 302650, fax 302651) and Avis (☎ 301263, fax 301265) are based at Beira airport.

Taxi There are taxis near Praça do Maquinino. A trip from the centre to Makuti costs about US$3.

CHIMOIO

☎ 051

Chimoio, capital of Manica Province, offers several nearby attractions. **Cabeça do Velho**, a large rock resembling the face of an old man at rest, is about 5km north-east of town past the market on Rua do Bárue. From the base, you can reach the top in about 10 minutes to enjoy the views.

About 35km west of Chimoio is the signposted turn-off for **Chicamba Real Dam**. It's a relaxing weekend getaway, and popular with Zimbabwean anglers. South-west of Chimoio on the Zimbabwean border is **Mt Binga** (2436m), Mozambique's highest peak. It's best climbed from Zimbabwe (see Chimanimani National Park in the Zimbabwe chapter for more details).

You can change travellers cheques at BCM on Avenida 25 de Setembro. LAM has a booking office for flights to Beira at Mafúia Comercial on Rua dos Operários.

Places to Stay & Eat

Pensão Flor de Vouga *(☎ 22027)* near the post office has basic rooms for US$12 and a restaurant. Better is the unrelated ***Residencial Flor de Vouga*** *(☎ 22469)* one block south above Banco Austral, with doubles for US$24 (US$36 with bathroom).

Motel Moinho *(☎ 23130)* about 2.5km outside town off the Beira road has decent rooms from US$16 and a restaurant.

Best in town is ***Executive Manica Hotel*** *(☎ 23135, fax 23129)*, signposted off the eastern bypass road, with clean, comfortable singles/doubles for US$40/60. There's parking, a restaurant, a pool and helpful staff.

Casa Msika *(☎ 011-603719 in Zimbabwe)* at Chicamba Dam has camping for US$3 per person, and three-bed rondavels for US$27 (US$20 for a double, and US$38 for six people). It's 4km south of the main road; the signposted turn-off is 45km west of Chimoio.

Take-Away at the eastern edge of town near the railroad tracks has meals from US$1 (closed Tuesday).

Maua in the Feira Popular has good local food. ***Elo 4*** opposite the government building on Avenida 25 de Setembro serves good Italian dishes from US$7. Also popular is ***Chicoteca***, 4km from town and signposted off the Zimbabwe road.

Getting There & Away

All transport leaves from near the train station. TSL buses depart at 5 am daily for Tete (US$5), and Oliveiras departs about 5 am for Vilankulo. There are frequent chapas to/from Manica (US$1) and the border, and frequent minibuses and chapas to/from Beira (US$2.50).

GORONGOSA NATIONAL PARK

About 65km east of Chimoio is the turn-off for Gorongosa National Park, once one of Southern Africa's best wildlife parks before it was destroyed by poaching and the war. Rehabilitation work has begun, but only basic infrastructure is in place. Little remains of the park's earlier wildlife populations, including the lion for which it was renowned, but you may still see impala, hippo and the occasional elephant. The park hosts rich birdlife, including several endemic species.

Entry costs US$16 per vehicle plus US$8 per person, which includes use of the park's camp site. You'll need to bring everything in with you, and your own 4WD.

MANICA

☎ 051

Tiny Manica, 70km west of Chimoio, lies in what was once the heart of the kingdom of Manica and also an important gold-trading area. About 5km from town, signposted from the town centre, are the **Chinamapere rock paintings**. Also nearby is **Vumba**, where Água Vumba mineral water is bottled.

Flamingo just west of the market and ***São Cristovão*** next door have lodging for US$8. About 1.5km further west and 500m south of the main road is ***Piscina***, with rooms for about US$12 and a ***restaurant***.

About 20km north of town (take the road behind the market) are the **Penha Longa Mountains**, which straddle the border with Zimbabwe. The area – home to the Shona people – offers pleasant scenery and good walking (but stick to the beaten path).

In the Mutombomwe area of Penha Longa is ***Casa Gaswa***, a simple but comfortable rondavel for US$12 (sleeps up to three). It's an ideal place for those with time who want to immerse themselves in local culture. For reasonable fees, the English-speaking caretaker can assist with meals (bring supplies from Manica market), and guides for hikes. For information on Casa Gaswa in Manica, contact Diniz Zandamela at Kwaedza Simukai Manica opposite the market (☎ 62217).

Chapas run frequently to/from Chimoio (US$1) and to the border, and several times daily from Manica market to Penha Longa (US$1). From the chapa terminus in Penha Longa, it's a 20-minute walk to Mutombomwe and Casa Gaswa (ask for John Machiri).

TETE

☎ 052

Tete was an important trading outpost well before the arrival of the Portuguese and today continues to be a major transport junction. The suspension bridge spanning the River Zambezi is an impressive sight.

BCM changes travellers checks. The immigration office is a few blocks uphill from Hotel Zambeze.

Places to Stay & Eat

For cheap lodging, try the ***Hotel Zambeze*** opposite BCM, with undistinguished singles/doubles for US$8/10 (US$16/20 with air-con). ***Piscina*** on the riverbank is a step up, with cramped rooms for about US$25.

Univendas *(☎ 23198)* near the immigration office rents spacious rooms above the shop for about US$28.

The most upscale place is ***Motel Tete*** *(☎ 23467, 23498)* on the river just past Piscina. Rooms with air-con and TV cost about US$50.

Piscina and Motel Tete have good ***restaurants***. For cheaper fare, try ***Pensão Central (Bar Melo)*** in the centre.

Getting There & Away

Air The LAM office (☎ 2055) is on Avenida 24 de Julho, several blocks up from Pensão Central. LAM flights connect Tete with Maputo (six weekly); Beira, Lichinga and Nampula (several weekly); and Quelimane (weekly). The airport is 6km out of town on the Moatize road. To get here, take any chapa heading to Moatize.

Bus & Chapa Chapas to Moatize leave frequently from the Moatize bus stand near immigration (US$0.15).

Chapas to Chimoio (US$5) depart from Mercado 1 de Maio.

The journey from Tete to Lichinga (US$28) via Blantyre and Mandimba is best done in stages.

For Malawi, chapas run frequently to Zóbuè and sporadically to Dedza from Mercado da OUA on the western side of town. At the border you'll need to change to Malawian transport. The daily TSL bus from Chimoio departs Hotel Kassuende in Tete about 10.30 am, continuing to Zóbuè. Alternatively, catch the bus that runs near Tete on its route between Harare and Blantyre.

For Harare, a few vehicles go direct to the border – otherwise take a chapa to Changara (US$2.50) and get transport from there. Departures are from Mercado 1 de Maio, 300m south of Hotel Kassuende. Alternatively, wait at the intersection of the bridge road and the road to Harare and try to catch one of the buses running between Blantyre and Harare, though this will be more expensive.

For Zambia, take a Moatize chapa over the bridge past the SOS compound to the petrol station, where you'll find chapas to Matema. From Matema, there's infrequent transport to Cassacatiza (on the border). There's no direct transport from Tete to the border town of Zumbo.

CAHORA BASSA DAM & SONGO

This dam, about 150km north-west of Tete near Songo, is one of the world's largest. It's at the head of a magnificent gorge in the mountains and makes a good excursion from Tete. You no longer need authorisation to visit the dam, though tours are possible only on certain days. For information, inquire at the Tete offices of Hidreléctrica de Cahora Bassa (HCB, pronounced ach-seh-beh) near the immigration office, a few blocks uphill from Hotel Zambeze.

In Songo, ***Pousada Sete Montes*** has basic rooms for about US$12, including hot running water, electricity and a ***restaurant***.

Chapas from Tete to Songo (US$3) depart a couple of times daily from Mercado 1 de Maio. From Songo, it's another 6km down to the dam; you'll have to walk or hitch.

QUELIMANE

☎ 04

Quelimane is the capital of Mozambique's densely populated Zambézia province and the centre of the Chuabo people. It stands on the site of an old Muslim trading settlement built on the banks of the Bons Sinais (Qua Qua) River in the days when it was linked to the River Zambezi. At one time it was the main entry port to the interior. Few traces of Quelimane's long history are evident today, and almost no old buildings remain. The main sights are the abandoned Portuguese **cathedral** on the waterfront, and the nearby **mosque**.

The BCM next to Hotel Chuabo changes travellers cheques.

Places to Stay

There are several cheap places; none appealing. ***Pensão Ideal*** on Avenida Samuel Magaia has accommodation for US$8 (US$13 with bathroom) and meals for about US$4. The ***Hotel 1 de Julho*** (*☎ 213067*) near Hotel Chuabo has grungy doubles for US$14. Opposite is ***Piscina Municipal de Quelimane*** with basic rooms for US$10 and a rooftop bar. ***Pensão Quelimane*** on Avenida Eduardo Mondlane has doubles from US$15 and meals from US$5.

The ***Hotel Zambeze*** on Avenida Acordos de Lusaka is better. Singles/doubles are US$15/20 (US$25/27 with bathroom), and meals cost about US$5.

A big step up from these places, and a Quelimane institution, is the ***Hotel Chuabo***

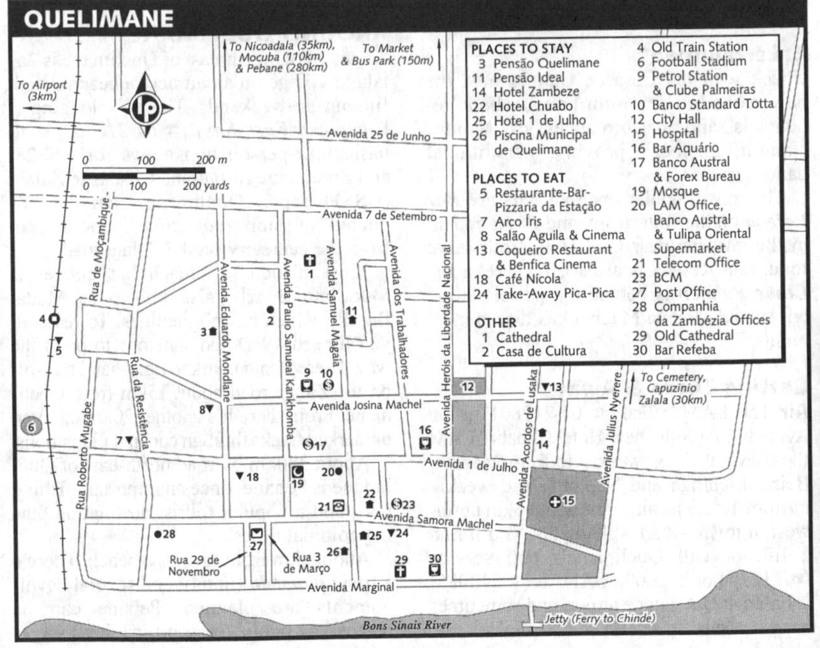

(☎ *213181, fax 213812)*. Large, comfortable rooms with TV, fridge and air-con cost US$85/115. It's probably the only place in Mozambique where you can still get your petticoat laundered (at least according to the laundry list).

Places to Eat

Cafes offering light meals from about US$3 include ***Cafe Nícola*** on Avenida 1 de Julho, ***Salão Aguila*** next to Cinema Aguila and ***Take-Away Piça-Pica*** opposite Hotel Chuabo. ***Arco Íris*** near the train station has air-con and a wider menu selection.

The best place for Zambézian dishes is Dona Guida's ***Coquinha*** 100m east of the Benfica cinema. For western fare, the best is ***Restaurante-Bar-Pizzaria da Estação*** near the train station, with a pizza oven and good-value Italian meals (closed Monday). The rooftop ***restaurant*** at Hotel Chuabo has good meals from US$6.

For self-caterers, ***Tulipa Oriental Supermarket*** next to the LAM office is well stocked.

Entertainment

Check with the Casa de Cultura near the new cathedral for information about rehearsals and performances of Montes Namúli, Zambézia province's traditional dance group.

The most popular open-air bars are ***Bar Refeba*** on the waterfront, and ***Bar Aquário*** in the gardens near City Hall. Both serve food, and Refeba is a disco on weekends. ***Clube Palmeiras*** behind the petrol station on Avenida Josina Machel has discos most nights.

Getting There & Away

Air The LAM office (☎ 04-212801) is on Avenida 1 de Julho near Hotel Chuabo. LAM flies several times weekly to/from Maputo, Beira, Lichinga and Nampula and weekly to/from Tete. The airport is about 3km north-west of town – start walking and you'll find a lift, or call Quelimane's taxi service (☎ 212704 or 212660). SANAir (☎ 213085) is based at Quelimane airport and sometimes has extra seats to sell on charter flights.

Bus & Chapa The bus park is near the market at the northern edge of town. Chapas run frequently to/from Nicoadala on the main highway (US$1). There's usually a direct bus to Nampula, departing between 4 and 5 am (US$10, one daily). Several vehicles run daily to Mocuba (US$2.50), for onward transport to Nampula via Alto Molócuè, or to Milange.

There's no direct southbound transport from Quelimane. If you want to go in stages, a bus departs Quelimane about 10 pm, arriving before dawn at the River Zambezi, where you'll need to wait until about 4 or 5 am when the first boats start crossing (or until 7 or 8 am for the ferry). On the other side at Caia, you'll find pick-ups and trucks for Beira. TSL buses go to Maputo (US$71, 48 hours, twice weekly) via Malawi and Tete.

Boat A ferry sails several times weekly to Chinde (US$8), near the mouth of the Zambezi.

AROUND QUELIMANE

About 30km north-east of Quelimane is **Zalala**, a village on an attractive beach which fills up on weekends. The only lodging is ***Complexo Kass-Kass*** *(☎ 04-212302)* with basic four-person bungalows for US$28, and a mediocre restaurant. Chapas to Zalala (US$1) depart Quelimane from the Capuchin mission *(capuzinio)*, about 1km from the cemetery on the Zalala road.

More difficult to reach but quieter is **Mundimo Beach** (also known as Madal Beach), which has no facilities. To reach it, you'll need 4WD and someone to point the way. There's an unmarked right-hand turn-off on the Zalala road about 15km from Quelimane. From there it's another 20km or so on unmarked tracks through coconut plantations.

About 280km by road north-east of Quelimane is **Pebane**, once an important fishing port, and a popular tourist destination during colonial times.

About 5km from town is a beach. There's a basic ***pousada*** (hotel), and several developments are planned. Pebane can be reached by public transport in (slow) stages via Namacurra, Olinga (Maganja) and Mucubela, or by 4WD.

MOCUBA

Mocuba is the junction town for travel from Quelimane to Nampula or Malawi. ***Pensão Cruzeiro*** on the main street has rooms for US$15 and meals from US$3.

Transport to Quelimane (US$2.50) leaves from the market. Transport to Nampula (US$10) leaves from the northern end of the main street. There are usually several vehicles daily between Mocuba and Milange (US$5.50), departing from the market, though you'll maximise your chances of a lift by walking west past the airstrip to the Milange road junction.

MILANGE

Milange is on the border with south-eastern Malawi. ***Pensão Esplanade*** has quite basic singles/doubles for US$7/14, and meals. The bank changes dollars and rand; moneychangers can help with Malawi kwacha. The road between Milange and Quelimane is fairly well travelled and finding a lift usually isn't a problem. (For more information on crossing the border, see Land in the Getting There & Away section of the Malawi chapter.)

GURÚÈ

Gurúè has a beautiful setting in the hills amid lush vegetation and tea plantations in one of the coolest, highest and rainiest parts of the country. There are some good walks in the surrounding area, starting with a stroll through the jacarandas on the northern edge of town. Gurúè is also the starting point for climbing Mt Namúli (2419m), Mozambique's second highest peak (see the boxed text 'Climbing Mt Namúli'). The town has no telephones, and the banks change cash only.

Places to Stay & Eat

Pensão Gurúè *(contact Gaia-Africa, e con struart.pp@teledata.mz, CP 109 Gurúè)* on the main street has reasonably clean rooms with bathroom (no running water) for US$14, and a ***restaurant***. Camping facilities are planned.

The other option is the friendly but very basic ***Complexo Sanzala*** one street eastward. Tiny rooms cost US$6; meals can be arranged.

Casa dos Noivos in the hills about 15km north-east of town has views over the surrounding countryside. Its one room, traditionally used for honeymooners, costs US$50. There's nothing here, not even electricity. To get here, follow the market road out of Gurúè to the first fork; turn left and continue for 2km through the jacarandas. Bookings must be made in advance through Companhia da Zambézia (☎ 04-213111, fax 213113 in Quelimane) or through their office about 2km north-west of Gurúè, past the market.

Getting There & Away

A few vehicles daily go to Quelimane, departing between 3 and 5 am from near the market (US$6). Otherwise go to Mocuba (US$3), where you'll find transport to Quelimane. There's at least one vehicle daily to Alto Molócuè, for onward transport to Nampula.

Most private vehicles to/from Alto Molócuè go via Nauela or a parallel shortcut road, while most public transport goes via Errego and the Nampevo junction (where you will most likely need to change vehicles).

The road to Cuamba is in decent shape, though there's little traffic. The best option to Cuamba is the train from Mutuáli. There is usually at least one chapa daily from Gurúè to Mutuáli, leaving in the morning, where you will have to wait at least several hours for the Nampula-Cuamba train to arrive. To Milange, it's usually fastest to go via Mocuba.

ALTO MOLÓCUÈ

This pleasant town is a refuelling point between Mocuba and Nampula.

If you need a place to stay, clean doubles at ***Pensão Santo António*** on the main square cost US$15; meals are about US$4. You can also sleep on the veranda.

Several vehicles daily go to/from Mocuba and Nampula.

Climbing Mt Namúli

Mt Namúli (2419m), which is the source or partial source for the Licungo (Lugela) and Malema Rivers, is considered sacred by the local Makua people. As travellers rarely hike up the mountain (due more to the fact that so few visitors come here, rather than to any technical difficulties posed by the climb), you should pay particular attention to respecting local customs and sensibilities.

According to tradition, before setting out, buy some *farinha de mapira* (sorghum flour) and some rice at the market in Gurúè. It should cost not much more than US$0.50 for everything. The climb begins about 6km outside Gurúè near UP5 (pronounced oo-pay-cinco), an old tea factory. To reach here, head south out of Gurúè along the Quelimane road. Go left after about 2km and continue several kilometres further to UP5. If you have a vehicle, you can drive to the factory and park there. With a 4WD it is also possible in the dry season to drive further up the mountain's slopes to Mugunha Sede, about 40km from Gurúè and the last village below the summit.

Shortly before reaching UP5 you will see a narrow but obvious track branching to the left. Follow this as it winds through unrehabilitated tea plantations and stands of bamboo and forest, until it ends in a high, almost alpine, valley about 800m below the summit of Mt Namúli. The views en route are superb. On the edge of this valley is Mugunha Sede, where you should seek out the *régulo* (chief) and request permission to climb the mountain. It would be helpful to have a person who can speak Portuguese or Makua, the local language, with you. If you have come this far with a 4WD, you will need to arrange to leave it here. The sorghum flour that you bought in Gurúè should be presented to the chief as a gift, who may save some to make traditional beer, and scatter the remainder on the ground to appease the ancestors who inhabit the area. The chief will then assign someone to accompany you to the top of the mountain, where another short ceremony may be performed for the ancestors.

Northern Mozambique

This section covers Mozambique's far north, including the provinces of Nampula, Niassa and Cabo Delgado. It's a scenic, topographically varied area, with Lake Niassa and the cool Lichinga Plateau to the west, dozens of massive and striking inselbergs between Cuamba and Nampula, and some of Africa's most idyllic beaches and islands along the coast. It's also fascinating culturally and historically – home to the large Makonde and Makua tribes, and birthplace of the Mozambican independence struggle.

As much of northern Mozambique is very remote – even most major towns have only minimal tourist infrastructure – travel here is mainly for the adventurous. More than elsewhere in the country, a basic knowledge of Portuguese (and, in the far north, Swahili) is essential. Places in this section are described roughly from south to north.

NAMPULA

☎ 06

Bustling Nampula is the commercial centre of northern Mozambique. The best bank for changing travellers cheques is Banco Internacional de Moçambique (BIM). Cheques can also be changed at BCM.

The excellent **National Ethnography Museum** is here, with explanations in English and Portuguese. It's open from 2 to 4.30 pm Tuesday to Saturday (until 6 pm on Friday) and 10 am to noon and 2 to 4 pm Sunday; entry is free but donations are welcome.

Other attractions include the **Sunday craft market** near Hotel Tropical, and the swimming pool and garden at the CFVM Piscina, which also has a bar and restaurant, plus music in the evenings (entry US$2.50). The large **cathedral** is a major landmark. In front is a large plaza.

Places to Stay

The cheapest places include: ***Pensão Central*** on Avenida Paulo Samuel Kankhomba near the train station; ***Pensão Marques*** on the same street; and ***Pensão Nampula*** just

Climbing Mt Namúli

About two-thirds of the way from the village is a spring where you can refill your water bottle, although it is considered a sacred spot and it may take some convincing to persuade your guide to show you where it is. Just after the spring, the climb becomes steeper, with some crumbling rock and places where you will need to use your hands to clamber up. Once near the summit, the path evens out and then gradually ascends for another 1.5km to the mountain's highest point. The top of Namúli is often shrouded in clouds, so it is likely you will have better views during the climb than from the summit itself. After descending the mountain, present the rice that you bought at the Gurúè market to the chief as thanks.

There is no public transport on the mountain's lower slopes. If you want to walk to Mt Namúli from either Gurúè or the UP5 warehouse, you will need to set out early and come fully equipped to camp. The best camping spot is in the high valley near Mugunha Sede. It is also possible to pitch a tent in the level area on the summit just below Namúli's highest point, although you may have to scratch around for a bit of earth. If you do this, the closest water source is the spring mentioned earlier, about a one-hour walk from the summit.

It is possible to do the climb in a long day from Gurúè if you drive as far as Mugunha Sede (allow about four hours), from where its another three hours on foot to the summit. The road to Mugunha Sede has been rehabilitated and is in rough but decent condition, but a few of the bridges are rickety and difficult to drive over. En route, about 20km from Gurúè, is a bridge which is not passable by even a 4WD (although a motorbike can make it over). During the dry season, you can negotiate this spot by going down through the riverbed.

Many thanks to Richard and Jacqueline Dove and to Rolf Gsell, who have provided most of this information.

off it. All are dingy, with singles/doubles from US$5/10 (Pensão Central) to US$8/20 (Pensão Marques).

Better are ***Pensão Parques*** on Avenida Paulo Samuel Kankhomba south of the market and ***Pousada Francisco*** near the traffic circle, both with rooms for about US$12/15.

The ***Hotel Brasília*** near BCM is a step up. Clean doubles with bathroom and running water cost US$12, and there's a restaurant.

The soulless ***Hotel Lúrio*** *(☎ 212520)* near Pensão Nampula has rooms with bathroom from US$28/46.

Nampula's best is the ***Hotel Tropical*** *(☎ 212232)* not far from the National Ethnography Museum, one block north of Avenida Eduardo Mondlane. It has helpful staff and its pricey but comfortable air-con rooms cost US$55/80, including a good buffet breakfast. Travellers cheques are accepted.

Places to Eat

There are numerous places with main dishes from about US$5. ***Cafe Carlos*** *(☎ 217960)* just off Rua dos Continuadores has Italian and other meals, and is one of the best. It's open daily, despite the sign to the contrary. There is a popular terrace ***restaurant*** at Hotel Tropical (see Places to Stay). Opposite is ***Copacabana***, with fresh pasta.

Other places include ***Restaurante Lord*** off Avenida Paulo Samuel Kankhomba, and ***Clube Tenis*** on Avenida Paulo Samuel Kankhomba, with pleasant outdoor seating. ***Almeida de Garrett*** off Avenida Eduardo Mondlane and ***Sporting Clube*** near Copacabana, are OK, and popular for lunch.

Nampula's best nonvegetarian dining is at ***Pinto's***, which features roast pig on Saturday, *bife pedra* (a popular meat dish) and similar fare. It's several kilometres outside town and you'll need your own transport to get there. Take the Quelimane road to the right-hand Ribáuè turn-off. Pinto's is 500m down the Ribáuè road on the right.

Also out of town is the popular ***Quinta de Gallo*** on a small lake. The restaurant is open only on the weekend during the day. Continue past Pinto's another couple of kilometres down the Ribáuè road. Turn left at the sign reading 'Araújo'; continue another few kilometres to the restaurant.

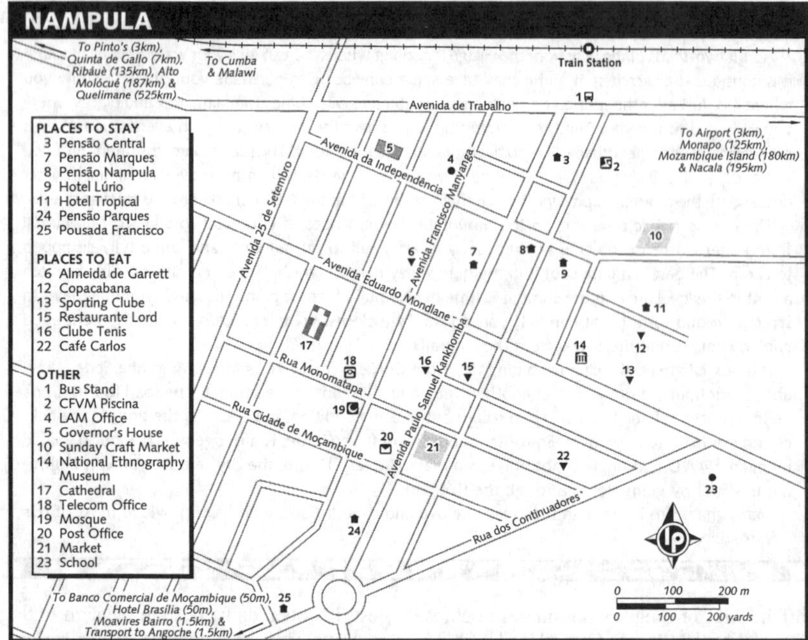

Getting There & Away

Air The LAM office (☎ 212801) is on Avenida Francisco Manyanga. LAM flies from Nampula to Maputo (daily), Beira, Lichinga, Quelimane and Tete (all several times weekly) and Pemba (weekly).

Bus & Chapa Transport to Monapo (US$1.60), Mozambique Island (US$2.50), Nacala (US$2.50) and Pemba (US$8) leaves from the train station. Transport to Ribáuè, Mocuba (US$8) and Quelimane (US$10) leaves from the same road about 2km west of the train station near the Ribáuè road junction. Transport to Angoche (US$3) leaves from Avenida das FPLM in Moavires bairro, about 2km south of the centre. Most transport departs between 5 and 7 am, and as early as 4 am to Quelimane. TSL buses to Maputo (US$80) via Malawi depart Monday and Thursday at 4 am.

Train A daily passenger train connects Nampula and Cuamba (see under Getting There & Away in the Cuamba section later in this chapter). There's a train three times weekly between Nampula and Nacala, though most people go by road (see under Getting There & Away in the Nacala section later in this chapter).

Car Rental Imperial Car Rental has an office at Nampula airport (☎/fax 216312).

MOGINCUAL

☎ 06

Mogincual, an old trading settlement 175km south-east of Nampula, sits near an estuary divided by a narrow finger of land from the sea. The only tourist facilities are at the self-contained ***Fim do Mundo*** *(☎ 526610 daytime, ask for Arthur; or 520017 evening)* on the estuary 3km from town, which offers camping for US$4 and chalet-style accommodation for US$50 per person, including full board. The area is good for birdwatching. Fishing, snorkelling and diving (bring your own equipment) can also be arranged, as can excursions to Mozambique Island. Advance reservations are essential. The camp is closed in February.

There's an airstrip at Mogincual for charter flights. Otherwise, road transfers can be arranged from Nacala and Nampula. Chapas run once or twice daily from the market in Monapo (US$3).

ANGOCHE

Angoche, an old Muslim trading centre dating from at least the 15th century, was one of the earliest settlements in Mozambique and an important gold- and ivory-trading post. Although it later declined, the town continued to play a significant role in coastal trade and in the 18th century was one of the major economic and political centres along the northern coast. Little remains from those days, although Angoche still has a certain charm. About 7km north of town is Praia Nova, a good beach. There are no facilities, and you'll need to walk or have 4WD. Hitching is easiest on weekends.

In town, there's a basic ***pensão*** with rooms for about US$8. More upscale is the ***casa tipo colonial*** (colonial-style house) overlooking the water. Book through CCA (☎ 06-7219, ext 2722, 06-212722). The cost is US$50 for the house, or US$25 per double room.

Occasional chapas connect Nampula and Angoche during the dry season, departing Nampula about 5 am. Access gets difficult during the rains.

MOZAMBIQUE ISLAND

☎ 06

Mozambique Island (Ilha de Moçambique) is about 2.5km long and about 3km off the mainland (linked by a bridge). It is one of the country's most fascinating destinations.

As early as the 15th century it was an important boat-building centre, and its history as a trading settlement – with ties to Madagascar, Persia, Arabia and elsewhere – dates back well before that. Vasco da Gama landed here in 1498 and in 1507 a permanent Portuguese settlement was established on the island. Unlike Sofala to the south, where the Portuguese established a settlement at about the same time, Mozambique Island prospered as both a trading station and a naval base. In the late 16th century, the sprawling fort of São Sebastião was constructed. The island soon assumed a role as capital of Portuguese East Africa – a status that it held until the end of the 19th century when the capital was transferred to Lourenço Marques (now Maputo).

Apart from its strategic and economic importance, Mozambique Island also developed as a missionary centre under the Portuguese, with numerous orders establishing churches here and Christians intermixing with the island's traditional Muslim population and its Hindu community. Various small waves of immigration over the years – from places as diverse as East Africa, Goa, Macau and elsewhere – contributed to the ethnic mix on the island. Today, its heterogeneity continues to be one of its most marked characteristics, although Muslim influence, together with local Makua culture, dominates.

Today, Mozambique Island is an intriguing anomaly – part ghost town and part active community. It's also a picturesque and exceptionally pleasant place to wander around. While many of its buildings are sadly dilapidated, several have been restored in recent years, particularly since 1991 when the island was declared a World Heritage Site by UNESCO.

Most of Mozambique Island's historic buildings – many of which date from between the 16th and 19th centuries – are located at its northern end (Stone Town), while the majority of residents live in the southern end in reed houses (Makuti Town).

Information

There's an excellent information office next to the museum (☎ 610081), open from 8.30 am to noon and 2 to 5 pm daily, with all sorts of information on things to do and see on and around the island. The staff are very helpful and can assist you with finding lodging, and arranging excursions to nearby destinations. They also offer guided tours of the fort, and bike rental for about US$4 per half day.

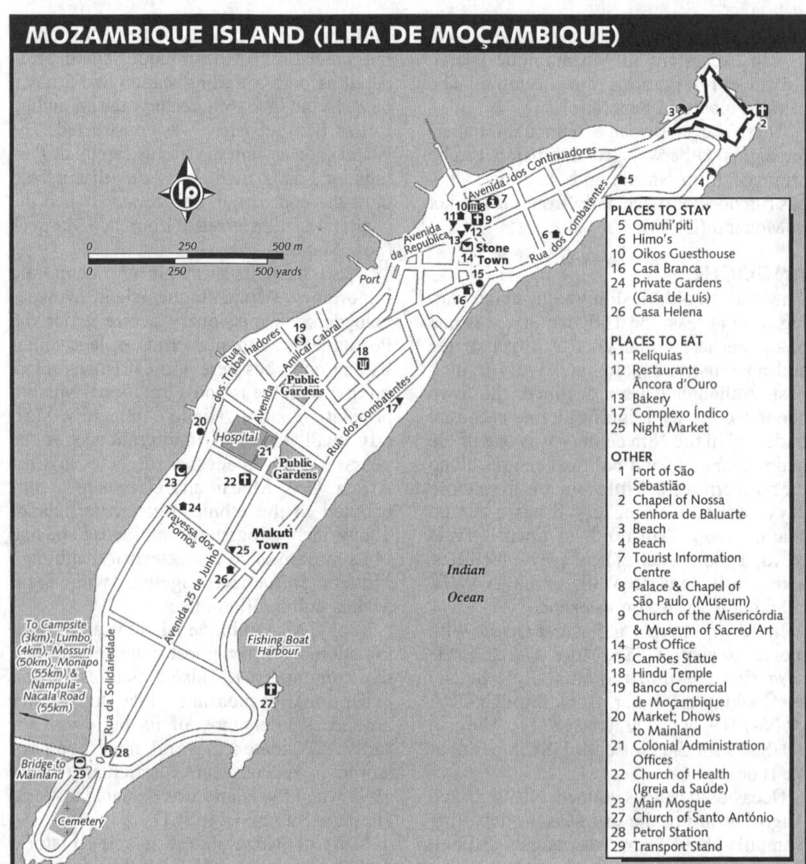

It is usually possible to change cash at BCM on the western side of the island. The closest places to change travellers cheques are Nampula and Nacala.

Things to See & Do

The main attraction is the **Palace and Chapel of São Paulo** – formerly the governor's residence – dating from 1610 and now a **museum** (☎ 610081, fax 610082, ilha@teledata.mz). Many rooms have been renovated to give a remarkable glimpse into what upper-class life must have been like during the island's heyday in the 18th century. In addition to a variety of ornaments from Portugal, Arabia, Goa, India and China, the museum contains much original furniture, including an important collection of heavily ornamented Indo-Portuguese pieces. In the chapel, note the altar and the pulpit (which was made in the 17th century by Chinese artists in Goa). On the ground floor of the building is a **Maritime Museum** documenting the island's relationship with the sea. Behind the palace are the **Church of the Misericórdia** and the **Museum of Sacred Art**, containing religious ornaments, paintings and carvings. The museum is housed in the former hospital of the

Holy House of Mercy, a religious guild which operated in several Portuguese colonies from the early 1500s, providing charitable assistance to the poor and sick.

The three museums on the island are open from 8 am to noon and 2 to 5 pm Wednesday to Sunday, although even on other days there's usually someone available who can show you around. Entry is free, but a small donation (in the box by the entrance) is appreciated.

At the northern end of the island is the **Fort of São Sebastião**, the oldest complete fort still standing in sub-Saharan Africa. It's open until about 5 pm daily; entry is free. Immediately beyond the fort, on the tip of the island, is the recently rehabilitated **Chapel of Nossa Senhora de Baluarte**, built in 1522 and considered to be the oldest European building in the southern hemisphere. At the southern end of the island is the **Church of Santo António.**

In the main town are several more recent buildings including the restored **bank** on Avenida Amilcar Cabral, and the ornate **colonial administration offices** overlooking the gardens east of the hospital. In the centre of the island is a **Hindu temple**, and on its western edge a fairly modern **mosque**. To the south is a **cemetery** with Christian, Muslim and Hindu graves.

An effort is being made to clean up the island's **beaches**, and you can now swim at the one just south-west of the fort, as well as on the north-eastern end of the island.

Places to Stay & Eat

For backpackers, the best place is ***Private Gardens***, also called Casa de Luís, on Travessa dos Fornos in Makuti Town, with accommodation for US$8 per person. There's also a ***camp site*** on the mainland next to the bridge (US$4); for details, inquire at Casa Helena or the tourist information office.

Otherwise, there's accommodation in several private guesthouses, most of which also have kitchen facilities. The best is ***Casa Branca*** (*☎ 610076*) on the island's eastern side near the Camões statue. Comfortable singles/doubles with excellent views cost US$16/24, including continental breakfast. ***Casa Helena*** also on the eastern side, and ***Himo's*** in the north-east near Rua dos Combatentes, have rooms for about the same price. ***Oikos*** guesthouse near the museum costs US$19/27.

The old pousada near the island's north-eastern tip has been renovated and is scheduled to open by early 2000 as the four-star ***Omuhi'piti*** (*☎ 526351, fax 526356*). Comfortable rooms with satellite TV will be priced from US$80/90, including breakfast.

The best restaurant on the island is ***Relíquias*** (closed Monday), with a pleasant ambience and good food from about US$4. It's on the western side, not far from the museum. ***Complexo Índico*** on the island's eastern edge is also good. The more basic ***Âncora d'Ouro*** near the museum has fish or chicken and rice dishes from about US$3, and there's a bakery nearby. For street food, there's a good ***night market*** near Private Gardens.

Getting There & Away

If you are driving, be aware that wide vehicles won't pass over the bridge and maximum weight is 1.5 tonnes.

Air There's an airstrip at Lumbo on the mainland for charter flights.

Bus & Chapa At least one bus and several chapas daily go to/from Nampula (US$2.50). All transport departs from the bridge. To get to Lumbo on the mainland costs US$0.30.

Boat There is no regular dhow transport to or from Lumbo (for details of boat connections between Mozambique Island and Chocas, see the following Chocas section).

CHOCAS

☎ 06

Chocas, opposite Mozambique Island near Mossuril, has a good beach and the pleasant ***Complexo Chocas-Mar*** (*☎ 212798*). Two-person cabins with bathroom cost US$27 (US$31 on weekends) and meals can be arranged.

Nearby are two villages formerly used as summer holiday spots by wealthy residents of Mozambique Island. **Cabaceira Grande,** the more interesting of the two, has a most well-preserved church dating from the late 16th century and ruins of the former governor general's palace dating to the mid-19th century. **Cabaceira Pequena** has a few old houses, an old Swahili-style mosque and the ruins of a cistern used as a watering spot by Portuguese sailors.

To reach Chocas by road, take any transport between Monapo and Mozambique Island, and get off at the signposted Mossuril junction 25km from Monapo. Chapas go from here to Mossuril (20km), from where it's another 12km or so (traversed sporadically by chapas) to Chocas. Hitching is fairly easy on weekends; at other times it's very slow.

From Chocas, it's about a 30-minute walk (at low tide) to Cabaceira Pequena, and an hour to 1½ hours to Cabaceira Grande. Alternatively, you can take a dhow from near the market on Mozambique Island to Cabaceira Pequena (US$0.20) and Cabaceira Grande (US$0.40). If there's no wind, the trip across the bay can take up to six hours. A better option for reaching Cabaceira Pequena from Mozambique Island is to contact the tourist information centre on the island (see Information under Mozambique Island earlier in this chapter), which can arrange dhow transport for US$10 per person (minimum two people).

NACALA

☎ 06

Nacala is northern Mozambique's busiest port. The main street runs from Nacala Porto (the area near the harbour and train station) to Nacala Alta (the higher town). BIM, just off the street, changes travellers cheques for US$5 commission.

Outside town are some beaches. The most popular are **Fernão Veloso** and **Relanzapo**. To get to both, take the turn-off for the airport and military base at the entrance to Nacala. Fernão Veloso is about 5km beyond the military base.

To reach Relanzapo, turn right on a dirt road before the base and continue 15km east. There's no public transport to either place. Hitching is possible on weekends; otherwise there is not much traffic. There are a few private homes at Fernão Veloso, but no tourist facilities, and nothing at Relanzapo.

Places to Stay & Eat

Cheapest is the ***pensão*** above the video shop just off the main street, with basic rooms for US$9 and dorms for US$5. ***Complexo Bela Vista*** *(☎ 520133)* in Nacala Alta is better, with singles/doubles for US$13/21 (US$30 for a double with bathroom) and a restaurant.

The ***Hotel Nacala*** on the main road has been renovated and is scheduled to open by early 2000 as the three-star ***Maiaia*** *(☎ 526351, fax 526356)*. Rooms will cost from US$70/80 with breakfast.

Restaurant Sandokan *(☎ 526740)* opposite Banco Standard Totta has good meals from US$5.

Getting There & Away

You can travel to/from Nampula by train (US$2, six hours, three times weekly), but most people go by road. Trains depart Nacala on Tuesday, Thursday and Sunday at 1.30 pm, and from Nampula on Tuesday, Thursday and Saturday at 5.30 am.

A couple of vehicles go direct to Nampula (US$2.50) daily, departing in the morning from below the market.

Chapas go frequently to Monapo (US$1.60), where you can get transport to Mozambique Island, Namialo (the junction for Pemba) and elsewhere.

Shipping offices (for trying to arrange passage to South Africa) are near the train station by the port (see also Sea & Lake in the main Getting There & Away section earlier in this chapter).

CUAMBA

☎ 071

Cuamba is a rail and road junction, and the economic centre of Niassa Province.

For inexpensive lodging, try ***Namaacha*** *(☎ 2549)* with singles/doubles from US$8/16 (plus US$1.60 for breakfast), or ***Pensão São Miguel*** *(☎ 2701)*, with rooms for US$15 (US$18 with bathroom), including breakfast.

Vision 2000 *(☎ 2632)* has comfortable rooms from US$20 (US$24 with TV and refrigerator) and a decent ***restaurant*** with slow service.

Other cheap dining options include ***Bar-Restaurante Escondidinho*** near the market, with xima and sauce for US$3 and the even cheaper ***Pensão Namúli*** on the street behind the market.

Getting There & Away

Bus & Chapa To/from Nampula, it's cheaper and more comfortable to travel by train. By road, the scenic route via Gurúè is in better shape than the direct route via Malema and Ribáuè. Public transport is scarce on both.

The best way to reach Gurúè is to take the train to Mutuáli, from where you can find onward transport, though you may have to wait several hours as chapas don't coordinate with the train.

To Lichinga, there's usually one vehicle daily departing about 6 am from Maçaniqueira market behind the rail yard. For other destinations, the best time to find transport is in the afternoon at the station when the train from Nampula arrives.

Road transport goes sporadically to Entre Lagos and costs US$2.50.

Train The Cuamba-Nampula train departs daily at 5 am from Cuamba and at 6 am from Nampula (US$31/8/4 for 1st/2nd/3rd class, 8½ hours). There's a dining carriage on alternate days. To transport your vehicle (about US$100), you'll need to load it on the train the night before and arrange a guard to be sure it's not tampered with. During the journey you can ride with your vehicle.

A slower train runs most days between Cuamba and Entre Lagos (US$1.50, 3rd class only, five hours); the schedule varies. For information about connections in Malawi, see Malawi in the main Getting There & Away section of the Mozambique chapter. The train service between Cuamba and Lichinga has been suspended.

MANDIMBA

The best place to stay in this border town with Malawi is ***Restaurante-Bar Ngame*** about 200m from the bus stand. Clean rooms with fan are US$8 per person. Several vehicles run daily between Mandimba and Lichinga. You can take a bicycle-taxi to the border, 7km away.

LICHINGA

☎ 071

Lichinga (formerly Vila Cabral) is the capital of Niassa province, the most remote and least visited part of Mozambique. It lies at about 1400m and the surrounding area, dotted with pine groves, is pleasant for walking and cycling. Niassa Province's well-known song and dance group, Massukos, perform here.

BCM in the town centre changes travellers cheques. The immigration office is just off the airport road, diagonally opposite Escola Industrial e Comercial Ngungunhane. Check at Radio Moçambique in the town centre for information on performance schedules of Niassa Province's well-known song and dance group, Massukos.

Places to Stay

The cheapest places are ***Hotel Chiwindi*** *(☎ 2345)* and ***Rival***, both near the market, with basic rooms for about US$8 per person.

Pousada *(☎ 2232, fax 2223)* has clean singles/doubles for US$12/16 (US$20 for a double with bathroom). It's conveniently located in the centre, but there's no running water.

Ponto Final *(☎ 2912)* at the north-eastern edge of town is better. Rooms with bathroom cost US$16/20 twin/double bed. There's running water for at least part of the day, and when it's not flowing, the staff are very helpful with arranging a hot bucket.

About 2km outside town in the forest is ***Quinta Capricórnio*** with camping for US$4 per person (US$6 if you want to use one of their tents). Full board in a four-person guesthouse costs US$16 per person. The owners have information about activities in the surrounding area and are planning a tourist information centre and notice board. They can also provide assistance with excursions to Meponda and boat trips on Lake Niassa. To get here, take the road heading west past the government building until the tarmac ends. Continue south-west through the forest for about 1.5km, staying left at the forks.

Places to Eat

The best restaurant – and one of the best in northern Mozambique – is ***O Chambo*** *(☎ 3354)* in the FEN complex next to the market. Great soups cost US$1 and well-prepared main dishes from US$4.

Other places in FEN include ***Hoyo Hoyo***, which can prepare Indian food given advance notice, and ***Euro-Treff***, which was scheduled to open by late 1999 with European-style dishes.

There is a good ***restaurant*** at Pousada (see Places to Stay). A full meal including soup, main dish and fruit costs US$6, and on Sunday there's a popular outdoor all-you-can-eat buffet from noon to 3 pm (US$12).

Lanchonete Modelo several blocks down from the BCM on the main street is good for hamburgers and snacks.

Quinta Capricórnio (see Places to Stay) sells home-made cheeses, yoghurt, jams and curries. It also offers meals, though for dishes other than local food you'll need to order in advance.

Comércio Geral (Nurbay's) on the main street is the best-stocked supermarket.

Getting There & Away

Air LAM (☎ 2434) is on Rua da LAM off the airport road. It has flights to/from Maputo (three times weekly, via Tete), Nampula (twice weekly) and Beira (weekly). Flights from Lichinga tend to be heavily booked; buy your ticket well in advance and arrive at the airport early.

Bus & Chapa All transport departs from next to the market, and buses/chapas to most destinations leave early – be there by 5 am. There's usually one minibus and one or two trucks daily to Cuamba (US$8, eight to 11 hours), several pick-ups to Metangula (US$4), and a couple daily to Meponda (US$2). To Mandimba, take a chapa (US$4, 4½ hours), or any transport heading to Cuamba. The road to Mandimba and Cuamba is unpaved, but in reasonable condition during the dry season.

It's also possible to reach Lichinga from Malawi, via Likoma Island and Cóbuè (see Mozimbique under Lake in the Getting There & Away section of the Malawi chapter; see also Boat in the Getting Around section of the same chapter).

AROUND LICHINGA

About 100km north of Lichinga is the so-called **Sanga Reserve** or Chipange Chetu (not gazetted), site of some interesting community development projects. For information about walks in the Sanga area, check at Quinta Capricórnio in Lichinga (see Places to Stay in the Lichinga section).

About 160km north-east of Lichinga on the Tanzanian border is the 42,000 sq km **Niassa Reserve**. It has significant numbers of elephant, buffalo, duiker, zebra and more, although because of their relatively low population densities, the reserve's vastness and the lack of roads, the best way to see them is by charter plane.

There's no official accommodation at present; a camp is being constructed. Until the reserve is further developed, visits are feasible only for the well heeled. For more information, contact the Sociedade Para a Gestão e Desenvolvimento da Reserva do Niassa (@ telemedia.3@online.no or gmadal@teledata.mz).

LAKE NIASSA

The Mozambican side of Lake Niassa (the Mozambican name for Lake Malawi) is much less developed than on the Malawian side. The main towns along the shore are Meponda, Metangula and Cóbuè.

Meponda

Meponda is a small village 60km south-west of Lichinga. ***O Pomar das Laranjeiras*** on the beach has one brick rondavel for US$4 per person, or you can camp. Food can be arranged with lots of advance notice. The other option is ***Restaurante-Bar Milagre IV da Praia*** nearby, which was building some basic huts when we passed through.

Boats to Malawi (US$5.50) depart from the tiny harbour in the centre of town (see the main Getting There & Away section of the Malawi chapter).

Metangula

Metangula is a district capital and the main town on the Mozambican shore of Lake Ni-

MOZAMBIQUE

assa. The main attraction for tourists is the beach at **Chuwanga**, 8km north of Metangula.

The friendly but basic ***Galeria Comercial de Mtendele Boma*** at the town's southern end has tiny rooms for US$4/5.50. Otherwise, you may be able to arrange something at ***Combinado Pesqueiro*** near the naval base.

Katawala's on the beach at Chuwanga has simple but comfortable bungalows for US$7/8, or US$16 for a four-person chalet. Camping costs US$4 per tent, and day use of facilities, including a grill, costs US$5. Meals are available for US$3 to US$4.

There's no regular public transport between Metangula and Chuwanga, but hitching is usually easy.

Cóbuè

Tiny Cóbuè is the immigration post for travellers heading to/from Malawi via Likoma Island (for details, see Sea & Lake in the main Getting There & Away section earlier in this chapter). ***Pensão San Miguel*** has rooms for US$3 per night; meals can be arranged with plenty of advance notice.

About 15km south of Cóbuè is the **Manda Wilderness Area** community development and conservation project. There's rustic bush-style ***camping*** at Mchenga Nkwichi on the lake for US$70 per person, including meals and guided walking safaris, plus a US$10 per night community development fee. No free camping is permitted. There is no telephone contact for this place in Mozambique, though you can try to email at mandawilderness@malawi.net. Otherwise, bookings can be made in Malawi through Tonga Tours (see Nkhata Bay in the Malawi chapter) or Ulendo Safaris (see Lilongwe in the Malawi chapter).

There are usually a couple of slow boats weekly between Cóbuè and Metangula (US$4), though don't be surprised if you get stuck in Cóbuè for up to a week; allow up to three days for the trip. You may be lucky and find a ride with one of the occasional speedboats doing business along the lakeshore. These boats take between six and eight hours, and are more easily arranged in Metangula than in Cóbuè. Otherwise, you'll need to walk (about two days) or cycle (with your own bike). There's no public transport by road.

PEMBA

☎ 072

Pemba (formerly Porto Amelia) lies on a peninsula jutting into the enormous Pemba Bay. It was established in 1904 as administrative headquarters for the Niassa Company and is now capital of Cabo Delgado province.

Orientation & Information

At the south-western tip of the peninsula is the low-lying baixa area around the port and old town, with traders and several banks along Rua do Comércio, the main street. East of here and up the hill is the town centre where there are a few hotels and restaurants, more shops, and offices.

There is a small tourist information centre at CeeBee Pemba (☎/fax 2743), on the airport road. BCM on Rua do Comércio changes travellers cheques. You can access the Internet at Inforline.net on the main road near Pastelaria Flor d'Avenida (US$15 per hour, or US$20 per month to send/receive emails via their account).

For assistance with car rentals, charter flights to the Quirimba Archipelago, LAM bookings and air tickets to Mtwara and Dar es Salaam (Tanzania), contact Viatur (☎ 3431, fax 2249, e viatur@emilmoz.com), on the main road in the plaza just up from Banco Standard Totta.

Things to See & Do

On Pemba's outskirts are several colourful and vibrant bairros, including the Muslim area of **Paquitequete** on the south-western edge of the peninsula and **Cariacó**, east of town, which has a good **market**.

The surrounding area offers beautiful palm-fringed beaches. Although tourism here is in its infancy, the industry is set for a boost, with new developments planned, including a top-end resort complex. Thus far, most activity has centred on **Wimbi Beach** (also spelled Wimbe), an attractive stretch of coast 5km east of town. Diving starts about 300m offshore, where the coastal shelf drops off steeply. There are many other sites nearby, most unexplored.

Climbing palm trees looks like fun, but you might want to leave it to the experts!

CI Divers (☎ 3520, fax 3717) is based at Complexo Naútilus (see Places to Stay) and offers a variety of excursions as well as full equipment rental and instruction. Jet skis, fishing boats, sailboards, windsurfing equipment and bicycles can also be hired. On the road between town and Wimbi Beach is a **Makonde carving workshop**. Closer to town is CeeBee Pemba (see Orientation & Information), with good-quality **crafts** from Cabo Delgado and elsewhere in Mozambique.

Places to Stay & Eat

Town Centre All the following places also offer food at prices which reflect their room rates. Cheapest is ***Pensão Marítimo*** on Rua do Comércio, with grubby singles/doubles for US$6/12. Much better is ***Pensão Baía*** *(☎ 2848)* in the upper part of town: it's clean, safe and friendly with simple rooms from US$12. Food can be arranged.

For more comfort, try the ***VIP Pemba Hotel*** *(☎ 2548, fax 2249)* on the hill near the governor's mansion. Good rooms – some small, others spacious – cost from US$20/30 with bathroom (from US$25/35 with air-con).

Down the hill and one block off the main street is the friendly ***Residencial Lys*** *(☎ 2951)* where doubles with fan cost US$20 (US$24 with air-con). The ***Hotel Cabo Delgado*** *(☎ 2558, ☎/fax 3552)* on the main street has comfortable but overpriced air-con rooms with bathroom for US$28/35.

For snacks and cheap meals, try ***Pemba Takeaway*** east of the Hotel Cabo Delgado, or the long-standing ***O Encontro*** on Rua do Comércio. ***Á Tasca*** on the main street is more expensive. ***Pastelaria Flor d'Avenida*** opposite Á Tasca is considered to be Pemba's best place to eat, with good meals from US$5.

Wimbi Beach About 2km beyond Complexo Naútilus along the beach road, ***Cashew Camp*** has camping for US$3 per tent and dinner for US$4. Shower blocks are being constructed. The camp ground is nothing special, but it's a good place to link up with other travellers and get the scoop on nearby destinations, road conditions etc.

Complexo Naútilus *(☎ 3520 or 2826, fax 3717, ⓔ nautilus@emilmoz.com)* on the beach has popular but cramped four-person bungalows for US$65, six-person bungalows cost US$75 and a two-person suite with TV and refrigerator costs US$80. Add a government tax of 17% to all these prices. Meals start from US$8. Despite the fact that the hotel is only about 20m from the sea, frozen seafood is the order of the day.

On the street behind the Naútilus is ***Complexo Caraçol***, with apartments (no cooking) for two to four people for US$55 plus tax (US$25/35 for smaller singles/doubles at the back). Book through Complexo Naútilus.

Dining options include ***Mar e Sol*** near the Naútilus and the popular ***Restaurante Wimbi***, another 100m further down the beach.

Getting There & Away

Air The LAM office (☎ 2434) is on Avenida 25 de Setembro near Banco Standard Totta. LAM flies three times weekly to/from Maputo (weekend special US$370 return) and weekly to/from Beira and Nampula.

Viatur (see Information earlier in this section) runs a flight most Fridays between Pemba and Mtwara in Tanzania (US$175/340 one way/return) connecting with Air Tanzania's Mtwara–Dar es Salaam flight. In Mtwara, book through Celestina at the parish office of St Paul's church in Majengo.

Bus & Chapa The best transport to Nampula is on the 'tanzaniano', which departs daily at 4 am from the *desportivo* in Pemba, opposite the seven-storey building near Hotel Cabo Delgado. Otherwise, several vehicles depart between 5 and 7 am from Embondeiro, Pemba's long-distance bus station on the Nampula road about 3km from the centre (look for the large baobab tree).

For points north, there's a 'tanzaniano' bus every second day to Moçimboa da Praia (US$8), departing between 3 and 3.30 am from the desportivo. Otherwise, you'll need to go to Embondeiro for a chapa; there are a couple daily, leaving early.

Transport to Metuge and other nearby villages, and some northbound transport, leaves from the shop of Osman Yacob ('Osman'), on the main road about 1.5km from the centre.

Boat The best place to arrange dhow transport to the Quirimba Archipelago or elsewhere is the beach behind the mosque at Paquitequete. Alternatively, contact Well En-Dhowed (☎ 3631) which runs dhow trips along the coast – ask for Mia, or go through CeeBee Pemba (see Orientation & Information).

QUIRIMBA ARCHIPELAGO

The Quirimba Archipelago consists of about a dozen islands plus numerous islets along the coastline between Pemba and the Rovuma River. Some, including Ibo and Quirimba Islands, have been settled for centuries and were already important Muslim trading posts when the Portuguese arrived in the 15th century.

The best-known of the islands is **Ibo** which was fortified as early as 1609, and which had become the second-most important town in Mozambique by the late 18th century, after Mozambique Island. It was a major slave trading post during this era, with demand spurred by French sugar plantation owners on Mauritius and elsewhere. Today, Ibo is a fascinating, almost surreal place with wide streets lined with dilapidated villas, and crumbling, moss-covered buildings. At its northern end is the star-shaped fort of São João dating from the late 18th century, known now for its silversmiths.

Other islands include **Quirimba**, which in the 16th century served as a centre for missionary work, and later was the site of a large coconut plantation; and **Matemo** and **Quisiva**, both sites of large Portuguese plantation houses. Tiny **Rolas Island** (Ilha das Rolas), between Matemo Island and Pangane, is uninhabited except for some seasonal fishing settlements.

All the islands can be visited, although many do not have fresh water, and most either have no facilities or only the most basic facilities. When travelling among the islands, remember that access (and exit) is tide-dependent and plan accordingly to avoid being stranded. Dense mangrove swamps connect some of the islands. Although channels were cut during Portuguese times, you'll need to take a guide along to navigate among them.

Places to Stay & Eat

On Ibo, most visitors stay at ***Casa de Janine***, with rooms for US$12, breakfast for US$2 and other meals for US$4. Camping costs US$1.60 per tent. The owner also has a slightly more expensive bungalow out of town on the beach. Also on Ibo, Telecomunicações de Moçambique has a ***guesthouse*** in the centre with doubles for about US$28. There's talk of dive operations opening on Ibo; check at CI Divers in Pemba for an update (see Things to See & Do in the Pemba section).

On Quirimba, there's a pleasant ***guesthouse***, with rates of US$50 per person for full board. There's a satellite number for reservations (☎ 00-9-873-761-670428). Otherwise, contact Pele or Isabel at the Pemba Takeaway (see Places to Stay & Eat in the Pemba section) for assistance with bookings. Don't expect to show up here and camp for free in the yard.

Several new places are planned. In Quissanga on the mainland, backpackers can ask around for Andre, a South African who's building a ***camp site*** on Quilaluia Island, south of Quirimba Island. A-frame ***cottages*** are planned for Quipaco, a tiny island halfway between Pemba and Quissanga, notable for its birdlife.

Getting There & Away

To reach Ibo or Quirimba, you'll need to go first to Quissanga, on the coast north of Pemba. There's a direct chapa to Quissanga daily from the fish market behind the mosque in Paquitequete in Pemba (US$3.50, five hours, departing about 4 am). Otherwise, there's usually another vehicle or two leaving Pemba in the morning from Embondeiro (Pemba's long-distance bus station on the Nampula road). From Quissanga, some vehicles continue to the village of Tandanhangue, where you can get dhows to Ibo (US$1) and Quirimba. Otherwise, you'll need to walk from Quissanga to Tandanhangue (one hour) – ask locals to show you the shortcut. If you're driving to Tandanhangue, take the dirt track to the left about 2km before Quissanga town. You'll need 4WD for the road from Pemba.

The dhow trip can take anywhere from one to six hours, depending on winds and tides. If you need help in Quissanga, ask for Iussuf, who can arrange meals while you're waiting for the tides to come in and will guard your vehicle for about US$1 per day. He also has an enclosed area where you can sleep.

An alternative to a dhow is the motorised boat of the District Health Directorate on Ibo (US$28 for the boat hire). Call the post office on Ibo (☎ 072-140, 440 2421 or 3240) in advance and ask the staff to have the hospital send the boat to Tandanhangue to fetch you.

From Pemba, *La Portino*, a fishing boat, sails once or twice weekly direct to Ibo, departing Paquitequete about 3 am. Those with larger budgets can arrange speedboat charter from Pemba direct to the islands. Ask at Complexo Naútilus or Cashew Camp (see Places to Stay in the Pemba section). Alternatively, you could arrange air charter through Viatur (see Information in the Pemba section).

MACOMIA

Macomia is the turn-off point for Pangane. ***Pensão Kwetu-Kumo***, about 1.5km from the main road, has basic rooms for US$6. There's only sporadic transport between Macomia and Mucojo, a few kilometres before Pangane; hitching is possible, but slow. If you're stranded here, a good place to ask for a lift is at Chung's Bar, on the main intersection.

About 40km north of Macomia is **Chai**, where Frelimo's military campaign against colonial rule began in 1964 with an attack on a Portuguese base.

PANGANE

Pangane is a long, palm-fringed beach just north of Mucojo, and about 50km off the main north-south road. There's a village here, with many seasonal fishermen from Nacala and points to the south, so the beach isn't always the cleanest though the setting is beautiful. There's a ***camp site***, for which you'll need to be self-sufficient, and ***Suki's Guesthouse*** with singles/doubles for about US$10.

There's sporadic transport to Macomia. You can also arrange a dhow to/from any of the islands from here, including Ibo.

MUEDA

Mueda, the main town on the Makonde Plateau, was built as an army barracks during the colonial era. In 1960, the town was the site of the infamous 'massacre of Mueda' (see The Independence War in the History section earlier in this chapter). There's a statue commemorating Mueda's role in Mozambican independence, and a mass grave for the 'martyrs of Mueda', at the western end of town. Just behind this monument is a ravine over which countless more Mozambicans were hurled to their deaths.

While Mueda itself is lacking in charm, its setting is attractive and there are good views from the escarpment along the southern and western edges of town. To see Makonde carvers at work, head to outlying villages.

Pensão Takatuka on the tar road has reasonably clean rooms for US$12 (US$16 in the annexe out the back) and a ***restaurant*** where you'll need to order well in advance.

There's at least one vehicle daily to Pemba (US$8), leaving Mueda at about 5 am from the main road opposite the market, and several vehicles to Moçimboa da Praia (US$2.50). There's usually one chapa daily from Mueda to Nangade (US$4), from where you may be able to cross the border into Tanzania (see under Land in the main Getting There & Away section earlier in this chapter). All transport from Mueda leaves early.

MOÇIMBOA DA PRAIA

Moçimboa da Praia is an important dhow port and the last major town before Rovuma River. If you leave or enter Mozambique here, have your passport stamped at the immigration office, near the police station in the eastern part of town. Tanzanian shillings are accepted at some places and a few words of Swahili will often get you further than Portuguese. To change cash, try Banco Austral or some of the Indian shop owners.

Places to Stay & Eat

The friendly ***Pensão Leeta*** *(☎ 072-2515 or 2326, ext 130 or 166)* at the entrance to town near the transport stand has clean, comfortable rooms with two beds and shared bathroom for US$14. Camping is possible in the grounds for US$4, and meals can be arranged. Manuel, the owner, is a good source of information on Moçimboa da Praia and the surrounding area.

Grupo Leeta, the owners of Pensão Leeta, is also building a ***camp ground*** on the beach, due to open by mid-2000. Camping will cost US$4 per tent, and there will be rooms in a house, as well as a ***restaurant*** and facilities for self-catering. Campers will be able to stow gear in the house during the day. Contact details are the same as for the pensão, above.

Complexo Miramar is another good place with a beachfront location at the end of the main road and clean, comfortable bungalow singles/doubles for US$14/16. The owners can arrange for the early morning chapa to the Rovuma River to pick you up. There's a ***restaurant*** with good, reasonably priced meals and surprisingly prompt service; a popular bar; and on weekends, a loud disco.

In the centre of town are a couple of basic places, including the ***Pensão Residencial Magid***, with rooms for US$6/12.

Getting There & Away

Two pick-ups daily go to/from the Rovuma River (US$12) via Palma (US$4), leaving Moçimboa da Praia between 3.30 and 5 am. Travelling from Moçimboa da Praia over the Rovuma to Mtwara in Tanzania takes about half a day.

If you're coming from Tanzania, be at Namoto by noon to avoid having to sleep at the border.

The best place to arrange dhow transport from Moçimboa da Praia to other destinations is at the small harbour on the eastern edge of town. For general information on dhow travel, see under Boat in the main Getting Around section.

PALMA

Palma is a large village nestled among coconut groves. There's some good basketware and mat-weaving here. The immigration office and the post office are in the upper part of town. Offshore are some idyllic islands. Dhow transport can be arranged from the small harbour near Hotel Palma. You'll need to take everything with you, including water.

The friendly but basic ***Hotel Palma*** is about 2km from the upper part of town along the sea. It has rooms for about US$6 and meals can be arranged with advance notice.

All transport in Palma leaves from the Boa Viagem roundabout at the entrance to town, about 3km from Hotel Palma. Travelling between Palma and Tanzania is described in the main Getting There & Away section earlier in this chapter. From Palma to the Rovuma River, chapas charge a special 'foreigners' price of US$8 (locals pay US$4). Transport from the Rovuma, south to Moçimboa da Praia, passes through Palma between 11 am and 2 pm. From Palma to Moçimboa da Praia costs US$4.

NAMIBIA MAP INDEX

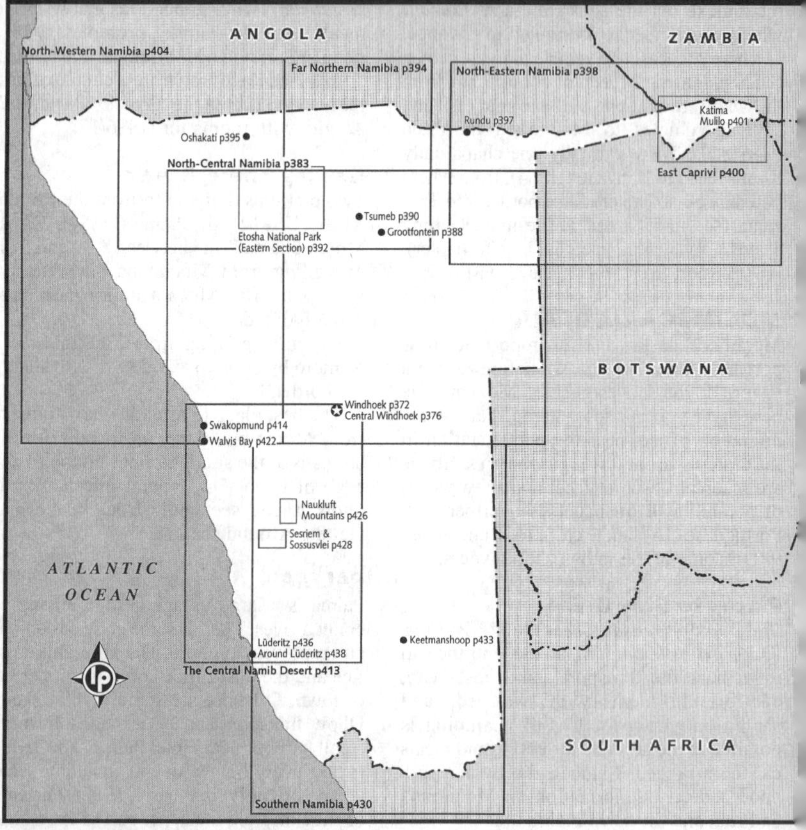

ANGOLA
ZAMBIA
North-Western Namibia p404
Far Northern Namibia p394
North-Eastern Namibia p398
Katima Mulilo p401
Rundu p397
Oshakati p395
East Caprivi p400
North-Central Namibia p383
Tsumeb p390
Grootfontein p388
Etosha National Park (Eastern Section) p392
BOTSWANA
Windhoek p372
Central Windhoek p376
Swakopmund p414
Walvis Bay p422
Naukluft Mountains p426
Sesriem & Sossusvlei p428
ATLANTIC OCEAN
Keetmanshoop p433
Lüderitz p436
Around Lüderitz p438
The Central Namib Desert p413
SOUTH AFRICA
Southern Namibia p430

ADRIEN VADROT

Damaraland

Namibia

Wedged between the Kalahari and the chilly South Atlantic, Namibia is a country of vast potential and promise. Rich in natural resources and spectacular beauty, it has also inherited from its colonial and African roots a solid modern infrastructure and a diversity of cultures and national origins: Herero, San, Khoikhoi, Owambo, Afrikaner, German, Asian and others. Its attractions are unparalleled in Africa and include fine bushwalking opportunities, rugged seascapes, appealing African and European cities and villages, and nearly unlimited elbow room.

NAMIBIA AT A GLANCE

Area: 825,000 sq km

Population: 1.73 million

Capital: Windhoek

Head of State: President Sam Nujoma

Official Language: English

Currency: Namibian dollar (N$)

Exchange Rate: US$1= N$6.35

Highlights

- Etosha National Park – see the incredible variety of African animals at one of the world's greatest wildlife-viewing venues
- Skeleton Coast – explore this lonely, ethereal coastline, studded with rusting shipwrecks
- Damaraland – visit rock engravings, and the Brandberg, Namibia's highest massif
- Fish River Canyon – marvel at the spectacular vistas while hiking through this enormous canyon
- Diverse cultures – learn about the many fascinating cultures of Namibia
- Namib Desert – wander amid this vast, dune-studded desert and discover a variety of desert wildlife

Facts about Namibia

HISTORY

It's generally accepted that Southern Africa's earliest inhabitants were San, nomadic people organised in extended family groups who had adapted to the severe terrain. Population densities were low and much movement took place. San communities came under pressure from Khoikhoi (Hottentot) groups (due to competition for territory, water and hunting grounds), the ancestors of the modern Nama, with whom they share a language group. The descendants of these Khoisan (the modern group comprising the San and Khoikhoi peoples) still live in Namibia, but few have retained their traditional lifestyles.

Between 400 and 300 BC, the first Bantu people appeared on the plateaus of south-central Africa. Their arrival marked the appearance of the first tribal structures in Southern African societies. Most of the San gradually disappeared from the scene – retreating to the desert or the swamps of the Okavango Delta to avoid enslavement by the dominant Bantu society.

Around AD 1600 the Herero people, who were Bantu-speaking pastoralists, arrived in Namibia from the Zambezi area and occupied the north and west of the country. This

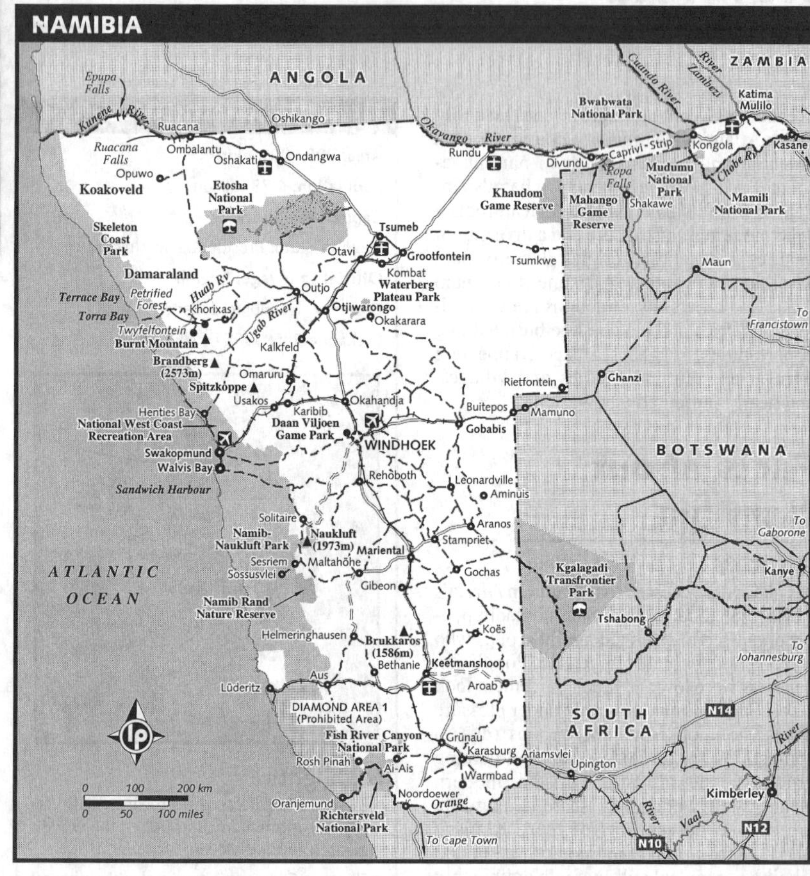

caused conflicts with the Khoikhoi, with whom they were competing for the best grazing lands and water holes. In what is now called Kaokoland, the more aggressive Herero displaced not only the Khoikhoi but also the few remaining San and the Damara people (whose origin is unclear).

It is thought that the Nama people of present-day Namibia are descended from South African Oorlam (bands of Khoisan people displaced from the Cape region by European encroachment) Khoikhoi groups who held out against the Herero through violent clashes in the 1840s to 1880s. In addition, another Bantu group, the Owambo, settled in the north along the Okavango and Kunene Rivers, and were probably descended from people who had migrated from eastern Africa over 500 years earlier. Their language is similar enough to that of the Herero that it's thought they were part of the same migration.

Because Namibia has one of the world's most barren and inhospitable coastlines, it was largely ignored by the European maritime nations until relatively recently. The first European visitors were Portuguese mariners seeking a way to the Indies in the late 15th century, but they confined their activities to erecting stone crosses along the shoreline as coastal navigational aids. It wasn't until the last-minute scramble for colonies towards the end of the 19th century that Namibia was annexed by Germany, except for the enclave of Walvis Bay, which was taken in 1878 by the British for the Cape colony. In 1904 the Herero launched a rebellion, and later that year were joined by the Nama, but it was quickly and brutally suppressed by the German colonists.

The Owambo living in the north of the country were luckier and managed to avoid conquest until after the start of WWI in 1914, when they were overrun by Portuguese forces fighting on the side of the Allies. In that same year the German colony abruptly came to an end when its forces surrendered to a South African expeditionary army also fighting on behalf of the Allies.

At the end of WWI, South Africa was given a mandate to rule Namibia (then known as South West Africa) by the League of Nations. The mandate was renewed by the United Nations (UN) following WWII but the UN refused to sanction the annexation of the country by South Africa.

Undeterred, the South African government tightened its grip on the territory, and in 1949 granted parliamentary representation to the white population. The bulk of Namibia's viable farmland was parcelled into some 6000 farms owned by white settlers, while male black workers with their families were confined to their 'reserves' and workplaces by labour and pass laws.

South African intransigence over Namibia was based on its fears of having yet another antagonistic government on its doorstep and on losing the income that it derived from mining operations there. Namibia is rich in minerals such as uranium, copper, lead and zinc, and is also the world's foremost source of gem diamonds. These were all mined by South African and western multinational companies under a generous taxation scheme that enabled them to export up to a third of their profits every year.

Forced labour had been the lot of most Namibians since the German annexation, and was one of the main factors that led to mass demonstrations and the development of nationalism in the late 1950s. Around this time, a number of political parties were formed and strikes organised, not only among workers in Namibia but also among contract labourers who had been sent to work in South Africa. Support was sought from the UN and by 1960 most of these parties had merged to form the South-West African People's Organisation (SWAPO).

SWAPO took the issue of South African occupation to the International Court of Justice in 1966. The outcome was inconclusive, but the UN General Assembly voted to terminate South Africa's mandate and set up the Council for South West Africa (renamed the Commission for Namibia in 1973) to administer the territory. The South African government responded to the UN demand by firing on demonstrators and arresting thousands of activists. At the same time, SWAPO launched its campaign of guerrilla warfare.

In 1975, the Democratic Turnhalle Alliance (DTA, named after the site of its meetings) was officially established as the dominant political party. Formed from a combination of white political interests and ethnic parties, it turned out to be a toothless debating chamber, which spent much of its time in litigation with the South African government over its scope of responsibilities. The DTA dissolved in 1983 after it had indicated it would accommodate SWAPO. It was replaced by yet another administration, the Multi-Party Conference, which had even less success than the DTA and quickly disappeared. Control of Namibia passed back to the South African-appointed administrator-general.

These attempts to set up an internal government did not deter South Africa from continuing its grip on Namibia. It refused to negotiate on a UN-supervised program for Namibian independence until the estimated 19,000 Cuban troops were removed from neighbouring Angola. In response, SWAPO intensified its guerrilla campaign, and as a result, movement in the north of the country became severely restricted.

In the end, it may not have been the activities of SWAPO or the pressure of international sanctions which forced the South Africans to the negotiating table. The white Namibian population was growing tired of the war and the economy was suffering badly. South Africa's internal problems also had a significant effect. The war was costing South Africa some R480 million per year by 1985 and conscription was widespread. Mineral exports which once provided around 88% of the country's GDP had plummeted to just 27% by 1984. This was due mainly to falling world demand and depressed prices, but also to fraud and corruption.

The stage was finally set for negotiations on Namibia's future. Under the auspices of the UN, the USA and the former USSR, a deal was struck between Cuba, Angola, South Africa and SWAPO, in which Cuban troops would be removed from Angola and South African troops removed from Namibia. UN-monitored elections were held in late 1989 on the basis of universal suffrage. SWAPO collected a clear majority of the votes, but voter support was insufficient to give it the sole mandate to write the new constitution.

Following negotiations between the various parties, a constitution was adopted in February 1990 and independence was granted the following month under the presidency of SWAPO leader, Sam Nujoma. Namibia's constitution is one of the few in Africa that provides for a democratically elected government and incorporates a series of checks and balances to ensure that things don't get out of hand.

President Sam Nujoma's policies are based on a national reconciliation program to heal the wounds left by 25 years of armed struggle and a reconstruction program based on the retention of a mixed economy and partnership with the private sector. At the time of research, Nujoma had almost served out his second (and constitutionally, his last) five-year term, but was attempting to change the constitution to allow him to run for a third term. This set off alarm bells among pro-democracy groups, and a coup attempt in north-eastern Namibia (see the boxed text 'Caprivi Woes') warned the government that all is not entirely well. Despite those glitches, Namibia's economy remains relatively stable, corruption is mostly contained and for most Namibians, hopes for the future remain high.

GEOGRAPHY

Namibia is predominantly an arid country of great geographical variation. Broadly speaking, its topography can be divided into four: the Namib Desert and coastal plains in the west; the eastward-sloping Central Plateau; the Kalahari Desert along the Botswana and South African borders; and the densely wooded bushveld of the Kavango and Caprivi regions.

CLIMATE

Namibia's climatic variations correspond roughly to its geographical subdivisions. The most arid region is the Central Namib, where summer daytime temperatures may climb to over 40°C, but can fall to below freezing during the night. Rainfall is heaviest in the north-east, which enjoys a subtropical climate and along the Okavango River, rainfall reaches over 600mm annually. The northern and interior regions experience two rainy seasons; the 'little rains' fall between October and December, while the main stormy period occurs from January to April.

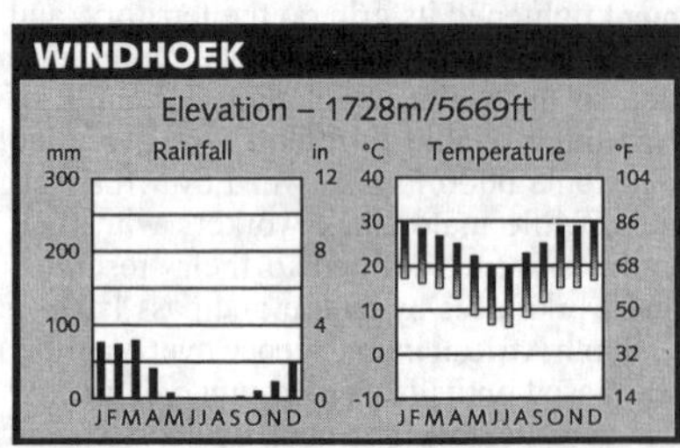

ECOLOGY & ENVIRONMENT

With a small human population spread over a large land area, Namibia is in better environmental shape than most African countries, but challenges remain. The Ministry of Environment & Tourism (MET) is largely a holdover from pre-independence days and, as a result, its policies strongly reflect those of its South African counterpart. Although changes are currently afoot, the country still lacks coherent environmental guidelines.

Caprivi Woes

On 2 August 1999 several rebels attempted to seize Katima Mulilo by attacking the Mpacha airport, as well as the television and police stations. The perpetrators were mainly members of Namibia's Lozi minority, who were dissatisfied with rule by the country's Owambo majority. In the end, none of the intended targets were captured. The rebels were very poorly trained – their one day of military instruction involved watching the video *Top Gun* – and after only a few hours, they were summarily put down by the Namibian Defence Force (NDF), which then set about arresting anyone else in the area who appeared to support the Caprivian separatist cause.

The leader of the revolt, Mishake Muyongo, is a former vice president of SWAPO (the South-West African People's Organisation – the ruling party in Namibia) and a proponent of Caprivian independence. He and 2000 followers crossed into neighbouring Botswana in 1998 to plot the August 1999 incursion.

The rather hysterical government reaction to the incursion was to close the Caprivi's Botswanan and Zambian borders for over a month and dispatch a rogue contingent of the Special Field Force (SFF). This unit, comprising former freedom fighters, set about intimidating and torturing suspected rebel sympathisers and zealously enforcing a 6 pm to 6 am curfew, which remained in place until early September 1999. Among the victims were: a bystander who was injured by rebels and then beaten by government soldiers as he sought treatment; former MP Geoffrey Mwilima, who was assaulted by government forces; an inebriated tourist from Windhoek, who was shot on the grounds of the Zambezi Hotel in Katima Mulilo; and a Katima Mulilo doctor who was shot dead as he responded to an emergency call (the injuries were to his chest area, but the killers claimed he was fleeing).

During the troubles, tourists, truckers and other motorists were intimidated at NDF roadblocks and many overseas tour companies cancelled their block bookings to Caprivi area lodges. The rebel leader Mr Muyongo escaped to Denmark, which has been required by international agreement to provide asylum. (As a result, there have been threats to Danish expatriates in Namibia, and Danes may want to check the current situation before travelling to Namibia.)

Although the Caprivi seems reasonably calm at present, travellers should check the current situation before visiting.

As yet, local people have seen few benefits from wildlife-oriented tourism and their encroachment on protected areas continues to affect local ecosystems. Many ranchers in the south view wildlife as a nuisance, while local people in the more densely populated north see wildlife reserves as potential settlement areas and wildlife itself as a food resource, and a threat to crops and human life.

Overfishing and the outbreak of red tide (an explosion of phyto-plankton density, sometimes toxic to fish and, indirectly, to humans) along the Skeleton Coast in the early 1990s have decimated sea lion populations, through starvation. Commercially inspired culling has also had a major impact.

Poaching in Damaraland, which is not an officially protected area, has caused declines in the populations of desert rhino, elephant and other species. Although the white rhino was wiped out in Namibia prior to 1900, some have now been reintroduced into Waterberg and Etosha and are doing relatively well. Namibia was a pioneer in using dehorning to protect its rhino, but, sadly, dehorned female rhino have been unable to protect their young from attack by hyaena. The nongovernmental Save the Rhino Trust (☎ 061-222281, fax 223077), PO Box 22691, Windhoek, promotes conservation education.

Although there's been a recent decrease in the lion population, Etosha's lion are free of two of the most serious causes of disease found in other parks: Feline Immunodeficiency Virus (a feline form of HIV) and Canine Distemper Virus (which has killed 30% of the lions in some Tanzanian parks).

Other major environmental issues involve projects designed to provide water and power resources for the country's growing industrial and human needs. Two major proposals with serious environmental impacts are the proposed dam and hydroelectric plant on the Kunene River in the Kaokoveld, and the pipeline from the Okavango River to provide water for Windhoek.

FLORA & FAUNA

As Namibia lies mostly within an arid zone, much of the flora is typical African dryland vegetation: scrub brush and succulents, such as *Euphorbia*. Some floral oddities found nowhere else include the *kokerboom* (quiver tree; see the boxed text 'Kokerbooms' in the Southern Namibia section later in this chapter), a southern Namibian species of aloe, and the bizarre welwitschia (see the boxed text 'Weltwitschia' in The Central Namib section later in this chapter). Along the coastal plain around Swakopmund lie the world's most extensive and diverse lichen fields (see the boxed text 'Lichen Fields' in the North-Western Namibia section later in this chapter); in dry weather, they appear to be merely plant skeletons, but with the addition of water they burst into colourful bloom.

Etosha, Namibia's greatest wildlife park, contains a variety of antelope species, as well as other African ungulates, carnivores and pachyderms. Damaraland, in the north-west, is home to antelope and other ungulates, and also harbours desert rhino, elephant and other specially adapted species. Hikers in the Naukluft Mountains may catch sight of the elusive Hartmann's mountain zebra, and along the desert coast live jackass penguins, flamingoes, Cape fur seals and the rare *strandwulf* (desert hyaena). (For more on Namibia's flora and fauna, see the colour section 'The Namib Dunes' in this chapter.)

National Parks

Despite its harsh climate, Namibia has some of the world's grandest national parks. They range from the world-famous wildlife park, Etosha, in North-Central Namibia, to the immense Namib-Naukluft Park, which protects vast dunefields, remote desert plains, wild mountains and unique flora. There are also the smaller wildlife reserves of the Caprivi region, the renowned Skeleton Coast parks and the awe-inspiring Fish River Canyon, which ranks among Africa's most spectacular sights.

Visiting the Parks Access to most wildlife-oriented parks is limited to enclosed vehicles only; no bicycles or motorcycles are allowed. For some parks, like the Etosha and Namib-Naukluft Parks, 2WD is sufficient, but you need 4WD in Mamili National Park and the Khaudom Game Reserve.

Namibian national parks are now operated by the semiprivate Namibia Wildlife Resorts (NWR; ☎ 061-236975, fax 224900, ⓔ reservations@iwwn.com.na), Private Bag 13267, Windhoek. Their office, at the corner of John Meinert and Moltke Sts, is open from 8 am to 3 pm weekdays. Most parks charge US$1.75 per person for day visits and US$15 per camp site per day (Etosha, however, charges US$5 per person for day visits and US$20 for a camp site; the Skeleton Coast parks also charge higher rates). Formal accommodation at Etosha now ranges from US$32 for a two-bed room at Namutoni fort to US$60 for a four-bed luxury bungalow at Okakuejo. Most other parks charge a bit less for similar facilities. Skeleton Coast Park transit permits for the Ugabmund-Springbokwater road are available at the park gates (US$3.40 per person, plus US$1.70 per vehicle).

When booking park camp sites or accommodation by fax (they unfortunately tend to ignore emails) include your passport number; the number of people in your group (including the ages of any children); your full address, telephone and fax numbers; the type of accommodation required; and dates of arrival and departure (including alternative dates). Bookings may be made by phone up to 11 months in advance, while written applications are taken up to 18 months in advance. The invoice will be sent to you by post; fees must be paid before the indicated due date. Full payment (by bank transfer – apparently they haven't yet heard of credit cards) is necessary before the booking will be confirmed.

Hiking For multiday, guided walks at Waterberg Plateau (US$15/34, unguided/guided), the Naukluft (US$15), the Ugab River (US$34), Daan Viljoen (US$10) or Fish River Canyon (US$15), the numbers of hikers are limited so book as far in advance as possible. These hikes are limited to groups of three to 12 people.

GOVERNMENT & POLITICS

Namibia is an independent republic, divided into 13 regions, each with its own regional government. The national president is elected by popular ballot for a maximum of two five-year terms; the legislative body, the National Assembly, is comprised of 72 members, who are elected by the people; and the independent judiciary is presided over by a chief justice.

Since independence on 21 March 1990 Namibia has been governed by a SWAPO-dominated National Assembly, which took 57% of the vote in the first national election. Namibia's current president is SWAPO leader, Sam Nujoma. The main opposition is the re-established DTA, the moderate 11-party alliance which took second place with 28% of the vote.

ECONOMY

The relatively prosperous Namibian economy is dominated by mining (diamonds and uranium), cattle and sheep herding, tourism and fishing, as well as subsistence agriculture. The economy faces some disadvantages – water shortages, lack of local fuel sources, vast distances and a widely scattered population – but the country's GDP is twice the African average and its population remains small and diverse. Over 80% of the food and manufactured goods are imported from South Africa, creating an unhealthy degree of economic dependence.

POPULATION & PEOPLE

Namibia has an estimated 1,727,000 people, which represents one of Africa's lowest population densities at approximately two people per sq km. This number comprises 11 major tribal groups, including Owambo (650,000 people), Kavango (120,000), Herero/Himba (100,000; see the boxed text 'The Himba' following and 'The Herero' in the North-Western Namibia section), Damara (100,000), Nama (60,000), Baster (35,000), Caprivian (80,000), German (20,000), Afrikaner (65,000), San (19,000; see the 'The San' section in the Botswana chapter), Tswana (8000). About 75% of the

The Himba

The distinctive Himba (or Ovahimba, meaning 'those who ask for things') of the Kaokoveld are descended from a group of Herero herders who were displaced by Nama warriors in the early 19th century. They fled to the remote north-west and continued their seminomadic lifestyle, raising sheep, goats and some cattle.

Himba women maintain their lovely and distinctive traditional dress of multilayered goat-leather miniskirts and ochre-and-mud-encrusted iron, leather and shell jewellery. To keep their skin looking young, they smear it with a mixture of butter, ash and ochre, which must work, for even elderly Himba women have beautifully smooth skin. Their plaited hair is also plastered with the same mixture, and the overall effect is truly stunning.

ADRIEN VADROT

people inhabit rural areas, but the uncontrolled urban drift in search of work or higher wages has resulted in increased homelessness, unemployment and crime in the capital and other towns.

ARTS

Although Namibia is still developing a literary tradition, its musical, visual and architectural arts are already established. The country also enjoys a wealth of amateur talent in the production of material arts, including carvings, basketware and tapestry, along with simple but resourcefully designed and produced toys, clothing and household implements.

Music

Namibia's earliest musicians were the San, whose music probably emulated the sounds made by their animal neighbours and was sung to accompany dances and storytelling. The early Nama, who had a more developed musical technique, used drums, flutes and basic stringed instruments, also to accompany dances. Some of these techniques were later adapted by Bantu peoples, who added marimbas, gourd rattles and animal-horn trumpets to the range. A prominent European contribution to Namibian music is the choir; the German colonists also introduced their traditional 'oom-pah-pah' bands, which feature mainly at German festivals.

Visual Arts

Most of Namibia's renowned modern painters and photographers are of European origin; they mainly interpret the country's colourful landscapes, bewitching light, native wildlife and diverse peoples. Names include François de Mecker, Axel Eriksson, Fritz Krampe and Adolph Jentsch, as well as colonial landscape artists Carl Ossman and Ernst Vollbehr. Non-European Namibians, who have concentrated mainly on the country's sculpture, carving and material arts, have recently begun to develop their own traditions. Township art, which develops sober themes in an expressive, colourful and generally light-hearted manner, first appeared in the townships of South Africa during the apartheid years. Names to watch out for include Tembo Masala and Joseph Madisia, among others.

Architecture

The most obvious architectural contribution in Namibia was made by the German colonists, who attempted to re-create late 19th-century Germany along the desert coast. In deference to the warmer climate, however, they added such features as shaded verandas, to provide cool outdoor living space. The best examples can be seen in Lüderitz, Swakopmund and Windhoek. The most ornate and monumental structures were done in Wilhelminischer Stil and Art Nouveau.

LANGUAGE

As a first language, most Namibians speak either a Bantu language, which would include Owambo, Kavango, Herero and Caprivian languages; or a Khoisan language, including Khoikhoi (Nama), Damara and San dialects, which are characterised by 'click' elements that make them difficult for the uninitiated to learn. At independence in 1990, the official language of Namibia was designated as English. However, the most widely used language of European origin is Afrikaans, which is the first language of over 100,000 Namibians of diverse ethnic backgrounds. German is also widely spoken but is the first language of only about 2% of the population. In the far north, many people also speak Portuguese. (See the Language chapter at the back of this book for some words and phrases useful in Namibia).

Facts for the Visitor

SUGGESTED ITINERARIES

If your time is limited, it's probably best to stick to the highlights, but also to include a lesser-known area or two, to give you a taste of the 'best of Namibia'. If you have just two weeks, perhaps begin in Windhoek and either hire a car or take an inexpensive organised tour to visit Etosha, Swakopmund, the Sossusvlei and the Namib Desert Park, plus the Skeleton Coast, Twyfelfontein and other Damaraland sites. If you have a month, cover those sites then either head south and add the Naukluft Mountains, Lüderitz and Fish River Canyon or thoroughly explore the north, taking in the Kaokoveld, Kavango and Caprivi areas.

PLANNING

When to Go

Most of Namibia enjoys a minimum of 300 days of sunshine a year, but generally, winter has the most pleasant climate, as November to March can be very hot. Owamboland, Kavango and Caprivi are generally more humid and receive more rain than the Central Plateau. Namibia experiences two rainy seasons: the 'little rains' from October to December and the main rainy period from January to April.

Note that some resort areas, including Ai-Ais Hot Springs, close for part of the year due to potential floodings.

It is important to note that all tourist areas get crowded and accommodation is frequently booked out during the school holiday periods (this includes the South African school holidays – see the South Africa chapter). Things get particularly busy over Christmas and Easter.

Maps

The *Shell Namibia 1994* map is probably the best reference for remote routes. Shell has also published a good map of north-western Namibia titled *Kaokoland-Kunene Region Tourist Map,* which depicts all routes and tracks through this remote area. It's available at bookshops and tourist offices for US$2 to US$3.

Aesthetically, the Macmillan *Namibia Travellers' Map*, at a scale of 1:2,400,000, is one of the nicest, with clear print and colour-graded altitude representation. However, minor back routes aren't depicted and it does contain some notable errors.

Government survey topographic sheets and aerial photos are available from the Office of the Surveyor General (☎ 061-2852332, 238110), Ministry of Justice, Private Bag 13267, Windhoek. The 1:250, 000 series maps cost US$2 each; the 1:50,000 maps are US$1.50.

TOURIST OFFICES

Local Tourist Offices

Windhoek has both city and national tourist offices, and Karibib, Usakos, Omaruru, Okahandja, Gobabis, Keetmanshoop, Lüderitz, Swakopmund, Grootfontein and Tsumeb all have private or municipal tourist information offices. Look for the useful publication *Welcome to Namibia – Tourist Accommodation & Info Guide*, which is distributed free by Namibia Tourism (☎ 061-284 2111, fax 284 2364) on the ground floor, Continental building, 272 Independence Ave (Private Bag 13346), Windhoek.

Tourist Offices Abroad

Germany

Namibia Verkehrsbüro: (☎ 069-1337 3620, fax 1337 3615, @ namibia.tourism@t-online.de) Schillerstrasse 42–44, D-60313 Frankfurt-am-Main

South Africa

Namibia Tourism: (☎ 011-784 8025, fax 784 8340) PO Box 78946, Sandton City, Sandton 2196

Namibia Tourism: (☎ 021-419 3190, fax 421 5840) Ground floor, Main Tower, Standard Bank Centre, Adderley St (PO Box 739), Cape Town 8000

UK

Namibia Tourism: (☎ 020-7636 2924, fax 7636 2969, @ namibia@globalnet.co.uk) 6 Chandos St, London W1M OLQ

USA

Kartagener Associates Inc: (☎ 212-465 0619, fax 868 1654) 12 W 37th St, New York, NY 10018

VISAS & DOCUMENTS

All visitors require a passport that is valid for at least six months after their intended departure date from Namibia, as well as an onward plane or bus ticket (note, however, that checks are rarely made). Most visitors do not need visas – including those from Australia, New Zealand, France, Germany, the UK, Ireland, Canada and the USA. Tourists receive entry for an initial 90 days, but extensions are available (for details on the immigration office in Windhoek, see that section).

Windhoek is useful for picking up visas for Zambia and Malawi, and is the best place in Africa to get Angolan visas.

Visas for Onward Travel

Although few neighbouring countries require visas for Europeans, North Americans or Australasians, several do. To obtain a visa, you'll need at least two passport photos, and it's best to arrive at the embassy early in the morning.

Angola Visas are issued in about a week.

Malawi Visas are generally available on the same day as application.

South Africa Visas are issued within 24 hours; many nationalities can get them at the border.

Zambia The high commission is open for applications, but most nationalities can get their visas at point of entry.

Zimbabwe The high commission processes applications, but visas are available at the border.

Hostel cards, student cards and senior cards are of little use in Namibia.

EMBASSIES & CONSULATES

Namibian Embassies

Namibia has embassies and high commissions in South Africa, Zambia and Zimbabwe (see the relevant country chapters). Namibian diplomatic representatives elsewhere include:

Angola
Embassy: (☎ 02-395483, fax 333923) Rua Dos Coqueiros (PO Box 953), Luanda
France
Embassy: (☎ 01 44 17 32 65, fax 44 17 32 73) 80 avenue Foch, F-75116 Paris
Germany
Embassy: (☎ 0228-346021, fax 346025) Mainzer St 47, D-53179 Bonn
UK
High Commission: (☎ 020-7636 6244, fax 7637 5694) 6 Chandos St, London W1M 0LQ
USA
Embassy: (☎ 202-986 0540, fax 986 0443) 1605 New Hampshire Ave NW, Washington DC 20009

If you need a visa for Namibia and can't get one in your home country, send your passport details along with an estimated length of stay to the Ministry of Home Affairs (☎ 061-292 2111), Private Bag X13200, Windhoek.

Embassies & Consulates in Namibia

All of the following are in Windhoek:

Angola
Embassy: (☎ 227535, fax 221498) Angola House, 3 Ausspann St, Ausspannplatz (Private Bag 12020)
Botswana
Embassy: (☎ 221941, fax 236034) PO Box 20359
France
Embassy: (☎ 229021, fax 231436) 1 Goethe St (PO Box 20484)
Germany
Embassy: (☎ 229217, fax 222981) 6th floor, Sanlam Centre, 154 Independence Ave (PO Box 231)
Kenya
High Commission: (☎ 226836) Kenya House, Robert Mugabe Ave (PO Box 2889)
Malawi
Consulate: (☎ 221391, fax 227056) 56 Bismarck St, Windhoek West (PO Box 23547)
South Africa
Embassy: (☎ 229765, fax 224140) RSA House, Jan Jonker St and Nelson Mandela Dr, Klein Windhoek (PO Box 23100)
UK
High Commission: (☎ 223022, fax 228895) 116A Robert Mugabe Ave (PO Box 22202)
USA
Embassy: (☎ 221601, fax 229792) 14 Lossen St, Ausspannplatz (Private Bag 12029)
Zambia
High Commission: (☎ 237610, fax 228162) 22 Sam Nujoma Dr at Republic Rd (PO Box 22882)
Zimbabwe
High Commission: (☎ 228134, fax 226859) Gamsberg Bldg, Independence Ave and Grimm St (PO Box 23056)

CUSTOMS

Any item from elsewhere in the Southern African Customs Union – Botswana, South Africa, Lesotho and Swaziland – may be imported duty free. From elsewhere, visitors can import duty free 400 cigarettes or 250 grams of tobacco, two litres of wine, one litre of spirits and 250 ml of eau de Cologne.

MONEY

Currency

The Namibian dollar (N$) equals 100 cents, and in Namibia it's pegged to the same value as the South African rand (in South Africa, it fetches only about R0.70). The rand is also legal tender here at a rate of 1:1. This can be confusing, given that there are three sets of coins and notes in use: old South African, new South African and Namibian.

To complicate matters further, the three coins of the same denomination are all different sizes! It takes a while to get the hang of it. Namibian dollar notes come in denominations of N$10, N$20, N$50, N$100 and N$200, and coins in values of 5, 10, 20 and 50 cents, and N$1 and N$5.

Exchange Rates

At the time of going to print, the Namibian dollar had the following values against other currencies:

country	unit		Namibian dollar
Australia	A$1	=	N$3.85
Canada	C$1	=	N$4.36
euro	€1	=	N$6.13
France	10FF	=	N$9.34
Germany	DM1	=	N$3.13
Japan	¥100	=	N$5.89
New Zealand	NZ$1	=	N$3.10
UK	UK£1	=	N$10.01
USA	US$1	=	N$6.35

Exchanging Money

There is no limit to the amount of currency or travellers cheques you can bring into Namibia. Major foreign currencies and travellers cheques may be exchanged at any bank (for up to 7% commission), but the latter normally fetch a better rate. When changing money, you can opt for either South African rand or Namibian dollars; to change leftover currency outside the country, you'll need to have rand.

Credit cards are widely accepted in most shops, restaurants and hotels, and credit card cash advances are available at banks and from BOB, the First National Bank's automatic teller system.

Costs

If you're camping or staying in backpackers hostels, cooking your own meals and hitching or using local minibuses, you'll get by on as little as US$15 per day. A plausible mid-range budget, which would include B&B or backpackers' doubles accommodation, public transport and at least one restaurant meal daily, would be around US$50 to US$80 per person (if accommodation costs are shared between two people). In the upper range, accommodation at hotels, meals in restaurants and escorted tours will cost upwards of US$300 per person per day.

To reach the most interesting parts of Namibia, you'll have to take an organised tour or hire a vehicle (see the Getting Around section). Car hire may be expensive for budget travellers, but if you can muster a group of four people and share costs, you can squeak by on an additional US$20/50 per day – that's assuming a daily average of around 200km in a 2WD/4WD vehicle with the least expensive agency, including petrol, tax and insurance.

Tipping & Bargaining

Tipping is expected only in upmarket tourist establishments, but many places add a service charge as a matter of course. Tipping is officially prohibited in national parks and reserves. Bargaining is only acceptable when purchasing handicrafts and arts directly from the producer or artist, but in remote areas, the prices asked do represent fair market value.

POST & COMMUNICATIONS

Post

Domestic post generally moves slowly, and it can take up to six weeks for a letter to travel from Lüderitz to Katima Mulilo, for example. Overseas airmail post is normally more efficient, and is limited only by the time it takes the letter to get from where you post it to Windhoek. Poste restante works best in Windhoek (Poste Restante, GPO, Windhoek, Namibia). Photo identification is required to collect mail.

Telephone

Telephone trunk dialling codes in Namibia are being greatly simplified, as large areas with many different codes are being consolidated into just a few three-digit codes. When phoning Namibia from abroad, dial the international access code (usually 00 or similar), then the country code (264), followed by the telephone code without the leading zero, and then the required number. To phone out of Namibia, dial 00 followed by the country code, area code without the leading zero and number. Telecom Namibia phonecards are sold at post offices and some retail shops, and most towns now have private fax bureaus where you can send and receive faxes. Many remote bush locations subscribe to a message service operated by Walvis Bay Radio (☎ 064-203581); messages are relayed by radio to individual subscribers.

Email & Internet Access

Both email and Internet access are available at backpackers hostels, Internet cafes and hotels in larger towns, and also at several tourist offices and remote lodges.

INTERNET RESOURCES

Check out the following Web sites for information on Namibia.

Horizon Available in both English and French, this site includes addresses for tourist services, booking information, recent news snippets and good links to other sites.
www.horizon.fr/Namibia.html

Namibia Wildlife Resorts (NWR, formerly MET) Provides information on booking national parks permits and accommodation.
www.iwwn.com.na/namtour/namtour.html

The Namibian Government This site details government functions, ministries and tourism promotion.
www.republicofnamibia.com

See also Internet Resources in the Regional Facts for the Visitor chapter for a more comprehensive listing.

BOOKS

Lonely Planet

For a more in-depth coverage of Namibia, see *Zimbabwe, Botswana & Namibia* as well as the *Zimbabwe, Botswana & Namibia Travel Atlas*.

Guidebooks

Guide to Backpacking and Wilderness Trails by Willie & Sandra Olivier. These guides cover hiking and backpacking routes in South Africa and Namibia, and are available locally.

Guide to Namibian Game Parks by Willie & Sandra Olivier. This book has the lowdown on the national parks, wildlife reserves and other conservation areas, with useful maps and advice on wildlife viewing. It's available locally.

Hiking Trails of Southern Africa by Willie & Sandra Olivier. This guide is an abridged version of the Olivier's two other titles (see earlier); it's distributed internationally.

Travel

Horns of Darkness – Rhinos on the Edge by conservationists Carol Cunningham and Joel Berger. This book describes a journey through the Namibian wilds to find and protect the country's remaining desert rhino.

The Sheltering Desert by Henno Martin. This Namibian classic recounts the adventures of German geologists Henno Martin and Hermann Korn, who spent two years in the Namib Desert avoiding Allied forces during WWII.

History & Politics

The Colonising Camera by Wolfram Hartmann (ed) et al. Part of the new historical writings, this book is an illustrated history of the country.

To Free Namibia: The Life of the First President of Namibia by Sam Nujoma. The president's autobiography.

Herero Heroes by JB Gewald. This book blends oral and written accounts to provide a fascinating history of Namibia's Herero people.

Namibia – the Struggle for Liberation by Alfred T Moleah. This is an account of SWAPO's independence struggle and describes the situation before success was certain.

General

The Burning Shore by Wilbur Smith. Probably the best tale set in Namibia, this novel is highly entertaining.

Journey through Namibia by Mohamed Amin, Duncan Willetts & Tahir Shah. This is a good collection of stunning photos, but the text does have some problems.

Kaokoveld – the Last Wilderness by Anthony Hall-Martin, J du P Bothma & Clive Walker. This compilation of beguiling photos is breathtaking and will have you heading for northwestern Namibia.

NEWSPAPERS & MAGAZINES

Most of Namibia's English-language newspapers are based in Windhoek: *The Namibian*, published weekdays; the *Windhoek Observer*, published on Saturday; and the government-owned *New Era*. *The Namib Times*, published in Walvis Bay, is issued twice weekly. German-language newspapers include the *Allgemeine Zeitung* and the *Namibia Nachrichten*. The monthly English-language *Namibia Review* is good for national political, cultural and economic issues; contact Namibia Review (☎ 061-222246, fax 224937), Ministry of Information & Broadcasting, Private Bag 11334, Windhoek.

RADIO & TV

The Namibian Broadcasting Corporation (NBC) operates nine radio stations broadcasting on different wavebands in 12 languages; the best pop station is Radio Wave, at 96.7FM in Windhoek.

NBC television broadcasts government-vetted programming in English and Afrikaans from 4 to 11 pm weekdays and later on Friday and Saturday. On Sunday, Christian programming is broadcast from 11 am to 1 pm and other programming from 3 pm. News is broadcast at 10 pm nightly. Also available are CNN, MNET and SATV, all via satellite.

HEALTH

Malaria is currently endemic in northern Namibia. For further information, see Dangers & Annoyances following, as well as the Health section in the Regional Facts for the Visitor chapter.

DANGERS & ANNOYANCES

Theft isn't particularly rife in Namibia, but in Windhoek and Swakopmund, avoid walking alone at night and conceal your valuables.

Don't leave anything in sight inside a vehicle or at camp sites, particularly in Tsumeb and Grootfontein; keep valuables inside your sleeping bag at night.

Kavango and Caprivi both have malarial mosquito problems, and bilharzia is present in the Kunene, Okavango and Kwando-Linyanti-Chobe River systems. In East Caprivi the tsetse fly is especially active at dusk, and all the northern rivers harbour crocodiles.

East of Lüderitz, keep well clear of the *Sperrgebiet*, the prohibited diamond area, as well-armed patrols can be overly zealous. The area begins immediately south of the A4 Lüderitz-Keetmanshoop road and continues to just west of Aus, where the off-limits boundary turns south towards the Orange River.

LEGAL MATTERS

Police and military officials are generally polite and on their best behaviour. However, during a national threat (such as the attempted coup in the Caprivi region), they can get quite aggressive and should be either avoided or treated with utmost deference.

BUSINESS HOURS

Normal business hours are from 8 am to 1 pm and 2.30 to 5 pm weekdays. In the winter, when it gets dark early, some shops open at 7.30 am and close at around 4 pm. Lunchtime closing is almost universal. Most city and town shops open from 8 am to 1 pm on Saturday. Banks, government departments and tourist offices also keep these hours, but some petrol stations, especially along highways, are open 24 hours.

PUBLIC HOLIDAYS & SPECIAL EVENTS

Resort areas are busiest over both Namibian and South African school holidays, which normally occur from mid-December to mid-January, around Easter, from late July to early August, and for two weeks in mid-October.

New Year's Day 1 January
Easter March/April – Good Friday, Easter Sunday, Easter Monday
Independence Day 21 March
Ascension Day April/May – 40 days after Easter
Workers' Day 1 May
Cassinga Day 4 May
Africa Day 25 May
Heroes' Day 26 August
Human Rights Day 10 December
Christmas 25 December
Family/Boxing Day 26 December

A major event to watch for is Maherero Day, on the weekend nearest 26 August, when the Red Flag Herero people gather in traditional dress at Okahandja for a memorial service to the chiefs killed in the Khoikhoi and German wars. A similar event, also at Okahandja, is staged by the Mbanderu or Green Flag Herero on the weekend nearest 11 June. On the weekend nearest 10 October, the White Flag Herero gather in Omaruru to honour their chief Zeraua.

Major social events, mainly among the European community, include: Windhoek Karnival (WIKA) in late April/early May; the Küska (Küste Karnival) at Swakopmund in late August/early September; the Windhoek Agricultural Show in late September; and the Windhoek Oktoberfest in late October.

ACTIVITIES

Hiking is a highlight in Namibia, and a growing number of private ranches are establishing wonderful hiking routes for their guests; the finest ones include Klein-Aus Vista, near Aus; Namibgrens Rest Camp, in the Khomas Hochland near the Namib-Naukluft Park; and the Fish River Lodge, south of Keetmanshoop. You'll also find superb routes in the national parks: Daan Viljoen, Naukluft, Fish River Canyon, Waterberg Plateau Park and the Ugab River area of the Skeleton Coast. For more about the latter, see Hiking under National Parks, earlier in this chapter.

A growing craze is sandboarding, which is commercially available in Swakopmund. In the same area, operators offer horse and camel riding, quad-biking, deep-sea fishing, sea kayaking, birdwatching and skydiving. White-water rafting is available on the Kunene River, but it's extremely expensive; more down-to-earth is the white-water canoeing is available through the canyons of the Orange River, along the South African border.

WORK

Lots of foreigners find work in Namibia, only to discover that work permits are scarcer than hen's teeth. The official policy is to accept only wealthy overseas business investors or those who can provide skills and expertise not available locally. If you are offered a job, you (or better, your prospective employer) must organise a temporary residence permit from the Ministry of Home Affairs (☎ 061-292 2111, fax 292 2185), Private Bag 13200, Windhoek (but don't hold your breath, as very, very few people are successful!).

ACCOMMODATION

Namibia has an exhaustive (and growing) array of hotels, rest camps, camping grounds, caravan parks, guest farms, backpackers hostels, B&Bs, guesthouses and safari lodges. Most places are very good, and while this book mentions some highly recommended ones, it would take an entire volume to list everything that's available. For exhaustive lists of what's on offer, look for the following annual publications, which are distributed at tourist offices: *Where to Stay – Namibia*, *Welcome to Namibia – Tourist Accommodation & Info Guide*, *Namibia Exclusive Safaris & Get-Aways* and *Namibia B&B Guide*.

Hotels and most other establishments are graded using a star system; awards are based on regular inspections carried out by the Ministry of Environment & Tourism. The accommodation rates listed in this chapter are rack rates for overseas bookings, and include the standard 11% GST; in most cases, you'll get better rates when booking from within Namibia.

Camping

Most towns have caravan parks with bungalows or *rondavels* (round African-style huts), as well as a pool, restaurant and shop. For information on camping in national parks, see National Parks Accommodation, later in this section. To camp on private or communal land, secure permission from the landowner or the nearest village.

Hostels & B&Bs

Several backpackers hostels now operate in Windhoek, Swakopmund, Walvis Bay and Lüderitz, and more are planned. They provide dorm accommodation and cooking facilities, which range from US$6 to US$10 per person. B&B establishments are also emerging around the country; for listings, contact the B&B Association, PO Box 90270, Klein Windhoek.

Hotels

The Namibian hotel-classification system rates everything from small guesthouses to four-star hotels. Most are locally owned and managed, and they always have a small dining room and a bar. The most luxurious hotels include the Kalahari Sands and Windhoek Country Club, both in Windhoek, and the Swakopmund Hotel & Entertainment Centre. Any hotel with a name that includes the word 'garni' lacks a full dining room, but does offer a simple breakfast.

National Parks Accommodation

Namibia Wildlife Resorts (NWR) oversees accommodation in the national parks and offers a range of camp sites, bungalows, chalets and 'bus quarters' (for bus tours). Most sites include access to a swimming pool, shop, kiosk, restaurant, *braai* (barbecue) facilities and well-maintained ablutions (amenities) blocks. During school holidays, visitors are limited to three nights at each of the three Etosha National Park camps and 10 nights at all other camps. Pets aren't permitted in any camp, but kennels are available at the gates of Daan Viljoen, Von Bach Dam, Gross-Barmen, Ai-Ais and Hardap Dam. For booking information, see under National Parks, earlier in this chapter.

Guest Farms

A growing number of private farms welcome guests, and provide insight into the rural white lifestyle. Many of these farms have also established hiking routes and set aside areas as wildlife reserves. In all cases, advance bookings are essential.

Safari Lodges

Most of Namibia's lodges offer luxury accommodation and superb international cuisine. Rates are very reasonable when compared to similar places in other countries in the region and there's little multi-tier pricing. Even around the popular Etosha National Park, you'll pay a third of what you'd pay for similar lodges in the Okavango Delta. Other areas are even more reasonably priced.

FOOD

Outside Windhoek and Swakopmund, you'll find few gourmet pretences. Most hotels serve three meals, but menus are usually meat-orientated and not very creative. For a treat, try one of the German-style *konditorei* (pastry shop) where you can pig out on *apfelstrüdel*, *sachertorte*, *Schwarzwälder kirschtorte* and other pastries and cakes. Gathemann's in Windhoek and Cafe Anton in Swakopmund are national institutions, and Windhoek, Swakopmund, Lüderitz and other towns have pleasant cafes and small coffee shops.

Small hotels normally provide a cooked breakfast with cereal and toast, and big hotels may include a buffet breakfast. In addition to

Traditional Namibian Foods

Each Namibian tribal group has its own pantry of preferred foods. For example, the staple for the Owambo people of the north is *mielie pap*, or cornmeal porridge. The second grain favoured in Owamboland is *mahango* (millet), which is made into a porridge, a soup or an alcoholic beverage. Both mielie and mahango are typically eaten with fish, goat, lamb or beef stew cooked in a *potjie*, a three-legged black pot. Pumpkins, peppers and onions also feature prominently in the Owambo diet.

The spiny *!nara* melon *(Acanthosicyos horrida)* is found in the lower reaches of the Kuiseb, and is popular with the Nama people, who make them into flour and cakes. Alternatively, the melons are mashed or fermented to yield a sweet beer.

Historically, the Herero subsisted mainly on milk products such as curds and butter and, while they still enjoy these staples to some extent, the Herero diet now revolves around mielie, meat and black beans.

The traditional diet of the San consists mainly of desert plants – wild fruits, nuts, berries and tubers – as well as birds' eggs (especially ostrich eggs), lizards, locusts and game hunted with small, poison-tipped arrows.

the usual English breakfast, they may offer kippers (smoked kingklip), porridge and a range of German breads, cold meats, cereal and fruit. Cooked breakfasts always include bacon and *boerewors* (farmer's sausages), steaks and often even curried kidneys.

For lunch, many people go for takeaway snacks, which may include fish and chips, meat pies and sandwiches in *brötchen* ('little bread'). Evening meals normally feature meat, and restaurants serve typically high-quality cuts. Fish (normally kingklip) is best eaten in Swakopmund or Lüderitz, where it's probably fresh. Chicken is often prepared with a fiery *peri-peri* sauce.

DRINKS

Nonalcoholic Drinks

Tap water is generally safe to drink, but in some places it may emerge salty or otherwise unappealing, especially in desert areas and around Etosha. Packaged fruit juices provide an alternative. Every cafe and takeaway serves coffee and tea – as well as the strong herbal tea known as *rooibos* (red bush).

Alcoholic Drinks

Namibia's dry heat means big sales for Namibia Breweries. The most popular drop is Windhoek Lager, a light and refreshing lager-style beer, but the brewery also produces the stronger and more bitter Windhoek Export, the slightly rough Windhoek Special, Windhoek Light and Das Pilsner. Guinness Extra Stout is also brewed under licence. Their main competitor is Hansa, in Swakopmund, which produces both standard and export-strength beer. South African beers like Lion, Castle and Black Label are widely available and you'll also find a range of typically excellent South African wines. Alcohol isn't available in supermarkets, but is sold in the *drankwinkel* (bottle store).

In the rural areas of Owamboland, people socialise in tiny makeshift bars, enjoying such traditional local brews as *mahango* (millet beer), *mataku* (watermelon wine), *tambo* (also called *mushokolo*, a beer made from small seeds) and *walende*, which is distilled from the makalani palm and tastes similar to vodka. Apart from walende, all of these rural confections are brewed in the morning and drunk the same day, and they're all dirt cheap – around US$0.10 per glass.

SHOPPING

Potential souvenirs range from kitsch African curios and airport art to superb Owambo basketware and Kavango woodcarvings.

Windhoek offers a good choice, but most of the items sold along Post St Mall are cheap curios imported from Zimbabwe and elsewhere. Along the highway between Rundu and Grootfontein, roadside stalls sell locally produced items, from woven mats and baskets to appealing wooden aeroplanes and helicopters, which are a Kavango speciality. In Rundu and the north-east, you'll find distinctive San material arts – bows and arrows, ostrich-egg beads, leather pouches and jewellery made from seeds and nuts.

The Namib Desert's pastel colours inspire artists, and galleries in Windhoek and Swakopmund specialise in local paintings and sculpture. Also, some lovely items are produced in conjunction with the karakul wool industry, such as rugs, wall hangings and textiles that are often made to order.

Minerals and gemstones also make popular purchases, either in the raw form or cut and polished as jewellery, sculptures or carvings. For fine work, see the Kristall Gallerie in Swakopmund, Henckert Tourist Centre in Karabib or the House of Gems near the corner of Stübel and John Meinert Sts in Windhoek.

Local postage stamps are also interesting and collectable; for information, contact Namibia Post Philatelic Services (☎ 061-201 3107, fax 259467, ⓔ philately@nampost.com.na), Private Bag 13336, Windhoek, or see their Web site: www.nampost.com.na

In Tsumeb, Windhoek and some other souvenir shops around Namibia look out for the Millenium Bugs – witty little model insects made from wire and small pieces of colourful cast-off metal such as bottle tops or bits of beer cans. These, and other model animals, are made by members of the Onankali Community Trust based in northern Namibia and make excellent lightweight souvenirs.

Getting There & Away

This section covers access into Namibia from neighbouring countries only. Information about reaching Southern Africa from elsewhere on the African continent and from other continents is provided in the Regional Getting There & Away chapter.

AIR

Airports & Airlines

South African Airways and Air Namibia (Web site: www.airnamibia.com.na) operate daily flights between Johannesburg (Jo'burg), Cape Town and Windhoek. A one-way fare from Windhoek to Jo'burg/Cape Town starts at around US$200. Air Namibia has daily flights from Windhoek's in-town Eros airport to and from Alexander Bay (South Africa), which is the airport for Oranjemund. It also flies twice weekly between Windhoek and Harare (Zimbabwe) for US$385, Victoria Falls for US$475, Lusaka (Zambia) for US$380, Maun (Botswana) for US$250 and Gaborone (Botswana) for US$247.

LAND

Angola

There are three border crossings to Angola, at Ruacana/Koaleck (open 6 am to 10 pm), Oshikango/Namacunda (6 am to 7 pm) and Rundu/Calai (7 am to 5 pm), but travellers need an Angolan visa permitting overland entry. These are available in Windhoek from the Angolan consulate (see earlier in this chapter). At Ruacana Falls, you can enter the border area temporarily without a visa; just sign in at the border post.

Botswana

The Trans-Kalahari Hwy crosses the border between Buitepos and Mamuno (7 am to 5 pm). Once weekly, the Star Line bus runs between Gobabis and Buitepos, then connects with a local Botswana bus to Ghanzi.

In the Caprivi, you can cross the border at Ngoma Bridge (6 am to 7 pm) or between Mahango and Mohembo (6 am to 7 pm). The border crossing between Mpalila Island and Kasane (7 am to 4 pm) is served by boat transfer from Kasane for guests of Impalila Island, Ichingo and King's Den Lodges.

South Africa

The Intercape Mainliner (☎ 061-227847) coach service from Windhoek to Cape Town (US$64) and Jo'burg (US$80) leaves on Monday, Wednesday, Friday and Sunday at 6 pm. In Windhoek, visit the office on Gallilei St or book through their agent, the Cardboard Box Travel Shop (☎ 061-256580, fax 256581, e namibia@bigfoot.com).

Most highway traffic between Namibia and South Africa passes through the 24-hour crossing between Noordoewer and Vioolsdrif; secondary routes include the crossings at Ariamsvlei, and between Aroab and Rietfontein. Consolidated Diamond Mines (CDM) allows no public access between Alexander Bay and Oranjemund without permission (this is normally only granted to individuals on official business). The border crossing is open from 6 am to 10 pm.

Zambia

From the border post at Wenela (about 6km west of Katima Mulilo town), it's a few hundred metres to the Zambian border post. From here you can cross the River Zambezi on a pontoon to reach Sesheke then continue east to Livingstone, or stay on the western side of the Zambezi and head north to Senanga and Mongu. If you're heading from Namibia into Zambia then north towards Mongu, there's no bank at the village of Katima Mulilo (on the Zambian side). You might find local moneychangers near the pontoon, or you can ask at the guesthouse. Rand and Namibian dollars are always in demand, as Zambians cross into Namibia for shopping; changing is hassle free. Alternatively, Namibian dollars (but not SA rand) are accepted in larger hotels, shops and petrol stations in Senanga. (Sesheke has a bank, so if you plan to cross the Zambezi and head for Livingstone this is no problem.) (For more details on these routes see the Zambia chapter.)

The only other route between Namibia and Zambia is to go east from Katima Mulilo to the border at Ngoma Bridge, then follow the Chobe National Park transit route through northern Botswana to the ferry at Kazungula. (For more details, see the main Getting There & Away section in the Botswana chapter.)

Zimbabwe

There's no direct border crossing between Namibia and Zimbabwe; the easiest access is via the Chobe National Park transit route from Ngoma Bridge through northern Botswana to Kasane and Kazungula, and from there to Victoria Falls. On Monday and Friday evening, Intercape Mainliner runs from Windhoek to Victoria Falls (US$71), via Grootfontein, Rundu and Katima Mulilo.

Getting Around

AIR

Air Namibia (☎ 061-298 2531) serves domestic routes out of Eros airport in Windhoek, including flights to and from Tsumeb; Rundu and Katima Mulilo; Keetmanshoop; Lüderitz and Alexander Bay (South Africa); and Swakopmund and Oshakati. There is no departure tax.

BUS

From Windhoek, Intercape Mainliner (☎ 061-227847, e info@intercape.co.za), with its main offices on Gallilei St, serves Swakopmund, Walvis Bay, Grootfontein, Rundu and Katima Mulilo. (For international services, see Getting There & Away, earlier in this chapter. Fares are outlined under Getting There & Away, in the Windhoek section.)

Trans-Namib runs its Star Line buses (☎ 061-298 2030, fax 298 2383), which access Lüderitz, Bethanie, Helmeringhausen, Gochas, Buitepos, Outjo, Kamanjab, Opuwo, Khorixas, Henties Bay, Gobabis, Grootfontein, Oshakati, Rundu, Mariental, Walvis Bay and other destinations.

Along major routes, long-distance minibuses depart when full. Fares work out to US$.03 per km, but there may be a charge of US$1.75 (N$10) per piece of luggage. From Windhoek, the minibus terminal is the Rhino Park petrol station. Services from Windhoek are most frequent on Friday afternoons, with return trips to Windhoek on Sunday afternoons.

TRAIN

Windhoek is the hub for the Trans-Namib rail lines, with four services: south to Rehoboth, Mariental and Keetmanshoop; north to Tsumeb; west to Swakopmund and Walvis Bay; and east to Gobabis. Note that on weekends (Friday to Monday), fares are normally double what they are during the week. Book through the Windhoek Booking Office (☎ 061-298 2030). Tickets must be collected by 4 pm on the day of departure.

The plush 'rail cruise' aboard the *Desert Express* (☎ 061-298 2600, fax 298 2601, e dx@transnamib.com.na) offers luxurious overnights between Windhoek and Swakopmund twice a week for US$134/216 for seats/couchettes.
Web site: www.transnamib.com.na/dx

The tourist-oriented *Shongololo Express* (☎ 061-298 2030, 021-556 0271 in South Africa, cell 0811 248 684, fax 021-557 1034, e shongo@hixnet.co.za), which journeys between Upington (South Africa) and Tsumeb, via Aus, Mariental, Swakopmund and Otjiwarongo, does an annual rail buffs' trip.
Web site: www.shongo.co.za

CAR & MOTORCYCLE

An excellent system of tar roads runs from Noordoewer in the south to Katima Mulilo in the north-east (soon to extend all the way to Ngoma Bridge). Similarly, tar spur roads connect the main north-south arteries to Gobabis, Lüderitz, Swakopmund and Walvis Bay. Most other towns and sites of interest are accessible on good gravel roads.

Vehicles keep to the left, with a general speed limit of 120km/h on open roads and 60km/h in built-up areas. Drivers and passengers in the front seat must use seat belts. Officially, foreign drivers need an International Driving Permit from their local Automobile Association, but in practice a valid driving licence from home will suffice. Note that motorcycles aren't permitted in the national parks, except along main transit routes.

Car & 4WD Hire

Car hire is the easiest way of seeing Namibia. If you're on a tight budget, this can be expensive, although if you get a group together to share costs it can still work out cheaper than joining an organised tour. But be warned that there's a chronic shortage of rental cars available. For that reason, you'll need to book your car well in advance. The least expensive companies charge US$45 to US$65 per day with unlimited kilometres (some have a minimum rental period) for a compact car. Most require a N$1000 (about US$155) deposit and won't hire to anyone under the age of 25. Note that it's normally cheaper to hire a car in South Africa and drive it into Namibia, but you need permission from the hirer and the proper paperwork. Be sure to verify what sort of repairs will be your responsibility; your liability should be limited to tyres and windows. The following agencies offer car and/or 4WD hire:

Andes Car Rental (☎ 081-129 1259, fax 061-228552, @ andescar@iafrica.com.na) 25 Boight St (Private Bag 13231), Windhoek
Web site: www.natron.net/tour/andes

Avis Car Hire
Swakopmund: (☎ 064-402527, fax 405881) Swakopmund Hotel
Tsumeb: (☎ 067-220520, fax 220821) Safari Centre, Jordaan St
Walvis Bay: (☎/fax 064-207527, fax 209150) Rooikop airport
Web site: www.avis.com
Windhoek: (☎ 061-233166, fax 223072) Hotel Safari, Aviation Rd (PO Box 2057)

Camping Car Hire (☎ 061-237756, fax 237757, @ carhire@iwwn.com.na) 36 Joule St, Southern Industrial Area (PO Box 5526), Windhoek
Web site: www.namibiaweb.com/cch

Caprivi Car Hire (☎ 061-232871, fax 232374, @ caprivi@iafrica.com.na) 8 Chopin St (PO Box 1836), Windhoek
Web site: www.caprivi.com.na

Enyandi Car Hire
Otjiwarongo: (☎ 061-303898, fax 303892, @ enyandi@lianam.lia.net) PO Box 264
Windhoek: (☎ 061-255103, fax 255477) PO Box 4490

Imperial Car Rental (☎ 067-220728, fax 220916, @ travelnn@tsu.namib.com) Travel North Namibia, 1551 Omeg Allee, Tsumeb

Into Namibia Car & 4x4 Hire (☎ 061-253591, cell 081-128 8899, fax 061-253593, @ intonam@iwwn.com.na) 76 Sam Nujoma Dr (PO Box 31551), Klein Windhoek
Web site: www.iwwn.com.na/intonam

Mpengu Car Hire (☎ 061-256946, fax 246945, @ mpengu@iafrica.com.na) 9 Tünchel St, Pioneerspark (PO Box 5207), Windhoek

Odyssey Car Hire (☎ 061-223269, fax 228911, @ odyssey@iwwn.com.na) PO Box 20938, Windhoek
Web site: www.iwwn.com.na/odyssey/odyssey.html

RK 4x4 Hire (☎ 061-256323, fax 256333, @ rk4x4@natron.net) PO Box 20274, Windhoek
Web site: www.natron.net/tour/rk4x4

Savanna Car Rental (☎ 061-227778, fax 223292, @ scr@iafrica.com.na) PO Box 5180, Windhoek
Web site: www.natron.net/tour/savanna/carrentd.htm

Tempest Car Hire (☎ 061-239164, fax 230722) 49 John Meinert St, Windhoek

Windhoek Car Hire (☎ 061-237935, fax 258972, @ wch@namib.com) PO Box 1038, Windhoek

HITCHING

Hitching is possible in Namibia, but it's illegal in national parks, and even main highways see relatively little traffic. On a positive note, it isn't unusual to get a lift of 1000km in the same car. Truck drivers generally expect to be paid, so agree on a price beforehand; the standard charge is US$1.50 per 100km. Lifts wanted and offered are advertised daily in Windhoek on the radio (☎ 061-291311) and at The Cardboard Box Backpackers. (For warnings about hitching, see the Getting Around the Region chapter.)

ORGANISED TOURS

Even if you normally spurn organised trips, independent travellers will find there's a good case for joining a tour in Namibia, as many highlights (like the Skeleton Coast, Damaraland, the Kaokoveld, the Kunene Valley, Owamboland, Fish River Canyon or the wild Namib Desert) are well off the beaten track – even for those in rental cars. For travellers on tight budgets, tours can be expensive, but there are several economic camping trips available, which help keep your costs to a minimum.

Tour companies include the following:

African Monarch Nature Trails (☎/fax 064-203599) PO Box 2451, Walvis Bay. Remote region hiking and 4WD tours through Kaokoveld and Damaraland, including the desert elephants, the Hoanib River, Ghowarib Ravine and Epupa Falls, starting at around US$150 per day.

Cardboard Box Travel Shop (☎ 061-256580, fax 256581, e namibia@bigfoot.com) PO Box 5142, Windhoek. This company, run by John Stewart, offers inexpensive safari bookings and advice, as well as excellent 10-day Himba Trails tours through the wildest bits of Kaokoveld (US$600) and seven-day circuits through Caprivi and the Okavango Delta (US$345), with optional transfers to Victoria Falls or Livingstone.
Web site: www.namibia.addr.com/travel

Chameleon Safaris (☎/fax 061-247668, e chamnam@namib.com or chamnam@chameleon.com.na) PO Box 21903, Windhoek. This budget safari company is geared to backpackers. For US$350, you can take a comprehensive spin around northern or southern Namibia. US$440 will get you to Victoria Falls in seven days, including the main sites en route, and for US$640, you'll have eight days in Owamboland, Kaokoveld (including Kunene River rafting and Epupa Falls) and Damaraland.
Web site: www.millennia.co.za/chameleon

Charly's Desert Tours (☎ 064-404341, fax 404821) 11 Kaiser Wilhelm St (PO Box 1400), Swakopmund. A variety of reasonably priced day tours around Swakopmund, including geology tours, the Spitzkoppe, Welwitschia Drive, Cape Cross and Sandwich Harbour.

Crazy Kudu Safaris (☎ 061-222636, cell 081-128 6124, fax 061-255074, e namibia.safaris@crazykudu.com) 11 Pinguin Rd, Hochland Rand (PO Box 99031), Windhoek. One of Namibia's friendliest and most economical safari companies, run by Mike Godfrey, organises 10-day all-inclusive 'Namibia Explorer' adventures through northern and central Namibia highlights (US$450), including the Waterberg, Etosha, the Skeleton Coast, Twyfelfontein and Sossusvlei; a six-day northern highlights tour (US$285); and a three-day Sossusvlei Express tour (US$150). There's also a Fish River option (US$167). These trips are one of the best deals around and there are guaranteed departures from Windhoek every Saturday; the Sossusvlei Express also leaves from Swakopmund.
Web site: www.crazykudu.com

Desert Adventure Safaris (☎/fax 064-404459, fax 404072) Namib Centre, Roon St (PO Box 1428), Swakopmund. This company operates inexpensive day tours around Swakopmund, the Spitzkoppe and Cape Cross, and longer tours to Damaraland and the Kaokoveld. It also runs Palmwag Lodge in Damaraland and the beautiful Serra Cafema Lodge on the Kunene River.
Web site: www.das.com.na

Eco-Marine Kayak Tours (☎/fax 064-203144, e jeannem@iafrica.com.na) PO Box 225, Walvis Bay. Jeanne Mientjes guides sea kayaking trips around the beautiful Walvis Bay wetlands, as well as trips to Pelican Point and Bird Island.

Inshore Safaris (☎ 064-202609, fax 202198, e inshore@gem.co.za) 12th Rd (PO Box 2444), Walvis Bay. This Walvis Bay operator does trips to Sandwich Harbour, the dunes, the nature reserves and Welwitschia Drive. It also does 10-day all-inclusive circuit tours of northern or southern Namibia for around US$1850.

Kaokohimba Safaris (☎/fax 061-222378, e kaohim@nam.lia.net) PO Box 11580, Windhoek. Kaokohimba organises cultural tours through Kaokoveld and Damaraland, wildlife-viewing trips in Etosha National Park and hiking around northern Namibia.

Lüderitzbucht Tours & Safaris (☎ 063-202719, fax 202863) PO Box 76, Lüderitz. In addition to Kolmanskop tours, this company also runs trips to other recently opened parts of the Sperrgebiet (Diamond Area 1) such as Elizabeth Bay, Atlas Bay and the Bogenfels. Tours are available in English, German or Afrikaans.

Mola-Mola Safaris (☎ 064-205511, cell 081-24 2522, fax 064-207593, e molamola@iwwn.com.na) PO Box 980, Walvis Bay. This water-oriented company runs half-day dolphin-watching cruises for US$38, seabird-watching trips for US$50 and day trips to Bird Island, Pelican Point and Sandwich Harbour, with a meal of Walvis Bay oysters, starting at US$75.

Muramba Bushman Trails (☎ 067-220659, e bushman@natron.net) PO Box 689, Tsumeb. This recommended company, owned by Reinhard Friedrich, provides a unique introduction to the Heikum San people. Participants experience the San traditions, lifestyles and natural pharmacopoeia.

Namib Sky Adventure Safaris (☎ 063-293233, fax 293241, e namibsky@iwwn.com.na) PO Box 197, Maltahöhe. For those who dream of looming over the dunes in a balloon, this company offers Namib desert balloon flights for US$246 per person. The early morning flight departs before sunrise, when not a breath of wind is stirring. This operator is affiliated with the Namib Rand Nature Reserve.

Okakambe Trails (☎ 064-402799) PO Box 1591, Swakopmund. This company gives riding lessons and runs horse-riding tours around Swakopmund, including an overnight Swakop River tour to Goanikontes.

Pleasure Flights (☎ 064-404500, cell 081-129 4500, fax 064-405325, ⓔ redbaron@iml-net.com.na) PO Box 537, Swakopmund. Pleasure Flights runs 'flightseeing' tours from the Skeleton Coast right down to Fish River Canyon. For an economical price, you need a group of five people.

Rhino Tours (☎/fax 064-405757) PO Box 4369, Vineta, Swakopmund. Rhino runs day tours around Swakopmund and longer safaris in the Namib, the Skeleton Coast, Damaraland and the Kaokoveld. Day tours cost from US$52 and longer tours average US$160 per day.

Skeleton Coast Fly-In Safaris (☎ 061-224248, fax 225713, ⓔ sksafari@iwwn.com.na) PO Box 2195, Windhoek. This company offers all-inclusive four-day tours of the Skeleton Coast and Kunene River region for US$1860; add Sossusvlei and it's US$2050. Five-day trips to the Skeleton Coast, the Kunene River, Etosha National Park and Sossusvlei are US$2280. Add the Namib Rand Nature Reserve and Lüderitz and it's US$2710. Tours accommodate four to 10 people.
Web site: www.iwwn.com.na/sksafari/brochure.html

Trans-Namibia Tours (☎ 061-221549, fax 298 2033, ⓔ tntours@iwwn.com.na) Shop 28, Gustav Voigts Centre, 123 Independence Ave (PO Box 20028), Windhoek. Trans-Namibia runs environmentally conscious day tours, hiking tours and fly-in safaris, as well as self-drive tour and longer itineraries to Namibia's highlights. One highlight is the Fish Eagle Hiking Trail in southern Namibia, which costs US$700 all inclusive.

Westcoast Angling Tours (☎ 064-402377, fax 402532) 9 Otavi St (PO Box 545), Swakopmund. This company specialises in fishing tours, from deep-sea fishing to rock and surf angling from the beach. Anglers can even try for copper sharks, which may be caught from the beach.

Wild Dog Safaris (☎ 061-257642, cell 081-124 6961, fax 061-240802 ⓔ safaris@wilddog.com.na) 19 Johann Albrecht St (PO Box 26188), Windhoek. This recommended budget operator does complete circuits through northern (US$320) and southern (US$320) Namibia, three days in Etosha or Sossusvlei (US$165), circuits through Sossusvlei and Botswana's Okavango Delta (US$1190) and fabulous 15-day hikes in northern/southern Namibia (US$1010/1170). For the hikes, physical fitness is required.
Web site: www.wilddog.com.na

Wilderness Safaris Namibia (☎ 061-225178, fax 239455, ⓔ nts@iwwn.com.na) The Namib Travel Shop, PO Box 6850, Windhoek. This company does camping safaris, rock-hounding/geology tours, Namib Desert tours and Etosha wildlife drives, as well as rafting trips on the Kunene. The Swakopmund office (☎ 064-405216, fax 405165) runs day tours around Swakopmund and Walvis Bay.

Windhoek

☎ 061

Namibia's central highlands are dominated by its small, German-flavoured capital, Windhoek. Set in the geographical heart of Namibia, it serves as the road and rail crossroads and the country's commercial nerve centre. At an elevation of 1660m and surrounded by low hills, it enjoys dry, clean air and a healthy highland climate, and its 160,000 people reflect the country's ethnic mix; on the streets, you'll see Owambo, Kavango, Herero, Damara, Caprivians, Namas, San, 'coloureds' and Europeans, all hurrying along together.

Windhoek has only existed for just over a century. The modern name Windhoek, or 'windy corner', was corrupted from the original 'Winterhoek' during the German colonial occupation. At that time, it became the headquarters for the German Schutztruppe, which was ostensibly charged with brokering peace between the warring Herero and Nama. For over 10 years around the turn of the 20th century, Windhoek served as the administrative capital of German South-West Africa.

Orientation

Maps Pick up topographic sheets from the Surveyor General (☎ 285 2332, 238110), in the Ministry of Justice building, opposite the clocktower on Independence Ave.

Information

Tourist Offices The friendly Windhoek Information & Publicity Office (☎ 391 2050, fax 391 2091) on Post St Mall answers questions and distributes local advertising.

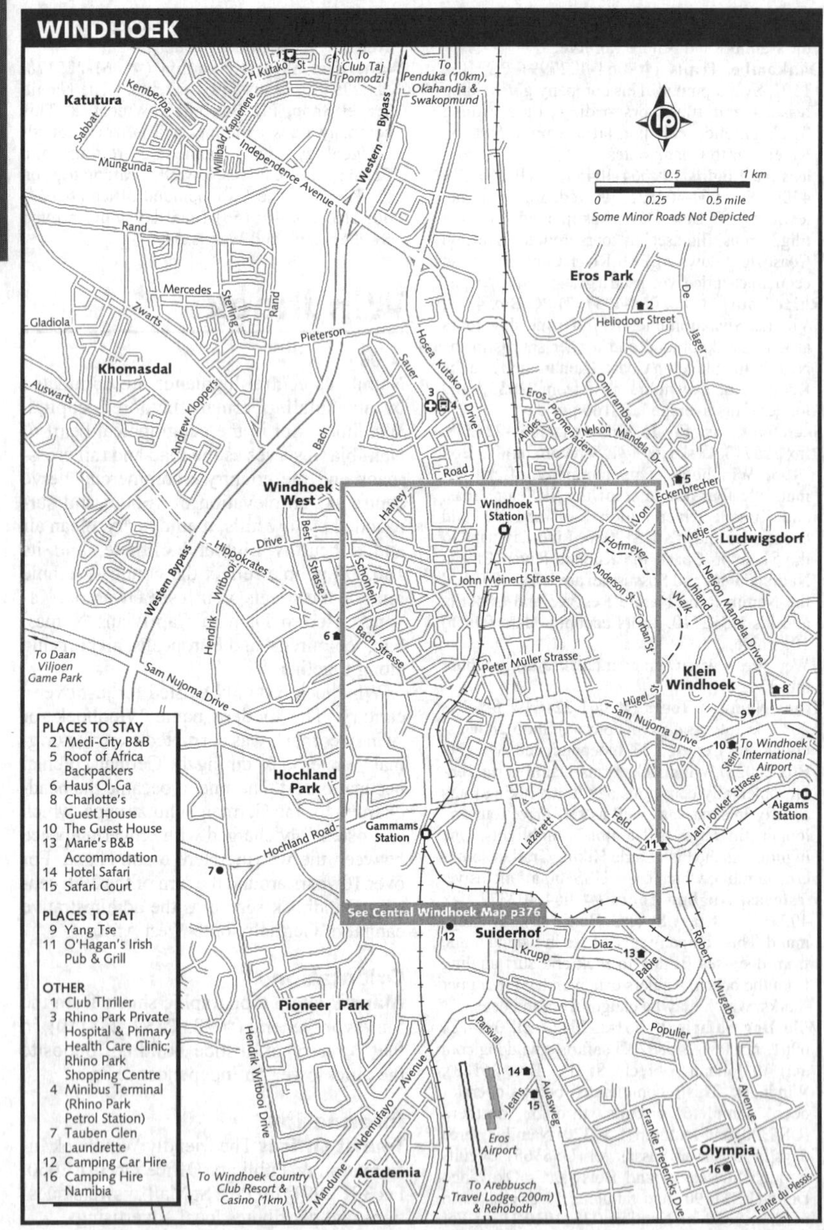

WINDHOEK
To Club Taj Pomodzi
To Penduka (10km), Okahandja & Swakopmund
Some Minor Roads Not Depicted
Katutura
Khomasdal
Eros Park
Windhoek West
Windhoek Station
Ludwigsdorf
Klein Windhoek
Hochland Park
Gammams Station
Aigams Station
Suiderhof
Pioneer Park
Olympia
Academia
Eros Airport
To Daan Viljoen Game Park
To Windhoek International Airport
To Windhoek Country Club Resort & Casino (1km)
To Arebbusch Travel Lodge (200m) & Rehoboth
See Central Windhoek Map p376
PLACES TO STAY
2 Medi-City B&B
5 Roof of Africa Backpackers
6 Haus Ol-Ga
8 Charlotte's Guest House
10 The Guest House
13 Marie's B&B Accommodation
14 Hotel Safari
15 Safari Court
PLACES TO EAT
9 Yang Tse
11 O'Hagan's Irish Pub & Grill
OTHER
1 Club Thriller
3 Rhino Park Private Hospital & Primary Health Care Clinic; Rhino Park Shopping Centre
4 Minibus Terminal (Rhino Park Petrol Station)
7 Tauben Glen Laundrette
12 Camping Car Hire
16 Camping Hire Namibia

There's also an information desk at the Grab-a-Phone bus terminal. The NWR office (☎ 236975) – formerly MET – in the Oode Voorpost on the corner of John Meinert and Moltke Sts, has detailed information on the national parks. It's open weekdays only.

Immigration Office Visa extensions are available from the 3rd floor of the Ministry of Home Affairs (☎ 292 2111) on the corner of Kasino St and Independence Ave. The office is open from 8 am to 1 pm weekdays.

Money The major banks, which are concentrated along Independence Ave, will change money and should have no problem giving you South African rand. The bureau de change on Post St Mall offers after-hours currency exchange at acceptable rates. The First National Bank ATM system, BOB, handles credit-card cash advances. Note that BOB (like everyone else) often runs short of cash at weekends.

Post & Communications The main post office (GPO) is on Independence Ave near Zoo Park. There are telephone boxes in the lobby and just up the hill is the Telecommunications Office, where you can make international calls and send or receive faxes on weekdays and Saturday morning. You'll also find convenient – albeit expensive – telephone services at Grab-a-Phone, which is the main bus terminal.

Email and Internet access are available at either The Cardboard Box, Rivendell Guest House or Roof of Africa Backpackers. There's also the Web Cafe (☎ 250540) on the corner of Robert Mugabe Ave and John Meinert St, which charges US$3.50 per hour for Internet access.

Travel Agencies A great place to look for advice on independent travel and book budget safaris is The Cardboard Box Travel Shop (☎ 256580, fax 256581, ⓔ namibia@bigfoot.com), PO Box 5142, Windhoek. They'll also arrange inexpensive car hire, adventure activities, flights, bus transport, and national park and lodge bookings. They'll customise your trip according to your budget, and can also (shamelessly!) recommend some fine ways to spend the money they save you. For full details, see their Web site www.namibia.addr.com/travel. Alternatively, see the helpful Trip Travel (☎ 236880, fax 225430) in the Levinson Arcade.

Bookshops The Windhoek Book Den (☎ 237976, ⓔ wbd@iwwn.com.na), between Post St Mall and the Levinson Arcade, is the best source of novels, European and African literature and travel books. On Peter Müller St is Der Bucherkeller, with novels, literature and travel books in English and German.

Laundry You'll find four self-service laundrettes: one near Ausspannplatz; the Rhino Park Laundrette in Rhino Park shopping centre; Tauben Glen in Village Square; and Laundraland, near the Mini-Markt in Klein Windhoek.

Medical Services Dr Rabie and Dr Retief (☎ 237213), who have offices on the corner of John Meinert and Stübel Sts, are recommended for consultations and hikers' health certificates. A good clinic is Rhino Park Primary Health Care Clinic (☎ 230926). Recommended hospitals include the Rhino Park Private Hospital (☎ 225434) in Windhoek North, and the Catholic Hospital (☎ 222 886).

Dangers & Annoyances By daylight, Windhoek is generally safe, but avoid going out alone at night, and stay wary of newspaper-sellers, who may shove the paper in your face as a distraction ruse. Parts of Katutura and other north-western suburbs, where boredom and unemployment are rife, should be avoided unless you have a local contact and/or a specific reason to go there.

Camping Gear You can hire camping equipment at Camping Hire Namibia (☎/fax 252995, ⓔ camping@nam.lia.net), 12 Louis Raymond St, Olympia. Gear for serious 4WD expeditions is sold at Safari Den (☎ 231931) at 20 Bessemer St. Gear for serious car camping and 4WD expeditions is available at

Gräber's (☎ 222732) on Bohr St in the Southern Industrial Area.

Hofmeyer Walk

The Hofmeyer Walk walking track through Klein Windhoek Valley starts from either Sinclair St or Uhland St and heads south through the bushland to finish at the point where Orban St becomes Anderson St. It takes about an hour and affords a panoramic view over the city, as well as a look at the *Aloe littoralis* aloes, which characterise the hillside vegetation. Hikers have recently been robbed along this route, so don't go alone and avoid carrying valuables.

Christuskirche

One of Windhoek's most recognisable landmarks, the 1907 Christuskirche stands at the top of Peter Müller St. This unusual building, constructed of local sandstone, was designed by Gottlieb Redecker in neogothic and Art Nouveau styles. To go inside, pick up the key during business hours from the church office on Peter Müller St.

Alte Feste & the Owela Museum

The whitewashed ramparts of Alte Feste, Windhoek's oldest surviving building, date from 1890–92. It originally served as the headquarters of the Schutztruppe, which arrived in 1889, but now houses the Historical Section of the State Museum. The other half of the State Museum, known as the Owela Museum, is on Robert Mugabe Ave; exhibits here focus on Namibia's natural and anthropological history. Both are open from 9 am to 6 pm weekdays and 3 to 6 pm weekends. Entry is free.

National Gallery

The National Gallery (☎ 231160), on the corner of Robert Mugabe Ave and John Meinert St, contains a permanent collection of works reflecting Namibia's historical and natural scene. It also hosts visiting exhibitions.

Tintenpalast

The Tintenpalast, now the Parliament building, was designed by architect Gottlieb Redecker and built in 1912–13 as the administrative headquarters for German South-West Africa. The name means 'ink palace', in honour of the ink spent on the typically excessive paperwork it generated. It has also served as the nerve centre for all subsequent governments, including the present one. On weekdays – except when the assembly is in session – you can take a 45-minute tour of the building. Reserve a place by phoning ☎ 229251. Also, take a look at Windhoek's first **post-Independence monument** on the lawn, which depicts Herero chief Hosea Kutako.

Other Historic Buildings

Near the corner of Lüderitz and Park Sts, take a look at the **Old Magistrates' Court**. It was built in 1897–98 as quarters for Carl Ludwig, the state architect, and now houses the Namibia Conservatorium. Heading down Park St towards Robert Mugabe Ave, you'll reach South-West Africa House, now called the **State House**. The site was once graced by the residence of the German colonial governor, but it was razed in 1958 and replaced by the present building. After independence, it became the official residence of the Namibian president.

Robert Mugabe Ave affords good city views and colonial architecture. The **Kaiserliche Realschule**, Windhoek's first German primary school, dates from 1907–08. The curious turret with wooden slats, which was part of the original building, was designed to provide ventilation. On the corner of Korner St and Robert Mugabe Ave is the **Old Supreme Court**, a gabled brick structure which dates from 1908.

Further south is the **Turnhalle**, which was designed by Otto Busch. It was built in 1909 as a gym, but on 1 September 1975, the first Constitutional Conference on Independence for South-West Africa (subsequently known as the Turnhalle Conference) was held here. In the 1980s, it was also the site of the political summits and debates which later resulted in Namibian independence.

On the corner of John Meinert and Moltke St, the classic 1902 **Oode Voorpost** originally held the colonial surveyors' offices. Early government maps were stored in fireproof archives. It was restored in 1988 and now houses the NWR reservations office.

Southward along Independence Ave are three colonial buildings designed by architect Willi Sander. The southernmost building was built in 1902 as the **Kronprinz Hotel**. In 1920, Heinrich Gathemann bought it and converted it into a private business, to adjoin **Gathemann House** next door, which he had built in 1913. The northernmost building is the **Erkrath building**, which dates from 1910.

Train Station & Trans-Namib Transport Museum

Windhoek's Cape Dutch–style train station dates back to 1912, and near the entrance sits the German steam locomotive *Poor Old Joe*, shipped to Swakopmund in 1899 and reassembled for the run to Windhoek. The small but worthwhile Trans-Namib Transport Museum, upstairs in the station, outlines the history of Namibian transport, particularly the railroads. It's open weekdays from 10 am to noon and 2 to 3.30 pm; entry is US$0.50.

Post Street Mall & Meteorite Exhibit

The throbbing heart of the Windhoek shopping district is the bizarrely colourful Post St Mall, which could have been a set for the film *Dick Tracy*. It's lined with vendors selling curios, artwork, clothing and other tourist items, and in the centre is a prominent display of 33 meteorites from the Gibeon meteor shower, which deposited at least 21 tonnes of mostly ferrous extraterrestrial boulders around Gibeon in southern Namibia.

Katutura

Unlike its South African counterparts, the black township of Katutura ('we have no permanent place', in Herero) is relatively safe by day if you stick to the northern areas or find a local who can act as a guide. Unfortunately, the lovely independence-theme murals that once graced Independence Ave have now been removed. A taxi from Windhoek centre to Katutura costs US$0.75.

Special Events

Windhoek's first big annual bash is the Mbapira/Enjando Street Festival, which is held in March around the city centre. It features colourful gatherings of dancers, musicians and people in ethnic dress. For information, call ☎ 225411. True to its partially Teutonic background, Windhoek stages its own Oktoberfest towards the end of October. Similarly, there's the German-style Windhoek Karnival (or WIKA), which

Frankie Fredericks

If Katutura has a favourite son, it's sprinting sensation Frankie Fredericks, who is probably Namibia's greatest role model for the youth and aspiring athletes. Fredericks was born in 1968 in Katutura, and began as a back-street football player. He was offered a place on the South African professional soccer team, the Kaizer Chiefs, but refused because he preferred track and field events.

Frankie credits his success to his mum, Riekie Fredericks, who financially supported his efforts at school and on the athletics track by working long hours as a seamstress. Her contribution was augmented by a Rössing Corporation scholarship that gave Frankie the opportunity to attend university in the USA (where he completed an MBA) and concentrate on his athletic training. Their efforts have apparently paid off, as Frankie Fredericks is now Africa's fastest sprinter, and won the silver for both the 100m and 200m sprinting events in the 1992 and 1996 Olympics in Barcelona and Atlanta. At the time of writing he was looking forward to a run for the gold at the 2000 Olympics in Sydney.

Currently, Fredericks trains in the USA for much of the year, but frequently returns to Windhoek, where a street has been named after him. He is also the patron of a charitable organisation in Katutura that promotes excellence for low-income youths. One of the secrets of his success, Fredericks claims, is that his religious convictions prevent him from touching drugs or alcohol.

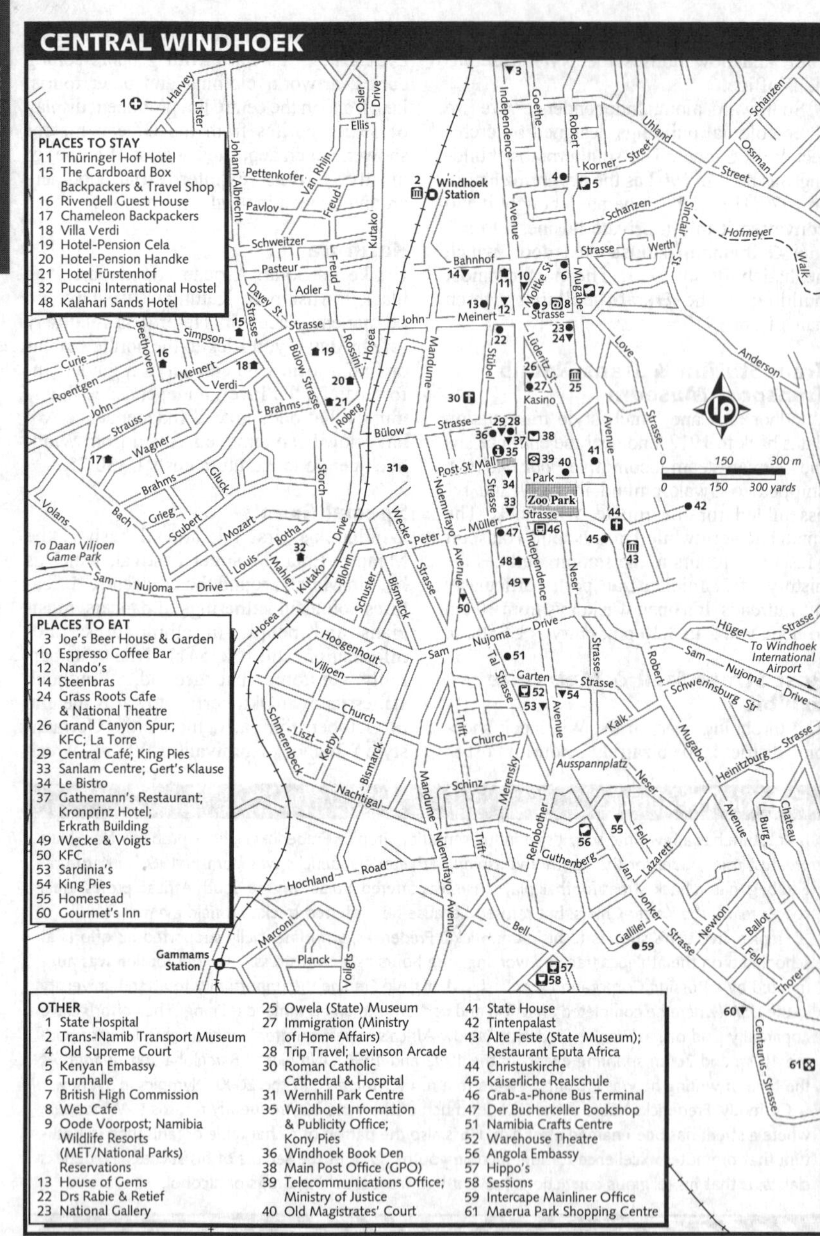
CENTRAL WINDHOEK
PLACES TO STAY
11 Thüringer Hof Hotel
15 The Cardboard Box Backpackers & Travel Shop
16 Rivendell Guest House
17 Chameleon Backpackers
18 Villa Verdi
19 Hotel-Pension Cela
20 Hotel-Pension Handke
21 Hotel Fürstenhof
32 Puccini International Hostel
48 Kalahari Sands Hotel
PLACES TO EAT
3 Joe's Beer House & Garden
10 Espresso Coffee Bar
12 Nando's
14 Steenbras
24 Grass Roots Cafe & National Theatre
26 Grand Canyon Spur; KFC; La Torre
29 Central Café; King Pies
33 Sanlam Centre; Gert's Klause
34 Le Bistro
37 Gathemann's Restaurant; Kronprinz Hotel; Erkrath Building
49 Wecke & Voigts
50 KFC
53 Sardinia's
54 King Pies
55 Homestead
60 Gourmet's Inn
OTHER
1 State Hospital
2 Trans-Namib Transport Museum
4 Old Supreme Court
5 Kenyan Embassy
6 Turnhalle
7 British High Commission
8 Web Cafe
9 Oode Voorpost; Namibia Wildlife Resorts (MET/National Parks) Reservations
13 House of Gems
22 Drs Rabie & Retief
23 National Gallery
25 Owela (State) Museum
27 Immigration (Ministry of Home Affairs)
28 Trip Travel; Levinson Arcade
30 Roman Catholic Cathedral & Hospital
31 Wernhill Park Centre
35 Windhoek Information & Publicity Office; Kony Pies
36 Windhoek Book Den
38 Main Post Office (GPO)
39 Telecommunications Office; Ministry of Justice
40 Old Magistrates' Court
41 State House
42 Tintenpalast
43 Alte Feste (State Museum); Restaurant Eputa Africa
44 Christuskirche
45 Kaiserliche Realschule
46 Grab-a-Phone Bus Terminal
47 Der Bucherkeller Bookshop
51 Namibia Crafts Centre
52 Warehouse Theatre
56 Angola Embassy
57 Hippo's
58 Sessions
59 Intercape Mainliner Office
61 Maerua Park Shopping Centre
Windhoek Station
Gammams Station
Zoo Park
Kasino
Ausspannplatz
To Daan Viljoen Game Park
To Windhoek International Airport
0 150 300 m
0 150 300 yards
Independence Avenue
Sam Nujoma Drive
Robert Mugabe Avenue
Hosea Kutako Drive
Mandume Ndemufayo Avenue
John Meinert Strasse
Bülow Strasse
Post St Mall
Peter Müller Strasse
Hochland Road
Hofmeyer Walk

is held in late April and features a series of events and balls lasting for about a week.

Places to Stay – Budget

Camping There is a popular camp site at ***Daan Viljoen Game Park***, 18km from town; prebook at Namibia Wildlife Resorts (see Tourist Offices earlier). For details of the camp and surrounds, see Around Windhoek, later in this chapter.

Just south of town is ***Arebbusch Travel Lodge*** *(☎ 252255, fax 251670, ⓔ atl@iwwn.com.na, PO Box 80160, Olympia)*, where camping here costs US$6.25 per person in a tent or caravan, and rooms for two or three people are US$50 and two- and four-bed chalets with bath cost US$46 and US$60 respectively. Taxis from the city centre cost around US$3.

Some of the hostels listed below also offer camping.

Hostels The favourite backpackers hostel is Aulden & Rachael Harlech-Jones' ***The Cardboard Box*** *(☎ 228994, fax 245587, ⓔ cardboardbox@bigfoot.com, PO Box 5142, 15 Johann Albrecht St)*. It's a 15-minute walk from the centre and dorms cost US$5, with use of the cooking facilities, swimming pool and lively bar. Double rooms start at US$15, but book in advance for any hope of getting one. There's a noticeboard for lifts, it's a great place to gather groups for car hire and email and Internet access is available. The lively atmosphere here is very enjoyable. Web site: www.ahj.addr.com

Chameleon Backpackers *(☎ 247668, cell ☎ 081-124 1567, PO Box 6107, 22 Wagner St, Windhoek West)* provides a friendly, lively atmosphere, thanks mainly to owner Jackie Burton and her various dogs and meerkats. Dorms cost US$5, including a sheet and pillow; private doubles are US$14 to US$17, with linen. Breakfasts, light meals and drinks are available on request, and guests have access to the pool, dart board, kitchen, video lounge and phone/fax facilities. For security purposes, Chameleon offers several daily shuttle trips to and from the centre.

The friendly and quiet ***Roof of Africa Backpackers*** *(☎ 254708, cell 081-124 4930, fax 248048, ⓔ roofofafrica@iwwn.com.na, 124 Nelson Mandela Ave)*, run by Terry and Torsten, makes a great haven away from the centre, but still lies within a 30-minute walk of the centre. Camping costs US$3.50, dorms US$7 and doubles US$20 to US$27. Email and Internet access is available, and there's a pick-up service from the Grab-a-Phone bus terminal for US$0.80.

Puccini International Hostel *(☎/fax 236355, 4 Puccini St)* has dorm places for US$6 to US$7, and doubles for US$17. Camping costs US$3.50 and use of the sauna is US$3.50 per hour. If you're walking from the Wernhill Park centre, watch your luggage, especially on the Mozart St bridge over the rail line.

Bed & Breakfast The friendly ***Marie's B&B Accommodation*** *(☎ 251787, fax 252128, ⓔ marie@maries.com.na, ⓔ brianhj@iafrica.com.na, 156 Diaz St)* has single/double rooms without bathroom starting at US$12/19 and double self-catering flats from US$25 to US$29. Amenities include phone, fax and email services, a braai, swimming pool, laundry and TV-and-video room.

The lovely ***Rivendell Guest House*** *(☎ 250006, fax 250010, ⓔ rivendell@toothfairy.com, PO Box 5142, 40 Beethoven St)*, which is affiliated with The Cardboard Box, provides quiet, comfortable accommodation within easy walking distance of the centre. In the main building, rooms with shared bathroom cost US$17, while spacious outside doubles with bath cost from US$22 to US$27. Rates include a continental breakfast and use of the pool. See its Web site for in-formation: www.rivendell-namibia.com. While you're there, don't miss the wall paintings at the corner of Beethoven and Simpson Sts.

The oddly named but friendly ***Medi-City B&B*** *(☎ 234249, 29 Heliodoor St, Eros Park)* is appropriately situated opposite the hospital. Singles/doubles cost US$19/34.

The industrial-looking ***Guest House*** *(☎ 255458, 29 Stein St, Klein Windhoek)* charges US$23/31 with shared bathroom and US$27/37 with bath.

The very friendly ***Haus Ol-Ga*** *(☎ 235853, 91 Bach St)*, where the name is formed from the owners' names – Gesa Oldach and Erno Gauerke, offers rooms in a nice, quiet garden atmosphere from US$20/30, with breakfast (if staying for just one night, add 10%).

Places to Stay – Mid-Range

One of the cheapest mid-range hotels, ***Hotel-Pension Handke*** *(☎ 234904, fax 225660, 3 Rossini St)* has 10 single/double rooms for US$30/42, with breakfast. Larger rooms accommodating three or four people cost US$18 per person. More upmarket is ***Hotel-Pension Cela*** *(☎ 226295, fax 226246, 82 Bülow St)*, which charges US$33/47, with breakfast. Amenities include TV, radio, telephone, fan, a swimming pool and fax service.

Charlotte's Guest House *(☎/fax 228846, @ cdunstan@mweb.com.na, PO Box 4234, 2A John Ludwig St, Klein Windhoek)*, offers pleasant rooms, tranquillity and healthy breakfasts for US$33/50.

On Independence Ave, the ***Thüringer Hof*** *(☎ 226031, fax 232981)*, famous for its beer garden, has rooms for US$54/71. The prominent ***Hotel Fürstenhof*** *(☎ 237380)* is also central and charges US$64/80.

Places to Stay – Top End

On Johann Albrecht St is the recommended ***Villa Verdi*** *(☎ 221994, fax 222574)*, a sort of Mediterranean-African hybrid, which charges US$59/97 for singles/doubles with telephone, TV and private bathroom. It also has a pool, bar and restaurant.

In the heart of the city is the four-star ***Kalahari Sands Hotel*** *(☎ 222300, fax 222260)*, a solid international-standard hotel, with rooms for US$89/102. The three-star ***Hotel Safari*** and attached four-star ***Safari Court*** *(☎ 240240, fax 235652)* have leafy gardens, a shady beer garden, a large pool and also a golf course next door. At the Hotel Safari single or double rooms cost US$79, including a buffet breakfast, and budget rooms cost US$66. It's probably the nicest of the big hotels. Safari Court charges US$93 for singles or doubles, with buffet breakfast.

The posh ***Windhoek Country Club Resort & Casino*** *(☎ 205 5911, fax 252797)*, built to host the Miss Universe pageant, is a Las Vegas-style hotel with standard rooms for US$105/125, but weekend specials are normally available. The fountains and green lawns seem as incongruous in the Namibian desert as they would in the deserts of Nevada.

Places to Eat

One of Windhoek's best takeaways is ***Steenbras***, on Bahnhof St near Independence Ave, which serves great fish, chicken burgers and spicy chips; all of which are memorably delicious. Windhoek also has the world's highest per capita concentration of pie shops (yes, really!); a good-value choice is ***King Pies***, with an outlet on Post St Mall and two on Independence Ave (at the corner of Garten St and the Levinson Arcade entrance). The outlets have a variety of filled meat and vegetable pies, and offer a super lunch deal: a large pie and a large soft drink for US$1.

Among the best chicken options is ***Nando's*** on Independence Ave, which does superb *peri-peri* chicken (fiery Portuguese-style dish), spicy rice, chips and other goodies. If you prefer the familiar, there are also two ***KFC*** outlets.

For brewed coffee, cappuccino and espresso, check out the ***Espresso Coffee Bar***, opposite the NWR booking office. Another recommended option for coffee, as well as meals and snacks, is ***Wecke & Voigts*** department store coffee bar in the Gustav Voigts Centre.

Le Bistro, a bit of a fishbowl on Post St Mall, is known for its breakfasts, pizza, salads and gyros. They serve breakfast from 7 to 11 am. The laid-back ***Central Cafe*** *(☎ 222659)* in the Levinson Arcade is open for lunch and dinner from Tuesday to Saturday. On Monday it's open for lunch only, and on Sunday from 8 am to midnight.

The decor at the ***Grass Roots Cafe***, between the National Theatre and the National Gallery, prominently features papier-mache, bottles, tins and razor wire – it's truly amazing. It serves light set lunches and dinners, as well as drinks and sweets, and you can frequently catch live performances.

An extremely popular spot for a large, meat-oriented evening meal – and prolonged drinking thereafter – is ***Joe's Beer House and Garden*** *(☎ 232457)*; reservations are requisite. ***Grand Canyon Spur*** *(☎ 231003)* on Independence Ave has a varied menu and appealing balcony seating. Don't miss the salad bar and renowned chocolate brownies. ***O'Hagan's Irish Pub & Grill*** *(cell ☎ 081-1241011)*, at the corner of Robert Mugabe Ave and Jan Jonker St, serves a range of popular dishes, but specialises in steak.

For pizza and basic Italian cuisine, there's ***Sardinia's***, on Independence Ave near Garten St.

A great splash-out is ***Gathemann's*** *(☎ 223853)*, in a prominent colonial building with a sunny terrace overlooking Independence Ave. In the morning and afternoon, it serves rich European-style gateaux and pastries, and downstairs there's a good sandwich takeaway. Another German-Namibian choice is the ***Homestead*** *(☎ 221958)* on Feld St east of Ausspannplatz. In the pleasant outdoor seating, you can enjoy a menu of herbs and vegetables fresh from their own garden. A bit finer is the recommended ***Gert's Klause*** *(☎ 235706)*, a quiet German-style bistro in the Sanlam Centre.

The best Chinese food is at ***Yang Tse*** *(☎ 234779)* on Sam Nujoma Dr near the petrol stations in Klein Windhoek. For a real splash-out, go to the ***Gourmet's Inn*** *(☎ 232360)*, on Jan Jonker St near Centaurus, which is a standard haunt of ambassadors, politicians and general power trippers. Reservations are essential but not easy to get.

Even African cuisine is available; the ***Restaurant Epata Africa*** *(☎ 247178)* in the Alte Feste, serves traditional dishes from all over the continent.

For the lazy, there's ***Dial-a-Meal*** *(☎ 220111)* – also known as Mr Delivery – which delivers orders from local restaurants for a service fee of US$1.50. Among the choices are ***Nando's***, ***Grand Canyon Spur*** and even the ***Pioneerspark Drankwinkel***!

Entertainment

A pleasant night spot for Wednesday, Friday and Saturday nights is ***The Warehouse Theatre*** *(☎ 225059)*, in the old South-West Breweries building on Tal St. This integrated club is friendly, secure and the cover charge averages at US$3.

In Katutura township is the wonderful ***Club Thriller*** (US$2.50 cover charge). Once you're past the weapons search at the door, the atmosphere is upbeat and secure. Don't carry valuables or walk around Katutura at night; always take a taxi. Less reliable is the tiny ***Club Taj Pomodzi*** in Katutura – a place specialising in *kwasa-kwasa* music from Congo (Zaïre), which is based on a rhumba beat (US$2.75 cover charge). It's great for an intimate taste of Windhoek's African scene, but is lost in the back streets of Katutura so it's hard to find without a taxi and local help (at night you need both of these, anyway).

In the Northern Industrial Area is ***Hippo's***, which attracts white, techno-oriented Namibians; next door is ***Sessions***, which features 70s and 80s pop music.

The ***Grass Roots Theatre*** offers down-to-earth cultural performances, and also a pleasant cafe. It has quite bizarre decor, including papier-mache furniture. Nearby, ***Joe's Beer Garden*** is probably *the* Windhoek bar hangout for young and trendy crowds of all persuasions. Other options are the ***Plaza*** at Maerua Park shopping centre, with easy-listening music, and ***O'Hagan's***, an Irish pub near Maerua Park, with mainstream music.

Shopping

Handicrafts stalls are a common sight in the main shopping areas; the stuff in Post St Mall is mostly brought in by the truckload from Zimbabwe and only a small percentage of it is worthwhile (especially if you're headed for Victoria Falls, where you'll find the same things for much less).

Better choices might be the locally made Herero dolls, sold outside the Kalahari Sands Hotel, or the baskets and woodcarvings sold around Zoo Park. The Namibia Crafts Centre (☎ 222236) at 40 Tal St sells an amazing variety of souvenirs. It's open from 9 am to 5.30 pm weekdays and 9 am to 1 pm Saturday. For raw minerals and gemstones, you'll find good deals – and an interesting mineralogy lesson – at Sid Pieters' House of Gems (e scrap@iafrica.com.na), at 131 Stübel St, near the corner of John Meinert St.

Getting There & Away

Air Air Namibia (☎ 298 2552, fax 221382) flies daily between Windhoek international airport (42km east of the city centre) to Cape Town and Jo'burg. There is also a twice-weekly service to and from London and Frankfurt; and several airlines offer services to and from Gaborone (Botswana, US$256), Maun (Botswana, US$250), Harare (Zimbabwe, US$385), Lusaka (Zambia, US$380) and Victoria Falls (US$475).

Domestic Air Namibia flights connect Eros airport, located to the south of the city centre, with Katima Mulilo, Keetmanshoop, Lüderitz, Oshakati, Rundu, Swakopmund and Tsumeb. If you're taking a taxi to the airport from Windhoek, make sure the driver knows which airport you want (ie, in-town Eros versus the more distant international airport).

Bus The Intercape Mainliner uses the Grab-a-Phone bus terminal on Independence Ave. It runs on Monday, Wednesday, Friday and Sunday to and from Cape Town (US$64) and Jo'burg (US$80), via Upington (US$42). Fares to places en route from Windhoek are: Rehoboth (US$5, one hour); Mariental (US$20, three hours); Keetmanshoop (US$30, five hours); and Grünau (US$34, seven hours). There are also daily services to Walvis Bay (US$20) via Swakopmund (US$19, four hours); and Monday and Friday departures to Victoria Falls (US$71, 18 hours) via Okahandja (US$12, one hour), Otjiwarongo (US$15), Grootfontein (US$34), Rundu (US$42) and Katima Mulilo (US$50, 12 hours).

Twice weekly, Trans-Namib's Star Line buses connect Windhoek with Katima Mulilo (US$21, 19 hours), via Otjiwarongo (US$5, four hours), Grootfontein (US$7, seven hours) and Rundu (US$10, 11 hours).

The cheaper local minibuses serve all the main routes and leave when full from the Rhino Park petrol station. There's also the Namib Travel Shop's Sossusvlei Shuttle (☎ 225178, fax 239455), which costs US$59 each way between Windhoek and Sesriem (you'll have to make your own way to Sossusvlei). It departs daily except Sunday and Tuesday from the Kalahari Sands, Safari Court and Windhoek Country Club, and returns on the same days.

Train The station booking office is open from 7.30 am to 4 pm weekdays; note that all fares quoted below double at weekends. Overnight trains run daily except Saturday between Windhoek and Keetmanshoop, leaving at 7.10/6.30pm southbound/northbound. Times and weekday business class fares from Windhoek are: Rehoboth (US$3, 2¾ hours), Mariental (US$4, six hours) and Keetmanshoop (US$6, 11½ hours).

The northern-sector line connects Windhoek with Tsumeb (US$4, 16 hours) via Okahandja (US$1.50, 2¼ hours) and Otjiwarongo (US$5, 10½ hours). At Otjiwarongo, this train connects with Star Line buses to Outjo, Khorixas, Kamanjab and Opuwo.

The other main lines connect Windhoek with Swakopmund (US$3.50, 3¾ hours) and Walvis Bay (US$3.50, five hours) daily except Saturday; and Windhoek with Gobabis to the east (US$4.25, eight hours) on Tuesday, Thursday and Sunday, on a very slow overnight run.

Getting Around

The airport shuttle (☎ 263211), which costs US$7, connects Windhoek international airport with Eros airport and the Grab-a-Phone bus terminal in the city centre. It leaves from town two hours and 10 minutes prior to international departures and from the airport an hour after the arrival of an international flight. Taxis between the international airport and the city centre cost around US$18.

City buses between the centre and townships charge US$.15, but as Windhoek is so small, most travellers opt for the relatively inexpensive taxis. The main taxi stand is the Grab-a-Phone bus terminal (☎ 237070). You'll find cheaper collective taxis at the Wernhill Park Centre, but they keep to set routes between the city centre and townships.

AROUND WINDHOEK

Penduka & Goreangab Dam

Penduka (☎/fax 061-257210, @ penduka@namib.com), which means 'wake up', operates a women's nonprofit needlework project at Goreangab Dam (Windhoek's water supply), 10km north-west of town. You can purchase baskets, carvings and fabric creations for fair prices and be assured that all proceeds go to the producers. It's open from 8 am to 5 pm daily except Sunday; day entry is US$10, including tea and a light lunch. There are also several hiking trails here. Backpacker ***dorm beds*** cost US$5 and single/double ***chalets*** cost US$20/26.

Take the Western Bypass north and turn left on Monte Cristo Rd, then left on Otjomuise Rd, right on Eveline St and right again on Green Mountain Dam Rd and follow the signs to Goreangab Dam/Penduka. There's no public transport, but Penduka provides lifts from town (cell ☎ 081-1294116) for a nominal fee.

Daan Viljoen Game Park

The beautiful Daan Viljoen Game Park sits in the Khomas Hochland about 18km west of Windhoek. Because there are no dangerous animals, you can walk to your heart's content through lovely desert-like hills and valleys. You'll almost certainly see gemsbok, kudu, mountain zebra, springbok, hartebeest and perhaps even eland. It's also known for its diversity of birds, with over 200 species recorded. Among them are the rare greenbacked heron and pin-tailed whydah. The park is open to day visitors from sunrise to 6 pm and day entry costs US$1.50.

The 3km **Wag-'n-Bietjie Trail** follows a dry riverbed from near the park office to Stengel Dam. A 9km circuit, the **Rooibos Trail**, crosses hills and ridges and affords great views back to Windhoek in the distance. The 34km **Sweet-Thorn Trail** makes a circuit of the empty eastern reaches of the reserve. One group of three to 12 people is allowed to do this trail each day and it costs US$10 per person, including accommodation in a shelter halfway along. Advance bookings through NWR are required.

Places to Stay & Eat At the ***rest camp*** on the shores of Augeigas Dam, camping costs US$15 for up to eight people, and single/double *rondavels* (huts) cost US$29/37. Prebook at NWR in Windhoek. The ***restaurant*** is open from 7.30 to 9 am, noon to 2 pm and 7 to 10 pm.

Getting There & Away There's no public transport to Daan Viljoen, but persistent hitchers will eventually get a lift. With your own vehicle, follow the C28 west from Windhoek. The park is clearly signposted about 18km from the city. No motorcycles are permitted.

Gobabis

☎ 062

Gobabis, the administrative centre for the Tswana people, lies 120km from the Botswana border at Buitepos. The name is Khoikhoi for 'the place of strife', although a slight misspelling ('Goabbis') would render it 'place of elephants', which most locals prefer (despite its lack of elephants). Gobabis isn't much to look at; the only historic building is the old military hospital, the **Lazarett**, which once served as a town museum. It's not officially open, but you can pick up a key at the library and have a look around.

The nicer of Gobabis' two hotels is the ***Gobabis Hotel*** *(☎ 562568)*, with singles/doubles for US$24/33. The hotel swimming pool, bar, restaurant and weekend disco are responsible for at least 80% of the town's action.

Slow overnight rail services run daily in either direction between Windhoek and Gobabis (US$4.25, eight hours). From Gobabis to Buitepos, the Star Line bus runs once weekly, and connects with a local bus to Ghanzi, Botswana.

Around Gobabis

☎ 062

The area between Gobabis and **Dordabis** is the heart of Namibia's karakul country. The weavery at **Farm Ibenstein** (☎ 573524), 4km down the C15 from Dordabis is open weekdays and Saturday morning.

Stephanie & Volker Hümmer's ***Eningu Clay House Lodge*** *(☎/fax 573580)* was painstakingly constructed of sun-dried adobe, and the result is an appealing African–American Indian architectural cross. This place really is beautiful, and activities include some wonderful hiking trails, wildlife viewing, archery and tours to a fabulous **sculpture studio** and nearby **Dorka Teppiche**, where you'll find superb original weavings. Rooms cost US$72 per person, including half board and wildlife drives. To get there, follow the D1458 for 63km south of Windhoek international airport and turn west on the D1471 for 1km to the Eningu gate.

Arnhem Cave Arnhem Cave, which at 2800m is the longest cave system in Namibia, was discovered by farmer DN Bekker in 1930 and was originally used as a source of bat guano fertiliser. Because the cave is dry there are few stalagmites or stalactites, but it is home to five species of bat and words can't describe the first view of the blue-cast natural light as you emerge from its depths. Entry costs US$9, plus US$3.50 to hire helmets and torches. Note that it gets extremely dusty, so wear old clothing and avoid wearing contact lenses. Advance booking is essential – contact Mr J Bekker (☎ 573585, ⓔ arnhem@iwwn.com.na).

Camping at ***Arnhem Cave Guesthouse*** costs US$7.50 per person, self-catering chalets are US$45 and double chalets cost US$32 with breakfast and US$40 with half board. To get there, turn south just east of the international airport on the D1458, towards Nina. After 66km, turn north-east on the D1506 and continue for 11km to the T-junction, where you turn south onto the D1808. The farm is 6km down this road.

Buitepos

Buitepos is essentially just a wide spot in the desert at the Namibia/Botswana border – little more than a petrol station, and a customs and immigration post. Here the oasis-like ***East Gate Service Station & Rest Camp*** *(☎ 560405, fax 560406)* rises from the desert like a mirage and the toilets are more than remarkable. Camping costs US$3.50, pre-erected tents are US$7 per person and four-bed bungalows are US$32. The toilets are more than remarkable. On Friday, a Star Line bus connects Buitepos and Gobabis. There are also connections to Botswana.

North-Central Namibia

Almost everything along the tourist trail in north-central Namibia is aimed at ushering visitors into Namibia's most popular destination, Etosha National Park, which is one of the world's pre-eminent wildlife areas.

OKAHANDJA

☎ 062

Okahandja, the Herero administrative centre, is best-known among travellers for its two immense craft markets – one near the junction of the B1 and B2, the other about 1km out on the B1 towards Windhoek – which sell a staggering number of mostly Zimbabwean curios.

At the southern end of Church St is Friedenskirche, the Rhenish mission church, which was consecrated in 1876. Both in the churchyard and over the road are the graves of several historical figures; these include Herero leader Willem Maherero; Nama leader Jan Jonker Afrikaner; and the father of Namibian independence, Hosea Kutako. A town museum is planned for the old German fort.

Okahandja's big events are Maherero Day in August and the gathering of the Green Flag Herero people in June. (For more information see Special Events in the Namibia Facts for the Visitor section earlier in this chapter.)

Gross Barmen

The former mission station of Gross Barmen (☎ 501091), 26km south-west of Okahandja, is Namibia's most popular hot-spring resort. Visitors come mainly for swimming and soaking, but there are also some nice walks and birdwatching around the dam and hillsides. Entry is US$1.75 per person and US$1.75 per vehicle. Camp sites cost US$15 for up to eight people, self-contained doubles are US$24 and two- and five-bed bungalows cost US$25 and US$45 respectively.

Book through Namibia Wildlife Resorts (NWR) in Windhoek.

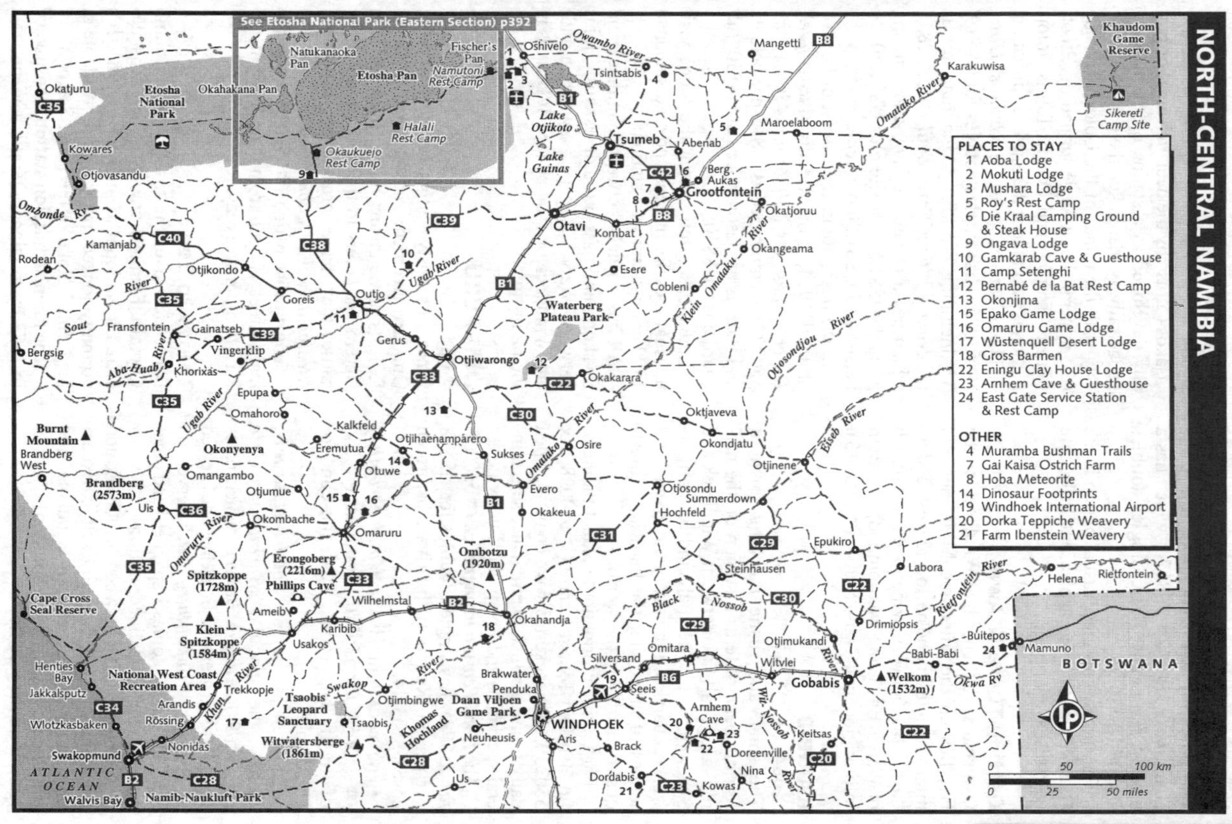
NORTH-CENTRAL NAMIBIA
See Etosha National Park (Eastern Section) p392
PLACES TO STAY
1 Aoba Lodge
2 Mokuti Lodge
3 Mushara Lodge
5 Roy's Rest Camp
6 Die Kraal Camping Ground & Steak House
9 Ongava Lodge
10 Gamkarab Cave & Guesthouse
11 Camp Setenghi
12 Bernabé de la Bat Rest Camp
13 Okonjima
15 Epako Game Lodge
16 Omaruru Game Lodge
17 Wüstenquell Desert Lodge
18 Gross Barmen
22 Eningu Clay House Lodge
23 Arnhem Cave & Guesthouse
24 East Gate Service Station & Rest Camp
OTHER
4 Muramba Bushman Trails
7 Gai Kaisa Ostrich Farm
8 Hoba Meteorite
14 Dinosaur Footprints
19 Windhoek International Airport
20 Dorka Teppiche Weavery
21 Farm Ibenstein Weavery
0 50 100 km
0 25 50 miles
BOTSWANA
ATLANTIC OCEAN
Etosha National Park
Etosha Pan
Natukanaoka Pan
Okahakana Pan
Fischer's Pan
Namutoni Rest Camp
Halali Rest Camp
Okaukuejo Rest Camp
Khaudom Game Reserve
Sikereti Camp Site
Waterberg Plateau Park
National West Coast Recreation Area
Cape Cross Seal Reserve
Namib-Naukluft Park
Daan Viljoen Game Park
Tsaobis Leopard Sanctuary
Khomas Hochland
WINDHOEK
Tsumeb
Grootfontein
Otavi
Otjiwarongo
Outjo
Omaruru
Okahandja
Gobabis
Swakopmund
Walvis Bay
Henties Bay
Usakos
Karibib
Brandberg (2573m)
Spitzkoppe (1728m)
Klein Spitzkoppe (1584m)
Erongoberg (2216m)
Ombotzu (1920m)
Witwatersberge (1861m)
Welkom (1532m)
Okonyenya
Phillips Cave
Burnt Mountain
Lake Otjikoto
Lake Guinas

Places to Stay & Eat

The only in-town accommodation is the ***Okahandja Hotel*** *(☎ 503024)* which has a modest restaurant. Basic singles/doubles start at US$15/23.

For meals, your best casual option is the ***Okahandja Bakery***, a pleasant little cafe with takeaway options.

Getting There & Away

Okahandja, 70km north of Windhoek on the B1, lies on the Intercape Mainliner and minibus routes to the north and west, and on the rail line between Windhoek and Tsumeb or Walvis Bay (via Swakopmund). For train information, call Trans-Namib (☎ 503315).

KARIBIB

☎ 064

The small and rustic ranching town of Karibib began life as a station on the narrow-gauge rail line between Windhoek and Swakopmund. The Palisandro marmorwerke quarries annually yield over 1200 tonnes of aragonite, the hardest, highest-quality marble in the world.

For tourist information, contact the helpful Henckert Tourist Centre (☎ 550028, fax 550230, @ henckert@iwwn.com.na), open daily from 8 am to 5.30 pm. It also sells mineral specimens and lovely local weavings.

The ***Hotel Pension Erongoblick*** *(☎ 550009, fax 550095)* has singles/doubles for US$18 per person. Rooms with private bathroom cost US$33/44.

The cool and shady ***Hotel Stroblhof*** *(☎ 550081, fax 550240)*, at the eastern end of town, has rooms with air-con for US$41/63.

As well as the two ***hotel restaurants***, there's the popular ***Springbok Cafe*** *(☎ 550094)*. ***Karibib Bakery***, which dates from 1913, is great for breakfast and brewed coffee, and ***Klippenburg Club*** serves up steak and chips, goulash, spaghetti and other popular lunch and dinner options.

All bus services between Windhoek and Swakopmund pass through Karibib. Except on Sunday, trains between Windhoek and Walvis Bay (via Swakopmund) stop at Karibib in the wee hours.

USAKOS

☎ 064

Usakos ('grasp by the heel' in Nama) originally developed as a station on the narrow-gauge railway that linked the port of Walvis Bay with the mines of the Golden Triangle (the mineral-rich triangle formed by Grootfontein, Tsumeb and Otavi). Tourist information is available at the Shell petrol station.

The clean but austere ***Usakos Hotel*** *(☎ 530259)* has singles/doubles for US$19/35, including breakfast. A popular stop is the ***Namib Wüste Farm Stall*** *(☎ 530283)*, which has a restaurant, shop and camping ground (US$1.50 per site plus US$1.50 per person and US$1.50 per vehicle).

In the bush, 70km south-west of Usakos on the D1914, is the friendly ***Wüstenquell Desert Lodge*** *(☎ 550266 or 430811, fax 550277)*. Camping costs US$5 per person, and B&B is modestly priced at US$30; full board costs US$50.

Lodge-based tours from the lodge visit unusual rock formations and an abandoned 1900 colonial railway station.

All bus services between Windhoek and Swakopmund pass through Usakos. Trains between Walvis Bay (via Swakopmund) and Windhoek or Tsumeb stop at Usakos in the night-time.

OMARURU

☎ 064

Omaruru's dusty setting beside the shady Omaruru riverbed lends it a real outback feel. Its name means 'bitter, thick milk' in Herero and refers to the milk produced by cattle that have grazed on bitterbush *(Pechuelloeschae leubnitziae)*.

The tourist office (☎ 570277), on the main street, is open from 8 am to 1 pm and 2.15 to 5 pm weekdays.

Things to See

For a view over the town, you can climb **Captain Franke's tower**, which was declared a National Monument in 1963. It's normally locked, but keys are available at the Central Hotel or the Hotel Staebe.

The **Rhenish mission station**, constructed in 1872 by missionary Gottlieb Viehe, now houses the town museum. Entry is free; pick up the museum keys from the tourist office.

Each year on the weekend nearest 10 October, the White Flag Herero people hold a **procession** in Omaruru (see Special Events in the Facts for the Visitor section earlier in this chapter).

Places to Stay & Eat

The leafy ***Omaruru Rest Camp*** *(☎/fax 570516)* charges US$5 per person for camping or birdwatchers' huts; two- or three-bed bungalows cost US$20; and self-catering four-bed chalets are US$30.

The German-run ***Hotel Staebe*** *(☎ 570035, fax 570450)* occupies a pleasant riverside green setting and charges US$35/50 for single/double rooms, including breakfast. At the more spartan ***Central Hotel*** *(☎ 570030, fax 570353)*, rooms cost US$25/30.

Omaruru Game Lodge *(☎ 570044, fax 570134)*, 16km north-east of town, presents a taste of the bush on a scenic, well-watered game farm. Rooms cost US$79/140, including breakfast.

Epako Game Lodge *(☎ 067-570551, fax 570533, ⓔ epako@iafrica.com.na)*, 20km from town on the Kalkfeld road, makes a nice wild getaway for US$73/84.

The cosy ***White House Cafe & Milky Bar*** on the main street is housed in a historic building dating from 1907. In addition to German baked goods, it offers 'farmhouse' breakfasts, lunches and snacks.

Getting There & Away

Trains between Windhoek and Tsumeb or Walvis Bay (via Swakopmund) pass through Omaruru. For train information, call TransNamib (☎ 570006).

OUTJO

☎ 067

Bougainvillea-decked Outjo, settled in 1880, was never a mission station, but in the mid-1890s it did a short, uneventful stint as a German garrison town. For visitors, it best serves as a jumping-off point for trips to Okaukuejo rest camp, in Etosha National Park.

Information, tour and accommodation bookings, snacks, curios, and fax, Internet and email services are available at the Setenghi information office (☎ 313445, fax 313447, ⓔ setenghi@iafrica.com.na). It's open from 8 am to 5 pm Monday to Saturday and 9 am to 5 pm Sunday.

One of Outjo's first buildings, the Franke House, was constructed in 1899 as a residence for the German commanders. It now houses the **Outjo Museum**, with exhibits on political and natural history. It's open from 10 am to 12.30 pm and 3 to 5 pm weekdays. At other times, pick up a key from the Setenghi information office. Entry is free.

Gamkarab Cave

This cave, about 50km north-east of Outjo, is replete with lovely stalagmites and stalactites. Charles and Sarita Dell (☎ 313827, fax 313318) offer cave tours for US$5; horse riding costs US$8.50 per hour (three-day horse tours are US$130); and hiking costs US$8.50 per day. With your own equipment, you can also go diving in the underground lake inside the cave for US$8.50.

Very basic ***accommodation*** is available for US$13 in two-bed rooms or US$20 in four-bed rooms. Camping costs US3.50 for up to six people. The showers are in the old charcoal ovens!

Places to Stay & Eat

The friendly ***Outjo Backpackers*** *(☎/fax 313470)*, run by Odette and Gerhard Labuschagne, makes a great place to hole up. Dorms cost US$7 (US$8 with breakfast) and camping US$3.50. Gerhard, who grew up in the area, runs great-value day trips (from US$77) and longer excursions to Etosha. Occasionally, he heads for the wildest parts of the Kaokoveld. Follow the road past the museum, up the hill; Outjo Backpackers is just past the water tower.

The ***Hotel Onduri*** *(☎ 313014, fax 313 166)* has singles/doubles with private facilities for US$32/45.

The ***Etosha Garten Hotel*** *(☎ 313130, fax 313419, ⓔ discovaf@iafrica.com.na)* charges US$33 per person, with breakfast.

The jacaranda-studded ***Ombinda Country Lodge*** *(☎ 313181, fax 313478)*, 1km south of town, has reed-and-thatch chalets for US$37/57, including breakfast. Camping costs US$5 per person.

The beautiful ***Camp Setenghi*** *(☎/fax 313445, @ setenghi@iafrica.com.na)*, run by Wayne and Ilvia MacAdam, lies on the Ugab Terrace, 4km south of town, then 4km along the Kalkfeld turn-off. Tented or natural stone bungalow accommodation costs US$50 per person, with breakfast. Camping costs US$6 per person and buffet dinners are US$11. There's also a lovely 10km-loop hike here.

The restaurants and bars at the town's hotels serve meals and snacks; Etosha Garten's ***Jacaranda*** is especially nice. The super little ***Outjo Cafe-Bäckerei*** serves chicken, schnitzels and burgers, and its bread and sweet treats are famous throughout the area.

Getting There & Away

Star Line buses to Otjiwarongo leave Outjo three times weekly (US$2, one hour). On Monday, there are connections from Outjo to Kamanjab and Opuwo; and on Thursday, to Khorixas, Henties Bay, Swakopmund and Walvis Bay. For hitchers, Outjo is a logical jumping-off point for Etosha National Park's Andersson gate, 105km away on the C38.

OTJIWARONGO

☎ 067

Otjiwarongo ('the pleasant place' in Herero) lies at the junction of the roads between Windhoek, Swakopmund, Outjo, Etosha and the Golden Triangle. The tourist office (☎ 303658, @ otjtc@iafrica.com.na) is opposite the Hamburger Hof Hotel.

At the train station sits **Locomotive No 41**, which was manufactured by the Henschel company of Kassel, Germany, in 1912 and was brought to Namibia to haul ore between the Tsumeb mines and the port at Swakopmund.

The **Otjiwarongo Crocodile Ranch**, beside the caravan park, is open from 9 am to 4 pm weekdays and 10 am to 1 pm weekends. Entry costs US$1.75.

Places to Stay

Acacia Caravan Park *(☎ 302231, fax 302098)* charges US$5 for tents and US$7 for caravans, plus US$1.50 per person.

The nearest thing to a backpackers hostel is ***Traveller's Inn*** *(☎ 303154, fax 304430, 44 Tuinweg)*, which charges US$14/20 for singles/doubles.

At the ***Hamburger Hof Hotel*** *(☎ 302 520, fax 303607)* – no, it's not a fastfood outlet – rooms start at US$30/40.

Karen Falk's friendly ***Falkennest B&B*** *(☎/fax 302616, @ otjbb@iafrica.com.na, 21 Industria Ave)* is a welcome mid-range option, and bird-lovers will appreciate the colourful aviary. Rooms with bathroom cost US$19/30.

Bush Pillow B&B *(cell ☎ 081-128 8420, @ fritz@iafrica.com.na)*, near the train station, has rooms for US$19/29.

Out of Africa *(☎ 303397, 304383, 94 Tuinweg)* provides a homely atmosphere with a pool, TV and comfortable rooms for US$20/30.

There's also a choice of farmstays and game ranches. One of the best-known is ***Okonjima*** *(☎ 304563, fax 304565, PO Box 793, Otjiwarongo)*. It offers superb birdwatching and the chance to interact with beef-loving leopard and cheetah which have been rescued from angry farmers and brought to the centre for rehabilitation. Bungalows cost US$200/340 in the high season, with full board and activities. Take the B1 south from Otjiwarongo. After 49km, turn west onto the D2515; after another 15km, turn left onto the farm road for the final 10km.

Places to Eat

The ***Hamburger Hof Hotel*** has a dining room and the ***Traveller's Inn*** prides itself on its pizza. On the main street are several takeaways and the excellent ***Carstensen's*** bakery. The ***Jäger Stube***, at 44 Tuin St, serves lunches and dinners, and the pleasant outdoor seating is great for an afternoon beer.

Getting There & Away

The Intercape Mainliner service between Windhoek and Victoria Falls (Zimbabwe) passes through Otjiwarongo. Minibuses between Windhoek and the north stop at the Engen petrol station. The weekly Star Line bus to Okakarara (US$2) can drop you within 21km of Bernabé de la Bat Rest

Camp in the Waterberg Plateau Park, while its Outjo bus runs three times weekly.

All train services between Tsumeb and Windhoek or Walvis Bay (via Swakopmund) pass through Otjiwarongo. A ticket to Windhoek costs US$5 (10½ hours).

WATERBERG PLATEAU PARK

This park takes in a 50km-long and 16km-wide Etjo sandstone plateau, which looms 150m above the plain. Around this sheer-sided 'lost world' is an abundance of freshwater springs, which support a lush mosaic of trees and an abundance of wildlife. The park is also known as a repository for rare and threatened species, including sable, roan antelope and white rhino.

Entry to the park costs US$1.75 per person plus US$1.75 per vehicle. Because visitors aren't permitted to explore the park in their own vehicles and tourist numbers are restricted, NWR arranges wildlife drives around the plateau in open 4WD vehicles (US$9, two daily, 3½ hours).

Hiking

There are nine short walking tracks around Bernabé de la Bat Rest Camp, including one up to the rim of the plateau at Mountain View.

A four-day, 42km unguided hike around a figure-eight track starts at 9 am every Wednesday from April to November. It costs US$15 per person and groups are limited to between three and 10 people. Hikers stay in basic shelters and don't need a tent, but must otherwise be self-sufficient.

Also from April to November, the four-day guided Waterberg Wilderness Trail operates every second, third and fourth Thursday of the month. These walks are open to groups of six to eight people for US$34 per person. Accommodation is in huts, but participants must carry their own food and sleeping bags. Both long-distance hikes must be prebooked through NWR in Windhoek (☎ 061-236975, fax 224900, ⓔ reservations@iwwn.com.na).

Places to Stay & Eat

At the pink sandstone ***Bernabé de la Bat Rest Camp***, tent or caravan sites cost US$15 for up to eight people. Three- or four-bed self-catering bungalows with fan, braai and outdoor seating areas cost US$39 and US$52 respectively; these are always preferable to the tour group 'bus quarters', which cost the same. The camp ***restaurant*** serves meals during limited hours and a shop sells staples in the morning and afternoon. The camp is open to day visitors all year from 8 am to 1 pm and 2 pm to sunset.

Getting There & Away

The nearest public transport is the weekly Star Line bus between Otjiwarongo and Okakarara, which will get you within 21km of Bernabé de la Bat. Taxis from Otjiwarongo cost at least US$25 one way. Note: bicycles and motorcycles aren't permitted in the park.

GROOTFONTEIN

☎ 067

With a pronounced colonial feel, Grootfontein (Big Spring) has an air of uprightness and respectability. Many of its buildings are constructed of local limestone and it boasts avenues of jacaranda trees that bloom in September. It was the spring that attracted the earliest travellers, and in 1885, the Dorsland (Thirst Land) trekkers set up the short-lived Republic of Upingtonia. By 1887, the settlement was gone, but six years later Grootfontein became the headquarters for the German South West Africa Company, thanks to the area's mineral wealth. In 1896, the German *Schutztruppe* (the imperial army) constructed a fort using local labour, and Grootfontein became a garrison town.

Grootfontein's marginally useful tourist office is in the municipal building.

German Fort & Museum

In 1968 it was only a last-minute public appeal that saved the old German fort from demolition, and in 1974 it was restored to house the municipal museum. It's open from 4 to 6 pm Tuesday and Friday, and 9 to 11 am Wednesday.

Gai Kaisa Ostrich Farm

The friendly Gai Kaisa Ostrich Farm (☎ 242277), run by Thekla and Udo Unkel,

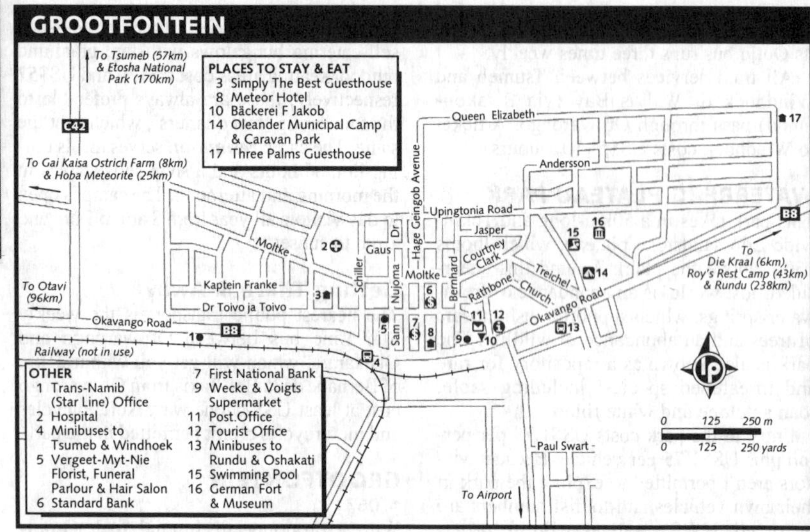

is 8km from Grootfontein on the D2859. It offers a worthwhile tour (US$1.75) which reveals the whole story about ostrich farming. Afterwards, you can have a meal (guess what's on the menu) or shop for ostrich-leather clothing or ostrich-eggshell jewellery.

Hoba Meteorite

Near the Hoba Farm, 25km west of Grootfontein, the world's largest meteorite was discovered in 1920 by hunter Jacobus Brits. This cuboid bit of space debris is composed of 82% iron, 16% nickel and 0.8% cobalt, along with traces of other metals.

No one knows when it fell to earth (it's thought to have been around 80,000 years ago), but since it weighs in at 54,000 kg, it must have made a hell of a thump. Entry is US$1.

Places to Stay

Oleander Municipal Camp & Caravan Park *(☎ 243101)* charges US$5 to US$7 for a camp site plus US$1 per person and US$1.50 per vehicle. Four-bed chalets cost US$19 to US$43. Note that this places suffers frequent security problems. A better choice for camping is ***Die Kraal*** *(☎ 240300)*, 6km north of town (phone for a lift), where camping costs US$3.50 and a flat is US$20 per person, including breakfast.

An excellent choice is the incredible ***Three Palms Guesthouse*** *(☎ 242054, fax 240044, e vistas@iafrica.com.na)*, where US$37/60 will get you a single/double room with breakfast and use of all the facilities: pool, tennis courts, sauna, jacuzzi and a phenomenal gym (nonguests can use the facilities for US$1.75 per hour). Meals are available.

At the friendly and pleasant little ***Simply the Best Guesthouse*** *(☎ 242431, 6 Weigel St)*, you'll pay US$20 per person. Check in at the Vergeet-Myt-Nie florist, funeral parlour and hair salon.

The old stand-by ***Meteor Hotel*** *(☎ 242 078, fax 243072)*, on the main Okavango road, has rooms starting from US$32/52.

Out of town on the Rundu road (the B8), opposite the Tsumkwe turn-off, is ***Roy's Rest Camp*** *(☎ 240302, fax 242759)*. Everything here is handmade and fabulously rustic, right down to the furniture in the bar and restaurant. Exotic-looking bungalows start at US$33/50 and camping costs US$2.50 per person. There are braai pits, picnic tables and a nice pool, and the owners run tours of their working cattle ranch.

Places to Eat

On Sunday, the ***Meteor Hotel*** dining room, which specialises in seafood, offers a buffet lunch from noon to 2 pm. On Fridays it serves pizza. For coffee, sweet treats and snacks throughout the day, try the renowned ***Bäckerei F Jakob*** *(☎ 312433)*, a bakery/coffee shop. The finest dining is at the homely ***Die Kraal*** *(☎ 240300)*, 6km north of town, which sizzles up Namibia's best – and most enormous – steaks. Reservations are essential.

Getting There & Away

Minibuses run frequently between Grootfontein and Tsumeb or Windhoek, and the Windhoek to Victoria Falls Intercape Mainliner bus also passes through. Star Line runs buses to Tsumkwe (US$7, 6½ hours), Rundu (US$12, four hours) and Katima Mulilo (US$14, 12 hours), each twice weekly.

TSUMEB

☎ 067

Tsumeb lies at the apex of the Golden Triangle of roads linking it with Otavi and Grootfontein. The town's name is derived from a melding of the San word *tsoumsoub* ('to dig in loose ground') and the Herero *otjisume* ('place of frogs'). The area isn't really known for its frogs; it's just that the red, brown, green and grey streaks created by minerals of the area resemble dried frog spawn (*paddaslyk*, in Afrikaans) and both the frogs and digging equipment appear on the town's crest.

Of the 184 minerals that have been discovered at Tsumeb, 10 are found nowhere else in the world, and mineral collectors justifiably rank the area as one of the world's great natural wonders.

Information

The friendly Travel North Namibia tourist office (☎ 220728, fax 220916, ⓔ travelnn@tsumeb.nam.lia.net, PO Box 799, Tsumeb), on Omeg Allee, is expertly run by Anita and Leon Pearson, who provide nationwide information, accommodation and transport bookings, as well as Imperial Car Rental (with special rates for Etosha National Park), fax services, email and Internet access (US$5 per hour), safe storage facilities, laundry and a range of other services. (They also run Travel North Backpackers.) They really go the extra mile here.

Things to See

Tsumeb's history is recounted in its small but worthwhile **Mining Museum**, in the 1915 Old German Private School. Entry costs US$1.50. It's open from 9 am to noon and 3 to 6 pm weekdays, and 3 to 6 pm Saturday.

Thanks to its soaring spire, the ultra-modern-styled **Otavi Minen- und Eisenbahn Gesellschaft Minenbüro** on 1st St is frequently mistaken for a church. It's probably the most imposing building in Tsumeb – and you'd never guess that this apparently modern structure dates back to 1907!

The **Tsumeb Cultural Centre**, on the Grootfontein road, presents Namibia's many cultures using artefacts, demonstrations and buildings from around the country. Entry costs US$1.75.

Lake Otjikoto, meaning 'deep hole' in Herero, lies about 24km north-west of Tsumeb, just off the B1. The lake was created when the roof of a 150m by 100m limestone sinkhole collapsed; the resulting 55m-deep lake and nearby Lake Guinas are the only natural lakes in Namibia. In 1915, during WWI, the retreating Germans dumped weaponry and ammunition into Lake Otjikoto – most of which is still there – to prevent the equipment falling into South African hands. Entry to the site is about US$1.

Muramba Bushman Trails

Muramba Bushman Trails (☎ 220659, ⓔ bushman@natron.net, PO Box 689, Tsumeb) is based on a large farm, 70km north-east of Tsumeb near Tsinstabis. It's a good place to learn about the culture and traditions of the San people (see 'The San' section in the Botswana chapter.)

You can follow, unguided, either of two main trails through woodland and grassy ranchland, but the most interesting walk is led by farmowner Reinhard Friedrich. While Reinhard's San colleagues are versed

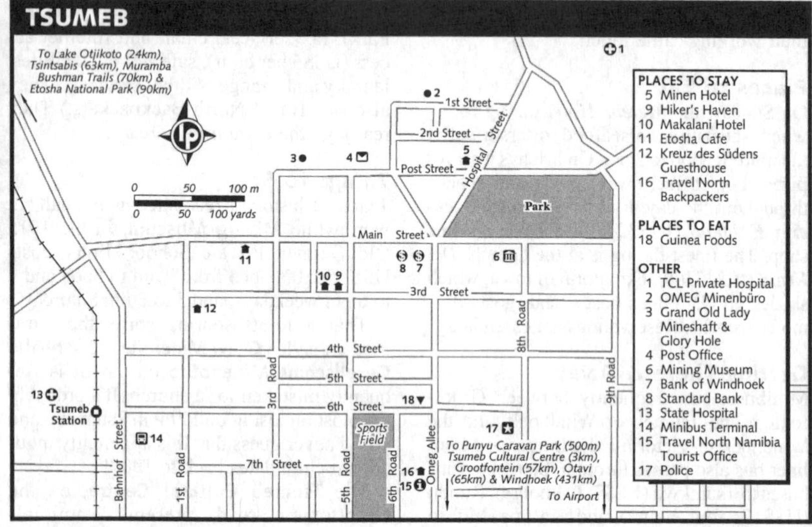

in traditional ways, their lifestyles are more modern than traditional. However, some examples of San huts and hunting traps have been built, and there's a small museum of implements and artefacts.

Guided morning walks are in English or German, and cost about US$20 per person, with lunch. Advance bookings are preferred.

You can ***camp*** (US$5 per site), or stay in delightful ***bungalows*** (US$15 per person). Self-catering facilities are provided or you can order meals. Access is difficult without your own car. Travel North Namibia (see Information earlier in this section) can provide more information.

Places to Stay & Eat

The only camping choice is ***Punyu Caravan Park*** *(☎ 221952)*, charging US$5 per tent and US$1.75 per person. It has an electrified fence, but it's wise to watch your belongings.

A great choice is ***Travel North Backpackers*** *(☎ 220728, or 220157 after hours, e travelnn@tsumeb.nam.lia.net)*, which has dorm beds for US$8.50 and singles/doubles with bathroom starting at US$20/24. The operators also run the Travel North Namibia tourist office.

For clean, inexpensive accommodation, try the friendly ***Etosha Cafe*** *(☎ 221207)* on Main St, which has rooms with shared facilities for US$17.50/30. It's also great for breakfast, lunch or a drink in the relaxed beer garden, and it brews up real filtered coffee.

Another small guesthouse is ***Kreuz des Südens*** *(☎ 221005, fax 221067, 500 3rd St)*. Simple rooms cost US$19/29.

The ***Makalani Hotel*** *(☎ 221051, fax 221575)* in the town centre is a good, clean choice at US$44/65, including breakfast, TV and phone. The hotel also runs the ***Hiker's Haven Hostel*** *(☎ 220420, fax 221575)*, where dorms cost US$8.50. Check in at the Makalani Hotel. At the ***Minen Hotel*** *(☎ 221 071, fax 221750)*, courtyard rooms with air-con start at US$39/52.

Guinea Foods, near Travel North Backpackers, offers quick takeaways, with burgers for less than US$1.

Getting There & Away

Air Namibia flies three times weekly between Tsumeb and Windhoek's Eros airport.

The Intercape Mainliner terminal for the twice-weekly buses between Windhoek and Victoria Falls (Zimbabwe) is the Minen Hotel.

Minibuses travel frequently from Tsumeb to Grootfontein, Oshakati and Windhoek.

On weekdays, Star Line buses connect Tsumeb with Oshakati (US$5, four hours), sometimes going on to Ruacana (US$8, six hours) and Opuwo (US$10, 10 hours).

Trains run three times weekly to and from Windhoek (US$6, 16 hours) and Walvis Bay (US$6, 17½ hours). For rail or Star Line bus information, contact Trans-Namib (☎ 220358).

ETOSHA NATIONAL PARK

Etosha National Park is undoubtedly one of the world's greatest wildlife-viewing venues, and few visitors will want to miss it. This vast park takes in over 20,000 sq km and protects 114 mammal species, as well as 340 bird species, 16 reptile and amphibian species, one fish species and countless insect species. The park's name, which means 'great white place of dry water', is taken from the vast white and greenish-coloured Etosha Pan. However, it's the surrounding woodlands and grasslands that provide habitats for the area's diverse communities of animals, birds and vegetation.

The first Europeans in Etosha were traders and explorers John Andersson and Francis Galton, who arrived by wagon at Namutoni in 1851. They were followed in 1876 by an American trader, G McKeirnan, who observed: 'All the menageries in the world turned loose would not compare to the sight I saw that day'.

However, Etosha didn't attract conservationists' interests until after the turn of the century, when the governor of German South West Africa, Dr Friedrich von Lindequist, became concerned about diminishing animal numbers and proclaimed 99,526 sq km, including Etosha Pan, as a reserve. In subsequent years the park's boundaries were altered several times, and by 1970 Etosha had been pared down to its present 23,175 sq km.

Information

The eastern two-thirds of Etosha is open to the public and the western third is reserved exclusively for organised-tour operators (but that is likely to change soon).

When you enter the park, check in at either von Lindequist or Andersson gate and pick up an entry permit (US$5 per person and US$1.75 per vehicle). This must then be presented at your reserved rest camp, where you pay fees for your prebooked camp site or other accommodation. Each of the three rest camps has an information centre, and the staff at either of the gates can sell you a map and point you in the right direction.

The best times for wildlife drives are at first light and late in the evening. All roads in eastern Etosha are passable in 2WD vehicles. Driving isn't permitted on the Etosha Pan itself, but there's a good network of gravel roads around the surrounding savanna grassland and mopane woodland. The park speed limit is set at 60km/h to protect plants and animals from the dust kicked up by vehicles.

Places to Stay & Eat

It takes at least three days to see Etosha, and most visitors stay at least a couple of nights in its three rest camps (Namutoni, Halali and Okaukuejo), which are spaced about 70km apart. Each camp has a different character, so it's worth visiting more than one.

At each camp you can choose between camping or self-catering accommodation. All three camps are open all year and each has a shop, a restaurant (open limited hours), a kiosk, picnic sites, a petrol station, a swimming pool and firewood.

Camping costs US$14 for a site accommodating up to eight people. Self-catering units include linen, towels, soap and kitchen facilities. You must arrive in the rest camps before sunset and you can leave only after sunrise; specific times are posted on the gates. There are also a number of safari lodges near the park.

Accommodation at the rest camps can be booked in advance through the NWR office in Windhoek.

Okaukuejo Okaukuejo (o-ka-**kui**-yo) has a pleasant pool area and restaurant, and a floodlit water hole where you have a good chance of seeing rhino, particularly between 8 and 10 pm.

ETOSHA NATIONAL PARK (EASTERN SECTION)

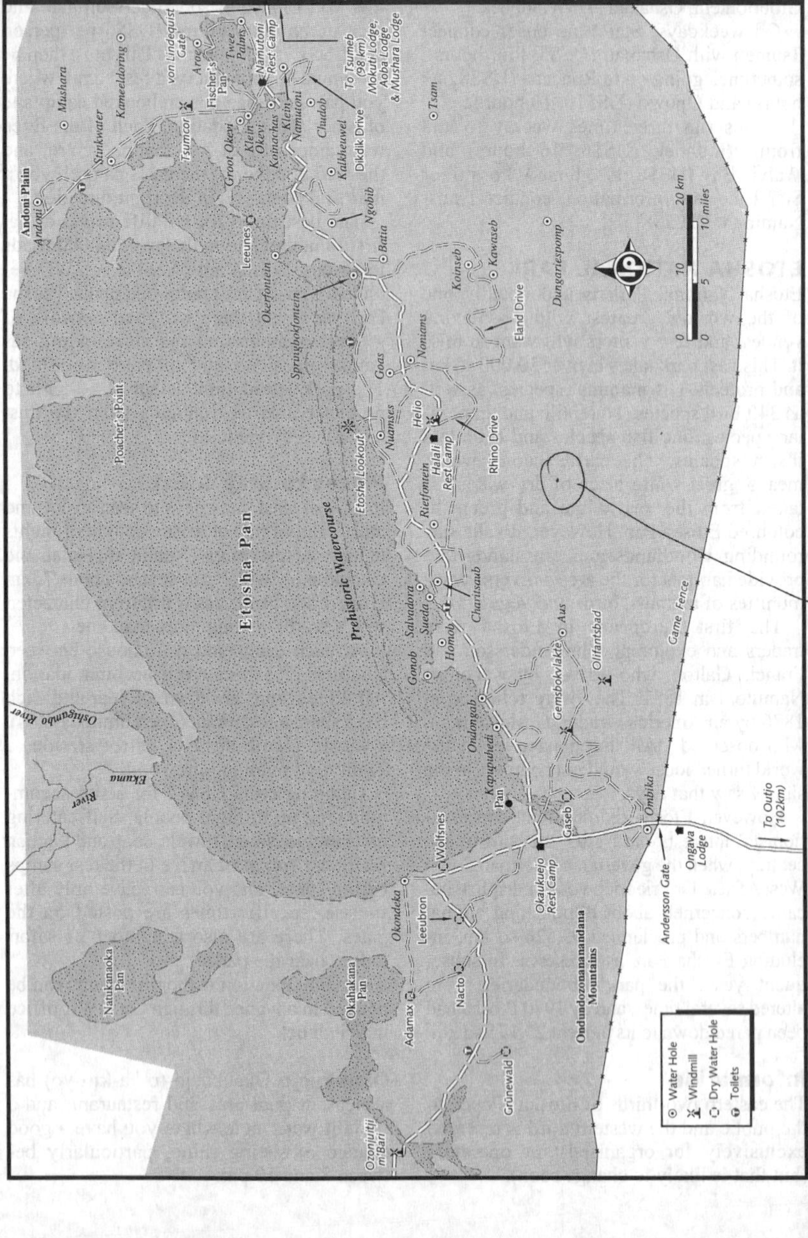

The dusty ***camping ground*** here is probably the least appealing of the three locations, but the self-catering accommodation is lovely.

Bungalows with kitchen, braai and bathroom facilities accommodate two/three/four people for US$37/47/54. 'Luxury' self-catering bungalows with four beds cost US$60. The ***restaurant*** and pool areas (three small pools and a nice bar) are open for breakfast, lunch and dinner, and also serve drinks.

Halali Halali, in the centre of the park, lies in a unique area that has several incongruous dolomite outcrops. It takes its name from a German term referring to the ritual blowing of a horn to signal the end of a hunt. The short Tsumasa walking track leads to the view from the summit of Tsumasa Kopje, the hill behind the camp, and a floodlit water hole extends wildlife viewing into the night. There is ***camping***, while self-contained double ***bungalows*** cost US$45 and four-bed units are US$50 and US$54.

Namutoni Namutoni was originally an outpost for German troops, and in 1899 the German cavalry built a fort from which to control the Owambo people. In the battle of 28 January 1904, seven German soldiers unsuccessfully attempted to defend it against 500 Owambo warriors. In 1956 the fort was restored to its original specifications, and two years later, it opened as tourist accommodation.

Beside the fort is a lovely limestone spring, the **King Nehale water hole**, which is clogged with reed beds and throngs of frogs. The viewing benches make a nice lunch spot and it's floodlit at night, but there are surprisingly few thirsty animals. If you're camping, watch out for midnight raids by potentially rabid jackals.

Two-bed ***rooms*** in the walls of the fort cost US$32 (US$47 with private facilities). Double ***rooms*** with bathroom and self-catering facilities cost US$47, and two-room, four-bed self-catering ***bungalows*** cost US$54.

Safari Lodges Etosha is surrounded by several privately run safari lodges. The luxurious ***Mokuti Lodge*** *(☎ 067-229084, fax 229091, ⓔ mokuti:@tsu.namib.com, PO Box 403, Tsumeb)* lies 2km down a side road from the von Lindequist gate. With nearly 100 rooms plus a pool and private game reserve, it's certainly accommoda ting. Prices start at US$77/109 for singles/doubles with half board, and it's almost worth the price for the restaurant alone. Etosha wildlife drives are also available. Web site: www.mokuti.namib.com

The ***Aoba Lodge*** *(☎ 067-229100, fax 229101, ⓔ aoba@tsu.namib.com, PO Box 469, Tsumeb)*, set on a private ranch of 70 sq km, accommodates up to 20 people in comfortable thatched bungalows. Rooms cost US$87/137, including half board. Wildlife drives into Etosha cost an additional US$75 per person.

Also great value is the ***Mushara Lodge*** *(☎ 067-230066, fax 230067, PO Box 1814, Tsumeb)*, 8km from von Lindequist gate. Here, comfortable bungalows cost US$75/134, including half board.

More upmarket is the ***Ongava Lodge*** *(☎ 061-225178, fax 239455, ⓔ info@nts.com.na, Namib Travel Shop, PO Box 6850, Windhoek)*, which sits on its own private wildlife reserve 3km south of Andersson gate, beside the tongue-teasing Ondundozonananandana Mountains. In addition to the luxurious main lodge, where you'll pay US$250/380, there's a more 'rustic' tented bush camp, which costs US$200/340. All rates include full board and wildlife-viewing activities.

Getting There & Away

Air Namibia connects Windhoek with Mokuti Lodge daily except Tuesday and Wednesday.

From Windhoek, it's possible to ride buses or minibuses as far as Tsumeb or Outjo, but from there, you'll only get to Etosha on a tour, or in a private vehicle or rental car. The best-value place to hire a car is Travel North Namibia in Tsumeb (see Information in the Tsumeb section earlier in this chapter). Note that walking, hitching, cycling and motorcycling are prohibited in the park.

To attempt hitching into the park, try petrol stations in Outjo or Tsumeb, but be sure that you're issued a separate park entry permit (as opposed to being included on the permit of your driver). Some officials may tolerate people discreetly seeking lifts from the rest camps to the highway outside the park gates, which is useful if you can't leave with the same driver.

Far Northern Namibia

During the war for independence, Owamboland, the home of the Owambo people, served as a base for the South-West African People's Organisation (SWAPO), and the villages of Oshakati, Ondangwa and Ombalantu were pressed into service as bases and supply centres for the occupying South African army. After the South Africans left, these new commercial centres attracted a growing number of entrepreneurs, many of who set up small businesses. Since then, the government has pumped money into the far northern area to develop housing, electricity services, roads, irrigation systems, healthcare and education.

Today, most Owambo follow subsistence agricultural lifestyles, growing staple crops and raising cattle and goats. The Owambo country is known for its high-quality basketware, sold at roadside stalls and in artists' homes for a fraction of what you'd pay in Windhoek. The designs are simple and graceful, usually incorporating a brown geometric pattern woven into the pale-yellow reed.

OSHAKATI

☎ 065

The Owambo capital, Oshakati, may be a friendly, bustling hive of activity, but the uninspiring commercial centre is little more than a strip of development along the highway. It lacks specific attractions, but you'll enjoy an hour wandering around the large covered market. Here you'll find a range of mostly unpleasant smells, along with clothing and baskets to *mopane* worms (caterpillars of the moth *Gonimbrasiabelina*, eaten as a delicacy) and glasses of freshly brewed *tambo*.

At the front of the market stands an odd monument: a dour figure standing with a

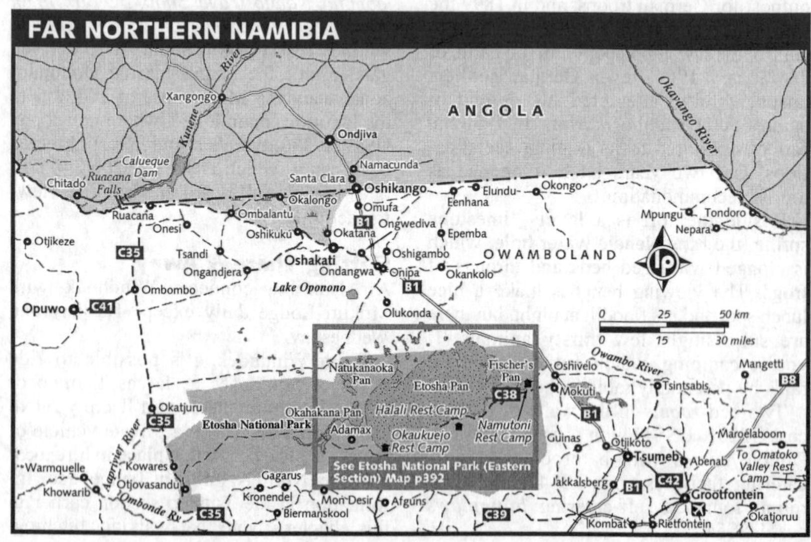

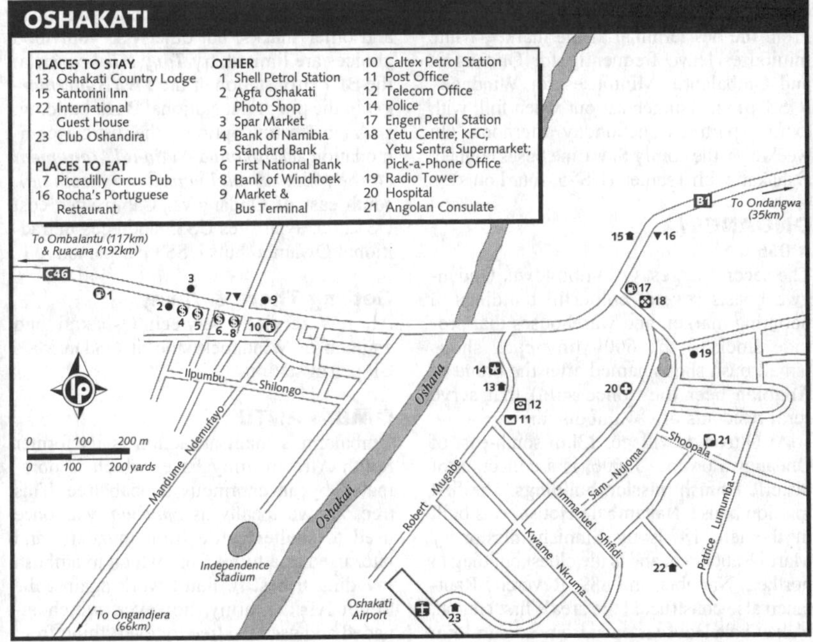

crashed plane (no one in town seems to be able to make a positive identification).

Information

Your best source for information is the Engen petrol station at the corner of the main road and Sam Nujoma Rd. For changing money, major banks are represented in the commercial centre. For phonecalls, go to Pick-a-Phone at the Yetu Centre or to the telecom office. You may be lucky enough to get an Angolan visa in Oshakati, but you'll normally fare better at the consulate in Windhoek. Fuji and Agfa slide and print film is available at the Agfa Oshakati Photo Shop. For car hire and travel bookings, see the Kunene Tourist Agency (☎ 220697, @ kta@osh.namib.com) on the main road.

Places to Stay & Eat

The ***Oshakati Country Lodge*** *(☎ 222380, fax 222384, @ countrylodge@osh.namib.com)* provides posh, heartless accommodation, mainly for business travellers and government officials; single/double rooms cost US$48/67.

The ***International Guest House*** *(☎/fax 220175)* charges US$48/54 for rooms with air-con.

If you want to feel like you've died and gone to Florida, stay at the ***Santorini Inn*** *(☎ 220506, @ santorini@osh.namib.com)*, on the main road north of town. This motel-style place has satellite TV, a pool, bar, restaurant, and an attached refrigeration shop, which ensures the air-con is working. Rooms start at US$48/64, with breakfast.

Club Oshandira *(☎ 220443, fax 221189)*, by the airport, charges US$40/49 for rooms, including breakfast. It has a pool, a bar, a restaurant, and green lawns.

Your best meal options are the ***Piccadilly Circus Pub***, ***Rocha's Portuguese Restaurant*** or the restaurants at the various hotels and lodges. There's also a ***KFC*** in the Yetu centre, as well as the ***Yetu Sentra Supermarket***.

Getting There & Away

From the bus terminal at the market, white minibuses leave frequently for Ondangwa and Ombalantu. Minibuses for Windhoek (US$16) via Tsumeb set out when full, with extra departures on Sunday afternoon. On weekdays, the comfy Star Line buses connect Oshakati with Tsumeb (US$5, four hours).

ONDANGWA

☎ 065

The second-largest Owambo town, Ondangwa boasts several colourful buildings, a booming market, and warehouses that provide stock to the 6000 tiny *cuca* shops (small bush shops named after the brand of Angolan beer they once sold) that serve rural residents of Owamboland.

At Olukonda village, 13km south-east of Ondangwa on the D3606, is a collection of historic **Finnish mission buildings**. The first mission house, **Nakambale House**, was built in the late 1870s by Finnish missionary Martti Rauttanen, and is the oldest building in northern Namibia. In 1889, Reverend Rauttanen also constructed the area's first church. Nakambale House is open from 8 am to 1 pm and 2 to 5 pm weekdays except Wednesday, 8 am to 1 pm Saturday and noon to 5 pm Sunday. Entry is US$0.20 and guided tours cost US$1. Accommodation is available in the village (see Places to Stay & Eat following).

Lost in the maze of routes and tracks south of Ondangwa lies **Lake Oponono**, a large wetland fed by the Culevai *oshanas* (underground river channels). After rains, the region attracts a variety of birdlife, including saddlebill storks, crowned cranes, flamingoes and pelicans. The edge of the lake lies 27km south of Ondangwa.

Places to Stay & Eat

Business travellers opt for the dingy ***Punyu International Hotel*** *(☎/fax 240556)*, 300m north of the Shell petrol station, where singles/doubles cost US$30/41.

The cluttered ***Ondangwa Rest Camp*** *(☎ 240310)* surrounds a fetid pond between the pink bank and the purple primary school. Camping costs US$5 per person. If there's no one around, check in at the Total petrol station. The attached cafe sells chips and other snacks, but otherwise your food choices are limited; try ***Tony's Takeaway*** at the BP petrol station or the ***Viva Supermarket*** in the pink First National Bank building.

An interesting option is the rustic accommodation at ***Olukonda National Monument*** *(☎ 884622, ⓔ elcinmus@iwwn.com.na)*, south-east of Ondangwa. Camp sites cost US$2, caravan sites US$3 and beds in traditional Owambo huts US$3 per person.

Getting There & Away

All bus services between Oshakati and Tsumeb or Windhoek stop at Ondangwa's BP petrol station.

OMBALANTU

Ombalantu's main attraction is its former South African army base, which is dominated by an enormous baobab tree. This tree, known locally as *omukwa*, was once used to shelter cattle from invaders, and later used as a turret from which to ambush invading tribes. It didn't work against the South African army, however, which invaded and used the tree for everything from a chapel to a coffee shop (a sign on the wall reads 'Die Koffiekamer Koelte', meaning 'The Coffee Chamber Cult'), a post office, a storage shed and an interrogation chamber for prisoners of war. It's now loosely described as the Omusati Region Museum, which also includes a nearby bomb shelter and a lookout tower dating from the South African days. The entrance is at the police station; if there's anyone around in uniform, respectfully ask permission to enter.

Minibuses link Oshakati and Ombalantu frequently. Minibuses also go to Ruacana.

RUACANA

☎ 065

The tiny Kunene River town of Ruacana takes its name from the Herero *orua hakahana* ('the rapids'). It was built as a company town to serve the 320-megawatt underground Ruacana hydroelectric project, which now supplies over half of Namibia's power.

The dramatic 85m-high **Ruacana Falls** was once a great natural wonder, but thanks to Angola's Calueque Dam, 50km upstream, the water flows only during the wettest seasons, when excess water is released over the dam and the weir (1km upstream from the falls). For a chance of seeing the falls flowing, visit in March or April. To enter the border area, visitors must sign the immigration register; from there, they can descend the 488 steps to the old power station in the Ruacana Gorge.

Beside the Hippo Pools oxbow lagoon, at the mouth of the Ruacana Gorge, is one of Namibia's worst camping grounds, ***Otjihampuriro***, where the toilets have never flushed and rubbish reigns supreme. It charges US$3 per person, but is probably better avoided.

The best accommodation is ***NAMPOWER Guesthouse*** *(☎/fax 270031)*, where rooms cost US$25/42, including breakfast; dinner must be prebooked and costs US$7.

Star line buses occasionally run to Tsumeb (via Oshakati) and to Opuwo. There are also minibuses to Oshakati.

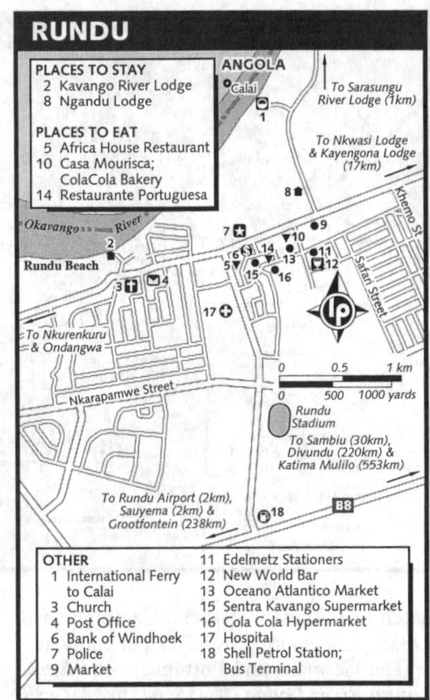

North-Eastern Namibia

The various regions of north-eastern Namibia, along with Owamboland in the far north, form the cultural heartland of Namibia.

The gently rolling Kavango region is dominated by the Okavango River and its broad flood plains. Here, people cultivate maize, sorghum and green vegetables along the bank, and supplement their diet with fish caught in woven funnel-shaped fish traps.

East of Kavango is the Caprivi Strip, Namibia's spindly appendage, where the flat, unexceptional landscape is characterised by expanses of forest. In fact, the difference between the highest and lowest points along the 500km-long Caprivi Strip, is only 39m.

South of Kavango, Bushmanland is starting to open up to visitors, thanks to increased interest in Kalahari cultures.

RUNDU

☎ 067

Rundu, occupying a lovely setting on the bluffs along the Okavango River, is a great spot for fishing, birdwatching and relaxing, but don't expect round-the-clock excitement.

At **Sambiu**, 30km east of Rundu, the Roman Catholic **mission museum** (☎ 251 111) exhibits traditional crafts and woodcarvings from southern Angola and Kavango; phone to arrange a visit.

Magazines, stationery and a few paperback books are sold by Edelmetz Stationers.

Places to Stay

The ***Kavango River Lodge*** *(☎ 255244, fax 255013, @ kavlodge@tsu.namib.com)*, with the best view in town, has basic single/double self-catering bungalows with air-con, TV and breakfast, from US$37/54. Its restaurant features Afrikaner country cooking.

The rather impersonal ***Ngandu Lodge*** *(☎ 256723, fax 256726, @ ngandu@tsu.namib.com)* provides convenient budget accommodation. Budget rooms with fan are US$17/30; standard rooms with air-con are US$27/42 and self-catering flats with

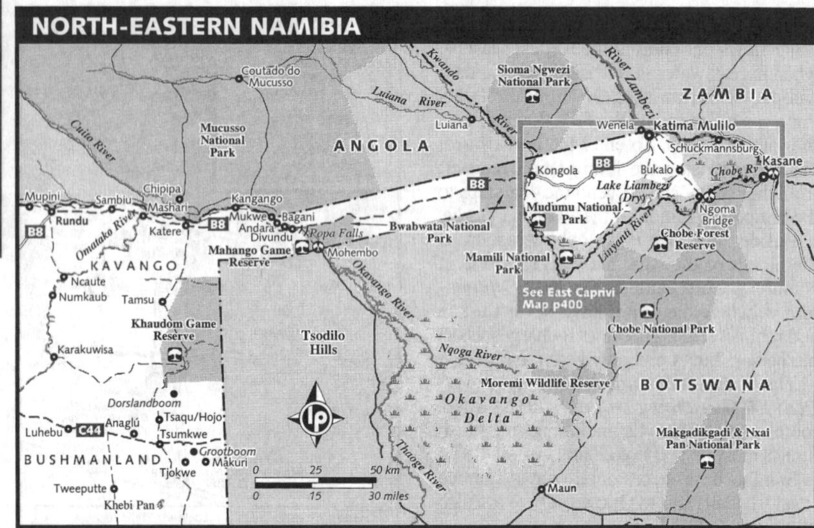

satellite TV cost US$45/54. Camping costs US$5 per person, plus US$2 per caravan.

The German- and Portuguese-run ***Sarasungu River Lodge*** *(☎ 255161, fax 256238, ⓔ sarasungu@tsu.namib.com)*, 4km from the town centre, offers camping for US$5 per person; the six bungalows, made from natural materials, cost US$52/67, including breakfast. The restaurant is well known for its pizza and pasta. Canoe rental, for pottering on the Okavango River, costs US$6 per person per hour. Phone for a pick-up from the bus terminal at the Shell petrol station.

The friendly and recommended ***Nkwasi Lodge*** *(☎/fax 255467, cell ☎ 081-127 4010, ⓔ nkwazi@iafrica.com.na)* offers a peaceful riverside retreat with a warm family atmosphere. Bungalows cost US$54/87, including breakfast, which is excellent value, given the standards and service. Camping is US$5 per person, including use of the swimming pool and bar. Lunch costs US$9 and dinner is US$13. The lodge lies about 13km east of Rundu, 4km north of the old River Road; transfers from the Shell petrol station (the bus terminal) cost US$9 per group. Don't miss the sunset cruise (US$5), the horse riding (US$13 per hour) or the incredible local dance program (US$3.50).

The same management also runs the ***Kayengona Lodge*** next door, which caters to overland groups, with simple bungalows costing US$14 (US$27 with bathroom), including breakfast.

Places to Eat

The popular ***Casa Mourisca*** serves excellent Portuguese specialities, as does the ***Restaurante Portuguesa***, both in the town centre.

The ***Africa House Restaurant***, run by two West African ladies, can fill you up with excellent, spicy dishes using recipes from their part of the world.

Self-caterers will find fresh fish, meat and other produce at the Portuguese-run ***Oceano Atlantico*** market. Full-service supermarkets include; ***Sentra Kavango Supermarket***; and ***Cola Cola Hypermarket***, which has a fine bakery a couple of blocks away.

Entertainment

The popular and pleasantly integrated ***Sauyema Night Club*** sits beside a large tree with lots of coloured lights in the suburb of Sauyema, south-west of town. On weekends, it rocks all night. If you're into sports on wide-screen TV with pizza, beer and billiards, visit the ***New World Bar***, behind Edelmetz Stationers.

Getting There & Away

The Star Line bus service between Windhoek (US$10, 11 hours) and Katima Mulilo (US$12, six hours) goes via Rundu, as does the Intercape Mainliner service from Windhoek ($US42, twice weekly) to Victoria Falls. When the border is open, access to Angola is via the Rundu-Calai international ferry.

KHAUDOM GAME RESERVE

The wild and undeveloped Khaudom Game Reserve, which covers 384,000 hectares on the border of Bushmanland, is like nowhere else in Africa. Along its meandering sand tracks you'll see roan, wild dog, elephant, zebra and almost everything you'd encounter at Etosha National Park, but in an unspoiled and untouristed context.

Namibia Wildlife Resorts asks visitors to travel in a convoy of at least two self-sufficient 4WD vehicles, equipped with food and water for three days; caravans, trailers and motorcycles are prohibited. The two camps, Khaudom and Sikereti (yes, it means 'cigarette'), offer basic four-bed ***huts*** for US$17. ***Camp sites*** cost US$14 (up to eight people). Accommodation must be prebooked at Windhoek, Rundu or Katima Mulilo. (For information on booking accommodation through NWR, see National Parks in the Facts about Namibia section earlier in this chapter.)

BWABWATA NATIONAL PARK

Namibia's newest park, established in late 1999, takes in the best of the former West Caprivi Game Reserve. It now consists of four zones: the 20,500-hectare West Caprivi Triangle, also known as the Kwando Core Area; the Mahango Game Reserve; the Buffalo Core Area, which lies on the Okavango River opposite the Mahango Game Reserve; and the Bagani/Omega agricultural areas.

Mahango Game Reserve

The 25,400-hectare Mahango Game Reserve occupies a broad flood plain north of the Botswana border and west of the Okavango River. It is best known for its dry-season concentrations of thirsty elephants. This is the only wildlife park in Namibia where visitors are permitted to walk on their own; winter is the best time for seeing wildlife and staying safely visible. Entry per day is US$1.75 per person plus US$1.75 per vehicle. The nearest NWR camp is Popa Falls, 15km north of Mahango.

Divundu

☎ 067

The nondescript settlement of Divundu is merely a creation of the highway junction; the real population centres are the neighbouring villages of **Mukwe**, **Andara** and **Bagani**. For travellers, Divundu offers a 24-hour petrol station; a fine supermarket; and a friendly tourist office (☎ 259042, fax 259041), with a small cultural museum, a curio shop, a cafe and Internet access (US$1.75 per 30 minutes).
Web site: www.audi-delta.com

Popa Falls

☎ 067

Near Bagani, the Okavango River plunges down a broad series of cascades known as Popa Falls. They're nothing to get steamed up about, but low water does expose a 4m drop. At the NWR rest camp, day entry costs US$1.75 per person and US$1.75 per vehicle. The kiosk sells the basics: tinned food, beer, candles and mosquito coils.

Places to Stay & Eat

For Mahango, ***Ngepi Camp*** *(☎ 267-660599 in Botswana, fax 259009, @ audicamp@info.bw)* is 4km off the road north of the Mahango gate. Camp sites cost US$3.50 per person and domed tents are US$5 per person. The staff can organise Mahango wildlife drives, as well as canoe trips on the Okavango River and *mokoro* (dugout canoe) trips in Botswana's Okavango Delta.
Web site: www.audi-delta.com

At the ***rest camp*** at Popa Falls, camp sites with braai pits cost US$14 for up to eight people; and four-bed huts are US$30.

The German-run ***Suclabo Lodge*** *(☎ 556 222, PO Box 894, Rundu)*, overlooking the

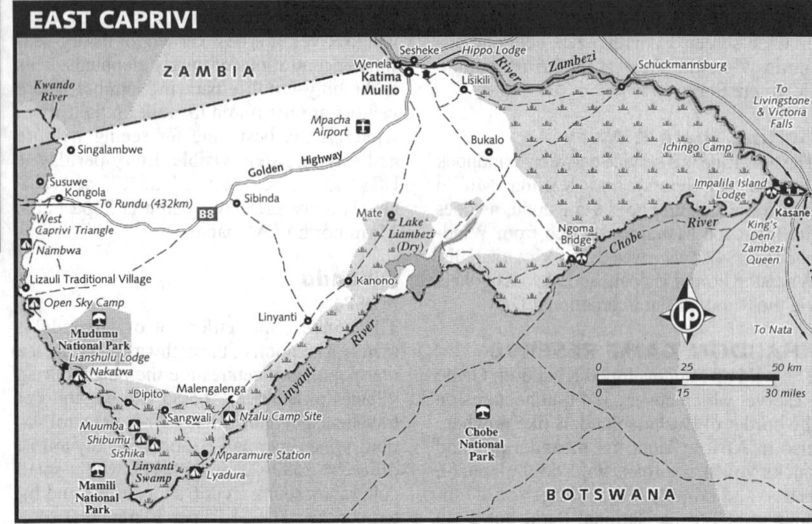

Okavango River 500m upstream from Popa Falls, has single/double bungalows for US$59/95. With full board and activities, the cost is US$85/124.

Getting There & Away

The gravel road between Divundu and Mohembo (on the Botswana border) is accessible by 2WD, and there's lots of traffic but no public transport. However, all buses and minibuses between Katima Mulilo and Runda pass through Divundu, where it's possible to hitch south to Mahango and Botswana. Driving through Mahango on the main road is free, but you'll have to pay the entry fee if you take the loop drives.

KATIMA MULILO

☎ 0677

Out on a limb at the eastern end of the Caprivi Strip lies Katima Mulilo, Namibia's most remote outpost. At 1200km from Windhoek, it's about as far from the capital as you can get in Namibia. This pleasant and very African town features lush vegetation and enormous trees, and was once known for the elephants that marched through. Nowadays little wildlife remains, apart from the River Zambezi hippos and crocodiles, but the ambience remains quite pleasant.

Information

On weekdays, the Bank of Windhoek, which sits beside the main square, changes cash and travellers cheques at an appropriately tropical pace. The post office is open from 8 am to 1 pm and 2 to 5 pm weekdays. For fax, email and Internet access, Cyber City (e cybercit@iafrica.com.na), in an incongruous hut near the market, delivers the bare minimum. It charges US$0.25 per minute (US$0.30 to send an email).

For travel information and bookings, your best option is Tutwa Tours, located on the main road west of the centre. Katima Mulilo also has a well-equipped hospital, including several VSO doctors and a pharmacy.

Caprivi Arts Centre

The Caprivi Arts Centre, run by the Caprivi Art & Cultural Association, is a good place to look for local curios and crafts, such as woodcarvings, baskets, bowls and traditional weapons. It's open from 8 am to 5.30 pm daily.

Places to Stay

The best-value place is ***Makusi Cabins*** *(☎/fax 3255)*, within easy walking distance of the centre, where budget cabins cost US$8 and singles/doubles with communal facilities are US$22/30, and units with bathroom are US$30/39. Meals are available.

A very basic backpackers' option, the ***Caprivi Travellers' Hostel*** *(☎ 3672, 2788)*, is a five-minute walk from the centre. Dorms cost US$4 and doubles cost US$17.

The relaxed ***Hippo Lodge*** *(☎/fax 3684)*, 6km downstream from town, offers camping for US$3.50 per person and rooms for US$37/55. The bar and restaurant have great sunset views and a frog chorus after dark.

The more upmarket ***Zambezi Lodge*** *(☎ 3203, fax 3631)* has self-catering bungalows for US$46/57, with breakfast. Camping in the flowery garden costs US$2.50 per person and US$1.75 per car. There's a pool, a restaurant and a floating bar on the Zambezi, as well as a nine-hole golf course.

Places to Eat

Coimbra Restaurant & Takeaways specialises in Portuguese-African food. For chicken-oriented snacks, there's ***Chicken Inn***, in the Kamunu Centre, east of the centre. The Zambezi Lodge's ***restaurant*** offers meals, but the most popular lunch and dinner spot is ***Mad Dog McGee's*** restaurant and bar, where the large menu includes a range of burgers, steaks, chicken, pasta and other dishes. If you're self-catering, try the ***Coimbra Supermarket & Takeaway***.

Getting There & Away

Air Namibia flies to Windhoek from Mpacha airport (18km south-west of town) daily except Tuesday, stopping at Mokuti Lodge (Etosha National Park) daily except Wednesday.

Star Line buses run between Windhoek and Katima Mulilo (US$21, 19 hours, twice weekly). The Intercape Mainliner passes through in both directions between Windhoek and Victoria Falls (Zimbabwe).

(For details about getting to Wenela, see under Land in the main Getting There & Away section of this chapter.)

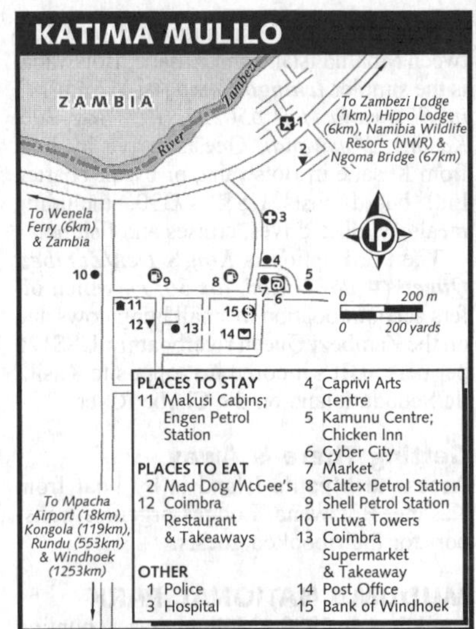

MPALILA ISLAND

Mpalila Island, driven like a wedge between Botswana and Zambia, sits at Namibia's outer eastern limits. The Kakumba sandbank, at its eastern end, actually reaches out and touches the western point of Zimbabwe, making it the one place in Africa where four countries meet. On a map, the area resembles Michelangelo's *Creation of Adam* on the ceiling of the Sistine Chapel (really – check it out!). In addition to that gratuitous distinction, the island is within easy reach of Victoria Falls and Chobe National Park.

The first two places to stay listed below appear on the Kasane & Kazungula map in the Chobe National Park section of the Botswana chapter.

The ***Impalila Island Lodge*** *(☎/fax 011-706 7207 in South Africa, fax 463 8251, ❷ info@impalila.co.za, PO Box 70378, Bryanston 2021, South Africa)*, overlooking the lovely Mombova rapids, makes an excellent upmarket getaway. The single/double rate of US$317/484 includes full board, boat transfers from the company's office in Kasane, Botswana (☎ 267-650795) and wildlife walks, drives and cruises.
Web site: www.impalila.co.za

Near the Mpalila immigration post (between Mpalila Island and Kasane, Botswana) is the simpler ***Ichingo Camp*** *(☎ 267-650143 in Botswana, fax 650223, PO Box 206, Kasane, Botswana)*. Guests arrive by boat from Kasane in Botswana, or by air charter. Full board costs US$264/330, including meals, wildlife drives, cruises and fishing.

The third option is ***King's Den/Zambezi Queen*** *(☎ 0677-3203, fax 3631)*, which offers accommodation in small bungalows and on the Zambezi Queen riverboat for US$125 per person. It's moored just opposite Kasikile/Sedudu Island on the Chobe River.

Getting There & Away

Access to Mpalila Island is by boat from Kasane, Botswana. Lodges organise transport for their booked guests.

MUDUMU NATIONAL PARK

Until the late 1980s, Mudumu was a hunting concession gone mad, and over the years the wildlife was depleted by both locals and trophy hunters. In 1989, Mudumu National Park and Mamili National Park were officially proclaimed in a last-ditch effort to rescue the area from environmental devastation.

In hopes of linking wildlife conservation and the sustainable use of natural resources around Mudumu with economic development in the local community, the former managers of Lianshulu Lodge and the local community established the **Lizauli Traditional Village**. Here, you can learn about the traditional Caprivian diet, fishing and farming methods, village politics, music, games, medicine basketware, tool-making etc. Tours cost US$5.50. To get there, follow the D3511, south of the Kongola petrol station.

Places to Stay & Eat

Mudumu's only official camping ground is at ***Nakatwa*** behind the Game Scout Camp 7km south-east of Lianshulu Lodge. It enjoys lovely views over the extensive riverine wetlands. In the lovely West Caprivi Triangle south of Kongola are a couple of NWR camping grounds; the most popular is ***Nambwa***, which may be booked at the Susuwe ranger station, north of Kongola.

At ***Open Sky Camp*** *(☎ 0677-2273)*, outside the park between Kongola and Lianshulu, riverside camping costs US$6 per site, chalets are US$24 per person and pre-erected double tents are US$19. Meals, wildlife drives and fishing trips are also available.

The ***Lianshulu Lodge*** *(☎ 061-214744, fax 214746, ⓔ mirages@iwwn.com.na, PO Box 142, Katima Mulilo)*, a private concession inside the park, is one of Namibia's most beautifully situated lodges. Just downstream lies the affiliated and equally lovely ***Lianshulu Bush Lodge***, which has an incredible riverview bar. Activities at both places include wildlife walks and drives in Mudumu, cruises in the pontoon *Jacana* and boat trips on the Kwando. Everywhere you're serenaded by an enchanting wetland chorus of insects, birds and frogs, and in the evening, hippos emerge to graze on the green lawns. Accommodation in single/double bungalows or A-frame chalets costs US$250/330, including all meals and two activities. Air transfers are available. To drive here, follow the D3511 for about 40km south of Kongola and turn west onto the signposted track to Lianshulu, 5km from the turn-off.

MAMILI NATIONAL PARK

Wild and little visited, Mamili National Park is Namibia's equivalent of the Okavango Delta, and when there's water, the park combines river channels, delightful wetlands and wildlife-rich islands. The forested areas brim with stands of sycamore figs, jackalberry, leadwood and sausage trees, and are fringed by *vleis* (low, open landscapes) and reed- and papyrus-choked marshes. Mamili's crowning glory is its birdlife and over 430 species have been recorded. The best time to visit is from September to early November.

Accommodation is limited to five wilderness camp sites: ***Lyadura*** and ***Nzalu*** in the east and ***Muumba, Shibumu*** and ***Sishika*** in the west. Camping permits are available from NWR in Windhoek. Access is limited to the 4WD tracks from Malengalenga north-east of the park and Sangwali village, which is north of the park.

EASTERN BUSHMANLAND

The flat, scrubby expanses of Eastern Bushmanland are cut by numerous meandering *omiramba* (fossil river channels), which support a rich ecosystem, including stands of camelthorn, red umbrella thorn and blackthorn acacia. Although the area lacks official protection, elephants roam freely, and in the dry season, antelope herds congregate around the panveld; when the rains come, they fan out to the west and north-west.

As the administrative capital, yellow-painted **Tsumkwe** is the only settlement of any size in this vast stretch of the Kalahari. It's also the service centre for the entire area, and you'll find basic groceries and snacks, and a tourist lodge (but no petrol).

Forming an arc north, east and south of Tsumkwe is a remote landscape of phosphate-rich natural pans, which are transformed into ephemeral wetlands after rains. The wetlands not only attract itinerant water birds – including throngs of flamingoes – but also provide a breeding habitat for ducks, spurwing geese, cranes, egrets and herons. The dry hard-crust landscape also supports baobabs, including several giants. The imaginatively named **Grootboom** (Big Tree) has a circumference of over 30m, and the historic **Dorslandboom** (Thirst Land Tree) bears carvings made by the Dorsland trekkers who camped here on their long trek to Angola in 1891. The immense **Holboom** (Hollow Tree) grows near the village of **Tjokwe**.

Information

Tourism in Eastern Bushmanland is regulated by the Nyae Nyae Conservancy (☎ 061-236327, fax 225997, e nndfn@iafrica.com.na), which also collects fees and activities charges from visitors. Entry costs US$3.50 per person per visit, and you can arrange activities such as hunting with the San (US$9) and gathering wild foods (US$4.50). Fees are per guide, and you'll usually be offered three or four – don't accept more than five! In the evening, you can experience traditional music and dancing by as many as 15 performers for US$37. Bookings should be made at Tsumkwe Lodge before you head into the bush; ask for Arno Oosthuysen.

Places to Stay & Eat

The conservancy has set up four official camp sites: the Holboom baobab at Tjokwe, south-east of Tsumkwe; Makuri village, a few kilometres east of that; Tsaqu/Hojo, north of Tsumkwe; and Khebi Pan, south of Tsumkwe, which is well out in the bush. The very basic sites cost US$2.50 per person.

Outside the conservancy, you have two choices. In Anaglú village, 11km west of Tsumkwe, you can stay at ***Camping /Anaglú/oo*** for US$2 per person. The ***Omatoko Valley Rest Camp***, at the junction of the C44 and D3306, has shady camping sites or thatched shelters for US$3 and four-bed bungalows for US$5 per person.

The ***Tsumkwe Lodge*** *(☎ 067-220117, radio ☎ 203581 and ask for 531, fax 067-220060, radio fax 264-207497 and ask for 528)* offers full board in single/double bungalows for US$64/107. To reach the lodge from Tsumkwe, go 1.5km south of the crossroads, turn right at the Ministry of Housing and continue for 500m. In Tsumkwe you can pick up limited supplies, but if you're heading for the bush you must be self-sufficient.

Getting There & Away

It's easy enough to get to Tsumkwe on the twice-weekly Star Line bus from Grootfontein (US$7, 6½ hours), but travel from there gets tricky. There are no tarred roads and only the C44, with good gravel, is open to low-clearance vehicles. Most roads require a 4WD. The only petrol is at the Hieromtrent 995 BP petrol station, which is 12km south of the C44 on the D2893, then 2km west on a ranch road. Unless you have reserves, it's an obligatory stop on the way to Tsumkwe.

North-Western Namibia

For many armchair travellers, Namibia is synonymous with the Skeleton Coast, a mysterious desert coast dotted with the corpses of ships run aground in sinister fogs. Namibia's desolate north-western corner also takes in the regions of Damaraland and

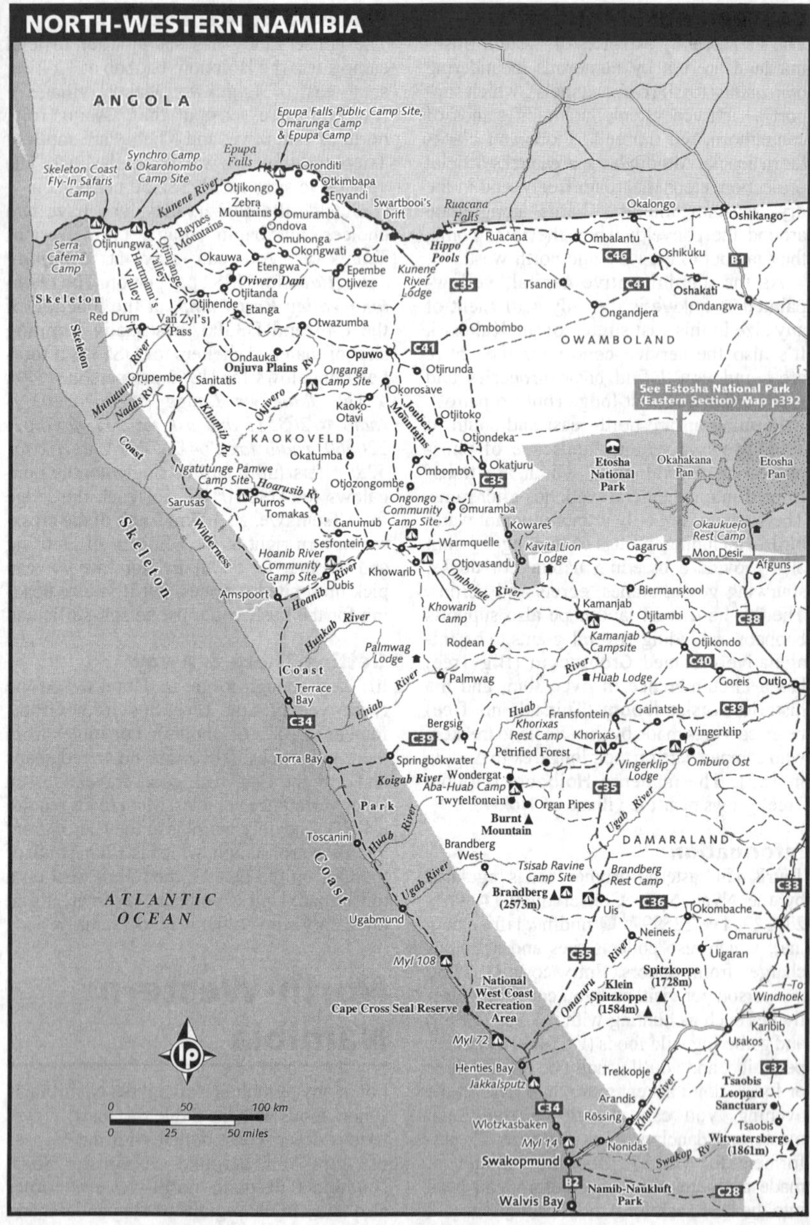
NORTH-WESTERN NAMIBIA
ANGOLA
Epupa Falls Public Camp Site, Omarunga Camp & Epupa Camp
Epupa Falls
Synchro Camp & Okarohombo Camp Site
Skeleton Coast Fly-In Safaris Camp
Kunene River
Oronditi
Otkimbapa
Enyandi
Otjikongo
Zebra Mountains
Omuramba
Swartbooi's Drift
Ruacana Falls
Okalongo
Oshikango
Baynes Mountains
Otjinungwa
Serra Cafema Camp
Hartmann's Valley
Otjinjange Valley
Ondova
Omuhonga
Okongwati
Otue
Kunene River Lodge
Hippo Pools
Ruacana
Ombalantu
C46
Oshikuku
B1
Okauwa
Etengwa
Epembe
Otjiveze
Ovivero Dam
Otjitanda
C35
Tsandi
C41
Oshakati
Skeleton
Otjihende
Etanga
Ondangwa
Ongandjera
Red Drum
Van Zyl's Pass
Otwazumba
Ombombo
OWAMBOLAND
Skeleton
Ondauka
Onjuva Plains
Opuwo
C41
Otjirunda
Orupembe
Sanitatis
Onganga Camp Site
Okorosave
See Estosha National Park (Eastern Section) Map p392
Munutum River
Nadas Rv
Khumib Rv
Otjivero Rv
Kaoko-Otavi
Joubert Mountains
Otjitoko
Coast
KAOKOVELD
Otjondeka
Okatumba
Etosha National Park
Okahakana Pan
Etosha Pan
Ngatutunge Pamwe Camp Site
Ombombo
Okatjuru
Otjozongombe
C35
Sarusas
Purros
Hoarusib Rv
Tomakas
Ongongo Community Camp Site
Omuramba
Skeleton
Wilderness
Ganumub
Kowares
Okaukuejo Rest Camp
Sesfontein
Warmquelle
Kavita Lion Lodge
Gagarus
Mon Desir
Hoanib River Community Camp Site
Otjovasandu
Afguns
Hoanib River
Dubis
Khowarib
Ombonde River
Biermanskool
Amspoort
Khowarib Camp
Kamanjab
Otjitambi
C38
Hunkab River
Kamanjab Campsite
Palmwag Lodge
Rodean
Otjikondo
C40
Coast
River
Huab Lodge
Goreis
Outjo
Terrace Bay
Palmwag
Uniab
Huab
Fransfontein
Gainatseb
C39
C34
Bergsig
Khorixas Rest Camp
Khorixas
Vingerklip
C39
Torra Bay
Springbokwater
Petrified Forest
Vingerklip Lodge
Omburo Öst
Koigab River
Wondergat
Aba-Huab Camp
C35
Park
Twyfelfontein
Organ Pipes
Ugab River
Burnt Mountain
Toscanini
Huab River
DAMARALAND
Coast
Brandberg West
Ugab River
Tsisab Ravine Camp Site
Brandberg Rest Camp
C33
ATLANTIC OCEAN
Brandberg (2573m)
Uis
C36
Okombache
Ugabmund
Neineis
Omaruru
Omaruru River
Uigaran
Myl 108
C35
Spitzkoppe (1728m)
Klein Spitzkoppe (1584m)
To Windhoek
National West Coast Recreation Area
Cape Cross Seal Reserve
Karibib
Usakos
Myl 72
Henties Bay
Trekkopje
C32
Jakkalsputz
Khan River
Tsaobis Leopard Sanctuary
Arandis
0 50 100 km
0 25 50 miles
C34
Rössing
Wlotzkasbaken
Tsaobis
Witwatersberge (1861m)
Myl 14
Nonidas
Swakop Rv
Swakopmund
B2
Namib-Naukluft Park
C28
Walvis Bay

Kaokoland (commonly known as The Kaokoveld), which have some of the country's most unusual natural features and fascinating cultures, including the Damara people and the enigmatic Himba people.

DAMARALAND

The territory between Skeleton Coast and Namibia's Central Plateau has traditionally been known as Damaraland, after the Damara people who make up much of its population. With lots of space and a negligible population, Damaraland has many natural attractions, including the **rock engravings** of Twyfelfontein and the **Brandberg**, Namibia's highest massif. Although it's not an officially protected area, Damaraland is home to many desert-adapted species, including giraffe, zebra, lion, elephant and rhino.

Spitzkoppe

The 1728m Spitzkoppe (Sharp Head), one of Namibia's most recognisable landmarks, rises mirage-like above the dusty pro-Namib plains (inland from the Namib Desert) of southern Damaraland. Its dramatic shape has inspired its nickname, the Matterhorn of Africa. Beneath an overhang in a large vegetated hollow known as Bushman's Paradise, there's a vandalised panel of ancient San paintings.

The community-based ***camping ground*** offers sites for US$2.50 per person plus US$1.25 per car. Following a well-publicised robbery attempt and fatal shooting in 1999, the local community, which relies on camping fees, has increased security in the hope of preventing further incidents. Water is scarce, so bring all you'll need.

There's no public transport, and although several Swakopmund tour agencies run day trips, you'll regret not allowing more time to explore this incredible place.

The Brandberg

The Brandberg (Fire Mountain) is named for the effect created by the setting sun on its western face, which causes the granite massif to resemble a burning slag heap. The Brandberg summit, Königstein, is Namibia's highest peak at 2573m.

The mountain's best-known attraction is the gallery of rock art in **Tsisab (Leopard) Ravine**, where you'll find the famous *White Lady of the Brandberg*. The figure, which isn't necessarily a lady, stands about 40cm high and has straight, light-coloured hair. The painting is a 45-minute walk from the car park and unofficial camping ground. Access is by private vehicle or organised tour.

Travellers who don't want to camp can stay in the company town of **Uis**, where there's a petrol station and the ***Brandberg Rest Camp*** *(☎/fax 504038)*. Single/double rooms cost US$27/45, and camping costs US$5 per person.

Brandberg Minerals (☎ 504036, fax 504091) runs geology tours and excursions to the Brandberg.

Khorixas

☎ 067

As the administrative capital of Damaraland, the decrepit town of Khorixas, might seem a good choice as a base for exploration. However, its atmosphere is less than welcoming, and as a result most travellers stop only long enough to refuel.

The bank opens only on weekday mornings. You may want to visit Khorixas Community Craft Centre, a self-help cooperative, which provides an outlet for local artists. The town holds an annual arts festival in May.

The convenient ***Khorixas Rest Camp*** *(☎ 331111, fax 331388, @ khorixas@iwwn.com.na, PO Box 2, Khorixas)* lies off the Torra Bay road, 3km north-west of town. Camping costs US$5 per person and fully furnished single/double bungalows are US$42/66. Amenities include a restaurant, braai area, swimming pool and general shop. Web site: www.iwwn.com.na/khorixas

The weekly Star Line bus between Otjiwarongo (US$5, 4½ hours), Outjo (US$3.50, three hours), Henties Bay (US$5, 4½ hours), Swakopmund (US$6.50, six hours) and Walvis Bay (US$8, 6½ hours) passes through Khorixas.

Petrified Forest

The Petrified Forest, 40km west of Khorixas, is an area of open veld scattered with petrified tree trunks up to 34m long and six metres around, which are estimated to be around 260 million years old. The original trees belonged to an ancient group of cone-bearing plants known as *gymnospermae*, which includes such modern plants as conifers, cycads and welwitschias. There's no official entry charge, but guides are compulsory and live only from tips; plan on US$1.25 per group for the 500m walking tour. Note that it's strictly forbidden to carry off even the smallest scrap of petrified wood.

Twyfelfontein

Twyfelfontein (Doubtful Spring), at the head of a grassy valley, is one of the most extensive galleries of rock art in Africa. The original name of this water source in the Aba-Huab Valley was /Ui-//Ais (Surrounded by Rocks), but in 1947 it was renamed by European settler D Levin, who deemed its daily output of one cubic metre of water insufficient for life in the harsh envi ronment. The 6000-year-old Twyfelfontein works aren't paintings but engravings, or petroglyphs, executed by cutting through the hard patina covering the local sandstone.

Entry costs US$1 per person plus US$1 per vehicle. Guides are available (plan on US$1 as a tip), but the route is easy and if you want more time than the guide is prepared to allow, you can usually arrange to walk alone. Note that some guides get lazy and omit the first part of the tour, so make sure that the first stops include the spring, the pump and the claw-like Wave Rock.

Nearby sites of interest include the **Wondergat sinkhole**, the volcanic **Burnt Mountain** and the **Organ Pipes** basalt columns. Access to these sites is only by private vehicle or organised tour.

Places to Stay The lovely ***Aba-Huab Camp***, near Twyfelfontein, is described as 'simple, rustic and natural'. Camping in tents or small open-sided A-frame shelters costs US$5 per person, and showers are normally available. Hot and cold drinks and basic groceries are sold on site, and simple meals are available if prebooked.

Kamanjab

☎ 067

The little town of Kamanjab, which sits in an area of lovely rock formations, functions as a minor service centre for northern Damaraland and the southern Kaokoveld.

The very friendly ***Oase Guesthouse*** *(☎/fax 330032)* has singles/doubles with half board for US$32/55. For meals, you're limited to the guesthouse (US$7/11 for lunch/dinner) or the bakery and takeaway. The new ***Kamanjab Campsite***, 3km from town in a beautifully rocky spot along the Torra Bay road, charges US$5 per person; it also offers a vehicle repair service.

Further out, 39km north-west of Kamanjab, lies Uwe and Tammy Hoth's very amenable ***Kavita Lion Lodge*** *(☎ 330 224, fax 330269, e logufa@namib.com)*, where injured or unruly lions find a home. In addition to guided wildlife walks and drives, the lodge offers a lovely walking track and excursions into Etosha and the Kaokoveld. Camping at the lodge's Otjombungu site costs US$7 per person and bungalows with full board are US$80 per person. Proceeds go to the Afri-Leo Foundation, which rescues problem lions from farming areas.

The acclaimed ***Huab Lodge*** *(☎ 312923)*, midway between Khorixas and Kamanjab, sits amid some of Namibia's most inspiring landscapes, and offers hiking, horse riding, wildlife viewing, and lazing in thermal springs beside the Huab River. Accommodation in thatched bungalows costs US$165 per person, including meals and activities.

The Star Line bus passes through Kamanjab twice weekly in each direction on the way to and from Otjiwarongo (US$7, 4½ hours), Outjo (US$6, three hours) and Opuwo (US$7, 5½ hours).

Vingerklip

The unusual Vingerklip lies on the Bertram farm, 54km east of Khorixas on the C39, then 21km south on the D2743. This towering 35m-high pillar of limestone is an erosional remnant of a plateau formed over 15 million years ago.

If you can stay at only one lodge in north-western Namibia, the ***Vingerklip Lodge***

(☎ 29031, fax 290319, ⓔ namdir@namib.com) would be an excellent choice. It enjoys spectacular views that include the Vingerklip itself. The panorama from above the bar is reminiscent of the famous scenes of Monument Valley in old John Ford westerns. Comfortable single/double bungalows cost US$105/137, including full board.

Palmwag

The Palmwag oasis lies amid stark red hills and plains in a surprisingly rich wildlife area. A super destination for day trips is the wildlife-rich **Van Zylsgat Gorge** on the Uniab River. Palmwag is also a good area to pick up carved pendants made from *uinidi* (vegetable ivory), the nut of the makalani palm, which cost around US$2.

The ***Palmwag Lodge*** *(☎/fax 064-404459, fax 404664, PO Box 339, Swakopmund)* is off the D3706, 157km north-west of Khorixas and 105km south of Sesfontein. Reed bungalows cost US$68/113; camping is US$8 per person. The watering hole for humans nuzzles against its elephantine counterpart, which attracts not only elephant but even black rhino. The place is run by Desert Adventure Safaris, which offers tours that include accommodation at the lodge.

Sesfontein

☎ 061

Sesfontein (Six Springs), which seems to belong in the Algerian Sahara, is built around a petrol station and a 1901 German fort. The fort has been converted into a lodge, ***Fort Sesfontein*** *(☎ 228257, fax 220103)*, where you can camp for US$6 per person or stay in a single/double for US$84/111. Web site: www.1023.com.na. If you're not eating at the lodge, there's a small shop selling staple goods.

Khowarib Camp, south of Sesfontein on the D3706, lies on a river bluff about 3km east of Khowarib village. Camp sites cost US$6 to US$14 per site plus US$3 per person, and accommodation in simple double huts costs from US$6.

Ongongo Community Camp Site lies 6km up the road from Warmquelle, on the road south from Sesfontein. For US$3 per person, you can camp within earshot of the paradisiacal Blinkwater falls and rock pool, created by a natural tufa formation.

Another community camp site, ***Hoanib River***, about 20km west of Sesfontein, offers great birdwatching, hiking trails and guided tracking of desert rhino and elephant. Camping costs US$5 per person.

To reach any of these sites, a vehicle with high clearance is required and a 4WD is recommended.

THE KAOKOVELD

You'll often hear the Kaokoveld described as 'Africa's last great wilderness'. Even if that isn't exactly accurate, this faraway corner of Namibia is certainly a beguiling and primeval repository of desert mountains and fascinating indigenous cultures. Being so isolated, even the wildlife of the Kaokoveld has specially adapted to local conditions. The most renowned example, of course, is the desert elephant, of which only about 35 remain. In addition, small numbers of black rhino survive here, alongside gemsbok, kudu, springbok, ostrich, giraffe and mountain zebra.

The easiest way to explore the Kaokoveld is with an organised camping safari, and several budget operators offer inexpensive packages (see Organised Tours in the Getting Around section earlier in this chapter). Otherwise, wait around the petrol stations in Ruacana or Opuwo and talk with passing expeditions. If you're a cook, a vehicle mechanic or a doctor you have the best chance of convincing someone you're indispensable.

The map to use here is the *Kaokoland-Kunene Region Tourist Map,* produced by Shell.

Opuwo

☎ 065

Although it's the Kaokoveld 'capital', Opuwo is little more than a dusty collection of commercial buildings ringed by traditional rondavels. You'll see lots of Himba and Herero people here, but the going rate for a 'people photo' is about US$1; please either respect local wishes or put the camera away. The brightly painted self-help curio shop sells Himba adornments and other local crafts.

Tourist information is available at the Kaoko Info Centre, which aims to soon offer email and Internet access. For vehicle repairs, the BP station poses the least risk, but don't break down here if you can possibly avoid it.

Ohakane Lodge runs half-day visits to Himba villages (US$57), day tours to Epupa Falls (US$450) and Epupa Falls transfers (US$337 for up to five people). For all tours, book at least one week in advance.

Places to Stay & Eat The ***Ohakane Lodge*** *(☎ 273031, fax 273025, ⓔ johans@iafrica.com.na, ohakane@iafrica.com.na)* charges US$68/ 90 for singles/doubles with bathroom, air-con and nice chunky furniture. There's also a swimming pool, a bar and a restaurant (guests only).

The ***Power Save Guesthouse*** has pleasantly cool dorms for US$13 a bed and camping for US$6. Guests may use the kitchen facilities. Coming from the south, turn left at the BP petrol station then take the next right; after passing the old hospital, turn left. It's several houses down on the right, beside a mobile home.

The amenable ***Kunene Village Rest Camp*** has a pleasant out-of-town location. Camp sites with braais cost US$4 and the proposed bungalows will probably never be finished. Follow the signposted turn-off from the Sesfontein road, 3km from town.

The French-owned ***Oreness Restaurant*** is the only decent restaurant choice in town, but the Ohakane Lodge does intend to open a public eatery. The Opuwo equivalent of quick culinary delights are available at the ***bakery*** beside the BP station, which sells doughnuts, pastries, yoghurt, beer, bread and delicious sausage rolls. The best-stocked supermarket is the ***Power Save***, and the ***drankwinkel*** next door sells soft drinks and alcohol.

Getting There & Away Star Line has buses from Otjiwarongo to Opuwo (US$11, 10 hours) on Sunday and Thursday, returning on Monday and Friday. There's also an intermittent Star Line service from Tsumeb, via Oshakati and Ruacana.

Swartbooi's Drift

☎ 065

From Ruacana, a 4WD track heads west along the Kunene River to Swartbooi's Drift, where a monument commemorates the Dorsland trekkers who passed here on the way to their future homesteads in Angola. The friendly ***Kunene River Lodge*** *(☎/fax 274300 or 240310, ⓔ kunenerl@osh.namib.com)*, 5km east of Swartbooi's Drift, makes an idyllic riverside stop. Camping costs US$5 per person, dorm beds are US$12 and single/double bungalows are US$27/30. You can hire canoes, fishing gear or mountain bikes, and organise white-water rafting trips (US$42 per person).

The Herero

The colourfully dressed Herero women, attired in their full-length Victorian-style finery on even the most stifling days, will be noticed by most visitors to northern Namibia. The unusual dress, which is now a tribal trademark, was forced upon them by prudish German missionaries in the late 19th century. The men, when traditionally dressed, wear a variation on the Scottish tartan kilt.

RICHARD I'ANSON

Epupa Falls

At this dynamic spot, whose name means 'falling waters' in Herero, the Kunene River fans out and is ushered through a 500m-wide series of parallel channels, dropping a total of 60m over 1.5km. The greatest single drop – 37m – is commonly identified as *the* Epupa Falls, where the river tumbles into a dark, narrow cleft. The river is in peak flow in April and May.

The pools above the falls make fabulous natural jacuzzis and you're safe from crocs in the eddies and rapids, but hang onto the rocks and keep away from the lip of the falls; once you're caught by the current, there's no way to prevent being swept over (as at least two people have learned too late). Swimming here isn't suitable for children. There's excellent hiking along the river west of the falls, and plenty of mountains to climb for panoramic views along the river and far into Angola.

Places to Stay & Eat The public ***camping ground*** at Epupa Falls can get very crowded, but it has showers and flush toilets which are maintained by the local community. Sites start at US$4 per person. Just upstream is Ermo Safaris' ***Omarunga Camp*** *(☎ 067-330220, fax 061-257123),* which operates through a concession granted by the local chief. Tented accommodation costs from US$42 per person. For US$120, you'll also get meals, airstrip transfers, visits to Himba villages and sundowner hikes.

Epupa Camp *(☎ 061-232740 for information, fax 249 876),* 800m upstream, was originally used by hydro project consultants and has now been converted into a luxury tourist camp. Tented accommodation with meals, drinks and activities (eg, Himba visits, sundowner hikes, river drives, trips to rock-art sites) costs US$130 per person.

Getting There & Away It's now possible to drive to Epupa Falls from Opuwo with 2WD, but the route is still very rough.

From Swartbooi's Drift, it's 93km to Epupa Falls via the Kunene River road. The area is known as the Namibian Riviera and it's among the loveliest places in Africa, but the route is challenging even with 4WD and can take up to 12 hours. The easier but less scenic 2WD route from Swartbooi's Drift goes via Otjiveze/Epembe.

The North-West Corner

West of Epupa Falls lies the Kaokoveld of travellers' dreams: stark, rugged desert peaks, vast landscapes, sparse scrubby vegetation, drought-resistant wildlife and nomadic bands of Himba people and their tiny settlements of beehive huts. This region, which is contiguous with the Skeleton Coast Park and Skeleton Coast Wilderness, is currently being considered for protection as the Kaokoland Conservation Area. From Okongwati, the westward route crosses the dramatic and treacherously steep Van Zyl's Pass into the **Otjinjange Valley**; this one-way road may only be taken from east to west.

Allow plenty of time to explore the wild, magical Otjinjange (perhaps better known as Marienflüss) and **Hartmann's Valley**, which lead to the Kunene River. The former ends at Kaokohimba Safaris' ***Synchro Camp*** on the Kunene River. The Hartmann's track ends at the ***Skeleton Coast Fly-In Safaris Camp***. Both these camps are open only to these safari companies' clients. (For more information on these and other safari companies, see Organised Tours in the main Getting Around section earlier in this chapter.)

At the community-run ***Okarohombo Camp Site***, at the end of the road at the mouth of the Otjinjange Valley, camping costs US$5. Facilities are limited to long-drop toilets and travellers must be self sufficient.

At ***Serra Cafema Camp***, at the mouth of Hartmann's Valley, access is limited to clients of Desert Adventure Safaris, based in Swakopmund. Note that no camping is permitted upstream in the Hartmann's or Otjinjange Valleys.

To foster sustainable tourism, the Integrated Rural Development and the World-wide Fund for Nature have established the ***Ngatutunge Pamwe Camp Site,*** near the confluence of the Hoarusib and Gamadommi riverbeds in Purros. Camping costs US$5 per person and facilities include showers and flush toilets. Campers may join guided hikes, donkey cart tours to Himba and Herero villages, and wildlife drives to observe desert-adapted wildlife and to learn about the natural pharmacopoeia.

SKELETON COAST

The term 'Skeleton Coast' properly refers to the stretch of coastline between the mouths of the Swakop and Kunene Rivers. The Skeleton Coast parks take in nearly two million hectares of gravel plains and sand dunes to form one of the world's most inhospitable waterless areas. The name is derived from the treacherous nature of the coast, which has long been a graveyard for unwary ships and their crews, hence its name. Once sailors were washed ashore in this desert wilderness, survival was out of the question.

The area is described from north to south.

National West Coast Recreation Area

☎ 064

The National West Coast Recreation Area, a 200km-long, 25km-wide strip from Swakopmund to the Ugab River, makes up the southern end of the Skeleton Coast. You don't need a permit to visit this area and the road is easily passable in a 2WD. This stretch of coast is extremely popular with anglers.

Most visitors head straight for **Cape Cross Seal Reserve**, a breeding reserve for thousands of Cape fur seals. It's open daily from 10 am to 5 pm all year. Entry costs US$1.75 per person plus US$1.75 per vehicle. There's a basic snack bar with public toilets. Note that no pets or motorcycles are permitted and visitors may not cross the low barrier between the seal-viewing area and the rocks where the colony lounges.

Places to Stay & Eat For information on places to stay in and around nearby Swakopmund, including ***Myl 4*** camping ground, see Swakopmund in The Central Namib section later in this chapter.

Along the salt road up the coast from Swakopmund, you'll find several bleak beach camping grounds set up mainly for sea anglers. ***Myl 14*** and ***Jakkalsputz*** have camp sites for US$12, while at ***Myl 72*** and ***Myl 108*** sites cost US$10, all for up to eight people. Myl 72 and Myl 108 each have a petrol station.

Supplies are available only at Henties Bay, where you'll also find ***Hotel De Duine*** *(☎/fax 500001, PO Box 1, Henties Bay).* Singles/doubles with bathroom cost US$36/50. Another option is the basic ***Die Oord Holiday Cottages*** *(☎ 500239, PO Box 92, Henties Bay).* Self-catering cottages for three/five/six people cost US$25/30/35. Bring your own towels.

For meals, the best place in Henties Bay is ***Spitzkoppe Restaurant & Pub*** *(☎ 500394),* which specialises in seafood (what else?) and boasts Namibia's longest bar.

Skeleton Coast Park

At Ugabmund, 110km north of Cape Cross, the salt road passes into the Skeleton Coast Park. Only the zone south of the Hoanib River is open to individual travellers, and everyone requires a permit. These cost US$3.50 per person plus US$1.75 per vehicle and require you to spend at least one night at either Torra Bay (open only in December and January) or Terrace Bay. To reach either camp, you must pass the Ugabmund gate before 3 pm or the Springbokwater gate before 5 pm.

Day visits are not allowed, but transit permits that allow you to drive on the road between the Ugabmund and Springbokwater gates are available at the Springbokwater and Ugabmund checkpoints. You must enter through one gate before 1 pm and exit through the other before 3 pm the same day; transit permits can't be used to visit Torra Bay or Terrace Bay.

Ugab River Hiking Trail The 50km Ugab River hiking trail takes in the coastal plain, then climbs into the hills and follows a double loop through fields of lichen and past caves, natural springs and unusual geological formations. This guided hike leaves from Ugabmund at 9 am on the second and fourth Tuesday of each month and accommodates groups of six to eight people. It costs US$34 per person and must be booked in advance through the NWR office in Windhoek (for

Lichen Fields

Neither plants nor animals, lichens actually consist of two components – an alga and a fungus – and provide perhaps nature's best example of symbiosis. The fungus portion absorbs moisture from the air, while the alga contains chlorophyll which produces sugar and starch to provide carbohydrate energy. Both algae and fungi are cryptogams, which means that they lack the sex organs necessary to produce flowers and seeds, and are therefore unable to reproduce as plants do.

Lichens come in many varieties. Perhaps the most familiar are the crustose varieties that form orange, black, brown or pale green ring patterns on rocks, but the gravel plains of the Namib support the world's most extensive fields of foliose lichens, which are free-standing. The lichens provide stability for the loose soil in this land of little vegetation. These fields are composed mostly of stationary grey lichen *(Parmelia hypomelaena)* and free-standing black lichen *(Xanthomaculina convoluta)*, but there's also a rarer orange variety *(Teleschistes capensis)*, an especially bushy lichen which grows up to 10cm high.

By day, the lichen fields very much resemble thickets of dead shrivelled shrubs, but with the addition of water the magic appears. On nights of heavy fog, the dull grey and black fields uncurl and burst into blue, green and orange 'bloom'. It's the fungus component that provides the lichens' root system and physical rigidity, absorbs the water droplets and draws limited nutrients from the soil. At the first light of dawn, however, before the sun burns off the fog and sucks out the moisture, the alga kicks in with its contribution: it uses the water droplets, light and carbon dioxide to photosynthesise carbohydrates for both itself and the fungus.

Lichens are incredibly fragile and slow-growing, and the slightest disturbance can crush them. Once that happens, it may take 40 or 50 years before any regeneration is apparent. Most of the damage to them is caused by thoughtless off-road driving.

The best places to observe the Namib lichens are south-west of Messum Crater, in scattered areas along the salt road between Swakopmund and Terrace Bay, and near the start of the Welwitschia Drive (see The Central Namib section later in this chapter).

contact information, see National Parks in the Facts about Namibia section earlier in this chapter). Hikers must provide and carry their own food and camping gear.

Torra Bay The Torra Bay camping ground is open only during December and January, to coincide with Namibian school holidays. ***Tent*** or ***caravan*** sites cost US$15 for up to eight people. Petrol, water, firewood and basic supplies are available, and campers may use the ***restaurant*** at Terrace Bay.

Terrace Bay The more luxurious Terrace Bay resort, 49km north of Torra Bay, is open all year. The area's main attraction is surf angling, but there's also a nice line of dunes to the north. Single/double ***accommodation*** at Terrace Bay costs US$67/90, including three meals and, of course, freezer space for the day's catch. The site has a ***restaurant***, shop and petrol station.

Getting There & Away The salt road which begins in Swakopmund and ends 70km north of Terrace Bay provides access to the National West Coast Recreation Area and the southern half of the Skeleton Coast Park. The park is also accessible via the C39 gravel road which links Khorixas with Torra Bay. Note that motorcycles are not permitted in the Skeleton Coast Park.

Skeleton Coast Wilderness

The Skeleton Coast Wilderness, between the Hoanib and Kunene Rivers, makes up the northern half of the Skeleton Coast Park. Here, seemingly endless stretches of foggy beach are punctuated by rusting shipwrecks and the cries of kelp gulls and gannets. The most commonly visited sites lie around Sarusas, historically a source of amethyst-bearing geodes, and include the coastal dunes, the **Cabo Frio seal colony**, the Clay Castles in **Hoarusib Canyon** and the **Roaring**

Sands. A lone park ranger who lives at **Möwe Bay** maintains a small museum of shipwreck detritus and newspaper clippings recounting the stories of shipwreck survivors.

The Skeleton Coast Wilderness is closed to individual travellers and access is only with fly-in safaris operated by the erratic official concessionaire, Olympia Reisen (ⓔ olympia@iafrica.com.na). However, the more recommended Skeleton Coast Fly-In Safaris operates tours within close proximity (see Organised Tours in the main Getting Around section earlier in this chapter).

The Central Namib

The Central Namib stretches over 2000km along the coast from the Oliphants River in South Africa to San Nicolau in southern Angola, and unlike the relatively well-vegetated Kalahari it gives an impression of utter barrenness. Much of its surface is covered by enormous linear dunes that roll back from the sea towards the inland gravel plains of the pro-Namib. Heading north, the dunes stop abruptly at the Kuiseb River, where they give way to flat, arid gravel plains interrupted by isolated ranges and hills known as inselbergs. The dunes may seem lifeless but they actually support a complex ecosystem capable of extracting moisture from the frequent fogs.

SWAKOPMUND

☎ 064

With palm-lined streets, seaside promenades and fine hotels, Swakopmund is popular with surfers, anglers and beach lovers from all over Southern Africa. For better or worse, the town reflects an overwhelmingly German heritage – indeed, some have said that it's more German than Germany. Thanks to its mild temperatures and negligible rainfall, Swakopmund generally enjoys a superb climate. However, there's a bit of grit in the oyster. When an easterly wind blows, the town gets a good sand-blasting, and in the winter, cold fogs produce a dreary, almost perpetual drizzle. This fog rolls up to 30km inland and provides moisture for desert-dwelling plants and animals, including 80 species of lichen.

Swakopmund gets very busy around Namibian school holidays in December and January, when temperatures average around 25°C, but in the cooler winter months, things are much quieter.

Information

Tourist Offices The helpful Namib i Information Centre (☎/fax 404827, ⓔ swainfo@iafrica.com.na), on Kaiser Wilhelm St, is open daily. Also useful is the Namibia Wildlife Resorts (NWR) office (☎ 404576), on Bismarck St, which sells Namib-Naukluft Park permits and is open on weekdays. After hours and on weekends, you can pick up permits from Hans Kriess Garage, on the corner of Kaiser Wilhelm and Breite Sts.

Money Swakopmund has branches of the major banks, which are open from 9 am to 3.30 pm weekdays, 8 to 11 am Saturday.

Post & Communications The GPO, on Garnison St, has a public telephone for international calls and a public fax office (☎ 402720). For fax services, Photographic Enterprises (☎ 405872, fax 405874), 55 Kaiser Wilhelm St, charges US$0.50 per page. Email and Internet access is available at the Alternative Space Backpackers; the Talk Shop Internet Cafe, on Moltke St; and the Swakopmund Adventure Centre.

Travel Agencies The Swakopmund Adventure Centre (☎ 406096, fax 405038, ⓔ swknadven@iafrica.com.na), on Roon St between Kaiser Wilhelm and Post Sts, is a central booking office for safaris, accommodation and adrenalin activities in Swakopmund and throughout Namibia. It also provides Internet and email access (US$3.50 for 30 minutes), and can book overland travel to South Africa, Botswana, Zimbabwe and beyond.

Bookshops CNA sells popular paperbacks and tourist publications. For literature, see the Swakopmunder Büchhandlung on Kaiser Wilhelm St. More esoteric works on art and local history are available at the Muschel Book & Art Shop, at 32 Breite St.

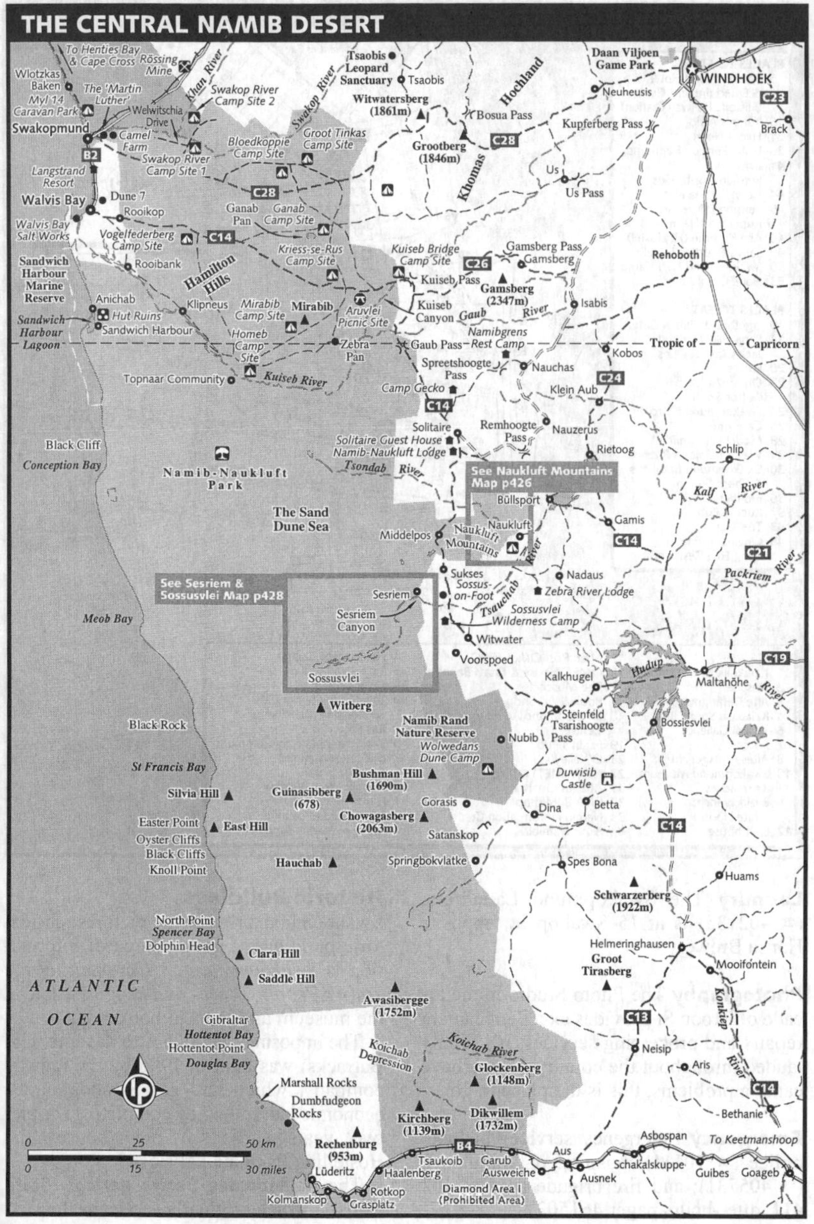
THE CENTRAL NAMIB DESERT
To Henties Bay & Cape Cross
Rössing Mine
Khan River
Wlotzkas Baken
The 'Martin Luther'
Myl 14 Caravan Park
Welwitschia Drive
Swakop River Camp Site 2
Swakop River
Swakopmund
Camel Farm
B2
Swakop River Camp Site 1
Bloedkoppie Camp Site
Groot Tinkas Camp Site
Langstrand Resort
C28
Walvis Bay
Dune 7
Rooikop
Walvis Bay Salt Works
Ganab Pan
Ganab Camp Site
Vogelfederberg Camp Site
C14
Kriess-se-Rus Camp Site
Sandwich Harbour Marine Reserve
Rooibank
Hamilton Hills
Anichab
Hut Ruins
Klipneus
Mirabib Camp Site
Mirabib
Sandwich Harbour Lagoon
Sandwich Harbour
Homeb Camp Site
Aruvlei Picnic Site
Zebra Pan
Topnaar Community
Kuiseb River
Tsaobis Leopard Sanctuary
Tsaobis
Witwatersberg (1861m)
Bosua Pass
Grootberg (1846m)
Khomas Hochland
C28
Daan Viljoen Game Park
WINDHOEK
Neuheusis
C23
Kupferberg Pass
Brack
Us
Us Pass
Rehoboth
Kuiseb Bridge Camp Site
C26
Gamsberg Pass
Gamsberg
Kuiseb Pass
Gamsberg (2347m)
Kuiseb Canyon
Gaub River
Isabis
Namibgrens Rest Camp
Gaub Pass
Tropic of Capricorn
Kobos
Spreetshoogte Pass
Nauchas
C24
Camp Gecko
Klein Aub
C14
Solitaire
Remhoogte Pass
Nauzerus
Solitaire Guest House
Namib-Naukluft Lodge
Rietoog
Schlip
Tsondab River
Black Cliff
Conception Bay
Namib-Naukluft Park
See Naukluft Mountains Map p426
Büllsport
Kalf River
The Sand Dune Sea
Naukluft
Gamis
Middelpos
Naukluft Mountains
C14
C21
Packriem River
Sukses
Sossus-on-Foot
Nadaus
See Sesriem & Sossusvlei Map p428
Sesriem
Zebra River Lodge
Sesriem Canyon
Tsauchab River
Sossusvlei Wilderness Camp
Meob Bay
Witwater
Voorspoed
C19
Hudup
Kalkhugel
Maltahöhe
River
Sossusvlei
Witberg
Steinfeld
Tsarishoogte Pass
Bossiesvlei
Black Rock
Namib Rand Nature Reserve
Nubib
Wolwedans Dune Camp
St Francis Bay
Bushman Hill (1690m)
Duwisib Castle
Silvia Hill
Guinasibberg (678)
Gorasis
Betta
Chowagasberg (2063m)
Dina
Easter Point
East Hill
C14
Satanskop
Oyster Cliffs
Black Cliffs
Knoll Point
Hauchab
Springbokvlatke
Spes Bona
Huams
Schwarzerberg (1922m)
North Point
Spencer Bay
Dolphin Head
Clara Hill
Helmeringhausen
Groot Tirasberg
Mooifontein
ATLANTIC OCEAN
Saddle Hill
Awasibergge (1752m)
Gibraltar
C13
Hottentot Bay
Hottentot Point
Koichab River
Koichab Depression
Neisip
Douglas Bay
Aris
Konkiep River
Glockenberg (1148m)
Marshall Rocks
C14
Dumbfudgeon Rocks
Dikwillem (1732m)
Kirchberg (1139m)
Bethanie
Rechenburg (953m)
Asbospan
To Keetmanshoop
B4
Tsaukoib
Garub
Aus
Schakalskuppe
Lüderitz
Haalenberg
Ausweiche
Ausnek
Guibes
Goageb
Rotkop
Diamond Area I (Prohibited Area)
Kolmanskop
Grasplätz
0 25 50 km
0 15 30 miles

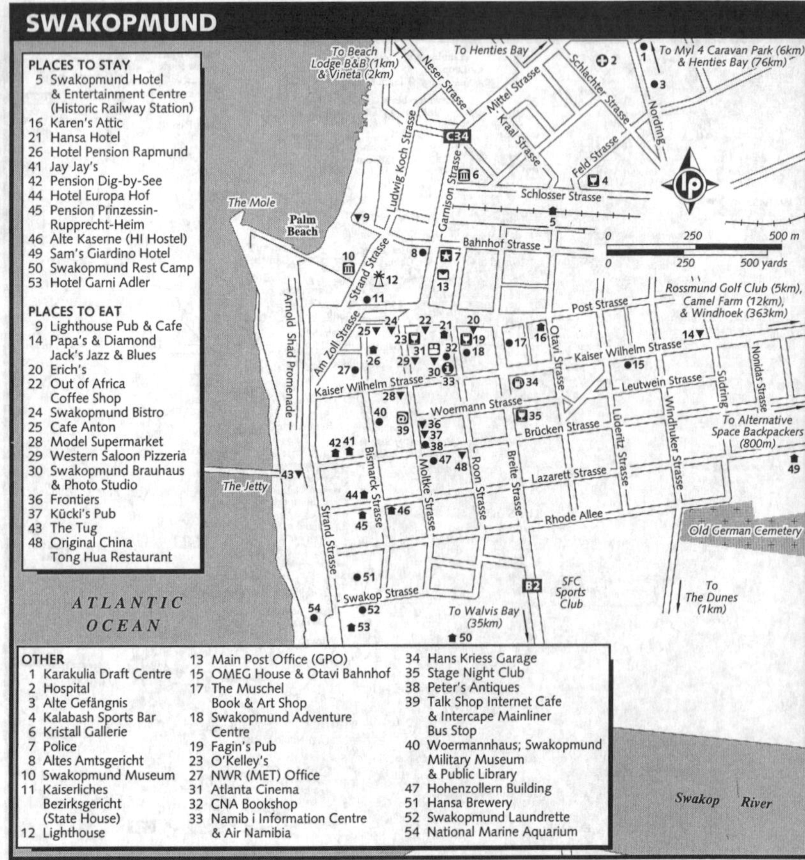

Laundry The Swakopmund Laundrette (☎ 402135) is at 15 Swakop St, opposite Hansa Brewery.

Photography The Photo Studio in the arcade off Roon St provides excellent camera repairs and processing services. It's highly lauded throughout the country; if you have camera problems, this is the place to go.

Emergency Emergency services include: police (☎ 10111); hospital or ambulance (☎ 405731); and fire brigade (day ☎ 402 411, after-hours pager 461503).

Historic Buildings

Swakopmund brims with picturesque historic buildings; a good source of information is *Swakopmund – A Chronicle of the Town's People, Places and Progress*, sold at the museum and in local bookshops.

The imposing, fort-like **Alte Kaserne** (Old Barracks) was built in 1906 by the railway company, which had got Swakopmund's economic ball rolling by completing the pier two years earlier. It now houses the Hostelling International Hostel.

The **Kaiserliches Bezirksgericht (State House)**, which originally served as the District Magistrate's Court, was designed by Carl Schmidt in 1901 and constructed the following year. It was extended in 1905 and a tower was added in 1945. After WWI, the building was modified to serve as an official holiday home of the territorial administrator. In keeping with that tradition, it's now the official Swakopmund residence of the executive president.

Designed by Otto Ertl, the gabled **Altes Amtsgericht** was constructed in 1908 as a private school. However, when the funds ran out, the government took over the project and requisitioned it as a magistrates' court. In the 1960s, it functioned as a school dormitory, and now houses municipal offices. Just so no one can doubt its identity, the words *Altes Amtsgericht* are painted across the front of the building.

The ornate **train station** (Bahnhof) was built in 1901 and declared a national monument in 1972. It was originally constructed as the terminus for the Kaiserliche Eisenbahn Verwaltung (Imperial Railway Authority) railway, which connected Swakopmund with Windhoek. When this state railway was closed in 1910, the building assumed the role as main station for the narrow-gauge mine railway between Swakopmund and Otavi. It now houses the Swakopmund Hotel & Entertainment Centre.

The excessively Baroque-style **Hohenzollern building**, on the corner of Moltke and Brücken Sts, is probably Swakopmund's most imposing and unusual structure. It dates back to 1906, and from its appearance you can probably guess that it was originally intended as a hotel. Its outlandish decor is crowned by a fibreglass cast of Atlas supporting the world, which replaced the rather precariously placed cement version, which graced the roof prior to renovations in 1988.

Especially picturesque is the 1905 **Woermannhaus**. It has, over the years, served as the main offices for the Damara & Namaqua Trading Company, a hostel for merchant sailors, a school dormitory, and now, the town library. The prominent Damara tower once served as a water tower and a landmark for ships at sea and traders arriving by oxwagon from the interior. When seen from the shore, the delightfully archetypal German structure stands out above the surrounding buildings and you'd be forgiven for assuming it's the town hall. In the 1920s, it fell into disrepair, but was declared a national monument and restored in 1976. It now contains the small **Swakopmund Military Museum** and a gallery of historic paintings, and affords a splendid panorama over the town; stop by the library and pick up a key.

The impressive **Alte Gefängnis** (Old Prison) was designed by architect Heinrich Bause and dates back to 1909. If you didn't know this building was a prison, you'd swear it was either an early German railway station or health-spa hotel. In fact, the main building was used only for staff housing, while the prisoners occupied less opulent quarters to one side. Note that it still serves as a prison and is considered a sensitive structure, so photography is not permitted.

The colonial company Otavi Minen- und Eisenbahn-Gesellschaft (OMEG) oversaw the rich mines around Otavi and Tsumeb in north-central Namibia. As there was a connection to the coast by a narrow-gauge railway in the early 1900s, the company also maintained an office in Swakopmund. Until 1910, the **OMEG House**, on Kaiser Wilhelm St, served as a warehouse. Next door is the **Otavi Bahnhof**, the old train station for the Tsumeb line.

Living Desert Snake Park

The Living Desert Snake Park (☎ 405100), at 15 Kaiser Wilhelm St, houses an array of serpentine sorts. The owner knows everything you'd ever want to know – or not know – about snakes, scorpions, spiders and other widely misunderstood creatures. She feeds them at 4 pm daily. Entry costs US$2.

National Marine Aquarium

The National Marine Aquarium, on the waterfront, provides an excellent introduction to the cold offshore world in the South Atlantic. Most impressive is the tunnel through the largest aquarium, which allows close-up views of graceful rays, toothy sharks (you can literally count the teeth!) and other marine beasties found on seafood platters around the country. The fish are fed daily at 3 pm, which makes for an interesting spectacle. The aquarium is open from 10 am to 6 pm Tuesday to Saturday and 11 am to 5 pm Sunday. It's closed on Monday unless there's a public holiday. Entry is US$1.50; pensioners pay half-price.

Kristall Gallerie

A new attraction in Swakopmund is the architecturally fascinating Kristall Gallerie (☎ 406080, fax 406084, e gems@kristallgalerie.com.na), which is a mineralogical museum featuring some of the most incredible crystal formations on earth, including the largest quartz crystal ever found. It's open daily except Sunday and entry costs N$15.

The adjacent shop features some lovely items, including mineral samples, crystal jewellery, and intriguing plates, cups and wine glasses carved from local stone.
Web site: www.kristallgalerie.com

Dunes

An interesting short hike will take you across the Swakop River bed to the large dune fields south of town. You can easily spend several hours exploring the dune formations and unique vegetation, and with a sheet of masonite, you can spend hours sledding down the slopes. Alternative Space Backpackers loans dune carts to its guests, and several tour companies offer sandboarding and quad-biking (see Activities, later in this section).

Swakopmund Museum

The superb Swakopmund Museum, at the foot of the lighthouse, displays exhibits on Namibia's history, ethnology and flora and fauna such as the !nara melon. It also contains a well-executed reconstruction of early colonial home interiors and an informative display on the Rössing Mine. The museum occupies the site of the old harbour warehouse, which was destroyed in 1914 by a 'lucky' shot from a British warship. It's open from 10 am to 12.30 pm and 3 to 5.30 pm; entry is US$1.50 (students pay half-price).

Hansa Brewery

Aficionados of the amber nectar will certainly want to visit the Hansa Brewery (☎ 405021), at 9 Rhode Allee, which is the source of Swakopmund's favourite drop. Free brewery tours – with ample opportunity to sample the product – run on Tuesday and Thursday, but must be prebooked.

Activities

Swimming in the sea is best done in the lee of the Mole (the seawall), although even in summer, the water is never warmer than 20°C. The best **surfing** is at Nordstrand or 'Thick Lip' near Vineta Point.

The par 72 Rössmund Golf Club (☎ 405644) accommodates anyone after 18 holes of desert **golf**; it's 5km east of Swakopmund on the main road. The course is open daily and you can hire equipment.

Swakopmund is trying to become a sort of waterless Victoria Falls, and has made some progress with its sandboarding, quad-biking, parachuting and other adrenalin boosters. **Sandboarding** is available from Alter Action (☎/fax 402737, cell ☎ 081-128 2737, e alteraxn@iafrica.com.na); contact them through Alternative Space Backpackers (see Places to Stay later in this section). For US$20, you get a sandboard, gloves, goggles, transport to the dunes and enough polish to ensure an adrenalin high. The highlight is a 60km/h *schuss* down a 120m mountain of sand. Slogging up the dunes can be rather taxing, so you need to be fit and healthy. For the less adventurous, Alter Action also arranges **birdwatching** tours to the salt pans, sewage works and Nonidas wetlands.

Jeff at Desert Explorers (☎ 408096, cell ☎ 081-129 2380, fax 405649) leads ecologically sensitive **quad-biking** tours on the dunes, which include instruction, helmets, goggles and lunch, for US$55. For more stomach-churning thrills, the Skydive Swakopmund parachute club (☎ 402841, cell ☎ 081-124 5167, e travel@ntc.com.na) does internationally recognised **parachuting** courses for US$90, including instruction, one jump and a logbook. Each additional jump costs US$30.

The Crazy Camel (cell ☎ 081-128 2670) offers 'mind-blowing' **climbing** and **abseiling** trips to the Spitzkoppe; you can choose between day and overnight expeditions.

Okakambe Trails (☎ 402799) runs overnight wilderness **horseback trips** along the Swakop River to the Goanikontes Oasis for US$70, including meals. Shorter trips are also available. Westcoast Angling Tours (☎ 402377, fax 402532), 9 Otavi St (PO Box 545, Swakopmund), and Blue Marlin (☎ 405070, cell ☎ 081-127 5070) organise deep-sea **fishing** trips for snoek, yellowtail and copper shark, as well as rock and surf angling from the beach; rates start at around US$70 per day. **Whale watching** and photography cruises cost US$40.

Balloon trips over the dunes are available from African Adventure Balloons (☎/fax 403455); champagne breakfast/sundowners trips cost US$125/200 per person.

Organised Tours

From Swakopmund, the only company to offer organised tours to Sossusvlei (US$150) is Crazy Kudu Safaris (see Organised Tours in the Getting Around chapter). Several other safari operators offer day tours and overnight trips. Among the most popular are Charly's Desert Tours (☎ 404341, fax 404821, ❷ charlydt@iwwn.com.na), 11 Kaiser Wilhelm St; Namibia Photo Tours (☎ 404561), 8 Roon St; and Nolte Adventure Safaris (☎/fax 405454, ❷ noltesaf@iafrica.com.na), web site www.horizon.fr/namibia/nolte.html; Rhino Tours (☎/fax 405757) PO Box 4369, Vineta; and Desert Adventure Safaris (☎ 404459, fax 404072, ❷ dassaf@iafrica.com.na, www.natron.net/tour/das/dash page2.htm).

Turnstone Tours (☎ 403123, fax 403290, ❷ 081-1292331) have been recommended for very good tours, with birdwatching and natural history slant.
Web site: www.swk.namib.com/turn

Half-day options with all these companies include Cape Cross (US$39); Rössing Mine gem tours (US$34); and Welwitschia Drive (US$31). Full-day trips run to the Spitzkoppe (US$42); the Kuiseb Delta and Walvis Bay Lagoon (US$50); sundowner tours on the dunes (US$22); and the Brandberg (US$55). Pleasure Flights (☎ 404500, fax 405325, ❷ redbaron@iml-net.ocm.na) offers 'flightseeing' tours over the colourful salt works, Sandwich Harbour, Welwitschia Drive, the Brandberg, the dunes, the Skeleton Coast and beyond; for a one-hour circuit, you'll pay US$50 per person.

Places to Stay

During the school holidays, from October to March (and especially December and January), Swakopmund accommodation is booked up well in advance, so either book early or come prepared to camp.

Places to Stay – Budget

The nearest camping is at ***Myl 4*** *(☎ 461781)*, on a cold and windswept beach north of town. Camp sites costs US$3 plus US$2 per person, and beach bungalows cost from US$11 to US$41; note that security can be a problem here.

The most atmospheric budget choice is the delightfully alternative ***Alternative Space Backpackers*** *(☎ 404027, ☎/fax 402713, ❷ thespace@iwwn.com.na, 46 Dr Alfons Weber St)*, on the desert fringe. Dorms cost US$7, including use of cooking facilities and a bizarre turret toilet. The main attractions here are the castle-like architecture, saturation artwork, its industrial-waste-recycling theme and the always friendly welcome from Frenus, Sybille and Rafael. Transport to/from town is free on request and it's just a 15-minute walk to a great sunset view from the dunes. Dune carts (free to guests) are guaranteed to provide a thrilling experience.

Swakopmund Rest Camp *(☎ 402807, fax 402076, Private Bag 5017, Swakopmund)* is so entangled in barbed wire that it has locally been dubbed 'Stalag 13'. You can choose from four-bed A-frame huts for US$35; two/four-bed 'fishermen's shacks' for US$12/19; four-bed flats for US$26; and self-contained six-bed bungalows/flats with TV, kitchen and bath for US$40/US$47. No animals or motorcycles are allowed.

Hostelling International Hostel *(☎ 404 164)*, in the Alte Kaserne, takes an appropriately military approach, and mature adults may feel cramped. Dorms are US$5 and private doubles cost US$11. Another backpackers' choice is ***Karen's Attic*** *(☎ 403 057, fax 405679, ❷ kattic@iafrica.com.na or petra@swk.namib.com)*, at the corner of Otavi and Post Sts. With good kitchen facilities and a TV lounge, it's a relatively plush place. Dorm places cost US$5 and single/double rooms are US$9/14.

Another inexpensive option is ***Jay Jay's*** *(☎ 402909)* on Brücken St, with simple rooms with bath for US$9/16, or with shared bathroom for US$7/13. Dorms cost US$5. It's clean and well located just half a block from the sea. On the ground floor there's a restaurant and typically noisy bar.

Places to Stay – Mid-Range

Pension Dig-by-See *(☎ 404130, fax 404170, 4 Brücken St)*, or just Digby's, has singles/doubles for US$26/37, with a large buffet breakfast. Rooms for three or four people cost US$18 per person and self-catering holiday flats cost US$80. Also near the beach is the ***Beach Lodge B&B*** *(☎ 500933, fax 400934, volkb@iafrica.com.na)*, where you'll get rooms with a sea breeze for US$28/45.

Pension Prinzessin-Rupprecht-Heim *(☎ 402231, fax 402019)*, housed in the former colonial hospital, has a lovely garden and charges US$25/42 for a room with bath. Small single rooms with shared facilities are US$8.50. All rates include breakfast.

The friendly ***Hotel-Pension Rapmund*** *(☎ 402035, fax 404524)* on Bismarck St charges US$30/34 for a room in the back and US$52/57 for a room with a sea view. All rates include breakfast, and this is among the most welcoming spots in Swakopmund.

Places to Stay – Top End

A good-value option is the ***Hotel Europa Hof*** *(☎ 405898, fax 402391, europa@iml-net.com.na)*, which resembles a Bavarian chalet, complete with colourful flower boxes and Alpine flags flying from the 1st-floor windows. Singles/doubles are US$48/68.

Another lovely European-style choice is ***Sam's Giardino Hotel*** *(☎ 403210, fax 403500, samsart@iafrica.com.na)*, which mixes Swiss and Italian-style hospitality and architecture. Rooms with a superb continental breakfast start at US$55/60.
Web site: www.giardino.com.na

Also nicely located is the ***Hotel Garni Adler*** *(☎ 405045, fax 404206, 3 Strand St)*, near the beach, where standard singles cost from US$50 to US$65 and doubles are US$72; there's a small surcharge for a sea view or use of the sauna.

At the charming ***Hansa Hotel*** *(☎ 400311, fax 402732, hansa@iml-net.com.na)*, which bills itself as 'luxury in the desert', standard rooms start at US$54/72, each of which is individually decorated. Rooms with a balcony and garden view cost US$66/88.

The ***Swakopmund Hotel & Entertainment Centre*** *(☎ 400800, fax 400801, shec@iafrica.com.na)*, in the renovated historic train station, houses a posh four-star hotel, the Platform One restaurant, the Captain's Tavern Pub, a casino, a large pool and a conference centre. Fortunately, much of the original train station has been left intact. Standard rooms are US$84/127, while luxury rooms cost US$150/167.

Places to Eat

At the wonderful ***Out of Africa Coffee Shop*** on Post St you'll find Namibia's best coffee – espresso, cappuccino, latte and other specialities – served up in French-style cups, and enormous and indescribably delicious muffins. Its motto is: 'Life is too short to drink bad coffee'. It's open daily except Sunday.

Pizza is also big in this town. Many locals reckon the best pizza in town comes from ***Papa's*** *(☎ 404747)*, in the Shop-Rite Centre, where large pizzas cost from US$4 to US$7. Also excellent is the ***Western Saloon*** *(☎ 464176)*, which has been transformed into a pizzeria; large pizzas go for US$3 to US$6. An ethnic alternative is the variable menu at the ***Original China Tong Hua Restaurant***, which also serves pizzas.

The ***Swakopmund Bistro*** *(☎ 402333)* does excellent and imaginative pub lunches and dinners, including a variety of salads, vegetarian specialities, crepes, gyros, steaks and seafood specials. It's open until 10 pm nightly. A place for one of Swakopmund's most sought-after commodities is the ***Swakopmund Brauhaus*** *(☎ 402214)*, a restaurant and boutique brewery in the arcade at 22 Kaiser Wilhelm St.

Several smaller restaurants specialise in seafood, including the upmarket ***Erichs*** *(☎ 405141)*, on Post St, which is open for lunch and dinner. It focuses on fish and steak dishes, and does a mean Tiroler knüdelsuppe. Another decent choice for fish is ***Tug*** *(☎ 402356)*, which is housed in the beached tugboat *Danie Hugo*, near the jetty.

The very popular ***Lighthouse Pub & Cafe*** *(☎ 400894)* features all sorts of good-value seafood including kabeljou, calamari, kingclip, lobster and a large seafood platter, as well as an appropriate view of the beach and crashing surf. Other specialities include burgers, salads, pasta, steaks, ribs and pizzas.

The rather pretentious ***Cafe Anton*** *(☎ 402 419)* does superb (albeit expensive and skimpy) coffee, *apfelstrüdel*, *linzertorte* and a host of other Deutsche delights. It's the best place for an afternoon snack in the sunshine.

You'll find great pub meals at ***Kücki's Pub*** *(☎ 402407)*, which is actually one of the best restaurants in town; don't miss the amazing seafood platter. Just north is the ***Frontiers*** steakhouse, with a popular dinner buffet for US$7.

At the ***Model Supermarket*** you can pick up groceries or have a snack at the coffee bar.

Entertainment

On Friday, ***Diamond Jack's Jazz & Blues*** *(☎ 404747)* at Papa's Pizzeria offers excellent jazz evenings. ***O'Kelley's***, which emphasises local disco music and dancing, is open from 8 pm until 4 am nightly. The popular ***Kalabash Sports Bar***, on Feld St, is the local hang-out for rugger and footie fanatics. Another local favourite is ***Fagin's Pub***, near the Atlanta Hotel on Roon St. The younger set generally prefers the ***Stage Night Club*** disco, in Hotel Grüner Kranz.

The ***Atlanta Cinema***, in the arcade on Kaiser Wilhelm St, screens several popular films nightly.

Shopping

Swakopmund has all sorts of places for tourists to deposit their holiday cash. One of the most unusual shops you'll ever see is Peter's Antiques, on Moltke St; in addition to all sorts of antiques – some rather politically incorrect – it has a bizarre collection of genuine relics and fetishes from around Africa. The Karakulia Craft Centre, on Knobloch St, produces and sells hand-woven rugs, carpets and wall-hangings made of karakul wool, and conducts tours of the spinning, dyeing and weaving processes. It also markets crafts from the Western Kunene area, which benefits the Save the Rhino Trust.

Getting There & Away

Air Namibia (☎ 405123) flies at least four times weekly between Swakopmund and Windhoek's Eros airport; you can also fly to/from Lüderitz, Alexander Bay and Cape Town.

Intercape Mainliner (☎ 061-227847) has daily bus services to Windhoek (US$19) and to Walvis Bay; its terminal is at the mall at the corner of Woermann and Moltke Sts. A new transport option between Swakopmund and Windhoek is the daily Wal-Wind Express (☎ 206365), which charges US$8.50 and picks up prebooked passengers at either the post office or the Alternative Space Backpackers. Alternatively, there's Pasedeno (☎ 406063), which charges the same rate and will pick up anywhere in Swakopmund; it departs between 9 and 10 am every second day. Either service will drop you off at any lodge in Windhoek. Star Line has a weekly service to Outjo via Henties Bay.

Overnight trains connect Windhoek with Swakopmund (US$9.50, 12½ hours) and Walvis Bay daily except Saturday. The three-times-weekly trains between Walvis Bay and Tsumeb (US$6, 17½ hours) also pass through Swakopmund. For rail information, call Trans-Namib (☎ 463538).

Hitching generally isn't difficult between here and Windhoek or Walvis Bay, but if you're heading for the Namib-Naukluft Park or Skeleton Coast, conditions can be rough and hitchers risk heat stroke, sandblasting and hypothermia – sometimes all in the same day!

AROUND SWAKOPMUND

The Martin Luther

In the desert east of Swakopmund sits a lonely and forlorn little steam locomotive. The 14,000kg machine was imported to Walvis

Bay from Halberstadt, Germany, in 1896 to replace the ox-wagons used to transport freight between Swakopmund and the interior. However, its inauguration into service was delayed by the outbreak of the Nama-Herero Wars, and in the interim, its locomotive engineer returned to Germany without having revealed the secret of its operation.

A US prospector eventually got it running, but it consumed enormous quantities of water, which wasn't available. It took three months to move it from Walvis Bay to Swakopmund and it survived just a couple of short trips before grinding to a halt just east of Swakopmund. Clearly, this particular technology wasn't making life easier for anyone, and it was abandoned and dubbed the *Martin Luther*, in reference to the great reformer's famous words to the Diet of Reichstag in 1521: 'Here I stand. May God help me, I cannot do otherwise'. It was restored in 1975 and declared a national monument.

Camel Farm

If you want to play Lawrence of Arabia in the Namib Desert, visit the Camel Farm (☎ 400363), 15km east of Swakopmund on the B2. Camel rides cost US$7 for 40 minutes. To book or arrange transport from town, phone and ask for Ms Elke Elb.

Rössing Mine

Rössing Uranium Mine (☎ 402046), 55km east of Swakopmund, is the world's largest open-cast uranium mine and certainly merits a visit. The scale of operations is staggering

Welwitschias

Among Namibia's many botanical curiosities, the extraordinary *Welwitschia mirabilis*, which exists only on the gravel plains of the northern Namib Desert, from the Kuiseb River to southern Angola, is probably the strangest of all. It was first noted in 1859, when Austrian botanist and medical doctor Friedrich Welwitsch stumbled upon a large specimen east of Swakopmund. He suggested it be named *tumboa*, which was one of the local names for the plant, but the discovery was considered to be so important that it was named after him instead. More recently, the Afrikaners have dubbed it *tweeblaarkanniedood* or 'two-leaf can't die'.

Welwitschias reach their greatest concentrations on the Welwitschia Plains east of Swakopmund, near the confluence of the Khan and Swakop Rivers, where they're the dominant plant species. Although these plants are the ugly ducklings of the vegetation world, they've adapted well to their harsh habitat. Although the plant gets some water from underground sources, most of its moisture is derived from condensed fog. Pores in the leaves trap moisture and longer leaves actually water the plant's own roots by channelling droplets onto the surrounding sand.

Welwitschias actually have only two long and leathery leaves, which grow from opposite sides of the corklike stem. Over the years, these leaves are darkened in the sun and torn by the wind into tattered strips, causing the plant to resemble a giant wilted lettuce.

Strangely, welwitschias are considered to be trees and are related to pines, but they also share some characteristics of flowering plants and club mosses. They're a dioecious species, meaning that male and female plants are distinct; females bear the larger greenish-yellow to brown cones, which contain the plant's seeds, while the males have smaller, salmon-coloured ones. Their exact method of pollination remains in question. It's thought that the large sticky pollen grains are carried by insects, specifically wasps.

Welwitschias have a slow rate of growth, and it's believed that the largest ones, whose tangled masses of leaf strips can measure up to 2m across, may have been growing for up to 2000 years. However, most mid-sized plants are less than 1000 years old. The plants don't even flower until they've been growing for at least 20 years. This longevity is probably only possible because they contain some compounds that are unpalatable to grazing animals, although black rhinos have been known to enjoy the odd plant.

and at full capacity the mine processes about one million tonnes of ore per week. Mine tours (4½ hours) leave from Cafe Anton at 8 am on Friday and cost US$3, including transport; all proceeds go to the museum. Book the tour the day before at the museum.

Welwitschia Drive & Moon Landscape

A worthwhile excursion by vehicle or organised tour is to Welwitschia Drive, east of Swakopmund. At Namibia Wildlife Resorts in Swakopmund, you can pick up an entry permit and leaflet describing the drive, with numbered references to 'beacons', or points of interest, along the route. The drive can be done in two hours, but you'll appreciate allowing more time. At the Swakop River crossing, there's a ***camp site***, which costs US$12 for up to eight people. Book through the NWR in Swakopmund.

WALVIS BAY

☎ 064

Architecturally uninspiring Walvis Bay, 30km south of Swakopmund, does have a sort of other-worldly charm (that may elude some visitors), but it survives mainly because it's the only decent port between Lüderitz and Luanda. That's thanks to the natural harbour created by the Pelican Point sand spit.

During the UN-sanctioned South African mandate over Namibia, the port of Walvis Bay was appended to South Africa's Cape Province, but when Namibia gained independence in 1990, its new constitution included Walvis Bay as part of its territory. Although South Africa stubbornly held its grip, the town's strategic and economic value made the issue of control over Walvis Bay a vital issue in Namibian politics. After much negotiation and deliberation, control finally passed to Namibia on 28 February 1994.

Orientation & Information

Although some streets are now being renamed after SWAPO luminaries, Walvis Bay streets, from 1st St to 15th St, run north-east to south-west. The roads, from 1st Rd to 18th Rd, run north-west to south-east. The helpful tourist office (☎ 205981) in the monumental civic centre is open from 8 am to 1 pm and 2 to 5 pm weekdays (until 4.30 pm Friday).

Things to See & Do

In a half-hour, you can visit the **Walvis Bay Museum**, in the library, which features the town's maritime and natural history and archaeology. It's open from 9 am to noon and 3 to 6 pm weekdays. Entry is free.

About 10km north of Walvis Bay on the Swakopmund road, look out to sea and you'll see the huge wooden platform known as **Bird Island**, which was built to provide a roost and nesting site for sea birds and to annually provide 1000 tonnes of smelly bird guano.

Dune 7 rises above the bleak expanses just off the C14, 8km north-east of town. Locals like to use it as a slope for sandboarding and skiing. Note that you must bring your own water here.

Three diverse wetland areas – the lagoon, the Bird Paradise and the salt works – together form the single most important coastal wetland for migratory birds in Southern Africa, and annually attract up to 150,000 transient birds. The 45,000-hectare **Walvis Bay Lagoon**, a shallow offshore area south-west of town, attracts half the flamingo population of Southern Africa. It also attracts pelicans, chestnut banded plovers and curlew sandpipers, and other migrants and waders. South-west of the lagoon is the **Walvis Bay Salt Works** (☎ 202376), a 3500ha salt pan complex that supplies over 90% of South Africa's salt. Phone to arrange a tour. Immediately east of town at the municipal sewage works is the **Bird Paradise**, that affords good birdwatching; it consists of a series of shallow artificial pools, fringed by reeds, with an observation tower to facilitate viewing.

Organised Tours

Inshore Safaris (☎ 202609, fax 202198, @ inshore@iafrica.com.na) runs half/full-day tours, cruises and adrenalin packages. Web site: www.inshore.com.na

The water-oriented Mola-Mola Safaris (☎ 205511, fax 207593, @ mola-mola@iafrica.com.na, 122 Sam Nujoma Ave) operates half-day dolphin-watching cruises

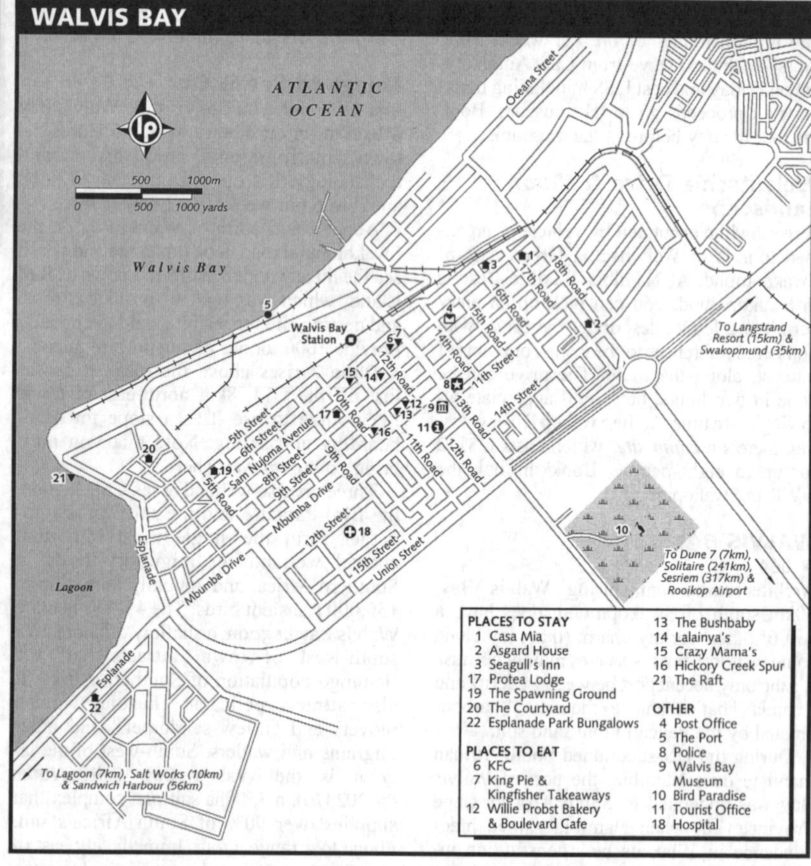

for US$38, birdwatching for US$50 and all-day cruises to Bird Island, Pelican Point and Sandwich Harbour, starting at US$75. All trips depart from the yacht club.

A new hit is sea kayaking with Jeanne Mientjes' Eco-Marine Kayak Tours (☎/fax 203144, @ jeannem@iafrica.com.na, PO Box 225, Walvis Bay). You can choose between paddles to shipwrecks, Pelican Point, Bird Island, seal and dolphin-watching spots and the oyster farm. Trips last three to five hours and cost from US$14 to US$34. Web site: www.namibianet.com/namibad venture

Places to Stay

The other-worldly ***Langstrand Resort*** *(☎ 293 134, fax 209714)* lies 15km north of town and looks like an archetypal desert mirage, especially in a fog or sandstorm. It charges US$8 per camp site plus US$1 per person, and two-/four-bed bungalows cost US$22/30.

Namibia's most oddly-named accommodation is the ***Spawning Ground*** *(☎ 205121, 55 6th St)*, and no, it's not a brothel. This lively backpackers lodge adds a welcome splash of colour in an otherwise drab part of town. Great, chunky wooden dorm beds cost US$7 and camping is US$5 per person.

The friendly ***Esplanade Park Bungalows*** *(☎ 206145, fax 209714)*, near the Esplanade, has five-/seven-bed self-catering bungalows for US$34/41. The motel-style ***Seagull's Inn*** *(☎ 202775, fax 202455, e discovaf@iafrica.com.na)* offers simple rooms for US$23/32, while self-catering rooms are US$32/36. The homely ***Asgard House*** *(☎ 209595, fax 209596, 72 17th Rd)* is a little family run place with rooms for US$30/41. The spotless ***Courtyard*** *(☎ 206 252, fax 207271, e courtyard@iafrica .com.na, 15 3rd Rd)*, offers comfortable accommodation with breakfast for US$32/45.

The ***Protea Lodge*** *(☎ 209560, fax 204097, e bay@iafrica.com.na)* isn't bad at US$65 for a double with breakfast. A more upmarket alternative is the friendly ***Casa Mia*** *(☎ 205975, fax 209565, e casancor@ iafrica.com.na)*, which charges US$56/68 for rooms, with breakfast.

Places to Eat

Crazy Mama's *(☎ 207364)* pizzeria has great service, atmosphere and prices. It serves fabulous pizzas, salads and vegetarian options.

The popular ***Raft*** *(☎ 204877)*, which sits on stilts offshore and looks more like a porcupine than a raft, serves excellent fare and you'll have a great front-row view of the ducks, pelicans and flamingoes in the lagoon, but the service isn't always top notch.

Bushbaby *(☎ 205490)* serves light bar lunches for US$2.20, as well as breakfast, milk shakes, waffles and ice cream. It's open from 8 am to 3 pm Monday to Saturday, and 5 pm to at least midnight on Sunday.

Hickory Creek Spur *(☎ 207990)*, of the ubiquitous South African chain, has a recommended salad bar. It's open from 11 am to 2 am daily. Posh ***Lalainya's*** *(☎ 202574)* on Sam Nujoma Ave serves upmarket dinners, including an excellent seafood platter.

You'll also enjoy the recommended ***Willie Probst Bakery & Boulevard Cafe***, which is always crowded at lunchtime. For a takeaway treat, try ***King Pie & Kingfisher Takeaways*** *(☎ 203477)*, on Sam Nujoma Ave, or for something more ordinary, ***KFC***.

Getting There & Away

Air Namibia (☎ 203102) has three weekly flights between Windhoek and Walvis Bay's Rooikop airport. Twice weekly, you can fly direct to or from Cape Town.

Intercape Mainliner (☎ 061-227847) has daily services between Windhoek (US$20) and Walvis Bay, via Swakopmund. Star Line's weekly bus between Walvis Bay and Mariental (US$11, 12 hours) leaves Mariental at 8 am Monday and Walvis Bay at 8.30 am Tuesday. It goes via Solitaire and Büllsport. (For details on rail services, see Getting There & Away in the Swakopmund section.)

NAMIB-NAUKLUFT PARK

The present boundaries of Namib-Naukluft Park, one of the world's largest national parks, were established in 1978 by merging the Namib Desert Park and the Naukluft Mountain Zebra Park with parts of Diamond Area 1 and bits of surrounding government land. Today, it takes in over 23,000 sq km of desert and semidesert, including the diverse habitats of the Namib Desert Park between the Kuiseb and Swakop Rivers, the Naukluft, the high dune field at Sossusvlei and the bird lagoon at Sandwich Harbour.

The main park transit routes, the C28, C14, D1982 or D1998, are open to everyone, but to turn off onto minor roads in the park or to visit picnic sites or sites of interest, park permits are required (note that some minor routes require 4WD). These are sold for US$1.75 at NWR offices in Windhoek, Swakopmund and Sesriem, and several petrol stations in Swakopmund and Walvis Bay.

Camp sites in the Namib Desert Park and Sesriem/Naukluft must be prebooked through the NWR offices in Windhoek or Swakopmund (see Places to Stay for more details). Permits for Sesriem/Sossusvlei and Naukluft hikes must be booked in Windhoek.

Sandwich Harbour

Sandwich Harbour, 50km south of Walvis Bay, historically served as a commercial fishing and trading port. Although the inlet has silted up in recent years, the northern end of the lovely lagoon continues to attract varying numbers of birds. The site is open between 6 am and 8 pm daily, but there are no visitor facilities – not even a camp site. Sandwich Harbour is accessible only with a sturdy 4WD high-clearance vehicle. The final 20km is a bit tricky, and depending on dune conditions may involve timing your arrival with low tide in order to run down to the sandy beach. The easiest access is with a tour; for some options (see Organised Tours under Walvis Bay earlier in this chapter).

Namib Desert Park

The relatively accessible Namib Desert Park lies between the canyons of the Kuiseb River in the south and the Swakop River in the north. Although it has a small area of linear dunes, it's characterised mostly by broad gravel plains punctuated by abrupt and imposing ranges of hills.

Although this area doesn't support a lot of large mammals, there is wildlife about. Along the road, you may see chacma baboons, as well as dassies, which like to bask on the kopjes. The **Kuiseb Canyon**, on the Gamsberg Route between Windhoek and Walvis Bay, is also home to klipspringer and even leopard. Spotted hyaena are often heard at night and jackal make a good living from the herds of springbok on the plains.

Places to Stay Namib Desert Park has nine basic camp sites, which cost US$12 and accommodate only one party of up to eight people at a time. These sites also function as picnic areas which may be used with a day-use permit. Sites have tables, toilets and braais, but you'll have to bring all the drinking water you'll need (some sites have brackish water suitable for cooking). Prebook these sites through NWR in Windhoek or Swakopmund. Camping fees are payable when your park permit is issued.

The shady ***Swakop River camp sites*** lie – not surprisingly – on the banks of the Swakop River, in the far northern reaches of the park. The southern area has five camp sites and is the better of the two locations, with lots of greenery – camelthorn, anaboom and tamarisk trees – while the northern one, which is beside a plain of welwitschias, is flat and treeless. The sites are accessible from Welwitschia Drive (see under Around Swakopmund earlier in this chapter).

The beautiful ***Bloedkoppie (Blood Hill) camp sites***, are among the most popular sites in the park. If you're coming from Swakopmund, they lie 55km north-east of the C28, along a signposted track. The northern sites may be accessed with 2WD, but they tend to attract ne'er do wells who drink themselves silly and get obnoxious. The southern sites are quieter and more secluded, but can be reached only by 4WD. The surrounding area offers some pleasant walking, and at Klein Tinkas, 5km east of Bloedkoppie, you'll see the ruins of a colonial police station and the graves of two German police officers dating back to 1895.

The ***camp site*** at Groot Tinkas must be accessed with 4WD and rarely sees much traffic. It enjoys a lovely setting beneath ebony trees and the surroundings are super for nature walks. During rainy periods, the brackish water in the nearby dam attracts a variety of birdlife.

The small ***Vogelfederberg camp site***, 2km south of the C14, makes a convenient overnight camp just 51km from Walvis Bay, but it's more popular for picnics or short walks. It's worth looking at the intermittent pools on the summit, which shelter a species of brine shrimp whose eggs hatch only when the pools are filled with rainwater. The only shade is provided by a small overhang where there are two picnic tables and braai pits.

The dusty, exposed ***Ganab camp site*** (the name is 'camelthorn acacia' in Nama) sits beside a shallow streambed on the gravel plains. It's shaded by hardy acacia trees, and a nearby bore hole provides water for antelopes.

The rather ordinary ***Kriess-se-Rus camp site*** occupies a dry stream bank on the gravel plains, 107km east of Walvis Bay on the Gamsberg Pass Route. It is shaded, but isn't terribly prepossessing and is best used simply as a convenient stop en route between Windhoek and Walvis Bay.

The shady ***Kuiseb Bridge camp site***, at the Kuiseb River crossing along the C14, is also a convenient place to break up a trip between Windhoek and Walvis Bay. The location is scenic enough, but the dust and noise from passing vehicles makes it less appealing than other camp sites. There are pleasant short canyon walks, but during heavy rains in the mountains the site can be flooded; in the summer months, keep tabs on the weather.

The pleasant ***Mirabib camp site***, which accommodates two parties at separate sites, is comfortably placed beneath rock overhangs in a large granite inselberg. There's evidence these shelters were used by nomadic peoples as much as 9000 years ago, and also by nomadic shepherds in the 4th or 5th century.

The scenic ***Homeb camp site***, which accommodates several groups, lies upstream from the most accessible set of dunes in the Namib Desert Park. Residents of the nearby Topnaar Khoikhoi village dig wells in the riverbed to access water beneath the surface, and one of their dietary staples is the !nara melon, which obtains moisture from the water table through a long taproot. This hidden water also supports a good stand of trees, including camelthorn acacia and ebony.

Getting There & Away The weekly Star Line bus between Mariental and Walvis Bay (US$11, 12 hours), via Maltahöhe and Solitaire, runs eastbound on Monday and the westbound on Tuesday. The bus passes close to the Vogelfederberg, Kriess-se-Rus and Kuiseb Bridge camp sites.

Naukluft Mountains

The Naukluft Massif, which rises steeply from the gravel plains of the central Namib, is mainly a high-plateau area cut around the edges by a complex of steep gorges, forming an ideal habitat for mountain zebra, kudu, leopard, springbok and klipspringer.

Hiking Most visitors to the Naukluft come to hike one of the area's two day walks, the Waterkloof Trail or the Olive Trail. These day hikes need not be booked, but are limited to campers at the Koedoesrus Camp Site, which must be prebooked. There are also two longer hikes – a four-day and an eight-day loop. Mostly due to high summer temperatures and potentially heavy rains, the hikes are available only from 1 March to 31 October on Tuesday, Thursday and Saturday of the first three weeks of each month. Groups must be comprised of three to 12 people. The price of US$15 per person includes accommodation at the Hikers' Haven hut near park headquarters on the day before and after the hike, as well as camping at basic shelters along the trail (with the exception of the comfortable mountain hut in Ubusis Canyon).

Due to the typically hot, dry conditions and lack of reliable natural water sources, you must carry at least 2L to 3L of water per person per day – and use it sparingly.

Waterkloof Trail The lovely 17km Waterkloof Trail begins at the Koedoesrus Camp Site and follows a counter-clockwise loop which takes about seven hours to complete. It first climbs up the Naukluft River past a weir, up a tufa waterfall and past a series of pools offering refreshing swimming. About 1km beyond the last pool, the trail turns west and starts traversing increasingly open plateau country. After the half-way mark, it climbs to a broad 1910m ridge that affords fabulous desert views in all directions before it descends steeply into the Gororosib Valley, past several inviting pools, filled with reeds and tadpoles, and climbs down an impressive tufa waterfall before meeting up with the Naukluft River. Here, it turns left and follows a 4WD track back to the park headquarters.

Olive Trail The 10km Olive Trail leaves from the car park about 4km north-east of the park headquarters and follows a four to five-hour triangular route. It begins with a steep climb onto the plateau, affording good views into the Naukluft Valley, then turns sharply east and descends a kloof, which grows deeper and steeper until it reaches a point where hikers must traverse a canyon wall past a pool using anchored chains. At the point where the river is joined by a major tributary, the trail crosses a jeep track, then angles to the south and follows the track to the car park.

Four-Day & Eight-Day Loops The four-day 60km loop is actually the first half of the eight-day 120km loop, combined with a 22km jaunt across the plateau back to park headquarters. Alternatively, you can finish

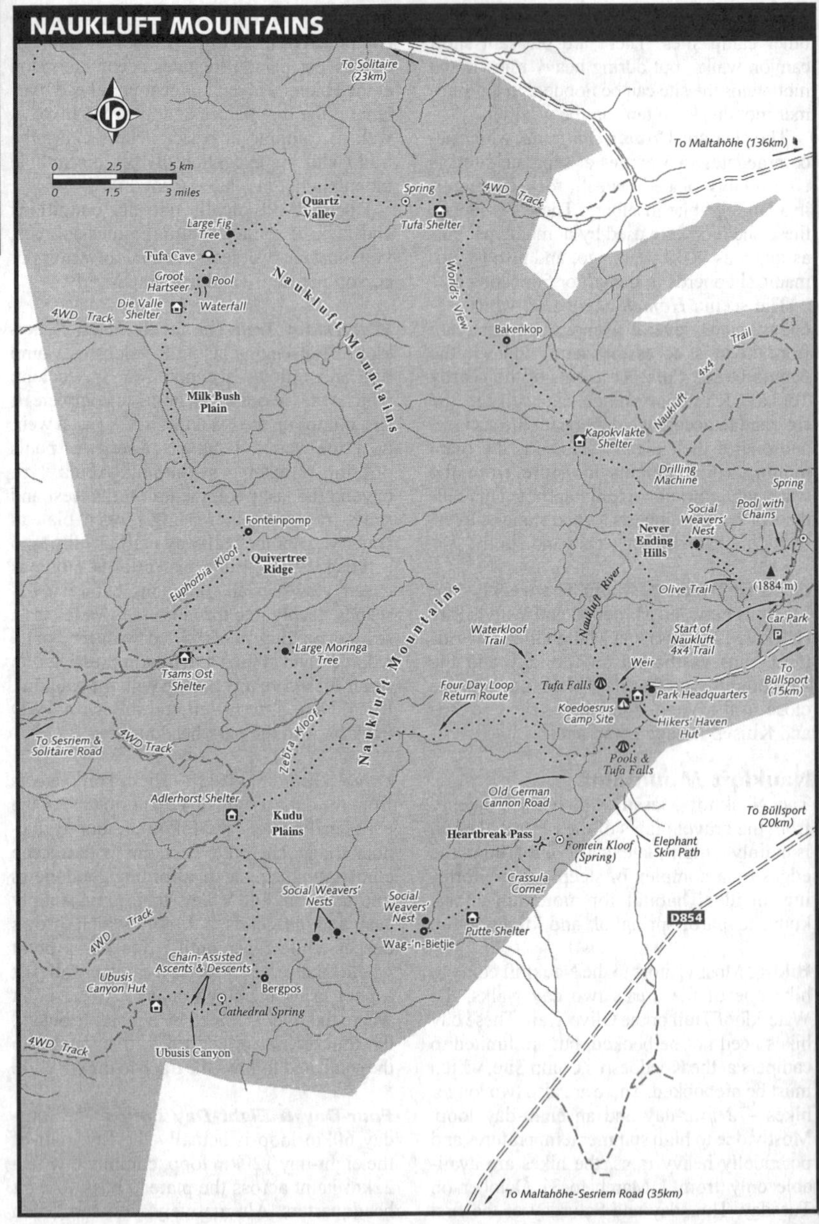
NAUKLUFT MOUNTAINS
0 2.5 5 km
0 1.5 3 miles
To Solitaire (23km)
To Maltahöhe (136km)
Quartz Valley
Spring
Tufa Shelter
4WD Track
Large Fig Tree
Tufa Cave
Groot Hartseer
Pool
Waterfall
Die Valle Shelter
4WD Track
Naukluft Mountains
World's View
Bakenkop
Trail
4x4
Naukluft
Milk Bush Plain
Kapokvlakte Shelter
Drilling Machine
Spring
Pool with Chains
Social Weavers' Nest
Never Ending Hills
Fonteinpomp
Euphorbia Kloof
Quivertree Ridge
Naukluft River
(1884 m)
Olive Trail
Car Park
Start of Naukluft 4x4 Trail
Waterkloof Trail
Large Moringa Tree
Naukluft Mountains
Tsams Ost Shelter
Weir
Tufa Falls
To Büllsport (15km)
Park Headquarters
Four Day Loop Return Route
Koedoesrus Camp Site
Hikers' Haven Hut
To Sesriem & Solitaire Road
4WD Track
Zebra Kloof
Pools & Tufa Falls
Old German Cannon Road
Adlerhorst Shelter
Kudu Plains
To Büllsport (20km)
Heartbreak Pass
Fontein Kloof (Spring)
Elephant Skin Path
Crassula Corner
Social Weavers' Nests
Social Weavers' Nest
D854
Putte Shelter
Wag-'n-Bietjie
4WD Track
Chain-Assisted Ascents & Descents
Bergpos
Ubusis Canyon Hut
Cathedral Spring
4WD Track
Ubusis Canyon
To Maltahöhe-Sesriem Road (35km)

the four-day route at Tsams Ost Shelter, mid-way through the eight-day loop, where a 4WD road leads out to the Sesriem-Solitaire Rd. However, you will have to arrange to leave a vehicle there before setting off from park headquarters. Note that hikers may not begin their hike at Tsams Ost.

The routes are marked by white footprints (except those sections that coincide with the Waterkloof Loop, where they're yellow), and water is reliably available only at overnight stops. If you're doing the eight-day circuit and don't want to carry eight days worth of food and stove fuel, you can drop off a supply cache at Tsams Ost Shelter prior to the hike.

In some places, such as the side trip down Ubusis Canyon and back up again, hikers must negotiate dry waterfalls and steep tufa (soft porous rock) formations with the aid of chains. Some people find this off-putting – especially with a heavy backpack – so be sure you're up to it.

Naukluft 4WD Trail Off-road enthusiasts can now exercise their machines on the new 73km Naukluft 4WD Trail, which costs US$34 per vehicle, including accommodation in a stone-walled A-frame at the 28km mark. Facilities include shared toilets, showers and braais. A maximum of four vehicles is permitted at a time. Book at NWR in Windhoek.

Places to Stay Pleasantly situated in a deep valley, ***Koedoesrus Camp Site*** has running water and ablutions blocks. Sites cost US$14 for a group, but space is limited so prebooking is required through NWR in Windhoek; the maximum stay is three nights.

In a beautiful setting amid the Tsaris Mountains is the friendly ***Zebra River Lodge*** *(☎ 063-293265, fax 293266, ⓔ zebra@mar.namib.com)*. It's run by Rob and Marianne Field, who bought their own Grand Canyon and set up this lodge to share it with visitors. The area is a real wonderland of desert mountains, plateaus, valleys and natural springs which are accessible on a network of hiking tracks. Single/double lodges with meals cost US$65/104. High clearance is necessary to approach the lodge, but if your vehicle falls short, they'll pick you up at the gate.

Getting There & Away The Naukluft is accessible only with a private vehicle. The Star Line bus between Mariental and Walvis Bay passes through Büllsport, which is within hitching distance of the Naukluft.

Sesriem & Sossusvlei

☎ 063

Welcome to Namibia's number one attraction! The name Sesriem means 'six thongs', which was the number of joined leather ox-wagon thongs necessary to draw water from the bottom of the gorge. Both Sesriem Canyon and Sossusvlei are open year-round between sunrise and sunset. If you want to witness the sunrise over Sossusvlei – as most people do – you must stay at Sesriem. Otherwise, you can't get through the gate early enough to reach Sossusvlei before sunrise.

Sesriem Canyon The 30m-deep Sesriem Canyon is 4km south of the Sesriem headquarters. Here the Tsauchab River has carved a 1km-long gorge through the 15-million-year-old deposits of sand and gravel conglomerate. There are two pleasant walks: you can hike upstream to the brackish pool at its head or 2.5km downstream to its lower end. Note the bizarre sphinx-like formation on the northern flank near the mouth of the canyon.

Sossusvlei The 300km-long and nearly 150km-wide sea of sand that covers over 32,000 sq km of western Namibia stretches from the Khoichab River in the south to the Kuiseb River in the north, and is reputed to contain some of the world's highest and most picturesque dunes. Sossusvlei, a huge ephemeral pan set amid 200m-high red sand dunes, is the most accessible part.

Along the 2WD road from Sesriem to Sossusvlei lies **Dune 45**, which rises over 150m above the surrounding plains and is flanked by several scraggly but picturesque trees.

At the end of the 2WD road is a car park, and only those with 4WD can drive the last 4km into the Sossusvlei pan itself. Those without 4WD can hike this last bit, or try to hitch, but the dunes that can be seen or reached from the 2WD car park are also very impressive.

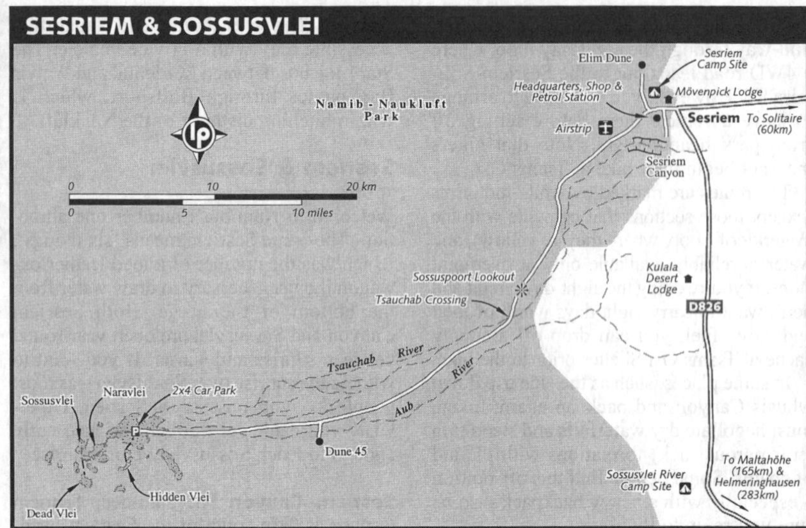

There's also a rewarding 4km return hike to **Hidden Vlei**, an unearthly dry vlei amid lonely dunes that makes a rewarding excursion; the route is marked by white-painted posts. Also, the rugged 6km return **Sossusvlei-Dead Vlei** walk is popular with those who think the former is getting a bit touristy.

An interesting way to visit Sossusvlei is with Sossus-on-Foot (☎ 293248), which guides strenuous three-hour dune and vlei hikes for US$25. It also shuttles between the 2WD car park and Sossusvlei for US$8.50 return. Tour companies run trips to Sossusvlei (see Organised Tours in the main Getting Around section).

Namib Sky (☎ 293233, fax 293241, @ namibsky@iwwn.com.na) offers early-morning balloon flights over the dune sea. It operates at Mwisho luxury tented camp (see Places to Stay); flights cost US$246.

Places to Stay & Eat There are many accommodation options in and around Sesrium.

Sesriem Sesriem is the most convenient ***camp site*** for Sossusvlei. Sites must be booked at NWR in Windhoek and cost US$22 (eight people maximum), but arrive before sunset or your site will be re-assigned on a stand-by basis. Anyone unable to book a site in Windhoek may get in on this nightly lottery. Failing that, you'll be relegated to the unappealing overflow camp outside the gates.

The luxury ***Mövenpick Lodge*** *(☎ 293223, fax 293231, @ sossusvlei@karoshotls.co.za)*, bears a strong resemblance to a toppled stack of coloured blocks. Singles/doubles in the cuboid bungalows costs US$135/172, with half board.

Around Sesriem A warm and friendly spot in the desert is ***Solitaire*** *(☎/fax 293387, Private Bag 1009, Maltahöhe)*, 65km north of Sesriem. Named after the dead tree that has become its renowned motif, it has recently been used in a Toyota Camry advert and might have provided the inspiration for the film *Baghdad Café*. Dusty camp sites cost US$3.50 per person and double aluminium rondavels are US$34. At the shop, the breakfasts and freshly baked 'Moose' bread can't be beaten.

Sossusvlei River Camp Site *(☎/fax 293236)*, which occupies a row of camelthorn acacias 20km south of Sesriem, offers a beautiful alternative to dealing with the Sesriem bureaucracy. Camping costs N$30 per person, and the sunrise over the spectacular multicoloured backdrop here is at least as grand as the one over the Sossusvlei dunes! If you don't have a 4WD, ask which route to take into the site or you may get bogged.

About 20km south on the D826 is the pleasantly unobtrusive ***Kulala Desert Lodge*** *(☎ 293234, fax 293235, ⓔ kulala@iwwn.com.na)*. This is the luxury option around Sossusvlei and from a distance, it actually resembles a Bedouin camp. Singles/doubles with bath cost US$135/158. Nearby, the beautiful new ***Sossusvlei Wilderness Camp*** *(☎ 061-225178, fax 239455)* offers delightful stone and thatch bungalows that melt into the stark landscape. Rooms start at US$350/450, with meals and activities.

Just south of Solitaire is the upmarket ***Namib-Naukluft Lodge*** *(☎ 061-263082 in Windhoek, fax 215356, ⓔ afex@afex.com.na)*. Accommodation costs US$80/125 with full board; tour packages from Windhoek or Swakopmund start at US$300.
Web site: www.natron.net/afex

A beautiful wildlife farm – and an attraction in its own right – is the ***Namibgrens Rest Camp*** *(☎/fax 062-572021, fax 061-234345, ⓔ rabie@namibnet.com or znam@iafrica.com.na, PO Box 21587, Windhoek)*, which is run by Mr JJ Rabie. Known for its hiking routes, it occupies a scenic position on the Spreetshoogte Pass (Namibia's steepest road, with a hair-raising 25% gradient!). Accommodation in the spacious old farmhouse costs US$31/59, with breakfast and use of kitchen facilities. Half board costs US$36/68. The one to three-day hiking routes form a ragged figure eight; accommodation along the routes is in basic huts where the loops cross. Hiking and/or camping costs US$5 per day, while nonhikers can take the soft option and tour the farm by vehicle for US$12.

The pleasantly located ***Camp Gecko*** *(☎ 061-572017 in Windhoek, fax 222266)* also lies on the Spreetshoogte Pass route (D1275). Activities include desert drives, farm drives, photographic tours and hiking trails. Tented accommodation with half board starts at US$42 and safaris are US$0.50 per kilometre.

South of Sesriem and west of the Maltahöhe road is the 140,000 hectare Namib Rand Nature Reserve (☎ 061-230616, fax 220102, ⓔ nrs@iafrica.com.na, PO Box 5048, Windhoek), the largest privately owned property in Southern Africa. Accommodation ranges from camp sites to fully catered packages at ***Mwisho luxury tented camp***; most people come for its early-morning balloon flights over the dune sea, operated by Namib Sky (see under Sossusvlei earlier). Full board and activities, with a balloon flight, costs US$341. Nights at ***Wolwedans Dune Camp***, with meals and scenic drives, are US$120 per person; accommodation at the ***Wolwedans Dune Lodge*** is US$160. On Die Duine Farm, within the reserve, is Mark and Elinor Dürr's ***Tok-Tokkie Guest House***, which offers inexpensive accommodation, one to four-day hikes and desert activities. Walking trips on the farm cost US$68 per night.

Getting There & Away Without your own transport you'll need to take a tour (see Organised Tours in the Getting Around section) or get a ride to get here.

You reach Sesriem via a signposted turnoff from the Maltahöhe-Solitaire road (C36). The 65km road south-west from Sesriem is good gravel (it's currently being tarred – with a special pink tar, believe it or not!) to within 4km of Sossusvlei, where it enters deep sand and requires 4WD. Visitors with lesser vehicles park at the 2WD Car Park and walk the remaining distance, which takes about 1½ hours. There's petrol at Solitaire, Sesriem and a bush BP station 93km south of Sesriem on the D826.

Southern Namibia

Southern Namibia takes in everything from Rehoboth in its north and areas south to the South African border, east to the Botswana border and west to the diamond coast. Set in the angle between South Africa's two most remote quarters, Namaqualand and the Kalahari, the bleak southern tip of Namibia exudes a sense of isolation. The desert

SOUTHERN NAMIBIA

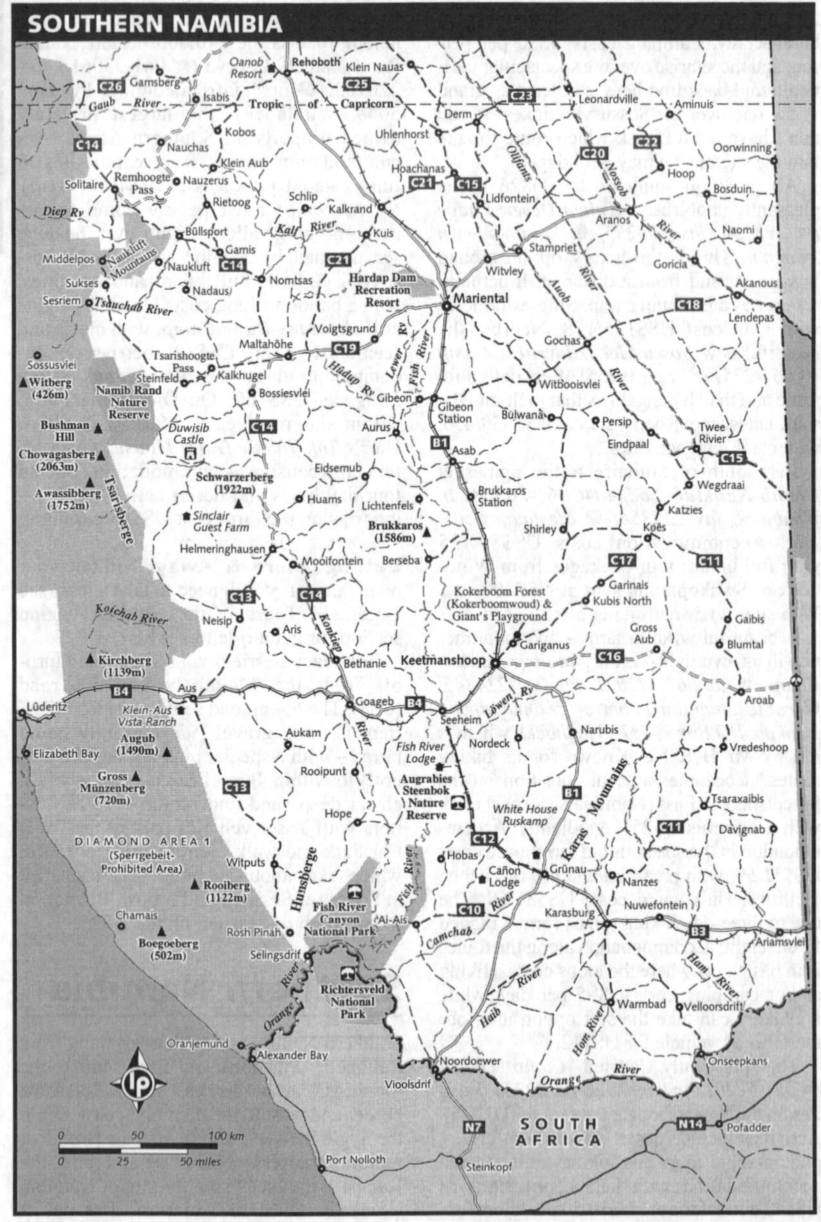

plains stretch to the horizon in all directions and seem to carry on forever. You can imagine, then, how surprising it is to suddenly encounter the gaping Fish River Canyon that forms an enormous and spectacular gash across the desert landscape.

Namibia's Central Plateau is characterised by wide open country, and the area's widely spaced, uninspiring towns function mainly as commercial and market centres. This is rich cattle-ranching country, and around Mariental, citrus fruit and market vegetables are grown under irrigation.

REHOBOTH

☎ 062

Rehoboth lies 85km south of Windhoek and just a stone's throw north of the Tropic of Capricorn. The original German mission was abandoned in 1864, but the town was revived in the early 1870s by the Basters, an ethnic group of mixed Khoikhoi/Afrikaner origin, who migrated north from the Cape under their leader Hermanus van Wyk.

The **town museum** (☎ 523954), which is dedicated to Baster heritage, is open from 10 am to noon and 2 to 4 pm weekdays, and Saturday morning. Accommodation is available at ***Reho Spa***, which is a hot-spring resort administered by NWR, and ***Lake Oanob Resort*** *(☎ 522369, fax 524112, ⓔ oanob@namib.com)*, with self-catering chalets and a watersports complex at Oanob Dam. Both places have inexpensive camping grounds.

HARDAP DAM RECREATION RESORT & GAME PARK

Hardap Dam, 15km north-west of Mariental, is a 25-sq-km dam, which offers good fishing, and a 25,000-hectare game park with 80km of gravel roads and a 15km hiking loop. It's also home to over 260 bird species.

Entry permits cost US$1.75 per person and US$1.75 per car, and entitle you to use the pool and picnic sites. Between sunrise and sunset, you can walk anywhere in the reserve, but camping is allowed only at the rest camp.

Camp sites at Hardap Dam cost US$15 for up to eight people, and two- and five-bed bungalows are US$24 and US$44 respectively. Other amenities include a shop, restaurant, kiosk, swimming pool and petrol station. The ***restaurant***, which sits on a terrace overlooking the lake, enjoys a wonderful view, as does the cliff-top pool.

There's no public transport to the dam. The Hardap Dam turn-off from the B1 is signposted 15km north of Mariental. From there, it's 6km to the entrance gate.

MARIENTAL

☎ 063

Mariental is a small administrative and commercial centre on the bus and rail lines between Windhoek and Keetmanshoop, and a popular petrol stop for drivers between Windhoek and South Africa. It lies in the midst of several agricultural endeavours, including large-scale irrigation and ostrich farming.

The nearest camping is at Hardap Dam. The recently upgraded ***Sandberg Hotel*** *(☎/fax 242291, fax 240738)*, which has a restaurant and bar, offers basic singles/doubles for US$30/47. The plusher ***Mariental Hotel*** *(☎ 242466, fax 242493)* has rooms for US$37/54. The cheapest place is the rather dingy ***Guglhupf Cafe*** *(☎ 240718)*, which charges US$24/30. It has a swimming pool, and the attached cafe serves excellent steaks and beef dishes.

For quick meals, try ***Bambi's Takeaways*** beside the central Engen petrol station, or the ***JC Ice Cream Parlour & Takeaway***, at the BP petrol station. Locals seem to love the ***Wimpy*** bar at the Engen petrol station on the Keetmanshoop road.

DUWISIB CASTLE

☎ 061

Duwisib Castle, a curious Baroque structure 70km south of Maltahöhe, was built in 1909 by Baron Captain Hans-Heinrich von Wolf. After the German-Nama Wars, he commissioned architect Willie Sander to design a home that would reflect his commitment to the German military cause. It resembles the Schutztruppe forts of Namutoni, Gibeon and Windhoek and now houses an impressive collection of 18th- and 19th-century antiques and armour. Open daily from 8 am to 1 pm, and 2 to 5 pm; entry costs US$1.75. Official guided tours are available.

The ***camping ground*** on the castle grounds costs US$14 per site (up to eight people) and there's a small snack bar beside the castle. The friendly ***Farm Duwisib*** *(☎/fax 223994)*, 300m from the castle, has self-catering rooms for two or four people from US$25/39 without/with half board.

There's no public transport.

MALTAHÖHE

☎ 063

Maltahöhe, in the heart of a ranching area, has little to recommend it, but thanks to its convenient location along the back route between Namib-Naukluft Park and Lüderitz, the area supports a growing number of guest farms and private rest camps. At the friendly and comfortable ***Hotel Maltahöhe*** *(☎ 293013, fax 293133, PO Box 20)*, single/double rooms cost US$25/41 and there's a ***restaurant*** and bar. It also organises inexpensive 4WD day trips to Sossusvlei.

The Star Line bus between Mariental (US$3, 3½ hours) and Walvis Bay (US$9, 8½ hours) passes Maltahöhe westbound on Monday and eastbound Tuesday.

HELMERINGHAUSEN

☎ 063

The tiny settlement of Helmeringhausen is little more than a homestead, hotel and petrol station; the homestead has been the property of the Hester family since 1919. The highlight is the idiosyncratic **Agricultural Museum**, established in 1984 by the Helmeringhausen Farming Association. It displays all sorts of farming implements collected from local properties. It's open daily; entry is free.

The friendly ***Helmeringhausen Hotel*** *(☎ 233083)*, run by Heinz and Altna Vollertson, has single/double rooms with breakfast for US$42/56. In the ***restaurant and bar*** the food is excellent, the beer is always cold and they keep a well-stocked cellar.

Star Line's bus between Keetmanshoop and Helmeringhausen (US$5, five hours) runs on Fridays.

BRUKKAROS

With a 2km-wide crater, this extinct volcano dominates the skyline between Mariental and Keetmanshoop. It was formed some 80 million years ago when a magma pipe encountered ground water about 1km below the earth's surface and caused a series of volcanic explosions. From the car park, it's a 3.5km hike to the crater's southern entrance; along the way, watch for the remarkable **quartz formations** embedded in the rock. From here, you can head for the otherworldly **crater floor** or turn left and follow the southern rim up to the abandoned **sunspot research centre**, which was established by the US Smithsonian Institute in the 1930s.

Camping is available in several spots along the road to the crater. The clear night skies make for a magical experience, but there's no water; so bring all you'll need. To get there you'll need a vehicle; follow the C98 west from Tses for 40km, then turn north on the D3904. It's then 18km to the car park.

KEETMANSHOOP

☎ 063

Keetmanshoop, with 15,000 people, is at the main crossroads of southern Namibia and is a centre for the karakul wool industry. It has more petrol stations per capita than any other town in Namibia, which may hint at its main function for travellers. The helpful Southern Tourist Forum (☎ 223316, fax 223818) in the municipal building is open weekdays during business hours (closed for lunch from 12.30 to 2 pm) and on Saturday morning.

Things to See

The free **town museum**, housed in the 1895 Rhenish Mission Church, outlines the history of Keetmanshoop with old photos, early farming implements, an old wagon and a model of a traditional Nama home. It's open from 7.30 am to 12.30 pm and 2 to 5 pm weekdays, and 9 to 11 am Saturday. There are also several fine examples of colonial architecture. The most prominent is the 1910 **Kaiserliches Postampt** (Imperial Post Office), on the corner of 5th Ave and Fenschelstraat.

Namibia's largest stand of the kokerbooms or quiver trees *(Aloe dichotoma)* lies at **Kokerboomwoud**, on Gariganus Farm, 14km north-east of town. Day entry and use of the picnic facilities is US$3 per vehicle

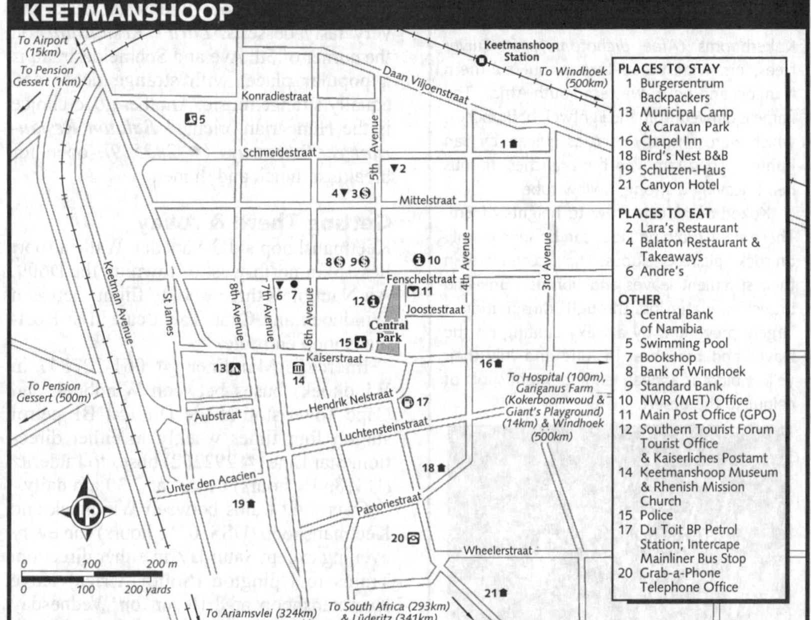

plus US$1.50 per person. This fee also includes the **Giant's Playground**, a bizarre natural rock garden 5km away.

Places to Stay

For camping, the bougainvillea-decked ***Municipal Camp & Caravan Park*** *(☎ 223316)* charges US$3 per vehicle, US$3 per site and US$4.25 per person. The budget ***Schutzen-Haus*** *(☎ 223400)*, 200m to the south, has single/double rooms for US$14/22. Backpackers accommodation is available at ***Burgersentrum Backpackers*** *(☎ 223454)*, where you'll pay US$5 for dorms.

There's also the plush new ***Lafenis Rest Camp*** *(☎ 224316)*, 5km south of town, where two-/four-bed bungalows cost US$25/34. Peripherals include a laundry, swimming pool, horse riding and mini-golf.

You can also stay at the Kokerboomwoud on ***Gariganus Farm*** *(☎ 222935)*, 14km east of town, which is run by Coenie Nolte. Camping costs US$5 per person and simple bungalows are US$20/30, with breakfast. With full board, they're US$32/49.

The homely and personable ***Chapel Inn*** *(☎/fax 223762, e frlodge@iafrica.com.na)*, Kaiserstraat, run by Louis and Riëtte Fourie, occupies a decommissioned church. Comfortable rooms start at US$24/41 and short tours to the Kokerboomwoud & Giant's Playground are N$10 per person. They offer transfers to the affiliated Fish River Lodge (see Fish River Canyon, later in this chapter).

Bird's Nest B&B *(☎ 222906, 16 Pastorie St, PO Box 460)*, Keetmanshoop, has homely accommodation for US$30/47. The popular ***Canyon Hotel*** *(☎ 223361, fax 223714)*, which is the standard mid-range option in Keetmanshoop, has rooms from US$49/75.

Heading south-west toward Lüderitz, you may want to take a break at the historic ***Seeheim Hotel*** *(☎ 250503, PO Box 1338, Keetmanshoop)*, at the Seeheim rail halt. It's full of antique furniture and offers good value,

Kokerbooms

Kokerbooms *(Aloe dichotoma)*, or quiver trees, are widespread throughout southern Namibia and north-western South Africa. The name is derived from the lightweight branches, which were formerly used as quivers by San hunters. They removed the branches' fibrous heart, leaving a strong, hollow tube.

Kokerbooms can grow to heights of 8m. These slow-growing aloes can be seen mainly on rocky plains or slopes. They store water in their succulent leaves and fibrous trunk and branches; water loss through transpiration is largely prevented by a waxy coating on the leaves and branches. In June and July their yellow blooms appear, lending bright spots of colour to the desert.

CHRIS BARTON

starting at US$20 per person, with breakfast. Undercover camping costs US$8.50 per person. This place is reputed to serve the best toasted sandwiches in Southern Africa, and that isn't far off the mark.

Places to Eat

Most Keetmanshoop folk will tell you that the new restaurant ***Andre's*** (☎ *222572)* is the best thing that's happened to the town in the past decade. This fabulous place specialises in pizza, but also does breakfasts, steaks and very tasty desserts. ***Lara's Restaurant***, on the corner of 5th Ave and Schmeidestraat, is a popular place, with strange decor and equally strange music. Another good choice is the Hungarian-oriented ***Balaton Restaurant & Takeaways*** (☎ *222539)*, open for breakfast, lunch and dinner.

Getting There & Away

Keetmanshoop's JG van der Wath airport lies 15km north-west of town on the D609. Air Namibia's three weekly flights between Windhoek and Cape Town call in at Keetmanshoop en route.

Intercape Mainliner (☎ 061-227847 in Windhoek) buses between Windhoek and Cape Town stop at the Du Toit BP petrol station four times weekly in either direction. Star Line (☎ 292202) buses to Lüderitz (US$8, 4¾ hours) depart at 7.30 am daily.

Overnight trains between Windhoek and Keetmanshoop (US$10, 11 hours) run every evening except Saturday, in either direction. Trains to Upington (South Africa) leave Keetmanshoop at 8.10 am on Wednesday and Saturday. For details, call Trans-Namib (☎ 292202).

Hitching isn't bad on the B1 between Keetmanshoop and Windhoek or Grünau, but there's less traffic between Keetmanshoop and Lüderitz. Hitchhikers bound for Fish River Canyon normally have better luck reaching Ai-Ais (from near Grünau) than Hobas (from Seeheim).

AUS

☎ 063

Aus, whose curious name means 'out' in German, is a tidy, tranquil little place 125km east of Lüderitz. After the Germans surrendered to the South African forces at Otavi on 9 July 1915, Aus became one of two internment camps for German military personnel. Military police and officers were sent to Okanjanje in the north and the noncommissioned officers went to Aus. After the Treaty of Versailles, the camp was dismantled and by May 1919 it was closed. Virtually nothing remains of the original camp, but some attempt has been made to reconstruct one of the brick houses.

The fabulous ***Klein-Aus Vista*** *(☎ 258021, fax 258021, ⓔ ausvista@ldz.namib.com)*, run by brothers Willem and Piet Swiegers, occupies a 10,000ha ranch along the Lüderitz road, 3km west of Aus. Hikers will love their magical four-day hiking route, which traverses some of Namibia's most incredible landscapes. Camp sites cost US$7 plus US$1 per person, and accommodation in the two wonderful hiking huts, range from US$16 per person for a dorm bed at ***Geister Schlucht hut*** to US$47/77 for a single/double room, with bedding, at the opulent ***Eagle's Nest hut***. Horseback tours are available for US$25 (two hours) to US$139 (overnight trip).

Aus and Klein-Aus Vista are on the main road, so access is via Star Line's Keetmanshoop-Lüderitz bus.

LÜDERITZ

☎ 063

Lüderitz is a surreal colonial relic – a Bavarian village on the barren, windswept Namib Desert coast, seemingly untouched by the 20th century. It has everything you'd expect of a small German town – delicatessens, coffee shops and Lutheran churches. Here, the icy but clean South Atlantic is home to seals, penguins and other marine life. The desolate beaches support flamingoes and ostrich.

Between Aus and the coast, the road crosses the desolate southern Namib; to the south lies the forbidden Diamond Area 1.

Information

The tourist office, run by Lüderitzbucht Tours & Safaris (☎ 202719), is currently the only place to get visitor permits for Kolmanskop. It's open from 8 am to 12.30 pm and 1.30 to 5 pm weekdays, 8 am to noon Saturday, and 8.30 to 10 am Sunday. It also sells curios, stamps and phone cards. The helpful NWR office is open from 7.30 am to 1 pm and 2 to 4 pm weekdays.

There are banks and a post office. The Club Internet Cafe, on the main street, provides email and Internet access.

Things to See

Lüderitz is chock-a-block with colonial buildings and every view reveals something interesting. The curiously intriguing architecture, which mixes German Imperial and Art Nouveau styles, makes this already bizarre little town appear even more otherworldly. Prominent buildings include the **colonial train station**, at the corner of Bahnhof and Bismarck St, and the **Goerke Haus**, which is open from 2 to 3 pm weekdays, and 4 to 5 pm weekends. Entry is US$1.50.

The prominent Evangelical Lutheran church, **Felsenkirche**, dominates Lüderitz from high on Diamond Hill. It was designed by Albert Bause, who implemented the Victorian influences he'd seen in the Cape. With assistance from private donors in Germany, construction began in late 1911 and was completed the following year. The stained-glass panel over the altar was donated by Kaiser Wilhelm II himself. You can visit from 6 to 7 pm (5 to 6 pm in winter) Monday to Saturday. This is the best time to see the late-afternoon sun shining directly through the extraordinary stained-glass work.

The **Lüderitz Museum** (☎ 202582), on Diaz St, has information on natural history, local indigenous groups, Bartolomeu Dias and local diamond-mining. It's open from 3.30 to 5 pm weekdays; entry is US$1. Large groups who prebook can also visit the *Lady Luck* **floating diamond museum** (☎ 204030), which occupies a ship in the harbour; tours are US$9 and cruises are US$17 per person.

Activities

A rewarding activity is to dig for the lovely **crystals** of calcium sulphate and gypsum known as sand roses, which develop when moisture seeps into the sand and causes it to adhere and crystallise into flowery shapes. NWR issues US$3 digging permits, which are valid for a two-hour dig and good for up to three sand roses or a total weight of 1.5kg. Diggers must be accompanied by an official from NWR.

Believe it or not, Lüderitz has a **golf** course; it may not be green and there is no shortage of sand traps, but the novelty value makes it worthwhile. It's open daily for golf, but the clubhouse only opens after 6 pm on Wednesday and Friday evening, and all day on Saturday.

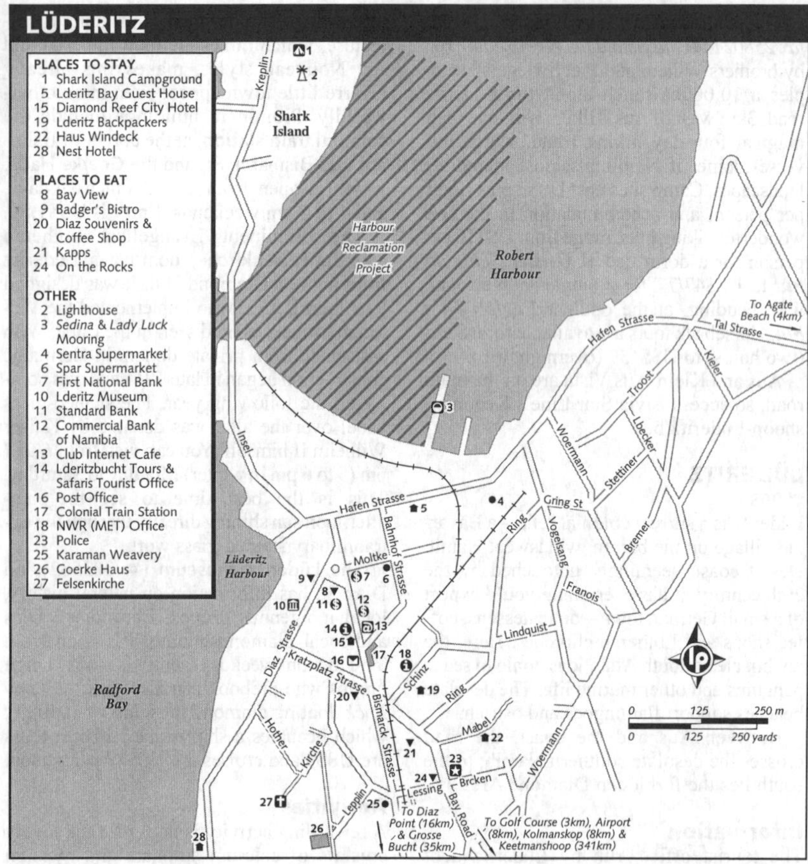

Organised Tours

Weather permitting, the schooner *Sedina* (☎ 204030) sails daily to the Cape fur-seal sanctuary at Diaz Point. The two- to three-hour trips cost US$20. When the seas are calm, it also visits the penguin sanctuary on Halifax Island. Be sure to take warm gear.

Tours of the area are offered by Lüderitzbucht Safaris & Tours (☎ 202719, fax 202863, ludsaf@ldz.namib.com), which runs the tourist office and organises trips to several areas of the Sperrgebiet, including Kolmanskop, Elizabeth Bay, the Atlas Bay seal colony, the 55m **Bogenfels** sea arch and Maerchental Valley, and the ghost towns of Kolmanskop, Bogenfels and Pomona).

Places to Stay

At the beautifully situated but aggravatingly windy ***Shark Island Campground***, operated by NWR, camping costs US$10 per site. It's connected to the town by a causeway, but thanks to the ongoing harbour reclamation project, Shark Island will soon be an integral part of the mainland.

Lüderitz Backpackers *(☎ 203632, fax 202000, toya@ldz.namib.com, 7 Schinz St)* has dorms for US$8 and doubles for US$18.

It's friendly and highly recommended. Mrs van Bach's rustic ***Haus Windeck*** *(☎ 203 370, fax 203306, 6 Mabel St)* has simple self-catering singles/doubles for US$25/30. The informal ***Kratzplatz*** *(☎/fax 202458, cell ☎ 081-129 2458, 5 Nachtigal St)*, run by Monica Kratz, charges US$14/24.

The friendly ***Lüderitz Bay Guest House*** *(☎ 203019)*, housed in a colonial building near the harbour, has homey German-style rooms with shared facilities, including use of a kitchen, starting at US$24/40. Right in the centre is ***Diamond Reef City*** *(☎ 202856, fax 202976)*, which charges US$25 per person, with breakfast. The bright new ***Nest Hotel*** *(☎ 204000, fax 204001, @ nest@ldz.namib .com)*, on the rocky coast south of the centre, features seaview rooms, a sheltered pool and a sauna. Rooms cost US$70/87.

Places to Eat

Many people opt for the hotel and guest-house ***restaurants***. If there has been a good catch that day, both the ***Bay View*** *(☎ 202 288)* and ***Kapps*** *(☎ 202345)* hotels both serve decent seafood dishes. Specialities include crayfish, local oysters and kingclip. The ***Diaz Souvenirs & Coffee Shop*** serves excellent toasted sandwiches, light meals, coffee and cakes until 5 pm daily. Although it's a bit noisy, a good spot for lunch or dinner, including seafood specials, is ***Badger's Bistro***, which has an attached bar. ***On the Rocks***, beside the Shell petrol station, specialises in local crayfish and beef dishes.

For self-catering, see the ***Spar*** and ***Sentra*** supermarkets.

Shopping

Karaman Weavery, on Bismarck St, is worth visiting for the high quality of its rugs and garments woven in desert pastel colours (Namibian flora and fauna are favoured designs). It's open from 8 am to 1 pm and 2 to 7 pm weekdays, and until noon Saturday.

Getting There & Away

Air Namibia flies between Windhoek, Swakopmund and Lüderitz three times weekly. Star Line (☎ 312875) buses from Keetmanshoop (US$8, 4¾ hours) leave at 8 am daily, returning from Lüderitz at 1 pm daily.

Lüderitz is worth the 300km detour from Keetmanshoop, via the tarred B4. The road crosses the desolate southern Namib, and to the south lies the forbidden Diamond Area 1. When the wind blows – which is most of the time – the final 10km into Lüderitz may be blocked by the barchan dune field which seems bent upon crossing the road. The drifts pile quite high before the road crews clean them off and conditions do get hazardous, especially if it's foggy.

AROUND LÜDERITZ

Kolmanskop

A popular trip from Lüderitz is the ghost town of Kolmanskop, which was once a substantial diamond-mining town. It was named after an early Afrikaner trekker, Jani Kolman, whose ox-wagon became bogged in the sand here. It once boasted a casino, skittle alley and theatre with fine acoustics, but the slump in diamond sales after WWI and the discovery of richer deposits at Oranjemund ended its heyday. By 1956 it was deserted. Several buildings have been restored, but many have already been invaded by the dunes and the ghost-town atmosphere remains.

Visitors' permits cost US$3.50 from the Lüderitz tourist office (see under Information earlier). Tours are conducted in English and German at 9.30 and 10.45 am Monday to Saturday, and at 10 am on Sunday. Visitors must either provide their own transport from town or you have to take a tour.

The Lüderitz Peninsula

The Lüderitz Peninsula, much of which lies outside the Sperrgebiet prohibited area, offers many interesting sites. The picturesque and relatively calm bay, **Sturmvogelbucht**, has a lovely beach and is viable for swimming, but the water temperature would only be amenable to a seal or a polar bear. A Norwegian whaling station was sited there in 1914, but is now a rusty ruin. The salty pan inland from Sturmvogelbucht actually appears to be iced over, and is worth a quick stop.

At **Diaz Point**, 22km south of Lüderitz, is a lovely, classic lighthouse and a replica of a

AROUND LÜDERITZ

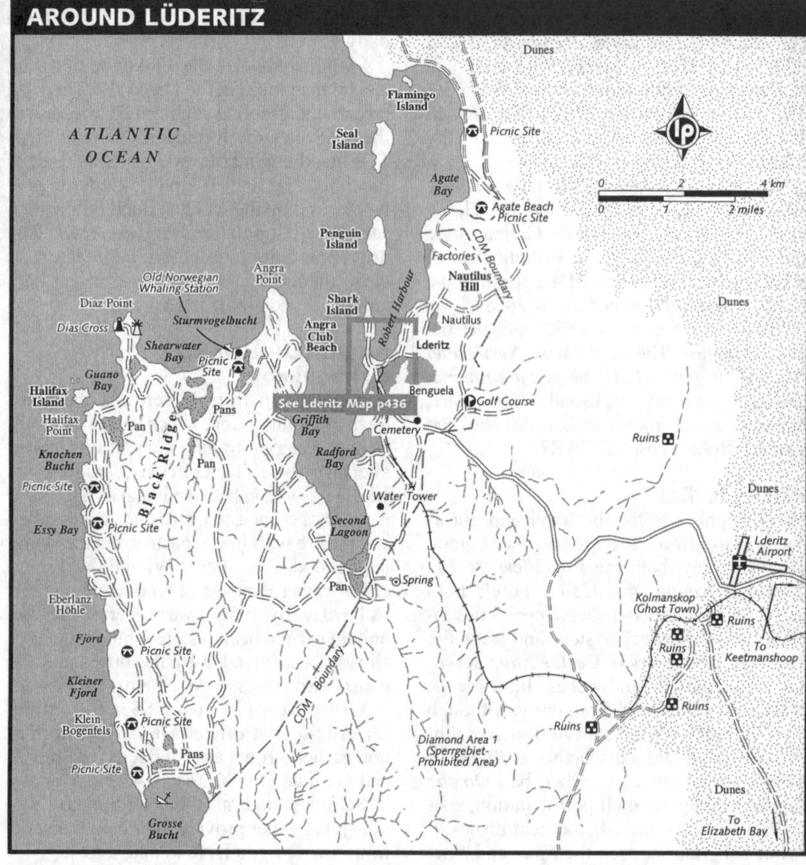

cross erected in July 1488 by Portuguese navigator Bartolomeu Dias on his return voyage from the Cape of Good Hope. From the point, there's a view to the nearby sea-lion colony, and jackass penguins are often seen frolicking, diving and surfing off the rocks. You can also observe cormorants, wading birds and even the occasional school of dolphins.

Grosse Bucht (Big Bay) at the southern end of the peninsula, is another wild and scenic beach. This normally cold, windy spot is favoured by flocks of flamingoes that feed in the tidal pools. It's also the site of a small but picturesque shipwreck on the beach. Just a few kilometres north lies the small seaside rock arch known as **Klein Bogenfels**.

GRÜNAU

☎ 063

For most travellers, Grünau is either the first petrol station north of the border or a place to settle while awaiting a lift to Ai-Ais, Fish River Canyon or points beyond.

The little-known **Augrabies-Steenbok Nature Reserve**, north-west of Grünau, protects not only steenbok, but also Hartmann's mountain zebra, gemsbok and klipspringer. ***Camping*** is allowed, but facilities are limited to basic toilets. To get there, follow the C12 for 59km north-west of Grünau, then turn west and continue 10km to the reserve. There's no entry charge.

Grünau Motors Rest Camp *(☎ 262026, fax 262003)* has camp and caravan sites, and simple rooms at the nicely upgraded ***Grünau Hotel*** *(☎ 262001, @ grunauhot@mar .namib.com)* cost US$23/30.

White House Ruskamp *(☎ 262061)*, 11km towards Windhoek then 4km to the west, offers safe, quiet, self-catering accommodation for US$13 per person, plus US$5/7 for breakfast/dinner. The petrol station on the main road has a shop, snack bar and takeaway.

FISH RIVER CANYON NATIONAL PARK

Nowhere else in Africa is there anything like Fish River Canyon. The Fish River, which joins the Orange River about 70km south of the canyon, has been gouging out this gorge for thousands of years and the result couldn't be improved upon. It's enormous – 160km in length, up to 27km wide and the dramatic canyon reaches a depth of 550m. But these figures convey little of the breathtaking vistas from various vantage points along its length.

The two main areas of activity are Hobas, near the northern end of the canyon, and Ai-Ais Hot Springs resort, in the south. Both are administered by NWR; all accommodation should be prebooked in Windhoek.

Hobas

☎ 061

The Hobas Information Centre, at the northern end of the park, is open from 7.30 am to noon and 2 to 5 pm daily. It's also the check-in point for the five-day Fish River Canyon Trail, which begins at **Hikers' Viewpoint**, 10km down a gravel road. This vantage point affords a fantastic view over the northern part of the canyon, but Main Viewpoint, a few kilometres further south, is probably the best – and most photographed – overall view. Both these views encompass the sharp river bend known as **Hell's Corner**.

Entry to the park costs US$1.75 per person and US$1.75 per vehicle; this permit is also good for Ai-Ais. Well-shaded ***camp sites*** cost US$15 for up to eight people. Facilities are clean and there's a kiosk and swimming pool, but no restaurant or petrol station.

The remarkable ***Cañon Lodge*** *(☎ 230066, fax 251863, @ nature.in@iwwn.com.na, PO Box 1847, Keetmanshoop)*, inside the 'Canyon Nature Park' and 10km south-east of Hobas, consists of 20 bungalows integrated into the red-rock backdrop and a restaurant housed in a restored 1910 farmhouse. B&B is good value at US$58/89 and camping costs US$5 to US$12 per person.

Fish River Hiking

The four- to five-day hike from Hobas to Ai-Ais is Namibia's most popular walk – with good reason. The magical 85km route, which follows the sandy bed of the river course (although in May and June, the river actually does flow), begins at Hikers' Viewpoint and ends at the hot-spring resort of Ai-Ais.

Due to flash flooding and heat in the summer months, the route is open only from 1 May to 30 September. Although groups of three to 40 people are allowed through every day of the season, this is a very popular hike so book well in advance. The permit costs US$15 per person but you must arrange your own transport and accommodation in Hobas and Ai-Ais.

(For an alternative hiking option, see Fish River Lodge, later in this section.)

Ai-Ais Hot Springs Resort

Ai-Ais (Scalding Hot, in Nama), a hot-spring oasis beneath towering peaks at the southern end of Fish River Canyon, is known for its thermal baths that originate beneath the riverbed. They're rich in chloride, fluoride and sulphur, and are reputedly salubrious for sufferers of rheumatism or nervous disorders. The hot water is piped to a series of baths, jacuzzis and an outdoor swimming pool.

Due to the flood risk, Ai-Ais is closed from 31 October to the second Friday in March. Entry costs US$1.75 per person and US$1.75 per vehicle (the permit is also good for visits to Hobas). Day visitors are welcome between sunrise and 11 pm.

Ai-Ais has a shop, restaurant, petrol station, tennis courts, post office and, of course, a swimming pool, spa and mineral baths. ***Camping***, with ablutions blocks, braai pits and use of all resort facilities costs the same as at Hobas. Two-bed self-catering ***flats*** are US$47, simpler four-bed flats are US$44 and basic four-bed ***bungalows*** cost US$30. Book through NWR in Windhoek.

The ***restaurant*** is open daily from 7 to 8.30 am, noon to 1.30 pm and 6 to 8.30 pm. The attached ***shop*** sells basic groceries.

Fish River Lodge

Fish River Lodge (*☎ 063-223762 or 266018, ⓔ frlodge@iafrica.com.na, PO Box 1840, Keetmanshoop*), also known as Canyon Adventures, makes a great outdoor-oriented backpackers' break. You can choose between dorms in 'the stable' for US$11 a bed and single/double rooms in the farmhouse for US$36/59. Meals are available but cost extra. Backpackers' packages, including self-catering accommodation, a trip into the canyon and return transport from Keetmanshoop, cost US$64/75/85 for one/two/three days (with a minimum of two people).

A highlight of this place is the bureaucracy-free access to Fish River Canyon on the lodge's own fabulous five-day, 85km Fish River Lodge Hiking Trail. The route, which takes in more diverse terrain than the NWR Fish River Canyon Trail, costs US$50 per person, including 4WD transport from the lodge to the trailhead and two nights in the lodge dormitory. On the 4th night, you can stay at the Koelkrans bush camp, which costs N$15 per person, including hot showers and cooking facilities. You can also opt for hikes of one to four days.

Web site: www.etosha.com/fish-river-lodge.htm

Getting There & Away

There's no public transport to either Hobas or Ai-Ais; if you don't have a vehicle consider taking the Fish River Lodge package which involves transfers from Keetmanshoop.

From mid-March to 31 October, hitchers should eventually be successful. Thanks to South African holiday traffic, the best travelled route is to Ai-Ais, via the turn-offs 20km north of Noordoewer or 30km south of Grünau. Once in Ai-Ais, most holidaymakers head for the viewpoints at the canyon's northern end, thus facilitating hitching between Ai-Ais, Hobas and the Hikers' Viewpoint trailhead.

ORANGE RIVER

☎ 063

The Orange River has its headwaters in the Drakensberg Range of Natal (South Africa), and forms much of the boundary between Namibia and South Africa. It was named not for its muddy colour, but after Prince William V of Orange, who was the Dutch monarch in the late 1770s.

Canoeing

Several companies offer three to six-day Orange River canoeing and easy rafting trips from Noordoewer to Selingsdrif, through the amazing canyons between Namibia's Fish River Canyon National Park and South Africa's Richterveld National Park. The trips aren't treacherous – the water is maximum class II – and the appeal lies mainly in the wild canyon country. Budget about US$170/200 for four/six days.

Felix Unite (☎ 27-021-683 6423 or 693 6433 in South Africa, fax 683 6488, ⓔ bookings@felix.co.za), 1 Griegmar House, Main Rd (PO Box 96), Kenilworth 7745, South Africa, organises a range of canoe trips and also hires canoes.

Namibian River Adventures (☎ 297161/283), PO Box 3, Noordoewer, is one of the few Namibian companies running canoe trips.

Orange River Adventures (☎ 27-021-419 1705) in South Africa

Wild Thing Adventures (☎ 27-021-461 1653, ⓔ wildthing@icon.co.za) in South Africa

Places to Stay

The ***Camel Lodge*** (*☎ 297171, fax 297143*) in Noordoewer has singles/doubles for US$24/38. Four-bed rooms cost US$45. On the South African side, 12km downstream from Vioolsdrif, is the relaxing ***Peace of Paradise Campsite*** (for details, see the Northern Cape Province section in the South Africa chapter).

The Namib Dunes

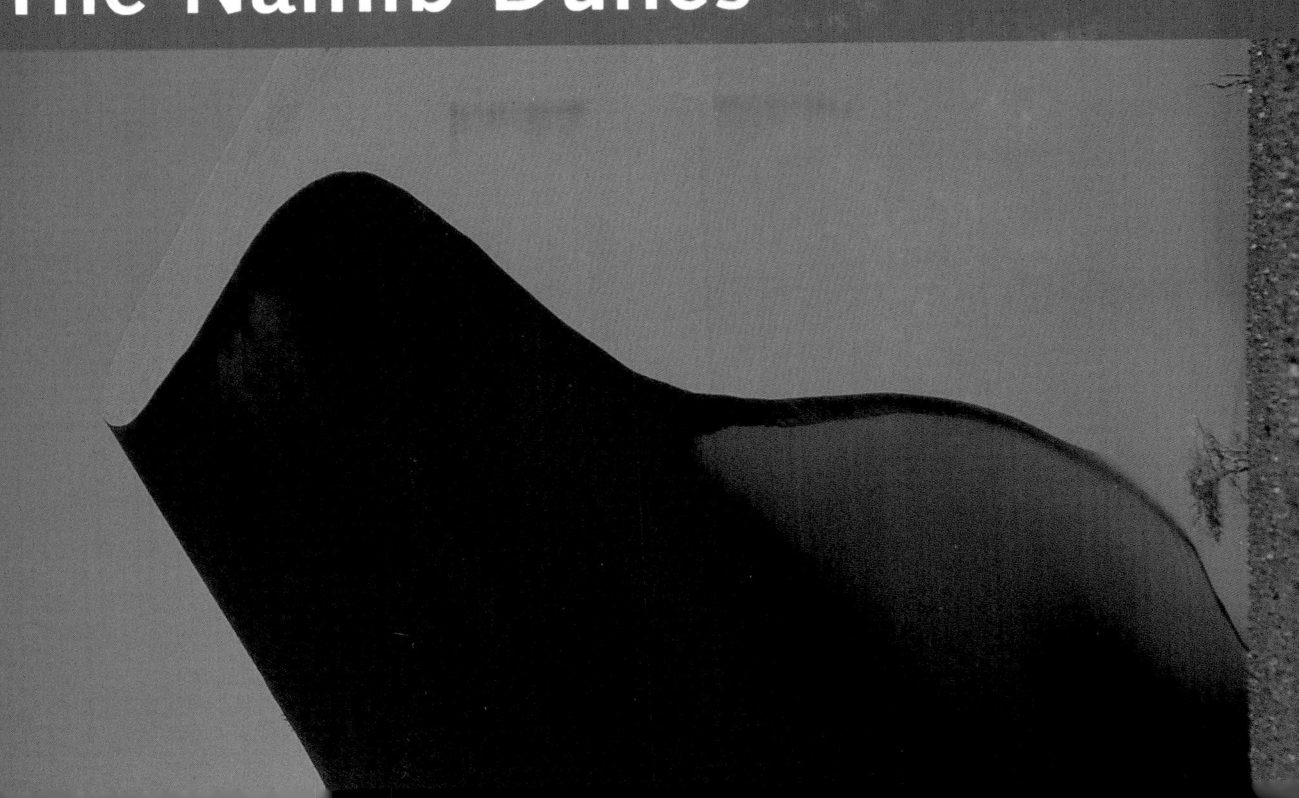

The Namib Dunes

The Namib's magnificent so-called Dune Sea stretches from the Orange River to the Kuiseb River in the south and from Torra Bay (in the Skeleton Coast Park) to Angola's Curoca River in the north. Its dunes are composed of colourful quartz sand and come in hues that vary from cream to orange, red and violet.

Unlike the Kalahari dunes, those of the Namib are dynamic. Over time, shifting winds sculpt them into a variety of distinctive shapes. The top portion of the dune, which faces the direction of migration, is known as a slipface. Wind-blown sand spills from the dune's crest and slips down the dune's face. It's where the majority of dune life is concentrated because plant and animal detritus also collect here, providing a food source.

Along the eastern area of the Dune Sea, including around Sossusvlei, the dunes are classified as parabolic or multi-cyclic and are the result of variable wind patterns. These are the most stable dunes in the Namib and are therefore the most vegetated.

Near the coast south of Walvis Bay, the formations are known as transverse dunes, which are long linear dunes lying perpendicular to the prevailing southwesterly winds. Their slipfaces, therefore, are oriented towards the north and north-east.

Between these two types of dunes – for example, around Homeb in the Central Namib – are the prominent linear or *seif* dunes, which are enormous north-west/south-east oriented sand ripples. These reach heights of 100m and are spaced about 1km apart and show up plainly

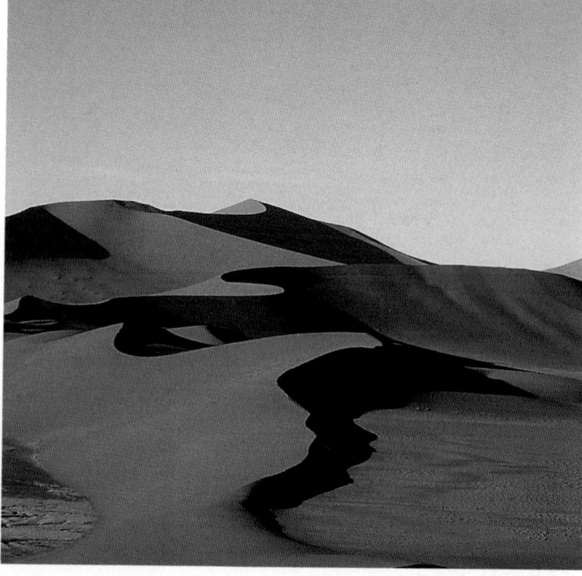

ANDREW VAN SMEERDIJK

Inset: The winds carve the dunes into intricate shapes. (Photo by Daniel Birks)

Left: Dune formations at Sossusvlei

on satellite photographs of the area. They're formed by seasonal winds; during the prevailing southerly winds of summer, the slipfaces lie to the north-east. In the winter, the wind blows in the opposite direction and slipfaces build up on the south-west.

In areas where individual dunes are exposed to winds from all directions, a formation known as a star dune appears. These dunes have multiple ridges and when seen from above may appear to have a star shape.

Considerably smaller are the tiny hump dunes, which build up around vegetation – mainly near water sources – and are only between 2m and 3m in height.

Around the southern portion of the Skeleton Coast Park and south of Lüderitz, barchan dunes prevail. These are the most highly mobile dunes of all, and are created by unidirectional winds. As they shift, these dunes take on a crescent shape, with the horns of the crescent aimed in the direction of migration. It is barchan dunes that are slowly devouring the ghost town of Kolkmanskop near Lüderitz. They're also known as 'roaring dunes' because of the rumbling sound they make as sand grains spill over their slipfaces. The roar is at its loudest on particularly large dunes or in especially warm weather.

Heading north, the dunes stop abruptly at the Kuiseb River, where they give way to flat, arid gravel plains interrupted by isolated ranges and hills known as inselbergs.

The Dune Community

Despite their barren appearance, the Namib dunes actually support a unique ecosystem. Life manages to survive the extreme conditions here thanks to grass seed and bits of plant matter deposited by the wind and the moisture carried in by fog.

The sand provides shelter for a range of small creatures, as even a short walk on the dunes will reveal. By day, surface temperatures may reach 70°C, but below, the spaces between sand particles allow air to circulate freely and provide a cool shelter. In the chill of a desert night, the sand retains some of the heat absorbed during the day and provides a warm place to burrow. When alarmed, most creatures can also use the sand as an effective hiding place.

Much of the dune community is comprised of beetles, which are attracted by the vegetable material on the dune slipfaces; indeed, the Namib supports 200 species of the Tenebrionid family alone. However, they're only visible when the dune surface is warm; at other times, they take shelter beneath the surface by 'swimming' into the sand.

The fog-basking beetle *(Onomachris unguicularis)*, which is locally known as a toktokkie, has a particularly interesting way of drinking. It derives moisture by condensing fog on its body – on foggy mornings, toktokkies line up on the dunes, lower their heads, raise their posteriors in the air and slide water droplets down their carapaces into their mouths. They can consume up to 40% of their body weight in water in a single morning.

The large dancing spider known as the 'white lady of the Namib' *(Orchestrella longpipes* – it sounds like a character in a children's novel!) lives in tunnels constructed beneath the dune surface. To prevent the tunnels from collapsing, they are lined with spider silk as they are excavated. This enormous spider can easily make a meal of creatures as large as palmato geckos.

The dunes are also home to the lovable golden mole *(Eremitalpa granti)*, a yellowish-coloured carnivore that spends most of its day buried in the dune. It was first discovered in 1837, but wasn't again sighted until 1963. The golden mole, which lacks both eyes and ears, doesn't burrow like other moles, but simply swims through the sand. Although it's rarely spotted, look carefully around tufts of grass or hummocks for the large, rounded snout, which often protrudes above the surface. At night, it emerges and roams hundreds of metres over the dune faces foraging for beetle larvae and other insects.

The shovel-snouted lizard *(Aporosaura anchitae)* uses a unique method of regulating its body temperature while tearing across the

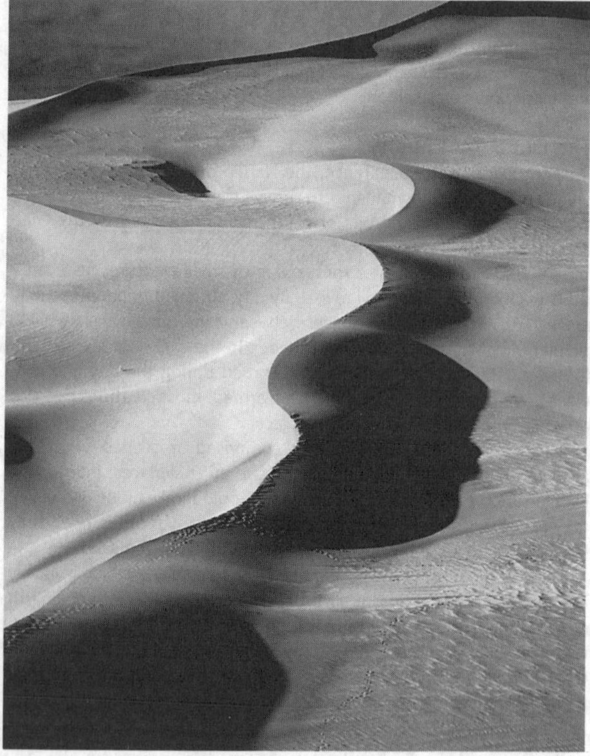

ADRIEN VADROT

Left: The Namib Desert dunes are continually sculpted by the wind.

scorching sand. This lizard can tolerate body temperatures of up to 44°C, but surface temperatures on the dunes can climb as high as 70°C. To prevent overheating, the lizard does a 'thermal dance', raising its tail and two legs at a time off the hot surface of the sand. When threatened, the lizard submerges itself in the sand.

Another unique creature is the rather appealing little palmato gecko *(Palmatogecko rangei)*, also known as the web-footed gecko after its unusual feet, which act as scoops for burrowing in the sand. This translucent, nocturnal gecko has a pinkish-brown colouration on its back and a white belly. It grows to a length of 10cm and has enormous eyes, which aid hunting at night. It's often photographed using its long tongue to clear its eyes of dust and sand. It also uses its tongue to collect condensed fog droplets from its head and snout. Other gecko species present in the dunes include the barking gecko *(Ptenopus garrulus)* and the large-headed gecko *(Chondrodactylus anguilifer)*.

Another dune lizard is the bizarre and fearsome-looking Namaqua chameleon *(Chamaeleo namaquensis)*, which grows up to 25cm in length and is unmistakable due to the fringe of brownish bumps along its spine. When alarmed, it emits an ominous hiss and exposes its enormous yellow-coloured mouth and sticky tongue, which can spell the end for up to 200 large beetles every day. Like all chameleons, its eyes operate independently in their cone-shaped sockets, allowing the chameleon to look in several directions at once.

The small, buff-coloured Namib sidewinding adder *(Bitis peringueyi)* is perfectly camouflaged on the dune surface. It grows to a length of just 25cm and navigates by gracefully moving sideways through the shifting sands. Because its eyes are on top of its head, the snake can bury itself almost completely in the sand and still see what's happening above the surface. When its unsuspecting prey comes along – normally a gecko or lizard – the adder uses its venom to immobilise the creature before devouring it. Although it is also poisonous to humans, the venom is so mild that it rarely causes more than an irritation.

The three species of Namib sand snakes *(Psammophis* sp.*)* are longer, slinkier and faster-moving than the adders, but hunt the same prey. These 1m-long back-fanged snakes grab their prey and chew on it until it's immobilised by venom, then swallow it whole. As with the adders, they're well camouflaged for life in the sand, ranging from off-white to pale grey in colour. The back is marked with pale stripes or a pattern of dots.

Several varieties of Namib skinks *(Typhlosaurus* sp.*)* are commonly mistaken for snakes. Because they propel themselves by swimming in the sand, their limbs are either small and vestigial or missing altogether, and their eyes, ears and nostrils are tiny and therefore well protected from sand particles. At the tip of their nose is a 'rostral scale', which acts like a bulldozer blade to clear the sand ahead and allow the skink to progress. Skinks spend most of their time burrowing beneath the surface, but at night emerge on the dune slipfaces to forage. In the morning, you'll often see their telltale tracks.

SOUTH AFRICA MAP INDEX

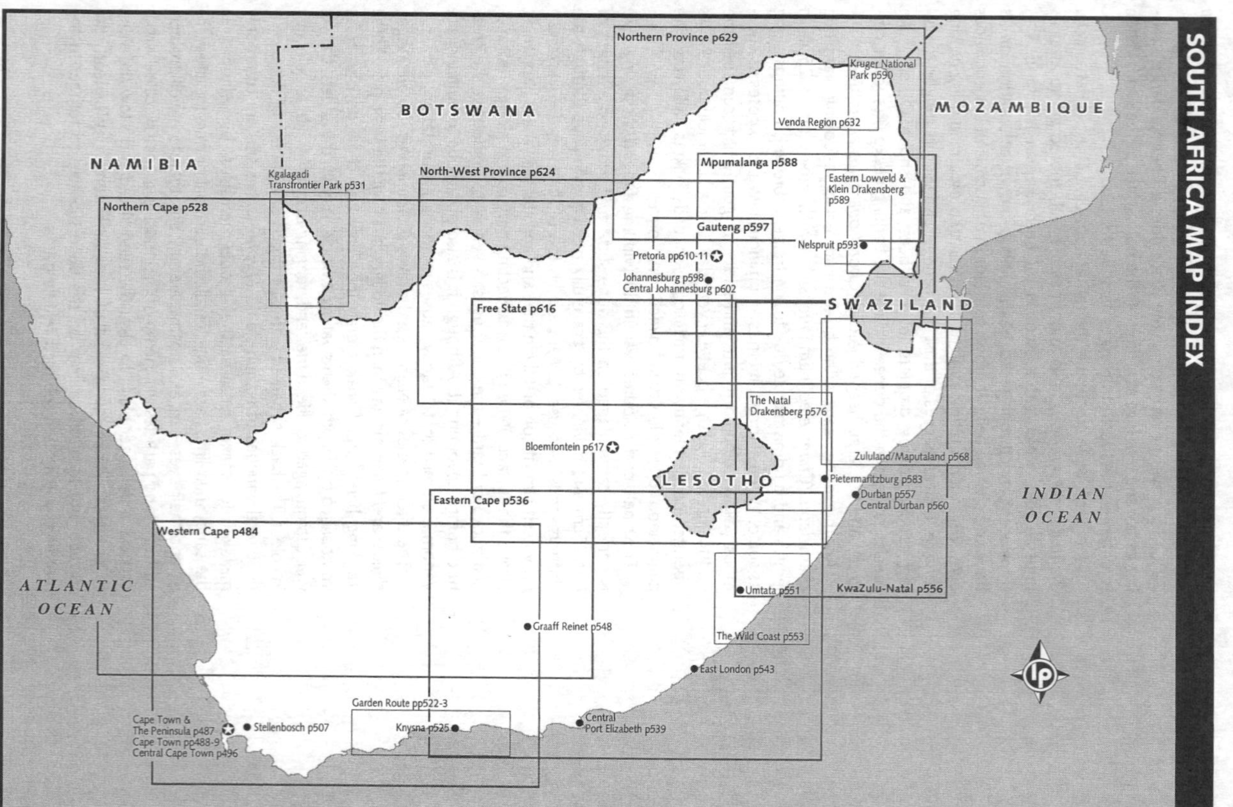

South Africa

South Africa, the southern gateway to the region and the whole vast continent, is an exhilarating, spectacular and complex country. Geographically, its extremes include the arid semidesert of the Karoo, the snowcapped peaks of the Drakensberg Range, the lush subtropical coast of KwaZulu-Natal and the fertile temperate valleys of Western Cape.

For tourists there are world-class attractions such as Kruger National Park, which has possibly the finest wildlife viewing in Africa. And then there's the staggering beauty of Cape Town – once seen, never to be forgotten – a city whose extraordinary location is dominated by the sheer cliffs of a mountain. The influx of foreign visitors in recent years has brought about an explosion of tours and activities: there is everything from abseiling off Table Mountain to sipping cocktails while watching lions.

The 'rainbow nation' is an economic powerhouse, and that is reflected in the outstanding and well-organised network of national parks and reserves. The road system is excellent and getting around is relatively easy: for budget travellers there are affordable backpackers hostels all over the country, and a bus service linking most of them.

With 11 official languages, it's obvious that South Africa's people are diverse, and since the amazingly peaceful transition to majority rule, that diversity is now respected. At one end of the country you can meet the Venda people, fabled iron-workers of mysterious origin; and at the other you can meet the Cape Muslims, with roots in South-East Asia.

South Africa is going through huge upheavals as it comes to grips with democracy, and in these terms it is a young country. Democracy has precipitated change, which is both good and bad – the dissolving of physical and psychological barriers built around skin colour at one end of the scale, and the well-publicised crime problem at the other. It is an exciting time to come to South Africa and observe this change blossoming at first hand.

SOUTH AFRICA AT A GLANCE

Area: 1,233,404 sq km

Population: 41 million

Capitals: Pretoria (administrative capital), Bloemfontein (seat of high court) and Cape Town (seat of parliament)

Head of State: President Thabo Mbeki

Official Languages: English, Afrikaans, Ndebele, South Sotho, North Sotho, Swati, Tsonga, Tswana, Venda, Xhosa and Zulu

Currency: rand (R)

Exchange Rate: US$1= R6.2

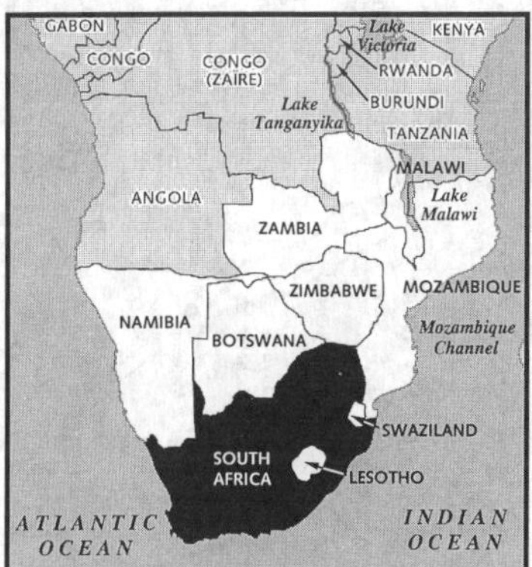

Highlights

- Cape Town – wander around one of the great cities of the world; close to Table Mountain and the Winelands
- Kruger National Park – perhaps the best wildlife viewing in Africa; a must-see!
- Drakensberg Range – hike through this rugged and spectacular escarpment
- Zululand – experience traditional Zulu culture, see important battlefields and visit outstanding national parks
- Transkei – revel in the solitude of this largely undeveloped area in the Eastern Cape, with its superb warm-water surf beaches and excellent hiking trails

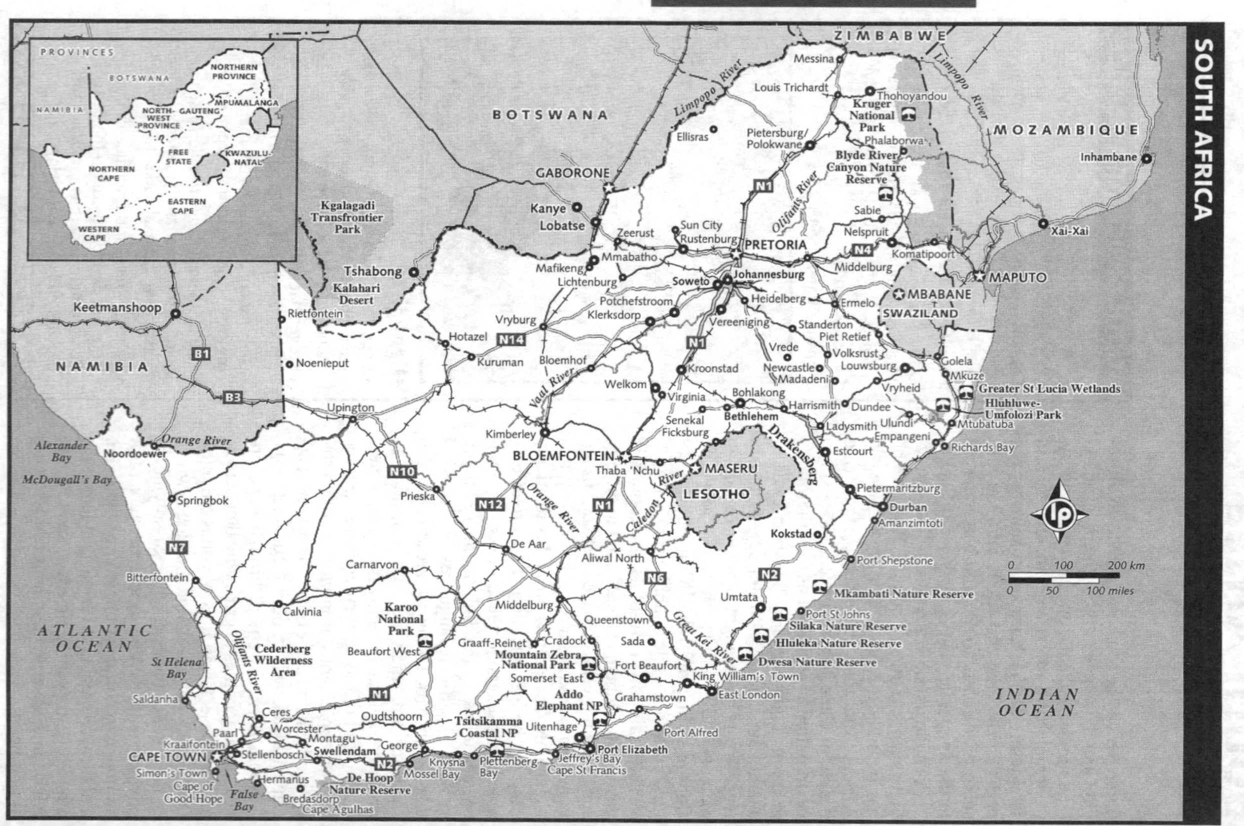
SOUTH AFRICA
PROVINCES
BOTSWANA
NAMIBIA
NORTHERN PROVINCE
MPUMALANGA
NORTH-WEST PROVINCE
GAUTENG
FREE STATE
KWAZULU-NATAL
NORTHERN CAPE
EASTERN CAPE
WESTERN CAPE
ZIMBABWE
BOTSWANA
MOZAMBIQUE
Limpopo River
Messina
Louis Trichardt
Thohoyandou
Kruger National Park
Phalaborwa
Ellisras
Pietersburg/Polokwane
Blyde River Canyon Nature Reserve
Olifants River
N1
Inhambane
GABORONE
Kanye
Lobatse
Sabie
Nelspruit
Xai-Xai
Zeerust
Sun City
Rustenburg
PRETORIA
N4
Komatipoort
Kgalagadi Transfrontier Park
Mafikeng
Mmabatho
Middelburg
MAPUTO
Tshabong
Lichtenburg
Soweto
Johannesburg
Kalahari Desert
Potchefstroom
Heidelberg
Ermelo
MBABANE
SWAZILAND
Keetmanshoop
Rietfontein
Klerksdorp
Vryburg
Vereeniging
Standerton
Piet Retief
Hotazel
N14
N1
Vrede
Volksrust
Golela
NAMIBIA
B1
Noenieput
Kuruman
Bloemhof
Kroonstad
Newcastle
Madadeni
Louwsburg
Mkuze
Vaal River
Welkom
Virginia
Bohlakong
Vryheid
Greater St Lucia Wetlands
B3
Upington
Harrismith
Dundee
Hluhluwe-Umfolozi Park
Senekal
Bethlehem
Ladysmith
Ulundi
Mtubatuba
Kimberley
Ficksburg
Empangeni
Alexander Bay
Orange River
Noordoewer
Drakensberg
Richards Bay
Estcourt
BLOEMFONTEIN
MASERU
Thaba 'Nchu
McDougall's Bay
N10
River
LESOTHO
Pietermaritzburg
Springbok
Prieska
N12
Orange River
N1
Durban
Caledon
Amanzimtoti
Kokstad
N7
De Aar
Aliwal North
Port Shepstone
0 100 200 km
0 50 100 miles
Carnarvon
N2
N6
Bitterfontein
Mkambati Nature Reserve
Umtata
Calvinia
Middelburg
Port St Johns
Karoo National Park
Queenstown
Silaka Nature Reserve
ATLANTIC OCEAN
Great Kei River
Cederberg Wilderness Area
Graaff-Reinet
Cradock
Sada
Hluleka Nature Reserve
Olifants River
Beaufort West
Mountain Zebra National Park
Dwesa Nature Reserve
St Helena Bay
Fort Beaufort
Somerset East
King William's Town
N1
Addo Elephant NP
East London
Saldanha
Grahamstown
INDIAN OCEAN
Ceres
Tsitsikamma Coastal NP
Oudtshoorn
Worcester
Uitenhage
Paarl
Montagu
Port Alfred
Kraaifontein
George
Port Elizabeth
CAPE TOWN
Stellenbosch
Swellendam
Knysna
Plettenberg Bay
Jeffrey's Bay
Simon's Town
N2
Mossel Bay
Cape St Francis
Hermanus
De Hoop Nature Reserve
Cape of Good Hope
False Bay
Bredasdorp
Cape Agulhas

Facts about South Africa

HISTORY

South Africa's history extends back to around 40,000 BC when the San people first settled Southern Africa. By the 3rd century AD, Bantu-speaking peoples were well established in South Africa. When the competing colonial powers arrived, the Cape was the main stage for their struggles, but widespread colonial settlement of South Africa did not begin until the 19th century (see History in the Facts about the Region chapter for a description of events leading up to the Great Trek).

The Great Trek

From the 1820s, groups of Boers dissatisfied with British rule in the Cape Colony trekked off into the interior in search of freedom. From the mid-1830s increasing numbers of Voortrekkers (Fore-trekkers, pioneers) abandoned their farms and crossed the Orange River in a decade of migration known as the Great Trek. Reports from early treks told of vast, uninhabited – or at least poorly defended – grazing lands.

Tensions between the Boers and the government had been building for some time, but the reason given by many trekkers for leaving was the 1833 act banning slavery.

The Great Trek coincided with the *difaqane* (forced migration, explained under History in the Facts about the Region chapter) and the Boers mistakenly believed that what they found – deserted pasture lands, disorganised bands of refugees and tales of brutality – was the normal state of affairs. This mistaken assessment gave rise to the Afrikaner myths (now dying hard) that the Voortrekkers moved into unoccupied territory or arrived at much the same time as the blacks.

The Voortrekkers Meet the Zulu The Great Trek's first halt was at Thaba 'Nchu, near modern Bloemfontein, where a republic was established. After a disagreement, trek leaders Maritz, Retief and Uys moved on to Natal, and Potgieter headed north to establish the Republics of Winburg (in the Free State) and Potchefstroom, later the Republic of Transvaal.

By 1837 Piet Retief's party had crossed the Drakensberg and wanted to establish a republic. Zulu king Dingaan (Shaka's successor) agreed to this and, in February 1838, Retief and some others visited his capital Mgungundlovu (near modern Ulundi) to sign the title deed. It was a trap. The deed assigning all Natal to the Boers was signed but immediately afterwards Dingaan's men massacred the entire party.

In December 1838 Andries Pretorius organised a revenge attack on the Zulus. Sarel Celliers climbed onto a gun carriage to lead the party in a vow that if they won the battle, the Boers would ever after celebrate the day as one of deliverance. Pretorius' party reached the Ncome River and on 16 December the Zulus attacked. After three hours of carnage the river ran red and was named Blood River by the Boers. Three Boers had slight injuries; 3000 Zulus had been killed.

After such a 'miraculous' victory (actually the result of good tactics and vastly superior weaponry) it seemed that the Boer expansion really did have that long-suspected stamp of divine approval, and the 16 December victory was celebrated as the Day of the Vow until 1994, when it was renamed the Day of Reconciliation.

Perhaps more miraculously, when the Boers pushed on to Mgungundlovu they found the remains of Retief and his party and the deed granting them Natal. Despite this, the British annexed the republic in 1843 and most of the Boers moved north into the Transvaal, carrying with them yet another grievance against the British.

The Boer Republics

Several short-lived Boer republics sprang up but soon the only serious contenders were the Orange Free State and the Transvaal.

The years between the Battle of Blood River (1838), and the conventions of Sand River (1852) and Bloemfontein (1854), which gave independence to the Transvaal and the Orange Free State, are full of confusion and

SOUTH AFRICA

conflict. The Boers knew what they wanted: land and freedom. The aims of the black tribes were similar, but the British government, which commanded the strongest forces in the area, wasn't at all sure of what it wanted. British officials in Africa often had no idea of whether they should be restraining Boers, protecting blacks, enforcing British treaties or carving out new British colonies.

The Orange Free State was intermittently at war with the powerful Basotho people – sometimes with British assistance, sometimes without. Finally, in 1871, the British annexed Basotholand. The Transvaal Republic's problems were mostly internal, with several leaders and breakaway republics threatening civil war until Paul Kruger (president of the Zuid-Afrikaansche Republiek [ZAR – South African Republic], 1883–1900) settled the issue with a short, sharp campaign in 1864.

The financial position of the republics was always precarious and their economies depended entirely on cattle. Most trade was by barter. Just when it seemed that the republics, with their thinly spread population of fiercely independent Boers, were beginning to settle into stable states, diamonds were discovered near Kimberley in 1869. Britain stepped in quickly and annexed the area.

The discovery of diamonds resulted in a rush of European immigrants and a migration of black labour. The Boers were disturbed by the foreigners, both black and white, and angry that their impoverished republics were missing out on the economic benefits of the mines.

Meanwhile, Britain became nervous about the existence of independent republics in Southern Africa, especially as gold had been found in the Transvaal. The solution, as usual, was annexation and in 1877 the Transvaal lost its independence.

Anglo-Boer Wars

After the annexation, the Transvaal drifted into rebellion and the First Anglo-Boer War, known by Afrikaners as the War of Independence, broke out. It was over almost as soon as it began, with a crushing Boer victory at the Battle of Majuba in early 1881, and the republic regained its independence as the ZAR.

With the discovery of a huge reef of gold in the Witwatersrand (the area around Johannesburg) in 1886 and the ensuing explosive growth of Johannesburg itself, the ZAR was suddenly host to thousands of *uitlanders* (foreigners), black and white.

With little experience of towns, none of cities, and a deep suspicion of foreign ways, Kruger's ZAR government did its best to isolate the republic from the gold rush. The foreigners paid taxes but were not allowed to vote.

In 1899 the British demanded that voting rights be given to the 60,000 foreign whites on the Witwatersrand. Kruger refused, demanding that British troops massing on the ZAR borders be withdrawn by 11 October – if they weren't, he asserted, he would consider the republic to be at war.

The British, confident that their vastly superior numbers of experienced troops would win swiftly, took him on. Shocked to find that the Boers were no pushover, the British were for a time in disarray. However, the British brought in more troops and new commanders, Lords Roberts and Kitchener. An army of 450,000 men was brought to bear on the 80,000 Boers from the ZAR, the Free State and the Cape. The Boers gave way rapidly and by 5 June 1900 Pretoria, the last of the major towns, had surrendered.

It seemed that the war was over but instead it entered a second, bitter phase. Commando raiders denied the British enemy control of the countryside. There was no possibility that the British could be defeated, but maintaining an occupying army would be an expensive proposition for them.

The British had no enemy army to face, just commandos who could instantly become innocuous farmers, and they decided to exact reprisals. If a railway line was blown up, the nearest farmhouse was destroyed; if a shot was fired from a farm, the house was burnt down, the crops destroyed and the animals killed. The women and children from the farms were collected and taken to concentration camps – a British invention. By the end of the war 26,000 people, mainly children, had died of disease and neglect in the camps.

On 31 May 1902 the Peace of Vereeniging was signed and the Boer republics became British colonies.

British Rule

The British response after their victory was a mixture of appeasement and insensitive imperialism. It was essential for the Boers and British to work together. The nonwhites were scarcely considered, other than as potential labour, despite the fact that they constituted about 80% of the combined population of the provinces.

Political awareness was growing, however. Mohandas (later Mahatma) Gandhi was working with the Indian populations of the Natal and Transvaal, and men like John Jabavu, Walter Rubusana and Abdullah Abdurahman laid the foundations for new nontribal, black political groups.

Hard-up Boers flooded into the cities to find a world dominated by the English and their language. Worst of all, they were forced to compete for jobs with blacks. Partly as a backlash to this, Afrikaans came to be seen as the *volkstaal* (people's language) and as a symbol of Afrikaner nationhood.

The former republics were given representative government in 1906–7, and moves towards union began almost immediately.

Union of South Africa

The Union of South Africa was established on 31 May 1910. The British High Commission Territories of Basotholand (now Lesotho), Bechuanaland (now Botswana), Swaziland and Rhodesia (now Zimbabwe) were excluded from the Union.

English and Dutch were made the official languages – Afrikaans was not recognised as the official language until 1925.

The first election was held in September 1910. The South African National Party (soon known as the South African Party, or SAP), a diverse coalition of Boer groups under General Louis Botha and the brilliant General Jan Smuts, won the election and Botha became the first prime minister of the Union.

The most divisive issues were raised by General Barry Hertzog, who championed Afrikaner interests, advocated separate development for the two white groups and independence from Britain. He and his supporters formed the National Party (NP).

Soon after the union was established a barrage of repressive legislation was passed. It became illegal for black workers to strike; skilled jobs were reserved for whites; blacks were barred from military service; and pass laws, restricting black freedom of movement, were tightened.

In 1912, Pixley ka Isaka Seme formed a national democratic organisation to represent blacks. It was initially called the South African Native Congress, but from 1923 it was known as the African National Congress (ANC).

In 1913 the Natives Land Act set aside 7.5% of South Africa's land for black occupancy. No black (and blacks made up over 70% of the population) was allowed to buy, rent or become a sharecropper outside this area. Thousands of squatters were evicted from farms and forced into increasingly overcrowded reserves, or into the cities.

In 1914 South Africa, as a part of the British Empire, found itself automatically at war with Germany and saddled with the responsibility of dealing with German South West Africa (now Namibia). South Africa's involvement on the British side prompted the last major violent Afrikaner rebellion – more than 300 men were killed. After the war, South West Africa became a part of South Africa under 'mandate' from the League of Nations.

Fusion

In 1924 the NP under Hertzog came to power, with an agenda that included promoting Afrikaner interests, independence and racial segregation. In the 1929 election the *swaartgevaar* (black threat) was made the dominant issue for the first time.

In reality, positions of the NP and the SAP were not so far apart and, in 1933, the two parties formed a coalition or fusion government, with Hertzog as the prime minister and Smuts as his deputy.

Fusion was rejected by Dr DF Malan and his followers. They formed the Purified National Party, which quickly became the dominant force in Afrikaner political life. The Afrikaner Broederbond, a secret ultranationalistic Afrikaner brotherhood, became an extraordinarily influential force behind the party. From 1948 to 1994 every prime minister and president was a member of the Broederbond.

At the far right, the Ossewa-Brandwag (Sentinels of the Ox-wagon, or OB) became a popular militaristic organisation with strong German sympathies and an obvious affinity with Hitler's doctrine of a master race.

Apartheid

The NP won the 1948 election on a platform of establishing *apartheid* (literally, the state of being apart). With the help of creative electoral boundaries it held power right up to the first democratic election in 1994.

Mixed marriages were prohibited and interracial sex was made illegal. Every individual was classified by race. The Group Areas Act enforcing the physical separation of residential areas was promulgated. The Separate Amenities Act created separate public facilities – separate beaches, separate buses, separate toilets, separate schools and separate park benches. The pass laws were further strengthened and blacks were compelled to carry identity documents at all times and were prohibited from remaining in towns, or even visiting them, without specific permission. Thanks to the Dutch Reformed churches, apartheid was even given religious justification.

Black Action

In 1949 the ANC for the first time advocated open resistance in the form of strikes, acts of public disobedience and protest marches. These continued intermittently throughout the 1950s, with occasional violent clashes.

In June 1955, at a congress held at Kliptown near Johannesburg, a number of organisations, including the Indian Congress and the ANC, adopted a Freedom Charter. This articulated a vision of a nonracial democratic state.

On 21 March 1960 the Pan African Congress (PAC) called for nationwide protests against the hated pass laws. When demonstrators surrounded a police station in Sharpeville police opened fire, killing 69 people and wounding 160. To people in South Africa and the rest of the world, the struggle had now crossed a crucial line – there could no longer be any doubts about the nature of the white regime.

Soon after, the PAC and ANC were banned and the security forces were given the right to detain people indefinitely without trial. Prime Minister Verwoerd announced a referendum on whether the country should become a republic. A slim majority of white voters gave their approval to the change and in May 1961 the Republic of South Africa came into existence.

Nelson Mandela became the leader of the underground ANC and Oliver Tambo went abroad to establish the organisation in exile. As more black activists were arrested, the ANC and PAC began a campaign of sabotage through the armed wings of their organisations, respectively Umkonto We Sizwe (Spear of the Nation; usually known as MK) and Poqo (Pure). In July 1963 Nelson Mandela, along with a number of other ANC and communist leaders, was arrested, charged with fomenting violent revolution and sentenced to life imprisonment.

The Homelands

Verwoerd was assassinated in parliament in 1966 (there was apparently no political motive) and was succeeded by BJ Vorster, who was followed in 1978 by PW Botha. Both men continued to pursue the insane dream of separate black Homelands and a white South Africa.

The plan was to restrict blacks to Homelands that were, according to the propaganda, to become self-sufficient, self-governing states on the traditional lands of particular tribal groups. In reality, these traditional lands had virtually no infrastructure and no industry and were therefore incapable of producing sufficient food for the burgeoning black population. They were based on the land that had been set aside for blacks in the

1913 Natives Lands Act. Under the plan, 13% of the country's total land area was to be the home to 75% of the population.

Blacks were to have no rights in South Africa and could not even be present outside their Homeland without a pass and explicit permission. There was intense and widespread suffering as a result.

The Homelands were first given internal self-government, and were then expected to accept a nominal independence. Power proved irresistible to the leaders of Transkei, Bophuthatswana, Venda and Ciskei. Between 1976 and 1981 the collaborators accepted 'independence', and they then proceeded to crush all resistance to their rule and that of the South African government.

International Conflict

In 1980 Robert Mugabe was elected prime minister of an independent Zimbabwe, and South Africa found itself the last white-controlled state in Africa. Increasing numbers of western countries imposed sanctions and the ANC and PAC received direct support from the governments of black Africa (with the exception of Malawi and Swaziland). South Africa increasingly saw itself as a bastion besieged by communism, atheism and black anarchy.

Soweto Uprising

On 16 June 1976 the Soweto Students' Representative Council organised protests against the use of Afrikaans (considered the language of the oppressor) in black schools. Police opened fire on a student march, starting a round of nationwide demonstrations, strikes, mass arrests and riots that, over the next 12 months, took more than 1000 lives.

Steve Biko, the charismatic leader of the Black Consciousness movement, which stressed the need for psychological liberation and black pride, was killed in September 1977. Unidentified security police beat him until he lapsed into a coma – he went without medical treatment for three days and finally died in Pretoria. At the subsequent inquest, the magistrate found that no one was to blame.

South Africa was never the same again – a generation of young blacks committed themselves to a revolutionary struggle against apartheid and the black communities were politicised.

After changes to the constitution in 1983, the powers of the state president were increased and coloureds (mixed race) and Indians were given a token role in government. Blacks were given no role at all.

Violent protest built up steadily over the next two years until, in 1985, the government declared a state of emergency that was to stay in force for the next five years. The media was strictly censored and, by 1988, 30,000 people had been detained without trial. Thousands were tortured.

Botha repealed the pass laws, but this failed to mollify black protesters and created a white backlash. Botha's reforms also failed to impress the rest of the world, and economic sanctions began to bite. In particular, foreign banks refused to roll over government loans and the rand's value collapsed. In late 1989 Botha was replaced by FW De Klerk.

Reform

At his opening address to the parliament on 2 February 1990 De Klerk announced that he would repeal discriminatory laws and that the ANC, PAC and Communist Party were legalised. Media restrictions were lifted, and De Klerk undertook to release political prisoners. On 11 February he released Nelson Mandela, 27 years after he had first been incarcerated. During 1990 and 1991 virtually all the old apartheid regulations were repealed.

On 21 December 1991 the Convention for a Democratic South Africa (CODESA) began negotiations on the formation of a multiracial transitional government and a new constitution extending political rights to all groups.

The CODESA negotiations did not proceed smoothly but it was apparent that both the NP and the ANC were determined that free elections would take place at some time. However, thrashing out the details was a complex process and the ANC suspected that the government was committed to drawing it out as long as possible.

By this stage the CODESA talks had become a straight negotiation between the NP

SARAH JOLLY

Nelson Mandela and Thabo Mbeki – past and present leaders of South Africa

and the ANC, excluding the smaller parties. The Zulu-based Inkatha movement (now called the Inkatha Freedom Party [IFP]) and some of the Homelands governments left CODESA, demanding a federal structure for the new constitution. Right-wing whites, who wanted a *Volkstaat* (literally People's State; a Boer Homeland), joined them in an unlikely alliance.

Now, with white support drifting to the right-wing parties, the National Party needed to hurry negotiations. A compromise was reached and both sides accepted an interim government of national unity to rule after the election for no more than five years.

Free Elections

Across the country at midnight on 26–27 April 1994, *Die Stem* (the old national anthem) was sung and the old flag was lowered. Then the new rainbow flag was raised and the new anthem, *Nkosi Sikelele Afrika* (God Bless Africa), was sung – once, people were jailed for singing this beautiful hymn.

The ANC won 62.7% of the vote, less than the 66.7% which would have enabled it to overrule the interim constitution. As well as deciding the national government, the election decided the provincial governments, and the ANC won in all but two of the provinces. The National Party won 20.4% of the vote, enough to guarantee it representation in cabinet.

Today

In 1999, after five years of learning about democracy, the country voted in another election. Issues such as economics and competence were raised and debated. There was some speculation that the ANC vote might drop with Nelson Mandela's retirement, but it didn't slide – the vote increased to put the party within one seat of the two-thirds majority that would allow it to alter the constitution.

The New National Party (NNP) lost two-thirds of its seats and lost official opposition status to the Democratic Party (DP); the United Democratic Movement (UDM) also fared poorly. The ANC retained all of its provincial governments.

Thabo Mbeki, who took over leadership of the ANC from Nelson Mandela, became president at the 1999 elections. Compared with Nelson Mandela, whose life has become the stuff of legend, Mbeki is not well known to the people.

Today, for white South Africans, crime is still the number one concern; blacks also suffer from crime, but then they have done so for a very long time. For black South Africans economic inequality is a huge problem, and although the apartheid system is dead, economic apartheid lives on.

GEOGRAPHY

South Africa is a big country, covering nearly 2000km from the Limpopo River in the north to Cape Agulhas in the south, and nearly 1500km from Port Nolloth in the west to Durban in the east. It's mostly dry and sunny, lying just to the south of the Tropic of Capricorn. The major influence on the climate is not the country's latitude, but its topography and the surrounding oceans.

The country can be divided into three major parts: the vast interior plateau (the highveld); the great escarpment at its edge (the Kalahari Basin); and a narrow coastal plain (the lowveld). Although Johannesburg is not far south of the tropics, its altitude (around 1700m above sea level) and its distance from the sea moderates its climate. It is 1500km further north than Cape Town, but its average temperatures are only 1°C higher.

South Africa is divided into nine provinces: Gauteng, Northern, Mpumalanga, Free State, KwaZulu-Natal, North-West, Northern Cape, Eastern Cape and Western Cape.

The Homelands no longer exist as political entities, but because of their different histories and economies it will be some time before there's a noticeable change when crossing one of the old borders. In this guide we sometimes refer to the old Homelands by name.

CLIMATE

The Western Cape has dry sunny summers with maximum temperatures around 26°C. It is often windy, however, and the south-easterly 'Cape Doctor' can reach gale force. Winters can get cold, with average minimum temperatures of around 7°C and maximum temperatures of around 17°C. There is occasional snow on the higher peaks.

The eastern plateau area (including Johannesburg) has a dry, sunny climate in winter with maximum temperatures around 20°C and crisp nights with temperatures dropping to around 5°C. Between October and April there are late afternoon showers often accompanied by spectacular thunder and lightning, but it rarely gets unpleasantly hot. Heavy hailstorms cause quite a lot of damage each year. It can, however, get very hot in the Karoo (the semidesert heart of all three Cape provinces) and the far north (the Kalahari).

The coast north from the Cape becomes progressively drier and hotter. Along the south

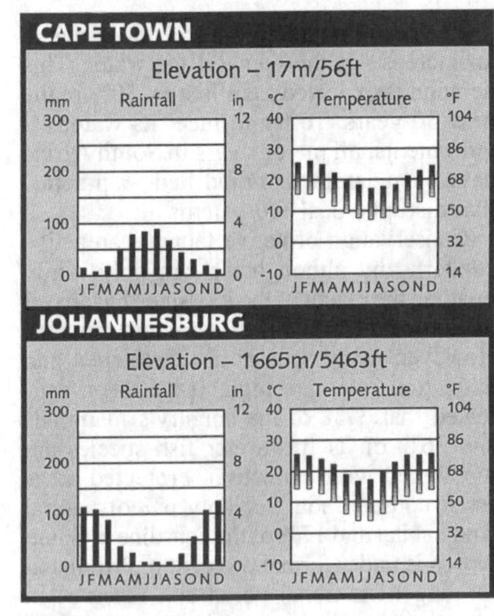

coast the weather is temperate, but further north the east coast gets increasingly tropical. KwaZulu-Natal and the Transkei region can be hot and very humid in summer, although the highlands are still pleasant; it's also a summer rainfall area. Mpumalanga and Northern Province lowvelds get very hot in summer, when there are spectacular storms. In winter the days are sunny and warm.

ECOLOGY & ENVIRONMENT

South Africa is ranked as the third most biologically diverse country in the world. A major environmental challenge for the government is to manage increasing population growth and urbanisation while protecting this diverse environment. The population is growing at 2% per year and is expected to top 80 million by 2024. With half of South Africa's people living in towns and cities, 30,000 hectares of farmland are being lost to the spread of urban centres annually.

This is putting more pressure on agricultural land, and overuse of woody vegetation for fuel, livestock grazing and soil cultivation have caused vegetation and soil degradation, particularly in former Homeland areas. Adding to the problem are both water and wind erosion, which are responsible for the loss of 500 million tonnes of topsoil each year.

The rising population also contributes to an increase in the demand for water. This demand is expected to inflate by 50% in the next 30 years. To try to meet its water requirements, all major rivers in South Africa have been dammed or modified – a practice that disrupts local ecosystems.

Conservation of native fauna is an active concern and although we can only dimly imagine the extent of the loss since the arrival of Europeans, a significant amount remains. However, many species are threatened and extinction rates are high. It has been estimated that 37% of the country's mammals and 36% of its freshwater fish species are threatened with extinction. Protected areas assist conservation, but only 6% of natural land habitat and 17% of the coastline in South Africa is under formal protection. Provincial funding of national parks and reserves in many areas of the country has been recently cut, making it harder for parks to provide services and protect their inhabitants.

FLORA & FAUNA

The world's flora is divided into just six floral kingdoms and South Africa is the only country with one of these kingdoms within its borders. This is the Cape Floral Kingdom in Western Cape with its characteristic *fynbos* (fine bush), primarily proteas, heaths and ericas. There are more than 8500 species, and the Cape Peninsula alone has more native plants than the entire British Isles.

In the drier areas there are succulents, dominated by euphorbias and aloes, and annuals, which flower brilliantly after spring rainfall (see Namaqualand in the Northern Cape Province section later in this chapter).

In contrast to this wealth, South Africa is very poor in natural forests. Although forests were more widespread in the past, they were never particularly extensive. Today, only a few protected remnants remain (see Flora & Fauna in the Facts about the Region chapter).

You probably have a better chance of seeing the 'big five' – buffalo, lion, leopard, elephant and black rhino – in South Africa than in any other African country. It is also home to the last substantial populations of black and white rhino (with horns intact). (For descriptions of fauna, see the colour Wildlife Guide.)

There is also a spectacular variety of birds in South Africa. They range from the largest in the world (ostrich) and the largest flying bird (the kori bustard), to spectacularly coloured sunbirds, flamingos and the extraordinary sociable weaver birds whose huge colonies live in 'cities' of woven grass.

National Parks & Reserves

National parks and reserves are among South Africa's premier attractions. The scenery is spectacular, the fauna and flora are abundant and the prices are extremely reasonable. Most people, especially those with private transport, will find that the parks are a highlight and are generally much more interesting than the towns and cities.

In addition to the South African National Parks Board, which is a countrywide organisation, the provinces also have conservation bodies. However, unless otherwise indicated, the following parks fall under the control of the National Parks Board. Please note that only a small selection is listed here.

In Kruger National Park (with exceptions) and Kgalagadi Transfrontier Park (formerly Kalahari-Gemsbok National Park), visitors are confined to vehicles so if you don't have a car, you'll have to take a tour. Probably the best way to get to and around the parks is to rent a vehicle (4WD is not necessary).

If you do want to walk in any of the other parks or reserves, it is necessary to get permits from the appropriate authorities in advance, and you are nearly always restricted to staying overnight in official camp sites or huts during your time there.

The national parks all have rest camps that offer a variety of good-value accommodation, from cottages to camp sites. Most of the camps have restaurants, shops and petrol pumps. Although it is not usually necessary to book camp sites (except at busy holiday times), it is necessary to book cottages.

Entrances to parks and reserves normally close around sunset. Listed here are some of the main booking addresses; for others see the individual park entries later in this book.

Cape Nature Conservation (☎ 021-483 4051) Private Bag X9086, Cape Town 8000. This organisation controls a surprisingly diverse range of reserves and wilderness areas in Western Cape.

Eastern Cape Tourism Board (☎ 040-635 2115) PO Box 186, Bisho, Eastern Cape for parks in the former Ciskei region. Nature Conservation Office (☎ 047-531 2711) corner of York and Victoria Sts, Umtata, Eastern Cape for parks in the former Transkei region.

Free State Dept of Environmental Affairs (☎ 051-403 3435) PO Box 264, Bloemfontein 9300

KwaZulu-Natal Nature Conservation (KNNC) (☎ 0331-845 1000) PO Box 662, Pietermaritzburg, runs all parks in KwaZulu-Natal

Mpumalanga Parks Board (☎ 013-759 5300) PO Box 1990, Nelspruit 1200

South African National Parks Board (☎ 012-343 1991, fax 343 0905) PO Box 787, Pretoria 0001; (☎ 021-422 2810, fax 424 6211) PO Box 7400, Rogge Bay, Cape Town 8012

There are many private game reserves and while entry to these generally costs more than entry to public parks and reserves, you can usually get closer to the animals. Before deciding which private reserve to visit, it's worth contacting a specialist travel agent to find out if there are any special deals going. Pathfinders Travel (☎ 011-453 1113/4, fax 453 1483), 17 Chaucer Ave, Senderwood, Bedfordview, Johannesburg, is very helpful.

Western Cape

Bontebok National Park Proclaimed to protect the last herds of bontebok, a beautiful antelope unique to the Cape, this park is small but pleasant. It is just south of Swellendam.

Cape of Good Hope Nature Reserve This reserve protects a dramatic coastline and the unique Cape Floral Kingdom, with some of the best examples of fynbos.

Cederberg Wilderness Area This area, administered by Cape Nature Conservation, comprises 71,000 hectares of rugged valleys and peaks (up to 2000m), characterised by extraordinary sandstone formations. The vegetation is predominantly mountain fynbos, and includes the rare Clanwilliam cedar. Mammals include baboon, rhebok, klipspringer and predators such as the honey badger and caracal.

De Hoop Nature Reserve De Hoop includes a scenic coastline, a freshwater lake and the Potberg Range. This is one of the best places to see both mountain and lowland fynbos. Fauna includes Cape mountain zebra, bontebok and a wealth of birdlife. The reserve covers 41,000 hectares to the east of Bredasdorp and is administered by Cape Nature Conservation.

Karoo National Park This park near Beaufort West encloses 32,000 hectares of classic Karoo landscape and a representative selection of its flora and fauna. There's a three-day hiking trail and excellent accommodation.

Northern Cape Province

Augrabies Falls National Park 120km west of Upington, this park features the dramatic Augrabies Falls, where the Orange River drops into a solid granite ravine.

Goegap Nature Reserve This reserve, which is 10km from Springbok, is famous for its extraordinary display of spring flowers and its nursery of more than 200 amazing Karoo and Namaqualand succulents. In addition to the flora, there are springbok, zebra and birds.

Kgalagadi Transfrontier Park The Kgalagadi Transfrontier Park (formerly Kalahari-Gemsbok National Park) is not as famous as many other African parks, but it is very important. It supports large populations of birds, reptiles, small mammals, springbok, gemsbok, blue wildebeest, red hartebeest and eland. These in turn support a large population of predators – lion, leopard, cheetah, hyaena, jackal and fox.

Richtersveld National Park This park protects 162,000 hectares of high-altitude, mountainous desert bordering Orange River in the province's north-western corner. The countryside and the flora are spectacular. The park is very rugged and it will be a while before it is easily accessible.

Eastern Cape

Addo Elephant National Park This park protects the last remnant of the great herds that once roamed the province. It is small, but the unusual bush (spekboom, sneezewood and guarri) supports a high density of elephants. You would be unlucky not to see one of the 316 elephants living in the park, which is north of Port Elizabeth.

Karoo Nature Reserve This reserve, just outside Graaff-Reinet, has extraordinary flora, with the weird Karoo succulents well represented. There's also wildlife, interesting birdlife and spectacular rock formations. There are a number of day walks and one two-day hike. The reserve is administered by Cape Nature Conservation.

Mountain Zebra National Park This park is only 6500 hectares in extent, and was proclaimed to ensure the survival of the Cape mountain zebra. It covers the rugged northern slopes of the

Bankberg Range and there are magnificent views across the mountains and the Karoo plains.

Transkei Area The Transkei coastline is largely untouched, but there are several conservation areas set aside. **Mkambati Nature Reserve** is a coastal reserve with some great scenery, including the Misikaba River Gorge. Other reserves include **Dwesa**, between Coffee Bay and Kei Mouth; **Hluleka**, on the Coffee Bay Trail; and **Silaka**, just south of Port St Johns.

Tsitsikamma Coastal National Park This coastal park encompasses a narrow band of spectacular coast between Plettenberg Bay and Jeffrey's Bay. It is traversed by one of the most famous walks in the country: the Otter Trail, which is an easy five-day, 41km trail along the coast.

KwaZulu-Natal

Drakensberg Reserves Along with Golden Gate Highlands National Park in Free State, there are two main reserves in the dramatic KwaZulu-Natal Drakensberg: **Giant's Castle Game Reserve** and **Royal Natal National Park**. Both have spectacular scenery, walking trails and good accommodation. In addition there are the Mkhomazi Wilderness Area, Mzimkulu Wilderness Area and Mzimkulwana Nature Reserve, all of which have excellent hiking.

Greater St Lucia Wetlands This complex of KNNC reserves centres on Lake St Lucia on the north coast. There are crocodile and hippo, as well as good fishing and hiking trails.

Hluhluwe-Umfolozi Park These large, adjoining game reserves have rhino, lion and elephant. Umfolozi offers guided hiking.

Itala Game Reserve With facilities rivalling much more expensive private reserves, this is the KNNC's flagship reserve and is worth visiting.

Ndumo Game Reserve On the Mozambique border about 100km north of Mkuze, this remote reserve has black and white rhino, hippo, crocodile, antelope and a wide range of birdlife.

Ntendeka Wilderness In the Zulu heartland, this is a beautiful area of grassland and indigenous forest, with some dramatic cliffs and hiking trails.

Mpumalanga

Blyde River Canyon Nature Reserve A spectacular 60km canyon follows the Blyde River down from the Drakensberg escarpment to the lowveld, and has a huge range of flora and fauna. Book the popular hiking trail through Blyde River Canyon Nature Reserve (☎ 013-759 4000), PO Box 1990, Nelspruit 1200.

Free State

Golden Gate Highlands National Park One of the spectacular Drakensberg reserves, this national park is close to the northern border of Lesotho.

QwaQwa Conservation Area This reserve is in the foothills of both the Maluti Mountains and the Drakensberg.

Northern Province

Kruger National Park Kruger is one of the best parks in Africa, if not the world. With all of the 'big five' animals, inexpensive accommodation and walking trails (book early), it's not to be missed.

Lapalala Wilderness This private reserve north in the Waterberg Mountains has white rhino, zebra, blue wildebeest and several antelope species, plus crocodile. The rivers are bilharzia-free.

Lesheba Wilderness In the Soutpansberg Range, this private reserve has dramatic and varied country and there are plenty of animals, including rhino.

Nwanedi National Park In the undeveloped Venda region, this park is on the northern side of the Soutpansberg Range and the country is in the lowveld rather than rainforest.

GOVERNMENT & POLITICS

South Africa's constitution was passed into law in 1996. South Africa has rejoined the (British) Commonwealth after withdrawing in 1961 when the country became a republic.

There are two houses of parliament: a National Assembly (400 members) and a Senate (90 members). Members of the National Assembly are elected directly (using the proportional representation method – there are no constituencies) but Senate members are appointed by the provincial legislatures. Each province, regardless of its size, appoints 10 senators.

The head of state is the president, currently Thabo Mbeki. The president is elected by the National Assembly (and thus will always be the leader of the majority party), rather than directly by the people.

There are also provincial legislatures, with memberships varying with population: Northern Cape is the smallest, with 30 members, and the largest is Gauteng, with 86. Each province has a premier. Provincial governments have strictly limited powers and are bound by the national constitution.

In addition to the Western-style democratic system there is a system of traditional leaders. There is a Council of Traditional Leaders, to which all legislation pertaining to indigenous law, traditions or customs must be referred. Although the council cannot veto or amend legislation, it can delay its passage. In each province where there have been recognised traditional authorities (every province except Gauteng, Western Cape and Northern Cape), a House of Traditional Leaders will be established. The house will have similar powers to the council.

ECONOMY

South Africa's economy is a mixture of First and Third World with a marked disparity in incomes, standards of living, lifestyles, education and work opportunities. On one hand there is a modern industrialised and urban economy; on the other there is a subsistence agricultural economy that has changed little over a century or more.

Within South Africa, wealth is concentrated in the Pretoria, Witwatersrand, Vereeniging (PWV) area centred on Jo'burg (now the province of Gauteng). It is claim-ed that this area accounts for about 65% of the country's gross domestic product (GDP) and no less than 25% of the entire continent's gross product.

Until the discovery of diamonds at Kimberley (1869) and the gold reef on the Witwatersrand (1886), the economy was exclusively agricultural. Since then, mineral wealth has been the key to development. Mining accounts for more than 70% of exports and 13% of GDP.

Both inflation and massive unemployment remain problems. Moreover, even if the economy recovers to its boom-time peak, almost the only people to immediately benefit will be whites. Nonwhites have never shared in the fruits of their labour and it will be very difficult for the government to ensure that they do so in the future. The economy is still geared to a limitless pool of nonwhite labour (who are paid Third World rates) and restructuring will be a long and slow process.

POPULATION & PEOPLE

Of the population of 41 million, some 32 million are black, five million white, three million 'coloured' (ie, mixed race) and one million of Indian descent. Some 60% of the whites are Afrikaner and most of the rest are of British descent.

Most of the 'coloured' population lives in Northern and Western Cape Provinces. Cape Muslims are South Africans of long standing. Although many were brought to the early Cape Colony as slaves, others were political prisoners from the Dutch East Indies. Most South Africans of Indian descent live in KwaZulu-Natal.

Northern Province, Mpumalanga and the Free State are the Afrikaner heartlands. People of British descent are concentrated in KwaZulu-Natal and Western and Eastern Cape Provinces.

Although the Homelands no longer have any political meaning and were never realistic indicators of the area's cultural diversity, it's useful to have some idea of where the Homelands were and who lived (and still live) in them. Zulus are the largest group (seven million), followed by the Xhosa (six million) and the various Northern Sotho peoples, most of whom are Tswana. The smallest group are the Venda (500,000).

The Homelands and their peoples were:

homelands	people
Bophuthatswana	Tswana
Ciskei	Xhosa
Gazankulu	Tsonga
KwaNdebele	Ndebele
KwaNgwane	Swazi
KwaZulu	Zulu
Lebowa	Lobedu
QwaQwa	South Sotho
Transkei	Xhosa
Venda	Venda

Superficially, urbanised European culture doesn't seem to differ much from that found in other western countries. However, the unique experience of the white people of Africa has given them a self awareness that has raised culture to an issue of central importance. Those of Afrikaner and British descent form distinct subgroups.

SOUTH AFRICA

Despite the strength of traditional black culture in the countryside, the mingling of peoples in South Africa's urban areas means that old cultures are fading and others are emerging. There is nothing new in this: culture is never static and always responds to external events.

San

The San (formerly Bushmen) culture did not survive the impact of white settlement. Introduced diseases and deliberate genocide by whites meant that they have virtually disappeared as a separate race. Many survivors inter-bred with other racial groups and their descendants are now considered to be a part of the coloured population.

There are small numbers of San at Twee Rivieren (Northern Cape Province), Kagga Kamma (Western Cape), and at Lake Chrissie (Mpumalanga).

Although their technology was simple, it worked well. Their main hunting weapon was the bow and poisoned arrows, and their tracking and hunting abilities were exceptional. Their principal cultural legacy is their extraordinary art. Rocks and caves were their canvas, and the whole country is covered with examples. There are quite a number of accessible sites in the Natal Drakensberg region, particularly around Giant's Castle Game Reserve in KwaZulu-Natal.

Khoikhoi

Like the San, the Khoikhoi (known as the Hottentots by the early European settlers) and their culture have been submerged in the Christianised and westernised coloured population of the Cape. Originally sheep and cattle herders who were closely related to the San, they have, at least according to official sources, entirely disappeared as a people.

The Khoikhoi were semi-nomadic and like the San, hunted with bows and arrows. They lived in easily transportable beehive huts made with saplings covered with woven mats and followed pasturage on a seasonal basis.

The Nama, one of the main tribes, still build the characteristic huts (these days using hessian) around Steinkopf (Northern Cape Province) on the north-west coast and are still small-scale pastoralists. Another group, the Griqua, settled around Kimberley (Northern Cape Province).

Nguni

Zulu The name Zulu (Heaven) comes from an early chief. His descendants were *abakwaZulu* (people of Zulu). Under a chief called Shaka the Zulu became a large and dominant tribe, and since that time the *inoksa* (king) has been the leader of all the people. Before Shaka there was a looser organisation of local chiefs and almost self-sufficient family groups.

The Zulu *kraal* (village) is usually circular, often with a defensive wall of dead saplings and branches. The huts are hemispherical and made of tightly woven grasses. Inside the hut the right-hand side is for the men and the left-hand side is for the women, with ancestral spirits allocated a space at the rear.

In common with other peoples, the important stages of life – birth, puberty, marriage and death – are marked by ceremonies. The clothes people wear reflect their status and age. For example, girls may not wear long skirts until they become engaged. Animal skins are worn to reflect status, with a leopard-skin cloak signifying a chief.

Dancing and singing are important and if you see an Inkatha Freedom Party (IFP) demonstration you'll feel something of the power of massed Zulu singing.

The Zulu traditionally believe that the creator of the world is Unkulunkulu (Old, Old Man), but his daughter uNomkubulwana is more important in day-to-day life as she controls the rain. Still more important are ancestors, who can make most things go well or badly depending on how assiduously a person has carried out the required sacrifices and observances.

Xhosa The Xhosa, many of whom maintain a traditional lifestyle, are known as red people because of the red-dyed clothing worn by most adults. Different subgroups wear different costumes, colours and arrangements of beads. The Tembu and Bomvana favour red and orange ochres in the dyeing of their clothing, and the Pondo and Mpon-

Zulu Beadwork

Zulu beadwork is worth looking out for. It takes many forms, from the small, square *umgexo*, a necklace which is widely available and makes a good gift; to the more elaborate *umbelenja*, a short skirt or tasselled belt worn by women at puberty, but before marriage. *Amadavathi* (bead anklets) are worn by men and women. Today beadwork is still common, but with the exception of traditional ceremonies, it is used mainly for decoration of people or objects; a common example is a beaded matchbox cover.

As in many other societies, beads were used for both decorations and as symbols to define status, but the Zulu people have also traditionally used them as a means of communicating messages, and especially as love letters. The colours and the arrangement of the beads give the message.

Some of the colours and their meanings are:

- red – passion or anger
- black – difficulties or night
- blue – yearning
- deep blue – elopement (refers to the flight of the ibis)
- white or pale blue – pure love
- brown – disgust or despondency
- green – peace or bliss

The more subtle meanings of the beads have been largely forgotten and there were always ambiguities. For example, a 'letter' predominantly red and black could be promising a night of passion or it could mean that the sender was annoyed.

Some bead sculptors make social and political comment in their work, often weaving elaborate tableaus; the most famous exponent was the late Sizakele Mchunu. The Durban Art Gallery has displays of Zulu beadwork and one of the best collections is in the KwaZulu Cultural Museum in Ondini.

domise use a very light-blue ochre (although chemical dyes are now much in use).

The Xhosa deity is known variously as uDali, Tixo and Qwamata. This deity also figured in the San religion and it is probable that the invading Xhosa adopted it from them. There are also numerous minor spirits

SARAH JOLLY

Married Xhosa women often whiten their faces with clay and wear large turban-like hats.

and a rich folklore that persists in rural areas. A belief in witches (male or female) is very strong and witch-burning still occurs. The Xhosa believe that most witchcraft is evil, and their main fear is that people will be possessed by depraved spirits. The main source of evil is the *tokoloshe* which lives in water but is also kept by witches.

The *igqirha* (spiritual healer) holds an important place in traditional society because he or she can deal with the forces of nature and the trouble caused by witches. The *ixhwele* (herbalist) performs some magic but is much more concerned with health issues. The *mbongi* are the holders and performers of a group's oral history and are something like a cross between a bard and a court jester.

While there is a hierarchy of chiefs, the structure of Xhosa society is much looser than that of the Zulus.

Puberty rituals figure heavily for both men and women, and marriage customs and rituals also play a significant role.

Beadwork and jewellery are important. The *danga* is a long turquoise necklace that identifies the wearer to his/her ancestors. The *ngxowa yebokwe* is a goatskin bag carried over the left shoulder on important occasions.

Ndebele The Ndebele are a Nguni group surrounded by Sotho groups in the Northern

Province, but their strikingly colourful painted houses and the women's elaborate costume and decoration make them stand out. Their beadwork is dazzling, and women can reach outstanding proportions as they load on an incredible 25kg of beads and jewellery. Some of the costume is so elaborate that it cannot be removed without being destroyed; the masses of copper rings on the ankles and neck are there for life, for example.

You can visit a Ndebele village in **Botshabelo Nature Reserve**, to the east of Johannesburg (Gauteng).

Northern Sotho

This is a broad classification that covers many unconnected groups. The various groups each have totem animals, which they must not kill. Traditional *kgoros* (villages) were large – the Tswana had towns of 15,000 people – and had a sophisticated political structure.

The Lobedu people are unique in that they have a Rain Queen, the Modjadji, who brings rain to the lush Lebowa area. The Modjadji is supposedly immortal, does not marry and thus theoretically has no children. In fact, the queen dies by ritual suicide and is then succeeded by a daughter. She is regarded with awe by her people and her reputation is widespread: even Shaka avoided attacking the Lobedu. Henry Rider Haggard's novel *She* is based on the story of the original Modjadji, a 16th-century refugee princess.

Venda

The Venda people are something of an enigma. No one is certain of their origin and there are signs that the Lemba subgroup is of Semitic origin. They do not eat pork or animals that have not been bled. The fact that their traditional economy was based on manufacture and trade rather than agriculture also sets them apart.

Traditional society is matriarchal, with female priests who supervise the worship of female ancestors. The *domba* (python dance) is a puberty rite performed by girls but the boys are included in the ceremony. Very few societies allow both sexes to attend puberty rituals.

The Venda people, especially the Lemba, mined, smelted and worked iron, copper and gold for centuries. They travelled throughout Southern Africa to trade their metal. Most of the lore was lost when cheaper European metal became available, but the quality of Venda iron is astonishingly high. Pottery is an important craft and fortunately the skills have survived.

Before the Venda region acquired 'independent Homeland' status (and a South African-supported dictator) there were about 30 independent chiefdoms, with no overall leader.

For more information, see the boxed text 'History of the Venda People' in the Northern Province section.

Afrikaner

The Boers' remarkable history and their geographical isolation, combined with often deliberate cultural isolation, has created a unique people – often called the white tribe of Africa.

The ethnic composition of Afrikaners is difficult to quantify, but estimates are 40% Dutch, 40% German, 7.5% French, 7.5% British and 5% other. Some historians have argued that the '5% other' figure includes a large proportion of blacks and coloureds – a claim that would still be seen as highly offensive by most Afrikaners.

The Afrikaners are a religious people and their brand of Christian fundamentalism based on 17th-century Calvinism is still a powerful influence.

European

Aside from the Afrikaners, the majority (around 1.9 million) of European South Africans are of British extraction. There is also a large and influential Jewish population (130,000); significant minorities of Portuguese (36,000), many of whom are refugees from Angola and Mozambique; Germans (34,000); Dutch (28,000); Italians (16,000); and Greeks (10,000).

The British have always had a slightly equivocal position in South African society. This is exemplified by a not-so-friendly Afrikaans term of abuse, *soutpiel* (literally salt dick), referring to a man with one foot in South Africa and one in Britain. The Afrikaners have often felt (rightly in many cases) that the English-speakers' commitment to Africa was at a completely different level to their own.

ARTS

Although South Africa is home to a great diversity of cultures, most were suppressed during the apartheid years. To an extent, the Homelands kept alive some of the traditional cultures, but in a static form. The day-to-day realities of traditional and contemporary cultures were ignored, trivialised or destroyed.

Many artists, black and white, were involved in the anti-apartheid campaign and some were banned. In a society where you could be jailed for owning a politically incorrect painting, serious art was forced underground and blandness ruled in the galleries and theatres. *Resistance Art in South Africa* by Sue Williamson gives an overview of South African art during these times.

It will take time for the damage to be undone, but there are hopeful signs. Many galleries are holding retrospective exhibitions of contemporary and traditional black artists, and musicians from around Africa perform in major festivals.

Jazz was about the only medium in which blacks and whites could interact on equal terms, and it remains tremendously important. Theatre was also important for blacks, both as an art form and as a way of getting political messages across to illiterate comrades. Jo'burg's Market Theatre continues to be the most important venue in the country.

Literature

Nadine Gordimer was awarded the Nobel Prize for Literature in 1991. Her first novel, *The Lying Days*, was published in 1953, and *The Conservationist* was the joint winner of the 1974 Booker Prize. Her more recent work explores the interracial dynamics of the country – look for *July's People* and *A Sport of Nature*.

JM Coetzee is another contemporary writer who has received international acclaim; *The Life & Times of Michael K* won the 1983 Booker Prize.

SOUTH AFRICA

Township Art

Western influences have given rise to a number of new forms of artistic expression among black peoples of South Africa, often characterised as 'township art'. The materials and iconography of much of this art is urban. Eclectic in scope, it ranges from complex articulated wirework 'toys' to prints and paintings. The often deceptively naive images employed in this art can embody messages that are far from simple.

BETHUNE CARMICHAEL

The political trauma that has reverberated throughout South Africa is reflected in the often violent themes of these works, and this trauma is also reflected in the theme of Christian forgiveness (religion and the spiritual exert powerful influences over contemporary art in this country). It is still possible to see and buy examples of township art from street sellers, though the best examples are now much sought after by museums and international collectors.

David Dorward

Alan Paton was responsible for one of the most famous South African novels, *Cry the Beloved Country*, an epic that follows a black man's sufferings in a white, urban society.

Indaba My Children is an interesting book of folk tales, history, legends, customs and beliefs, collected and told by Vusamazulu Credo Mutwa. Published literature by nonwhite authors is in short supply but that situation will change.

LANGUAGE

South Africa's official languages were once English and Afrikaans but nine others have been added. These are: Ndebele, South Sotho, North Sotho, Swati, Tsonga, Tswana, Venda, Xhosa and Zulu. The most widely spoken are English, Afrikaans, South Sotho, Xhosa and Zulu. (For more information on the official languages of South Africa and for some useful words and phrases, see the Language chapter at the back of this book.)

Facts for the Visitor

SUGGESTED ITINERARIES

In a country as large and diverse as South Africa, it's very tempting to plan a long trip. If you only have a limited amount of time, you will have some tough decisions to make – not where to go but what to leave out. The following presumes you are starting from around either Cape Town or Jo'burg and is far from exhaustive. In particular, don't forget the Transkei and the Wild Coast in Eastern Cape, which is well worth a detour.

Two Weeks

You could easily spend a week exploring beautiful and relaxed Cape Town with its vibrant nightlife and mouth-watering cuisine. Stunning Table Mountain right in the middle of the city is accessible via the cableway or good old-fashioned climbing. With two weeks you could go further afield to explore the unique flora in the Cape of Good Hope Nature Reserve; and then head to the Winelands to taste world-class vintages around gracious Stellenbosch and cosy Franschhoek.

If you enter the country via Jo'burg, you could spend a few days in the city where the change – good and bad – in South Africa is happening first. Nearby Pretoria is also worth a look and is a lot more relaxed. Kruger National Park is only a four-hour drive from Jo'burg and is South Africa's premier attraction with perhaps the best wildlife viewing in Africa. Remember to book your accommodation well in advance, especially in the high season. A week inside the park and a few days meandering along the scenic Blyde River Canyon in the Klein Drakensberg will have you planning your return trip.

One Month

Starting with two weeks around Cape Town, if you had a month you could extend your trip further to include some whale watching at Hermanus and then potter along the Garden Route with its magnificent scenery and buzzing towns such as Knysna and Plettenberg Bay. You may even get as far as Port Elizabeth – the friendly city.

Alternatively, after spending time around Kruger, you could head down to KwaZulu-Natal where you'll find magnificent national parks, glimpses of Zulu culture and the subtropical city of Durban, where you can replenish yourself with sun, surf and jazz; plenty to keep you busy for a month. If you do have any time left, then there's the spectacular Drakensberg Escarpment, a magnet for hikers.

PLANNING

When to Go

In many places, especially the lowveld, summer (December to February) can be uncomfortably hot. The warm waters of the east coast make swimming a year-round proposition. Spring (September to December) is the best time for wildflowers in the Northern and Western Cape provinces and they are at their peak in Namaqualand (Northern Cape) from mid-August to mid-September. Winter (June to August) is mild everywhere except in the highest country, where there are frosts and occasional snowfalls. Summer brings warmer weather but also rain and mist to the mountains.

Many people take their annual holidays from mid-December to late January, with several overlapping waves of holiday-makers streaming out of the cities. Then, as well as during the other school holidays, resorts and national parks are heavily booked and prices on the coast can more than double. The KwaZulu-Natal coast,especially south of Durban, is packed. The absolute peak time is from Christmas to mid-January.

Maps

Good maps are widely available. Lonely Planet's *Southern Africa Travel Atlas* is a handy companion to this book. For a sturdy and helpful map of Cape Town, see Lonely Planet's *Cape Town City Map*.

The South African Tourist Corporation (Satour) can supply you with a reasonable map of the country to peruse while you are planning your trip, and good maps are widely available in South Africa. The Map Studio series is recommended and, as always, Michelin maps are excellent.

The Map Office (☎ 011-339 4941), 3rd floor, Standard Bank building, 40 De Korte St, Braamfontein (Jo'burg), sells government topographic maps for about R25 a sheet. The Map Office's postal address is Box 207, Wits 2050, Gauteng.

TOURIST OFFICES

Satour handles international promotion, while the provincial authorities have their own tourist boards for local information.

Local Tourist Offices

Some of the provincial organisations are very new at the job and have little practical information. Just about every town in the country has a tourist office.

Tourist Offices Abroad

Satour produces some glossy guides, which can be fairly useful. They are free outside the country but expensive within South Africa.

Satour offices abroad include:

Australia
(☎ 02-9261 3424, fax 9261 3414) Level 6, 285 Clarence St, Sydney, NSW 2000

France
(☎ 01 45 61 01 97, fax 01 45 61 01 96) 61 Rue La Boëtie, 75008 Paris

Germany
(☎ 69-929 1290, fax 28 0950) Alemannia Haus, An der Hauptwache 11D-60313 Frankfurt/Main 1, Postfach 101940, 60019 Frankfurt

UK
(☎ 020-8944 8080, fax 8944 6705) 5 Alt Grove, London SW19 4DZ

USA
New York: (☎ 1800 822 5368 toll free, fax 212-764 1980) 500 Fifth Ave, 20th floor, New York, NY 10110
Los Angeles: (☎ 1800 782 9772 toll free, fax 310-641 5812) Suite 1524, 9841 Airport Blvd, Los Angeles, CA 90045

VISAS & DOCUMENTS

Visas

Entry permits are issued free on arrival to nationals of many Commonwealth countries and other countries, including Ireland, France, Germany and the USA. You are entitled to a stay of 90 days, but officials usually write the date of your flight home as the date of expiry.

Other nationalities may need a visa. Visas are usually free, but are not issued at the border, so you must get one in advance – South Africa has consular representation in most countries, but outside Southern Africa allow at least a couple of weeks for the process.

On arrival you might have to satisfy an immigration officer that you have sufficient funds for your stay in South Africa. If you arrive by air, you must have an onward ticket of some sort. An air ticket is best but overland travel seems to be acceptable. If you come by land, things are more relaxed.

Visa Extensions Apply for a visa extension or a re-entry visa at the Department of Home Affairs (☎ 012-324 1860) Sentrakor Bldg, Pretorius St, Pretoria; or (☎ 021-462 4970), 56 Barrack St, Cape Town; or in Jo'burg or Durban.

Driving Licence & Permit

You can use your own driving licence if it has your photo, otherwise you'll need an

SOUTH AFRICA

Visas for Onward Travel

In South Africa you can get visas for the following neighbouring countries (for exceptions, see under Visas earlier). All embassies are open weekday mornings (for opening times, see Embassies & Consulates later in this section). To obtain a visa, it's best to arrive at the embassy early in the morning.

Botswana Visas cost R33.25 and take between four and 14 days to issue; no photos are required.

Lesotho Visas cost R20 and take 24 hours to issue; you'll need to take one photo.

Mozambique Visas cost R75 and usually take about a week to issue; you'll need to take two photos. You can also get a visa in Swaziland (see that chapter for details).

Namibia Visas cost R138 and take two to three days; no photos are required. Namibia Tourism in Cape Town and Jo'burg also issues visas.

Swaziland Visas cost R40 and are issued on the day of application. Apply for a visa in the morning and collect it in the afternoon; no photos are required.

Zimbabwe Visas cost R140 and take between one and two weeks; no photos are required.

International Driving Permit, obtainable from a motoring organisation in your country.

Student Card

A student card can be useful as some attractions, such as museums, particularly around Cape Town, charge a student entry price.

If you plan on going to a South African cinema, you should also be eligible for a cheaper ticket. Try to get an international student card (inquire at your educational institution) before you leave home, otherwise you may have to convince a doubting ticket-seller about the legitimacy of your card.

Other Documents

If you have travelled through the yellow fever zone in Africa or South America (including Brazil), you must have a vaccination certificate to show you've been immunised against yellow fever.

EMBASSIES & CONSULATES

South African Embassies & High Commissions

South Africa has embassies and high commissions in the following African countries: Kenya, Lesotho, Malawi, Mozambique, Namibia, Swaziland, Zambia and Zimbabwe. (Embassies for countries in this book are listed in the relevant country chapters).

Elsewhere in the world, places with a South African embassy or high commission include:

Australia
High Commission: (☎ 02-6273 2424, fax 6273 3543) Rhodes Place, Yarralumla, Canberra, ACT 2600

Belgium
Embassy: (☎ 02-285 4400, fax 02-285 4455) Wetstraat 26, Box 7/8, Brussels 1000

Canada
High Commission: (☎ 613-744 0330, fax 741 1639) 15 Sussex Dr, Ottawa, K1M 1M8

France
Embassy: (☎ 01 53 59 23 23, fax 01 53 59 23 33) 59 Quai d'Orsay, 75343 Paris

Germany
Embassy: (☎ 030-825 2711) Friedrichstrasse 60, Berlin 10117

Ireland
Embassy: (☎ 1-661 5553) 2nd floor, Alexandra House, Earlsfort Centre, Dublin 2

Netherlands
Embassy: (☎ 70-392 4501, fax 346 0669) Wassenaarseweg 40, The Hague

Sweden
Embassy: (☎ 08-243 950, fax 660 7136) Linnégatan 76, 115 23 Stockholm

UK
High Commission: (☎ 020-7451 7299, fax 7451 7284) South Africa House, Trafalgar Square, London WC2N 5DP

USA
Embassy: (☎ 202-232 4400, fax 265 1607) 3051 Massachusetts Ave NW, Washington DC 20008 (also consulates in Chicago, Los Angeles and New York)

Embassies & Consulates in South Africa

Most countries have their main embassy or high commission in Pretoria, with an office or consulate in Cape Town that becomes the official embassy during Cape Town's parliamentary sessions. However, many countries also maintain consulates (which can arrange visas and passports) in Jo'burg.

Many consulates are only open in the morning. For a full list, see the Yellow Pages. Embassies in Pretoria and Johannesburg include:

Australia
High Commission: (☎ 012-342 3470) 292 Orient St, Arcadia, Pretoria. Open from 8.45 am to 12.30 pm weekdays.

Belgium
Consulate: (☎ 011-447 6434) Smuts Bldg, 158 Jan Smuts Ave, Rosebank, Johannesburg (also represented in Pretoria and Cape Town). Open from 9 am to noon weekdays.

Botswana
Trade Mission: (☎ 011-403 3748) Futura Bank House, 122 De Korte St, Braamfontein, Johannesburg (also a consulate in Cape Town). Open from 8 am to 1 pm weekdays.

Canada
High Commission: (☎ 012-422 3000) 1103 Arcadia St, Hatfield, Pretoria. Open from 8 am to noon weekdays.

France
Consulate: (☎ 011-778 5600) 3rd floor, Standard Bank Bldg, 191 Jan Smuts Ave (corner of Seventh Ave), Rosebank, Johannesburg (also represented in Pretoria and Cape Town). Open from 8.30 am to 1 pm weekdays.

Germany
Embassy: (☎ 012-427 8999) Block B, 1st floor, Embassy House, 1267 Pretorius St, Hatfield, Pretoria (also a consulate in Cape Town). Open from 7.30 to 11 am weekdays, except Wednesday when it's open from 9 to 11.30 am.

Ireland
Embassy: (☎ 012-342 5062) 1234 Church St, Arcadia, Pretoria. Open from 8.30 am to 1 pm weekdays.

Lesotho
Embassy: (☎ 012-467 648, fax 467649) 391 Anderson St, Menlopark, Pretoria. Open from 9 am to 4.30 pm weekdays.

Mozambique
Embassy: (☎ 012-343 0959) 199 Beckett St, Arcadia, Pretoria (also consulates in Jo'burg, Cape Town and Durban). Open from 8.30 am to 12.30 pm weekdays.

Namibia
Embassy: (☎ 012-344 5992) 702 Church St, Arcadia, Pretoria. Open from 8.30 am to 12.30 pm weekdays.

Netherlands
Embassy: (☎ 012-344 3910) 825 Arcadia St, Arcadia, Pretoria (also a consulate in Cape Town and an honorary consul in Durban). Open from 9 am to noon weekdays.

Swaziland
Embassy: (☎ 012-342 5782) 715 Government Ave, Arcadia, Pretoria (also a consulate in Jo'burg). Open from 9 am to 12.30 pm and 2.30 to 4 pm weekdays.

UK
High Commission: (☎ 012-483 1400) Liberty Life Place, Block B, 1st floor, Grey St, Hatfield, Pretoria (also represented in Jo'burg and Cape Town). Open from 8.45 am to noon weekdays.

USA
Embassy: (☎ 012-342 1048) 877 Pretorius St, Arcadia, Pretoria (also represented in Jo'burg and Cape Town). Open from 8 am to noon weekdays.

Zimbabwe
High Commission: (☎ 011-838 2156) 17th floor, CCMA Bldg, 20 Anderson St, Marshalltown, Johannesburg (also a high commission in Pretoria). Open from 8.30 am to noon weekdays, except Wednesday.

CUSTOMS

South Africa, Botswana, Namibia, Swaziland and Lesotho are all part of the South African Customs Union, which means the internal borders are effectively open from a customs point of view. When you enter the union, however, you're restricted in the normal way to personal effects: 1L of spirits, 2L of wine and 400 cigarettes. Motor vehicles must be covered by a triptyque or carnet. For information contact the Department of Customs & Excise (☎ 012-284 308) in Pretoria.

MONEY

Currency

The unit of currency is the rand (R), which is divided into 100 cents. There is no black market.

South Africa has introduced new coins and notes. The only old note you're likely to see is the R5 (which has been replaced by a coin). The coins are: 1, 2, 5, 10, 20 and 50 cents; 1, 2 and 5 rand. The notes are: 10, 20, 50, 100 and 200 rand. The R200 note looks a lot like the R20 note, so take care. There have been forgeries of the R200 note and some businesses are reluctant to accept them.

Exchange Rates

At the time of going to print, the currency exchange rates were as follows:

country	unit		rand
Australia	A$1	=	R3.85
Canada	C$1	=	R4.36
euro	€1	=	R6.13
France	FF10	=	R9.34
Germany	DM1	=	R3.13
Japan	¥100	=	R5.89
New Zealand	NZ$1	=	R3.10
UK	UK£1	=	R10.01
USA	US$1	=	R6.35

Exchanging Money

The Thomas Cook agent is Rennies Travel, a large chain of travel agencies, and there are American Express offices in the big cities. Neither charges commission on its own travellers cheques. Nedbank is associated with American Express. The First National Bank and Nedbank are associated with Visa and are supposed to change Visa travellers cheques free of fees, but many branches don't seem to know this. Most other banks change travellers cheques in major currencies, with various commissions.

Keep at least some of the receipts you get when changing money as you'll need to show them to reconvert your rands when you leave.

Credit cards, especially Visa and MasterCard, are widely accepted. Most ATMs give cash advances.

Costs

Although South Africa is certainly not as cheap to travel in as many poorer countries, it is very good value by European, US and Australian standards.

Shoestring travellers will find that camping or staying in hostels, on-site caravans or bungalows where they can self-cater are the cheapest options, often working out to around R40 per person. Sit-down meals in restaurants (without getting into *haute cuisine*) consistently work out to between R35 and R60 per person, and less in pubs.

Mid-range travellers will find accommodation in self-catering cottages, B&Bs and hotels for between R180 and R320 – the standard is normally very good.

Distances are large, so transport can be infrequent and expensive; hiring or buying a car can be worthwhile both for convenience and economy (see the Getting Around section later in this chapter, and the Getting Around the Region chapter).

Tipping

Tipping is pretty well mandatory because of the very low wages. Around 10% to 15% is usual.

Taxes & Refunds

There is a Value Added Tax (VAT) of 14%, but foreign visitors can reclaim some of their VAT expenses on departure. This applies only to goods that you are taking out of the country; you can't claim back the VAT you've paid on food or car rental, for example. Also, the goods have to be bought at a shop participating in the VAT Foreign Tourist Sales scheme.

To make a claim you need the tax invoices (usually the receipt, but make sure the shop knows that you want a full receipt). They must be originals – no photocopies. The total value of your purchases must exceed R250.

When you depart you'll have to fill out a couple of forms and show the goods to a customs inspector. At airports make sure you have the goods checked by an inspector before you check in your luggage. You pick up your refund cheque after you've gone through immigration.

POST & COMMUNICATIONS

Post

South Africa has reasonably good post and telecommunications facilities. Most post offices are open from 8.30 am to 4.30 pm weekdays and 8 am to noon on Saturday.

Aerograms and postcards cost R1.30 to send. Airmail letters cost R1.60 per 10g (R1.10 to Southern African countries). Internal letters cost R0.70. Internal delivery can be very slow and international delivery isn't exactly lightning fast.

Telephone

Local telephone calls are timed, although you get a decent amount of time for each R0.40 unit. Phonecards are widely available (see under eKno Communication Card later in this section).

Long-distance and international telephone calls are very expensive. There are private phone centres where you can pay cash for your call without feeding coins into the slot. Unfortunately, their rates are about double those of public phones. Calls from hotels are also charged at exorbitant rates.

All South African telephone books give full details of service numbers and codes.

The following are useful directory service numbers within South Africa:

Directory inquiries (local)	1023
Directory inquiries (national and international)	1025
Reverse-charge calls (national)	0020
Reverse-charge calls (international)	0090

When dialling overseas from South Africa, add 09 before the country code (see the list of codes under Post & Communications in the Regional Facts for the Visitor chapter). When making calls to South Africa from outside the country, dial the international access code, then 27, then the area code in South Africa (dropping the zero), and then the telephone number.

International calls are cheaper after 8 pm on weekdays and between 8 pm Friday and 8 am Monday.

To avoid high charges when calling home, dial your 'Country Direct' number, which puts you through to an operator in your country. You can then either place a call on your 'phone home' account, if you have one, or place a reverse-charge call. To find out your Country Direct number, call a major telecommunications company in your country.

South African Telephone Codes

Area codes are still changing in South Africa and codes that have more than three numbers (eg, Beaufort West) are likely to have changed by the time you read this. When an area code is updated, the individual phone number in the area changes as well. However, if you call the old area code and phone number, there is a good chance you'll get a recorded message from Telkom with the new area code and phone number. If not, try directory inquiries.

Cell Phones The cell (mobile) phone network covers most of the country and cell phone ownership is very widespread among those who can afford it. Hiring a cell phone is very cheap, although call charges are high. It costs about R12 a day plus call charges and you normally pay a deposit that is refundable. Some rental car places offer deals on cell phones when you rent a car, and it can be useful to have one if you're driving around the country. It's also possible to hire a cell phone at Jo'burg international airport and at some Vodacom shops.

eKno Communication Card

As we go to print, within the region you can only access eKno services from South Africa. You can join online at www. ekno .lonelyplanet. com, or by phone from South Africa by dialling 080-099 7286. Once you have joined, to use eKno from South Africa, dial 080-099 2921. (For more information on Lonely Planet's eKno card, see Post & Communications in the Regional Facts for the Visitor chapter.)

Fax

You can fax most organisations and businesses. Phone books list fax numbers. You can send faxes from private phone centres.

Email & Internet Access

There is an increasing number of Internet cafes mushrooming throughout South Africa, and more and more hostels are offering email facilities. Most places charge between R20 and R30 per hour for online access.

INTERNET RESOURCES

The following Web sites are worth a surf. (For regional listings, see also Internet Resources in the Regional Facts for the Visitor chapter)

Baz Bus Transport specifically geared towards budget travellers (see also Bus in the Getting Around section later in this chapter).
www.bazbus.com

Intercape Mainliner Coaches operating throughout Southern Africa (see also Bus in the Getting Around section later in this chapter).
www.intercape.co.za

National Parks Board Information and bookings for national parks around the country.
www.ecoafrica.com/saparks

Powerzone South Africa's largest music gig guide.
www.powerzone.co.za

Satour The government-run tourism organisation that operates only outside South Africa.
www.satour.co.za

Womensnet A government-sponsored women's Internet resource.
www.womensnet.org.za

BOOKS

This section covers books specific to South Africa. (For information on books about the whole Southern Africa region, see Books in the Regional Facts for the Visitor chapter.)

Guidebooks

The Automobile Association (AA) publishes some handy paperback guides to caravan parks and hotels; these are available in most bookshops.

History & Politics

Election '94 South Africa edited by Andrew Reynolds. An excellent overview of recent events in the country.

Foundations of the New South Africa by John Pampallis. A partisan but nonetheless accurate view of South Africa. The book was originally written as a history textbook for exiled South African students in Tanzania and gives South African history from the ANC's point of view.

Long Road to Freedom by Nelson Mandela. There are some books that seem to have such a powerful sense of place they become compulsory reading for foreign visitors to a country – there can be no more obvious or important example than this autobiography.

The Mind of South Africa by Allister Sparks. The best introduction to white South African history.

South Africa Belongs to Us by Francis Meli. This book outlines the history of the ANC.

Tomorrow is Another Country by Allister Sparks. His most recent book, this is the inside story of the CODESA (Convention for a Democratic South Africa) negotiations.

General

Exploring Southern Africa on Foot: Guide to Hiking Trails by Willie & Sandra Olivier. This book doesn't cover all the trails (there are so many!) but otherwise it's simply outstanding. Highly recommended.

John Platter's South African Wine Guide. Updated annually and incredibly detailed, covering all available wines.

My Traitor's Heart by Rian Malan. An outstanding autobiography of an Afrikaner attempting to come to grips with his heritage and his future. It gives a disturbing, white perspective on the apartheid years.

Namaqualand in Flower by Sima Eliovson. A detailed book on the flora of Namaqualand. It has excellent colour plates.

Western Cape Walks by David Bristow. One of many small books detailing walks in various areas of the country – it covers 70 walks of varying length and standard.

Whale Watching in South Africa by Peter Best. This book contains handy information about the leviathans you have a good chance of seeing.

NEWSPAPERS & MAGAZINES

Major English-language newspapers are published in the cities and sold across the country, although in Afrikaans-speaking areas and the ex-Homelands they may not be available in every little town.

The *Sowetan* is the biggest-selling paper in the country and its background of support for the Struggle makes it interesting reading. Despite catering to a largely poorly educated audience, it has a much more sophisticated political and social outlook than the major white papers.

The best newspaper or magazine for investigative journalism, sensible overviews and high-quality columnists, not to mention a week's worth of Doonesbury and a good entertainment section, is the *Weekly Mail & Guardian*. It also includes a shortened version of the international edition of the British

Guardian, which includes features from *Le Monde* and the *Washington Post*.

RADIO & TV

The monolithic and conservative South African Broadcasting Corporation (SABC) was the mouthpiece of the government, and although times have changed you'll still find most of its fare rather timid. The mainstream SABC radio stations (AM and FM) play dreary music and offer drearier chat about recipes and the like, but the stations geared to a black audience often play good music.

TV is even worse than radio, with daytime US soap operas playing in prime time, and local programs broadcast in many languages but without subtitles.

As well as the SABC there is the pay-TV channel M-Net, which shows some good movies.

PHOTOGRAPHY & VIDEO

Films, cameras and accessories are readily available in larger towns. Processing is generally of a high standard. Negative film (24 exposures) costs about R50 plus R45 for processing.

HEALTH

Apart from malaria and bilharzia in some areas and the possibility of hikers drinking contaminated water, there are few health problems for visitors. Good medical care is never too far away except in the remote areas, where air evacuation of emergency cases is routine. Make sure you have enough insurance (for more details, see Travel Insurance in the Regional Facts for the Visitor chapter).

Problem Areas

Malaria is mainly confined to the eastern part of the country (Northern Province, Mpumalanga, northern KwaZulu-Natal) and Swaziland, especially on the lowveld. Kgalagadi Transfrontier Park and parts of the North-West Province might also be malarial. Bilharzia is also found mainly in the east but outbreaks do occur in other places, so you should always check with knowledgeable local people before drinking water or swimming in it.

While hiking in the ex-Homelands or wherever you find yourself drinking from streams (even if there is no bilharzia), make sure that there isn't an upstream village. Typhoid is rare but it does occur. Industrial pollution is common in more settled areas.

WOMEN TRAVELLERS

Many South African men, whatever their colour, have sexism in common. Modern ideas such as equality of the sexes haven't filtered through to many people, especially those away from the cities. There's a very high level of sexual assault and other violence against women in South Africa; as usual most victims (an estimated 60%) know their attackers. For most female visitors, paternalistic attitudes are the main problem rather than physical assault. There have been incidents of female travellers being raped, but these cases are rare and isolated, and cause outrage in local communities.

A large part of the problem in South Africa is the leniency of the judicial system which repeatedly lets perpetrators of sex offences off with short prison sentences. This, particularly in recent times, has had women's groups around the country voicing concern, and judges have been called before the South African parliament to explain extraordinarily light sentences for sexual assault offenders. It has even been suggested that judges take 'sensitivity lessons' to make them more perceptive of the victims' suffering.

(For more information, see Dangers & Annoyances later in this section, and Women Travellers in the Regional Facts for the Visitor chapter.)

GAY & LESBIAN TRAVELLERS

South Africa's new constitution guarantees freedom of sexual choice and there are small but active gay and lesbian communities and scenes in Cape Town (see Entertainment in Cape Town in the Western Cape section), Jo'burg and Durban. However, the new constitution is a radical legislative move and it will be a while before the more conservative sections of society begin to accept it.

Check out the GaySA Web site, which has entertainment and travel listings, but be

warned that it also contains links to explicit erotic images.
Web site: www.gaysa.co.za

The Gay & Lesbian Organisation of Pretoria (☎ 012-344 6501), 133 Verdoorn St, Sunnyside, has been recommended. As well as a gay map of Pretoria it has loads of information such as listings of guesthouses and tour companies.
Web site: www.glop.co.za

DISABLED TRAVELLERS

For information on travelling in South Africa with a disability, try the Web site www.access-able.com. (For more information, see Disabled Travellers in the Regional Facts for the Visitor chapter.)

The following tour companies can assist disabled travellers:

Titch Travel (☎ 021-689 4151, fax 689 3760, @ MandiJ.titch@galileosa.co.za), 26 Station Rd, Rondebosch 7700, Cape Town, specialises in tours for visually impaired and physically disabled travellers. It has tailor-made itineraries according to the interests and disabilities of travellers and has specialised equipment such as a coach fitted with a hydraulic lift for wheelchairs. It also hires cars fitted with hand controls, specifically designed for disabled people. Contact Mandi Johnson-Aliverti for more information.
Web site: www.titchtravel.co.za

Wilderness Wheels (☎ 011-648 5737, fax 648 6769), 117 St Georges Rd, Observatory 2198, Johannesburg, caters for disabled travellers and has been recommended by readers. Most of its tours are in and around Kruger National Park and guided tours depart on Wednesday and return on Saturday. It can also arrange tours in other parts of South Africa but requires notice and a minimum of five people. Contact Mrs Roberts for more information.

DANGERS & ANNOYANCES

Some specific things to watch out for are listed here. Also keep in mind the natural dangers, from freezing storms in the Drakensberg to crippling heat on the lowveld. (For more-detailed information. see Warnings or Dangers & Annoyances at the start of some area sections, and for general advice see Dangers & Annoyances in the Regional Facts for the Visitor chapter.)

Animals

Crocodile occur in lowveld rivers and streams. Hippo can also be very dangerous. If you meet one (most likely on and near the KwaZulu-Natal north coast), do not approach it and be prepared to run away or up a tree very fast. You are very unlikely to encounter lion, rhino and elephant when you are walking, but do not leave your vehicle while in a wildlife reserve (for more information see the boxed text 'Close Encounters' in the Regional Facts for the Visitor chapter).

Crime

Crime is the national obsession, although the perception that crime rates rose from low levels following the ANC's first election victory is wrong. This has always been a violent country. The big difference since 1994 is that the white community is now suffering from the crime that has long plagued nonwhites.

Be very careful at night and also during the day; daylight muggings are not uncommon in parts of Jo'burg, and that city's Metro train system has had a problem with violent crime. Generally, the CBD areas of all bigger cities should be avoided at night; if you need to go through the CBD at night grab a taxi – don't walk.

It would be unwise for an outsider of any race to venture into a township except with a trusted guide or as part of a tour.

Cape Town is reasonably safe and there are few places around the city that are off-limits during the day. As in all the big cities, the situation changes at night; ask around to find out the current situation.

Most ATMs have security guards. If there's no guard around when you're withdrawing cash, watch your back or, better yet, get someone else to watch it for you.

If you're driving around the country try to avoid driving at night, keep your windows up and doors locked when driving through cities, and consider hiring a cell phone. Leave your car in secure parking at night and don't leave anything valuable in the car when you're not in it.

Incidents such as taxi wars (between rival minibus taxi companies) have led to massacres. Once again, it's a matter of knowing the current situation and avoiding being in the wrong place at the wrong time. There are very, very few wrong places and times.

Incidents of violent crime are far worse in Jo'burg than other cities and extra precautions are necessary (for more information, see Dangers & Annoyances in the Jo'burg and Pretoria sections later in this chapter).

EMERGENCIES

The countrywide contact numbers for emergency services are: ambulance (☎ 10177) and police (☎ 10111).

LEGAL MATTERS

Marijuana was an important commodity in the Xhosa's trade with the San. Today *dagga* or *zol* is illegal but widely available. There are heavy penalties for use and possession but it's estimated that the majority of black men smoke the drug. The legal system doesn't distinguish between soft and hard drugs, which are increasingly available.

BUSINESS HOURS

Banking hours vary, but are usually from 9 am to 3.30 pm weekdays; many branches are also open 8.30 to 11 am Saturday. Post offices usually open from 8 am to 4.30 pm weekdays and 8 am to noon Saturday. Banks and post offices close for lunch in smaller towns.

Most shops are open from 8.30 am to 5 pm weekdays, and on Saturday morning. Bars usually close around 11 pm, except in the major cities (where the closing times vary).

PUBLIC HOLIDAYS & SPECIAL EVENTS

South Africa's public holidays include:

New Year's Day 1 January
Human Rights Day 21 March
Good Friday March/April
Family Day 17 April
Constitution Day 27 April
Workers' Day 1 May
Youth Day 16 June
Women's Day 9 August
Heritage Day 24 September
Day of Reconciliation 16 December
Christmas Day 25 December
Day of Goodwill 26 December

South African (and Namibian) school holidays normally occur from mid-December to mid-January; around Easter; from late July to early August; and for two weeks in mid-October.

ACTIVITIES

With increasing numbers of foreign visitors, many outfits aimed at the 'adventure' or 'eco' market are appearing. They offer a range of activities, such as hiking, canoeing and rafting, and some have trips into other African countries. There are plenty of options, so shop around. Two of the larger 'alternative' South African companies are African Routes (☎ 031-304 6358, fax 304 6340) based in KwaZulu-Natal and Drifters (☎ 011-888 1160, fax 888 1020) based in Gauteng.

In addition to longer trips there are a lot of smaller outfits offering day trips and these can be excellent. Hostels often take bookings for adventure activities and travel, but remember that a particular hostel might have an agreement with a particular company.

Hiking

South Africa has an excellent system of hiking trails, usually with accommodation available. They are popular and most must be booked well in advance (for more details see Hiking under Activities in the Regional Facts for the Visitor chapter). Satour's brochure on hiking is useful and if you plan to do a lot of hiking pick up a copy of Jaynee Levy's *Complete Guide to Walks & Trails in Southern Africa*.

There are also many hiking clubs – contact the Hiking Federation of South Africa (☎ 011-886 6524, **e** sahiker@cis.co.za). Several of the adventure travel outfits offer organised hikes.

Most trails are administered by the National Parks Board or the various Forest Regions, although the KwaZulu-Natal Nature Conservation (KNNC) controls most trails in KwaZulu-Natal. Some of the best-known trails and their booking details are:

Western Cape

Otter Trail: Five days on the coast of the Garden Route; contact the National Parks Board (☎ 021-422 2810 or 012-343 1991).

Outeniqua: Up to eight days in indigenous forest near Knysna; contact the Forestry Department (☎ 044-382 5446).

Eastern Cape

Amatola: Up to six days in the former Ciskei Homelands; contact the Eastern Cape Tourism Board (☎ 040-635 2115), PO Box 186, Bisho, Eastern Cape.

Wild Coast: Three five-day sections along the Transkei coast; contact the Nature Conservation Department (☎ 047-531 2711), Private Bag X5002, Umtata, Eastern Cape.

KwaZulu-Natal

Giant's Cup: Up to five days in the southern Drakensberg; contact KNNC (☎ 0331-845 1000), Queen Elizabeth Park, Pietermaritzburg. There are also 'wilderness trails and guided walks' in Umfolozi, Mkuzi and Greater St Lucia National Parks; contact KNNC.

Mpumalanga

Blyde River Canyon Trail: Up to five days in this spectacular area; contact Blyde River Canyon Nature Reserve (☎ 013-759 4000), PO Box 1990, Nelspruit 1200.

Kruger National Park: There are 'wilderness trails and guided walks'; contact the National Parks Board (☎ 021-422 2810 or 012-343 1991).

Free State

Rhebok: Two days in Golden Gate Highlands National Park; contact the National Parks Board (☎ 021-422 2810 or 012-343 1991).

Northern Province

Mabudashango: Four days in former Venda Homelands; contact the Department of Agriculture & Forestry (☎ 0159-31001), Private Bag X2247, Sibasa 0970.

Soutpansberg: Up to two days in the Soutpansberg Range; contact the South African Forestry Company Ltd (SAFCOL; ☎ 013-764 1058).

Mountain Biking

South Africans have discovered mountain biking and taken to it in a very big way. Some nature reserves and national parks are putting in mountain-bike trails, and some outfits offer trips.

Rock Climbing

There are some challenging climbs, especially in the KwaZulu-Natal Drakensberg. Contact the Mountain Club of South Africa (☎ 021-465 3412) at 97 Hatfield St, Cape Town 8001 for addresses of regional clubs. In Johannesburg there's the South African Climbers Club at 71 12th St, Parkhurst 2153.

Surfing

South Africa has some of the best and least-crowded surfing in the world. Most surfers will have heard of Jeffrey's Bay, but there are myriad alternatives, particularly along the east and south coasts. The best time of the year for surfing on the coasts is from April to July.

Boards and surfing gear can be bought in most of the big coastal cities. New boards sell for around R1000; good quality second-hand boards for R350 to R800. A Rip Curl steamer sells for about R650. It's now out of print but you might find a second-hand copy of *Surfing in Southern Africa* by Mark Jury, which has excellent practical information on when and where to go. If you plan to surf Jeffrey's Bay you'll need a decent-sized board – it's a big, very fast wave.

Canoeing & Rafting

South Africa is a dry country and it has few major rivers by international standards. This limits the canoeing and rafting potential, but there are, nonetheless, some interesting possibilities. The Orange River is the giant among South African rivers, running west across the country for 2340km. Other major rivers include the Tugela (KwaZulu-Natal), the Komati (Mpumalanga) and the Olifants, Berg and Breede (Western Cape).

Rafting and canoeing trips on the Orange River in the far north-west, where it forms the border with Namibia, have become very popular. The main attraction is that you float through a beautiful desert wilderness; the rapids are not demanding.

The Tugela offers rather more challenging rafting, although it is highly variable depending on the rainfall. It is at its best from late December to mid-March.

One of the biggest operators is Felix Unite, with offices in Jo'burg (☎ 011-803 9775) and in Cape Town (☎ 021-762 6935).

Diving

The KwaZulu-Natal north coast, particularly around Sodwana Bay, offers excellent warm-water diving and there are some good reefs. Most resort towns along Western Cape's Garden Route have diving schools.

A Zulu witchdoctor in his beaded finery

A rickshaw driver on Durban's beachfront

Bones laid out for sale at a Soweto street market

Bags of herbs at a Durban market

Basketware and *mbira* (thumb piano)

Colourful beadwork makes a good souvenir

ALL PHOTOGRAPHS BY RICHARD I'ANSON

ALL PHOTOGRAPHS BY RICHARD I'ANSON

South Africa **Clockwise from Top Left:** Cape Town's popular Waterfront complex; the village of Franschhoek, nestled in a beautiful Winelands valley; a Xhosa village in Transkei; fynbos vegetation in the Cape of Good Hope Nature Reserve; part of the Drakensberg Range of KwaZulu-Natal

Shark Diving Currently popular with visitors, this involves being lowered in a cage and seeing sharks up close. Though mainly offered in Western Cape, it's a hit, so copycat operators will probably spring up all along the coast. There are, however, some ecological downsides to shark diving and you might want to think twice before doing it. The most obvious problem is that operators use bait to attract sharks, which means that South African sharks are being trained to associate humans with food. Not a pleasant scenario.

Birdwatching

With hundreds of endemic species, South Africa is a paradise for birdwatchers. The regional variation is huge so keen birdwatchers should aim to cover a range of habitats – Kruger National Park is particularly renowned. Even those with a passing interest will find that binoculars and a field guide are worthwhile investments. There are birdwatching clubs in the major cities.

WORK

The best time to look for work is from October to November, before the high season starts and before university students begin holidays. Due to high unemployment and fears about illegal immigration from the rest of Africa, there are tough penalties for employers taking on foreigners without work permits. So far this doesn't seem to have stopped foreigners getting jobs in restaurants/bars in tourist areas, but this might change. Don't expect decent pay – about R12 per hour plus tips (which can be good) is usual.

ACCOMMODATION

Both hostels and self-catering cottages (usually on farms) have become boom budget accommodation industries. If you're prepared to camp or pay a little more for a pub or a B&B, accommodation is even more plentiful and generally of a high standard.

Many places such as caravan parks, have seasonal rates. The high season is usually the summer school holidays, especially around Christmas and the New Year, and Easter. Prices can double or triple and there might be a minimum stay of a week. The other school holidays are often high season also.

Camping

Most towns have an inexpensive municipal caravan park or resort close to the centre of town. You'll probably pay about R30 to R35 for a site at a caravan park, and anything up to R60 a site (more in high season) at a resort. Many backpackers hostels have space for a few tents and usually charge around R15 to R25 per site. In some rural backwaters of the ex-Homelands (where there are few official camp sites) you can still free-camp. *Always* ask permission from the nearest village or home before setting up your tent. This is not just good manners; you are at serious risk of robbery or worse if you ignore local sensibilities.

Self-Catering Cottages

The cheapest self-catering accommodation is usually in farm cottages, which can be great value. You might find something for about R100 a double, although most start around R120. Information centres in small towns are the best places to find out about farm cottages. To confuse things a little, self-catering cottages are also called chalets, cabins and rondavels (circular, often thatched, huts).

Hostels

There has been an explosion in the number of backpackers hostels in the past few years. Nearly all hostels are of a high standard and a dorm bed costs about R40 to R50 a night. Many hostels also offer private rooms, which cost about R100/130 a single/double.

B&Bs & Guesthouses

The distinction between a B&B and a guesthouse is usually pretty vague. Even places offering a number of guest rooms are usually private houses, and the service is always on a very personal level. There is an enormous number of B&Bs and on the whole the standard is extremely high.

Hotels

Until the boom in B&B accommodation began, almost every town in the country had at least one hotel offering reasonable accommodation and meals. Now, many of the cheaper places have found that they can't compete and have either lifted standards and prices or have stopped offering accommodation altogether.

FOOD

Despite the fact that South Africa produces some of the best meat, fresh produce and seafood in the world, the food is often disappointing. The British can take most of the blame. Large steaks (admittedly, usually excellent), overboiled vegetables and fried chips seem to be the staple diet for whites. In pubs and steakhouses, steak or fish dishes cost between R35 and R50.

Since the influx of foreign visitors in 1994, things are changing, particularly in the cities where there is some variety being offered on menus. The Winelands and Cape Town are easily the best places for cuisine.

Boerewors (farmers' sausage) is the traditional sausage and it's sold everywhere. Even committed carnivores can find this unappetising but that's partly because what you're being sold sometimes isn't boerewors but *braaiwors*, an inferior grade.

There are a few restaurants serving African dishes, most of which don't originate in South Africa. The staple for most blacks is rice or *mielie* (maize) meal, served in a variety of forms. Although it isn't especially appetising, it's cheap. Servings of rice and stew are sold for about R5 around minibus taxi parks.

DRINKS

Pubs

Surprisingly, there are few bars and pubs in South Africa. Durban, Pretoria, Bloemfontein and Cape Town have a decent range of drinking places, but in most other towns and cities the situation is dire. Most towns have at least one hotel, but they are usually not very social places.

For beer drinkers there are a number of lagers: Castle is probably the most popular (and usually the cheapest), but Amstel and Carlsberg are considered superior brews. In the Cape, look out for Mitchell's Beers, which come from a couple of small breweries around the area. A beer costs between R6 to R15 depending on the drinking establishment.

The Mint Yardstick

A good guide to the quality of dining establishments in South Africa is the free mouth-cleansing mints offered after every meal. Whether it's a burger joint or an upmarket restaurant, the quality of the mint (which comes with the bill) often reflects the standard of the cuisine!

Wine

Wine was first made in South Africa in 1659. It is now an enormous industry, employing around 30,000 people in Western Cape. The wine is of a high standard, and it is very reasonably priced. If you buy direct from a vineyard you can get bottles for as little as R10, but in a bottle store R25 and up is a more realistic price. Most restaurants have long wine lists and stock a few varieties in 250ml bottles, which is very handy if you want to try a few different wines or you're eating alone.

There is a range of excellent dry whites made from sauvignon blanc, riesling, colombard and chenin blanc. The most popular red cultivars are cabernet sauvignon, pinotage (an interesting local cultivar crossed from pinot and cinsaut, which was known as Hermitage), shiraz, cinsaut and pinot noir.

SPECTATOR SPORTS

Soccer is the most popular sport among blacks. South Africa won the prestigious Africa Cup in 1996 (helped, perhaps, by Nigeria's boycott of the event), thus making three important victories in the three major sports since the country's readmittance to world sport.

Cricket fans tend to be English-speakers, but after South Africa's return to international sport in the 1992 World Cup, cricket occupied centre stage. The euphoria following South Africa's surprising success in the competition probably helped the Yes vote in the referendum on constitutional reform.

Rugby (Union, not League) was traditionally the Afrikaners' sport until the 1995

World Cup, which was hosted and won by South Africa. The entire white and coloured population went rugby mad – the black population was officially part of the celebrations but its response was a little muted.

In tennis, South Africa won the Hopman Cup in 2000.

There are traditional Afrikaner games, the most popular of which is *jukskei*. This game is something like horseshoe-tossing but uses items associated with trek wagons. Kroonstad (in the Free State) is the centre for national competition.

SHOPPING

Crafts

Indigenous crafts are on sale everywhere, from expensive galleries to street corners. There's a lot of junk but also a lot of quality items. See what's available in a good shop in a big city, then see if you can get a better price as you travel around the rural areas.

As well as traditional crafts there are also items available known collectively as 'township crafts'.

These are the product of extreme poverty and vivid imaginations. Items such as boxes made from oil tins, flowers made from soft-drink cans and toys made from wire all make great gifts.

Antiques & Collectables

South Africa's long isolation from the outside world means that there are troves of old goods (everything from Beatles paraphernalia to 18th-century furniture) for sale at very reasonable prices. Cape Town's numerous antique and junk shops are the best places to browse.

Getting There & Away

This section covers access into South Africa only from neighbouring countries. Information about reaching Southern Africa from elsewhere on the African continent and from other continents is outlined in the regional Getting There & Away chapter.

AIR

South Africa is the major air link in Southern Africa. (For more information, including discount travel agents around the world, see Air in the regional Getting There & Away chapter.)

Airports & Airlines

The main international airport remains Jo'burg International Airport (JNB), between Jo'burg and Pretoria, but there are an increasing number of international flights to Cape Town and to Durban.

South Africa is serviced by about 25 international carriers. The national carrier, South African Airways (SAA), has a good safety record and its service is generally of a high standard.

Departure Tax

There's an airport departure tax of R46 for flights to regional (Southern African) countries and R78 for all other international flights.

Southern Africa

There are several flights to other countries within Southern Africa. Air Botswana has flights between Jo'burg and Gaborone for R890.

SAA flies frequently between Moshoeshoe International Airport, 18km from Maseru in Lesotho, and Jo'burg in South Africa.

The one-way fare from Jo'burg is R450. There are some deals on return flights (about R620).

SAA flies between Jo'burg and Maputo in Mozambique for about R720. Comair and Air Namibia fly between Windhoek (Namibia) and Jo'burg or Cape Town for about R1180.

Royal Swaziland Airways flies from Mbabane to Jo'burg most days for R430 one way.

Air Zimbabwe flies from Jo'burg to Harare for R1800. There are also flights to Bulawayo and Victoria Falls. Some flights leave from Durban.

(For details on flying to places beyond Southern Africa, see the regional Getting There & Away chapter.)

LAND

South Africa shares borders with Botswana, Lesotho, Mozambique, Namibia, Swaziland and Zimbabwe. Jo'burg is a major hub for road and rail transport.

Fares given are one way.

Botswana

Border Crossings Most land border crossings between Botswana and South Africa are open between 7 or 8 am and 4 pm. The main border crossings are Ramatlabama/ Mmabatho, north of Mafikeng, open from 7 am to 8 pm; Skilpadshek, north-west of Zeerust, open from 7 am to 7 pm; and Tlokweng Gate/Kopfontein, north of Zeerust, open from 7 am to 10 pm.

Bus Intercape Mainliner (☎ 011-333 2312) runs from Jo'burg/Pretoria to Gaborone daily for R150. Minibus taxis run from Mafikeng (North-West Province) to Gaborone for about R30 (for more travel information, see the Getting There & Away section in the Botswana chapter).

Train The *Bulawayo* runs once a week from Pretoria to Gaborone (and on to Bulawayo). It costs R225 in 1st class.

Lesotho

There are no direct buses between South African cities and Maseru. Take a bus to Bloemfontein or Ladybrand and catch a minibus taxi from there. Bloemfontein to Maseru is about R25.

For information on land routes and border crossings and regional sections for details on hiking and horse trails through the Drakensberg into South Africa, see the Getting There & Away section in the Lesotho chapter.

Malawi

Intercape Mainliner makes the run from Jo'burg to Blantyre three times a week for R460. Translux does the same trip at the same price twice a week.

Mozambique

Bus Translux (☎ 011-774 3333) runs daily from Jo'burg/Pretoria to Maputo for R150. Intercape Mainliner also makes the run but it is slightly more expensive.

Train The *Komati* runs between Jo'burg and Komatipoort, on the Mozambique border (R155/110/65 in 1st/2nd/3rd class). From here you need to change trains for Maputo (about R30, 150km). The *Trans Lubombo* runs between Durban and Maputo, but check for current schedules as there have been recent disruptions to this train service (for more travel information, see the Getting There & Away section in the Mozambique chapter).

Namibia

Border Crossings The main crossing west of Upington is at Nakop (Ariamsvlei), open 24 hours. The main crossing on the west coast is between Vioolsdrif and Noordoewer and that is also open 24 hours. You can't cross the border between Namibia and South Africa in the Kgalagadi Transfrontier Park. The nearest alternative is to cross between Rietfontein and Klein-Menasse, which is open from 8 am to 10 pm.

Bus Intercape Mainliner (☎ 021-386 4400) runs between Cape Town and Windhoek four times a week for R350. You can travel between Windhoek and Jo'burg (R480) with Intercape, but you will probably have to stay overnight in Upington. (For more travel information, see the Getting There & Away section in the Namibia chapter.)

Swaziland

The Baz Bus (☎ 021-439 2323, fax 439 2343, bazbus@icon.co.za) runs from Jo'burg/Pretoria to Durban via Mbabane and Manzini, four times a week for R180.

For details on land routes and border crossings, see the Getting There & Away section in the Swaziland chapter

Zambia

Intercape Mainliner (☎ 011-333 2312) buses run from Jo'burg to Lusaka three times a week for R330. Translux (☎ 012-334 8000) does the same trip from Pretoria twice a week for the same price.

Zimbabwe

Border Crossings The only border crossing between Zimbabwe and South Africa is at Beitbridge on the Limpopo River, which is open between 5.30 am and 8.30 pm. Lengthy waits are not uncommon, particularly going from South Africa to Zimbabwe. Car drivers pay a toll at the border crossing to use the Limpopo Bridge when entering/leaving South Africa.

Bus Translux (☎ 021-449 3333) runs four services each week from Jo'burg/Pretoria to Harare for R250. Greyhound and Intercape Mainliner do the same run, but Greyhound (☎ 012-323 1154) also has a useful service four times a week from Pretoria to Bulawayo for R200. Route 49 (☎ 021-426 5593) runs from Cape Town to Victoria Falls for R700 (R320 from Jo'burg); check out its Web site: www.route49.liveshop .com. The Baz Bus also does these routes.

For more travel information, see under Getting There & Away in the Zimbabwe chapter.

Train The *Bulawayo* runs weekly between Pretoria and Bulawayo (via Jo'burg and Gaborone) for R225 in 1st class.

SEA

South Africa's Safmarine (☎ 021-408 6911, fax 408 6660) is actively seeking passengers for its container ships, which sail to many of the world's major ports. Fares are expensive (eg, from US$2200/3000 a single/double between Cape Town and the UK), however they are negotiable. Also fares *from* South Africa seem to be lower than fares *to* South Africa.

You can take a ship between Cape Town and Durban (from US$310/420 a single/double) and Port Elizabeth and Durban (from US$160/210).

Web site: www.safmarine.co.uk

ORGANISED TOURS

For tour and safari companies based outside of Southern Africa that run trips around the region, see Organised Tours in the regional Getting There & Away chapter.

Getting Around

South Africa is geared towards travel by private car, with some very good highways but limited and expensive mainstream public transport. If you want to cover a lot of country in a limited time, hiring or buying a car might be necessary. If you don't have much money but have time to spare, you can hitch to most places, and if you don't mind a modicum of discomfort there's the extensive network of minibus taxis, and 3rd-class train seats.

AIR

South African Airways (SAA) is a domestic as well as an international carrier. To most destinations there are plenty of daily flights. Fares aren't cheap, but if you plan to do a lot of flying in South Africa check with a travel agent before you leave home for special deals on advance purchase tickets. Once you're in South Africa there are a few discount options. For example, there's a 15% discount if you book and pay 14 days in advance and 50% off for one-month advance purchases.

Domestic destinations covered include Jo'burg, Cape Town, Durban, Port Elizabeth, East London, Bloemfontein, Upington, Kimberley Nelspruit, Springbok and Alexander Bay.

SAA flights can be booked at travel agents, or at SAA offices in Jo'burg (☎ 011-978 1111), Cape Town (☎ 021-936 1111) and Durban (☎ 031-250 1111) in major cities. Destinations include: Cape Town to Jo'burg (R1083); and Cape Town to Durban (R1117).

Comair (☎ 011-921 0222 in Jo'burg, ☎ 021-936 9000 in Cape Town) is an airline operating in conjunction with British Airways. Comair destinations include Cape Town, Durban, Jo'burg and Port Elizabeth. Destinations include: Jo'burg to Cape Town (R1070); and Durban to Jo'burg (R590).

There are also several regional airlines, including Nationwide, Sun Air and National Airlines.

There is an airport departure tax of R22 for domestic flights within South Africa. It's usually included in the ticket price.

BUS

Translux, part of the semi-privatised government transport service, runs long-distance buses between most major towns. The other main national operator is Greyhound. With the exception of City to City (a poor relation of Translux) and local services competing with minibus taxis, bus travel isn't cheap.

In the western half of the country Intercape Mainliner has useful services at fares a little lower than Translux.

Translux

Translux runs express services on the main routes. Tickets must be booked 24 hours in advance. You can get on without a booking if there's a spare seat, but you won't know that until the bus arrives. You usually can't book a seat to a nearby town, but prices for short sectors are exorbitant anyway – you're better off catching a local bus or a minibus taxi.

Computicket takes bookings, as do many travel agents and some train stations. There are also reservations offices around the country including:

Cape Town	☎ 021-449 3333
Durban	☎ 031-308 8111
Jo'burg	☎ 011-774 3333
Port Elizabeth	☎ 041-507 1333

Note that fares increase in the high season.

Translux services include:

Jo'burg-Cape Town via Bloemfontein Daily, 19 hours (overnight). Stops (with fares from Jo'burg/Cape Town) include: Bloemfontein (R155/245); Beaufort West (R210/160); Worcester (R290/75); and Cape Town (R320).

Jo'burg-Cape Town via Kimberley Five a week, 18½ hours (overnight). Stops (with fares from Jo'burg/Cape Town) include Kimberley (R115/250).

Jo'burg-Durban Several daily, eight or nine hours (daylight and overnight). Stops (with fares from Jo'burg/Durban) include: Harrismith (R100/110); Pietermaritzburg (R110/30); and Durban (R110).

Jo'burg-East London Daily, 14 hours (overnight). Stops (with fares from Jo'burg/East London) include: Bloemfontein (R150/185); Queenstown (R165/65); King William's Town (R220/65); and East London (R220).

Jo'burg-Knysna Daily, 17½ hours (overnight) via Kimberley or Bloemfontein. Stops (with fares from Jo'burg/Knysna) include: Bloemfontein (R155/200); Kimberley (R115/210); Oudtshoorn (R220/50); Mossel Bay (R220/50); George (R220/40); and Knysna (R235).

Jo'burg-Port Elizabeth Daily, 15 hours (overnight) via Cradock or Graaff-Reinet. Stops (with fares from Jo'burg/Port Elizabeth) include: Bloemfontein (R155/180); Cradock (R205/165); Graaff-Reinet (R195/140); and Port Elizabeth (R220).

Jo'burg-Umtata Four a week, 13½ hours (overnight). Stops (with fares from Jo'burg/Umtata) include: Pietermaritzburg (R110/120); Kokstad (R155/80); and Umtata (R170).

Cape Town-Durban Daily, 20 hours. Stops (with fares from Cape Town/Durban) include: Paarl (R75/265); Bloemfontein (R245/140); Bethlehem (R265/100); Pietermaritzburg (R265/30); and Durban (R265).

Cape Town-East London Daily, 15 hours (overnight). Stops (with fares from Cape Town/East London) include: Graaff-Reinet (R210/200); Cradock (R215/180); Queenstown (R220/65); King William's Town (R230/65); and East London (R230).

Cape Town-Port Elizabeth via Coastal Route Daily, 10½ hours (daylight). Stops (with fares from Cape Town/Port Elizabeth) include: Swellendam (R75/130); Mossel Bay (R100/100); Oudtshoorn (R130/100, overnight); George (R130/90); Knysna (R135/70); Plettenberg Bay (R140/60); Storms River (R155/55); and Port Elizabeth (R155).

Cape Town-Port Elizabeth via Mountain Route Daily, 12 hours (overnight). Stops (with fares from Cape Town/Port Elizabeth) include: Robertson (R75/140); George (R130/90); Knysna (R135/70); Plettenberg Bay (R140/60); and Port Elizabeth (R155).

Durban-Port Elizabeth Daily, 14 hours (daylight). Stops (with fares from Durban/Port Elizabeth) include: Port Shepstone (R65/190); Kokstad (R90/175); Umtata (R125/135); East London (R160/90); Grahamstown (R190/65); and Port Elizabeth (R200).

Greyhound

Greyhound offers services on much the same routes as Translux at much the same prices, although special deals are sometimes available. One of Greyhound's Jo'burg-Durban services runs through parts of Zululand to Richards Bay, then down the coast to Durban, which is handy.

Book through a travel agent or the following Greyhound offices:

Bloemfontein	☎ 051-447 1558
Cape Town	☎ 021-418 4310
Durban	☎ 031-309 7830
Nelspruit	☎ 013-753 2100
Port Elizabeth	☎ 041-585 8648

Intercape Mainliner

Intercape Mainliner (☎ 021-386 4400 in Cape Town) is a major line in the western half of the country and generally charges less than Translux. Routes include: Port Elizabeth–East London (R90); Cape Town–Port Elizabeth (R140); Cape Town– Upington (R185); Jo'burg-Upington (R190); Upington-Windhoek (Namibia) (R210); and Cape Town–Windhoek (R350).

City to City (Transtate)

City to City has taken over Transtate routes, although you sometimes still see buses painted with the Transtate sign. Unfortunately, services have been wound back and City to City stops and offices are few and can be difficult to find. Buses often stop at train stations (ask about the 'railways bus') – try asking there. It's worth using City to City (because they are generally far cheaper than the major bus companies) but it's difficult to find current and reliable information about them.

Baz Bus

The Baz Bus (☎ 021-439 2323, fax 439 2343, **e** bazbus@icon.co.za) is an excellent alternative to the major bus lines. Most hostels take bookings, or you can phone. While it's aimed at backpackers, its routes, organisation and service levels make it very useful for travellers on any budget.

The Baz Bus offers hop-on, hop-off fares and door-to-door service between Cape Town and Jo'burg via the Northern Drakensberg, Durban and the Garden Route. It also does a very useful loop from Durban up through Zululand and Swaziland and back to Jo'burg, passing close by Kruger National Park. No other mainstream transport options cover this route.

MINIBUS TAXI

If there's no bus, and you don't have a car, the only way to get between many places is to take a minibus taxi or hitch (see Hitching later in this section).

Minibus taxis tend to run on relatively short routes, generally only to neighbouring towns, although you'll nearly always find a few running to a distant big city. As well as the usual 'leave when full' taxis, there's a small but increasing number of door-to-door services, which you can book. These tend to run on the longer routes and, while they cost a little more, they're convenient.

Away from the big cities, robbery on taxis is not much of a problem. There have been isolated outbreaks of 'taxi wars' between rival companies, and crowded taxis have been machine-gunned, but given the number of taxis the incidence of attacks is very low if you avoid problem areas. Cape Town's taxi war flares regularly and a few other areas have had trouble, including East London. The government has been threatening to clean up the industry for a long time. Read the newspapers and ask around.

A bigger problem is driver fatigue and if you are concerned about safety you're better off using a bus or train for long-distance trips (eg, Jo'burg to Cape Town).

TRAIN

Trains are a good way to get between major cities and travel in 3rd class is very cheap.

The Blue Train

Some people come to South Africa just to ride on the famous *Blue Train*. The original train ran between Pretoria/Jo'burg and Cape Town, offering 25 hours of luxury. Even more luxurious trains have replaced the original train, and more routes have been added.

If you can't afford to take an entire trip, consider taking just a section. For example, a 40-hour trip from Cape Town to Port Elizabeth along the Garden Route costs from R6100/8100 in single/double suites. Low-season fares apply between the beginning of May and the end of August.

Blue Train bookings can be made in Jo'burg (☎ 011-773 7631), Cape Town

(☎ 021-449 2672), Pretoria (☎ 012-334 8459) and Durban (☎ 031-361 7550). Some travel agents in South Africa and in other countries take bookings.
Website: www.bluetrain.com.za

Name Trains

Passenger services are all on 'name trains'. On overnight trips the fare includes a sleeping berth (more expensive private compartments can also be hired), but there's a R25 charge for bedding hire. Meals are a la carte.

First and 2nd class must be booked at least 24 hours in advance; you can't book 3rd class. Most stations and some travel agents accept bookings.

Routes & Fares Return fares are simply double the one-way fares (given here in 1st/2nd/3rd class). Note that these are most of the lines, however there are other lines with routes that double-up on some of the stops listed following. Call the station at Cape Town (☎ 021-449 5770) or Pretoria (☎ 012-334 8475) for more information.

***Algoa* Jo'burg-Port Elizabeth** Daily, 19 hours. Departs from Jo'burg and Port Elizabeth at 2.30 pm. Stops include: Kroonstad (R60/40/25 from Jo'burg, R205/135/85 from Port Elizabeth); Bloemfontein (R105/70/45, R165/110/70); Cradock (R200/135/85, R75/50/30); and Port Elizabeth (R265/180/110).

***Amatola* Jo'burg-East London** Daily, 20 hours. Departs from Jo'burg 12.45 pm, departs from East London at noon. Stops include: Kroonstad (R60/40/25 from Jo'burg, R205/135/85 from East London); Bloemfontein (R105/70/45, R165/110/70); Queenstown (R195/130/80, R60/40/25); and East London (R235/165/100).

***Bosvelder* Jo'burg-Messina** Daily, 15 hours. Departs from Jo'burg at 6.50 pm, departs from Messina at 2.45 pm. Stops include: Pretoria (R25/20/10 from Jo'burg, R135/90/55 from Messina); Pietersburg/Polokwane (R90/65/35, R75/50/30); Louis Trichardt (R125/85/50, R45/30/15); and Messina (R150/105/60).

***Diamond Express* Pretoria-Bloemfontein via Kimberley** Daily except Saturday, 15 hours. Departs from Pretoria at 6.35 pm, departs from Bloemfontein at 5 pm. The fare between Jo'burg and Kimberley is R125/85/50.

***Komati* Jo'burg-Komatipoort** Daily, 12 hours. Departs from Jo'burg at 5.45 pm, departs from Komatipoort at 6.07 pm. This service theoretically connects with a train to Maputo in Mozambique. There is also a shuttle bus that runs from Komatipoort to Maputo daily. Stops include: Pretoria (R25/20/10 from Jo'burg, R115/85/45 from Komatipoort); Middelburg (R60/45/25, R80/60/35); Nelspruit (R110/75/45, R40/30/15); and Komatipoort, (R155/110/65).

***Southern Cross* Cape Town-Port Elizabeth** Weekly, 24 hours. Departs from Cape Town every Friday, departs from Port Elizabeth on Sunday. Stops from Cape Town include: Swellendam (R60/45/25); George (R95/70/40); Oudtshoorn (R105/75/45); and Port Elizabeth (R235/165/95).

***Trans Karoo* Jo'burg-Cape Town** Daily, 27 hours. Departs from Cape Town at 9.20 am, departs from Jo'burg at 12.30 pm. Stops include: Kimberley (R130/85/50 from Jo'burg, R240/165/100 from Cape Town); Beaufort West (R235/160/100, R135/95/60); and Cape Town (R360/260/150).

***Trans Natal* Jo'burg-Durban** Daily, 13½ hours. Departs from both Jo'burg and Durban at 6.30 pm. Stops include Newcastle (R85/60/35 from Jo'burg, R110/70/45 from Durban); Ladysmith (R115/75/45, R85/55/35); Pietermaritzburg (R155/105/65, R40/25/15); and Durban (R180/120/80).

***Trans Oranje* Cape Town-Durban** Weekly, 30½ hours. Departs from Cape Town on Monday at 6.50 pm, departs from Durban on Thursday at 5.30 pm. Stops include: Wellington (R30/25/15 from Cape Town, R430/290/185 from Durban); Beaufort West (R135/95/60, R330/225/140); Kimberley (R240/165/100, R230/160/100); Bloemfontein (R270/180/115, R190/130/85); Kroonstad (R310/210/130, R150/105/60); Ladysmith (R385/255/165, R75/55/30); Pieter maritzburg (R430/290/180, R40/25/15); and Durban (R470/315/195).

Metro Trains

There are Metro services in and around several cities. Make sure you get local advice before using a Metro train – violent robbery is always a possibility, particularly between Pretoria and Jo'burg.

CAR & MOTORCYCLE

Most major roads are excellent and carry relatively little traffic, and off the big roads there are some interesting back roads to explore.

The country is crossed by national routes (eg, the N1), and some sections of these are freeways. A toll of between R3 and R18 is payable on some of these.

Petrol stations are often open 24 hours and fuel costs have increased substantially in recent times (now about R2.72 a litre). Unleaded petrol is widely available.

Road Rules

South Africans drive on the left-hand side of the road. The main local road rule is the 'four-way stop', which can occur even on major roads. When you arrive at a four-way stop, you must stop. If there are other vehicles at the intersection, those that arrived before you cross first.

Hazards

South Africa has a horrific road fatality rate, caused mostly by dangerous driving. Hundreds of people die whenever there's a long weekend and the annual death toll is pushing 10,000. A further 150,000 people are injured on the roads annually. With a population of about 41 million – the vast majority of whom don't own cars – that's appalling.

Animals & Pedestrians In rural areas, particularly in the Eastern Cape, slow down and watch out for people and animals on the roads.

Crime Carjacking is a problem in Jo'burg and to a lesser extent in the other big cities (people have been killed for their cars). Stay alert and keep windows wound up at night.

Other Drivers On highways, fast cars coming up behind you will expect you to move over into the emergency lane to let them pass, and will sit on your tail until they can pass. The problem is that there might be pedestrians or a slow-moving vehicle already in the emergency lane. Don't move over unless it's safe. It is becoming common for an overtaking car to rely on *oncoming* traffic to move into the emergency lane! This is sheer lunacy and you must remain constantly alert. Drivers on little-used rural roads often speed and they often assume that there is no other traffic. Be careful of oncoming cars at blind corners on country roads. Drink-driving is another major hazard.

Car Guards

Parked cars are easy targets in crime-plagued South Africa and you'll see car guards in towns and cities across the country. Although probably incapable of stopping a gang of determined car thieves, the guards are good visible deterrents.

When you step out of your car you'll be handed a ticket with the name of your guard and a note explaining that donations are gratefully received, as the guards are volunteers organised by local councils.

You may come back to your vehicle without sighting the guard (and we certainly caught them napping on more than one occasion), but you can be sure they will pop up before you have the chance to zoom off.

Give them back their card and a couple of rand if you've been away from your car for half an hour or more. These people are providing a valuable service and it's all part of a campaign with a slogan you will come across often in this country – fight crime together!

Roads In the ex-Homelands beware of dangerous potholes, wash outs, unannounced hairpin bends and the like.

You don't have to get very far off the beaten track anywhere in the country to find yourself on dirt roads. Most are regularly graded and reasonably smooth and it's often possible to travel at high speed – don't!

If you're travelling along a dirt road at 100km/h and you come to a corner, you won't go around that corner, you'll sail off into the veld. If you put on the brakes to slow down you'll probably spin or roll. If you swerve sharply to avoid a pothole you'll go into an exciting four-wheel drift, then find out what happens when your car meets a telegraph pole. Worst of all you could lose control as you move to the side of the road to avoid an approaching car, and have a head-on collision. As a rule, treat dirt like ice.

Rental

The major international companies, such as Avis (☎ 0800 021 111 toll free) and Budget

(☎ 0800 016 622 toll free), are represented. They have offices or agents across the country. Their rates are high, but if you book through your local agent at home before you arrive they will be significantly lower – but still higher than the cheaper companies in South Africa.

Local companies come and go, but currently the larger companies include Imperial (☎ 0800 131 000 toll free) and Tempest (☎ 0800 031 666 toll free). They have agents in the main cities and a few other places.

A step down from these are smaller and cheaper outfits that regularly burst onto the scene, and in a lot of cases fade just as rapidly. They normally offer very competitive rates. Tourist information offices are the best places to begin your inquiries.

For budget travellers, hostels can often organise a rental car deal through a broker with one of the major companies (such as Budget or Europcar) at far better rates than if you approached the company directly. For a small car (such as a 1.6L Toyota Corolla) you can expect to pay around US$27 to $US32 a day with insurance and other costs included. This is a bargain if there is a group of you. Try Zebra Crossing in Cape Town or North South Backpackers in Pretoria (see Places to Stay in the Western Cape and Gauteng sections respectively).

Camper Vans One way around South Africa's high accommodation and transport costs is to hire a camper van. Note that one-way rentals might not be possible with these vehicles.

One company with a range of deals is Leisure Mobiles (☎ 011-792 1884) in Jo'burg at 2 Sambreelboom Ave, Randparkridge, Gauteng. It has been in business for quite a while and its rates are good. As well as Toyota Landcruiser campers they have cheaper 'bakkie' campers, which sleep two in the back of a canopied pick-up. These include all the necessary camping gear.

Motorcycle Renting a bike isn't cheap but the idea of riding around South Africa is attractive. For more information, see Car & Motorcycle under Cape Town & the Peninsula in the Western Cape section.

Purchase

An increasing number of travellers buy a car to tour South Africa, or the entire region, then sell it again after their trip. Cape Town and Jo'burg are the two main places for this (for more information, see the regional Getting Around chapter).

BICYCLE

South Africa is a good country to cycle around, with a wide variety of terrain and climate, plenty of camping places and many good roads, most of which don't carry a lot of traffic.

However, parts of South Africa are very hilly and even on main roads gradients are steep.

Away from the big cities you might have trouble finding specialised parts, although there are basic bicycle shops in many towns. Theft is a problem – bring a good lock and chain.

There is a boom in mountain biking (usually with support vehicles, *braais* (barbecues) and beer – see Activities in the Regional Facts for the Visitor chapter), so mountain bikes are sold everywhere. Touring bikes are harder to come by except in the major cities.

HITCHING

Hitching is never entirely safe in any country, and it's not a form of travel we can recommend. People who decide to hitch should understand that they are taking a small but potentially serious risk. They will be safer if they travel in pairs and let someone know they are going.

However, hitching is sometimes the only way to get to smaller towns, and even if you're travelling between larger ones the choice is sometimes to wait a day or two for a bus or hitch. Make it obvious that you're a clean-cut foreign visitor. You might have to wait a while for a lift, especially on major roads, but when you get one there's a good chance that you'll be offered other hospitality. It helps to carry a sign stating your destination.

Hitching always involves a degree of risk, but this is particularly so in and around major cities. You are advised to catch public transport well beyond the city limits before you start to hitch.

LOCAL TRANSPORT

Getting around in towns isn't easy, and many of them sprawl a long way. This is a major pain if you're hitching, especially if the town is bypassed by the freeway. The big cities and some of the larger towns have bus systems. Services often stop running early in the evening.

In Durban and some other places you'll find that mainstay of Asian transport, the tuk-tuk (motorised three-wheel vehicle), which run mainly in downtown or tourist areas.

ORGANISED TOURS

Air

Various operators offer 'fly-in' tours of Kruger National Park, arriving at the park's airstrip at Skukuza. Sepunga Safaris (☎ 011-475 9904, ⓔ sepunga@global.co.za) offers flights to/from Jo'burg and three nights in the park, including wildlife drives, for R6500 a double.

Bus

One of the major long-distance coach tour operators is Connex (☎ 011-884 8110, fax 884 3007) in Jo'burg. It has a wide range of fairly expensive tours covering popular routes, as well as day tours. It caters particularly well for senior travellers.

Train

Union Ltd Steam Rail Tours (☎ 021-449 4391, fax 449 4395, ⓔ SteamSA@Transnet.co.za), a division of Spoornet, runs restored steam trains. The six-day Golden Thread tour, for example, runs from Cape Town along the coast to Oudtshoorn and back; it's a leisurely trip. It costs R3800/7600 a single/double, including meals and bedding.

Also doing similar tours is Rovos Rail (☎ 012-315 8258, ⓔ reservation@rovos.co.za), which runs superbly restored old trains within South Africa and elsewhere.
Web site: www.rovos.co.za

Western Cape

Western Cape takes in the south-western corner of the old Cape Province. With its diverse and spectacular flora, winelands and simply magnificent mountain scenery it's a highlight of any visit to South Africa.

The province is home to the so-called 'coloureds' – people who have diverse origins and who didn't fit neatly into the apartheid system's pigeonholes. Most people who were classified as coloured are descended from a mixture of backgrounds, including the Khoisan, Xhosa, slaves (from Asia and Africa) and Europeans.

CAPE TOWN & THE PENINSULA

☎ 021

Cape Town, or Kaapstad, is one of the most beautiful cities in the world. About 40km from the Cape of Good Hope, near the southern tip of Africa, it is one of the most geographically isolated of the world's great cities. Dominated by a 1000m-high mountain with virtually sheer cliffs, it's surrounded by mountain walks, vineyards and beaches.

Cape Town is the most open-minded and relaxed city in South Africa and has nothing like the sense of tension that pervades Johannesburg. It is the capital of Western Cape and the parliamentary capital of the republic.

History

The first European to round the Cape (in 1487) was Portuguese sailor Bartholomeu Dias. He named it Cabo da Boa Esperanca (Cape of Good Hope). At this time the Cape was occupied by the Khoikhoi, relatives of the San people, who were seminomadic sheep and cattle pastoralists.

By the late 16th century the English and Dutch were starting to challenge the Portuguese, and the Dutch East India Company (VOC) established a base where ships could stock up on supplies. Jan van Riebeeck was chosen to lead an expedition and barter with the Khoikhoi for meat. He reached Table Bay on 6 April 1652, built a mud-walled fort and planted gardens that have now become the Botanical (Company's) Gardens.

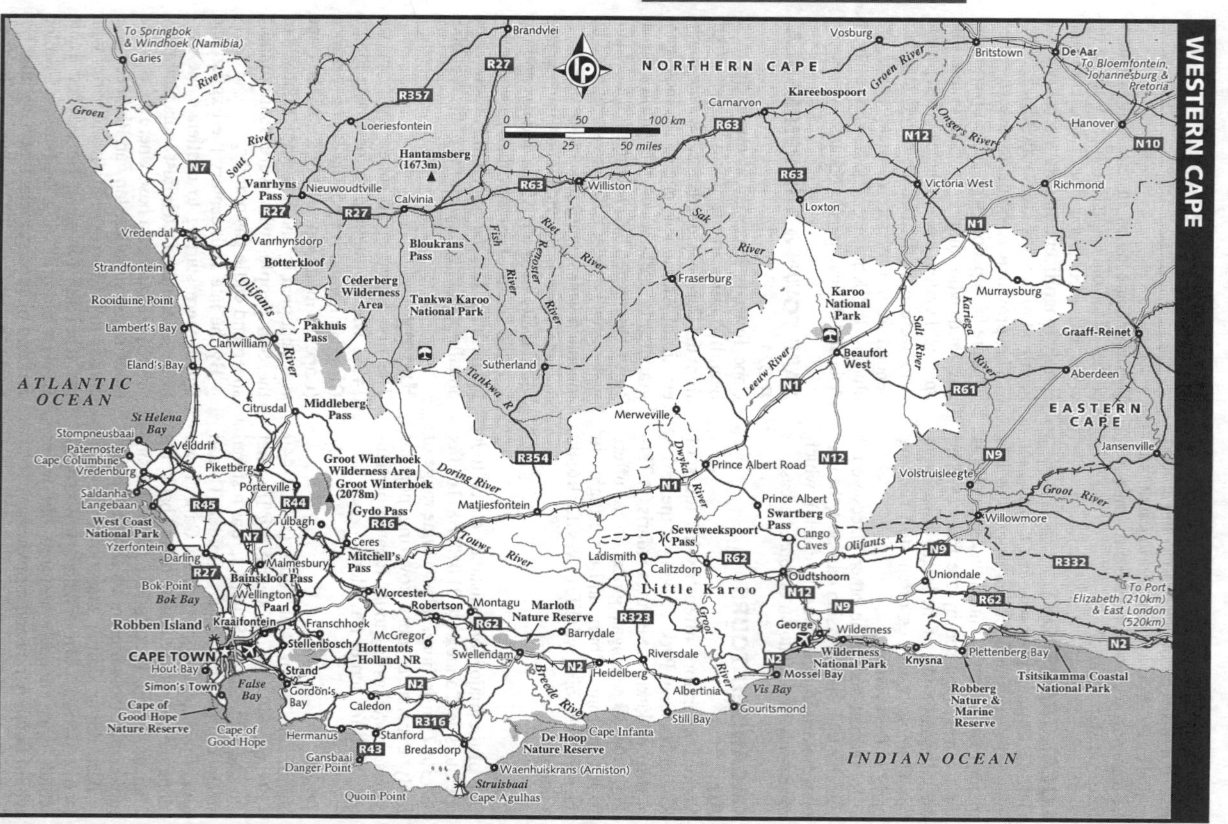
WESTERN CAPE
NORTHERN CAPE
EASTERN CAPE
ATLANTIC OCEAN
INDIAN OCEAN
0 50 100 km
0 25 50 miles
To Springbok & Windhoek (Namibia)
Garies
Groen River
Sout River
N7
Vanrhyns Pass
Nieuwoudtville
R27
Vredendal
Vanrhynsdorp
Strandfontein
Botterkloof
Rooiduine Point
Lambert's Bay
Clanwilliam
Olifants River
Eland's Bay
Citrusdal
St Helena Bay
Stompneusbaai
Paternoster
Cape Columbine
Velddrif
Vredenburg
Piketberg
Porterville
Saldanha
Langebaan
R45
West Coast National Park
Yzerfontein
Darling
Bok Point
Bok Bay
Robben Island
Kraaifontein
CAPE TOWN
Hout Bay
Simon's Town
False Bay
Cape of Good Hope Nature Reserve
Cape of Good Hope
Strand
Gordon's Bay
Hermanus
Gansbaai
Danger Point
R43
Stanford
Quoin Point
Bredasdorp
R316
Struisbaai
Cape Agulhas
Waenhuiskrans (Arniston)
De Hoop Nature Reserve
Cape Infanta
Breede River
Still Bay
Gouritsmond
Vis Bay
Mossel Bay
George
Wilderness
Wilderness National Park
Knysna
Robberg Nature & Marine Reserve
Plettenberg Bay
Tsitsikamma Coastal National Park
Brandvlei
R357
Loeriesfontein
Hantamsberg (1673m)
Calvinia
Bloukrans Pass
Cederberg Wilderness Area
Tankwa Karoo National Park
Pakhuis Pass
Middleberg Pass
Groot Winterhoek Wilderness Area
Groot Winterhoek (2078m)
R44
Gydo Pass
R46
Tulbagh
Ceres
Mitchell's Pass
Malmesbury
Bainskloof Pass
Wellington
Paarl
Franschhoek
Stellenbosch
Hottentots Holland NR
Worcester
McGregor
Robertson
Montagu
Marloth Nature Reserve
Barrydale
Swellendam
Caledon
Heidelberg
Riversdale
Albertinia
Groot River
R323
Ladismith
Calitzdorp
Little Karoo
Seweweekspoort Pass
R62
Oudtshoorn
Cango Caves
Swartberg Pass
Prince Albert
Prince Albert Road
Dwyka River
Merweville
Matjiesfontein
Touws River
Doring River
R354
Sutherland
Tankwa R
Fish River
Renoster River
Riet River
Williston
R63
Fraserburg
Sak River
Carnarvon
Kareebospoort
Loxton
Vosburg
Groen River
Britstown
Ongers River
N12
Victoria West
De Aar
To Bloemfontein, Johannesburg & Pretoria
Hanover
N10
Richmond
N1
Leeuw River
Beaufort West
Karoo National Park
Salt River
Murraysburg
Kariega River
Graaff-Reinet
Aberdeen
R61
Jansenville
N9
Volstruisleegte
Groot River
Willowmore
Olifants R
Uniondale
R332
To Port Elizabeth (210km) & East London (520km)
N2

The colony was short of labour, so van Riebeeck imported slaves from East Asia.

Cape Town thrived, and was known as the Tavern of the Seas, a riotous port used by every navigator, privateer and merchant travelling between Europe and the East.

The population of whites did not reach a thousand until 1745, but small numbers of free (meaning non-VOC) burghers had begun to drift inland, driving the Khoisan (San and Khoikhoi peoples) from their lands.

By the end of the 18th century, Dutch power was fading and the British took the Cape in 1806. The slave trade was abolished in 1808 and the remaining Khoisan were given the explicit protection of the law in 1828, a move that contributed to Afrikaner dissatisfaction and the Great Trek (1834–40).

With the discovery of diamonds and gold in the centre of South Africa in the late 1800s and the ensuing growth of Johannesburg, Cape Town was no longer the single dominant metropolis in the country; as a major port it was, however, a beneficiary of this mineral wealth.

Orientation

The city centre lies to the north of Table Mountain and east of Signal Hill, and the inner city suburbs of Tamboerskloof, Gardens and Oranjezicht are within walking distance of it. This area is referred to as the City Bowl. On the western side of Signal Hill, Sea Point is another inner suburb, densely populated with high-rise apartments, hotels, restaurants and bars.

Some suburbs and surrounding towns cling to the coast, such as exclusive Clifton and Camps Bay and, further south, Llandudno, Hout Bay and Kommetjie. The False Bay towns from Muizenberg to Simon's Town can be reached by rail from the centre.

Most of the population lives in sprawling suburbs on the eastern side of Table Mountain; whites close to the mountain and blacks and coloureds on the bleak plain known as the Cape Flats (which includes Guguletu, Nyanga, Philippi, Mitchell's Plain and Khayelitsha).

The Cape of Good Hope (70km by road south of the city centre) is the meeting point for the cold Benguela Current, which runs up the west (Atlantic) side of the Cape, and the warm Agulhas Current, which runs along the east coast.

Information

Tourist Offices Cape Town Tourism (☎ 426 4267, e captour@iafrica.com) has a new office on the corner of Castle and Burg Sts. It's an efficiently run place with knowledgeable staff and is open daily. There's also a Western Cape Tourism desk here, a Baz Bus booking desk and an Internet cafe.

National Parks & Reserves Offices The National Parks Board (☎ 422 2810, fax 424 6211) has an office on the corner of Long and Hout Sts. It's open from 9 am to 4.45 pm weekdays.

Cape Nature Conservation (☎ 483 4051) at 1 Dorp St controls several reserves in the province.

Immigration Office For visa extensions, apply at the Department of Home Affairs (☎ 462 4970) at 56 Barrack St.

Embassies & Consulates Most countries have their main embassy in Pretoria, with an office or consulate in Cape Town (this becomes the official embassy during Cape Town's parliamentary sessions). Check the Yellow Pages under Consulates & Embassies for your country's consulate. Many are open in the morning only.

Money Money can be changed at any bank; they're open from 9 am to 3.30 pm weekdays, and on Saturday morning.

American Express is at Thibault Square (☎ 421 5586) at the top end of St George's Mall, and also at the Victoria & Alfred Waterfront (☎ 419 3917). The Waterfront office is open from 10 am to 5 pm daily.

Rennies Travel is the agent for Thomas Cook. It has branches at 101 St George's Mall (☎ 423 7154); 182 Main Rd, Sea Point (☎ 439 7529); and at the Waterfront (☎ 418 3744). All branches are open on weekdays and the St George's Mall branch is also open on Saturday morning.

Post & Communications The GPO is on the corner of Darling and Parliament Sts and is open from 8 am to 4.30 pm weekdays, and on Saturday morning. It has a poste restante counter.

The public phones in the GPO are open 24 hours, but they're often busy. There are plenty of privately run public phone businesses where you can make calls (and usually send faxes) without coins. They cost considerably more than public phones.

Many hostels have email facilities. Some of the better Internet cafes are: Connection Internet C@fe, Shop 4, Heerengracht Centre, Foreshore; Virtual Turtle, upstairs at the Purple Turtle, on the corner of Long and Shortmarket Sts; and in the Cape Town Tourism office (see Tourist Offices earlier), which charges R15 for half an hour.

Travel Agencies STA Travel (☎ 418 6570) on the corner of Riebeeck and Loop Sts offers competitive airfares. Several hostels take bookings for tours and overland trips. Check out the Africa Travel Centre (☎ 423 5555, fax 423 0065) at The Backpack Hostel, 74 New Church St.

Bookshops Exclusive Books (☎ 419 0905), situated at the Waterfront, has an excellent range and is open daily. The main mass-market bookshop/newsagency is CNA, with numerous shops around the city. Ulrich Naumann's (☎ 423 7832), at 17 Burg St, has a good range of German-language books.

Medical Services Doctors are listed under Medical in the Yellow Pages, and they generally arrange for hospitalisation, although in an emergency you can go directly to the casualty department of Groote Schuur Hospital (☎ 404 9111), at the intersection of De Waal (M3) and the Eastern Boulevard (N2) to the east of the city. Phone the police (☎ 10111) to get directions to the nearest hospital.

The Glengariff Pharmacy, Main Rd (corner of Glengariff), Sea Point, is open until 11 pm daily.

Emergency The phone numbers for emergency services are:

ambulance	☎ 10177
fire brigade	☎ 461 4141
police	☎ 10111
tourist police	☎ 418 2852
Automobile Association (AA)	☎ 0800 10101 toll free
Lifeline	☎ 461 1111
Rape Crisis	☎ 447 9762

Dangers & Annoyances Cape Town is one of the most relaxed cities in Africa but common sense is still required. There has been a substantial increase in street crime in recent years. Take care in Sea Point late at night; walking to or from the Victoria & Alfred Waterfront is not recommended day or night; and seek local advice before walking around the city centre at nights.

The townships on the Cape Flats have an appalling crime rate and unless you have a trustworthy guide, they are off limits.

There has recently been an ATM scam operating in Cape Town. Some ATMs accept your card but don't give it back because they have been jammed with a piece of paper. While you're away getting help, your card and cash mysteriously disappear! Try to use ATMs attached to a bank and do this during business hours, so help is on hand. Outside business hours, a queue in front of an ATM is a good sign.

Swimming at all of the Cape beaches is potentially hazardous, especially for those inexperienced in surf. Check for signs warning of rips and rocks, and swim in patrolled areas.

The mountains in the middle of the city are no less dangerous just because they are in the city. Weather conditions can change rapidly, so warm clothing and a good map and compass are necessary. Also watch out for ticks here.

Museums

Bo-Kaap Museum The small but interesting Bo-Kaap Museum (☎ 424 3846) at 71 Wale St gives an insight into the lifestyle of a prosperous, 19th-century Muslim family. The house itself was built in 1763. It's open from 9.30 am to 4.30 pm Monday to Saturday; entry is R3.

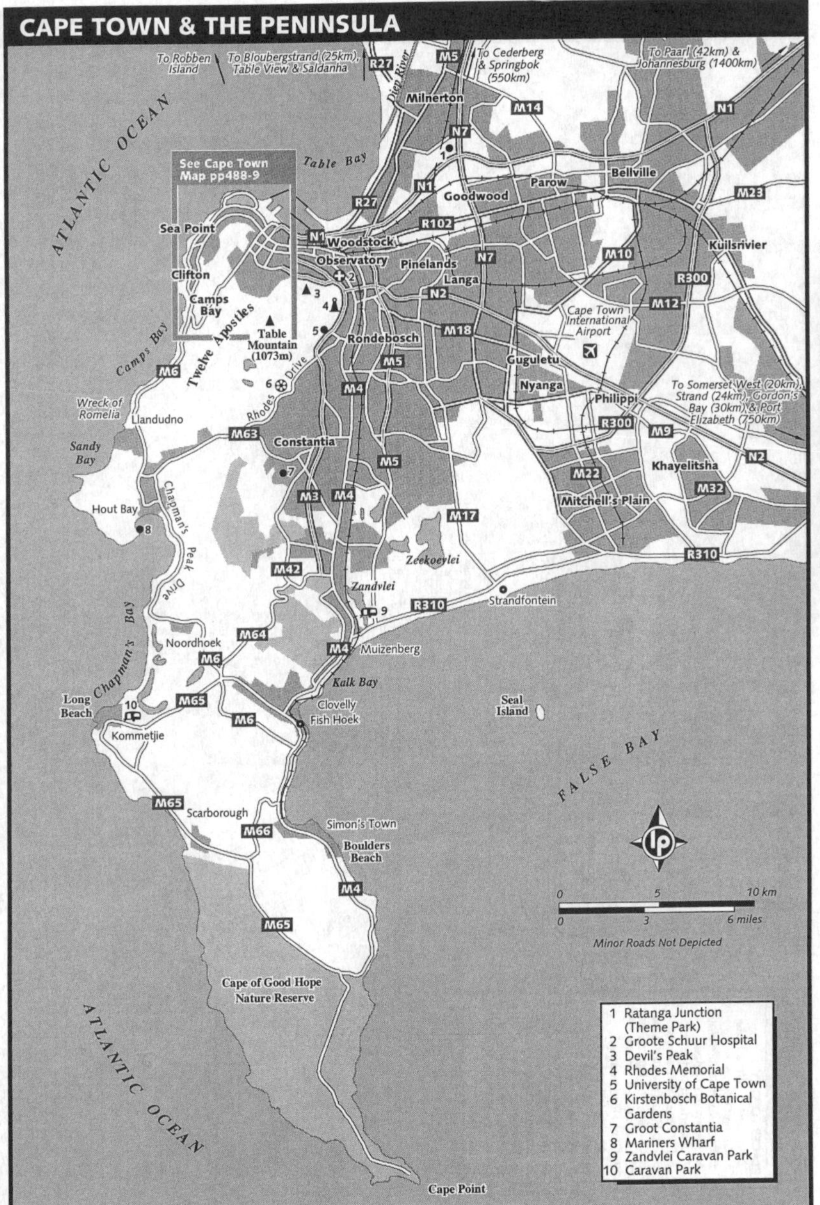

CAPE TOWN & THE PENINSULA
To Robben Island
To Bloubergstrand (25km), Table View & Saldanha
To Cederberg & Springbok (550km)
To Paarl (42km) & Johannesburg (1400km)
ATLANTIC OCEAN
Table Bay
Diep River
Milnerton
See Cape Town Map pp488-9
Sea Point
Clifton
Camps Bay
Twelve Apostles
Table Mountain (1073m)
Woodstock
Observatory
Pinelands
Langa
Goodwood
Parow
Bellville
Kuilsrivier
Rondebosch
Cape Town International Airport
Guguletu
Nyanga
Philippi
To Somerset West (20km), Strand (24km), Gordon's Bay (30km) & Port Elizabeth (750km)
Khayelitsha
Mitchell's Plain
Camps Bay
Rhodes Drive
Wreck of Romelia
Llandudno
Sandy Bay
Constantia
Hout Bay
Chapman's Peak Drive
Zeekoevlei
Zandvlei
Strandfontein
Chapman's Bay
Noordhoek
Muizenberg
Kalk Bay
Long Beach
Kommetjie
Clovelly
Fish Hoek
Seal Island
FALSE BAY
Scarborough
Simon's Town
Boulders Beach
Cape of Good Hope Nature Reserve
ATLANTIC OCEAN
Cape Point
R27
M5
M14
N1
N7
R102
M23
M10
R300
M12
N2
M18
M63
M4
M3
M9
M22
M32
M17
M42
R310
M64
M6
M65
M66
0 5 10 km
0 3 6 miles
Minor Roads Not Depicted
1 Ratanga Junction (Theme Park)
2 Groote Schuur Hospital
3 Devil's Peak
4 Rhodes Memorial
5 University of Cape Town
6 Kirstenbosch Botanical Gardens
7 Groot Constantia
8 Mariners Wharf
9 Zandvlei Caravan Park
10 Caravan Park
SOUTH AFRICA

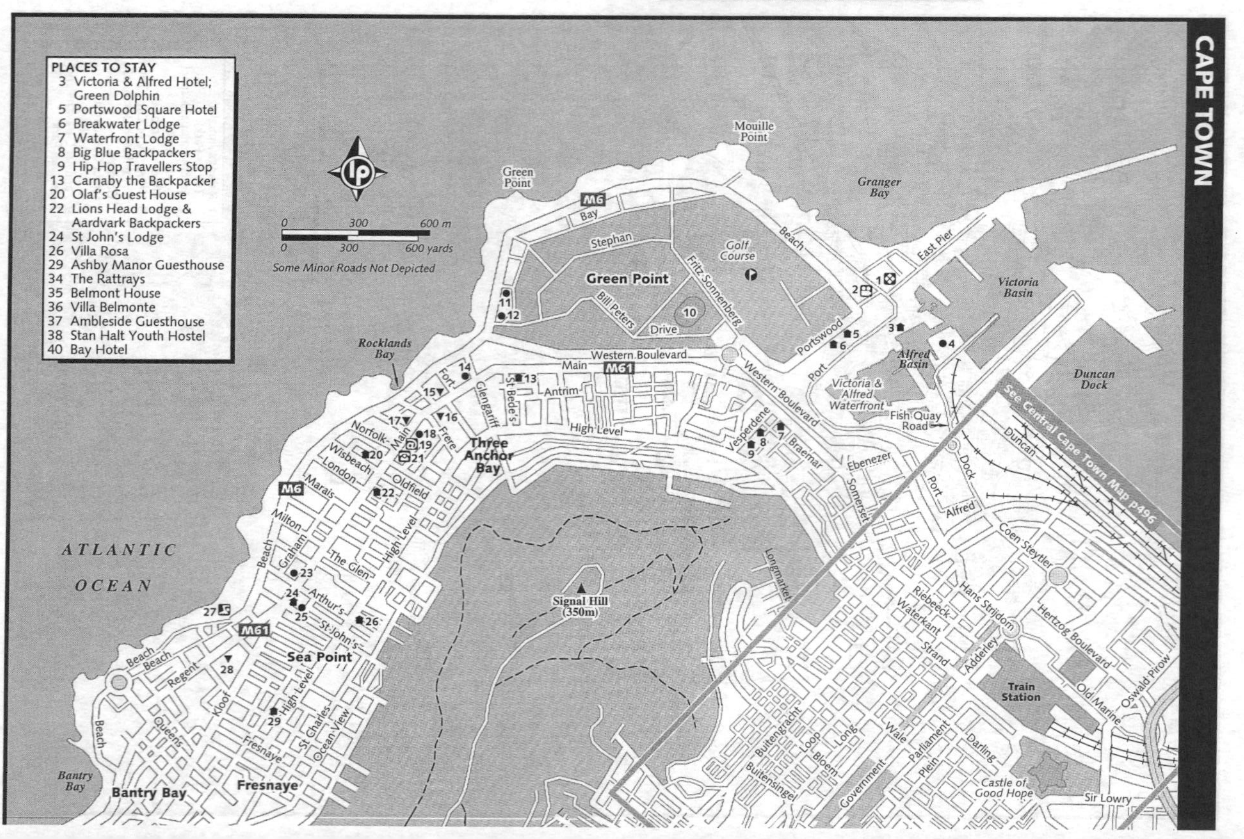
CAPE TOWN
PLACES TO STAY
3 Victoria & Alfred Hotel; Green Dolphin
5 Portswood Square Hotel
6 Breakwater Lodge
7 Waterfront Lodge
8 Big Blue Backpackers
9 Hip Hop Travellers Stop
13 Carnaby the Backpacker
20 Olaf's Guest House
22 Lions Head Lodge & Aardvark Backpackers
24 St John's Lodge
26 Villa Rosa
29 Ashby Manor Guesthouse
34 The Rattrays
35 Belmont House
36 Villa Belmonte
37 Ambleside Guesthouse
38 Stan Halt Youth Hostel
40 Bay Hotel
0 300 600 m
0 300 600 yards
Some Minor Roads Not Depicted
ATLANTIC OCEAN
See Central Cape Town Map p496
Green Point
Mouille Point
Granger Bay
Victoria Basin
Duncan Dock
Alfred Basin
Victoria & Alfred Waterfront
Golf Course
Rocklands Bay
Three Anchor Bay
Signal Hill (350m)
Sea Point
Fresnaye
Bantry Bay
Train Station
Castle of Good Hope

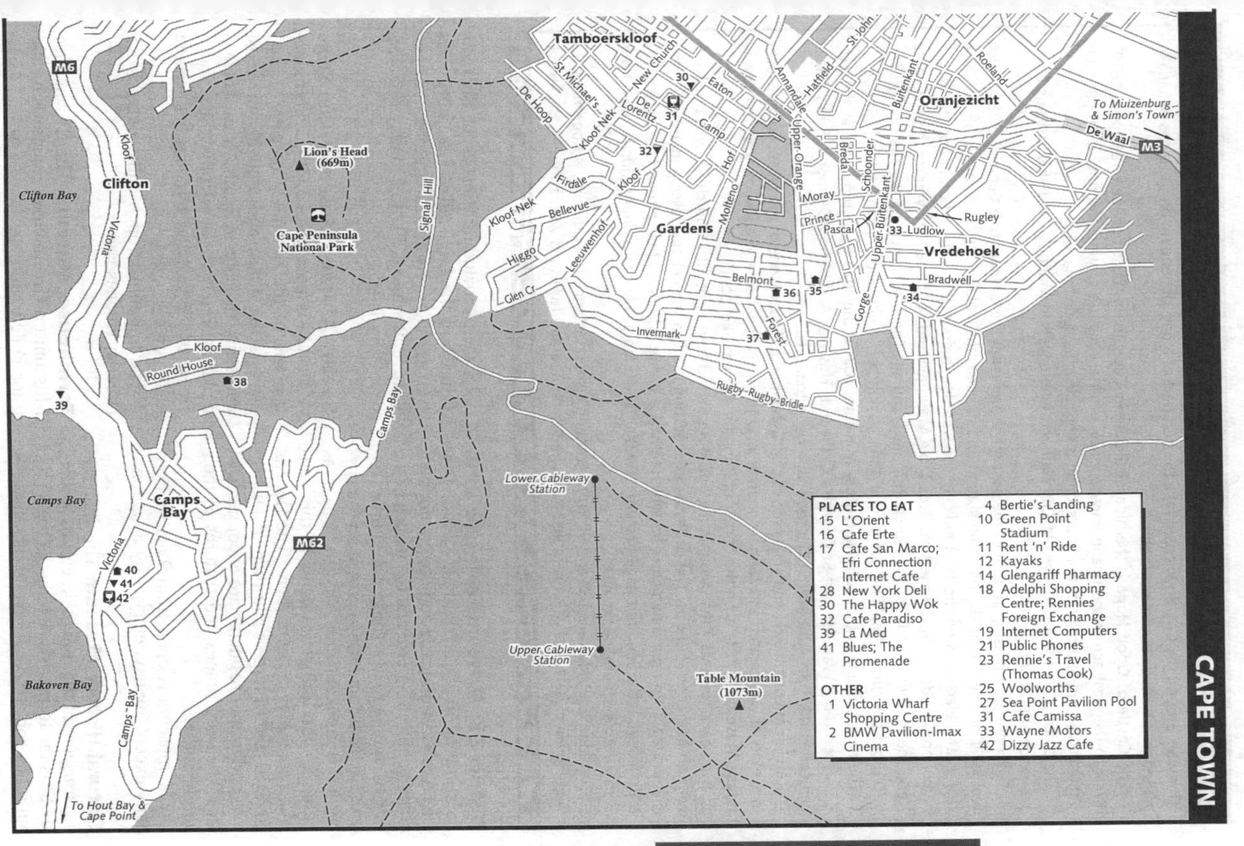
CAPE TOWN
PLACES TO EAT
15 L'Orient
16 Cafe Erte
17 Cafe San Marco; Efri Connection Internet Cafe
28 New York Deli
30 The Happy Wok
32 Cafe Paradiso
39 La Med
41 Blues; The Promenade
OTHER
1 Victoria Wharf Shopping Centre
2 BMW Pavilion-Imax Cinema
4 Bertie's Landing
10 Green Point Stadium
11 Rent 'n' Ride
12 Kayaks
14 Glengariff Pharmacy
18 Adelphi Shopping Centre; Rennies Foreign Exchange
19 Internet Computers
21 Public Phones
23 Rennie's Travel (Thomas Cook)
25 Woolworths
27 Sea Point Pavilion Pool
31 Cafe Camissa
33 Wayne Motors
42 Dizzy Jazz Cafe
Tamboerskloof
Oranjezicht
Gardens
Vredehoek
To Muizenburg & Simon's Town
De Waal
M3
M6
M62
Clifton
Clifton Bay
Camps Bay
Camps Bay
Bakoven Bay
Lion's Head (669m)
Cape Peninsula National Park
Signal Hill
Lower Cableway Station
Upper Cableway Station
Table Mountain (1073m)
Kloof
Round House
Victoria
Kloof Nek
To Hout Bay & Cape Point

City Sights & Walking Tour

This walk around the City Bowl could take the best part of a day, depending on the stops you make, although it is only about 6km long.

The **Castle of Good Hope** is the oldest building in Cape Town (built between 1666 and 1679). Walk to the west across the **Grand Parade**, once a military parade ground and now a car park. On Wednesday and Saturday morning a section is kept clear for a flea market.

The balcony on the impressive old **City Hall** was where Nelson Mandela made his first public appearance after being freed.

Turn right after passing in front of the post office and enter the **Golden Acre Centre** (1978), which was built on the site of the old train station and dubbed 'the golden acre' because of its valuable real estate. Black tiles on the floor indicate the waterline before land reclamation in the 1930s.

Exit onto Adderley St, turn left towards Table Mountain and continue until you reach the **Groote Kerk**, the mother church for the Dutch Reformed Church. The first church on the site was built in 1704, but the current building dates from 1841. A number of early notables have tombs inside.

The next building is the **Cultural History Museum**. Follow the road as it turns right at the gardens (becoming Wale St) past **St George's Cathedral**. This was Archbishop Desmond Tutu's Anglican cathedral. Turn right into St George's St, a pedestrian mall.

Turn left at Longmarket and you come out on **Greenmarket Square**, one of the most pleasant spots in the city. It was created as a farmers' market in 1710 and is now home to a flea market. The **Townhouse Museum** (1761) is on the corner of Burg and Longmarket Sts.

Walk back towards Table Mountain along Burg St and turn right into Church St, which is lined with art and antique shops. The pedestrianised section is a flea market specialising in antiques and bric-a-brac. Turn right down **Long St**, which retains a strong historical atmosphere. One of the oldest buildings is the **Sendinnestig Museum** (1802) at No 40, originally a missionary church (open from 9.15 am to 4.15 pm weekdays).

Continue until you reach Strand St. Turn right and a short distance on your right is **Koopmans de Wet House** (1701), a classic example of a Cape townhouse and furnished with antiques. Backtrack

District Six Museum During the apartheid era the lively mixed-race suburb District Six was bulldozed and the government changed the street grid and the names of the few remaining roads. Today, the simple District Six Museum (☎ 461 8745) on the corner of Buitenkant and Albertus Sts is as much *for* the former residents of this vanished area as it is about them. The floor is covered with a large-scale map of District Six, and former residents are encouraged to label their old homes and features of their neighbourhood.

The museum is open from 9 am to 4 pm daily except Sunday; entry is by donation.

Cultural History Museum This interesting museum at the mountain end of Adderley St is the former slave lodge of the VOC, but it has gone through several incarnations since then – including stints as the Supreme Court and the Legislative Assembly – as well as major physical alterations. It's open from 9.30 am to 4.30 pm Monday to Saturday; entry is R5.

South African Museum The South African Museum (☎ 424 3330), at the mountain end of the Botanic (Company's) Gardens, is the oldest and arguably the most interesting museum in South Africa. There is a planetarium here – a visit may help northerners understand the southern hemisphere night sky.

The museum is open daily; entry is R5 (free on Wednesday).

Townhouse Museum The Townhouse Museum on Greenmarket Square is an old Cape Dutch building.

City Sights & Walking Tour

along Strand St passing, on the right-hand side in the block before Buitengragt, the old **Lutheran Church**, which was converted from a warehouse in 1780.

Cross Buitengragt, and you enter the old **Cape Muslim Quarter**, the historical residential suburb for the descendants of the Asian slaves and political prisoners imported by the Dutch. The steep streets, some of which are still cobbled, and 18th-century flat-roofed houses and mosques are still home to a strong Muslim community.

Turn left down Rose St, which after a couple of hundred metres forms a T-intersection with Wale St. Here you will find a restored house, the **Bo-Kaap Museum**, which gives an insight into the lifestyle of a 19th-century Muslim family.

Walk down the hill, cross Buitengragt and keep going until you reach Long St. Turn right into Long St and follow it until it becomes Orange St. The **Long St Baths** on the corner are still in operation. Turn left into Orange St, and left again into Grey's Pass, which takes you past the excellent **South African Museum**.

From here, you enter the top end of the **Botanical Gardens**, also known as the Company's Gardens. This is the surviving six hectares of van Riebeeck's vegetable garden which provided fresh produce for the VOC's ships. The gardens are open from 9.30 am to 4 pm daily.

On the southern side of Government Ave (Wale St end), are the **Houses of Parliament**. Continue towards the mountain, and past **De Tuynhuys**, the president's office, which has been restored to its 1795 appearance. Next on the left, on the south-eastern side of the gardens, is the **South African National Gallery**.

Leave the gardens by Gallery Lane and turn left into St Johns (towards the bay), take the next left and then next right into Parliament St. This takes you through to **Church Square**, where the burghers would unhitch their wagons while they attended the Groote Kerk. Slaves were auctioned under a tree in the square.

Continue down Parliament, keeping your eyes open for the Art Deco details on the buildings. Turn right on Darling St and you're back at the Grand Parade where you started. Phew!

It houses dour Dutch and Flemish art from the 16th and 17th centuries. The museum is worth visiting for the views from the balcony overlooking the bustling square. It is open from 10 am to 5 pm daily; entry is free.

National Gallery

This small but exquisite gallery (☎ 465 1628) in the Botanical Gardens has some interesting exhibitions which begin to redress the imbalance from the apartheid days. There is a shop and a cafe. The gallery is open from 10 am to 5 pm daily except Monday; entry is free.

Houses of Parliament

On the southern side of Government Ave (Wale St end) are the Houses of Parliament (☎ 403 2911), which were opened in 1885. During the parliamentary session (usually January to June) gallery tickets are available; overseas tourists may have to present their passports.

During the recess (usually July to January) there are free guided tours (☎ 403 2198) at 11 am and 2 pm weekdays. Go to the Old Parliament building entrance on Parliament St.

Castle of Good Hope

The Castle of Good Hope was constructed between 1666 and 1679 and is one of the oldest European structures in Southern Africa.

It is still a military base but visitors are welcome. There are a couple of museums with collections of furniture, paintings and interesting temporary exhibitions. Guided tours leave at 11 am, noon and 2 pm; entry (from Grand Parade) is R12.

Robben Island

A tour of Robben Island, where former president Nelson Mandela was held prisoner for 27 years, is an unforgettable experience.

Tours (☎ 419 1300) run from Jetty 1 at the Waterfront. A high speed boat leaves on the hour between 9 am and 3 pm daily. You should get to the ticket office (near the Clocktower) early on the day you want to go, as tours are popular.

What makes this tour special are the prison guides who are ex-political prisoners; many of them were held here during Mandela's imprisonment. Our guide, when asked how many years he had been in prison, answered 5,590 days (about 15 years). The guides are happy to answer any questions you ask them about their personal experiences. Their answers are direct, personal and shocking: there is no tourist gimmick at work here.

Amazingly, the guides are without bitterness. They wish to keep the history of the prison and its criminal past alive for reconciliation, not for the sake of revenge. After the prison, a bus ride around the island reveals an interesting history, including the remnants of a leper colony, some WWII bunkers and two 19th-century churches. The view of Cape Town and Table Mountain from the island is stunning.

The tour takes three hours and costs R100.

Noon Gun & Signal Hill

Signal Hill separates Sea Point from the City Bowl. There are magnificent views from the 350m-high summit, especially at night. At noon (daily except Sunday) a cannon is fired, and can be heard throughout the city. Head up Kloof Nek Rd from the city and take the turn-off to the right at the top of the hill.

Table Mountain & Cableway

You *must* go up the mountain! The views from the top are phenomenal and there are some excellent walks on the flat summit.

Cable cars don't operate when it's dangerously windy, and there's not much point going up if you're going to be wrapped in cloud. To see if they're operating call ☎ 424 8181. They run from about 7.30 am to 9 pm; the return fare is about R60. If you don't like heights keep in mind that the cableway took its 10 millionth passenger up the mountain a few years ago and there has never been a fatality.

There's a small ***restaurant*** and shop at the top. To get to the lower cableway station, catch the Kloof Nek bus from outside OK Bazaars in Adderley St to the Kloof Nek terminus and connect with the cableway bus. By car, take Kloof Nek Rd and turn off to the left (signposted).

Victoria & Alfred Waterfront

The Victoria & Alfred Waterfront is pitched at tourists, but it's atmospheric, buzzing and packed with restaurants, bars and interesting shops. There is an information centre (☎ 418 2369), which is open daily.

A **cruise** into Table Bay should not be missed. Go to Waterfront Charters (☎ 418 0134), Port Captain's building, Pier Head (across from Bertie's Landing) for a variety of cruises, including a half-hour cruise for just R10.

The **aquarium** is well worth a visit. The kelp forest tank is astounding, and it will make you wonder why you've never done a dive course. It's open from 9.30 am to 6 pm daily; entry is R34.

Shuttle buses run from Adderley St up Strand St, with a stop near the Intercontinental Hotel, to the centre of the Waterfront. They also leave from near the Pavilion Pool in Sea Point. Departures are half-hourly from early to late and cost R1.20.

Kirstenbosch Botanical Gardens

The Kirstenbosch Botanical Gardens (☎ 762 1166) on Rhodes Dr, Constantia, is one of the most beautiful gardens in the world. In 1895, Cecil Rhodes purchased the eastern slopes of Table Mountain; he bequeathed the property to the nation on his death in 1902.

The gardens are devoted almost exclusively to indigenous plants and have about 9000 of Southern Africa's 22,000 plant species. The information office (open daily) has maps and gives advice on various walks.

The gardens are open year-round from 8 am, closing at 7 pm from September to March, and 6 pm from April to August; entry is R10.

Groot Constantia

Groot Constantia is the oldest vineyard in the Cape, and one of the grandest. It was built by Governor Simon van der Stel in 1692. In the 18th century, Constantia wines were exported around the world and were highly acclaimed. Fine wines are still produced here.

Though a bit of a tourist trap, it's still worth visiting. For R10 you can taste five wines; there are also cellar tours (R9; tastings are free if you do the tour).

A visit to Groot Constantia could easily be combined with a visit to Kirstenbosch Botanical Gardens. Unfortunately there is no direct public transport to either.

Atlantic Coast

The Atlantic coast here has some of the most spectacular scenery in the world. The beaches include the trendiest on the Cape, with the emphasis on sunbaking rather than swimming – the water comes straight from the Antarctic.

For the areas south or west of the City Bowl, buses and minibus taxis run along Victoria Rd from the city to Hout Bay.

Bloubergstrand & Table View Bloubergstrand, 25km to the north of the city on Table Bay, is the site of the 1806 battle between British and Dutch forces that resulted in the second British occupation of the Cape. This is also the spot with the most dramatic (and photographed) view of Table Mountain.

Unfortunately, you'll need a car. Take the R27 north from the N1.

Sea Point Sea Point is a bustling residential suburb and Main Rd is lined with restaurants and shops. The coast is rocky and swimming is dangerous but there are four tidal swimming pools. The Sea Point Pavilion Pool (at the end of Clarens St) is open from 8.30 am to dusk; entry is R4.

Clifton There are four linked beaches at Clifton accessible by steps from Victoria Rd. They're the trendiest, busiest beaches on the Cape. Fourth Beach, at the Camps Bay end, is the most accessible and is popular with families. First Beach is the place to be seen.

Camps Bay Camps Bay is often windy and is not as trendy as Clifton, but it is more spectacular. The Twelve Apostles running south from Table Mountain tumble into the sea above the broad stretch of white sand. There are no lifesavers, but strong surf, so take care.

Hout Bay Hout Bay has a stunning setting and still retains something of its village atmosphere. The southern arm of the bay is an important fishing port.

The information centre (☎ 790 4053) is in the Trading Post store on the main road. The ***Mariners Wharf complex*** is the best place to eat, drink and buy fresh seafood.

Buses to Hout Bay (R5.30) leave from outside OK Bazaars. There are several before 9 am, a few in the middle of the day and several between 2.15 and 5.30 pm.

Chapman's Peak Drive This 10km drive is cut into the side of sheer mountain walls. There are great views over Chapman's Bay and back to the Sentinel and Hout Bay. It is one of the world's great scenic drives.

Kommetjie This is just a smallish crayfishing village but it's the focal point for surfing on the Cape, offering an assortment of reefs that hold a very big swell. There's a ***caravan park*** here.

False Bay

False Bay lies to the south-east of the city. Although the beaches on the east side of the peninsula are not quite as scenically spectacular as those on the Atlantic side, the water is much warmer.

During October and November, False Bay is a favoured haunt for whales and their

Apartheid & the Townships

In 1948 the newly elected National Party declared the western half of the Cape Province a 'coloured preference area', which meant no black could be employed unless it could be proved there was no suitable coloured person for the job. No new black housing was built. As a result, illegal squatter camps mushroomed on the sandy plains to the east of Cape Town. Government bulldozers would flatten the shanties, and their occupants were dragged away and dumped in their Homelands. Within weeks, the shanties would rise again.

District Six, just to the east of the city centre, was the suburb that, more than any other, gave Cape Town its cosmopolitan atmosphere and life. It was primarily a coloured ghetto, but people of every race lived there. It was a poor, overcrowded, but vibrant community. The streets were alive and jazz was its lifeblood.

This state of affairs did not appeal to the government so, in 1966, District Six was classified as a white area. Fifty thousand people, some of whose families had been there for five generations, were evicted and dumped in bleak townships such as Athlone, Mitchell's Plain and Atlantis.

The government tried for decades to eradicate the squatter towns, such as Crossroads, which were focal points for black resistance to apartheid. In its last attempt between May and June 1986, an estimated 70,000 people were driven from their homes and hundreds were killed.

calves; southern right, humpback and bryde (**bree**-dah) whales are the most commonly sighted.

On weekdays trains run between Cape Town and Fish Hoek via Muizenberg every half hour to 9 pm; every hour one continues through to Simon's Town. On weekends nearly all trains run through to Simon's Town, and they're more or less hourly. Cape Town to Muizenberg is R6.50/3.50 in 1st/3rd class, Simon's Town is R8/4.

Simon's Town (Simonstad) Named after Simon van der Stel, an early governor, this town was the VOC's winter anchorage. The British turned the harbour into a naval base in 1814 and it has remained one ever since.

There's an information bureau (☎ 786 2436) at the Simon's Town Museum (off the main road about 600m south of the train station); both are open daily. Next door is the Navy Museum, open from 9 am to 4 pm daily. **Seaforth Beach** is the nearest to Simon's Town and a good family swimming spot. A bit further on is the **Boulders**, an area with attractive coves among large boulders.

Cape of Good Hope Nature Reserve

This is a beautiful peninsula. There are numerous walks, beaches, the Cape's unique flora (*fynbos*) as well as baboon, antelope and abundant birdlife.

The reserve (☎ 780 9526) is open from 7 am to 6 pm daily; entry is R10 per person. Maps and firewood are available at the gate, and there are picnic places, a kiosk and restaurant.

The only public transport to the Cape is with Rikki's (which runs those Asian-style mini-minibuses). They run from Simon's Town and cost about R70 per hour. Numerous tours include Cape Point on their itineraries. Day Trippers (☎ 531 3274) and possibly other backpacker-oriented companies take along mountain bikes.

Cape Flats

For the majority of Cape Town's inhabitants, home is in one of the grim townships on the Cape Flats: Guguletu, Nyanga, Philippi, Mitchell's Plain, Crossroads or Khayelitsha. Visiting without a companion who has local knowledge would be foolish. If a black friend is happy to escort you, you should have no problems, and tours have operated safely for years (see Organised Tours later in this chapter).

Diving

Cape Town has a wide variety of diving possibilities as the Agulhas and Benguela

Currents create a unique cross section of marine conditions. There are several dive operators, such as Sheer Blue Adventures (☎ 439 3710) at 152 Main Rd, Sea Point. A certificate course costs about R900.

Surfing

The Cape Peninsula has fantastic surfing possibilities: from gentle shorebreaks ideal for beginners to monsters for experts only.

In general, the best surf is along the Atlantic side, and there is a string of breaks from Bloubergstrand through to the Cape of Good Hope. Most of these breaks work best in south-easterly conditions.

The Surf Centre (☎ 423 7853) at 70 Loop St in the city centre has a good stock of wetsuits and second-hand boards; it also hires boards and wetsuits.

Hiking & Walking

There are some fantastic hikes around the peninsula. Shirley Brossy's *Walking Guide to Table Mountain* (R35) details 34 routes. Mike Lundy's *Best Walks in the Cape Peninsula* (R45) is also useful. Cape Town Tourism also has information about various guided walks.

Walking up (or down) Table Mountain is definitely possible. It's safe enough if you are properly prepared with warm clothing and emergency food and water, and if you stick to the path. The trouble is, thick mists can make the paths invisible, and you just have to wait until they lift. Always tell someone where you are going and never walk alone. None of the routes are easy, but the Platteklip Gorge walk on the City Bowl side is at least straightforward. You can get a one-way ticket back down on the cableway.

Serious technical climbers should get in touch with the Mountain Club of South Africa (☎ 465 3412) at 97 Hatfield St.

Other Activities

Several **canoeing** operators run short trips from Cape Town (as well as their regular longer trips). Felix Unite (☎ 762 6935) is the major operator and has a good reputation.

Abseiling off Table Mountain (or Chapman's Peak, depending on the weather) with Abseil Africa (☎ 424 1580) costs R195 (plus the cableway fare, if applicable). On Thursday and Saturday they also have day tours to **'Kamikazi Kanyon'** (R350), which include hiking, kloofing and abseiling through a waterfall.

Hostels are usually a good source of information on most activities and budget tour companies. Day Trippers (☎ 531 3274) gets excellent feedback.

Organised Tours

For a quick orientation on a fine day, you can't beat Topless Tours (☎ 448 2888), which runs a roofless double-decker bus. The two-hour city tour (R40) between Dock Rd at the Waterfront and the train station departs six times a day.

Major tour companies include Springbok Atlas Tours (☎ 417 6545) and Hylton Ross (☎ 511 1784). There are many others: ask at Cape Town Tourism.

One City Tours (☎ 387 5351) runs highly recommended township tours of the Cape Flats and we've had very positive feedback about township tours conducted by Legend Tours (☎ 448 0625).

Tana-Baru Tours (☎ 424 0719, fax 423 5579) offers a two-hour walk or drive through Bo-Kaap (the Malay quarter). Shereen Habib lives in the area and is an excellent guide. Tours cost R70.

Court Helicopters (☎ 425 2966) has 20-minute flights from near the Waterfront to Hout Bay then back to Table Mountain and down over the City Bowl. The flights are spectacular and there are various deals – you could end up paying just R300 per person for a front seat. There is also a sunset flight.

For information on boat cruises, see the Victoria & Alfred Waterfront section earlier.

Places to Stay

There is a huge number of options in Cape Town and most people will easily find something that suits their pocket; keep in mind that in the high season – basically December to Easter – prices can double and many places are fully booked.

There is a huge and increasing range of cheap hostels aimed at backpackers. Listed

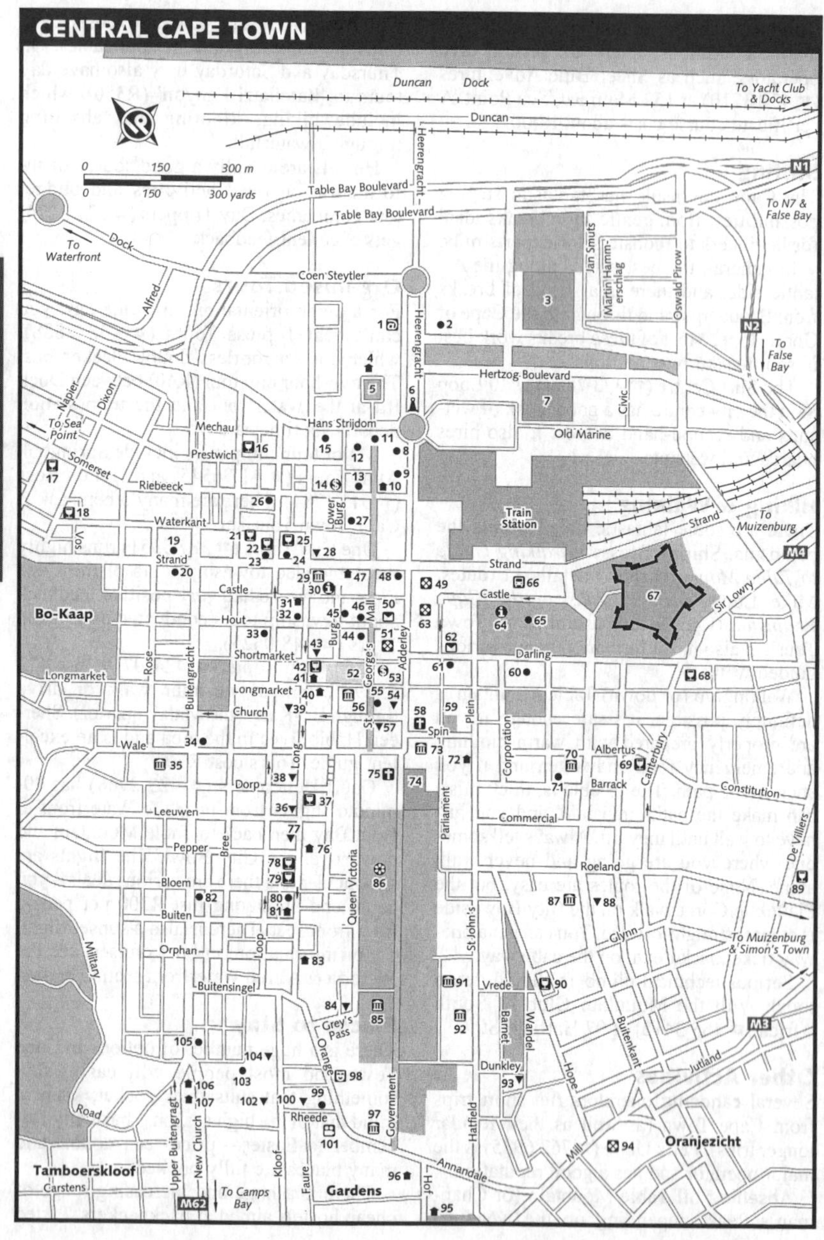
CENTRAL CAPE TOWN
Duncan Dock
Duncan
To Yacht Club & Docks
0 150 300 m
0 150 300 yards
Table Bay Boulevard
Table Bay Boulevard
Heerengracht
To N7 & False Bay
To Waterfront
Dock
Coen Steytler
Alfred
Jan Smuts
Martin Hammerschlag
Oswald Pirow
To False Bay
Hertzog Boulevard
Civic
Old Marine
Napier
Dixon
To Sea Point
Mechau
Hans Strijdom
Prestwich
Somerset
Riebeeck
Waterkant
Lower Burg
Train Station
Strand
To Muizenburg
Strand
Strand
Castle
Castle
Sir Lowry
Vos
Bo-Kaap
Hout
Shortmarket
Burg
St George's Mall
Adderley
Darling
Longmarket
Longmarket
Rose
Buitengracht
Church
Spin
Plein
Corporation
Wale
Long
Albertus
Canterbury
Barrack
Constitution
Dorp
Leeuwen
Commercial
Parliament
De Villiers
Pepper
Bree
Queen Victoria
Roeland
Bloem
Buiten
Loop
Glynn
To Muizenburg & Simon's Town
Orphan
St John's
Military
Buitensingel
Vrede
Grey's Pass
Barnet
Wandel
Buitenkant
Orange
Jutland
Dunkley
Hope
Road
Rheede
Government
Hatfield
Mill
Oranjezicht
Upper Buitengragt
New Church
Kloof
Faure
Annandale
Hof
Tamboerskloof
Carstens
To Camps Bay
Gardens
N1
N2
M4
M3
M62
1 2 3 4 5 6 7 8 9 10 11 12 13 14 15 16 17 18 19 20 21 22 23 24 25 26 27 28 29 30 31 32 33 34 35 36 37 38 39 40 41 42 43 44 45 46 47 48 49 50 51 52 53 54 55 56 57 58 59 60 61 62 63 64 65 66 67 68 69 70 71 72 73 74 75 76 77 78 79 80 81 82 83 84 85 86 87 88 89 90 91 92 93 94 95 96 97 98 99 100 101 102 103 104 105 106 107

CENTRAL CAPE TOWN

PLACES TO STAY
4 Diplomat Holiday Flats
10 Holiday Inn Garden Court St George's Mall
31 Metropole Hotel
40 Tudor Hotel
41 Holiday Inn Garden Court Greenmarket Square
47 Intercontinental Hotel
72 Townhouse Hotel
76 Long St Backpackers
81 Travellers Inn
83 Cat & Moose
95 Ashanti Lodge
96 Mount Nelson Hotel
106 The Backpack & Africa Travel Centre
107 Zebra Crossing

PLACES TO EAT
28 Spur Steakhouse
36 Sooz Baguette Bar
38 Yellow Pepper
39 Cafe Mozart
43 Nino's
54 Off Moroka Cafe Africaine
57 Mark's Coffee Shop
77 Mr Pickwicks Deli
84 Kaapse Tafel Restaurant
88 Perseverance Tavern
93 Roxy's Coffee Bar
100 Mario's Coffee Shop
102 Cafe Bar Deli
104 Rozenhof

ENTERTAINMENT
3 Nico Malan
16 Brunswick Hotel
17 The Bronx
18 Cafe Manhattan
21 Crow Bar
22 The Drunken Springbok
25 The Rockin' Shamrock; Bourbons
37 169 on Long
42 Purple Turtle; Virtual Turtle; Sturk's Tobacconist
68 District Six Cafe
69 The Fringe
78 Mama Africa
79 The Lounge
89 The Shed
90 Stag's Head Hotel
98 Little Theatre
101 Labia Cinema

MUSEUMS
29 Koopmans de Wet House
35 Bo-Kaap Museum
56 Townhouse Museum
70 District Six Museum
73 Cultural History Museum
85 South African Museum
87 Rust-en-Vreugd
91 National Gallery
92 Jewish Museum
97 Bertram House

OTHER
1 Connection Internet C@fe
2 Broadway Centre
5 Tulbagh Square
6 Jan & Maria van Riebeeck Statues
7 Civic Centre
8 British Airways Travel Clinic
9 Trustbank Centre
11 American Express; Trustbank Centre
12 Thibault Square
13 Southern Life Centre
14 Rennies Foreign Exchange
15 BP Centre
19 Budget
20 Avis
23 Hertz
24 Imperial Car Rental
26 STA Travel
27 Namibia Trade & Tourism
30 Cape Town Tourism; Western Cape Tourism; Baz Bus Booking Office; Internet Cafe
32 National Parks Board Office
33 Surf Centre
34 Tempest Car Rental
44 Pezulu
45 Ulrich Naumann's
46 Rennies Travel (Thomas Cook)
48 Woolworths
49 Golden Acre Centre
50 Post Net
51 Stuttaford's Town Square
52 Greenmarket Square; Cycles
53 BOB (First National Bank)
55 Rennies Travel
58 Groote Kerk
59 Church Square
60 Town Hall
61 Lite Kem Pharmacy
62 GPO
63 OK Bazaars
64 Bus Information Kiosk
65 Grand Parade
66 Main Bus Station
67 Castle of Good Hope
71 Department of Home Affairs
74 Houses of Parliament
75 St George's Cathedral
80 The Junk Shop
82 Alisa Car Rental
86 Botanical (Company's) Gardens
94 Gardens Centre; Holiday Flats
99 Spar Supermarket
103 Le Cap Motorcycle Hire
105 Afrogem

below are a few favourites. You'll find brochures about the rest at Cape Town Tourism.

Places to Stay – Budget

Caravan Parks There are no central caravan parks. In Muizenberg, the ***Zandvlei Caravan Park*** *(☎ 788 5215)* on The Row is about 2km from Muizenberg train station and about 1km from the beach. Sites cost R70 for two people.

Hostels – City Bowl One of the best hostels in town is ***The Backpack*** *(☎ 423 4530, ⓔ backpack@gem.co.za, 74 New Church St)*. Dorms are R50, and spacious doubles are R150. Check out its Web site at www.backpackers.co.za, which also includes information on tours and activities available from the Africa Travel Centre (based at the hostel). The hostel is a short walk from the train station, or you can catch the Kloof Nek bus from outside OK Bazaars.

SOUTH AFRICA

A few doors up is the friendly ***Zebra Crossing*** *(☎/fax 422 1265, 82 New Church St)*, which is smaller, quieter and more personal. It's also slightly cheaper.

There are loads of hostels springing up on Long St. One we recommend is ***Long St Backpackers*** *(☎ 423 0615, 209 Long St)*. This bustling place is in the thick of things on this busy strip and it's very friendly; a dorm is R50 and a double is R110.

A bit further down Long St, ***Cat & Moose*** *(☎ 423 7638)* near the Long St Baths is a dizzy warren of rooms, set around a garden courtyard in a 1791 historic building. Dorms are R35 and doubles are R100.

The ***Ashanti Lodge*** *(☎ 423 8721, 11 Hof St, Gardens)* is in a huge rambling mansion that includes a travel centre for backpackers. There's a bar and cafe upstairs and a terrific view of Table Mountain. Dorms are R50 and doubles are R130.

Hostels – Waterfront & Sea Point Areas Not too far from the Waterfront and the city, the ***Waterfront Lodge*** *(☎ 439 1404, 6 Braemar Rd)* is a pleasant spot. There's a good bar (also doing teas, coffees and snacks), and a couple of swimming pools. Dorms are R45 and double/triple rooms are R145 per person.

Hip Hop Travellers Stop *(☎ 439 2104, 11 Vesperdene Rd, Green Point)* describes itself as being on the Waterfront. It isn't, but it *is* one of the closest hostels to the Waterfront. The hostel also describes itself as lively – and it is that. Dorms are R40 and doubles are R120.

Close by and still to define its character is the new ***Big Blue Backpackers*** *(☎ 439 0807, 7 Vesperdene Rd, Green Point)*. This imposing 1905 mansion, complete with chandeliers, has grand staircases leading up to 22 rooms. It has great potential and the owners are busy upgrading and renovating the facilities. Huge triple rooms cost R120.

Carnaby the Backpacker *(☎ 439 7410)* on the corner of Main Rd and St Bede's St, Sea Point, is a large, converted, old hotel. It's cheap and pretty good, if a bit impersonal. Dorms cost R50; singles/doubles (most with bathroom, TV and phone) are from R90/140.

Hostels – Camps Bay A national monument in a beautiful position with a great view, the ***Stan Halt Youth Hostel*** *(☎ 438 9037)* at The Glen, Camps Bay, is very easygoing. Dorms (only) are R35 and meals are available. This would be a good place to spend a few days recuperating from an overdose of nightlife. Take the Kloof Nek bus from outside OK Bazaars (R2.60) to the top of Kloof Nek, then take the road to the right.

Guesthouses Perhaps over-trading on its old world charm is the ***Travellers Inn*** *(☎ 424 9272, 208 Long St)*, in one of the gracious wrought-iron decorated buildings. There is, however, a fantastic balcony overlooking Long St. Rooms start at R130/160 in the low season, including a get-your-own breakfast.

Places to Stay – Mid-Range

The Bed 'n Breakfast organisation (☎ 683 3505, fax 683 5159) has members around the Cape Peninsula. Prices start at around R110/140 per person in the low/high seasons. You can pay a lot more than this. Alternatively try the accommodation booking service at Cape Town Tourism.

There are several agencies letting furnished houses and flats, including Cape Holiday Homes (☎ 419 0430, PO Box 2044, Cape Town 8000), 31 Heerengracht.

Most of the good-value hotels are in and around the city centre.

City Bowl A small but comfortable guesthouse overlooking the City Bowl, ***Belmont House*** *(☎ 461 5417, 10 Belmont Ave, Oranjezicht)* charges from R120/200. There are kitchen facilities.

A place that prides itself on its peaceful ambience – staff will bring you breakfast in bed – is the ***Ambleside Guesthouse*** *(☎ 465 2503, 11 Forest Rd, Oranjezicht)*. There are comfortable singles/doubles and family rooms. Doubles start at R190.

The Rattrays *(☎ 461 2116, 8 Bradwell Rd, Vredehoek)* has large rooms with kitchenettes. Its friendly hosts charge about R200 a double. Book early as it's popular.

Diplomat Holiday Flats *(☎ 419 5150)* is on Tulbagh Square near the train station.

The flats are old-fashioned and a bit grubby but central and cheap. There is a huge array of rates and seasons, but basically the low season rate for a single-bedroom self-catering flat is R150 a double.

Gardens Centre Holiday Flats (*☎ 461 8000)* is in the distinctive multistorey building on Mill St, Gardens. The single-bedroom self-catering flats start at about R200 a double, doubling in price in peak times.

With a great position right in the middle of town, the ***Tudor Hotel*** (*☎ 424 1335)*, on Greenmarket Square, is small and could do with renovation but it's OK. Rooms start at R195/260, including breakfast.

The ***Metropole Hotel*** (*☎ 423 6363, 38 Long St)* is a charming old-style hotel that has recently been revamped and has clean rooms (with TV, phone and bathroom) at R176.75. There are also executive rooms for about R60 extra, but the standard rooms are better value. There's secure parking at night for an extra R6 – well worth it.

Waterfront Area The ***Breakwater Lodge*** (*☎ 406 1911)* on Portswood Rd has a great location but it's a renovated tertiary institution and the rooms are *tiny*. Rates start at R180/215.

Sea Point ***St John's Lodge*** (*☎ 439 9028, 9 St John's Rd)* on the corner of Main Rd is a bargain, with doubles for R130 and dorms for R40.

Ashby Manor Guesthouse (*☎ 434 1879, fax 439 3572, 242 High Level Rd, Fresnaye)* at the corner of Disandt Ave is a rambling old house on the slopes of Signal Hill above Sea Point. All rooms have a fridge and hand basin and there is a communal kitchen. Doubles go for about R160, and some rooms have great balconies.

Villa Rosa (*☎ 434 2768, 277 High Level Rd)* has well-equipped rooms starting at R195/280 and rising to R245/350 in the peak season.

Excellent value is the efficiently run ***Lions Head Lodge*** (*☎ 434 4163, 319 Main Rd)*, which has rooms and self-catering apartments. The nightly rate in rooms is R190 a double and apartments start at R220 a double out of season. The rates might fall if you stay longer than a day or so and it often has specials. There is also a pub and restaurant here.

Hout Bay In Hout Bay, the ***Chapman's Peak Hotel*** (*☎ 790 1036)* has rooms from R180/300. The rooms aren't flash but it's a relaxed place.

The Beach House Hotel (*☎ 790 4228)*, on Royal Ave, charges R270 a double, including breakfast. No children under 14 allowed.

Places to Stay – Top End

City Bowl Staying at the ***Mount Nelson Hotel*** (*☎ 483 1000, 76 Orange St)* is like stepping back in time to the grand days of the British Empire. Dating from 1899, the hotel is set in seven acres of parkland, a short walk through the Company's Gardens to the city. Don't forget your wallet – mid-season rates start at about R2400!

In complete contrast, the five-star ***Intercontinental Hotel*** (*☎ 488 5100)* on Strand St is a large, modern hotel in the middle of the city with double rooms for R618; there are weekend specials.

Less expensive but still good is the four-star ***Townhouse Hotel*** (*☎ 465 7050, 60 Corporation St)*, which charges from R391/523. Rooms with numbers ending in six have good views of the mountain.

There are a few hotels that are part of the ***Holiday Inn Garden Court*** (*☎ 419 0808, fax 419 7010)* chain, including the one on the corner of Riebeeck St and St George's Mall, where rooms are R359/508.

As well as the hotels, there are some outstanding top-end guesthouses, such as ***Villa Belmonte*** (*☎ 462 1576, fax 462 1579, 33 Belmont Ave, Oranjezicht)*. It's an ornate Italianate villa charging from R670/890.

Waterfront Area The ***Victoria & Alfred Hotel*** (*☎ 419 6677, fax 419 8955)* is right in the middle of the Waterfront. It should definitely be your first choice if you have the money and swimming is not a priority; rooms start at R770/1190.

On the Green Point side of the Waterfront, the ***Portswood Square Hotel*** (*☎ 418 3281,*

SOUTH AFRICA

fax 419 7570) on Portswood Rd is a classy four-star hotel. Rates start at R550.

Sea Point & Camps Bay If you want to be close to a beautiful beach, consider the five-star ***Bay Hotel*** *(☎ 438 4444)*, across the road from the Camps Bay beach. Rooms start at R340 per person in the low season. For a sea view, you'll pay more.

Olaf's Guest House *(☎/fax 439 8943, 24 Wisbeach Rd, Sea Point)* is spotless and very serene; you feel relaxed as soon as you walk in. The owner speaks German and there are doubles starting at R590.

Places to Eat

Cape Town could easily claim to be the gastronomic capital of Southern Africa.

The two main restaurant zones are Main Rd in Sea Point and the Victoria & Alfred Waterfront. Most of the inner neighbourhoods in the City Bowl also have an increasing number of good places to eat.

City Centre On Church St, near the corner of Long St, is the buzzing ***Cafe Mozart***, open from 7am to 3 pm weekdays and on Saturday morning. It's popular with locals at lunchtime and has live music

Mark's Coffee Shop *(105 St George's Mall)* on the corner of Church St has good coffee and reasonably priced light meals.

If it isn't too busy, ***Cycles*** has a pleasant terrace outside the Holiday Inn, overlooking Greenmarket Square. There's a large menu and prices aren't too bad.

Mr Pickwicks Deli *(158 Long St)* is a licensed, deli-style cafe that stays open very late for good snacks and meals. It's just the place to recuperate in a civilised atmosphere after a night out at the clubs.

Not far away, ***Sooz Baguette Bar*** *(150 Long St)* has inexpensive snacks and excellent rolls with a choice of tasty fillings.

At ***Off Moroka Cafe Africaine*** *(120 Adderley St)* near Church St you can eat inexpensive African food in a good atmosphere.

If you're looking for a pleasant place to have lunch in the city centre, try ***Squares*** in Stuttaford's Town Square, overlooking St George's Mall. A good meal will set you back about R50.

Nino's *(☎ 424 7466)*, Greenmarket Square, is a good, Italian-run restaurant and pizzeria. Pizzas start at R26, veal campagnola is R37 and scrumptious foccacias are R20.

Kaapse Tafel Restaurant *(☎ 423 1651, 90 Queen Victoria St)* is a pleasant little restaurant that serves a variety of traditional Cape dishes. There are entrees such as Cape pickled fish (R18), and main courses (mostly R38 or R42) include Malay chicken biryani, *bobotie* (curried mincemeat with a topping of egg) and vegie dishes.

Yellow Pepper *(138 Long St)* has a casual atmosphere and interesting food, with main courses priced under R20. It's worth trying and is open during the day (closed Sunday) and also from 7.30 pm on Friday and Saturday.

Gardens & Tamboerskloof There's a batch of interesting places south of the city centre.

Not far from several hostels, ***Mario's Coffee Shop*** on Rheede St is small and simple but has very cheap meals. A big breakfast is R15.50 and a ridiculously big breakfast is R19.50.

Roxy's Coffee Bar *(☎ 461 4092)* on the corner of Wandel and Dunkley Sts is self-consciously bohemian and serves good coffee and light meals for about R20. It's open from noon to 2 am weekdays, and from 7 pm Saturday. There are free movies on Monday nights and live music on Wednesday nights.

Perseverance Tavern *(☎ 461 2440, 83 Buitenkant)* is a Cape Town gem. It's an old pub built in 1808 and licensed since 1836. In addition to beer (some draught) and an excellent range of wines, they serve decent pub food; pie and mash is R15.

In a recycled building on Kloof St near the corner of Rheede St is the big, snappy ***Cafe Bar Deli***. Open daily except Sunday from breakfast until late and it's usually packed. The food is not only excellent, with an emphasis on fresh and healthy dishes, but it's very good value. Tapas are around R8, pasta R25 and salads R24.

Rozenhof *(☎ 424 1968, 18 Kloof St)* is one of the best restaurants in town, with small but interesting seasonal menus. Despite the good quality it isn't too expensive. Starters and salads are about R26 and most main courses cost about R48.

Cafe Paradiso on the corner of Kloof and Malan St is a trendy but informal upmarket cafe. Pastas are about R30. There's a relaxed bar area as well.

Waterfront Area The quality of the food here is excellent, especially the seafood, and it's a great place to eat outside on a warm evening.

There are loads of good places for coffee and breakfast in the Victoria Wharf shopping centre. One of our favourites is ***Charly's***, where a formidable breakfast (with bottomless coffee) will set you back R25. It also specialises in German cakes and pastries

Upstairs in the same centre, ***Musselcracker Restaurant*** is the perfect place to gorge yourself on a great seafood buffet (R85).

There's also the relaxed, adjoining ***Musselcracker Oyster Bar***, a good place for a quiet drink and some cheaper seafood. Oysters cost R60 a dozen.

Green Dolphin *(☎ 421 7480)* beneath Victoria & Alfred Hotel is a good jazz venue and popular restaurant. It's the only place on the Waterfront with live music nightly. There's a cover charge of R15 (R12 if you don't have a view of the stage). Starters are about R30 and mains about R50.

One of the cheap and cheerful options is ***Ferryman's Tavern*** adjoining Mitchell's Waterfront Brewery. The emphasis is on an interesting variety of freshly brewed beers and good-value pub meals. To give you an idea, a calamari starter is R18, fish and chips cost R25 and steaks are about R40.

Cafe San Marco *(☎ 418 5434)* is the offspring of the San Marco restaurant in Sea Point (see below), and here you can sample some of the famed Italian cooking at lower prices. Pasta costs from R18.

Sea Point A stroll along Main Road will reveal a wide selection of places that will tempt most palates.

On Main Rd near the corner of Frere, ***Café Erté*** is a relaxed and gay-friendly bar and cafe open from 11 am to 5 am. The food is inexpensive and fresh.

There are some good ***coffee shops*** at the Adelphi shopping centre, across the road from San Marco, as well as a ***Falafel King***, and even a ***biltong bar*** for those of you game enough!

A good restaurant with fairly genuine Malaysian and Indonesian dishes is ***L'Orient*** *(☎ 439 6572, 50 Main Rd)*. Most main courses start at around R50. It's open for dinner daily (except Sunday).

San Marco *(☎ 439 2758, 92 Main Rd)* is an excellent formal Italian restaurant. Prices match the quality, with entrees from R25, pasta from R35 and main courses between R40 and R90. It's open daily except Tuesday for dinner, plus lunch on Sunday. The gelataria in front of the restaurant has delicious takeaway gelati and other ice cream.

Further toward Bantry Bay is ***New York Deli*** *(☎ 439 7523, 51 Regent St)*. The food is very fresh and it's a great spot for breakfast or dinner. You're allocated a charge card on arrival and the food that you select (from a central food court) is charged to the card – a novel way of ensuring you forget how much money you've spent.

Camps Bay Upstairs in the Promenade centre, ***Blues*** *(☎ 438 2040)* on Victoria Rd is in a large, airy room overlooking the beach. This is a place to be seen. The menu is interesting and the prices (from about R45) are surprisingly reasonable.

La Med *(☎ 021-438 5600)* is another casual but upmarket place. It's at the Glen Country Club and often has live music.

Entertainment

You can't do without the entertainment guide in the *Weekly Mail & Guardian* (R5). For bookings, contact Computicket (☎ 430 8010). It has outlets in the Golden Acre Centre on Strand St, at the Waterfront and at many other places.

Pubs & Bars Several pubs and bars are listed under Places to Eat.

SOUTH AFRICA

At the Waterfront, ***Cantina Tequila*** is very popular, and the ***Quay 4 Bar*** is nearly always crowded.

The gathering at ***The Lounge*** *(194 Long St)*, a small and relaxed place, tends to the alternative. ***District Six Cafe*** on the corner of Sir Lowry Rd and Darling St is similar but more down-to-earth.

Purple Turtle on Shortmarket St, around the corner from Greenmarket Square, has a relaxed and student pub-like atmosphere. There are meals and bands.

Travellers have recommended ***The Rockin' Shamrock*** on Loop St, particularly if you like dancing on the bar! ***The Drunken Springbok*** across the road is worth a look as well.

Away from the centre but not too far by Rikki's minibus or taxi, ***The Shed*** on De Villiers St, Gardens, is a bar and pool hall that attracts an interesting crowd.

The ***Stag's Head Hotel*** *(71 Hope St, Gardens)* is a very popular grungy pub. It's one of the few English/Australian-style hotels in South Africa.

Clubs Wednesday, Friday and Saturday are the big nights in the clubs. In the city centre, the blocks around Bree, Loop and Long Sts and Waterkant are incredibly lively all night long on summer weekends. The actual entertainment rarely matches this level of activity (most clubs play techno to young suburbanites), but it's a good buzz. Cover charges are about R15.

Clubs in these areas come and go quite rapidly, but some, such as ***Bourbons*** (formerly Cafe Comic Strip) on Loop St, seem to survive.

Around here you'll find other places, such as the wall-shaking ***Crow Bar*** on Waterkant St. ***The Fringe*** *(46 Canterbury St, Gardens)* is a popular club/pub with a student clientele.

Gay & Lesbian Venues There's quite a vibrant gay scene in Cape Town, although exclusively gay and lesbian places can be hard to find. Your first stop should be Cape Town Tourism, where you can pick up a copy of the *Pink Map*.

The Bronx is a small bar and cabaret venue on the corner of Somerset Rd and Napier St between the city and Green Point.

Nearby on Main Rd, ***Angels*** is a mixed dance venue. Not far away is the excellent and gay-friendly ***Cafe Manhattan*** bar and restaurant on the corner of Waterkant and Dixon.

In the city, the ***Brunswick Hotel*** *(17 Bree St)* has drag shows.

Live Music Several music venues are listed under Places to Eat.

Dizzy Jazz Cafe *(☎ 438 2686)* on The Drive, just off Victoria Rd, Camps Bay, has live music from 9 pm nightly. It's a good place to party and the crowd gets cranked. The cover charge is R10 and there's everything from soulful blues to knee-slapping Peruvian pipes, depending on the night.

Mama Africa on the corner of Long and Pepper Sts is a snappy restaurant/bar. There's live African music on the weekends. The music is better than the food.

A good live jazz venue is ***169 on Long***. It's upstairs on the buzzing Upper Long St strip.

Cafe Camissa *(80 Kloof St, Gardens)* is a funky little venue that hosts local bands, often African jazz, on Wednesday and Sunday night. It's a good place to meet locals and travellers and is open late every night.

One of the best venues is a long way from the city. The ***River Club*** *(☎ 448 6117)* near the corner of Station Rd and Liesbeek Parkway, Observatory, often hosts big-name bands. It has a cover charge of about R10.

For classical music, see what's on at the ***City Hall*** *(☎ 462 1250)*, where the Cape Town Symphony has regular concerts. The ***Nico Malan*** complex also has classical music (see Cinema & Theatre later).

Cinema & Theatre The best cinema for 'mainstream alternative' films is the ***Labia Cinema*** *(☎ 424 5927, 68 Orange St, Gardens)*. At the Waterfront there are ***Nu-Metro cinemas*** for commercial fare, a giant-screen ***IMAX cinema*** and in the old Pumphouse, ***Cyberworld***, which has 3D movies for R30.

The ***Baxter Studio*** *(☎ 685 7880)* on Woolsack Rd, Rosebank, and the ***Little Theatre***

(☎ *480 7100)* on Orange St, Gardens are venues for nonmainstream theatre productions.

The various theatres in the *Nico Malan* complex on the foreshore host ballet, opera and more-mainstream theatre.

Shopping

You'll find most things you need at shops in the city centre, but if you hunger for a suburban mall, try stylish Cavendish Mall, off Protea Rd in Claremont.

Crafts There are craft shops all over town, but don't forget that few items come from this area. For traditional crafts you're better off looking in the part of the country from which they originate. There are, however, some township-produced items, such as recycled tin boxes and toys, which make great gifts for family and friends.

The Siyakatala stall in the craft market at the Waterfront sells items made by self-help groups in the townships, and the quality is as good as anywhere. African Image on the corner of Church and Burg Sts has a very interesting range of new and old craftworks and artefacts. Prices are reasonable, eg, flowers made from aluminium cans cost R8 – you can pay R20 elsewhere.

Markets In addition to the specialised markets (see under Crafts) there are markets in Greenmarket Square (daily) and at Green Point (between the Waterfront and Sea Point) on Sunday.

Antiques & Collectables The Junk Shop, on the corner of Long and Bloem Sts, has some intriguing junk from many eras. In the same area there are several good second-hand and antiquarian bookshops. Not far away, in Church St between Long and Burg Sts, is a pedestrian mall where a flea market is held on Thursday, Friday and Saturday (daily in summer). There are also several antique shops around here.

Wine The many wines produced in the Cape are of an extremely high standard and they are very cheap by international standards. Several companies will freight wine home for you, including Vaughan Johnson's Wine Shop (☎ 419 2121, fax 419 0040) at the Waterfront.

Getting There & Away

Air Cape Town has an increasingly busy international airport. Domestically, SAA flies between Cape Town and major centres (see the South Africa Getting Around section).

There are many international airlines with offices in Cape Town. Following is a short list; for others, see the Yellow Pages:

Air France (☎ 421 4760) Golden Acre Centre
British Airways (☎ 683 4203) Noewich Oval, Oakdale Rd, Claremont
KLM-Royal Dutch Airlines (☎ 421 1870) Main Tower, Standard Bank Centre, Heerengracht
Lufthansa (☎ 425 1490) Southern Life Centre, 8 Riebeeck St
Qantas (☎ 683 4203) Norwich Oval, Oakdale Rd, Claremont
SAA (☎ 936 1111, 24 hours) Cape Town airport

Bus All long-distance buses leave from the main train station. Don't forget the Baz Bus (☎ 439 2323), which picks up from hostels; there's a booking desk at Cape Town Tourism. The main bus lines are:

Translux (☎ 449 3333, fax 449 2545) The Translux office is on the Adderley St side of the station block.
Greyhound (☎ 418 4310, fax 418 4315) Runs fewer routes from Cape Town than Translux, and prices are a bit higher.
Intercape Mainliner (☎ 386 4400) Runs some extremely useful services, including along the west and south coasts. Can be a little cheaper than the major companies.

Johannesburg Translux, Greyhound and Intercape run to Jo'burg at least once every day for about R320/350/325 respectively, via either Bloemfontein or Kimberley. Intercape also runs to Johannesburg via Upington for R325.

Garden Route Translux runs at least once daily to Port Elizabeth (R155, 11 hours) via Swellendam (R75), Mossel Bay (R100), Oudtshoorn (R130 – not all services stop here), George (R130), Knysna (R135),

Plettenberg Bay (R140) and Storms River (R155).

Intercape runs the Garden Route twice daily at slightly lower fares. Even cheaper is the weekly Chilwans Bus Services (☎ 934 4786) to Port Elizabeth. It departs from the upper deck of the train station on Friday and returns on Sunday.

If you plan to visit several Garden Route towns, check out the options on the Baz Bus.

Mountain Route Like the Garden Route, the mountain route takes you east from Cape Town, but inland for the first half of the trip. Translux runs to Port Elizabeth (R155) three times a week via Robertson (R75) and Oudtshoorn (R130).

Munnik Coaches (☎ 637 1850) departs from the upper deck at the train station and runs to Montagu via Robertson thrice-weekly for about R50.

Eastern Cape & Durban Translux services to Port Elizabeth (R155, 11 hours) connect with a daily bus to Durban via East London and Umtata. The total trip takes about 24 hours – consider finding a discount air ticket.

A slightly faster Translux service runs to Durban (R265) via Bloemfontein (R245). Greyhound has a direct bus.

West Coast & Namibia Intercape runs to Upington (R185) via Citrusdal (R110) and Clanwilliam (R120). From Upington you can get an Intercape bus to Windhoek (Namibia) for R210. Intercape also has a direct service between Cape Town and Windhoek (R350), running via Springbok (R230).

Minibus Taxi Most long-distance minibus taxis start picking up passengers in a distant township and make a trip into the train station's taxi ranks only if they need more people, so your choices can be limited. Not all townships are off-limits but the situation is volatile and changes very quickly. *Do not* go into a township without accurate local knowledge, and preferably go with a black friend.

A minibus to Jo'burg costs about R170, but it's a long, uncomfortable trip.

Train The local area Metro service is the best way to get to the wineries area (see the following Getting Around section).

Several long-distance trains run to/from Cape Town (☎ 449 3871 for information and bookings). The *Blue Train* and *Trans Karoo* run to Pretoria via Kimberley; the *Trans Oranje* goes to Durban via Kimberley and Bloemfontein; and the *Southern Cross* goes to Port Elizabeth via some Garden Route towns (for fares and other details, see the main Getting Around section in this chapter).

If you can't afford the time or money to take the expensive *Blue Train* all the way to Jo'burg, consider taking a sector. For example, the cheapest fare to Matjiesfontein, where you can stay in the wonderful Lord Milner Hotel, is R990, including lunch.

Car & Motorcycle Major international companies such as Avis (☎ 0800 021 111 toll free) at 123 Strand St, and Budget (☎ 0800 016 622 toll free) at 120 Strand St, are represented.

The larger local companies, such as Imperial (☎ 0800 131 000 toll free), on the corner of Loop and Strand Sts, and Tempest (☎ 0800 031 666 toll free), on the corner of Buitengragt and Wale St, offer comparable service to the major companies at slightly lower rates.

The smaller, cheaper local companies come and go – at the time of writing a prominent one was Panther (☎ 386 5051, fax 386 5058) on Main Rd, Sea Point. You'll find plenty of brochures at Cape Town Tourism and at hostels – read the small print!

Le Cap Motorcycle Hire (☎ 423 0823, ⓔ lecap@dockside.co.za) at 3 Carisbrook St hires motorbikes and also runs longer tours. If you're looking for cheap transport, you'd be much better off hiring a car, but it's very tempting to explore South Africa by motorcycle. You need to be aged over 23 and have held a motorcycle licence for two years to rent one of the Kawasaki KLR650s.

Hitching Although we do not recommend hitching, if you are planning on using your thumb, either start in the city centre or catch public transport to one of the outlying towns – the idea is to miss the surrounding suburbs and townships.

In the city centre, make a sign and start at the foreshore near the train station where the N1 (to Jo'burg), the N7 (to Windhoek) and the N2 (to the Garden Route) converge.

Lift Net (☎ 785 3802) connects drivers with passengers. It's a lot more expensive than hitching but is still cheaper than most other forms of transport. Hostel notice boards often have offers of lifts.

Getting Around

To/From the Airport The Back Packers Bus (☎ 082 809 9185) picks up at City Bowl hostels and runs to the airport for R45. If you are travelling with others, it's cheaper with CA Shuttle & Tours (☎ 552 6028), which charge R80 for one person, R90 for two, R100 for three and R120 for four.

You can pay up to R150 for a taxi.

Bus The main local bus interchange is on Grand Parade, where there's an information office (☎ 461 4365).

A bus (off-peak fares) to Sea Point costs R1.60, to Camps Bay R2.10, and to Hout Bay about R4.20. Travelling short distances, most people wait at the bus stop and take either a bus or a minibus taxi – whichever arrives first.

Minibus Taxi Minibus taxis cover most of the city with an informal network of routes. They are a cheap and efficient way of getting around the city, and cost about the same as the municipal buses. The main rank is on the upper deck of the train station, accessible from a walkway in the Golden Acre Centre, or from stairways on Strand St. In the suburbs, you just hail them from the side of the road – point your index finger into the air.

Rikki's Rikki's runs its tiny, open vans in the City Bowl and nearby areas for low prices. Telephone Rikki's (☎ 423 4888) or just hail one on the street – you can pay a shared rate of a few rand or more if you phone for the whole van. They run between 7 am and 7 pm daily except Sunday and go as far afield as Sea Point and Camps Bay. From the train station to Camps Bay a single-person trip will cost about R14; to Tamboerskloof will cost about R6. Rikki's also operates out of Simon's Town (☎ 786 2136).

Train The information office for Metro (local) trains (☎ 0800 656 463 toll free) is in the main train station near the old locomotive opposite Platform 23. Note that services have been cut back recently.

Local trains have 1st- and 3rd-class carriages. It's reasonably safe to travel in 3rd class (check the current situation), but don't do it during peak hours (crowds offer scope for pickpockets), on weekends (lack of crowds offer scope for muggers) or when carrying a lot of gear.

Probably the most important line for travellers is the Simon's Town (Simonstad) line that runs through Observatory (R3.50/2.50 in 1st/3rd class) and then around the back of the mountain through upper-income white suburbs such as Rosebank, down to Muizenberg (R6.50/3.50) and along the False Bay coast to Simon's Town (R8/4).

Local trains run some way out of Cape Town to Strand (on the eastern side of False Bay) and into the Winelands to Stellenbosch (R10/5) and Paarl (R12/6).

Taxi There is a taxi rank at the Adderley St end of Grand Parade, or call Star Taxis (☎ 419 7777), Marine Taxis (☎ 434 0434) or Sea Point Taxis (☎ 434 4444). There are often taxis near the Holiday Inn on Greenmarket Square and outside the Cape Sun on Strand St. Taxis cost about R4.50 per kilometre and are a particularly good idea at night.

Bicycle Many hostels hire bicycles and some of them are in reasonable condition. For a trouble-free bike, contact Mike Hopkins (☎ 423 2527) at 133A Bree St, near the corner of Wale St; or Day Trippers (☎ 531 3274).

WINELANDS

The wine-producing region around Stellenbosch, sometimes known as the Boland, is only one of the important wine-growing

SOUTH AFRICA

places in South Africa, but it is the oldest and most beautiful.

Although Jan van Riebeeck had planted vines and made wine, it was not until the arrival of Simon van der Stel in 1679 that wine-making seriously began. From 1688 to 1690, 200 French Huguenots arrived in the country. They were granted land in the area, particularly around Franschhoek (French Corner) and they gave the infant industry fresh impetus.

It is possible to see Stellenbosch and Paarl on day trips from Cape Town. Both are accessible by train, but Stellenbosch is the easiest to get around if you don't have a car. If you want to explore the wine routes, you'll need wheels; bicycle wheels will do.

Stellenbosch

☎ 021

Stellenbosch was established as a frontier town on the banks of the Eerste River by Governor van der Stel in 1679. It's the second-oldest town (after Cape Town) in South Africa, and one of the best preserved. The town is full of architectural and historical gems, and is shaded by oak trees.

The presence of the University of Stellenbosch, with over 12,000 students, means there is a thriving nightlife here.

Information The Stellenbosch Tourism Bureau (☎ 883 3584) at 36 Market St is open from 8 am to 6 pm weekdays, 9 am to 5 pm Saturday and 9.30 am to 4.30 pm Sunday. The staff are extremely helpful. There are also Internet facilities here for R10 per half hour. Pick up *Discover Stellenbosch on Foot* (also available in German) and *Stellenbosch & its Wine Route*, which gives opening times and tasting information about the three dozen or so nearby wineries.

You can also check your emails at Java Internet Cafe on Ryneveld St.

Rennies Travel (☎ 886 5259) has an office on the 1st floor of the De Wet Centre, on the corner of Bird and Kerk (Church) Sts.

Village Museum The Village (Dorp) Museum is a group of restored houses dating from 1709 to 1850. The main entrance, on Ryneveld St, leads into the oldest of the buildings, the Schreuderhuis. The museum is open from 9.30 am to 5 pm Monday to Saturday, and 2 to 5 pm Sunday; entry is R10.

The Braak The Braak (Town Square) is an open stretch of grass surrounded by important buildings. In the middle is the **VOC Kruithuis** (Powder House), built in 1777 to store the town's weapons and gunpowder. On the north-western corner the **Burgerhuis** was built in 1797 and is a fine example of the Cape Dutch style.

Bergkelder This should be your first stop if you are interested in the area's wines. For R10 you get a slide show, a cellar tour and tastings of up to 12 wines. The Bergkelder (☎ 888 3016) is a short walk from the train station; tours are held at 10 am, 10.30 am (in German) and 3 pm.

Stellenryck Wine Museum This small wine museum has some old furniture and wine-making paraphernalia; the most impressive item is the huge wine press which you can see on the corner of Blersch and Dorp. The museum is open daily (except Sunday).

Activities There are 90 **walks** in the Stellenbosch region – the Tourism Bureau has details.

Amoi Horse Trails (☎ 082 681 4285) offers tailor-made **horse rides**. There are no minimum numbers and they'll match you with a horse to suit your skill level.

Places to Stay The ***Backpackers Inn*** *(☎ 887 2020, ⓔ bacpac1@global.co.za)* is upstairs on the corner of Kerk and Bird Sts. It's central, clean and very friendly, and dorms cost R45 per person.

The ***Stumble Inn*** *(☎ 887 4049, 14 Mark St)* is a good hostel offering lots of activities and information. Dorms are R45 and doubles are R140, while camping will set you back R30.

De Goue Druif *(☎ 883 3555, 110 Dorp St)* is a rambling old house built in 1811 with very comfortable suites. Rooms are

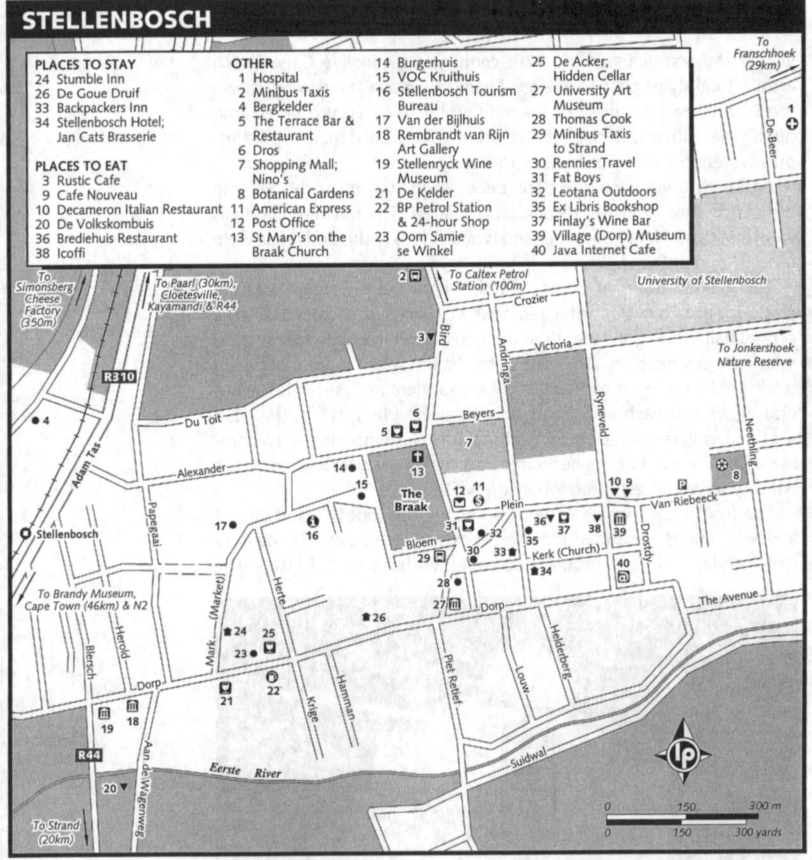

from R180 per person, including an excellent breakfast.

The ***Stellenbosch Hotel*** (☎ *887 3644)* on the corner of Dorp and Andringa Sts is a rather idiosyncratic country hotel, but it is also very comfortable. A section dating from 1743 houses the excellent Jan Cats Brasserie, a bar and dining room. The accommodation is in a modern section. Singles/doubles cost from R349/499.

Places to Eat Keep in mind that several of the nearby vineyards have good restaurants or cafes.

The ***Rustic Cafe***, off Bird St to the north of the Braak, stays open until 4 am.

Funky ***Icoffi*** on Ryneveld St has a great menu – the service is a little slow, but the pancakes (R16), toasted sandwiches (R12) and salads (R18) are excellent.

Good for a pit stop and a lunch-time beer is the trendy ***Cafe Nouveau*** on the corner of Ryneveld and Plein Sts.

Brediehuis Restaurant on Plein St has an outdoor area and occasional live music. Good size meals are R25 and salads about R15.

[Continued on page 510]

CAPE DUTCH ARCHITECTURE

During the last years of the 17th century, a distinctive Cape Dutch architectural style began to emerge. Thanks to Britain's wars with France, the British turned to the Cape for wine, so the burghers prospered and, during the 18th and 19th centuries, were able to build many of the impressive estates that can be seen today.

Although there is no direct link between the Cape Dutch style and the Dutch style, they are recognisably related. The building materials were brick and plenty of plaster and wood (often teak), and reeds were used to thatch the roof.

The main features of a Cape Dutch manor are the *stoep* (a raised platform, the equivalent of a veranda) with seats at each end, a large central hall running the length of the house, and the main rooms symmetrically arranged on either side of the hall. Above the front entrance is the gable, the most obvious feature, and there are usually less elaborate gables at each end. The house is covered by a steep, thatched roof and is invariably painted white (a traveller with an eye to commerce reckoned that if you wanted to make your fortune in South Africa you would get a monopoly on white paint).

The front gable, which extends up above the roof line and almost always contains an attic window, most closely resembles 18th century Dutch styles. The large ground floor windows have solid shutters. The

RICHARD I'ANSON

Left: Groot Constantia, Cape Town

graceful plaster scrolls of the gable are sometimes reflected in the curve on the top of the front door (above which is a fanlight, often with elaborate woodwork), but sometimes the door has neoclassical features such as flat pillars or a simple triangle above it. This combination of styles works surprisingly well.

Inside, the rooms are large and simply decorated. The main hall is often divided by a louvred wooden screen, which probably derives from similar screens the Dutch would have seen in the East Indies. Above the ceilings many houses had a *brandsolder*, a layer of clay or brick to protect the house if the thatching caught fire. The roof space was used for storage, if at all.

Perhaps the loveliest of all the manors is **Boschendal**, between Franschhoek and Stellenbosch, although **Groot Constantia** in Cape Town is also very fine. Other good examples of Cape Dutch architecture include **Reinet House** in Graaff-Reinet and **Burgerhuis** in Stellenbosch. To see the slightly different style of the Cape Dutch townhouse, visit **Koopmans de Wet House**, now a museum in the centre of Cape Town. To get an idea of how pervasive this indigenous style is, just travel around the country and see the many, many imitation Cape Dutch houses, walls, gates etc.

One of the best books on Cape Dutch architecture is the modern facsimile edition of the 1900 book *Old Colonial Houses of the Cape of Good Hope*, by Alys Fane Trotter. Only 1500 copies of the facsimile edition were printed, but you have a reasonable chance of finding one in an antiquarian bookshop in Cape Town.

RICHARD I'ANSON

Right: Boschendal, near Franschhoek

[Continued from page 507]

For good, genuine Italian food, try the ***Decamaron Italian Restaurant*** on Van Riebeeck St. Two courses, wine and coffee could cost well over R80, but it's worth it.

De Volkskombuis *(☎ 887 2121)* on Aan de Wagenweg, to the south of town, is one of the best places in the Cape to sample traditional cuisine. Try the Cape country sampler (four traditional specialities) for R49.50. Bookings are advisable.

Entertainment It's relatively safe to walk around at night, so think about checking a few of the options before you settle.

On Alexander St, facing the Braak, is ***Dros*** – dark, panelled, pubbish and a good place for a drink. There's sometimes live music. Next door, ***The Terrace Bar & Restaurant*** has pub food from R18.

De Kelder *(63 Dorp St)* has a nice atmosphere and is popular with German backpackers.

De Acker on the corner of Dorp and Herte Sts is a pub – a classic student drinking hole with cheap grub from R25.

On Plein St, ***Finlay's Wine Bar*** is a boisterous, cheerful place. ***Fat Boys***, upstairs on the corner of Plein and Bird Sts, plays everything from trance to Little Richard.

Getting There & Away Buses to Cape Town are expensive (about R20 with Translux) and you can't book this short sector. Translux stops here on the Mountain Route run between Cape Town and Port Elizabeth (see under Getting There & Away in the Cape Town section).

Metro trains run the 46km between Cape Town and Stellenbosch; 1st/3rd class is R10/5 (no 2nd class) and the trip takes about one hour. For inquiries phone Stellenbosch train station (☎ 808 1111).

A minibus taxi to Strand (and thus the beach) can cost as little as R4.50. A minibus taxi to Paarl is about R7, but you'll probably have to change minibus en route.

Getting Around Green Tri See Call pedal service (☎ 082-899 1067) uses nothing but pedal power to get you around – a fun, ecofriendly way to see Stellenbosch. The rate is 80 cents per person per minute.

Moto (☎ 887 9965) on Ryneveld St rents scooters.

Boschendal

Boschendal lies between Franschhoek and Stellenbosch on the Pniel Rd (R310). The **Cape Dutch homestead** (open from 9.30 am to 5 pm daily), winery buildings and vineyard are almost too beautiful to be real. Sales and tastings (free) are not available on Saturday afternoon or Sunday.

Franschhoek

☎ 021

Franschhoek, about 30km north-east of Stellenbosch, is nothing more than a village, but it's nestled into arguably the most beautiful valley in the Cape.

The information centre (☎ 876 3603) is in a small building on the main street. Pick up a map of the area's scenic walks. In season the centre is open daily.

There is an interesting **museum** (entry R4) commemorating the French Huguenots who settled in the area, and there are good wineries and restaurants nearby.

Places to Stay The information centre will tell you about B&Bs and other accommodation in town and the district. Farm B&Bs in the area offer the best value, but you'll need wheels.

The ***Dartrey Lodge*** *(☎ 876 3530, 5 Dirkie Uys St)* is a cheap guesthouse with good-value rooms from R130 per person, including breakfast.

The ***Hotel Huguenot*** *(☎ 876 2092)* on Huguenot Rd in the centre of town is a rather garish old-style country hotel that has been refurbished. Each room is self-catering and has a private bathroom; the rate is about R200/300 a single/double.

Auberge Bligny *(☎ 876 3767, 28 Van Wijk St)* is one of the town's oldest houses and is now a guesthouse with six tastefully decorated guest rooms. Rooms per person cost from R190 with breakfast, or R230 with TV as well.

Places to Eat ***Dominic's Country Pub & Restaurant*** is on the main street and has a pleasant lawn where you can have coffee, pastries or meals.

Further along the main street, ***Le Quartier Francais*** *(☎ 876 2248)* is a highly acclaimed restaurant. If it's beyond your budget, there's also the bistro and deli for takeaways and lighter meals.

Getting There & Away It's possible, if you're fit, to cycle between Stellenbosch and Franschhoek, otherwise taxis are the best way of getting between towns.

Paarl

☎ 021

Paarl is a large commercial centre on the banks of the Berg River, surrounded by mountains and vineyards. There are actually vineyards and wineries within the sprawling town limits, including the huge Kooperatieve Wijnbouwers Vereniging (better known as the KWV), a cooperative that regulates and dominates the South African wine industry.

The town is less touristy than Stellenbosch, in part because it is not as compact and historically coherent.

Information Paarl Tourism (☎ 872 3829) is at 216 Main St on the corner of Auret St. The office is open from 9 am to 5 pm weekdays, 9 am to 1 pm Saturday and 10 am to 1 pm Sunday.

Paarl Museum The old parsonage (1714) on Main St houses a collection of Cape Dutch antiques and relics of Huguenot and early Afrikaner culture. It's open from 9 am to 1 pm and 2 to 4 pm weekdays. Entry is by donation.

Paarl Mountain Nature Reserve This popular reserve is dominated by three giant granite domes which loom over the town on its west side. The domes apparently glisten like pearls if they are caught by the sun after a fall of rain – hence 'Paarl'.

A map (R5) showing walking trails is available from Paarl Tourism.

Places to Stay If you're a backpacker, you could consider the big, rather drab ***Manyano Centre*** *(☎ 863 2537)* on Sanddrift St. There's a fair chance that you'll be the only guest. Beds cost R40 and you'll need a sleeping bag.

Backpackers should also check out a place called ***Tourist Junction*** *(91 Main St)*, which offers several services, including backpacker accommodation.

Queenslin Guest House *(☎ 863 1160, 2 Queen St)* has a couple of rooms in a modern house overlooking the valley. Rates are about R130 per person, including breakfast. The price drops if you stay a few days.

The Berghof *(☎ 871 1099)* describes itself as not quite a guesthouse, not quite a hotel. Whatever it is, it's pleasant. You'll definitely need a vehicle to get there, as it's a long way up the side of the valley, with excellent views down over the town. Rooms cost from R295/450 for singles/doubles.

Mountain Shadows *(☎ 862 3192)* is a magnificent place to stay just outside Paarl. B&B rates start from about R395/550, rising in the peak season. From the N1, exit at Drakenstein (R101) and turn right at the BP petrol station.

Places to Eat Several of the vineyards around Paarl have restaurants and they are probably the best places to eat if you're sightseeing.

There's plenty to choose from at the Omni Park building on the corner of Main and Zion Sts, including ***Saddles*** (if you're after a steak) and ***Chellos Pizza & Pasta***.

Kontrehuis *(193 Main St)* has good-value meals, with Cape Malay bobotie for R30. In a courtyard next door is ***Squirrels***, a stylish place good for escaping the busy streets. A tasty chicken surprise sandwich (whatever the chef feels like putting in it) is R17.50.

Getting There & Away Several bus services come through Paarl but the bus segment between Paarl and Cape Town is much more expensive and inconvenient than the train, so take a train to Paarl and then link up with the buses.

Paarl is on Translux's Mountain Route between Cape Town and Port Elizabeth. Paarl to Port Elizabeth costs R155. Translux and Greyhound buses running between Cape Town and Jo'burg/Pretoria also stop in Paarl.

There are a reasonable number of weekday Metro trains between Cape Town and Paarl but they are sparser on the weekends. A 1st/3rd-class ticket from Cape Town to Paarl is R12/6 and the trip takes about 1¼ hours.

You can travel by train from Paarl to Stellenbosch, but you have to take a Cape Town-bound train and then change at Muldersvlei.

Bainskloof Pass

Bainskloof, north of Wellington (which adjoins Paarl), is one of the great mountain passes. Andrew Bain developed the road and pass between 1848 and 1852.

Tweede Tol Caravan Park *(021-889 1566),* which is halfway along the pass, is a magical spot and there are walks nearby. It's open only between October and May and costs R35 for a camp site. The gates are open from 7.30 am to 6 pm.

WEST COAST & SWARTLAND

The area immediately to the north of Cape Town that straddles the N7 highway is often further divided into two contiguous vicinities: the West Coast and Swartland.

The coast, because of its relative barrenness and cold water, has only recently been discovered by Capetonian holiday-makers.

Most public transport through this area travels from Cape Town north along the N7, either going all the way to Springbok and Windhoek (Namibia), or leaving the N7 at Vanrhynsdorp and heading through Calvinia to Upington. Intercape Mainliner services both these routes.

West Coast National Park

The West Coast National Park is one of the few large reserves along South Africa's coastline. It runs north from Yzerfontein to just short of Langebaan, surrounding the clear, blue waters of the Langebaan lagoon.

The park protects wetlands of international significance, as well as important seabird breeding colonies. The park is famous for its wildflower display, which usually occurs between August and October.

It's worth starting your visit at Langebaan so you can get a map and details of where you can go.

There's no accommodation in the park but Langebaan has several municipal ***caravan parks***. They have chalets but don't allow tents.

Die Strandloper *(☎ 022-772 2490)* is an open-air restaurant on the beach, specialising in seafood. It gets good reviews. You must book. Bring your own alcohol.

No public transport runs to Langebaan. Saldanha is the nearest town with public transport to/from Cape Town.

Olifants River Valley

There are some acclaimed wineries on the intensively cultivated valley floor of the Olifants River. The eastern side is largely bounded by the spectacular Cederberg Range and the whole area is famous for spring wildflowers.

Cederberg Wilderness Area The Cederberg is a rugged area of valleys and peaks extending roughly north-south for 100km between Citrusdal and Vanrhynsdorp. Part of it is protected by the 71,000-hectare Cederberg Wilderness Area.

The Cederberg offers excellent hiking. This is a genuine wilderness area – you are *encouraged* to leave the trails and little information is available on suggested routes. It's up to you to survive on your own.

There is a buffer zone of conserved land between the wilderness area and the farmland, where activities such as mountain biking are allowed. Pick up a copy of the mountain biking trail map (R35) from the Citrusdal information centre (see Information following).

Information The main office is at Citrusdal. There's also an office at the Algeria Camping Ground. Entry to the Wilderness Area costs R8. The Algeria entrance closes at 4.30 pm (9 pm on Friday). You won't be allowed in if you arrive late. Permits must be collected during office hours, so if you're arriving on Friday evening you'll need to make arrangements.

Hiking permits, which cost R7 per day, must be booked through the Chief Nature Conservator, Cederberg (☎ 027-482 2812 during office hours), Private Bag XI, Citrusdal 7340. The minimum group size is three; 12 is the maximum.

Places to Stay In a beautiful spot alongside the Rondegat River is ***Algeria Camping Ground***. Camp sites cost about R35, more in peak periods. There's another good camping ground in ***Kliphuis State Forest*** near Pakhuis Pass on the R364, about 15km north-east of Clanwilliam.

You'll need to book either of these camping grounds through the Chief Nature Conservator, Cederberg. There are basic huts for hikers in the wilderness area.

Getting There & Away The Cederberg Range is about 200km from Cape Town. It is accessible from Citrusdal and Clanwilliam but the easiest route is from the signposted turn-off from the N7 north of Citrusdal.

Public transport into Algeria is nonexistent, so you might want to go to Citrusdal and start walking from there. It takes about two days to walk from Citrusdal to Algeria, entering the wilderness area at Boskloof. The Chief Nature Conservator's office in Citrusdal has information on this route.

Citrusdal

☎ 022

This small town makes a good base for exploring the Cederberg Range. The Sandveldhuisie Country Shop & Tea Room (☎ 921 3210) on Kerk St is also the information centre and it's very helpful. Not far away is the office of the Chief Nature Conservator for the Cederberg Wilderness Area.

Much of the accommodation is out of town and there are plenty of farmstays in the area, either B&Bs or self-contained cottages. Contact the information centre for recommendations.

Intercape stops at a petrol station on the highway just outside town; Translux comes into town and stops at the Cederberg Hotel. Minibus taxis to Cape Town and Clanwilliam stop at the Caltex petrol station.

Clanwilliam

☎ 027

A popular little weekend resort, the attraction here is the town itself (which has some nice examples of Cape Dutch architecture) and the proximity to the Cederberg Range. Accommodation can be expensive and scarce in the spring wildflower season.

Clanwilliam Dam Municipal Caravan Park & Chalets (☎ *482 2133*) is good, with camp sites (R54) and chalets (about R165 a double).

The very comfortable ***Strassberger's Hotel Clanwilliam*** (☎ *482 1101*) is good value at R165/290 (R235/415 in flower season), including breakfast.

All the buses that pass through Citrusdal also come through Clanwilliam. It's about 45 minutes between the two towns. Minibus taxis running between Springbok and Cape Town also pass through Clanwilliam.

BREEDE RIVER VALLEY

This area lies to the north-east of the Winelands on the western fringes of the Little Karoo. Though dominated by the Breede River Valley, it's mountainous country and includes some smaller valleys. The valley floors are intensively cultivated with orchards, vineyards and wheat.

The headwaters of the Breede (sometimes called the Breë), in the beautiful mountain-locked Ceres basin, escape via Mitchell's Pass, flowing south-east for over 300km before meeting the Indian Ocean at Whitesands.

Look out for the *Cape Fruit Routes* map in information centres. It covers places in the Breede River Valley and also around the Winelands and east to the Montagu area.

Tulbagh

☎ 023

Tulbagh is one of the most complete examples of an 18th and 19th-century village in South Africa, although many of the buildings were substantially rebuilt after earthquakes in 1969 and 1970.

Although most of Tulbagh's surviving buildings date from the first half of the 19th century, the Tulbagh Valley was first settled in 1699. The village began to take shape after the construction of a church in 1743.

The town's main street, Van der Stel St, is parallel to Church St, in which every building has been declared a national monument. A visitor's first port of call should be 4 Church St (☎ 230 0506), part of the Old Church Folk Museum, which has an information counter.

Oude Kerk Volksmuseum The Old Church Folk Museum is made up of four buildings. Start at No 4; then visit the beautiful Oude Kerk itself (1743); follow this with No 14, which houses Victorian furniture and costumes; and then No 22, which is a reconstructed town dwelling from the 18th century.

The complex is open from 9 am to 5 pm weekdays, and 10 am to 4 pm weekends. Entry is R5.

Places to Stay On the edge of town is the ***Kliprivier Park Resort*** *(☎ 230 0506)*, quite a pleasant spot with reasonable modern chalets from R255 a double on weekends and slightly less during the week.

De Oude Herberge *(☎ 230 0260, 6 Church St)* is a guesthouse surrounded by old buildings and built in traditional Cape style. Rooms cost R150 per person (no smoking and no children under 12).

Ask at the information centre for other B&Bs and guesthouses (averaging about R200 a double) and farmstays (from R70 per person self-catering).

Places to Eat The ***Paddagang Restaurant*** is in a beautiful old homestead with a vine-shaded courtyard. It serves snacks and light meals. The restaurant is open for breakfast (R25 and very good), lunch and dinner.

Die Oude Herberge restaurant is open during the day, with breakfast (R22), light lunches (R24 for smoked trout) and snacks. Dinner is also available but you must book by 4 pm – on a weekend it would pay to book well in advance.

Getting There & Away Most minibus taxis leave from the 'location' (black residential area), on the hill just outside town, but you might find one at Tulbagh Toyota (the Shell service station) on the main street.

Robertson

☎ 023

Robertson is an attractive, prosperous, rather complacent little town. It's the centre for one of the largest wine-growing regions in the country and is also famous for horse studs.

The tourist bureau (☎ 626 4437) on the corner of Piet Reteif and Swellendam Sts is open from 9 am to 5.00 pm weekdays and on Saturday morning. Ask about 'overnight' hiking trails (ie, more than one day) which take you into the mountains above Robertson, offering great views.

Places to Stay The tourist bureau can tell you about accommodation, including self-catering farm cottages which start at about R80 per person.

The ***Grand Hotel*** *(☎ 626 3272, 68 Barry St)* on the corner of White St has a friendly atmosphere. There are a couple of cheerful bars downstairs, and excellent food. Singles/doubles go for R180/280.

Getting There & Away Translux Mountain Route buses to Port Elizabeth stop at the train station (for more details see under Getting There & Away in the Cape Town section). Munnik Coaches (☎ 021-637 1850) runs to Cape Town and Montagu on weekends.

The weekly *Southern Cross* train between Cape Town and Port Elizabeth via George and Oudtshoorn stops here.

Minibus taxis running between Cape Town (R30) and Oudtshoorn (R80) stop at the Shell petrol station on the corner of Voortrekker and Barry Sts. These minibuses also run through Montagu (R29).

McGregor

☎ 023

McGregor feels as if it has been forgotten. It's one of the best-preserved mid-19th century villages in the country, with thatched cottages surrounded by orchards, vegetable gardens and vineyards. There are about 30 wineries within half an hour's drive.

On the road between Robertson and McGregor is **Vrolijkheid Nature Reserve**, with about 150 species of bird to see. It has bird hides and there's an 18km, circular walking trail in the reserve.

The **Boesmanskloof Hiking Trail** begins at Die Galg, about 15km south of McGregor, and winds 14km through the Riviersonderend mountains to the small town of Greyton. For permits, contact Vrolijkheid Nature Reserve (☎ 023-625 1621).

Places to Stay Guesthouses are the major industry in this village and more are opening all the time. There are also self-catering cottages on nearby farms (the information centre in Robertson has a complete list).

Old Mill Lodge *(☎ 625 1841)* is a beautiful old building surrounded by a clutch of modern cottages. Half board costs R215 per person.

The lovely ***McGregor Country Cottages*** *(☎ 625 1816)* is a complex of seven cottages surrounding an apricot orchard. The cottages are fully equipped and cost R450 a double – great value.

THE OVERBERG

The Overberg (literally, Over the Mountains), is the area west of the Franschhoek Range and south of the Wemmershoek and Riviersonderend Ranges, which form a natural barrier with the Breede River Valley.

This area's wealth of coastal and mountain fynbos is unmatched; most species flower somewhere in the area between autumn and spring.

Coming from Cape Town by car, head to Gordon's Bay, from where the R44 skirts a magnificent stretch of coast facing out onto False Bay. It's a spectacular drive.

Hermanus

☎ 028

Hermanus is a popular seaside resort 122km from Cape Town. It was originally a fishing village, and still retains vestiges of its heritage, including an interesting **museum** at the old harbour. It's best known as a place for **whale-watching** close to the shore.

The Hermanus Tourism Bureau (☎ 312 2629) at 105 Main Rd is helpful. It's open from 9 am to 5 pm weekdays, and on weekends during the whale season (June to November) and in December.

There's an Internet & Information Cafe (☎ 313 0249) on the corner of Main and Park Sts.

Whales Between June and November, southern right whales *(Eubalaena australis)* come to Walker Bay to calve. There can be 70 whales in the bay at once. Humpback whales *(Megaptera novaeangliae)* are also sometimes seen.

Whales often come very close to shore and there are some excellent vantage points from the cliff paths that run from one end of Hermanus to the other. The best places are Castle Rock, Kraal Rock and Sievers Point.

Sharks Shark watching has been highly recommended by readers. There are several

Hermanus during the Holidays

Hermanus is a favourite spot for South Africans as well as overseas travellers.

We were here over the Heritage Day weekend, which coincided with the Moby Dick Hermanus Whale Festival (24 Sept–2 Oct). The narrow streets were jam-packed with people and horn-blaring BMWs. There was a line of cars on the R43 highway stretching all the way to Fisherhaven, crawling into the already overflowing town.

Parking was a challenge and accommodation was impossible to find without a booking. Nevertheless, the festival, described as an 'enviro-arts experience', was a whale of a time with loads of events, including rocking jazz shows, magic exhibitions for the kids, dancing (the tourism bureau sells programs for R8) and, of course, plenty of opportunity for whale-watching.

However, if you want the whales to yourself, avoid visiting at local holiday times!

SOUTH AFRICA

operators who run trips to Dyer Island, near Gansbaai, where Great White sharks patrol the waters. You'll get within metres of the sharks and it costs about R300 for the day – ask at the Tourism Bureau for more information.

Places to Stay In a huge, manic house, ***Hermanus Backpackers*** *(☎ 312 4293, 26 Flower St, Westcliff)* is a bustling place, and the friendly vibe is fed by the enthusiastic owners. There's a big kitchen and a great lounge area. Dorms are R55 and doubles go for about R130.

The ***Zoete Inval Traveller's Lodge*** *(☎ 312 1242, 23 Main Rd)* has dorms for R45 and comfortable doubles for R170. Renovations have added a new coffee bar, kitchen and lounge area.

The tourism bureau has listings of B&Bs (from R100) and self-catering cottages (from R150) or you can book through the Hermanus Accommodation Centre (☎ 083-651 0001) on Church St.

The ***Windsor Hotel*** *(☎ 312 3727)*, Marine Dr, is a large old place which seems to make its living from coach tours. Low-season rates are R150 per person, with breakfast; sea-facing rooms are more.

On Main Rd, the ***Marine Hotel*** *(☎ 313 1000)* is a grand, old-style hotel that has been superbly renovated. It's very comfortable and is in a great spot. Rooms cost from R800.

Places to Eat A stroll along Main St and around Village Square will quickly turn up a place suitable for your palate.

St Tropez *(☎ 312 3221, 28 Main Rd)* has good-value lunches for under R20, although it is more expensive at night (closer to R30).

Tucked in between Main and Marine Sts, ***Trattoria*** is a great little spot on St Peter's Lane; pasta is about R25 and wafer-thin garlic focaccia is R14.50.

Burgundy Restaurant *(☎ 312 2800, 16 Harbour Rd)* is one of the most acclaimed restaurants in the province. Main courses are about R35 to R65.

There are a couple of interesting possibilities on High Street, which runs parallel to Main Rd. For example, ***Rossi's Pizzeria & Italian Restaurant*** *(☎ 312 2848, 10 High St)* has a pleasant and relaxed atmosphere. It has a range of pasta dishes (about R30), pizzas (from R25) and steak or line fish (from R40).

Getting There & Away Chilwans (☎ 021-905 3910 in Cape Town) has an evening service from Cape Town to Gansbaai via Hermanus on Friday and Saturday for about R25.

Bernardus Niehaus (☎ 083-658 7848) runs a 24-hour private shuttle service between Hermanus and Cape Town.

The taxi park is behind the tourism bureau, but there aren't many minibus taxis.

Cape Agulhas

Cape Agulhas is the southernmost point of the African continent. On a stormy day it real-ly looks like the next stop is the South Pole, but otherwise it isn't especially impressive.

There isn't much in the hamlet of Cape Agulhas, but **Struisbaai**, about 6km east, is a little larger and has a ***caravan park***. There's also the luxurious ***Arniston Hotel*** *(☎ 028-445 9000)* in **Waenhuiskrans** (also called Arniston), with rooms for R285 per person.

De Hoop Nature Reserve

De Hoop (**huu**-op) is worth visiting. It includes a scenic coastline with lonely stretches of beach, rocky cliffs, a freshwater lake and the Potberg Range.

This is one of the best places to see both mountain and lowland fynbos and a diverse range of coastal ecosystems. Fauna includes the Cape mountain zebra, bontebok and a wealth of birdlife. The coast is an important breeding area for the southern right whale.

There is hiking and good snorkelling along the coast, and since it is to the east of Cape Agulhas, the water is reasonably warm.

Cottages for four people start at R100 and ***camp sites*** are R45; these must be booked in advance, so contact ☎ 028-542 1126.

Swellendam

☎ 028

As well as being a very pretty town with a real sense of history, Swellendam offers those with transport a good base for exploring quite a range of country. The Breede River Valley and the coast are within easy reach, as is the Little Karoo.

Swellendam is dotted with old oaks and on its southern side is surrounded by beautiful rolling wheat country, but it backs up against a spectacular ridge of the Langeberg Range.

Swellendam dates from 1746 and is the third-oldest European town in South Africa.

Information Swellendam Tourist Office (☎ 514 2770) in the old mission, or Oefeninghuis, on Voortrek St is open from 9 am to 1 pm and 2 to 5 pm weekdays, and on Saturday morning.

The Bramble Bush Cafe has Internet terminals – see Places to Eat following.

For permits to walk in **Marloth Nature Reserve** in the Langeberg Mountains contact the Nature Conservation Department (☎ 514 1410). There are one-day, two-day and week-long hikes.

Drostdy Museum The centrepiece of this museum is the beautiful *drostdy* (the former official government residence), which dates from 1746. There is also the Old Gaol; part of the original administrative buildings; the Gaoler's Cottage; a water mill; and Mayville, a residence dating from 1853. Some distance away, **Morgenzon**, 16 Van Oudtshoorn Rd, is an annexe of the museum. It was built in 1751 as a house for the secretary of the *landdrost* (an official representative of the colony's governor).

The complex is open from 9 am to 4.45 pm weekdays, and 10 am to 3.45 pm weekends; entry is R10.

Places to Stay ***Swellendam Caravan Park*** *(☎ 514 2705)* is in a lovely spot near the Morgenzon museum, a 10-minute walk from town. Camp sites are expensive at about R50 per site.

Serene and comfortable, ***Swellendam Backpackers*** *(☎ 514 2648, 5 Lichtenstein St)* is a good place to unwind, with a large grassed area out the back; dorms are R45, doubles R130 or you can pitch a tent for R30. They also organise horseback and mountain bike trails.

A friendly little guesthouse is ***Roosje Van de Kaap*** *(☎ 514 3001, 5 Drostdy St)*, which has four guest rooms overlooking a small pool. They cost about R150 per person with breakfast and there is a restaurant here.

Moolmanshof *(☎ 514 3258, 217 Voortrek St)* is a beautiful old home dating from 1798. The garden is superb and the house is furnished with period furniture. B&B is a very reasonable R125 per person per night.

Klippe Rivier Homestead *(☎ 514 3341)*, a kilometre or so south-west of town just across the Keurbooms River, is an exceptional place to stay. Built on land granted in 1725, the Cape Georgian manor is a superb building. There are six guest suites overlooking an oak-shaded lawn, costing from R800 a double.

Places to Eat The homely ***Bramble Bush Cafe***, on the corner of Voortrekker and Andrew Whyte Sts, has a shady outdoor area. Toasted sandwiches are R13.50 and the carrot cake is sensational. There are also Internet terminals for R20 per hour.

Mattsen's Steak House on Voortrek St near the tourist office is popular. A big dinner costs about R60 and there are light meals and snacks.

Zanddrift Restaurant adjoins the Drostdy Museum and is in a building that dates from 1757. Breakfast is a must: R30 gets you a huge platter of omelette, ham, cheese, pate, fruit and so on.

Getting There & Away Intercape runs to Cape Town and Port Elizabeth. Destinations include: Cape Town (R75); Mossel Bay (R80); Knysna (R100); and Port Elizabeth (R130). Swellengrebel Hotel is the Intercape agent.

Translux has a similar service at higher prices. Some Translux buses also run to Oudtshoorn (R100).

Minibus taxis stop at the Caltex petrol station on Voortrek St, opposite Swellengrebel

Hotel. There's a daily service to Cape Town for R40 and to Mossel Bay for a little more.

The weekly *Southern Cross* train between Cape Town and Port Elizabeth via George and Oudtshoorn stops here.

Bontebok National Park

Bontebok National Park, 6km south of Swellendam, is a small chunk of land protecting the bontebok, an unusually marked antelope. As a nice place to relax, it's hard to beat.

Entry is R15 per vehicle. There are six-berth 'chalavans' for R100 plus R16 per person (book through the National Parks Board) and pleasant camp sites for R40 a double.

THE LITTLE KAROO

The Little (or Klein) Karoo is bordered in the south by the Outeniqua and Langeberg Ranges, and in the north by the Swartberg Range. It runs east from Montagu for about 300km to Uniondale, and is more fertile and better watered than the harsher Karoo to the north. The Little Karoo is renowned for ostrich and wildflowers and for the spectacular passes that cut through the mountains.

Most people travelling between Cape Town and the Garden Route use the N2, but there's an interesting alternative: the Mountain Route running via Robertson, Montagu, Oudtshoorn and George.

Montagu

☎ 023

Montagu, founded in 1851, lies just outside the Breede Valley – once you pop through the Kogmanskloof Pass near Robertson you are in a very different world. It's a good place to go if you want to escape the 20th century and get a brief taste of the Little Karoo.

The information office (☎ 614 2471) has information on accommodation (including a range of B&Bs and self-catering cottages), walks, hikes and organised tours of Zolani township (R40).

Montagu Museum & Joubert House The Montagu Museum is in the old mission church on Long St, and includes interesting displays and some good examples of antique furniture. Joubert House, also on Long St, is the oldest house in Montagu (built in 1853) and has been restored to its Victorian finery.

Montagu Hot Mineral Springs The springs are about 3km from town; they are hot (45°C), radioactive and renowned for their healing properties.

Places to Stay On the edge of town, ***De Bos*** *(☎ 614 2532)* is a guest farm with camp sites (R20), a backpackers' barn (R30) and a bungalow (R60) per person; there's a double room with private bathroom for R100.

The ***Mimosa Lodge*** *(☎ 614 2351)* on Church St is a good, if expensive, guesthouse in a beautifully restored old building. Its room charges are from R440/700 for half board.

The information office has details on several B&Bs from about R90 per person. There are also cheap self-catering farmhouses and cottages.

Out at the springs, the ***Avalon Springs Hotel*** *(☎ 614 1150)* has mineral springs, warm pools, massages and gyms. Double rooms start at R275.

Right up on top of the Langeberg Range, Niel Burger (☎ 614 2471) offers several accommodation options, including ***cottages*** for R160. Niel also runs popular tractor trips up the mountain.

Places to Eat Locals say that the best pizzas are to be found at ***Da Vinci's Pizzeria***, out at Avalon Springs Hotel.

Something Special is a craft/coffee shop in a beautiful old Cape Dutch building; you can sit indoors or outdoors.

The ***Montagu Country Inn*** has a restaurant, but no longer serves food in the bar.

Getting There & Away Munnik Coaches (☎ 021-637 1850 in Cape Town) has buses three times a week between Cape Town and Montagu (about R50).

Minibus taxis running between Oudtshoorn (about R45) and Cape Town (R65) stop near the police station.

Oudtshoorn

☎ 044

Oudtshoorn is the tourist capital of the Little Karoo. It's a large, sedate place with some nice old buildings built on the profits from the boom in ostrich feathers at the turn of the century. The boom collapsed but Oudtshoorn's claim to fame is still the ostrich industry. It is also well situated as a base for exploring the very different environments of the Little Karoo, the Garden Route and the Great Karoo.

Oudtshoorn Tourism Bureau (☎ 279 2532) is on Baron van Rheede St near Queen's Hotel. It's open from 8 am to 6 pm weekdays, and on Saturday morning.

Ostrich Farms There are three ostrich show farms, each open daily, which offer guided tours of about two hours: Safari Ostrich Farm (☎ 272 7311), 6km from town on the Mossel Bay road; Highgate Ostrich Farm (☎ 272 7115), 10km from town, signposted from the Mossel Bay road; and Cango Ostrich Farm (☎ 272 4623), 14km from town on the Cango Caves road. Entry is about R18 to R25.

Cango Caves These impressive caves are 30km from town. There's a ***restaurant*** and curio complex and three tours, costing R15, R30 and R40.

If you continue on past the Cango Mountain Resort (on the way to the caves) up the dirt road for 8km, you'll come to the pretty **Rust en Vrede Waterfall**, which runs year-round.

Places to Stay On Park Rd, ***NA Smit Caravan Park*** *(☎ 272 4152)* has camp sites for R45 in the low season (R70 in the high season) and rondavels from R100 for doubles in the low season (R265 in the high season).

Backpackers Oasis *(☎ 279 1163, 3 Church St)* is in a large and relaxed house with a good-sized yard and a decent pool. The staff arrange budget tours to the ostrich farms and some good activities. Dorm beds are R50, doubles are R140 and camp sites are R30 per person.

Backpackers Paradise *(☎ 272 0725)* on the corner of Baron van Rheede and Victoria Sts is an impressive hostel with dorms for R45 and doubles for R140. Travellers have recommended their bike tour (R75, bike included), starting at the top of Swartberg Pass.

A worthwhile place to stay is ***La Pension*** *(☎ 279 2445, 169 Church St)*. It has a pool, a sauna and a large garden. There's a range of accommodation, from standard B&B to a two-bedroom unit. Prices start at about R110/140. The ***Bisibee Guesthouse***, next door, is just as good.

The ***Queen's Hotel*** *(☎ 272 2101)* on Baron van Rheede St is an attractive, old-style country hotel charging from R200/350, with breakfast.

Places to Eat Between the tourism bureau and Queen's Hotel, ***Cafe Brule*** does open sandwiches and tasty baguettes from R15 to R22.

Most places serve ostrich in one form or another. ***Godfather*** *(61 Voortrekker St)* is a bar and restaurant open daily for dinner only. As well as standards such as pasta and pizza, you can try Springbok steaks or exotic dishes such as ostrich antipasto.

Headlines on Baron van Rheede St is pleasant enough in a kitsch sort of way. Soups cost R14, stuffed mushrooms are R16 and chicken dishes are from R29.

Getting There & Away Translux runs the Mountain Route three times a week. Fares from Oudtshoorn include: Knysna (R55; stand-by available only); Port Elizabeth (R100); and Cape Town (R130).

Translux also stops in Oudtshoorn on its run between Knysna and Jo'burg/Pretoria. Fares from Oudtshoorn include: Bloemfontein (R175) and Jo'burg (R220).

Minibus taxis aren't easy to find – try Union St near the Spar supermarket, or contact the tourism bureau.

The weekly *Southern Cross* train between Cape Town and Port Elizabeth via George stops here.

THE KAROO

Although some of the Karoo is in Western Cape, it sprawls into Eastern and Northern

Cape provinces as well. The section of the Karoo around the lovely town of Graaff-Reinet is possibly the most interesting (see the Eastern Cape section).

The term Karoo describes most of the interior of the old Cape Province, an area of semidesert which covers almost one-third of South Africa.

Prince Albert

☎ 023

Prince Albert is a beautiful little town, dozing on the edge of the Karoo at the foot of the astounding **Swartberg Pass**. You can easily visit on a day trip from Oudtshoorn or the coast. Alternatively, stay in Prince Albert and make a day trip to Oudtshoorn.

The town was founded in 1762 and there are some interesting examples of Cape Dutch, Victorian and Karoo styles of architecture.

Places to Stay & Eat On the southern (Swartberg Pass) edge of town, Elaine Hurford's ***Dennehof Karoo Guesthouse*** *(☎ 541 1227)* is in the town's oldest house (1835). There are self-contained cottages for R115 per person.

The ***Swartberg Hotel*** *(☎ 541 1332, 77 Church St)* is a pleasant old pub. Rates include breakfast and start at R235/390 a single/double.

Sampie se Plaasstal on the main street is a farm produce stall that is much, much better than most. It sells nuts, game meat, biltong, dried fruit (including *meëbos*, parchment-like sheets) and some delicious home-made pastries.

Getting There & Away The nearest Intercape, Translux and Greyhound stop (on the run between Cape Town and Jo'burg/Pretoria) is at Laingsburg, about 120km away, but you can arrange to be dropped at Prince Albert Road, the rail halt. Some places to stay in Prince Albert will collect you from here.

The nearest train station is Prince Albert Road, 45km north-west of Prince Albert. The daily *Trans Karoo* between Cape Town and Jo'burg via Kimberley stops there.

Beaufort West

☎ 0201

Beaufort West is the archetypal stopover town. Most people will be happy to snatch a cold drink, petrol and perhaps a sleep. In summer Beaufort West is a sluice gate in the torrent of South Africans heading for the coast.

Places to Stay & Eat There are many places offering 'overnight rooms'. The best deal is at ***Donkin House*** *(☎ 4287, 14 Donkin St)*. It's fairly basic but friendly and rooms cost just R65 per person.

Ye Olde Thatch *(☎ 2209, 155 Donkin St)* has secure parking and four guest suites from R200 a double. The ***restaurant*** here is very pleasant, specialising in Karoo dishes.

Getting There & Away Beaufort West is a junction for many bus services. Most buses stop on Donkin St outside Oasis Hotel, which is the Translux agent.

Most minibus taxis stop at the BP station at the southern end of Donkin St, not far from the caravan park. Destinations include: Oudtshoorn (R45); King William's Town (R80); and Cape Town (R90).

The daily *Trans Karoo* train, which runs to Cape Town and Jo'burg via Kimberley, stops here.

Karoo National Park

The Karoo National Park, north of Beaufort West, protects 33,000 hectares of impressive Karoo landscapes. The park has 61 species of mammal, the most common of which are dassie and bat-eared fox. A rhino or two have been reintroduced.

The entrance gates are open from 7 am to 6 pm (entry costs R10/5 for adults/children). There are two short nature trails and an 11km day walk, plus the three-day **Springbok Hiking Trail**. There are also 4WD guided trails, for one day or longer. There's a shop and a ***restaurant***.

Hikers stay in ***huts***, and the cost is R150 per person. Book accommodation through the National Parks Board (☎ 021-422 2810 in Cape Town). There's an inexpensive ***caravan park*** and a variety of other accommodation, starting at R300 a double in a bungalow.

Matjiesfontein

☎ 0230

Matjiesfontein (sounds like 'Mikeys...') is a small railway siding that has remained virtually unchanged for 100 years; its impressive buildings seem incongruous in the bleak Karoo landscape.

As well as the attractive **old buildings** there's a **museum** in the train station.

The grand ***Lord Milner Hotel*** *(☎ 551 3011)* is a period piece with B&B rooms from R201/320 (no children under 12).

The daily *Trans Karoo* train between Cape Town and Jo'burg stops here.

GARDEN ROUTE

The heavily promoted Garden Route encompasses a beautiful bit of coastline from Still Bay in the west to just beyond Plettenberg Bay in the east.

The narrow coastal plain is often forested, and is mostly bordered by lagoons which run behind a barrier of sand dunes and superb beaches. Inland, its boundary is the Outeniqua and Tsitsikamma Ranges.

Although the Garden Route is beautiful, it is also heavily (and tackily) developed. Prices normally jump by at least 30% in mid-season (late January to May) and more than double over the high season (December, January and Easter).

Getting There & Away

Translux (☎ 021-449 3333 in Cape Town) and Intercape (☎ 021-386 4400 in Cape Town) run at least daily from Cape Town to Port Elizabeth via the main Garden Route towns. Translux also runs a service from Jo'burg to Knysna via some Garden Route towns. (For fares and main destinations, see the main Getting Around section in this chapter.) If you plan to travel around the area, don't forget the Baz Bus, which drops/picks up at hostels along the Garden Route.

The weekly *Southern Cross* train between Cape Town and Port Elizabeth stops in some Garden Route towns (see the main Getting Around section earlier in this chapter).

Mossel Bay

☎ 044

Mossel Bay (or Mosselbaai) is a fairly sleepy country town on a beautiful bay.

The first European to visit the bay was the Portuguese explorer Bartholomeu Dias in 1488. From then on, many ships stopped to take on fresh water and to barter for provisions with the Gouriqua Khoikhoi who lived in the area.

The efficient information centre (☎ 691 2202) is on Market St.

Mossel Bay is off the highway and buses don't come into town – they'll drop you at the Voorbaai Shell petrol station, 7km from town. The hostels can usually collect you if you give notice.

Bartholomeu Dias Museum Complex

The highlight of this complex is the replica of the vessel that Dias used on his 1488 voyage of discovery. The replica was built in Portugal and sailed to Mossel Bay in 1988 to commemorate the 500th anniversary of Dias' trip.

Boat Trips There are boat trips to Seal Island for about R40 on the *Romonza*, which leaves from the harbour behind the train station. In late winter and spring it's not unusual to see whales on the trip. Whale-watching trips and shark cage diving is available from several operators in town – ask at the information centre.

Places to Stay There are two adjacent municipal caravan parks, ***Bakke*** and ***Santos***, on the pretty Dias Strand. You can contact these places on ☎ 691 2915. Both have chalets (R160) and camp sites (R50 per site).

Barnacles Ecno-Lodge *(☎ 690 4584, 112 High St)*, with its entrance off Hill St, is a big house with superb views over the bay. It's very clean and you won't see better doubles (R130) in a backpackers. There are also dorms for R45.

Dolphin House Backpackers *(☎ 691 4317, 15 Marsh St)* is a friendly place in a great spot near pubs and restaurants. They have an agreement with O'Hagans next door, and you get good meal deals. Dorm beds are R45 and doubles are R120.

SOUTH AFRICA

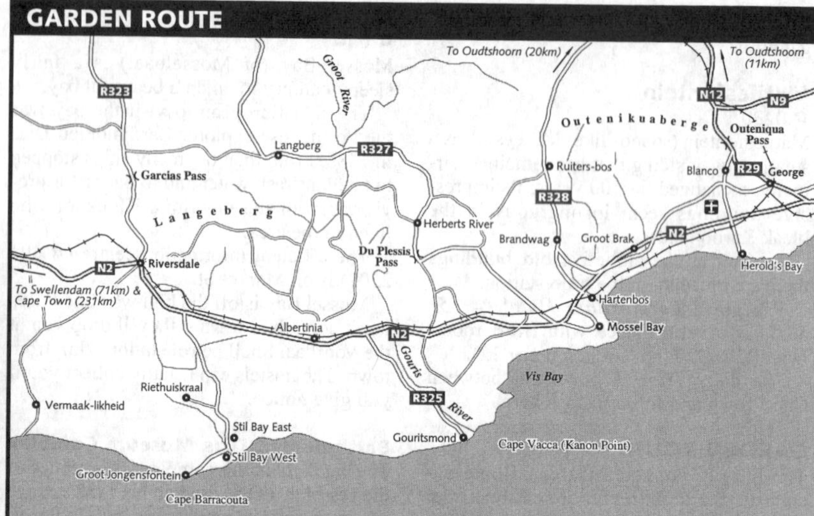

Not far away, the ***Mossel Bay Backpackers*** *(☎ 691 3182, 1 Marsh St)* has dorms for R40 and doubles for R120 (R140 with bathroom). You can also rent mountain bikes and boogie boards here.

Not far from the museum, the ***Old Post Office Tree Guesthouse*** *(☎ 691 3738)* is a very comfortable set up, more like a hotel than a guesthouse in size. Singles/doubles start at about R225/350, including breakfast.

The ***Diving Dolphin Beach Hotel*** *(☎ 082-449 0882)* on the R102 as you come into town from George, is a huge garish monolith from the outside, but has extremely good-value rooms; doubles with TV and phone are R149 and a family room is R199.

There are many other guesthouses and B&Bs; the information centre has a list.

Places to Eat ***Gannet Restaurant*** in the Old Post Office Tree Guesthouse specialises in seafood and has a bright and informal atmosphere. Mouth-watering crayfish is R70 and baby cob costs R37.

The Pavilion is right on Santos Beach, in a 19th-century bathing pavilion. There are snacks for about R20; line fish start at R43, and steaks at R42.

On Marsh St at the corner of Kloof St is ***Bay Tavern***, a local pub in a renovated sandstone building. It serves reasonable pub food.

George

☎ 044

George is a large town that bills itself as the capital of the Garden Route. It was founded in 1811 and lies on a coastal plateau at the foot of the Outeniqua Range. The town is not especially interesting and unless you have a car it's too far from the coast.

The tourist office (☎ 801 9295) at 124 York St has lots of information and some handy maps.

Outeniqua Choo-Tjoe Steam Train

One of the reasons to visit George is the famous *Outeniqua Choo-Tjoe*, a steam train running along a spectacular line to Knysna. The trip takes 2½ hours; fare to Knysna is R40 one-way; R50 return (six months validity). For more details, contact Transnet (☎ 801 8288).

Places to Stay About a 20-minute walk from the centre, the ***George Tourist Resort*** *(☎ 874 5205)* is a large caravan park on

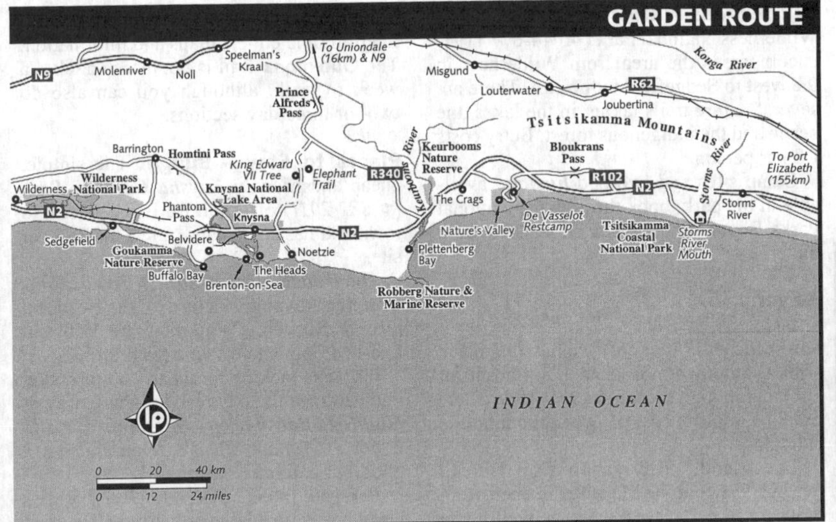

York St. Camp sites start at R50 per site. Rondavels cost from R127 a double and there are also more expensive chalets (R165).

The ***George Backpackers Hostel*** *(☎ 874 7807, 29 York St)* is quite a long walk south of the centre of town. It's under new management, who are giving the place a much-needed facelift. Dorms are R45 and doubles are R110.

The ***George Lodge International*** *(☎ 874 6549, 86 Davidson Rd)* is very much an overnight stop, but it's not bad. Singles/doubles cost about R149/179.

The comfortable ***Protea Foresters Lodge*** *(☎ 874 4488, 123 York Rd)* has specials from R259 per room.

Places to Eat The ***Keg & Lourie*** does tasty pub lunches and serves an excellent, creamy pint of Kilkenny.

Hop Inn *(70 Courtenay St)* is a friendly restaurant with a bar and a young crowd. There is no shortage of meat on the menu, with the odd seafood dish thrown in. Also on Courtenay St, ***The Kingfisher*** is the place for seafood and pasta at reasonable prices.

Wilderness

☎ 044

Wilderness is no longer an apt description for this popular holiday village. Still, it is on a beautiful stretch of coast with a lush mountain hinterland.

The Wilderness Eco-Tourism Association (☎ 877 0045) runs the information centre and can help with accommodation bookings. It's open daily except Sunday.

Places to Stay Right on the N2 and therefore a bit noisy, ***Wild Welcome Backpackers*** *(☎/fax 877 1307, 10 The Avenue)* has bike hire and organises loads of activities. Dorms are R40 and doubles cost R120.

Fairy Knowe Backpackers *(☎ 877 1285)*, one of the best hostels on this stretch of coast, is set on four hectares and you can canoe into town! Accommodation is in a converted farmhouse (dorms R45, doubles R120). Follow signs to Fairy Knowe Hotel – the hostel is just over the railway line.

The ***Fairy Knowe Hotel*** *(☎ 877 1100)*, on Dumbleton Rd, is on the banks of the Touw River; take Waterside Rd from Wilderness. There are luxury riverside rooms and thatched rondavels. Doubles start at R140.

Wilderness National Park

Wilderness National Park (☎ 044-877 1197) encompasses the area from Wilderness in the west to Sedgefield in the east. There are several nature trails taking in the lakes, the beach and the indigenous forest. Entry costs R8 per person.

Camp sites and two-bed ***huts*** are available in the park; book through the National Parks Board. The park is signposted from the N2.

Knysna

☎ 044

Knysna (the 'k' is silent) is a bustling place with a holiday atmosphere. It's a beautiful spot, but in high season the crowds are horrendous and the cost of accommodation is ridiculous.

The friendly Knysna Tourism Bureau (☎ 382 5510) at 40 Main Rd is open from 8.30 am to 5 pm weekdays, as well as on Saturday morning. You can't miss the office, as there's an elephant skeleton out the front.

Cyber Perk Internet Cafe (R20 per hour) is in the Spar Centre on Main Rd.

Mitchell's Brewery Those who have been in the country for a while, particularly in Cape Town, may well have come across Mitchell's excellent beers. There are free tours of the brewery on weekdays at 10.30 am. Tastings are available during the brewery's weekday opening hours.

Activities Travellers have highly recommended the nearby **Township Trail Tour** (about R130), which includes Xhosa dancing and a visit to a *sangoma* (witchdoctor); ask at the tourism bureau for details.

The MV *John Benn* (☎ 382 1693) offers **cruises** on the lagoon for R35. Bookings are essential.

Diving in the lagoon is interesting and there's a wreck to explore. Beneath Tapas Jetty you might meet the unique Knysna seahorses. Waterfront Divers (☎ 384 0831) at East Head charges about R850 for an openwater certificate course. It also rents gear.

The Forestry Department (☎ 382 5446), in an office upstairs on Main Rd opposite Memorial Square, is where you book walking trails and collect maps and information. The **Outeniqua Trail** is popular and takes a week to walk, although you can also do two- or three-day sections.

Places to Stay – Budget The simple, cheap and friendly ***Knysna Caravan Park*** *(☎ 382 2011)* off Main Rd is the closest to town and has camp sites (only) for R55 per site.

The ***Woodbourne Resort*** *(☎ 384 0316)* is a pretty caravan park close to The Heads on George Rex Dr. Camp sites are R50 and two-bedroom chalets cost from R180.

If you're looking for a party atmosphere, you can rage the days (and nights) away at ***Highfield Backpackers Guesthouse*** *(☎ 382 6266, 2 Graham St)*. It's clean and has a pool, bar and braai area.

Peregrin *(☎ 382 3747, 37 Queen St)* is a clean hostel on a large property with a great view over the bay. Dorms are R45, doubles are R110 and camp sites cost R35; these prices include breakfast.

Knysna Backpackers Hostel *(☎ 382 2554, 12 Newton St)* is a large Victorian house on the hill a few blocks up from Main Rd; its prices are the same as Peregrin and also include breakfast.

Places to Stay – Mid-Range & Top End In a great location near East Head, ***Under Milk Wood*** *(☎ 384 0745)* on George Rex Dr is a group of high-quality chalets with a small but pretty lagoon beach. There are canoes and small boats. They also have B&B rooms for R150 per person. The well-equipped chalets cost from R450 a double but can sleep four.

Fair Acre Guest House *(☎ 382 2242)* in Thesen's Hill has stunning views and large grounds, with B&B from R85 per person.

The ***Yellowwood Lodge*** *(☎ 382 5906, 18 Handel St)* is a beautiful old house with very comfortable double rooms from R320, with breakfast.

The ***Knysna Log Inn*** *(☎ 382 5835)* on Grey St lays claim to be the largest log building in the southern hemisphere and perhaps helps account for South Africa's lack of

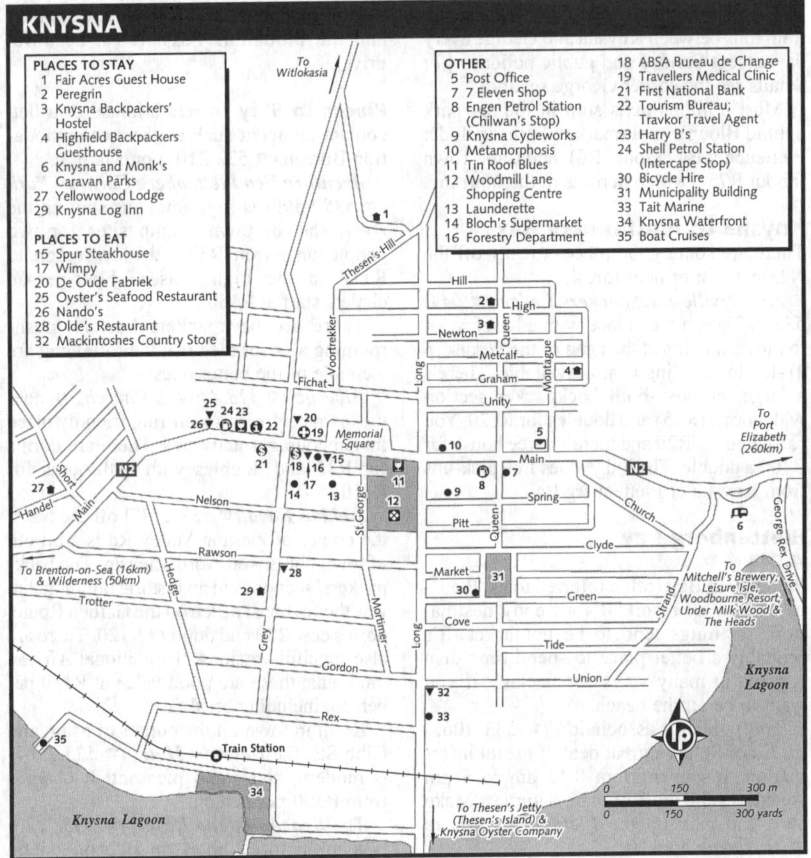

forests. Double rooms go for about R390 per person. There's a pub and restaurant.

Places to Eat There are plenty of snack and coffee places in town. For some cheap, fresh oysters, head to ***Knysna Oyster Company*** on Thesen's Island.

There's a ***Wimpy***, a ***Spur Steakhouse*** and a ***Nando's*** on Main Rd to satisfy the fast food junkies.

De Oude Fabriek, on the corner of Main Rd and Grey Sts, has a cafe, a restaurant and an informal courtyard. There are some interesting South African dishes on the menu.

Olde's Restaurant *(14 Grey St)* offers a seven-course buffet for just R40.

Out at the Heads and in a beautiful setting, ***Paquita's*** has a coffee shop and does inexpensive snacks and lunches. Paquita's is also a bar and restaurant, serving pasta from R21 and steaks from R40; it also does great soups.

Getting There & Away Travkor, behind the tourism bureau, sells bus tickets. Translux stops at the bus station, Intercape stops on Main Rd at the Shell petrol station and Chilwans stops on Main Rd at the Engen petrol station.

The historic *Outeniqua Choo-Tjoe* steam train runs between Knysna and George every day except Sunday and public holidays (for details see the earlier George section).

Most minibus taxis stop in the car park behind Bloch's supermarket. Fares include: Plettenberg Bay (about R6); and Cape Town (about R75), which departs in the morning.

Knysna to Plettenberg Bay

There are some good places to stay off the N2, many in or near forest.

Harkerville Backpackers Lodge *(☎ 044-532 7777)* is a nice place with a lot of room to move, and it's at the head of the Perdekop Trail. Horse riding is also available. There's a large, purpose-built backpacker section with dorms (R45) and doubles for R120. You can camp for R20 and there's a tree house for R100 a double. The lodge does free pick-ups from Knysna or Plettenberg Bay.

Plettenberg Bay

☎ 044

Plettenberg Bay (often referred to as 'Plett') is a beautiful resort. It's a trendy destination, so things tend to be upmarket. It's probably a better place to spend time than Knysna in many ways – especially if you want to be on the beach.

The publicity association (☎ 533 4065) on Kloof St has a great deal of useful information. It's open from 8.15 am to 5 pm weekdays and until 1 pm on Saturday. Make sure you pick up the *Plettenberg Bay to Tsitsikamma* booklet.

Activities For information on the surrounding **nature reserves and walks** contact Nature & Environmental Conservation (☎ 533 2125) at 7 Zenon St. Ask the staff about **canoeing** on the Keurbooms River.

Mountain-bike trails are being developed in the area: the publicity association has details. Equitrailing (☎ 533 0599) offers **horse riding**.

Places offering **diving** include Diving International (☎ 533 0381) and Beyond the Beach (☎ 533 1158).

If you have your own vehicle, the road running east of Plett is brilliant. Don't take the toll road, but turn off to Nature's Valley and the **Bloukrans Pass**. It's a beautiful drive.

Places to Stay To rent a house or a flat, contact an agent such as the Accommodation Bureau (☎ 533 2101) on Main St.

Aventura Eco Plettenberg Caravan Park *(☎ 535 9309)* is in a gorgeous spot on the river, east of town. Camp sites for two people range from R53 in the low season, to R111 in the high season. Four-person chalets start at R150.

There are backpackers hostels mushrooming all over the area; the following are a couple of the better ones:

Albergo *(☎ 313 4434, 8 Church St)*, near the town centre, is a well-run, friendly place that encourages activities. There are dorms for R35 and doubles with bathrooms for R110.

Weldon Kaya *(☎ 533 2437)* off the N2 at the corner of Piesang Valley Rd is a bit out of town but is well worth the trip. The backpackers' section is in an historic building that was the first post office on the Garden Route; dorms cost R30 and doubles R120. There are also fanciful versions of traditional African mud huts; these are good value at R150 per person, including breakfast.

Right in town on the corner of Main and Gibb Sts, the ***Bayview Hotel*** *(☎ 533 1961)* is modern, small and pleasant. It charges from R300 per person.

The ***Beacon Island Resort*** *(☎ 533 1120)* is a multistorey hotel on Beacon Island (linked to the rest of Plett by a causeway). The position is spectacular and so is the price. Expect to pay about R950 a double.

Places to Eat A popular place with locals, surfies and visitors is ***The Boardwalk***. It's an excellent cafe with soup for R12.50 and main courses starting at about R25.

If you're lucky, you may see dolphins playing in the surf at ***The Lookout***, by the beach near Lookout Rocks. Mains cost about R35.

Blue Bay Cafe does a good breakfast for R15, and you can sit outside on the balcony overlooking Main St while you sip your coffee. Their dinners are also excellent; the Thai green prawn and chicken curry (R38) is delicious.

Cranzgot's Pizzeria has excellent pizzas for about R30 and steaks for about R40.

Tivoli Continental Coffee Bar in Sun Plaza is good.

Getting There & Away Buses and long-distance minibus taxis stop at or near the Shell Ultra City on the highway. Minibus taxis to Knysna (about R6) leave from the corner of Kloof and High Sts.

Robberg Nature & Marine Reserve

This reserve (☎ 044-533 3424) is 9km south-east of Plettenberg Bay. From Piesang Valley follow the airport road until you see signs to the reserve. Robberg protects a peninsula with a rugged coastline of cliffs and rocks. The peninsula acts as a sort of marine speed bump to larger sea life, with mammals and fish spending time here before moving on.

Northern Cape Province

Northern Cape is by far the largest but one of the least populated of South Africa's provinces. The mighty Orange River is a lifeline that runs through this area that becomes desert-like on the fringes of the Kalahari and in the Karoo. The Orange and its tributary, the Vaal, combine to create the longest and largest river in South Africa.

Along the river there are intensely cultivated, irrigated farms. To the north of the river, bordering Botswana, are sparsely wooded savanna and grasslands – cattle-ranching country. To the south, there's the Karoo with woody shrubs and succulents – sheep-farming country.

The Orange flows west to form the border between South Africa and Namibia, and this area is spectacularly harsh country. South of here is the Namaqualand region, world-famous for its spring flowers.

KIMBERLEY

☎ 053

Kimberley, the capital of Northern Cape, would never have existed had it not been for a human fascination for things that glitter. This was where the De Beers company began and Cecil Rhodes and Ernest Oppenheimer made their fortunes.

Diamonds were discovered in the area in 1869, and by 1872 there were 50,000 miners in the vicinity. In 1871 diamonds were discovered at a small hill, which came to be known as **Colesberg Kopje** and later as Kimberley, and the excavation of the Big Hole commenced.

After a long trip across the Karoo, the relatively bright lights of Kimberley are a welcome sight.

Orientation & Information

The town centre is a tangle of streets inherited from the days when Kimberley was a rowdy shantytown.

The city's most noticeable tall building is Harry Oppenheimer House, south of the centre, where South Africa's diamonds are graded and valued.

The well-stocked Diamantveld Visitor Centre (☎ 830 6277) is near the corner of Bultfontein and Lyndhurst Rds and is open weekdays and Saturday morning. There is a branch of Northern Cape Tourism (☎ 832 2657) at 187 Du Toitspan Rd.

The Big Hole & Kimberley Mine

The 180m-deep Big Hole is the largest hole in the world dug entirely by manual labour.

Kimberley Mine, which took over after opencast mining could no longer continue, went to a depth of around 1100m. It closed in 1914. Altogether, 14.5 million carats of diamonds are believed to have been removed from under Colesberg Kopje. In other words, 28 million tonnes of earth and rock was removed for three tonnes of diamonds.

Kimberley Mine Museum

This excellent open-air museum is on the western side of the Big Hole. Forty-eight original or facsimile buildings form a

SOUTH AFRICA

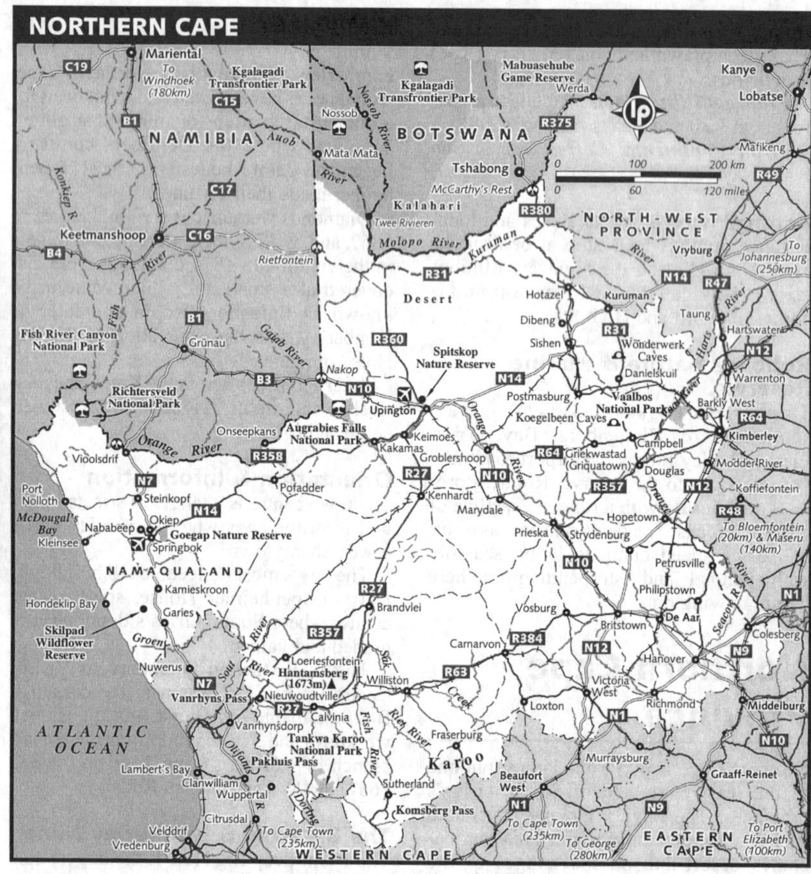

reconstruction of Kimberley in the 1880s and De Beers Hall has a collection of diamonds. The museum (☎ 833 1557) is open from 8 am to 6 pm daily; entry is R15.

Duggan-Cronin Gallery

The Duggan-Cronin Gallery (☎ 842 0099) on Egerton Rd in the suburb of Belgravia features a collection of photographs of black tribes taken in the 1920s and 30s – before many aspects of traditional life were lost. The gallery is open from 9 am to 5 pm weekdays, 9 am to 1 pm Saturday, and 2 to 5 pm Sunday; entry is R3.

De Beers Tours

De Beers Tours runs tours of the Bultfontein Mine's treatment and recovery plants, departing from the visitors centre at the mine gate. They cost R7 and start at 9 and 11 am weekdays. Underground tours (☎ 842 1321) are at 7.45 am weekdays (9.30 am Tuesday). Tours cost R40 and you have to be over 16 years.

Places to Stay

Open Mine Caravan Park** (☎ 830 6322)* is central and attractive but has little shade. Tent sites are R14 plus R8 per person. If you have your own transport, ***Kimberly

Cecil Rhodes

Cecil John Rhodes (1853–1902), the sickly son of an English vicar, was sent to South Africa in 1870 to improve his health. By 1887 he had founded the De Beers Consolidated Mines Company and could afford to buy Barney Barnato's Kimberley Mine for UK£5,000,000. By 1891, De Beers owned 90% of the world's diamonds and Rhodes also had a stake in the fabulous reef of gold discovered on the Witwatersrand (near Johannesburg).

Rhodes was not satisfied with merely acquiring personal wealth and power. He personified the idea of empire and dreamed of 'painting the map red' by building a railway from the Cape to Cairo (running through British territory all the way) and even of bringing the USA back under British rule. The times were right for such dreams and in 1890 he was elected prime minister of the Cape Colony.

Rhodes was successful in establishing British control in Bechuanaland (later Botswana) and the area that was to become Rhodesia (later Zimbabwe), but the gold mines there proved to be less productive than those on the Witwatersrand.

The Transvaal Republic in general, and Paul Kruger in particular, had been causing Rhodes difficulty for some time. It irked Rhodes that Kruger's republic of pastoralists should be sitting on the richest reef of gold in the world, and the republic was also directly in the path of British expansion.

The miners on the Witwatersrand were mainly non-Boers, who were denied any say in the politics of the republic. This caused increasing resentment, and in late 1895 Captain Leander Jameson led an expedition into the Witwatersrand with the intention of sparking an uprising among the foreigners.

The Jameson raid was a fiasco. All the participants were either killed or captured and Jameson was jailed. The British government was extremely embarrassed when it became apparent that Rhodes had prior knowledge of the raid and probably encouraged it. He was forced to resign as prime minister and the British government took control of Rhodesia and Bechuanaland, his personal fiefdoms. Rhodes' empire-building days were over.

After his death in 1902, Rhodes' reputation was largely rehabilitated by his will, which devoted most of his fortune to the Rhodes Scholarship. This still sends winning students from the Commonwealth and other countries to study at Oxford University.

Caravan Park about 4km from the centre on Hull St (the road towards the Youth Hostel), is friendly, secure and similarly priced.

Kimberley Youth Hostel *(☎ 832 8577)*, also known as Gum Tree Lodge, is about 5km from town at the intersection of Hull St and the Bloemfontein road. It's a large, pleasant place with shady lawns, a pool and a cafe. Dorms cost R35; singles or twins in fairly basic flats with stove and fridge cost from R50 per person.

Stay-A-Day *(☎ 832 7239, 72 Lawson St, New Park)* is big, clean, central and exceptional value. Doubles with bathroom, TV and tea and coffee making facilities are R160, twin rooms are R100 and dorms R35. Proceeds go to the local children's home, so please respect the facilities.

The ***Horseshoe Motel*** *(☎ 832 5267)* on Memorial Rd (look for the giant Caltex sign) is a comfortable motel with a swimming pool. Singles/doubles with TV, aircon and telephone start at R165/230.

Holiday Inn Garden Court *(☎ 833 1751)* on Du Toitspan Rd is a large hotel delivering high standards at a reasonable price; rooms start at R294/318. Next door is the comfortable ***Diamond Protea Lodge*** *(☎ 831 1281)* with rooms for R290 (R225 on weekends).

Places to Eat

If you're looking for something cheap and delicious, ***Panino Bakery*** on the corner of Jones St and Old Main Rd has a selection of cakes, biscuits, pies and bread.

Overlooking Market Square, ***Safari Steakhouse*** upstairs on the corner of Old Jones St and Main Rd, is highly regarded by locals. The service is good and the steaks are the best in town. At the old-style and atmospheric ***Star of the West Hotel*** on North Circular Rd there are cheap pub meals.

The ***Keg & Falcon*** conveniently located next to the Northern Cape Tourism office has tasty, affordable meals for around R25. The ***Halfway House*** on Du Toitspan Rd near the corner of Egerton Rd is an atmospheric watering hole in a historic building.

Getting There & Away

Bus Many services run to/from Jo'burg, which is about six hours from Kimberley. The cheapest is Greyhound's daily service for R120. The trip from Kimberley to Cape Town with Translux costs R250. Translux also runs to Knysna (11 hours) via Oudtshoorn, Mossel Bay and George. The fare to any of these is R210.

Northern Cape Bus Service (☎ 831 1062), 5 Elliot St, is the Greyhound agent in Kimberley. Greyhound, Intercape and Translux buses stop at the Shell Ultra City on the N12 – you'll have to get a bus, taxi or hitch there.

Minibus Taxi The minibus taxi area is around the Indian shopping centre on Duncan St. Destinations include: Bloemfontein (R40); Jo'burg (R80); Upington (R80); and Cape Town (R120).

Train For information on trains, contact Spoornet (☎ 838 2100) or check out its Web site: www.spoornet.co.za.

The *Trans Karoo* runs daily to Cape Town and Jo'burg/Pretoria.

The *Diamond Express* runs to Jo'burg/Pretoria and Bloemfontein. The *Trans Oranje* between Cape Town and Durban also stops here.

Getting Around

A minibus taxi around town costs about R1.40. For a taxi from the pub, there is AA Taxi (☎ 861 4015) and Rikki's Taxi (☎ 082 461 8818).

An antique tram runs hourly between the mine museum (departing on the hour) and the town hall (departing at quarter past). The one-way fare is R3.

UPINGTON

☎ 054

Upington is on the banks of the Orange River and is the principal town in the far north. It's an orderly, prosperous place, full of supermarkets and chain stores.

The surrounding area is intensively cultivated thanks to the limitless sunlight and irrigation water.

The helpful tourist office (☎ 332 6064) is in the Kalahari Orange Museum.

Places to Stay

The ***Eiland Holiday Resort*** *(☎ 334 0286)* is a fair walk from town on the southern bank of the Orange River; cross the bridge signposted for Prieska at the northern end of town. There are pleasant tent sites for R17 per person and four-bed rondavels at R176, plus a range of huts and chalets.

Yebo Guesthouse & Backpackers *(☎ 331 2496, 21 Morant St)* is in a pleasant spot with a swimming pool, kitchen and tidy rooms. Dorms are R50, more comfortable rooms are R85/200.

There are a number of guesthouses that charge from R100, such as ***Three Gables*** *(☎ 331 1220, 34 Bull St)*; the tourist office has a full list of the others.

The two Protea hotels stand opposite each other on the corner of Lutz and Schroder Sts. The ***Oasis Protea Lodge*** *(☎ 331 1125)* is a comfortable if characterless place with rooms for R299. The older ***Upington Protea Hotel*** *(☎ 332 4414)* charges R295. Both hotels have weekend specials.

Getting There & Away

Air SAA flies to/from Jo'burg and Cape Town. One-way fares include: Cape Town (R855, daily except Saturday) and Jo'burg (R900, daily). Note there is no public transport between the airport and Upington.

Bus The Intercape bus office (☎ 332 6091) is on Lutz St. The trip from Jo'burg costs R190 and takes 8½ hours. This bus connects with one to Windhoek, taking 10 hours and costing R210. Intercape also has buses running to/from Cape Town (R185, 10½ hours).

Minibus Taxi You'll find minibus taxis near Checkers supermarket on the corner of Mark and Basson Sts.

Upington taxis can take a long time to fill but there is generally at least one per day to major destinations including Kimberley (R95), Cape Town (R130), Jo'burg (R140) and Windhoek (R160).

Car If you want to see the Kgalagadi Transfrontier Park and are short of time, it makes sense to fly to Upington and hire a car. There's an Avis agent (☎ 332 4746) at the airport. The Oasis Protea Lodge rents 4WD vehicles.

KGALAGADI TRANSFRONTIER PARK

In April 1999, South Africa's Kalahari-Gemsbok National Park and Botswana's Mabuasehube-Gemsbok National Park merged and are now collectively known as the Kgalagadi Transfrontier Park. The South African area of this park is not as well known as many other Southern African parks but it is well worth visiting. The accessible section of the park lies in the triangular segment of South Africa between Namibia and Botswana. This area covers 959,103 hectares. However, the protected area continues on the Botswana side of the border (there are no fences) where there are another 1,807,000 hectares. Together, the two sections make up one of the largest protected areas in Africa. If you want to venture into the Botswana side of the park, you will need to make arrangements with Botswana Department of Wildlife & National Parks (☎ 09-267-660376) in Maun.

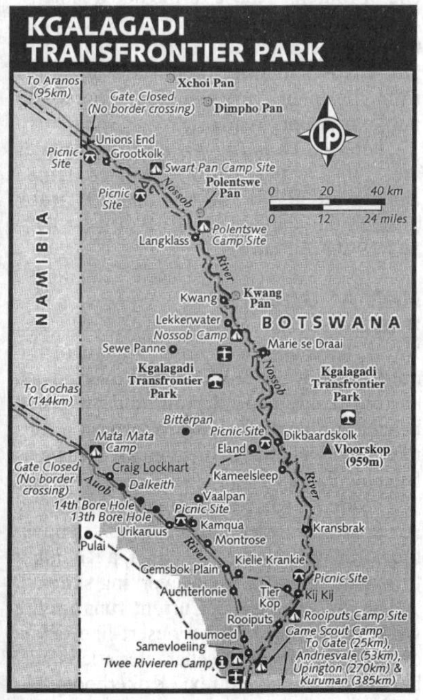

Although the countryside is semidesert it is richer than it appears and supports large populations of birds, reptiles, small mammals and antelopes. These in turn support a large population of predators.

The Nossob and Auob Rivers (usually dry) run through the park and meet at Twee Rivieren. Much of the wildlife is concentrated in these riverbeds, where there are water holes. This makes wildlife viewing here remarkably successful.

Information

The best time to visit is in June and July when the weather is coolest (below freezing at night) and the animals have drawn in to the water holes along the dry riverbeds.

From September to October is the wet season and if it does rain, many of the animals scatter out across the plain to take advantage of the fresh pastures. November is quiet, and daily temperatures start to increase. Despite the fact that temperatures frequently reach 45°C in December and January, the chalets in the park are often fully booked.

Entry is R36/18 for adults/children. All the rest camps have shops where basic groceries, soft drinks and alcohol can be purchased (no fresh vegetables). Petrol and diesel are available at each camp.

The entrance gate opening hours generally open from around 6.30 am to 6.30 pm depending on the time of year.

Fauna

There have been 215 species of bird recorded in the park, including the secretary bird, the kori bustard and the sociable weaver.

There are 19 species of predator, including the dark-maned Kalahari lion, cheetah, leopard, wild dog, hyaena, jackal, bat-eared fox and suricate. The most numerous species is the springbok.

Places to Stay

There are rest camps at ***Twee Rivieren***, ***Mata Mata*** and ***Nossob***; all have a range of fully equipped cottages (from R240 for four people) and there are huts with shared facilities at Mata Mata and Nossob for R105 for three people. All the rest camps have camp sites without electricity, for R40 for up to six people. All accommodation, including tent sites, must be booked through the National Parks Board (☎ 012-343 1991) in Pretoria.

There are a number of places, mainly farms, which offer accommodation en route between Upington and Kgalagadi Transfrontier Park. The tourist office in Upington has details.

Getting There & Away

There is no public transport to the national park. By car, it's a five- or six-hour drive from Twee Rivieren to Kuruman (385km) or Upington (358km) and you have to cover a significant distance on dirt, although the road is being sealed. Be careful driving on the dirt sections and if you stop, don't pull too far off the road or you might become stuck in the sand.

No petrol is available between Upington and Twee Rivieren, so make sure you start with a full tank. It's important to carry water, as you might have to wait a while if you break down – you can rapidly become dangerously dehydrated when the temperature is over 40°C.

UPINGTON TO SPRINGBOK

West from Upington the road at first follows the course of the Orange River and passes through oases of vineyards and the pleasant little towns of **Keimos** and **Kakamas**. The turn-off to Augrabies Falls National Park, 40km north of the road, is at Kakamas.

From Kakamas to **Pofadder** things are considerably duller, but then you enter a wide, bleak valley and, as you approach Springbok, dramatic piles of boulders litter the landscape – you have entered Namaqualand.

Augrabies Falls National Park

Augrabies Falls National Park (☎ 054-451 0050) is more than just an impressive waterfall.

Certainly the falls can be spectacular but the most interesting facet of the park is the fascinating desert and riverine environments on either side of the river.

The three-day **Klipspringer Hiking Trail** runs along the southern bank of the river. Hikers must supply their own sleeping bags and food. Booking in advance is advised; the per-person charge is R70. The walk is closed from the middle of October to the end of March because of the hot weather.

The entry charge per vehicle is R12, and the entrance gate is open from 6.30 am to 10 pm. Maps and information are available from the main park complex. There's no public transport available.

There's a ***camping ground*** where sites are R40 for two people. Self-contained chalets are R290 for two people. Book through the National Parks Board (☎ 012-343 1991) in Pretoria.

NAMAQUALAND

☎ 027

Namaqualand is a rugged plateau in the north-west of the province that overlooks a narrow, sandy coastal plain and the bleak beaches of the west coast. In the east it runs into the dry central plains that are known as Bushmanland.

The area is sparsely populated, mainly by Afrikaans-speaking sheep farmers, and in the north-west by the Namaqua, a Khoikhoi tribe famous for its metal-working skills.

The cold Benguela Current runs up the west coast and creates a desert-like environment. You'll see the characteristic kokerboom (see the boxed text 'Kokerbooms' in the Southern Namibia section in the Namibia chapter), an aloe that can grow to a height of 4m. In the north you'll see 'halfmens' or elephant trunk *(Pachydodium namaquanum)*, weird tree-like succulents topped by a small 'face' of foliage. They always look to the north, and there's a legend that they are the transformed bodies of Khoikhoi who were driven south during a war. Those who turned around to look towards their lost lands were turned into trees.

Namaqualand can get cold in winter (average minimums around 5°C) and hot in summer (average maximums around 30°C).

Alluvial Diamonds

In 1925 a young soldier found a glittering stone near Port Nolloth. Prospectors converged on the area and it soon became clear (notably to Ernest Oppenheimer of De Beers) that an enormously rich resource of diamonds had been discovered.

Eventually all major mines were brought into the De Beers fold and all production was brought under the control of a worldwide cartel, the Central Selling Organisation (CSO).

The diamonds are harvested from gravel beds on the sea floor and from beneath the sandveld, a narrow, sandy plain between mountains and sea that was itself once under the sea.

Despite strict security and laws, it's believed that substantial quantities of diamonds still find their way to illegal traders beyond the reach of the CSO. You may meet locals who offer to sell you cheap diamonds – this is highly illegal, and you're likely to end up with a *slenter* (fake diamond).

The bleak landscape and the presence of diamond miners and divers contribute to a frontier atmosphere. If you want to check it out, the best place to go is **Port Nolloth**; stay at the friendly ***Bedrock*** *(☎ 851 8865)*, which has B&B, guesthouse and backpacker accommodation.

Wildflowers

Although the wildflowers of the Western Cape are spectacular, they are overshadowed by the brilliance of the world-renowned Namaqualand displays. Generally the Namaqualand flowers bloom a couple of weeks earlier than those further south.

The optimum time to visit varies from year to year, but your best chance of seeing the flowers at their peak is between mid-August and mid-September.

The Namaqualand flora, which is part of the Palaeotropical kingdom, begins north of Vanrhynsdorp in Western Cape. There can be flowers on the plains between Nuwerus and Garies, but the major spectacle begins around Garies and extends to Steinkopf in the north. Springbok is considered the flower capital.

Another zone can be found in the Kamiesberg Range, which is to the east of Kamieskroon. The plain to the east of Springbok and north to Vioolsdrif produces more brilliant annuals.

The flower season brings hordes of people to the area and accommodation becomes scarce and expensive. In Cape Town you can call the Flower Line (☎ 021-418 3705) for information on flower viewing.

Getting There & Away

Aside from buses on the N7 and R27 (between Vanrhynsdorp and Upington) public transport is sparse. The major operators offer tours of Namaqualand from Jo'burg and Cape Town, but if you really want to see the area you'll need your own vehicle.

Kamieskroon

Kamieskroon is perched high in the mountains and is surrounded by boulder-strewn hills. There are some beautiful drives and walks in the area. For information contact the Kamieskroon & Sandveld Tourism Forum (☎ 672 1627).

About 18km north-west of Kamieskroon is the **Skilpad Wildflower Reserve**.

The ***Kamieskroon Hotel*** *(☎ 672 1675)* is a very civilised hideaway. Singles/doubles are R110/180 for B&B and more in flower season. You can also camp for R40.

Springbok

Springbok considers itself the capital of Namaqualand, and it lies in a valley among

SOUTH AFRICA

harsh, rocky hills that explode with colour in the flower season.

The first European-run copper mine was established on the town's outskirts in 1852, and from a rough-and-tumble frontier town, Springbok has been transformed into a busy service centre for the copper and diamond mines in the area.

Orientation & Information The town is quite spread out, but most places are within walking distance of the small *kopje* (isolated hill) in the elbow of the main street's right-angled bend.

Springbok Lodge (☎ 712 1321) on the main street is the best place in town to collect information on the area (including where the best flowers are). There's also an official information centre (☎ 712 2071) in the old church next to the post office. You can get online access at Melkboschkuil Travel Shop (see Places to Eat in this section).

Springbok Museum In the 1920s Springbok had a large Jewish population. Most have moved away, however, and their synagogue has been converted into an interesting local museum. It's open on weekday mornings.

Places to Stay During the flower season accommodation in Springbok can fill up and prices rise. The information centre can tell you about overflow accommodation in private homes.

Springbok Caravan Park *(☎ 718 1584)* is 2km from town on Goegap Rd, the road to the nature reserve. Occasional buses run past, otherwise it's a long walk. Tent sites are R15 per person.

Recommended by readers' letters is ***Annie's Cottage*** *(☎ 712 1451, 4 King St)*, which has backpacker accommodation (R50) as well as B&B for R120 per person.

Namastat *(☎ 712 2435)* has accommodation in traditional woven Namaqua 'mat' huts *(matjiehuis* in Afrikaans), similar in shape to Zulu 'beehive' huts. Each hut has two beds and costs R45 per person, R30 if you have your own bedding. The Namastat is about 3km south of town and on the Cape Town road (not the N7).

The ***Springbok Lodge*** *(☎ 712 1321)* has rooms and cottages behind the cafe. The cottages have been steadily upgraded over the years and are simple but pleasant. Rates start at R90 per person and cost more for self-catering units.

The best hotel option is the ***Springbok Hotel*** *(☎ 712 1161)*, a plain, old-style hotel with a certain antiquated charm. Singles/doubles are R127/202.

Places to Eat Light meals and good coffee are available at ***Melkboschkuil Travel Shop***, which also has an Internet service. Travellers have recommended ***BJ's***, a licensed steakhouse with an extensive menu; a burger with chips and salad is R15.

For something informal and fun, the ***Springbok Restaurant*** at the Springbok Lodge can't be beaten. The menu is large and includes grills from R30, breakfast, snacks and salads. Avoid the pizza.

Getting There & Away There are weekday flights from Springbok to Cape Town (R730) with National Airlines. Call ☎ 712 2061 in Springbok, or ☎ 021-934 0350 in Cape Town.

Intercape's bus service from Windhoek (Namibia) to Cape Town runs through Springbok. The fare from Springbok to Cape Town is R175; Springbok to Windhoek costs R245.

Van Wyk's Busdiens (☎ 713 8559) runs a daily door-to-door taxi to Cape Town for R100. You'll find ordinary minibus taxis to Cape Town (also R100) at the Caltex garage, near the traffic light on Voortrekker St, or at the taxi rank at the rear of the First National Bank near the kopje.

Ask at the Springbok Lodge or the tourism information centre about car hire from local garages.

Goegap Nature Reserve

This reserve is about 8km from Springbok and is famous for its spring flowers and its nursery of amazing Karoo and Namaqualand succulents. In addition to the flora, there is springbok, ostrich, zebra and birdlife. The reserve is open from 8 am to 4 pm weekdays and on weekends during the flower season. Entry is R5 per vehicle plus R4 per person.

Vioolsdrif

Vioolsdrif, on the N7 677km north of Cape Town, is the border crossing for traffic going to/from Namibia (the border is open 24 hours), and is the gateway to Richtersveld National Park.

The drive from Steinkopf is spectacular and at Vioolsdrif there are great views of the Orange River carving its way through the desolate mountains with the narrow strip of farmland along its banks.

For more border crossing information, see under Land in the main Getting There & Away section earlier in this chapter.

Peace of Paradise camp site occupies a lovely setting 23km downstream along the river road from the border crossing. Sites cost US$5 per person and canoes are available for guests.

Richtersveld National Park

Richtersveld National Park is a big park in the northern loop of the Orange River to the north-west of Vioolsdrif and the N7. The park is the property of the local Namaqua people who continue to lead a semitraditional, seminomadic pastoral existence.

The area is a mountainous desert and the hiking possibilities, though demanding, are excellent. Despite its apparent barrenness, the territory has a rich and prolific variety of succulent plants.

Most of the park is virtually inaccessible without a properly equipped expedition and local guides. For more information, call ☎ 831 1506 or write to Richtersveld National Park, PO Box 406, Alexander Bay 8290.

Eastern Cape

Eastern Cape is a diverse and largely undeveloped province. It includes the former Homelands of Ciskei and Transkei, so most of its population is Xhosa-speaking.

The long coastline extends from Tsitsikamma Coastal National Park, through Port Elizabeth and the Sunshine Coast to the Shipwreck Coast of the former Ciskei region. It then continues past East London and into the spectacular subtropical Wild Coast of the former Transkei.

Inland, the rolling green hills around Grahamstown are known as Settler Country, after the British migrants who settled the area in the early 19th century. Further north and on the plateau is the semidesert Karoo.

Warning

Although many of the roads within the former Ciskei and Transkei regions are of a reasonable standard, there is a real likelihood of children and livestock straying onto them.

NATURE'S VALLEY TO THE KEI RIVER

Tsitsikamma Coastal National Park has beautiful forests, while the coast between Cape St Francis and East London is best known for its surf. The coast between the Great Fish River (east of Port Alfred) almost to East London was once part of Ciskei and is less developed.

Tsitsikamma Coastal National Park

The park protects the 100km of coast east of Plettenberg Bay. The Cape clawless otter is found in the park; there are also baboon, monkey and small antelope. Diving and snorkelling here are rewarding.

Orientation & Information The park gate is 6km off the N2. It's open from 5.30 am to 9.30 pm, and day visits cost R14/7 for adults/children. It's 2km from the gate to the Storms River Mouth Rest Camp; there's a shop and restaurant here.

Nature's Valley Nature's Valley is a small settlement in the west of Tsitsikamma Coastal National Park. The surrounding hills are forested with yellowwood, and the 5km beach is magnificent. The only shop in the area is painted a lovely pink and yellow!

Otter Trail The five-day Otter Trail hugs the coastline from Storms River Mouth to

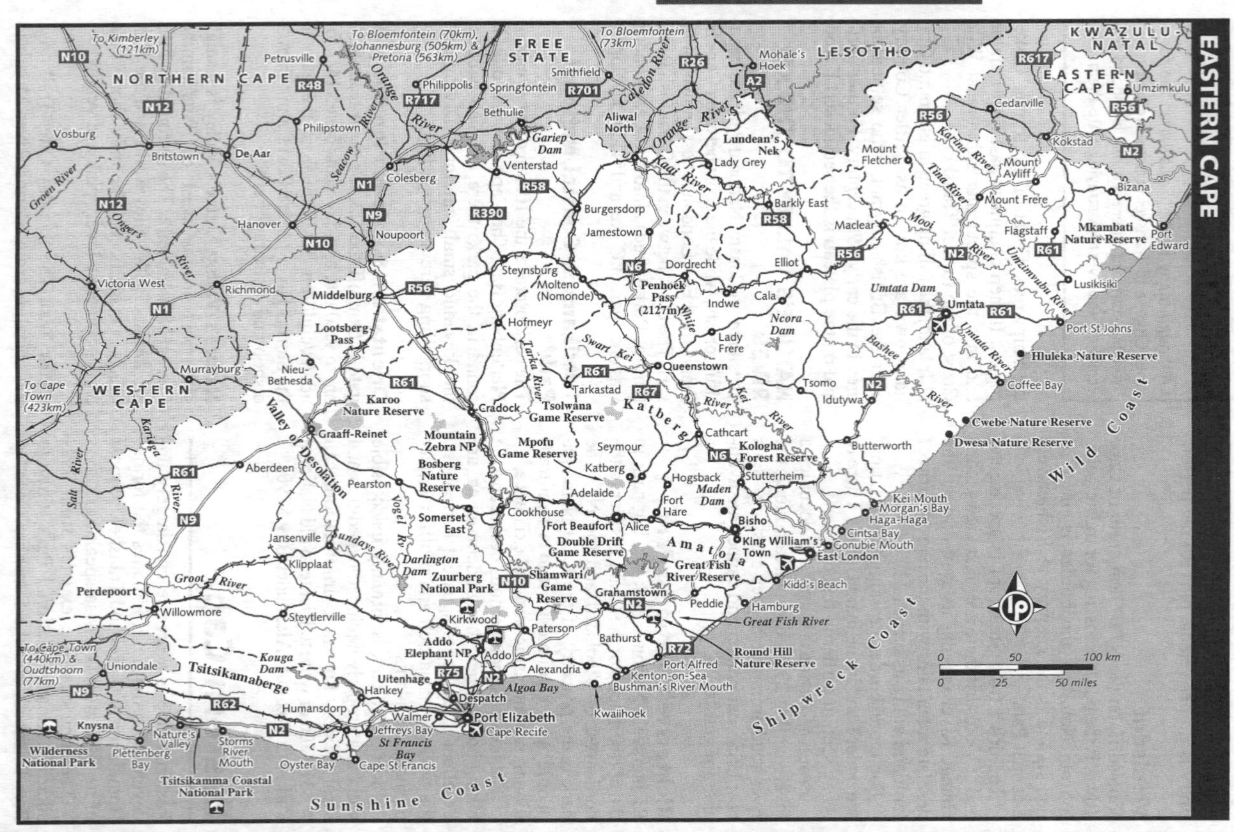
EASTERN CAPE
LESOTHO
FREE STATE
NORTHERN CAPE
WESTERN CAPE
KWAZULU-NATAL
EASTERN CAPE
Wild Coast
Shipwreck Coast
Sunshine Coast
Umtata
Port St Johns
Coffee Bay
Hluleka Nature Reserve
Cwebe Nature Reserve
Dwesa Nature Reserve
Mkambati Nature Reserve
Kokstad
Bizana
Port Edward
Umzimkulu
Lusikisiki
Flagstaff
Mount Ayliff
Mount Frere
Cedarville
Mount Fletcher
Maclear
Elliot
Barkly East
Lady Grey
Lundean's Nek
Mohale's Hoek
Aliwal North
Burgersdorp
Jamestown
Dordrecht
Indwe
Cala
Queenstown
Penhoek Pass (2127m)
Lady Frere
Tsomo
Idutywa
Butterworth
Kei Mouth
Morgan's Bay
Haga-Haga
Cintsa Bay
Gonubie Mouth
East London
Kidd's Beach
King William's Town
Bisho
Stutterheim
Kologha Forest Reserve
Cathcart
Hogsback
Fort Hare
Alice
Fort Beaufort
Seymour
Katberg
Adelaide
Cookhouse
Somerset East
Bosberg Nature Reserve
Mountain Zebra NP
Cradock
Tarkastad
Tsolwana Game Reserve
Mpofu Game Reserve
Double Drift Game Reserve
Great Fish River Reserve
Shamwari Game Reserve
Grahamstown
Bathurst
Peddie
Hamburg
Round Hill Nature Reserve
Port Alfred
Kenton-on-Sea
Bushman's River Mouth
Kwaaihoek
Alexandria
Paterson
Kirkwood
Addo
Addo Elephant NP
Zuurberg National Park
Darlington Dam
Despatch
Uitenhage
Port Elizabeth
Cape Recife
Algoa Bay
Walmer
Jeffreys Bay
St Francis Bay
Cape St Francis
Oyster Bay
Humansdorp
Hankey
Kouga Dam
Tsitsikamaberge
Storms River Mouth
Tsitsikamma Coastal National Park
Nature's Valley
Plettenberg Bay
Knysna
Wilderness National Park
Uniondale
Willowmore
Steytlerville
Klipplaat
Jansenville
Pearston
Aberdeen
Graaff-Reinet
Valley of Desolation
Karoo Nature Reserve
Nieu-Bethesda
Lootsberg Pass
Middelburg
Hofmeyr
Steynsburg
Molteno (Nomonde)
Venterstad
Gariep Dam
Bethulie
Springfontein
Smithfield
Philippolis
Colesberg
Noupoort
Petrusville
Philipstown
De Aar
Hanover
Richmond
Murrayburg
Britstown
Victoria West
Vosburg
Perdepoort
Orange River
Caledon River
Kaai River
Tarka River
Swart Kei
White
Kei River
Great Fish River
Sundays River
Groot River
Kariga
Salt River
Seacow River
Ongers River
Groen River
Umzimvubu River
Umtata River
Umtata Dam
Bashee River
Tina River
Karina River
Mooi River
Ncora Dam
Maden Dam
Vogel Rv
Katberg
Amatola
To Bloemfontein (73km)
To Bloemfontein (70km), Johannesburg (505km) & Pretoria (563km)
To Kimberley (121km)
To Cape Town (423km)
To Cape Town (440km) & Oudtshoorn (77km)
0 50 100 km
0 25 50 miles

Nature's Valley. The river crossings can be quite difficult, so it is essential that your gear is stowed in waterproof bags.

Accommodation is in ***huts***; no camping is allowed. The cost of walking the trail is R275 per person and bookings should be made through the National Parks Board in Pretoria (☎ 012-343 1991) or Cape Town (☎ 021-422 2810). Unfortunately, the trail is booked up months ahead.

Tsitsikamma Trail The five-day Tsitsikamma Trail parallels the Otter Trail but takes you inland through the forests. Accommodation is in ***huts***. You should have little difficulty getting a booking. Book through the Forestry Department (☎ 044-382 5466) in Knysna or contact De Vasselot Nature Reserve near Nature's Valley.

Places to Stay A National Parks Board camping ground, the ***De Vasselot Restcamp***, can be found on the river east of the town of Nature's Valley. Camp sites cost a steep R65 for two people, plus R20 for each additional person. There's a 20% discount between May and August. Forest huts cost R120 and if you stay in one you can use a canoe for no charge.

The Xhosa

Most of Eastern Cape is populated by groups of Nguni peoples (Zulu, Xhosa and Ndebele) who occupied the coastal savanna of South Africa, but those living west of the Great Fish River are relatively recent arrivals. There is no satisfactory explanation for the differences between the coastal Nguni and the Sotho of the highveld, or when the distinction came about. It is believed that Iron Age Bantus had reached the Great Kei River by AD 1000.

The Xhosa first came into contact with Boers in the 1760s. Both groups were heavily dependent on cattle, and both coveted the grazing land in the area known as Zuurveld (the coastal strip from Algoa Bay to the Great Kei River).

In 1771, Governor van Plettenberg convinced some chiefs to consider the Great Fish River as the boundary between the Dutch East India Company's territory and the Xhosa's. Conflict was inevitable, and the first of nine major frontier wars broke out in 1779 – skirmishes and brigandage (by blacks and whites) were virtually continuous for the next century.

By the beginning of the 19th century, the Xhosa were under pressure in the west from white expansion, and in the east and north from peoples fleeing from the *Difaqane* (forced migration). After the Sixth Frontier War (1834–35) the British declared the land between the Great Kei and Keiskamma Rivers the Province of Queen Adelaide, and allowed a limited degree of independence. In 1846, however, white colonialists invaded, beginning the Seventh Frontier War. In its aftermath, British Kaffraria was established, with King William's Town as its capital.

In 1840 the great leader Sandile had become the paramount chief of the Rharhabe (or Ciskei) Xhosa, and he was to mobilise the Xhosa in their last increasingly desperate attempts to retain their land and resist white influence. He was a key figure in the Seventh, Eighth (1850–53) and Ninth Frontier Wars.

He was also involved in the 'Great Cattle Killing', the Xhosa suicide of 1857. A young girl, Nongqawuse, had visions that described how the Xhosa could reconcile themselves with a spirit world that allowed the theft of their lands and destruction of their culture. According to her visions, the spirits required the sacrifice of cattle and crops – in return the whites would be swept into the sea. The Xhosa followed Nongqawuse's visions and it is estimated that of a Xhosa population of 90,000 in British Kaffraria, 30,000 died of starvation and 30,000 were forced to emigrate as destitute refugees.

In 1866, British Kaffraria became part of the Cape Colony. The Xhosa had been devastated by years of struggle, but in 1877–78 they once again fought for their independence in the Ninth Frontier War.

The ***Storms River Mouth Rest Camp*** in the park has camp sites that cost R65 for two people, plus R20 for each additional person. There are 20% seasonal discounts on tent sites. Various types of cottages cost from R290 a double, with breakfast; all are equipped with kitchens (including utensils), bedding and bathrooms. Forest huts are also available for R120. The reception office is open from 7 am to 7.45 pm.

Bookings for both of these camps should be made through the National Parks Board in Pretoria (☎ 012-343 1991) or Cape Town (☎ 021-422 2810).

Hikers' Haven *(☎ 531 6805, 411 St Patrick's Rd)* in Nature's Valley is a cosy place with good facilities. B&B costs R95 per person and dorms under thatch cost R49.

Getting There & Away Buses running between Cape Town and Port Elizabeth will drop you off at the signposted turn-off on the N2, from where it's an 8km walk to the Storms River Mouth Rest Camp.

Storms River

☎ 042

There can be some confusion between Storms River, and Storms River Mouth in the Tsitsikamma Coastal National Park. The Storms River signpost is 4km east of the park turn-off (despite what some maps show) and leads to a different place entirely: a tiny village with tree-shaded lanes.

Storms River Adventures (☎ 541 1836, ⓔ adventure@gardenroute.co.za) is based here and offers a huge range of activities, including black-water tubing (R250), abseiling (R65) and snorkelling (R110).

The world's highest bungee jump (216m) is at the Bloukrans River Bridge (☎ 281 1450), 21km west of Storms River. For R500 you can have one hell of an adrenalin rush. It may be the world's highest jump but it is not the longest – you don't fall anywhere near the 216m.

The ***Stormsriver Rainbow Lodge*** *(☎ 541 1530)* is a comfortable place with a friendly owner and a range of accommodation. Dorms are R45, doubles cost R100 and well-appointed B&B rooms are R100 per person.

Jeffrey's Bay

☎ 042

Surfing is the reason to come here! Few would disagree that 'J Bay' has the best waves in Southern Africa and among the best in the world. Supertubes can be better than a three-minute ride from Boneyards to the end. Development is raging at a furious pace, but so far the local board-waxing vibe has been retained, and the town is still a laid-back place.

Information The small publicity association (☎ 293 2588) in the municipal buildings is open on weekdays and Saturday morning. The Network Internet Cafe is opposite the publicity association (R20 per hour).

Places to Stay The friendly, well-run ***Jeffrey's Bay Backpackers*** *(☎ 293 1021, 12 Jeffreys St)* has four-bed dorms for R35 per person; private rooms are just R45 per person. Your third night is free. It also rents surfboards for about R10 per hour and organises surfing lessons for around R15 per hour.

A very short walk from the beach, the ***Beachfront Backpackers*** *(☎ 082-892 1689, 36 Diaz Rd)* is great value at R30 per person in comfortable dorms. There's parking for the Kombi out the front.

A bit out of town (follow the signs) but worth the trip is ***Island Vibe Backpackers*** *(☎ 293 1625)*. It has panoramic views of the bay and if you were any closer to the surf, you'd be in it; dorms cost R35, doubles R100.

There are loads of B&Bs around town. We recommend ***Bay Cove*** *(☎ 296 2291)* on the corner of Poplar St and Da Gama Rd, which costs R80 per person – excellent value.

The ***Savoy Protea Hotel*** *(☎ 293 1106)* is OK, but nothing flash. Expect to pay around R220/310 for singles/doubles in the low season.

Places to Eat Good places for coffee are the ***cafes*** in the Seafront Mall, and the ***Coffee Mill*** at the museum opposite the mall. ***O'Hagans*** is an Irish pub on Da Gama St offering good pub lunches and dinners. Also on Da Gama St, ***Trawlers*** has good food, especially calamari, at low prices.

The Breakers *(☎ 293 1975, 23 Diaz Rd)*, overlooking the water, is a good place to go for a bit of a splurge. The menu offers mainly seafood, from R40, as well as pizza.

Getting There & Away The Baz Bus (☎ 021-439 2323) stops at the hostels. A trip from Jeffrey's Bay to Cape Town costs R385; to Port Elizabeth R55. Sunshine Bus Services (☎ 293 2221) runs to Port Elizabeth for R40. It's a door-to-door service.

Minibus taxis depart from Bloch's supermarket; the fare to Humansdorp is R5.

Port Elizabeth

☎ 041

Port Elizabeth's city centre is on steep hills overlooking Algoa Bay. It has pleasant beaches, parks and some interesting historical architecture, which is unfortunately crumbling because of neglect. Port Elizabeth (commonly known as PE) bills itself as the 'Friendly City', and it's a genuinely friendly place.

There are some enormous townships around PE and Uitenhage, and all the problems associated with poverty and violence are well represented.

Orientation The train station (for trains and buses) is just north of the Campanile, the bell tower, which you can climb for a donation. Walk up the steep hill to Donkin Reserve to orient yourself. The beaches are to the south.

Information Tourism Port Elizabeth (☎ 585 8884) is in the lighthouse building in Donkin Reserve. It is open daily.

American Express (☎ 365 1225) has an office in Pamela Arcade, Second Ave, Newton Park. Rennies Travel (☎ 374 3536) is in the Murray & Roberts building, 48/52 Ring St, Greenacres.

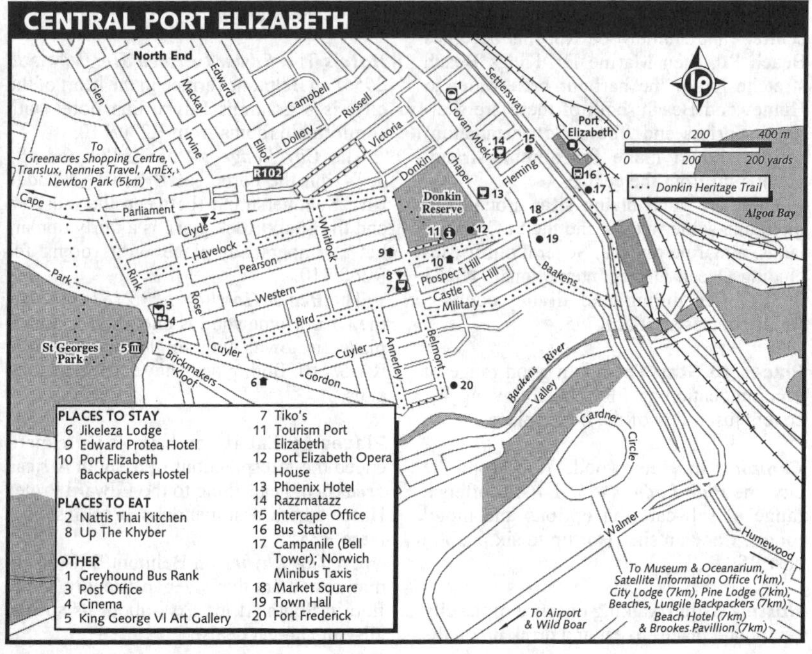

Things to See & Do Although **Settlers' Park** is virtually in the centre of the city, it includes 54 hectares of cultivated and natural gardens in the valley of the Baakens River. The main emphasis is on native plants and flowers, so it's also a good place for birdlife. The main entrance is on How St (off Park Dr, which circles St George's Park and its sporting fields).

The **Port Elizabeth Museum** is one of the best in the country. There are some interesting anthropological exhibitions; a tropical house and snake park; and an oceanarium, complete with performing dolphins. The complex is open daily from 9 am to 5 pm. Entry is R3 to the museum and R15 to the oceanarium.

Travellers have recommended the day and night **township tours** offered by Walmer Township Tours (☎ 082-970 4037). Daytime or nighttime visits to a local township cost about R120. Contact the company directly or ask at the Jikeleza Lodge for details (see Places to Stay later in this section).

The **beaches** are to the south of the city centre. Take Humewood Rd; this becomes Beach Rd, then Marine Dr. Kings Beach stretches from the harbour breakwater to Humewood Beach; both of these are sheltered. Surfers and *Hobie Cat* (catamaran) sailors should make for Summerstrand, about 5km from the centre.

There are good **diving sites** around PE, including some wrecks and the St Croix Islands, a marine reserve. Several outfits, including Ocean Divers International (☎ 363 0035) offer diving and diving courses. PADI courses start at R795.

Places to Stay There is a good range of accommodation in PE. The following list covers just a few of the better places.

Camping In Humewood, 7km from the city, the ***Pine Lodge*** *(☎ 583 4004)* offers a range of self-catering options and motel rooms. Caravan sites (for up to six people) cost R80.

Hostels Within walking distance of the city centre and places to eat and drink up on the headland, is the sociable ***Port Elizabeth Backpackers Hostel*** *(☎ 586 0697, 7 Prospect Hill)*. It offers free trips to the beaches. Dorms cost R40 and double rooms are R120.

The ***Jikeleza Lodge*** *(☎ 586 3721, 44 Cuyler St)* is an excellent hostel. It's small and clean and the owners are a veritable gold mine of information on PE – ask about local township tours. Prices are the same as at Port Elizabeth Backpackers.

Lungile Backpackers *(☎ 582 2042, 12 La Roche Dr, Humewood)* offers value for money. It's on the beachfront and surfboards are available; you'll fork out the same as at the hostels above.

B&Bs & Guesthouses Tourism Port Elizabeth makes B&B bookings. Most places charge between R100 and R150 per person.

The ***Fundani Township Lodge*** *(☎ 463 1471, 69 Theko St, KwaMagxaki)* offers the rare opportunity to stay in a township. Rooms with private bathroom cost R90/140, including a township walk and *ubuntu* (Xhosa hospitality).

Hotels The ***Edward Protea Hotel*** *(☎ 586 2056)* on Belmont Terrace in the heart of the city, is a gracious Edwardian hotel with comfortable rooms from R270/310.

The ***City Lodge*** *(☎ 586 3322, fax 586 3374)* on the corner of Beach and Lodge Rds, Summerstrand (between the museum and the Shark Rock pier), is a fairly upmarket if impersonal place with rooms for R260/310.

The ***Beach Hotel*** *(☎ 583 2161)* on Marine Dr in Humewood is one of the classiest places in town, with singles/doubles from R335/410. Both places have weekend specials.

Places to Eat If you haven't yet experienced the full splendour of a South African ***breakfast***, head along to the Edward Protea Hotel where a stupendous breakfast is a mere R35.

Up The Khyber on Belmont St is an Indian restaurant that's vegan-friendly, a rare find in South Africa. Ask about its special all-you-can-eat deals.

According to locals, ***Nattis Thai Kitchen*** on Clyde St is one of the best places to eat in PE, with meals costing around R35.

Brookes Pavillion at Humewood Beach has several eateries; ***Caffe Raphaels*** (open 8 am until late) is good.

Wild Boar *(3, 3rd Ave, Walmer)* near the airport has been recommended by travellers for its interesting, well-priced cuisine, which includes ostrich, kudu and wild boar.

Entertainment The ***Phoenix Hotel*** on Chapel St is a grungy little pub which can get rough; it has live music some nights. ***Razzmatazz*** on Morgan St is a black club that has live jazz. (Be careful in this area at night.) ***Tiko's***, on Belmont St next to Up the Khyber, goes all night and has live music; it's popular with backpackers.

Getting There & Away BA Comair (☎ 0800 011 747 toll free) has daily flights between Jo'burg and Port Elizabeth. SA Airlink (☎ 507 1111) flies from Port Elizabeth to Jo'burg on Saturday only, to Bloemfontein weekdays, to East London daily, and to Cape Town.

Buses stop at the train station or the Greenacres shopping centre, which is a better place to disembark at night. PE has regular connections to the major South African cities. The Translux office (☎ 507 1333) is on Ring Road in Greenacres. The Intercape office (☎ 586 0055) is on Fleming St, behind the old post office. You can book Greyhound tickets through Computicket (☎ 374 4550).

Most minibus taxis leave from the townships surrounding PE and can be difficult to find.

The *Algoa* train runs daily to Jo'burg via Bloemfontein and the *Southern Cross* runs to Cape Town via some Garden Route towns.

All the big car-rental operators have offices in PE or at the airport: Avis (☎ 581 4291), Budget (☎ 581 4242) and Imperial (☎ 581 4214). Alternatively, try Economic Car Hire (☎ 581 5826), 104 Heugh Rd, Walmer.

Getting Around There's no public transport to the airport; a taxi costs around R30.

For local bus information, call ☎ 080 142 1444 toll free. Bus No 2 leaves from platform 5 at the bus station and runs along the beachfront to Happy Valley. No 55 leaves from platform 7 for Greenacres.

For taxis, contact Supercab (☎ 457 5590) or Hurter's Radio Cabs (☎ 585 5500).

Addo Elephant National Park

☎ 042

Addo is 72km north of Port Elizabeth near the Zuurberg Range in the Sundays River Valley. It's a park of 15,000 hectares (it was recently expanded), which protects the remnants of the huge elephant herds that once roamed Eastern Cape. There are about 316 elephants in the park and you'd be unlucky not to see some. Those without transport can take a tour from Port Elizabeth – contact Tourism Port Elizabeth for suggested operators.

Information The entrance gate is open from 7 am to 7 pm. The park's roads are dirt and can become impassable after heavy rain, so call ahead (☎ 640 0556) if the weather is wet. Day visitors are charged R12/6 per adult/child. A well-stocked shop is open from 8 am to 7 pm daily.

Places to Stay & Eat The ***camping area*** has sites for R36 for two people, plus R11 per additional person. It also has a range of other accommodation, from R220 for two in a rondavel. Book through the National Parks Board in Cape Town or Pretoria. There's a communal kitchen and a ***restaurant***.

Port Alfred

☎ 046

Port Alfred is a pleasant holiday village being developed into a bustling resort. For surfers there are good right breaks at the river mouth, and for golfers there's a famous course, one of the four 'royal' golf courses in South Africa.

The Tourist Information Centre (☎ 624 1235), near the municipal buildings, is open weekdays. It sells brochures detailing accommodation, walks and canoe trails.

Things to Do Kowie Dive (☎ 083-512 3437) at the Halyards Hotel has **dive courses** for R1200, a resort course for R300 and an introductory pool dive for R100.

The two-day **Kowie Canoe Trail** is a fairly easy paddle upriver from Port Alfred. Phone (☎ 624 2230) well in advance for bookings and canoe hire.

Places to Stay The ***Willows Caravan Park*** *(☎ 624 5201)* is near the bridge over the Kowie River. Camp sites start at R30.

Port Alfred Backpackers *(☎ 624 4011, 29 Sports Rd)* has a self-catering kitchen; dorms cost R40 and doubles R100. Take the first turn to the left off the R72 as you approach the marina and follow the resort security fence; the hostel is on your left.

Ferrymans *(☎ 624 1122)* on the riverbank is the closest hotel to the beach and has singles/doubles from R135/230, including breakfast.

An excellent choice is the ***Royal Alfred Marina Hotel*** *(☎ 624 2410)* at Royal Alfred Marina on Albany Rd, overlooking the harbour. Rooms cost from R225/398, including dinner and breakfast.

Places to Eat For great lunch specials, check out ***CJ's Bistro*** on Campbell St. ***Buck & Hunter*** has sizzling seafood dishes from R35.

Butlers Pub & Restaurant, on the riverbank, is a pleasant place for a beer, a snack or a good meal. Most dishes on the pub menu are under R30 and are available from 11 am to 11 pm. A vegetarian platter costs R25.

Getting There & Away The Baz Bus stops at Port Alfred Backpackers on its run between Port Elizabeth (R70) and Durban (R390).

The Shipwreck Coast

This unspoiled stretch of coast, the graveyard for numerous ships, was once part of the Ciskei Homeland.

Sherwood Shack Backpackers Haven *(☎ 046-675 1090, @ src@imaginet.co.za)* is near Seafield/Kleinmond. The cheerful owners offer dorms for R40 and doubles for R110 and does pick-ups from the R72 and Port Alfred. If driving, the turn-off is 22km past Port Alfred (look for Trappes Valley/Shaw Park); Sherwood is 2km up this road.

Mpekweni Sun *(☎ 040-676 1026)* is 11.5km east of the Great Fish River, beside the sea; there's a restaurant, several bars and a pool. Single/double two-night weekend packages start at R500/690. Intercape services between East London and Port Elizabeth stop here.

Shipwreck Hiking Trail This hiking trail from the Great Fish River to the Ncera River is 64km long, but it is possible to do any section. This is one of the few walking areas in South Africa where hikers can set their own pace, camp more or less where they choose and light fires.

The trail must be booked with the Department of Forestry (☎ 043-642 2571) in King William's Town; it costs R20 per person per night.

Hamburg The small village of Hamburg is at the wide river flats at the mouth of the Keiskamma River, near empty beaches. The flats are home to many birds, especially migrating waders in summer. They also offer good fishing.

The ***Hamburg Hotel*** *(☎ 040-678 1061)* is a family hotel with half board for R99 per person.

There's a daily minibus taxi between Hamburg and East London, about 100km east. The Baz Bus also goes through here to Port Alfred (R40) and East London (R60).

East London

☎ 043

This bustling port with 175,000 residents has a good surf beach and a spectacular bay which curves around to huge sand hills. The main downtown street is Oxford St, with the city centre extending from about Argyle St south to Fleet St.

Information Tourism East London (☎ 722 6015) on Argyle St behind the city hall, has loads of information on the area. It's open

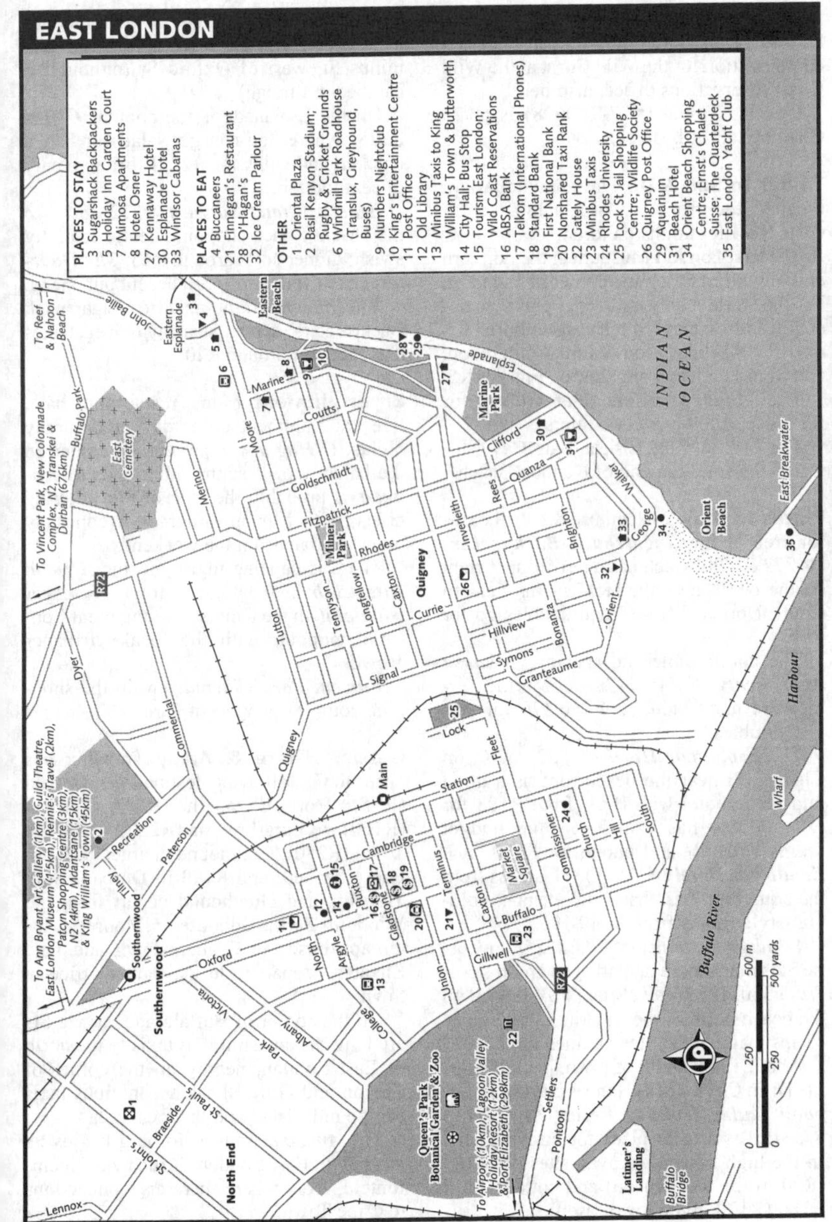
EAST LONDON
PLACES TO STAY
3 Sugarshack Backpackers
5 Holiday Inn Garden Court
7 Mimosa Apartments
8 Hotel Osner
27 Kennaway Hotel
30 Esplanade Hotel
33 Windsor Cabanas
PLACES TO EAT
4 Buccaneers
21 Finnegan's Restaurant
28 O'Hagan's
32 Ice Cream Parlour
OTHER
1 Oriental Plaza
2 Basil Kenyon Stadium; Rugby & Cricket Grounds
6 Windmill Park Roadhouse (Translux, Greyhound, Buses)
9 Numbers Nightclub
10 King's Entertainment Centre
11 Post Office
12 Old Library
13 Minibus Taxis to King William's Town & Butterworth
14 City Hall; Bus Stop
15 Tourism East London; Wild Coast Reservations
16 ABSA Bank
17 Telkom (International Phones)
18 Standard Bank
19 First National Bank
20 Nonshared Taxi Rank
22 Gately House
23 Minibus Taxis
24 Rhodes University
25 Lock St Jail Shopping Centre; Wildlife Society
26 Quigney Post Office
29 Aquarium
31 Beach Hotel
34 Orient Beach Shopping Centre; Ernst's Chalet Suisse; The Quarterdeck
35 East London Yacht Club
To Ann Bryant Art Gallery (1km), Guild Theatre, East London Museum (1.5km), Rennie's Travel (2km), Patcyn Shopping Centre (3km), N2 (4km), Mdantsane (15km) & King William's Town (45km)
To Vincent Park, New Colonnade Complex, N2, Transkei & Durban (676km)
To Reef & Nahoon Beach
To Airport (10km), Lagoon Valley Holiday Resort (12km) & Port Elizabeth (298km)
Queen's Park Botanical Garden & Zoo
East Cemetery
Milner Park
Marine Park
Eastern Beach
Eastern Esplanade
Esplanade
INDIAN OCEAN
Orient Beach
East Breakwater
Harbour
Buffalo River
Wharf
Latimer's Landing
Buffalo Bridge
Southernwood
North End
Quigney
Main
Market Square
R72
0 250 500 m
0 250 500 yards

from 8.30 am to 4.30 pm weekdays and 8.30 to 11 am Saturday. You can book accommodation for the Wild Coast at the Wild Coast reservations office, also here.

Rennies Travel (☎ 726 0698) is at 23 Chamberlain Rd, Berea.

Things to See & Do The small **aquarium** on the beachfront is worth a look; entry costs R8/4 for adults/children.

The **East London Museum** at the northern end of Oxford St, on the corner of Lukin St, has the world's only dodo egg, plus a coelacanth and displays on Xhosa culture. It's open on weekdays, on Saturday afternoon, and from 11 am to 4 pm Sunday. Entry is R5.

The *Albatross* offers **river cruises** for R25, departing every two hours.

The best **surfing** is near Bats Cave, towards the southern end of Nahoon Beach.

Places to Stay You can use the surfboards for free at the ***Sugarshack Backpackers*** *(☎ 722 8240)*, which has a terrific spot right on the beach near the Holiday Inn Garden Court. Dorms cost R35 and doubles go for R90.

The comfortable and spacious ***Mimosa Apartments*** *(☎ 743 3433)* on Marine Terrace are good value at R140/170 for singles/doubles.

The ***Esplanade Hotel*** *(☎ 722 2518)*, on Clifford St near the beachfront, is a good mid-range hotel with B&B from R198 for two. It also has excellent-value budget rooms with TV and phone for R100. The ***Kennaway Hotel*** *(☎ 722 5531)*, across from the aquarium, has charming, elegant, colonial-style rooms from R140/190.

Windsor Cabanas *(☎ 743 2225)* on Currie St is much more upmarket and rooms cost R295/340. The ***Hotel Osner*** *(☎ 743 3433)* on the beach north of the aquarium, has breezy rooms that are ideal for families for R230.

About 12km south of town, just off Marine Dr in Cove Rock, is the picturesque ***Lagoon Valley Holiday Resort*** *(☎/fax 736 9753)*. It is a great place for birdwatchers. In the high season, caravan sites cost R65 (R20 in the low season) and cottages cost R180 (R130 in the low season).

Places to Eat For cheap pub lunches (R15), try ***Finnegan's Restaurant*** on Terminus St, west of Oxford St (although it can be a bit rough).

On the Esplanade is the popular ***O'Hagan's***, where you can get salads or half a chicken and chips for R22. It offers plenty of seafood too.

Ernst's Chalet Suisse *(☎ 722 1840)* in the Orient Beach shopping centre is pretty swish; dinner costs around R45. ***The Quarterdeck*** next door offers a decent pub menu.

Buccaneers, right next to Sugarshack Backpackers, serves steak with vegetables and chips for around R20.

Entertainment Many restaurants have live entertainment on Friday or Saturday nights. ***O'Hagan's*** is perfect for a beer on the balcony on a sunny afternoon. ***Buccaneers*** is probably the pick of the watering holes, with a happy hour on Wednesday night and bands on the weekends.

There is dancing nightly in the ***African Nite Club*** in the Beach Hotel. ***Numbers Nightclub*** in the King's Entertainment Centre is popular with the local Afrikaner crowd.

Vincent Park Cinemas are in the shopping complex at Vincent Park.

Getting There & Away Translux has buses to the following destinations: Umtata (R75); Port Elizabeth (R90); Durban (R160); Jo'burg/Pretoria (R220); and Cape Town (R230). Greyhound charges R100 to Port Elizabeth and R170 to Durban. Both Translux and Greyhound depart from the Windmill Park roadhouse on Moore St. Intercape buses to Grahamstown and Port Elizabeth depart from the tourist office in town.

On the corner of Buffalo and Argyle Sts are long-distance minibus taxis to the north of East London; nearby on the corner of Caxton and Gillwell Sts are minibus taxis for the old Ciskei and the local area.

The *Amatola* train to Jo'burg begins its journey in East London. It runs via Bloemfontein, from where there are connections to Cape Town.

Getting Around Most city buses stop at the City Hall on Oxford St. For information call Amatola Regional Services (☎ 722 1251).

There's a taxi rank (☎ 722 7901) on Union St on the corner of Oxford St.

East London to the Kei River

☎ 043

There are many resorts on the coast north of East London and a couple of good backpackers hostels in Cintsa. The East Coast Resorts turn-off from the N2 will get you to most of them.

The first beaches to the north are centred on Gonubie Mouth, which has caravan parks and the ***Gonubie Mouth Hotel** (☎ 740 4010)*. Good-value singles/doubles here cost R110/155.

The next concentration of beaches is around Haga-Haga, a small village about 70km from East London. The tip of the very scenic Cape Henderson Nature Reserve adjoins Haga-Haga.

North-east of Haga-Haga, reached by turning off the N2 onto the R349, are Morgan's Bay and Kei Mouth. Kei Mouth is the last resort before the Wild Coast. ***Kei Mouth Backpackers & Surfaris** (☎ 841 1238)* is a good spot to chill and get over those hard days on the road. Dorms cost R35, doubles R90, and camping is R25 per person. A pick-up from the Baz Bus on the N2 costs R10.

Independent travellers will probably have heard about ***Buccaneers Backpackers** (☎ 734 3012)* in Cintsa long before they get to this part of the world. Many consider it to be the best in South Africa. You can use the canoes, surfboards and paddle-skis for free. It also organises many activities as well as trips around the area. Dorms are R40, doubles are R100 and camping is R25. Buccaneers has a daily shuttle service to East London. If you're driving from East London, take exit 26 from the N2; coming the other way take the Cintsa/Cefani exit.

Strandloper Hiking Trail This five-day trail between Gonubie and Kei Mouth costs R37/45 to walk unguided/guided. It is managed by the Strandloper Ecotourism Board (☎ 841 1888). The Wildlife Society (☎ 743 9409) in East London's Lock St Jail has a useful booklet (R5). You'll need tide tables, as it's dangerous to cross the estuaries when the tide is flowing out. *What's On In East London*, available at the tourist office and some hotels, includes the monthly tide tables.

Camping on the beach is prohibited but the coast is littered with resorts, most of which have camp sites.

SETTLER COUNTRY & AROUND

This section covers the area around Grahamstown, the heart of Settler Country, as well as most of the old Ciskei Homeland.

Grahamstown

☎ 046

Grahamstown is the capital of Settler Country and the Borders and it still feels like a strange English transplant. The large student population breathes life into this otherwise conservative, Victorian-era town.

Information The efficient Tourism Grahamstown (☎ 622 3241) on Church Square is open from 8.30 am to 5 pm weekdays (to 4 pm on Friday) and Saturday morning.

GBS Travel (☎ 622 2235) at 84 High St handles bookings for local travel.

Albany Museum The museum has four components and entry to all of them costs R5/4 for adults/children. The most interesting is the wonderfully eccentric Observatory Museum, on Bathurst St. The National History Museum, on Somerset St, has some interesting Xhosa artefacts. The 1820 Settlers Memorial Museum, also on Somerset St, is devoted to the English settlers. Fort Selwyn, built in 1836 as a semaphore station, has been fully restored.

Fort Selwyn is open by appointment (☎ 622 2312); the other places are open from 9.30 am to 1 pm and 2 to 5 pm weekdays.

Dakawa Art & Craft Project Begun in the ANC's Dakawa refugee camp in Tanzania, the project moved to Grahamstown in 1991 when the ban on the ANC was lifted. The project aims to teach participants skills and to provide an outlet for their work,

SOUTH AFRICA

which is mainly weaving, graphic art and textile printing. Dakawa (☎ 622 9303) is at 4–11 Froude St.

Grahamstown Festival The town hosts the very successful National Festival of Arts and an associated Fringe Festival. The festival runs for 10 days, beginning at the end of June; accommodation at this time can be booked out a year in advance. For more information, contact the 1820 Foundation (☎ 622 7115).

Places to Stay The tranquil ***caravan park*** *(☎ 603 6072)* is in a beautiful spot, although it's a bit of a trek from town. Camp sites cost R30; basic rondavels with no bedding are R80 for four people.

Old Gaol Backpackers *(☎ 636 1001)* on Somerset St is in one of the town's many National Monument buildings; clean and cheap dorms are R30 and double rooms cost R90.

The ***Graham Protea Hotel*** *(☎ 622 2324, 123 High St)* is characterless but comfortable enough and is in the centre of town. Singles/doubles cost R299/359, with breakfast.

The ***Cock House*** *(☎ 636 1287, 10 Market St)* is a cosy guesthouse in a National Monument building dating back to 1826. The thoughtful hosts arrange activities around town and the exquisite rooms are worth the cost of R250/440, which includes a sumptuous breakfast.

Tourism Grahamstown can put you in touch with B&Bs.

Places to Eat Grahamstown has loads of cafes; check out the buzzing ***Mad Hatters*** on High St, where good meals are under R20.

Redwood Spur Steak House is a decent example of the genre.

La Galleria *(☎ 622 3455)* on New St is an Italian place that has been recommended. The pseudo-British ***Rat & Parrot***, also on New St, serves the usual pub meals. It's a good place for a beer and attracts a student crowd most nights.

The ***restaurant*** at the Cock House is superb, with meals on an ever-changing menu from R25 to R50.

Getting There & Away Translux stops on the corner of Bathurst and High Sts on the run from Port Elizabeth (R65, standby only) to Durban (R190, 11 hours), via King William's Town (R65), East London (R80) and Umtata (R130). Greyhound stops here on the same run.

Minilux runs between Port Elizabeth and East London, stopping in Grahamstown. The Bee Bus (☎ 082-651 6646) runs to Port Elizabeth (R60) and has been recommended; ask at the Cock House for details.

You'll find minibus taxis on Raglan St but most leave from Rhini township. Fares include: King William's Town (R29); East London (R30); and Port Elizabeth (R30).

King William's Town

☎ 043

Established by the London Missionary Society in 1826, King William's Town (KWT) became an important military base in the interminable struggle with the Xhosa. After the Seventh Frontier War (1846–47), British Kaffraria was established with King William's Town as its capital. KWT remains the area's commercial and shopping capital.

The library (☎ 642 3450) has some tourist information.

At the Grahamstown entry to town, ***King William's Town Caravan Park*** *(☎ 642 3160)* is OK but a bit noisy; camp sites cost R22. For ***hotels***, you're better off in East London.

Bisho

☎ 040

Bisho, once the capital of Ciskei and now the administrative capital of Eastern Cape, was originally the black 'location' for nearby King William's Town. The centre of Bisho was built to house Ciskei's bureaucrats and politicians, so there is a compact bunch of suitably grandiose and ugly public buildings.

The Eastern Cape Tourism Board (☎ 635 2115) is opposite the post office; it has brochures and handles bookings for hiking trails in the old Ciskei region.

For accommodation, you should go to East London.

Amatola & Katberg Mountains

The area north and west of King William's Town is partly degraded grazing land and partly rugged mountains with remnant indigenous forest. It has some good walks, all of which must be booked with the Department of Forestry (☎ 043-642 2571) in King William's Town. Accommodation is in ***huts*** with braai facilities and the fee for adults/students is R28.50/22.80 per night.

The six-day **Amatola Trail** begins at Maden Dam, 23km north of King William's Town, and ends at the Tyumie River near Hogsback. It is pretty tough.

The two-day **Evelyn Valley Loop Trail** starts and ends at Maden Dam. The scenery includes magnificent forests and numerous streams. It's a fairly easy hike.

The two-day **Zingcuka Loop Trail** begins and ends at the Tyumie River near Hogsback. It's fairly easy but there are some steep sections on the second day.

Hogsback Hogsback is a small resort area high in the beautiful Amatola Mountains about 100km north-west of Bisho. There are some great walks and drives in the area. You can buy booklets detailing walks from the Hogsback store.

Near the forestry station above town is ***Hogsback Caravan Park*** *(☎ 045-962 1055)*. Pleasant sites cost R30, plus R7 per person. The office is a long walk from the camping area.

Away with the Fairies *(☎ 045-962 1031)* is a majestic little getaway with a superb view of Hogsback Ridge. Dorms are R40 and doubles a little more. There are mountain bikes for hire and Sugarshack in East London can get you here.

The ***Hogsback Mountain Lodge*** *(☎ 045-962 1005)*, also known as ***Arminel***, has pleasant cottages, a swimming pool and a huge, beautiful garden. Half board is good value at R115/180 per person for a standard/deluxe room.

Katberg 110km north-west of Bisho, Katberg is a small town at the foot of a wooded range. The surrounding countryside is still very much as it was when this area was part of Ciskei – overworked, underfunded and almost medieval.

It's an interesting drive from Hogsback, 27km to the east. The road over the Katberg Pass is unsealed, so make sure you check locally before tackling it after a lot of rain, and definitely think twice if it has been snowing (which happens a couple of times each winter).

The luxurious ***Katberg Hotel*** *(☎ 040-864 1010)* is 8km uphill from the village. Singles/doubles start at around R150/272, including meals (more on weekends).

Tsolwana Game Reserve

Tsolwana is 57km south-west of Queenstown, near Fort Beaufort. It protects a rugged Karoo landscape south of the spectacular Tafelberg (1965m), adjoining the Swart Kei River. The reserve has rolling plains interspersed with valleys, cliffs, waterfalls, caves and gullies.

There is a similarly diverse range of animals, including herds of antelope, rhino, giraffe and mountain zebra. The largest four-legged predator is the Cape lynx.

The park is managed in conjunction with the local Tsolwana people, who benefit directly from the jobs and revenue produced. There are ***lodges*** and ***huts*** here.

The Eastern Cape Tourism Board (☎ 040-635 2115) in Bisho administers the reserve; entry costs R10/5 for adults/children.

THE KAROO

The Karoo, a vast semidesert, lies on the great Southern African plateau. It's a dry, hot and inhospitable area, but is fascinating for its sense of space.

Mountain Zebra National Park

Mountain Zebra National Park, about 30km from the small town of Cradock, is on the northern slopes of the 2000m Bankberg Range and has magnificent views over the Karoo. It's a small park protecting one of the rarest animals in the world – the mountain zebra *(Equus zebra)*.

In addition to the zebra, there are many antelope species. The largest predator is the caracal (or lynx).

There's a relatively limited network of roads around the park and visitors have to drive themselves. The Mountain Zebra Hiking Trail is closed.

Information The entrance gate is open from 1 October to 30 April between 7 am and 7 pm, and from 1 May to 30 September between 7.30 am and 6 pm. Day visits cost R10/5 for adults/children. The main camp has a shop and restaurant.

Places to Stay The most interesting place to stay in the national park area is the restored historic farmhouse ***Doornhoek***, which was built in 1836 and is hidden in a secluded valley. Doornhoek costs R475 for up to four people.

There are also ***camp sites*** (R40 for two people) and cottages (from R270 for two people). Book through the National Parks Board in Pretoria or Cape Town (see earlier for contact details).

Graaff-Reinet

☎ 049

Graaff-Reinet is the quintessential Karoo town – it is often referred to, justifiably, as the gem of the Karoo. If you visit only one inland town in Eastern Cape, make it this one.

The fourth-oldest European town in South Africa, its outstanding architectural heritage has been restored through the recognition of 220 National Monument buildings – more than any other town in South Africa.

History In 1786 a *landdrost* was despatched to establish order in the lawless Cape interior. In 1795 the citizens of Graaff-Reinet drove out the landdrost and established a short-lived independent republic.

Between 1824 and 1840, the Boers' continuing dissatisfaction with Cape Town's control led to the Great Trek, and Graaff-Reinet became an important stepping stone for Voortrekkers heading north.

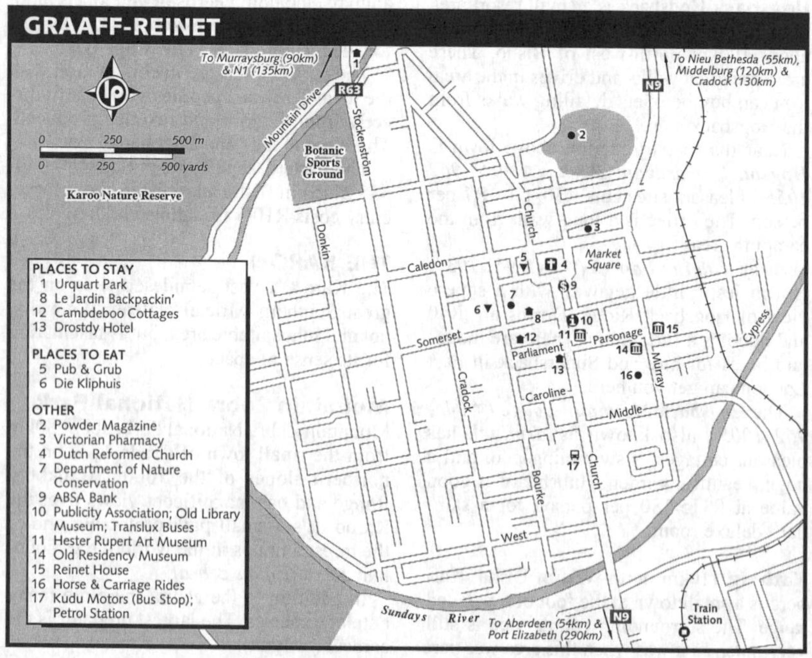

Orientation & Information The town lies within a bend of the Sundays River, overshadowed by the rocky Sneeuberg. The centre of town is easy to get around on foot.

The publicity association (☎ 892 4248) on the corner of Church and Somerset Sts is worth a visit, but the staff are disinterested and seem to have pre-recorded answers to most inquiries. The association is open from 8 am to 12.30 pm and 2 to 5 pm weekdays, and 9 am to noon weekends.

Museums On the corner of Church and Somerset Sts, the **Old Library** houses paintings, Karoo fossils and a collection of photos and clothing from the 19th century.

The **Hester Rupert Art Museum** exhibits contemporary South African art.

Reinet House on Murray St is a beautiful example of Cape Dutch architecture. It is furnished with 18th- and 19th-century furniture.

The **Old Residency** in Parsonage St is another well-preserved 19th-century house, displaying a large collection of historical firearms.

All museums are open from 9 am to 12.30 pm and 2 to 5 pm weekdays, and in the morning on weekends. Entry is about R5.

Places to Stay To the north of town, ***Urquart Park*** *(☎ 892 2136)* has camp sites for R40 and other accommodation, starting at R60 for two people in a rondavel (less if you don't need bedding).

Le Jardin Backpackin' *(892 3326, 50 Somerset St)* is a simple place; rooms with shared bathroom cost R50 per person.

The modest but charming ***Cambdeboo Cottages*** *(☎ 892 3180, 16 Parliament St)* are restored Karoo cottages – all are National Monuments. The rate is R170 a double.

There are plenty of other B&Bs and guesthouses – ask at the publicity association.

The ***Drostdy Hotel*** *(☎ 892 2161, 30 Church St)* is simply outstanding. The main part of the hotel is in the beautifully restored drostdy, built in 1806, and the accommodation is in old Karoo workers' cottages (originally slaves' quarters). Singles cost R280 and doubles range from R380 to R460. Suites, some of them whole cottages, start at R620.

Places to Eat ***Die Kliphuis*** *(46 Bourke St)* serves a tasty breakfast from R10.50 and decent coffee.

For pub fare, try ***Pub & Grub*** on the corner of Muller St, opposite the Dutch Reformed Church; a filling serve of steak and chips costs R25.

The dining room at the ***Drostdy Hotel*** is an unmissable experience. When was the last time you dined in an 18th-century room illuminated by candelabra? Set-menu dinners cost R73. You can also order a la carte. You don't have to stay here to use the dining room.

Getting There & Away The publicity association is the Translux agent. Translux stops here on the run between Cape Town and East London. The trip from Cape Town takes eight hours and costs R210. The trip to East London takes 7 hours and costs R200, stopping at Cradock (R140) and King William's Town (R180) along the way.

Minibus taxis leave from Market Square. Major destinations are Port Elizabeth, Cape Town and Jo'burg. For more information try calling J Kane (☎ 892 4390).

Karoo Nature Reserve

This reserve, which virtually surrounds Graaff-Reinet, protects mountainous veld and its flora is a highlight. Ask about its hiking trails and wildlife viewing at the Karoo Nature Reserve office (☎ 049-892 3453), upstairs in the provincial administration building on Bourke St in Graaff-Reinet.

The road overlooking the **Valley of Desolation** has simply outstanding views.

Owl House

In the tiny and isolated village of **Nieu Bethesda** is the extraordinary Owl House – home, studio and life's work of artist Helen Martins (1898–1976). Concrete and glass are the materials used in her creations. Whether the Owl House is a monument to madness or a testament to the human spirit is difficult to say.

Owl House Backpackers (*☎ 049-841 1642*) is an ecofriendly lodging. Dorms cost R40, double rooms in the cottage are R100 and camping is R15 per person.

The drive here is interesting (there are several turn-offs from the N9 between Graaff-Reinet and Middelburg), but remember that you can't buy petrol in Nieu Bethesda.

NORTH-EASTERN HIGHLANDS

This area is surrounded on three sides by the former Transkei and it also has a short border (but no crossing point) with Lesotho. It's high country, in the southern tail of the main Drakensberg. It's a bleak but atmospheric place.

Tiffindell

The centre for skiing is Tiffindell (2800m), an area of breathtaking mountain scenery near Rhodes, and with snow-making facilities it guarantees a season of a hundred or so days.

Tiffindell's ***mountain hut*** (*☎ 011-454 0660*) offers full board from R175 per person in summer. Summer activities include mountain cycling, horse riding, grass-skiing and rock climbing. In winter, it costs from R400 to R750, including lift pass, equipment hire and emergency medical facilities.

Nearby is **Ben Macdhui** (3001m), where there are ski lifts.

Aliwal North

☎ 0551

Aliwal North is a largish town popular for its mineral baths and hot springs. For information on the local area, drop by the North-East Cape Tourism Association (☎ 41362).

At the ***spa complex*** (*☎ 2951*) there are camp sites for R25, plus R10 per person. There are several other places to stay nearby.

If you crave African-style food, ***Ezibeleni*** on the corner of Grey and Murray Sts, has *samp* (maize porridge) and fish balls for about R10.

A daily City to City bus stops here on the Jo'burg to Queenstown run. Translux, Greyhound and Intercape stop at Nobby's Restaurant. The minibus taxi and local bus stop is on Grey St, near the corner of Somerset St.

TRANSKEI

With natural boundaries (the Kei River and the Drakensberg), Transkei was at least a logical subdivision of the country, unlike most of the Homelands.

Transkei's major attraction is its coastline, where you'll find superb warm-water surf beaches and lush subtropical vegetation.

Nelson Mandela was born in Transkei, in the village of Mvezo on the Mbashe River. He spent most of his childhood in **Qunu**, 31km south of Umtata. There is a museum and cultural centre built on the site of Mandela's former school in Qunu, which details his life and struggle against apartheid.

Summers on the coast are hot and humid. Inland, summers can be hot, but many areas have winter frosts. Most rain falls in March and spring also sees heavy rains. Unsealed roads can be impassable after rain, especially near the coast.

History

The Xhosa peoples living east of the Kei River (that is, living trans-Kei from the Cape Colony) came under the domination of the Cape Colony government from about 1873, but it was not until 1894, with the defeat of Pondoland, that the whole of modern Transkei came under European rule.

In 1976, Transkei became an 'independent Homeland'. If its independence had been internationally recognised it would have been classified as one of the world's poorest countries and one of Southern Africa's most densely populated regions.

Umtata

☎ 047

Umtata, the main town in Transkei, was founded in 1871 when Europeans settled on the Umtata River at the request of the Thembu tribe to act as a buffer against Pondo raiders. Today, Umtata is more like an oversized village, with the same violent crime problems that plague most South African cities. It isn't pretty but it's refreshingly free of racism and has a raw, African edge which is missing from most cities in South Africa.

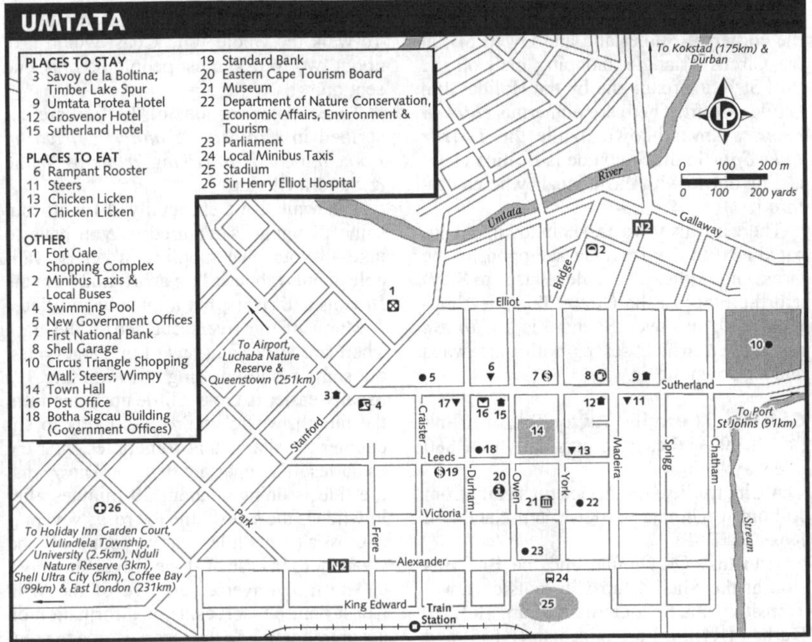

Information The helpful Eastern Cape Tourism Board (☎ 531 5290/2, ✉ ectbwc@icon.co.za) is at 64 Owen St. Unfortunately, you can't book Wild Coast hiking trails with these friendly and efficient people – you have to deal with the less than enthusiastic staff at the Department of Nature Conservation, Economic Affairs, Environment & Tourism (☎ 531 2711), also known as the Nature Conservation Department, on the corner of York and Victoria Sts. Maps of the coastal trails cost R3 and you should also buy *A Guide to the Coast & Nature Reserves of Transkei*.

Wild Coast Central Reservations (☎ 532 5344, fax 523 3766, 3 Beaufort St) books the various hotels and resorts on the coast.

There is a Standard Bank and a First National Bank. Do your banking here before heading to the Wild Coast.

Things to See The small **museum** opposite the Nature Conservation Department displays traditional costumes and beadwork. It's open from 8 am to 4.30 pm weekdays (3.30 pm on Friday), and entry is by donation.

Places to Stay The cheapest option is the crummy ***Sutherland Hotel*** *(☎ 531 2281)* on Sutherland St, which charges R90 per person. You're much better off at the colonial-era ***Grosvenor Hotel*** *(☎ 531 2118)* on the corner of Sutherland and Madeira Sts. Its room rate is R100 per person.

Savoy de la Boltina *(☎ 531 0791)*, out on the Queenstown bypass, is a big airy place, and is good mid-range value at R168/195 for singles/doubles. There are more-luxurious rooms in the courtyard at the rear.

The overpriced ***Umtata Protea Hotel*** *(☎ 531 0721, 36 Sutherland St)* has rooms for R320/400. ***Holiday Inn Garden Court*** *(☎ 537 0181)*, out of town on the East London side of the N2, charges R324/408.

Places to Eat There's almost nowhere to sit down and have a coffee. Noisy ***Wimpys***

can be found in the Munitata Building, on the corner of Sutherland and Owen Sts; at the Circus Triangle shopping mall on the Port St Johns road; and by the Holiday Inn Garden Court. There are numerous ***chicken eateries*** around town, while the ***Timber Lake Spur*** in the Savoy de la Boltina Hotel is a favourite with those locals who can afford it.

There are also two ***Steers*** in town, one located next to the Total Garage opposite the Grosvenor Hotel (see under Places to Stay) and the other in the Circus Triangle shopping mall. In Owen St there is a ***Chinese restaurant***, which serves both takeaways and sit-down meals.

Getting There & Away SAA Airlink (☎ 536 0024) flies to Jo'burg daily for R880 one way.

A City to City bus service runs daily from Jo'burg to Umtata via KwaZulu-Natal and Kokstad (R95).

Translux, Greyhound and the Baz Bus stop at the Shell Ultra City outside town. Translux runs to Pietermaritzburg (R120), Durban (R125), Port Elizabeth (R135) and Jo'burg/Pretoria (R170).

Local buses and also minibus taxis to Transkei destinations, stop at the taxi park near Bridge St (a minibus taxi to Port St Johns costs R17).

Avis (☎ 536 0066) is based at the airport.

The Wild Coast

The Transkei coast is notoriously dangerous for ships. Shipwrecked sailors were the first Europeans to visit this part of the world, and few were rescued or completed the harrowing journey to Cape Town or Lourenço Marques (now Maputo, Mozambique).

About 40,000 hectares of indigenous forest survives along the coast. While there is plenty of birdlife (and butterflies galore), the numbers of animals are dwindling.

Wild Coast Hiking Trail A walk along this trail is an unforgettable experience – see bottlenose dolphins frolicking out at sea, meet the locals who welcome you into their villages as you wait for ferries and experience the hauntingly quiet, starry nights. To walk the whole Wild Coast would take about two weeks; most people do only one section.

Three major sections of the trail are described in *Exploring Southern Africa on Foot: the Guide to Hiking Trails* by Willie & Sandra Olivier.

The walk isn't especially difficult, but some planning is required as you have to take all your own supplies. Water is available at huts (about 12km apart) and from the streams and rivers, but it must be purified.

Many of the rivers cut across the trail. There are ferries at a few of the larger ones, but some require wading or swimming. It's usually easier to cross a little upstream from the mouth, where you're less likely to encounter the sharks that sometimes enter the estuaries. It's important that you know what the tide is doing – about 30 minutes after low tide is the safest time to cross. Never try to cross a river while wearing your pack, and wear shoes in case of stone fish or stingrays.

The trail traverses all five of the Wild Coast nature reserves. (For information on accommodation in the reserves, see the section following.) In addition, there are ***trail huts*** and ***camping*** areas, most of which share basic facilities. Costs vary but most sites are around R20.

Bookings for the trail must be made at the Nature Conservation Department (☎ 047-531 2711) in Umtata. The trail must be walked from north to south. There's currently a fee payable only for the five-day section from Port St Johns to Coffee Bay (R45). Good maps of the trail sections are available at the department for R3 each.

The trail also passes near the backpackers hostels, hotels and resorts scattered along the coast. Check with Wild Coast Reservations (☎ 047-532 5344) in Umtata.

Wild Coast Nature Reserves There are five coastal reserves and the Wild Coast Trail traverses them all. There is self-catering ***accommodation*** at Mkambati, Silaka, Hluleka and Dwesa Reserves, and there are ***camp sites*** at Cwebe and Dwesa. Sites cost about R20 and ***chalets*** around R40 per person, although during peak holiday times you might have to book a whole chalet for about R120.

Camp sites and accommodation must be booked at the Nature Conservation Department (☎ 047-531 2711) in Umtata, which can also provide current information on roads into the reserves.

Mkambati You can canoe up the Msikaba River, and there are walking trails too. Entry to the reserve is R5. A shop sells basic food. You get here from Flagstaff (also known as Siphaqeni), 65km south of the N2 – take the turn-off to Holy Cross Hospital just north of Flagstaff. Buses run from Port St Johns to Msikaba on the southern edge of the reserve.

Silaka Just south of Port St Johns, Silaka runs from Second Beach to Sugarloaf Rock. There are often Cape clawless otters on the beach, and white-breasted cormorants clamber up onto Bird Island. Magic!

Hluleka A scenic reserve combining sea, lagoons and forest, Hluleka is between Port St Johns and Coffee Bay. The coast is rocky, although there's a quiet lagoon flanked by a saltmarsh. To get here take the road from

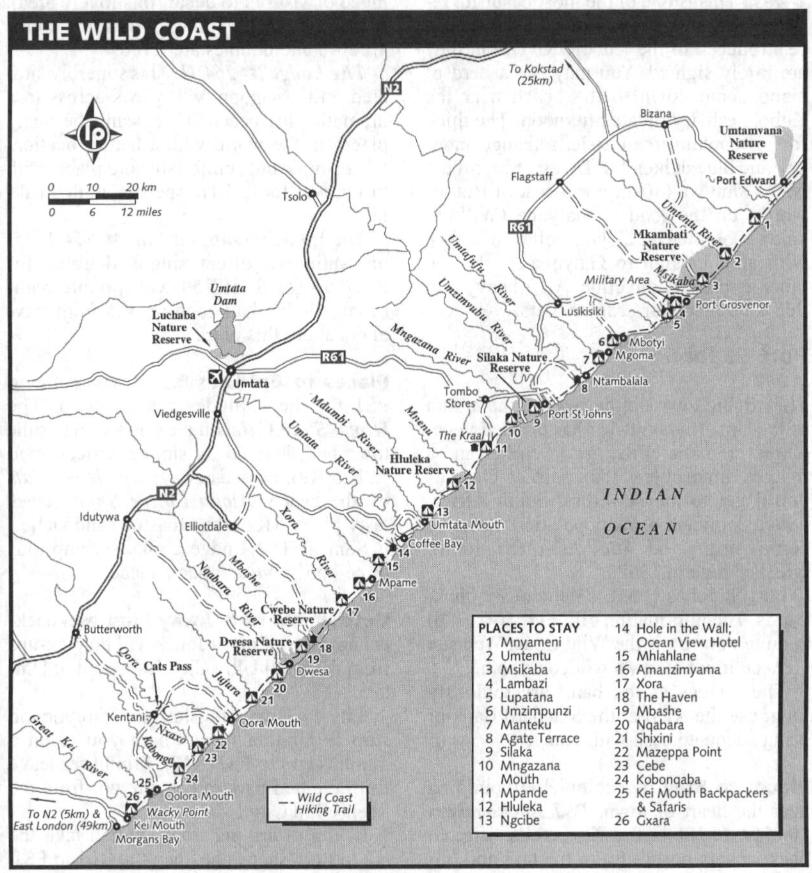

Umtata towards PSJ, but turn off to the right at Libode, about 30km from Umtata. The reserve is about 90km further on.

Cwebe Cwebe Reserve is adjacent to Dwesa Reserve, about midway between Coffee Bay and Kei Mouth. It has tracts of forest as well as good beaches and hiking trails. You can walk to the Mbanyana Falls or to the lagoon, where you might see a Cape clawless otter in the late afternoon. To get to Cwebe take the Xhora (Elliotdale) turn-off from the N2. The reserve is 65km further on.

Dwesa This is one of the most beautiful reserves in South Africa. Crocodile have been reintroduced to the Kobole River, but they are rarely sighted. You may see a herd of eland come down to the beach near the Kobole estuary in late afternoon. The thick forests contain tree dassie, samango monkey and blue duiker. For Dwesa, turn off the N2 at Idutywa (40km north-east of Butterworth) on the road to Gatyana (Willowvale). Continue until you come to a fork with another sign to Gatyana – take the other, unmarked direction. After heavy rain this is no place for ordinary cars.

Port St Johns

☎ 047

This idyllic town on the coast at the mouth of the Umzimvubu River has tropical vegetation, dramatic cliffs, great beaches and a relaxed atmosphere. It's about as close as you'll get to the new rural South Africa, with a dominant black population. Its name comes from the *São João* (St John), wrecked here in 1552.

Port St Johns (PSJ) is deliciously backwards. The information office (☎ 564 1206) is quite new. So is the Wild Coast Web site – check it out at www.wildcoast.com.

The queues at the bank are tediously long; use the ATM at the Standard Bank or bring adequate cash with you.

Places to Stay In a colonial-era building near the heart of town, ***PSJ Backpackers*** *(☎ 564 1517)* is the Transkei's original backpackers hostel. From the taxi and bus stops, walk along the main road parallel to the river, and take the fourth road on the right past the post office. You can camp for R20 or sleep in the dorm for R40. Doubles cost R100.

In the rambling Mtumbane township is ***Mama Constance's Place*** *(☎ 564 1517)*. Traditional meals are included in the price of R50 per person and you'll probably be invited to the local shebeen. Get directions and transport from PSJ Backpackers.

Amapondo Backpackers *(☎ 564 1582)* at Second Beach advertises itself as the 'home of Pondo fever' (Pondo fever is the reluctance of visitors to depart this lovely area). It has a point. Camping costs R25, dorms are R40 and doubles are R100.

The Lodge *(☎ 564 1171)* is superbly situated on the lagoon with views across to a dramatic surf beach. There can't be many places in the world with a better location. It's a simple but comfortable old place, with tidy rooms for R110 per person, with breakfast.

The friendly ***Outspan Inn*** *(☎ 564 1345)* on Main Rd offers singles/doubles for R85/150 (or R135/250 with private bathroom). We've had good reports from travellers about this place.

Places to Eat Let's face it, you came to PSJ for the solitude, not the food. The ***Hippo Store Cafe***, on the same street as the town hall, is good for simple African food (R7 to R9). For takeaways try ***Neat's Eats*** by the beach. ***Aloha Coffee Shop*** serves tasty pizzas (R20) and toasted sandwiches.

Sam at The Lodge cooks scrumptious three-course ***meals***; book ahead.

Getting There & Away Most backpackers hostels in Port St Johns will do pick-ups from the Shell Ultra City, just south of Umtata.

City to City, Translux and Greyhound stop in Umtata from where you catch a minibus taxi to PSJ (R17). Minibuses leave from the taxi park in Umtata, not from the Shell Ultra City.

If you're driving from Durban take the N2 to Port Shepstone, then the R61 to PSJ.

There is a good sealed road to Lusikisiki and then 17km of dirt road. Watch out for maniacal drivers on blind corners and for hidden speed dips. The scenic part of the R61 (from Umtata to Port St Johns) is sealed; watch out for police speed traps.

The ferry (R1.50) is the quickest way across the river to Agate Terrace even though there is a bridge upstream.

Coffee Bay

☎ 047

Coffee Bay is just a tiny hamlet but it's relaxed and is becoming popular with travellers. There is a theory that a ship wrecked here in 1863 deposited its cargo of coffee beans on the beach; hence the name. Coffee Bay's Xhosa name, *Tshontini*, refers to a dense wood nearby.

Three rivers flow into the sea near Coffee Bay: the Henga (Place of the Whale); the Mapuzi (Place of Pumpkins); and the Bomvu (Red).

Places to Stay & Eat Set in a large garden area, ***Woodhouse Backpackers*** *(☎ 575 2029)* has a great bar/restaurant serving vegetarian and seafood meals (mussels and rice for R30). Camping costs R20, dorms are R40 and the mosquito-ridden loft is R30.

Coffee Bay Backpackers *(☎ 575 2004)* is good value, even if it doesn't look too flash from the outside. Camping costs R20 and a bed in a dorm is R40. There are surfboards and a windsurfer, and horse riding can be arranged.

The bungalow-style accommodation at the ***Ocean View Hotel*** *(☎ 575 2005)* is just metres from the beach. There is a restaurant in the hotel. Half board costs R210 per person (R250 in the high season).

Getting There & Away The backpackers hostels will collect you (free) from the Shell Ultra City in Umtata. A minibus taxi from Umtata to Coffee Bay costs R17 and takes about an hour.

To get to Coffee Bay by vehicle, take the sealed road that leaves the N2 at Viedgesville, south of Umtata.

KwaZulu-Natal

Despite being a relatively small province, KwaZulu-Natal manages to cram in most of the things visitors come to South Africa to see.

There's the spectacular Drakensberg Range in the south-west, a long coast of subtropical surf beaches, remote lowveld savanna in the far north, and historic Anglo-Boer War and Anglo-Zulu War battlefields. In the middle of it all is the Zulu heartland. The KwaZulu-Natal Nature Conservation (KNNC) organisation has many excellent parks and Durban is a city with a holiday atmosphere and, in parts, an Indian flavour.

History

Just before the 1994 elections, Natal Province was renamed KwaZulu-Natal, in a belated recognition of the fact that the Zulu heartland of KwaZulu comprises a large part of the province.

Natal was named by Vasco da Gama, who sighted the coast on Christmas Day 1497. It was not until 1843 that Natal was proclaimed a British colony, and in 1845 it was made part of the Cape Colony.

In 1856 Natal was again made a separate colony. With the introduction of Indian labour in the 1860s and the development of commercial agriculture, and with railways linking Durban's port with the booming Witwatersrand in 1895, the colony began to thrive.

The recorded history of the province until the Union of South Africa is full of conflict: the difaqane, the Boer-Zulu and the Anglo-Zulu Wars; and the two wars between the British and the Boers.

DURBAN

☎ 031

Durban is a big subtropical city on a long surf beach. It is a major port, but it is better known as a mecca for holiday-makers. The weather (and the water, thanks to the Agulhas Current) stays warm year-round. Over summer the weather is hot and very humid, with spectacular thunderstorms.

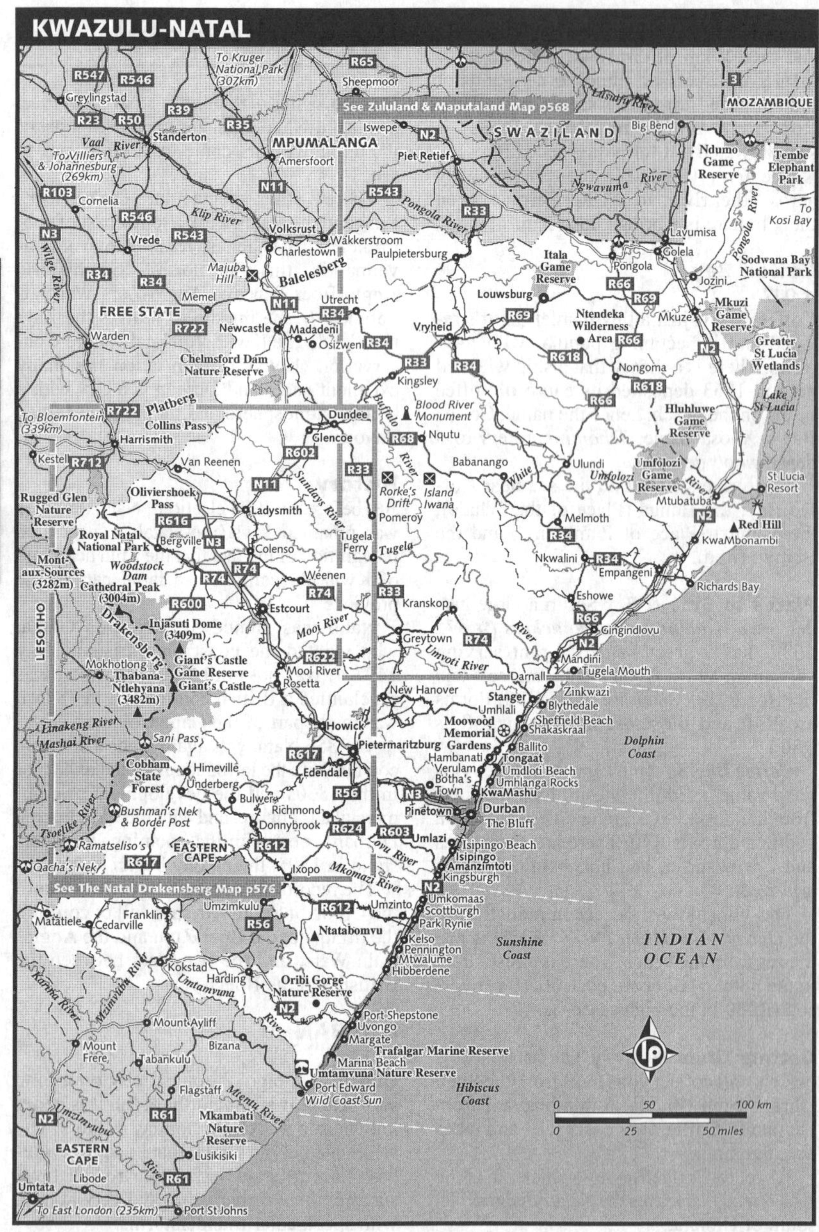
KWAZULU-NATAL
To Kruger National Park (307km)
R65
Sheepmoor
R547
R546
Greylingstad
See Zululand & Maputaland Map p568
MOZAMBIQUE
Usutu River
R23
R50
R39
R35
Iswepe
N2
SWAZILAND
Big Bend
Vaal River
Standerton
MPUMALANGA
To Villiers & Johannesburg (269km)
Amersfoort
Piet Retief
Ndumo Game Reserve
Tembe Elephant Park
Ngwavuma River
N11
R103
Cornelia
R543
Pongola River
R33
To Kosi Bay
R546
Klip River
Volksrust
Wakkerstroom
Lavumisa
N3
Vrede
R543
Charlestown
Paulpietersburg
Golela
Wilge River
Majuba Hill
Balelesberg
Itala Game Reserve
Pongola
Sodwana Bay National Park
R34
R34
Memel
Utrecht
R66
R69
Jozini
FREE STATE
N11
R34
Louwsburg
R69
Mkuze
Mkuzi Game Reserve
R722
Newcastle
Madadeni
Osizweni
R34
Vryheid
Ntendeka Wilderness Area
R66
Warden
R618
N2
Greater St Lucia Wetlands
Chelmsford Dam Nature Reserve
R33
R34
Kingsley
Nongoma
R618
R66
Lake St Lucia
Platberg
R722
Dundee
Blood River Monument
Hluhluwe Game Reserve
To Bloemfontein (339km)
Collins Pass
Glencoe
Buffalo River
Harrismith
R68
Nqutu
R602
Kestell
R712
Van Reenen
R33
Babanango
White
Ulundi
Umfolozi
Umfolozi Game Reserve
St Lucia Resort
N11
Sundays River
Rorke's Drift
Island Iwana
Rugged Glen Nature Reserve
Olivershoek Pass
Ladysmith
Pomeroy
River
Mtubatuba
R616
Melmoth
N2
Red Hill
Royal Natal National Park
Bergville
N3
Tugela Ferry
Tugela
R34
KwaMbonambi
Mont-aux-Sources (3282m)
Woodstock Dam
Colenso
R74
Nkwalini
R34
Empangeni
Cathedral Peak (3004m)
R74
Weenen
Richards Bay
R74
R33
R600
Estcourt
Kranskop
Eshowe
Drakensberg
Injasuti Dome (3409m)
Mooi River
R66
LESOTHO
Greytown
R74
River
Gingindlovu
N2
Giant's Castle Game Reserve
Mokhotlong
R622
Umvoti River
Mandini
Thabana-Ntlehyana (3482m)
Giant's Castle
Mooi River
Tugela Mouth
Rosetta
Darnall
Zinkwazi
New Hanover
Stanger
Blythedale
Umhlali
Linakeng River
Moowood Memorial Gardens
Sheffield Beach
Shakaskraal
Howick
Mashai River
Sani Pass
Dolphin Coast
Pietermaritzburg
Ballito
Cobham State Forest
Himeville
R617
Hambanati
Tongaat
Verulam
Umdloti Beach
Edendale
Umhlanga Rocks
Underberg
R56
Botha's Town
N3
KwaMashu
Bulwer
Pinetown
Durban
Bushman's Nek & Border Post
Richmond
The Bluff
Tsoelike River
Donnybrook
R624
R603
Ramatseliso's
Umlazi
Isipingo Beach
EASTERN CAPE
R612
Lovu River
Isipingo
Amanzimtoti
R617
Qacha's Nek
Ixopo
Mkomazi River
Kingsburgh
See The Natal Drakensberg Map p576
N2
Umkomaas
Umzimkulu
R612
Umzinto
Scottburgh
Franklin
Matatiele
Cedarville
R56
Park Rynie
Ntatabomvu
Kelso
Sunshine Coast
INDIAN OCEAN
Pennington
Mtwalume
Hibberdene
Kokstad
Mzimvubu River
Harding
Umtamvuna
Oribi Gorge Nature Reserve
Kinira River
N2
River
Port Shepstone
Mount Ayliff
Uvongo
Margate
Mount Frere
Tabankulu
Bizana
Trafalgar Marine Reserve
Marina Beach
Umtamvuna Nature Reserve
Flagstaff
Mtentu River
Port Edward
Wild Coast Sun
Hibiscus Coast
0
50
100 km
0
25
50 miles
N2
Umzimvubu
R61
Mkambati Nature Reserve
EASTERN CAPE
Lusikisiki
River
Libode
R61
Umtata
To East London (235km)
Port St Johns

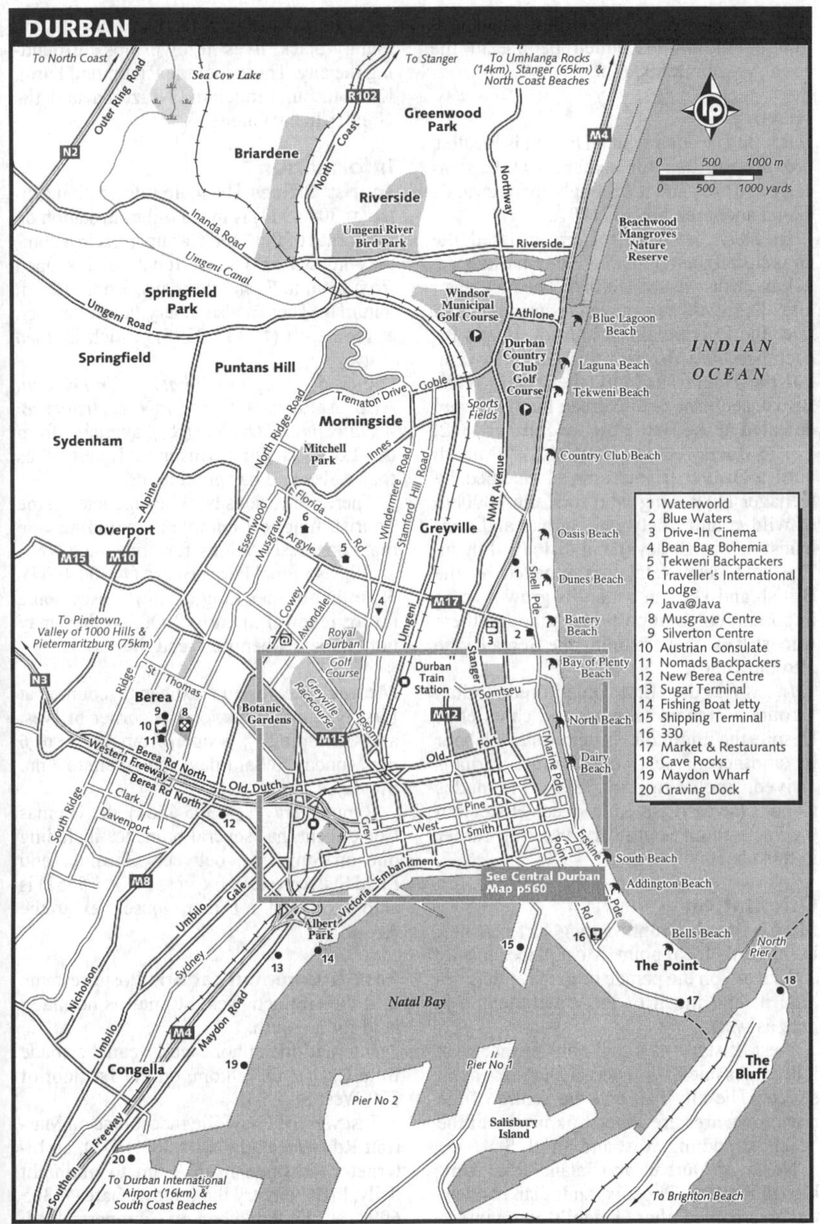
DURBAN
To North Coast
Sea Cow Lake
Outer Ring Road
To Stanger
To Umhlanga Rocks (14km), Stanger (65km) & North Coast Beaches
R102
Greenwood Park
Briardene
Riverside
Umgeni River Bird Park
North Coast
Northway
Beachwood Mangroves Nature Reserve
Inanda Road
Umgeni Canal
Riverside
Springfield Park
Umgeni Road
Windsor Municipal Golf Course
Athlone
Blue Lagoon Beach
Springfield
Puntans Hill
Durban Country Club Golf Course
INDIAN OCEAN
Laguna Beach
Tekweni Beach
Goble
Trematon Drive
Sports Fields
Morningside
North Ridge Road
Sydenham
Mitchell Park
Innes
Country Club Beach
Windermere Road
Stamford Hill Road
NMR Avenue
Alpine
Essenwood
Florida Rd
Musgrave
Argyle
Overport
Greyville
Oasis Beach
Snell Pde
Dunes Beach
Cowey
Avondale
Umgeni
To Pinetown, Valley of 1000 Hills & Pietermaritzburg (75km)
Royal Durban Golf Course
Battery Beach
Stanger
Bay of Plenty Beach
Durban Train Station
Greyville Racecourse
Ridge
St Thomas
Berea
Botanic Gardens
Somtseu
Epsom
North Beach
Western Freeway
Berea Rd North
Old Dutch
Old Fort
Marine Pde
Dairy Beach
Clark
South Ridge
Davenport
Pine
West
Smith
Grey
Point
Erskine
Embankment
Victoria
South Beach
See Central Durban Map p560
Addington Beach
Umbilo
Gale
Albert Park
Rd
Pde
Bells Beach
North Pier
The Point
Nicholson
Sydney
Natal Bay
Maydon Road
The Bluff
Congella
Pier No 1
Pier No 2
Salisbury Island
Southern Freeway
To Durban International Airport (16km) & South Coast Beaches
To Brighton Beach
N2
N3
M4
M8
M10
M12
M15
M17
0 500 1000 m
0 500 1000 yards
1 Waterworld
2 Blue Waters
3 Drive-In Cinema
4 Bean Bag Bohemia
5 Tekweni Backpackers
6 Traveller's International Lodge
7 Java@Java
8 Musgrave Centre
9 Silverton Centre
10 Austrian Consulate
11 Nomads Backpackers
12 New Berea Centre
13 Sugar Terminal
14 Fishing Boat Jetty
15 Shipping Terminal
16 330
17 Market & Restaurants
18 Cave Rocks
19 Maydon Wharf
20 Graving Dock
SOUTH AFRICA

Durban is home to the largest concentration of Indian-descended people in the country – about 800,000.

History

Natal Bay, around which Durban is located, provided refuge for seafarers at least as early as 1685, and it's thought that Vasco da Gama anchored here in 1497.

In 1837 the Voortrekkers crossed the Drakensberg and founded Pietermaritzburg, 80km north-west of Durban. The next year, after Durban was evacuated during a Zulu raid, the Boers claimed control. It was reoccupied by a British force later that year, but the Boers stuck by their claim. The British sent troops to Durban but they were defeated at the Battle of Congella in 1842.

The Boers retained control for a month until a British frigate arrived (fetched by teenager Dick King who rode the 1000km of wild country between Durban and Grahamstown in 10 days) and dislodged them. The next year Natal was annexed by the British and Durban began its growth as an important colonial port city, although there were still elephant roaming the Berea Ridge into the 1850s.

In 1860 the first indentured Indian labourers arrived to work the canefields. Despite the iniquitous system – slave labour by another name – many more Indians arrived, including, in 1893, Mohandas Gandhi (see British Rule under History in the Facts about South Africa section earlier in this chapter).

Orientation

Marine Parade, fronting long surf beaches, is Durban's focal point. Most places to stay and eat are on the parade or in the streets behind it, and much of the entertainment is here as well.

West St starts as a mall, but further west it becomes one of downtown Durban's main streets. The city hall and the centre of the downtown area are about 1.5km west of the beach, straddling West and Smith Sts.

North of Durban and inland from Umhlanga Rocks is Phoenix, an Indian residential area named after Gandhi's commune.

A fair proportion of Durban's population, mainly black, lives in townships surrounding the city. These include Richmond Farm, KwaMashu, Lindelani, Ntuzuma and the Greater Inanda area.

Information

Tourist Offices The main information centre (☎ 304 4934) is in the old train station on the corner of Pine and Gardiner Sts in a complex known as Tourist Junction. It's open from 8 am to 5 pm weekdays, 9 am to 2 pm Saturday. There's also a very helpful branch at the beach (☎ 332 2595), which is open daily.

Pick up a copy of *What's on in Durban*. Also useful is *A Guide to the History & Architecture of Durban* (R4), available from the Local History Museum. It describes four walks and has good maps.

There are various booking agencies in the Tourist Junction complex, including one that takes reservations for both the KNNC and the National Parks Board (☎ 304 4934). Note that the booking agency leases come up for renewal in early 2000, so they may not be there when you read this.

Money The foreign exchange counter at First National Bank, on the corner of West and Gillespie Sts, is open from 11 am to 6 pm Monday to Saturday, and 10 am to 3 pm Sunday.

Rennies Travel (☎ 305 6561), the Thomas Cook agent, has several branches including one on Smith St, between Gardiner and Field Sts. American Express (☎ 301 5551) is across the road in Denor House, next to the AA office.

Post & Communications Poste restante is at the GPO on West St; mail is normally held for a month.

International phone calls can be made from Cash Call Telkom, on the 1st floor of 320 West St.

Just west of Greyville racecourse on Marriott Rd is Java@Java (☎ 309 1575), an Internet cafe, open from 9 am to midnight daily. In the city try the Internet Cafe (☎ 305 6998) at The Workshop on Commercial Rd.

SOUTH AFRICA

Emergency Contact numbers for emergencies are: ambulance (☎ 10177), or for a private service call St Johns (☎ 305 6588); and police (☎ 10111 or 300 3333).

Dangers & Annoyances Many areas can be unsafe at night, especially in the Indian area (see Indian Area later in this section). At night, most people head to the restaurants in the northern suburbs such as Morningside or the big hotels and clubs along the beachfront.

The crowded beachfront Promenade has been a happy hunting ground for pickpockets, and violent robberies have occurred here at night. At the time of research, security along the beachfront had considerably improved; get the local word when you're there.

Beachfront

Durban's prime attraction is its long string of surf beaches. Lifesavers patrol the beaches between 8 am and 5 pm – always swim in the patrolled area between the flags. Durban's 'Golden Mile' is actually 6km long; shark nets protect the warm-water beaches all the way from Blue Lagoon Beach (at the mouth of the Umgeni River) south to Addington Beach on The Point.

The revamped **Promenade** fronts the surf. It's a good place to watch the crowds and there are a number of things to do. Near West St is **Seaworld** (☎ 337 4079), open from 9 am to 9 pm daily. The fish are hand-fed daily by divers (sharks are fed on Tuesday, Thursday and Sunday). There are dolphin and seal shows daily. Entry is R30/20 for adults/children.

There are about a dozen **rickshaws** in Durban, which are usually found on the beachfront near Seaworld. A five-minute ride costs R7.50 plus R4 for the mandatory photo.

The **Snake Park** (☎ 337 6456) on Snell Pde, North Beach, has daily venom-milking demonstrations; entry is R12.

City Centre

The impressive **city hall** (1910) is worth a look inside and out. In the city hall building is the **Natural Science Museum** (enter from Smith St), which is open from 8.30 am to 4 pm Monday to Saturday, and 11 am to 4 pm Sunday. Upstairs is the **Art Gallery**, which houses a good collection of contemporary works; especially good are the arts and crafts of Zululand. Entry is free. The **Local History Museum** is in the courthouse (1863) behind the city hall (enter from Aliwal St). It has interesting displays on colonial life and a useful bookshop; entry is free.

On the eastern side of the GPO is **Church Square**, with its old vicarage and the 1909 **St Paul's Church** at the rear on Pine St.

The Workshop, a shopping centre on Commercial Rd, and the Tourist Junction complex nearby are in interesting former train station buildings. The excellent **KwaMuhle Museum** (in the former Bantu Administration building on Ordnance Rd) has a permanent display with good oral history tapes on the 'Durban System' by which whites historically subjugated blacks.

Indian Area

The **Victoria Indian Street Market**, at the western end of Victoria St on the corner of Prince Edward St, has replaced the old Indian Market, which burned down. It is the main tourist attraction of the area but a walk through the nearby bustling streets is equally interesting – watch out for pickpockets.

Grey St, between Victoria and West Sts, is the main shopping area. Prices are low and you can bargain. Most Muslim shops close between noon and 2 pm on Friday.

The big **Juma Mosque** on the corner of Queen and Grey Sts is open to visitors on weekdays and Saturday morning; call for a guided tour (☎ 304 0326). The **Alayam Hindu Temple** is the oldest and biggest in South Africa. It's away from the main Indian area, north of the centre on Somtseu Rd, which runs between Snell Parade and NMR Ave. It is open from 7 am to 6 pm daily.

Berea

The Africana Museum at 220 Marriot Rd, near the corner of Musgrave Rd, in Berea, is an old home preserving an important collection of Zulu craft, art, furniture and paintings. Entry is R15.

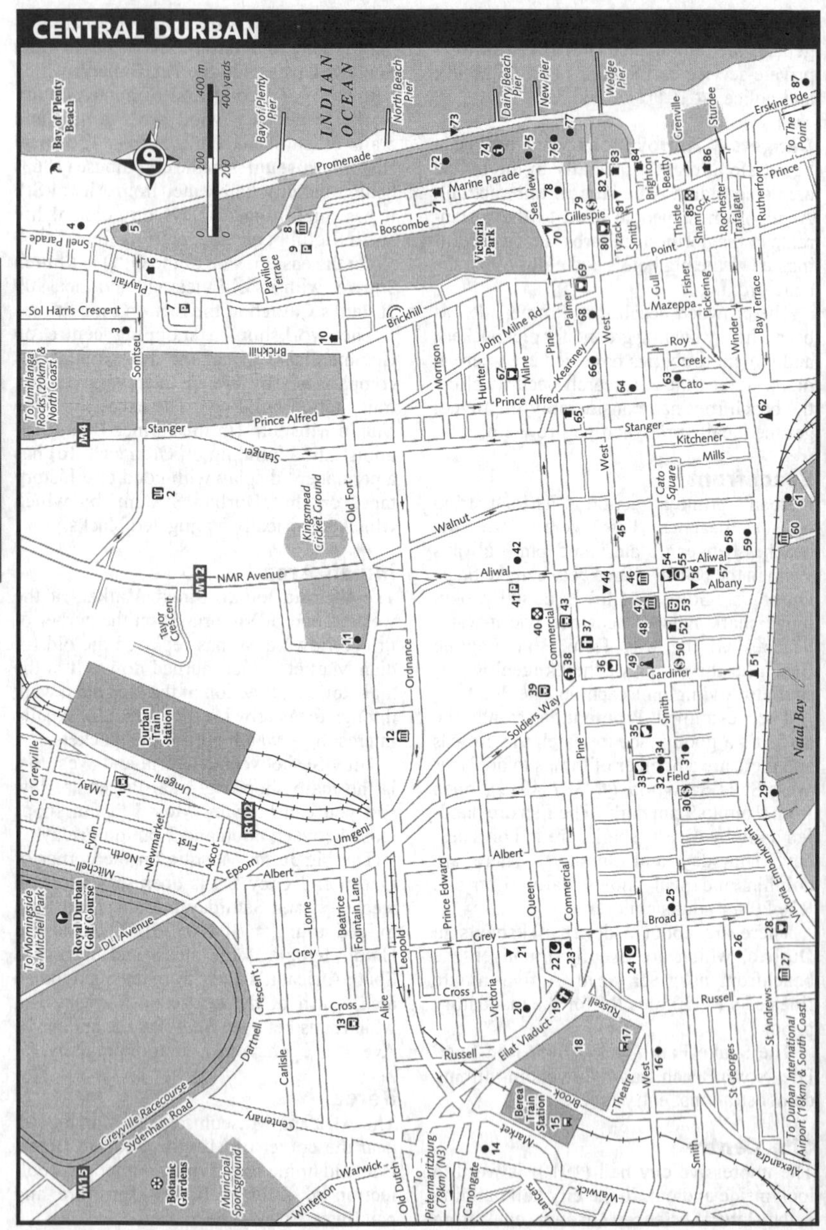
CENTRAL DURBAN
INDIAN OCEAN
Bay of Plenty Beach
Bay of Plenty Pier
North Beach Pier
Dairy Beach Pier
New Pier
Wedge Pier
400 m
400 yards
Promenade
Marine Parade
Snell Parade
Playfair
Sol Harris Crescent
Somtseu
Pavilion Terrace
Boscombe
Victoria Park
Brickhill
Sea View
Gillespie
Erskine Pde
To The Point
Grenville
Sturdee
Brighton
Beatty
Tyzack
Smith
Point
Thistle
Shamrock
Rochester
Trafalgar
Rutherford
Prince
Gull
Fisher
Pickering
Mazeppa
Winder
Bay Terrace
Roy
Creek
Cato
Palmer
John Milne Rd
Morrison
Hunter
Milne
Pine
Kearsney
West
Prince Alfred
Stanger
Kitchener
Mills
Cato Square
To Umhlanga Rocks (20km) & North Coast
M4
Old Fort
Kingsmead Cricket Ground
Walnut
NMR Avenue
M12
Aliwal
Albany
Commercial
Ordnance
Tayor Crescent
Durban Train Station
Gardiner
Soldiers Way
Field
Natal Bay
Umgeni
R102
May
To Greyville
Fynn
Newmarket
First
North
Ascot
Mitchell
Epsom
Albert
To Morningside & Mitchell Park
Royal Durban Golf Course
DLI Avenue
Lorne
Beatrice
Fountain Lane
Leopold
Prince Edward
Queen
Broad
Victoria Embankment
Grey
Cross
Victoria
Alice
Dartnell Crescent
Carlisle
Russell
Ellat Viaduct
St Andrews
To Durban International Airport (18km) & South Coast
St Georges
Theatre
Brook
Berea Train Station
Market
Greyville Racecourse
Sydenham Road
Centenary
M15
Botanic Gardens
Municipal Sportsground
Warwick
Winterton
Old Dutch
To Pietermaritzburg (78km) (N3)
Canongate
Lancers
Alexandra

CENTRAL DURBAN

PLACES TO STAY
6 Holiday Inn Garden Court North Beach
10 City Lodge
45 Tudor House Hotel
52 Royal Hotel; Ulundi; Royal Carvery; Royal Grill
57 Durban International Backpackers
65 Banana Backpackers
71 Parade Hotel; The Big Blue
83 Tropicana
84 Holiday Inn Garden Court South Beach
86 Impala Holiday Flats

PLACES TO EAT
21 Victory Lounge
44 Medwood Gardens Cafe; Swimming Pool
56 The Cat & The Fiddle
70 Thatcher's
73 Joe Kool's
81 The Haven
82 Lord Prawn

OTHER
1 Long-Distance Minibus Taxis
2 Alayam Hindu Temple
3 Ocean City (Theatre & Ice Rink)
4 Snake Park
5 Mini Town
7 Parking
8 Military Museum; Sunday Flea Market
9 Parking
11 Old Fort; Warriors Gate
12 KwaMuhle Museum
13 Bus Depot
14 Fruit & Vegetable Market
15 Minibus Taxis
16 The Mansions
17 Minibus Taxi to Lusikisiki (Transkei)
18 Cemetery
19 Emmanuel Cathedral
20 Victoria Street Indian Market
22 Juma Mosque
23 Madrassa Arcade
24 West St Mosque
25 Medical Centre, Pharmacy & Internet
26 AA Office
27 Old House Museum
28 Le Plaza Hotel
29 Yacht Mole
30 First National Bank
31 Rennies Travel; US Consulate
32 AA Office
33 US Consulate
34 American Express
35 German Consulate
36 GPO
37 St Paul's Church
38 Tourist Junction
39 Local Buses to Umhlanga Rocks; Old Railway Station; African Art Centre
40 The Workshop
41 Parking
42 Durban Exhibition Centre
43 Local Bus Terminus
46 Local History Museum
47 Natural Science Museum; Municipal Library; Art Gallery
48 City Hall
49 Francis Farewell Square
50 Standard Bank
51 Dick King Statue
53 The Natal Playhouse
54 Italian Consulate
55 Airport Bus
58 The Movies
59 Hilmark Car Rental
60 Natal Maritime Museum; Boat Cruises
61 BAT Centre
62 Vasco Da Gama Clock
63 Cycle Logic
64 Bavarian Deli
66 Fairport Market
67 Cool Runnings
68 Mike Lamont Surf Shop
69 Odessy
72 Surfboad Hire
74 Information Kiosk
75 Amusement Park
76 U-Tour Coach Company; Rennies Travel; Rickshaws
77 Seaworld
78 Laundrette
79 First National Bank
80 Palm Beach; London Town Pub
85 The Wheel Shopping Centre; Cinemas
87 Al's Bike Hire

Diving

Simply Scuba (☎/fax 309 2982), Marriott Rd, Berea, offers PADI or NAUI courses. Blue Dolphin offers a two- to three-hour dive on KwaZulu-Natal reefs and wrecks for R350, including equipment.

Surfing

There's a multitude of good beaches with any number of breaks. The bi-monthly *Zigzag* magazine has some information crammed in between glossy ads.

Sailing

Durban is a great place to learn how to sail. Readers have recommended the Ocean Sailing Academy (☎ 082-553 1467, ⓔ academy@oceansailing.co.za) at 38 Fenton Rd. It offers a five-day course for aspiring yacht hands/skippers for R2000/R2400.

Organised Tours

Durban Africa (☎ 304 4934) conducts several walking tours of the city; the R25 cost is well worthwhile. Tours leave from the Tourist Junction at 9.45 am on weekdays; you must book in advance.

The Durban Rickshaw Bus does tours of the city in an open-top, double-decker bus. They depart from outside U-Tours (☎ 368 2848) on the beachfront, just north of West St, at 2pm on Tuesday, Thursday and Sunday. They cost R40/20 for adults/children and give visitors an excellent overview of the city.

SOUTH AFRICA

Readers recommend mountain-bike tours of the city by registered tour guide Cynthia Meintsma (☎ 564 0730).

Hostels are good places to organise budget tours and activities. The largest range is offered by Tekweni Eco-Tours, part of Tekweni Backpackers (see Places to Stay – Budget following).

Places to Stay – Budget

***Queensburgh Caravan Resort** (☎ 464 5800)* is about 12km west of the city in Northdene. Camp sites are R40 per person in low season. To get there, take the M7 west and exit at Bellville Rd/Old Main Rd/M5. Travel west on the M5 for some way and just after the civic centre turn right onto St Augustine Rd then right onto Haslam Rd.

***Banana Backpackers** (☎ 368 4062, 1st floor, 61 Pine St)* on the corner of Prince Alfred, is 1km from the beach. It's a big, friendly and relaxed place that gets good feedback from readers. Dorms are R40, singles R60, twins R100 and small doubles R140.

***Durban International Backpackers** (☎ 305 9939, 31 Aliwal St)* has grungy dorms and doubles for R35. The rooms are small but it's in the city centre.

***Tekweni Backpackers** (☎ 303 1433, 167 Ninth Ave)* is a popular place a manageable distance north of the centre in trendy Morningside. Dorms are R45, doubles cost R120 or there are bargain doubles (with private bathroom) in a building next door for R150. Tekweni Eco-Tours is also here. Not far away is another good place, ***Traveller's International Lodge** (☎ 303 1064, 743 Currie Rd)*. Prices are about the same as at Tekweni, but it's smaller and more laid-back.

***Nomad Backpackers** (☎ 202 9709, 70 Essenwood Rd, Berea)* run by a friendly Kiwi is another good option. Dorms are R40 and large, clean doubles cost R120.

Places to Stay – Mid-Range

Most of the mid-range to top-end places are listed in the *Natal Accommodation Guide* (R4), available at Tourist Junction. There's an accommodation booking desk in the complex, and the staff should be able to find you a B&B from about R150/200 a single/double.

The streets near the beach, especially Gillespie St, are the places to look for cheaper hotels and apartments. Good value in the low season is ***Impala Holiday Flats** (☎ 332 3232, 40 Gillespie St)*, with tidy three- or four-bed flats from R175.

***The Parade Hotel** (☎ 337 4565, 191 Marine Parade)* is typical of the comfortable beachfront hotels with singles/doubles for R110/180 in the low season.

The ***Tudor House Hotel** (☎ 337 7328)* on West St, east of Aliwal St, is away from the beach but great value. Elegant, pub-style double rooms with air-con, phone and TV are R180 with breakfast.

Places to Stay – Top End

Many top-end places line the beachfront. ***Blue Waters** (☎ 0800 312 044 toll free)* north of the centre is a bit further way from the crowded Promenade and has singles/doubles for R220/320 with breakfast.

***Tropicana** (☎ 368 1511, fax 332 6890)* on Marine Parade south of West St is comfortable and has rooms for R295/390.

***Holiday Inn Garden Court South Beach** (☎ 337 2231, fax 337 4640)* nearby has great views; double rooms are R280. There is another branch a bit further along at North Beach.

The ***City Lodge** (☎ 332 1447, fax 332 1483)* on the corner of Brickhill and Old Fort Rds has free, secure parking and luxury, generic doubles for R292 on weekends (R356 on weekdays).

You have to leave the beachfront to find Durban's best hotel, the extravagant ***Royal Hotel** (☎ 304 0331, fax 304 5055, 267 Smith St)*, which is opposite the city hall. Rates start at R225 per person on the weekend.

Places to Eat

Beachfront Many hotels around the beachfront have cheap meals.

If you head north along North Beach Promenade, you get to an enclave of eating places that overlook the sea. ***Joe Kool's*** is a night (and day) spot that serves great 'recovery' breakfasts for R18.

Thatcher's, in a block of apartments on the corner of Gillespie and Sea View Sts, is a sedate place with surprisingly inexpensive dishes. ***Lord Prawn***, in the Coastlands building (2nd floor) on the corner of West St and Marine Pde, is open daily for seafood feasts.

The Haven restaurant and bar is a small place on Tyzack St that has steaks and seafood. The seafood curry (R45) is good.

City Centre Takeaways around the city have good Indian snacks, including bunny chow (a hollowed-out loaf of bread filled with curry). ***Victory Lounge***, upstairs on the corner of Grey and Victoria Sts, is an excellent cafe, which is open during the day; *biryanis* are R17. Another place on Grey St is the Gujarati-style ***Patel's Vegetarian*** (closes 3 pm).

Medwood Gardens Cafe on West St, near the GPO, is inexpensive, outdoors and a good place to read your snail mail. It's open from 8.30 am to 4 pm Monday to Saturday.

The Cat & the Fiddle, on Albany Grove near Smith St, serves decent pub meals and the kitchen is open all afternoon. Bangers and mash costs R14, while burgers are around R20.

The five-star ***Royal Hotel*** on Smith St has a variety of excellent restaurants. Most have a Sunday lunch deal where a buffet or set menu costs around R60 plus drinks (see Places to Stay – Top End earlier).

Roma Revolving Restaurant *(☎ 332 3337)* is on the 32nd floor of John Ross House on Victoria Embankment. The view is amazing and the Italian food isn't horrifyingly expensive: three courses with coffee and wine costs around R75.

Greyville & Morningside On Florida Rd in Morningside are several places to eat and drink. ***Christina's Kitchen*** near the corner of Eighth St has pre-prepared gourmet dishes, and next door is ***Christina's Restaurant***, with main courses such as roast duck for about R40. Nearby is the British-style ***Keg & Thistle*** serving filling pub lunches.

Bean Bag Bohemia (the sign says 'BBB') on Windermere Rd at the corner of Campbell Ave (near the Florida Rd junction) serves excellent food in the light, healthy and spicy Australian/Californian style.

The downstairs cafe and bar is open from 9 am daily. Baguettes with tasty fillings start at around R24, with larger main courses around R45. Crisp, fresh salads are R25.

Entertainment

Durban is a good place to party, with a range of venues. Many events can be booked with Computicket (☎ 304 2753).

Pubs & Clubs Near the beachfront try the ***London Town Pub*** (in the Palm Beach Hotel) complete with double-decker bus. ***The Big Blue*** in the Parade Hotel has a band most nights.

Cool Runnings, between the beach and the city centre on Milne St, is the place for reggae.

No 330 on Point Rd is *the* place for Durban groovers. It's basically a dance club but masquerades as an 'alternative' club on Friday night. The regular beat includes techno, hip-hop, acid house and garage.

The ***Octagon Jazz Forum*** is a popular jazz club on the corner of Field and Queen Sts – catch a taxi here at night, as the area can be dangerous. Other well-known jazz venues include ***Bassline*** on Rutherford St.

The ***Rainbow*** *(23 Stanfield Lane, Pinetown)* is a monthly Sunday jazz venue attracting top musicians (around R25 entry). One reader reports seeing the African Jazz Pioneers, Ladysmith Black Mambazo, and Sakhile (with jazz-fusion king Sipho Gumede) here.

The ***BAT Centre*** *(☎ 332 0451)* on the Victoria Embankment is a funky little venue and recommended for African music on the weekends. We saw some outstanding West African drumming for a cover charge of R20 – fantastic! Call ahead to find out what's on.

The Florida Rd precinct of Morningside also attracts a late-night crowd, with several pubs and places to eat (see Greyville & Morningside under Places to Eat earlier in this section).

Gay & Lesbian Venues There's a small gay scene in Durban. ***Axis*** on the corner of Gillespie and Rutherford Sts is a popular gay nightclub. The ***Riviera Hotel*** on the corner of Victoria Embankment and Field St is probably the best place to meet people and ***The Bar*** here is Durban's oldest gay club, open every night. There's a small cover charge.

Classical Music, Theatre & Dance A variety of musicians and exceptional gospel choirs play and sing on the city hall steps on Wednesday at 1 pm.

The University of Natal's Music Department has free lunchtime concerts on Monday in ***Howard College*** (concerts also in the evenings).

The ***Natal Playhouse***, opposite the city hall on Smith St, has dance, drama and music most nights.

Cinemas There are cinemas in ***The Wheel*** shopping centre on Gillespie St; there are more in ***The Workshop*** (Commercial Rd) and at the ***BP Centre***, across the road from the Tudor House Hotel.

Getting There & Away

Air Durban international airport is off the N2, about 15km south of the city. SAA (☎ 250 1111) is based at the airport.

Bus Most long-distance buses leave from the rear of the Durban train station. Translux (☎ 308 8111) is here and Greyhound's office (☎ 309 7830) is nearby. You can also book Translux and Greyhound on the beachfront at U-Tours (☎ 368 2848 or 337 6474).

The Baz Bus (☎ 021-439 2323 or book through hostels) service between Cape Town and Jo'burg runs via Durban and the Garden Route.

Amanzimtoti Enbee (☎ 039-979 5447) runs several services to Amanzimtoti from the Dick King Statue (Victoria Embankment) on weekday afternoons and 1.30 pm on Saturday.

Bloemfontein Greyhound runs to Bloemfontein (R165) via Bethlehem (R125) and Welkom (R125).

Cape Town Translux has a daily service (R265) via Bloemfontein (R140).

Jo'burg Translux (R110) and Greyhound (R140) run at least daily.

Margate The Margate Mini Coach (☎ 039-312 1406) runs between Margate and Durban daily (R50, same-day return R65). Some services run all the way down to the Wild Coast Sun Casino (just over the border in Eastern Cape).

Pietermaritzburg Cheetah Coaches (☎ 342 0266) runs to Pietermaritzburg daily (R30), call for current departure times. The bus leaves from Aliwal St outside the Local History Museum.

Port Elizabeth Translux runs a daily service (R200) via Umtata (R125) and East London (R160).

Richards Bay Stallion Coaches (☎ 403 7725) runs to Richards Bay weekdays at 7 am and 4.30 pm (R60, three hours). There are also weekend services. The bus departs outside St Paul's church on Pine St.

Umhlanga Rocks Umhlanga Express (☎ 561 2860) leaves from a number of stops, including Pine St, Commercial Rd and the corner of Brickhill and Somtseu Rds. The fare is R12.

Minibus Taxi Some long-distance minibus taxis leave from ranks in the streets opposite the Umgeni Rd entrance to the Durban train station. Routes include the Swaziland border (R70) and Jo'burg (R75).

Other minibus taxis, running mainly to the south coast and the Transkei region in Eastern Cape, leave from around the Berea train station.

Train Durban train station (☎ 308 8118) is on Umgeni Rd. The daily *Trans Natal* (Durban to Jo'burg via Newcastle and Ladysmith) and the weekly *Trans Oranje* (Durban to Cape Town via Bloemfontein and Kimberley) run from here. There are also commuter trains running down the coast as far as Kelso near Pennington and north to Stanger.

Car Avis (☎ 462 3282), Budget (☎ 304 9023) and Imperial (☎ 337 3731) have offices here. There are smaller companies with lower rates, including Tempest (☎ 307 5211) and Hilmark (☎ 332 9455). Forest Drive (☎ 562 8433) claims to be the cheapest.

Getting Around

To/From the Airport A bus (☎ 211 1333) runs to the airport from near the corner of

Aliwal and Smith Sts for R20. Some hostels can get discounts and pick-ups for backpackers on the return trip. By taxi, the same trip costs nearly R200!

Bus The main bus terminus and information centre is on Commercial Rd across from The Workshop. Mynah is a small bus company that covers the central and beachfront areas. All trips cost around R3.50. There are also less-frequent full-size buses running more routes and travelling further from the city centre than Mynah. At off-peak times the most you will pay is R4.

Taxi A taxi fare between the beach and the train station costs around R20. Bunny Cabs (☎ 332 2914) runs 24 hours – the drivers we met were friendly. Other taxi companies are Eagles (☎ 337 8333) and Aussies (☎ 309 7888).

Rickshaw Rickshaws (Asian-style three-wheelers) congregate on the beachfront near Palmer St. Over short distances their fares are lower than taxis.

AROUND DURBAN

The **Valley of 1000 Hills** (also known as the Umgeni Valley) runs from the ocean at Durban to Nagle Dam, east of Pietermaritzburg. The rolling hills and traditional Zulu villages are the main reason visitors drive through here, usually on the R103, which begins in Hillcrest, off the M13.

PheZulu (High Up) and the adjacent **Assegay Safari Park**, which features reptiles, are both on the R103. These places are open daily and have touristy cultural displays.

SOUTH OF DURBAN

There are some good beaches on the south coast between Durban and Transkei. There are also shoulder-to-shoulder resorts for much of the 150km, and in summer there isn't much room to move.

Commuter trains run from Durban down the coast as far as Kelso, on the northern edge of Pennington. (For details of the Margate Mini Coach, see also Getting There & Away in the Durban section).

Sunshine Coast

The Sunshine Coast stretches about 60km from Amanzimtoti to Mtwalume. All of the beaches are easily accessible from the N2, but the area suffers from its proximity to Durban.

The main town is Amanzimtoti (Sweet Waters), a high-rise jungle of apartment blocks. It merges into Kingsburgh to the south. **Winklespruit**, **Illovo** and **Karridene** beaches are nearby. The friendly visitors centre (☎/fax 031-903 7493) is in Amanzimtoti on Beach Rd, not far from the Inyoni Rocks.

Further south are Umkomaas, Scottburgh, Park Rynie, Kelso and Pennington. Scottburgh has a publicity association (☎ 039-976 1364).

Inland from Park Rynie, off the R612 past Umzinto, the **Vernon Crookes Nature Reserve** has a few animal species and some indigenous forest. If you walk through the reserve beware of ticks. There are two-bed ***huts*** for R75 per person; entry to the reserve is R8. Unlike most KNNC reserves, it can be booked locally (☎ 0323-42222, between 8 am and 7 pm).

Places to Stay In Amanzimtoti, ***Ocean Call Caravan Park*** *(☎ 031-916 2644)*, 1.5km from Winklespruit train station, has camp sites for R35 per adult (R45 with electricity). ***Illovo Beach Caravan Park*** *(☎ 031-916 3472)* has camp sites for R80 in the high season (R60 in the low season). ***Villa Spa*** *(☎ 031-916 4939)*, also on Illovo Beach, has camp sites for R30 per adult (R15 per child). It also has chalets for R250 a double.

Further south in Scottburgh, the amiable ***Blue Marlin*** *(☎ 039-978 3361, fax 976 0971, 180 Scott St, Scottburgh)* costs about R195/285 for singles/doubles with DB&B.

There are plenty of B&Bs and in the low season you may get away with R80 per person – ask at the various information centres.

Hibiscus Coast

This section of the south coast includes the seaside towns of Hibberdene, Port Shepstone, Shelly Beach, St Michaels-on-Sea, Uvongo, Margate, Ramsgate and Marina Beach. Port Shepstone is an unattractive industrial centre and Margate is a large, tizzy resort town. You can get information on these places from the South Coast Publicity Association (☎ 03931-22322) at Main Beach, Margate.

The **Oribi Gorge Nature Reserve** is inland from Port Shepstone, off the N2. The spectacular Oribi Gorge on the Umzimkulu River is one of the highlights of the coast. As well as the scenery there are many animals and birds. Entry costs R8. The KNNC has huts and cottages. The ***Oribi Gorge Hotel*** *(☎ 039-687 0253)*, near a viewing site overlooking the gorge, has B&B for R150 per person.

The **Trafalgar Marine Reserve** off the coast near Margate protects ancient fossil beds, but for most visitors it is the surfing and especially sailboarding here that are the attractions.

Places to Stay In Margate there are many hotels, resorts and self-catering apartments. It's a good idea to book something through an agency such as Beach Holidays (☎ 03931-22543, fax 73753) or the Information Centre for Holiday Accommodation (☎ 03931-50265).

De Wet *(☎ 03931-21022)* at St Andrews Ave on the beach only has a few camp sites (about R35). You could try the ***Margate*** *(☎ 03931-20852)*, opposite the police station and sandwiched between the R620 and Valley Rd. ***Sunlawns*** *(☎ 03931-21078)*, on Uplands Rd, is a cheap hotel, which charges R125 per person for DB&B.

In Anerley ***Villa Siesta*** *(☎ 039681-3343)* has sites for R130 in the high season (R65 in the low season). Four-person chalets cost from R250 in the high season and from R125 in the low season.

Port Edward

☎ 039

Port Edward adjoins the Transkei region of Eastern Cape. Just south of town is the interesting **Mzamba Village market** where a range of Xhosa crafts are sold.

Old Pont *(☎ 313 2211)* is a good family resort, offering caravan and camp sites from R80 in the high season.

Vuna Valley Backpackers *(☎ 303 2532)* not far from Port Edward is a large, mellow place. Camp sites are R25, dorms R40 and doubles R100. To get there from the highway at Port Edward, turn right onto Old Pont Rd and follow the signs.

NORTH OF DURBAN

The stretch of coast from Umhlanga Rocks north to Tugela Mouth is less developed than the south coast, and the beaches are better. With lots of time-shares and retirement villages, things aren't very lively.

Umhlanga Rocks

☎ 031

This big resort town (the name means Place of Reeds) is about 15km north of Durban.

There's an information kiosk (☎ 561 4257) on the mall, near the intersection of Lagoon Dr and Lighthouse St.

The **Natal Sharks Board** (☎ 566 1017) is a research institute dedicated to studying sharks and their danger to humans. It's open daily (call for the latest times); entry is R12/7 for adults/children. The board is about 2km out of town, up the steep Umhlanga Rocks Drive (the M12 leading to the N3).

A minibus service (☎ 561 2860) runs from the information kiosk in Umhlanga Rocks to Durban five times a day (R12).

Places to Stay & Eat Umhlanga's many holiday apartments fill up in the high season, when you'd be lucky to rent one for less than a week, but otherwise it's possible to rent one for as few as two days. A two-bedroom apartment costs from R190 per night in the low season (R380 in the high season), and three-bedroom apartments cost from R210 in the low season (R400 in the high season). Contact Umhlanga Accommodation (☎ 561 2012).

Most hotels charge about R300/500 a single/double. Along Lagoon Dr are ***Umhlanga Rocks*** *(☎/fax 561 1321)* and ***Umhlanga Sands*** *(☎ 561 2323, fax 561 4408)*.

Most of the hotels have restaurants. Vegetarians are catered for at ***Health Nut*** in the Village Centre, on Chartwell Dr.

Dolphin Coast

☎ 032

The Dolphin Coast starts at Umdloti Beach and stretches north to the Tugela River. It includes Tongaat, Ballito, Shaka's Rock, Umhlali (Salt Rock), Blythdale, Stanger, Zwinkwazi and Tugela Mouth. The coast gets its name from the pods of bottlenose dolphins that frolic offshore.

The Dolphin Coast Publicity Association (☎ 946 1997) is near the BP service station, just where you leave the N2 to enter Ballito.

Places to Stay In Ballito, the colourful ***Dolphin Coast Backpackers*** *(☎ 946 1644, 10 Edward Place, Ballito)* on the beachfront has dorms for R40 and doubles for R120.

Rainbow Backpackers *(☎ 946 2710, 3B Jack Powell Rd, Ballito)* is close to shops and has bodyboard hire; dorms are R40 and doubles R110.

Rental agencies in Ballito include Coastal Holiday Letting (☎ 946 2155); a typical three-room flat costs R130 a night (R300 in the high season).

Tugela Mouth The Tugela River, once an important natural boundary for local tribes, enters the sea here to end its journey from Mont-aux-Sources in the Drakensberg. There are several major battlefields near the mouth.

The **Ultimatum Tree**, where the British presented their demands to Cetshwayo's representatives, is nearby. At this site in 1878, the British demanded that by mid-January 1879 the Zulu pay taxes and return all the cattle they had stolen. The cattle were not returned, precipitating the Anglo-Zulu War, which raged until August 1879 when Cetshwayo was captured (for more on Cetshwayo, see the boxed text 'The Zulu after Blood River' later in this chapter). Across the river there is a collection of war graves on the site of Fort Pearson.

ZULULAND

Zululand covers much of central KwaZulu-Natal. The area east of the N2 and north of the Mtubatuba–St Lucia road is known as Maputaland and is covered later in this chapter.

This area is dominated by one tribal group, the Zulu. The name Zulu (Heaven) comes from an early chief. His descendants were known as *abakwaZulu*, or people of Zulu.

Warning

There is malaria in Zululand and other places in the north of KwaZulu-Natal, and bilharzia in some waterways and dams.

Richards Bay

☎ 0351

This town feels as though it was meticulously planned for a boom that hasn't happened yet. It's spread out, with tourist-oriented facilities far from what passes for the centre. Unless you have business here there's not much for visitors to do. The publicity association (☎ 31111, fax 31897) at 48 Anglers Rd has information on things to do in the area.

Empangeni

☎ 035

Empangeni (m'pan-**gay**-nee) started out as a sugar town, but the huge eucalypt plantations nearby are rivalling the cane in importance to the town's economy. It's a jumping-off point for the coast and the inland areas of Zululand.

Enseleni Nature Reserve is 13km northeast of Empangeni on the N2.

Harbour Lights *(☎ 196 6239)* is a caravan park off the N2 between Empangeni and Richards Bay with sites for R30. The friendly ***Imperial Hotel*** *(☎ 192 1522, 52 Maxwell St)* has singles/doubles for R230/370, or R165/220 with shared bathroom. There is also a plethora of B&Bs in the area.

There's a ***Portuguese restaurant*** next to the old Royal Hotel and it's known for its prawn *piri-piri* (chilli prawns). You'll also find a ***Spur*** and a ***Mike's Kitchen*** in town.

Eshowe

☎ 0354

This town is inland in the misty Zululand hills. The name Eshowe is said to be the sound the wind makes when passing through trees. Eshowe was Cetshwayo's stronghold before he moved to Ondini, and like Ondini, Eshowe was destroyed during the Anglo-Zulu War. The British built Fort Nongqai in 1883, establishing Eshowe as the administrative centre of their newly captured territory.

The helpful Eshowe Publicity Association (☎ 41141) provides information.

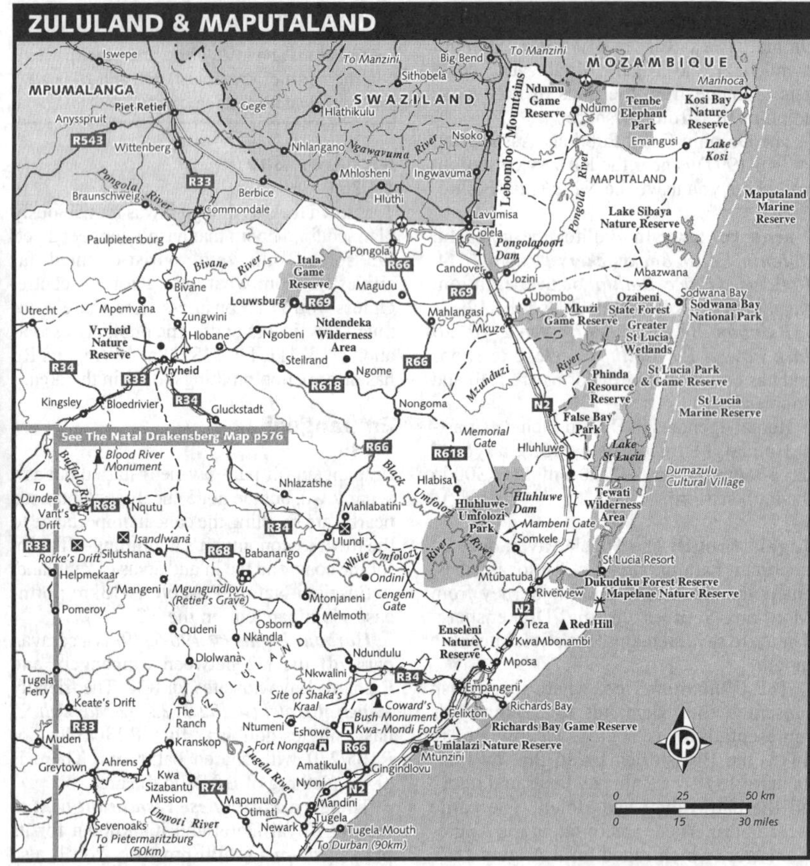

Things to See & Do In the mud-and-brick Nongqai Fort is the **Zululand Historical Museum**, open from 9 am to 5 pm daily; entry is R6. From the museum you can walk to **Mpushini Falls**, but don't swim or drink the water as bilharzia is present.

The **Dlinza Forest Reserve** is a 200-hectare stand of dense rainforest – on a misty day this is an eerie place. There are a few animals, rich birdlife and walking trails.

Places to Stay *Eshowe Caravan Park* (☎ *741759)* costs around R35 per site. It's some way from the town centre but close to Dlinza Forest Reserve.

Zululand Backpackers *(☎ 742894)* is a separate part of the George Hotel. There is a great range of activities, and the owner has some good Zulu contacts. Dorms are R45 and doubles are R130.

The ***George Hotel*** *(☎ 74919)* has singles/doubles for R166/210 with breakfast. The hotel was undergoing extensive renovations at the time of research.

Getting There & Away Minibus taxis depart from the car park at the Kwik Spar on

The Zulu After Blood River

After the disaster of Blood River (for more details, see The Great Trek under History in the Facts about South Africa section), Zulu king Dingaan fled to Swaziland, where he was killed in 1840. During the reign of his successor, Mpane, much Zulu land was lost. He was succeeded by his son Cetshwayo in 1873.

Cetshwayo inherited a kingdom under threat from the land-grabbing Boers in the Transvaal. The British agreed that Boer encroachment was illegal but they gave little assistance to the Zulu, largely because they had a plan of their own – a British wedge into Africa heading north from Durban. The Zulu kingdom was directly in the way. In January 1879 the British invaded the kingdom in a dispute over cattle and taxes (see Tugela Mouth in the Dolphin Coast section earlier in this chapter), beginning the Anglo-Zulu War.

The Zulu decisively defeated the British at the Battle of Isandlwana but failed to capture the small station at Rorke's Drift, despite overwhelming superiority in numbers. After that things went downhill and on 4 July at Ulundi, Cetshwayo was defeated.

In 1887 the British annexed Zululand. Dinizulu, Cetshwayo's son and the last independent Zulu king, was exiled. In 1897 the British handed Zululand over to the colony of Natal.

During the apartheid era, the Zulu resisted attempts to turn their lands into one of the 'independent' Homelands, thanks to the political skills of Chief Mangosuthu Buthelezi, leader of Inkatha (now the Inkatha Freedom Party, IFP) and great-grandson of Cetshwayo. However, Inkatha was manipulated by the apartheid regime into becoming an enemy of the ANC, and this almost derailed the march to democracy.

The current Zulu monarch is King Goodwill Zwelithini.

the main street. A taxi fare to Empangeni costs R16. If you want to head deeper into Zululand, take a taxi to Melmoth (about R9).

Washesha Buses (☎ 74504) runs several services in the area, including a scenic but rough trip through forest to Nkandla (R15). There's no accommodation at Nkandla but you can get a taxi from there to Melmoth, where there's a hotel. A bus from Eshowe to Empangeni (R12) also runs along a dirt road through rural areas. For more information ask at the office, behind KFC on the main street.

Nkwalini Valley

KwaBulawayo, Shaka's *kraal* (hut village), once loomed over this beautiful valley but today the valley is regimented into citrus orchards and canefields rather than *impis* (military regiments). A marker shows where the kraal was. Across the road is **Coward's Bush**, where warriors who returned from battle without their spears or who had received wounds in the back were executed.

To get to Nkwalini Valley from Eshowe, head north for about 6km on the R68, turn off to the right onto the R230, and then keep going for about 20km.

Shakaland Created as a set for the telemovie *Shaka Zulu* and managed by the Protea chain, this isn't exactly a genuine Zulu village. The Nandi Experience (Nandi was Shaka's mother) is a display of Zulu culture and customs, which is held daily at 11 am and 12.30 pm and costs R115. The 'experience' plus accommodation costs R575/900 for single/double DB&B.

Shakaland (☎ 0800 119 000 for bookings) is at Norman Hurst Farm, Nkwalini, a few kilometres off the R68 and 14km north of Eshowe.

KwaBhekithunga Zulu Kraal This craft centre on the road into Nkwalini *is* a genuine Zulu village, although it doesn't look much like a traditional one. A live-in 'Zulu Experience' is offered here too, but only for large groups. Make a booking

(☎ 0354-600644, fax 600867) if you can muster 15 or more people. Even if you can't, it's worth visiting for the crafts.

Ulundi

☎ 0358

Tiny Ulundi was the capital of the KwaZulu Homeland, and it may replace Pietermaritzburg as the capital of KwaZulu-Natal. The town is fairly new but this area has been the stronghold of many Zulu kings, and several are buried in the nearby Valley of the Kings. The town itself offers little to see, but there are important historical sites in the area. For information go to the KwaZulu Monuments Council (☎ 702 050) in Ondini.

Close to Ulundi are **Fort Nolela**, near the drift on the White Umfolozi River where the British camped before attacking Ondini in 1879; and **KwaGqokli**, where Shaka celebrated victory over the Ndwandwe in 1818. Another place of great significance to the Zulu is eMakhosini, **Valley of the Kings**. The great *makhosi* (chiefs) Nkhosinkulu (Zulu), Senzangakhona (father of Shaka, Dingaan and Mpande) and Dinizulu are buried here.

Ulundi Holiday Inn Garden Court *(☎ 701 012)* has singles/doubles from R374/458, and weekend specials.

Ondini

☎ 0358

Ondini (High Place) was established as Cetshwayo's capital in 1873, but it was razed by British troops after the Battle of Ulundi (4 July 1879). It took the British nearly six months to defeat the Zulu impis but the Battle of Ulundi went the way of most of the campaign, with the number of Zulu deaths 10 to 15 times higher than the number of British deaths.

The **royal kraal** section of the Ondini site was still being rebuilt at the time of research, but you can see the floors of identifiable buildings. Also at Ondini is the **KwaZulu Cultural-Historical Museum** (entry R9), with good exhibits on Zulu history and culture.

DB&B accommodation *(☎ 702050)* in traditional *umuzi* ('beehive' huts) costs R160 per person.

To get to Ondini, take the airport turn-off from the highway just south of Ulundi and keep going for about 5km on a dirt road. This road continues on to Hluhluwe-Umfolozi Park. Minibus taxis occasionally pass Ondini. The minibus taxi rank is opposite the Holiday Inn. Routes include: Vryheid (R15); Eshowe (R20); and Jo'burg (about R65).

Itala Game Reserve

Itala in northern Zululand has all the trappings of a private game reserve but at much lower prices. Entry costs R8 per person plus R30 per vehicle.

Animals include black and white rhino, elephant, nyala, hyaena, buffalo, baboon, leopard, cheetah and crocodile. The diverse habitats support over 320 species of bird.

Ntshondwe (☎ 0388-75239 for accommodation bookings) is the main centre, with superb views of the reserve below. Accommodation starts at R163 for a unit with communal kitchen and R185 for a chalet. There are a few basic camp sites for R16 per person.

Itala is entered from Louwsburg, about 65km east of Vryheid on the R69, and about the same distance south-west of Pongola via the R66 and the R69.

MAPUTALAND

Maputaland is one of the wildest and most fascinating areas of South Africa. It takes its name from the Maputo River, which splits, on the border of Mozambique and South Africa, into the Usutu and Pongola Rivers. Maputaland is sparsely settled and much of it is protected in parks and reserves. It contains coral reefs, many game reserves, the country's last wild elephants in Tembe Elephant Park, and three huge lakes, including the Greater St Lucia Wetlands.

KwaMbonambi

☎ 035

KwaMbonambi is a tiny but lush and beautiful town off the N2 about 30km north of Empangeni and the same distance south of Mtubatuba. There would be no reason to stop here, except that it has two excellent hostels, making it an ideal base for travellers exploring St Lucia, Hluhluwe-

Umfolozi and other attractions in northern Zululand and Maputaland.

Cuckoo's Nest *(☎ 580 1001/2, 28 Albezia St)* is a cheerful, carefree hostel with few rules and lots of activities. Dorms are R40 and doubles are R100, or R110 in outside huts. It offers trips to Sodwana Bay and Hluhluwe-Umfolozi Parks, or excursions (sometimes free) to a secluded stretch of beach where camping is available.

The ***Amazulu Lodge*** *(☎ 580 1009, 5 Killarney Place)* is in a beautiful setting among tall eucalypts, next to a golf course and only a short walk from minibus taxis to Richards Bay. Dorms are R40 (R45 with air-con) and doubles are R110. There's a pool, spa, sauna and other luxuries. The lodge arranges pick-ups from Durban and Richards Bay.

Mtubatuba

☎ 035

This is a trading town which is busy on weekends; the main reason to visit Mtubatuba is because local buses and minibus taxis run through here on the way south to Durban and west into Zululand. Coming from those destinations, Mtubatuba is the stop for St Lucia, which is about 25km east; the trip costs R6 by minibus taxi.

The ***Paradiso Hotel*** *(☎ 550 0153)* is friendly and was undergoing a serious facelift at the time of research. Singles/doubles cost R100/170 with shared bath (R120/200 with private bath), including breakfast. The ***Paradiso Guesthouse*** is next door.

Across the road from the Sundowner on Celtis Dr are two good B&Bs: ***Mtubatuba*** *(☎ 550 0558)* is R150 per person; and ***Celtis*** *(☎ 083 440 6489)* next door is a bit cheaper at R125 per person.

Dumazulu Cultural Village

☎ 035

Probably the best of the 'Zulu experience' villages, Dumazulu (☎ 562 2260 for bookings) is east of the N2, north of Mtubatuba. Four shows are held daily for about R60 and lunch and dinner are available. There's DB&B accommodation for about R440 per person.

Isinkwe *(☎ 562 2258)* is arguably one of the best backpackers hostels in South Africa. It's next to Dumazulu Cultural Village, off the N2 south of Hluhluwe (take the Bushlands exit). It's on a large, beautiful patch of virgin bush and has small but comfortable cabins, 'rustic' huts, tents and a dorm, all in a pleasant garden. There's a good kitchen and bar. The cabins cost R50 per person and all the other accommodation costs R40 per person.

Hluhluwe-Umfolozi Park

The two reserves of Hluhluwe (shlu-shlu-ee and Umfolozi were first proclaimed in 1897 and today they are among the best in Soutl Africa. They don't adjoin, but a 'corridor between them allows animals to move fron one park to the other. Both reserves havı lion, elephant, many rhino (black and white) giraffe and a host of other animals and birds

Several tours include Hluhluwe-Umfoloz Park. One inexpensive option is the three day trip with Tekweni Eco-Tours (contac Tekweni Backpackers in Durban), whicl also takes in the Greater St Lucia Wetlands

Entry to each reserve costs R8 per persoı plus R30 per vehicle.

Wilderness Trails In Hluhluwe there are driving trails but no walking trails except for a short one around the camp.

In Umfolozi, one of the main attractions is the trail system in a 24,000-hectare wilderness area. Accompanied by an armed ranger and donkeys to carry supplies, hikers spend three days walking in the reserve. You need a party of eight people (no children under 12). Bookings are accepted up to six months in advance and it's advisable to book early, with alternative dates if possible. The cost is R1200 per person, including all meals and equipment. On weekends there is a two-night trip which costs R650 per person.

Places to Stay & Eat In Hluhluwe, ***Hilltop Camp*** has stupendous views and is the best place to stay. Huts cost from R130 per person and self-catering chalets are R250 per person. ***Mpunyane Restaurant*** serves game dishes at reasonable prices. There are bush lodges at ***Muntulu***, perched high above the Hluhluwe River, and at ***Munyawaneni***, which is secluded and self-contained. These sleep eight and cost a minimum of R1375.

In Umfolozi, accommodation at ***Mpila*** and ***Masinda*** costs from R95 per person (minimum R190) in four-bed huts. There are also eight-bed bush camps (including your own ranger and cook) for R180 per person (minimum R720) or a bush lodge (minimum R1100).

Book all accommodation through the KNNC in Pietermaritzburg or its agent in Durban (for contact numbers, see the Durban and Pietermaritzburg sections of this chapter).

Getting There & Away The main entrance to Hluhluwe, at Memorial Gate, is about 15km west of the N2, about 50km north-west of Mtubatuba. Alternatively, just after Mtubatuba, turn left off the N2 onto the R618 to Nongoma and take the right-hand turn to the reserve after 17km.

The Mambeni gate on the eastern side of Umfolozi is 30km from Mtubatuba. Petrol is available at Mpila Camp in the park.

Greater St Lucia Wetlands

☎ 035

One of the world's great ecotourism destinations stretches for 80km from Sodwana Bay, in the north of Maputaland, to Mapelane Nature Reserve at the southern end of Lake St Lucia. The area is gradually being consolidated as the Greater St Lucia Wetlands, and satisfies the criteria for listing as a UNESCO world heritage area.

The park protects five interconnected ecosystems: marine (coral reefs, beaches); shore (barrier between lake and sea); Mkuze reed and sedge swamps; the lake (the largest estuary in Africa); and western shores (fossil corals, sand forest, bushveld and grasslands).

The main walks are the four-night guided St Lucia Wilderness Trail and the three-day Mziki Trail, both in the Cape Vidal area (see Tewati Wilderness Area later in this section), and the Dugandlovu Hiking Trail in False Bay Park (see False Bay Park later in this section). There are also day walks, detailed in KNNC literature available at the St Lucia Resort office.

WARNING

This is a malarial area. You should also be aware of crocodile and hippo – both are potentially deadly. Be careful at night, as hippo roam. In more remote areas hippo may be encountered on shore during the day – treat them with respect and retreat quietly. Sharks sometimes venture up the St Lucia estuary.

All the parks and reserves in the area are administered by the KNNC, but there is also private accommodation at St Lucia Resort, which is a sizeable holiday village.

Organised Tours St Lucia Tours & Charters (☎ 590 1259), next to the Dolphin supermarket, can organise just about anything in the area, including night drives for R95. Bibs Hostel (see Places to Stay & Eat later) has loads of organised activities such as snorkelling at Cape Vidal for R150 and hippo tours on the estuary for R60.

One of the highlights is the trip on the *Santa Lucia*. It leaves from the wharf on the west side of the bridge on the Mtubatuba road at 8.30 and 10.30 am and 2.30 pm daily (R45).

St Lucia Resort St Lucia Resort is the main centre for the area, with KNNC offices, shops, boat hire and other services, as well as a lot of private accommodation.

There are two ATMs in town: at the First National Bank next to the Dolphin supermarket, and at the Standard Bank.

About 2km north of St Lucia Resort on the road to Cape Vidal is the **Crocodile Centre** where there are displays on the ecosystems in the area and other information; entry is R8.

Places to Stay & Eat There are three KNNC camping areas: ***Sugarloaf***, ***Eden Park*** and ***Iphiva***. Camp sites cost R45; make bookings on ☎ 590 1340.

Bibs Hostel *(☎ 590 1056, @ kgb@mega.co.za)* is a huge barn converted into backpacker and guesthouse accommodation. Dorms are R40, and doubles R110. It has online terminals and organises heaps of activities (see Organised Tours earlier in this section). There are regular braais.

On the road between Mtubatuba and St Lucia Resort is the colourful ***African Tales Backpackers*** *(☎ 550 4300)*, a great place to hang out for a day or two. Accommodation options include genuine umuzi ('beehive' huts) for R100 per hut.

St Lucia Wilds *(☎ 590 1033)* is one of the real bargains in town: apartments sleeping six cost from R65 per person; ask in town for directions. Next door is the ***Kingfisher Lodge*** *(☎ 590 1015)*, an upmarket B&B we've had excellent feedback about from readers.

St Pizza has a shaded outdoor area. For seafood try the upmarket ***Lake View*** and the pricey ***Quarterdeck***.

Mapelane Nature Reserve South across the estuary from St Lucia, this popular fishing spot will probably become the visitors centre for Mhlatuze State Forest when that area is developed for recreational use.

Entry costs R8 and ***camp sites*** are R38; there are also ***log cabins*** for R130.

Although it's across the estuary from St Lucia, travel between the two centres is circuitous unless you have a boat. Mapelane is reached by 40km of sandy and sometimes tricky road from KwaMbonambi, off the N2 south of Mtubatuba. Follow the 'Kwa Mbonambi Lighthouse' sign.

Tewati Wilderness Area (Cape Vidal) The Tewati Wilderness Area takes in the land between the lake and the ocean north from Cape Vidal. The Eastern Shores State Forest runs south from Cape Vidal to St Lucia, and is administered as part of the Cape Vidal State Forest; entry is R8 per person plus R30 per vehicle.

The Cape Vidal KNNC office is the starting place for the four-night **St Lucia Wilderness Trail**, a guided walk costing R1200 per person (minimum four people). Walks are available only from April to September.

The 38km, three-day **Mziki Trail** (R40) is in the Mfabeni section, north of St Lucia Resort (entry costs R8 plus R30 per vehicle). The base camp for this trail is Mt Tabor, inland just north of Mission Rocks and accessible from the road running between St Lucia and Cape Vidal. The trail is part of a system that will eventually link St Lucia with Cape Vidal.

In the ***Bhangazi*** complex *(☎ 590 1404)* there are camp sites for R40 per person, log cabins from R137 per person (minimum R411), dorm cabins for R75 (minimum R600) and an eight-bed bush lodge for R180 (minimum R900).

From St Lucia Resort head north past the crocodile centre and through the entrance gates. Cape Vidal is about 30km further on.

False Bay Park False Bay Park runs along the western shore of Lake St Lucia; entry is R8 per person. As well as the lake's hippo and crocodile, the park has several antelope species and other animals.

Walking trails include the easy two-day **Dugandlovu Hiking Trail**. Book this trail through the KNNC in Pietermaritzburg or Durban. In the northern part of False Bay Park is the **Mpophomeni Trail**, divided into two routes, which are suitable for families.

There are ***camp sites*** (R32 per person) and rustic four-bed huts (R65 per person; minimum R130) on the Dugandlovu Trail, about 9km from the entrance gate; you can drive there. Book both of these direct on ☎ 562 0425.

The main road into the park runs east from Hluhluwe village (not Hluhuwe-Umfolozi Park) off the N2. Hluhluwe village is also the nearest place to buy fuel and supplies.

St Lucia Park & Game Reserve This takes in the lake, the islands and Mapelane Nature Reserve. Lake St Lucia is in fact a huge and meandering estuary with a narrow sea entrance. It is mainly shallow and the warm water is crowded with fish, which in turn attract huge numbers of water birds. However, the area is best known as a crocodile and hippo reserve (see the boxed text 'Warning' at the start of this section).

St Lucia & Maputaland Marine Reserves These reserves combined cover the coastal strip and three nautical miles out to sea, running from Cape Vidal right up to

Snorkelling & Diving

The coastline near Sodwana Bay is a diver's paradise. Predominantly soft coral over hard, the reef has one of the world's highest recorded numbers of tropical fish species. All of these wonders can be seen using scuba or snorkelling equipment, and excellent visibility and warm winter waters allow for diving year-round.

Popular snorkelling spots are Cape Vidal; Two-Mile Reef off Sodwana Bay; Mabibi; and the Kosi Mouth with its famous 'aquarium', so named because of the diversity of fish. Scuba divers should head for Tenedos Shoal, between the Mlalazi River and Port Durnford, and Five-, Seven- and Nine-Mile Reefs. Courses are held at Two-Mile Reef.

Sodwana Bay Lodge specialises in NAUI diving packages (see its listing under Sodwana Bay).

Mozambique. The reserves include the world's most southerly coral reefs, especially around Sodwana Bay, and nesting sites of leatherback and loggerhead turtles.

Sodwana Bay
☎ 035

Sodwana Bay's appeal is in its isolation, the accessibility of Africa's most southerly coral reef, its walking trails, fishing and its magic coastal scenery.

The small **Sodwana Bay National Park** is on the coast east of Mkuze Game Reserve. There are some animals and the dunes and swamps are worth visiting, as are the offshore coral reefs. Over Christmas there are turtle-viewing tours.

For a more peaceful look at a similar ecosystem, head south to the adjoining Sodwana State Forest, now called **Ozabeni**, which runs all the way down to Lake St Lucia. North of the lake is a prohibited area. Birdwatchers will go wild, as over 330 species have been recorded here.

There is KNNC ***accommodation*** *(☎ 571 0051/2)* at Sodwana Bay, with cabins from R130 per person (minimum R390) and camp sites for R45. There is a shop and fuel in this resort; entry is R8. ***Sodwana Bay Lodge*** *(☎ 571 0095)* is a private resort with single/double DB&B for R385/664. This place specialises in diving packages (see the boxed text 'Snorkelling & Diving').

There are ***camp sites*** *(☎ 571 0011)* at Ozabeni.

Tongaland
☎ 035

The area north of Hluhluwe-Umfolozi Park up to the Mozambique border was once known as Tongaland, as it was settled by Mozambique's Tonga people. It's a distinct ecological zone: flat and hot with sandy soil and sluggish rivers harbouring crocodile and hippo. Inland are forests of huge figs, especially along the Pongola River; nearer the coast, palms grow among salt pans and thornveld.

Mkuze A small town on the N2 and the Mkuze River, Mkuze is west of a pass over the Lebombo Mountains. The road through the pass is one route to Sodwana Bay. **Ghost Mountain**, south-east of the town, was an important burial place for the Ndwandwe tribe and has a reputation for eerie occurrences.

The ***Ghost Mountain Inn*** *(☎ 573 1025)* is an upmarket place with singles/doubles for R315/530; it has bargain weekend specials of R295 per room.

Mkuzi Game Reserve This KNNC reserve lacks lion and elephant but just about every other sought-after animal is represented, as well as over 400 species of bird. The hides at the pans and water holes offer some of the best wildlife viewing in the country.

Entry costs R8 per person and R30 per vehicle. The reserve is open daily between sunrise and sunset. It's possible to arrange guided walks (R45) and night drives (R65).

Self-contained ***chalets*** cost from R155 per person (minimum R310) and the ***safari camp*** costs from R135 (minimum R202). ***Camp sites*** *(☎ 573 0003)* cost R35 per person.

Ndumo Game Reserve On the Mozambique border, about 100km north of Mkuze, Ndumo has black and white rhino, hippo, crocodile and antelope species, but it is the birdlife that attracts visitors. Guided walks and vehicle tours are available. You can't camp but there are self-catering ***cottages*** (R200 per person). Entry is R8 and R35 per vehicle.

Tembe Elephant Park South Africa's last free-ranging elephants are protected in the sandveld forests of this park on the Mozambique border. There are about 100 elephant as well as white rhino and leopard.

Getting to the park requires a 4WD; entry costs R8 plus R30 per vehicle. There is private ***accommodation*** *(☎ 031-202 9090)* in the park.

Coastal Forest Reserve

This reserve stretches from Mozambique in the north to Sodwana Bay in the south, and includes Lake Sibaya, Kosi Bay, Bhanga Nek, Black Rock, Rocktail Bay, Manzengwenya, Mabibi and Nine-Mile Beach. The reserve is administered by the KNNC.

Lake Sibaya Nature Reserve The largest freshwater lake in South Africa is home to hippo, crocodile and a large range of birds. The lake is popular for fishing – you can hire boats (complete with skipper) for fishing trips.

There is accommodation in cabins at ***Baya Camp*** for R130 on the south side of the lake. The main route here is via the village of Mbazwana, south of the lake, either from Mkuze or from Mhlosinga, off the N2 north of Hluhluwe village.

Kosi Bay Nature Reserve On the coast near the Mozambique border, this remote reserve encompasses fig and raffia palm forests, mangrove swamps and freshwater lakes. There are pristine beaches and a coral reef with great snorkelling.

There are antelope species in the drier country and hippo, Zambezi shark and some crocodile in the lake system. A research station here studies the leatherback turtle.

You can arrange a four-night guided walk around the Kosi estuarine system (R250), stopping each night in remote camps that focus on different aspects of the reserve.

You can camp or stay at the privately run ***Rocktail Bay Lodge*** *(☎ 011-884 1458 for bookings)*.

To get here, take the Jozini turn-off from the N2 and head towards Ndumo Game Reserve, but turn hard right (east) just before Ndumo village – you might need a 4WD.

THE NATAL DRAKENSBERG

The awesome Drakensberg Range is a mountainous basalt escarpment forming the border between KwaZulu-Natal and Lesotho, and continuing a little way into Free State.

Drakensberg means Dragon Mountains; in Zulu named it's Quathlamba (Battlement of Spears). The Zulu word is a more accurate description of the sheer and jagged escarpment, but the Afrikaans name captures something of its otherworldly atmosphere. People have lived here for thousands of years – there are many San rock-art sites to testify to this fact; yet some of the peaks and rocks were first climbed by Europeans less than 50 years ago.

Orientation The Drakensberg is usually divided into three sections, although the distinctions aren't strict. The northern Drakensberg runs from the Golden Gate Highlands National Park in the Free State (covered in that section) to the Royal Natal National Park. Harrismith (Free State) and Bergville are sizeable towns in this area.

The central Drakensberg's main feature is Giant's Castle Game Reserve, the largest national park in the area. North-west of Giant's Castle are Cathedral Peak and wilderness areas. Bergville, Estcourt and Winterton are all adjacent to the central Drakensberg.

The southern Drakensberg runs down to the Transkei region of Eastern Cape. This area is less developed than the others but is no less spectacular. There's a huge wilderness area and the Sani Pass route into southern Lesotho. In the hills are some pleasant little towns, notably Underberg and Himeville.

Information As well as the various KNNC offices in the reserves, the Drakensberg Publicity Association (☎/fax 036-448 1557), which covers the northern and central Drakensberg, is based in Bergville. The Southern

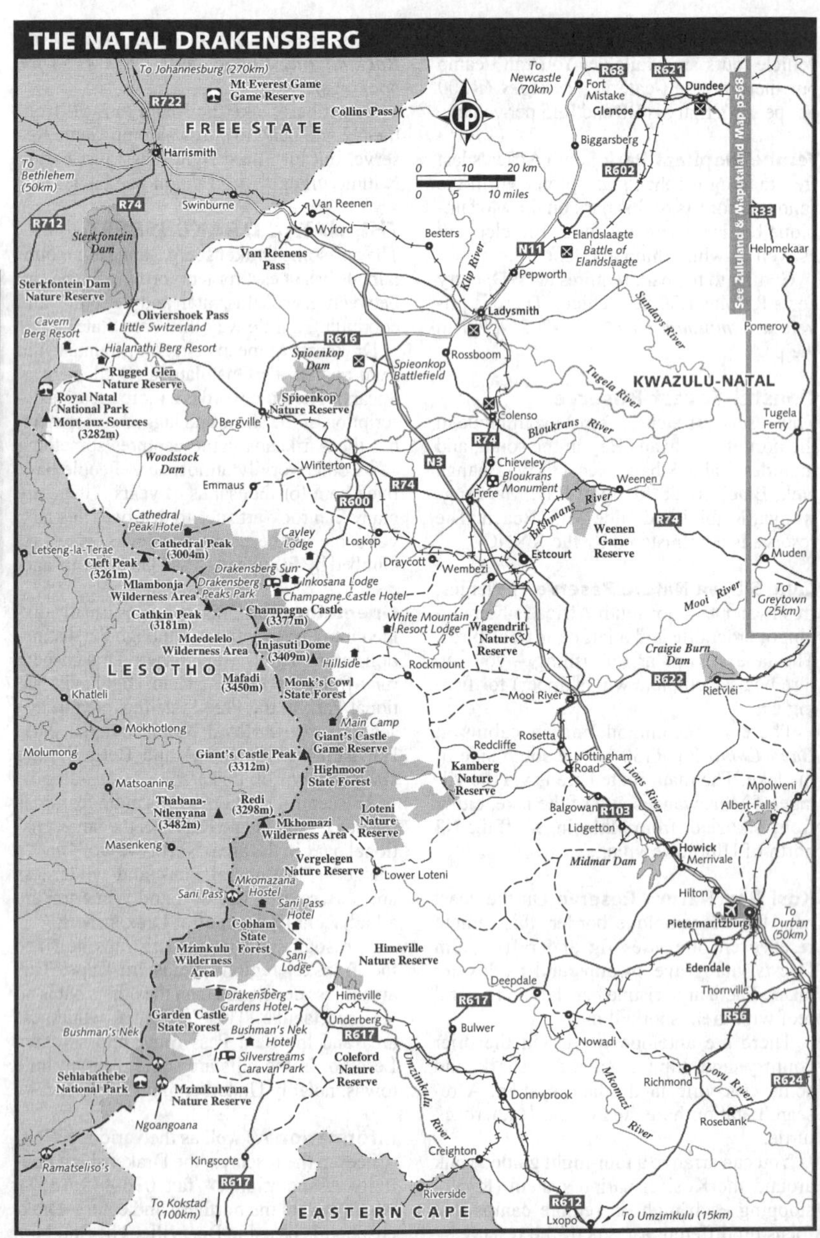
THE NATAL DRAKENSBERG
To Johannesburg (270km)
Mt Everest Game
Game Reserve
R722
FREE STATE
Collins Pass
To Newcastle (70km)
R68
R621
Fort Mistake
Dundee
Glencoe
See Zululand & Maputaland Map p568
Biggarsberg
R602
0
10
20 km
0
5
10 miles
Harrismith
To Bethlehem (50km)
R74
Swinburne
R712
Sterkfontein Dam
Van Reenen
Wyford
Van Reenens Pass
Besters
Klip River
Elandslaagte
Battle of Elandslaagte
N11
R33
Helpmekaar
Pepworth
Sterkfontein Dam Nature Reserve
Olivershoek Pass
Little Switzerland
Cavern Berg Resort
Hlalanathi Berg Resort
Rugged Glen Nature Reserve
Royal Natal National Park
Mont-aux-Sources (3282m)
Ladysmith
Sundays River
Pomeroy
R616
Spioenkop Dam
Spioenkop Battlefield
Rossboom
Tugela River
KWAZULU-NATAL
Spioenkop Nature Reserve
Bergville
Colenso
Bloukrans River
Tugela Ferry
Woodstock Dam
Winterton
R74
N3
Chieveley
Bloukrans Monument
Weenen
Emmaus
R74
Frere
Bushmans River
R600
Cathedral Peak Hotel
Cayley Lodge
Loskop
Weenen Game Reserve
R74
Letseng-la-Terae
Cathedral Peak (3004m)
Cleft Peak (3261m)
Draycott
Wembezi
Estcourt
Muden
Drakensberg Sun
Mlambonja Wilderness Area
Drakensberg Peaks Park
Inkosana Lodge
Champagne Castle Hotel
Mooi River
To Greytown (25km)
Cathkin Peak (3181m)
Champagne Castle (3377m)
White Mountain Resort Lodge
Wagendrift Nature Reserve
Mdedelelo Wilderness Area
Injasuti Dome (3409m)
Hillside
Craigie Burn Dam
LESOTHO
Mafadi (3450m)
Rockmount
R622
Monk's Cowl State Forest
Mooi River
Rietvlei
Khatleli
Main Camp
Mokhotlong
Giant's Castle Game Reserve
Rosetta
Redcliffe
Molumong
Giant's Castle Peak (3312m)
Nottingham Road
Kamberg Nature Reserve
Lions River
Matsoaning
Highmoor State Forest
Thabana-Ntlenyana (3482m)
Redi (3298m)
Mpolweni
Balgowan
R103
Albert Falls
Loteni Nature Reserve
Mkhomazi Wilderness Area
Lidgetton
Masenkeng
Howick
Merrivale
Vergelegen Nature Reserve
Lower Loteni
Midmar Dam
Mkomazana Hostel
Sani Pass
Sani Pass Hotel
Hilton
Pietermaritzburg
To Durban (50km)
Cobham State Forest
Mzimkulu Wilderness Area
Sani Lodge
Himeville Nature Reserve
Edendale
Himeville
Deepdale
Drakensberg Gardens Hotel
Thornville
R617
Garden Castle State Forest
Underberg
R56
Bulwer
Bushman's Nek
Bushman's Nek Hotel
R617
Nowadi
Silverstreams Caravan Park
Coleford Nature Reserve
Umzimkulu River
Mkomazi River
Richmond
Lovu River
R624
Sehlabathebe National Park
Mzimkulwana Nature Reserve
Donnybrook
Rosebank
Ngoangoana
Creighton
Kingscote
Ramatseliso's
R617
Riverside
R612
To Kokstad (100km)
EASTERN CAPE
Lxopo
To Umzimkulu (15km)

Drakensberg Publicity Association (☎ 033-701 1096) is on Main St, Underberg.

Climate If you want to avoid most of the sharp frosts and, on the heights, snowfalls, you should visit in summer, although this is when most of the rain falls and views can be obscured by low cloud. However, what you lose in vistas you'll gain in atmosphere, as the stark and eerie peaks are at their best looming out of the mist.

Much of the rain falls in sudden thunderstorms so you should always carry wet-weather gear. Cold snaps are possible even in the middle of summer.

Getting There & Away There is little public transport in the northern and central Drakensberg. The main jumping-off points are on or near the N3. See the entries for Estcourt, Mooi River, Winterton and Bergville later in this chapter.

Sani Pass is the best-known Drakensberg route into Lesotho.

Many roads in the Drakensberg area are unsealed and after rain some are impassable.

Royal Natal National Park

☎ 036

Despite covering only 8000 hectares, Royal Natal has some of the Drakensberg's most dramatic and accessible scenery. The southern boundary is formed by the Amphitheatre, an 8km stretch of cliff that is spectacular from below and even more so from the top. Here the Tugela Falls drop 850m in five stages (the top one often freezes in winter). Looming up behind is **Mont-aux-Sources**, so called because the Tugela, Elands and Western Khubedu Rivers rise here – the latter eventually becomes the Orange River and flows all the way to the Atlantic. The **Rugged Glen Nature Reserve** adjoins the park on the north-eastern side.

The park's visitors centre is about 1km from the main gate. There's a bookstore here where you can pick up the KNNC's excellent booklet *Royal Natal National Park*. A good 1:20,000 topographical map, *Mont-aux-Sources,* is also available. Entry is R8 per person. Fuel is available.

Flora & Fauna Broadly speaking, much of the park is covered in grassland. At lower altitudes there are valleys of small yellowwood forests. At higher altitudes grass yields to heath and scrub.

Of the six species of antelope, the most common is the mountain reedbuck. Most other animals, including otter, jackal and mongoose, are shy and not often seen. More than 200 bird species have been recorded.

Rock Art There are several San rock-art sites, although Royal Natal's are fewer and not as well preserved as those at Giant's Castle. The notable sites are Sigubudu Shelter, north of the road just past the main gate; and Cannibal Caves, on Surprise Ridge, outside the park's northern boundary.

Hiking Trails Except for the walk to Mont-aux-Sources, all of the 30-odd walks are day walks. Only 50 day visitors and 50 overnighters are allowed on Mont-aux-Sources each day. There are two ways to approach the summit. The easiest way is to drive to the Sentinel car park on the road from Phuthaditjhaba in the Free State (see QwaQwa Area in the Free State section of this chapter). By doing this it's possible to get to the summit and back in a day. Otherwise, you walk up to Basotho Gate then take the road to the Sentinel car park.

If you plan to camp on the mountain, you should book with the Free State Agriculture Department (☎ 058-713 4444, fax 713 4342) in Phuthaditjhaba. Otherwise, there's a basic hut on the escarpment near Tugela Falls.

Climbing The park is a mecca for technical climbers and mountaineers. You must apply for a permit from the KNNC office before you attempt a climb. Take your passport if you plan to venture into Lesotho.

Places to Stay The main camp is ***Tendele***, where there are a variety of chalets from R180. At ***Mahai*** *(☎ 438 6303)* there's a camping ground with sites for R35 per person, and at Rugged Glen Nature Reserve, on the north-eastern edge of the park, there are camp sites for the same price.

The ***Royal Natal National Park Hotel*** *(☎ 438 6200, fax 438 6101),* also in the reserve, is privately run and near the visitors centre. Rooms cost about R295 per person, including meals.

The following places are outside the park. ***Little Switzerland*** *(☎/fax 438 6220),* just off the R74, near Oliviershoek Pass, is a large place with chalets sleeping four for about R125 per person. It also has hotel-style rooms for R340 per person, including meals.

Hlalanathi Berg Resort *(☎ 438 6308),* off the road into Royal Natal from the R74, has camp sites for about R50, and chalets from R228 a double.

Isibongno Lodge & Backpackers *(☎ 438 6707)* is about 15km from the park and has backpacker accommodation at the usual prices.

Getting There & Away The only road into Royal Natal runs off the R74, about 30km north-east of Bergville and about 5km from Oliviershoek Pass (for information on a route to Mont-aux-Sources, see also Hiking Trails earlier in this section).

Bergville

☎ 036

This small town is a handy jumping-off point for both the northern Drakensberg and the Midlands – if you have a car. The Drakensberg Publicity Association has an office here (☎ 448 1557).

On the third Friday of each month there are cattle sales and this sleepy town takes on an altogether different atmosphere.

The ***Hotel Walter*** *(☎ 448 1022)* in town has reasonable rooms for R140/240, with breakfast. The ***Sanford Park Lodge*** *(☎ 448 1001, fax 448 1047),* a few kilometres out of Bergville off the R616 to Ladysmith, has good rooms in thatched rondavels or in a big old farmhouse for about R315/550, with meals.

None of the long-distance buses run very close to Bergville. You'll probably have to get to Ladysmith and take a minibus taxi from there. Translux's Jo'burg/Pretoria-Umtata and Jo'burg/Pretoria-Durban services stop at Montrose. The daily Greyhound bus stops at Estcourt, Swinburne (Free State) and Ladysmith.

Minibus taxis run into the Royal Natal National Park area for about R10 but few run all the way to the park entrance. The taxi rank is behind the Score supermarket.

Central Berg

☎ 036

In some ways the Central Berg is the most attractive part of the range with some of the most challenging **climbs**: Cathkin Peak (3181m), Monk's Cowl (3234m) and Champagne Castle (3377m). The central area also includes the grand Giant's Castle Peak (3314m). Midway between Cathedral and Cathkin Peaks is Ndedema Gorge, where there is some fine **San rock art**.

The area between Cathedral Peak and Giant's Castle Game Reserve, in the Central Berg, comprises two wilderness areas: Mlambonja and Mdedelelo. Grey rhebok, klipspringer and mountain reedbuck can be found here.

Winterton This pretty little town is the gateway to the Central Berg and is not too far from the northern end.

There is a great little **museum** on Kerk St which concentrates on the geology, flora and fauna of the Drakensberg. It is open Wednesday and Friday afternoon and Saturday morning.

The ***Bridge Hotel*** *(☎ 488 1554)* is a friendly local pub with singles/doubles for R150/245.

Ntabeni Backpackers *(☎ 488 1773)* is on a farm 5km from Winterton and charges R35 for a dorm and R90 for a double.

Minibus taxis run to Bergville (R6), Cathedral Peak State Forest (R8) and Estcourt (R8).

Cathedral Peak State Forest Cathedral Peak (3004m) lies between Royal Natal National Park and Giant's Castle Game Reserve, west of Winterton. Entry to the reserve costs R8. It's part of a small chain of peaks that jut out east of the main escarpment. Cathedral Peak is a long day's climb but no special ability or equipment is required, although you need to be fit.

A trail begins near the hotel and the forest office is also nearby. Entry costs R7, and hikes of more than one day cost R16 per person per night.

The KNNC has ***camp sites*** *(☎ 488 1880)* for R24 per person. The ***Cathedral Peak Hotel*** *(☎/fax 488 1888)*, some 42km from Winterton, is close to the escarpment. Doubles cost from R500 including meals. The hotel will collect you from Estcourt.

Monk's Cowl State Forest (Champagne Castle) The office (☎ 468 1103) is 3km beyond the Champagne Castle Hotel. Entry, camping and hiking fees are the same as for Cathedral Peak State Forest.

The ***Inkosana Lodge*** *(☎ 468 1202)* has very good information about hiking and is a useful base for treks. It has dorms (R75), doubles (R190) and a suite (R250); all rates include breakfast and pick-up from Winterton.

Dragon Peaks Park *(☎ 468 1031, fax 468 1104)* is a Club Caravelle resort with the usual maze of prices and minimum stays that depend on seasons and school holidays.

The ***Champagne Castle Hotel*** *(☎/fax 468 1063)* is one of the best-known resorts and it's well located, right in the mountains at the end of the R600 to Champagne Castle. There are cottages, rondavels and units, costing from R275 per person, meals included.

Giant's Castle Game Reserve

This reserve was established in 1903. It's in high country: the lowest point is 1300m and the highest tooth of the Drakensberg in the reserve is the 3409m Injasuti Dome. With huge forest reserves to the north and south and Lesotho's barren plateau over the escarpment to the west, it's a rugged and remote place, despite the number of visitors it attracts.

There's an entry fee of R8 per person. Limited supplies (including fuel) are available at Main Camp and there's a basic shop near the White Mountain Lodge, but otherwise the nearest shops are in Estcourt, 50km away. There are three main areas, as well as trail huts and caves for hikers. Note that nowhere in the park are you allowed to cut or collect firewood, so bring a stove. Litter must be carried out, not burned or buried.

Flora & Fauna The reserve is mainly grassland, wooded gorges, high cliffs with small forests in the valleys, and some protea savanna. In spring there are many wildflowers.

The reserve is home to 12 species of antelope and altogether there are about 60 mammal species. The rare lammergeyer, or bearded vulture *(Gypaetus barbatus)*, which is found only in the Drakensberg, nests in the reserve. **Lammergeyer Hide** is the best place to see the vultures. The fee for using the hide is R75 per person (minimum R300), and you must book.

Rock Art The reserve is rich in San rock art, with at least 50 sites. It is thought that San people still lived here at the turn of the 19th and 20th centuries.

The two main sites are Main Cave and Battle Cave, both of which have an entry fee of R8. Main Cave is 2km south of Main Camp.

The cave is open on weekends and holidays from 9 am to 3 pm; on weekdays you have to go with a tour, which departs from the camp office at 9 am and 3 pm. Battle Cave is near Injasuti and must be visited on a tour, which leaves the camp daily at 9 am. It's an 8km walk each way.

Hiking Trails There are many walking trails, most of them loops from either Main Camp or Injasuti or one-way walks to the mountain huts. There are also walks between huts, so you can string together several two-day hikes, but you need to pre-book the huts through the KNNC. The reserve's booklet *Giant's Castle Game Reserve* gives details and has a basic map of the trails.

Before setting out on a long walk you must fill in the rescue register; if you plan to go higher than 2300m you must report to the warden.

Places to Stay ***Main Camp*** has a range of accommodation from R120/180 a single/double in bungalows. You can't camp here.

Hillside *(☎ 0363-24435)*, in the reserve's north-eastern corner, is a long way from Main Camp, let alone the escarpment. Entry costs R8 and camp sites are R22 per person.

Injasuti Hutted Camp *(☎ 036-488 1050)* is a pleasant and secluded spot on the northern side of the reserve. Entry is R8; camp sites cost R22 per person, and chalets cost from R75 per person.

Berg Backpackers *(☎ 0333-32214)* is on a large property just outside Giant's Castle Game Reserve. Camp sites cost R20 per person, dorms R35, doubles R90. Call for directions or a pick-up from Mooi River (R25). The Baz Bus, Greyhound and trains stop at Mooi River.

Getting There & Away The best way into Main Camp is via the dirt road from Mooi River, although the last section can be impassable when wet. It's also possible to get here by following the route for Hillside, taking the Hillside turn-off. However, until the road is sealed don't attempt it in wet weather.

To get to Hillside, take the Giant's Castle road from Estcourt, signposted at the Anglican church. Turn left at the White Mountain Lodge junction and after 4km turn right onto the Hillside road. Take the right turn at the two minor intersections that follow. Minibuses run between Estcourt and Mahlutshini – ask to be let off at the signposted Hillside Camp junction. From the junction it's about a 5km walk to the camp site.

Infrequent minibuses run between Estcourt and the villages near the main entrance (KwaDlamini, Mahlutshini, KwaMankonjane), but these are still several kilometres from Main Camp.

Injasuti is accessible from the township of Loskop, north-west of Estcourt; the road is signposted.

Southern Drakensberg Wilderness Areas

☎ 0333

Four state forests – Highmoor, Mkhomazi, Cobham and Garden Castle – run from Giant's Castle south beyond Bushman's Nek, to meet Lesotho's Sehlabathebe National Park. The big Mkhomazi Wilderness Area and the Mzimkulu Wilderness Area are in these state forests.

The wilderness areas are close to the escarpment, with the Kamberg, Loteni, Vergelegen and Mzimkulwana Nature Reserves to the east of them, except for a spur of Mzimkulwana that follows the Umkomazana River (and the road) down from Sani Pass, separating the two wilderness areas.

The wilderness areas are administered by the KNNC. Entry to each is R8 per person and hiking costs R16 per night.

Kamberg Nature Reserve South-east of Giant's Castle and a little away from the main escarpment area, this small KNNC reserve (2232 hectares) has a number of antelope species. The country in the Drakensberg foothills is pretty, but it's trout fishing that attracts most visitors.

Entry to the reserve costs R8 per person and hiking costs R16 per night. The cheapest accommodation is in ***rest huts***, at R88 per person.

Take either road (west off the N3) from Rosetta or Nottingham Road.

Highmoor State Forest Part of the Mkhomazi Wilderness Area is in Highmoor. The forest office (☎ 0333-37240) is off the road between Rosetta and Kamberg; turn off to the south just past the sign to Kamberg, 31km from Rosetta. Camp sites with limited facilities cost R16.

Loteni Nature Reserve This reserve has a **Settlers Museum** and good day walks. There are ***camp sites*** *(☎ 702 0540)* for R25 and a variety of other accommodation (from R85). Entry is R8 and the fee for hiking is R16 per night.

The access road runs from the hamlet of Lower Loteni, about 30km north-east of Himeville or 65km south-west of Nottingham Road. The roads aren't great and heavy rain can close them.

Mkhomazi State Forest This is the southern part of Mkhomazi Wilderness Area. The 1200-hectare **Vergelegen Nature Reserve** is along this road; the entry fee is R8 and there are no established camp sites. The turn-off to the state forest is 44km from

Nottingham Road, off the Lower Loteni/Sani Pass road, at the Mzinga River. From here it's another 2km.

Cobham State Forest The **Mzimkulu Wilderness Area** and the **Mzimkulwana Nature Reserve** are both in Cobham. The forest office (☎ 702 0831) is about 15km from Himeville on the D7 and it's a good place to get information on the many hiking trails in the area. Entry costs R8 and basic ***camp sites*** (and overnight hiking) cost R16 per night.

Garden Castle State Forest The reserve's headquarters (☎ 712 1722) are 3km further on from the Drakensberg Gardens Resort Hotel, 30km west of Underberg. No camping is allowed at the headquarters, but there is a hut nearby on the Giant's Cup Hiking Trail (see later in this section), which you can use if it's not fully booked by hikers. Otherwise, there's a camp site at the ***Drakensberg Gardens Resort Hotel,*** or if you walk at least 3km into the reserve, pitching a tent counts as wilderness camping (for which you pay R8).

Sani Pass This steep route into Lesotho, the highest pass in South Africa and the only road between KwaZulu-Natal and Lesotho, is one of the most scenic parts of the Drakensberg. At the top of the pass, just beyond the Lesotho border crossing, is Sani Top chalet (for details see the Sani Pass section of the Lesotho chapter). Various operators run 4WD trips up to the chalet – contact the information centres in the nearby towns of Underberg and Himeville.

Khotso Horse Trails (☎ 701 1502) has rides and treks in the area and has been highly recommended by readers.

There are two budget places at the bottom of the pass. ***Sani Lodge*** *(☎ 702 1401)*, 19km from Underberg, is small and quiet. Camping costs R25, dorms R40, and doubles R100. This place is run by Russel Suchet, a good source of information on the many hiking (one day or longer) possibilities that exist in this area.

Mkomazana *(☎ 702 0340/313)* another 5km along the road, is much larger. It's an old farm and in a beautiful spot – the only privately owned property in KwaZulu-Natal in a national park – and there's good walking in the area. Dorms cost R35, singles/doubles are R75/90 and there are self-contained cottages from R95/150. (This place has had various names in recent years, including Sani Pass Youth Hostel.)

Giant's Cup Hiking Trail The five-day, 60km Giant's Cup Trail runs from Sani Pass to Bushman's Nek and is one of the great walks of South Africa. It's designed so that any reasonably fit person can walk it, so it's very popular. Early booking (up to nine months ahead, through the KNNC) is advisable. The usual precautions for the Drakensberg apply – expect severe cold snaps at any time of the year.

Camping is not permitted; accommodation in shared ***huts*** costs R43 per person per night. No firewood is available so you'll need a stove and fuel. Sani Lodge (see its listing under Sani Pass earlier in this section) is near the trailhead; arrange for the lodge to pick you up from Himeville or Underberg.

Bushman's Nek This is one of the border crossings into Lesotho. From here there are hiking trails up into the escarpment, including to Lesotho's Sehlabathebe National Park. You can walk in or hire a horse and trot across the border for R50!

The ***Bushman's Nek Hotel*** *(☎ 701 1460)*, east of the border, has rooms for R185 per person in the high season (meals included) and four-person self-catering chalets from R195.

Underberg

☎ 033

This quiet little town in the foothills of the southern Drakensberg is the centre of a farming community. The Underberg hiking club is a good source of information on the excellent hiking in the area. The KNNC has an office in the main street.

The ***Underberg Hotel*** *(☎ 701 1412)* is archaic; rooms cost R120 per person, with breakfast. To rent B&Bs and cottages contact Sani Pass Tours (☎ 701 1064).

The frilly ***White Cottage Cafe*** is in the shopping centre and the ***Bull & Tankard*** restaurant is on the southern edge of town.

The ***Drakensberg Garden Hotel*** *(☎ 701 1355),* west of Underberg on the Garden Castle State Forest station road in a magnificent valley, is a resort-style place with B&B singles/doubles from R275/390.

Getting There & Away Sani Pass Carriers (☎ 701 1017) runs a shuttle bus daily between Underberg and Pietermartizberg (R65), and three times weekly to/from Durban (R95).

Minibus taxis run between Underberg and Himeville (R2) and Pietermaritzberg (R20), and occasionally to the Sani Pass Hotel.

The main routes to Underberg and nearby Himeville are from Pietermaritzburg on the R617 and from Kokstad on the R626, but it's possible to drive here from the north-east via Nottingham Road on an unsealed road.

Himeville
☎ 033

Not far from Underberg, this smaller but nicer town is above 1500m so winters are coolish.

There's a KNNC ***camping ground*** in Himeville Nature Reserve (entry R8, sites R24 per person) not far from town. The ***Himeville Arms*** *(☎/fax 702 1305)* has good singles/doubles from R195/370, with breakfast.

Minibus taxis to Underberg (R2) and twice-daily KZT buses to Pietermaritzburg are about the only regular transport from Himeville.

THE MIDLANDS

The Midlands run north-west from Durban to Estcourt and skirt Zululand to the north-east. This is mainly farming country with not a lot to interest visitors. The main town is Pietermaritzburg – KwaZulu-Natal's capital.

West of Pietermaritzburg there is pretty, hilly country, with horse studs and plenty of European trees. The various art galleries and potteries in this area are linked in a tourist route called the *Midlands Meander*. Pick up a brochure from one of the larger tourist offices.

Pietermaritzburg
☎ 0331

After the defeat of the Zulu at the Battle of Blood River, the Voortrekkers began to establish their republic of Natal. Pietermaritzburg (PMB) was named in honour of leader Pieter Mauritz Retief, and was founded in 1838 as the capital. Here in 1841 the Boers built their Church of the Vow to honour the Blood River promise (see History in the Facts about South Africa section earlier in this chapter). The British annexed Natal in 1843 and retained Pietermaritzburg as the capital.

PMB rightly bills itself as 'the heritage city', as it has numerous historic buildings and a British colonial air.

Orientation The central grid of PMB contains most places of interest and is easy to get around. The northern end of the city, beyond Retief St, is a largely Indian commercial district. North of here is the Indian residential area of Northdale. To the south-west of the city is Edendale, the black dormitory suburb.

Information The helpful publicity association (☎ 451348, fax 943535) is at 177 Commercial Rd, on the corner of Longmarket St.

Rennies Travel (☎ 941571) is at 35 Park Lane Centre. American Express (☎ 425829) is on the 2nd floor of the Nedbank building on Church St.

KwaZulu-Natal Nature Conservation (KNNC) Office This is the office (☎ 845 1000) where you book most of the accommodation and walks for KwaZulu-Natal parks; it's a long way north-west of the town centre, in Queen Elizabeth Park. You can make phone bookings with a credit card but it's better to visit to collect the literature. It's open from 8 am to 4 pm weekdays.

To get to the office, head out to the Old Howick Rd (Commercial Rd) and after some kilometres you'll come to a roundabout – don't go straight ahead (to the Hilton), but take the road veering to the right. This road has a very small sign directing you to 'QE Park', which is 2km further on. Some minibus taxis running to the Hilton pass this roundabout.

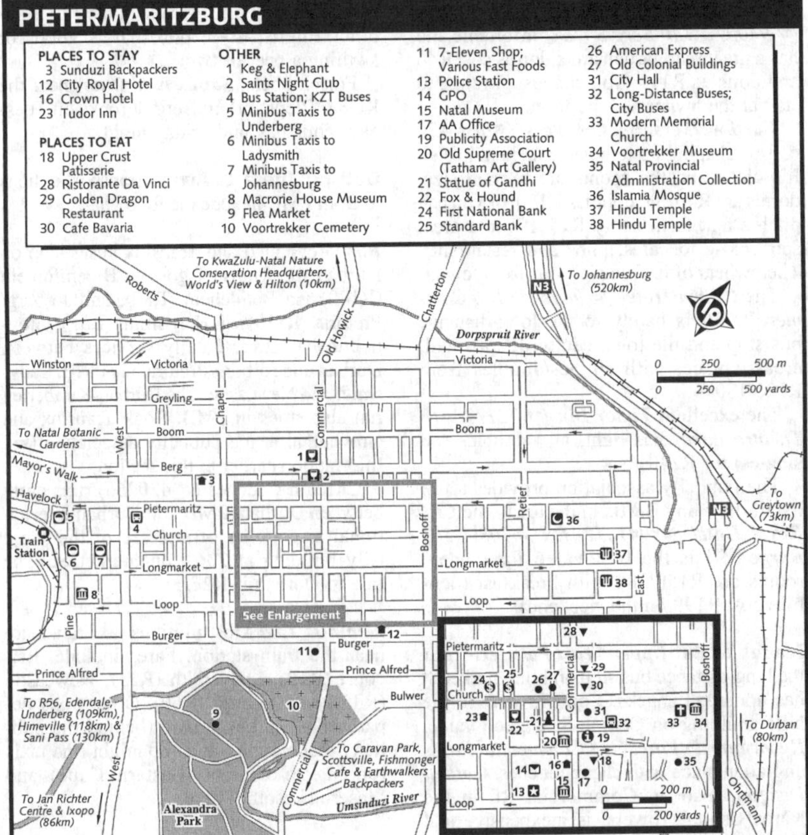

Things to See & Do Two of the town's best features are its avenues of huge old **jacaranda trees**, and the maze of narrow pedestrian **lanes** running between Church and Longmarket Sts off the mall. There are a number of colonial-era buildings. The massive red brick **city hall**, on the corner of Church and Commercial Sts, is a good example, as is the old **supreme court** across the road.

The **Macrorie House Museum**, on the corner of Loop and Pine Sts, displays items related to early British settlement. It's open from 9 am to 1 pm Tuesday to Friday, and 11 am to 4 pm Monday. The **Natal Museum** has a range of displays, including African ethnography. It's on Loop St, south-west of Commercial St; entry is R4.

The **Tatham Art Gallery**, housed in the old supreme court, is open from 10 am to 6 pm daily (except Monday). It has a collection of French and English 19th- and early 20th-century works.

The **Natal Provincial Administration Collection** at 330 Longmarket St has some of the finest examples of indigenous art, including beadwork, pottery and weaving. It is open by appointment only (☎ 453201).

Places to Stay ***Sunduzi Backpackers*** *(☎ 940072, 140 Berg St)* is comfortable and has a great rear garden area; dorms cost R40 and doubles R110. You can also arrange to stay at the owner's game farm.

Earthwalkers Backpackers *(☎/fax 420 653)* is shaping up to be an excellent hostel. It's clean and the rooms are a good size; dorms are R40 and doubles R100, or you can pitch a tent for a paltry R15. It's in a great spot, close to cafes, pubs and restaurants. The owners offer free pick-ups from town.

The ***Crown Hotel*** *(☎ 941601, 186 Commercial St)* is handy to the long-distance bus stop and the town centre. It's a small, creaky place, with singles/doubles from R120/180.

The excellent ***Tudor Inn*** *(☎ 421778, 18 Theatre Lane)* has light, airy doubles (no singles) for R240.

The publicity association provides a full list of the many B&Bs in the area. The ***City Royal Hotel*** *(☎ 947072, fax 947080, 301 Burger St)* is the best value for money; rooms are R150/280 with breakfast (doubles cost R199 on the weekend).

Places to Eat ***Upper Crust Patisserie*** near the long-distance bus stop on Longmarket St has upmarket snacks. ***Café Bavaria*** in the NBS building on Church St is good value. ***Ristorante da Vinci*** *(117 Commercial Rd)* is an Italian place with cheap lunches. ***Golden Dragon***, also on Commercial Rd in the Karos Capital Towers, is inexpensive and has been recommended by locals.

Pakeesa's, on the corner of Naidoo and Greytown, north of the centre in the Indian suburb of Raisethorpe, serves up excellent Indian food.

The Fishmonger Cafe *(☎ 450615, 40 Durban Rd)* south-east of the centre has superb lashings of seafood at very reasonable prices. Mains start at about R25 and a mouth-watering seafood platter (for two) is R59.

Entertainment ***Ristorante da Vinci*** (see under Places to Eat earlier) is a popular nightspot. The ***Keg & Elephant*** *(80 Commercial Rd)* is not far away and is an atmospheric watering hole. The ***Fox & Hound*** down Perks Arcade in the city is another English-style pub that is good for swilling a beer or two.

For clubbers, ***Saints Nite Club*** (near the Keg & Elephant) on Berg St rocks on Tuesday, Thursday and Friday night.

Getting There & Away Transport options to/from PMB include the following:

Bus Greyhound and Translux buses stop on Durban Rd. Translux goes to Bloemfontein (R140) via Bethlehem (R80), and Jo'burg/Pretoria (R110) via Harrismith (R55). Greyhound has several daily services between Durban and Jo'burg/Pretoria via PMB, Ladysmith and Newcastle. The Durban-Kimberley run also stops in PMB. Book Translux and Greyhound at the publicity association (see Information earlier in this section).

Cheetah Coaches (☎ 420266) runs daily between Durban, PMB and Durban international airport; its offices are in the Main City building at 206 Longmarket St. The fare to Durban is R27.

Minibus Taxi Most minibus taxi ranks are near the train station. Fares include: Estcourt (R19); Ladysmith (R25); Newcastle (R35); and Jo'burg (R60). Other taxis depart from Market Square (behind the publicity association), and you might find taxis running to Umtata (Eastern Cape) and Maseru (Lesotho) here.

Train The weekly *Trans Oranje* (Durban-Cape Town) and the daily *Trans Natal* (Durban-Jo'burg/Pretoria) stop here (for more information, see the South Africa Getting Around section earlier in this chapter).

Car If you're driving and heading north, a nicer route than the N3 is the R103, which runs through pretty country between Howick and Mooi River.

Avis (☎ 454601), Budget (☎ 428433) and Imperial (☎ 942728) have agents in Pietermaritzburg.

Getting Around The main rank for city-area buses is in the area behind the publicity association office on the corner of Longmarket St and Commercial Rd.

For a taxi, call Springbok (☎ 424444), Junior (☎ 945454) or Unique (☎ 911238).

Mooi River

☎ 0332

Mooi River is a nondescript town, but the surrounding countryside, especially to the west, is worth exploring. It's horse-stud country on rolling land dotted with old European trees.

***Riverbank** (☎ 632144)* is a caravan park in town. The ***Argyle Hotel** (☎ 631106)* is inexpensive with singles/doubles for R85/140.

However it's the country guesthouses in the area that visitors come for. One of the better-known places is ***Granny Mouse's Country House** (☎/fax 344532)*, near the village of Balgowan, south of Mooi River. Luxury B&B costs from around R390 per person.

Greyhound buses between Durban and Jo'burg/Pretoria stop at the big truck stop on the Rosetta road near the N3, 1km from the centre.

The *Trans Oranje* and *Trans Natal* trains stop here. Book tickets at the goods office, across the tracks from the old station.

Estcourt

☎ 0363

Estcourt is close to the central Drakensberg resorts and Giant's Castle Game Reserve, and it's on the Durban-Jo'burg/Pretoria bus route. It also has good train and minibus taxi connections.

About 30km north-east of Estcourt is the **Weenen Game Reserve**, which has black and white rhino, buffalo, giraffe and several antelope species. There are two good walking trails; entry costs R8 per person and R15 per vehicle.

The municipal ***caravan park** (☎ 523000)* is inexpensive and close to the town centre on Lorne St. ***Lucey's Plough Hotel** (☎ 523 040, fax 522580, 86 Harding St)* has singles/doubles for R135/220, with breakfast.

Greyhound buses leave from the information centre on the main street, as do Translux buses on the Durban-Jo'burg/Pretoria route.

Both the *Trans Oranje* and the daily *Trans Natal* trains stop here.

The main minibus taxi rank is at the bottom of Phillips St, downhill from the post office. Taxis beside the post office are for the local area only. Destinations include: Winterton (R8); Ladysmith (R14); Pietermaritzburg (R22); Durban (R30); and Jo'burg (R60).

THUKELA

History buffs will be happy in Thukela, in the north-west of KwaZulu-Natal. The area is often described as the Battlefields Route as some of the more important conflicts in South Africa's recent history took place in the area. They include the Siege of Ladysmith, the Battle of Spioenkop, the defeat of the British by the Zulu at Isandlwana, the heroic Defence of Rorke's Drift and the battles of Majuba Hill and Blood River.

Colenso

☎ 03622

There are several Anglo-Boer War battlefields near Colenso, a small town about 20km south of Ladysmith. Colenso was the British base during the Relief of Ladysmith, and there is a **museum** relating to the Battle of Colenso (15 December 1899). The museum is in the toll house adjacent to the bridge. You can pick up the keys from the police station between 8 am and 6 pm.

There is a municipal ***caravan park** (☎ 2737)* and the ***Old Jail Lodge** (☎ 2594)*, which has a restaurant.

Spioenkop Nature Reserve

This 6000-hectare KNNC reserve is handy to most of the area's battlefield sites and not too far from the Drakensberg for day trips. Animals in the two small game reserves include white rhino, giraffe and zebra. There's a swimming pool, and horse riding and tours of the Spioenkop battlefield are available. Entry costs R8.

Ntenjwa has accommodation in an eight-bed bush camp for R100 per person.

Camp sites at ***iPika*** cost R28 per person and the four-bed bush camp costs R100 per person. Book both of these on ☎ 036-488 1578.

Ladysmith

☎ 036

Ladysmith (not to be confused with Ladismith in Western Cape) was named after the wife of Cape governor Sir Harry Smith. The town achieved fame during the 1899–1902 Anglo-Boer War, when it was besieged by Boer forces for 118 days.

The information office (☎ 637 2992) is in the town hall on Murchison St and is open on weekdays during office hours. Ask here about guided tours of the battlefields.

Things to See & Do The good **Siege Museum** is next to the town hall in the Market House (built in 1884), which was used to store rations during the siege. The museum is open from 8 am to 4.20 pm weekdays and until noon Saturday.

Outside the town hall are two guns, **Castor** and **Pollux**, used by the British in the defence of Ladysmith. Nearby is a replica of **Long Tom**, a Boer gun capable of heaving a shell 10km.

Across the river on the west side of town (there's a footbridge) is a **Sufi Mosque**, built by the Muslim community, which has been in Ladysmith almost since the town's inception.

South of town, near the junction of the N11 and R103, is an area generally known as **Platrand** (or Wagon Hill). There is an unusual monument to the Boers who died attempting to wrest Wagon Hill from the British on 6 January 1900.

Places to Stay The municipal ***caravan park*** *(☎ 637 6050)* is on the northern side of town; follow Poort Rd over the hill, where it becomes the Harrismith road.

Near the town hall, on Murchison St, there are two venerable old hotels. The ***Crown*** *(☎ 637 2266)* has single/double B&B for R297/367 and the ***Royal*** *(☎/fax 637 2176)* is a bit cheaper at R253/343.

The information office has details of farmstays and B&Bs. Prices start at around R170 a double.

Getting There & Away Translux buses leave from the train station and run to Durban (R80) and Bloemfontein (R140). Greyhound has daily services to Jo'burg/Pretoria and Durban. Book at the Shell service station on the corner of Murchison and King Sts, or at Destinations Travel (☎ 631 0831).

Both the *Trans Oranje* and the daily *Trans Natal* trains stop here.

The main minibus taxi rank is south of the centre near the corner of Queen and Lyell Sts. Taxis for Harrismith and Jo'burg are nearby on Alexandra St. Destinations include: Harrismith (R12); Durban (R30); and Jo'burg (R55).

Majuba Hill

The first Anglo-Boer War ended abruptly 40km north of Newcastle, with the British defeat at **Majuba Hill** in 1881. The site has been restored and a map is available; there is a small entry fee.

Peace negotiations took place at **O'Neill's Cottage** in the foothills near Majuba. The cottage, used as a hospital during the battle, has been restored and has a photographic display; it is open daily.

Isandlwana, Rorke's Drift & Fugitive's Drift

☎ 0358

Isandlwana should not be missed. At the base of this sphinx-like rock there are many graves and memorials to those who fell in battle on 22 January 1879, when the Zulu wiped out a British army. The Isandlwana museum, with artefacts taken from the battlefield, is in St Vincent's, just outside the site.

At **Rorke's Drift**, 42km from Dundee, 100 British soldiers held off 4000 Zulu, winning 11 Victoria Crosses for their efforts. There is a splendid museum, a trail around the battlefield, several memorials and the ELC Zulu craft centre. The rugs and tapestries woven here are world-renowned and not cheap: a small wall-hanging costs over R1000.

About 10km south of Rorke's Drift is **Fugitive's Drift**. Two British officers were killed here attempting to prevent the Queen's Colours from falling into Zulu hands.

Places to Stay About 20km east of Islandwana is the small town of Babanango. The ***Babanango Hotel*** *(☎ 350029)* is rough round the edges but exudes atmosphere, with B&B from R200 per person.

The ***Babanango Valley Lodge*** *(☎ 350 062, fax 350160)* is outside the town and way up in quality. Singles/doubles cost R485/630 with breakfast. It is run by John and Meryn Turner, who are extremely friendly hosts. You need a car to get there: turn north off the R68 about 4km west of Babanango and continue on for about 12km (stay left at the fork).

Getting There & Away The battlefields are south-east of Dundee. Isandlwana is about 70km from Dundee, off the R68; Rorke's Drift is about 40km from Dundee, also accessible from the R68 or the R33 (the R33 turn-off is 13km south of Dundee). The road to Isandlwana is sealed but the roads to Rorke's Drift and Fugitive's Drift can be dusty and rough.

Blood River Monument

For information on the Battle of Blood River, see History in the Facts about South Africa section earlier in this chapter. The Blood River battlefield is marked by a full-scale re-creation of the 64-wagon *laager* (wagon circle) in bronze.

The cairn of stones was built by the Boers after the battle to mark the centre of their laager. The monument is 20km south-east of the R33.

Mpumalanga

Mpumalanga takes in both highveld and lowveld, with the dramatic Klein Drakensberg escarpment in between.

Down on the lowveld is the world-famous Kruger National Park, which is bordered by a host of luxurious private game reserves.

Mpumalanga was once part of the Transvaal (it was called Eastern Transvaal for the first couple of years of the new South Africa). For more information on history, see the Gauteng and Northern Province sections.

Warning

Beware of bilharzia and, on the eastern lowveld, malaria.

EASTERN LOWVELD

To the north the lowveld is hot – extremely so in summer, when there are storms and high humidity. Further south the temperatures are more moderate and the scrubby terrain gives way to lush subtropical vegetation around Nelspruit and the Crocodile River. South of here, around Barberton, the dry country resumes with a vengeance – gold prospectors last century dubbed it the Valley of Death.

Much of the eastern lowveld is taken up by Kruger National Park and the private game reserves that border it.

Kruger National Park

Kruger National Park is one of the most famous wildlife parks in the world. It's also one of the biggest and oldest. Sabie Game Reserve was established in 1898 by the president of the South African Republic (ZAR), Paul Kruger. The reserve, since renamed and much expanded, is now nearly two million hectares in extent (about the size of Wales).

The park boasts the greatest variety of animals of any park in Southern Africa (and perhaps the whole of Africa), with lion, leopard, elephant, buffalo and rhino (the 'big five') as well as cheetah, giraffe, hippo and many varieties of antelope and smaller animals. Altogether, these include 147 mammals, more than 500 birds, 114 reptiles and 49 species of fish.

Unlike some of the parks in Southern Africa, Kruger does not offer a true wilderness experience. The infrastructure is too highly developed and organised. However, this means that you can explore at leisure, without having to depend on organised tours or guides.

Orientation Kruger stretches almost 350km along the Mozambique border and has an average width of 60km. There are eight entrance gates (*heks* in Afrikaans): Malelane and Crocodile Bridge on the southern edge, accessible from the N4 (the

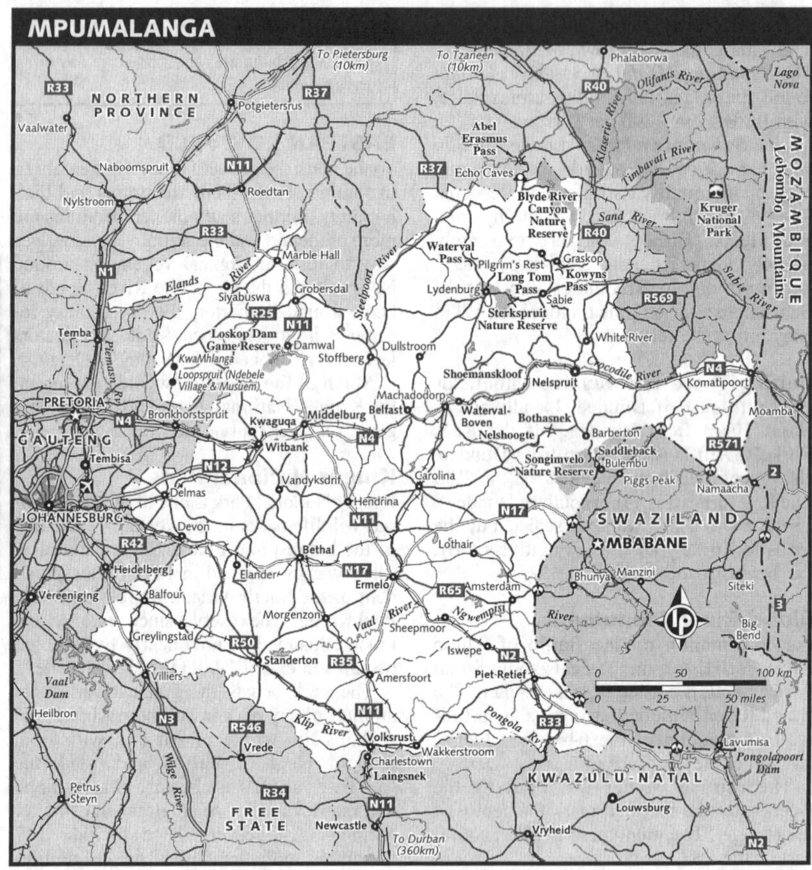

quickest direct route from Jo'burg); the Numbi and Paul Kruger Gates, accessible from White River and Hazyview (turn off the N4 just before Nelspruit); Orpen, which is convenient if you have been exploring Blyde River; Phalaborwa, accessible from Pietersburg/Polokwane and Tzaneen; Punda Maria, accessible from Louis Trichardt; and Pafuri, accessible from the Venda region of Northern Province.

Information The National Parks Board has an informative Web site: www.ecoafrica.com/saparks.

While you're in the area, listen to Radio Safari (94.4 FM) which broadcasts interesting programs about the park and its animals.

Maps and publications are sold at the larger rest camps.

Bookings Accommodation (except camp sites) can be booked through the National Parks Board (☎ 012-343 1991, fax 343 0905, ⓔ reservations@parks-sa.co.za), PO Box 787, Pretoria 0001. There are also offices in Cape Town (☎ 021-22 2810, fax 24 6211) and at the Tourist Junction in Durban (☎ 031-304 4934) which take bookings.

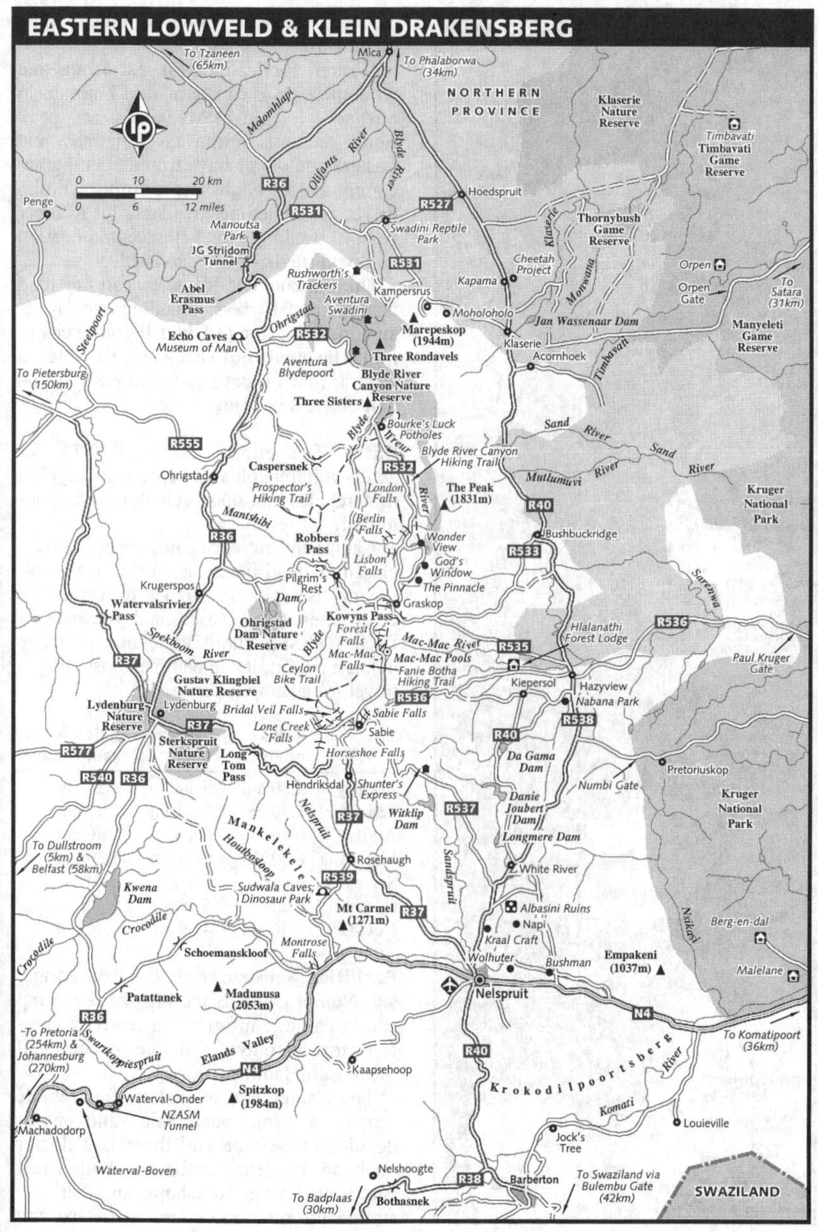
EASTERN LOWVELD & KLEIN DRAKENSBERG
To Tzaneen (65km)
Mica
To Phalaborwa (34km)
NORTHERN PROVINCE
Klaserie Nature Reserve
Timbavati
Timbavati Game Reserve
Hoedspruit
Swadini Reptile Park
Thornybush Game Reserve
Penge
Manoutsa Park
JG Strijdom Tunnel
Rushworth's Trackers
Cheetah Project
Kapama
Kampersrus
Orpen
Orpen Gate
To Satara (31km)
Abel Erasmus Pass
Aventura Swadini
Moholoholo
Marepeskop (1944m)
Jan Wassenaar Dam
Manyeleti Game Reserve
Echo Caves
Museum of Man
Three Rondavels
Klaserie
Acornhoek
Aventura Blydepoort
Blyde River Canyon Nature Reserve
To Pietersburg (150km)
Three Sisters
Bourke's Luck Potholes
Blyde River Canyon Hiking Trail
Sand River
Mutlumuvi River
Ohrigstad
Caspersnek
Prospector's Hiking Trail
London Falls
The Peak (1831m)
Kruger National Park
Berlin Falls
Bushbuckridge
Robbers Pass
Wonder View
God's Window
The Pinnacle
Lisbon Falls
Pilgrim's Rest
Krugerspos
Graskop
Watervalsrivier Pass
Ohrigstad Dam Nature Reserve
Kowyns Pass
Forest Falls
Mac-Mac River
Hlalanathi Forest Lodge
Mac-Mac Falls
Mac-Mac Pools
Fanie Botha Hiking Trail
Paul Kruger Gate
Ceylon Bike Trail
Gustav Klingbiel Nature Reserve
Kiepersol
Hazyview
Nabana Park
Lydenburg Nature Reserve
Lydenburg
Bridal Veil Falls
Sabie Falls
Sabie
Lone Creek Falls
Sterkspruit Nature Reserve
Long Tom Pass
Horseshoe Falls
Da Gama Dam
Pretoriuskop
Hendriksdal
Shunter's Express
Numbi Gate
Danie Joubert Dam
Witklip Dam
Kruger National Park
Mankelekele
Longmere Dam
To Dullstroom (5km) & Belfast (58km)
Rosehaugh
White River
Kwena Dam
Sudwala Caves; Dinosaur Park
Albasini Ruins
Mt Carmel (1271m)
Napi
Kraal Craft
Berg-en-dal
Schoemanskloof
Montrose Falls
Wolhuter
Bushman
Empakeni (1037m)
Malelane
Nelspruit
Patattanek
Madunusa (2053m)
To Pretoria (254km) & Johannesburg (270km)
Elands Valley
To Komatipoort (36km)
Kaapsehoop
Krokodilpoortsberg
Waterval-Onder
Spitzkop (1984m)
NZASM Tunnel
Machadodorp
Jock's Tree
Louieville
Waterval-Boven
Nelshoogte
Barberton
To Swaziland via Bulembu Gate (42km)
To Badplaas (30km)
Bothasnek
SWAZILAND
0 10 20 km
0 6 12 miles

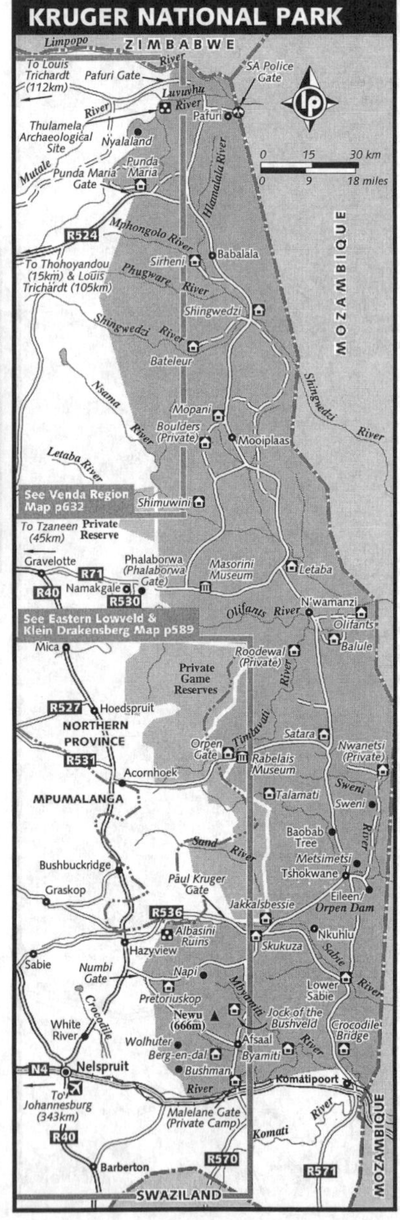

You can make a phone booking with a credit card.

Written applications for rest camps and wilderness trails can be made 13 months in advance. Except at weekends and peak times (school holidays, Christmas and Easter) you won't have trouble getting accommodation. Night and morning wildlife drives are sometimes available for R70 per person. Bookings for both accommodation and wildlife drives are advisable.

During school holidays you can stay for a maximum of 10 days, including five days at any one rest camp (10 days if you're camping). The number of visitors is restricted, so at peak times it pays to arrive early if you don't have a booking.

Entry The entry cost is R30/15 for adults/children, plus R24 for a car (bicycles, motorcycles and open vehicles are not admitted).

Camps and entrance gates are opened and closed at fixed times, as shown in the following list. It is an offence to arrive at a camp after it has closed, and you may be fined. With speed limits of 50km/h on tar and 40km/h on dirt, it can be time-consuming to travel from camp to camp.

	gates open	camps open	gates & camps close
January	5.30 am	5 am	6.30 pm
Feb–Mar	5.30 am	5.30 am	6.30 pm
April	6 am	6 am	5.30 pm
May–Aug	6.30 am	6.30 am	5.30 pm
September	6 am	6 am	6 pm
October	6 am	5.30 am	6 pm
Nov–Dec	5.30 am	4.30 am	6.30 pm

Facilities Skukuza, near the Paul Kruger and Numbi gates, is the biggest rest camp and has a large information centre with interesting displays and the exceptional Stevenson-Hamilton library.

There's an AA workshop for vehicle repairs, a bank, post office and photo-developing service and there is a doctor on hand as well. Letaba and Satara rest camps also have workshops, and there are staffed information centres at Letaba and

Berg-en-dal. All camps have telephones and first-aid centres.

The larger camps have restaurants and shops that stock a range of essentials (including cold beer and wine), but if you are planning to do your own cooking it is worth stocking up outside the park.

Climate Summers are very hot with violent thunderstorms, and temperatures average 30°C. The park is in a summer rainfall area, with the rainfall generally decreasing as you go north. In winter, nights can be cold (sometimes falling below 0°C) and the days are pleasant.

Fauna Kruger takes in a variety of ecosystems. Most mammals are distributed throughout the park, but some show a preference for particular areas.

Impala, buffalo, Burchell's zebra, blue wildebeest, kudu, waterbuck, baboon, vervet monkey, cheetah, leopard and smaller predators are all widely distributed. Birdlife is prolific along the rivers, and north of the Luvuvhu River at the northern extremity of the park.

The south-western corner between the Olifants and Crocodile Rivers, where the rainfall is highest (700mm a year), is thickly wooded. This terrain is favoured by white rhino and buffalo, but is less favoured by antelope and, therefore, by predators.

The eastern section to the south of the Olifants River, on the plains around Satara and south to the Crocodile River, has large expanses of good grazing. This favours large populations of impala, zebra, wildebeest, giraffe and black rhino. Predators, particularly lion, prey on the impala, zebra and blue wildebeest.

North of Olifants River the rainfall drops below 500mm and the veld's dominant tree is mopane, a favoured diet of elephant, which are most common north of the Olifants.

Perhaps the most interesting area is in the far north around Punda Maria and Pafuri. This has a higher rainfall than the mopane country and supports a wider variety of plants (baobabs are particularly noticeable) and a higher density and greater variety of animals.

Wilderness Trails There are seven guided trails, offering a chance to walk through the park with knowledgeable armed guides. Most trails last two days and three nights, departing on Sunday. Accommodation is in huts and you don't need to provide food or equipment (bring your own beer and wine).

Wilderness trails cost R1075 per person and must be booked well in advance. See Bookings earlier in this section for booking information.

Places to Stay Most visitors stay in ***rest camps***. These have a wide range of facilities. Their restaurants are good and prices are reasonable. Most have shops, phones and fuel. The accommodation varies, but usually includes huts and self-contained cottages. Camping facilities are also available at most camps.

Bushveld camps are smaller, more remote camps without shops and restaurants, and ***private camps*** cater for groups which must take the entire camp. Bookings are essential for both these types of camps.

All huts and cottages are supplied with bedding and towels. Most have air-con or fans, and fridges. If you are staying in accommodation with a communal kitchen you have to supply your own cooking and eating utensils. Most tent sites are not equipped with power points.

As a guide to prices: camping costs R40 to R70 for two people, plus R16 for each additional person; most huts with communal bathroom and kitchen cost between R80 and R150 for two people; huts with private bathroom and shared kitchen cost between R275 and R380 for two; most self-contained chalets, rondavels and huts cost at least R330 for two; and the average price for a self-contained cottage sleeping six is about R750, more if you want a cottage with two bathrooms.

Getting There & Away There are several transport options to/from Kruger National Park.

Air SA Airlink flies daily from Jo'burg to Skukuza for R525, Nelspruit for R660 and Phalaborwa for R809; all fares are one way.

Bus & Minibus Taxi Nelspruit is the most convenient large town near Kruger, and it's well served by buses and minibus taxis to and from Jo'burg. However, from Nelspruit you still have a fair way to go to get into the park. Near Nelspruit and closer to Kruger (15km from Numbi Gate) is the small village of Hazyview, where there are a couple of backpackers hostels that pick up from Nelspruit.

City to City buses make the run from Jo'burg to Hazyview for R65. A minibus taxi from Hazyview to Skukuza costs about R8.

Train The *Komati* runs from Jo'burg to Komatipoort (via Nelspruit), about 12km from Crocodile Bridge Gate.

Car Skukuza is about 500km from Jo'burg and can be reached in about six hours. Punda Maria is about 620km from Jo'burg and can be reached in about eight hours. Rental cars are available at Skukuza, Nelspruit and Phalaborwa.

Private Game Reserves

The area just west of Kruger contains a large number of private reserves, usually sharing a border with Kruger and thus sharing most of the animals. They are often extremely pricey – R700 per person is only mid-range – but with an economic stake in their guests getting close to animals, they have good viewing facilities. It is possible to find cheaper places, and these may be more enjoyable because accommodation is in bush camps.

It's worth talking to a travel agent to help you decide on a reserve, as there are sometimes special offers. The better-known reserves include those within the large Sabi Sand conservation area (such as Sabi Sabi), Idube, Londolozi and Mala Mala.

Nelspruit

☎ 013

Nelspruit, in the Crocodile River Valley, is the largest town in Mpumalanga's steamy subtropical lowveld, and is the provincial capital. Its growth began only in the 1890s, when the ZAR decided to put a railway through to Delagoa Bay (Maputo) so it would have access to a non-British port.

Information The helpful Nelspruit Publicity Association (☎ 755 1988/9) is in the Promenade Centre. It's open from 8 am to 5 pm weekdays and 9 am to 4 pm weekends.

Places to Stay Tranquil ***Safubi River Lodge & Caravan Park*** *(☎ 741 3253, 45 Graniet St)* is a long way from the town centre. Sites cost R60 for two people and chalets cost from R195. To get there head west on the N4, go past Agaat St and turn left at the Caltex station.

Funky Monkey Backpackers *(☎/fax 744 0534, 102 Van Wijk St)* is a large, well-run hostel with a pool and a small bar area. Dorms are R45 and doubles are R110. Ask the owners about the best nightspots in town.

Nelspruit Backpackers *(☎ 741 2237, e nelback@hotmail.com, 9 Andries Pretorius St)* is laid-back and in their words 'attitude-free'. It offers free pick-ups and charge R40 for a dorm and R120 for a double.

On the corner of General Dan Pienaar and Koorsboom Sts, the ***Road Lodge*** *(☎ 741 4490)* has good-value rooms that sleep three for R155. Breakfast is R16. The more upmarket ***Town Lodge*** with similar facilities is next door.

The ***Hotel Promenade*** *(☎ 753 3000)* is in the recycled town hall. It's a pleasant place and charges R265/340 for B&B. Rooms come with bathroom, TV and phone.

For other B&B accommodation contact the Publicity Association.

Places to Eat On Louis Trichardt St, ***Nando's*** and ***Pappa's Pizza*** are the pick of the fastfood places.

In the Promenade Centre is ***Cafe Mozart*** where a tasty breakfast costs around R20 and toasted sandwiches go for R15. It is licensed and also does lunch and dinner.

Harper's Restaurant, Coffee Shop & Takeaway on Brown St does cheap, healthy rolls.

Villa Italia *(☎ 752 5780)* on the corner of Louis Trichardt and Paul Kruger Sts is a

NELSPRUIT

1 Bus & Minibus Taxi Park
2 Promenade Centre; Nelspruit Publicity Association; Cafe Mozart
3 Hotel Promenade
4 Standard Bank
5 Harper's Restaurant, Coffee Shop & Takeaway
6 Villa Italia
7 ABSA Bank
8 Parking
9 Nando's
10 Pappa's Pizza
11 Mozambique Embassy (CVA Building)
12 Municipal Buildings
13 Joshua Doore Centre; Translux
14 Nel Forum Medical Centre
15 Keg & Jock Pub
16 Road Lodge; Town Lodge
17 Village Mall; Laundromat; Bottle Store; Tavern; Spar Supermarket
18 Nelspruit Backpackers

popular place; delicious pasta meals cost around R35.

Getting There & Away The airport is 8km south of town on the Kaapsche Hoop road. SA Airlink (☎ 752 5257) flies daily to Jo'burg (R513 one way) and Durban (R638 one way).

Bus Translux runs daily to Jo'burg and Pretoria for R115, and to Maputo for R90. Greyhound has a daily service to Jo'burg for R120. Translux and Greyhound depart from the Promenade Centre.

The City to City Shuttle runs direct from Nelspruit to Durban for R220, three times a week. Book at Lowveld Promotions (☎ 752 5134) in the Joshua Doore centre for City to City and Translux services.

Minibus Taxi The main minibus taxi park is near the end of Brown St, although others stop near the train station. Destinations include: Barberton (R7); Hazyview (R10); Sabie (R15); Komatipoort (R30); and Jo'burg (R70). A daily service to Maputo leaves from near the train station.

Train The *Komati* runs between Jo'burg and Komatipoort daily, via Nelspruit.

Car Avis (☎ 741 1087), Budget (☎ 741 3871) and Imperial (☎ 741 2834) have offices at the airport.

Hazyview

☎ 013

Hazyview is a small village with large shopping centres. It is close to Kruger National Park's Numbi Gate (15km) and Paul Kruger Gate (43km).

For tourist information, Original Tourism Consultants (☎ 737 7715) in the grounds of the Numbi Hotel is very helpful; it's open from 8.30 am to 5 pm Monday to Saturday.

Places to Stay About 2km south of Hazyview, just past the White River turn-off, ***Kruger Park Backpackers*** *(☎ 737 7224)* has Zulu-style huts for about R60 per person. It organises tours of Kruger.

The genial ***Big 5 Backpackers*** *(☎ 083-524 6615)* is 3km up the hill from the intersection of R40 and R538. There are superb views to Kruger. It has dorms for R45 and doubles for R120.

Not far from the main junction is the peaceful ***Numbi Hotel*** *(☎ 737 7301)*, which has singles/doubles for R235/380. A camp site costs R65 a double.

Getting There & Away City to City has a daily service to/from Jo'burg (R65). Minibuses go to Nelspruit (R15) and Sabie (R15).

SOUTH AFRICA

Komatipoort
☎ 013

This border town is at the foot of the Lebombo Mountains near the confluence of the Komati and Crocodile Rivers. It is only 10km south of Crocodile Bridge into Kruger.

Border Country Inn *(☎ 790 7328)* is on the N4 close to the Mozambique border crossing and Kruger; B&B costs R200/300 for singles/doubles.

It is now fairly easy to cross the border here. Visas for Mozambique are available in Jo'burg, Cape Town, Durban and Nelspruit. If you have a car you will need a breakdown warning triangle, seat belts and the relevant vehicle papers, especially for rental cars.

Barberton
☎ 013

Barberton, about 50km south of Nelspruit, is a quiet town in the harsh but interesting lowveld country of De Kaap Valley. It had South Africa's first stock exchange. The very helpful information centre (☎ 712 2121) in Market Square on Crown St is open on weekdays (closed between 1 and 2 pm) and Saturday morning. The information centre has a brochure detailing the various **restored houses**. Not far from town is an umbrella thorn tree known as **Jock's Tree**.

The aerial cableway brings asbestos down from a mine in Swaziland, carrying coal in the other direction as counterweight.

Places to Stay At the ***caravan park*** *(☎ 712 3323)*, tent sites cost R45 for up to three people, and chalets with kitchens start at R160 for two people.

A good place to stay is ***Fountain Baths Guest Lodge*** *(☎ 712 2707)*, also called FB Holiday Cottages, at the southern end of Pilgrim St. Self-contained rooms cost R100 per person. Built in 1885, it used to be Barberton's public baths and swimming pool; it's popular so book ahead.

The ***Hillside Lodge*** *(☎ 712 4466, 62 Pilgrim St)* is a comfortable guesthouse with magnificent views and lovely gardens; B&B costs R120 per person.

The ***Phoenix Hotel*** *(☎ 712 4211)* on the corner of Pilgrim and President Sts is a clean, old-style country pub, exuding a certain faded elegance that dates from 1882. Rooms cost R140/250, including breakfast.

Places to Eat The ***Gold Mine*** next to the Checkers supermarket covers most tastes; bar meals cost R25.

Cocopan on Crown St opposite the museum is a casual place with ***John Henry's Pub*** attached. The ***Victorian Tea Garden*** near the tourist office is a great place to relax; light meals cost R25.

Getting There & Away The scenic R40 from here to Swaziland (via the Bulembu border crossing) is unsealed and rough. Do not attempt the journey in a 2WD in the wet. The border closes at 4 pm.

There is a minibus taxi rank by Emjindini, about 3km from town on the Nelspruit road, or you can find taxis in town. The fare to Nelspruit is R7 and to Badplaas it costs R11.

KLEIN DRAKENSBERG

The highveld ends suddenly at this escarpment which tumbles down to the eastern lowveld.

The Klein (Small) Drakensberg (as opposed to the main Drakensberg Range in KwaZulu-Natal) is not so much peaks as cliffs, and there are stunning views. As it is prime vacation territory there's a lot of accommodation, but it fills up at peak times. The population density is low, so there's little public transport.

Winters are cold, with occasional snowfalls. Summers are warm, but after the sweltering lowveld it's a relief to get up here.

Blyde River Canyon
☎ 013

The Blyde River Canyon Nature Reserve snakes north for almost 60km from Graskop, following the escarpment and meeting the Blyde River as it carves its way down to the lowveld. The Blyde's spectacular canyon, nearly 30km long, is one of South Africa's scenic highlights.

The following description, from north to south, begins near the Manoutsa Cliffs at the junction of the Tzaneen road (R36) and the R527 (sometimes marked on maps as a continuation of the R531).

Following the R36 as it turns south and climbs up from the lowveld through the Strijdom Tunnel and scenic Abel Erasmus Pass, you pass the turn-off to the R532 and come to the village of Mogaba and the turn-off to the **Museum of Man**. This archaeological site has rock paintings and other finds on show between 8 am and 5 pm daily.

If you return to the R532 junction and proceed east along the R532 you come to the Aventura Blydepoort resort. There is a good view of the **Three Rondavels** from within the resort. The Rondavels are huge cylinders of rock with hut-like pointy 'roofs' rising out of the far wall of the canyon.

Bourke's Luck Potholes are weird cylindrical holes carved into the rock by whirlpools in the river. They are interesting, although nothing mind-boggling. There is a good visitors centre with information on the geology, flora and fauna of the canyon. It costs R10 to see the potholes.

The R532 follows the Treur River south to its source, and further on is a turn-off to the R534 loop road. This road leads to the spectacular viewpoints of **Wonder View** and **God's Window**. A few kilometres on you pass the **Pinnacle**, an impressive rock formation which juts out from the escarpment. The R534 rejoins the R532 about 3km north of Graskop.

Hiking Trails There are several great hiking trails in the area. The visitors centre at the Bourke's Luck Potholes is the best place to get maps and information. The Graskop information centre is also helpful. Fees on the overnight trails (the only way to get to the canyon floor) are R30 per person per night. Book well in advance (☎ 769 6019).

Places to Stay As well as accommodation in the towns on top of the escarpment, there are several places to stay close to the canyon.

Aventura Blydepoort *(☎ 769 8005)* is a large resort with all the usual facilities. Tent sites cost about R20, plus R16 per person; two-bed chalets cost from R300 and standard four-bed chalets are R325.

At the bottom of the escarpment, on the eastern side but still on the Blyde River, is ***Aventura Swadini*** *(☎ 015-795 5141)*; camping and four-bed units cost about the same as at Blydepoort.

Also at the bottom of the escarpment, to the north of Swadini (and actually in Northern Province) is ***Rushworth's Trackers*** *(☎ 015-795 5033)*, which takes in the strikingly different ecosystems of the highveld and the lowveld. The reserve caters mainly to educational groups, but individuals are welcome. Basic camping costs R20; a cottage costs R65 per person or R140 for DB&B.

To get to Trackers take the R527 west from Hoedspruit and after about 20km turn south onto the small Driehoek road, just after you cross the Blyde River. After 6.5km you will see the Trackers signpost.

Graskop

☎ 013

Graskop is on the edge of the Drakensberg escarpment, at the top of Kowyns Pass. Nearby are some spectacular views of the lowveld, almost 1000m below. The town is well situated for visiting the area's highveld attractions and is less than 60km from Kruger National Park.

There is an information centre (☎ 767 1833) next to the Spar supermarket.

Places to Stay The ***Municipal Holiday Resort*** *(☎ 767 1126)* has tent sites at R25/35 for one/two people and chalets from R125. A walking trail that includes places described in *Jock of the Bushveld* starts at the resort.

Colourful ***Graskop Backpackers*** *(☎ 767 1761, 69 Eeufees St)* is in a bizarre, castle-like building on the other side of town from the railway line. This is the best place to ask about walks in the area. Dorms are R35, doubles R80 and camping R25 for two people. A tip – try the homemade pizzas!

Panorama Rest Camp *(☎ 767 1091)* is about 2km east of town on the road to Kowyns Pass. It's stunningly situated and the small swimming pool is right on the edge of the berg. Camp sites cost R50 for two people. Chalets with breathtaking views start at R125 for two people.

The spacious ***Graskop Hotel*** (☎ *767 1244)* on the main street charges R150/250 a single/double for B&B. There are also family rooms and a good coffee shop.

Places to Eat Well geared to the area's tourism, the gastronomic delights of Graskop include ***Harry's Pancake Bar*** on Louis Trichardt St. It's been recommended by Jo'burg's Chosen Few motorcycle gang, and pancakes cost about R25. A bit further along is the ***Lonely Tree Pancake Cabin***, highly recommended by us. ***Leonardo's Trattoria*** (☎ *767 1078)* across the road will satisfy those pizza and pasta cravings.

Getting There & Away The Baz Bus is now the only major bus service covering the area. Jo'burg to Graskop costs R110.

Sabie

☎ 013

Sabie is a fairly small town, but it's the largest in this area. Tourists come for the cool climate, trout fishing and the extensive pine and eucalypt plantations, but if you prefer your forests wild these aren't much of an attraction.

Sondelani Travel & Info (☎ 764 3492) has tourist information; it's next to the Woodsman on the corner of Mac-Mac Rd and the R536. It's open daily except Sunday.

Things to See & Do The **Forestry Museum** has displays on the local forests. It's open daily; entry costs R5/3 for adults/students.

There are several waterfalls in the area. Off the R532 are the **Mac-Mac Falls** (named because of the number of Scottish names on the area's mining register) and **Forest Falls**, 10km from Graskop and reached by a walk through the forest.

There are several **nature walks** near Sabie and two excellent **mountain bike trails**. Sondelani Travel & Info can provide details.

Places to Stay Out of town off Old Lydenburg Road is ***Merry Pebbles*** (☎ *764 2266)*. It has camp sites for R35 (low season) plus R10 per person, as well as self-contained chalets from R200 a double.

The newly opened ***Sabie Backpackers***, on Main Rd near the corner of Simmons St, has dorms for R40 and doubles for R120 in a clean little house with cooking facilities.

Sabie Vallée Inn (☎ *764 2182)* on Tenth St has backpacker dorms for R40. Self-catering log cabins and comfortable hotel rooms cost R155 per person (less if you stay two nights); the hotel rate includes DB&B.

The area has a number of B&Bs. ***Sabie Townhouse*** (☎ *764 2292)* on Power St is *the* place in town for a well-earned indulgence. Book ahead as it gets popular; singles/doubles cost R260/470 and there are separate rates for families.

South-east of Sabie, on the R537 to White River, is ***Shunter's Express*** (☎ *764 1777)* which has B&B for R170 per person in 1930s railway coaches.

Places to Eat At ***Zeederburg Coach House*** a smoked trout with salad costs R24, and pasta dishes are also available. The ***Woodsman*** has main meals for between R30 and R40, and a great Greek menu. Near Sabie Falls, ***Loggerhead*** is a good steakhouse where you'll pay about R45 for a meal.

Getting There & Away Baz Bus runs four times a week to and from Jo'burg for R110.

Sabie's minibus taxi park is behind the Spar supermarket on Main St. Most taxis run only in the local area. The fare to Hazyview is R18; to Nelspruit it's R25.

Mt Sheba Nature Reserve

☎ 013

To see how the area looked before most of the indigenous forest was destroyed, visit this reserve, 15km off the R533 and about 10km west of Pilgrim's Rest. With its plentiful rain and mists, it's an evocative place. There are day walks in the area; pick up a brochure and map at the Mt Sheba Hotel, the Sondelani Travel & Info Centre in Sabie or from Pilgrim's Rest.

The luxurious ***Mt Sheba Hotel*** (☎ *768 1241)* in the nature reserve has great views. Singles/doubles cost R592/790 for DB&B.

Pilgrim's Rest

☎ 013

Gold was discovered here in 1873 and for 10 years the area buzzed with diggers working small-scale alluvial claims. When the big operators arrived in the 1880s, Pilgrim's Rest became a company town, and when the gold finally fizzled out in 1972 the town was sold to the government as a ready-made historical village.

The information centre on the main street is open from 9 am to 12.45 pm and 1.15 to 4.30 pm daily. There are three **museums** and entry to all three costs R5; buy tickets at the information centre. The **nature reserve** that surrounds the town is a good place for a walk.

The restored ***District Six Miner's Cottages*** *(☎ 768 1211)* are your cheapest accommodation option at R160 for two people in a four-bed cottage. The Victorian-era ***Royal Hotel*** *(☎ 768 1100)* has ornate singles/doubles for R480/660.

Gauteng

Gauteng (Place of Gold, in Sotho) takes in the area once known as the PWV – Pretoria,

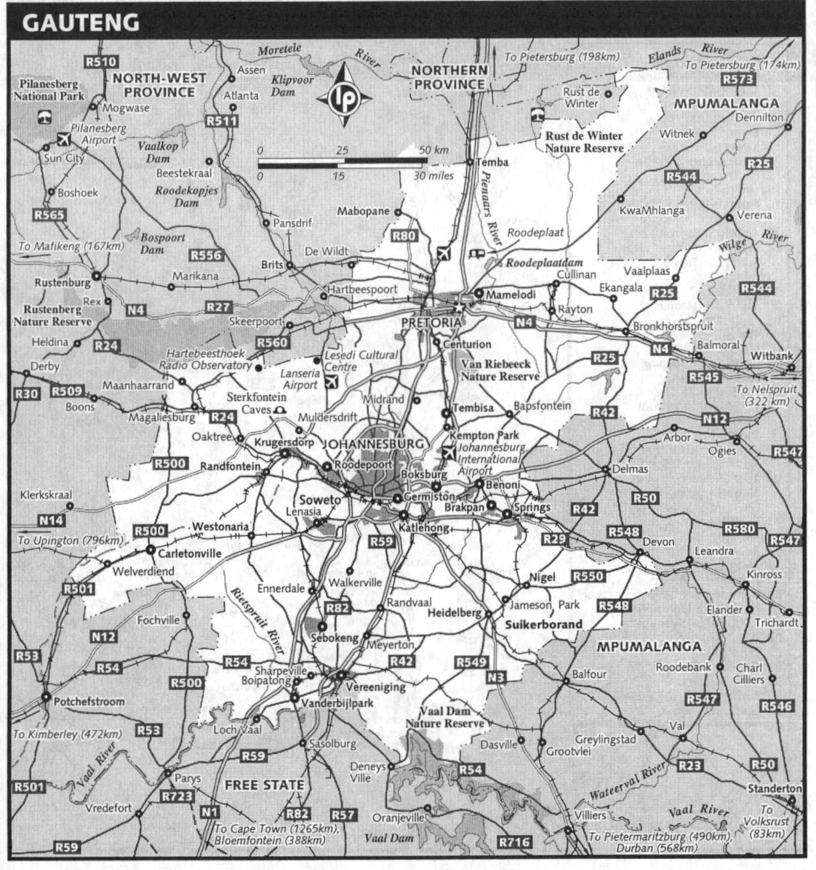

Witwatersrand and Vereeniging. The Witwatersrand (literally, Ridge of White Waters), is often shortened to 'the Rand'. The ridge contains the world's richest reef of gold.

Gauteng is the smallest South African province (about 19,000 sq km) but with around 10 million people it has the largest population. It has been claimed that Gauteng accounts for 25% of the gross product of the whole of Africa.

The area is rich in history, but for most visitors a quick visit to the crime-plagued Johannesburg (Jo'burg), and perhaps Pretoria, will be enough.

JOHANNESBURG

☎ 011

Jo'burg's sole reason for existence is the reef of gold that lies under the *highveld* (high open grassland), and its inhabitants are single-minded in their pursuit of the rand. Cultural assets (including good bars and restaurants) are pitifully thin on the ground.

This is the heart of the new South Africa, and this is where change – both good and bad – is happening first.

Unfortunately, it's the bad that gets most of the press and, to an extent, it's warranted

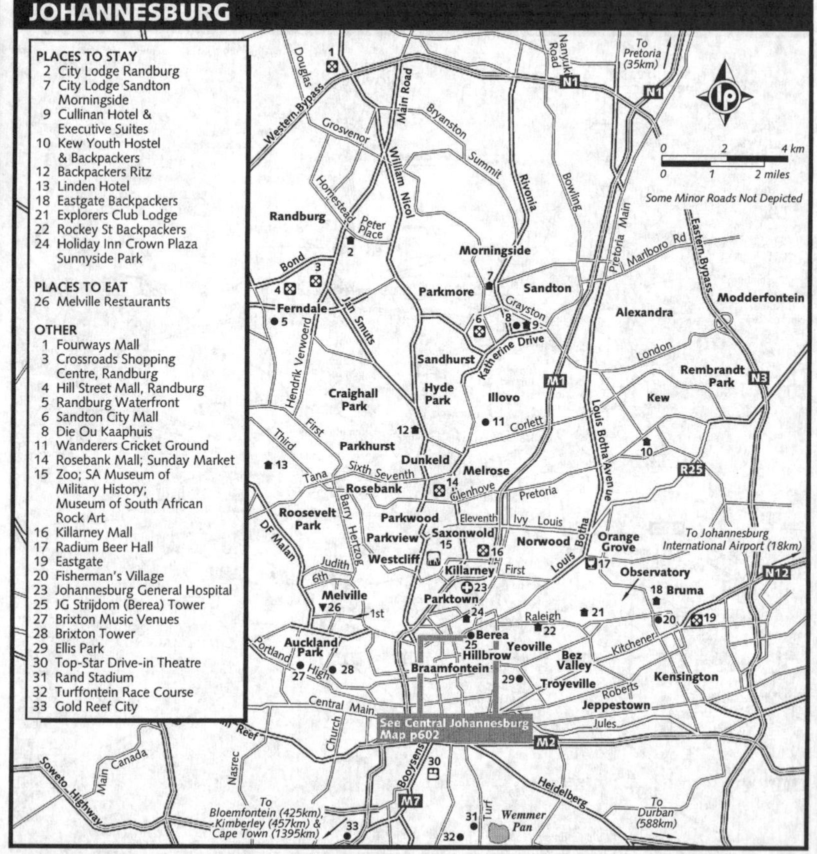

– violent crime is rampant in the city centre and the inner suburbs of Hillbrow and Berea.

The statistics are simply horrifying. Businesses have fled to the suburbs (particularly north) and that's where you'll find most accommodation, bars and restaurants.

History

In 1886 George Harrison, a prospector, found traces of gold on the highveld. He didn't realise it, but he had stumbled on the only surface outcrop of the world's richest gold-bearing reef. He sold his claim for £10.

Thousands of diggers soon descended on the site and by 1889 Jo'burg was the largest town in Southern Africa. After the 1899–1902 Anglo-Boer War, which saw Jo'burg become a virtual ghost town, the city recovered quickly and huge new mines were developed.

Under black leadership, the vast squatter camps that sprung up around Jo'burg became well-organised cities, despite the atrocious conditions. In the late 1940s many of the camps were destroyed by the authorities and the people were moved to new suburbs known as the South-Western Townships, now shortened to Soweto.

Orientation

Two communication towers on the ridges to the north of the city centre make good landmarks: the Hillbrow Tower; and the Brixton Tower, to the north-west of the city.

The city centre is laid out on a simple grid. Many people arrive in Jo'burg by bus or train at or near Park Station on the northern edge of the city centre. The northern suburbs are white middle-class ghettos.

Soweto (to the south-west) is the main township outside the city, but there are also large developments at Tokoza (south of Alberton), Kwa-Thema and Tsakane (south of Brakpan), Daveyton (east of Benoni), Tembisa (to the north-east) and Alexandra (inside the N3 freeway to the north).

Information

Tourist Offices Info Africa Passenger Services Centre (☎ 390 9000) at the airport has information and some useful books.

The Gauteng Tourism Association is hopeless; their office is in the city centre (☎ 331 2041) on the corner of Market and Kruis Sts, next to the former Carlton Centre.

To make bookings for parks run by the National Parks Board, you'll need to contact the board's office in Pretoria (☎ 012-343 1991 – for more contact details, see the Pretoria section later).

Money Banks are open from 9 am to 3.30 pm weekdays and 8.30 to 11 am Saturday. There are foreign exchange counters at the airport.

American Express (AmEx) offices are in the northern suburbs: in Sandton (☎ 883 1316) at 78A Sandton City Mall; in Randburg (☎ 789 9491) at Shop 107, Randburg Waterfront; and the efficient Rosebank office (☎ 880 8382), located at Nedbank Gardens, 33 Bath Ave.

Rennies Travel is the agent for Thomas Cook. They have foreign exchange outlets at 35 Rissik St (☎ 492 1990), Jo'burg International Airport (☎ 390 1040) and Sandton City Mall (☎ 884 4035).

Post & Communications The GPO is on Jeppe St, between Von Brandis St and Smal St Mall. It's open from 8.30 am to 4.00 pm weekdays and 8 am to noon Saturday.

There are plenty of commercial phone services around the city. Check the rates before making a long-distance call. Most backpackers hostels have email facilities.

Travel Agencies There's a branch of the South African Students' Travel Service (SASTS) in the Student Union building of the University of Witwatersrand (☎ 716 3045), open on weekdays. You don't have to be a student to use their services.

Rennies Travel has several offices around Jo'burg (see Money earlier).

Pathfinders Travel (☎ 453 1113/4, fax 453 1483), at 17 Chaucer Ave, Senderwood, Bedfordview, is a small agency that specialises in ecotourism and personalised itineraries.

Medical Services Doctors are listed under 'Medical' in the Yellow Pages. If urgent

Soweto

For the majority of Jo'burg's inhabitants, home is in one of the black townships surrounding the city – probably Soweto. Most white South Africans are completely ignorant of life in the townships and very few have ever been inside one. Their picture of the area is one of unmitigated hostility, and a nightmare environment of drugs, superstition, tribal warfare, depravity and violent crime.

In fact, some suburbs within the townships are quite acceptable and not all that far removed from suburbs anywhere, while others are as bad as any Third World slum.

In descending order of wealth, there's a tiny wealthy elite that live in comfortable bungalows; the privileged who live in monotonous rows of government-built three-room houses; the lucky who have been provided with a block of land, a prefabricated toilet and a tap; the fortunate who live in shacks erected in backyards; the squatters who build wherever they can and have virtually no facilities at all; and at the bottom of the pile, the men who live in dorms in vast, dilapidated hostels.

It is striking how neat and clean the houses, shacks and yards are. Unfortunately, the streets and open places are buried under a blizzard of plastic bags and rubbish because each house only gets one rubbish bin, which is emptied once a week. This may be adequate when one family lives in a house, but it is hopelessly inadequate when three or four additional families live in the backyard, and it's irrelevant if you are a squatter.

The townships played a crucial role in the struggle against apartheid. This was a struggle against a government that routinely used bullets; tear gas; bombs; imprisonment without trial; torture; and summary execution of men, women and children. Soweto was in a virtual state of war from 1976, when the first protesting school students were killed, until the 1994 elections. During that time many thousands died. No one is quite sure exactly how many. The struggle is graphically depicted in a photographic exhibition, temporarily housed in old shipping containers that surround the Hector Pieterson monument. The photographs by Pulitzer Prize winner, Peter Magubane, have been removed from display because of an ongoing dispute over royalties.

Given the townships' recent history, the friendliness that is generally shown to white visitors is almost embarrassing.

Most people have entirely reasonable aspirations – they want a job, decent housing, affordable education and an opportunity for their children to better themselves.

Although outsiders, including whites, are *not* automatically targeted, the townships are still in a state of acute social trauma, and violent crime is commonplace. Visiting without a companion who has local knowledge is likely to be disastrous. If a trustworthy black friend is happy to escort you, you should have no problems, and tours have operated safely for years.

Visiting a large township is an unforgettable experience. It may seem grotesque treating these places as a tourist attraction, but to get any kind of appreciation for South African reality, you have to visit them.

Most Soweto tours are designed to be educational experiences, so they can be earnest and a little dry. You should plan to see the poignant Hector Pieterson monument, a squatter camp, Vilakazi St (Winnie Madikizela-Mandela's house, Nelson Mandela's old house, Walter Sisulu's residence and Desmond Tutu's house), Regina Mundi Square, Soweto 'architecture' (including shacks, brick palaces, and – if you can – the inside of a shack) and the Freedom Charter on the side of a shipping container in Kliptown. If you are lucky, Avalon Cemetery with the graves of Helen Joseph and Joe Slovo, and the 'Never, Never Again' monument, may be visited.

Max Maximum Tours (☎ 938 8703 or 082-533 1587) is highly recommended. Max is a longtime Soweto resident, a nice bloke and a good guide. He charges about R150; there are also overnight tours for about R300, which include B&B with a local family.

Packers (☎ 012-343 9754 in Pretoria, ⓔ ptaback@hotmail.com) also run Soweto trips.

medical attention is required go direct to the casualty department of Johannesburg General Hospital (☎ 488 4911) less than 1km north of Hillbrow. Otherwise ring the Police Flying Squad (☎ 10111) to get directions to the nearest hospital.

The Yeoville Medical Centre on Rockey St stays open every night until 9 pm. There is a pharmacy (☎ 883 7520) in Sandton City Mall that is open until 10.30 pm daily.

Emergency The emergency numbers in Jo'burg are: ambulance (☎ 403 4227); fire brigade (☎ 999); and police (☎ 10111).

The phones at the Battered Women and Rape Crisis Centre (☎ 642 4345) are staffed daily from 6 am to 10 pm. There's a Lifeline service (☎ 728 1347).

Dangers & Annoyances Personal security in Jo'burg is an issue on the minds of most travellers coming in and out of the city. The amount of violent crime is pretty scary; to avoid getting paranoid don't read the statistics in the local newspapers! Daylight muggings in the city centre and other inner suburbs, notably Hillbrow, are not uncommon and you must be constantly on your guard. You'd be crazy to walk around central Jo'burg at night – if you arrive after dark and don't have a car, catch a taxi to your final destination.

Yeoville has taken on a much seedier edge in recent times and the 'far east' end of Rockey St is definitely dodgy; avoid it if you can.

Follow the usual rules: never advertise your wealth or your tourist status; look as if you know where you are going; don't carry anything (even in a money belt) that can't easily be replaced; and use your hotel or hostel safe.

If you have a car, make sure your doors are locked and your windows wound up and when you're at traffic lights leave a car's length between you and the vehicle in front so that you can drive away if necessary. Avoid driving at night and fork out the extra cash to put your car in a secure parking area.

If you do get held up, don't be a hero. If your skin is white, the muggers will assume that you are a South African, that you are carrying a gun and that you will try to kill them. Don't scare them into shooting you first.

If you want (or have) to spend some time in Jo'burg, talk to hostel/hotel managers and, of course, other travellers. Educate yourself on what places are OK and what places are off-limits. As a general rule avoid the city centre for at least the first couple of days you are here.

Remember that anyone can get unlucky, but if you use a bit of common sense you'll significantly reduce your chances of becoming a statistic in the newspapers.

Museum Africa

The museum (☎ 833 5624) at 121 Bree St, next to the Market Theatre, has outstanding exhibitions on Jo'burg's recent history, a large collection of rock art, and various other exhibits.

It is open daily except Monday and entry is R5/2 for adults/children.

Johannesburg Art Gallery

This gallery (☎ 725 3180), on the Klein St side of Joubert Park, is housed in a lovely little building and has exhibitions featuring contemporary work and retrospectives of black artists. There's a good coffee shop. Entry is free and it's open from 10 am to 5 pm daily, except Monday.

Market Theatre

The Market Theatre complex (☎ 832 1641) on Bree St, to the west of the city centre, has live theatre venues, an art gallery, a coffee shop, some interesting shops, a pleasant pub and Kippie's Bar (an excellent jazz venue).

There's usually some interesting theatre here – check out the *Weekly Mail & Guardian* entertainment section for more information.

Places to Stay

Some of the places to stay in central Jo'burg are excellent value but that's because crime has scared away customers; unless you need to stay in the city centre, you're better off in the 'burbs.

An alternative, particularly if you plan on spending some time in Jo'burg, is house

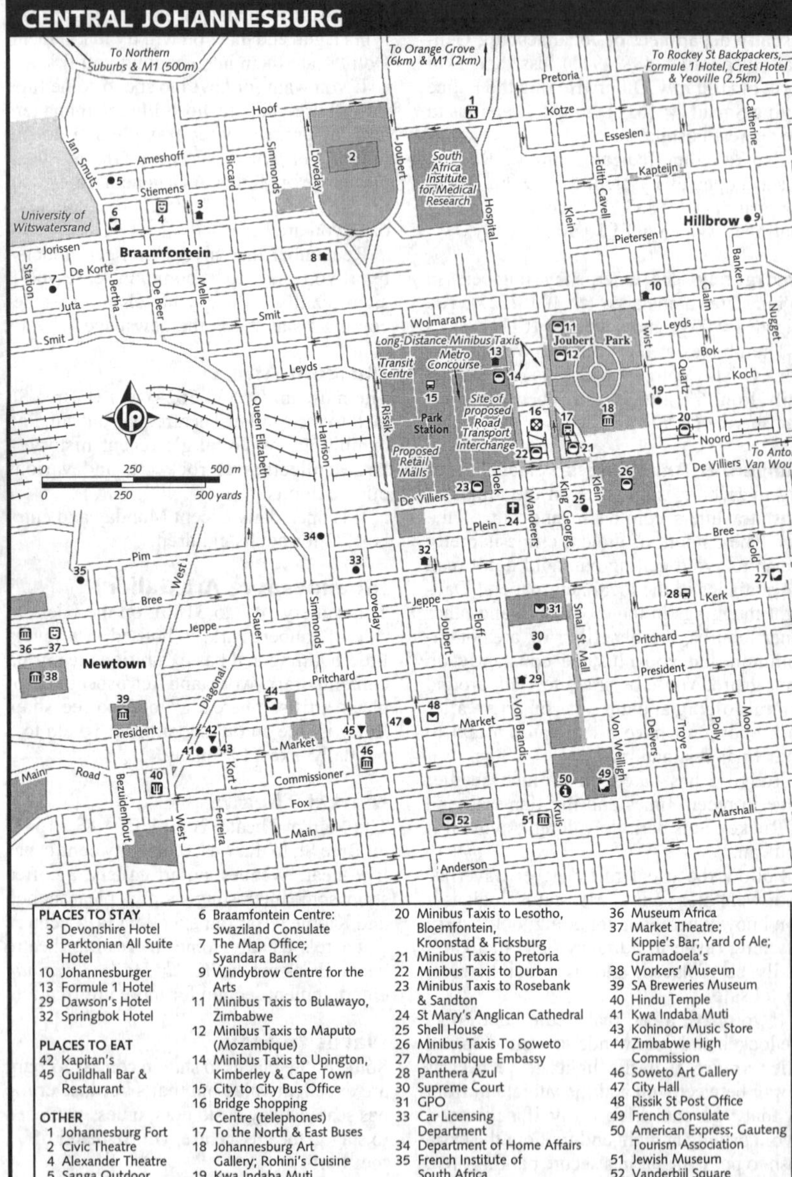

CENTRAL JOHANNESBURG
To Northern Suburbs & M1 (500m)
To Orange Grove (6km) & M1 (2km)
To Rockey St Backpackers, Formule 1 Hotel, Crest Hotel & Yeoville (2.5km)
Pretoria
Kotze
Hoof
Esselen
Kapteijn
Ameshoff
Stiemens
Jan Smuts
Biccard
Simmonds
Loveday
Joubert
South Africa Institute for Medical Research
Hospital
Edith Cavell
Klein
Catherine
University of Witswatersrand
Hillbrow
Pietersen
Jorissen
Braamfontein
De Korte
Station
Juta
Bertha
De Beer
Melle
Smit
Banket
Claim
Nugget
Wolmarans
Long-Distance Minibus Taxis
Metro Concourse
Transit Centre
Joubert Park
Twist
Leyds
Bok
Koch
Quartz
Rissik
Park Station
Site of proposed Road Transport Interchange
Proposed Retail Malls
Queen Elizabeth
Harrison
Noord
To Anton Van Wouw
De Villiers
0 250 500 m
0 250 500 yards
Hoek
Wanderers
King George
Plein
Bree
Gold
Pim
West
Kerk
Jeppe
Sauer
Eloff
Small St Mall
Pritchard
President
Newtown
Diagonal
Market
Von Brandis
Von Weilligh
Delvers
Troye
Polly
Mooi
Main Road
Commissioner
Kort
Bezuidenhout
Fox
Main
Ferreira
Kruis
Marshall
Anderson
PLACES TO STAY
3 Devonshire Hotel
8 Parktonian All Suite Hotel
10 Johannesburger
13 Formule 1 Hotel
29 Dawson's Hotel
32 Springbok Hotel
PLACES TO EAT
42 Kapitan's
45 Guildhall Bar & Restaurant
OTHER
1 Johannesburg Fort
2 Civic Theatre
4 Alexander Theatre
5 Sanga Outdoor
6 Braamfontein Centre: Swaziland Consulate
7 The Map Office; Syandara Bank
9 Windybrow Centre for the Arts
11 Minibus Taxis to Bulawayo, Zimbabwe
12 Minibus Taxis to Maputo (Mozambique)
14 Minibus Taxis to Upington, Kimberley & Cape Town
15 City to City Bus Office
16 Bridge Shopping Centre (telephones)
17 To the North & East Buses
18 Johannesburg Art Gallery; Rohini's Cuisine
19 Kwa Indaba Muti
20 Minibus Taxis to Lesotho, Bloemfontein, Kroonstad & Ficksburg
21 Minibus Taxis to Pretoria
22 Minibus Taxis to Durban
23 Minibus Taxis to Rosebank & Sandton
24 St Mary's Anglican Cathedral
25 Shell House
26 Minibus Taxis To Soweto
27 Mozambique Embassy
28 Panthera Azul
30 Supreme Court
31 GPO
33 Car Licensing Department
34 Department of Home Affairs
35 French Institute of South Africa
36 Museum Africa
37 Market Theatre; Kippie's Bar; Yard of Ale; Gramadoela's
38 Workers' Museum
39 SA Breweries Museum
40 Hindu Temple
41 Kwa Indaba Muti
43 Kohinoor Music Store
44 Zimbabwe High Commission
46 Soweto Art Gallery
47 City Hall
48 Rissik St Post Office
49 French Consulate
50 American Express; Gauteng Tourism Association
51 Jewish Museum
52 Vanderbijl Square

sitting. House & Home Sitting Services (☎ 789 1250, fax 787 6645, ⓔ housesit@netactive.co.za), at 17 Sylvan Place, 96 Hendrik Verwoerd Dr, Ferndale, provides an excellent and affordable service. It costs R70 to join and then R15/23 per day for one/two people, for sits of up to three months. A deposit is also required. Backpackers are accepted.

Places to Stay – Budget

Hostels Many hostels will pick you up from the airport or Park Station. If you make an arrangement to be picked up, make sure you stick to it so the hostel people don't make a wasted journey. The Baz Bus (see Getting There & Away later in this section) drops off at most hostels. The list below is a small selection; there are plenty more to choose from.

Rockey St Backpackers *(☎ 648 8786, fax 648 8423, 34 Regent St, Yeoville)* isn't on Rockey St, but it is just a short and (during the day) safe walk away. The management is friendly and very knowledgeable, the atmosphere is good and it's clean. Dorms go for R40 and great double rooms cost from R120.

The ***Explorers Club Lodge*** *(☎ 648 7138, 9 Innes St, Observatory)* is recommended. It's an old place with a large garden and swimming pool. A dorm bed is R45 and singles/doubles cost R100/120; add R20 for a private bathroom. You can also pitch a tent for R30.

One of the best places around, if a little far from the city, is ***Backpackers Ritz*** *(☎ 325 7125, 1A North Road, Dunkeld West)*, an imposing mansion with spacious grounds, friendly staff and a good bar. This place is huge! Excellent dorms cost R45 and rooms are R90/130.

Kew Youth Hostel & Backpackers *(☎ 887 9072, 5 Johannesburg Rd, Kew)* has a good pool room and separate male/female dorms (the female dorms have private bathrooms). A bunk bed will set you back R40, a double R120, or you can camp for R35 per tent.

A short walk from Bruma Lake, ***Eastgate Backpackers*** *(☎ 616 2741, 41 Hans Pirow Rd)* draws a groovy travelling clique; you come here to shoot pool, play tunes and chill out. Dorms are R30 and doubles R90 (R120 with bathroom).

Hotels The ***Crest Hotel*** *(☎ 642 7641, 7 Abel Rd, Berea)* right on the edge of Hillbrow is comfortable. The well-maintained rooms have phones and there is secure parking. Singles/doubles cost only R75/105 – a real bargain.

Formule 1 *(☎ 484 5551, 1 Mitchell St, Berea)* off Louis Botha Ave is a good overnight stop. This chain of hotels is devoid of character but offers exceptional value, particularly if there are three of you. The price is R149 for one, two or three people. There is another Formule 1 at Park Station.

On the corner of Von Brandis St, ***Dawson's Hotel*** *(☎ 337 5010, 117 President St)* is an old-style hotel with a restaurant and a couple of bars. Rooms start at just R100 from Sunday to Thursday and R140 on weekends.

Places to Stay – Mid-Range

B&Bs The Bed & Breakfast organisation (☎ 482 2206/7, fax 726 6915) has members in and around the wealthy northern suburbs. The accommodation is exceptionally good value – prices start at about R160/260.

The Portfolio organisation (☎ 880 3414, fax 788 4802) also lists high-quality B&Bs in the northern suburbs.

Hotels In the city centre, one of the few old-style small hotels to maintain standards is the ***Springbok Hotel*** *(☎ 337 8336)*, on the corner of Joubert and Bree Sts. It offers frilly singles/doubles for R130/230.

Johannesburger *(☎ 725 3753, 60 Twist St)* is under new management and they're keen to attract business; ask if they have any special deals going. When we dropped by, rooms were R120 and luxury suites R250.

North-west of the city centre, the ***Linden Hotel*** *(☎ 782 4905)* on the corner of Seventh St and Fourth Ave, Linden, is a charming hotel, seemingly out of place in the 21st century. Rooms start at R250/290 with breakfast. They also have frequent specials.

The ***Duneden Protea Hotel*** *(☎ 453 2002, 46 Van Riebeeck Ave, Edenvale)* is close to shops and the airport but not to the city; rooms go for R295/315.

There are good-value places in the City Lodge group, which charges about R304/370 for rooms. These include: ***City Lodge Sandton Morningside*** *(☎ 884 9500)* on the corner of Rivonia and Hill Rds, Sandton, close to shops; ***City Lodge Randburg*** *(☎ 706 7800)* on the corner of Main Rd and Peter Place, Bryanston West, Randburg; and ***City Lodge JIA*** *(☎ 392 1750),* out near the airport on Sandvale Rd, Edenvale. Check out the City Lodge Web site: www.citylodge.co.za.

Also look out for the comfortable and cheaper ***Town Lodges*** (about R246/284 for rooms), administered by the same group.

Places to Stay – Top End

The ***Parktonian All Suite Hotel*** *(☎ 403 5740, 120 De Korte St, Braamfontein)* charges R485/570 for singles/doubles, including breakfast. There are weekend specials if you stay more than one night.

The ***Devonshire Hotel*** *(☎ 339 5611)* on the corner of Melle and Jorissen Sts is a comfortable, medium-sized hotel with undercover parking. Rooms cost about R340/390, including breakfast. There are weekend specials available.

The four-star ***Holiday Inn Crowne Plaza Sunnyside Park*** *(☎ 643 7226, 2 York Rd, Parktown)* is recommended. The entrance is actually off Carse O'Gowrie Rd. It's an old-style hotel in attractive gardens. Rooms go for R535/610. It's not far from the city, so basing yourself here and getting around by taxi wouldn't be too expensive.

The ***Cullinan Hotel & Executive Suites*** *(☎ 884 8544)* on Katherine Drive is luxurious and not bad value; standard rooms cost R465/560 and luxury rooms cost R640/840.

Places to Eat

Jo'burg is packed with places to eat but unfortunately for visitors, especially those without cars, most are in the northern suburbs.

City Centre There's a shortage of cafes and cheap eating places in the city. Just finding somewhere to sit down is a major problem.

Guildhall Bar & Restaurant *(☎ 836 5600)* on the corner of Harrison and Market Sts has tables on a balcony, offering a chance to get off the streets and do a spot of people-watching.

At one of the few remaining Indian streets, ***Kapitan's*** *(☎ 834 8048, upstairs 11A Kort St)* is a cheerful, old-fashioned restaurant serving authentic Indian food. Vegetable curry is R20, meat curries are R25 and chicken vindaloo or biryani is R32.

Vegetarians can try ***Rohini's Cuisine*** in the Jo'burg Art Gallery.

Gramadoela's *(☎ 838 6960)* in the Market Theatre complex is probably the best restaurant in the city. The menu is superb, with Cape Dutch/Malay specialities. Expect to pay about R60 for a filling meal.

Yeoville With crime worsening, most places in Yeoville have either moved or closed and the trendy restaurant scene has been driven out to Melville.

On the corner of Fortesque Rd and Raleigh St, at the back of the courtyard, is ***Charros Curry***, a good place to eat simple but authentic Indian food. Curries are about R20 (vegetarian R16).

Fisherman's Village It's worth considering an expedition to Fisherman's Village, a kitsch South African version of a Mediterranean village, beside Bruma Lake. There are a number of popular, though relatively pricey restaurants. Fisherman's Village is about 4km east of Yeoville.

Melville Just north-west of Braamfontein, Melville is the hip place to see and be seen. You'll find a good selection of restaurants on Seventh St.

Between Second and Third Aves, ***Bass Line*** *(☎ 482 6915)*, a fine jazz venue, has meals for about R25, or R35 for steaks.

Global Wrapps serves vegetarian pittas such as teriyaki vegetable for R11 and milano rice and salad with pesto sauce for R12.

Not far away, ***Horatio's*** *(☎ 726 2247, 10 Seventh St)* has great seafood meals for about R50. It's open for lunch and dinner on weekdays and for dinner on Sunday nights.

Koala Blu *(☎ 482 2477, 9C 7th St)* actually serves Thai food, so don't expect to see kangaroo on the menu! Tasty mains at R45 are good value.

Entertainment

The best guide to entertainment is the *Weekly Mail & Guardian* (R5); you can't do without a copy.

For entertainment bookings, contact Computicket (☎ 445 8000). Since it has everything on its system, staff can also give advice about what's on.

Pubs & Bars There are late-night bars and music venues in Yeoville, mostly on Rockey St and the western end of Raleigh St; this area is still the best place for 'alternative' music.

Rockerfella's, a standard watering hole, is one place where the less conservative citizens hang out.

On a hot evening the courtyard in the ***Time Square Courtyard***, on the corner of Fortesque Rd and Raleigh/Rockey St, is a good place for a beer.

Radium Beer Hall *(282 Louis Botha Ave, Orange Grove)* is one of the few neighbourhood pubs left in Jo'burg.

In the city centre, the classic ***Yard of Ale*** in the Market Theatre complex has reopened and is worth checking out.

Music & Dancing At the Market Theatre complex, ***Kippie's Bar*** *(☎ 833 3316)* is one of the best places to see South African jazz talent; entry is R30.

The ***Bass Line*** *(☎ 482 6915)* on Seventh St in Melville has jazz nightly except Sunday. On Friday and Saturday the emphasis is on blues and the cover charge is R15.

To join a student crowd, check out ***Wings Beat Bar*** *(☎ 339 4492, 8 Ameshof St, Braamfontein)*. There are tunes Tuesday to Sunday and entry is a paltry R10.

One of the best venues for interesting music and a mixed crowd is the ***House of Tandoor*** *(☎ 487 1569)* at the east end of Rockey St, Yeoville.

There's usually something on Wednesday and Saturday nights, with a cover charge of about R15 to R30. It is also a fine bar; if there isn't a band playing, head upstairs.

Jahnito's Live House, further down at 43 Rockey St, is free and has a wide range of music, both recorded and live.

Theatre The ***Market Theatre*** *(☎ 832 1641)* complex on Bree St is the most important venue for live theatre. A visit is worthwhile – some of the productions are outstanding.

Shopping

Shopaholics would do well to start in the Smal St Mall, but if you're a serious buyer, make an expedition to Rosebank Mall in Rosebank or Sandton City Mall in Sandton, an enormous and plush shopping centre a half-hour drive north of the city centre.

A handy shopping centre is the big Eastgate Mall, off the N12 just east of Bruma Lake.

One of the best places to buy ethnic/African music is Kohinoor; there are a number of branches, including one at 54 Market St.

If you want to remind yourself that you're still in Africa, visit one of the *muti* (traditional medicine) shops, which sell herbs and potions prescribed by a *sangoma* (witchdoctor). Kwa Indaba is at two locations: 14 Diagonal St, and also on the corner of Koch and Twist St, opposite the Art Gallery.

Crafts There are some good shops where you can buy traditional carvings, beadwork, jewellery and fertility dolls, although prices in Jo'burg are high.

Street vendors set up on the footpaths around town. There's some awful rubbish, but there's good stuff as well. Bargaining is expected. At Bruma Lake there's lots of craft sellers but they mostly sell kitsch.

Gold Reef City Arts & Crafts at Gold Reef City, south of Jo'burg, has a fine collection of interesting crafts and antiques from all over Africa, and they're well priced. It's along the street from the more obvious Egoli Village craft shop.

The market in the northern suburb of Rosebank, held every Sunday in the upper-level car park of the Rosebank Mall, is good for all kinds of things, but especially for traditional crafts. There is a stall selling San crafts and genuine mohair products from Lesotho (at very reasonable prices) that you won't find anywhere else.

Getting There & Away

Air Johannesburg International Airport (JIA; ☎ 333 6504, 975 9963 for flight inquiries) is South Africa's major international and domestic airport (for details on domestic fares and destinations, see the South Africa Getting Around section).

Numerous international airlines have offices in Jo'burg and the following list is a small sample – check the Yellow Pages for other addresses.

Air France (☎ 880 8055) 1st floor, Oxford Manor, 196 Oxford Rd, Illovo
Air Namibia (☎ 442 4461) Lower Mezzanine, Level South, JIA
British Airways (☎ 441 8600) 158 Jan Smuts Ave, Rosebank
KLM-Royal Dutch Airlines (☎ 881 9600) Sable Place, 1A Stan Rd, off Grayston Drive, Sandton
Qantas Airways (☎ 884 5300) 3rd floor, Village Walk, on the corner of Rivonia Rd and Maude Sts, Sandown
SAA (☎ 978 1111 reservations, 978 3370 international terminal, 978 3119 domestic terminal)

Bus International bus services leave Jo'burg for Botswana, Zambia, Mozambique and Zimbabwe (for more details, see South Africa's Getting There & Away chapter).

The main long-distance bus lines (national and international) depart from and arrive at the Park Station transit centre. There are booking counters for Translux (☎ 774 3313), Greyhound (☎ 830 1301) and Intercape (☎ 333 2312) and a Jo'burg information desk (☎ 337 6650) in the station. City to City, the inexpensive government bus service, leaves from behind the Formule 1 Hotel.

Don't forget the Baz Bus (☎ 021-439 2323 in Cape Town or book through hostels). One major advantage of the Baz Bus in Jo'burg is its door-to-door service, dropping at most hostels. This avoids the hassle (and danger) of finding your way to a hostel from the bus station.

North Several services run north up the N1 via Pretoria. For example, Translux has at least one bus each day to Beitbridge (and on to Harare) via Pietersburg/Polokwane (R105), Louis Trichardt (R115) and Messina (R125).

City to City runs daily to Venda (Sibasa) for R60, and also to Giyani/Malamulele via Pietersburg (R55). These services also stop at the major towns along the N1.

North Link Tours (☎ 015-291 1867 in Pietersburg/Polokwane) runs a bus service between Jo'burg and Phalaborwa (R140) via, Pietersburg/Polokwane and Tzaneen.

Kruger National Park The nearest large town to Kruger is Nelspruit, and Greyhound runs there daily (R120, five hours). Translux also stops at Nelspruit (R115) on its run to Maputo (Mozambique).

City to City runs a slow service to Nelspruit for R45. The trip takes about seven hours and continues on to Acornhoek via Hazyview (R60, eight hours). Hazyview is much closer to Kruger than Nelspruit, and the backpackers hostels there organise trips into Kruger.

KwaZulu-Natal Greyhound has four daily buses to Durban (R140, seven hours). It also has a useful service running to Durban via Zululand and Richards Bay on the KwaZulu-Natal north coast. Translux has at least one daily bus running down the N3 to Durban (R110, 7½ hours).

South Coast Translux runs from Jo'burg/ Pretoria to East London (R220, 11 hours) daily and also has five services weekly to Port Elizabeth (R220, 10 hours). Greyhound has overnight buses from Jo'burg to Port Elizabeth (R250, 14½ hours).

Translux runs to Knysna (R235, 17 hours) via Kimberley or Bloemfontein then Oudtshoorn (R220), Mossel Bay (R220) and George (R220).

City to City runs to Umtata, the closest large town to Port St Johns and Coffee Bay daily at 6 pm (Tuesday and Friday at 7 pm) for R95.

Cape Town Translux has at least one bus daily running from Jo'burg/Pretoria to Cape Town (R320, 18 hours) via Bloemfontein.

Also, five services (not Tuesday and Thursday) run via Kimberley (17½ hours to Cape Town). From Jo'burg to Bloemfontein costs R155; to Kimberley it's R160.

Greyhound has buses daily to Cape Town via Bloemfontein (R350). From Jo'burg to Bloemfontein costs R180. Greyhound also has a daily express bus to Kimberley (R120).

Intercape has four services a week to Upington (R200, 9½ hours). From Upington there is a connection to Cape Town (R160, nine hours).

West City Link (☎ 333 4412) runs twice a day to Mafikeng for R70. Another option to Mafikeng is Explorer Coachlines (☎ 012-328 3231 in Pretoria).

Intercape runs to Upington and from there to Windhoek (Namibia). There is no direct connection between the two services.

Minibus Taxi The main long-distance minibus taxi ranks are between Park Station and Joubert Park, mainly on Wanderers and King George Sts. Despite the apparent chaos, the ranks are well organised – ask for the queue marshal.

Some destinations and approximate fares from Jo'burg include: Pretoria (R12); Manzini in Swaziland (R65); Nelspruit (R70); Pietersburg/Polokwane (R70); Maseru in Lesotho (R75); Durban (R80); Kimberley (R80); and Cape Town (R190).

As well as these minibus taxis, which leave when they are full, there are a few door-to-door services which you can book. Durban (about R130 from Jo'burg) is well served. Ask about these at hostels.

Train Trains from Jo'burg's Park Station travel to most of South Africa's major cities as well as to Gabarone (Botswana), Bulawayo (Zimbabwe) and Maputo (Mozambique; change at Komatipoort). For more details, see the Getting Around section in this chapter.

There are sometimes 25% discounts available on train tickets, making them very competitive with the major bus services. Contact Main Line Passenger Services (☎ 773 2944) for information.

On the main concourse at Jo'burg station there's a Spoornet Information Office, but it doesn't have any information; go to the Main Line ticket office further along. It's open from 7.30 am to 5 pm weekdays and until 1 pm Saturday.

The station's left-luggage department is open from 6 am to 7 pm daily (7 am to 6 pm on Sunday). For more information on trains from Jo'burg, see the Getting Around section in this chapter.

Car The major companies have counters at the airport and offices around the city. Operators and their toll-free numbers include: Avis (☎ 0800 021 111); Budget (☎ 0800 016 622); Imperial (☎ 0800 131 000); Europcar (☎ 0800 011 344); and Tempest (☎ 0800 031 666).

There aren't many budget-priced rental companies; your best bet is to ask at a hostel, which will often negotiate special deals on your behalf. This can be a lot cheaper than going to the rental agencies themselves.

For details on purchasing a car, see the Getting Around the Region chapter.

Hitching Hitching is *not* recommended, especially around Jo'burg, but inevitably some will do it anyway. Heading north, a popular place to begin hitching is on the N1 near the Killarney Mall shopping centre, a couple of kilometres north-west of Yeoville. The N12 running east towards Kruger National Park begins just east of Eastgate Mall. Heading south on the N1 (to Cape Town, for example) you could try your luck on one of the freeway on-ramps.

Also check on hostel notice boards for details of free or shared-cost lifts.

Getting Around

To/From the Airport Between 5 am and 10 pm, buses run every half-hour between Johannesburg International Airport and Park Station transit centre. Journey time is about 25 minutes and the fare is about R40. There's also the Magic Bus (☎ 884 3957) which costs more but drops off at the more expensive hotels. Hire taxis aren't cheap (around R100).

Buses also run from the airport to Pretoria. See Getting There & Away in the Pretoria section for details.

Bus For inquiries about local bus services, call ☎ 838 2125, or visit the information counter on Vanderbijl Square. Most services stop by 7 pm and most fares are about R4. Route Nos 5 (Parktown, Houghton, Rosebank and Illovo), 22 (Yeoville and Bruma) and 75 (Braamfontein, Auckland Park and Melville) are useful.

The buses that run out to Sandton are not part of the municipal fleet; they're operated by Padco (☎ 474 2634). The Padco buses leave the city centre from the corner of Kruis and Commissioner Sts.

Minibus Taxi Fares differ depending on the route, but R3 will get you around the inner suburbs and the city centre. It's easy to get a minibus taxi into the city centre and, if you're waiting at a bus stop, a minibus will probably arrive before the bus does. Getting a minibus taxi home from the city is more difficult. If you're heading for Yeoville, try Eloff St.

Train For inquiries about Metro trains, call ☎ 773 5878 or visit the information office in the Park Station concourse. There has been a serious problem with violent crime on the metropolitan system, mostly on lines connecting with black townships. In recent times the line between Pretoria and Jo'burg has been particularly bad. Be careful.

Taxi There are hire taxi ranks in the city centre, at the airport and on Kenmere St near the corner of Rockey St in Yeoville. Taxis have meters but once you get an idea of how much a trip should cost, try agreeing on a price rather than using the meter. Flash Taxis (☎ 886 6816) is a reputable company.

PRETORIA

☎ 012

Although the two cities are less than 60km apart, Pretoria's history bears no relation to Jo'burg's and they have very different atmospheres. Pretoria is the administrative capital and is a more relaxed place that in recent times has been shedding its conservative image. The Sotho-speaking citizens call the city *Tshwane*.

History

The Great Trek reached its logical conclusion in the early 1850s when the British granted independence to the Zuid-Afrikaansche Republiek (ZAR; South African Republic) north of the Vaal River, and to the Free State between the Orange and Vaal Rivers.

In 1853 two farms on the Apies River were bought as the site for the republic's capital. The ZAR was a shaky institution though. There were ongoing wars with the black tribes and violent disputes among the Boers themselves. Pretoria, which was named after Andries Pretorius, hero of the Battle of Blood River, was the scene of fighting during the 1863–69 Boer Civil War.

The discovery of gold on the Witwatersrand in the late 1880s revolutionised the situation. A small community of farmers suddenly controlled some of the richest real estate in the world.

Orientation

The main east-west road is Church (Kerk) St which, at 26km, is claimed to be one of the longest straight streets in the world. Fortunately most of the sights, decent hotels and restaurants in the city centre are not far apart. Church St runs through Church Square (although traffic is diverted), the historic centre of the city, and east to the suburb of Arcadia, home of most of the hotels and embassies, as well as the Union buildings.

Information

Tourist Offices The excellent Pretoria Tourism information centre (☎ 337 4337) is on Church Square and is open from 7.30 am to 4 pm weekdays. Check out its Web site at www.pretoria.co.za; also try www.pta-online.co.za. The information centre can be hard to spot as it has no external sign. Ask at Cafe Riche, as it's only a few doors up from there. The old Tourist Rendevous has closed.

The National Parks Board head office (☎ 343 1991, fax 343 0905, PO Box 787, Pretoria 0001) is at 643 Leyds St, Muckleneuk, not far from the university to the south-east of the city centre.

Immigration Office Applications for visa extensions should be made to the Department of Home Affairs (☎ 324 1860) in the Sentrakor building on Pretorius St (near Church Square).

Money AmEx (☎ 320 0665) is in the Tramshed complex on the corner of Van der Walt and Schoeman Sts. There's also a Nedbank here. Rennies Travel (☎ 320 2240) has a few branches, including one in the Sanlam Centre on the corner of Andries and Pretorius Sts and another in Brooklyn shopping centre.

Post & Communications The GPO is on the corner of Pretorius and Van der Walt Sts, and is open from 8.00 am to 4.30 pm weekdays, and 8 am to noon Saturday.

Odyssey Internet Cafe at 1066 Burnett St, Hatfield, has email access for R8 per hour. Word of Mouth backpackers (see Places to Stay later in this section) also has online terminals.

Travel Agencies There is a list of agencies in the free *Pretoria: Window on Africa,* available at the Pretoria Tourism Information Centre. The hostels in Pretoria take bookings for many budget tours; recommended are Word of Mouth and North South Backpackers (see Places to Stay later in this section). Another possibility is Rennies Travel (see Money earlier in this section).

Medical Services Pretoria Academic Hospital (☎ 354 1000) is north-west of the Union buildings on Dr Savage Rd. There are numerous chemists around town. The pharmacy on the north-western corner of Esselen and Collings Sts stays open until 10 pm.

Emergency The emergency phone numbers in Pretoria are: ambulance (☎ 10177); fire brigade (☎ 326 0111); police (☎ 10111); and Life Line (☎ 343 8888).

Dangers & Annoyances Pretoria is definitely safer and more relaxed than Jo'burg, but it's a big city so reasonable precautions should be observed. The square roughly formed by Pretorius, Boom, Andries and du Toit Sts has a bad reputation for mugging.

Due to concern that Pretoria was going the same way as Jo'burg, the Tourist Protection Unit (☎ 082-653 3039) was introduced. Measures such as these give the impression of a greater degree of safety on the streets.

Church Square

Church Square, the heart of Pretoria, is surrounded by imposing public buildings. In the centre, Paul Kruger looks disapprovingly at office workers lounging on the grass. In the early days, Boers from the surrounding countryside would gather in the square every three months for *achtmaals* (communion).

Union Buildings

The Union buildings are an impressive red sandstone construction surrounded by gardens. They are the government's administrative headquarters. The buildings are quite a long walk from the city centre, or you can catch just about any bus heading east on Church St and walk up through the gardens.

Museums

Paul Kruger House A short walk west of Church Square, on Church St, the residence of Paul Kruger has been turned into a museum. Some of the rooms have been restored to their original form, and others chronicle his extraordinary life and times.

The house is open from 8.30 am to 4 pm Monday to Saturday and 9 am to 4 pm Sunday. Entry is R7/5 for adults/children.

Transvaal Museum of Anthropology and Geology This museum has traditional static displays of animals and birds. If you are interested in South Africa's fauna, particularly its birdlife, a visit is worthwhile. The museum is on Paul Kruger St between Visagie and Minnaar Sts. It's open from 9 am to 5 pm Monday to Saturday and 11 am to 5 pm Sunday; entry is R6/3.50 for adults/children.

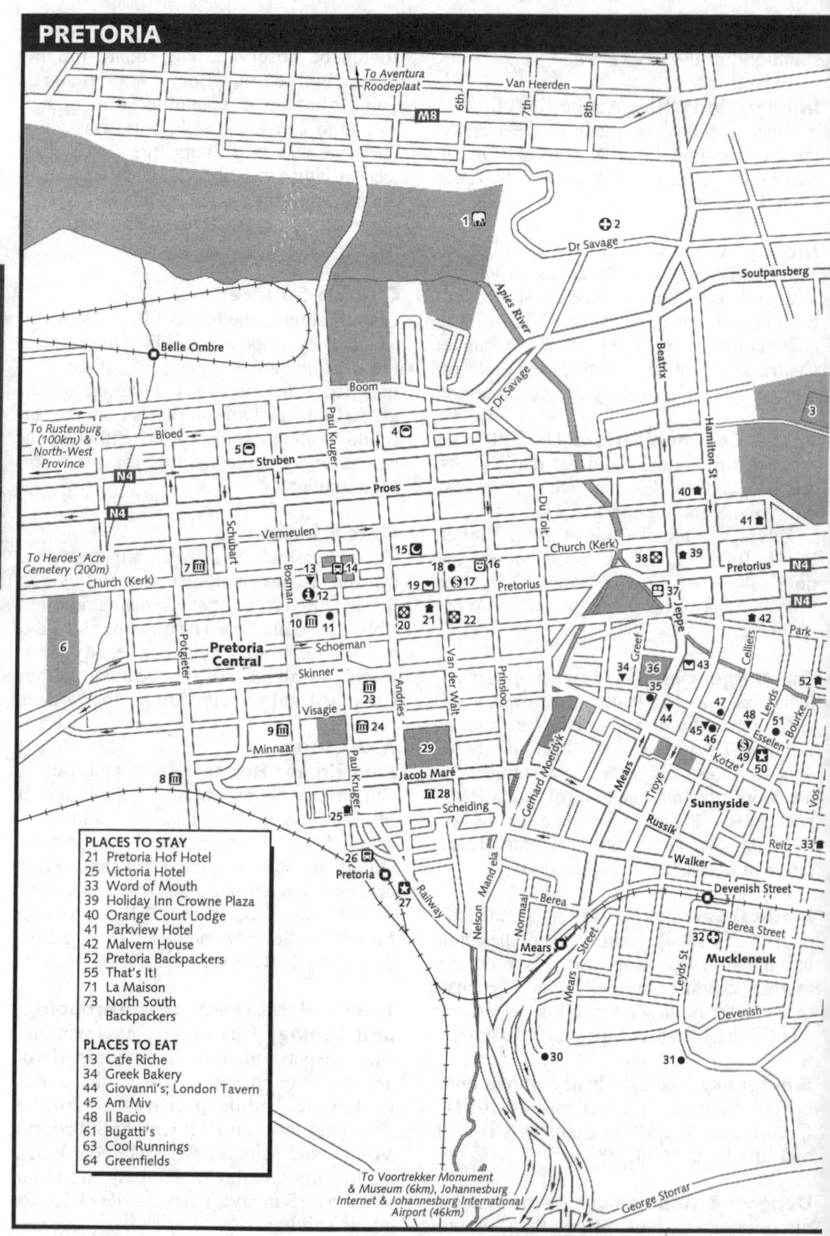

PRETORIA
To Aventura Roodeplaat
Van Heerden
M8
6th
7th
8th
Dr Savage
Soutpansberg
Apies River
Belle Ombre
Beatrix
Dr Savage
Boom
Hamilton St
To Rustenburg (100km) & North-West Province
Bloed
Struben
Paul Kruger
N4
Proes
Du Toit
Schubart
Vermeulen
Church (Kerk)
Pretorius
To Heroes' Acre Cemetery (200m)
Church (Kerk)
Bosman
Pretorius
Jeppe
Park
Celliers
Pretoria Central
Schoeman
Skinner
Van der Walt
Prinsloo
Greef
Potgieter
Visagie
Andries
Leyds
Bourke
Esselen
Minnaar
Paul Kruger
Gerhard Moerdyk
Mears
Troye
Kotze
Jacob Maré
Scheiding
Sunnyside
Russik
Reitz
Vos
Walker
Pretoria
Railway
Mandela
Nelson
Normaal
Berea
Devenish Street
Berea Street
Mears
Mears Street
Muckleneuk
Leyds St
Devenish
To Voortrekker Monument & Museum (6km), Johannesburg Internet & Johannesburg International Airport (46km)
George Storrar
PLACES TO STAY
21 Pretoria Hof Hotel
25 Victoria Hotel
33 Word of Mouth
39 Holiday Inn Crowne Plaza
40 Orange Court Lodge
41 Parkview Hotel
42 Malvern House
52 Pretoria Backpackers
55 That's It!
71 La Maison
73 North South Backpackers
PLACES TO EAT
13 Cafe Riche
34 Greek Bakery
44 Giovanni's; London Tavern
45 Am Miv
48 Il Bacio
61 Bugatti's
63 Cool Runnings
64 Greenfields

PRETORIA

OTHER

1 National Zoological Gardens
2 Pretoria Academic Hospital
3 Union Buildings
4 Long-distance Minibus Taxis
5 Long-distance Minibus Taxis
6 Showgrounds
7 Paul Kruger House
8 Correctional Service Museum
9 National Museum of Culture
10 Police Museum
11 Department of Home Affairs
12 Pretoria Tourism Information Centre
14 Church Square; Local Bus Terminus
15 Mosque
16 State Theatre
17 ABSA Bank
18 JG Strijdom Square
19 GPO
20 Sanlam Centre; Rennies Travel
22 Tramshed Complex; AmEx; Curry Palace
23 Science & Technology Museum
24 Transvaal Museum of Anthropology & Geology
26 Greyhound, Translux Intercape Terminal
27 Police Station
28 Melrose House
29 Burgers Park
30 UNISA
31 National Parks Board Head Office
32 Zuid Afrikaans Clinic
35 Metro Cine 1,2,3; Camping Centre (Backpack & Tent Repair)
36 Sunnypark Shopping Centre
37 Sterland Cinemas
38 Dion Shopping Centre
43 Post Office
46 Duplica Printing
47 Pharmacy
49 ABSA Bank
50 Police Station
51 Shoprite
53 Pretoria Art Museum
54 Swaziland Embassy
56 US Embassy
57 Australian Embassy
58 Loftus Versfeld
59 University of Pretoria
60 Petrol Station
62 Hatfield Galleries: Odyssey Internet Cafe; Tings & Times
65 STA Branch
66 ABSA Bankteller
67 Hatfield Square; McGinty's
68 Post Office
69 Tequila Sunrise
70 Hatfield Plaza
72 New Zealand Embassy
74 Sophiatown Jazz Cafe
75 Magnolia Dell 'Moonlight' Market
76 Austin Roberts Bird Sanctuary
77 Tinseltown
78 Brooklyn Shopping Centre; Rennies Travel

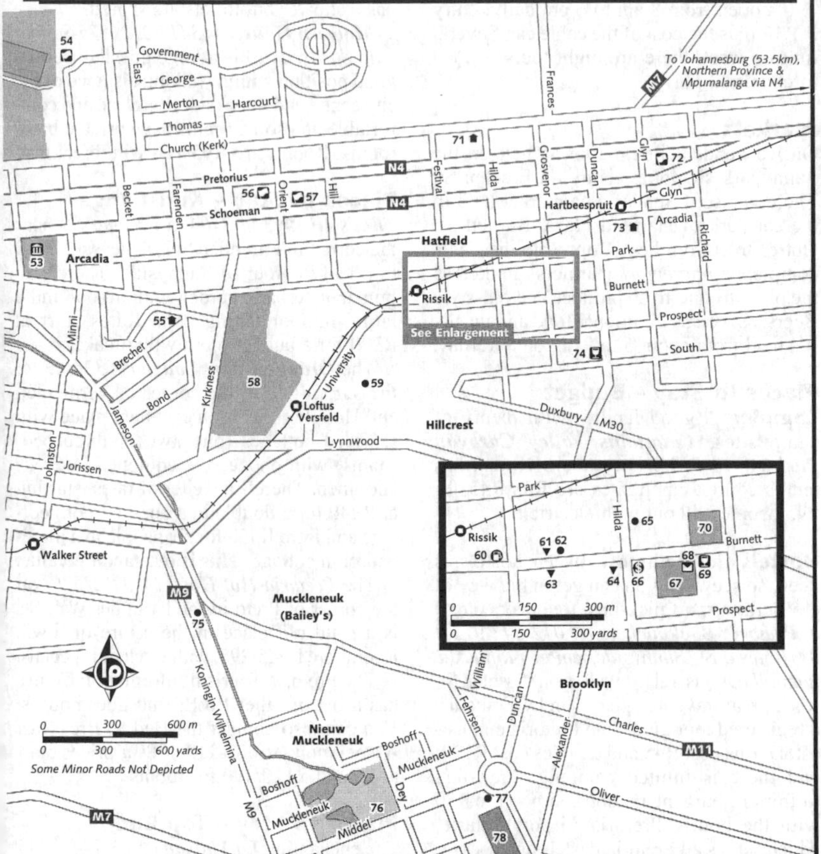

To Johannesburg (53.5km), Northern Province & Mpumalanga via N4

See Enlargement

0 150 300 m
0 150 300 yards

0 300 600 m
0 300 600 yards

Some Minor Roads Not Depicted

Pretoria Art Museum In Arcadia Park, off Schoeman St a kilometre or so east of the centre, this museum (☎ 344 1807) displays South African art from all periods. It's open from 10 am to 5 pm Tuesday to Saturday (8 pm on Wednesday) and noon to 5 pm Sunday. Entry is R3.

National Zoological Gardens

The zoo is quite impressive and the highlight is the cable car that runs up to the top of a *kopje* (isolated hill) overlooking the city. The entrance is near the corner of Paul Kruger and Boom Sts.

It's open from 8 am to 6 pm daily; entry is R17 plus the cost of the cable car. Several times a week there are night tours – BYO torch (flashlight).

Markets

On weekends a flea market is held in the Sunnypark shopping centre on Esselen St. There is also a Sunday flea market held in the car park of Hatfield Plaza, Burnett St. Out of town, on the N4 opposite the CSIR complex, a *boeremark* (farmers' market) is the place to find fresh produce and old-style Boers, as well as traditional food and music. It's held from about 6 to 9 am on Saturday.

Places to Stay – Budget

Camping A good facility with plenty of camp sites, ***Fountains Valley Caravan Park*** *(☎ 44 7131)* is on the M18 and has tennis courts; camp sites are R38/R45 for two people without/with electricity.

Hostels Competition between hostels is keen, so see what you can get in the way of (Jo'burg) airport pick-ups, free beers etc.

Pretoria Backpackers *(☎ 012-343 9754, 34 Bourke St, Sunnyside, email ptaback@hotmail.com)* is a short walk from Esselen St. It's a great travellers place run by François, a registered tour guide and Pretoria enthusiast. Dorms cost R45 and doubles cost R130; and there is limited camping. Transfers to/from Jo'burg international airport are R50 with the hourly Pretoria Airport Shuttle, which serves all Pretoria hostels and accommodation. There is an excellent backpackers travel agency attached to the hostel; it organises great tours to an Ndebele village.

North South Backpackers *(☎ 362 0989, 355 Glyn St, Hatfield)* is an excellent, recommended hostel. It's an easy walk to buzzing Burnett St, and the helpful owners can organise tours and bargain rental car deals. Clean dorms are R45 and doubles cost R130.

Hotels & Guesthouses The ***Parkview Hotel*** *(☎ 325 6787, 179 Zeederberg St)* opposite the Union buildings gardens is dingy but very clean and cheap, with small single/double rooms for R50/80. Each room has a shower but toilets are shared.

Malvern House *(☎ 341 7212, 575 Schoeman St, Arcadia)* is a large guesthouse in a good position within walking distance of the city centre and Sunnyside. It's clean and comfortable and some rooms have private bathrooms. Rooms are R95/140 with breakfast.

Places to Stay – Mid-Range

That's It! *(☎ 344 3404, 5 Brecher St)* near the corner of Farenden St is a pleasant B&B in a leafy corner of Sunnyside. There's an immaculate back garden with a pool and a large outdoor eating area. Rates start at R200 for a budget room with breakfast.

The ***Orange Court Lodge*** *(☎ 326 6346, fax 326 2492)* on the corner of Vermeulen and Hamilton Sts is an excellent place with serviced cottages (one, two or three bedrooms) with phone, TV, equipped kitchens and linen. There's a welter of rates, starting at R240 for a double in a one-bedroom cottage and from R350 for six people in a three-bedroom cottage. This is outstanding value.

The ***Pretoria Hof Hotel*** *(☎ 322 7570)* on the corner of Pretorius and Van der Walt Sts is a solid old place in the centre of town. Rooms are R225/295, with weekend specials.

The Pretoria Tourism Information Centre has a list of other B&Bs and guesthouses. You can also contact the Bed & Breakfast Association (☎ 083-212 1989); prices start at around R120/190 for rooms.

Places to Stay – Top End

The enchanting ***La Maison*** *(☎ 43 4341, 235 Hilda St, Hatfield)* has three beautiful guest rooms in a historic house. The owner is a cordon bleu chef. Singles/doubles are R369/502.

The gracious ***Victoria Hotel*** *(☎ 323 6052, fax 323 0843)* on the corner of Paul Kruger and Scheiding Sts, opposite the train station, was built in 1896. There are 10 rooms costing from R660/825, with a good breakfast.

The ***Holiday Inn Crowne Plaza*** *(☎ 341 1571)* on the corner of Beatrix and Church Sts is well positioned – the city centre is about a 15-minute walk away. Rooms offering the usual comforts are R450/R500.

Places to Eat

City Centre The best spot in the city for people watching is ***Cafe Riche*** *(☎ 328 3173, 2 Church St)*, a swanky place full of suit-wearing yuppies proudly comparing the latest in cell phone technology. The food is pretty good too.

An old favourite, Roberto's Italian, has closed and in its place is the ***Curry Palace*** *(☎ 322 6786)*, in the Tramshed complex. Locals have told us that their curries are pretty good.

Sunnyside Esselen St, to the south-east of the city, has numerous restaurants and take-away joints. Go for a stroll and see what takes your fancy.

Il Bacio is popular with travellers. It has all-you-can-eat-and-drink deals for R35 on selected days.

Am Miv, between Celliers and Troye Sts, is an Israeli place where you can get a felafel for R10 or a quarter roast chicken for R6. For good value Italian food, ***Giovanni's*** is upstairs across from the Sunnypark shopping centre. Pasta is about R25 and a decent salad will set you back R15. Downstairs, the ***London Tavern*** has bar meals.

Hatfield Burnett St is blossoming into a swinging restaurant and cafe area. Recommended is ***Greenfields***, very popular with the locals, and ***Bugatti's***, which is good for breakfast. ***Cool Runnings*** makes a great stop during the day for a cheap, filling meal costing about R17.

Entertainment

Pubs & Bars The nightlife scene is progressively heading east, escaping the crime-ridden city centre. Even Esselen St has taken on an air of seediness in recent times.

Steamers, near the train station, is a gay-friendly club.

Sophiatown Jazz Cafe *(☎ 362 988, 525 Duncan St)* is open mainly on weekends and is arguably the best spot around for black music.

Hatfield Square on Burnett St is where hip, young Afrikaner style-cats showcase themselves. There's outdoor dining and drinking, and some of the cafes such as ***Square Time*** often have live music. Despite the trendiness it's a genuinely good spot to either get a little boisterous or relax with a quiet drink, especially on a warm evening. ***McGinty's***, an Irish pub, is open daily from 11 am until late.

A short stroll away is ***Tequila Sunrise***, which has bands on Friday nights. ***Cool Runnings*** and ***Tings & Times*** are two funky reggae joints close by.

Cinemas & Theatre There are several enormous cinema complexes. The largest is ***Sterland*** on the corner of Pretorius and Beatrix Sts, which has 13 cinemas and the worst decor we've seen in South Africa.

There's quite a range of high culture (opera, music, ballet and theatre) offered at the ***State Theatre*** (☎ 322 1665), on the corner of Prinsloo and Church Sts. Check local newspapers for listings. Computicket has an office in the Tramshed complex.

Getting There & Away

Bus Most interprovincial and international bus services commence in Pretoria unless they are heading north (for details see the Getting There & Away section in this chapter). Most buses leave from the forecourt of Pretoria train station on Paul Kruger St.

Most Translux (☎ 334 8000) and Greyhound (☎ 323 1154) services running from Jo'burg to Durban, the south coast and Cape Town originate in Pretoria (for more information, see the earlier Johannesburg Getting There & Away section in this chapter).

Translux and City to City services running north up the N1 also stop here.

Examples of Translux fares from Pretoria are: Durban (R110); Kimberley (R115); Nelspruit (R115); Messina (R125); Beitbridge (R140); Bloemfontein (R155); Knysna (R220); Port Elizabeth (R220); and Cape Town (R320).

Intercape (☎ 654 4114) has services to Upington (R220), connecting with a service to Cape Town. From Upington you can also get an Intercape bus to Windhoek (Namibia), but there isn't a direct connection.

North Link Transport (☎ 315 2333) runs north to Pietersburg/Polokwane and Phalaborwa.

Train Pretoria has direct train connections with many major South African cities and also with Gabarone (Botswana), Bulawayo (Zimbabwe) and Maputo (Mozambique; change at Komatipoort). However, for many train services, it will be necessary to get to Jo'burg first (for further details see the Getting Around section of the South Africa chapter).

The train station (☎ 315 2757) is about a 20-minute walk from the city centre; all Main Line services can be booked here. Buses run along Paul Kruger St to Church Square, the main local bus terminus.

There have recently been many violent robberies on the Metro system to Jo'burg, so be careful. A 1st-class train ticket to Jo'burg is R15. The journey takes about 1¼ hours. On weekdays, trains run half-hourly early in the morning then hourly until 10 pm. On weekends trains run about every 1½ hours. To find out the exact times, call ☎ 315 2007 in Pretoria or ☎ 011-773 5878 in Jo'burg.

Car The larger local and international companies are represented. You can make bookings at the Pretoria Tourism office (see Information earlier in this section).

Getting Around

To/From the Airport Pretoria Airport Shuttle (☎ 323 0904) operates between Jo'burg airport (departing outside domestic arrivals) and the corner of Vermeulen and Prinsloo Sts in the city. The journey takes a bit under an hour and costs R55; more if you want to be picked up from another location.

Bus The inquiry office (☎ 308 0839) and main terminus for local buses is on the south-eastern corner of Church Square. Some services, including the one to Sunnyside, run until about 10.30 pm. The standard minibus fare around town is R3.

Taxi There are ranks on the corner of Church and Van der Walt and at Vermeulen and Andries Sts, or call Five Star (☎ 320 7513/4). You'll pay about R3 per kilometre.

AROUND PRETORIA

☎ 012

Doornkloof (Smuts' House)

General JC Smuts was a brilliant scholar, Boer general, politician and international statesman. He was one of the architects of the Union of South Africa. His home, south of Pretoria, is now an excellent museum. The house (☎ 667 1176) is open daily from 9.30 am to 1 pm and 1.30 to 4.30 pm (until 5 pm weekends); entry is R5, free to the garden.

There's a small ***cafeteria*** with an outdoor tea garden, and a pleasant ***caravan park*** *(☎ 667 1176)*. Camp sites cost R30.

There is no access by public transport. The house is signposted from both the N1 freeway (R28) and the R21.

Cheetah Research & Breeding Centre (De Wildt)

Just outside Pretoria, the Cheetah Research & Breeding Centre (☎ 504 1921) has excellent half-day tours for about R70. As well as cheetah you'll probably see wild dogs, meerkats, honey badgers and lots of birds.

The only way to reach this centre is by car. It's about a 45-minute drive from Pretoria and is located just off the R513.

Pretoria National Botanical Gardens

The botanical gardens cover 77 hectares and are planted with indigenous flora from around the country. They are 11km east of the city centre and are open from 8 am to 5.30 pm daily; entry is free on weekdays and R2 on weekends.

To get there, catch the Meyerspark or Murrayfield bus from Church Square. By car, head east along Church St (R104) for about 9km, then turn right into Cussonia Rd; the gardens are on the left-hand side.

Voortrekker Monument & Museum

The enormous Voortrekker Monument was built in 1938 to commemorate the Boers who trekked north into the heart of the African *veld* (open grassland). A staircase leads to the roof and a panoramic view of Pretoria and the highveld.

Below the car park is a small museum that reconstructs the lives of the trekkers. Entrance to the monument is R5 and to the museum it's also R5. There's a ***restaurant*** and a ***cafe*** here too.

The monument is 6km south of the city, just to the east of the N1 freeway. It is possible to catch the Voortrekkerhoogte or Valhalla bus from Kruger St, near the corner of Church Square. Ask the driver to let you off at the entrance road to the monument, from where it is a 10-minute walk uphill.

Free State

The Free State consists largely of the plains of the Southern African plateau. The east of the province is highland with weirdly eroded sandstone hills.

The Free State's borders reflect the role it has played in South African history (for more details, see under History in the Facts about South Africa section earlier in this book). To the south is the Orange River, which the Voortrekkers crossed to escape the Cape colony during the Great Trek. The northern border is defined by the Vaal River, which was the next frontier of Boer expansion. To the east, across the Mohokare (Caledon) River, is Lesotho, where mountains and Moshoeshoe the Great's warriors halted Boer expansion. To the south-east, the Free State spills across the Caledon River as the mountains dwindle to grazing land, which was harder for Moshoeshoe to defend.

BLOEMFONTEIN

☎ 051

Bloemfontein (literally, Fountain of Flowers), known as 'Bloem', is the provincial capital and South Africa's judicial capital. As well as the legal community there is a university and a large military camp, so you can meet a wide range of people. Most of the blacks still live in the enclaves they were shunted into during the apartheid days. Botshabelo, on the Thaba 'Nchu road, is one of the largest 'locations' in the country.

History

In 1854 the Orange Free State was created, with Bloemfontein as the capital, and in 1863 Johannes Brand began his 25-year term as president. During Brand's presidency, Bloemfontein grew from being a struggling frontier town, in constant danger of being wiped out by Moshoeshoe the Great's warriors, to a wealthy provincial capital with railway links to the coast.

Orientation & Information

The central area is laid out on a grid and Hoffman Square is the centre of the downtown area. To the north-east is Naval Hill, from where there are good views of the town and surrounding plains.

Tourist information can be found at the friendly Bloemfontein Tourist Centre (☎ 405 8490) at 60 Park Rd, where there is also a Free State tourist office, STA Travel and a Copy Centre with cheap Internet and email access at R15 per hour.

Rennies Travel (☎ 430 2361) is on Voortrekker Rd.

Museums

The **National Museum** on the corner of Charles and Aliwal Sts is open daily from 8 am to 5 pm (1 to 6 pm on Sunday); entry is R5. The most interesting display is a recreation of a 19th-century street.

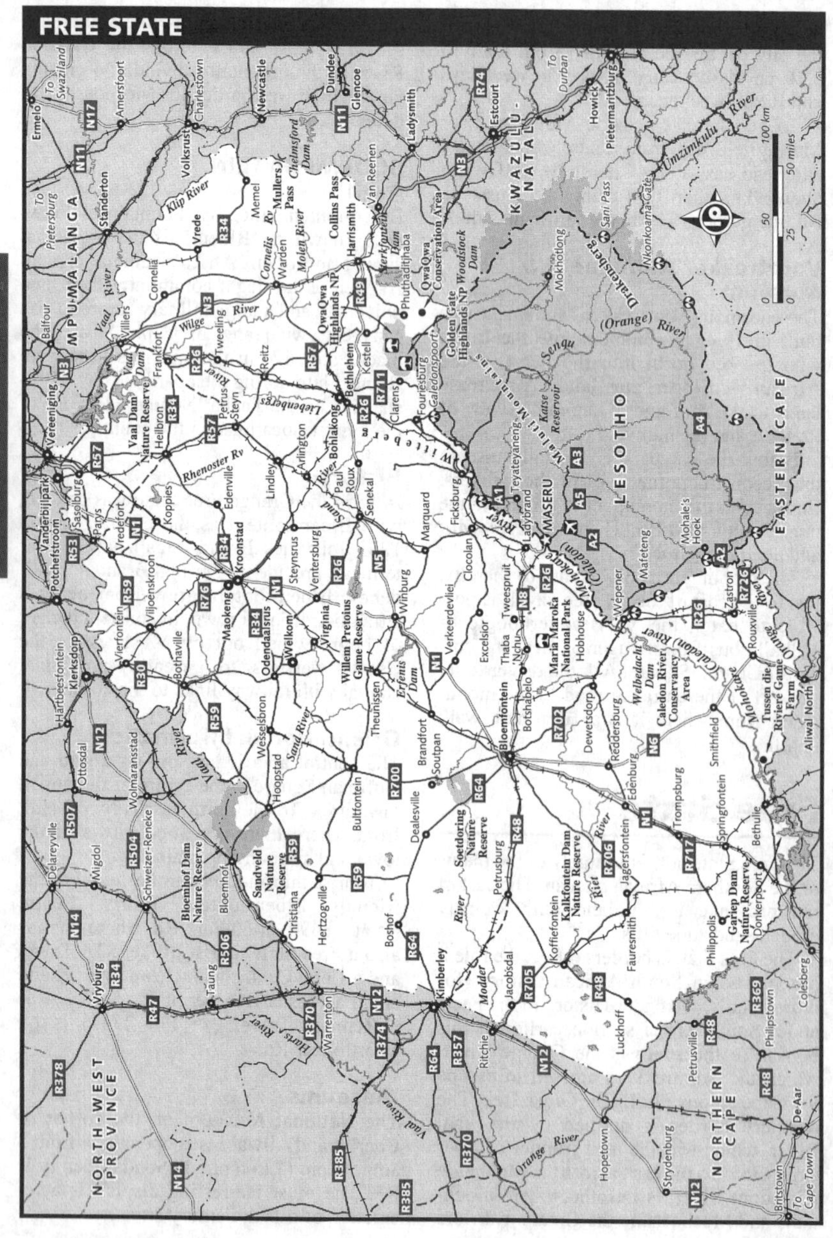
FREE STATE
MPUMALANGA
KWAZULU-NATAL
LESOTHO
EASTERN CAPE
NORTHERN CAPE
NORTH-WEST PROVINCE
To Swaziland
To Pietersburg
To Durban
To Cape Town
Ermelo
Amersfoort
Charlestown
Volksrust
Newcastle
Dundee
Glencoe
Ladysmith
Estcourt
Howick
Pietermaritzburg
Standerton
Balfour
Vereeniging
Vanderbijlpark
Sasolburg
Potchefstroom
Klerksdorp
Hartbeesfontein
Ottosdal
Delareyville
Migdol
Vryburg
Taung
Schweizer-Reneke
Wolmaransstad
Bloemhof
Christiana
Warrenton
Kimberley
Ritchie
Jacobsdal
Koffiefontein
Luckhoff
Hopetown
Strydenburg
Petrusville
Philipstown
De Aar
Bristown
Colesberg
Philippolis
Springfontein
Bethulie
Donkerpoort
Smithfield
Trompsburg
Edenburg
Reddersburg
Dewetsdorp
Jagersfontein
Fauresmith
Petrusburg
Bloemfontein
Botshabelo
Thaba 'Nchu
Tweespruit
Hobhouse
Wepener
Zastron
Rouxville
Aliwal North
Mafeteng
Mohale's Hoek
MASERU
Teyateyaneng
Ladybrand
Clocolan
Ficksburg
Marquard
Excelsior
Verkeerdevlei
Brandfort
Soutpan
Dealesville
Boshof
Hertzogville
Bultfontein
Hoopstad
Wesselsbron
Theunissen
Winburg
Welkom
Virginia
Odendaalsrus
Ventersburg
Steynsrus
Senekal
Paul Roux
Bohlokong
Bethlehem
Clarens
Fouriesburg
Kestell
Phuthaditjhaba
Harrismith
Van Reenen
Warden
Memel
Vrede
Cornelia
Villiers
Frankfort
Tweeling
Reitz
Petrus Steyn
Heilbron
Lindley
Arlington
Edenville
Koppies
Vredefort
Parys
Kroonstad
Maokeng
Viljoenskroon
Vierfontein
Bothaville
Mokhotlong
Sani Pass
Nkonkoama Gate
Caledonspoort
Vaal Dam Nature Reserve
Willem Pretoius Game Reserve
Erfenis Dam
Maria Maroka National Park
Soetdoring Nature Reserve
Kalkfontein Dam Nature Reserve
Sandveld Nature Reserve
Bloemhof Dam Nature Reserve
Caledon River Conservancy Area
Welbedacht Dam
Gariep Dam Nature Reserve
Tussen die Riviere Game Farm
QwaQwa Highlands NP
Golden Gate Highlands NP
QwaQwa Conservation Area
Woodstock Dam
Sterkfontein Dam
Chelmsford Dam
Katse Reservoir
Collins Pass
Mullers Pass
Maluti Mountains
Drakensberg
Witteberge
Liebenbergs
Vaal River
Klip River
Wilge River
Cornelis Rv
Molen River
Rhenoster Rv
Sand River
Modder River
Riet River
Harts River
Orange River
(Orange) River
Sengu
Mohokare (Caledon) River
Umzimkulu River
N1
N3
N5
N6
N8
N11
N12
N14
N17
R26
R30
R34
R47
R48
R49
R53
R57
R59
R64
R74
R76
R357
R369
R370
R374
R378
R385
R504
R506
R507
R700
R702
R705
R706
R711
R717
R726
A1
A2
A3
A4
A5
0 25 50 100 km
0 50 miles

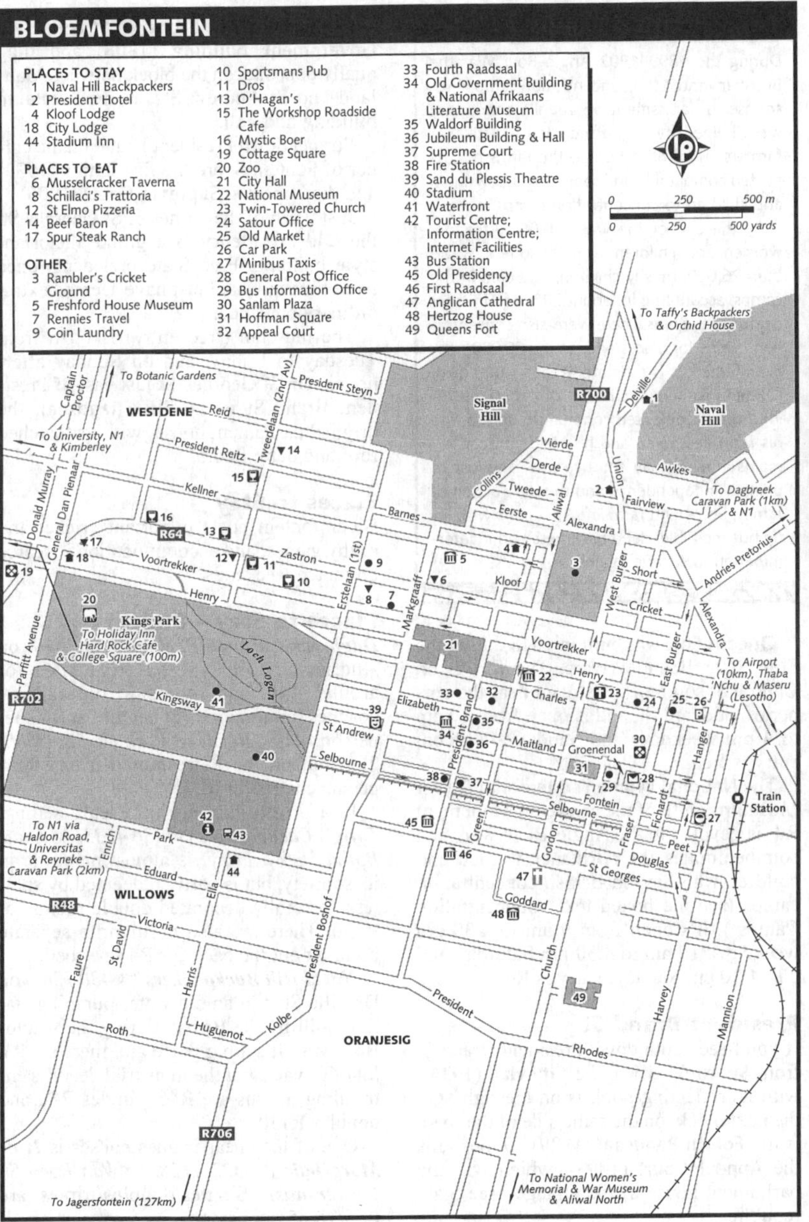

BLOEMFONTEIN
PLACES TO STAY
1 Naval Hill Backpackers
2 President Hotel
4 Kloof Lodge
18 City Lodge
44 Stadium Inn
PLACES TO EAT
6 Musselcracker Taverna
8 Schillaci's Trattoria
12 St Elmo Pizzeria
14 Beef Baron
17 Spur Steak Ranch
OTHER
3 Rambler's Cricket Ground
5 Freshford House Museum
7 Rennies Travel
9 Coin Laundry
10 Sportsmans Pub
11 Dros
13 O'Hagan's
15 The Workshop Roadside Cafe
16 Mystic Boer
19 Cottage Square
20 Zoo
21 City Hall
22 National Museum
23 Twin-Towered Church
24 Satour Office
25 Old Market
26 Car Park
27 Minibus Taxis
28 General Post Office
29 Bus Information Office
30 Sanlam Plaza
31 Hoffman Square
32 Appeal Court
33 Fourth Raadsaal
34 Old Government Building & National Afrikaans Literature Museum
35 Waldorf Building
36 Jubileum Building & Hall
37 Supreme Court
38 Fire Station
39 Sand du Plessis Theatre
40 Stadium
41 Waterfront
42 Tourist Centre; Information Centre; Internet Facilities
43 Bus Station
45 Old Presidency
46 First Raadsaal
47 Anglican Cathedral
48 Hertzog House
49 Queens Fort
0 250 500 m
0 250 500 yards
To Taffy's Backpackers & Orchid House
To Botanic Gardens
To University, N1 & Kimberley
To Dagbreek Caravan Park (1km) & N1
To Airport (10km), Thaba 'Nchu & Maseru (Lesotho)
To Holiday Inn Hard Rock Cafe & College Square (100m)
To N1 via Haldon Road, Universitas & Reyneke Caravan Park (2km)
To National Women's Memorial & War Museum & Aliwal North
To Jagersfontein (127km)
Signal Hill
Naval Hill
Kings Park
Loch Logan
WESTDENE
WILLOWS
ORANJESIG
Train Station
R700
R64
R702
R48
R706
Captain Proctor
President Steyn
Reid
Tweedelaan (2nd Av)
President Reitz
Kellner
Barnes
Zastron
Voortrekker
Henry
Kingsway
St Andrew
Selbourne
Park
Eduard
Victoria
Roth
Huguenot
Kolbe
President
Rhodes
Donald Murray
General Dan Pienaar
Parfitt Avenue
Enrich
Ella
St David
Harris
Faure
President Boshof
Erstelaan (1st)
Markgraaff
President Brand
Elizabeth
Green
Gordon
Church
Fraser
Fichardt
Harvey
Mannion
Hanger
East Burger
West Burger
Union
Aliwal
Collins
Delville
Vierde
Derde
Tweede
Eerste
Awkes
Fairview
Alexandra
Andries Pretorius
Short
Cricket
Kloof
Charles
Maitland
Groenendal
Fontein
Peet
Douglas
St Georges
Goddard

Concentration Camps

During the 1899–1902 Anglo-Boer War the British invented the concentration camp in response to harassment by guerilla bands that were helped by – and included – Afrikaner farmers. The British burned the farms of suspected combatants and sent Afrikaner women and children to concentration camps.

By the end of the war 200,000 Afrikaner women and children were prisoners. More than 26,000, mostly children, had died in the camps, accounting for about 70% of Afrikaner deaths in the war. There were also concentration camps for blacks and, of the 80,000 people interned, it is estimated that 14,000 died.

For Afrikaners, the image of a man returning from his defeated commando unit to find his farm destroyed and his children dead remains a powerfully emotive one. The loss of political independence and the destruction of family, home and farm left Afrikaners with little but the Bible, deep bitterness and a determination to survive against any odds.

Queens Fort was built in 1848 during the Free State–Basutho Wars. The fort is on Church St south of the stream near the corner of Goddard St, and is open from 10 am to 4 pm weekdays and Sunday afternoon; entry is free.

The **National Women's Memorial & War Museum**, south of the centre on Monument Rd, is devoted to the Anglo-Boer Wars and commemorates the Afrikaner women and children who died in British concentration camps (see the boxed text 'Concentration Camps'). It's open from 9 am to 4.30 pm weekdays, 10 am to 4.30 pm Saturday and 2 to 4.30 pm Sunday; entry is R4.

President Brand St

If you head south down President Brand St from Voortrekker Rd, the **City Hall** (1934), with its reflecting pool, is on the right. On the next block, on the same side of the road, is the **Fourth Raadsaal** (1929). Opposite is the **Appeal Court** (1893), which was the parliament house of the Orange Free State republic.

On the corner of Elizabeth St is the **Old Government building** (1908) and diagonally opposite, on the block between Maitland and St Andrew Sts, is the **Jubileum building and hall**.

Further down President Brand on the corner of Fontein St are the fire station (1933) and the imposing **Supreme Court** (1906).

Just north of the corner of St Georges St, the **Old Presidency** is a grand Victorian-style building. Free State presidents once lived here in what must have seemed extraordinary opulence.

The museum (free entry) is open from Tuesday to Friday, and on Sunday afternoons. On St Georges St just east of President Brand St is the **First Raadsaal**, the original parliament house, with its thatched roof and dung floors.

Places to Stay

Bloemfontein hosts important cricket and rugby games, and accommodation is scarce on match weekends.

Places to Stay – Budget

Dagbreek Caravan Park *(☎ 433 2490)* on Andries Pretorius St has tent sites for around R40, and rooms in old railway coaches (minimum eight people) at R40 per person. Also, ***Reyneke Park*** *(☎ 523 3888)* 2km out on the Petrusburg Rd has four-person chalets for R270.

In a private home with a leafy setting, ***Taffy's Backpackers*** *(☎ 436 4533, 18 Louis Botha St, Waverley)* is almost monastic in its sobriety, but is partly redeemed by spotless, tastefully decorated double rooms for R130. There are also dorms in a separate building out the back for R45 per bed.

Naval Hill Backpackers *(☎ 430 7266)* on Delville St is in an old water-pumping station built by the British during the Anglo-Boer War. It's a big place and there's not a lot of privacy, but the industrial decor is enthralling; dorms are R45, singles R80 and doubles R130.

One of the cheaper guesthouses is ***Huis Margrietje*** *(☎ 522 4128, 28 Van Rooy St, Universitas)*. Singles/doubles/triples are R55/78/65 per person.

The ***Stadium Inn*** *(☎ 474 747)* on Park St across from the tourist centre has self-catering flats that are very good value. Rooms are R95/120, and the flats on the fifth floor are the best.

Places to Stay – Mid-Range & Top End

The ***Kloof Lodge*** *(☎ 447 7603, fax 447 7746)* on the corner of Kellner and Kloof Sts is a comfortable guesthouse with spacious singles/doubles that come with bathroom, TV and phone for R215/230; there's a cosy bar downstairs.

The three-star ***President Hotel*** *(☎ 430 1111, fax 430 4141, 1 Union Ave, Naval Hill)* is out of the centre, but reasonable value with rooms for R299/342.

Guesthouses don't come much better than the enchanting ***Hobbit House*** *(☎ 447 0663, 19 President Steyn St, Westdene)*. The owners pride themselves on their faultless service and impeccable facilities. The original property was built in 1924. Rooms are R350/450 and a three-course dinner is R90. Forget the bill and spoil yourself!

The ***City Lodge*** *(☎ 444 2974)* on the corner of Voortrekker Rd and Parfitt Ave has rooms for R279/326, with the usual businessperson facilities. There is also a ***Holiday Inn*** *(☎ 444 1253)* next to the Hard Rock Cafe on Zastron St with rooms for R334/378; ask about weekend specials.

Places to Eat

Steak-lovers have the usual wide choice for their R40, including ***Spur Steak Ranch*** on Zastron St and ***Beef Baron*** (perhaps the best of them all) on Tweedelaan (2nd Ave) St.

Schillaci's Trattoria on Zastron St is a good Italian restaurant. Main courses start at R30 and there are midweek specials. There are a few places around the corners of Tweedelaan (2nd Ave) and Zastron Sts, including a ***St Elmo Pizzeria***.

There are loads of places to eat at the Cape Town-style Waterfront (yes, believe it or not, landlocked Bloemfontein has a Waterfront!). There are many of the usual chain restaurants but the trendy ***Jazztime Cafe*** stands out.

The menu is brilliant and the service enthusiastic, perhaps the best we came across in South Africa. Try the *zivas* (R25), a Yemeni-style dough, stuffed with a variety of fillings (such as Cajun chicken, feta and avocado) rolled and toasted – delicious!

The ***Musselcracker Taverna*** on the corner of Zastron and Msarkgraaf Sts is a small airy restaurant with excellent seafood – a mini seafood platter is R40.

Entertainment

Being a university town, Bloem has a fair range of places to drink and, sometimes, to hear music. The ***Mystic Boer*** on Zastron St is pretty good.

You could also try the ***Workshop Roadside Cafe***, corner of Tweedelaan (2nd Ave) and President Reitz Sts; ***Dros*** on the corner of Tweedelaan (2nd Ave) and Zastron Sts; or ***Cantina Tequila*** in the College Square centre on Zastron St.

If you're up for a boogie, the best place to carve up the dance floor according to locals is ***Barney's*** at the Waterfront – there's a decent-sized room and bands on the weekend. If you want to shoot some pool ***Bulldogs***, also at the Waterfront, is a good place.

Getting There & Away

Bus Long-distance bus services arrive and leave from the tourist centre on Park Rd. Translux (☎ 408 3242) runs to Durban (R160), Jo'burg/Pretoria (R175), Port Elizabeth (R195), East London (R200), Knysna (R230) and Cape Town (R285).

Greyhound (☎ 447 1558) has similar services. Intercape Mainliner (☎ 447 1435) runs to Jo'burg (R155) and Cape Town (R245).

Minibus Taxi Most minibus taxis leave from opposite the train station. A taxi to Kimberley costs R30, and to Maseru (Lesotho) it's R25.

Train For train information call ☎ 408 2946; for bookings call ☎ 408 2941.

The *Diamond Express* (Bloemfontein to Pretoria via Kimberley), the *Trans Oranje* (Durban-Cape Town), the *Amatola* (Jo'burg-

East London) and the *Algoa* (Jo'burg- Port Elizabeth) all stop in Bloemfontein.

Car Rental companies in Bloemfontein include Avis (☎ 433 2331), Budget (☎ 433 1178) and Imperial (☎ 433 3511).

Getting Around

To/From the Airport The airport is 10km from the city centre. There's no public transport so you'll have to take a taxi (around R100).

Buses & Taxis There's a public bus system, although services stop early in the evening. All buses run through Hoffman Square, and the bus information office (☎ 405 8135) on St Andrew St has timetables. To get to Naval Hill take bus No 2 to Union Ave and walk from there.

For taxis, try Rosestad Taxis (☎ 451 1022) or Silver Leaf Taxis (☎ 430 2005).

NORTHERN FREE STATE & GOLDFIELDS

The Free State goldfields produce more than a third of the country's total gold output. The goldfields are centred on Welkom, Virginia and Odendaalsrus.

Kroonstad

☎ 0562

Kroonstad on the N1 is a typical large rural town, dating back to 1855. Sarel Celliers (of the Blood River Vow) was one of the first settlers (for more details see History in the Facts about South Africa section).

The **Old Market building**, opposite the pretty **Magistrate's building** on the corner of Mark and Murray Sts, is a national monument. Upstairs in the library there's the small **Sarel Celliers Museum**, and some tourist information.

Places to Stay & Eat Across the river from the town centre, ***Kroon Park*** *(☎ 319 42)* is more like a resort than a municipal caravan park. It has sites from R23 plus R15 per person and chalets from R230.

The hotels are poor – you're better off hunting out B&Bs and farmstays.

Angelo's Trattoria in Reitz St is good for Italian food, with pasta from R22. ***Sleepers*** is a steakhouse with a selection of beers on tap, and there's a ***Spur Steak Ranch*** in Buitekant St.

Getting There & Away Translux services between Jo'burg/Pretoria and East London, Knysna and Port Elizabeth stop at the Shell Ultra City on the highway, as does Greyhound's Jo'burg/Pretoria–Port Elizabeth service.

The *Amatola* (Jo'burg-East London) and *Algoa* (Jo'burg-Port Elizabeth) trains stop here. The minibus taxi park is opposite the train station.

Welkom

☎ 057

This modern town is a showpiece at the centre of the goldfields. There is plenty of money here – Welkom has the highest per capita income in the country.

Orientation & Information The 'publicity tower' (☎ 352 9244) is in the clock tower at the civic centre on Stateway, the main street.

Not far from here is Mooi St, which encloses most of the central shopping area in its horseshoe curve.

Things to See & Do Approximately once a month, free tours of a **mine**, including a gold pour, are organised. Contact the tourist office in the publicity tower for more information.

The area's mine evaporation pans are home to a wide variety of **birdlife**, including flamingoes. A good site is Flamingo Pan off the R30, just west of the town.

Places to Stay & Eat About 2km north of the town centre is ***Sirkel Caravan Park*** *(☎ 53987, 281 Koppie Alleen Rd, Reitz Park)* with sites for R30.

The ***Welkom Lodge*** *(☎ 357 2291, 162 Stateway)* is a cheap guesthouse with singles/doubles for R140/160. The ***Welkom Inn*** *(☎ 357 3361)* on Stateway at the corner of Tempest Rd a few blocks east of the centre is a bit more upmarket, with rooms from about R265.

Giovani's Pizzaghetti (15 Mooi St) has pasta and pizza from R22 as well as steak and seafood. There are plenty of ***steak-houses*** in town.

Getting There & Away Being a mining town, Welkom is a major depot for City to City buses, with a few services to Jo'burg/Pretoria and more south-east to QwaQwa, Lesotho and Transkei. Several Translux services stop on Buiten St on the way to destinations such as Bloemfontein (R60) and Jo'burg (R130). Greyhound buses stop at the Orange Hotel on Stateway. Book for either bus line at Rennies Travel in Sanlam Plaza.

The taxis in the supermarket car park in town are mainly for the local area, but you might find long-distance taxis here in the early morning.

SOUTHERN FREE STATE

The Southern Free State is dusty, harsh and dry, and the many windmills are reminiscent of parts of the Australian landscape.

Tussen Die Riviere Game Farm

This reserve (☎ 051-762 2803) has more animals than any other in the Free State, including white rhinos and hippos. Between May and the end of August the reserve is closed for the annual cull. For keen hikers, there are the Middelpunt (7km), the Klipstapel (12km) and the Orange River (16km) **hiking trails**; water must be carried on all of them.

There are ***tent sites*** and cheap ***chalets*** but no food is available. The entrance gate is on the road between Bethulie and Smithfield (R701), about 65km east of the N1.

Stokstert Hiking Trail

This overnight trail is in the Caledon River Conservancy Area, near Smithfield. This huge area includes the land of more than 60 farmers who have adopted conservation-based techniques. To book hikes write to: The Secretary, Caledon River Conservancy Area, PO Box 71, Smithfield 9966.

EASTERN HIGHLANDS

This is the most beautiful part of the Free State and stretches from Zastron in the south to Harrismith in the north-east. Roughly, it is the area which fringes the R26 and the R49 east of Bethlehem to Harrismith.

As well as being tremendously scenic, the Eastern Highlands are archaeologically and historically important.

Zastron

☎ 051

Zastron on the R726 is a quiet little town at the foothills of the Aasvoëlberg and Maluti Mountains. There are some **San paintings** in the area; the best are in the Seekoei and Hoffman Caves.

The ***caravan park*** *(☎ 673 1397)* is a few kilometres out of town; tent sites are R40. It's a nice walk down a wooded gorge.

Ladybrand

☎ 051

Ladybrand on the R26 is the closest South African town to the main border crossing (16km from Ladybrand) into Lesotho.

Zabi's Coffeeshop opposite the post office on Church St is the best place to get tourist information.

There are some nice **sandstone buildings**, including the town hall and the Old Magistrate's Court. The **Catharina Brand Museum** has rock paintings and Stone Age tools.

The two-day **Steve Visser Hiking Trail** starts at the Leliehoek Holiday Resort; book at the town hall (☎ 924 0654).

Places to Stay & Eat The peaceful ***Leliehoek Holiday Resort*** *(☎ 924 0260)* 2km south of the town hall has camp sites (about R50) and chalets from R150.

Ladybrand's one hotel is the old-style ***Country Lodge*** *(☎ 924 3200, 23 Joubert St)*, which charges R155/189 for singles/doubles, including breakfast.

There are plenty of B&Bs in town to choose from, including the friendly ***My Housy*** *(☎ 924 1010, 17A Prinsloo St)*, which has secure parking and charges from R180/270.

Getting There & Away Minibus taxis can be found near the church on Piet Retief St. Most run to the nearby areas, including Ficksburg (R18). For a wider choice of destinations, take a taxi to Maseru Bridge (at the Lesotho border) for R4 and find a long-distance taxi in the big taxi rank there.

Ficksburg

☎ 051

This town is in sandstone country and there are some fine buildings, including the town hall, the NG Kerk and the post office.

Ficksburg is the centre of the Free State's cherry industry and the **Cherry Trail** is a tourist route around the district. There are several orchards to visit, art and craft shops, some guest farms and hiking trails. The library near Hotel Hoogland has tourist information.

Thom Park *(☎ 083-592 1267)*, the municipal caravan park, is on Voortrekker Rd and has sites for R30, plus R5 per person. The ***Hoogland Hotel*** *(☎ 933 2214)* on Market Square near Voortrekker Rd has rooms for R180/300, more during the week. The dining room in the hotel has a reasonable menu with main dishes from R30.

You can get to Ficksburg by taking a minibus taxi from Jo'burg to Bethlehem. At Bethlehem change buses for Ficksburg.

Rustler's Valley

☎ 051

This remote valley in the heart of the conservative Free State is in the vanguard of the 'dare to be different' movement in the new South Africa. ***Rustler's Valley*** *(☎/fax 933 3939)*, a resort in the valley of the same name, attracts a diverse crowd – yuppies from Jo'burg, remnant hippies from all parts of the continent and 'ideas' people from all over the globe.

You can walk up onto sandstone escarpments, climb imposing Nyakalesoba (Witchdoctor's Eye), ride into the labyrinthine *dongas* (steep-sided gullies) on a horse, or discuss existentialist philosophy in the bar with the valley's semipermanent residents.

Rustler's has a variety of accommodation, including single/double for R100/140. There is backpacker space for R30 per person and ***camping*** is encouraged (R10 per person).

Getting There & Away If you've got wheels, the main turn-off is about 25km south of Fouriesburg on the R26 to Ficksburg. Head west on a dirt road that crosses the railway line. From the turn-off it is about 12km to Rustler's.

Alternatively, you can get to Ficksburg by taking a minibus taxi from Jo'burg to Bethlehem. At Bethlehem change buses for Ficksburg and call Rustler's to see if they can pick you up (they charge a small fee for this).

Fouriesburg

☎ 058

This is another town on the scenic R26, only 10km from the Calendonspoort border post into Lesotho and 50km from the Golden Gate Highlands National Park.

The **Brandwater Hiking Trail** is a five-day circular walk from the Meiringskloof Caravan Park, 3km from Fouriesburg, through varied sandstone country.

The ***Meiringskloof Caravan Park*** *(☎ 223 0067)* 3km from town has sites for R40 plus R10 per person. There are also chalets from R150 a double. The ***Fouriesburg Hotel*** *(☎ 223 0207)* has singles/doubles for R130/240, including breakfast.

Golden Gate Highlands National Park

Golden Gate preserves the spectacular scenery of the foothills of the Maluti Mountains. There are also several animal species in the park, including grey rhebok, eland, oribi, Burchell's zebra, jackal and baboon.

Winters can be very cold here, with frost and snow; summers are mild but there's a good chance of rain and cold snaps are possible – if you're walking take warm clothing.

Rhebok Hiking Trail This circular, one-day trail (26km) is a great way to see the park. There are some steep sections so hikers need to be reasonably fit. The trail must be booked through the National Parks Board (for contact details, see Flora & Fauna in the

Facts about South Africa section) or by calling ☎ 058-256 1471; there's a fee of R40.

Places to Stay & Eat At ***Brandwag Camp*** singles/doubles cost from R165/285, with breakfast, and there's a restaurant.

At ***Glen Reenen*** three-bed bungalows start at R150 for two people. A camp site costs R50. Book accommodation through the National Parks Board.

Getting There & Away The R711 is a tar road into the park from Clarens, between Bethlehem and Fouriesburg. Alternatively, midway between Bethlehem and Harrismith on the R49 (N5), head south on the R712 and after a few kilometres turn west on a dirt road, or continue south on the R712 and head west about 7km before Phuthaditjhaba, QwaQwa.

QwaQwa

☎ 058

QwaQwa (master the 'click' pronunciation and you'll win friends) was once a small and extremely poor Homeland east of Golden Gate Highlands National Park.

Phuthaditjhaba, adjacent to the town of Witsieshoek and about 50km south of Harrismith, has an information centre (☎ 713 5093). Here, you can pick up the QwaQwa tourist pamphlet, which details hiking trails in the area. The **QwaQwa Conservation Area** covers 30,000 hectares in the foothills of both the Maluti Mountains and the Drakensberg. There are three excellent hiking trails: the Sentinel, the Fika Patso and the two-day Metsi Matsho.

Places to Stay & Eat The ***QwaQwa Hotel*** *(☎ 713 0903)* in Phuthaditjhaba is clean and well equipped; singles/doubles are R145/155, including breakfast.

About 25km south of Phuthaditjhaba is the ***Witsieshoek Mountain Resort*** *(☎ 713 6361)*, said to be the highest hotel (in altitude) in South Africa. It charges from R185 per person for DB&B.

Getting There & Away Minibus taxis to Harrismith cost R12 and to Bethlehem the fare is R30.

Bethlehem

☎ 058

Voortrekkers came to this area in the 1840s and Bethlehem was established in 1864. It's now a pleasant, large town and the main centre of the eastern Free State.

The tourist office (☎ 303 5732) is in the civic centre on Muller St, near the corner of Roux St.

As usual for this area, there are some impressive sandstone buildings, including the **Old Magistrate's Office** on the corner of Louw and Van der Merwe Sts, and the **NG Moederkerk** in the centre of town.

Places to Stay & Eat The tourist office has a full list of B&Bs.

About 3km from the town centre, the ***Loch Athlone Holiday Resort*** *(☎ 303 4981)* charges R50 for a site plus R10 per person. Single/double chalets are from R180/250.

The ***Park Hotel*** *(☎ 303 5191, 23 Muller St)* on the corner of High St has rooms with TV and bathroom from R155/200.

The ***Royal Hotel*** *(☎ 303 5448, 9 Boshoff St)* is reasonable value at R150/190, including breakfast.

Nix Pub on Kerk St opposite the church is a cosy place for a drink and next door is the ***Wooden Spoon*** restaurant. ***Beef Baron*** at the Loch Athlone Holiday Resort is shaped like the mail ship *Athlone Castle* and is full of memorabilia.

Getting There & Away Translux runs to Durban (R100) and Cape Town (R265), as does Greyhound, with similar fares. Both bus lines stop at Top Grill, on the corner of Church and Kerk Sts.

The weekly *Trans Oranje* (Cape Town–Durban) train stops here.

North-West Province

The North-West Province is an area of wide, hot plains. It was once covered entirely in scrub vegetation and thorn trees, but is now an important agricultural territory. The

Warning

If you're travelling in the North-West Province, you need to take precautions against bilharzia and malaria (for details about these two serious diseases, see the Health section in Regional Facts for the Visitor).

dominant crop is *mielies* (maize). The world's largest platinum mines are in the Rustenburg region.

San **rock art** attest to the original inhabitants of the area, but when the first white missionaries arrived in the 1830s the area was settled by Batswana. The Batswana were dispersed by Ndebele, who were themselves swept up in the wave of disruption unleashed during the difaqane (for more details see History in the Facts about South Africa section).

As part of the apartheid regime's Homeland policy, the Batswana were relocated to Bophuthatswana (known as Bop); North-West Province takes in most of the area once covered by Bop.

RUSTENBURG

☎ 014

Rustenburg is a large and prosperous town at the western edge of the Magaliesberg Hills. Founded by Voortrekkers in 1841, it is the third-oldest town north of the Vaal River.

There's a good information centre (☎ 594 3194) in the museum, on the corner of Plein and Burger Sts, behind the Civic Centre. It's open on weekdays.

Things to See & Do

The **museum** is small but interesting, concentrating on the early Boer settlers. The original flag of the Zuid-Afrikaansche Republiek (ZAR; South African Republic) is on display. The museum is open from 8.30 am to 4.30 pm weekdays, 9 am to 1 pm Saturday and 3 to 5 pm Sunday.

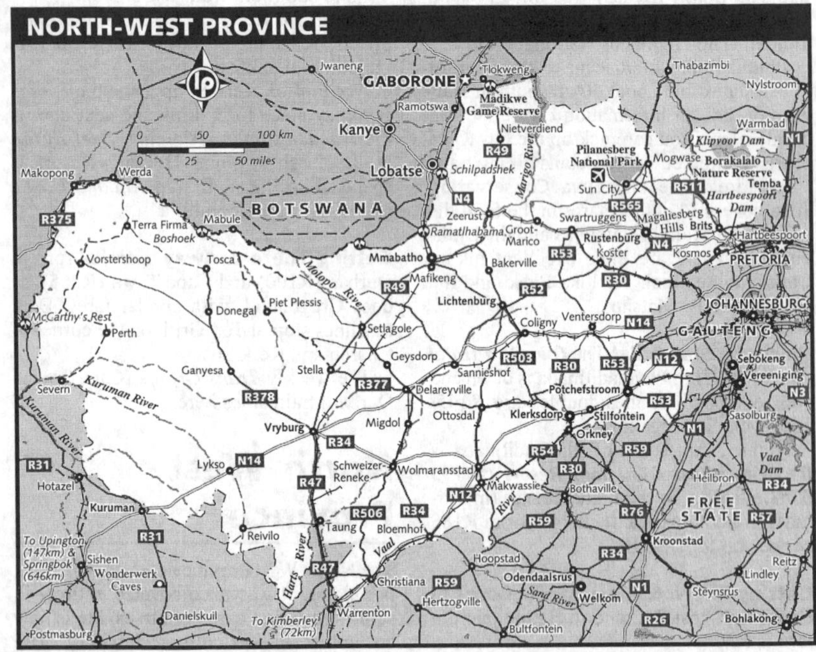

Paul Kruger's farm, **Boukenhoutfontein**, just north of town, is worth visiting. A small section of the farm and several buildings have been preserved. These include a pioneer cottage built in 1841 and the main family homestead built in 1875, which is a fine example of Colesberg Cape Dutch style.

The **Rustenburg Nature Reserve**, at the western end of the Magaliesberg, is dominated by rocky ridges and wooded ravines.

Places to Stay & Eat

The ***Hunter's Rest Hotel** (☎ 537 2140)* is an attractive resort 14km south of Rustenburg on the R30. There's a swimming pool and sports facilities, including horse riding. Rooms are R200 per person.

The ***Ananda Country Lodge** (☎ 537 1966)* has singles/doubles for R150/280 and there are camping facilities. The lodge is 7km from town, close to a spectacular, looming *kloof* (ravine). Contact the owners for detailed directions.

There are a few fastfood places that cater to the passing traffic. If you are peckish, the ***Rustenburg Bistro & Brewery*** on the R30 is worth a look.

Getting There & Away

Rustenburg is not well served by South Africa's buses. Intercape runs from Jo'burg/Pretoria to Rustenburg (en route to Windhoek) for R80 four times a week.

SUN CITY

☎ 014

Sun City is an extraordinary creation, based on gambling and mildly risque shows, plus excellent golf courses, swimming pools, sports facilities, restaurants and high-quality accommodation. It exists because Bop was considered by the apartheid regime to be an independent country and could provide the sort of 'immoral' entertainment that was banned at that time in South Africa.

Entry to Sun City costs R40. This includes 'chips' worth R30. You don't have to use these for gambling; you could put them towards a meal or entry to the Valley of the Waves, for example.

The Batswana

Bantu-speaking peoples had settlements on the highveld by AD 500. These were Iron Age communities and their inhabitants grew crops and kept domestic animals. Linguistic and cultural distinctions developed between the Nguni people, who lived along the coast, and the Sotho-Tswana, who lived on the highveld.

The Batswana (also called the Tswana), in common with the rest of the Bantu-speaking peoples, formed clans within a larger tribal grouping. Oral tradition describes a number of dynastic struggles, often with competing sons splitting clans on the death of the old chief. This segmentation often occurred peacefully, partly because there was sufficient land available for people to move on to new areas.

By the 19th century, Batswana tribes dominated much of present-day Northern Province, North-West Province, Northern Cape and large parts of Botswana. Fresh pastures were now hard to find, and all hell broke loose during the *difaqane* (forced migration).

Such was the devastation when the first whites crossed the Vaal River in the 1830s that they believed the land was largely uninhabited. However, as the Boers moved further north, the Batswana fought back. They also petitioned the British for protection. Eventually, in 1885, the British established the British Protectorate of Bechuanaland, which later became Botswana. Mafeking (now Mafikeng) was the capital of Bechuanaland, even though it was in South Africa – giving unintended recognition to the fact that the protectorate did not include all Batswana land.

The Batswana outside Bechuanaland found themselves in the Union of South Africa when it was created after the Boer War.

Information

There's a Welcome Centre (☎ 557 1000) at the entrance to the Entertainment Centre where you can get maps and information.

Things to See & Do

The **Entertainment Centre** is a gambling venue aimed primarily at day-trippers and slot-machine addicts. It's pretty tacky. There is also a bank, bingo hall, a number of reasonably priced restaurants, cinemas, shops and the 7000-seat Superbowl. The **Sun City Hotel** has a more sophisticated casino area, ranks of slot machines, restaurants and nightclubs.

The spectacular centrepiece of Sun City is **The Lost City**, an extraordinary piece of kitsch. There's also the **Valley of the Waves** where there is (surprise!) a large-scale wave machine. This is probably the best reason for nongamblers to come to Sun City. Entry costs R40.

Golf at the superb **Gary Player Country Club** (☎ 557 1528) is R120 for 18 holes if you're a resident (or member), R150 for day visitors. A caddy is compulsory and costs R60; club hire is R75. Prices are slightly higher at the **Lost City Golf Course** (☎ 557 3700) and you have to take a cart (R130) rather than a caddy.

Waterworld on the shores of a large artificial lake has facilities for parasailing, water-skiing and windsurfing. Alternatively, you can play bowls (indoor and outdoor), go horse riding, work out in a gym, or play tennis or squash.

Places to Stay & Eat

The cheapest accommodation is at the laid-back ***Sun City Cabanas***. Standard rooms start at R755.

The lively ***Sun City Hotel*** is the oldest and least expensive of the five-star hotels. Standard rooms start at R1250. ***The Palace*** is the top place to stay at Sun City and is suitably opulent – and expensive. Standard rooms start at around R2090, and a night in a suite starts at R3050. These hotels can be booked through Sun City (☎ 557 1000, fax 4277) or Sun International central reservations (☎ 011-780 7800 in Jo'burg).

All the hotels have a selection of ***restaurants***. In the ***Entertainment Centre***, expect to pay from R45 to R60 for a straightforward meal.

Getting There & Away

Pilanesberg airport is about 9km north-west of the entrance to Sun City. SA Airlink (☎ 011-978 1111 in Jo'burg) has daily flights from Jo'burg (R342).

Sun City Buses (☎ 657 3382) has weekend buses from Rustenburg to Sun City for R30. Several tour operators make the trip from Pretoria and Jo'burg; ask at your hostel to find out what's on offer.

Sun City is surprisingly poorly signposted. From Jo'burg it's around a two-hour drive, depending on which route you take. The most straightforward route is via Rustenburg on the R565.

PILANESBERG NATIONAL PARK
☎ 014

Pilanesberg National Park surrounds Sun City. It protects more than 500 sq km of an unusual complex of extinct volcanoes. The countryside is attractive, with rocky outcrops, ridges and craters, mostly covered in sparse woodland.

The park is home to white and black rhino, elephant, giraffe, hippo, buffalo, a wide variety of buck, zebra, leopard, jackal, hyaena and even a few cheetahs.

Orientation & Information

Signposting in this area is less than terrific but you can't really go wrong once you get to Sun City, because the Pilanesberg are the only significant hills in the area.

Information is available at the Manyane Gate. The office is open from 7.30 am to 8 pm daily, closed between 1 and 2 pm. If you are planning on staying overnight in the park, unless you are staying at Kwa Maritane, Tshukudu or Bakubung Lodge, you must enter the park through this gate.

The entrance fee is R15/10 for adults/children. Gates into the park proper (ie, beyond the Manyane Complex) are closed from 6 pm to 6 am from April to August and from 7 pm to 5.30 am from September to March.

Gametrackers Wildlife Adventures (☎ 552 1561) runs trips into the park for R90/60 for adults/children.

Places to Stay & Eat

Manyane Complex & Caravan Park near the Manyane Gate has expensive sites at R130 (in the low season) for up to four people and chalets from R175 per person. There's also a shop and restaurant.

Mankwe Camp is a smaller place, overlooking Mankwe Lake. There are self-catering bungalows and safari tents, with communal washing and kitchen facilities (including fridges). The bungalows sleep two adults and two children and cost R300. The tents (bedding provided) sleep two and cost R165.

You can book at the Manyane Complex and Mankwe Camp through Golden Leopard Resorts (☎ 555 6135, @ goldres@iafrica.com).

Kwa Maritane *(☎ 557 1820)* and the ***Bakubung Lodge*** *(☎ 557 1861)* are a couple of upmarket time-share resorts that also have hotel accommodation. Rates at both of these places start at around R730/1130 for singles/doubles, more if you stay on weekends.

MAFIKENG & MMABATHO

☎ 018

Until recently Mafikeng and Mmabatho were twin towns about 3km apart. Mafeking, as it was known, is most famous for its role in the 1899–1902 Anglo-Boer War, when British forces under Colonel Baden-Powell were besieged by the Boers. Mmabatho was built as the capital of Bophuthatswana and became capital of North-West Province after 1994. It was developed as Bop's showcase and has some suitably grandiose (and ugly) buildings.

The two towns have now been combined and Mmabatho is part of Mafikeng.

Orientation & Information

It's easy to get around Mafikeng on foot. Most shops and banks are grouped around the central bus and car park. It's a hot and dusty 5km walk from the centre to the Megacity shopping mall in Mmabatho; you're better off catching one of the numerous local buses.

The North-West Province tourist office (☎ 384 3040), Borekelong House, Dr James Maroka Drive, Mmabatho, is open on weekdays but is not very helpful.

First National Bank has a branch in Mafikeng, on Robinson St between Main and Shippard Sts.

Lotlamoreng Dam & Cultural Village

Small traditional villages and kraals have been developed on the banks of the Lotlamoreng Dam to give an all-too-rare insight into traditional cultures. Although the village is still here, there's not much in the way of cultural activity. The complex is open from 7 am to 5 pm; entry is R10.

Places to Stay

The ***Cooke's Lake Camping Ground*** is dusty and unattractive but cheap at R10 per site. You can sometimes get a bed (R50) in ***St Joseph's Centre*** at St Mary's Mission *(☎ 383 2646)* in Lomanyaneng, about 2km south of the train station.

If you have the money, it's definitely worth considering one of the Sun hotels in Mmabatho. The ***Molopo Sun*** *(☎ 392 4184)*, Dr Mokhobo Ave (University Drive), charges from R300 for singles, with occasional specials in the low season.

The ***Manyane Game Lodge*** *(☎ 381 6021)*, which is about 6km out of town on the Zeerust road offers single/double chalets for R180/220.

Places to Eat

Cafe Farma *(☎ 381 6099)* on Nelson Mandela Dr is good for breakfast and light meals. ***Cafe Society Coffee & Tea Garden*** *(☎ 083-477 8485, 43 Nelson Mandela Dr)* is the perfect place to relax and enjoy lunch.

There is an ***O'Hagan's Irish Pub & Grill*** on the corner of Tillard and Gemsbok Sts; mains are around R30.

Getting There & Away

People often come through Mafikeng on their way to/from Botswana. Ramatlabama, 26km to the north, is the busiest border crossing and lies on the main route to/from Lobatse and Gaborone.

City Link (☎ 381 2680) runs daily buses between Megacity shopping mall in Mmabatho and Jo'burg (R70).

The Bulawayo train runs from Jo'burg/Pretoria to Bulawayo via Mafikeng and Gaborone. Contact the station (☎ 392 8259) for information.

Minibus taxis leave from the forecourt of the Mafikeng train station. As usual, most leave early in the morning. You can take one to the border crossing at Ramatlabama (about R5) or all the way to Gaborone (R30). Taxis to Jo'burg cost about R50.

Getting Around

Numerous city buses go between Mafikeng (from the corner of Main St and Station Rd) and Mmabatho (Megacity shopping mall) for a few rand. Buses also run out to Lotlamoreng.

Northern Province

Northern Province is a combination of highveld and lowveld but most of it is savanna. It is very hot in summer. This is the Afrikaner frontier and conservative values remain strong.

A large part of Kruger National Park is in Northern Province, but the park is covered as a whole in the Mpumalanga section earlier in this chapter.

History

This area was not densely populated but it was, and still is, home to a considerable number of different peoples, including the Ndebele (north of Pretoria), the Venda (in the north-east), the Langa (in the Waterberg) and the Batswana of the Sotho group (in the south-west).

The Voortrekkers first crossed the Vaal River (which forms the northern border of Free State) in 1836 and bloody conflicts between blacks and whites followed. In 1852 the British granted independence to the trekkers north of the Vaal River, and in 1853 the name Zuid-Afrikaansche Republic (ZAR; South African Republic) was adopted.

THE N1 HIGHWAY

The N1 highway from Jo'burg and Pretoria to the Zimbabwe border divides Northern Province. Along this artery are the main towns, including the provincial capital Pietersburg/Polokwane, as well as some smaller places, such as **Warmbaths** (or Warmbad), which has a hot springs complex and plenty of accommodation options. Translux, Greyhound and City to City buses run along the N1, and the *Bosvelder* train stops at towns along the N1.

Warning

Take precautions against both malaria and bilharzia while in Northern Province (for more information about these two serious diseases, see the Health section in Regional Facts for the Visitor). Lowveld waterways can harbour crocodile, especially in the Venda region.

Nylsvley Nature Reserve

This reserve is about 20km south of Naboomspruit. It's a great place to see birds, especially in spring and summer. The reserve is open from 6 am to 6 pm daily and there's a basic ***camp site***, which you must book (☎ 014-743 1074). From Naboomspruit, head south on the N1 for 13km and turn left on the road to Boekenhout.

Potgietersrus

☎ 015

This conservative town was settled by early Voortrekkers. The **Arend Dieperink Museum**, open weekdays, tells their story. The **Potgietersrus Game Breeding Centre** (☎ 491 4314) has a wide variety of native and exotic animals. It's open from 8 am to 4 pm weekdays and 8 am to 6 pm weekends; entry is R8/5 for adults/children. Potgietersrus has a ***caravan park*** *(☎ 491 7201)* and other accommodation.

Pietersburg/Polokwane

☎ 015

Pietersburg/Polokwane, the provincial capital, was founded in 1886 by Voortrekkers who had to abandon a settlement further north because of malaria and 'hostile natives'. Today, the town is a big, sedate place serving agricultural and mining communities.

There's a helpful tourist office at the Pietersburg Marketing Company (☎ 290 2010) in the park on the corner of Vorster St (the main road) and Landdros Mare St.

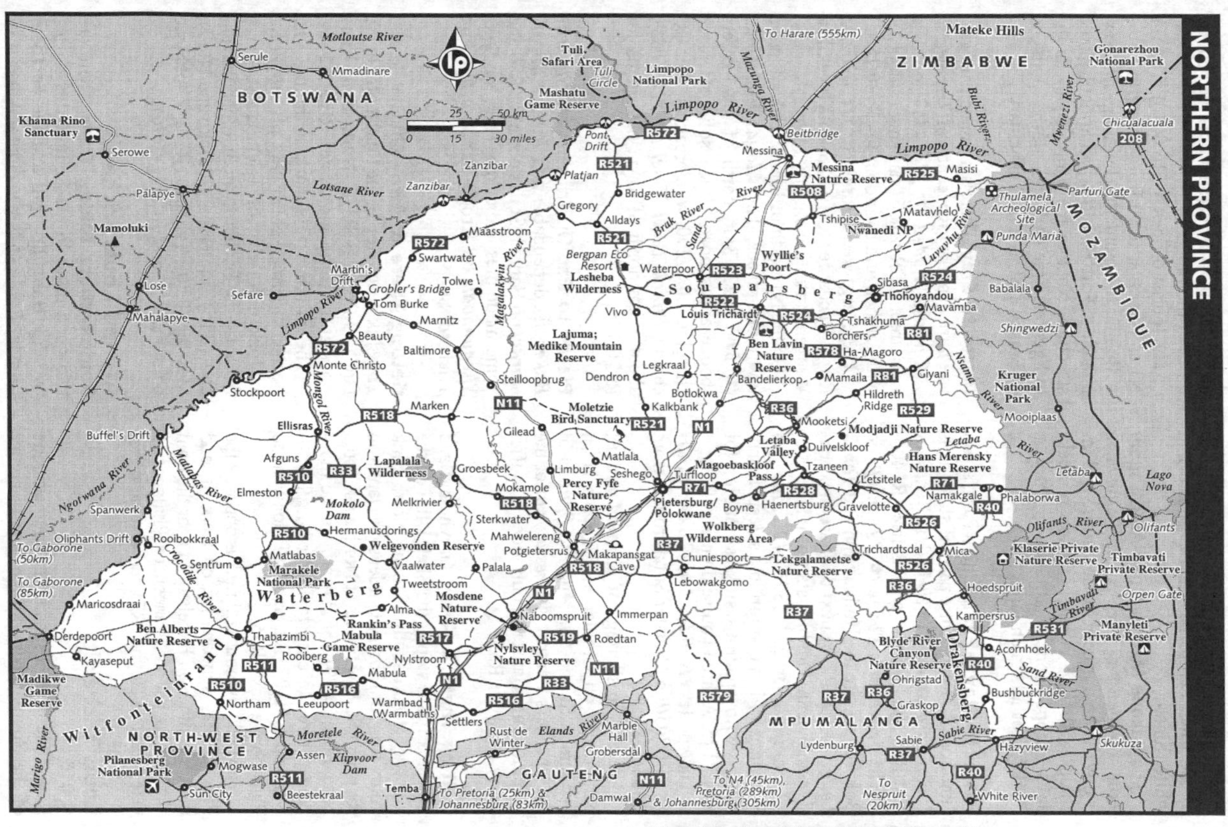
NORTHERN PROVINCE
ZIMBABWE
BOTSWANA
MOZAMBIQUE
SOUTH AFRICA
MPUMALANGA
GAUTENG
NORTH-WEST PROVINCE
Soutpansberg
Waterberg
Drakensberg
Witfonteinrand
Limpopo River
Bubi River
Mwenezi River
Luvuvhu River
Shingwedzi
Letaba River
Olifants River
Sand River
Sabie River
Magalakwin River
Mongol River
Matlabas River
Crocodile River
Elands River
Moretele River
Marigo River
Ngotwana River
Lotsane River
Motloutse River
Mazunga River
Nsama River
Brak River
Timbavati River
Gonarezhou National Park
Chicualacuala
Mateke Hills
To Harare (555km)
Beitbridge
Messina
Messina Nature Reserve
Parfuri Gate
Thulamela Archeological Site
Punda Maria
Babalala
Kruger National Park
Mooiplaas
Phalaborwa
Letaba
Lago Nova
Olifants
Timbavati Private Reserve
Klaserie Private Nature Reserve
Manyleti Private Reserve
Orpen Gate
Skukuza
Hazyview
White River
Hoedspruit
Acornhoek
Bushbuckridge
Kampersrus
Blyde River Canyon Nature Reserve
Ohrigstad
Graskop
Sabie
Lydenburg
To Nespruit (20km)
To N4 (45km), Pretoria (289km) & Johannesburg (305km)
Masisi
Matavhelo
Nwanedi NP
Tshipise
Sibasa
Thohoyandou
Mavamba
Giyani
Tshakhuma
Ha-Magoro
Hildreth Ridge
Modjadji Nature Reserve
Hans Merensky Nature Reserve
Namakgale
Mica
Gravelotte
Letsitele
Trichardtsdal
Mooketsi
Duivelskloof
Tzaneen
Letaba Valley
Haenertsburg
Magoebaskloof Pass
Wyllie's Poort
Ben Lavin Nature Reserve
Louis Trichardt
Bandelierkop
Botlokwa
Kalkbank
Borchers
Mamaila
Waterpoor
Legkraal
Pietersburg/Polokwane
Turfloop
Boyne
Wolkberg Wilderness Area
Chuniespoort
Lekgalameetse Nature Reserve
Lebowakgomo
Limpopo National Park
Tuli Safari Area
Tuli Circle
Mashatu Game Reserve
Pont Drift
Platjan
Bridgewater
Alldays
Gregory
Bergpan Eco Resort
Lesheba Wilderness
Vivo
Dendron
Lajuma; Medike Mountain Reserve
Moletzie Bird Sanctuary
Matlala
Seshego
Limburg
Percy Fyfe Nature Reserve
Makapansgat Cave
Immerpan
Roedtan
Naboomspruit
Nylsvley Nature Reserve
Potgietersrus
Mahwelereng
Mokamole
Groesbeek
Gilead
Steilloopbrug
Maasstroom
Zanzibar
Swartwater
Tolwe
Marnitz
Baltimore
Marken
Tom Burke
Grobler's Bridge
Martin's Drift
Beauty
Monte Christo
Lapalala Wilderness
Melkrivier
Sterkwater
Palala
Welgevonden Reserve
Vaalwater
Tweestroom
Mosdene Nature Reserve
Alma
Rankin's Pass
Mabula Game Reserve
Mabula
Nylstroom
Warmbad (Warmbaths)
Settlers
Rust de Winter
Marble Hall
Grobersdal
Damwal
Temba
To Pretoria (25km) & Johannesburg (83km)
Klipvoor Dam
Mokolo Dam
Hermanusdorings
Ellisras
Afguns
Elmeston
Matlabas
Marakele National Park
Thabazimbi
Rooiberg
Leeupoort
Northam
Assen
Beestekraal
Mogwase
Sun City
Pilanesberg National Park
Stockpoort
Sefare
Mmadinare
Serule
Palapye
Serowe
Khama Rino Sanctuary
Mamoluki
Lose
Mahalapye
Buffel's Drift
Rooibokkraal
Sentrum
Ben Alberts Nature Reserve
Spanwerk
Oliphants Drift
To Gaborone (50km)
To Gaborone (85km)
Maricosdraai
Kayaseput
Derdepoort
Madikwe Game Reserve
0 25 50 km
0 15 30 miles
N1 N11 R37 R36 R40 R71 R81 R508 R510 R511 R516 R518 R519 R521 R522 R523 R524 R525 R526 R528 R529 R531 R572 R578 R579 R33 R517 208

The **nature reserve** in Union Park south of the town centre has zebra, giraffe and white rhino.

The **Bakone Malapa Open-Air Museum** 9km south-east of Pietersburg/Polokwane is devoted to northern Sotho culture and includes a 'living' village. It is open weekdays except Monday afternoon; entry is R3/1.50 for adults/children.

Places to Stay & Eat In Union Park, about 3km from the town centre past the stadium, is ***Union Caravan Park*** *(☎ 295 2011)*. Tent sites cost R35 and there are chalets from R140.

The ***Traveller's Lodge*** *(☎ 291 5511)* on Bok St opposite the Holiday Inn and ***Tom's Lodge*** *(☎ 291 3798)* next door are inexpensive and clean. Doubles start at R150.

Arnotha's *(☎ 291 3390, 42 Hans van Rensburg St)* is a comfortable salespersons' refuge with spacious singles/doubles for R145/175. A three-course dinner is R18.

The spotless ***Holiday Inn Garden Court*** *(☎ 291 2030)* on Vorster St has rooms from R304/328.

There is no shortage of ***fastfood outlets***, particularly on Grobler St. ***Nando's*** is on Schoeman St and ***San Antonio Spur*** is in the Checkers Centre. The ***restaurant*** at the Holiday Inn Garden Court does a buffet every night for R55.

Getting There & Away Greyhound and Translux buses stop at the Shell Ultra on the highway, 10km south of town. North Link Tours stops at Library Gardens on Hans van Rensburg St. Buy tickets at North Link Tours head office (☎ 291 1867) nearby in the shopping centre. Jo'burg to Pietersburg/Polokwane costs R105; Pietersburg/Polokwane to Phalaborwa costs R75.

The main minibus taxi rank is opposite the Pick 'n' Pay supermarket on Kerk St, and there's another on Excelsior St near the train station. To get to Tzaneen or Phalaborwa take a taxi to Boyne (R7) and change there.

Louis Trichardt

☎ 015

Louis Trichardt nestles in the southern side of the Soutpansberg Range, and is cooler and wetter than the harsh thorn-tree country north of the range.

The tourist office (☎ 516 0040) is on the N1 as you enter town from the north.

Behind the municipal buildings on Erasmus St is **Fort Hendrina**, an armour-plated structure. Next to the caravan park is the **Indigenous Tree Park** and, off the south end of Erasmus St, is a **bird sanctuary**.

Places to Stay There's a municipal ***caravan park*** near the town centre off Grobler St.

Carousel Lodge *(☎ 516 4482)* down a side street off Rissik St has singles/doubles with kitchen and bathroom for R120/180.

The ***Bergwater Hotel*** *(☎ 516 0262, 5 Rissik St)* charges R210/285, with breakfast. Weekend rates are slightly lower.

On the N1 north of Louis Trichardt are a few more places. The ***Clouds End Hotel*** *(☎ 517 7021)* 3km north of town offers 'booze and snooze'. It's a solid old place charging R170/290, with breakfast. The excellent ***Punch Bowl Hotel*** *(☎ 517 7088)*, about 11km north of town, has rooms for R120/176.

Places to Eat On Trichardt St, ***Gateway Bakery*** is dependable and ***Ricky's Supermarket*** on Baobab St has pizza for R20 and home-made pies and cakes. There's a ***Spur Shenandoah*** on Krogh St and a ***KFC*** on Trichardt St.

Getting There & Away Greyhound and Translux buses stop at the tourist office; the fare to Jo'burg is R115. North Link Tours stops at the Bergwater Hotel, Rissik St.

The minibus taxi park is in the OK Bazaar supermarket car park off Burger St, a block north-east of Trichardt St. Fares from Louis Trichardt include: Thohoyandou (R15); Pietersburg/Polokwane (R17); Messina (R20); Tzaneen (R20); Zimbabwe border (R20); and Jo'burg (R70).

Around Louis Trichardt

Soutpansberg Hiking Trails There are two good hikes in the Soutpansberg – the two-day **Hangklip Trail** and the **Entabeni Circular Route** (52km), about 40km east of

Louis Trichardt. Trail fees are from R40 per person per day. To book either of these hikes, contact the Sabie Forestry Office (☎ 013-764 2279).

Lesheba Wilderness On the top of the western Soutpansberg Range, Lesheba Wilderness is home to white rhino, leopard, baboon and zebra. This is dramatic, varied country, with grassland and forests, plains and the cliffs of the Sand River Gorge.

There are 4WD tours and 10 well-marked walking trails. Accommodation is in self-catering ***cottages*** starting at R105 per person or in the ***guesthouse***. You have to book (☎ 593 0076, fax 593 0076) and the minimum stay is two nights.

Ben Lavin Nature Reserve This reserve (☎ 015-516 4534) has four marked hiking trails, all of which are rewarding. The Tabajwane Trail (8km) is good for wildlife viewing and the Fountain Trail follows the Doring River; there are hides at water holes.

The reserve is open from 6 am to 6 pm daily. Entry (day visitors only) is R25. ***Tent sites*** are R30, or you can stay in ***luxury tents*** for R65, ***huts*** for R85 or the ***lodge*** for R110. All rates quoted are per person.

Messina

☎ 015

The closest town to the Zimbabwe border, Messina is hot and dusty, with a frontier feel. The border is 12km away at Beitbridge and is open from 5.30 am to 8.30 pm.

You can change money at the First National Bank, open from 9 am to 12.45 pm and 2 to 3.30 pm weekdays and 8.30 am to 1 pm Saturday.

Places to Stay The ***caravan park*** *(☎ 534 3504)* is on the southern outskirts of town. Sites cost R25, plus R12 per person. Next door, the ***Impala Lielie Motel*** *(☎ 534 0127)* has a pool and restaurant; single/double/triple rondavels are R150/170/190.

The ***Limpopo River Lodge*** *(☎ 534 0204)* has singles/doubles with TV, air-con and bathroom for R105/140.

Getting There & Away Translux buses stop at the Limpopo River Lodge and Beitbridge on the other side of the border; Greyhound stops at Beitbridge. Translux fares from Jo'burg are R125 to Messina and R140 to Beitbridge.

Taxis between the border and Messina can cost as little as R5. There are a few taxis to Sibasa for R25. There are many more minibus taxis at the border than in Messina. If you're coming from Zimbabwe and want to take a minibus taxi further south than Messina, it's better to take one from the border.

THE VENDA REGION

The Venda region, once the Homeland of the Venda people, is a fascinating place to visit for its cultural insights and scenery. The Soutpansberg Range is covered by rainforest, which is strikingly lush compared with the hot, dry lowveld in the north of the area.

A good way to see the area is to take a tour. Several interesting tours run from Acacia Park (☎ 014-736 3649; see Places to Stay & Eat in the following section) in Thoyandou. A half-day/full-day tour costs R120/R150 per person (minimum of three people). The highlight of the Southern Venda day tour is meeting Noria Mabasa, a woman who sculpts traditional Venda characters in clay and wood. The Mzuri Hostel (☎ 012-343 7782) in Pretoria also arranges tours.

Thohoyandou/Sibasa

☎ 015

Created as the capital of the Venda Homeland, Thohoyandou has a casino, some impressive public buildings, a shopping mall and not much else.

The town of Sibasa is a few kilometres north and most public transport arrives and leaves from here.

Places to Stay & Eat Neither Thohoyandou or Sibasa has much in the way of accommodation. ***Acacia Park*** *(☎ 014-736 3649)* has chalets for R130 a double and you can camp for R35 per site.

The motel-style ***Bougainvillea Lodge*** *(☎ 962 4064)* is located about 1km from

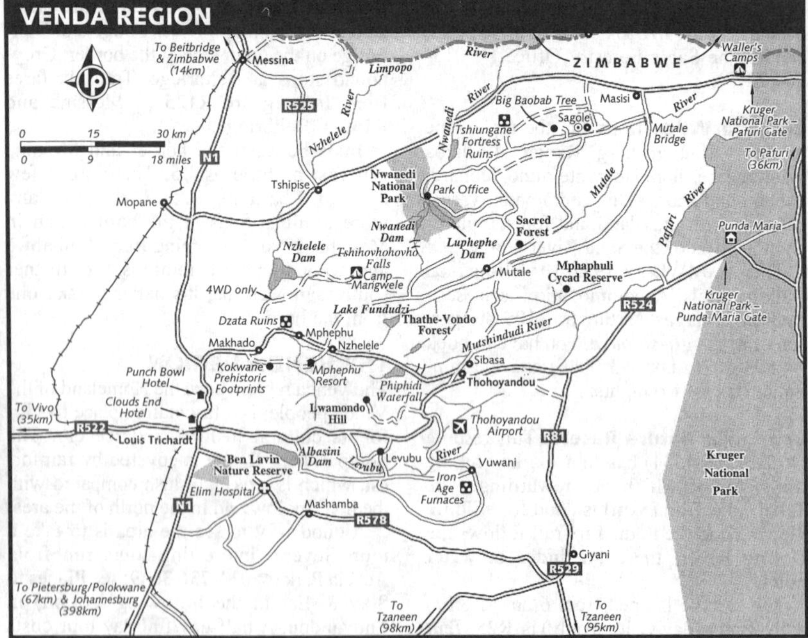

Thohoyandou, up the hill towards Sibasa. It's friendly, clean and comfortable; singles/doubles start at R160/190, with breakfast. The ***Venda Sun Hotel** (☎ 962 4600)* in the centre of Thohoyandou has rooms from R335/450, and a casino.

Getting There & Away City to City buses run daily between Pretoria and Thohoyandou/Sibasa (R60). The Magweba company has a daily bus from Sibasa to Sagole (R8).

In Thohoyandou minibus taxis congregate in the car park opposite the Venda Sun Hotel. The fare to Sibasa is R2.50. The main taxi park is in Sibasa. Fares include: Mphephu Resort (R4.50); Sagole Spa (R8); Punda Maria (R14); Louis Trichardt (R15); Messina (R18); and Jo'burg (R65).

Nwanedi National Park

The main attraction of this park is fishing and there's a walk to the scenic Tshihovhohovho Falls. You may spot white rhino and blue wildebeest; there are also lion and cheetah kept in enclosures.

Tent sites cost R40 and four-person ***chalets*** are from R130. Basic supplies are available and there's a ***restaurant***.

You can get to the park from Thohoyandou via the Nwanedi Gate, but there's a good chance of getting lost. It's simpler to come via Tshipise, and enter from the west. Tshipise is the nearest place to buy fuel.

Sagole

This Venda town is near the hot springs spa of the same name. To the north-west are the ruins of the **Tshiungane stone fortifications** and nearby, in caves, are the remains of dwellings with clay grain bins built into the rocky walls. What is believed to be the biggest **baobab** in Africa is in the same area.

Sagole Spa has cottages with plunge pools fed by the nearby hot spring for R230, and tent sites are R25. Make bookings

The Venda People

Just when the Venda people arrived in the Soutpansberg Range, and where they came from, are matters of dispute among historians. They share aspects of Zimbabwean culture, and mining and metalworking have long been important elements in their economy and culture. The Lemba people, another group living in Venda, appear to have had contact with Islam.

What is known is that in the early 18th century a group of Senzi and Lemba, led by Chief Dimbanyika, crossed the Limpopo River and located a tributary they called the Nzhelele (Enterer). They moved up the Nzhelele and into the Soutpansberg, calling their new land Venda, believed to mean Pleasant Land.

At Lwandali they set up a chief's kraal and called it Dzata. When Dimbanyika died some of his people moved south down the Nzhelele where they established another Dzata. Under the new chief, Thohoyandou, the Venda flourished. When Thohoyandou disappeared mysteriously, this Dzata was abandoned and there was a period of unrest as his offspring fought for succession.

Several invaders then tried to take over the Venda lands. First came the Boers under Paul Kruger, then the Swazis, the Pedi and the Tsonga. The Venda, however, managed to avoid being overrun throughout the 19th century, and did not even admit missionaries into their territory. Their relative isolation was partly due to the geography of the Soutpansberg, which made attack difficult, and partly to the tsetse fly, which made this area unattractive to graziers.

It was not until 1898 that a Boer army conquered Venda. If the Venda had been able to hold out for another year, the defeat of the Boer republics in the 1899–1902 Anglo-Boer War may have given them time to negotiate a place in the Union of South Africa. Instead, Venda was absorbed into the Transvaal, and was granted 'independent Homeland' status in 1979. Today the area is part of Northern Province but retains its unique culture.

through Acacia Park (☎ 014-736 3649) in Thohoyandou.

Mphephu Area

☎ 015

Known for its hot springs, ***Mphephu Resort*** is 34km west of Thohoyandou. There are chalets from R130. Book at Acacia Park (☎ 014-736 3649) in Thohoyandou. There is a licensed ***restaurant*** in the resort.

The peaceful ***Land of Legend Backpackers*** *(☎ 583 0033)* on the R524 about 31km north-east of Louis Trichardt organises loads of activities in the Venda region, including an arts and crafts tour where you can see local pottery and silk-screen printing. A dorm at the backpackers is R40 and twin rooms are R100.

It's best to bring your own food, although meals can be provided.

Lake Fundudzi

This lake is held sacred, as its water is believed to come from the great sea that covered the earth before land was created. The python god, who holds an important place in the rites of Venda's matriarchal culture and once required human sacrifice, lives here. The lake is 35km north-west of Thohoyandou but you can't visit it without permission (which is unlikely to be granted) from the lake's priestess.

Near the lake is **Thathe-Vondo Forest**, or Sacred Forest, where a spirit lion guards the burial grounds of Venda chiefs.

Vuwani & Mashamba

South of Vuwani, you can see the remains of Iron Age furnaces where the Venda smelted high-grade iron for centuries. Many of their metalworking skills have been lost, but pottery making continues. Mashamba village also has several metal-casting foundries.

THE WATERBERG

The wild Waterberg, west of the N1, gets its name from the many swamps, springs and streams in the range. It stretches from Thabazimbi in the south to the Lapalala

River in the north-east. The area's main town is **Vaalwater**.

From Vaalwater, there's a very scenic circular drive on a dirt road. Head north-west on the R517 for 10km, then turn south for 37km. At the prominent junction turn right for 20km to the **Palace of the Vultures**, a colony of Cape vultures *(Gyps coprotheres)*. Return to the junction but continue straight ahead over Rankin's Pass. Here, take the Tweestroom road back to the R517 and turn left to Vaalwater or right to Nylstroom.

North-east of Vaalwater is the pleasant little town of **Melkrivier** (Milk River) on the banks of the Lapalala.

The Waterberg is a great place for **horse riding.** Equus Trails, within the Touch Stone Game Ranch (☎ 014-765 0230), is south-east of Marken off the R518.

There are several private game reserves. **Lapalala Wilderness** (☎ 011-453 7645 for bookings) is one of the best and has a wilderness area where you can hike. To get there from Nylstroom, take the R517 to Vaalwater and from there head to Melkrivier.

THE EAST

The eastern Northern Province is culturally rich, being the traditional home of the Tsonga-Shangaan and Lobedu people. It's also popular for a north-south traverse through Kruger National Park, or a visit to one of the many private reserves in the Hoedspruit area.

Letaba District

The Letaba Valley is east of Pietersburg/Polokwane, between two chunks of the former Lebowa Homeland.

Tzaneen is the main town in the area and most places of interest are easily reached by car from there. The valley is subtropical and lush, with tea plantations and tropical fruits, while on the hills are mainly plantation forests.

The Magoebaskloof

The Magoebaskloof (ma-**ghoo**-bas-kloof) is the escarpment on the edge of the highveld, and the road here drops quickly down to Tzaneen and the lowveld. There are waterfalls in the area, including **Debengeni Falls** in the De Hoek State Forest. You are able swim in the pool at the bottom but be careful, as many people have drowned here. To get there, turn west off the R71 at Bruphy Sawmills.

The **Woodbush State Forest** is the largest indigenous forest in the Northern Province. It is home to leopard, among other animals.

There are several challenging **hiking trails**, through some beautiful country in this area. Two trails we recommend are the two-day Debengeni Falls Trail (21km) and the three-day Dokolewa Waterfall Trail (37km); both are rated moderately difficult. Book through South African Forestry Company Ltd (SAFCOL, ☎ 013-764 1058) in Sabie.

Places to Stay The ***Magoebaskloof Hotel*** *(☎ 276 4276)* has singles/doubles from R310/420, including breakfast. ***Lakeside Chalets*** *(☎ 276 4245)* located 32km from Tzaneen on the R71 has caravan sites for R50 and six-bed chalets for R200 for two people.

Tzaneen

☎ 015

Tzaneen, the largest town in the Letaba region, is a good place to base yourself. The helpful tourist centre (☎ 307 1294, ❷ tzaneen_tourism@tzaneen.co.za) is at 25 Danie Joubert St.

Clarke's Trips & Tours (☎ 307 4065) arranges tours in the area.

Places to Stay & Eat On the George's Valley road (the R528), the ***Satvik Backpackers Village*** *(☎ 082-853 6645, ❷ satvik@pixie.co.za)* has farm accommodation in converted workers' cottages. Dorms/doubles cost R40/100 or there is an expensive self-contained cottage for R250.

Fairview Caravan Park *(☎ 307 2679)* is 1km from the town centre, after a turn-off from either the Phalaborwa road or Danie Joubert St. Camp sites are R50 and a basic chalet is R150.

In the Arbour Park Shopping Centre, on the corner of Soetdoring and Geelhout Sts,

***Arbour Park Travel Lodge** (☎ 307 1831)* has singles/doubles for about R195/270.

The ***Coach House*** offers an excellent five-course set menu for R140.

Getting There & Away North Link Tours runs to Jo'burg (R125) and Pietersburg/Polokwane (R45).

The minibus taxi park is located behind the OK Centre, off the main street in the centre of town. To get to Pietersburg/Polokwane (R15), take a taxi to Boyne and change there; to get to Louis Trichardt (R20) take a taxi to Duivelskloof and change there.

Wolkberg Wilderness Area

South of Tzaneen in the northern tail of the Drakensberg Range, this wilderness area (☎ 295 9713 for information) has hiking trails and, in the valleys to the south and east, strands of indigenous forest. Book the hiking trails (a permit is essential) through SAFCOL (☎ 013-764 1058) in Sabie.

There is a ***camp site*** on the western side of the Serala Forest Station. You can't drive in the wilderness area, so plan your trip well. Fires aren't permitted – you'll need a gas or fuel stove.

The ***Coach House** (☎ 015-307 3641)*, about 15km south of Tzaneen, near the New Agatha Forest, is a refurbished old hotel with good views. Rates for singles/doubles start at R295/520.

Hans Merensky Nature Reserve

This nature reserve is bordered by the Letaba River but you risk contracting bilharzia if you swim in the river, not to mention the risk from larger denizens – crocodile and hippo. You'd have to be lucky to see a lion or a leopard, but there is plenty of other wildlife.

There are several **hiking trails** of up to four days. To book the trails write to the reserve at Private Bag X502, Letsitele 0885, or call ☎ 015-386 8632/5.

Modjadji Nature Reserve

This small nature reserve protects forests of the ancient Modjadji cycad. In the summer mists this place takes on an ethereal atmosphere.

Take the Ga-Kgabane turn-off from the R36 about 10km north of Duivelskloof; the turn-off to the reserve is a few kilometres further on.

Phalaborwa

☎ 015

Phalaborwa is a clean and planned town. There is an interesting mix of cultures – Tsonga, Shangaan, Pedi, Sotho, Venda, Afrikaners. The majority of blacks live in the nearby townships of Namakgale, Lulekani, Majeje and Namakushan.

Phalaborwa is a **copper-mining** town, and the metal has been mined here for at least 1200 years. You can tour the current mine, a big open-cut operation, on Friday at 9 am. Call ☎ 780 2911 to book.

The Phalaborwa Gate into Kruger National Park is 3km from town. The amiable Phalaborwa Tourist Association (☎ 781 6770) is near the gate and is open from 6.45 am to 3 pm weekdays, 9 am to 1 pm Saturday and noon to 1.30 pm Sunday.

Places to Stay & Eat ***Elephant Walk*** *(☎ 781 2758, 082-495 0575, 30 Anna Scheepers St)* provides friendly, clean, budget accommodation. A dorm bed will set you back R50/60, without/with breakfast, and a tent site costs R20. It also offers self-catering cottages. The owner, Christa, also organises various tours.

The ***Allin's Travel Lodge** (☎ 781 3805)* is on Palm Ave just north of the shopping centre. The large singles/doubles with TV and air-con cost R145/200.

The colourful ***Daan & Zena's Guesthouse** (☎ 781 6049, 15 Birkenhead St)* is a good B&B with rooms for R120/150.

The tranquil ***Selati Lodge** (☎ 789 2021)* on Rooibos St costs from R230/310, less on weekends. ***Tiffany's***, one of Phalaborwa's better dining places, is here.

Getting There & Away North Link Tours has buses daily except Saturday between Phalaborwa and Jo'burg (R140). In Phalaborwa, you can buy tickets from Turn Key Travel (☎ 781 2492) near the Impala Protea Inn.

There aren't many minibus taxis in this area. Most run to Tzaneen (R18) and south as far as Hoedspruit (R16). There's a taxi park near the corner of Sealene Rd and Mellor Ave, about 300m south-west of the town centre.

If you are looking to rent a car, Avis (☎ 781 3169) has an office in town.

Cheetah Breeding Project

South of the small town of Hoedspruit on the R40, the Hoedspruit Research and Breeding Centre (☎ 793 1633) is both a breeding station and study centre. It is open from 8 am to 4 pm daily except Sunday; entry is R30, which includes a video and guided tour.

Private Reserves

The area just west of Kruger National Park has a large number of private reserves, many of which share a border with Kruger. These reserves are often extremely expensive but they have excellent wildlife-viewing facilities. Travel agents take bookings for many of these private reserves and will know of any special deals.

The best-known private reserves are just north of the Kruger Gate in Mpumalanga (see the Mpumalunga section earlier in this chapter).

Around Hoedspruit and Kruger National Park's Orpen and Phalaborwa Gates, there is another group of private reserves, which are generally cheaper than those to the south. Better-known reserves include **Manyeleti** near Orpen Gate; **Klaserie** east of Hoedspruit, which contains similar fauna to Kruger; and **Timbavati**, known for its white lion population.

Swaziland

Swaziland, one of the few remaining African monarchies and the smallest country in the southern hemisphere, is a friendly place. It's worth visiting for its parks and handicrafts, and it makes a relaxing stopover on the trip between Mozambique and South Africa.

SWAZILAND AT A GLANCE

Area: 17,363 sq km

Population: 860,000

Capital: Mbabane

Head of State: King Mswati III

Official Languages: Swati, English

Currency: lilangeni (E); fixed at a value equal to the South African rand

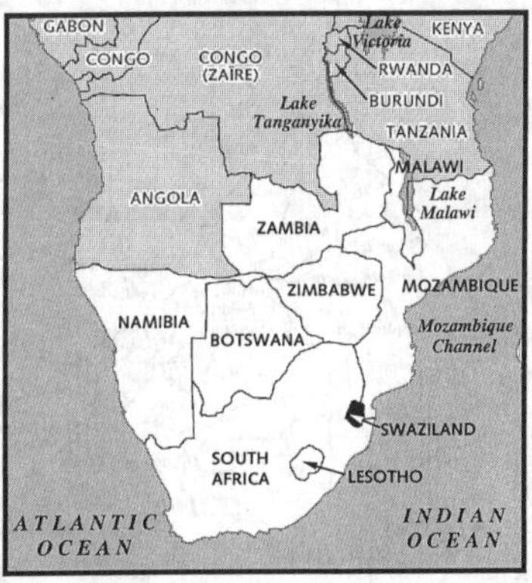

Highlights

- Mkhaya Game Reserve – see the rare black rhino in the wild
- Usutu River – shoot white-water rapids, including a 10m waterfall
- Ezulwini Valley – spend time in the centre of Swazi royalty and culture
- Piggs Peak – shop around for souvenirs in an area known for its traditional handicrafts
- Malolotja Nature Reserve – hike in a genuine, unspoiled wilderness

Facts about Swaziland

HISTORY

The area that is now Swaziland has been inhabited for a long time – in eastern Swaziland archaeologists have discovered human remains dating back 110,000 years – but the Swazi people arrived relatively recently.

During the great Bantu migrations into Southern Africa, one group, the Nguni, moved down the east coast. A clan settled in the area near what is now Maputo in Mozambique, and a dynasty was founded by the Dlamini family. (For detailed information on the Bantu migrations, see the History section in the Facts about the Region chapter.)

In the mid-18th century increasing pressure from other Nguni clans forced King Ngwane III to lead his people south to lands by the Pongola River, in what is now southern Swaziland. Today, Swazis consider Ngwane III to have been the first king of Swaziland.

Clan encroachment continued and the next king, Sobhuza I, also came under pressure from the Zulu. He withdrew to the Ezulwini Valley, which remains the centre of Swazi royalty and ritual today. Trouble with the Zulu continued though the next king, Mswazi (or Mswati), managed to unify the whole kingdom and by the time he died in 1868, a Swazi nation was secure. Mswazi's subjects called themselves people of Mswazi, or Swazis.

European Interference

During the same period the Zulu were coming under pressure from both the British and the Boers, and this created frequent respites for the Swazis. However, the presence of European caused a number of other problems. From the mid-19th century Swaziland attracted increasing numbers of European hunters, traders, missionaries and farmers.

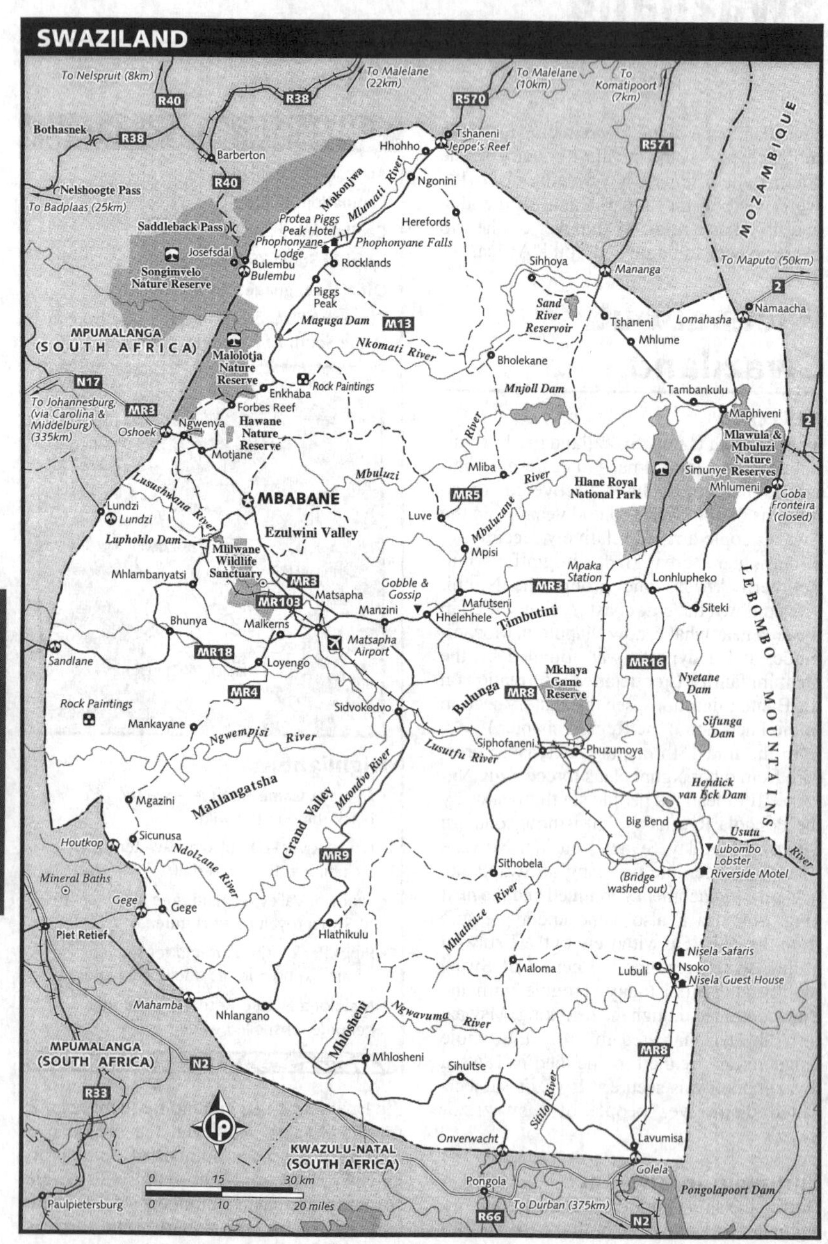

SWAZILAND
To Nelspruit (8km)
To Malelane (22km)
To Malelane (10km)
To Komatipoort (7km)
R40
R38
R570
R571
MOZAMBIQUE
Bothasnek
Barberton
Tshaneni
Jeppe's Reef
Hhohho
Makonjwa
Mlumati River
Ngonini
Nelshoogte Pass
To Badplaas (25km)
Saddleback Pass
Protea Piggs Peak Hotel
Phophonyane Lodge
Phophonyane Falls
Herefords
Josefsdal
Songimvelo Nature Reserve
Bulembu
Rocklands
Sihhoya
Mananga
To Maputo (50km)
Piggs Peak
Sand River Reservoir
Namaacha
Maguga Dam
M13
Tshaneni
Lomahasha
Mhlume
MPUMALANGA (SOUTH AFRICA)
Malolotja Nature Reserve
Nkomati River
Bholekane
N17
Rock Paintings
Enkhaba
Mnjoll Dam
Tambankulu
To Johannesburg, (via Carolina & Middelburg) (335km)
MR3
Forbes Reef
Maphiveni
Oshoek
Ngwenya
Hawane Nature Reserve
River
Mlawula & Mbuluzi Nature Reserves
Motjane
Mbuluzi
Mliba
Simunye
Hlane Royal National Park
Mhlumeni
Lusushwana River
River
Goba Fronteira (closed)
Lundzi
MBABANE
MR5
Luve
Ezulwini Valley
Luphohlo Dam
Mbuluzane
Mlilwane Wildlife Sanctuary
Mpisi
LEBOMBO MOUNTAINS
Mhlambanyatsi
Mpaka Station
Lonhlupheko
MR3
Gobble & Gossip
MR103
Matsapha
Mafutseni
Siteki
Manzini
Hhelehhele
Bhunya
Malkerns
Timbutini
Matsapha Airport
Sandlane
MR18
Loyengo
MR16
Nyetane Dam
MR4
Mkhaya Game Reserve
Rock Paintings
MR8
Bulunga
Sidvokodvo
Sifunga Dam
Mankayane
Ngwempisi River
Siphofaneni
Phuzumoya
Lusutfu River
Mkondvo River
Mahlangatsha
Hendick van Eck Dam
Mgazini
Grand Valley
Big Bend
Usutu River
Sicunusa
Houtkop
Ndolzane River
MR9
Lubombo Lobster
Sithobela
Riverside Motel
Mineral Baths
(Bridge washed out)
Gege
Gege
Mhlathuze River
Piet Retief
Hlathikulu
Nisela Safaris
Maloma
Lubuli
Nsoko
Nisela Guest House
Mahamba
Nhlangano
Mhlosheni
Ngwavuma River
MPUMALANGA (SOUTH AFRICA)
N2
Mhlosheni
MR8
Sihultse
R33
Sitilo River
Onverwacht
Lavumisa
KWAZULU-NATAL (SOUTH AFRICA)
Golela
0 15 30 km
0 10 20 miles
Pongola
Paulpietersburg
To Durban (375km)
Pongolapoort Dam
R66
N2

Mswazi's successor, Mbandzeni, inherited a kingdom rife with European carpetbaggers, and more and more land was being leased to Europeans.

The Boers' South African Republic (ZAR) decided to extend its control to Maputo. Swaziland was in the way, so the ZAR decided to annex the kingdom, but before this could happen, the ZAR itself was annexed by the British in 1877.

The Pretoria Convention of 1881 guaranteed Swaziland's 'independence', but also defined its borders, and Swaziland lost large chunks of territory. 'Independence' in fact meant that both the British and the Boers had responsibility for administering their various interests in Swaziland, and the result was chaos. The Boer administration collapsed with the 1899–1902 Anglo-Boer War and afterwards the British took control of Swaziland as a protectorate.

During this troubled time, King Sobhuza II was only a young child but Labotsibeni, his mother, acted ably as regent until her son took over in 1921. Throughout the regency and for most of Sobhuza's long reign, the Swazis sought to regain their land, a large portion of which was owned by foreign interests. Labotsibeni encouraged Swazis to buy the land back, and many sought work in the Witwatersrand mines (near Johannesburg) to raise money. By the time of independence in 1968, about two-thirds of the kingdom was again under Swazi control.

Independence

In 1960, King Sobhuza II proposed the creation of a legislative council composed of elected Europeans, and a national council formed in accordance with Swazi culture. One of the Swazi political parties formed at this time was the Mbokodvo (Grindstone) National Movement, which pledged to maintain traditional Swazi culture but also to eschew racial discrimination. When the British finally agreed to elections in 1964, Mbokodvo won a majority and, at the next elections in 1967, won all the seats. Independence was achieved on 6 September 1968.

The country's constitution was largely the work of the British. In 1973 the king suspended it on the grounds that it did not accord with Swazi culture. Four years later the parliament reconvened under a new constitution which vested all power in the king. Sobhuza II, then the world's longest-reigning monarch, died in 1982.

The young Mswati III ascended the throne in 1986 and continues to represent and maintain the traditional way of life. This reflects the main concern of most Swazis, namely that Swazi culture survives in the face of modernisation.

GEOGRAPHY

Swaziland, although tiny, has a wide range of ecological zones, from rainforest in the north-west to savanna scrub in the east.

The western edge of the country is highveld, consisting mainly of short, sharp mountains. There are large plantations of pine and eucalyptus. The mountains dwindle to middleveld in the centre of the country, where most of the people live. The eastern half is scrubby lowveld, lightly populated because of malaria, which is still a risk, but now home to sugar estates. To the east, the harsh Lebombo Mountains form the border with Mozambique.

CLIMATE

Most rain falls in summer, usually in torrential thunderstorms and mostly in the western mountains. Summers on the lowveld are very hot, with temperatures often over 40°C; in the high country the temperatures are lower and in winter it can get cool. Winter nights on the lowveld are sometimes very cold.

The rains usually begin around early December and last until April. May to August are the coolest months, with frosts in June and July.

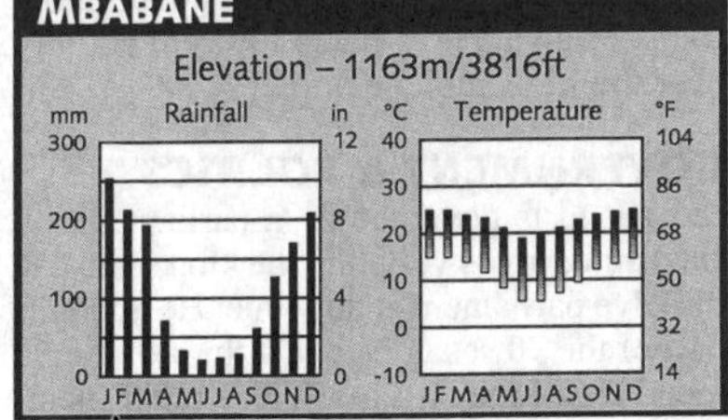

FLORA & FAUNA

Although small in size, Swaziland is rich in flora and accounts for 14% of the recorded plant life in Southern Africa. The remoteness of parts of the countryside means there are probably species that have not yet been brought to the attention of botanists. Nature reserves, particularly those administered by the National Trust Commission, help to conserve indigenous plants.

Swaziland has about 121 species of mammal, representing a third of nonmarine mammal species in Southern Africa. These days the larger animals are restricted to the nature reserves and private wildlife reserves dotted around the country. Many species (such as elephant, warthog, rhino and lion) have been reintroduced. Mongoose and the large-spotted genet are common throughout the country, while hyaena and jackal are found in the reserves. Leopard are present, but you'd be lucky to see one.

The most common of the 19 recorded species of bat is the little free-tailed bat, which can be found roosting in houses in the lowveld and middleveld.

National Parks & Reserves

The five main reserves reflect the country's geographical diversity. Easiest to get to is Mlilwane Wildlife Sanctuary in the Ezulwini Valley. Hlane Royal National Park and Mkhaya Game Reserve are also well worth visiting. These three reserves are privately run as part of the Royal Swazi Big Game Parks organisation (☎ 404 4541, ⓔ biggame@realnet.co.sz).

The office of the National Trust Commission (☎ 416 1178/9) is in the National Museum near Lobamba. It runs Malolotja and Mlawula Nature Reserves. Malolotja is a highlands reserve with some good hiking trails. Mlawula is in harsh lowveld country near the Mozambique border.

GOVERNMENT & POLITICS

Swaziland is governed by a parliament but final authority is vested in the king, who can dissolve parliament at any time. He appoints half of the 30 senators, and a third of the 60 members of the Assembly. The other members of the Assembly are elected in the constituencies, first by a show of hands and then by ballot. These members elect the other half of the Senate. The real power is vested in the king and the 16-person Council of Ministers.

Opposition parties remain illegal, but the main players, Pudemo (People's Unite Democratic Movement) and Swayoco (Swaziland Youth Congress), are achieving some success in convincing the king to move to a more democratic system.

ECONOMY

Swaziland is a poor country but it is by no means in crisis. The major export is sugar, and forest products are also important. Nearly 75% of the population works in agriculture, mostly at a subsistence level, but the country is not self-sufficient in food.

POPULATION & PEOPLE

Almost all of the 860,000 people are Swazi. The rest are Zulu, Tsonga-Shangaan and European. There are also a number of Mozambican refugees, of both African and Portuguese descent. About 5% of Swazis live and work in South Africa.

The dominant clan is the Dlamini and you'll meet people with that surname all over the country. There's a good chance you'll meet a prince in Swaziland. There are a lot of princes and they come from all walks of life.

LANGUAGE

The official languages are Swati and English, and English is the official written language. For some useful words and phrases in SwatiSee the Language chapter.

Facts for the Visitor

SUGGESTED ITINERARIES

One Week

With a week at your disposal, a day in Mbabane is plenty; drop into the Indingilizi Gallery with its displays of traditional crafts. Spend a few days poking around the pretty Ezulwini Valley and Lobamba, the heart of the royal valley, and make a trip into the Mlilwane Wildlife Sanctuary, where there is

Swazi Culture & Society

The rich and vigorous culture of the Swazi people is vested in the monarchy: the king (Ngwenyama – the lion) rules in conjunction with the queen mother (Ndlovukazi – the she-elephant). The queen mother may be the King's natural mother, which is presently the case, or, on her death, a senior wife.

The identity of the Swazi nation is maintained by a system of age-related royal regiments. Boys graduate from regiment to regiment as they grow older. These regiments help to minimise the potentially divisive differences between clans while emphasising loyalty to the king and nation.

The Swazi people's forebears were a clan living on the coast in modern Mozambique, and even today their most important ritual, the Incwala (see the boxed text 'Swazi Ceremonies' later in this section), involves the waters of the Indian Ocean.

Mkhulumnchanti is the Swazi deity. Respect for ancestors and the aged also plays a large part in the complex structure of traditional Swazi society.

good walking; you'll probably see zebra, giraffe, many antelope species and a variety of birds. If you have time and you want to see the rare black rhino in the wild, continue east to Mkhaya Game Reserve.

Two Weeks

With two weeks you'd have plenty of time to do the above as well as take in some more wildlife at the extensive Hlane Royal National Park and Mlawula Nature Reserve. On your circular route back to Mbabane, you could drop in to Piggs Peak, an area known for its handicrafts, before doing some hiking in Malolotja Nature Reserve, an unspoiled wilderness area. Alternatively you could do this route clockwise, starting in Mbabane and heading north to Malolotja.

PLANNING

Maps

The free maps available in various brochures and at Mbabane's tourist office are good enough for getting around this tiny country. A good 1:250,000 scale map is available from the Surveyor-General's office at the Ministry of Works in Mbabane (PO Box 58). If you're serious about hiking, there are also 1:50,000 scale maps.

VISAS & DOCUMENTS

Most people don't need a visa to visit Swaziland. Anyone staying for more than 60 days must apply for a temporary residence permit from the Chief Immigration Officer (☎ 404 2941) PO Box 372, Mbabane.

No vaccination certificates are required unless you have recently been in a yellow-fever area.

Hostel cards, student cards and senior cards are of little use in Swaziland.

EMBASSIES & CONSULATES

Swazi Embassies

Swaziland has diplomatic representation in Kenya, Mozambique and South Africa (embassies for countries in this book are listed in the relevant country chapters). Elsewhere in the world, places with Swazi diplomatic representation include:

Canada
High Commission: (☎ 613-567 1480) 130 Albert St, Ottawa, Ontario KIP 5G4

Germany
Consulate: (☎ 0213-377 010)

UK
High Commission: (☎ 020-7630 6611) 20 Buckingham Gate, London SW1E 6LB

USA
Embassy: (☎ 202-362 6683) Suite 3M, 3400 International Dr, Washington DC 20008

Embassies & Consulates in Swaziland

The Mozambique embassy in Mbabane issues one-month visas for E80 (considerably less than you would pay in Johannesburg). They usually take a week to issue. You will need two photos. Other diplomatic representation in Swaziland includes:

Belgium
Consulate: (☎/fax 528 3180) PO Box 124, Malkerns. Inquiries and visas handled in Johannesburg, South Africa.

Denmark
Consulate: (☎ 404 3547) Ground floor, Sokhamlilo Bldg, Johnson St, Mbabane. Open from 8 am to noon and 2 to 5 pm weekdays.
Germany
Embassy: (☎ 404 3174) 3rd floor, Dhlan'ubeka House, Walker (Mhlonhlo) St, Mbabane. Inquiries and visas handled in Maputo, Mozambique.
Mozambique
Embassy: (☎ 404 3700) Princess Dr, Mbabane. Open from 9 am to 1 pm weekdays.
The Netherlands
Consulate: (☎ 404 5178) Business Machine House, Gilfillan St, Mbabane. Open from 8.30 am to 12.30 pm weekdays.
South Africa
High Commission: (☎ 404 4651) The Mall, PO Box 2597, Mbabane. Open from 8.30 am to 12.30 pm weekdays.
UK
High Commission: (☎ 404 2581) Allister Miller St, Mbabane. Open from 8 am to 1 pm weekdays.
USA
Embassy: (☎ 404 6441) Central Bank Bldg, Warner St, Mbabane. Open from 8 am to 12.30 pm Wednesday and Friday.

CUSTOMS

Customs regulations are similar to those for South Africa. (See Customs under Facts for the Visitor in the South Africa chapter for more information.)

MONEY

Currency

The unit of currency is the lilangeni (the plural is emalangeni – E), which is fixed at a value equal to the South African rand. Rands are accepted everywhere in Swaziland and there's no need to change them, although many places will not accept South African coins. Emalangeni are difficult to change for other currencies outside Swaziland. (For more details on exchange rates, see Facts for the Visitor in the South Africa chapter.)

Exchanging Money

Several banks change travellers cheques. Barclays Bank has branches in Mbabane (☎ 404 2691), Manzini (☎ 505 2411), Nhlangano (☎ 207 8377), Piggs Peak (☎ 437 1100) and Big Bend (☎ 367 4100).

Opening times differ slightly between banks, but generally, they are open from 8.30 am to 2.30 pm weekdays, and until 11 am Saturday. There's a bank at Matsapha airport, near Manzini, open for flights.

A number of ATMs accept various (but not all) credit cards.

Costs

Costs are similar to those in South Africa, although food is a little cheaper. The wildlife reserves here are particularly good value.

POST & COMMUNICATIONS

Post offices are open from 8 am to 4 pm weekdays, and until 11 am Saturday.

There are no area codes within Swaziland. The international country code is 268; to call Swaziland from South Africa dial the prefix 09-268. You can make international calls (but not reverse-charge calls) at the Mbabane post office.

The only public Internet facility in the country is the Internet Cafe in the Omni Centre (near La Casserole restaurant) in Mbabane. A couple of backpacker hostels in Ezulwini Valley have Internet facilities for their guests.

INTERNET RESOURCES

A couple of Web sites worth a surf include:

The Ministry of Tourism Useful details about Swaziland's hotels, restaurants and other facilities.
www.mintour.gov.sz/szcomplete
Swaziland National Trust Commission A helpful site with information about Malolotja and Mlawula Nature Reserves as well as Swaziland's cultural heritage.
www.sntc.org.sz

(For a more comprehensive listing, see also Internet Resources in the Regional Facts for the Visitor chapter.)

BOOKS

All the King's Animals: The Return of Endangered Wildlife to Swaziland by Cristina Kessler and Mswati III. This book contains some terrific photography. It's the story of the conservationist Ted Reilly and the successful reintroduction of endangered wildlife into the kingdom.

SWAZILAND

The Kingdom of Swaziland by D Hugh Gillis. This is a history (to independence) of the kingdom seeking to maintain its traditional way of life in the face of overwhelmingly European influence. It portrays the personalities and politics of the time.

Swaziland Jumbo Tourist Guide by Hazel Hussey. This book has some useful information between a lot of glossy ads.

NEWSPAPERS & MAGAZINES

There are two English-language daily newspapers – the *Times of Swaziland* and the *Swazi Observer*.

PHOTOGRAPHY & VIDEO

Film and photographic accessories are available in Mbabane and Manzini.

Don't take photos of soldiers, police, airports and government buildings.

HEALTH

Beware of both bilharzia and malaria. (For more information on how to avoid contracting these potentially deadly diseases, see Health in the Regional Facts for the Visitor chapter.)

If you need medical assistance there is the Mbabane Clinic Service (☎ 404 2423), the Mbabane Government Hospital (☎ 404 2111), the Raleigh Fitkin Hospital in Manzini (☎ 505 2211) and the Piggs Peak Government Hospital (☎ 437 1111).

PUBLIC HOLIDAYS & SPECIAL EVENTS

Public holidays observed in Swaziland are:

New Year's Day 1 January
Easter March/April – Good Friday, Holy Saturday and Easter Monday
King Mswati III's Birthday 19 April
National Flag Day 25 April
King Sobhuza II's Birthday 22 July
Umhlanga Dance Day August/September
Somhlolo Day (Independence) 6 September
Christmas Day 25 December
Boxing Day 26 December
Incwala Day Late December/early January

Sibhaca dancing developed fairly recently, but it is very popular and there are national competitions at the Manzini Trade Fair – it's practically a team sport. Local competitions are held frequently, and the Mbabane tourist office has details. The Sun hotels in the Ezulwini Valley sometimes have performances.

The most important cultural events in Swaziland are the Incwala ceremony, held sometime between late December and early January, and the Umhlanga (Reed) dance held in August or September (see the boxed text 'Swazi Ceremonies'). The venue for both is near Lobamba in the Ezulwini Valley. Ask at the tourist office in Mbabane for exact dates. Photography is not permitted at the Incwala but it is at the Umhlanga dance.

ACTIVITIES

Although Swaziland is a small country, there are enough activities to keep you going for a few days. White-water rafting near Mkhaya Game Reserve is popular and there are some opportunities to go horse riding.

As well as walking trails in several parks, especially Malolotja Nature Reserve, there are countless tracks that are generations old, so you can set out to explore the country on foot.

ACCOMMODATION

There are few designated camp sites in Swaziland except in some of the national parks and reserves. Away from the population centres it's usually possible (and safe) to pitch a tent, but *always* ask permission from local people, who will probably have to seek permission in turn from their local leader.

In Swaziland there are hostels in Mbabane, at Mlilwane Wildlife Sanctuary and near Manzini. If you're stuck for a room in rural areas, you could try the local school, where you'll probably be welcomed.

Many of the country's hotels are geared towards South African tourists and are expensive.

SHOPPING

Swaziland's handicrafts are worth looking out for. Many items are made for the local market as much as for tourists.

Woven grasswares such as *liqhaga* (grassware 'bottles', so well made that they are used for carrying water) and mats are popular, as are wooden items, ranging from bowls to knobkerries. Jewellery, pottery, weapons and implements are also available.

Swazi Ceremonies

Incwala The *Incwala* (sometimes Ncwala) is the most sacred ceremony of the Swazi people. During this 'first fruits' ceremony the king gives permission for his people to eat the first crops of the new year.

Preparation for the Incwala begins some weeks in advance, according to the moon. *Bemanti* (learned men) journey to the Lebombo Mountains to gather plants, other groups collect water from Swaziland's rivers and some travel across the mountains to the Indian Ocean (where the Dlamini clan lived long before the Swazi nation came into being) to skim foam from the waves. Meanwhile, the king goes into retreat.

On the night of the full moon, young men all over the kingdom harvest branches of *lusekwane*, a small tree, and begin a long trek to the Royal Kraal at Lobamba. They arrive at dawn and their branches are used to build a *kraal* (a hut village). If a branch has wilted it is a sign that the young man bearing it has had illicit sex. Participants sing songs prohibited during the rest of the year, and the bemanti arrive with their plants, water and foam.

On the third day of the ceremony a bull is sacrificed. On the fourth day, in response to the pleadings of all the regiments of Swaziland, the king breaks his retreat and dances before his people. He eats a pumpkin, the sign that Swazis can eat the new year's crops. Two days later there's a ritual burning of all items used in the ceremony, after which the rains are expected to fall.

Umhlanga Not as sacred as the Incwala, the *Umhlanga* (Reed) dance serves a similar function in drawing the nation together and reminding the people of their relationship to the king. It is something like a week-long debutante ball for marriageable young Swazi women, who journey from all over the kingdom to help repair the queen mother's home at Lobamba.

SARAH JOLLY

After arriving at Lobamba they spend a day resting, then set off in search of reeds, some not returning until the fourth night. On the sixth day they perform the reed dance and carry their reeds to the queen mother. They repeat the dance the next day, some carrying the torches they used to search for reeds by night. Those with red feathers in their hair are princesses. The reed dance is also a showcase of potential wives for the king. As with the Incwala, there are signs that identify the unchaste, a powerful incentive to avoid premarital sex.

The trade fair held in Manzini each year from the end of August is a showcase for handicrafts as well as industrial products.

Getting There & Away

This section covers travel between Swaziland and its neighbours, South Africa and Mozambique. (For information on reaching Swaziland from elsewhere on the African continent and from other continents, see the regional Getting There & Away chapter.)

AIR

Royal Swazi Airlines (☎ 518 6155) operates out of Matsapha airport, north of Manzini. Schedules and tickets often refer to the airport as Manzini. Royal Swazi flies to Johannesburg (E430 one way), and a number of other Southern African cities. A departure tax of E20 is levied at Matsapha airport.

LAND

Swaziland's border crossings are all with South Africa, with the exception of the one between Namaacha and Lomahasha in the extreme north-east, which is the entry point to Mozambique.

This border crossing is open from 7 am to 8 pm. Another crossing to Mozambique further south, Goba Fronteira, is due to open soon.

The main border crossings with South Africa are Oshoek/Ngwenya (open from 7 am to 10 pm), Mahamba (7 am to 10 pm), Golela/Lavumisa (7 am to 10 pm) and Josefsdal/Bulembu (8 am to 4 pm).

Bus & Minibus Taxi

There is a twice-weekly bus service from Mbabane to Maputo (Mozambique); inquire at the tourist office.

The Baz Bus (☎ 021-439 2323 in South Africa) runs from Jo'burg/Pretoria to Durban via Mbabane and Manzini four times a week (E180), returning the next day.

City to City is safe, relatively comfortable and rarely crowded. It has a couple of useful routes to Johannesburg, but check at the tourist office to see if they are still running.

Minibus taxis operate directly between Mbabane and Johannesburg for about E55.

Train

The passenger train *Trans Lubombo* runs between Durban and Maputo (Mozambique), via Swaziland; the trip takes 21 hours. It departs Durban on Tuesday and Friday at 7.35 pm, reaching Swaziland the following morning and departs Maputo on Thursday and Sunday at 11.20 am reaching Swaziland in the afternoon. Recently there have been a few disruptions to this service, so check at the station for current details.

The *Komati* runs near Swaziland from Pretoria to the Mozambique border at Komatipoort.

Car & Motorcycle

There's an E15 road tax for vehicles entering Swaziland.

Getting Around

BUS & MINIBUS TAXI

There's a good system of buses, some express, running regular routes, but not very frequently. Manzini to Sitegi, for example, costs E8. Minibus taxis usually run shorter routes at prices a little higher than the bus prices.

There are also nonshared taxis in some of the larger towns.

CAR & MOTORCYCLE

Most roads are quite good and there are also some back roads through the bush that are satisfyingly rough. Drive slowly on the gravel roads (see Car & Motorcycle under Getting Around in the South Africa chapter for more advice). Driving down the Ezulwini Valley has improved substantially with the addition of the MR3 dual carriageway.

Away from the few population centres, the main dangers are people and animals on the road. Wearing seat belts is compulsory. If an official motorcade approaches, you must pull over and stop. The speed limit is

80km/h on the open road and 60km/h in built-up areas.

Many petrol stations are open 24 hours and the price of petrol is similar to that of South Africa. There are Automobile Association (AA) agents in Manzini, Mbabane and Piggs Peak.

Rental

Swaziland is so small that hiring a car for a couple of days will give you a good idea of the whole country. Rates are similar to those in South Africa.

Both Avis (☎ 518 6226) and Hertz (☎ 518 4393) are at Matsapha airport, near Manzini. Hertz also has an agent in Mbabane (☎ 404 1384). The minimum age for hiring a car with these companies is 23.

HITCHING

Hitching is easier here than in South Africa because the skin colour of the driver and the hitchhiker aren't factors in the driver's decision to offer a lift. You might wait a long time for a car on back roads, and everywhere you'll have lots of competition from locals.

Mbabane

Mbabane (if you say mba-baa-nay you'll be close enough) is the largest town in Swaziland, with about 50,000 people. There isn't much to see or do here – the adjacent Ezulwini Valley has the attractions – but Mbabane is a relaxed place in a nice setting in the Dlangeni Hills.

The hills make Mbabane cooler than Manzini, and that's one reason why the British moved their administrative centre here from Manzini in 1902.

Orientation

Despite recent development, Mbabane is still a pleasant town. The main street is Allister Miller St. Off Western Distributor Rd is Swazi Plaza, a large, modern shopping centre with most services and a good range of shops; it's also a good landmark. Across Plaza Mall St (or OK Rd) is the Mall.

Information

The tourist office (☎ 404 2531) is in Swazi Plaza. The staff are friendly and knowledgeable. Pick up a copy of the free monthly *What's On?* for current information.

For trustworthy information on Royal Swazi Big Game Parks (☎ 404 4541, @ biggame@realnet.co.sz) inquire at its office in the Mall.

Money There is a Standard Bank in Swazi Plaza, and a First National Bank in the Mall. The Standard Chartered Bank at 21 Allister Miller St has a 24-hour ATM.

Post & Communications You can make international calls (but not reverse-charge calls) at the post office between 8 am and 4 pm weekdays and until noon Saturday. There are often long queues.

There is an Internet Cafe in the Omni Centre on Allister Miller St, open Monday to Saturday.

Emergency The contact numbers for emergency services are: fire (☎ 43333); Mbabane Clinic Service (☎ 404 2423); Mbabane Government Hospital (☎ 404 2111); and police (☎ 404 2221).

Dangers & Annoyances Mbabane is becoming unsafe at night, so don't walk around by yourself away from the main streets. The back streets can be a bit dodgy even during the day. Street kids can be a real hassle.

Places to Stay – Budget

Laid-back, friendly and the only backpackers hostel in town, ***The Chillage*** *(☎ 404 8854, 18 Mission St)* is a great place to kick back. Dorms and doubles go for E40 and E120 respectively; camping is E30. E20 will buy you a home-made dinner most nights.

If there's no room at The Chillage, try the ***Thokoza Church Centre*** *(☎ 404 6681)* on Polinjane Rd; simple rooms cost E70 with private bathroom and E60 with shared bathroom. To get here from Allister Miller St turn east onto Walker St, cross the bridge at

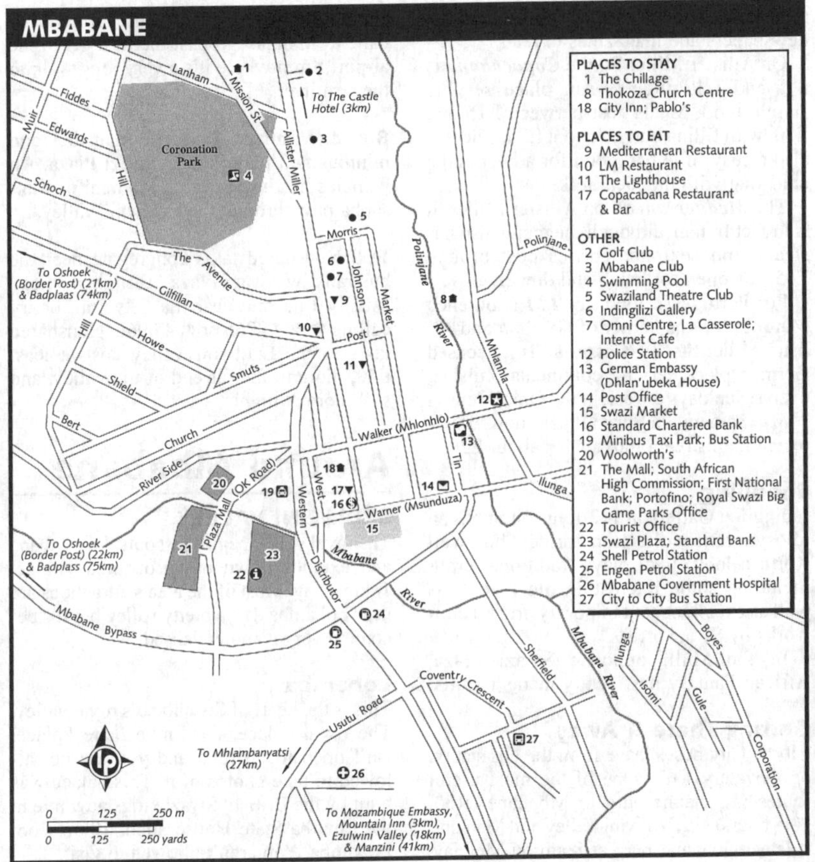

the bottom of the hill, turn left at the police station and head along a dirt road up the hill for about 10 minutes. The main drawback is that it's some way from the centre of town and walking back at night isn't safe.

Places to Stay – Mid-Range & Top End

A long-time travellers' favourite is the ***City Inn*** *(☎ 404 4278/2406)* on Allister Miller St. Singles/doubles cost from E160/230 with private bathroom or E90/120 with shared bathroom, including breakfast. Older double rooms with TV and telephone cost R190, which is good value. (They won't tell you about them unless you ask.)

The plush ***Mountain Inn*** *(☎ 404 2781)* has a great view over the Ezulwini Valley and is only 4km south of the centre. Rooms cost E336/456, with breakfast; cheaper poolside double rooms go for about E300.

Places to Eat & Entertainment

A good breakfast option is ***Portofino*** in the Mall. Large servings cost between E16 and E20 and toasted sandwiches are E8.50.

Next to the City Inn is ***Pablo's*** – the decor and food are Wimpyesque, with some steak dishes added to the menu. There are newspapers and magazines to read.

On Allister Miller St, the ***Copacabana*** is a friendly Portuguese-run place serving simple food. Meals cost between E15 and E30, with filling curries about E25. There is also a cosy little bar, good for a beer and a chin-wag with the local folk.

The ***Mediterranean*** on Allister Miller St is in fact Indian, although the menu also has steaks and seafood; curries cost around E35. It's open for lunch and dinner.

For Portuguese food, try ***LM*** (Lourenco Marques) on the corner of Gilfillan and Allister Miller Sts. ***La Casserole*** is a licensed German place serving continental cuisine, open seven days a week in the Omni Centre.

Maxi cinema in Swazi Plaza shows fairly recent mainstream movies for about E20.

Shopping

Indingilizi Gallery at 112 Johnson St has an idiosyncratic collection, pricey but well worth a look. It displays traditional craft, including some interesting old pieces, as well as excellent contemporary art and craft works by Swazi artists.

In the Mall, opposite Swazi Plaza, African Fantasy has locally made T-shirts.

SWAZILAND

Getting There & Away

City to City buses leave from the bus station on Coventry Cres. One of the most useful routes is Johannesburg to Mbabane (R60, 10½ hours) via Ezulwini Valley and Manzini. It leaves Johannesburg at 8 am on Monday, Wednesday and Friday, returning the same day. City to City services are being wound back, though, so you should ask for the latest information on existing routes at the tourist office in Swazi Plaza. (For details on the Baz Bus, which stops at The Chillage hostel, see Getting There & Away earlier in this chapter.)

Minibus taxis to South Africa leave from the taxi park near Swazi Plaza, where you'll also find buses and minibus taxis to destinations in Swaziland.

Getting Around

To/From the Airport A nonshared taxi from Mbabane to Matsapha airport costs about E80. Buses and minibuses from Mbabane to Manzini go past the turn-off to the airport, from where it's a very long walk to the terminal.

Bus & Minibus Taxi The main bus and minibus taxi park is near Swazi Plaza. All vehicles heading towards Manzini or Matsapha pass through the Ezulwini Valley.

Taxi Nonshared taxis congregate near the bus rank by Swazi Plaza. At night you can usually find one near the City Inn, or try calling ☎ 404 0965 or 404 0966. Nonshared taxis to the Ezulwini Valley cost at least E40, more to the far end of the valley, and still more at night.

Around Mbabane

EZULWINI VALLEY

The royal valley begins just outside Mbabane and extends down past Lobamba village, 18km away. Most of the area's attractions are near Lobamba. It's a pretty valley but it's becoming very commercialised.

Lobamba

This is the heart of Swaziland's royal valley. The royal palace, the Embo State Palace, isn't open to visitors, and you are not allowed to take photos of it. This palace was built by the British; Swazi kings now live in the Lozitha State House about 10km from Lobamba. You aren't allowed to visit.

You can see the monarchy in action at the **Royal Kraal** in Lobamba during the Incwala ceremony and the Umhlanga dance (see the boxed text 'Swazi Ceremonies' earlier in this chapter). The nearby **Somhlolo National Stadium** hosts big sports events (mainly soccer) and important state occasions.

The **National Museum** has some interesting displays on Swazi culture and a traditional beehive village. The National Trust Commission office (☎ 416 1178/9), where you can make bookings for Mlawula and Malolotja Nature Reserves, is here. The museum is open daily; entry costs E10 for foreigners.

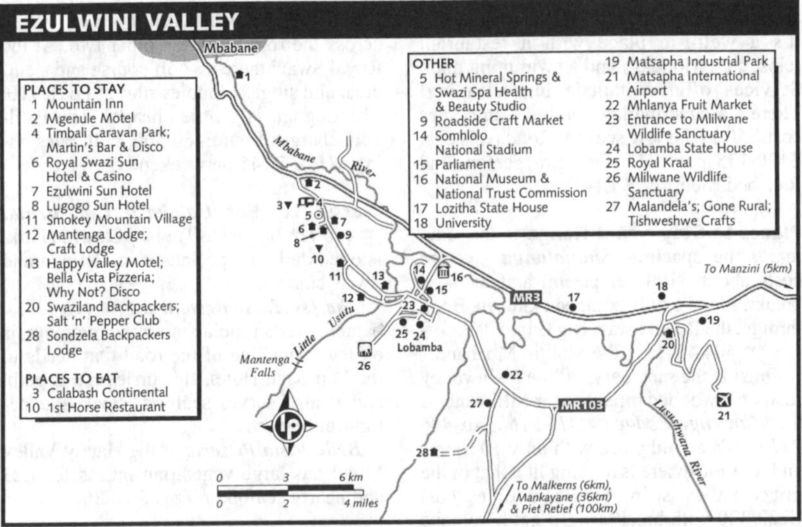

Next to the museum is the **parliament**, which is sometimes open to visitors. Across the road from the museum is a memorial to King Sobhuza II, the most revered of Swazi kings, and a small **museum** devoted to him.

Mlilwane Wildlife Sanctuary

This sanctuary, near Lobamba, is a private reserve created by Ted Reilly on his family farm in the 1950s. Reilly went on to open Mkhaya Game Reserve, and he also supervised the establishment of Hlane Royal National Park. The reserve is dominated by the precipitous Nyonyane (Little Bird) peak, and there are several nice walks around it.

Zebra, giraffe, many antelope species, crocodile, hippo and a variety of birds can be seen; in summer, these include the black eagle *(Aquila verreauxii)*.

There are plenty of guided trips through the reserve: walks cost E15 per hour, mountain biking costs E40 per hour and horse riding costs E60 per hour; there are also night drives. Watching the hippos from the restaurant is great entertainment, especially at feeding time (3 pm).

Entry to the reserve costs E17.50 for adults and E9 for children. The new entrance is 2km south-east of the Happy Valley Motel on the old Mbabane-Manzini road; it is signposted from the turn-off.

At the entry point you can get a sanctuary map and ask about night access via an alternative gate.

Places to Stay – Budget In Mlilwane Wildlife Sanctuary, camping and caravanning (no electricity) costs E30 per person. Beehive huts in the sanctuary's ***Main Camp*** cost E80 per person. More-luxurious rest camp huts with bathroom and fridge cost E170 per person. Book through the Royal Swazi Big Game Parks office (☎ 404 4541) in the Mall in Mbabane.

Also in the sanctuary, south of the camp, is the luxurious ***Sondzela Backpackers (HI) Lodge*** *(☎ 528 3117)*, which has dorms for E45 and private singles/doubles for E70/140. It's roomy, with a large veranda offering great views. The pick-up point is Malandela's restaurant in Malkerns, where the Baz Bus stops; this is about 2km west of the Mahlanya fruit market on the old Manzini-Mbabane road.

Outside the sanctuary, ***Timbali Caravan Park*** *(☎ 416 1156)* has camp sites and accommodation in rondavels and caravans. It's a well-run place with a restaurant (closed on Monday) and a swimming pool. Services offered include tent cleaning! There's a supermarket nearby. Camp sites cost E50 in the low season. Rondavels cost E120/135 plus E15 per extra person, and four-bed rooms cost E147.

Places to Stay – Mid-Range In the sanctuary, the spacious ***Shonalanga Cottage*** costs about E190 per person and includes breakfast and a fully equipped kitchen. Book through the Royal Swazi Big Game Parks office (☎ 404 4541) in the Mall in Mbabane.

Outside the sanctuary, off the main valley road on a wooded hillside near Mlilwane, is the ***Mantenga Lodge*** *(☎ 416 2168, fax 416 2516)*. It's an old place with only 10 rooms and its atmosphere is nothing like that of the glitzy valley strip. Singles/doubles cost E220/320 with breakfast. To get here, take the turn-off from the highway at Lobamba for Mlilwane Wildlife Sanctuary, but turn right rather than left at the T-intersection (look out for the Matenga Craft Centre sign); the hotel is 400m along.

The ***Mgenule Motel*** *(☎ 416 1041)* is quite close to Mbabane. Doubles cost from E168 on weekdays and E180 on weekends. There's a pool and a tandoori restaurant.

Smokey Mountain Village *(☎ 416 1291)* has 18 self-contained A-frame chalets costing E150/200/250 for singles/doubles/triples, and up to E380 for six people. The chalets are excellent value, especially for families, and they each have a bathroom, a kitchenette and a good porch for coffee in the morning. There is a bar and a swimming pool. Parking at reception is a challenge!

The ***Happy Valley Motel*** *(☎ 416 1061)* has rooms from E180/235. All rooms have cable TV and the cost includes breakfast and free entry to the Why Not? disco (see Entertainment).

Places to Stay – Top End At the top of the scale are three of the Sun group's hotels: the ***Royal Swazi Sun & Casino*** *(☎ 416 1001)*, the ***Lugogo Sun*** *(☎ 416 1101)* – which is in the grounds of the Royal Swazi – and the ***Ezulwini Sun*** *(☎ 416 1202)*, across the road from the other two. At the Royal Swazi there's a golf course and a cinema, and singles/doubles start at E570/710. The Lugogo is a little cheaper. The Ezulwini charges from E460/560, with rates rising to E615/745 on weekends.

Places to Eat ***Calabash Continental*** *(☎ 416 1187)*, next to Timbali Caravan Park, is open daily. It specialises in German and Swiss cuisine.

The 1st Horse Restaurant *(☎ 416 1137)*, named after an Indian mounted regiment, is on the south side of the road that heads to the Yen Saan Hotel. Its curries are superb, and it also serves seafood, steak and delightful desserts.

Bella Vista Pizzeria at the Happy Valley Motel has large vegetarian pizzas for E23 and hearty seafood pizzas for E30.

Entertainment The best-known nightspot in the area is the ***Why Not?*** disco at the Happy Valley Motel. Entry costs E30, or E40 on weekends, when there are shows that are mainly of the stripping variety.

The ***Ezulwini Sun*** has music, food and drinks in the beer garden every Tuesday from 1 pm.

Martin's Bar & Disco near the Timbali Caravan Park seems to buzz most nights.

Getting There & Away During the day you could get on a Manzini-bound bus, but make sure that the driver knows you want to get off in the valley. Even some non-express buses aren't keen on stopping. Nonshared taxis from Mbabane cost at least E40, and from E60 if you want to go to the far end of the valley. At night you'll have to negotiate.

MALKERNS

About 7km south-east of Lobamba there is a turn-off to the fertile Malkerns Valley, known for its art and craft outlets. At Tishweshwe Crafts (☎/fax 528 3336), 1km from the turn-off, *lutindzi* grass is woven into baskets and mats. Swazi Candles is based near Malkerns, and Baobab Batik is near Nyanza Stables on the Manzini road.

MANZINI

Manzini is now the country's industrial centre, but between 1890 and 1902 it was the combined administrative centre for the squabbling British and Boers. During the Anglo-Boer War a renegade Boer commando burnt it down.

Downtown Manzini isn't large but it feels like a different country from easygoing rural Swaziland. There are reckless drivers, city slickers and a hint of menace. Be careful walking around at night. For police, call ☎ 505 2221.

The market on Thursday and Friday mornings has been highly recommended. Get there at dawn if possible, as the rural people bring in their handicrafts to sell to retailers.

Apart from the market, there's not much to keep travellers here for long.

Places to Stay & Eat

Swaziland Backpackers *(☎ 518 7225, ⓔ info@swazilandbackpackers.com)* is a well-run, clean place, adjacent to the Salt 'n Pepper Club. It has a fully equipped kitchen, a bar, laundry service and email facilities. Camping costs E25, dorms E40 and doubles E100. This is one of the overnight stops for the Baz Bus.

The ***Mozambique Hotel*** *(☎ 505 2489)* on Mahleko St is overtrading on its old-world charm. Distinctly average singles/doubles cost E90/150. There is a dingy but good bar and a popular Portuguese restaurant.

The ***Park Royal Hotel*** *(☎ 505 7423)*, not part of the Park Royal chain of hotels, has disinterested staff but decent rooms with small balconies, TV and phone for E155/195.

There's a load of takeaways in Bhunu Mall, including ***Chicken Licken***, ***King Pie*** and ***Steers***. At Hhelehhele, 8km east of Manzini, is the ***Gobble & Gossip***, a fun place where there is always great *braai* (barbecue) food and, occasionally, live music.

Getting There & Away

A nonshared taxi to Matsapha airport costs around E60. The main bus and minibus taxi park is at the northern end of Louw St. Buses run up the Ezulwini Valley to Mbabane for E2.

MHLAMBANYATSI

Mhlambanyatsi (literally, Watering Place of the Buffalo) is 27km from Mbabane. The popular ***Foresters Arms*** *(☎ 467 4177, fax 467 4051)* has rooms for about E340 per person. It is likely to be full of locals on the weekend, when they drift here from Mbabane for homemade bread and Sunday lunch. You can go sailing, windsurfing or canoeing on the nearby **Lupholho Dam**, on the Mbabane road, or relax in the Foresters Arms library.

North-Western Swaziland

NGWENYA

Ngwenya (Crocodile) is 5km east of the Oshoek border crossing on the road to Mbabane. At the **Ngwenya glass factory**, recycled glass is used to create African animals and birds as well as vases and tableware. The showroom is open from 8 am to 5 pm daily. **Endlotane Studios** (☎ 444 5447) is 1km further up the road. Its tapestries are hung in galleries throughout the world; the studio is open from 8 am to 5 pm daily.

MALOLOTJA NATURE RESERVE

This reserve in the hilly north-west has mainly antelope species. Over 280 species of bird have also been recorded here, a number of them rare. Wildflowers and rare plants feature, and several of the plants are found only in this part of Africa, including the woolly Barberton and Kaapschehoop cycads. The Komati River cuts a gorge through the park and continues east in a series of falls and rapids until it meets the lowveld.

The reserve has one of the world's oldest known mines, dating from 41,000 BC. You can visit the mine by vehicle, but you must be accompanied by a ranger; arrange one day in advance.

Entry to the reserve costs E15 per person. Camping costs E18 at the established ***camp***

sites and E13 on the trails. There are fully equipped ***cabins***, which sleep six people for E250, or E350 on weekends. Book through the National Trust Commission (☎ 416 1178/9) in the National Museum, Lobamba.

The park entrance is about 35km from Mbabane on the Piggs Peak road; the gates are open from 6 am to 6 pm in summer, and from 6.30 am to 6 pm in winter.

Hiking Trails

The reserve is a true wilderness area, rugged and in most parts unspoiled. There are hiking trails, from short day-walks to a week-long trail, extending from Ngwenya in the south to the Mgwayiza Range in the north.

For the extended trails, you must obtain a free permit and map from the reserve office. You need to bring all your own food and a camp stove as fires are not permitted outside the base camp.

PIGGS PEAK

This small town is the centre of Swaziland's logging industry and there are huge pine plantations in the area. The town was named after a prospector who found gold here in 1884.

West of Piggs Peak is **Bulembu** and the Havelock asbestos mine. The aerial cableway carries the asbestos to Barberton, 20km away in South Africa.

As well as its scenery, including the **Phophonyane Falls** about 8km north of town, this area is known for its handicrafts. At the Highlands Inn in Piggs Peak, Tintsaba Crafts displays a good range; there are several other craft centres in the district.

Places to Stay

The only place to stay in town is the ***Highlands Inn*** *(☎ 437 1144)*, about 1km south of the town centre on the main road. Singles/doubles cost from E125/250, with breakfast. The rooms are clean enough, but aren't great value. There's a pleasant garden area with views.

In the area is one of Swaziland's nicest places to stay. The ***Phophonyane Lodge*** *(☎ 437 1319, fax 434 4246)* is in its own nature reserve of lush forest on the Phophonyane River, where you can swim in rock pools. This isn't a malarial area but there are plenty of mosquitoes in summer, so bring repellent. Cottages cost from about E198 per person and tents from E143 per person. On weekends the minimum stay is two nights, and prices rise during holidays. There are cooking facilities or you can eat in the tiny restaurant. Day visitors are charged E10.

About 10km north-east of Piggs Peak, on the road to the Jeppe's Reef border crossing, is the upmarket ***Protea Piggs Peak Hotel*** *(☎ 437 1104)*. Room rates start from around E465/532.

Getting There & Away

Roads in the north-west of the country are mainly dirt, but they're in reasonable condition. If you're driving, beware of buses between Piggs Peak and Tshaneni – they speed and hog the gravel road.

There's an express bus to Mbabane for E10. The bus and minibus taxi rank is next to the market at the top end of the main street.

There are a few nonshared taxis in Piggs Peak. The fare to Mbabane is E130.

Eastern Swaziland

The north-eastern corner of Swaziland is a major sugar-producing area. It's hot and in the arid foothills of the Lebombo Mountains, the scenery approaches what most people think of when you say 'Africa'.

This area has three notable parks and reserves: Hlane, Mlawula and Mkhaya. The towns of Tshaneni, Mhlume, Tambankulu and Simunye are the main population centres in the country's north-east. **Simunye** is a showpiece and is worth a look. It describes itself as a village but that's being coy. It's a neat, lush town with excellent facilities.

The Sand River Reservoir, west of Tshaneni, has no facilities, but you can camp there. Don't swim in the water or drink it untreated, as it's full of bilharzia.

SITEKI

This trading town isn't really on the way to anywhere any more, but it's a nice enough

Rhino Wars

White rhino were re-established in the kingdom in 1965 after an absence of 70 years, and since then there has been an ongoing battle to protect them from poachers. At the forefront of this battle have been Ted Reilly and a band of dedicated, hand-picked rangers. This defence has not been easy as the poachers have received hefty financial backing from Taiwanese interests.

Poaching escalated in the late 1980s and there were determined efforts to toughen Swaziland's laws relating to rhino poaching. As a result of the poaching, rhinos were dehorned and confined to enclosures for their own protection. After poachers armed with AK-47s attacked Hlane in January 1992, the rangers armed themselves. With the rhinos dehorned at Hlane, the poachers shifted to Mkhaya. The battle commenced.

Three months later, rangers captured some poachers in a shoot-out at Mkhaya. Not long after, two poachers were killed in a big shoot-out at Big Bend.

The last rhino, the majestic bull Mthondvo, was killed for its horn in December 1992, while the Swazi courts were still agonising over the Big Bend incident. The young king, Mswati III, intervened on behalf of Reilly's rangers and poaching declined dramatically.

The Taiwanese government made a donation in 1996 of enough money to purchase six black rhino: a gesture of good faith that was welcomed with open arms.

The rangers still wait with their rifles at the ready. You can help – your presence at any one of the big wildlife parks assists in rhino conservation.

little place and a bit cooler than down on the plains. There are good views from the steep road on the way up here.

The town was originally named when Mbandzeni (great-grandfather of the present king) gave his frontier troops permission to marry – Siteki means Marrying Place.

The ***Siteki Hotel*** *(☎ 343 4126)* has half board for E130 per person, and the host, Graham Duke, knows a lot about the surrounding area.

HLANE ROYAL NATIONAL PARK

This park (Hlane means Wilderness) in the north-east is near the former royal hunting grounds. There are white rhino and many antelope species. Elephant and lion have been reintroduced but they are kept in an enclosure. There are guided walking trails (E15) in the park.

For more information, the park sells copies of the *History & Significance of Hlane Royal National Park*, published in 1994 to celebrate the return of lion to the kingdom.

The park entrance is about 4km from Simunye. Entry to the reserve costs E17.50/9 for adults/children.

Places to Stay

Camping (no electricity) costs from E30 per person.

Thatched huts with communal facilities and no electricity at ***Ndlovu Rest Camp*** cost from E130 per person. Self-contained huts with electricity at ***Bhubesi Rest Camp*** also cost from E130 per person (more on weekends). Book for both through the Royal Swazi Big Game Parks office (☎ 404 4541) in the Mall in Mbabane.

MLAWULA NATURE RESERVE

Mlawula (pronounced something like mull-oo-way) is an 18,000-hectare reserve in harsh but beautiful country, taking in both plains and the Lebombo Mountains. Walking trails are being established through the reserve, which has shy hyaena in remote areas as well as antelope species. Snakes include the deadly trio of black mamba, puff adder and spitting cobra. Aquatic dangers include both crocodiles and bilharzia. Watch out for ticks, too.

The reserve's entrance is about 10km north of Simunye. Entry costs E15 plus E6 per vehicle.

Camping costs E18 for adults and E10 for children. ***Tented accommodation*** is also available from E120 per tent. Call for bookings (☎ 383 8885, e mlawala@sntc.org.sz), or see the National Trust Commission in Lobamba.

MKHAYA GAME RESERVE

Mkhaya (☎ 404 4541) is a private reserve off the Manzini-Big Bend road, near the hamlet of Phuzumoya.

The reserve is on cattle farms that have been rehabilitated, although the area had always been popular with hunters. Mkhaya takes its name from the mkhaya tree (or knobthorn, *Acacia nigrescens)*, which abounds on the reserve. Mkhayas grow only on fertile land, and are valued not only for their fruit, from which Swazis brew beer, but for the insects and birdlife they support.

Although small, Mkhaya has a wide range of animals, including white and black rhino, roan and sable antelope, and elephant. The reserve boasts a better chance of you meeting a black rhino in the wild here than anywhere else in Africa. There are also herds of the indigenous and rare Nguni cattle (see the boxed text 'Nguni Cattle') which make the reserve economically self-supporting.

Nguni Cattle

Mkhaya started in 1979 as a stud-breeding program for indigenous Nguni cattle. The Nguni is an old breed, and centuries of natural selection have made it heat tolerant, disease immune, self-sufficient and, importantly, tick resistant. It was and still is highly prized by the Nguni tribes who led these cattle south during the *difaqane* (forced migration). The Zulu king has a herd of Royal White Nguni *(Inyonikayiphumuli)* near Ulundi in KwaZulu-Natal.

Nguni cattle are small and were interbred with larger foreign breeds to increase beef production. This led to a degeneration of their gene pool, hence the attempts at Mkhaya to preserve their purity. When supplemental feeding of other breeds became expensive, the Nguni came into its own as an effective beef producer and it is now highly valued. Conservation activities at Mkhaya are funded entirely by the sale of these cattle.

Wildlife Drives

The game reserve organises a couple of good-value day tours. A one-day drive in a 4WD, with lunch, costs E175; a half-day costs E125. The minimum number of people for the tour is two.

White-Water Rafting

One of the highlights of Swaziland is white-water rafting on the Usutu River. The river is usually sluggish and quite tame, but near the reserve it passes through the narrow Bulungu Gorge which separates the Mabukabuka and Bulungu Mountains, generating rapids.

At one stage you'll have to portage a 10m waterfall. The second half of the day is a sedate trip through scenic country with glimpses of the 'flat dogs' (crocodiles) sunning on the riverbanks.

The trips are operated by Swazi Trails (☎/fax 416 2180, e tours@swazitrails.co.sz) in two-person 'crocodile rafts'. They take a full day and cost E250 per person (minimum of four people) or E1000 for groups of less than four people. Prices include lunch and all equipment.

Places to Stay

Mkhaya is worth staying at for at least a night. ***Stone Camp*** provides safari tents which start at E520 per person sharing, and the price includes three meals, wildlife drives and walks.

The camp is like a comfortable 19th-century hunting camp. The floors of the tents are on sand, allowing you to see ant trails and the tracks of the small animals that come in at night. The food is simple and good, with traditional methods and ingredients used.

There is also ***Nkonjane*** (Swallow's Nest), a luxurious stone cottage, also at E520 per person sharing (more on weekends). Book accommodation through the Royal Swazi Big Game Parks office (☎ 404 4541) in the Mall in Mbabane.

Note that you can't visit without having booked, and even then you can't drive in alone; you'll be met at Phuzumoya at a specified pick-up time.

SWAZILAND

BIG BEND

Big Bend is a neat sugar town on, not surprisingly, a big bend in the Lusutfu River. It's quite a picturesque spot. Book your accommodation ahead as places fill up quickly around here – it's a popular stopover with South Africans.

The ***New Bend Inn Hotel*** *(☎ 363 6725)*, on a hill just south of town and with great views across the river, is good value at E150/180 for singles/doubles. There's a restaurant and a pleasant outdoor bar overlooking Big Bend.

The friendly ***Riverside Restaurant & Motel*** *(☎ 363 6012)* is a 10-minute drive south of Big Bend on the road to KwaZulu-Natal; rooms with breakfast cost E136/180. Nearby, next to the Lumpopo Restaurant, is the new ***Lismore Lodge*** *(☎ 363 6019)* with small, comfortable doubles for E150, which is good value.

One of Swaziland's best restaurants, the ***Lebombo Lobster***, is a few kilometres south of Big Bend. If you are going to splash out on a meal in Swaziland, do it here. The food is superb – you won't taste better calamari. Highly recommended is the seafood curry for E56, enough for three people. They also do crayfish, priced according to size; expect to pay about E85.

ZAMBIA MAP INDEX

CONGO (ZAÏRE)
TANZANIA
ANGOLA
South Luangwa National Park p694
MALAWI
Kafue National Park p712
Lower Zambezi National Park p692
Lusaka p678
Lochinvar National Park p708
Siavonga & Kariba Dam p707
Livingstone p699
NAMIBIA
ZIMBABWE
MOZAMBIQUE

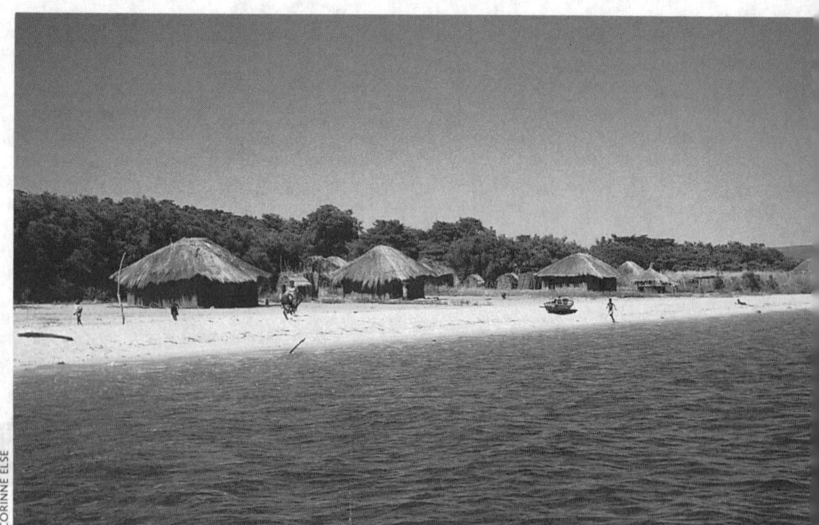

CORINNE ELSE

Village on the southern shore of Lake Tanganyika, near Mpulungu

Zambia

For independent travellers, Zambia is a challenge. Distances between major towns or places of interest are long, and getting around by car or public transport takes persistence – particularly once you get off the main routes. But for many people, this challenge is Zambia's main attraction. This is the 'real' Africa; something different or authentic in a region that has been (and still is) considerably influenced by the west.

For wildlife fans, Zambia has several genuinely wild national parks, and for visitors with less time and more money, Zambia also has some of the finest safari lodges in the whole of Southern Africa. On top of this, the country shares (with Zimbabwe) Victoria Falls and part of the River Zambezi – two of the region's tourist highlights.

After many years of failing to cash in on these attractions, Zambia is now changing. Until recently, Zambia was often regarded as a place to avoid, or to 'get through' as quickly as possible. But those days have gone; Zambian people are incredibly welcoming and an increasing number of visitors, on all budgets, are staying longer – to sample Zambia's rather specialised delights.

There's still a long way to go though, so if you like your travel trouble-free or your wilderness neatly bundled then much of Zambia may not appeal – you'd better go further south. But if you enjoy a raw edge, Zambia could be just the place you're looking for.

ZAMBIA AT A GLANCE

Area: 752,615 sq km

Population: 9.6 million

Capital: Lusaka

Head of State: President Frederick Chiluba

Official Language: English

Currency: Zambian kwacha (ZK)

Exchange Rate: US$1=ZK2800

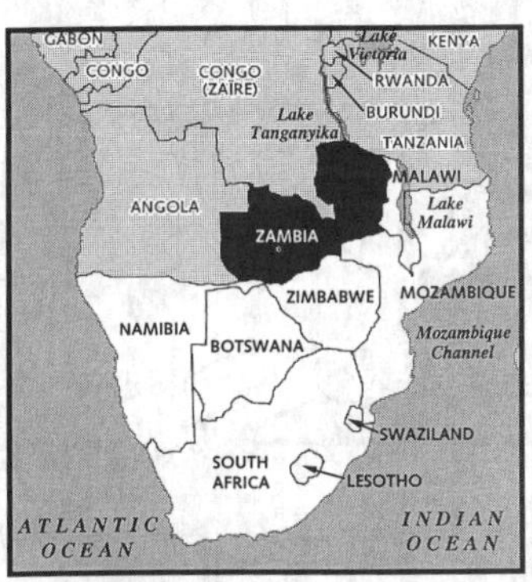

Highlights

- Victoria Falls – go rafting, bungee jumping or microlighting at the mother of all waterfalls
- South Luangwa National Park – take a walking safari through one of Africa's finest wildlife areas
- Barotseland – visit the fascinating home of the Lozi people
- River Zambezi – watch elephants lolling on the bank and fish eagles soaring overhead; perfect for canoeing
- Kafue National Park – explore this vast classic wildlife country on a night drive
- Northern Zambia – discover rolling hills, lakes, wetlands and waterfalls with rarely another tourist in sight

Facts about Zambia

HISTORY

The precolonial history of the area that became Zambia, along with the rest of Southern African, is covered in the History section of the Facts about the Region chapter.

The Slave Trade & Early Europeans

The first Europeans to enter the area now called Zambia were Portuguese explorers. In

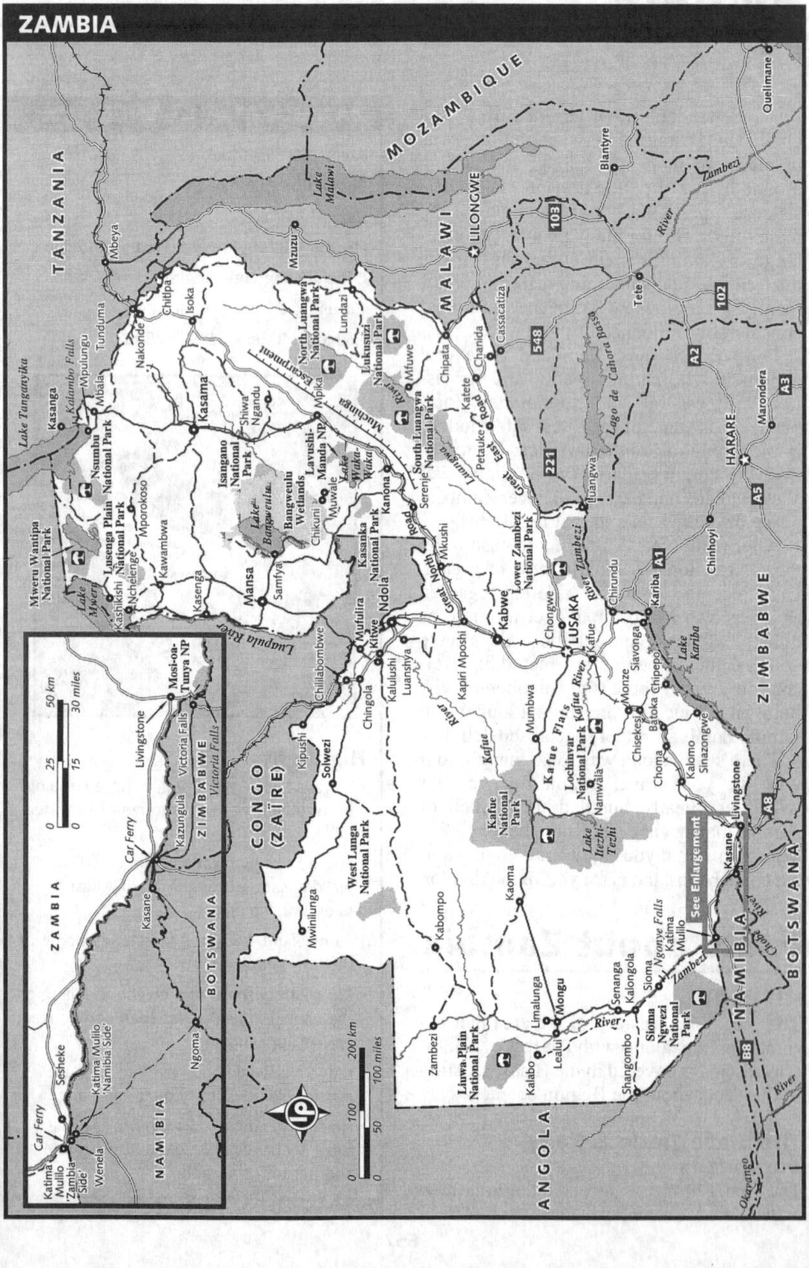
ZAMBIA
TANZANIA
MOZAMBIQUE
MALAWI
ZIMBABWE
BOTSWANA
NAMIBIA
ANGOLA
CONGO (ZAÏRE)
LUSAKA
LILONGWE
HARARE
Lake Tanganyika
Lake Mweru
Lake Malawi
Lake Bangweulu
Lake Kariba
Lago de Cahora Bassa
Lake Itezhi-Tezhi
Lake Waka-Waka
Kasanga
Kalambo Falls
Mpulungu
Mbala
Tunduma
Mbeya
Nakonde
Chitipa
Isoka
Nsumbu National Park
Mweru Wantipa National Park
Lusenga Plain National Park
Kasama
Mporokoso
Kawambwa
Nchelenge
Kashikishi
Kasenga
Mansa
Samfya
Bangweulu Wetlands
Isangano National Park
Lavushi-Manda NP
Shiwa Ngandu
Mpika
Muchinga Escarpment
North Luangwa National Park
Lukusuzi National Park
South Luangwa National Park
Lundazi
Mzuzu
Mfuwe
Chipata
Chanida
Cassacatiza
Katete
Petauke
Great East Road
Luangwa
Serenje
Kanona
Chikuni
Muwale
Kasanka National Park
Mkushi
Great North Road
Kabwe
Lower Zambezi National Park
Chongwe
Chirundu
Kariba
Kafue
Siavonga
Ndola
Mufulira
Kitwe
Luanshya
Kalulushi
Chililabombwe
Chingola
Kapiri Mposhi
Kafue River
Mumbwa
Kafue Flats
Lochinvar National Park
Namwala
Monze
Chisekesi
Batoka
Chipepo
Choma
Kalomo
Sinazongwe
Livingstone
Kipushi
Solwezi
Kafue National Park
West Lunga National Park
Mwinilunga
Kabompo
Kaoma
Zambezi
Liuwa Plain National Park
Limalunga
Mongu
Lealui
Kalabo
Senanga
Kalongola
Sioma
Ngonye Falls
Sioma Ngwezi National Park
Shangombo
Katima Mulilo
Kasane
See Enlargement
Chobe River
Zambezi River
Okavango
Luapula River
Blantyre
Quelimane
Tete
Marondera
Chinhoyi
Mozambique
103
102
548
221
A1
A2
A3
A5
A8
B8
0 100 200 km
0 50 100 miles
Car Ferry
Katima Mulilo 'Zambia Side'
Katima Mulilo 'Namibia Side'
Wenela
Sesheke
Ngoma
Kazungula
Victoria Falls
Mosi-oa-Tunya NP
0 25 50 km
0 15 30 miles

the 1790s, several of them travelled from Angola as far as the headwaters of the Zambezi. Around the same time another group pushed inland from Mozambique to Lakes Mweru and Bangweulu.

The Portuguese generally followed routes established many centuries earlier by Swahili-Arab slave-traders who had penetrated the region from their city-states on the east coast of Africa. Often in collaboration with the chiefs of powerful tribes, the slave-traders captured many people from what is now Zambia. They were taken across Lake Malawi and through Mozambique or Tanzania to be sold in the slave markets of Zanzibar. For more details on the slave trade, see the boxed text 'The Horrors of Slavery' in the Facts about the Region chapter.

In the 1820s the effects of the *difaqane* (see the History section of the Facts about the Region chapter) rippled through to Zambia. Matabele migrants entered western Zimbabwe and threatened the Makololo, who moved into southern Zambia, displacing the Tonga people and threatening the Lozi people on the upper Zambezi.

The celebrated British explorer David Livingstone travelled up the River Zambezi in the early 1850s, searching for a route to the interior of Africa, hoping to introduce Christianity and the principles of European civilisation to combat the horrors of the slave trade. In 1855, Livingstone reached the giant waterfall that he christened Victoria Falls.

Livingstone's work and writings inspired missionaries to come to the area north of the Zambezi, and close on their heels came explorers, hunters and prospectors searching for whatever the country had to offer. The 'new' territory did not escape the notice of Cecil John Rhodes, who was already establishing mines and a vast business empire in South Africa. (See the boxed text 'Cecil Rhodes' in the Northern Cape Province section of the South Africa chapter.) Rhodes' British South Africa Company (BSAC) laid claim to the area in the early 1890s and was backed by the British government in 1895, partly to help combat slavery and also to prevent further Portuguese expansion in the region.

The Colonial Era

For the next few decades, like many other parts of Southern Africa, Zambia's history was largely influenced by BSAC activities. Two territories were initially created: North-Western Rhodesia and North-Eastern Rhodesia, but these were combined in 1911 to become Northern Rhodesia. In 1907 the town of Livingstone became the capital.

At around the same time, vast deposits of copper were discovered in the area now called the Copperbelt. The indigenous people had mined here for centuries, but now large European-style opencast pits were established, and local Africans were employed as labourers. They may have had little choice: they needed money to pay the hut tax which had been introduced, and their only other source of income had gone when their farmland was appropriated by European settlers.

In 1924 the colony was put under direct British control and in 1935 the capital was moved to Lusaka. In the following years, settlers pushed for closer ties with Southern Rhodesia and Nyasaland (Malawi), to make them less dependent on colonial rule, but various interruptions (including WWII) meant the Federation of Rhodesia and Nyasaland did not come about until 1953.

Nationalist Resistance

Meanwhile, African nationalism was becoming a more dominant force in the region. The United National Independence Party (UNIP) was founded in the late 1950s by Kenneth Kaunda; he spoke out against the Federation on the grounds that it promoted the rights of white settlers to the detriment of the local African population.

Through the early 1960s, as many other African countries gained independence, Zambian nationalists opposed the colonial forces, culminating in a massive campaign of civil disobedience and a small but decisive conflict called the Chachacha Rebellion.

The Federation was dissolved in 1963 and Northern Rhodesia became independent in 1964, taking the name Zambia. By this time the British government had generated huge sums from Northern Rhodesia, yet it had spent only a small part of this money on the colony, investing instead in Southern Rhodesia. Today, Zambia still suffers from the effects of this staggering loss of capital.

Independence

After gaining independence, Zambia inherited a British style multiparty political system. Kenneth Kaunda, as leader of the majority UNIP, became the new republic's first president. The other main party was the African National Congress, led by Harry Nkumbula. But Kaunda disliked opposition. In 1972, in one neat move, he disbanded the Zambian ANC, created the 'second republic', declared UNIP the sole legal party and made himself sole presidential candidate.

Kaunda remained in power for the next 27 years, and his rule in Zambia was based upon 'humanism' – his own mix of Marxist ideals and traditional African values. The civil service was increased and nearly all private business (including the copper mines) were nationalised. But corruption and mismanagement, exacerbated by a fall in the world copper price, meant that by the end of the 1970s Zambia was one of the poorest countries in the world.

Another problem was the closure of landlocked Zambia's trade routes to the coast through neighbouring countries (especially Rhodesia and South Africa) in retaliation against Kaunda's support for several liberation movements in the region – including the ANC (South Africa), the Zimbabwe African People's Union (ZAPU), the Zimbabwe African National Union (ZANU), Frelimo (Mozambique), and Namibia's South West African People's Organisation (SWAPO).

The 1980s

By the early 1980s Rhodesia had become Zimbabwe, allowing Kaunda to take his country off a war footing, and the TAZARA railway to Dar es Salaam (Tanzania) had been completed, giving Zambia access to the sea. Despite these improvements things were hardly rosy. The economy was on the brink of collapse, foreign exchange reserves were almost exhausted, and there were serious shortages of food, fuel and other basic commodities, while crime and unemployment rates had risen sharply. The constant threat of saboteurs and spies had left its mark too – foreign travellers passing through Zambia in the 1980s were regularly hassled at roadblocks by underpaid and ill-disciplined officials.

In 1986 an attempt was made to diversify the economy and improve the country's balance of payments. Zambia received economic aid from the International Monetary Fund (IMF), but its conditions were severe, and included cutting basic food subsidies. The resultant price rise led to serious countrywide riots in which many people lost their lives, forcing Kaunda to restore subsidies.

Turning Point

The winds of change blowing through Africa and the world in the late 1980s, coupled with Zambia's disastrous domestic situation, meant something had to give. Following another round of violent street protests against increased food prices in mid-1990, which quickly transformed into a general demand for the return of multiparty politics, Kaunda was forced to accede to public opinion.

He attempted to fob off the population with a snap referendum in late 1990 but, as protests grew more vocal, he was forced to legalise opposition parties and set full presidential and parliamentary elections for October 1991. These went ahead, and Kaunda and the UNIP were resoundingly defeated by Frederick Chiluba, a former trade union leader, and the Movement for Multiparty Democracy (MMD). Kaunda stepped down without complaint, which some analysts say saved Zambia from descending into anarchy.

President Chiluba moved quickly to encourage loans and investments from the IMF and World Bank. Exchange controls were liberalised to attract investors, particularly from South Africa, but tough austerity measures were also introduced. Once again, food prices soared. The civil service was rationalised, state industries privatised or simply closed, and thousands of people lost their jobs. For many Zambians the IMF and World Bank made things even worse than they'd been in the 1980s.

By the mid-1990s the lack of visible change in Zambia allowed Kaunda to confidently re-enter the political arena. He attracted strong support and again became UNIP leader. Leading up to the elections, the MMD was worried, and passed a law forbidding those with foreign parents from standing (Kaunda's parents were from Malawi). Despite intercessions from western aid donors and world leaders like Nelson Mandela, not to mention accusations that Chilumba's parents were from Congo (Zaïre), the law was not repealed, and elections went ahead in November 1996. The UNIP withdrew all their candidates in protest, and there was a very low turn-out. Chiluba and the MMD won easily and remained in firm control.

Shortly after the election, Chiluba ordered the arrest of two independent monitors who claimed the elections were rigged. Two days later, some journalists were suspended from their jobs, apparently because their reports of the MMD's election victory lacked sufficient enthusiasm.

But overall most Zambians accepted the result, even if they knew it was rigged, many in the hope it would at least help Zambia remain peaceful. International donors showed concerns at continuing corruption and human rights abuses, but some aid money slowly flowed back into the country – mainly to nongovernmental organisations.

Modern Times

In October 1997 a bungled coup attempt allowed Chiluba to announce a state of emergency, and many opposition figures were arrested. Kaunda said the coup was a set-up and an excuse, but he was placed under house arrest until March 1998, which only endeared him further to UNIP supporters and MMD opponents.

Throughout 1998 and 1999 political parties continued to trade insults while both UNIP and the MMD were torn by internal rivalries. Several government ministers and senior civil servants were sacked, and another was mysteriously assassinated. Edith Nawakwi, the outspoken and controversial finance minister, was fired in July 1999, possibly in an attempt to placate major donors.

Despite such moves, the sad fact is that with ineffectual government, a continued debt crisis, high unemployment and a rapidly growing population, Zambia's troubles are far from over.

GEOGRAPHY

Landlocked Zambia is one of Africa's most eccentric legacies of colonialism. Shaped like a contorted figure-of-eight, its borders do not correspond to any tribal or linguistic area.

Zambia sits on an undulating plateau, sloping to the south. Areas of high ground include the Copperbelt Highlands and the Nyika Plateau on the border with Malawi. In the far north the plateau drops steeply to Lake Tanganyika, one of the Rift Valley lakes, which Zambia shares with Tanzania, Burundi and Congo (Zaïre).

Zambia's main rivers are the Zambezi, which rises in the west of the country and forms the border between Zambia, Namibia, Botswana and Zimbabwe; the Kafue, which rises in the highlands between Zambia and Congo, and flows into the Zambezi south of Lusaka; and the Luangwa, which rises in the north and also flows into the Zambezi, to the east of Lusaka.

CLIMATE

Zambia's altitude creates a temperate climate. There are three distinct seasons: cool and dry from May to August; hot and dry from September to October; and rainy from November to April. Rainfall is higher in the north of the country than in the south.

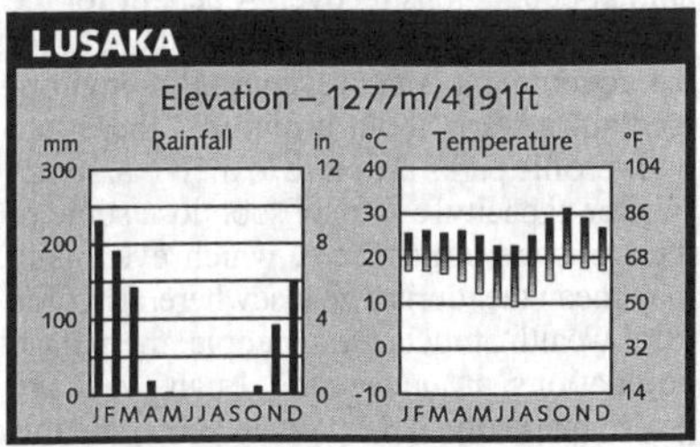

ECOLOGY & ENVIRONMENT

Although Zambia's human population is growing rapidly, it is still relatively sparse, and many of the environmental issues associated with overpopulation suffered by neighbouring countries are not encountered here. Having said that, around the main urban areas – Lusaka, Livingstone and the Copperbelt – the denudation of local vegetation is apparent, and unsustainable deforestation (and associated soil erosion) may become a problem in the future.

Zambia's national parks and wildlife areas are discussed later in this section, but they neatly illustrate a major environmental issue which confronts parks in many parts of Southern Africa. During the 1970s and 1980s, many Zambian parks were effectively abandoned and poaching became a major problem. Then, under pressure from donor and conservation organisations, the government slowly realised that tourism could be a major money-earner for the country (and for local people), and that this depended on healthy national parks. Through the 1990s, some former state-run lodges were privatised, and tour companies were awarded 'concessions' to build camps and run safaris. The process is slow, and despite success in some parks, poaching, poor management and low tourism numbers still remain major problems in some areas.

Improvements have been most noticeable in South Luangwa and Lower Zambezi national parks, which today are thriving. A benefit for visitors is that these parks are easier to visit, and there are more facilities. A benefit for wildlife is the presence of tourists and guides, which deters poachers and helps animal populations recover. A benefit for the local people is jobs and money. A benefit for the government is tax revenue. But environmentalists warn about a minus – these two high-profile parks are close to their maximum 'visitor-capacity' and may soon lose some of their pristine atmosphere, which eventually may mean the tourists go elsewhere. Also, the local wealth attracts more people; the village populations around South Luangwa have grown markedly in the past ten years, and this puts pressure on natural resources.

For true success, a balance has to be struck between tourism growth and environmental destruction – in other words, all development has to be sustainable. Only then can the people of Zambia genuinely benefit in the long term from the wildlife resource sitting on their doorstep.

FLORA & FAUNA

An overview of Southern Africa's vegetation zones is given in the Facts about the Region chapter, and the colour Wildlife Guide discusses the region's indigenous animals.

Zambia's main vegetation zones are various types of miombo woodland, which covers the plateau areas (about 60% the country), mopane woodland in the hotter lower parts of the country such as the Zambezi and Luangwa Valleys, and smaller patches of acacia woodland and semi-evergreen forest – mostly in the south and west. Zambia's many rivers and lakes give the country some of the most extensive wetlands in Southern Africa.

Zambia's diversity of landscape, its plentiful water supplies and its position between east, southern and central Africa mean there's a huge diversity of animal species. The rivers, of course, support huge populations of hippo and croc, and the associated grasslands provide plenty of grazing for huge herds of plains wildlife such as zebra, impala and puku – an antelope common in Zambia but more unusual elsewhere. Other antelope occurring in Zambia include waterbuck and lechwe. Near Lake Bangweulu you can see vast herds of the rare black lechwe subspecies, and in the area around the Kafue River there's another endemic, the Kafue lechwe. Kasanka National Park is one of the best places in Africa to see sitatunga – another rare water-loving antelope. Other endemics are the Thornicroft giraffe and Cookson's wildebeest, both found in South Luangwa. In the bush you'll also see waterbuck, bushbuck and smaller antelope such as duiker and klipspringer.

The plains grazers naturally attract predators, and most parks contain lion, leopard and hyaena (which you'll probably see) and cheetah (which are harder to spot). Wild dog, a rare and very endangered species, is encountered occasionally. Other big draws are buffalo and of course elephant, both found in huge herds in the main national parks.

Birdwatchers can go crazy in Zambia. Over 750 species have been recorded here, and birders used to the 'traditional' Southern African species listed in the *Roberts* and *Newman's* fieldguides will spend a lot of time identifying unusual species – especially in the northern and western parts of the country. Most notable of the Zambian specials is the shoebill stork, found in the Bangweulu Wetlands, and reliably in only one other place in Africa.

National Parks

Zambia's parks have been called Southern Africa's best-kept secret, but in the past few years their cover has been blown and wildlife aficionados now come from all over the world to see the impressive populations of birds and animals, or to take part in the walking safaris for which Zambia's parks are particularly well known.

Zambia has 19 national parks – an impressive total – but after decades of poaching, clearing and general bad management, many are just lines on the map which no longer protect (or even contain) much in the way of wildlife. Parks with healthy stocks of wildlife and good tourist facilities (the so-called high profile parks) are South Luangwa, Lower Zambezi, Kafue and Mosi-oa-Tunya (Victoria Falls) – all highly recommended. Also very good, but less often visited, is North Luangwa. More obscure are Liuwa Plain, Sioma Ngwezi and Nsumbu, although they all feature in the itineraries of exclusive safari companies. In a scheme unique in Zambia (and unusual in Africa), the management of Kasanka National Park has been leased to a private operator, and this park is now functioning very well after being overlooked for many years. It is hoped that in the future this scheme may be extended to other parks.

Zambia also has 31 game management areas (GMAs) acting as 'buffer zones' around the national parks, used mostly for commercial hunting. National parks and GMAs are administered by the semi-autonomous Zambia Wildlife Authority, which took over from the National Parks & Wildlife Service (a government department) through 1999 and 2000.

Entrance Fees Entry for tourists to South Luangwa and Lower Zambezi National Parks is US$20 per person per day. North Luangwa and Lochinvar are US$15. Kafue and Nsumbu are US$10. Kasanka costs US$5, Mosi-oa-Tunya (Victoria Falls section) US$3 and Mosi-oa-Tunya (Game Park) costs US$3. Vehicle entry costs US$15. Camping at a national park camp site costs US$5. Zambian residents pay cheaper rates. For most other parks, where there are no facilities, or if you're in transit, there's no charge.

> **National Park Maps**
>
> The maps of national parks in this Zambia chapter show main access routes only. It is not possible to show all minor roads and tracks in the parks: many original tracks have gone back to bush and simply disappeared; some tracks are lost after heavy rains and rebuilt the following year in another position; and several new routes will be built as part of planned rehabilitation schemes. Therefore, please use the national park maps in this chapter as guides only. More detailed maps may be available in the parks themselves or in Lusaka.

GOVERNMENT & POLITICS

Zambia is a parliamentary democracy, with elections for president and members of parliament held every five years. There are several political parties, although all politics in the country are dominated by the Movement for Multiparty Democracy (MMD), the ruling party led by President Frederick Chiluba, and the United National Independence Party (UNIP), the main opposition led by Kenneth Kaunda. There are 150 seats in the parliament, and in the 1996 elections the MMD won 130 of these. The next elections are due in 2001.

ECONOMY

Zambia's economy is dominated by agriculture, with 50% of produce from subsistence farmers, and the rest from large commercial farms, although the country still needs to import a lot of its food requirements.

Industry is dominated by copper mining, which employs about 5% of the population. Since the copper price slump of the 1970s, the industry has plunged into severe debt, effectively taking the country with it.

The economy is very largely dependent on aid, and in the last two decades has received billions of US dollars from donor countries and in loans from major institutions such as the World Bank and the IMF. Despite this, in the mid-1990s GNP was declining, inflation was running at 80% and the World Bank reported that poverty was affecting 90% of rural people. By 1999 things looked slightly better – inflation was down to 18% and the privatisation of many formerly state-owned companies had reportedly led to a small increase in GNP, although for most Zambians poverty remains a very real problem. A notable growth industry is tourism, which earns the country about US$30 million per year.

POPULATION & PEOPLE

Zambia's population is estimated at about 9.6 million, and its population density is about 12.8 people per sq km, making Zambia one of the most thinly populated countries in Africa. More than 50% of the population is concentrated in urban areas (mostly Lusaka and the cities of the Copperbelt) – very unusual for a developing country. This is noticeable as you travel through rural areas. You can go for hours sometimes without seeing more than a couple of small villages.

ARTS

Music & Dance

All Zambia's ethnic groups have their own musical traditions. The Lozi of western Zambia are famous for their large drums played during the famous Kuomboka ceremony, which is described in detail in the Western Zambia section of this chapter. The Bemba people are also drummers, and have several different types. Other traditional musical instruments include large wooden xylophones, often with gourds underneath the blocks for resonance, and tiny thumb pianos, with just a few keys made from flattened metal.

The most notable traditional dance is the *makishi*, in which male dancers wear masks of stylised human faces with grass skirts and anklets. It probably originated in the Congo (Zaïre) region and was brought to north-

SARAH JOLLY

The *makishi*, performed by men, is the most notable traditional dance in Zambia.

western Zambia by the Luvale or Luchasi people, then adopted by some other ethnic groups. It is now found in many parts of the country, mainly at boys' initiation ceremonies, but any local celebration seems to be a good excuse.

Contemporary musicians who have achieved some international fame include Larry Maluma and Ricki Ilonga, both exponents of a traditional style called *kalindula*. Other popular musicians who play traditional styles include the Sakala Brothers from Eastern Province, and Mpunda Mutale from Northern Province.

Younger Zambians prefer reggae – both the hard Jamaican style and a softer version popular in Zambia and Malawi. There are many Zambian reggae bands; a good one to look out for in Lusaka is Real African. Also very popular is Congo-style rhumba music – also called *kwasa kwasa* – invariably played long and loud at local bars and nightclubs.

Visual Arts

Zambian artists produce a fine range of wares, including the skilfully woven baskets of Barotseland, malachite jewellery from the north, and the famous wood carvings from Mukuni village near Livingstone. Much of this craft is sold in markets around the country. (For more details see Shopping in the sections on the main cities.)

Zambia has a thriving contemporary art scene. One of the country's most famous and respected painters is the late Henry Tayali; his works (described by critics as 'crowded social realism') have inspired many other painters and enjoyed a popular following among ordinary Zambians. If you're keen on finding out more about the local art scene, the studio and exhibition centre named after him in Lusaka is worth a visit.

Other internationally recognised artists include Agnes N'Gambi Yombwe, who works with purely natural materials and uses traditional ceramics and textile designs in her striking sculptures; and the sculptor Eddie Mumba. Starry Mwaba and Mulenga Chafilwa produce realistic urban paintings; Jack Chande sculpts in stone; and Friday Tembo produces fantastical figures from wood.

Literature

Well-known Zambian poets and novelists are thin on the ground. The main names in home-grown literature still date from the 1960s – Fwanyanga Mulikita's collection of short stories *A Point of No Return* – and the 1970s – writer-politician Dominic Mulaisho's novels *The Tongue of the Dumb* and *The Smoke that Thunders*. In the 1980s one of Zambia's most widely read and distributed books was *Zambia shall be Free*, the personal manifesto of President Kenneth Kaunda.

Theatre

Lusaka's theatre scene is thriving, with plenty of local writers producing plays and other dramas, from slapstick comedy to hard political comment. There's nearly always something on at the Lusaka Playhouse, and a visit can be very entertaining and revealing (see Entertainment in the Lusaka section).

LANGUAGE

There are about 35 different ethnic groups (or tribes) in Zambia, all with their own language, although the actual number varies according to definition. Main groups and languages include Bemba in the north and centre, Tonga in the south, Nyanja (which is very similar to Chichewa, spoken in Malawi) in the east, and Lozi in the west. English has become an essential national and official language; it's widely spoken across the country, even in quite remote areas. See the Language chapter at the back of this book for some useful words and phrases in Chichewa.

Facts for the Visitor

SUGGESTED ITINERARIES

Zambia is a large country, and its geography makes neat circuits tricky, so unless you've got a lot of time it's better to concentrate on one area than try to do everything. Where you go will also depend on your own interests, but Zambia's major draw is undoubtedly its wildlife, so most visitors' itineraries tend to work around a visit to at least one national park. Another major factor is your method of travel – backpackers simply cannot get to some places that are easily reached by car drivers.

Two to Three Weeks

A trip of two to three weeks might start at Livingstone, just north of Victoria Falls – the main centre for adventure and activities in Southern Africa. You could easily spend a week here, white-water rafting, bungee jumping, canoeing, abseiling and microlighting. From Livingstone you could head straight for Lusaka, but if you're not in a rush and you like getting off the beaten track you could loop through western Zambia to Sesheke and Mongu, then go to Lusaka via Kafue National Park. From Lusaka you could go to Siavonga on Lake Kariba, or arrange a trip to Lower Zambezi National Park, then return to Livingstone, possibly stopping off in Choma on the way. Birdwatchers with their own wheels may like to branch off to Lochinvar National Park.

Three to Four Weeks

Added to the itinerary outlined above, with more time you could go from Lusaka up the Great East Road, and branch off at Chipata to visit South Luangwa National Park, easily reached by backpackers. Alternatively, you could cut the western loop and go to the north of Zambia, to Samfya, Lake Bangweulu and Kasanka National Park (also quite accessible for backpackers), or to Kasama, Mbala and Mpulungu on the beautiful and dramatic southern tip of Lake Tanganyika.

With a car, several more options open up. You can go beyond the Copperbelt and reach the Chimpanzee Sanctuary at Chimfunshi, or on the road to Lake Tanganyika, you could stop off at the incongruous colonial mansion and beautiful hot springs of Shiwa Ngandu. The adventurous could even consider a visit from here to North Luangwa National Park.

Six Weeks

With six weeks or more you could choose 'all of the above' and really start to get to know Zambia. Tying in Lake Tanganyika is especially good for north-bound long-distance travellers, as there is a ferry that travels from Mpulungu to Kigoma in Tanzania. Or you could finish off your visit with a safari in South Luangwa National Park, ideal if you're heading on to Malawi, then return to Lusaka and Livingstone.

PLANNING

When to Go

Zambia has three seasons. In May to August, after the rains, conditions are dry and cool, and the landscape is green and lush. In August vegetation becomes brown and more sparse, and is better for wildlife viewing. From September to October temperatures are uncomfortably hot, although wildlife viewing is good. November to April is the rainy season – many rural roads are impassable and most national parks are closed. The best time for birdwatching is from November to December, but conditions are good through the rest of the year too.

Maps

Zambia, published by International Travel Maps at 1:1,500,000, includes most roads and has topographic shading. Even better is Macmillan's *Tourist Map of Zambia* (1:2,200 000); the main map is good for planning and travel on the main routes, and on the reverse are detailed maps of several cities, national parks and other tourist areas. If you want more detail you can get survey maps at various scales from the Map Sales Office in Lusaka.

TOURIST OFFICES

In Zambia there are tourist offices in Lusaka and Livingstone. Outside of Africa, the main office of the Zambia National Tourist Board is in Britain, at 2 Palace Gate, Kensington, London W8 5NG (☎ 020-7589 6343, fax 225 3221, e znttb@aol.com). In reply to general inquiries, this office will send brochures and leaflets to most parts of the world. You can also get up-to-date ZNTB information on the Web (see Internet Resources later in this section).

VISAS

All independent visitors need visas, except those from Ireland and some Commonwealth countries (visitors from Britain and New Zealand do need visas). The price varies according to nationality, but most people pay US$25 for a single-entry visa (maximum stay three months). British citizens pay US$50. Multiple-entry visas are also available. As always, regulations can change, so check the latest requirements before you enter Zambia.

If you're coming from Zimbabwe and you don't have a visa in advance, you can get one at the Kariba, Chirundu or Victoria Falls border crossing. If you come by boat on Lake Tanganyika, visas are available at Mpulungu.

Getting a visa at the border is normally no hassle, but sometimes only seven-day transit visas (US$10) are issued, extendable in Lusaka at the immigration office in Memaco House on Cairo Rd. Going beyond the three-month minimum is tricky and very expensive. It's easier to leave the country and re-enter on a new visa.

You do not need a visa if you go to Zambia on an organised tour. This can be of any length – even a day – and the visa period may be longer than the tour. Entering Zambia from Zimbabwe at Victoria Falls, you'll find several places to stay in Livingstone that organise 'tours' which include accommodation and are still cheaper than a visa (see the Livingstone section for details).

EMBASSIES & CONSULATES

Zambian Embassies & High Commissions

Zambia has embassies or high commissions in the following African countries: Angola, Botswana, Kenya, Malawi, Mozambique, Namibia, South Africa, Tanzania and Zimbabwe. (Embassies for countries in this book are listed in the relevant country chapters.) Elsewhere in the world, places with Zambian diplomatic representation include:

Australia
Consulate: (☎ 02-9299 8880) 36 Clarence Street, Sydney, NSW 2000
France
Embassy: (☎ 01 44 95 97 56) 34 Ave de Messine, 75008 Paris
UK
High Commission: (☎ 020-7589 6655) 2 Palace Gate, London W8 5NG
USA
Embassy: (☎ 202-265 9717) 2419 Massachusetts NW, Washington DC 20008

Embassies & High Commissions in Zambia

The following countries have embassies or high commissions in Zambia (all are in Lusaka):

Australia
High Commission: Memaco House, Cairo Rd
Botswana
Embassy: (☎ 250555) Haile Selassie Ave
Canada
High Commission: (☎ 254176) 5199 United Nations Ave
Congo (Zaïre)
Embassy: (☎ 229044) Parirenyetwa Rd
Kenya
High Commission: (☎ 227938) United Nations Ave
Malawi
High Commission: (☎ 265765) Bishops Rd, Kabulonga
Mozambique
Embassy: (☎ 290451) Chozi Rd, Northmead
Namibia
Embassy: (☎ 252250) Kabanga Rd, off Addis Ababa Dr
Netherlands
Embassy: (☎ 253590) United Nations Ave
South Africa
High Commission: (☎ 260999) Cheetah Rd, Kabulonga
Tanzania
High Commission: (☎ 253320) United Nations Ave
UK
High Commission: (☎ 251133) Independence Ave
USA
Embassy: (☎ 250955) Independence Ave
Zimbabwe
High Commission: (☎ 254006) Haile Selassie Ave

CUSTOMS

There are no restrictions on the amount of foreign currency that tourists can bring in or

Visas for Onward Travel

If you need visas for neighbouring countries, it's always best to go the embassy or high commission between 9 am and noon. You will need two photos. Visa conditions are as follows:

Congo (Zaïre) One-month single-entry visas cost US$20 and you'll need a 'letter of introduction' from your own embassy. If you apply early you can get the visa the same day.

Mozambique Transit visas cost US$6. Single-entry one-month visas cost US$10. Three-month multiple-entry visas cost US$20. Visas are ready in two days, but for a 20% extra fee you can get same-day service.

Tanzania Visas cost US$50. Apply before noon, and the visa is ready later the same day.

Zimbabwe Single-entry visas cost US$30. The process takes seven days. However, most nationalities can get visas on the spot at the border, so it's not essential to come to the embassy.

take out of Zambia. Import or export of Zambian kwacha is technically forbidden, but if you bring in a small amount (say, US$20 worth) it's unlikely to be a problem.

MONEY

Currency

Zambia's unit of currency is the Zambian kwacha (ZK). Bank notes include ZK10,000, ZK5000 ZK1000, ZK500, ZK100 and ZK50. Despite the exchange rate, in 1999 a new batch of ZK20 notes was issued. These are worth less than US$0.01 and many market traders refuse to accept them. The kwacha is divided into 100 ngwee, but the value of the kwacha is so low that ngwee are worthless.

Inflation is high in Zambia, so quoting costs of transport, hotels etc in kwacha is not helpful, as prices will have undoubtedly changed by the time you arrive. Therefore we have used US dollars (US$) throughout this chapter. Although the actual exchange rate will have changed by the time you reach Zambia, the cost of things in US$ (or any other hard currency) will not have altered much. Most tourist places in Zambia quote prices in US$, and some hotels and tour operators will only accept payment in this currency. Even at places that will accept kwacha, it's usually easier (and no more expensive) to pay in US$. National parks quote entrance fees in US$, but some will accept payment in kwacha at the current rate of exchange, which can sometimes be to your advantage, but in reality it's usually easier to pay in dollars.

Exchange Rates

As a guide here are some exchange rates from early 2000:

country	unit		kwacha
Australia	A$1	=	ZK1800
Canada	C$1	=	ZK2000
euro	€1	=	ZK2800
France	10FF	=	ZK4200
Germany	DM1	=	ZK1400
Japan	¥100	=	ZK2600
New Zealand	NZ$1	=	ZK1400
South Africa	R10	=	ZK4500
UK	UK£1	=	ZK4600
USA	US$1	=	ZK2800

Exchanging Money

In Lusaka and big towns, you can change cash or travellers cheques at branches of Barclays Bank and Standard Chartered Bank. In smaller towns around the country, the Zambia National Commercial Bank is by far the best. Charges at all banks are normally around 1% (minimum US$2 to US$4) of the transaction amount.

There are foreign exchange (forex) bureaus in most large towns, with rates generally around 5% better than the banks. Service is also faster here.

There's no black market. You might get a few kwacha more on the street, but the chances of con-tricks or robberies make this a bad risk. However, if you get stuck when banks and bureaus are closed, try changing at a hotel, or a shop that sells imported items.

Travellers Cheques When you change travellers cheques at a bank, and at some foreign exchange bureaus the staff will check your original purchase receipt.

You can pay for many items (such as tours, activities, hotels and lodges) directly with travellers cheques, but a few places and operators have a nasty habit of adding a surcharge for this.

Credit & Debit Cards You can get cash with a Visa card (but not reliably with other cards) at banks in Lusaka and some other main towns, but it can be an all-day process. If you go early, things seem to work better, and if there's a hitch you can leave your card while the system trundles along, then come back to pick up your cash later in the day.

Some mid-range and top-end hotels, lodges, shops and restaurants accept international credit and debit cards – Visa seems to be the most readily recognised – but many add a surcharge of 5% to 10% to your bill. You're probably better off using your card to draw cash and paying with that.

Costs

If you're travelling on a budget, you may find Zambia a tad more expensive than some other countries in the Southern African region. Camping and dorm beds in backpacker hostels cost around US$5, and reasonable double rooms in simple hotels cost from US$10 to US$15. Local-style meals from cheap restaurants are available for less than US$1, and you can get western-style takeaways and snacks from US$1.50.

Public transport can seem expensive too, but that's mainly because the distances in Zambia are so long. Generally, the cost of bus travel per 100km is only slightly higher than elsewhere, at about US$1 to US$1.50 on ordinary buses, or up to US$2 per 100km for luxury or express services.

Even if your budget is not restricted, you'll still find that the cost of accommodation, restaurants and independent travel by charter plane or rental car is more expensive than it is in some other countries in the region, such as Zimbabwe or South Africa. It's worth remembering, however, that the premium you're paying is often for wilder and more remote locations or for a more exclusive experience.

More details are given in the Accommodation, Food and Getting Around sections later in this chapter.

POST & COMMUNICATIONS

Post

Letters under 20g cost US$0.30 to Europe and US$0.40 to the USA or Australia. Sending international letters from Lusaka is surprisingly quick (three or four days to Europe), but from elsewhere in the country it's less reliable and much slower. Parcels up to 1kg to Europe or the USA cost US$10 by airmail, US$7 by surface mail.

If you're sending something urgent, try the post service offered by Mercury Couriers (☎ 01-231137, e mercury@zamnet.zm) on Joseph Mwilwa Rd in Lusaka. It also has agents in large towns around the country. Letters under 50g cost US$1 to Britain, US$1.50 to mainland Europe and US$2.50 to anywhere else in the world. It also handles packages up to 2kg.

Poste restante service is available at the main post office in Lusaka, on the corner of Cairo and Church Rds. To pick up mail costs US$0.40.

Telephone & Fax

There are public phone and fax bureaus in Lusaka and in most large towns. From these, calls within the country cost about US$0.50 per minute; international calls to Europe or Australia cost about US$25 for three minutes (minimum charge). From the business centres in Lusaka's top-end hotels (not from the rooms), calls to Europe or the USA cost around US$10 per minute; Australia and New Zealand cost around US$12. Reverse charge (collect) calls are not available from Zambia. Phone rates might come down in future as Zambia's phone service is due to be deregulated.

Zambian phone numbers starting with 7 or 8 are cell phones and more expensive to call. If you're phoning from another country, Zambia's country code is ☎ 260.

Email & Internet Access

There are Internet bureaus in Lusaka and Livingstone (see Information in those sections). Elsewhere some hotels let guests send and receive email for a nominal fee.

INTERNET RESOURCES

Zamnet Links to the *Lusaka Lowdown* magazine, all the major national newspapers and several other useful sites.
www.zamnet.zm

Zambia Online Has several of its own webzines, plus news summaries, pictures of Lusaka, the latest news on the national football team and links to many other sites, including Tourisma for information on hotels, tour operators and travel agents.
www.zambia.co.zm

Africa Insites A good Zambia section from the Zambia National Tourist Board.
www.africa-insites.com/zambia/travel

BOOKS

This section covers books specific to Zambia. Titles on the whole Southern Africa region are covered under Books in the Regional Facts for the Visitor chapter. Literature by Zambian writers is discussed under Arts in the Facts about Zambia section earlier.

Lonely Planet

Malawi, Mozambique & Zambia and ***Africa on a shoestring*** both have coverage of Zambia.

Guidebooks

Zambia by Chris McIntyre. A good recent book if you're driving your own vehicle or spending a lot of time in the national parks.

General

The Africa House by Christina Lamb. This book tells the story of Stewart Gore-Brown and his grand plans for a utopian fiefdom in a remote part of Zambia during the 1920s. His country mansion at Shiwa Ngandu still stands and is described in the Northern Zambia section of this chapter.

Kakuli by Norman Carr. The author spent a lifetime working with animals and people in the South Luangwa National Park (for more details, see that section later in this chapter). Although this book is a personalised selection of observations on wildlife and humans made over a decade, it also raises deeper issues, and suggests some practical solutions to today's conservation problems.

Spirit of the Zambezi by Jeff & Fiona Sutchbury. A large-format book worth looking out for. This personal and knowledgeable account of three decades living and working in, on and around the great river between Zambia and Zimbabwe is illustrated with beautiful photos.

Survivor's Song by Mark & Delia Owens. The authors rose to fame with their Botswana-based book *Cry of the Kalahari*; this more recent title picks up their story in Zambia's North Luangwa National Park, where they launch themselves single-mindedly (some say arrogantly) into the hard fight against elephant poachers, putting their lives and their relationship seriously on the line.

Zambia by Richard Vaughan. A highly recommended large-format book, with photographs by Ian Murphy. It covers the natural beauty of Zambia's landscape and wildlife, but also the less 'touristy' aspects such as city life and mining, to create a complete and fascinating picture. Both this book and *Spirit of the Zambezi* (mentioned above) are too big to carry while travelling but make excellent trip souvenirs.

NEWSPAPERS & MAGAZINES

Zambia has several national newspapers; main titles include the *Daily Times* and *Daily Mail*, but look out for the *Post* ('the paper that digs deeper'), which contains reasonable coverage of home news and political events, plus limited overseas news.

The *Lusaka Lowdown* is aimed mainly at expats and well-off residents, but it contains a lot of useful information for tourists, such as restaurant reviews, news from national parks, forthcoming local events and attractions, handy adverts and analysis of local news.

RADIO & TV

The Zambia National Broadcasting Corporation has two main radio stations, both offering music, news and chat shows in English and some local languages. The large cities also have commercial music stations. There is a national TV service, although only a small proportion of Zambians have TV sets, and international satellite channels are far more popular.

PHOTOGRAPHY

In Lusaka, slide and print film can be bought at a couple of photo shops on Cairo Rd. Prices for a 36 exposure print film (Fuji, Kodak or Agfa) range from US$3 to US$5. Slide film is US$9. Developing and printing costs US$6. Passport photos cost US$3 for four.

In Zambia, possibly more than any other country in the region, officials do not like you photographing public buildings, bridges, airports or anything else that could be considered strategic. If in doubt, ask – or better still, save your camera for the national parks.

HEALTH

General aspects of health are covered under Health in the Regional Facts for the Visitor chapter, and most of these apply to Zambia. Generally speaking, medical facilities in Zambia are poor, and state-run hospitals suffer from severe shortages. In cities and large towns there are pharmacies, and private clinics and hospitals for those who can pay (and this includes you – see the section on Travel Insurance in the Regional Facts for the Visitor chapter). More details are given in the Lusaka section of this chapter.

DANGERS & ANNOYANCES

Some general warnings and safety tips are given under Dangers & Annoyances in the Regional Facts for the Visitor chapter. Generally, Zambia is a very safe country for travellers, although in the cities and tourist areas there is always a chance of visitors being targeted by robbers or con-artists. More details are given in the Lusaka and Livingstone sections of this chapter. As always, you can reduce the risk considerably by being sensible.

All recreational drugs are illegal in Zambia, as are buying, selling and possession. In 1999 two Kiwi travellers got six months in jail with hard labour after being caught with a relatively small amount.

BUSINESS HOURS

Offices are open from 8 or 9 am to 4 or 5 pm weekdays, with an hour for lunch sometime between noon and 2 pm. Shops keep the same hours Monday to Saturday. Some supermarkets in Lusaka open from 9 am to 1 pm on Sunday mornings.

Banks are open from around 8 am to 2 pm Monday to Saturday, except Thursday (when they close at noon) and Saturday (when they close at 11 am or noon).

Post offices are open from 8 or 9 am to 4 or 4.30 pm weekdays, and until noon on Saturday in Lusaka.

PUBLIC HOLIDAYS & SPECIAL EVENTS

The following days are public holidays:

New Year's Day 1 January
Youth Day March – second Monday
Good Friday & Easter Monday March/April
Workers' Day 1 May
Africa Day 25 May
Heroes' Day July – first Monday
Unity Day July – first Tuesday
Farmers' Day August – first Monday
Independence Day 24 October
Christmas Day 25 December
Boxing Day 26 December

ACTIVITIES

This section provides a brief overview of what's available in Zambia. More information is given in the relevant sections.

At Livingstone you can arrange a bewildering array of activities in and around Victoria Falls; **white-water rafting** in the gorge below the Falls is the most famous activity, but **river-boarding** is another option, and **canoeing** on the quieter waters above the Falls is also very popular. Canoeing is also possible on the Lower Zambezi, and can be arranged in Lusaka or Siavonga. **Bungee jumping** is another classic adrenaline surge available at Victoria Falls, or you can try **abseiling**, highwiring, cable swings and **rock climbing**. For something a little less scary but just as dramatic, **hiking** and **horse riding** are available in the Livingstone area. **Microlighting**, rides in a **helicopter** and **parachuting** are also possible.

Fishing on the River Zambezi is very popular – the tigerfish here are reckoned to give the best fight in the world. Fishing, boating and some other **water sports** are also possible on Lakes Kariba, Bangweulu and Tanganyika.

Several tour companies in Livingstone arrange short **wildlife drives** in Mosi-oa-Tunya National Park, and in Lusaka or Livingstone you can arrange longer **safaris** to wildlife areas all over Zambia. In some national parks (eg, Kasanka and South Luangwa), you can turn up and arrange wildlife drives or **bush walks** on the spot. Zambia is excellent for **birdwatching** (see the 'Birds of Southern Africa' section earlier in this book).

ACCOMMODATION

This section covers information specific to Zambia. For accommodation information applicable to the whole Southern Africa region, see Accommodation in the Regional Facts for the Visitor chapter.

For travellers on a tight budget, most towns have government resthouses, which are cheap (around US$2 to US$4) but in a bad state of repair. Some have been renovated by the Hostels Board and are now clean, with good food and facilities. Naturally, prices have also gone up (around US$15), but they are still fair value.

Many budget hotels charge by the room. Thus two, three or even four people travelling together can get some real, if crowded, bargains. Solo travellers may find some prices steep, although negotiation is always a possibility.

In Lusaka and the major tourist areas there are also camp sites and backpackers hostels, ideal for budget travellers, although in Zambia these places charge a bit more than similar places elsewhere in the region.

Expect to pay US$5 for camping and US$6 for a dorm bed at a backpackers hostel. Some places offer double rooms for US$10 per person. Simple chalets at camping grounds go from US$10 to US$30.

In cities and towns, mid-range hotels charge from about US$20 to US$50, and top-end hotels are usually US$100 or more. All but the cheapest hotels include breakfast in their overnight rate.

In national parks, accommodation used to be state-run, and just about everything was in bad condition and poor value. Today nearly all parks accommodation is managed by commercial companies, and although prices have risen, facilities have definitely improved. Mid-range lodges charge about US$100 per person, and as quality and exclusivity gets higher, rates go up to US$300 or more (this price is for full board and usually includes activities such as wildlife viewing).

In this book, for national parks accommodation (in fact, for all accommodation) we have quoted high (dry) season rates. Most lodges close during the rains. Those that stay open offer considerable discounts. Except for the camp sites and self-catering chalets, it's usually necessary to book accommodation in advance, either directly with the lodge, or through an agent in Lusaka or abroad.

Many upmarket lodges in remote areas have satellite communications, which are expensive to call (or call from), but rigged to a computer they make email easy and cheap, so you can contact many places this way, even if they can't be reached by fax or phone.

FOOD

At markets and bus stations simple food stalls serve tea and bread for US$0.15. Some stalls and basic local restaurants serve meals of beans and *nshima* (maize meal) for about US$0.30. In slightly fancier local restaurants these meals will cost US$0.80, and you may also get fish or chicken with rice or chips (fries) for about US$1.50. In cities and larger towns, local meals are a bit more expensive, and some restaurants offer things like T-bone steak or curry and rice. Prices are around US$2 to US$4, depending on the surroundings as much as the food itself, and whether you eat in or takeaway. Most also serve cheaper snacks, such as sandwiches or sausage rolls, for US$1 to US$2. Pie shops are a big thing too, with meat or veg pies from US$0.50 to US$1.50.

Mid-range hotels and restaurants in cities and tourist areas serve European-style food: steaks, chicken or fish served with vegetables, chips or rice usually goes for between US$5 and US$10. More elaborate French, British or Italian cuisine is also available from such hotels. Several restaurants in Lusaka serve Chinese and Indian food. At most top-end establishments, main courses range from around US$8 to US$15.

Taxes are added to meals in smarter restaurants: 10% for service (which technically means tipping is not required) plus a whopping 17.5% VAT government tax, which many restaurants round up to a handy 20%. What's more, they add the 20%, get the total, then add 10% to that. Extortionate! Wherever possible in this book we've quoted rates with tax, but it's always worth checking the menu before ordering.

DRINKS

You can buy tea in many places, from the lowliest eating house to upmarket hotels and restaurants (which also serve coffee). International fizzy drinks, such as Coke and Pepsi, are widely available.

Most beers in Zambia are lager-type, although the main locally produced brews, Mosi and Rhino, are good quality and have more taste than some of the imported beers available (notably Castle from South Africa). In Lusaka, some British-style 'bitters' are also available.

Getting There & Away

This section covers access into Zambia from neighbouring countries only. Information about reaching Southern Africa from elsewhere on the African continent and from other continents is provided in the regional Getting There & Away chapter.

AIR

Airports & Airlines

Zambia's international airport is in Lusaka, although some regional and domestic flights serve Livingstone (near Victoria Falls), or Mfuwe (South Luangwa National Park).

Departure Tax

If you're flying out of Lusaka, departure tax for international flights is US$20; payable in US dollars cash only. (For more details about Lusaka's airport, see Getting Around in the Lusaka section.)

Southern Africa

Zambia is linked to most other parts of the region by air. All fares quoted are one way. Return fares cost double, but excursion fares can be cheaper.

From Lusaka there are flights to: Harare on Aero Zambia and Air Zimbabwe (US$130); Johannesburg (Jo'burg) on Aero Zambia and SAA (US$300); and Nairobi on Aero Zambia and Kenya Airways (US$380). Each route is served by five flights per week.

Air Namibia flies from Lusaka to Windhoek (US$300, three flights weekly), and Air Malawi flies from Lusaka to Lilongwe (US$170, three flights weekly).

LAND

Border Crossings

Zambia shares borders with eight other countries so there's a huge number of crossing points. Most border crossings are open from 6 am to 6 pm (8 pm at Victoria Falls). If you're bringing a car into Zambia without a carnet, a temporary import permit is free, and compulsory third-party insurance (available at the border or at the nearest large town) costs US$6 per month.

Botswana

The only crossing point between Zambia and Botswana is the pontoon (car ferry) across the River Zambezi at Kazungula, about 65km west of Livingstone, and 11km south of the main road between Livingstone and Sesheke. There's a bus at least once per day from Livingstone to Sesheke, plus minibuses, which sometimes loop off the main road and drop you by the ferry. Other times (ie, when there aren't enough passengers) you're dropped at the ferry turn-off, then walk the 11km to the terminal (although you'll probably be able to hitch, as there's a lot of traffic on this route). The Zambian border crossing is on the northern bank. The Kazungula pontoon carries cars for US$15/R60, 4WDs for US$25/R90, and foot passengers for free. It also carries trucks, and accepts payment in pula. The Botswana post is on the southern bank, and just beyond here roads lead to Kasane, Maun, Nata and Francistown.

An easier way to reach Botswana from Zambia is to go from Livingstone to Victoria Falls in Zimbabwe first, then get one of the many tourist transfer services from there to Kasane or Maun. The Route 49 backpackers bus goes from Victoria Falls through Botswana on its way to South Africa. (For more information see Bus in the Getting Around the Region chapter.)

Congo (Zaïre)

The main Zambia-Congo (Zaïre) border crossing is on the main road between Ndola and Lubumbashi. There is a daily bus from Lusaka and minibuses from Ndola to Chililabombwe, from where minibuses run to the border. You'll have to walk from the border to Kasumbalesa; from Kasumbalesa to Lubumbashi there are pick-ups and taxis.

Malawi

The main border crossing between Zambia and Malawi is 30km east of Chipata, on the main road between Lusaka and Lilongwe. There are direct buses most days between Lusaka and Lilongwe, but these are slow, so most travellers do this trip in stages. Express buses go most days between Lusaka and Chipata, and ordinary buses every day.

From the BP petrol station on the main street in Chipata, regular minibuses run the 30km to the Zambian border crossing (US$1). The distance between the two border crossings is 12km, but share-taxis and pick-ups shuttle up and down for US$1.20 per person, or US$7 for the car. From the Malawi border crossing, 2km west of Mchinji, minibuses run to Lilongwe for US$2.50. A new Malawi border crossing is being built only a few metres from the Zambia border. When this is completed, transport will probably run from here straight to Lilongwe.

Mozambique

The main Zambia-Mozambique crossing is between Chanida and Cassacatiza, in southeastern Zambia, but very few travellers take this route as most go through Malawi.

Namibia

The only border crossing between Zambia and Namibia is at Katima Mulilo (Zambia), on the western bank of the River Zambezi, near Sesheke. The Namibian border crossing is called Wenela, near the Namibian town of Katima Mulilo. (The geography here is complicated, with four countries meeting at the River Zambezi, and two places with the same name. Locals refer to 'Katima Mulilo Zambia side' and 'Katima Mulilo Namibia side' – see the Zambia country map.)

If you're doing the trip from Zambia to Namibia in sections, there's at least one bus per day from Livingstone to Sesheke (US$4), plus several minibuses, and the trip takes seven hours (there are bad potholes between Kazungula and Sesheke). The bus may terminate in Sesheke or continue another 5km to the pontoon (car ferry) on the eastern bank of the Zambezi.

The pontoon carries cars for US$15 or R60, 4WDs for US$25 or R90, and foot passengers for nothing. If the pontoon isn't running, passengers pay US$0.20 to cross by dugout canoe.

On the western bank, it's 500m south to the Zambia border crossing, and then less than 1km to the Namibia border crossing (Wenela). From here to Katima Mulilo (Namibia side) is 5km; there's no bus, but a lift in a pick-up costs about US$0.50.

If you need direct transport between Zambia and Namibia, an option from Livingstone is to cross to Victoria Falls (Zimbabwe), from where the Intercape Mainliner bus runs twice weekly to Windhoek (US$71), via Katima Mulilo (Namibia side), Rundu and Grootfontein. Another option is the Nam-Vic Shuttle, a tourist minibus service that runs from Victoria Falls to Windhoek every Sunday (US$110). You can book at Backpackers Bazaar in Victoria Falls (see Information in the Victoria Falls section of the Zimbabwe chapter), and all the backpacker hostels in Livingstone can give you details. Finally, it's always worth asking around at the tour companies in Livingstone about safaris going to Namibia, which sometimes end in Windhoek (some start in Vic Falls). Even if the safari only goes to northern Namibia, you could always jump off here at the end of the trip and continue to Windhoek by bus. If there's enough interest, some tour companies also run direct minibus services from Livingstone to Windhoek or northern Namibia.

South Africa

If you need to get to South Africa quickly and cheaply, there are five services a week direct from Lusaka to Jo'burg, some with Translux and some with Intercape, for about US$50 (see Getting There & Away in the South Africa chapter for more details).

Tanzania

The main Zambia-Tanzania border crossing is between Nakonde and Tunduma. It is used by the Great North Road and the TAZARA railway line. Most travellers use the train, since international bus rides on this route can be very long and slow, and often involve changing at the border anyway.

Train There are usually two international express trains per week in each direction between Kapiri Mposhi and Dar es Salaam, although trains are sometimes cancelled and the timetable is subject to change. Express trains go from Kapiri Mposhi at 2.30 pm every Tuesday and Friday; the trip takes 36 hours. The fare is US$60/40/24 in 1st/2nd/3rd class (1st and 2nd are sleeping compartments). The fare between Kapiri Mposhi and Mbeya is US$33/22/13. With a student card you can get a 50% discount on these prices.

You can buy tickets on the spot at the TAZARA station in Kapiri Mposhi. If you're coming from Lusaka, you can book your ticket (more than three days in advance) at the TAZARA office there (see the Lusaka section later in this chapter). The system works! If there are no more seats left at the Lusaka office, don't despair – we've heard from travellers who bought tickets on the spot at Kapiri Mposhi without trouble.

You'll be visited by border officials on the train (visas are essential for most tourists entering Tanzania). You'll also be disturbed by moneychangers. If you're sure of the rates, it's worth changing, but take care – these guys are sharks. The train buffet uses the correct currency in each country.

There are also slower ordinary trains departing from Kapiri Mposhi every Monday, Thursday and Saturday at 5.45 pm for the border at Nakonde, with fares slightly lower than on the express trains. On the Tanzanian side, there are ordinary trains between the border and Dar es Salaam.

There are plans for the TAZARA service to be extended to Lusaka, which will be handy for travellers, but it will pretty much wipe Kapiri Mposhi off the map.

Zimbabwe

The main crossings between Zambia and Zimbabwe are Chirundu, on the main road between Lusaka and Harare; Kariba, about 50km upstream from Chirundu; and Vic Falls.

From Lusaka's main bus station there are direct buses to Harare, via Chirundu, four times per day for US$13.50. Slower buses cost US$9 and take nine hours. Alternatively, you can take a minibus from Lusaka to Siavonga, walk across Kariba Dam, then go by bus from Kariba to Harare.

The most popular crossing for travellers is at Victoria Falls. Take a bus or train from Lusaka to Livingstone, and then a minibus or taxi from Livingstone to the Zambian border crossing. Walk across the spectacular bridge overlooking Victoria Falls to reach the Zimbabwe border crossing. (For more details see the Lusaka and Livingstone sections later in this chapter). On the Zimbabwe side there's regular transport between Victoria Falls town and Bulawayo. (For more details see Getting There & Away in the Victoria Falls section of the Zimbabwe chapter.)

LAKE

Tanzania & Burundi

A ferry called the *Liemba* on Lake Tanganyika links the Zambian port of Mpulungu with Kigoma and various other smaller places in Tanzania, as well as Bujumbura (Burundi). The timetable is flexible, but the ferry normally arrives in Mpulungu early Friday morning, then leaves around 2 pm the same day to reach Kigoma on Sunday. The fare from Mpulungu to Kigoma is US$50 for 1st class (two-bed cabin), US$40 for 2nd class (six-bed cabin) and US$35 for economy class (lower deck). Fares must be paid in Zambian kwacha or Tanzanian shillings. To take a car on the ferry from Mpulungu to Kigoma costs around US$100, plus US$20 for loading at each port. Meals are available on the boat.

Getting Around

AIR

Several small airlines, including Roan Air, Eastern Air, TIAC and Proflight, offer domestic flights around Zambia. Fares are pretty much the same with each company, but timetables change constantly, so you have to buy your ticket from an agent with up-to-date schedules. To give you an idea, some sample one-way fares from Lusaka are: Kitwe or Ndola (US$80); Livingstone (US$120); Mfuwe (South Luangwa) (US$120). Return fares are double. All the above flights go at least once daily (less often to Mfuwe outside the tourist season). Most travel agents in Lusaka and Livingstone can also arrange air charters.

BUS & MINIBUS

Travelling around Zambia by bus can be hard and tiring. Many roads are badly potholed and journeys are often slow. All main routes are served by ordinary long-distance buses. These either run on a fill-up-and-go basis, or have fixed departures (these are called 'time buses'), although arrival times can still be a little unpredictable. Even though the buses may be run by different companies, fares are normally standardised. Some ordinary bus services from Lusaka include: Ndola (US$5.20, 325km); Livingstone (US$6, 475km); and Chipata (US$8, 600km).

Two companies, Euro-Africa and Virgin-Lux, run comfortable European-style long-distance express buses on the main routes between Lusaka, Livingstone and the Copperbelt. Their fares are about 10% to 20% more than the ordinary bus fares.

Many routes are also served by minibuses, which always leave when full and in rural areas have very unpredictable journey times. Their fares can be more or less than the bus fares (about 25% either way) depending on the route. In remote areas the 'bus' is often a truck or pick-up carrying goods as well as people.

TRAIN

The TAZARA railway runs between Kapiri Mposhi and Dar es Salaam in Tanzania (see the Getting There & Away section earlier in this chapter). Zambia's other main line runs from Kitwe in the north to Livingstone in the south, via Lusaka.

From Lusaka to Livingstone, express trains depart Monday, Wednesday and Friday at 7 pm, arriving the next morning between 6 am and noon. From Livingstone to Lusaka they depart Tuesday, Thursday and Saturday at 6.30 pm, arriving the next morning. Fares are US$12/10/7/4.50 in sleeper/1st/2nd/3rd class. The train used to be the best way to go between Lusaka and Livingstone, but these days buses are quicker (although not necessarily safer). An ordinary train also runs daily each way between Lusaka and Livingstone; it's cheaper by about 25% but very slow.

From Lusaka to Kitwe there are ordinary trains only; they depart daily at 9 pm, arriving the next morning. Fares are US$8 for a sleeper, and US$4 for standard (2nd) class. This train goes via Kapiri Mposhi, where you can change to the TAZARA line. The two services don't actually connect, so you're better going by bus if you want the TAZARA service.

Tickets for sleeper, 1st and 2nd class can be bought in advance. On express trains, a sleeper is a compartment for two people; 1st class is a sleeping compartment for four; 2nd class is a sleeper for six people; 3rd class is seats only. On ordinary trains, standard (2nd) class is a reclining seat.

Conditions on the trains vary, but generally range from slightly dilapidated to ready for scrap. Most compartments have no lights or locks – take a torch and something to secure the door at night. Beware of bogus ticket collectors, and of 'double bookings', which can be sorted out for a small fee.

CAR & MOTORCYCLE

It is possible to get around Zambia by car or motorbike, although many sealed roads are in bad condition and dirt roads can range from bad to impassable, especially after the rains. If you haven't driven in Africa before, this is no place to start.

Petrol costs US$0.60 per litre, diesel around $0.50. Distances between main towns with filling stations are long and supplies are not always reliable, so fill up whenever you can. (More information for those in their own vehicle is given in the regional Getting There & Away and Getting Around the Region chapters.)

Rental

If you need to hire a car to tour Zambia, there are car rental outfits in Lusaka, Livingstone, Kitwe and Ndola. Avis (☎ 01-251652), based at the Holiday Inn in Lusaka, charges US$50 per day for a small saloon car, plus US$0.60 per km. Voyagers Travel in Lusaka (☎ 01-253048, @ voytrav@zamnet.zm) and Ndola (☎ 02-617062, @ voyagers@zamnet.zm) is the agent for Imperial Car Rental, with rates slightly lower than Avis. Zungulila Car Hire (☎ 227730, @ zung@zamnet.zm) in Taz House, on Chiparamba Rd, off Cairo Rd, Lusaka, is a small independent outfit which often undercuts the big boys, and may negotiate a little on rates. Self-drive saloon cars start at US$35 per day, plus US$0.25 per km. It also has 4WD vehicles, with driver, from US$65 per day. The Zambian Safari Company (☎ 01-228682, @ reservations@zamzaf.co.zm) on Cairo Rd in Lusaka represents several car rental firms and can arrange self-drive saloon cars from US$35 per day or self-drive 4WDs from US$85 per day, plus US$0.50 per km.

In Livingstone, Foley's Hire (☎ 03-320888, ⓔ foley@zamnet.zm) has 4WDs from $100 per day or US$180 for a fully equipped 'safari prepared' vehicle with insurance and unlimited milage.

To all of the above rates, add 20% to 25% tax, plus collision damage waiver of US$10 to US$20 per day. If you don't want to self-drive it's easy to arrange a driver. You pay a daily allowance, but not insurance or collision damage waivers, so the price is about the same. Most companies offer better rates for rentals over five days.

HITCHING

Hitching can be good in Zambia, although just because we say hitching is possible doesn't mean we recommend it (see the general warning under Hitching in the Getting Around the Region chapter). Some drivers, particularly expats, give lifts for free in the usual western hitching way. You should expect to pay for lifts with local drivers (normally about the same as the bus fare, depending on the comfort of the vehicle). In such cases it's usual to agree on a price beforehand.

LOCAL TRANSPORT

Cities and large towns have minibuses on local routes. Private hire taxis operate in cities and main towns. You can find them outside bus stations, supermarkets or hotels. There are no meters, so rates are negotiable, particularly on airport runs. Check the price at the start of the journey. (For more details, see the individual city sections.)

ORGANISED TOURS

Tours and safaris around Zambia invariably focus on the national parks. Since many of these are hard to visit without a vehicle, joining a tour might be your only option, and if you've got some cash to spare it would be a very good investment.

Some tour companies cater for budget travellers, while others are select and specialised, offering mainly 'tailor-made' tours aimed squarely at the top end of the market. The budget operators run scheduled trips, or can arrange things on the spot, and they can usually be contacted through backpackers hostels or camp sites. The upmarket companies prefer to take bookings in advance (you can contact them direct or go through an agent in your home country), but can arrange things on the spot with a few days' notice if required.

Companies running tours around Zambia as part of wider trips of Southern Africa are listed in the regional Getting There & Away chapter. Tours of Zambia are also organised by some tour companies based in Malawi (for details, see under Travel Agencies & Tour Operators in the Lilongwe section). Many of Zambia's tour companies are based in Lusaka (see under Travel Agencies & Tour Operators in the Lusaka section) and Livingstone (see the boxed text 'Adventure Activities in Livingstone' and also Organised Tours in the Southern Zambia section).

Lusaka

☎ 01

Lusaka is the capital of Zambia – a big city, part modern and part traditional African, where dusty markets sit alongside high-rise blocks. Although Zambia is a fascinating country, it has to be said that Lusaka will never be a highlight for tourists; there's little in the way of grand buildings, monuments or other sights. But Lusaka is not quite as bad as it's often painted. Compared to some other capitals in the region, it's a very lively city with a very African feel. The markets are fascinating, there's a healthy arts scene and the nightlife throbs at weekends. If you have to be here for a while (eg, to get a visa), you'll have no trouble passing the time pleasantly enough.

Orientation

Lusaka city centre's main street is Cairo Rd, lined with shops, cafes, supermarkets, travel offices, banks, exchange bureaus and two landmark traffic circles: North End Roundabout and South End Roundabout. East of Cairo Rd, across the railway tracks, are the

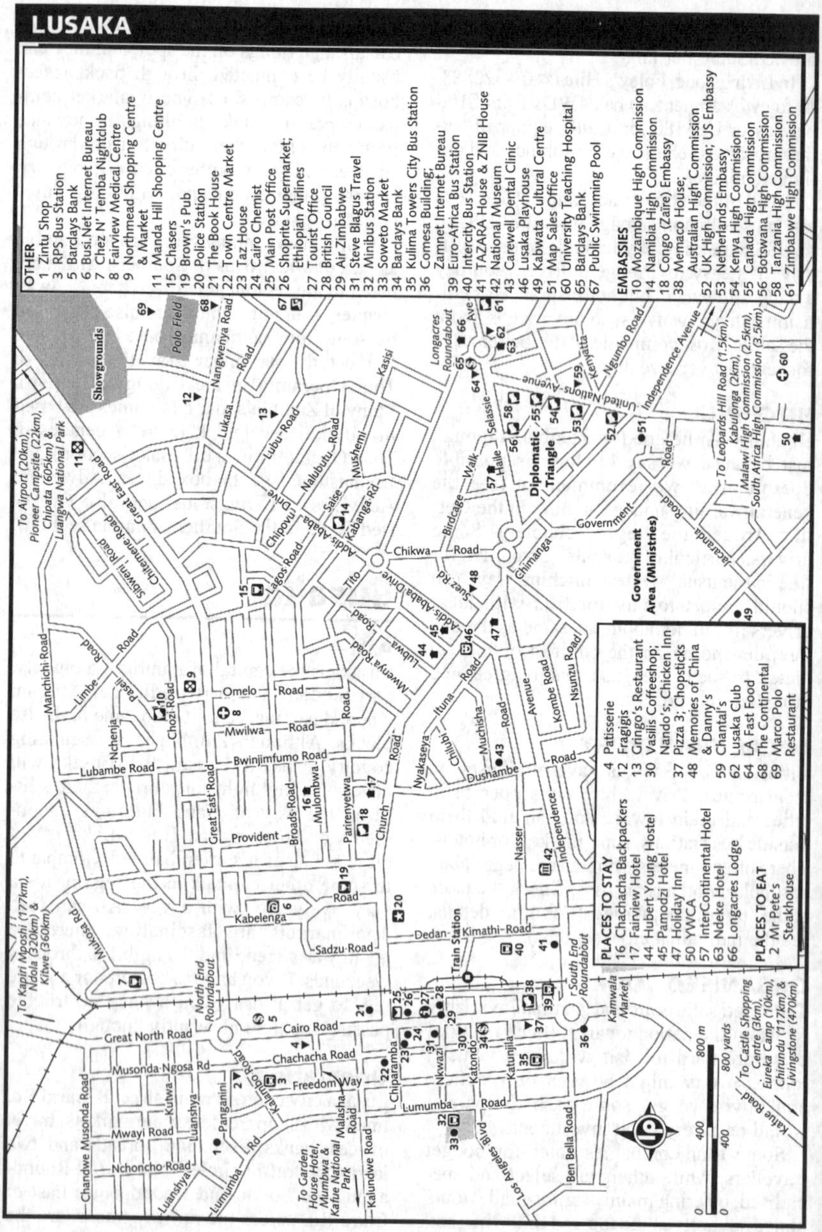

LUSAKA

PLACES TO STAY
16 Chachacha Backpackers
17 Fairview Hotel
44 Hubert Young Hostel
45 Pamodzi Hotel
47 Holiday Inn
50 YWCA
57 InterContinental Hotel
63 Ndeke Hotel
66 Longacres Lodge

PLACES TO EAT
2 Mr Pete's Steakhouse
4 Patisserie
12 Fragigis
13 Gringo's Restaurant
30 Vasilis Coffeeshop; Nando's; Chicken Inn
37 Pizza 3; Chopsticks
48 Memories of China & Danny's
59 Chantal's
62 Lusaka Club
64 LA Fast Food
68 The Continental
69 Marco Polo Restaurant

OTHER
1 Zintu Shop
3 RPS Bus Station
5 Barclays Bank
6 Busi.Net Internet Bureau
7 Chez N' Temba Nightclub
8 Fairview Medical Centre
9 Northmead Shopping Centre & Market
11 Manda Hill Shopping Centre
15 Chasers
19 Brown's Pub
20 Police Station
21 The Book House
22 Town Centre Market
23 Taz House
24 Cairo Chemist
25 Main Post Office
26 Shoprite Supermarket; Ethiopian Airlines
27 Tourist Office
28 British Council
29 Air Zimbabwe
31 Steve Blagus Travel
32 Minibus Station
33 Soweto Market
34 Barclays Bank
35 Kulima Towers City Bus Station
36 Comesa Building; Zamnet Internet Bureau
39 Euro-Africa Bus Station
40 Intercity Bus Station
41 TAZARA House & ZNIB House
42 National Museum
43 Carewell Dental Clinic
46 Lusaka Playhouse
49 Kabwata Cultural Centre
51 Map Sales Office
60 University Teaching Hospital
65 Barclays Bank
67 Public Swimming Pool

EMBASSIES
10 Mozambique High Commission
14 Namibia High Commission
18 Congo (Zaïre) Embassy
38 Memaco House; Australian High Commission
52 UK High Commission; US Embassy
53 Netherlands Embassy
54 Kenya High Commission
55 Canada High Commission
56 Botswana High Commission
58 Tanzania High Commission
61 Zimbabwe High Commission

To Kapiri Mposhi (177km), Ndola (320km) & Kitwe (360km)
To Airport (20km), Pioneer Campsite (22km), Chipata (605km) & Luangwa National Park
To Garden House Hotel, Mumbwa & Kafue National Park
To Castle Shopping Centre (3km), Eureka Camp (10km), Chirundu (117km) & Livingstone (470km)
To Leopards Hill Road (1.5km), Kabulonga (2km), Malawi High Commission (2.5km), South Africa High Commission (3.5km)

0 400 800 m
0 400 800 yards

intercity bus station and train station. East of here, wide streets lead to the government area (which contains many ministries), the diplomatic triangle (which contains most embassies) and the smarter residential suburbs. To the west are the 'high density housing zones' (read 'townships').

Maps The Map Sales Office is behind the Geological Survey Department, near the junction of Government and Nationalist Rds. Survey maps of all parts of Zambia, plus maps of some cities and national parks, cost US$3.

Information

Tourist Office The tourist office is on Cairo Rd. The staff are friendly enough, but the information they have is fairly limited.

Money Barclays has two branches on Cairo Rd (the one near the North End Roundabout is quieter and quicker); they change travellers cheques (with 1% commission) and cash (no charge), and give cash on a Visa card (no fee). Standard Chartered Bank and Stanbic Bank also change cash and travellers cheques. There are several exchange bureaus on Cairo Rd, including Delta Change Bureau, opposite Shoprite, and several more near the banks. Rates are good for cash, but lower than the banks for travellers cheques.

Post & Telephone The main post office is on the corner of Cairo and Church Rds. The poste restante is located here (it costs US$0.40 to pick up mail). The telephone office (for international calls and faxes) is upstairs. (For more information, see Post & Communications in the Facts for the Visitor section earlier in this chapter.)

Email & Internet Access Internet bureaus include: Busi.Net on Kabelenga Rd, off Church Rd, open from 8 am to 7 pm weekdays, and 10 am to 4 pm weekends (US$6 per 30 minutes); Internet Cafe on Katondo Rd, off Cairo Rd (US$5 per 30 mins); and Zamnet in the Comesa Building near South End Roundabout, open from 8 am to 1 pm and 2 to 5 pm weekdays (US$3.50 per 30 mins).

Travel Agencies & Tour Operators Along Cairo Rd are several travel agencies selling international and domestic flights, including Steve Blagus Travel (☎ 225178, ⓔ sblagus@zamnet.zm) on Nkwazi Rd, off Cairo Rd – also the agent for Busanga Trails camps in Kafue National Park.

Zambian Safari Company (☎ 228682, fax 222906, ⓔ reservations@zamsaf.co.zm), behind Farmers House on the corner of Cairo and Church Rds, sells flights, arranges hotels, lodges, car rental and air charter, and also puts together tailor-made safaris covering the whole country, specialising in northern Zambia.

Voyagers Travel (☎ 253048, ⓔ voytrav@zamnet.zm), near the Holiday Inn, arranges flights, hotel reservations and car hire.

Africa Tour Designers (☎ 274883, ⓔ atd@zamnet.zm), located in Castle shopping centre on Kafue Rd, outside the city centre, is a switched-on booking service for hotels, safaris and activities all over the country.

At Kachelo Travel (☎ 263973, ⓔ kachelo@zamnet.zm), in the suburb of Kabulonga, the friendly and knowledgeable team can arrange flights, reserve hotels and lodges, and put together tours around Zambia.

Bookshops By far the best in Lusaka is The Book House, on the junction of Cairo and Church Rds, with paperback fiction, guidebooks, maps, coffee-table books, magazines and foreign newspapers.

Libraries & Cultural Centres The British Council library is on Heroes Place, just off Cairo Rd, but is open only to members. The US Information Service library, in the Comesa Building near South End Roundabout, is open to tourists on Monday morning, Tuesday all day, Thursday afternoon and Friday morning.

Medical Services At the University Teaching Hospital (UTH), conditions are not good and medical supplies are scarce, but there are several other options for those who can afford to pay (and that includes tourists with insurance). For straightforward matters, such as consultations or blood tests,

Fairview Medical Centre (☎ 225477), on Great East Rd near Northmead shopping centre, is recommended. The best pharmacy in Lusaka is Cairo Chemist, on Chiparamba Rd just off Cairo Rd.

For serious illness or injury, go to the Health International Clinic (☎ 236644) behind Barclays Bank at the northern end of Cairo Rd. This place has highly trained staff and good facilities, and is run in conjunction with the Medical Rescue Service, which has air and road ambulances, but you must pay in advance or have proof of insurance before they'll treat you. For bone injuries, the Italian Orthopaedic Hospital (☎ 254601) on Los Angeles Blvd is also recommended.

Dangers & Annoyances As in any city, pickpockets take advantage of crowds, so be alert in Lusaka's markets and bus stations and in the busy streets west of Cairo Rd. There are occasional reports of people being jostled by youths while leaving banks on Cairo Rd, so take care when you change money here, but in general there are enough people around during the day to dissuade muggers from going for an outright attack. At night, things are different. The streets are dark and often empty. Even if you're on a tight budget, Lusaka is a place where you should seriously consider taking taxis after sunset.

Things to See & Do

The **National Museum** is open daily and costs US$2. Downstairs is an impressive display of contemporary Zambian paintings and sculpture. Upstairs are traditional exhibits; don't miss the curator's cryptic comments about the witchcraft items.

For more paintings and sculpture, head for the laid-back **Henry Tayali Visual Arts Gallery** at the showgrounds, where local artists meet, work and display their art. Entry is free. The best display of contemporary Zambian art is at **Namwande Gallery**, the private collection of a Zambian businessman and patron of the arts, John Kapotwe, next to his house on Leopards Hill Rd, about 5km beyond the suburb of Kabalonga. Minibuses run only part way along Leopards Hill Rd, so it's better to get a taxi. The gallery is open from 9 am to noon and 2 to 4 pm Tuesday to Friday, plus weekend mornings.

For something more lively, **Town Centre Market** off Chachacha Rd is well worth a stroll around. This is where Zambians get their bargains – fruit and veg, and new and second-hand hardware, tapes and clothes. It's relaxed, and tourists don't get hassled. It also has lots of cheap-eats stalls. (Latest news is that this market may close and a shopping mall be built here instead.)

Kamwala Market south-east of the centre is similar and also good, but the re-built **Soweto Market** lacks the traditional atmosphere of the others.

A healthy local performing arts scene means there's nearly always something on at the **Lusaka Playhouse**, on Church Rd. Look for flyers locally. A seat costs around US$3. Cultural performances also take place at **Zambili d'Afrique** (for details, see Shopping later in the Lusaka section).

Animal fans should visit the well-stocked and informative **Kalimba Reptile Park** near the airport. Or try the **Munda Wanga** zoo and botanical garden, formerly a perfect advert for closing all zoos, but now undergoing sensitive renovation; it's on Kafue Rd about, 15km from the centre.

At the Pamodzi Hotel, **squash courts** are open to nonguests for US$2, and the swimming pool is US$1 (including a towel). The public **swimming pool**, east of Addis Ababa Dr, is spotlessly clean with a pleasant grassy, shaded area; a good place to pass the day. Entry costs US$1 and it's closed on Monday.

Places to Stay – Budget

By far the most popular place with budget travellers is ***Chachacha Backpackers*** *(☎ 222257, @ cha@zamtel.zm)* on Mulombwa Close (off Bwinjimfumo Rd), east of the centre. Camping costs US$3, dorms are US$6 and you can have a double room for US$14. There's a garden, bar and lounge, self-catering kitchen, baggage store, public phone and email service. Hot drinks, breakfasts, snacks and excellent evening meals are also available. It has to be said this place isn't fancy, but manager Wade and his staff are very friendly and have all the latest info on bus and train times, cheap car hire and so on. Some budget tour companies start and finish their safaris here.

Chachacha can also arrange for you to stay with local families in villages about 50km outside Lusaka; this is cheap (about US$4), but firmly intended as a cultural experience rather than a money-saving exercise. It's very popular – travellers who have gone for a night have stayed for three or four.

For budget accommodation with a local feel, the ***YWCA*** *(☎ 252726)* on Nationalist Rd takes men and women, charging US$24 for both singles and doubles. It's basic but very clean and friendly, and often full. The shared bathrooms have hot water. There's also a restaurant.

The ***Emmasdale Lodge*** *(☎ 243692)* on Great North Rd, 2.5km from North End Roundabout, has acceptable double rooms with private bathroom for US$16. Flats sleeping one to four people, with bathroom and equipped kitchen, cost US$24 – a real bargain if you're in a group. Cheap food is available, and the bar gets crowded some nights.

Hubert Young Hostel *(☎ 250538)* on Church Rd is safe and friendly with simple single/double rooms with shared bathroom for US$4/6.50, and nice rooms with private bathroom for US$5/8, going up to US$14. Breakfast costs US$1 and local-style meals are also available.

Eureka Camp *(☎/fax 272351, @ eureka@zamnet.zm)*, about 10km south of the city, is an ideal stop-off. Simple cabins with shared showers cost US$10 per person, double cabins with a bathroom cost US$30, plus US$10 for an extra bed, and camping is US$5. Security is good, and there's a swimming pool, a bar (which sells snacks), and firewood for sale. Minibuses from the city go past the gate. If you need supplies, the minibuses pass Castle shopping centre, which has a supermarket, cafe, petrol station and snack bar.

Pioneer Campsite *(☎ 771936, @ pioneer@zamnet.zm)* is signposted 5km south of Great East Rd, 18km east of the city centre. Double chalets cost US$20, a bed in the dorm is US$8 and camping costs US$5. There's a bar and meals, or you can self-cater in the kitchen. The friendly owners run a free lift service to and from town on weekdays. They pick up at 4.30pm from Busi.Net Internet cafe on Kabelenga Rd.

Places to Stay – Mid-Range

All rooms in this price range have private bathroom, and prices include breakfast.

The ***Longacres Lodge*** *(☎ 254847)* off Haile Selassie Ave is a revamped government hostel, where functional rooms cost US$26 (with double bed) or US$32 (two single beds).

Up in price is the ***Ndeke Hotel*** *(☎ 252779)* off Los Angeles Blvd. Doubles cost US$50 (after 6 pm they're half-price). There's a bar, restaurant and pool. Less spartan is ***Fairview*** *(☎ 212954)* on Church Rd, which has small comfortable rooms for US$60/70. An evening meal costs US$6, and there's a terrace bar.

Chasers *(☎ 752659)* on Lagos Rd is primarily a pub, with a few decent rooms upstairs for US$20 per person. There's food and safe parking. It's friendly, but could be loud at weekends.

Outside the centre, the ***Wayside B&B*** *(☎ 273439)* has well-appointed rooms for US$40/50. Meals are available. To get here turn north off Kafue Rd near Castle shopping centre, onto Makeni Rd, and continue for 2km. The ***Makeni Guesthouse*** *(☎ 274667)* is another 800m along the road. Straightforward and friendly, it charges US$30 for doubles (US$20/25 with shared bathroom).

On the Mongu road, 6km west of the centre, the large and spacious ***Garden House Hotel*** *(☎ 289328)* has doubles for US$32 (half-price after 6 pm).

Places to Stay – Top End

All places in this bracket accept credit cards. All rooms have private bathroom, and rates include breakfast. The three hotels have business centres (secretarial services, photocopiers, faxes, email etc), swimming pools, hair salons, boutiques, travel desks and bookshops.

The ***Holiday Inn*** *(☎ 251666, @ holinn@zamnet.zm)* on Church Rd has singles/doubles for US$115/140. On the ground floor are the Golden Spur Restaurant and

McGinty's Pub – both, despite their titles, are South African chains. There are also two smarter restaurants and a garden terrace, where snacks cost US$5 to US$8, and full meals around US$12.

The ***InterContinental Hotel*** *(☎ 250000, ✉ lusaka@interconti.com)*, on Haile Selassie Ave, charges US$130/150. You can get snacks on the terrace, there's a brasserie doing light meals from US$6, and the restaurant has a la carte meals from US$10. This place was dull, soulless and a bit tatty when we visited, and seemed poor value, but a recent change of owner and a promised multimillion-dollar facelift should improve things.

Pamodzi Hotel *(☎ 254455, ✉ pamodzi@zamnet.zm)* on Addis Ababa Drive charges US$130/150, and we've heard good reports about the quality of rooms, food and service here. The restaurant serves main courses for around US$8 and evening buffets for US$15.

If you don't need to be in the city, one of Lusaka's finest options is the ***Lilayi Lodge*** *(☎ 228682, ✉ reservations@zamsaf.co.zm)*, in a private wildlife reserve 8km off Kafue Rd, 11km south of the centre. Very comfortable bungalows cost from US$80/90, and a four-course evening meal is US$20. Buffet lunches are served at weekends. The pool is lovely. Full board, including transfers from town or the airport, costs US$150/230.

Places to Eat

Food Stalls & Cafes For very cheap meals, there are basic eating houses at the bus stations, but those at Kamwala and Town Centre Markets are more appealing. Or you can take advantage of a splendid Lusaka institution: the petrol station snack bar. Try the Caltex (open until 5 pm) near North End Roundabout, or the Mobil (open to midnight) on the corner of Church and Kabelenga Rds, where burgers, pies and chips start at about US$1. The BP petrol station at Castle shopping centre has similar offerings.

Cairo Rd offers hungry travellers a huge choice. Going from north to south, on the western side of the street, your first stop for a splurge might be the ***Patisserie***, with decent coffee for US$0.80, croissants and donuts for US$0.50, and a huge range of pies, sandwiches, cakes and gateaux. A few blocks down is ***Vasilis Coffeeshop***, with cakes and pastries from US$0.35 to US$0.60, burgers and steak sandwiches from US$2. Nearby, ***Nando's*** serves western-style takeaways. Next door are ***Chicken Inn*** (fried chicken and burgers from US$1.20) and ***Pizza Inn*** (pizzas from US$2). Further along are ***Pizza 3*** with small pizzas from US$2.50; and ***Chopsticks***, with snacks like spring rolls from US$0.80, and other dishes from US$2.

On the other side of Cairo Rd, behind the Indo-Zambia Bank building, ***Sichuan Food Corner*** serves local meals like *nshima* and beef, plus burgers, chips and Chinese snacks, from US$1 to US$2.

If you're waiting for a visa to be processed, visit ***LA Fast Food*** on Haile Selassie Ave at the apex of the diplomatic triangle.

Restaurants The top-end hotels listed in Places to Stay have ***restaurants*** and ***coffee shops*** that welcome nonguests. Of the restaurants in town, a perennial favourite is ***Mr Pete's Steakhouse*** on Panganini Rd, where big meals cost around US$5 to US$8.

Shehnai Indian Restaurant, at Northmead shopping centre, offers starters for US$1 to US$2, main courses for US$4 to US$8, and rice or nan for US$2; the menu is so big it has an index!

Jaylin *(☎ 252206)* at Lusaka Club in Longacres is open to nonmembers. It's not much to look at, but the food (especially steak) is excellent and good value, with main meals around US$5 to US$8.

Memories of China & Danny's *(☎ 253 787)* near the Holiday Inn is a combined Chinese and Indian restaurant. Ordering samosas followed by *egg foo yung* is amusing, but the Chinese food is poor, and we recommend you stick to the Indian food.

Much better for Chinese is the ***Sichuan Restaurant*** *(☎ 253842)*, somewhat bizarrely situated in a warehouse at the showgrounds. But inside, the food is excellent and prices are fair, with starters such as deep-fried crocodile meat at US$2.50, and mains like Sichuan pork for US$3.75 or teppenyaki sizzling chicken for US$5.50.

Near the showgrounds, the ***Marco Polo Restaurant*** (☎ *250111*) is a very smart place with Italian specialities for around US$10 to US$15 and a terrace overlooking the polo field. Opposite is the ***Continental***, less fancy, with shady outdoor seating, burgers from US$4, and good grilled meat, fish or chicken from US$6. Nearby is ***Fragigi's***, an austere restaurant with genuine Italian cuisine: pastas from US$4, sauces from US$4, pizzas from US$4, main courses US$6 to US$10.

Entertainment

For a local urban flavour, try ***Sam's Sports Cafe*** on Malasha Rd, off Cairo Rd. In Northmead, ***Alpha Bar*** is good and has pool tables. ***Brown's***, on Kabelenga Rd, is a British-style pub, popular with South Africans and other expats, and has darts, video jukebox, live music some evenings (no cover charge for local bands, up to US$2 for big names), and real pints of draught. For a pub with a more mixed crowd, go to ***Chasers*** on Lagos Rd; it also serves snacks and evening meals.

For music and dancing, the ***Continental*** (see Places to Eat earlier in this section) has live bands or discos at weekends (US$1 to US$2 cover charge, free if you eat). A bit more hot and sweaty is ***8000 rpm***, a bar in Northmead with dancing and music – mostly rave. Nearby is a good nightclub called ***Zenon***.

The best nightclub in town is ***Chez N'Temba***, busy on Thursday and Sunday, doubly so on Friday and Saturday. The music is hardcore rhumba; the place warms up at midnight, then rocks until dawn. Entry is US$2. For more-western sounds the ***Cage*** nightclub on Panganini Rd has also been recommended. As anywhere, nightclubs sometimes attract a rough crowd, but bouncers at the door generally frisk men for weapons.

At ***Mike's Car Wash*** on Kafue Rd south of the centre, you really can get your car cleaned, but there are also a couple of bars, serving beers and snacks, and another popular rhumba nightclub at weekends for which most people come by taxi.

For a more serene experience, ***Zambili d'Afrique*** (see Shopping following) arranges regular cultural nights, with contemporary and traditional music and dance performances.

Shopping

The Shoprite supermarket on Cairo Rd has a huge stock of imported and local goods, including fresh bread and a surprisingly good selection of cassettes. There's an even bigger Shoprite and many other stores at the glitzy Manda Hill shopping centre on Great East Rd. Northmead shopping centre, also on Great East Rd, has a more local feel, with smaller supermarkets and shops, a market selling fresh fruit and veg, plus a good selection of craft stalls.

Also good for crafts is Kabwata Cultural Centre, a scruffy collection of huts and stalls (although a renovation is promised) off Burma Rd, south-east of the centre. Prices are reasonable and you can buy direct from the workers who live here.

Completely different is Zambili d'Afrique (☎ 779846), a smart souvenir shop with a wide choice and lots of imaginative items made for western tastes which you won't find on the street. Musical events are held here (phone for details), and there's also a cafe. It's on Lufubu Rd in the suburb of Kalundu, off Great East Rd, about 4km from the centre.

You can buy locally made goods at Zintu Shop, on Panganini Rd, which has a small but good selection of Congo cloth, basketwork and traditional pottery, and you can see some things being made.

Lusaka's markets are covered in the Things to See & Do section earlier in this chapter.

Getting There & Away

Air Getting to and from the airport is covered in Getting Around later in this section. For details on flights, see Getting There & Away and Getting Around earlier in this chapter. The following airline offices are useful if you have reservations to confirm, but for buying a ticket you may be better off going to a travel agent as prices are usually the same and it saves you a lot of shopping around.

Aero Zambia (☎ 226111) ZNIB House, behind TAZARA House, Independence Ave
Air France (☎ 264930) 8 Chindo Rd, Woodlands
Air Malawi (☎ 228121) ZNIB House, behind TAZARA House, Independence Ave
Air Zimbabwe (☎ 225431) Kariba House, Chachacha Rd
British Airways (☎ 254444) Holiday Inn, Church Rd
Ethiopian Airlines (☎ 223835) Cairo Rd
KLM & Kenya Airways (☎ 255147) Pamodzi Hotel, Addis Ababa Drive
Royal Swazi (☎ 224222) Farmers House, Cairo Rd
South African Airways (☎ 254327) InterContinental Hotel, Haile Salassie Ave

Bus & Minibus City Bus Station, near Kulima Towers at the southern end of Freedom Way, is for local services and surrounding towns such as Kafue (US$1), Chirundu (US$3), Siavonga (US$3.50) and Kapiri Mposhi (US$4). Minibuses also go from Soweto Market.

The Intercity Bus Station on Dedan Kimathi Rd is for long-distance routes, and several different companies run buses from here. Some sample routes and fares include: Kapiri Mposhi (US$4 minibus, about three hours); Ndola (US$5); Kitwe (US$6 minibus); Livingstone (US$6 ordinary bus); Mongu (US$6.50 ordinary bus, US$8 'time bus'); and Chipata (US$8 ordinary bus, US$10 express bus). It's worth checking times and trying to buy your ticket the day before on long-distance routes if you have time.

If you're going to Kapiri Mposhi to transfer to the TAZARA train, make sure you get a bus going all the way to the TAZARA station, which is about 2km outside Kapiri Mposhi town.

A bus company called RPS has its station on Freedom Way. Buses go twice weekly to Kashikishi via Serenje (US$7.50) and Samfya (US$9). There are ordinary buses daily to Mongu (US$10) and to Chipata (US$10), and 'luxury express' buses (slightly faster and more comfortable) twice a week to the same destinations (US$11.50, eight hours to Mongu, 10 hours to Chipata). An ordinary bus goes three times a week (fastest on Thursday) to Mpulungu (US$14) via Mpika (US$11), Kasama (US$12) and Mbala (US$13). All RPS buses depart at 7 am.

A bus company called Euro-Africa has its station near South End Roundabout, on the back street between Cairo Rd and the railway. Express buses go three times weekly to Livingstone (US$7, six hours). Other days it's an ordinary bus (US$6). Buses go four times daily to Ndola (US$5) and Kitwe (US$6, three hours).

Virgin-Lux express buses depart 500m north of Euro-Africa's station: to Ndola (every hour); Livingstone (one daily); and Chipata (one daily). Prices are the same as Euro-Africa's. Most Virgin-Lux and Euro-Africa buses leave between 6 am and 7 am. You can buy tickets in advance or on the day.

A final option worth considering is the Post Bus service, which carries mail and people between Lusaka and other main centres. The bus is comfortable and quite fast. The most useful services are from Lusaka to Kasama (every Monday, US$11) and from Lusaka to Chipata (Thursday and Saturday, US$9). You can buy tickets in advance at the depot behind the main post office on Cairo Rd, open from 7 am to noon daily (11 am at weekends).

Train Lusaka's train station, on Dedan Kimathi Rd, deals with reservations and tickets for trains to Livingstone and Kitwe (via Kapiri Mposhi and Ndola). For more details see the Getting Around section earlier in this chapter.

Trains on the TAZARA railway between Kapiri Mposhi and Dar es Salaam (Tanzania) currently do not run to Lusaka, but you can make reservations at TAZARA House on Independence Ave. (For more details, see the main Getting There & Away section earlier in this chapter.)

Hitching Although we don't recommend hitching, the place to wait if you're heading along the Great East Road is the bus stop just beyond the airport turn-off (where you can retreat to Pioneer Campsite if it gets late). Heading south, it's best to get to the junction 10km beyond Kafue town, where the roads to Chirundu and Livingstone divide; if you get stuck, a petrol station takeaway and a basic local resthouse are nearby.

Getting Around

To/From the Airport Lusaka's international airport is about 20km east of the city centre. Taxis from the airport cost about US$15, plus a 10% tip. From town to the airport costs around US$10. There's no airport bus, but the big hotels send courtesy buses to meet international flights, and you might be able to arrange a ride into town with the driver.

Bus Local minibuses run along Lusaka's main roads, but there are no route numbers or name boards, so the system is difficult to work out. The main routes for travellers are: from South End Roundabout along Independence Ave to Longacres Roundabout, then along Los Angeles Blvd to Kabulonga; and from South End Roundabout along Kafue Rd, past Castle shopping centre and Eureka Camp, then on to Kafue town. Fares from the centre include: Longacres US$0.20; Eureka Camp US$0.30; and Kabulonga US$0.50.

Taxi Taxis can be identified by the numbers painted on the doors, but there are lots of unofficial taxis cruising the streets. There are ranks at the main hotels, near markets and outside Shoprite on Cairo Rd, and you can also hail a cab in the street. Fares are negotiable, but as a guide, from the city centre to Holiday Inn or Pamodzi costs US$1 to US$2, and from the centre to Kabulonga costs US$3. Always check the fare before your journey.

AROUND LUSAKA

From Lusaka, the Great North Road aims, not surprisingly, north through the towns of Kabwe and Kapiri Mposhi. Just beyond Kapiri Mposhi it splits: left to the Copperbelt and Congo (Zäire); right to northern and eastern Zambia, and eventually to Tanzania.

About 40km from Lusaka, the luxurious ***Chisamba Safari Lodge*** *(☎ 01-226589, ⓔ chisamba@zamnet.zm)*, on a wildlife farm, has comfortable double chalets for US$95 with breakfast.

More affordable is friendly ***Fringilla Farm*** *(☎ 01-611199)*, about 50km from Lusaka. Comfortable chalets with two or three beds and private bathroom cost US$35. Family rooms with four/six beds cost US$48/58, smarter double cottages are US$48, and camping is US$5. Simple chalets on the camp site cost US$7. There's a restaurant selling snacks and meals, plus a post office, bank, clinic and shop. Buses between Lusaka and Kapiri Mposhi pass the farm entrance, and this place is well worth considering if you're heading to Lusaka and don't want to arrive late in the day.

Kapiri Mposhi

☎ 05

Kapiri Mposhi is a small but busy town at the southern end of the TAZARA railway from Dar es Salaam (Tanzania), and it's also on the line between Lusaka and Kitwe. The Lusaka-Kitwe line station is in the centre of town, but the station for the TAZARA train is about 2km from the centre.

If you're coming from Tanzania, there's a passport check before you can get out of the station, then a mad rush for buses going to Lusaka and elsewhere. When a train comes in, most buses leave from right outside the station. Thieves and pickpockets love the crowds and confusion, so take great care here. If you're coming from Lusaka, make sure you get a bus or minibus straight to the TAZARA station. Coming from elsewhere you'll probably be dropped in the centre and have to walk or take a taxi to the TAZARA station. If you get stuck, there are some local resthouses on the main street.

Mkushi

☎ 05

This small town, also called Mkushi Boma, is 95km east of Kapiri Mposhi on the Great North Road. ***Forest Inn*** *(☎ 362003)* is on the eastern side of the road, about 30km south of Mkushi and 65km from Kapiri Mposhi. Set in a patch of shady woodland, very comfortable chalets with private bathroom cost US$25/35, and camping on the flat grassy site is US$5. There's a bar and good-value ***restaurant***, with three-course dinner for US$10. The friendly owners are a good source of information on places to visit in the surrounding area.

The Copperbelt

The Copperbelt is the industrial heart of Zambia, although since the world copper market slumped during the 1970s, the vast open-cast mines have cut back on production, creating high unemployment in this area. The main cities are Ndola and Kitwe, while other large towns include Chingola and Mufulira – all rarely visited by tourists.

NDOLA

☎ 02

Ndola is the official capital of the Copperbelt. Cheap places to stay are limited, and most hotels cater for business visitors. By far the best value in town is the ***Travellers Lodge*** *(☎ 621840, ⓔ travell@zamnet.zm)* on Vitanda St, just north of the centre, charging US$20/30 for single/doubles with aircon, fridge, TV and breakfast. Up a grade, the ***Savoy Hotel***, in the centre, charges US$32/45 and has a nice terrace bar.

The airport is on the edge of town, and there are daily flights to and from Lusaka. For details on buses and trains from Lusaka, see that section.

KITWE

☎ 02

Kitwe is the centre of Zambia's mining business, seemingly even busier than Ndola, although the centre is compact.

Cheap places to stay include the friendly ***YMCA*** *(☎ 211710)* on Independence Ave, north of the centre, with basic doubles for US$10 (US$12 with bathroom and breakfast). ***Lothian House*** *(☎ 222889)* on Chandamali Rd, a former government hostel, has musty but clean rooms at US$16/18 with breakfast and bathroom.

In the same area as the Lothian, the small and friendly ***Sherbourne Guesthouse*** *(☎ 222168)* charges US$55/70 for good rooms, or US$45/60 in the annex. The nearby ***Mukwa Lodge*** *(☎ 224266)* is similar in price and quality, and both places serve excellent food. In the town centre, the high-rise ***Edinburgh Hotel*** *(☎ 222444)* is nothing special but fair value at US$32/60.

CHIMFUNSHI CHIMPANZEE SANCTUARY

If this place wasn't so remote, it would be a major tourist attraction. On a farm about 50km west of Chingola, the Siddel and Forbes families have built a chimpanzee sanctuary, home to about 60 adult and young chimps confiscated from poachers and traders in nearby Congo (Zaïre) or brought from other parts of Africa and zoos all over the world.

Currently, one cohesive group of adults and young can be seen in a large enclosure, while it's possible to walk and interact with younger chimps when they're taken to a nearby forest for exercise. A visit here is not a natural wildlife experience, but it's still fascinating to observe the chimps as they feed, play and socialise. We knew that chimps and humans were something like 98% the same, but until we went for a walk in the woods with Alfie and his friends we didn't realise just how amazingly similar the two species are.

There are long-term plans to make a large (10,000 hectare) wildlife farm here, where the chimps can roam through the bush, and visitors can walk and observe them. A luxury lodge is also planned. In the meantime, visitors are welcome at the simple ***camp site*** (US$5), which also has some basic huts, and food supplies for sale. You have to come here first to arrange to visit the sanctuary, which is only open to visitors in the morning. To see the chimps in the enclosure costs US$5. To go into the forest with the young chimps is US$25. People with a genuine interest in chimpanzee research and rehabilitation will need to stay for several days and set things up in advance, and may also be able to arrange more comfortable accommodation.

Chimfunshi is hard to reach without a car, as the sanctuary is 19km off the main road between Chingola and Solwezi. Independent travellers can just turn up, but advance notice is preferred. To make arrangements, phone Ian Forbes' house in Chingola (☎ 02-311255); the people there are in radio contact with Chimfunshi. If you're already in Lusaka, you can get more details from a tour agent or from Chachacha Backpackers.

Northern Zambia

Northern Zambia starts once you've passed the 'Pedicle' – the great tongue of Congo territory that almost splits Zambia in two. It's a beautiful and sparsely populated area of hills, valleys, lakes, rivers, wetlands and waterfalls, where you rarely meet another tourist. Distances between towns are long, and some sights are way off the main routes, so visitors with a car or motorbike will find getting around easier. But public transport is not hard to find, and we've heard from several hardy travellers who used buses, trains and boats here, and had an unforgettable trip. Places are described from south to north.

SERENJE

Serenje is an unremarkable town, but you may find yourself changing buses or refuelling here. The centre is 3km north of the Great North Road, with a TAZARA train station and some unappealing resthouses. You're better off at the junction on the main road, which has a petrol station, shop, local ***restaurant*** and the ***Siga-Siga Motel*** with basic but clean doubles for US$6, and a friendly manager who can advise on local transport.

Buses from Lusaka to Mpika, Kasama and Mansa (for Samfya and Kasanka) all stop here. The TAZARA train also stops here.

KASANKA NATIONAL PARK

Kasanka is Zambia's only privately managed national park, and it's highly recommended. Highlights include taking a boat ride and watching iridescent kingfishers under a beautiful canopy of riverine forest, or watching from a hide 18m up in a tree as the semi-aquatic sitatunga graze in the reed beds (Kasanka is one of the best places in Africa to see this shy antelope). Bush walks, canoeing and trips to villages can also be arranged.

Between Kasanka and Lake Waka-Waka, fans of culture and history can divert to **Chief Chitambo's Palace** at the village of Chalilo, or to the **David Livingstone Memorial**, which marks the spot where the famous explorer died.

Places to Stay

The only places to stay are ***Wasa Camp*** (e *kasanka@aol.com)*, which is also the park headquarters, and ***Luwomba Camp***. At both, simple rondavels with shared bathroom cost US$20 per person. Smarter chalets with bathroom and veranda are planned (US$30). You can bring all your own food and the friendly kitchen staff will prepare it, or you can get a good-value all-inclusive deal with accommodation, meals, drives, walks, boat trips, soft drinks and beers for about US$100 per person – ideally this should be booked in advance. Revenue from visitors staying at these camps goes directly into management, conservation and local community projects.

Getting There & Away

The park is easy to reach with a vehicle and can also be reached by public transport. From the Great North Road, 1km east of Serenje, turn left (north) onto the road towards Mansa. After about 50km, the entrance to Kasanka is on your left (west). You pay entrance fees here (see National Parks in the Facts for the Visitor section earlier in this chapter). From here to Wasa Camp is 12km, passable by car all year.

Alternatively, minibuses for Mansa will pick you up from the junction by Serenje and drop you off at the park gate. From there you can radio Wasa Camp for a lift (US$10 for the vehicle) or walk through the beautiful woodland.

BANGWEULU WETLANDS

To the south and east of Lake Bangweulu, this vast seasonally flooded area (sometimes called the Bangweulu Swamps) is a fascinating and very rarely visited part of Zambia. The wetlands support a scattered human population that lives mainly by subsistence fishing, and are also an excellent area for wildlife (designated as a Game Management Area or GMA). The area is particularly noted for the vast herds of black lechwe antelope which cover the plains literally as far as the eye can see, and the extremely rare shoebill stork. The best place for viewing wildlife and birds is where the wetlands meet the plains, and the best time to come for birdwatching is April to June, when the water is high, although July and August (when the waters are still up) are pretty good, and better for seeing the lechwe.

Places to Stay

Nsobe Camp is on the edge of the plains about 5km north of the village of Muwale, with friendly helpful management and spotless grass huts with simple private bathroom for US$30 per person. At quiet times discounts are sometimes available, but please remember all revenue goes to the local community. Camping is US$2. You must bring all your food, and the kitchen staff will prepare it. Wildlife walks, boat rides and village visits can all be arranged.

Further north is ***Shoebill Camp***, with large walk-in safari tents for US$40 per person (bring your own food for the staff to prepare). It's not cheap, but you're paying for the splendid position, seemingly in the heart of the wetlands, with only birds, hippo, lechwe and the occasional passing fisherman for company. The price includes boating with skilful guides to help you spot the shoebill stork. Camping costs US$10 per person, and you pay extra for boat trips. Meals can be provided with advance warning. You can make bookings with agents in Lusaka, or through the Kasanka National Park email address – essential if you want meals, and handy if you need to be taken to the camp by boat.

Getting There & Away

This place is restricted to drivers (and chartered planes), as there's no public transport. From near Kasanka (where you can get help with directions), dirt roads lead via Lake Waka-Waka (where there's a camp site), Chiundaponda and Muwale to Nsobe Camp. About 5km beyond Nsobe is Chikuni GMA ranger post, from where you can drive to Shoebill Camp if it's dry. If it isn't dry, you'll have to do the last 5km by boat – and it saves a lot of time if you arrange this in advance.

SAMFYA

On the western shore of beautiful Lake Bangweulu, the small town of Samfya is about 10km east of the main road between Mansa and Serenje. It's a trading centre and a lake transport hub, small enough in which to get to know people, and big enough to have resthouses, restaurants and bars – just the type of place to slow down and become a local for a few days. To cap it all, just outside town is a wonderful white sandy beach.

Cheap places to stay include the ***Transport Hotel*** at the port, with basic rooms for US$2.50. Or ask around about the ***camp site*** being built by Dirk Snyman on a beach 7km from town. He also plans a smarter lodge in town, and runs ***Tigerfish Haven***, a fishing camp, near Twingi, south of Samfya. Samfya is served by minibuses running between Mansa and Serenje.

SHIWA NGANDU

The vast estate of Shiwa Ngandu was established in the 1920s by Stewart Gore-Brown, a paternalistic British aristocrat. At its heart is the incongruous mansion of **Shiwa House** (described in *The Africa House*, which is listed under Books in the Facts for the Visitor section earlier in this chapter). Now almost abandoned, Shiwa House is slowly being reclaimed by the surrounding vegetation, and already looks several hundred years old. It's about 90km north of Mpika, on the dirt road that links the Great North Road to the Mpika-Kasama road, and is easily reached by car (there's no public transport). Tours cost US$1.

About 20km west of Shiwa House, still on the Shiwa Ngandu estate, is **Kapishya Hot Springs**, where the ***lodge*** has comfortable chalets for US$30 per person, and ***camping*** for US$5. Bring your own food for the staff to prepare, or the friendly management can provide meals for around US$6 to US$10. There's a wonderful pool at the hot springs where you can swim to your heart's content – the water never gets cold! Walking, fishing and canoeing trips are offered, or take a safari into North Luangwa National Park (see the Eastern Zambia section of this chapter). You can make reservations for the chalets and safaris at the Zambian Safari Company in Lusaka.

KASAMA

☎ 04

You might find yourself overnighting in this small busy town if you're travelling between Lusaka and Mpulungu, or switching from TAZARA train to local bus. Places to stay near the TAZARA station (5km from the town centre) include the friendly ***Elizabeth Guesthouse***, where doubles cost US$7 with shared bathroom, and the ***Kapongolo Resthouse*** with small but clean doubles for US$9, including private bathroom and breakfast. Between the station and the centre is the large ***Modern Kwacha Relax Hotel*** where reasonable singles/doubles cost US$9.50/12, including private bathroom and breakfast.

The ***Thorntree Guesthouse*** *(☎/fax 221615,* e *kansato@zamnet.zm)*, in the southern suburbs (ask for directions at the Caltex petrol station in the town centre), has very nice rooms for US$17.50 per person, and cottages with private bathroom for US$30 (single or double). A three-course dinner costs US$10. It's owned by the Powell family, who are very friendly and knowledgeable about the surrounding area.

Minibuses between the TAZARA train station and the centre cost US$0.20. A private taxi is US$2. For more details on the TAZARA train, see the main Getting There & Away section earlier in this chapter. Minibuses to Mpulungu cost US$4.50, via Mbala. Buses to Lusaka are US$12, via Mpika and Serenje.

MBALA

☎ 04

Mbala is a small town perched on the edge of the Great Rift Valley. From here the road north drops over 1000m in less than 40km down to Mpulungu and Lake Tanganyika.

The main reason to come to Mbala is to visit the **Moto Moto Museum**, about 3km outside town, a huge and fascinating collection of artefacts relating to the Bemba tribe and surrounding area.

The old colonial ***Arms Hotel*** charges US$4.50 for grotty rooms. The ***Grasshopper Inn***, about 750m off the main street, is much better, with simple rooms for US$6 (US$8 with private bathroom), bar, garden and an airy restaurant where meals cost US$2. On the main street, ***Old Soldier's Restaurant*** offers good company and local food from US$1. The owner is also planning a camping ground on nearby Lake Chila.

KALAMBO FALLS

About 40km north-west of Mbala, on the border between Zambia and Tanzania, is Kalambo Falls – the second-highest single drop waterfall in Africa (after Tugela Falls in the Drakensberg). From spectacular viewpoints near the top of the falls, you can see the River Kalambo plummeting off a steep V-shaped cliff cut into the Rift Valley escarpment into a deep valley covered in dense vegetation, which then winds down towards Lake Tanganyika. A walk from the falls to the escarpment edge overlooking the lake is also wonderful.

From Mbala, the falls can be reached by car, and if you don't have your own, Mr Jasper Luchembe at Old Soldier's Restaurant will take you in his for a negotiable US$20 per person, or rent you a bike for the whole day (also negotiable).

Alternatively, the energetic and adventurous can reach the falls by boat from Mpulungu. You can take the daily taxi boat that serves villages along the lakeshore east of Mpulungu, but be aware that just getting to Nyamba village (the start of the walk) can take all day. It's better to hire a boat: this will cost US$10 to US$20, plus fuel (around US$12 to US$15).

From Nyamba, it's a two-hour walk to the falls; a local guide is useful and costs US$1.20 to US$1.50. The heat means an early start is essential, so arrange your boat the day before. Don't forget water and a sunhat.

MPULUNGU

☎ 04

Mpulungu is the Zambian terminal for the Lake Tanganyika ferries serving Tanzania and Burundi (see the main Getting There & Away section earlier in this chapter). It's a busy crossroad between East, Central and Southern Africa with a lively atmosphere. It's also very hot.

Places to Stay

Places to stay include a couple of local ***resthouses*** in the town centre, but a long-time favourite is the ***Nkupi Lodge***, on the eastern side of town, with camping (US$2.50) and basic rondavels (US$8). Near the port is the ***Harbour Inn***, with the most popular bar in town. Nice rooms with private bathroom are very good value at US$8. The owner has fancy speedboats for hire, for fishing or trips to Kalambo Falls.

About 6km west along the coast is the ***Tanganyika Lodge*** in a splendid position on the lakeshore, reached by turning off the main road about 5km before the town (signposted). Backpackers can get a taxi boat from near Mpulungu market, going towards Kasakalabwe village, that passes the lodge (US$0.60). Camping is US$3, and clean, simple chalets cost US$10 per person. There's a bar, and meals are available. The manager can help you arrange a local fishing boat for a trip to Kalambo Falls.

When we passed through, Luke Powell was planning a place called ***Mishemba Beach***, about 20km east of Mpulungu, with tents on wooden platforms under palms for US$20 per person. It sounds great – ask around when you arrive.

Getting There & Away

Long-distance direct buses tie in with the ferry. The RPS bus goes every Thursday from Lusaka to Mpulungu (US$14) and returns on Friday. The sector from Mpulungu to Kasama costs US$3.50. There are two other services each week, but they're slower. Minibuses are faster and more regular; they depart from near the BP petrol station to Mbala (US$1.40) and Kasama (US$4.50), from where you can get onward transport to Lusaka.

NSUMBU NATIONAL PARK

This remote and frequently overlooked park covers a beautiful area of hilly grassland and escarpment, cut by several rivers and wetland zones, on the southern shore of Lake Tanganyika, west of Mpulungu. Like many other parks in Zambia, Nsumbu was virtually abandoned in the 1980s, and suffered from poaching, but in recent years conditions have improved, and herds of elephant and buffalo are seen here once again. Other animals include bushbuck, waterbuck and puku. Lion and leopard prey upon the puku, although these big cats are rarely seen.

Most visitors fly in to Nsumbu. The park airstrip is near the ***Kasaba Bay Lodge*** which costs US$200 per person for full board and caters mainly for anglers. Another option is the ***Nkamba Bay Lodge***, which charges US$65 per person including breakfast.

The ***Ndole Bay Lodge*** (*☎ 02-711150 in Kitwe, ⓔ ndolebay@coppernet.zm*) receives the best reports. It's on the lakeshore just outside the western boundary of the park. Chalets for up to four people cost US$125 per person (half price for children) including all meals. Camping costs US$15 per person, and you can eat at the lodge if you like. You can also arrange boat hire for wildlife viewing or angling (from US$40 per day), local bird walks (free), wildlife drives in the park ($40 for the vehicle) and various water sports. If you fly to Kasaba Bay, a boat will then take you to the lodge.

Eastern Air flies from Lusaka to Kasaba Bay (US$180, twice weekly). You reach Nsumbu from Mpulungu by lake; the lodges arrange speedboat transfers. Hardy overlanders can drive, but you must approach from the west, via Mporokoso, and the roads are bad. It's very rare for visitors to simply turn up at Nsumbu. You must make a reservation and arrange air or boat transfers at the same time, which is easiest through a travel agent or tour operator in Lusaka.

NAKONDE

Nakonde is on the southern side of the border between Zambia and Tanzania. It's full of hustlers, and worth avoiding by getting through transport if you can. If you have to change buses here, try and do it during daytime. If you get stuck, Nakonde has two unappealing local ***resthouses***, but these often fill on the nights before and after the TAZARA train goes through.

Eastern Zambia

This section covers the area to the east of Lusaka, including the border towns of Chirundu and Chipata, plus the Lower Zambezi and South Luangwa National Parks – the two finest in the country. Places are described from west to east.

CHIRUNDU

☎ 01

This border town on the main road between Lusaka and Harare has shops, a few truckers' bars, a bank and a clutch of moneychangers.

The ***Nyambadwe Motel*** has grotty doubles for US$10, and some slightly better ones with bathroom for US$16.

The best place to stay is the ***Gwabi Lodge*** *(☎ 515062, e gwabi@zamnet.zm)* 11km from Chirundu towards the Lower Zambezi National Park. Comfortable chalets cost US$30 per person, including full breakfast, and camping costs US$5. The lodge has marvellous lush grounds, although the camping area is a bit dusty, plus a bar that sells snacks, a restaurant, swimming pool and terrace with one of the best views in Africa. Boat rides are available. The owners are tireless conservationists, involved in wildlife education schemes in the surrounding area.

Minibuses between Lusaka and Chirundu cost US$3. To reach the Gwabi Lodge, head north through the truck park just before the border, then along the dirt road for 11km. Unless you've got your own wheels, you'll have to hitch or walk.

LOWER ZAMBEZI NATIONAL PARK

The Lower Zambezi National Park covers some 4000 sq km on the western bank of the River Zambezi, opposite Zimbabwe's Mana Pools. Overlooked for many years, this is now one of Zambia's premier parks, with a beautiful flood plain alongside the river, dotted with acacias and other large trees, and flanked by a steep escarpment on the northern side, covered with thick miombo woodland. The best wildlife viewing is on the flood plain and along the river itself, so boat rides are a major feature of all the camps and lodges here. Seeing groups of elephant swim across the river, or hundreds of colourful bee-eaters nesting in the steep sandy banks, could be the highlight of your trip.

The main gate is at Chongwe, on the western boundary, where you pay park fees (see National Parks in the Facts about Zambia section earlier in this chapter). The south-western sector is the easiest to reach, and has excellent wildlife viewing, so it's the most popular. To the east the park ends at the Mpata Gorge.

Places to Stay

The park has a wide choice of places to stay, and we list a selection here. For most places, it's usually necessary to book in advance, either directly or through an agent in Lusaka or overseas. The prices listed here are all per person in the high season for double rooms. Single supplements usually cost 30% more. Places are described from west to east.

The ***Kayila Lodge***, run by Safari Par Excellence (e *safpar@harare.iafrica.com*), is about 35km east of the Kafue River, with thatched chalets, a twin-bedded treehouse and plunge pool for US$240, all inclusive.

The ***Royal Zambezi Lodge*** *(☎ 01-223952, e royalzam@zamnet.zm)* a few kilometres west of the Chongwe gate has luxurious walk-in tents with private bathroom, a restaurant overlooking the river and splendid aerial bar built around the branches of a tree, costing US$185 for full board and activities. There's also a self-catering camp for US$35, and you can arrange wildlife drives or boat rides on the spot (US$25).

The ***Chongwe Camp*** *(☎ 01-262717, e chongwe@zamnet.zm)* is a beautiful camping ground in a great position, just outside the park. To avoid crowding, it has just four spacious pitches, each big enough to take several cars and tents, which can be booked for US$15 per person. Reservations are preferred, directly or through Africa Tour Designers in Lusaka (see under Travel Agencies & Tour Operators in the Lusaka section). Boat trips and wildlife drives are available.

The ***Chiawa Camp*** *(☎ 01-261588, fax 262683, e chiacamp@zamnet.zm)* is a

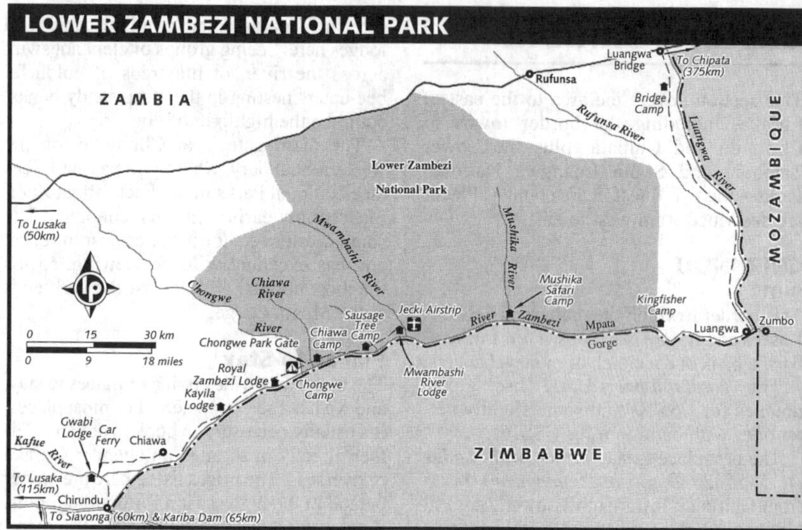

luxurious lodge inside the park at the confluence of the Chiawa and Zambezi Rivers. The owners are pioneers in this area. Their expertise is highly regarded – and has to be paid for: US$295 per person, fully inclusive of accommodation in large walk-in tents with pine-clad private bathroom, top-quality food, park fees, boat trips, wildlife drives and walks. The bar and lounge has an upstairs deck with great views over the river.

Further downstream is the ***Sausage Tree Camp***, part of the exclusive and unconventional Tongabezi group *(☎ 03-323234, ⓔ tonga@zamnet.zm)*. True to form, traditional safari decor is rejected, and tents are cool and elegant Bedouin-style, each in its own private clearing, with minimal furniture and open-air bathrooms which continue the North African theme. Rates are US$330.

Just outside the park's east boundary, 25km upstream from Luangwa, is the ***Kingfisher Camp***, run by the indestructible Alistair Gellatly. The wildlife viewing is good, as is the fishing, and you can also go by boat to the spectacular Mpata Gorge.

The camp is undergoing renovation, so you can get more details from an agent in Lusaka.

Getting There & Around

There's no public transport to the gate, hitching is very difficult, and you need a vehicle to enter the park anyway. Most people visit the park as part of a tour, and stay at a lodge that provides wildlife drives and boat rides as part of the deal.

The best option for budget travellers is to join a cheap tour that stays at Chongwe Camp and includes wildlife drives. You can get more details from Chachacha Backpackers in Lusaka.

Most of the top end lodges and camps arrange transfers for guests, either by air, or by boat from Gwabi Lodge. Unless you're pushed for time, the latter option is highly recommended, and costs from US$100 per person.

Drivers can reach the park independently, and a track runs from the gate roughly parallel to the Zambezi, although it's in very bad condition east of the airstrip. There are also several wildlife-viewing loops, but these change from year to year, and getting around is unlikely to be rewarding without the knowledge of a guide.

Another way to see the park is from a canoe. Several operators run canoe trips here, stopping for two or three nights at seasonal camps along the Zambezi, or simply pitching tents and mosquito nets on the midstream islands. You can get more details from tour agents in Lusaka and Livingstone.

LUANGWA BRIDGE

The Great East Road crosses the Luangwa River on a large suspension bridge about halfway between Lusaka and Chipata. On the western side of the river, 3km south of the main road, is the ***Bridge Camp*** (*e rshenton@zamnet.zm*), an excellent place to break the long journey, or to base yourself for a couple of days of rest and relaxation. Camping costs US$3, and single/double chalets cost US$15/25. There are hot showers, cooking facilities, meals and snacks. Food and supplies are available from the market on the main road. Canoe trips for a few hours or a few days can be arranged. From the camp you can also visit Luangwa town (where a vehicle-carrying pontoon means Zimbabwe and Mozambique are easily reached) and the eastern side of Lower Zambezi National Park, or go hiking – all on a backpacker budget. You can get more details from Chachacha Backpackers in Lusaka.

CHIPATA

☎ 062

Chipata is on the main road near Zambia's eastern border with Malawi. It's a lively, friendly town, with a big market and some nice bars and cafes. It's also the main jumping off point for travellers heading for South Luangwa National Park. Many people try to rush through, but as neat bus connections are unlikely, it's worth considering two nights and a day of rest here. Other facilities include shops, petrol stations, a telephone office and banks.

Places to Stay

Shoestringers enjoy the ***Kapata Resthouse***, near the bus station and market, 1km from the main street; it's safe and fairly clean and doubles cost US$6. Food is available. About 1.5km from the bus station, the ***camping ground*** run by the Zambian Wildlife Conservation Society charges US$2.50 per person. To get here, turn off the main street at the BP station, and continue for two blocks. The nearby friendly ***Kamocho Guesthouse*** has doubles for US$20 (US$24 with private bathroom).

If you're driving or hitching, about 3km west of town, where the road to Luangwa turns off, is the faded but friendly ***Chipata Motel***. Clean doubles with bathroom and breakfast cost US$10 to US$15. Down the road, 10km from Chipata, ***Katutu Lodge*** offers good clean singles/doubles with bathroom and breakfast for US$15/20, and good-value meals. Camping is US$5.

About 10km east of town, 1.5km off the main road towards the border, is the ***Sunnyside Farm Campsite*** (signposted), with a nice grassy site by a small lake, for US$2.50 per person. Bring all the food you need – and watch out for the mosquitoes in the toilet.

Getting There & Away

Buses to Lusaka go from the main bus station and cost US$8 (US$9.50 for the express or 'time bus'). Small minibuses leave from near the mosque in the town centre and cost US$6.50. For information on reaching South Luangwa National Park, see Getting There & Away in the following section.

SOUTH LUANGWA NATIONAL PARK

☎ 062

For scenery, variety of animals, accessibility and choice of accommodation, South Luangwa is the best park in Zambia, and one of the best in Africa. Vegetation ranges from dense woodland to open grassy plains, and mammals include lion, buffalo, Cookson's wildebeest and the endemic Thornicroft's giraffe. The park also contains large herds of elephant and is noted for leopard. Antelope species include bushbuck, waterbuck, impala and puku. The birdlife is tremendous.

The wide Luangwa River is the lifeblood of the park. It flows all year, and gets very shallow in the dry season, when vast midstream sandbanks are exposed – usually covered in groups of hippo or croc, basking in the sun. Steep exposed banks mean animals prefer to drink at the park's numerous oxbow lagoons, formed as the river continually changes its course, and this is where wildlife viewing is often best. Thus, unlike other parks in Zambia, South Luangwa doesn't feature boat trips, but all camps and lodges run excellent wildlife drives (day or night) and walking safaris.

The focal point is Mfuwe, where there's a large village (with shops and a market), the main gate into the park, a bridge over the river, and several lodges and camps in the surrounding area. This part of the park can get quite busy with vehicles, but only because it's the best wildlife-viewing area. And in Zambia everything is relative; if you've suffered rush-hour-rally-style safaris in places like Kenya you'll find it positively peaceful here.

Although South Luangwa is hard to visit on the cheap, there are more options for the budget-conscious here than in other Zambian parks. Having said that, some shoestring travellers who hitch in get a nasty surprise at the lack of real bargains. By the time you've paid for accommodation, park fees and a couple of wildlife-viewing drives, you're looking at about US$100. If you haven't got that, you won't get much from your visit, so it's probably not worth coming.

For details on entrance fees, see National Parks in the Facts about Zambia section.

Activities

All the places to stay arrange wildlife-viewing drives and **walks**. At the top-end lodges these are included in your accommodation fee. At the cheaper places you can arrange things on the spot. A morning or evening **wildlife drive** normally costs US$25. A night drive is US$30. This is based on three or four people in the car, and you should be able to team up with others, but don't bank on it. For one person alone, a drive will cost US$45 minimum. You also have to pay park fees, but only once per 24 hours, so this covers two drives.

There's more to South Luangwa than animals. If you want to meet local people too, most lodges can arrange a visit to Kawaza, a real village (not a touristy set-up), where a highly recommended night in the guest hut, eating, drinking and socialising Zambian-style, costs US$40.

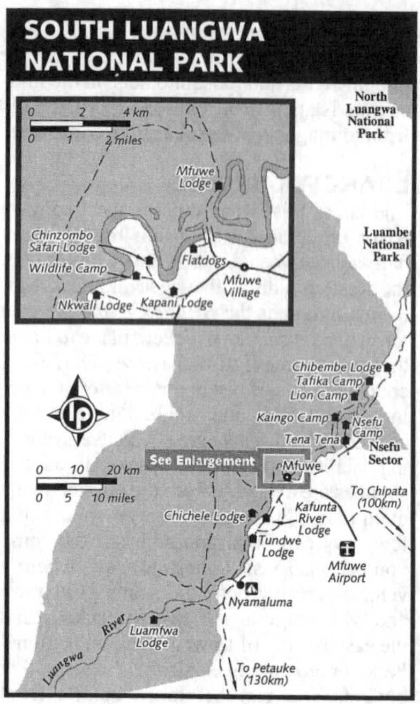

Places to Stay

South Luangwa offers a wide range of places to stay, from camp sites and budget huts through mid-range chalets to highly luxurious lodges, and we list a selection here.

In the past few years there has been a move towards larger lodges in the park, catering for around 30 or 40 guests, instead of around 10, which had been the norm at top end places until recently. When you're deciding where to stay, consider the size of the lodge. It's not necessarily a question of quality – more one of atmosphere. Some visitors prefer the intimate exclusive feel of the smaller places; others prefer the facilities and livelier atmosphere of the larger places.

Most lodges and camps in South Luangwa are on the banks of the river or an oxbow lagoon. Several lodges also have smaller 'bush camps' deep in the park, where they operate walks or drives away from the busier areas. Despite the rustic title most bush camps are very comfortable, with large tents, private bathrooms and excellent food. Walking for a few days from one bush camp to the next is popular, and a wonderful way to really experience the sights, sounds and smells of the bush.

Except for the chalets and camp sites, it's usually necessary to book accommodation in advance, either directly or through an agent in Lusaka or overseas. When deciding where to stay, it's worth considering how long a lodge or camp has been operating in the park. Recent arrivals may have less experience when it comes to hospitality or, particularly, wildlife viewing.

Several places are just outside the park boundary, so you don't pay park fees until you go into the park. Note that some are open only in the high season – April/May to October/November – but those around Mfuwe are open all year, and rates are reduced in the low (or 'green') season. The prices listed here are all per person in the high season for double rooms. Single supplements usually cost 30% more.

Places to Stay – Budget & Mid-Range

Some budget travellers stay at the local ***Cobra Resthouse*** in Mfuwe village. This is particularly useful if you arrive after dark or need to catch a crack-of-dawn minibus out. (Lots of wild animals in the area makes walking around at night very dangerous.)

Flatdogs *(e moondog@super-hub.com)*, just outside the park near Mfuwe gate, overlooking the river, gets consistently good reviews. There are separate camp sites with excellent facilities for overlanders, self-drivers and backpackers, all US$5 per person. Small 'cottage tents' with bed and mosquito net cost US$10 per person. Imaginative and surprisingly luxurious self-catering chalets cost US$20 per person. There's a restaurant, shop, bar and quiet thatched shelters away from the camp where you can relax or watch wildlife. For families, a kids' menu and nanny service are provided. This place is run by a guy called Jake who understands backpackers and is a good source of information.

About 6km west is the spacious and efficient ***Wildlife Camp*** *(☎ 45026, e miles@super-hub.com)*, with quiet and secluded self-catering chalets (sleeping up to three) for US$22 per person. Camping costs US$5, and there's a four-bed dorm or family room for US$16.50 per person. The bar serves snacks and meals.

South of here is the quiet and under-used ***Tundwe Lodge*** with self-catering chalets for US$25 per person; you must bring all your own food and drinks.

Near Nyamaluma ranger post (on the eastern bank of the river) is a pontoon which carries vehicles over to the southern part of the park, plus a ***camp site*** and some seldom-used ***chalets***, handy for drivers using the rough back road from Petuake.

Places to Stay – Top End

South of Mfuwe gate, just outside the park on the river's eastern bank, are three well-established top-end lodges. Most famous is ***Kapani Lodge*** *(☎ 45015, e kapani@super-hub.com)*, a classic Luangwa camp, built by Norman Carr (see the boxed text 'Norman Carr & South Luangwa' later in this section) with thatched cottages overlooking a lagoon frequented by weed-munching hippo. Rates are US$290 per person, all inclusive. Kapani has three bush camps in the park and runs highly rated walking safaris.

Further along is the ***Chinzombo Safari Lodge*** *(☎ 45053, e chincamp@zamnet.zm)*, very close to the riverbank with excellent views and comfortable bungalows for US$260, all inclusive. The lodge has two bush camps and also runs walking safaris.

The ***Nkwali Lodge*** *(☎ 45090, e rps@super-hub.com)*, run by Robin Pope Safaris, has tastefully designed walk-in tents with delightful open-air bathrooms. The bar and restaurant overlook the river and the camp's private water hole; rates are US$250, all inclusive. This company also offers highly regarded walking safaris in the Nsefu sector and in the seldom visited northern reaches of the park. Robin Pope leads many personally, and guests say his feel for the wilderness is addictive. Sometimes these safaris are booked up years in advance. But all addictions are expensive: you'll pay from US$300 to US$470 per person per day.

A few kilometres further south, the ***Kafunta River Lodge*** *(☎ 45026, ⓔ miles@super-hub.com)* has cool, airy chalets and a vast restaurant-lounge-deck area offering a wonderfully open panoramic view over the river; the rate is US$280, all inclusive.

Just inside the park, near the main gate, is the ***Mfuwe Lodge*** *(☎ 45041, ⓔ mfuweloj@zamnet.zm)*. This former state-run place was bought by Malawi-based Club Makokola in 1998, and was completely rebuilt. The results are impressive: a central restaurant and bar area, with gigantic thatched roof and open sides, leading out onto a deck with swimming pool and splendid views over a lagoon where animals come to drink. The lodge sleeps around 36 people, with hotel-standard rooms in cottages (each for two or three people) with private verandas along the lagoon. It also has two bush camps in the southern section of the park, and offers a range of walking and vehicle safaris. Rates are US$300 per person. The lodge's main reservation centre is Ulendo Safaris in Malawi (ⓔ ulendo@malawi.net).

South of Mfuwe village, on the western bank of the river, is the ***Chichele Lodge***, under construction when we passed through, with rooms for 40 guests in the US$180 to US$240 range when it opens.

North of Mfuwe gate are some well-established top-end places. On the eastern bank are ***Tena Tena*** and ***Nsefu Camp***, both run by Robin Pope Safaris and both overlooking beautiful wide bends in the river. Tena Tena has a calm and exclusive atmosphere, and just four large walk-in tents under shady trees, each with veranda and private view. Nsefu was the first camp in Luangwa, and the six double bungalows, although completely renovated, retain their historic atmosphere. This area is the Nsefu sector, the only part of the park on the eastern bank of the river, which gives the lodges here some extra exclusivity, although this has to be paid for: US$300 at Nsefu, US$325 at Tena Tena, all inclusive.

On the western bank of the Luangwa is ***Kaingo Camp*** *(ⓔ shensaf@satmail.bt.com)*, run by the highly respected safari guide Derek Shenton, owner of Shenton Safaris (☎ 062-45064, 05-362188). This place is small, exclusive, relaxed and friendly, with five delightful cottages surrounded by bush overlooking the river. Skilled guides operate walks and wildlife drives, and there's also a bush camp which can be reached on a walking safari from the main camp. As always, quality comes at a price: US$300 per person, all inclusive.

North of here is the ***Chibembe Lodge***, a new top end place, and ***Lion Camp*** – under development when we passed. The well-established ***Tafika Camp*** *(☎ 45018, ⓔ remote.africa@satmail.bt.com)* is a touch less fancy than some other places in the Luangwa, with very experienced management, charging around US$300 per person, and also offering boat trips.

Places to Eat

All the places to stay provide meals, from simple snacks at the camping grounds to haute cuisine at the top end lodges. There are also a couple of local eating houses in Mfuwe village.

If you're travelling by air, or with your own vehicle, take time to visit the unlikely but splendid ***Moondogs Cafe*** next to Mfuwe airport, where good coffee, cold beers, tacos, waffles and salads grace the menu. It also has a radio link with Flatdogs and the other lodges.

Shopping

Most of the lodges and camps have souvenir shops selling the usual array of carvings. Also look out for ceramics and elephant-dung paper from Malawi, and the splendidly decorated fabrics from a local organisation called Tribal Textiles. On the road between Mfuwe and the airport is Mango Tree Crafts, and there are a couple of souvenir shops at the airport itself.

Getting There & Away

Most people reach South Luangwa by air. Mfuwe airport is about 20km from the main gate, and served by chartered and scheduled flights most days from Lusaka and Lilongwe. A one-way flight from Lusaka is US$120, and can be easily arranged with

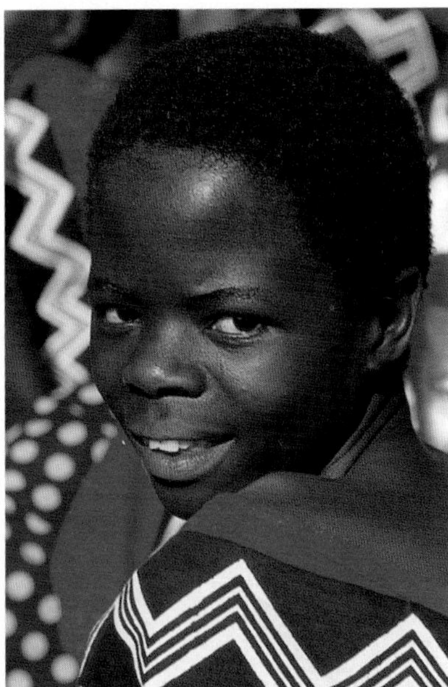

ALL PHOTOGRAPHS BY RICHARD I'ANSON

Swaziland **Top Left:** A sugarcane worker in the Ezulwini Valley **Top Right:** A Swazi child in a colourful traditional outfit **Bottom:** Swazis have many ceremonial dances, including the sod-cutting dance

DAVID WALL

DENNIS JOHNSON

Zambia **Top:** The leopard carries its kill into trees to keep it from other predators (South Luangwa National Park). **Bottom:** The famous Victoria Falls as seen from the Zambian side of the mighty River Zambezi

any agent in Lusaka. Lodge vehicles meet clients who have reservations.

If you have your own vehicle, Mfuwe gate and the surrounding camps are easily reached from Chipata. In the dry season the dirt road is usually in poor to reasonable condition, and the drive takes about three hours. In the wet season, it can take all day (or be impossible).

For backpackers, local minibuses run daily to Mfuwe village from Chipata main bus station. They cost US$4 plus US$0.40 for a backpack, and leave when full (which may take several hours). From Mfuwe village you can walk the 1km to Flatdogs or hitch to the Wildlife Camp (we repeat – don't do this at night). Some travellers hitch all the way from Chipata: the junction by the Chipata Motel is the best place to wait for a lift.

If you're in a group, consider chartering your own minibus for a negotiable US$80. Or consider flying; we've heard from lots of travellers who weighed up US$120 and an hour of sheer joy, against US$40 (bus fares, food, accommodation) and two days of hell. Many took the former option! Air Malawi flies to Mfuwe from Lilongwe (Malawi) twice weekly (US$109). It's also worth chartering a plane from there – if you get a small group together to charter your own five-seater plane it should cost less than US$150 each.

To leave Mfuwe, minibuses to Chipata depart very early. Hitching with other tourists in their own vehicle is another possibility. It's also worth asking around to see if any of the camps are sending supply vehicles to Chipata or Lusaka.

A final option for budget travellers is to join a tour – several cheap outfits in Lilongwe run safaris to South Luangwa. (For details, see Information in the Lilongwe section of the Malawi chapter.)

Norman Carr & South Luangwa

The history of South Luangwa National Park is inextricably linked with the story of Norman Carr, a leading wildlife figure sometimes known as the 'George Adamson of Zambia' because he raised two lions and returned them to the wild. But his influence and his contribution to conservation in Africa go much deeper than this.

In 1938, the North and South Luangwa Game Reserves were created to protect and control wildlife populations, notably elephant. A year later Norman Carr became a ranger here. With the full backing of the area's traditional leader, Carr created Chief Nsefu's Private Game Reserve in 1950, and opened it to the public (until this time reserves had been for the animals only). All visitor fees were paid directly to the chief, thus benefiting both wildlife and local people. Thirty years later 'community involvement' became a buzz word, as conservationists finally realised that the survival of habitats and animals depends on the cooperation of local people.

Norman Carr was years ahead of his time in other fields too. He built Nsefu Camp, the first tourist camp in the country, and developed walking safaris, a totally new concept then, to introduce visitors to African bush conditions away from the sometimes more restricting confines of vehicles.

In the following decades, other game reserves were created, more tourists came to the Luangwa and more camps were built along the river, including Chinzombo – owned by Norman Carr's increasingly busy safari company. In 1972, Nsefu and several game reserves were combined to form the South Luangwa National Park. Despite the new title, poaching of elephant and rhino became an increasing problem in the mid-1970s. In 1980, Norman Carr and several other people founded the Save the Rhino Trust; funds raised helped the government parks department combat poachers.

In 1986, Norman Carr opened yet another camp, Kapani Lodge, and continued operating safaris from this base. He retired from 'active service' in the early 1990s, but continued living in the Luangwa Valley, and met guests at Kapani most days – a highlight of many people's visits.

Norman Carr died in April 1997, aged 84.

NORTH LUANGWA NATIONAL PARK

This park is large, wild, remote and spectacular, with a set-up for visitors very different from its southern namesake's. Despite the proximity of the two parks, road access between North and South Luangwa is not easy; most guests on exclusive organised tours fly in on chartered planes. For drivers, it's possible to reach North Luangwa from the Great North Road near the village of Luana River, about 65km north of Mpika. But this is no doddle – the track is rough and rarely used, and plunges steeply down the Muchinga Escarpment into the Luangwa Valley. High clearance and a 4WD are essential.

Base Camp costs US$40 per person, self-catering. ***Buffalo Camp*** costs US$200 per person, including meals, drinks and park entry (Shiwa Safaris runs both places). For both camps, you can arrange things in advance at the lodge at Kapishya hot springs (see Shiwa Ngandu in the Northern Zambia section earlier in this chapter) or through the Zambian Safari Company in Lusaka (see Information in the Lusaka section). The only other place is the top end ***Mwaleshi Lodge***, run by Remote Africa Safaris.

If you don't have your own car (or even if you do), lifts to Buffalo Camp and Base Camp are provided free of charge (for groups of four people) from Kapishya hot springs. It takes five hours to cover the 160km between Shiwa and the camps, so a minimum of three nights in the park is recommended. From the camps, wildlife drives cost US$20 and bush walks are US$10. An onward transfer by vehicle to South Luangwa is US$150.

Southern Zambia

This section covers the area between Livingstone and Kafue National Park, and includes Victoria Falls and Lake Kariba. Places are described roughly south to north.

LIVINGSTONE

☎ 03

Livingstone is Zambia's tourist capital, and a major hub for travellers in Southern Africa. The town lies a short distance north of the River Zambezi, where the river drops over world-famous Victoria Falls, and is within easy distance of some high-quality national parks. Within a few hours, or at most a day, you can go rafting, canoeing, microlighting or bungee jumping, watch rhino and lion in dry savanna, or get soaked in lush rainforest.

Information

Tourist Office The friendly tourist office (☎ 321404) on Mosi-oa-Tunya Rd is fine for information on happenings in Livingstone and can arrange bookings for hotels, tours and activities. The panoramic picture on the wall is useful for orientation.

Money Barclays Bank on Mosi-oa-Tunya Rd changes cash and travellers cheques, and the Union Bank nearby changes cash only. Next to the post office is Falls Bureau de Change, open weekdays and Saturday morning, with helpful staff who try to beat any other rate in town. They will also give cash on a Visa card, but have to charge for a long-distance call to verify your details.

Post & Communications The post office is on Mosi-oa-Tunya Rd, and you can make international calls from Zamtel next door. Nearby, Zamnet in Liso House offers Internet access. The funky Cyberian Outpost at the Livingstone Adventure Centre charges US$2 for 10 minutes of Internet access, and US$3.70 per minute for phone calls to Europe (cheaper at weekends/evenings).

Things to See

The **National Museum** has a good collection of archaeological relics, but more interesting are the Tonga ritual artefacts and crafts, the life-size model African village, the collection of David Livingstone items, memorabilia from the Chachacha Rebellion (including Kenneth Kaunda's motorcycle) and a display of maps dating back to 1690. Entry for foreigners is US$5.

The **Railway Museum** on the south-western edge of town contains a charmingly motley collection of locos, rolling stock and rail-related antiques.

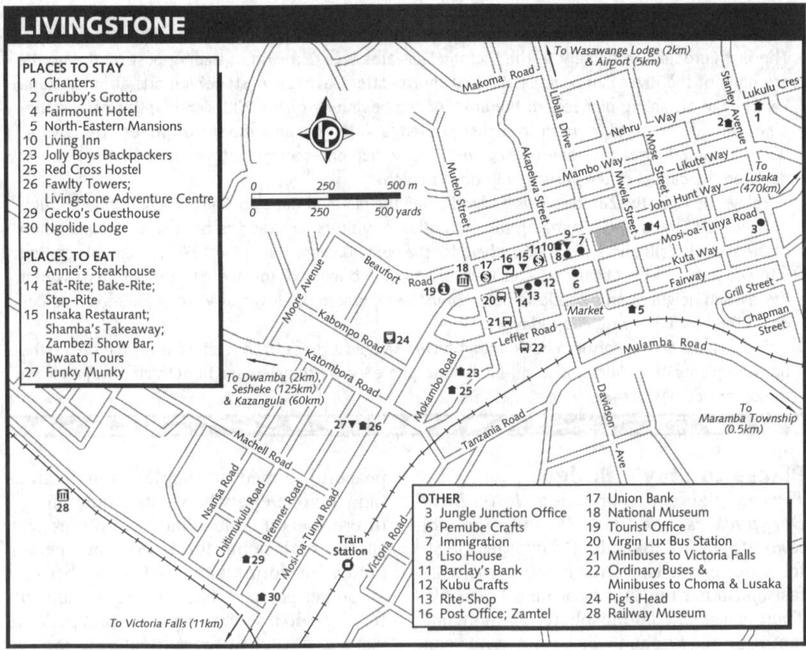

The museum is open from 8.30 am to 4.30 pm daily. Entry is US$5 and unless you're a ravenous railway buff, it isn't worth it. However, if you're genuinely interested and short of cash, it's often possible to work out some sort of discount.

About 5km south of Livingstone, the **Maramba Cultural Centre** stages traditional dances every Saturday between 3 and 5 pm. The performance is quite low-key, but enjoyable and more authentic than glitzy stage shows put on by big hotels.

A popular destination for tours is **Makuni village**, where the locals welcome visitors for a small fee (which goes to projects like water tanks and a clinic), and you can take photos, chat to people, and not get pestered by kids. Most of the carvers around Livingstone come from this village.

Organised Tours

Several companies offer short wildlife drives in the Game Park section of Mosi-oa-Tunya National Park. These include Livingstone Safaris, run by knowledgeable Dave Lewis of Gecko's Guesthouse. The charge is US$25 per person for a three-hour drive (morning or evening).

AJ Car Hire (☎ 322090) at Liso House, Mosi-oa-Tunya Rd, offers a car and driver for tours to Victoria Falls (US$20), for wildlife drives (US$25), and for half-day tours to Vic Falls and Makuni village (US$55, or US$80 if you take in the Game Park too).

A boat ride with drinks ('booze cruise') is a very popular option. Sunset cruises cost US$25 including all drinks, and less-riotous lunch and dinner cruises are US$30. Book at your hotel or with any agent.

Bwato Tours (☎ 324227) on Mosi-oa-Tunya Rd offers booze cruises, wildlife drives, tours and canoeing, or you can take an all-inclusive canoe-drive-cruise package for US$100.

Livingstone & the Pendulum of History

The first European settlement in the Victoria Falls area was Old Drift, a trading post on the northern bank of the River Zambezi, established shortly after David Livingstone's reports about Victoria Falls began attracting pioneers to the area. At the beginning of the 20th century, this basic settlement shifted about 10km north to higher ground, and this became the site of present-day Livingstone – named after the famous explorer. The settlement became a town, and in 1911 it was declared the capital of the Northern Rhodesia colony.

Below the Falls, the Zambezi was bridged when the planned Cape-to-Cairo railway came through between 1902 and 1904, bringing the first influx of visitors. Livingstone became the tourism hub of the Victoria Falls area – a position it held for the next 60 years. But in the 1970s, as Zambia cruised into economic and political chaos, tourism dried up, and most visitors went to the southern side of the river in neighbouring Rhodesia (later Zimbabwe), where the town of Victoria Falls grew to become the bustling centre it is today.

Today, back on the northern bank, things have changed again and Livingstone is once more on the up, with plenty of facilities and a laid-back atmosphere – a welcome escape from the tourist jungle on the other side of the river.

Places to Stay – Budget

The popular and pioneering ***Jolly Boys Backpackers*** *(☎ 324278, ⓔ jboys@zamnet.zm)* on Mokambo Rd charges US$6 for a dorm and US$3 for camping. Breakfast and other meals cost around US$2.50. There's a relaxed atmosphere, good swimming pool, kitchen, bar, and you can arrange all activities. If you're coming from Vic Falls (Zimbabwe), ask at Backpackers Bazaar about the Jolly Boys transfer service: for US$10 you get a lift to Livingstone, a visa, a bed for the night, an evening meal, a beer and entrance to the Falls.

For a more local feel, the friendly ***Red Cross Hostel*** *(☎ 322473)*, also on Mokambo Rd, has clean double rooms with communal facilities for US$3.50.

New on the scene, but already making a big impression, is ***Fawlty Towers*** *(☎/fax 323432, ⓔ ahorizon@zamnet.zm)*, at the Livingstone Adventure Centre on Mosi-oa-Tunya Rd. Camping is US$3, dorms US$6 and double rooms US$20. There's a big garden, swimming pool, lounge, kitchen, bar, restaurant, a booking desk for all activities, and free transfers to and from Victoria Falls twice a day. If you come from Vic Falls, they offer a 'backpacker special' including transfer, visa, dorm, meal and drink for US$10.

Gecko's Guesthouse *(☎ 322267, ⓔ gecko@zamnet.zm)* is clean, friendly and peaceful, aimed at couples, and families (and anyone else who wants a quiet night), offering good double and twin rooms with shared bathrooms for US$10 per person (and a few dorms with three or four beds for US$6 per person). There's free tea and coffee, a garden, swimming pool, safe parking, bar and a kitchen for self-catering, or you can order breakfast from US$0.40 and other meals for around US$3.50. Camping is US$3 per person. If you arrange a transfer from Vic Falls, they can help you avoid the visa fee.

Living Inn *(☎ 324204)* on John Hunt Way, one block north of Mosi-oa-Tunya Rd, has good clean singles/doubles for US$12/25, plus US$2 for a full breakfast. Nearby, ***Grubby's Grotto*** on Mambo Way caters exclusively for overland trucks.

The ***Nyala Lodge*** *(☎ 322446, ⓔ eland@acacia.smamr.co.zw)* is outside town on the road to the game park, with camping for US$3, four-bed chalets for US$30, luxury twin rooms for US$40 and US$60, and a pool, bar and restaurant.

Livingstone Overnight *(☎ 320371)*, about 3km outside Livingstone on the road to Victoria Falls, has a well-organised camping ground for US$5 per person, and nice cabins with private bathroom for US$35. Just 1km further along, the relaxed ***Maramba River Lodge*** *(☎/fax 324189, ⓔ maramba@*

Adventure Activities in Livingstone

The range of activities on offer in and around Livingstone is mind-blowing, and the choice is bound to be even bigger by the time you arrive. Many tour companies and agents operate here, and there's a lot of cross-over between them, so it doesn't really matter which agent you book through, as the prices will be the same. Having said that, it's always worth looking out for the special deals which only a few outfits will offer.

Abseiling For fun on a rope, Abseil Zambia (☎ 323454, @ abseil@outpost.co.zm) offers abseiling plus high-wiring, rock climbing and cable swings in a scenic canyon off the Zambezi Gorge. For US$95 (including lunch) you can come to this playground for the entire day and do as much as you like.

Bungee Jumping The jump from the Zambezi Bridge is among the highest in the world and certainly the most spectacular. African Extreme (☎ 324231, @ extreme@zamnet.zm) runs the show but you can make bookings anywhere. A jump costs US$90.

Canoeing Bundu Adventures (☎ 324407, @ zambezi@zamnet.zm) offers canoeing on the Zambezi upstream from Vic Falls, as does Makora Quest (☎ 324253, @ quest@zamnet.zm) in the Livingstone Adventure Centre. Both offer half-day trips for US$70 and full-day trips for US$85 to US$90, including lunch.

Flying For views from the air, microlighting is very highly rated, from US$50 for 15 minutes. Flying directly over Vic Falls with almost nothing between your butt and the maelstrom below is totally exhilarating. The pilot will take pictures for you with a camera fixed to the wing. If you like to keep your exhilaration to controllable levels, helicopter rides are available at the same price. The operator is Batoka Sky (☎ 320058) and you can book at any tour agent.

Hiking If you'd rather see the dramatic gorge with your feet on the ground, Taita Falcon Lodge (☎/fax 321850, @ taita.falcon@outpost.co.zm) organises one-day hikes around the lodge, and four-day hikes downstream from Vic Falls.

River-Boarding This latest craze to hit Vic Falls was instigated by Serious Fun (☎ 323912, @ seriousfun@zamnet.zm) from the Livingstone Adventure Centre. Other operators are Safari Par Excellence (@ safpar@harare.iafrica.com) and the smaller, more flexible Bundu Adventures (☎ 324407, @ zambezi@zamnet.zm). 'Waterfall surfing', as it's been called, will cost you from US$85 for a half day and around US$130 for a full day.

White-Water Rafting Safari Par Excellence and Bundu Adventures (contact details earlier) operate white-water rafting – the best-known activity in the Vic Falls area – through huge rapids in the dramatically zigzagging gorge downstream from the Falls, some of the best rafting conditions in the world. Only from the Zambian side of the river can you run all the rapids. A full day costs US$95, and a double shot of rafting and boarding costs US$135. You can arrange rafting at any tour agent in town. For a rundown on rafting seasons and the rapids you'll encounter, see Activities in the Victoria Falls section of the Zimbabwe chapter.

zamnet.zm) has double chalets for US$30, large safari tents with beds for US$10 per person and camping for US$5. The lodge is well known for the elephants that often wander harmlessly through the site.

Places to Stay – Mid-Range

At the western end of Mosi-oa-Tunya Rd, *Ngolide Lodge (☎ 321092)* has a big thatch roof, airy courtyard and motel-style single/double rooms, complete with TV and coffee-making facilities, for US$32/36, including breakfast.

The old colonial ***Fairmount Hotel*** *(☎ 320723)* on Mosi-oa-Tunya Rd is unappealing from the outside, but the rooms are OK, though a touch pricey at US$34/41, including breakfast

Chanters is a small and homey place with rooms around US$40. The attached restaurant serves good food from around US$4, and is recommended locally for its fish.

Livingstone Overnight (see Places to Stay – Budget) also has smart chalets and walk-in tents separate from the camping ground, with bar and restaurant, at US$65 per person for DB&B.

The ***Taita Falcon Lodge*** *(☎/fax 321850, ⓔ taita.falcon@outpost.co.zm)* is about 15km from Livingstone, downstream from the Zambezi Bridge, perched right on the edge of the gorge, with splendid views of the river (and white-water rafters) far below. Full board in simple airy huts with private bathroom costs from US$95 per person including transfers from Livingstone. The resident guide, who is very knowledgeable about birds and snakes, leads short informative bush walks, and the lodge can also set up longer hikes in the area.

Places to Stay – Top End

Most of the top end hotels and lodges in the Livingstone area are outside the town, and described in The Zambezi Waterfront section later in this chapter.

Songwe Point Village *(☎ 323659, 013-3211 in Zimbabwe, ⓔ saflodge@saflodge.co.zw)* has luxurious African-style huts with private bathroom overlooking the gorge about 5km downstream from Vic Falls. The aim is to give visitors (who would otherwise miss it) the chance to meet local people and learn something about their culture and traditions. It costs US$140 including transfers, all meals and a visit to Mukuni village. Some of this money goes to a community trust fund, and we've heard positive reports from people who have stayed here. Book in advance directly or through an agent.

Places to Eat

There are several cheap cafes and takeaways along Mosi-oa-Tunya Rd. ***Eat-Rite*** is OK for lunches, but next door ***Bake-Rite*** is cleaner and quieter, with good cheap cakes, snacks and meals. Also good is ***Annie's Steakhouse***, a block off Mosi-oa-Tunya Rd, with filling local meals from US$1.

Near the post office, ***Shamba's Takeaway*** has nice shady outdoor seating, burgers for US$0.40 and meals like meat and rice for US$0.60. Next door the smarter ***Insaka Restaurant*** and the ***Zambezi Show Bar*** sell drinks and snacks at slightly higher prices.

The ***Funky Munky***, behind the Livingstone Adventure Centre, is open for lunch and dinner. The food is excellent, with soups for US$1, quiche, sandwiches and pasta dishes around US$2.50, and main courses such as venison kebabs, chicken satay or steak and chips from US$3 to US$4. In the same price range is the genteel, English country-style ***Pilgrims Tea Room***, on the edge of town towards Vic Falls, especially good for breakfast and light meals.

If you're self-catering, ***Rite-Shop*** supermarket has a good selection. There are also several smaller shops along Mosi-oa-Tunya Rd. Livingstone's main market for food and goods is at Maramba Township, south of the centre.

Entertainment

Jolly Boys Backpackers and ***Fawlty Towers*** (see Places to Stay – Budget) both have bars that are very popular with backpackers. ***The Pig's Head*** is an English-style pub, complete with photos of drunk cross-dressed regulars. It's very lively at weekends, and also offers food.

For music and dancing with a local feel at weekends, ***Step-Rite***, behind Rite-Shop, is a popular open-air place. The disco at the ***Fairmount Hotel*** regards itself as a more upmarket affair. There's also a bar with pool tables, but it's pretty dreary.

Shopping

The smartest souvenir shop is African Visions at the Livingstone Adventure Centre, with good quality fabrics and crafts from all over Africa; it accepts Visa cards. Kubu Crafts on Mosi-oa-Tunya Rd has a good selection of locally made items. You can also buy carvings and other crafts at the stalls in Mukuni Park – there's no hassle or hard sell.

Getting There & Away

Air Roan Air flies twice weekly between Livingstone and Lusaka (US$110 one way). Eastern Air also flies twice weekly (US$120) – once per week via Mongu.

Bus Between Livingstone and Lusaka, there are express buses for US$7 and ordinary buses for US$6. Ordinary buses and minibuses leave from the bus station south of Mosi-oa-Tunya Rd. The Virgin-Lux bus station is nearby. Euro-Africa buses leave from outside the post office.

Buses from Maramba township go to Kazungula (US$1.60, once daily) and Sesheke (US$4, once daily). A taxi from Livingstone to the bus stop in Maramba township costs US$0.50. Also from Maramba township, there's a bus to Mongu via Senanga, which leaves late in the evening every Monday and Thursday (sometimes it leaves late: around 2 am on Tuesday and Friday). It goes through Sesheke early on Tuesday and Friday and gets to Mongu later the same day. The fare to Mongu is US$10.

Minibuses to Sesheke leave from Dambwa, on the main road 3km west of Livingstone centre. You must get there around 7 am, although transport may not leave until noon. A taxi from Livingstone to the bus stop in Dambwa costs US$0.50.

Train For schedules and fares of trains between Lusaka and Livingstone, see the main Getting Around section earlier in this chapter. There's also a train across the famous Zambezi Bridge, between Livingstone and Victoria Falls town in Zimbabwe (for details, see the Zimbabwe chapter), twice per day in each direction. You can get the latest schedule from the train station. (For details of the more touristy Victoria Falls Safari Express steam train, see under Activities in the Victoria Falls section of the Zimbabwe chapter.)

Organised Tours Short tours and adventure activities are covered earlier in the Livingstone section (see the earlier boxed text 'Adventure Activities in Livingstone'). For longer journeys, the Botswana Bus (☎/fax 323432, ⓔ ahorizon@zamnet.zm), based at Fawlty Towers, offers excellent inexpensive tours to Botswana's Chobe National Park and the Okavango Delta Panhandle. All-inclusive tours of seven/10 days cost US$345/495. Pioneer Trails, part of the same organisation, offers budget tailor-made trips for small groups to any part of Zambia, from around US$50 per day. Jolly Boys Backpackers (see Places to Stay – Budget in the earlier Livingstone section) also offers popular budget trips to the Okavango Delta.

The southern section of the huge, wild Kafue National Park can be reached easily from Livingstone. Livingstone Safaris at Gecko's Guesthouse (see Places to Stay – Budget in the Livingstone section) runs four and five-day safaris from around US$200. Jolly Boys Backpackers also operates safaris to Kafue.

VICTORIA FALLS

Over the years, Zimbabwe has cashed in heavily on Victoria Falls – or Vic Falls as it's commonly known – and the Zambian side is sometimes forgotten. (Having said that, our map of Victoria Falls is in the Zimbabwe chapter of this book.) But the Zambian side of the Falls provides an entirely separate experience from its Zimbabwean counterpart, and if you possibly can you should visit both sides of this most spectacular natural wonder.

On the Zambian side you follow narrow footpaths through the forest or cross a dramatic footbridge to reach spectacular viewpoints almost touching the falling water. The panoramas may not be as picture-postcard perfect as those in Zimbabwe, but they do allow closer observation of the mesmerising water, while the less manicured surroundings create a pristine atmosphere. In Zambia, you can view the Falls from upstream and downstream, from above and from below, and at least two visits are required just to take in the sheer size, force and majesty of it all.

If you can't visit both sides, at least make sure you *do* get to the Falls. We've heard about some visitors who came here on a tight timetable; by the time they'd done their rafting, canoeing, bungee jumping and booze cruising, it was time to move on, and the Falls themselves got scrubbed from the itinerary.

Mosi-oa-Tunya National Park

Zambia's smallest national park, Mosi-oa-Tunya, is comprised of two sections: the Victoria Falls area; and the Game Park, further west along the riverbank. Entry to each section of the park is US$3.

Victoria Falls Area From the park entry gate, a network of paths leads through the thick vegetation to the various viewpoints. You can walk upstream a little on a path mercifully free of fences and warning notices (although take care!), to watch the Zambezi waters glide smoothly through rocks and little islands towards the lip of the Falls.

For close-up shots of the Eastern Cataract, nothing beats the hair-raising (but perfectly safe) walk across the footbridge, through swirling clouds of mist, to a sheer buttress called Knife Edge Point. If the water is low or the wind favourable, you'll be treated to a magnificent view of the Falls, as well as the yawning abyss below. Otherwise, your vision (and your clothes) will be drenched by spray.

Other highlights are the viewpoints overlooking the Zambezi Bridge and the first 'zig' of the massive zigzagging gorge that carries the river away from the Falls. After that you can walk down a steep track to the banks of the great river itself to see the huge whirlpool called the Boiling Pot.

Near the Falls is a small **museum** built on an archaeological site, with some displays from the excavation, providing evidence that humans have inhabited this region for 2½ million years. Next door is a small cafe, and a line of **curio stalls** with an excellent selection of crafts – cheaper than equivalents on the Zimbabwe side. The traders here are always keen to barter; as usual, T-shirts with slogans, caps and trendy training shoes are always in demand.

Game Park Upriver from the Falls, the little Game Park is easy to reach and ideal if you're unable to reach any other national parks. OK, it's not South Luangwa, but this park has a nice feel and a surprisingly good range of animals. You can easily spot zebra, giraffe, and various antelope, and there's nowhere else in Zambia where you're almost guaranteed to see white rhino.

You can walk to the park entrance and arrange a walking safari with one of the rangers at the gate, but most people without their own car join a wildlife drive organised in Livingstone (for details, see Organised Tours in the Livingstone section).

Places to Stay & Eat

Hotel InterContinental and ***Rainbow Lodge*** overlooking the Falls were closed in 1998 and this prime site, unbelievably, stood empty for more than a year. In 2000 construction started on a luxury hotel and villa complex owned by the Sun International hotel chain, so expect big changes by the time you arrive.

Other choices are in Livingstone and on the Zambezi Waterfront (for details, see those sections).

Getting There & Away

Victoria Falls is 11km from Livingstone along the main road. A minibus costs US$0.40, but there aren't many. You're better off hiring a taxi, which costs US$3 to US$4 each way, not bad if you share with others. Your other option might be walking, but some people have been mugged between Livingstone and the Falls, so it's not advisable.

Livingstone Island

Livingstone Island is the big chunk of rock that splits Victoria Falls into two. Thanks to Tongabezi Lodge, you can now enjoy a three-course champagne lunch here at the world's most exclusive picnic spot. Even if you're not staying at the lodge, you can arrange to join a picnic through any tour agent in Livingstone. The price of US$80 includes transfers, meal, drinks and park fees.

Day Trips to Zimbabwe If you're based in Zambia and want to pop over to the Zimbabwe side of Victoria Falls, you still have to queue through immigration formalities at the border crossings. An early start is advisable. If you don't have a multiple-entry visa to come back into Zambia, make this clear to the officials, who will give you a temporary exit stamp.

Most people walk between the border crossings and get great views of the Falls from the Zambezi Bridge.

THE ZAMBEZI WATERFRONT

Upstream of Victoria Falls the Zambia shore of the River Zambezi is fast becoming one of the country's major tourist areas. Widely spread over about 50km are plenty of places to stay, with something for every taste and budget, all overlooking the river, and reached from the main road that runs between Livingstone and Kazungula. It's usually necessary to book accommodation in advance, either directly or through an agent in Lusaka or overseas. Most places to stay are shown on the Western Zimbabwe map in the Zimbabwe chapter.

Places to Stay – Budget & Mid-Range

About 50km from Livingstone and 8km from Kazungula is the ***Jungle Junction*** on a lush island in the Zambezi. There really is nothing else like this place anywhere in Africa, and everyone who stays (from budget backpackers to yuppies with credit cards) just loves the palm trees, the hammocks, the slow pace and the all-round mellow atmosphere. To stay here you pay a one-off cover charge of US$50, which includes road transfers from Livingstone or the Vic Falls border, plus canoe activities. On top of this you pay US$5 per night for camping, or US$15/20 for a single/double hut (with mattress and mosquito net), each in a private clearing in the forest. There's a bar and small shop ('so well stocked you never need to leave'), or you can order meals (breakfast from US$1, lunch around US$2, dinner US$3). There's even a communication service that takes letters, postcards, faxes and emails to Livingstone for transmission. Owners Dave, Brett and Gremlin can organise village visits, sightseeing and fishing trips with locals in traditional canoes, and they take care to ensure local people benefit directly from tourism. You can make bookings or get information at any hostel or tour company in Livingstone, or go straight to the Jungle Junction office (☎ 03-324127, ⓔ jungle@zamnet.zm) on Mosi-oa-Tunya Rd in Livingstone. You can pay by credit card or with just about any currency including travellers cheques.

Places to Stay – Top End

The following places are described from east to west.

About 10km outside Livingstone and 2km off the main road is the ***Thorntree Lodge***. Comfortable chalets and large walk-in tents provide a front-row view of elephant crossing the Zambezi, and the bar overlooks a watering hole where animals from the game park often come to drink. All-inclusive rates are US$220.

About 5km further west is the ***Tongabezi Lodge*** *(☎ 03-323234, ⓔ tonga@zamnet.zm)*, one of the most imaginative and talked-about hotels in the region. The large luxury tents (US$300 per person, all inclusive) and secluded houses (US$375) are completely open to views across the river. For something really different, try the honeymoon suite, set atop a cliff with its own private garden, a sunken bathtub and a romantic four-poster bed, or the Tree House, with the bed cradled in the branches of a giant mahogany, and the bathroom downstairs almost within touching distance of the Zambezi. Tongabezi also runs ***Sindabezi Camp***, on a tiny mid-river island just downstream.

The River Club, just downstream from Tongabezi, has luxurious chalets on stilts among trees overlooking the river, although the deliberate officers'-mess atmosphere of the restaurant might be a touch too formal for some tastes. Rates are US$275 per person.

About 7km further upstream, 2km off the main road, is the ***Chundukwa River Camp*** *(☎ 03-324006, ⓔ chunduka@zamnet.zm)*, a small and friendly lodge charging US$145, which includes all meals and drinks, plus an evening boat trip. You can also arrange canoeing, horse riding and trips to Kafue National Park.

About 25km from Livingstone, 5km off the main road, is the popular and long-standing ***Kubu Cabins*** *(☎ 03-324093, ✉ kubu@zamnet.zm)*, also called the Livingstone Explorers' Club. You can chose from comfortable walk-in tents or delightful thatched cabins, all with private bathroom, for US$150/220, or go wild in the honeymoon suite with a river-view bathtub and one side open to the African skies for US$310. The rates include full breakfast and excellent dinner on the broad deck overlooking the river. The relaxed and friendly management can arrange birdwatching, canoeing, walking and all the activities at Victoria Falls.

Next along is the ***Royal Chundu Lodge*** *(☎ 03-321772, ✉ chundu@icon.co.za)*, a tortuous 12km off the main road, with pleasant chalets for US$125 including all meals and boat rides. Fishing is a speciality, although this lodge lacks the relaxed atmosphere of some other places along the river. Full board including transfer from the airport, fishing and lots of activities costs US$250. Treehouses on the river's edge cost US$75 for DB&B; they have a better view but a longer walk to the bathroom!

CHOMA

☎ 032

The small town of Choma (capital of Southern Province) is on the main road between Livingstone and Lusaka. Most visitors pass through at high speed, but it's easy enough to hop off the bus, and for drivers Choma makes a good stopover and useful base for touring southern Zambia.

For anyone interested in history, the excellent **Choma Museum** is well worth a visit. In a former school dating from the 1920s (one of the oldest preserved colonial buildings in Zambia), the exhibits concentrate on the Tonga people, most of whom were forcibly relocated when Kariba Dam was built. There's also a contemporary art exhibition, and a craft shop.

Gwembe Safaris *(☎ 20169, ✉ gwemsaf@zamnet.zm)* at Brooks Farm is 1km south of town, 2km off the road. Pleasant chalets cost US$35/55, breakfast costs US$5 and dinner is US$10. Camping is US$5; the grassy site has a shelter, electric lights, and spotless bathrooms. Meat, milk, eggs etc are available. Security is no problem: a sign on the gate says 'Beware of the Crocodiles'.

LAKE KARIBA

Lake Kariba is described in the Northern Zimbabwe section of the Zimbabwe chapter, and most tourists go to the Zimbabwe side. But the Zambia side of Kariba also has its attractions, although these are typically Zambian in nature: authentic, a bit rough around the edges, off the beaten track and more appealing to aficionados than to the seekers of instant gratification.

Sinazongwe

This small town is the centre of Zambia's lake-fishing industry. The ***Lake View***, in a wonderful setting on the shore, has chalets at US$55 per person including meals, or US$35/55 (single/double) if you self-cater (ie, bring food for the staff to prepare). Camping costs US$5. This place is run by the Brooks clan at Gwembe Safaris (where you can arrange bookings – see the earlier Choma section) and aimed at drivers. For travellers without a car, minibuses go to Sinazongwe from Choma via Batoka, or you might be able to arrange a lift.

Chikanka Island

This beautiful private island, about 10km from Sinazongwe, has very good self-catering ***chalets*** for US$35/55 single/double, and ***camping*** on a separate site for US$5 (exclusivity for a bargain price). Fishing boats can be hired and boat transfers go from Sinazongwe. Reservations are essential through Gwembe Safaris (see the Choma section, earlier).

Chipepo

This small fishing village is linked by local ferry to Siavonga but it has no official place to stay. Minibuses run to Chipepo a few times per day from Monze, via Chisekesi.

Siavonga

☎ 01

Siavonga sprawls along the banks of Lake Kariba just a few kilometres from the massive Kariba Dam, and is the nearest most Zambians get to the seaside. On the opposite shore is the town of Kariba, with a fancy yacht marina, hotels, restaurants and fishing-tackle shops. (Kariba town and the accompanying map are included in the Northern Zimbabwe section of the Zimbabwe chapter.) In comparison, Siavonga is quiet and low-key, and therefore preferred by some travellers, especially those who want to feel they are in Africa rather than a place that desperately pretends to be anything but.

Places to Stay & Eat East of town is the highly recommended ***Eagle's Rest*** *(☎ 511 168, e eagles@zamnet.zm)*, with chalets with bathroom and kitchen for US$23.50 per person. Bring your own food and cooking gear (if you're travelling light the friendly owner can loan you a saucepan or two). Camping costs US$6.50. Snacks and meals are available in the restaurant. Exciting and good-value canoe trips are also arranged, for one day in Kariba Gorge, or for three days between Chirundu and Chongwe. For details, contact a tour operator in Lusaka.

Nearby is the large hotel-style ***Manchinchi Bay Lodge*** *(☎ 511599)*, where singles/doubles with air-con, private balcony and TV cost around US$40 per person.

In Siavonga town, you have several more choices. The Leisure Bay Lodge has a pebbly beach on the lakeshore and straightforward rooms for US$20/36 (half price after 6 pm). The Lake View Council Resthouse has a local feel and basic rooms for US$10. Toward the western end of town, the Lake Safari Lodge and the Lake Kariba Inn are mid-range places aimed mainly at the conference market.

The ***Sandy Beach*** is a secluded camp 14km west of the road between Siavonga and Chirundu, with camping for US$6 and chalets for US$30 per person (US$60 with full board). Drivers should look for the sign 20km north of Siavonga, near a group of local shops called Kariba Stores. Transfers by car or boat can be arranged at Eagle's Rest.

Getting There & Away Minibuses leave from the market, headed for Chirundu (US$0.50) and Lusaka (US$3.50). For the adventurous, a local ferry runs twice weekly between Siavonga and Chipepo (US$6). In both directions it leaves at 6 am and arrives at 5 pm.

LOCHINVAR NATIONAL PARK

This small park, north of Monze, consists of grassland, low wooded hills, and the seasonally flooded **Chunga Lagoon** – part of a huge flood plain called the **Kafue Flats**. Lochinvar was virtually abandoned in the 1980s, but plans to rehabilitate the park and the accommodation were announced in 1999, although they had not materialised when we passed through. If there are improvements, Lochinvar will be worth a visit, so ask around in Lusaka or Livingstone.

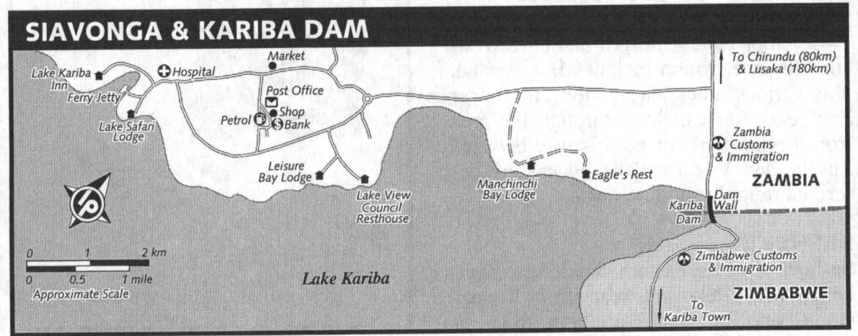

Currently, the network of tracks is overgrown, with only the track from the gate to Chunga Lagoon open. Mammals include buffalo, wildebeest, zebra, kudu, and large herds of Kafue lechwe (a subspecies of this rare antelope), but they are skittish and their numbers have been depleted by poaching. Lochinvar is a major draw for birdwatchers, with more than 400 species recorded. An excellent selection of wetland birds (including wattled crane) occurs in the area where the main park track meets Chunga Lagoon.

Despite this attraction, the ridiculously high entry fees (see National Parks in the Facts about Zambia section) might put you off coming until things improve.

Places to Stay

Lochinvar Lodge is an empty shell, although it's in a spectacular position, and may be renovated in the future. The only ***camp site*** (US$5) is a few kilometres from the park gate; facilities are minimal.

Getting There & Away

By car from Monze, take the dirt road towards Namwala. After 15km, just past Nteme village, turn right and continue along narrow dirt roads for 13km. Near a village called Kembe, then turn left and continue for another 13km to reach the park entrance. In the dry season, Chunga Lagoon can be reached without 4WD. For those without wheels, minibuses go to Namwala, but after the first junction you'd have to walk.

Western Zambia

This section covers most of Zambia's Western Province, which includes Barotseland, plus various other places along the upper Zambezi. You can loop through the area from Livingstone, or go this way between Lusaka and Victoria Falls. Places are described roughly south to north.

SESHEKE

Sesheke is on the eastern bank of the Zambezi, about 200km upstream from Livingstone, opposite the Namibian town of Katima Mulilo. The ***Council Resthouse*** has basic double rooms for US$4, or US$10 with private bathroom. Meals are available, the garden overlooks the Zambezi, and the bar sells cold beers to accompany wonderful views at sunset.

For information on reaching Sesheke from Livingstone by minibus or overnight bus, see Getting There & Away in the Livingstone section earlier in this chapter. You can also reach Sesheke from Katima Mulilo in Namibia.

Katima Mulilo (Zambia Side)

This small village is on the western bank of the Zambezi about 6km from Sesheke (not to be confused with Katima Mulilo town in Namibia). The border with Namibia is just south of the village.

The friendly ***Mulatiwa Guesthouse***, near the pontoon (car ferry), has basic rooms from US$4, good rooms from US$8, and 'VIP' rooms with private bathroom for

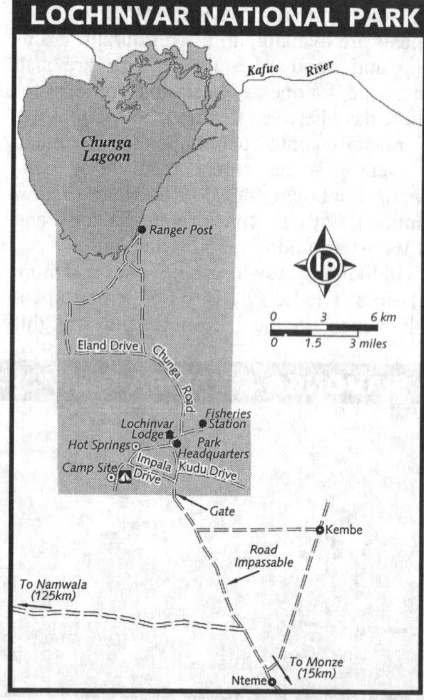

US$18. The staff can advise on changing money, and on buses to Mongu.

The pontoon carries cars for US$15 or R60, 4WDs for US$25 or R90, and foot passengers free of charge. If the pontoon isn't running, passengers pay US$0.20 to cross by canoe.

NGONYE FALLS

Ngonye Falls (also called Sioma Falls) is a 1km-wide chain of waterfalls, rapids and rocky islands cutting across the River Zambezi. It's beautiful and very impressive, and if it wasn't for Victoria Falls about 300km downstream, Ngonye would be a major attraction. On most days you'll probably have the entire place to yourself.

The falls are less than 1km east of the main dirt road between Sesheke and Senanga. For drivers, access is easy. Without your own wheels, ask to be dropped by the falls turn-off (look for the Wildlife Department sign). Or stay at the ***Maziba Bay Lodge*** (e *mirages@iwwn.com.na*), 7km south of the falls, where luxurious chalets cost US$110 per person, including meals, trips to the falls, and other activities such as fishing, walking, boat trips and white-water rafting. Advance bookings are preferred. Camping costs US$10 (large groups not allowed).

Other lodges in this area include ***Mutemwa***, with all-inclusive rates around US$240, and ***Zambolozi***, where chalets cost US$60 per person, including meals and activities. You may be able to get information on these lodges in Lusaka, but if you're coming from Namibia, an agent called Tutwa Tours in Katima Mulilo (Namibia side) has details.

SENANGA

If you're coming from Lusaka, Senanga has an 'end of the line' feel. The tar runs out, and the dusty dirt road that continues south towards Namibia and Zimbabwe is quiet and rarely travelled by tourists.

The ***Council Resthouse*** has simple rooms, but a better option is ***Senanga Safaris***, which charges US$16 for comfortable double rondavels with bathroom and breakfast. Camping is US$5. There are splendid views over the Zambezi plains – spoilt only slightly by the giant satellite dish in the garden. The bar has cold beer and the restaurant serves expensive meals, but there are several good-value local restaurants nearby along the main street.

Minibuses and pick-ups run between Senanga and Mongu (US$2.75). South of Senanga, at Kalongola, a pontoon carries vehicles across the Zambezi. Bus passengers don't pay. For cars the fare is US$15 or R60; for 4WDs it's US$25 or R90.

MONGU

☎ 07

Mongu is the largest town in Barotseland, and the capital of Western Province, on high ground overlooking the flat and seemingly endless Liuwa Plain. The town itself is spread out, and has a pleasant lively feel, so a walk along the main street is always interesting. From a harbour on the outskirts of town, an 8km canal runs westwards to meet a tributary of the Zambezi. Around the harbour is a lively and fascinating settlement of reed and thatch buildings, where local fishermen sell their catch, and passenger boats take people to outlying villages.

Mongu really comes alive once a year, when thousands of people come here for the annual **kuomboka ceremony**, which takes place between the palaces just outside Mongu (see the boxed text 'The Kuomboka Ceremony'). Hotel prices rocket at this time.

Places to Stay & Eat

Near the bus station, the friendly ***Lumba Guesthouse*** has basic singles for US$8, and better doubles with bathroom for US$12. Dinner costs US$3 and full breakfast is US$2. A favourite is the ***Winters Resthouse***, at the northern end of town, where basic rooms for one or two people cost US$4, or US$6 with private bathroom. The bar gets loud in the evenings, so get a room at the far end of the yard. Nearby the friendly ***Kombahari Guesthouse, Steakhouse & Bar*** has dingy rooms for US$4 and very good local meals from US$1. At ***Vliex's Guesthouse***, behind the Bata shop, double rooms are OK but a bit pricey at US$12.

Barotseland History

For many Zambians, Western Province *is* Barotseland – the kingdom of the Lozi people, who migrated here in the 17th century from the central Congo area. They settled the fertile flood plains of the upper Zambezi, and over the next century established a stable and well-organised system of rule and administration.

In the early 19th century, the effects of the *difaqane* (described in the History section of the Facts about the Region chapter) disrupted the Lozi culture, and Barotseland was occupied by the Makololo people for around 40 years.

The Lozi people regained control of their kingdom in the mid-19th century, and reinstated their *litunga* (king). At around the same time the explorer Livingstone came to the area, blazing the way for the arrival of other Europeans. In 1871 a trader called George Westbeech advised the litunga, named Lewanika, to invite French Catholic missionaries to Barotseland, an event which had profound effects on the Lozi people.

The 1880s brought the European 'Scramble for Africa'. The Portuguese wanted the upper Zambezi region to link their colonies of Angola and Mozambique, but the British South Africa Company had designs on the mineral rights in the area. Lewanika was feeling increasingly threatened by the neighbouring Matabele, so he requested British support, and in 1900 Barotseland became a British protectorate, later incorporated into the colony of Northern Rhodesia, despite Lozi hopes that they might regain some autonomy.

When Zambia became independent, the new government maintained control over Barotseland. This has fuelled an ongoing Lozi bitterness towards central government, and self-rule for Barotseland remains high on the political agenda.

In the *boma* part of town, near Mongu Lodge, the ***Travellers Lodge*** *(☎ 221435, 221302)* is two converted houses, well worth searching out, with friendly management and clean double rooms for US$8 (US$10 with private bathroom). In the same area, the slightly run-down ***Lyamba Hotel*** has double rooms for US$12, including breakfast. There's a wonderful view of the plain – but unfortunately you have to sit in the car park to fully appreciate its beauty. Up a grade from here, the ***Mongu Lodge*** has good-value 'executive' doubles with bathroom, air-con and breakfast for US$20.

The ***Ngulu Hotel*** *(☎ 221258)* 2km south of the centre has clean rooms (single/double) with bathroom, hot water, fan and breakfast for US$45, which is a bit steep for what you get, although the staff are friendly. Evening meals cost around US$5, and there's a bar.

Getting There & Away

The bus station for transport to Lusaka is on the eastern edge of town, behind the Catholic church. Several companies run buses to Lusaka for US$6.50; the RPS express is US$10. Look out for the JR 'time bus' (US$8), which parks for the night outside Winters Resthouse – you can get on very early in the morning before it goes to the bus station for its 6 am departure.

A bus goes to Livingstone (US$10) twice per week, departing at 3 am (you can get on the evening before) via Senanga, Kalongola and Sesheke (US$8).

Minibuses and pick-ups leave on a fill-up-and-go basis from near the Caltex filling station for Senanga (US$2.75), where you can find onward transport to Sesheke or the Namibia border.

KAFUE NATIONAL PARK

Kafue National Park, about 200km west of Lusaka, covers more than 22,000 sq km, making it the largest park in Zambia, and one of the largest in the world. Vegetation includes: riverine forest around Lake Itezhi-Tezhi and around the Kafue River and its main tributaries (the Lunga and Lufupa); areas of open mixed woodland; and the vast seasonally flooded grasslands of the Busanga Plains on the northern edge.

This is classic wildlife country. Elephant and buffalo are often seen in the wooded areas, particularly around Chungu and south of Ngoma Lodge in the southern part of the park. Carnivores include lion and hyaena, and the northern part of the park is noted for

The Kuomboka Ceremony

The *kuomboka* (literally 'to move to dry ground') is probably one of the last great Southern African ceremonies, and celebrates the move of the *litunga* (the Lozi king) from his dry-season palace at Lealui to his wet-season palace on higher ground at Limulunga. It usually takes place in late March or early April, and sometimes ties in with Easter.

Central to the ceremony is the royal barge, the *Nalikwanda,* which carries the litunga. This is a huge wooden canoe painted with black and white stripes. It is considered a great honour to be one of the hundred or so paddlers on the *Nalikwanda*, and each paddler wears a head-dress of a scarlet beret with a piece of lion's mane, and a knee-length skirt of animal skins.

Drums also play a leading role in the ceremony. The most important are the three royal war drums, *kanaona*, *munanga* and *mundili*, each more than 1m wide and said to be at least 170 years old.

The journey from Lealui to Limulunga takes about six hours, the drums playing continuously. The litunga begins the day in traditional dress, but during the journey changes into the full uniform of a British admiral, complete with all regalia and ostrich-plumed hat. The uniform was presented to the litunga in 1902 by the British King Edward VII, in recognition of treaties signed between the Lozi and Queen Victoria.

The kuomboka does not happen every year. In 1994, 1995 and 1996 the floods were not extensive enough to require the litunga to leave Lealui, or to allow the passage of the *Nalikwanda*.

Visiting the Palaces

Limulunga

At Limulunga you can see the litunga's palace from the outside (although no photos are allowed), but of more interest is the museum, containing exhibits about the Lozi, the litunga and the kuomboka. Minibuses run between Mongu and Limulunga throughout the day for US$0.70.

Lealui

The litunga's low-water palace is on the plain about 15km north-west of Mongu. It takes a bit more effort to reach, but the journey by boat (along a canal from Mongu to a branch of the Zambezi, then upstream to Lealui) is very interesting. You go through the flat grassland of the plains, passing local people on dugouts and other boats. The birdlife is amazing. Avoid visiting at weekends, when the litunga's *kotu* (court) is closed, because you need permission from his *indunas* (advisors) to get a close look at the palace, or take photos. Public longboats go between Mongu harbour and Lealui once or twice per day (US$1.50). Alternatively, if you're in a small group, you can charter a good fast longboat to Lealui for US$60, or a smaller slower boat for about US$20. Prices include fuel and are negotiable.

its leopard. The rivers contain great numbers of crocodile and hippo. Antelope species include impala, roan, kudu, sable and red lechwe, plus sitatunga in the wetlands. Birdlife is also prolific, with more than 400 species recorded. Most camps and lodges arrange foot safaris, but you are not allowed to walk in the park without a ranger.

As with all parks in Zambia, the situation here is fluid. Under a new management plan, improvements will be made: lodges and camps are under construction, and new camp sites are planned. Expect some changes (even to the road layout) by the time you arrive. For details on entry fees, see National Parks in the Facts about Zambia section.

The main road between Lusaka and Mongu runs though the park, dividing it into northern and southern sectors. You don't pay park fees if you're in transit.

Places to Stay

Kafue has a wide choice of places to stay, and we list a selection here.

Except for camp sites and chalets, it's usually necessary to book in advance, either directly or through an agent in Lusaka or overseas. Several lodges are just outside the park, so you don't pay entrance fees until you go in.

Southern Sector On the north-eastern bank of the Kafue River, just outside the park and easy to reach, is the ***Mukambi Safari Lodge*** *(☎ 01-251564, ✉ mukambi@zamnet.zm)* with stylish well-designed cottages with private bathroom for US$70 per person for DB&B.

On the western bank at the park headquarters is the ***Chunga Safari Lodge***, run by Njovu Safaris *(☎ 01-272307)*, in a beautiful spot overlooking a bend in the river. Basic rondavels cost US$15 per person and camping is US$5. The shared showers are hot. If you bring food, staff will prepare it in the kitchen. A lot of animals come to the vicinity of the camp, but if you want to go a bit further, there are wildlife-viewing loops for drivers, or you can arrange a walk in the bush with a ranger.

South from here, on the eastern bank, is the remote and beautifully located ***Puku Pan Lodge***, reached from the Itezhitezhi road. Although originally intended as an exclusive place, it remains seldom-visited, and costs a bargain US$85 per person for full board, plus park fees, wildlife drives and boat rides. Self-catering accommodation costs around US$40. For details contact Africa Tour Designers (see under Travel Agencies & Tour Operators in the Lusaka section earlier in this chapter).

Near Lake Itezhi-Tezhi, the ***New Kalala Lodge*** has chalets for US$28 per person for DB&B, and camping for US$8. Nearby is the ***Musungwa Lodge*** *(☎ 01-273493)*, a larger place, originally built as a lakeside resort, complete with gardens, big swimming pool, boats, tennis and squash courts. Comfortable singles/doubles with verandas overlooking the lake are US$32/56 (about 12% more at weekends) for DB&B. Camping is US$10. The lodge has vehicles for wildlife-viewing trips into the park for about US$15 per person, plus park fees. Nearby, ***David Shepherd Camp***, administered by Musungwa Lodge, offers self-catering chalets for US$8 per person. It's a

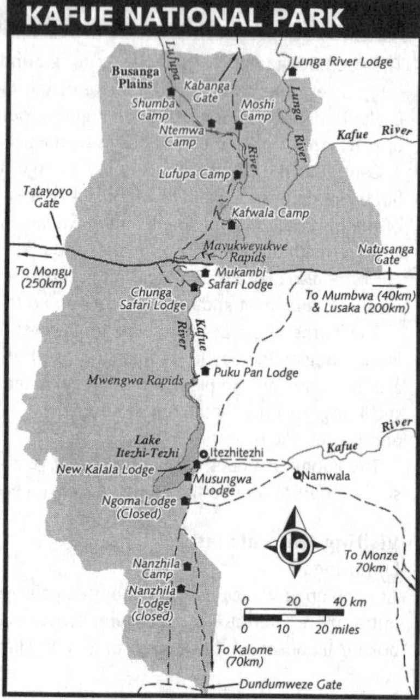

bit run-down these days, but you'll almost certainly have the place to yourself.

In the far south of the park, the old state-run ***Ngoma Lodge*** and the ***Nanzhila Lodge*** are closed but due (one day) for renovation. In the same area, the very comfortable ***Nanzhila Camp*** is a base for safaris run from Livingstone by Chundukwa River Camp (see the Zambezi Waterfront in the Southern Zambia section earlier in this chapter).

Northern Sector At the confluence of the Lufupa and Kafue Rivers, ***Lufupa Camp*** is a large place in a lovely position. Full board in straightforward but comfortable rondavels with private bathrooms costs US$90 per person. Camping is US$6, and there's a swimming pool. From the camp you can take boat rides (US$18), wildlife-viewing walks (US$18) and wildlife-viewing drives (day US$25, night US$30). The guides are particularly adept at locating leopard. At

Lufupa you can also find out about the self-catering ***Kafwala Camp***.

Further north, in the heart of the spectacular Busanga Plains, is ***Shumba Camp***, which costs US$94 per person. Lufupa, Kafwala and Shumba are all operated by Busanga Trails, which also runs safaris from Lusaka. These include vehicle transfers and three to five days at the lodges. For more information contact the Busanga agent in Lusaka, Steve Blagus Travel (see Information in the Lusaka section earlier in this chapter). Busanga's main agent outside Africa is Sunvil Discovery in the UK (see the regional Getting There & Away chapter).

Further north and higher up the luxury scale is the remote and exclusive ***Lunga River Lodge***, with rates around US$250 per person. The former state-run ***Ntemwa Camp*** has been taken over by a top end operator and should be open in 2000, along with ***Kapinga Tented Camp*** on the Busanga Plains. ***Moshi Camp*** is due for renovation and re-opening by 2001. You can get details from a travel agent in Lusaka or overseas.

Getting There & Away

The top end lodges use airstrips and their guests fly in. As advance reservations are essential at these places, transfer information is provided when you book.

For drivers, the main road into Kafue National Park is from Lusaka. About 60km beyond Mumbwa, a road leads south-west towards Lake Itezhi-Tezhi. The tar is terribly potholed, but passable with care in any vehicle. At Itezhitezhi town, there's a checkpoint and the road crosses Itezhitezhi Dam to New Kalala and Musungwa Lodges.

Alternatively, from Lusaka, if you continue west on the main road, about 10km before Kafue Bridge is the turn-off to Mukambi Safari Lodge (signposted). On the western side of the bridge, the main track into the northern sector of the park turns off right (towards Lufupa, Moshi and Ntemwa camps). There is a small guard post where you pay park fees, unless you have a lodge booking where this is included. About 6km west of the bridge, a dirt road leads south-east to Chunga, the park headquarters (21km from the main road).

There's no public transport in the park, but you could get off the bus between Lusaka and Mongu to reach Mukambi Safari Lodge, or get off at the Chunga junction and try your luck waiting for a lift to the park headquarters and Chunga Safari Lodge.

Alternatively, by public transport from Lusaka you could head for Itezhitezhi town (which has houses and facilities for workers at the dam). There's a slow bus most days for US$4.50, and regular minibuses for US$5.50. From the bus stop it's about 1km to the checkpoint, then a 7km walk across the dam to the New Kalala Lodge and a further 1.5km to the Musungwa Lodge.

A final alternative: several tour companies in Livingstone organise relatively cheap safaris into the southern sector of Kafue National Park. Try those based at Jolly Boys Backpackers or Gecko's Guesthouse (see Places to Stay – Budget in the Livingstone section earlier in this chapter).

ZIMBABWE MAP INDEX

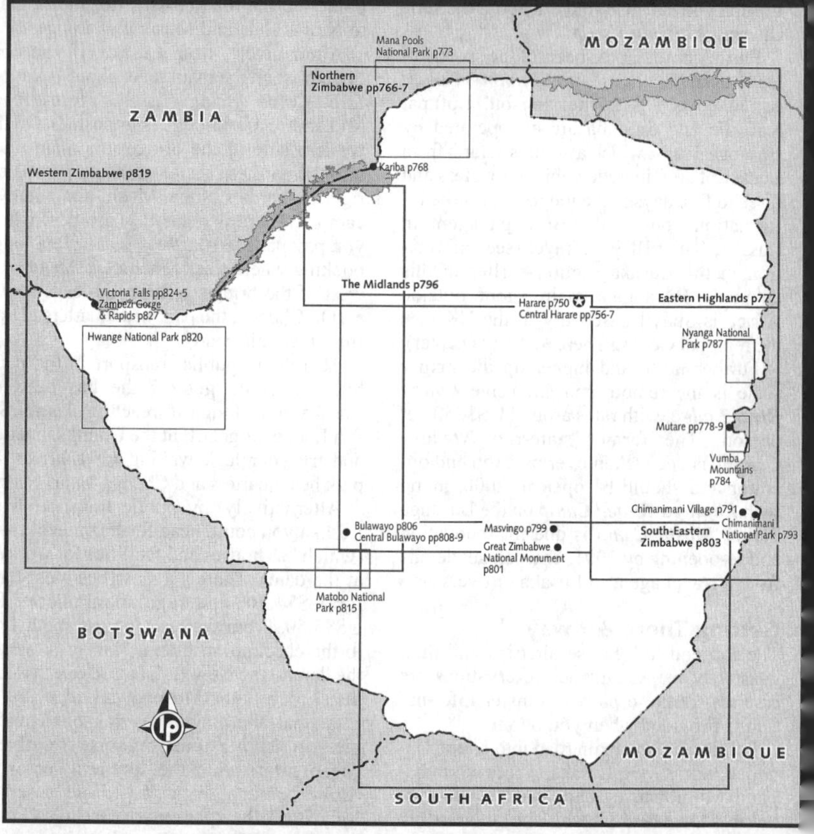

ZAMBIA

MOZAMBIQUE

BOTSWANA

SOUTH AFRICA

MOZAMBIQUE

RICHARD I'ANSON

Hut decoration at Victoria Falls Craft Village

Zimbabwe

Tradition, culture and soul combine with the best infrastructure on the continent outside South Africa to make Zimbabwe an almost perfectly packaged African destination.

The Africa that most travellers envisage is all around: in the *kopje*-studded landscape; in face-to-face encounters with the 'big five'; and in the spray of the 'Smoke that Thunders', Victoria Falls. Unfortunately, few allow enough time to include the haunting shores of Lake Kariba and the River Zambezi or the mist-shrouded, lush green Eastern Highlands. Like explorers before them, many fail to realise that the greatest sub-Saharan structure, Great Zimbabwe – still not fully understood – lies only a stone's throw away.

Of course, the country has its well-publicised problems. It's impossible to ignore the devastation that AIDS and corruption have wrought on the morale of the people and on the infrastructure.

Despite this, a visit to Zimbabwe remains hugely rewarding and relatively safe (the increased security is reassuring without being overbearing). Most importantly, the people remain friendly and good natured and it is they who will get under your skin and leave you yearning for more.

ZIMBABWE AT A GLANCE

Area: 390,580 sq km

Population: 11.2 million

Capital: Harare

Head of State: Robert Gabriel Mugabe

Official Language: English

Currency: Zimbabwe dollar (Z$)

Exchange Rate: US$1 = Z$38.3

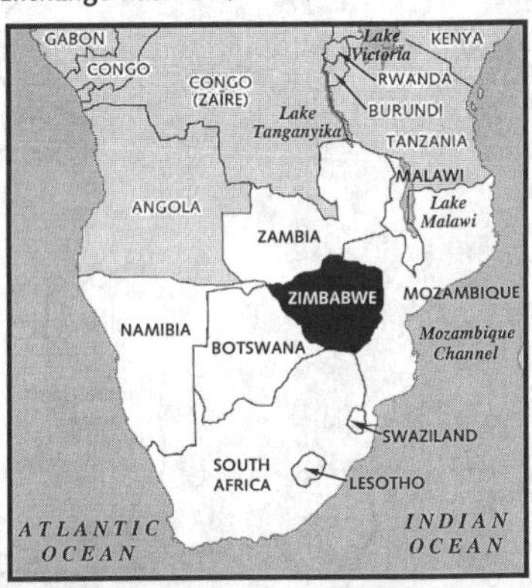

Highlights

- Harare and Bulawayo – dance at a *pungwe*, overload your luggage with souvenirs and take in some cultural sites
- Mana Pools National Park – either on foot or by canoe, you'll encounter wildlife
- Chimanimani National Park – camp in caves and swim in the waterfalls of this stunningly rugged park
- Great Zimbabwe – explore the ruins of sub-Saharan Africa's greatest archaeological site
- Matobo National Park – savour an African sunset over the *kopje*-studded terrain
- Hwange National Park – don your safari suit and prepare to see the 'big five'
- Victoria Falls – ride the rapids below the Falls or simply laze above them

Facts about Zimbabwe

HISTORY

The Shona Kingdoms & The Portuguese

The early history of the people of Southern Africa is covered in the Facts about the Region chapter. It's generally believed that in the 11th century, the Great Zimbabwe society encountered Swahili traders who had been plying the Mozambique coast for over four centuries. They traded gold and ivory for glass, porcelain and cloth from Asia, and Great Zimbabwe became wealthy and powerful. However, by the 15th century, its

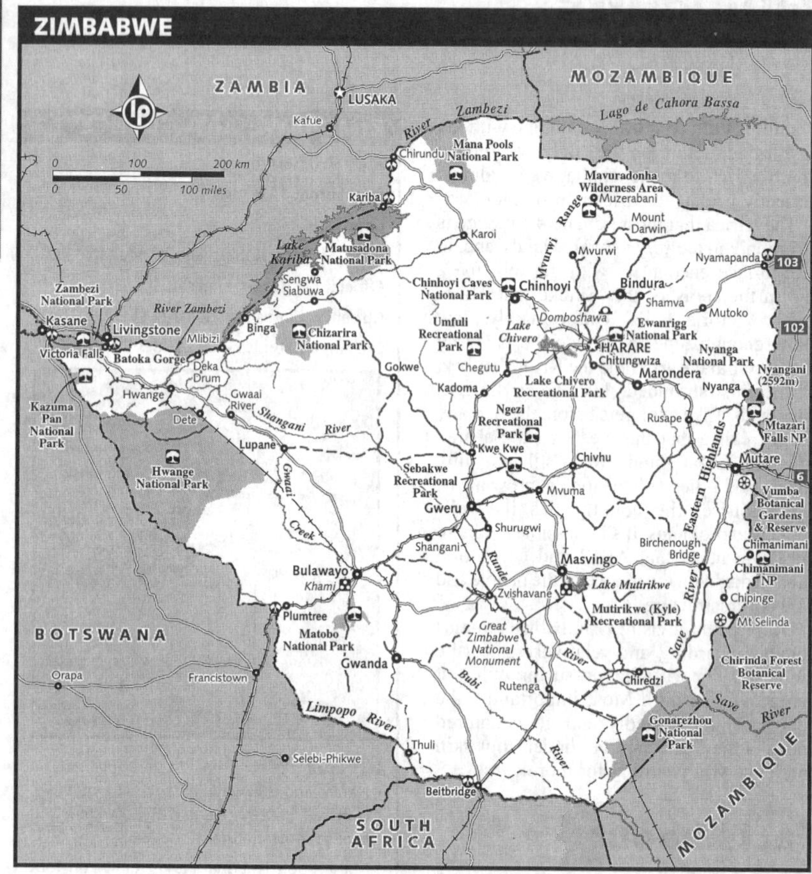

influence was in decline, for reasons including overpopulation, overgrazing, political fragmentation and uprisings.

During Great Zimbabwe's twilight period, Shona dynasties fractured into autonomous states. In the 16th century, Portuguese traders arrived in search of riches and golden cities in the vast empire of Mwene Mutapa (Monomatapa to the Europeans), where they thought they would find King Solomon's mines and the mysterious land of Ophir.

Alliances between Shona states led to the creation of the Rozwi state, which encompassed over half of present-day Zimbabwe and continued until 1834 when Ndebele (Those who Carry Long Shields) raiders under the command of Mzilikazi invaded from the south and assassinated the Rozwi leader. Upon reaching the Matobo Hills, Mzilikazi established a Ndebele state. After Mzilikazi's death, in 1870, his son Lobengula ascended the throne and relocated the Ndebele capital to Bulawayo.

Lobengula soon found himself face to face with the British South African Company (BSAC). In 1888, Cecil Rhodes, the company's founder, got him to sign the Rudd Concession, granting foreigners mineral rights in exchange for 10,000 rifles, 100,000 rounds of ammunition, a gunboat and £100 each month.

A series of misunderstandings followed. Lobengula sent a group of Ndebele raiders to Fort Victoria (or Masvingo) to prevent Shona interference between the British and the Ndebele. The British mistook this as aggression, launching an attack on Matabeleland. Lobengula's *kraals* (hut villages) were destroyed and Bulawayo was burned. A peace offering of gold sent by Lobengula to the BSAC was commandeered by company employees. Ignorant of this gold token, the vengeful British sent the Shangani River Patrol to track down the missing king and finish him off. In the end, it was the patrol that was finished off – in spectacular fashion (see the Matobo National Park section later in this chapter). Shortly after, Lobengula died in exile of smallpox.

Without their king, the Ndebele continued to resist the BSAC and foreign rule. In the early 1890s, they allied themselves with the Shona, and guerrilla warfare broke out in the Matobo Hills. When Rhodes suggested a negotiated settlement, the Ndebele, with their depleted numbers, couldn't really refuse.

Meanwhile, finding little gold, the colonists appropriated farmlands on the Mashonaland plateau. By 1895, the new country was being called Rhodesia after its heavy-handed founder, and a white legislature was set up. European immigration began in earnest and by 1904 there were some 12,000 settlers in the country, and double that again by 1911.

The First Chimurenga

The government of Rhodesia was set up 'for, by and of' the whites. The Ndebele had effectively been quashed, but trade between the Shona and the Europeans continued until it became apparent that the colonists intended to control both African and Rhodesian interests. Spotting weakness in the BSAC army, the Ndebele came back with a vengeance, gathering forces and single-mindedly attempting to drive the enemy from their land forever. This warlike spirit proved contagious; the Shona, traditional enemies of the Ndebele joined in and by 1896 the First Chimurenga, the War for Liberation, had begun.

Although the revolt gained some momentum, it was stalled in 1897 when its leaders were captured and subsequently hanged. One leader's parting words, 'my bones will rise again', prophesised the Second Chimurenga, which led to Zimbabwean independence, described later in this section.

Beginnings of Nationalism

Conflicts between black and white came into sharp focus after the 1922 referendum in which the whites chose to become a self-governing colony rather than join the Union of South Africa. Although Rhodesia's constitution was in theory nonracial, suffrage was based on British citizenship and annual income, so few blacks qualified. In 1930, white supremacy was legislated in the form of the Land Apportionment Act, which excluded black Africans from ownership of the best farmland, and a labour law that excluded them from skilled trades and professions. Poor wages and conditions eventually led to rebellion and by the time Southern Rhodesia, Northern Rhodesia and Nyasaland were federated in 1953, mining and industrial concerns favoured a more racially mixed middle class as a counterweight to the radical elements in the labour force.

Two African parties emerged – the Zimbabwe African People's Union (ZAPU) under the leadership of Joshua Nkomo, and the Zimbabwe African National Union (ZANU), a breakaway group under the leadership of Ndabaningi Sithole. Following the federation's break-up in 1963 – which paved the way for the independence of Northern Rhodesia (Zambia) and Nyasaland (Malawi) – both ZAPU and ZANU were banned and their leaders imprisoned.

Ian Smith & the Second Chimurenga

In 1964, Ian Smith took over the Rhodesian presidency and began pressing for independence. British prime minister Harold Wilson countered by outlining conditions to be met before Britain would cut the tether: a guarantee of racial equality, a course towards majority rule, and majority desire for independence. Smith realised whites would never agree, and in 1965 he made a Unilateral Declaration of Independence (UDI).

Britain reacted by declaring Smith's action illegal and imposed economic sanctions, which were also adopted by the UN in 1968. However, they were ignored by most western countries and even British companies. Sanctions also provided incentives to increase and diversify domestic production and the Rhodesian economy prospered.

By this stage, both ZANU and ZAPU had opted for guerrilla warfare. Their raids struck deeper and deeper into the country with increasing ferocity, and whites, most of whom had been born in Africa and knew no other home, abandoned their property. It finally struck Smith that all might not be well.

On 11 December 1974, South Africa's John Vorster and Zambia's Kenneth Kaunda persuaded Smith to call a ceasefire and release high-ranking nationalists – Nkomo, Sithole and Robert Mugabe among them – and begin peace negotiations. The talks, however, broke down; ZANU split; Nkomo fell out with South Africa's African National Congress (ANC); and Mugabe went to Mozambique. The following year, ZANU chairman Herbert Chitepo was assassinated in Lusaka by Rhodesian intelligence.

Nationalist groups fragmented and reformed in an alphabet soup of 'Z' acronyms. ZANU and ZAPU were induced to form an alliance known as the Patriotic Front (PF), but the hoped-for spirit of cooperation was never realised. Similarly, ZIPRA and ZANLA (the military arms of ZAPU and ZANU respectively) combined to form the Zimbabwe People's Army (ZIPU) under Rex Nhongo.

At this point, Smith faced wholesale white emigration and a collapsing economy and was forced to try a new ploy – an 'internal settlement'. Both Sithole and the leader of the ANC, Abel Muzorewa, joined a so-called transitional government in which whites were guaranteed 28 out of the 100 parliamentary seats; a veto over all legislation for 10 years; a guarantee of white property and pension rights; and white control of the armed forces, police, judiciary and civil service. An amnesty was declared for PF guerrillas.

The effort was a dismal failure. Indeed, the only result was an escalation of the war, now known as the Second Chimurenga. To salvage the settlement, Smith entered into secret negotiations with Nkomo, offering to ditch both Sithole and Muzorewa, but Nkomo proved to be intransigent. Finally, Smith was forced to call a general, nonracial election and hand over leadership to Muzorewa, but on much the same conditions as the 'internal settlement'.

Independence

In 1979 it was decided that any new constitution must be satisfactory to Britain and be ratified in free elections. On 10 September 1979, delegations met at Lancaster House, London, to draw up a constitution favourable to both the PF of Nkomo and Mugabe, and the Zimbabwe-Rhodesian government of Muzorewa and Smith. Mugabe, who wanted ultimate power, initially refused to make any concessions, but after 14 weeks the Lancaster House Agreement was reached. It guaranteed whites (3% of the population) 20 of the 100 parliamentary seats.

In the carefully monitored election of 4 March 1980, Mugabe prevailed by a wide margin and Zimbabwe and its majority-rule government joined the ranks of Africa's independent nations.

Despite the long, bitter struggle, Mugabe kept vengeful tendencies at bay. The economy soared, wages increased, and basic social programs – notably education and healthcare – were initiated. However, the initial euphoria, unity and optimism quickly faded. A resurgence of rivalry between ZANU (mostly Shona) and ZAPU (mostly Ndebele) escalated into armed conflict and the ZAPU leader Nkomo was accused of plotting against the government. Guerrilla activity resumed in ZAPU areas of Matabeleland, and Mugabe deployed the North Korean-trained Fifth Brigade in early 1983 to quell the disturbances. Instead, the brigade launched an orgy of killing; innocent villagers were gunned down and prominent members of ZAPU were eliminated in order to root out dissidents – 20,000 people are believed to have died.

Land Reform

When Rhodes and his Pioneer Column (private army) advanced into Zimbabwe, freely making land grants, they no doubt thought they were securing investments for future generations. Today the legacy left by this land seizure is one that many would prefer not to have.

How to fairly resolve the issue in a country where an estimated seven million people eke out a subsistence on poor soils while a few reap the rewards of the prime land? Although their forefathers 'stole' the land, today 'white' farms form the backbone of the economy. To simply redistribute this profitable land to subsistence farmers, who lack the skills to utilise it, would have serious implications.

When independence was declared, the Lancaster House Agreement guaranteed that private landholdings could not be nationalised without fair compensation. This was reviewed in 1990, and in 1996, after written assurances that the takeover would be handled in a 'rational' way, the IMF promised to finance any shortfalls as long as President Mugabe put his own house in order first.

In November 1998, the government announced it would seize 1503 white-owned farms. Promising compensation, amid rumours of US$2 million being spent each day defending the regime in Congo (Zaïre), the government then stated it could only afford to compensate farmers for improvements (houses, barns and other structures) made during their ownership, not for the full value of the farms. This led to breakdowns in negotiations with the IMF, and while some farmers freely gave their land back, for others the compensation (or lack of it) was unfair and lawsuits followed.

In early 2000, Mugabe, wishing to consolidate his powers, held a referendum on rewriting the antiquated constitution. Even though he included a land-reform sweetener and was supported by an estimated US$50 million (taxpayer-funded) advertising campaign, Mugabe was shocked to receive the first 'No' in his political career. Although shaken, Mugabe remained confident that land reform would bring in the votes for him and published his own constitutional clause to allow for the seizure of farms. This gave many approval to invade and reclaim white properties. At the time this book went to print, armed assailants had occupied many commercial farms owned by white Zimbabweans and violence betweeen the two groups had resulted.

Nkomo, meanwhile, fled to England until Mugabe (realising the strife threatened to erupt into civil war) publicly relented and guaranteed his safe return. Talks resulted in a ZAPU-ZANU confederation and amnesty for the dissidents, thereby masterfully sweeping the matter, but not the underlying discontent, under the rug.

The late 1980s were characterised by scandal and government corruption. Some MPs and cabinet ministers were loudly professing socialism while privately amassing small fortunes. In 1988, student protests against 'dirty government' were suppressed by cutting university funding and forcing dissidents to admit their 'mistake'.

Increasing Taxes & Tensions

Despite tragic experiments with one-party socialism in neighbouring countries, President Mugabe's Marxist dream remained alive. In 1988, the long-overdue abolition of the law that guaranteed 20 parliamentary seats to whites, and the imposition of strict controls on currency, foreign exchange and trade, were steps in this direction.

In the 1990 elections, ZANU was challenged by the newly formed Zimbabwe Unity Movement (ZUM) under Edgar Tekere, which promoted free enterprise and a multiparty democratic state. A gerrymander engineered by Mugabe, however, enabled ZANU to post a landslide victory. Soon afterwards, Patrick Kombayi, a ZUM candidate, was wounded in an assassination attempt and those with ZUM ties immediately sought a low profile. In 1990, despite Mugabe's persistence, members of parliament voted against the implementation of Marxism in Zimbabwe.

In 1995, with his popularity waning and elections due, Mugabe revealed a US$160 million 'anti-poverty program'. Predictably, he also promised land reform and a reduction in unemployment. The election, however, was characterised by general apathy and voter turnout was poor. Mugabe won.

In 1996 it emerged that government officials had ripped off the War Victims' Compensation Fund. Veterans began demonstrating and demanding their rightful compensation; their demands culminated in a confrontation with Mugabe at the 1997 Heroes' Day rally. Mugabe hastily promised money for the veterans, and soon afterwards, an increase in income and fuel taxes was announced.

In the same year, Mugabe married his 32-year-old former secretary, Grace Marufu, in front of 20,000 guests. Disgruntled public workers viewed the lavish affair as an affront and walked off the job in protest – they were sacked, which further eroded support for the government.

Already heavily burdened by excessive taxes, the normally passive Zimbabweans found the new tax levies unsustainable. They rebelled, and boycotted work. Throughout the country, all colours united in a peaceful demonstration of disapproval, but in Harare, police attempted to halt the demonstration by firing tear gas into the crowds. It was parliament that saw reason and rejected the proposed income-tax increase, and mandated that the fuel price be dropped. The president and his ministers were incensed.

Meanwhile, the Zimbabwe dollar lost over 50% of its value. The increased cost of imports caused immediate price hikes for most goods, including basic foodstuffs. In Harare, protesters again took to the streets and rioting ensued, costing millions in damage. The police and the army were called in and a number of people were killed. Even so, the government refused to reduce the sales taxes or even to discuss alternative measures.

The Zimbabwe Congress of Trade Unions (ZCTU) called on the government to address and right the problems or face a two-day work stoppage. The government simply threatened 'stern action' if the boycott went ahead. Undaunted, workers stayed home on 3 and 4 March 1998. Trade worth millions was lost. Riot police came out in force and waited for a demonstration that never happened.

In 1999, thousands attended a ZCTU rally to launch the Movement for Democratic Change (MDC). Morgan Tsvangirai, the secretary general, stated he would lead a social democratic party fighting for workers' interests in the 2000 parliamentary elections. Opposition parties have traditionally lost votes in rural areas to the wealthier and better-organised ruling ZANU-PF. However, in a country where inflation runs at 50% and unemployment reaches over 70%, the MDC, with a strong trade union network, is a very real threat to the ruling party.

GEOGRAPHY

Landlocked Zimbabwe lies within the tropics and consists of highveld and middleveld plateaus lying between 900m and 1700m above sea level. Its area is 390,580 sq km, roughly half the size of Australia's New South Wales or the size of the UK with an extra Scotland thrown in. A low ridge running north-east to south-west across the country marks the divide between the Zambezi and Limpopo-Save River systems.

The north-west consists mostly of plateaus, characterised by bushveld dotted with small rocky outcrops called kopjes and bald knob-like domes of smooth rock known as *dwalas*. The hot, dry lowveld of southern Zimbabwe is mainly the level savanna of the Save Basin, sloping almost imperceptibly towards the Limpopo.

The main mountainous region is the Eastern Highlands, which straddles the Zimbabwe-Mozambique border from Nyanga in the north to Chimanimani in the south. Zimbabwe's highest peak, Nyangani, rises to 2592m near the northern end of the range.

CLIMATE

Zimbabwe stretches over a high plateau and, during the dry season, enjoys a pleasantly temperate climate. The cooler months (May to October) are similar to the Mediterranean summer, with warm, sunny days and cool, clear nights. It never snows, not even in the Eastern Highlands, though overnight frosts and freezing temperatures are not uncommon.

The lowveld and the Zambezi Valley experience hotter and more humid tempera-

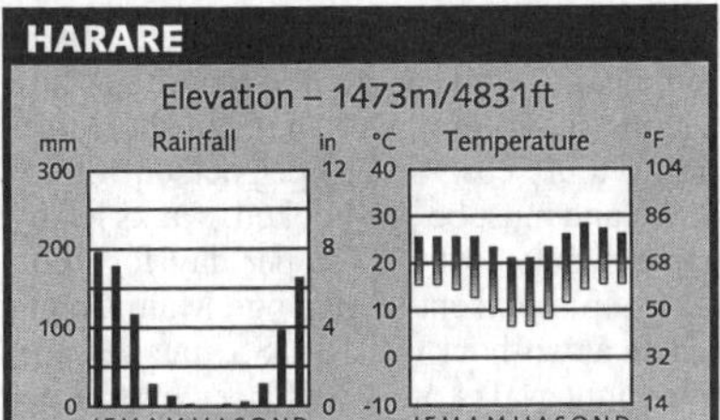

tures, but in winter there's still very little rainfall. Most of Zimbabwe's rain falls in brief afternoon deluges and electrical storms in the relatively humid warm-weather months (November to April).

ECOLOGY & ENVIRONMENT

The Elephant 'Problem'

With a population of over 65,000, Zimbabwe's elephants are not endangered, but according to many, the country faces ecological disaster from their destructive habits. Zambezi Valley elephants have already proven a menace by destroying thousands of hectares of crops.

It has been suggested that numbers could be reduced by culling and trophy hunting. Currently, hunters pay up to US$20,000 to shoot a bull elephant, providing badly needed revenue. On the other hand, many conservation groups contend that the elephant population is sustainable and it's all part of a grand, natural cycle. (The issues of ivory sales and elephant conservation are discussed in more detail under Ecology & Environment in the Facts about the Region chapter.)

Conservation Efforts

In 1989, increasing disquiet over the government's 'shoot to kill' policy to combat poaching gave rise to the CAMPFIRE program (the Communal Areas Management Programme for Indigenous Resources). This channelled revenue from hunting on communal lands, where wildlife had become a nuisance to subsistence farmers, back into the communities. Since its inception, CAMPFIRE participation has prospered and the amount of land in Zimbabwe dedicated to conservation has more than doubled. Poaching has slowed and populations of endangered species – including rhino – are rising. About 90% of CAMPFIRE's revenue is derived from leases on sport hunting and tourism concessions to commercial safari operators, with large contributions from foreign sources.

Control of wildlife on private ranches has been ceded to ranchers since 1975, but the Ministry of Environment & Tourism hopes to place it under the care of the district councils and CAMPFIRE. However, alleged government mismanagement of elephant and rhino translocation projects, the policy of 'indigenisation' (granting new licences only to black Zimbabweans) of the safari industry, and government attempts to take over white-owned lands have cast a veil of uncertainty over private conservation.

FLORA & FAUNA

Much of Zimbabwe's natural vegetation is comprised of *msasa* and mopane woodland, but the drier parts of the country also nurture a variety of bizarre aloes, as well as euphorbias, cycads and palms.

Wildflowers bloom in spring (September to November) as do the jacarandas lining city streets. Information on the region's animals and birds is given in the colour Wildlife Guide section.

National Parks & Wildlife Reserves

Thirteen per cent of Zimbabwe's surface area is protected or semiprotected, either in national parks or safari areas. This doesn't include privately protected areas such as game ranches and nature conservancies. The following is a list of national parks and botanical reserves:

Chimanimani Roadless park with great bushwalking through dramatic mountains.

Chizarira Zimbabwe's wildest park blends stunning scenery and a relatively undisturbed wildlife habitat.

Gonarezhou Formerly home to some of Africa's largest elephant, the 'abode of elephant' is still worth a visit for its grand scenery and increasing wildlife.

Hwange The country's largest, most wildlife-packed and most accessible park is a favourite with visitors.

Kazuma Pan The centrepiece of this wild and little-visited park is a large grassy pan surrounded by teak and mopane forest. It contains Zimbabwe's only gemsboks and is also home to the rare oribi antelope.

Mana Pools Lovely Zambezi landscapes popular for canoe trips and walking safaris. The only wildlife park where visitors may walk without a guide.

Matobo The hills and balancing rock kopjes form Zimbabwe's most bizarre landscape, and the attached Whovi Game Park has healthy rhino populations.

Matusadona High and wild mountain country, contrasting with Lake Kariba; known for elephant, buffalo and lion.

Nyanga This former estate of Cecil Rhodes contains lovely highlands, picturesque waterfalls, great fishing and Mt Nyangani, Zimbabwe's highest mountain.

Vumba Botanical Reserve High, misty forests and botanical gardens.

Zambezi (Victoria Falls) 40km of River Zambezi frontage backed by wildlife-rich mopane forest and savanna. The area includes the Falls themselves, the zigzag Zambezi Gorge downstream of the Falls, and a small rainforest reserve.

Visiting the Parks In 1999, a 300% hike in fees caused outrage. Tourists refused to pay these inflated rates, choosing instead national parks in neighbouring countries. Visitor numbers deteriorated and tourism operators fiercely protested. Bowing to pressure, the authorities reset the day fee to a reasonable US$10. Even so, the fees are still under review, tourism operators continue to lobby for lower fees, and debates on the discrepancies between fees charged to foreigners and locals rage on.

For foreigners, day entry to most parks is US$10 (or US$20, valid for seven days, if you wish to stay overnight). Cars are charged less than US$2. Unfortunately, very little of the revenue collected returns to the parks. As a result, some parks face constant budget problems: artificially pumped water holes often go dry, facilities are becoming increasingly shabby and the reservations system has its difficulties.

Organised activities are limited, but in some parks, you can go horse riding or hire a game scout for a walk in the bush. Horse-riding tours cost US$20 per person for 1½ hours and must be pre-booked. Walks led by game scouts cost US$22 per day for up to six people (except at Hwange Main Camp, where a two-hour walk is US$5 per person); overnight walks are US$40 per person per day and US$15 per day thereafter. For details on accommodation (and the tedious booking system), see Accommodation in the Facts for the Visitor section in this chapter.

Note that hitching is forbidden in parks, although park officials realise not everyone has a vehicle and usually tolerate discreet or informal hitching outside the park entrances. Cats and dogs are forbidden.

GOVERNMENT & POLITICS

The Republic of Zimbabwe's legislative body consists of the president and a parliament. The president is, in theory, elected by national popular vote every five years, and is the official head of state and commander-in-chief of the armed forces.

Of the 150 members of parliament, 120 are elected by the people, one from each of

Women in Society

Following a high court decision that effectively branded women as having the rights of minors, the rewriting of the constitution has become a major issue for Zimbabwe's female population. At present the constitution fails to protect women from violence and strips them of their property rights. It was the latter issue that led to a well-publicised ruling that caused one Vennia Magaya to be evicted from her family home in favour of her younger half-brother, even though she was the eldest child. As well as equal rights of inheritance, the Zimbabwean women's movement is campaigning for equality in all aspects of society (such as prohibition of gender discrimination and the right to equal pay). One major target is the removal of section 23 of the constitution, which allows women to be discriminated against as part of traditional or customary law.

the 120 constituencies in the country. Eight members are provincial governors and 10 are chiefs, who are elected by an electoral college of other chiefs (although only the president can authorise the title of 'chief'). The remaining 12 members are directly appointed by the executive president.

Zimbabwe is divided into eight provinces, each with its own local government headed by a state-appointed governor.

ECONOMY

Zimbabwe's temperate climate, ample natural resources and increasingly skilled workforce are all positive economic factors. Despite economic stagnation during the Second Chimurenga, the effects of industrial diversification during the international sanctions are still felt, and the country has a reasonably sound industrial base. However, during the first decade of independence, the economy suffered setbacks under strict isolationist policies: an artificially valued Zimbabwe dollar, strict currency controls, corruption and crippling import duties. Despite this, inflation sometimes runs as high as 70% and the annual monthly wage is less than US$60.

In late 1991 the government collaborated with the World Bank and the IMF to implement the Economic Structural Adjustment Program (ESAP), which was intended to liberalise Zimbabwe's economy. ESAP lifted price controls and import restrictions, with the aim of stimulating trade and turning the country into an international player. Unfortunately, the resultant price increases were initially devastating, particularly for the country's poorest people.

About 70% of Zimbabwe's population depends on agriculture, but it's mostly at the subsistence level and accounts for only 20% of the GNP. The staple food crop is maize, while cotton, coffee, tea, tobacco, wine grapes and sugar cane are the main cash crops. Livestock, the main indicator of wealth in precolonial Zimbabwe, remains a major commodity and the country is nearly self-sufficient in its by-products. Mining accounts for 40% of exports; gold is the greatest earner. Coal, chromite, nickel, asbestos, copper, iron ore and tin are also exported in significant quantities. Forestry is an up-and-coming venture, especially in the Eastern Highlands. Manufacturing comprises only a small sector of the economy and is dominated by textiles, including spinning, weaving and dyeing. Tourism is thriving, as visitors are sure to notice.

POPULATION & PEOPLE

Zimbabwe has an estimated population of 11.2 million, with a growth rate of 2.4%. Of these, 65% live permanently in rural areas and 40% are under 18 years of age. Only a few years ago, the average life expectancy was nearly 60 years; today, with the onslaught of AIDS it is closer to 35.

Most Zimbabweans are of Bantu origin: 76% belong to various Shona groups (Ndau, Rozwi, Korekore, Karanga, Manyika and Zezuru), occupying the eastern two-thirds of the country; 18% are of Ndebele stock (including the Kalanga), living primarily in south-western Zimbabwe; and the remainder are divided between the Tonga (or Batonga) of the upper Kariba area (2%), the Shangaan or Hlengwe of the lowveld (1%), the Venda of the far south (1%), and the Europeans and Asians scattered around the country (2%). The European population stands at around 100,000. There are also 25,000 people of mixed European and African descent and 10,000 Asians, mainly Indians.

ARTS

Visitors are often surprised by the degree of artistic talent Zimbabweans take for granted. Even the most humble pot or basket created in a remote village displays artistic sensitivity and attention to detail. Artists are highly esteemed in Zimbabwean society and make much more trade than in most other countries. Arts centres seek out promising talents for special training, for which there is abundant competition.

Literature

Although oral traditions perpetuated a large body of stories, legends, songs and poetry, the first written works by black authors didn't appear in print until the publication (in Shona) of *Feso*, by S Mutswairo, in 1956.

Traditional Medicine

In Zimbabwe, traditional healers and folk practitioners *(n'anga* or *chiremba)* are shamans, whose powers are thought to be derived from two types of spirit. The first type, *midzimu*, are ancestral protective spirits and are bestowed by a direct ancestor of the healer. The second type, *shave*, are the spirits of deceased strangers who lived nearby and were not properly buried. This powerful entity honours the recipients by selecting them to be shamans. In rural Zimbabwe, about one person in 1000 practices the profession.

Although some shamans are called as children, callings are most often accompanied by a chronic mental or physical sickness which occurs during young adulthood, together with dreams of herbal remedies and 'medical' practices. The cause of this distress is usually diagnosed by someone who's already a shaman and, if the elected person agrees to accept the calling, he or she is initiated in a special ceremony.

Like most physicians, n'anga have three main aims: preventing illness, finding the cause of illness and working out a cure. For some ailments, a n'anga may simply prescribe herbs, but if the patient suggests that the ailment is derived from a spell or magic, some form of divining may be necessary to isolate the cause of the problem and make a prognosis for survival. This is often done by consulting with the spirits or reading the *hakata* (wooden divining bones, used in central Mashonaland), *shoro* (animal bones, used mainly in eastern Zimbabwe) or *mungomo* (seeds, used in Matabeleland).

Often, the problem is determined to be an intervening spirit, such as a *muroyi* (witch), *ngozi* (avenger) or a shave, which is affecting the protection normally afforded by the patient's *mudzimu* (singular of 'midzimu'). It may also be determined that the patient brought on the illness by failing to perform a required ritual, such as observing a special holiday, or by breaking a taboo, such as eating one's totem animal. The n'anga then decides on an appropriate *muti* (treatment). This may involve powders, ointments, teas or scarification. The disease may be determined to have been caused by an *uroyi* (evil spirit) or *muroyi* (witchcraft), willed upon the patient. Historically, a perpetrator – most often a woman – would have been identified and punished, but this practice is now illegal in Zimbabwe and is rare.

If the person has been possessed, the n'anga exorcises the spirit and casts it into an animal, which carries it away. If the victim has been jinxed by a witch, treatment normally involves the ingesting of herbs. Alternatively, the bad luck may be lured into a specially prepared bottle and left in the bush; the spell is then cast upon the person who finds it.

Currently, traditional healers are gaining increased credibility and patronage among the masses. This is largely due to rising health costs, which place much western medicine out of reach of most Zimbabweans.

The first Ndebele novel, published in 1957, was *Umthawakazi*, by PS Mahlangu.

Subsequent works dealt with precolonial traditions, myths and folk tales and focused on the experiences of blacks under a white regime. Although numerous protest pieces were written during the following 10 years, the first serious treatise on the topic was Stanlake Samkange's 1966 *On Trial for my Country*.

Since independence, Zimbabwean literature has focused on the liberation effort and the struggles to build a new society. The 1992 Commonwealth Prize for Literature went to Zimbabwean writer Shimmer Chinodya for *Harvest of Thorns*, his epic novel of the Second Chimurenga. Another internationally renowned writer is Chenjerai Hove, who wrote the war-inspired *Bones*, the tragic *Shadows*, and the rather humorous *Shebeen Tales*.

Tsitsi Dangarembga's *Nervous Conditions* is highly acclaimed and shouldn't be missed. Set in eastern Zimbabwe, it's the tale of a young woman attending a mission school in 1960s Rhodesia.

Also worthwhile are the works of Charles Mungoshi, who masterfully captures the despair of black Africans in pre-independence Rhodesia. His most highly acclaimed work is *Coming of the Dry Season*.

Established and emerging names in Zimbabwean literature are published by Heinemann, in its African Writers Series; by Longman, in its African Classics series; and in a couple of locally published series.

For information on books about Zimbabwe, see Books in the Facts for the Visitor section in this chapter.

Traditional Crafts

Traditional African crafts, though utilitarian, demonstrate ancient traditional values and the spirituality of the culture. Women in particular have perpetuated African themes and shapes by integrating them into everyday items, while men have focused on woodcarving, iron sculpture and architecture in the context of tool-making and home construction.

Even before Arab traders brought cloth from India, Zimbabweans were spinning and weaving garments from wild cotton that grew on the plateau. They were also making blankets, mats and clothing from strands of the soft and pliable tree bark known as *gudza*.

Although they aren't traditional arts, Zimbabwean women have developed crocheting, batik, tie-dyeing and clothing design skills.

Pungwes

The exact origin of the word *pungwe* is unknown but is believed to be derived from the word *ngwe*, meaning 'from darkness to light'. It was first used in the 1960s and referred to all-night discos. However, during the Second Chimurenga (1972–80), all-night celebrations of nationalistic unity between villagers and guerrillas, accompanied by morale-inspiring song and dance, came to be known as pungwes. Nowadays, any sort of event may be advertised as a pungwe, meaning it begins in the evening and carries on through the night. There's usually a big name playing in a stadium at least once every couple of months; entry is usually US$4.

Shona Sculpture

A relatively recent addition to Zimbabwe's cultural arts, Shona sculpture has garnered most of the laurels as far as international recognition is concerned, although it has no functional or ceremonial value. The Shona tribe has no exclusive rights to the genre, which welds African themes and ideas with European artistic training, and smaller tribal groups are participating as well.

Pieces represent stylised animals, gods, spirits, ancestors and totems as well as humans. A recurring theme is the metamorphosis of man into beast, the prescribed punishment for violation of social interdictions – such as eating one's totem animal.

RICHARD I'ANSON

Pottery, another traditional female activity, has been an enduring art form.

Intricately designed pots have always played a practical role in everyday life – they are used for storage, cooking, serving, carrying, preparing curdled milk and even brewing yeast beer.

[Continued on page 730]

MUSIC IN ZIMBABWE

Traditional Music

Music has always been an important part of traditional Zimbabwean culture. In common with music throughout Southern Africa, the melody and rhythm of repetitive chanting becomes a mesmerising declaration of unity between the singers, while the individuality of the various parts is sustained by harmonisation. Shared song has served as an evocation and confirmation of solidarity in common struggles, whether battle with a neighbouring tribe, cooperation on a successful harvest or confrontation with natural disaster. Moreover, African stories and legends are punctuated by musical choruses in which the audience participates, and social events (such as weddings, funerals, religious ceremonies, harvests and births) are accompanied by unique songs.

Like the traditional musical instruments of all Southern African countries, those of Zimbabwe, usually fashioned from natural materials on hand, produce an array of effects. The best known is the *marimba*, a wooden xylophone that creates tones similar to those in western music and is often used for pieces with strong European influences. The keys of the best marimbas are made from the hardwood of the *mwenje* tree of northern Mozambique, which produces an optimum resonance. Sound boxes are normally made of dried gourds.

Another instrument that enjoys popularity among souvenir hunters as well as musicians is the *mbira*, known in English as a thumb piano. It was originally used to accompany historical epics set to music. Although there are several variations, most mbira consist of 22 to 24 narrow iron keys mounted in rows on a wooden sound board. The player plucks the ends of the keys with the thumbs or special thumbnails. An accomplished mbira player is known as a *gwenyambira*.

Percussion instruments include an array of rattles and drums. Rattles can be made of gourds and contain seeds or even bottle caps. *Hosho* rattles (maracas) are held in the hands, while *magagada*, *majaka*, *madare* (bells) and Ndebele *mahlwayi* rattles are attached to the legs and ankles of dancers. The *ngoma*, a tapered cylindrical drum made from the *mutiti*

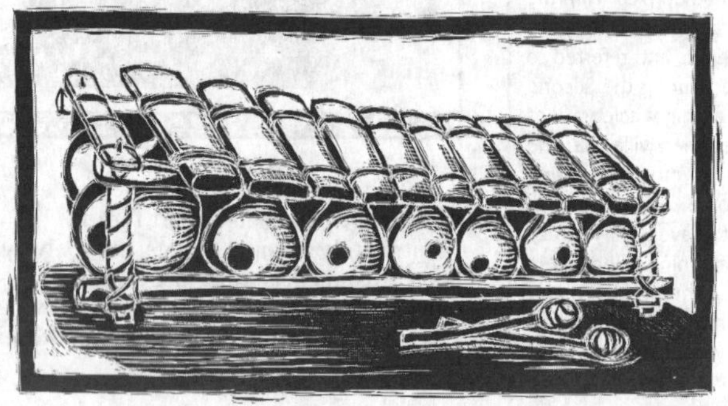

SARAH JOLLY

Left: You'll see the *marimba*, a wooden xylophone, used in musical ensembles all over Southern Africa.

or lucky bean tree, comes in all sizes. Although the standard skin covering is cowhide these days, the optimum skins are considered to be zebra and *leg-uaan* (a water-loving lizard). For maximum resonance, drums are treated with beeswax and dried over a flame before a performance.

Probably the oddest percussion instrument ever used in Zimbabwe was the *mujejeje*, or stone bells. Many of the stones in granite kopjes found around the country have exfoliated in such a way that when struck, they'll resound with a lovely bell-like tone (Zimbabwe's first rock music?). Historically, special occasions were held around these stones in order to take advantage of this novel musical opportunity. The most famous of these can be seen today at the Khami Ruins near Bulawayo.

The woodwind group is represented by several types of flute, including pan pipes and the *nyanga* or horn, which is, logically, fashioned from animal horn. Although traditional string instruments (mostly bow-shaped like the Shangaan *makweyana*) have been used historically in Zimbabwe, they are rarely played these days.

Popular Music

In Zimbabwe, as in most Southern African countries, music is incorporated into almost every aspect of life (and will accompany you on most of your travels). Through traditional songs, stories are told, games are played

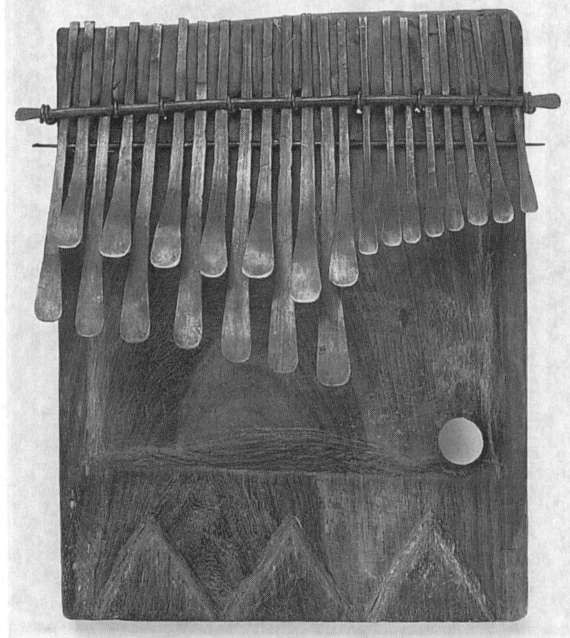

DENNIS WISKEN/SIDEWALK GALLERY

Right: The *mbira* (sometimes called a 'thumb piano') is a traditional instrument found throughout Southern Africa.

and important lessons are passed from generation to generation. These songs use the traditional rhythmic structures of Zimbabwean music and are often accompanied by various percussion instruments (such as dried gourd rattles and skin drums), the mbira, marimbas and the nyanga.

In the period between WWII and the start of Zimbabwe's war of independence in the early 1970s, little attention or even interest was afforded by the music industry to these traditional musical forms. Musically, Zimbabwe was inundated with foreign material – from swing in the 1940s through to South African pennywhistle in the 1950s to Otis Redding and other US soul musicians in the 1960s. Many local musicians, including some of today's famous names such as Thomas Mapfumo and Oliver Mtukudzi, began their careers doing Beatles and Elvis covers.

To the great benefit of Zimbabwean music lovers, the war of independence inspired musicians to write, perform and record original

SARAH JOLLY

Left: Drums play an important role in Zimbabwean music.

RICHARD I'ANSON

DANIEL BIRKS

RICHARD I'ANSON

RICHARD I'ANSON

Zimbabwe Clockwise from Top Left: Locals race to buses to sell their wares – snacks, drinks and cabbages; cotton is one of Zimbabwe's main cash crops; a vendor at the buzzing Mbare market, the largest in Zimbabwe; the Harare skyline

RICHARD I'ANSON

RICHARD I'ANSON

DANIEL BIRKS

Zimbabwe **Top:** Balancing rocks, Matobo National Park **Middle:** The Great Enclosure and other ruins at the Great Zimbabwe National Monument **Bottom:** Moonrise over the Mazowe River valley, north of Harare

protest songs, which were based on traditional Shona sounds, transposed onto western instruments. These songs, known as *chimurenga*, form the musical basis for much of Zimbabwean popular music today, mostly with Shona lyrics.

Some of the best musicians have been snapped up by overseas audiences, but the majority are still in Zimbabwe. This, and the fact that so many foreign bands include Zimbabwe on their tours, combine to make Harare one of Africa's great musical centres. One way to tap into what's current and popular is to take your own radio and tune in to one of the Shona stations that play great local and not-so-local music.

As well as the popular Shona and Shangaan styles, there is a strong market for Congalese (Zaïrean) *kwasa kwasa* music, which tends to be based on the rhumba beat. In fact, so admired is the rhumba that Zimbabwean record shops have made it a category for African music. The recorded music you will generally hear in pubs and discos will be a mix of mainstream American artists (eg, Mariah Carey and Michael Jackson), dance, funk and pop.

Groups & Musicians

Some of Zimbabwe's better known music names include: Thomas Mapfumo & the Blacks Unlimited, Oliver Mtukudzi, Simon Chimbetu, Andy Brown, Steve Dyer, the Real Sounds of Africa, the Khiami Boys, the Ngwenya Brothers, Leonard Dembo, Black Umfolosi, John Chibudura and the Tembo Brothers.

Bands, however, are constantly breaking up, changing members and changing names, so don't be discouraged if you can't find a group you know of – those helpful and enthusiastic people in the record shop can be a useful source of information. Or just keep your eye out for posters to get an idea of who's around.

Further Information

A good source of information on Zimbabwean music is *Dandemutande Magazine & Calendar*, published by Paul Novitski (☎ 206-323 6592, fax 329 9355), 1711 East Spruce St, Seattle, WA 98122-5728, USA. The calendar lists events worldwide and the quarterly magazine has articles on trends, personalities and hints on making and playing traditional instruments. Web site: www.dandemutande.com

The Zimbabwe Entertainment Directory Web site features all the latest on Harare's music scene. It can be reached through the Web site of The Tube nightclub: thetube.cybergate.co.zw (don't insert www)

The Kunzwana Trust (☎/fax 04-301519), 73 Quorn Avenue, Mt Pleasant, Harare, is a nonprofit organisation that aims to help Zimbabwean musicians and instrument makers become commercially self-sufficient. It also sponsors the fabulous annual Houses of Stone music festival in Harare. Write for advance information and specific dates.

For information on books about Zimbabwean music, see under Books in the Facts for the Visitor section of the Zimbabwe chapter.

[Continued from page 725]

Traditionally, tools like hoes, axe handles, ladles, bowls and *umncwado* (penis sheaths) were all carved from wood in simple and practical designs. Spear, knobkerrie and dagger handles were decoratively rendered and shields were mounted on a carved wooden frame. Even small canoes were typically hewn out of a single piece of wood.

Carved *mutsago* and *umqamelo* (Shona and Ndebele words for 'headrests') were considered emblematic of family responsibility, and those of distant ancestors were passed down male lines and called upon to ceremonially evoke the spirits of earlier owners.

Wooden stools, whose intricate decorations reach their highest level in the Tonga culture of western Lake Kariba, are carved from a single piece of wood. Historically, only men were allowed to sit on them and male heads of households used them as 'thrones' from which to oversee family affairs.

LANGUAGE

The official language of Zimbabwe – that used in government, legal and business proceedings – is English, but it is a first language for only about 2% of the population. The rest of the people are native speakers of Bantu, the two most prominent dialects of which are Shona, spoken by 76% of the population (mainly in the centre and east), and Ndebele, spoken by 18% (mainly in the west). Another dialect, Chilapalapa, is actually a pidgin version of Ndebele, English, Shona and Afrikaans, and isn't overly laden with niceties – stick to English. For more information on the indigenous languages of Zimbabwe and some useful words and phrases in Shona and Ndebele, see the Language chapter at the back of this book.

Facts for the Visitor

SUGGESTED ITINERARIES

Two Weeks

Two weeks will allow time to see the main sights. Spend two days in Harare – sample the nightlife, have lunch in the gardens, suss out Shona sculpture at a garden gallery. Then head for Masvingo and the Great Zimbabwe National Monument and spend a full day exploring the ruins and cruising on Lake Mutirikwe at sunset. Dedicate two days to Bulawayo, spending one day wandering around town and another in the Motobo Hills, then board the overnight train to Victoria Falls and, over three days, do an adrenalin-pumping activity, take a safari to Hwange National Park and sink a few beers on a boat above the Falls. Next, spend a lovely cruisey day on a ferry between Mlibizi and Kariba, and a day checking out the Zimbabwe Riviera at Kariba. Spend four days on a Chirundu-to-Mana-Pools canoe safari searching for wildlife while gliding along the Zambezi; and, finally, return to Harare.

One Month

One month will allow for a thorough exploration of Zimbabwe, although there will still be plenty left unseen for a return visit. Follow the above itinerary, perhaps allowing an extra day in the main centres and a few days safari in Mana Pools, and supplement it with the following: two to three days in Chimanimani, where you can chill out in the village before tackling the mountains, then chill out again at a secluded waterfall; two days in Vumba, walking the gardens and enjoying cake at Tony's Coffee Shop; two days in Kwe Kwe, joining in a game of polocrosse or horse riding through the bush; two days in Binga, discovering a traditional African community; and three to four days on a walking safari in Chizarira, Zimbabwe's most scenic park.

PLANNING

When to Go

Most of Zimbabwe enjoys a more temperate climate than its latitude would otherwise suggest. Generally, the dry winter months are the most comfortable for travelling, but you'll miss the green landscapes that characterise the hotter and wetter summer season. In winter, night-time temperatures can fall below freezing.

Winter can be the best season for wildlife viewing because animals tend to concentrate close to water holes and are therefore easily observed. At this time, though, some animals may be in distress as water and food sources become scarce. It gets crowded during South African and Namibian school holidays (see the Facts for the Visitor sections in the South Africa and Namibia chapters). June is a cool and relatively quiet month.

Maps

City plans of larger towns are available at Publicity Associations; Harare and Bulawayo sell large-scale atlas-style maps of their respective cities. Lonely Planet's *Southern Africa Travel Atlas* complements this guide with detailed road and park maps. The best detailed national map is *Zimbabwe Relief, 1:1,000,000*, published by the Surveyor General (☎ 04-794545) Electra House, Samora Machal Ave, Harare, and costs US$5.

The Surveyor General also sells 1:50,000 ordnance survey topographic sheets, and a range of thematic maps, such as national parks maps and a large-scale Harare street plan.

TOURIST OFFICES

Local Tourist Offices

Publicity associations can be found in most Zimbabwean towns. Some are considerably more helpful than others, but they all distribute brochures and can try to answer queries. For details, see Information under individual cities and towns.

Tourist Offices Abroad

Germany (☎ 069-920 7730) Schillerstrasse 3, D-60313 Frankfurt
South Africa (☎ 011-622 5741, fax 622 5757) Finance House, Oppenheimer Rd, Bruma Park, Johannesburg
UK (☎ 020-7836 7755, fax 240 5465) Zimbabwe High Commission, 428 The Strand, London WC2
USA (☎ 212-332 1090) Rockefeller Centre, Suite 412, Avenue of the Americas, New York, NY 10020

VISAS & DOCUMENTS

Visas

Visas are required by nationals of all countries, except for those from Canada, Ireland, Sweden and the UK, and everyone needs a valid passport.

Visas can be obtained at your point of entry. Single-entry visas cost US$30; multiple-entry visas cost US$55.

Visa requirements sometimes change, so if you're not sure whether you need one, inquire at the Zimbabwe embassy or high commission in your home country or to the Chief Immigration Officer, Private Bag 7717, Causeway, Harare, Zimbabwe. Alternatively, try this Web site: www.travel.com.au/tools/visa.html

Unless you're arriving by car, immigration officials may be immovable about you having to have an onward ticket to your home country – a ticket out of a neighbouring or other African country will usually suffice; they rarely ask to see cash/credit cards. Miscellaneous Charge Orders aren't acceptable.

On the immigration form, in the space asking for your hotel or address in Zimbabwe, enter a mid-range hotel at your destination, whether you've booked it or not.

Visas for Onward Travel

In Harare you can get visas for the following neighbouring Southern African countries. For specific opening times and addresses, see Embassies & Consulates in Zimbabwe. To obtain a visa, you'll normally need at least two passport photos, and it's best to arrive at the embassy early in the morning.

Botswana Visas cost US$2.70 and can be processed by the next working day.

Mozambique Transit visas cost US$11/24/35 when issued within three days/24 hours/the same day. Tourist visas (valid for one month) cost US$15/23 when issued the same day or within three days.

Namibia Visas cost US$24 and are issued within 48 hours.

Zambia Single/multiple entry visas cost US$60/75 for UK citizens and US$25/40 for others. They take two days to process.

Visa Extensions The maximum length of stay is normally 90 days, but this can be extended to a maximum of six months at immigration offices. The catch is that you can extend for only one month at a time. The procedure is normally hassle-free; just fill in a form and demonstrate that you have enough money for the extended stay. In general, the Harare office has the biggest backlog and therefore the longest waits.

Other Documents

Yellow fever vaccination certificates are required if you're entering from an infected country. A driving licence from your home country is sufficient to drive in Zimbabwe provided it's in English. Otherwise, you'll need an authenticated translation plus a photograph.

It's worth bringing a youth, student and seniors card with you to Zimbabwe as public transport companies, Internet cafes, museums and other tourist services offer discounts to card holders. An international hostel card isn't necessary.

EMBASSIES & CONSULATES

Zimbabwean Embassies & High Commissions

Zimbabwe has embassies and high commissions in Botswana, Mozambique, Namibia, South Africa and Zambia (see those country chapters for details), as well as in:

Australia
High Commission: (☎ 02-6286 2281, fax 6290 1680) 11 Culgoa Circuit, O'Malley, Canberra, ACT 2606

Canada
High Commission: (☎ 613-237 4388, fax 563 8269) 332 Somerset St West, Ottawa, Ontario K2P OJ9

France
Embassy: (☎ 01 53 81 90 10, fax 01 53 81 90 190) 5 rue de Tilsit, Paris 75008

Germany
Embassy: (☎ 0228-356071, fax 356309) Villichgasse 7, 5300 Bonn 2

Kenya
High Commission: (☎ 02-721071) 6th floor, Minet ICDC Bldg, Mamlaka Rd (PO Box 30806), Nairobi

Tanzania
High Commission: (☎ 51-116789, fax 46260) 6th floor, New Life House, Sokaine Dr, Ohio St (PO Box 20762), Dar es Salaam

UK
High Commission: (☎ 020-7836 7755, fax 7379 1167) 429 The Strand, London WC2R 0SA

USA
Embassy: (☎ 202-332 7100, fax 438 9326) 1608 New Hampshire Ave NW, Washington, DC 20009

Embassies & High Commissions in Zimbabwe

Harare is one of the best places in the region to pick up visas for other African countries. Requirements are constantly changing but nearly all require a fee (some must be paid in US dollars) and multiple passport-sized photos. Following are some of the embassies and high commissions based in Harare.

Australia
High Commission: (☎ 04-757774) 4th floor, Karigamombe Centre, 53 Samora Machal Ave. Open from 8 am to 12.30 pm and 1.30 to 4.30 pm Monday to Thursday, 8 am to 12.30 pm Friday.

Botswana
Embassy: (☎ 04-729551) 22 Phillips Ave, Belgravia. Open from 8 am to 12.30 pm Monday, Wednesday and Friday.

Canada
High Commission: (☎ 04-252181) 45 Baines Ave, corner of Moffat St (PO Box 1430). Open from 9 am to 1 pm Monday to Thursday, and 9 am to noon Friday.

France
Embassy: (☎ 04-704393) 74-76 Samora Machal Ave, Old Reserve Bank. Open from 8.30 am to 1 pm and 2 to 4.30 pm weekdays.

Germany
Embassy: (☎ 04-708535) 14 Samora Machal Ave (PO Box 2168). Open from 9 am to noon weekdays.

Israel
Embassy: (☎ 04-756898) Anchor House, 54 Jason Moyo Ave. Open from 9.30 am to 4.30 pm weekdays.

Italy
Embassy: (☎ 04-498190) 7 Bartholomew, Greendale. Open from 9 am to 1 pm weekdays.

Malawi
Embassy: (☎ 04-705611) Malawi House, 42–44 Harare St (PO Box 321).

Mozambique
Embassy: (☎ 04-253871) 152 Herbert Chitepo Ave. Open from 8 am to noon weekdays.

Namibia
Embassy: (☎ 04-304856) 31A Lincoln Rd, Avondale. Open from 8 am to 1 pm and 2 to 5 pm weekdays.

New Zealand
High Commission: (☎ 04-759221) 8th floor, Green Bridge, Eastgate Centre. Open from 8 am to 4.30 pm Monday to Thursday, and 8 am to 1.30 pm Friday.

South Africa
High Commission: (☎ 04-753147) 7 Elcombe Ave, Belgravia. Open from 8 am to noon and 1.15 to 3 pm weekdays.

UK
High Commission: (☎ 04-772990) 7th floor, Corner House, corner of Leopold Takawira St and Samora Machal Ave. Open from 8 am to 12.30 pm and 1.30 to 4.30 pm Monday to Thursday, and 8 am to noon Friday.

USA
Embassy: (☎ 04-794522) Arax House, 172 Herbert Chitepo Ave (PO Box 3340). Open from 7.30 am to 12.15 pm and 1 to 5 pm Monday to Thursday, and 8 am to 12.30 pm Friday.

Zambia
High Commission: (☎ 04-773777) 6th floor, Zambia House, Union Ave (PO Box 4698). Open from 8 am to 12.30 pm and 2 to 4.30 pm weekdays.

CUSTOMS

Visitors may import a maximum of US$250 in nontrade items, excluding personal effects. Travellers over 18 years of age can also import up to 5L of alcohol, including 2L of spirits. Firearms must be declared at the border and temporary import permits should officially be completed for cameras etc.

Motor vehicles may be imported temporarily, as long as they bear current number plates and are licensed, registered and titled in the home country. For more information, see Car & Motorcycle in the Getting Around section of this chapter.

If you're travelling with a pet or a guide dog (unless you reside inside the Southern African Customs Union), you'll need a permit issued by the Director of Veterinary Services, PO Box 8012, Causeway, Harare, Zimbabwe. Applications take a minimum of three months to process. T… antine laws regarding pe… mit, all animals need va… and a clean bill of health fro… veterinary office in their home co…

MONEY

Currency

The unit of currency is the Zimbabwe dollar (Z$1 = 100 cents). Notes come in denominations of two, five, 10, 20, 50 and 100 dollars. Coins are valued at one, five, 10, 20 and 50 cents, and Z$1 and Z$2.

The import of Zimbabwean banknotes is limited to Z$500 per person per visit and export is limited to the equivalent of US$200, although it's unlikely you'll be able to exchange it outside of Zimbabwe. For hotels and organised activities such as rafting or canoeing, nonresidents must pay in foreign currency, although this often isn't enforced.

Exchange Rates

Bank rates at the time of going to print were as follows:

country	unit		Zim dollar
Australia	A$1	=	Z$22.9
Canada	C$1	=	Z$26.3
euro	€1	=	Z$36.5
France	10FF	=	Z$55.7
Germany	DM1	=	Z$18.7
Japan	¥100	=	Z$36.3
New Zealand	NZ$1	=	Z$19.1
South Africa	R10	=	Z$58
UK	UK£1	=	Z$60.5
USA	US$1	=	Z$38.3

Exchanging Money

Banks are open from 8 am to 3 pm Monday, Tuesday, Thursday and Friday. On Wednesday, they close at 1 pm and on Saturday they're open from 8.30 to 11.30 am. The exchange desk at Harare airport is open whenever there's an incoming flight, but often limits transactions to US$100. Hotel reception desks will sometimes exchange currency but the service is normally reserved for guests and includes a large commission.

All brands of travellers cheques in US dollars or UK pounds may be easily exchanged

…Zimbabwe dollars at any bank or bureau …change, but you may have to fill out an 'Application for Permission to Sell Foreign Exchange to an Authorised Dealer'. Major currencies are also welcomed, but due to rampant counterfeiting US$50 and US$100 notes probably won't be accepted. It's almost impossible to buy foreign currency in Zimbabwe. To exchange travellers cheques, Zimbank charges 2% commission, while Barclays and Standard Chartered Bank charge 1%. Barclays offers the best rates on Visa travellers cheques, but you must show proof of purchase – you know, the piece of paper they tell you to keep separate from your cheques. Bureau de change offices generally charge no commission, but they too are increasingly asking to see purchase receipts.

ATMs Bank cards with a Visa logo may use Barclays Bank ATMs, and MasterCard and Cirrus logo cards can be used at Standard Chartered Bank ATMs.

Credit Cards American Express, Diner's Club, MasterCard and Visa, as well as Eurocheques, are accepted by establishments catering to tourists and business people. Many businesses (ie shops, hotels, restaurants) have the technology to process visa transactions electronically. However, connections can be incredibly slow, which makes this service impossible to rely on.

With a credit card, you can buy as many Zimbabwe dollars as your limit will allow. Petrol credit cards aren't accepted at all.

Black Market In the late 1980s, strict currency controls created a thriving black market in Zimbabwe, but the Economic Structural Adjustment Program (ESAP) and relaxation of import regulations have ended it. Informal currency exchange is illegal and the difference in the rates – just a few cents – means it's not worth the considerable risks. If you use street changers, they'll either turn you in to the police or attempt to separate you and your money; many travellers wind up with a wad of clipped newspaper sandwiched between two notes.

Costs

Many hotels, national parks and tour operators employ a two-tier (or three-tier) pricing system, in which foreigners pay considerably more for goods and services than residents. However, Zimbabwe is still not expensive unless you're using international-class hotels, fine restaurants and/or package safaris, in which case the sky's the limit. Fortunately, it's possible to find hotels, hostels, camping grounds and caravan parks in most cities and towns for under US$10 per night.

Food is reasonably priced and a meal of the Zimbabwean staple, *sadza ne nyama* (cooked cob of maize, or *mealies*, with meat relish), in a local eatery costs less than US$1.50, and big hotels put on all-you-can-eat buffets – good value at US$4 to US$12. A bottle of beer costs US$0.70 and a bottle of local wine in a restaurant is US$5.

Due to a shortage of foreign exchange, some imported items are expensive, but Zimbabwe-produced goods are affordable. Consumer taxes – 16% on retail items, excluding food, and 19% on 'luxury' goods – are normally included in the price of the item. A 15% tourist tax is usually added to the price of hotel rooms, safari and other tourist services. A further 2% tourist levy may also apply.

Tipping & Bargaining

Tips of approximately 10% are expected by taxi drivers and tourist-class hotel and restaurant staff. Some establishments automatically add a 10% service charge to the bill, replacing the gratuity. When out shopping at markets and street stalls most prices will be negotiable – taking things you own to trade with will drop prices even lower.

POST & COMMUNICATIONS

Postal Rates

At the time of writing, airmail postage cost the following:

	rest of world (US$)	Europe (US$)
postcard	0.32	0.43
letter (10g)	0.26	0.33
parcel (under 100g)	0.86	0.93
1kg to 2kg	2.76	3.30

Sending five 2kg parcels works out cheaper than sending one 10kg parcel; the small registration fee is probably worth the peace of mind it brings.

Sending Mail

In spite of long queues at service windows, the Zimbabwean postal system is generally quite good, especially in larger cities and towns. When joining a queue, check the notice over the teller, it lists services available there and the time it shuts for lunch.

Freight forwarders can offer an inexpensive option for getting all those heavy stones home. They handle all sorts, from packages to containers full of furniture. DHL, Fedex and the other big names have representatives. A recommended local company is Trans Freight (☎ 04-773817, fax 773816) 1 Union Ave, Harare.

Receiving Mail

Poste restante services are available in all major cities and towns but Harare is probably the best and most efficient. Have mail sent to you c/o Poste Restante, GPO, Inez Terrace, Harare, Zimbabwe. The address for American Express Customer Mail is PO Box 3141, Harare.

Telephone

The Zimbabwean telephone system may be the butt of jokes but it's improving – or so they say. Local calls are the most notorious. Although there are lots of public telephones, glitches in the local service, for example, mean long queues and bad connections.

As a result, the cell-phone network is flourishing and if you have international roaming it's possible to purchase prepaid calls for your mobile at city phone shops. Cell-phone numbers are prefixed with 011 or 019. Another option is to hire a cell phone for the duration of your stay. GSM Renta Fone (☎ 04-790797, @ gsm@hireit.co.zw) hires cell phones starting at US$4 per day. You can reserve one directly or through the Europcar network.

To make overseas calls, your best bet is to use phonecards, which are sold at post offices for Z$30, Z$50, Z$100 and Z$200. Otherwise, find a private telephone (hotels charge double or triple the official rates) or carry a huge stack of coins. Reverse-charge calling is available but, if possible, it's much better value to wear the cost while in Zimbabwe.

Dialling codes and services include the following:

country code (drop the leading 0 from the internal trunk code)	263
international access code	00
international operator	966
national operator	962

International direct operators can be reached for the following countries:

Australia	00-896
Canada	00-897
New Zealand	00-894
UK	00-898
USA	00-899

Fax

Public fax services are available at post offices in larger towns. If you wish to receive faxes there, advise correspondents to clearly mark your name, contact address and telephone number on them. There's no fee charged for receiving faxes and the post office should contact you when they arrive.

Email & Internet Access

Internet cafes are springing up all over Zimbabwe, although connections can be slow. Costs average around US$3 to US$4 per half hour. It's a good idea to try and restrict your surfing to times outside business hours.

INTERNET RESOURCES

For up-to-date information on Zimbabwe, try the following Web sites:

Samara Services Accommodation and tourist-related services and information.
www.samara.co.zw

Sunshinecity Useful site with accommodation, travel and general Harare and Zimbabwe information.
www.sunshinecity.net

Zimbabwe Independent An online version of the newspaper of the same name.
www.samara.co.zw/zimin/

Zimbabwe Network Good starting point for planning a visit to Zimbabwe, with information on business, tourism and entertainment.
www.zimbabwe.net

Other useful addresses are given throughout this chapter. For a more comprehensive listing, see also Internet Resources in the Regional Facts for the Visitor chapter.

BOOKS

This section covers books specific to Zimbabwe. For details on books about the whole Southern Africa region, see Books in the Regional Facts for the Visitor chapter. For books written by Zimbabwean authors, see Arts in the Facts about Zimbabwe section.

Lonely Planet

Songs to an African Sunset: A Story of Zimbabwe by Sekai Nzenza Shand. An excellent introduction to Shona traditions and culture. Shand tells of her childhood in Zimbabwe, and of her return to the country after spending many years living in the west. Packed with cultural information about rural life, it also gives an insight into the lives of middle-class urban Zimbabweans. *Songs* is one of the many titles in Journeys, Lonely Planet's travel literature series.

Zimbabwe, Botswana & Namibia provides more in-depth coverage of Zimbabwe.

Guidebooks

Great Zimbabwe Described & Explained by Peter Garlake. This guidebook attempts to sort out the history, purpose and architecture of the ancient ruins at Great Zimbabwe.

The Painted Caves – An Introduction to the Prehistoric Art of Zimbabwe by Peter Garlake. Major prehistoric rock-art sites in Zimbabwe are uncovered in this guide.

History & Politics

If you're interested in colonial history, look for the biographies and diaries of Robert Moffat, David Livingstone, Cecil John Rhodes, Frederick Courteney Selous, Leander Starr Jameson, etc, which are available in libraries. Other titles include:

The Great Betrayal, by Ian Smith. The autobiography of colonial Rhodesia's most controversial leader, it chronicles a tumultuous, emotion-charged period in modern Zimbabwean history.

An Introduction to the History of Central Africa – Zambia, Malawi and Zimbabwe, by AJ Wills. More than just an 'introduction', this 500-page work is generally considered the best on the history of the region.

Mapondera 1840-1904 by DN Beach. The biography of Kadungure Mapondera, a descendent of the Changamire and Mutapa dynasties, who resisted settler encroachment in north-eastern Zimbabwe.

Mugabe by Colin Simpson & David Smith. A biography of Robert Mugabe, which traces his rise to the presidency.

Mukiwa – A White Boy in Africa by Peter Godwin. A sensitive and delightfully nonpolitical account of Rhodesian life in the 1960s.

The Struggle for Zimbabwe: the Chimurenga War by David Martin & Phyllis Johnson. A popular history of the Second Chimurenga, the tragic war that led to the country's independence.

Art

Life in Stone by Oliver Sultan. Outlines the 15 top-rated Zimbabwean sculptors, with a short biography of each and brilliant black and white photos.

The Material Culture of Zimbabwe by H Ellert. The most complete coverage of all aspects of Zimbabwe's material crafts cultures, both ancient and modern, including weapons, musical instruments, tools, pottery, jewellery, basketware and so on.

Music

Making Music – Musical Instruments in Zimbabwe Past & Present by Claire Jones. This book outlines teaching, playing and construction of Zimbabwean musical instruments.

Roots Rocking in Zimbabwe by Fred Zindi. Zimbabwe's pop-music scene, including background information on the music itself, is covered in this book, plus data on all the major players.

The Soul of Mbira – Music & Traditions of the Shona People of Zimbabwe by Paul F Berliner. A scholarly treatise on the mbira and marimba musicians, with instructions on how to build and play a mbira.

NEWSPAPERS & MAGAZINES

The two daily papers – the Bulawayo *Chronicle* and the Harare *Herald* – are both long on local, national and especially sports news; international events get short shrift. Two journalists from a similar weekly, the *Standard*, were detained and tortured in 1999 following publication of a story about an alleged coup plot against the government.

Of much greater interest – and a better source of world news – is the politically vocal and controversial *Zimbabwe Independent* (for Web site details see Internet Resources earlier), which is run by Zimbabweans, both black and white, with a decidedly antigovernment editorial stance. It comes out on Friday.

Hotel gift shops often stock international newspapers.

The monthly *Parade* is Zimbabwe's most popular magazine with something for everyone, from politics and beauty competitions to tabloid headlines and sport.

RADIO & TV

Radio and television broadcasting are overseen by the Zimbabwe Broadcasting Corporation (ZBC). There are two television stations and four radio stations in Zimbabwe. Television broadcasts a stream of really, really old repeats from the likes of the BBC and Australian commercial stations, or morning talk shows and religious broadcasts. The government-funded TV 2 and Radio 4 are commercial-free and education-oriented. Radio 1 broadcasts talk programs in English and emphasises classical music. Radio 2 focuses on African music and broadcasts primarily in Shona, but also in Ndebele. Radio 3 broadcasts mainly in English and plays popular western top 40-style music.

The Voice of America and BBC World Service broadcast two and four times daily, respectively. With ideal atmospheric conditions you can also pick up Radio Australia's South East & North Asian service.

HEALTH

Both Harare and Bulawayo have excellent general hospitals, but for potentially serious problems or complications, it's probably best to go home or go to Johannesburg (Jo'burg), where there's a full range of medical services. Doctor's are listed in the front of telephone directories.

It is estimated that one in four people in Zimbabwe have HIV/AIDS. In hospitals and private clinics, medical equipment is well sterilised and blood products are carefully screened, so there's little chance of infection from needles or transfusions. However, bush clinics operate on limited budgets and proper equipment may not always be available, especially in emergency situations. To ease any concerns, carry a couple of sterile syringes (for more information, see Predeparture Planning under Health in the Regional Facts for the Visitor chapter).

In Zimbabwe, cases of malaria rose by nearly 200% from 1997 to 1998. Danger areas are Binga, Chipinge, Chiredzi, Kariba and Mt Darwin, although you should take the usual precautions countrywide. Take prescribed prophylactics and consider investing in a mosquito net from the Malaria Self Help Project, Newlands shopping centre, Harare, or Shop 4, Nagrani Building, Lobengula St, Bulawayo.

Pharmacies and chemists are found in all major towns, but they won't dispense any medicines and drugs without a doctor's prescription. Zimbabwe is also blessed with an outstanding natural pharmacopoeia; you'll find everything from sausage tree *(Kigelia africana)* cream, which is used as a remedy for basal cell carcinoma (skin cancer), to natural sunblocks made from extracts of sausage tree cream, Zimbabwean aloes *(Aloe excelsa)* and lavender trees *(Heteropyxis dehniae)*. These may also be found at pharmacies around the country.

GAY & LESBIAN TRAVELLERS

Although homosexual activities are certainly present in Zimbabwe, they are officially scorned – and technically illegal – and discretion is strongly advised. The Reverend Canaan Banana has been investigated for alleged homosexual offences and Robert Mugabe has conducted a very high-profile antihomosexuality campaign and is on record as saying that: '...gays can never, ever stand as something we approve in Zimbabwe'. In 1999, gay activists retaliated by trying to perform a citizens' arrest on Mugabe while he was visiting London. They were removed by the police amid protests that they had the wrong person. Meanwhile the Gays and Lesbians of Zimbabwe (GALZ), Private Bag A1631, Avondale, Harare continue to fight for equal rights.

DANGERS & ANNOYANCES

Some specific things to watch out for are listed here. For more detailed information see under Warnings or Dangers & Annoyances throughout this chapter, especially the Eastern Highlands section. For some general advice, see Dangers & Annoyances in the Regional Facts for the Visitor chapter.

Zimbabwe remains one of Africa's safest countries, although the frustrations of its people can spill out onto the streets. Your embassy should be able to advise you accordingly. There's no call for paranoia, remain alert and you'll avoid the worst of it.

Con Artists & Scams

A 1995 poverty assessment survey classified 74% of Zimbabweans as poor. Adept con artists take tourists for staggering amounts of money. Often the victims don't even realise they've been conned. 'Sponsorship scams', whereby you're approached for donations for anything from a church fund to a kidney transplant, are rife – don't fall for ridiculous stories.

More sinister scams are thankfully not so common. Sometimes, someone may claim to have seen you smoking *ganja* (marijuana) or changing money illegally and threaten to report you to the police. Sometimes this ploy is merely used to distract you from your belongings. At other times, especially if you are guilty, it's simply attempted extortion.

Theft

During the early 1990s drought forced many people to migrate to the cities in search of employment, but most lacked marketable skills and few were successful. Some turned to crime which has conversely created a reassuring security presence, particularly at banks, hotels and shops.

Don't walk around at night in the cities; have change handy for small purchases; and never pull out a stash of cash in the streets. Remove all valuable jewellery before going out and keep your passport in a safe place.

Places that warrant special caution are bus terminals, markets, crowded discos and parks. Camping grounds and caravan parks have guards posted to watch over campers' belongings, but occasionally things go missing. Always use the safes and baggage storage available at your accommodation. If you have a car, park in well lit areas at night and don't leave any tempting items in sight.

Racism

Although Zimbabwe has been independent for some time now, visitors will notice that racism still exists. However, the issue is not merely a black and white one; the longstanding animosity between the Shona and the minority Ndebele has also caused untold grief.

Drinking

Most Zimbabweans are paid on the last Friday of each month. As with pay day throughout the world, almost immediately thousands flock to the nearest beer hall or *pungwe*. Unfortunately, in Zimbabwe this invariably brings parts of the country to a complete standstill the next day as staff are too drunk or hungover to work. Needless to say, lone women should be especially vigilant at this time of month. Drunk drivers are also a serious problem – avoid driving too late in the day.

Beggars

Being a third world country, Zimbabwe has plenty of beggars in its city streets, and even in rural areas you'll find toddlers asking for a dollar or pen. If you do want to give something back to the people who made your trip so great, consider donating a cash sum at the end of your trip. Charity collection boxes can be found in the departure lounge of Harare airport. Alternatively, you can chose to donate directly to:

Harare Street Childrens' Organisation (☎ 04-721805) PO Box 6952, Harare
Help Age (☎ 04-795500) PO Box 19, Harare
Salvation Army (☎ 04-736666) PO Box 14, Harare

EMERGENCIES

In an emergency, the following services are available: ambulance (☎ 994); fire brigade (☎ 993); and police (☎ 995).

The Medical Air Rescue Service (MARS) is a private rescue service providing air evacuation and ambulance services. Phone details are listed under Emergencies in the Harare, Mutare and Victoria Falls sections.

LEGAL MATTERS

The police presence in Zimbabwe is more reassuring than threatening, and if you're white you're quite likely to receive a bit of respect from them.

Zimbabwe takes speeding and drink-driving very seriously. Speed traps are set up around the country and on the spot fines apply – make sure you get a ticket or receipt.

Although you're likely to be blatantly offered *ganga* (marijuana) on the streets, it, along with other drugs, is an illegal substance – if you're caught, the penalties will be severe.

Some authorities may be susceptible to bribes – you'll need to weigh up the risk of getting yourself into even more trouble (and further corrupting the system) against the punishment you could face should things go further. Should you encounter an officer behaving unprofessionally, note their name and ID number. If the offence is serious, report it to the Public Relations Officer at the Harare Central Police Station.

BUSINESS HOURS

Shops are generally open from 8 am to 1 pm and 2 to 5 pm weekdays (with early closing on Wednesday), and 8 am to noon Saturday. Petrol stations are open from 6 am to 6 pm, although some open 24 hours. Banks are open from 8.30 am to 2 pm weekdays, except Wednesday when they close at noon, and 8.30 to 11 am Saturday. Postal services are available from 8.30 am to 4 pm weekdays and 8.30 to 11.30 am Saturday.

PUBLIC HOLIDAYS & SPECIAL EVENTS

The following public holidays are observed in Zimbabwe:

New Year's Day 1 January
Easter March/April – Good Friday, Easter Sunday, Easter Monday
Independence Day 18 April
Workers' Day 1 May
Africa Day 25 May
Heroes' & Defence Forces Day 11 & 12 August
National Unity Day 22 December
Christmas Day 25 December
Boxing Day 26 December

In Zimbabwe, the most pleasant cultural events will be those you run across incidentally: a rural fair, a school production, a wedding or a town anniversary. Most Zimbabweans will be pleased that strangers are interested in their special events, and you'll almost certainly be welcomed to share in festivities.

ACTIVITIES

In Zimbabwe, the scope for activity tourism grows daily, and in Victoria Falls alone you'll find a wide range: white-water rafting, abseiling, kayaking, microlighting, parachuting, wildlife viewing, horse riding, cycling and bungee jumping. The Mavuradonha Wilderness and the national parks of the Eastern Highlands offer superb hiking. You can white-water raft on the Pungwe River; Kariba offers sailing, house-boating and other water activities; the middle Zambezi is ideal for long-distance canoeing; and the Midlands has several horse-riding ranches. Golf is popular and green fees are some of the world's least expensive – if you're into it, a round is a must.

WORK

It isn't impossible to get a work permit, but neither is it easy; officials definitely prefer that you organise it in your home country. However, if you've run out of money and have a skill that's in demand, your best bet is to seek an employer, secure a solid job offer and then set about arranging a permit with the prospective employer's help. Average wages are about US$60 per month.

Upper or A-level teachers, especially science teachers, engineers, computer experts and medical personnel, will fare the best. Those in professions which have sufficient qualified Zimbabweans, such as nursing or primary teaching, will have limited success. Teachers may teach up to the level they have completed, although those with a degree will command higher salaries. You can improve your job chances by requesting a rural posting. Normal teaching contracts are negotiated for an extendable two years. Private colleges pay better than government schools, but teachers must at least hold a four-year degree.

With special permission, some people may export up to one-third of their salaries.

ACCOMMODATION

Most visitors are pleasantly surprised by accommodation standards and prices (15% government bed tax is included in quoted rates). Bedding is generally included, even in dorms, but it's worth bringing a sheet sleeping bag, too. Some accommodation may require foreigners to pay in foreign currency.

Camping

All large cities and towns have clean, well-maintained caravan parks with ablutions. In many cases, hotels and backpackers hostels will also allow you to camp and use their facilities for a fee. Don't leave anything outside your tent – the wildlife isn't picky and will take anything, from cooking utensils to underwear left out to dry.

Camping in rural areas or on communal lands is generally discouraged and often prohibited. However, if you are caught without accommodation, ask property owners or village chiefs before setting up camp.

Hostels

Happily, there is a growing number of backpackers hostels. Most offer dorm beds, double rooms and camping space as well as a wide range of services: bars, swimming pools, tourist information, Internet access, transfers to and from transport terminals and budget tour bookings. Some also offer meals for a small fee. However, it's still a good idea to carry some packet soup or something similar, in case of emergencies.

B&Bs

Zimbabwe has an association of home and farmstay B&Bs. For the latest listings and information, contact The Town & Country Association of Zimbabwe (☎ 04-7481270) 19 Drummond Rd, Harare.

Hotels

If you want a cheap and quiet place to crash, you can discount most cheap hotels. Their regular patrons are normally more interested in sex and swill than sleep, and the noise level remains fairly constant. Single women should probably suss the cheaper hotels out for security and atmosphere before committing themselves to staying there.

Mid-range accommodation is comfortable, adequate and in most cases reasonably priced. Middle to upper-range hotels are rated on a zero to five-star scale based on an elaborate points system. In some four- and five-star hotels, foreigners pay considerably more than Zimbabwean and regional residents.

Game Ranches

Private game ranches are a rapidly growing sector. Most are owned by white Zimbabweans, who have converted commercial farms and cattle ranches into bushland and stocked them with wildlife.

Some ranches operate as hunting reserves and the accommodation is incidental to the hunting trip. In others, the emphasis is on wildlife viewing and photography, and the accommodation and catering will be the main draw cards. Find out the orientation of a game ranch before you book.

Game ranches aren't generally budget options, although several have opened up camping areas or basic, inexpensive cottages. For more information, contact Zimbabwe Safari Farms (☎ 04-733573) PO Box 592, Harare.

National Park Accommodation

Zimbabwe's national parks' accommodation is relatively well organised, with over 250 chalets, cottages and lodges, plus well-appointed camp sites.

Chalets, often the most basic accommodation option, provide fridges, pots and pans (but no crockery or cutlery), bedding and towels. Cooking and ablutions are communal. Cottages have kitchens and bathrooms. Lodges are fully self-contained and

Booking for National Parks Accommodation

In Harare
The Department of National Parks and Wildlife Management, Central Booking Office (☎ 04-706078), National Botanic Gardens, corner of Borrowdale Rd and Sandringham Dr (PO Box CY826), Harare. Open from 7.45 am to 4.45 pm weekdays.

In Bulawayo
The Bulawayo Booking Agency (☎ 09-63646), corner of Herbert Chitepo St and Eleventh Ave, Bulawayo. Open from 7.45 am to 4.45 pm weekdays.

serviced by National Parks staff. All options have at least two beds per bedroom.

Some parks also offer exclusive camps which accommodate groups. Campers here have access to *braai* pits, hot showers and sometimes special grassy areas for tents.

Bookings are essential for National Park accommodation, but the reservations system isn't exactly a well-oiled machine, so book early and hang on to your receipt. They're most reliably made through the Central Booking Office in Harare, but there is also an office in Bulawayo (for contact details, see the boxed text 'Booking for National Parks Accommodation').

Bookings are available up to six months in advance. Those sought for January, April, May, August, September and December are handled on a draw basis; for other months, on a first-come basis (except Matusadona National Park exclusive camps, which are always on a draw basis). If they tell you everything is full, don't despair; the reservation system accepts bookings without payment and there are lots of no-shows. The catch is that, although you should get to your destination as early as possible, you must wait until 5.30 pm to have accommodation confirmed. Have an alternative plan in case you're turned away. If you've paid for accommodation and can't arrive before 5.30 pm, inform the attendant or you'll forfeit the booking.

FOOD

Zimbabwean cuisine is mostly the legacy of bland British fare combined with stodgy African dishes. The dietary staple is *sadza* – the white maize meal porridge most locals are brought up on. The second component is meat (or *nyama*); *Sadza ne nyama* is plentiful and inexpensive.

Zimbabwe is one of the world's great beef producers and meat is available nearly everywhere. Game meat, such as crocodile, kudu and impala, can be found in restaurants. Popu-lar fish include bream and the whitebait-like dried *kapenta*, both from Kariba. Trout is a speciality in the Eastern Highlands and is superb. Most mid- to upper-range restaurants offer decent vegetarian options, with well-rounded combinations, not just chips and soya mince. If you're self-catering, note that eggs and groundnuts, both good sources of protein, are readily available. Lots of backpackers hostels offer cooked meals, invariably with a vegetarian option.

At bus and train stops, vendors thrust their wares at you, generally fruit or puffed maize, providing a healthy snack option. In the cities, especially around transport terminals, you'll find lots of small eating halls which serve up plain but filling fare – usually sadza ne nyama, chips, sausage rolls, meat pies, sandwiches, burgers – for just a dollar or two. More institutionalised fast food is available from Chicken Inn, Baker's Inn, Creamy Inn, Pizza Inn and Wimpy.

Central business districts offer a variety of coffee houses and international cuisine. All tourist hotels harbour expensive restaurants serving European dishes – mostly the meat and two veg variety – and a handful of elegant places are successful with gourmet cuisine. For hearty appetites, nothing beats the hotel buffets. Breakfast/lunch/dinner buffets allow for a complete pig-out, with a huge selection, for about US$5/6/9 – one of these should keep you going all day.

Dress restrictions can apply in bars and restaurants after about 6 pm, but the definition of 'smart casual dress' varies. At the least, it means no shorts, jeans, T-shirts or thongs (flip-flops).

DRINKS

Nonalcoholic Drinks

In towns and cities, the water is treated and safe to drink. Boxed fruit juices and cola drinks are widely available. Pasteurised milk comes in a plastic bag-like container.

Although both tea and coffee are grown in the Eastern Highlands, the best of it is for export. An increasing number of cafes and restaurants serve real local or imported coffee. At others you'll get a revolting blend made of 10% instant coffee and 90% chicory.

Although it isn't the optimum-quality stuff, Nyanga tea is acceptable and is available throughout the country.

Alcoholic Drinks

The tipple of the masses is *chibuku*, which is, as its advertising asserts, 'the beer of good cheer'. Served up in large plastic containers which, after the Gulf War, came to be known as *scuds*, it has the appearance of vomit, the consistency of thin gruel and a deceptively mellow build up to the knockout punch. It's shared mainly in roadside and township beer halls – a distinctly male social scene.

The beer you will more commonly see is lager, which is always served cold – or as cold as they can get it. The most popular brand is the South African owned Castle, followed by Lion and the misnamed Black Label. Domestic beers are the excellent Zambezi and Bollinger Lagers.

Although Zimbabwe's climate isn't ideal for grapes, it sustains a limited wine industry centred east and south-east of Harare. The largest and most renowned winery is Mukuyu, near Marondera.

SHOPPING

One of the most frustrating things about a trip to Zimbabwe is reconciling your baggage allowance with the amazing range of souvenirs you can choose from. From wire helicopters with rotating rudders to life-size carvings – you'll find it all. What's more, most of it is dirt cheap (bargaining is expected – down to around 40% of the initial asking price), and even when you've broken the bank you can still get more by trading anything and everything, from half a tube of toothpaste to a broken pen.

Realising that many tourists love to shop, the Zimbabwe people have set up stalls all over, from busy city parks to remote roadsides, where the last thing you expect to see is a youngster thrusting a basket at you as you speed by in your car. Also increasing are the number of cooperatives and self-help programs, such as Jairos Jiri, with branches countrywide.

Getting There & Away

This section covers access into Zimbabwe only from neighbouring countries. Information about reaching Southern Africa from elsewhere on the African continent and from other continents is outlined in the regional Getting There & Away.

AIR

Airports and Airlines

Harare international airport (☎ 04-575111) lies 15km south-east of the city, and handles all international traffic.

Both Air Zimbabwe and Zimbabwe Express Airlines have frequent services between Harare, Victoria Falls, Jo'burg and other South African cities. Air Zimbabwe and Air Botswana have nonstop flights between Harare and Gaborone. Air Zimbabwe, Air Namibia and Lufthansa fly between Harare and Windhoek.

Other regional destinations covered by Air Zimbabwe include Lusaka (twice a week), Durban (once a week) and Lilongwe, Malawi (three times weekly).

International air services also connect Bulawayo and Victoria Falls; South African Airways has flights between Bulawayo, Victoria Falls and Jo'burg. Air Namibia's service between Windhoek and Victoria Falls calls in at Tsumeb, Rundu and Katima Mulilo (Mpacha). Air Botswana covers the Maun–Victoria Falls route (via Kasane).

Departure Tax

The US$20 airport departure tax is simple enough to pay for at the bureau de change opposite the airport check-in. Note that only US or Zimbabwe dollars are accepted.

LAND

Border Crossings

Unless stated otherwise, international bus services from Harare depart from the Roadport (☎ 04-702828) on the corner of Fifth St and Robert Mugabe Rd.

When crossing borders by train, customs and immigration formalities are handled on board. Arrivals from Botswana pass through immigration at the Plumtree border, but must clear customs at Bulawayo train station.

When booking international rail tickets from Zimbabwe, you'll have to show your passport. (Note that Zimbabwe dollars aren't accepted on international trains, so have some hard currency before setting out.)

For temporary entry to Zimbabwe with a hired vehicle registered in the Southern African Customs Union, you'll need a sheet known as a Blue Book, detailing the vehicle's particulars, as well as proof of insurance in the vehicle's registered country. At the border, you must get a temporary import permit, which must be presented on departure.

Botswana

There are two major border crossings for travellers going from Zimbabwe to Botswana – between Kazungula and Kasane (open 6 am to 6 pm) and between Plumtree and Ramokgwebana (6 am to 8 pm or whenever a train passes through). There's also a minor crossing at Pandamatenga, west of Hwange National Park (6 am to 4 pm).

Bus A UTC bus runs between Victoria Falls and Kasane via the Kazungula border, and costs US$39 each way. It leaves the UTC office at 7.30 am and 2.30 pm.

Local buses to Francistown leave the Renkini bus terminal in Bulawayo daily.

Train There's a daily train between Bulawayo and Gaborone, which departs Bulawayo at 2.30 pm and arrives the following morning at 8.30 am. The fares are US$30/25/9 in 1st/2nd/economy class.

Hitching Mornings are best for hitching into Botswana. Hitching between Bulawayo and Francistown via the Plumtree border crossing is fairly easy. From Victoria Falls to the Kazungula border crossing, wait at the Kazungula Rd turn-off.

Mozambique & Malawi

The most direct route between Zimbabwe and Malawi is through Mozambique (via Nyamapanda; open 6 am to 6 pm). A second route runs via Machipanda (6 am to 6 pm) on the Beira-Harare road. Everyone needs a transit visa for Mozambique, even if you're heading straight to Malawi. Even so, a border tax of US$5 (hard currency only) is also payable.

Bus It's quite easy to hitch all the way, but you'll also find minibuses between Nyamapanda and Tete in Mozambique, and between Tete and Zóbuè on the border with Malawi.

The direct bus between Harare and Blantyre takes nine to 14 hours – depending on border delays – and costs about US$17. ZUPCO (☎ 04-793171) operates buses from Mbare and Rezende terminals at 6.45 am on Tuesday and Thursday. Stagecoach Malawi buses leave Harare on Wednesday, Friday and Sunday at 6.30 am. Shoestring Shuttle (☎ 04-691966) and Munororama (☎ 04-751234) have twice weekly 'luxury' services. The latter also has not-quite-so-luxurious buses leaving Mbare daily at 6 am.

Namibia

There's no direct overland connection between Zimbabwe and Namibia. The most straightforward route is between Victoria Falls and Katima Mulilo (in the east of the Caprivi Strip). This entails driving or hitching to Botswana via Kazungula and then across the free transit route through Chobe

National Park (you won't be subject to park fees unless you turn off onto a tourist route) to the Namibian border at Ngoma Bridge.

From there, it's a short drive or hitch to Katima Mulilo. For details on the route between Victoria Falls and Kazungula, see Botswana earlier in this section.

Intercape has two services a week from Victoria Falls to Windhoek. The Nam-Vic Shuttle minibuses runs to Windhoek on Sunday at 11 am (US$110). Book through Backpackers Bazaar in Victoria Falls.

South Africa

The only direct border crossing between Zimbabwe and South Africa is at Beitbridge. Car drivers pay a toll (at the border post) to use the Limpopo Bridge when entering/leaving South Africa this way.

Going north, Zimbabwean officials are keen to catch local travellers trying to smuggle in South African goods without paying duty, but foreign travellers encounter few problems beyond long queues.

Bus Luxurious options to Jo'burg have TVs, videos, reclining seats, air-con, toilets and even first-aid trained attendants who serve drinks; fares from Bulawayo/Harare are around US$35.50/42.

Greyhound buses (☎ 04-729514) to Jo'burg (☎ 011-830 1301) leave Harare on Sunday, Tuesday, Wednesday and Friday at 10 pm. From Bulawayo (☎ 09-65548) they leave the Blue Arrow office on Monday, Wednesday, Friday and Sunday at 4 pm. Connections with Greyhound services in South Africa are available.

Express Motorways (☎ 04-720392, fax 737438) has three weekly services from Harare to Jo'burg via Masvingo and Bulawayo. Trans Zambezi Express (☎ 04-722163, e transzam@iafrica.com) also has daily services between Harare and Jo'burg.

Translux has a daily service from the Blue Arrow office in Bulawayo (☎ 09-65548, fax 65549) to Jo'burg at 5 pm.

There are also daily minibus taxis running from Harare and Bulawayo to Jo'burg. They depart when full from the Crown Plaza Hotel in Harare (US$24) and the City Hall Car Park bus terminal in Bulawayo (US$22) and operate to no fixed schedule. You could wait 30 minutes or six hours.

Baz Bus (cell ☎ 011 704242, e info@bazbus.com) and Route 49 (☎ 09-61189 in Bulawayo, 013-2189 in Victoria Falls, e zimcaper@dockside.co.za) offer door-to-door services between hostels in South Africa and Zimbabwe. For more details, see the Getting Around the Region chapter.

Train Bulawayo-Jo'burg/Pretoria services leave at 9 am on Thursday, arriving the next day. The 1st/2nd-class fares are US$42/30; advance bookings are recommended.

Zambia

Between Zimbabwe and Zambia, there are three main border crossings: Chirundu (open 6 am to 6 pm), Kariba (6 am to 6 pm) and Victoria Falls (6 am to 8 pm).

Daily buses leave Mbare for Lusaka (via Chirundu) at 6 am, but the buses get crowded, so arrive early. The trip takes nine hours and costs US$14. ZUPCO has services to Lusaka leaving at 7 am on Monday, Wednesday and Friday (US$12). For a bit more comfort, Power Coach Express (☎ 04-720829) has daily services from Mbare at 10 am.

Most travellers cross at Victoria Falls; the Zimbabwe border post is 1km from Victoria Falls town. It's a further 1km walk between the Zimbabwe and Zambia border posts, but you're rewarded with great views of the Falls from the Zambezi Bridge. For full details, see Victoria Falls later in this chapter, and the main Getting There & Away section in the Zambia chapter.

ORGANISED TOURS

For information on all-inclusive organised tours arranged and booked outside Zimbabwe, see Organised Tours in the regional Getting There & Away chapter.

Getting Around

The land-hungry colonists left good rail links between all major centres in Zimbabwe and a superb network of tarred roads which, although they've deteriorated, are still among Africa's best.

The problem for independent travellers is that public transport runs only where there's demand. To strike out into the country's wilder areas – national parks, for instance – you'll have to find alternative means of transport. The masses aren't going that way.

Avoid travelling on weekends after pay day (last Friday of the month) or at the beginning and end of school holidays, when it's pandemonium at every bus station in the country.

AIR

Air Zimbabwe, the national carrier, and Zimbabwe Express Airlines fly domestic routes between Harare, Kariba, Bulawayo, Hwange and Victoria Falls. Foreigners can purchase domestic tickets with Zimbabwe dollars.

BUS

Zimbabwe has two types – express bus and local bus (the latter is commonly known as 'African' or 'chicken' bus). A third option is overland trucks: see Overland Tours in the regional Getting There & Away chapter.

Express Buses

Express buses are relatively efficient, operating according to published timetables and making scheduled snack and toilet stops along the way. The best services between major cities and towns are operated by Blue Arrow and Express Motorways. Other luxury options are the hotel transfer services such as UTC and Zimbabwe Sun Hotels' Sabi Star.

Local (African) Buses

Local buses go just about anywhere people are living. They're good value, and between main centres services are frequent. Most companies are upgrading their buses – making for fractionally less diesel fumes – and levels of service and reliability vary, but they're often just as quick as the express services.

Buses are also fairly crowded, and despite major hikes in fuel prices they remain cheap. You're more likely to meet Zimbabweans on a local bus than on an express bus. The excitement of having a foreigner aboard will scarcely be containable for many people.Local buses normally depart from the *musika* (or *renkini* in Ndebele), the market outside the town centre. Larger cities and towns also have a city centre or 'in-town' bus terminus, where you can be picked up or dropped off. The problem will be finding a seat – or even standing space – once the bus has left the terminus. Commuter 'omnibuses' also cover intercity routes, but are far more cramped and uncomfortable (see the Local Transport section later in this chapter).

Although you'll hear vague murmurings about average numbers of buses per day, they follow no real timetables. Don't get flustered if no one seems to have specific information or touts are pressuring you. Between major population centres, buses depart when full throughout the day, usually until mid or late afternoon, but if you're unsure about departures or heading for a small town or village, turn up as early as possible. Sometimes the only bus of the day leaves at 5.30 am!

Warning

A crash in the value of the Zimbabwean dollar (among other factors) has created a fuel shortage that threatens to last until at least the end of 2000. Be aware, especially if you plan to rent a car, that there are fuel rations in place and long queues at petrol stations. Ask around for the latest situation upon your arrival.

TRAIN

Zimbabwe has a good railway network connecting Harare, Bulawayo, Victoria Falls, Mutare and Chiredzi. Trains are very cheap, especially in 3rd (economy) class.

Zimbabwean rolling stock includes 1920s passenger cars, complete with beautiful brass and wood-trimmed interiors, even in 2nd class. Newer trains have showers in 1st class and blaring video screens in 2nd class (on an emptier train you can ask the conductor to turn it off – which is a good way to ensure some privacy, as your fellow travellers will then head for a compartment where it's turned on).

Most Zimbabwean trains run at night, and because of the relatively short distances covered, move very slowly in order to arrive at a convenient hour. However, despite the excruciating time they allow, trains regularly run late. Sleeping (1st- and 2nd-class) compartments, with bedding, are inexpensive and comfortable.

Sexes are separated at night, unless you say you're married or reserve a family or two-person compartment in advance, for an additional charge. Second-class compartments hold six adults, but children under seven years are not counted and most Zimbabwean women have at least one child.

Trains have buffet cars, serving passable, inexpensive food and drink. You even have a private coupe (which can be locked by the conductor and opened by anyone else with a credit card); leave someone to watch your gear or take it with you.

For domestic trains, bookings open 30 days ahead and although you can often book and travel the same day, book as early as possible.

A 20% peak-period surcharge applies to travel on Friday and Sunday; the following fares are for off-peak travel.

Timetables

Harare to Mutare The 1st/2nd/3rd-class fares are US$8.50/6/3. Trains run daily, leaving Harare at 9.30 pm, stopping at Marondera, Rusape and Nyazura, arriving in Mutare at 6 am the next day. In the opposite direction, trains leave Mutare at 9 pm, arriving in Harare at 6 am the next day.

Bulawayo to Harare The 1st/2nd/3rd-class fares are US$15/9/5. Trains leave Bulawayo at 9 pm, stopping at Gweru, Kwe Kwe and Kadoma, arriving in Harare at 6.55 am the next day. From Harare, trains leave at 9 pm, arriving in Bulawayo at 7 am the next day.

Bulawayo to Victoria Falls The fares for 1st/2nd/3rd classes are US$15/9/5. Trains for Victoria Falls depart from Bulawayo at 7 pm, stopping at Dete (for Hwange National Park) and Hwange, arriving at 7 am the next day. From Victoria Falls, trains leave at 6.30 pm, arriving in Bulawayo at 7 am the next day.

Train de Luxe The 1902 *Train de Luxe* (☎ 09-75575, e railsaf@acacia.samara.co.zw) PO Box 2536, Bulawayo, offers luxurious train travel from Harare to Bulawayo, Victoria Falls and Jo'burg. There are three classes, the lowest of which isn't much different from 1st class on the state trains. Here though you're getting five-star service with all meals and some tours thrown in. The one-way fare in Ivory cabins, the mid-range choice, from Harare to Bulawayo/Victoria Falls is US$220/550.

CAR & MOTORCYCLE

Main roads are generally good for cars and motorcycles, but the latter aren't permitted in national parks.

Foreign-registered vehicles (including rentals) can be imported temporarily free of charge, and third-party insurance – albeit expensive – is available at the border if you're not already covered. Hire cars can be brought in with permission from the hire company, but at the border you'll need to secure a temporary export permit from the vehicle's home country and a temporary import permit for Zimbabwe. Ask the hire company to provide the relevant paperwork.

Use of seat belts is technically compulsory in the front seat and motorists must use headlights between 5.30 pm and 5.30 am every day of the year. If you see the presidential motorcade, identifiable by the accompanying police motorcycles with sirens and blue flashing lights, pull over and wait for it to pass before proceeding. In wildlife-oriented national parks you can't drive after sunset.

Speed traps operate in Zimbabwe, seemingly for no other purpose than as a tidy piece of revenue raising. Fines are reasonably inexpensive, but always be on your guard for a scam.

Petrol or 'blend' (petrol blended with sugar cane ethanol) can cost from around US$0.50 per litre.

Rental

Hiring a vehicle in Zimbabwe can be expensive, so if you're on a tight budget, you'll need to be part of a group to make it worthwhile.

All drivers must have a valid driving licence. The minimum driving age varies, but it's usually between 23 and 25 years. The maximum age is usually 65 years.

The larger companies will probably insist on a credit card as a deposit; smaller companies will most often accept a cash deposit.

With all rental agencies, collision damage waiver (CDW) insurance (normally with an excess of around US$500) of US$9 per day is charged on top of the hire rate and if you opt not to take it, you'll be responsible for all damage. Having said that, no CDW policy covers 2WD vehicles in Mana Pools or on remote gravel roads. For that, you'll have to hire a 4WD.

Zimbabwe has both the international and local rental agencies. When you're hiring from an unknown agency, read the fine print carefully before accepting a car. Vehicles may not be well maintained, and in the case of a breakdown, few provide rescue service or replacement vehicles. They may even try to charge for routine repairs.

For the cheapest Group A car (normally a Mazda 323 or similar), the big companies charge around US$28 per day plus US$0.25 per kilometre. If you hire for a longer period – normally more than five days – you'll pay US$55 per day with up to 250 or 300 free km. Smaller firms charge less, averaging US$20 per day plus US$0.20 per kilometre. Baby seats are available from bigger companies for US$5.50 per day.

The following are the main offices of some of the rental agencies in Zimbabwe:

Bright Eyes (☎ 013-5833) Jays Spar, 1st floor, Victoria Falls
Club Car Hire (☎/fax 020-62108, fax 60467) corner of Herbert Chitepo St and Fifth Ave, Mutare
Elite Car Rental (☎ 04-738325, fax 738327) 95 Belvedere Rd, Harare
Hertz (☎ 04-727209, fax 792794) 4 Park St, Harare
Parkend Cars (☎ 04-707632, fax 707635, @ parkend@harare.iafrica.com) 140 Samora Machal Ave (PO Box CY1118), Harare
Thrifty (☎ 04-736587, fax 746123) 10 Samora Machal Ave, Harare
Truck and Car Hire (☎/fax 04-721388) corner of Nelson Mandela and Fifth Sts, Harare

BICYCLE

Most major routes in Zimbabwe are surfaced and in excellent repair, and road shoulders are often sealed and separated from vehicular traffic by painted yellow lines, so they may be used as bicycle lanes. Although there are certainly rough hilly sections, the relatively level landscape over much of the country (including the cities) further facilitates long-distance cycling. Note, however, that bicycles are not permitted in wildlife parks. The predictable climate helps cyclists considerably.

The best cycle shops in Harare are: Zacks, on Kenneth Kaunda Ave opposite the train station; and Manica Cycles, nearby on Second Ave. Bicycle hire is available from most hostels.

HITCHING

Hitching is never entirely safe, and travellers who do hitch must realise that they're taking a small but potentially serious risk. However, many people do hitch, and the following advice should help to make their journeys as fast and safe as possible.

Hitching is relatively easy in Zimbabwe and is many locals' main means of transport. It also offers good opportunities to meet Zimbabweans, and many travellers consider hitching more reliable than public transport. To hitch a ride, don't use your thumb western or South Africa style – stick your hand out at a 45° angle from your body. Many drivers charge passengers, to help pay for fuel. Ask about charges before you climb in; the rate should never exceed the local bus fare.

Although it's best to hitch in pairs, it's possible for women to hitch alone if there are women and/or children in the car – it's not worth the risk of accepting a lift from a car full of men. It's also best to ascertain the driver's degree of sobriety; drink-driving is a serious problem in Zimbabwe, especially on weekends and public holidays. Hitching at night is not advisable, and hitching isn't permitted in national parks.

BOAT

Since Zimbabwe is a landlocked country, the only boats of consequence are the ferries on Lake Kariba between Kariba and

Binga or Mlibizi. They're handy especially if you want to do a circular tour of Zimbabwe without retracing your steps between Victoria Falls and Bulawayo.

The more popular and comfortable option is Kariba Ferries, whose two-car ferries each run twice weekly between Kariba and Mlibizi. The more basic DDF ferry connects Kariba with Binga and Gache Gache. The Binga ferry departs fortnightly and stops overnight in Chalala and Sengwa. There are also weekly runs to Tashinga and Gache Gache, For details on both ferries, see under Kariba in the Northern Zimbabwe section later in this chapter.

LOCAL TRANSPORT

Bus

In the cities, bus services connect the centre with suburban areas. Try to board at the terminus, otherwise it will be packed to overflowing. Once people are hanging out the windows and doors, the driver won't bother to stop to pick up more. Local bus fares are currently less than US$0.40.

Commuter Omnibuses

Minibuses called 'commuter omnibuses' serve city centres and suburbs, and some rural destinations. They originate at bus terminals or on city streets and can be flagged down by the roadside. Destinations are written on the pavement-facing back panel or in the windscreen, and they generally leave when full (officially they carry 15 but the conductors are adept at squeezing a few more bodies on). They are frequent and cheap but you can't take any luggage with you – and don't think you can squeeze it on your lap or under your seat because you're going to be uncomfortable enough without it.

Taxi

By anyone's standards, city and suburban taxis are inexpensive – generally less than US$2 anywhere in the city centres and US$4 to US$5 into the Harare or Bulawayo suburbs. Most legal taxis are metered, but drivers will often forego the meter and offer competitive fixed prices. If you think you're going to be overcharged, insist on using the meter. Unlicensed taxis aren't actually any cheaper than licensed taxis (they're constantly having to pay fines and bribes).

If you're out at night and need a taxi, ask the staff at your bar or restaurant to call you one. The taxi companies listed in this chapter are reputable and should be safe, but it does no harm to take some precautions – note the taxi's number plate and, especially at night, insist on being dropped right at your door.

ORGANISED TOURS

Tours of all sorts – bushwalking, rail tours, canoe and raft trips, sightseeing, wildlife viewing, birdwatching and even all-inclusive lounging around – are available from local tour operators and agencies. In many cases, to save money, it's advisable to book tours on the spot rather than in advance through an overseas agent, although if you're short of time the latter option can be more convenient. The companies listed below cover the whole country. Tours of specific areas are described in more detail in the relevant sections.

Black Rhino Safaris (☎/fax 09-41662, ⓔ blckrhino@hotmail.com) PO Box FM 89, Famona, Bulawayo. This group specialises in excellent day trips to Matobo National Park and longer trips to Mana Pools and Hwange National Parks from US$110 per person per day.

Khangela Safaris (☎ 09-49733, fax 68259, ⓔ scott@gatorzw.com) PO Box FM 296, Famona, Bulawayo. Khangela has walking, camping and wilderness trips through Chizarira, Hwange, Chimanimani, Matusadona and Gonarezhou national parks. You can take day walks from semipermanent base camps and trek through the wilderness for US$130 per day.

United Touring Company (UTC, ☎ 04-770623, fax 770643, ⓔ utczim@harare.iafrica.com) 4 Park St (PO Box 2914), Harare. With tentacles all over Africa, UTC runs a range of day trips in Harare, Kariba, Bulawayo, Hwange National Park and Victoria Falls.

Wildlife Adventures (☎ 04-490738, fax 498552, ⓔ wildlif@id.co.zw). This budget safari company specialises in mobile safaris with the maximum possible interest along the way. For US$595, it will take you on a round trip of Zimbabwe from Victoria Falls, taking in highlights such as Great Zimbabwe, Hwange, Chimanimani and Motopos. You can also join en route. The price includes transport, meals and activities.

Safari operators and lodges will have some kind of affiliation with a regulating body. The Zimbabwe Association of Tour and Safari Operators, the Zimbabwe Professional Hunters and Guides Association and Inbound Tour Operators of Zimbabwe (☎ 04-708878, fax 794015) PO Box 7240, Harare, can send you their member lists. If you have a complaint against an operator, these bodies will investigate it for you. The government-run contact is the Ministry of the Environment and Tourism, PO Box CY286, Causeway, Harare.

Harare

☎ 04

Harare (population 1.6 million) is the capital and heart of the nation in nearly every respect. Bequeathed a distinctly European flavour by its colonisers, it continues to be Zimbabwe's showpiece city and the country's commercial centre, with high-rise buildings, traffic and all the attendant bustle.

Chitungwiza, Harare's massive 'satellite' (though effectively a city in its own right), lies south of the airport. It is home to an additional one million people.

History

The first Shona inhabitants of the marshy flats near the Kopje called themselves Ne-Harawa after their regional chief, whose name meant 'the one who does not sleep'. The Mbare, under the rule of the lower Chief Mbare, controlled the Kopje. Later, another small clan led by Chief Gutsa settled in what is now Hillside, south-east of the city centre. When the inevitable clash came, it was Gutsa who emerged victorious; Chief Mbare was killed and his people were sent into the rugged north-western plateaus above the Zambezi Valley.

On 11 September 1890 another intruder arrived. The BSAC's Pioneer Column, led by Major Frank Johnson, saw Chief Gutsa's Kopje and decided it was ideal for agriculture and expropriation by the colonists. He even suggested to Leander Starr Jameson that the Kopje was destined to become the modern capital of the country they were founding.

The Union Jack was raised at what is now African Unity Square and the settlement was named Fort Salisbury, after the then British prime minister Robert Cecil, the Marquis of Salisbury. The next winter brought the first influx of white settlers from the south, arriving to collect on promises of fertile farm lands and gold claims along the Zambezi.

Salisbury was officially proclaimed a municipality in 1897 and was recognised as the colonial capital in 1923. In 1935 it was granted city status. It languished through WWII and the following decades of unrest, sanctions and war, but after gaining independence in 1980 it was made the capital of the new Republic of Zimbabwe and was renamed Harare, a mistransliteration of Ne-Harawa.

In recent years the city has seen riots spill on to its streets, but it remains a manageable and relatively safe city to visit.

Orientation

Central Harare is formed by the collision of two grids, and further confused by a one-way traffic system. On the main grid, stretching from Samora Machal Ave to Kenneth Kaunda Ave and from Fourth St to Julius Nyerere Way, streets run north-south, while avenues run east-west. On the Kopje grid, west of Julius Nyerere Way, streets run in both directions, except where they are extensions of avenues from the main grid.

The city is compact, making it a breeze to get around on foot. The trendy central shopping area is on the main grid. Cheaper shops and hotels and much of central Harare's nightlife are concentrated in the bustling Kopje area.

The rest of Harare sprawls outward in both high and low-density suburbs. The industrial area is in the south-western suburbs.

Construction in Harare continues despite the economic crises, and as newer, flashier premises become available, organisations (including those listed here) move. If this is the case, there's generally helpful security

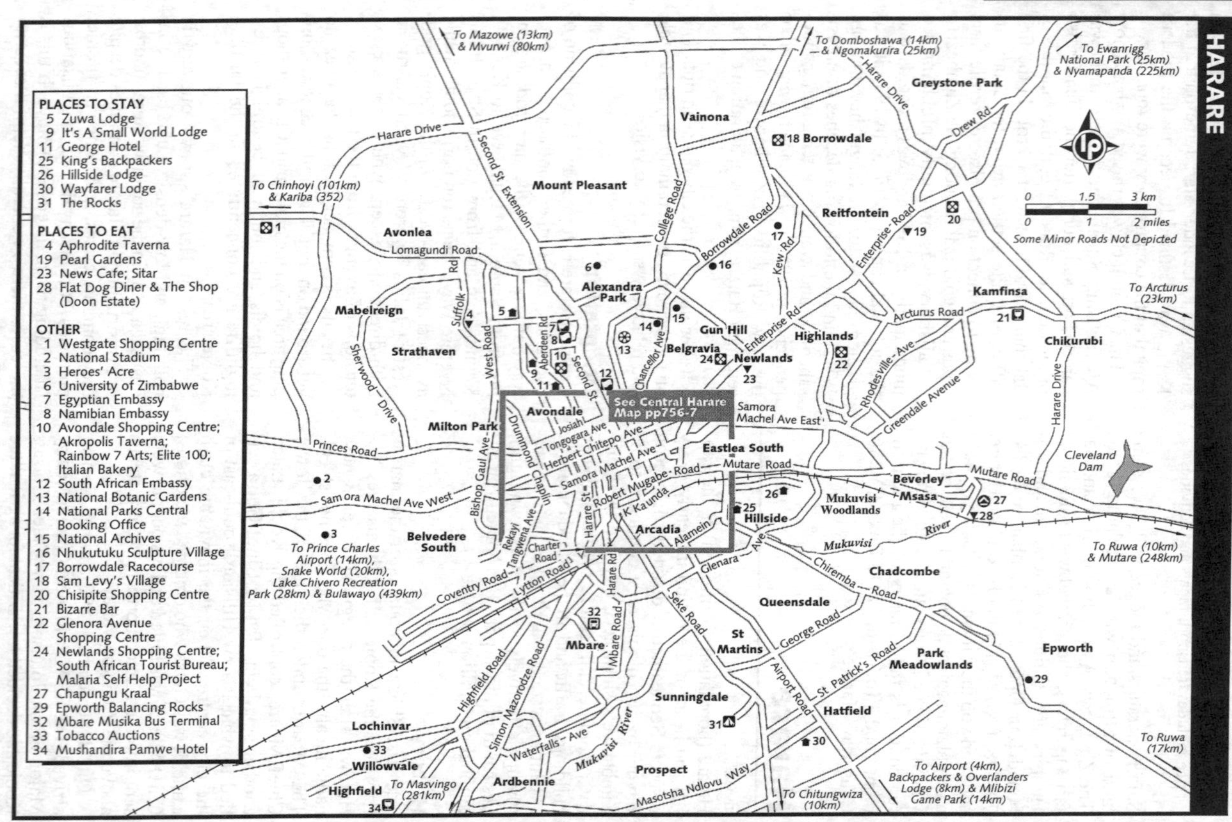
HARARE
PLACES TO STAY
5 Zuwa Lodge
9 It's A Small World Lodge
11 George Hotel
25 King's Backpackers
26 Hillside Lodge
30 Wayfarer Lodge
31 The Rocks
PLACES TO EAT
4 Aphrodite Taverna
19 Pearl Gardens
23 News Cafe; Sitar
28 Flat Dog Diner & The Shop (Doon Estate)
OTHER
1 Westgate Shopping Centre
2 National Stadium
3 Heroes' Acre
6 University of Zimbabwe
7 Egyptian Embassy
8 Namibian Embassy
10 Avondale Shopping Centre; Akropolis Taverna; Rainbow 7 Arts; Elite 100; Italian Bakery
12 South African Embassy
13 National Botanic Gardens
14 National Parks Central Booking Office
15 National Archives
16 Nhukutuku Sculpture Village
17 Borrowdale Racecourse
18 Sam Levy's Village
20 Chisipite Shopping Centre
21 Bizarre Bar
22 Glenora Avenue Shopping Centre
24 Newlands Shopping Centre; South African Tourist Bureau; Malaria Self Help Project
27 Chapungu Kraal
29 Epworth Balancing Rocks
32 Mbare Musika Bus Terminal
33 Tobacco Auctions
34 Mushandira Pamwe Hotel
0 1.5 3 km
0 1 2 miles
Some Minor Roads Not Depicted
See Central Harare Map pp756-7
To Mazowe (13km) & Mvurwi (80km)
To Domboshawa (14km) & Ngomakurira (25km)
To Ewanrigg National Park (25km) & Nyamapanda (225km)
To Chinhoyi (101km) & Kariba (352)
To Arcturus (23km)
To Prince Charles Airport (14km), Snake World (20km), Lake Chivero Recreation Park (28km) & Bulawayo (439km)
To Ruwa (10km) & Mutare (248km)
To Ruwa (17km)
To Airport (4km), Backpackers & Overlanders Lodge (8km) & Mlibizi Game Park (14km)
To Chitungwiza (10km)
To Masvingo (281km)
Greystone Park
Vainona
Borrowdale
Mount Pleasant
Reitfontein
Avonlea
Alexandra Park
Mabelreign
Kamfinsa
Gun Hill
Highlands
Chikurubi
Strathaven
Belgravia
Newlands
Milton Park
Avondale
Eastlea South
Cleveland Dam
Beverley
Msasa
Mukuvisi Woodlands
Belvedere South
Arcadia
Hillside
Chadcombe
Queensdale
Mbare
St Martins
Park Meadowlands
Epworth
Sunningdale
Hatfield
Lochinvar
Willowvale
Prospect
Ardbennie
Highfield
Harare Drive
Second St Extension
College Road
Borrowdale Road
Kew Rd
Enterprise Road
Drew Rd
Lomagundi Road
Suffolk Rd
Aberdeen Rd
Second St
Chancellor Ave
Enterprise Rd
Arcturus Road
Sherwood Drive
West Road
Rhodesville Ave
Greendale Avenue
Samora Machel Ave East
Josiah Tongogara Ave
Herbert Chitepo Ave
Samora Machel Ave
Drummond Chaplin
Princes Road
Bishop Gaul Ave
Mutare Road
Robert Mugabe Road
K Kaunda
Sam ora Machel Ave West
Harare St
Rekayi Tangwena Ave
Alamein
Charter Road
Coventry Road
Lytton Road
Harare Rd
Glenara Ave
Mukuvisi River
Chiremba Road
Seke Road
George Road
Mbare Road
Highfield Road
Simon Mazorodze Road
Airport Road
St Patrick's Road
Waterfalls Ave
Masotsha Ndlovu Way

guards around office building entrances who should be able to redirect you.

Harare International Airport is 15km south-east of the centre.

Maps The Publicity Association (see Information) sells the *Street Map of Harare*, an indexed large-scale map of the city centre and suburbs. The Surveyor General (☎ 794545), on the ground floor of Electra House, Samora Machal Ave, sells a good *Central Harare* map for US$2.50.

Information

Tourist Offices The Harare Publicity Association (☎ 705085) PO Box 1483, Causeway, Harare, is in African Unity Square. It's only marginally helpful, but it's worth picking up their monthly publication, *What's on in Harare* for US$0.15, as well as pamphlets and advertising about local attractions. It's open from 8 am to noon and 1 to 4 pm weekdays, 8 am to noon Saturday.

Nationwide information is more reliably obtained from the Zimbabwe Tourist Development Authority (☎ 793666, fax 758828) on the 9th floor of Kopje House, located at 1 Jason Moyo Ave.

You can pick up national parks information and make bookings at the National Parks Central Booking Office (☎ 706078) on Sandringham Dr, near the northern end of the National Botanic Gardens. It's open from 7.45 am to 4.45 pm weekdays.

Immigration Office You can pick up visa and length-of-stay extensions at the Department of Immigration Control (☎ 791913), 1st floor, Liquenda House, Nelson Mandela Ave (between First and Second Sts).

Money There are exchange desks at the airport (open for international arrivals), Roadport bus terminus and train station. There are bureaus de change and banks throughout the city.

Post & Communications The main post office is on Inez Terrace. Stamp sales and poste restante are upstairs in the arcade, while the parcel office is in a separate corridor downstairs. The poste restante and stamp-sales counters are open from 8.00 am to 4 pm weekdays and until 11.30 am on Saturday. You can also buy stamps on the ground floor between 4 and 5 pm weekdays.

There are several clean and functional telephone boxes in the First St Mall, and it's more pleasant to queue here than at the GPO. The public fax number is ☎ 731901.

Email & Internet Access Internet Village (☎ 732518), opposite the train station on the corner of Second St, has a good number of fairly speedy Internet terminals available for US$3 per ½ hour. It's open from 7 am to 10 pm daily. The Internet Cafe, next to the food court on the first floor of the Eastgate Centre, charges the same.

If those are busy, you can also try ClicNet Internet in Batani Gardens on the corner of First St and Jason Moyo Ave. It's open from 8 am to 8.30 pm Monday to Saturday and 2 to 6 pm Sunday.

Travel Agencies Thomas Cook and American Express are represented by Manica Travel (☎ 704012) in the Eastgate Centre.

Also located in the Eastgate Centre is the slightly more independent Wacko Travel Co (☎ 250210, ⓔ wacko@internet.co.zw).

For overland trips, international flights, adventure-safari bookings, adrenalin activities and information on inexpensive tours and transfers, visit Worldwide Adventure Travel (☎ 72092, fax 704794 ⓔ wwathre@internet.co.zw) on the third floor of the Travel Centre at 93 Jason Moyo Ave.

On the fifth floor of the Travel Centre, Safaris Incorporated (☎ 728255, fax 792932, ⓔ safaris@harare.iafrica.com) offers backpacker information and bookings.

Bookshops Kingston's has the best selection. Its outlets are in the Parkade Centre, which is on First St between Samora Machal and Union Aves, and on the corner of Second St and Jason Moyo Ave. For used books, check out Treasure Trove at 26C Second St, which is an Ali Baba's cave full of second-hand books, used clothing and sports and camping gear.

The bookshop attached to the Book Cafe (see Places to Eat later in this section) has a great selection of African literature and reference material.

Photography Strachan's Photo Chemist at 66 Nelson Mandela Ave, near Second St, does one-hour photo processing and sells a range of film, including slide film. Film and processing services are also available at Photo Inn outlets throughout the city.

Camping Equipment Limited camping equipment, including butane Camping 'gaz' canisters, is available at Fereday & Sons, on Robert Mugabe Rd.

Laundry If you're too nice to unleash your crusty jocks and smelly socks on the staff at your hostel or hotel, the coin-operated Fife Avenue Laundrette, in the Fife Avenue shopping centre, is open daily.

Left Luggage Most hostels will let you leave your gear with them while you're off on safari. If you're only in town for a day and want somewhere to dump your stuff, try the train station. Alternatively, ask the guys at Safaris Incorporated, on the fifth floor of the Travel Centre at 93 Jason Moyo Ave, to look after it for you.

Medical Services Parirenyatwa is the main and most central hospital. Hostels and hotels will be able to recommend a doctor should you need one. Night pharmacies are listed in the *Herald*.

Emergency For nonemergency police calls, dial ☎ 733033. The Medical Air Rescue Service (MARS) number is ☎ 737086.

Dangers & Annoyances The city has countered an alarming increase in violent crime by drastically increasing its police force and posting officers on virtually every street corner. There are still problems – especially in quieter areas around the avenues and the crowds of Mbare – but things have vastly improved. However, never walk around the city at night and only use official taxis.

Warning

Be aware that Chancellor Ave (a short stretch of the street known in the city as Seventh St and further out as Borrowdale Rd) is the site of the Executive President's residence and the State House. It's off limits and barricaded between 6 pm and 6 am. Don't wander in there between these hours; the guards are under orders to fire without questioning.

National Archives

Founded in 1935 by the Rhodesian government, the National Archives is the repository for the history of both Rhodesia and modern Zimbabwe. It has colonial artefacts and photos, accounts of early explorers and settlers and a display on the Second Chimurenga. It's open 8.30 am to 4 pm weekdays and 8 am to noon on Saturday; entry is free.

Take the Borrowdale or Domboshawa bus from the Market Square terminal. The archives, 3km from the city on Ruth Taylor Rd, are well signposted from Borrowdale Rd.

Zimbabwe Museum of Human Sciences

The best thing about this small and easily digestible history of life and rocks in Zimbabwe is the appealing concrete chameleon, praying mantis, pangolin and snail standing guard out front. Although not as good as its Bulawayo counterpart, the fossils and dioramas are well done and worth an hour or so. Zimbabwean adults/children pay US$0.15/0.10, while foreigners pay US$2/1.

The museum (☎ 751797) in the Civic Centre complex between Pennefather Ave and Raleigh St is open from 9 am to 5 pm daily, except public holidays.

National Gallery of Zimbabwe

This collection is the final word on art and culture from around the continent. Founded in 1957 around a core of works by European artists, it's been augmented by an African sculptors' workshop. The small indoor sculpture exhibit and crowded outdoor sculpture garden showcase some of the genre's best work. On the ground floor are drawings and paintings from Europe and the late colonial and post-colonial eras. On the first floor is a vibrant display of earthy African art and cultural material, a storehouse of insight into tradition, religion and mythology.

The gallery on the south-eastern side of Harare Gardens is open from 9 am to 5 pm Tuesday to Sunday. Entry is US$0.40/0.10/free for adults/students/under 12s, and free for all on Sunday.

Harare Gardens

Harare Gardens, the city's largest park, is a popular picnic spot and a haven from the city bustle just a block to the south. It's also a live-music venue and home to Harare's Theatre in the Park, a small crafts market, and Sherrol's in the Park (see Places to Eat later in this section) – a favourite spot for watching couples posing for photos. While you're in the gardens look for the island-like stand of rainforest with its miniature Victoria Falls and Zambezi Gorge, complete with Zambezi Bridge. At Christmas time there are also lights and nursery characters to get you in the festive spirit.There's no cycling allowed and despite its peaceful atmosphere, Harare Gardens is notorious for crime. Avoid short-cutting through here at night and watch your belongings carefully by day.

The Kopje

Rising above the south-western corner of central Harare is the Kopje. This granite hill was once Chief Mbare's capital, and at its foot pioneers first set up their businesses. Access to the summit, where the Eternal Flame of Independence was lit on 18 April 1980, is from Skipper Hoste Drive and Rotten Row. Unfortunately, the Kopje is no longer the safest place to walk, even by day, so don't climb it alone or carry valuables here.

National Botanic Gardens

The 58-hectare National Botanic Gardens contain examples of the diverse flowers and greenery that thrive in Harare's pleasant climate. Most Zimbabwean species are represented, as are specimens from elsewhere, and it's a great place for relaxing, birdwatching and spending a day losing yourself.

The gardens are open daily between sunrise and sunset. Entry is free. Take a north-bound bus along Second St Extension and get off at Downie Ave, from where the gardens are signposted.

Historic Buildings

Many colonial buildings remain on Robert Mugabe Ave. For background on Harare's colonial architecture, look out for a copy of *Historical Buildings of Harare* by Peter Jackson.

The **market hall**, built in 1893, is at the Market Square bus terminus near the corner of Bank and Mbuya Nehanda Sts. It has been renovated and still serves as a market.

Parliament, on the corner of Nelson Mandela Ave and Third St, was originally conceived as a hotel in 1895, but was commandeered for army barracks. It has undergone several renovations – in 1969 it grew to six storeys – but is still used by the Senate and Legislative Assembly for official proceedings. For a guided tour, or to sit in on sessions, apply to the Chief Information Officer (☎ 700181), Parliament of Zimbabwe, PO Box 8055, Causeway.

The **Town House** on Julius Nyerere Way, near the main post office, dates back to 1933 and serves as Harare's town hall. This primarily Italian Renaissance-style structure houses the mayoral, city council and town clerk's offices. The centrepiece of the gardens is a colourful floral clock. Also check out the Coca-Cola clock on the house tower. For a look around the interior, make an appointment by calling ☎ 706536.

Mukuvisi Woodlands

The nearest thing to a zoo in Harare is Mukuvisi Woodlands (☎ 747152), a 265-hectare woodland reserve 7km east of the city. Of the total area, 156 hectares are natural msasa parkland for picnics, walking and birdwatching. The remaining area is a game park where antelope, zebra, giraffe and warthog roam free.

It's open from 7 am to 5 pm daily. Entry costs US$2.15/0.50 for adults/children. Guided one-hour foot safaris at 2.30 pm on weekends cost US$2/1 for adults/children. You can also explore from the (dis)comfort of a walking horse at 8.30 am and 3 pm daily. There's a coffee shop, craft shop and braai facilities.

Mukuvisi Woodlands is a 20-minute walk from Coronation Park along Glenara Ave South. From the city centre, take the Msasa bus from Market Square or the Greendale bus from the Rezende St terminus, and ask to get off as near to Mukuvisi as possible.

Chapungu Kraal

The Chapungu Kraal and Shona village (☎ 486648) at Doon Estate, 1 Harrow Rd, Beverley East, Msasa, is an attempt to create a cultural theme park for tourists. Sculptural displays are accessible in a half-hour guided tour, which leads you through the motivation behind the granite, jasper and verdite works of Zimbabwe's most renowned artists. It's open from 8 am to 6 pm daily and entry is US$0.50. The sculpture garden and weekend African dance performances are also worth seeing. There's a tea garden here, but it's worth detouring to the Flat Dog Diner next door (see Places to Eat, later in this chapter).

Take the Greendale bus from the Rezende St terminus to Coronation Park, then walk east on Mutare Rd past the Beverley shopping centre and Chicken Inn. Turn right into the industrial area and after a sharp right turn, pass through the security gate at the Sorbaire sign.

Heroes' Acre

On a hill overlooking Harare, the dominating obelisk of Heroes' Acre serves as a monument to the ZIPRA and ZANLA forces (see the History section at the start of this chapter) who died during the Second Chimurenga. Among other heroes entombed here are Joshua Nkomo and Mugabe's first wife. Apply for a visitor's permit from the Ministry of Information, Liquenda House, Nelson Mandela Ave which, if you're a foreigner, will normally be issued immediately.

Heroes' Acre lies 5km from the city centre, off the Bulawayo Rd. Catch the Warren Park bus from the terminus just west of Chinhoyi St along Samora Machal Ave. Entry and guided tours are free.

Tobacco Auctions

Zimbabwe is one of the world's largest producers of tobacco, a large foreign-exchange earner, and Harare serves as the tobacco-trading centre of Southern Africa. The world's largest tobacco auction floor, on Gleneagles Rd in Willowvale, 8km from the centre, holds daily sales between April and October (depending on the harvest) from 8 am to noon. Take the Highfields bus from the Fourth St bus terminus.

Mbare

Mbare, 5km from the centre, is probably the only Harare suburb worth visiting in its own right. Activity centres on the Mbare musika, Zimbabwe's largest market and busiest bus terminal. Between 6 am and 6 pm it hums constantly with shoppers, travellers and traders. Being so busy, it's not a great idea to come here alone. And you should definitely leave your valuables at home.

Shoppers can find everything from second-hand clothing and appliances to herbal remedies, African crafts and jewellery. Fresh fruit and vegetables can be bought at a fraction of supermarket prices.

To get there, take a taxi or any Mbare-bound bus.

Special Events

Harare hosts a few festivals and cultural events. These include an Arts Festival (April), Zimbabwe International Book Fair (late July/early August), Zimbabwe Agricultural Society Show (August) and an International Film Festival (September). Check the press and advertising around town for details.

Music lovers will enjoy the annual Houses of Stone Music Festival, a celebration of traditional Zimbabwean music. Contact the Kunzwana Trust at 3 Maxwell Rd, Groombridge, for dates and information.

Activities

The Olympic-sized Les Brown **swimming** pool, between Harare Gardens and Crowne Plaza Hotel, is open from 10 am to 6.30 pm daily. Entry is US$0.30/0.15 (adults/children) and you must have proper swimwear – there's not that many women here. Alternatively, there's **Water Whirld**, with water slides and an artificial beach, 2km east of the centre on Samora Machal Ave. Both pools advertise dance parties in the press.

There are seven **golf** courses around Harare, including the internationally acclaimed Royal Harare Golf Club on Josiah Tongogara Ave, just north of the city centre.

Organised Tours

Several companies operate Harare-area day tours, including museums and historical buildings, as well as trips outside the city.

Tour companies include Jacaranda Tours and Travel (☎ 019-346142, fax 758779) Roadport; Lisma Tours and Safaris (☎/fax 727339) 3rd floor, Kodak House, 86 Samora Machal Ave; and United Touring Company (UTC, ☎ 770623, fax 770641) at 4 Park St. Additionally, most accommodation will operate tours in line with their clientele's tastes and budgets.

Places to Stay – Budget

The ***Possum Lodge*** *(☎ 726851, fax 722803, e possum@zol.co.zw, 7 Deary Ave)* is perfect if you're flying into Harare, as it offers free airport pick ups. Amenities include meals, a tiny pool, a TV lounge and a largish outdoor bar with pool tables and table tennis. It's a pleasant 20-minute walk from the centre through Harare Gardens, but don't walk through at night. Camping costs US$3 per person, dorms US$5 and doubles US$12.

Hillside Lodge *(☎ 747961, e hillside91@hotmail.com, 71 Hillside Rd),* in an old colonial home surrounded by jacarandas, has a pool, cooking facilities (breakfast is available), email and Internet access and a sociable bar. Singles/doubles cost US$8/11, dorm beds/mattresses are US$4.30/4, camping in the large garden costs US$2.70, and there's even tree houses for US$11. Bike hire is US$5 per day. They will pay for a taxi to get you there or you can take the Msasa, Tafara or Mabvuku bus from the corner of Speke Ave and Julius Nyerere Way. Get off at the Children's Home and cross the train tracks and turn left into Hillside Rd.

Still in Hillside, ***King's Backpackers*** *(☎ 743552, e kingsbackpack@hotmail.com, 1 Dean Simmons Ave)* is a small, clean and cosy place with swimming pool, lounges and cooking facilities. Dorms/doubles cost US$4/10 and camping in the well-tended garden costs US$2.

Between Eighth and Ninth Sts, the ***Sable Lodge*** *(☎ 726017, 95 Selous Ave)* is friendly, clean and central. Guests have access to cooking facilities and the pool is nice to laze around. Camping costs US$3.30, dorms cost US$3.50 and doubles are US$15.

The pleasant ***Wayfarers' Lodge*** *(☎ 572 125, e wayfarer@icon.co.zw, 47 Jesmond Rd, Hatfield)* is out of town, but has free transfers from the GPO (3.30 pm daily) and airport. Camping costs US$3, dorms US$5 and double-thatched chalets US$6/12. It has cooking facilities, but also offers meals, TV, swimming pool, bar area and safe boxes.

The Cosmic Gap *(☎ 011-204209, 20 Vincent Ave, Belvedere)* has been repeatedly recommended and can be booked through Safaris Incorporated *(☎ 728255, fax 792 932, e safaris@harare.iafrica.com)* on the 5th floor of the Travel Centre. For US$7 you have access to a swimming pool, bar, pool table and TV room.

The Rocks *(☎/fax 576371, e rocks@icon.co.zw, 18 Seke Rd)*, an overlanders stop (it's a good place to connect with trucks to Malawi or Kenya), is set in 2.5 hectares of bushland. Camping costs US$3 (tents are available for hire), basic dorms are US$4 and doubles cost US$12. The place revolves around an immense outdoor bar where there's always someone to drink with. From the Mobil station on the corner of Robson Manyika Ave and Julius Nyerere Way, take a Hatfield minibus, or the Zengeza or St Mary's bus from the Angwa St terminus. The Rocks is a five-minute walk from Seke Rd.

A potentially interesting option available to women only is ***Bromley House*** *(☎ 724 072, 182 Herbert Chitepo Ave)*. This place caters mainly to young Zimbabwean women working in the city and charges US$7, including meals.

Near Harare International Airport South of the Ruwa crossing is ***Backpackers & Overlanders*** *(☎ 5074115, 932 Delport Rd)*,

CENTRAL HARARE

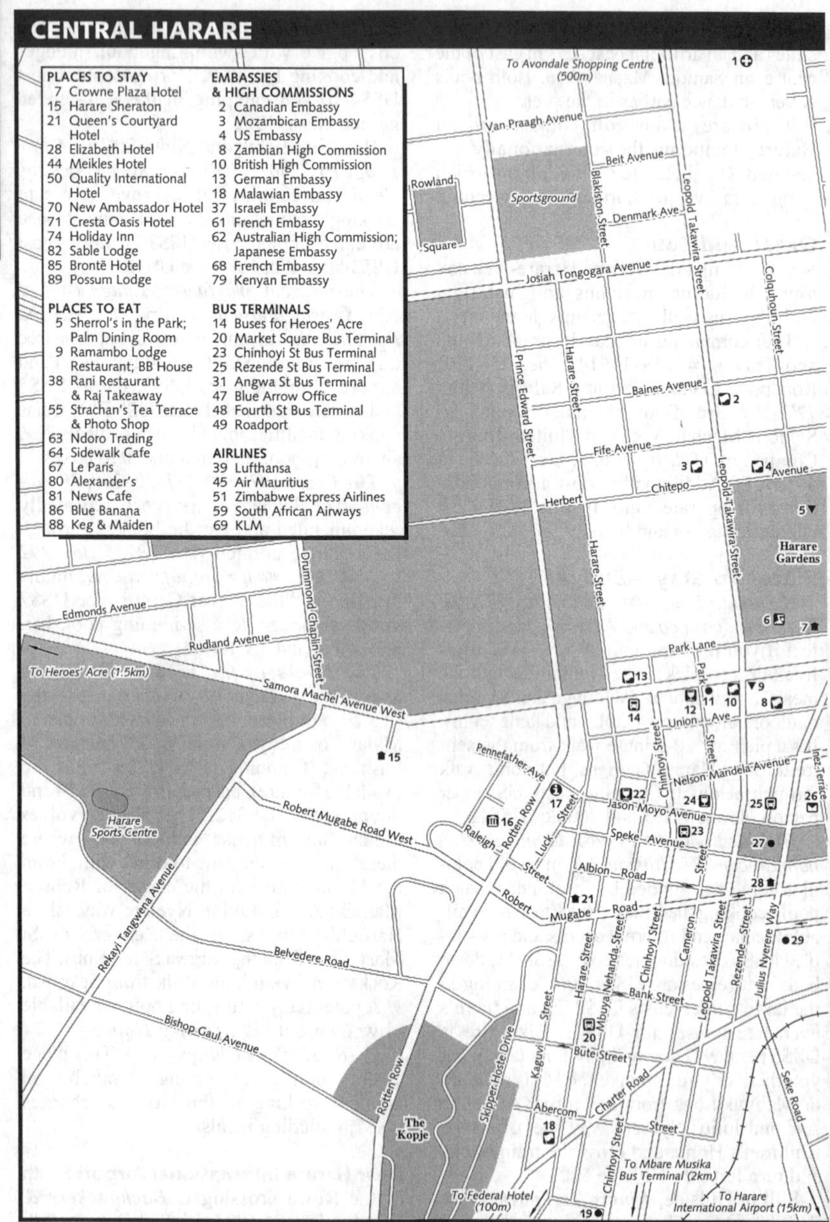
PLACES TO STAY
7 Crowne Plaza Hotel
15 Harare Sheraton
21 Queen's Courtyard Hotel
28 Elizabeth Hotel
44 Meikles Hotel
50 Quality International Hotel
70 New Ambassador Hotel
71 Cresta Oasis Hotel
74 Holiday Inn
82 Sable Lodge
85 Brontë Hotel
89 Possum Lodge
PLACES TO EAT
5 Sherrol's in the Park; Palm Dining Room
9 Ramambo Lodge Restaurant; BB House
38 Rani Restaurant & Raj Takeaway
55 Strachan's Tea Terrace & Photo Shop
63 Ndoro Trading
64 Sidewalk Cafe
67 Le Paris
80 Alexander's
81 News Cafe
86 Blue Banana
88 Keg & Maiden
EMBASSIES & HIGH COMMISSIONS
2 Canadian Embassy
3 Mozambican Embassy
4 US Embassy
8 Zambian High Commission
10 British High Commission
13 German Embassy
18 Malawian Embassy
37 Israeli Embassy
61 French Embassy
62 Australian High Commission; Japanese Embassy
68 French Embassy
79 Kenyan Embassy
BUS TERMINALS
14 Buses for Heroes' Acre
20 Market Square Bus Terminal
23 Chinhoyi St Bus Terminal
25 Rezende St Bus Terminal
31 Angwa St Bus Terminal
47 Blue Arrow Office
48 Fourth St Bus Terminal
49 Roadport
AIRLINES
39 Lufthansa
45 Air Mauritius
51 Zimbabwe Express Airlines
59 South African Airways
69 KLM
To Avondale Shopping Centre (500m)
Van Praagh Avenue
Beit Avenue
Rowland Square
Sportsground
Blakiston Street
Denmark Ave
Leopold Takawira Street
Josiah Tongogara Avenue
Colquhoun Street
Prince Edward Street
Harare Street
Baines Avenue
Fife Avenue
Chitepo Avenue
Herbert
Harare Gardens
Drummond Chaplin Street
Edmonds Avenue
Rudland Avenue
Park Lane
To Heroes' Acre (1.5km)
Samora Machel Avenue West
Park Street
Union Ave
Chinhoyi Street
Inez Terrace
Nelson Mandela Avenue
Pennefather Ave
Jason Moyo Avenue
Robert Mugabe Road West
Raleigh Street
Rotten Row
Luck Street
Speke Avenue
Albion Road
Robert Mugabe Road
Harare Sports Centre
Rekayi Tangwena Avenue
Belvedere Road
Mbuya Nehanda Street
Cameron Street
Rezende Street
Julius Nyerere Way
Bank Street
Bishop Gaul Avenue
Kaguvi Street
Skipper Hoste Drive
Bute Street
Charter Road
Seke Road
Abercorn Street
The Kopje
To Mbare Musika Bus Terminal (2km)
To Federal Hotel (100m)
To Harare International Airport (15km)

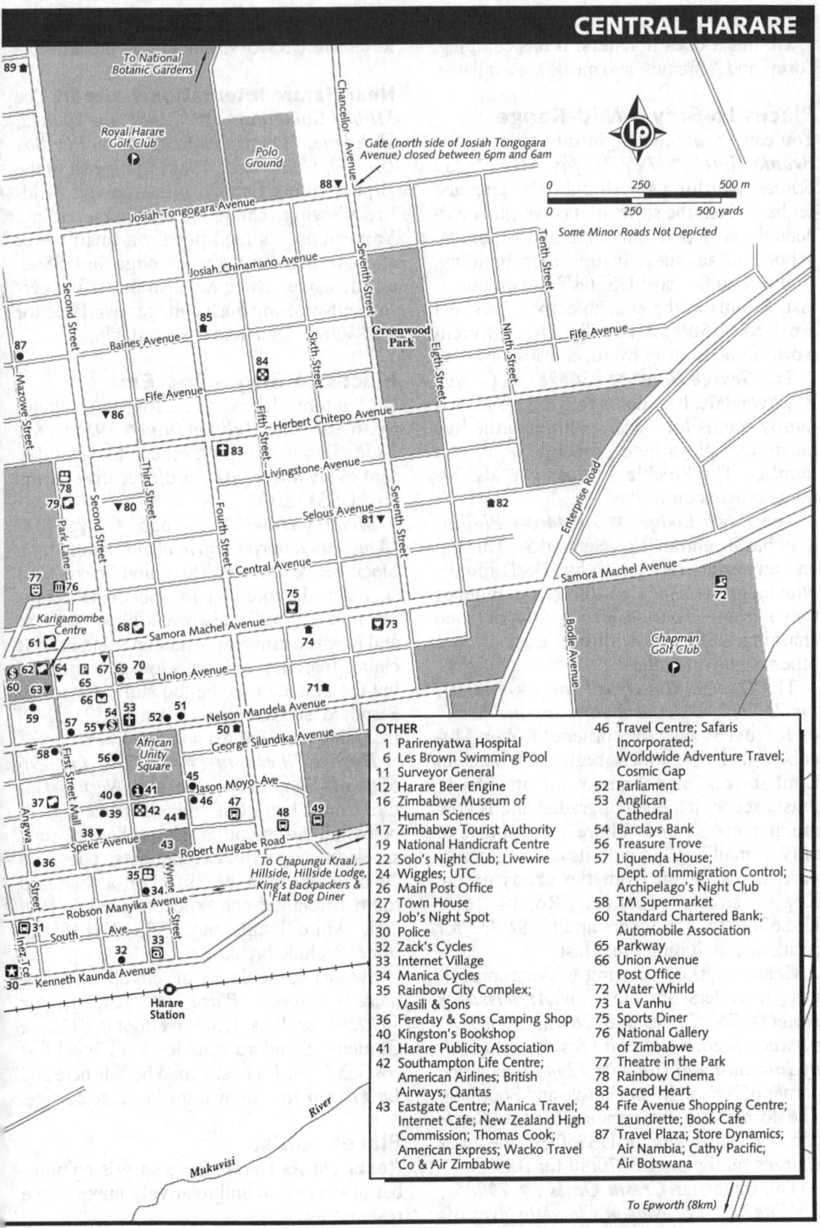
CENTRAL HARARE
To National Botanic Gardens
Royal Harare Golf Club
Polo Ground
Gate (north side of Josiah Tongogara Avenue) closed between 6pm and 6am
0 250 500 m
0 250 500 yards
Some Minor Roads Not Depicted
Chancellor Avenue
Josiah Tongogara Avenue
Josiah Chinamano Avenue
Seventh Street
Tenth Street
Second Street
Greenwood Park
Baines Avenue
Fife Avenue
Sixth Street
Eigth Street
Ninth Street
Mazowe Street
Fifth Street
Herbert Chitepo Avenue
Livingstone Avenue
Third Street
Enterprise Road
Selous Avenue
Park Lane
Fourth Street
Central Avenue
Samora Machel Avenue
Karigamombe Centre
Union Avenue
Bodle Avenue
Chapman Golf Club
Nelson Mandela Avenue
George Silundika Avenue
African Unity Square
Jason Moyo Ave
First Street Mall
Angwa Street
Speke Avenue
Robert Mugabe Road
To Chapungu Kraal, Hillside, Hillside Lodge, King's Backpackers & Flat Dog Diner
Wynne Street
Robson Manyika Avenue
South Ave
Inez Tce
Kenneth Kaunda Avenue
Harare Station
Mukuvisi River
To Epworth (8km)
OTHER
1 Parirenyatwa Hospital
6 Les Brown Swimming Pool
11 Surveyor General
12 Harare Beer Engine
16 Zimbabwe Museum of Human Sciences
17 Zimbabwe Tourist Authority
19 National Handicraft Centre
22 Solo's Night Club; Livewire
24 Wiggles; UTC
26 Main Post Office
27 Town House
29 Job's Night Spot
30 Police
32 Zack's Cycles
33 Internet Village
34 Manica Cycles
35 Rainbow City Complex; Vasili & Sons
36 Fereday & Sons Camping Shop
40 Kingston's Bookshop
41 Harare Publicity Association
42 Southampton Life Centre; American Airlines; British Airways; Qantas
43 Eastgate Centre; Manica Travel; Internet Cafe; New Zealand High Commission; Thomas Cook; American Express; Wacko Travel Co & Air Zimbabwe
46 Travel Centre; Safaris Incorporated; Worldwide Adventure Travel; Cosmic Gap
52 Parliament
53 Anglican Cathedral
54 Barclays Bank
56 Treasure Trove
57 Liquenda House; Dept. of Immigration Control; Archipelago's Night Club
58 TM Supermarket
60 Standard Chartered Bank; Automobile Association
65 Parkway
66 Union Avenue Post Office
72 Water Whirld
73 La Vanhu
75 Sports Diner
76 National Gallery of Zimbabwe
77 Theatre in the Park
78 Rainbow Cinema
83 Sacred Heart
84 Fife Avenue Shopping Centre; Laundrette; Book Cafe
87 Travel Plaza; Store Dynamics; Air Nambia; Cathy Pacific; Air Botswana

known for its partying. It's a long way from town, but it does transfers. It has camping, dorms and A-frames, and meals are available.

Places to Stay – Mid-Range

You can't beat the delightfully olde-worlde ***Brontë Hotel*** *(☎ 796631, fax 721429, 132 Baines Ave)* for a splash-out. It's clean and set back from the street in its own quiet gardens. It has a pool and a bar and is popular – book in advance. In the main building, singles/doubles cost US$68/88, with breakfast. Rooms in the annexe across the street are US$48.50/66. It really is a different world in here, drop by for a drink or meal.

The ***George Hotel*** *(☎ 336678)* on George Rd, Avondale, has rooms for US$23/32, and family rooms for US$51, although the live music that plays here probably won't suit families. The Freckle & Phart pub also attracts crowds on Friday.

The ***Zuwa Lodge*** *(☎ 705446, 9 Phillips Ave)* has its entrance on Second St. This big and airy converted house has B&B rooms, with bathrooms for US$40/65 (minimum of two nights). There's also a budget zone charging US$15/35 with breakfast; it does other meals on request.

The ***Queens Courtyard Inn*** *(☎ 759508, fax 759382, @ qcourt@africaonline.co.zw)* on Kaguvi St, near the corner of Robert Mugabe Rd, is the oldest registered hotel in Zimbabwe. Once known for its rowdy music scene, it's been upgraded and is now much more serene. There's no pool and only a small bar, but with its covered courtyard it's a haven from the chaos of the Kopje streets outside. Rooms cost US$63/83 for foreigners and US$27/32 for residents, including breakfast.

Central options catering to African business travellers are the ***New Ambassador Hotel*** *(☎ 708121, fax 708126)* on Union Ave, between Second and Third Sts and the ***Quality International Hotel*** *(☎ 729439)*, near the corner of Nelson Mandela Ave and Fourth St. The former has the popular ***Bird & Bottle*** carvery, and rooms for US$60/80; the latter charges foreigners US$70/80 for B&B.

The three-star ***Cresta Oasis*** *(☎ 790861, fax 704217, 124 Nelson Mandela Ave)* offers high standards and a quiet location. Rates are US$75/95, including breakfast.

Near Harare International Airport The ***Mlibizi Game Park*** *(☎ 572886, fax 700812, @ johnpar@mbizizim.icon.co.zw, PO Box UA 358, Union Ave)*, 10km south-east of the airport, offers fishing, birdwatching, wildlife viewing, canoeing and horse riding. You can use its facilities for a small fee or stay overnight in the main lodge for US$90, all inclusive. There are also three/five person self-catering bush cottages available for US$40/80. Transfers are available.

Places to Stay – Top End

On Samora Machal Ave between Fifth and Sixth Sts is the ***Holiday Inn*** *(☎ 795611, fax 735695)*, which is pretty much like Holiday Inns everywhere. Standard/executive rooms cost US$128/133.

Meikles Hotel *(☎ 795655, fax 707754, @ meikles@harare.iafrica.com)* taking up a block between Jason Moyo and Speke Aves served as the foreign correspondents' watering hole during Zimbabwe's liberation war and boasts a range of restaurants and bars. It claims five stars and caters to high standards, but the attitude may be too stuffy for some. Standard singles/doubles are US$210/240, including morning tea and breakfast.

Harare Sheraton *(☎ 729771, fax 796 678)* off Samora Machal Ave West is Harare's most luxurious and expensive digs. It boasts all the amenities: shops, hairdressers, snack bars, gourmet restaurants, pubs and 24-hour Internet access. For a standard room, foreigners can expect to pay US$190/205, while locals pay US$120/135; all prices include breakfast.

Size-wise, the daddy of 'em all is the immense ***Crowne Plaza*** *(☎ 704501, fax 791920)*, on Park Lane overlooking Harare Gardens. Standard doubles with breakfast cost US$196. There are good buffets here and ***La Francaise*** is known for its haute cuisine.

Places to Eat

Restaurants Harare has a surprising number of very good and relatively inexpensive restaurants.

The Book Cafe *(☎ 728191)* at the Fife Avenue shopping centre is a great place to relax over a drink or delicious home-cooked food. Open from 10 am to 10.30 pm daily, it's fully licensed and most nights has a theme. Wednesday is Africa night, with appropriate food and music, and on Saturday afternoon it has jazz and blues. The cafe has Internet access and the attached bookshop has a good range of African literature and nonfiction.

Flat Dog Diner *(☎ 480883, 5 Harrow Rd)* has good pub grub, with seafood a specialty. It serves 28g of prawns for US$4 on Wednesday and Saturday night. You can sit in the lush garden, on the veranda or on colourful indoor seating. Combine it with a visit to the Chapungu Kraal next door.

Perhaps in emulation of Nairobi's renowned Carnivore restaurant, the ***Ramambo Lodge Restaurant*** *(☎ 775334, fax 775334)* serves a spread of wild game dishes, from impala and warthog to ostrich steak. If that's not your bag, they also do 'normal' dishes. As you'd expect, the decor reflects the 'safari lodge' theme, and you can almost forget you're in Harare. Lunches are backed by a marimba band and dinner is accompanied by a 'traditional dance cabaret', including a very traditional song about telephones. You'll find it upstairs in BB House, on the corner of Samora Machal Ave and Leopold Takawira St. It's open daily for lunch and dinner.

The Keg & Maiden at the Harare Sports Club is in an unbeatable location overlooking the cricket oval. Chain-steakhouse-type food is served with a 'choice of starch'. It's a bit overpriced, but it does have vegetarian choices. Smart casual dress is a good idea.

The Newlands shopping centre has a branch of the South African ***News Cafe*** chain, which serves up a delicious range of cuisines from noodles to pasta. ***Alexander's*** *(☎ 700340, 7 Livingstone Ave)* serves fairly high-priced continental cuisine, but many say it's the best in town.

The ***Rani Restaurant*** and ***Raj Takeaway*** *(☎ 729242, 56 Speke Ave)* does Mughlai and tandoori dishes. If you don't go to them, the ***Sitar Restaurant*** *(☎ 746215, 39A Newlands shopping centre)* will deliver curry to you.

Pearl Gardens *(☎ 495199)* on Enterprise Rd serves excellent Chinese food under bright lights. Aromatic Thai food is available at the ***Blue Banana*** *(☎ 702613, 109 Fife Ave)* between Second and Third Sts.

Breakfast, Lunch & Snacks Many backpacker hostels serve breakfast for a small fee. Extravagant buffet breakfasts and lunches at the big hotels (usually included with accommodation) will satisfy for most of the day.

If you can't face anything until you've had a decent coffee, try ***Vasili & Sons*** with outlets in the Rainbow City complex, Robert Mugabe Rd and Newlands shopping centre; it also does some fine pastries and breakfast. Other options are ***Ndoro Trading*** *(Unity Court, First St)* or the ***Italian Bakery*** in the Avondale shopping centre.

Le Paris on Samora Machal Ave, near Second St, serves great full breakfasts for US$4, while ***Strachan's Tea Terrace*** *(66 Nelson Mandela Ave)* serves the same or a healthy muesli, yoghurt and fresh juice breakfast from Monday to Saturday. Strachan's also serves home-baked muffins, baguettes, quiche, cakes and scones on a pleasant shaded terrace.

The ***Sidewalk Cafe*** on First St is central, with pavement seating and breakfasts, burgers, chicken, salads, sweets and vegetarian dishes. It's open from 8.30 am to 8 pm Monday to Saturday and until 4.30 pm Sunday.

If you want to sit in the sun, drink coffee and spend a couple of hours writing postcards or people watching, go to the laid-back ***Sherrol's in the Park*** *(☎ 725535)* in Harare Gardens, which serves excellent light lunches (salads, toasted sandwiches and pies) daily. The attached Palm Dining Room serves Mediterranean lunches from Tuesday to Friday, and dinner from Tuesday to Saturday.

Other outdoor seating can be found at ***Cafe Afrique*** by the Cresta Oasis Hotel's pool. It offers a diverse range of dishes in its indoor buffet, but you can eat from the outdoor braai for half the price.

Around the city centre you'll find takeaways selling chips, burgers, 'samoosas', soft drinks and other fast fare as well as the usual motley crew of fastfood chains. If you're after cheap and filling fast food or African fare, the takeaways in the Kopje grid are good value.

Self-Catering There are TM and OK supermarkets across the city, including a ***TM supermarket*** on Nelson Mandela Ave between First and Angwa Sts. The supermarket at the Fife Ave shopping centre is open until 6.30 pm Monday to Saturday and until 11.30 am Sunday. Vendors around the town and the bus terminals sell fruit and vegetables.

Deliveries If you're too lazy to go out, Dial-a-Delivery *(☎ 336336)* will deliver orders from Harare restaurants between noon and 9 pm. Your hostel or hotel should also be able to provide you with menus and numbers for pizzas etc. The delivery person's white shirt and bow tie are a nice touch.

Entertainment

Harare is great for African music – both live and disco – as well as music catering to European and American tastes. For information on upcoming events, check the daily listings in the *Herald* and billboards around town.

Most pubs, hotel bars and nightclubs are open during lunch (and onwards) as well as in the evenings when conservative and 'smart casual' dress rules may apply. Remember – don't walk to, or from, any of these late-night spots after dark; take a taxi right to your door.

Bars & Clubs All hotels have a bar of some description. Some are pretty good and popular. The ***Harare Beer Engine*** at the Jameson Hotel brews its own beer. You can see the workings of the brewery and sample its products. If you miss the golden days of empire, check out the ***Explorers' Club*** at Meikles Hotel.

The ***New Horizon Cafe*** on Julius Nyerere Way is a good place to meet the local Rastafarian crowd, as is the ***Book Cafe***. Hostels such as the ***Possum Lodge*** and ***The Rocks*** have popular bars, which are good places to hook up with other travellers before setting out into the night. The ***Bizzare Bar*** out in Kamfinsa is popular with young Rhodeys out to have some wacky fun.

Archipelago's at Liquenda House, on Nelson Mandela Ave, rocks until the early hours most nights. ***Solo's***, on the corner of Jason Moyo Ave and Harare St, is in a converted synagogue, which makes for a beer-hall atmosphere. There's also a shaded beer garden with a braai and stage, although it sometimes has to compete with the ragamuffin beats pumping out of ***Livewire*** next door.

The dance scene has (kind of) arrived in Harare. Places to try for a bit of doof are ***Wiggles*** on the corner of Jason Moyo and Park Sts, and ***La Vanhu*** on Samora Machal Ave.

Amambo Cultural Tours and Safaris (☎ 7773882, ⓔ wamambo@telconet.co.zw) offers those who would otherwise be stuck alone the opportunity to paint Harare red with guided night trips to see local performers.

Live Music Lots of people interested in local music want to attend a *pungwe*. There's usually a big-name play every couple of months – look around the Kopje for advertising.

The best places to catch local bands are the ***George***, ***Quality International*** or ***Elizabeth*** hotels on Friday and Saturday night. You do get the occasional dud, but sometimes a well-known name may drop by for a session. They're good places to meet and party with locals. The ***Nyagonzera Skyline Motel*** *(☎ 67588)*, at the 19km mark along the Beatrice-Masvingo road, also attracts superb talent, but as it's not serviced by public transport at night it's a long and expensive taxi ride to get there.

For a better chance at hearing such greats as the Bhundu Boys, Thomas Mapfumo & the Blacks Unlimited or Ilanga, try weekend gigs at ***Job's Night Spot*** in the Wonder Shopping Centre on Julius Nyerere Way between Kenneth Kaunda and Robson Manyika Aves.

Star Studio at the Sheraton, and the ***Sports Diner*** *(134 Samora Machal Ave)* have live acts (such as Andy Brown) during the week. For the more intrepid, the three nightclubs in Highfields – ***Machipisa***, ***Club Saratoga*** and the ***Mushandira Pamwe Hotel*** – have live bands on weekends and at least one should be offering something of interest.

Cinemas In the afternoon and evening, Harare cinemas run screenings of regional and US films. Cinemas include the ***Rainbow*** chain *(☎ 705901)*, with theatres on Park Lane and Robert Mugabe Rd, between Second and Third Sts, and the ***Elite 100*** *(☎ 339995)* at the Avondale shopping centre. The entry price averages around US$1.30. Check the daily *Herald* or call for listings.

Theatre Harare doesn't have much in the way of theatre, although touring companies do visit; for information check the *Herald*.

The ***Theatre in the Park*** *(☎/fax 774945, ⓔ theatreinthepark@mango.zw)* in Harare Gardens showcases local and touring drama. The rondavel-styled hut makes for some intimate theatre. Tickets can usually be bought at Ndoro Trading on First St. Look for advertising around town or as you're passing the gardens. Student and pensioner discounts apply.

The ***Rainbow 7 Arts*** *(☎ 302772)* theatre in Avondale is a popular live venue for comedians such as Edgar Langeveldt, whose political satire is merciless and hugely popular.

Spectator Sports

Sporting events are held regularly at the National Stadium, west of the city off the Bulawayo road. On weekends, horse racing is at the track in the 'mink and manure' suburb of Borrowdale. Check the *Herald* for details.

Shopping

Harare is packed with shops and galleries selling gifts, curios and souvenirs. While these shops are convenient, they're not the cheapest, and similar or superior items can be found at informal markets and outlets.

For real works of art, particularly Shona sculpture, the National Gallery and several commercial galleries offer a variety of names and prices. Stone Dynamics at Travel Plaza, 29 Mazowe St, specialises in serpentine and verdite works by older, established artists. Vhikutiwa Gallery, 2km north of town on the corner of Harvey Brown Ave and Blakiston St, has sculptures by well-known and new artists. Matombo Gallery at 114 Leopold Takawira St emphasises big names, but also devotes space to emerging talent.

If you're after something a bit more inspired (and pricey) visit the National Handicraft Centre on the corner of Grant and Chinhoyi Sts in Kopje. It offers musical instruments, crafts and textiles. It's open from 9.30 am to 5 pm daily. There's a restaurant and tea garden where you can sample traditional food.

There are shopping malls in most Harare suburbs, all following the same formula with shops, cinemas, restaurants, delis etc, but Sam Levy's, in Borrowdale, goes one better and features English-style bobbies.

Getting There & Away

Air Air Zimbabwe and Zimbabwe Express Airlines have daily services between Harare and Bulawayo, Kariba, Hwange National Park and Victoria Falls. These depart and arrive at Harare international airport, 15km south-east of the centre. Charter flights and light aircraft operate out of Charles Prince airport, 18km west of Harare.

Main airline offices in Harare include:

Air Botswana (☎ 733836) Travel Plaza, 29 Mazowe St
Air Mauritius (☎ 735738) 13th floor, Old Mutual Centre, corner Third St and Jason Moyo Ave
Air Namibia (☎ 729835) Travel Plaza, 29 Mazowe St
Air Zimbabwe (☎ 794481, fax 796039) 2nd floor, Red Tower, Eastgate Centre
American Airlines (☎ 733071) 8th floor, Southampton Life Centre, 77 Jason Moyo Ave
British Airways (☎ 747400, fax 575140) 5th floor, Southampton Life Centre, 77 Jason Moyo Ave
Cathay Pacific (☎ 732091) Travel Plaza, 29 Mazowe St
KLM (☎ 705690) 1st floor, Finsure House, corner Union Ave and 2nd St
Lufthansa (☎ 793861) 99 Jason Moyo Ave
Qantas (☎ 751228) 5th floor, Southampton Life Centre, 77 Jason Moyo Ave
South African Airways (☎ 738922) 2nd floor, Takura House, 69-71 Union Ave
Swissair (☎ 704411) Travel Plaza, 29 Mazowe St
Zimbabwe Express Airlines (☎ 705923, ⓔ zexpro@samara.co.zw) Kurima House, 89 Nelson Mandela Ave

Bus The Roadport (☎ 702828) on Fifth St, between Jason Moyo and Robert Mugabe, has representatives from Greyhound, Express Motorways, Trans-Zambezi and Munorurama, and there's room for more. Most cross-border bus services originate/terminate here; there's a foreign exchange bureau on site.

Blue Arrow (☎ 729514, fax 729572), at Chester House, Speke Ave, connects Harare and Bulawayo (US$18). Services run at least once daily, travelling either via Chivhu (six hours) or Kwe Kwe (6¼ hours). On Wednesday, Friday and Sunday it also has services to Mutare (US$11, 4¼ hours).

Express Motorways (☎ 720392, fax 737438) has daily services to Mutare (US$12.50) and Bulawayo (US$21). The booking office and terminal are at the Roadport.

Shoestring Shuttle (☎ 691966) has a 6 am departure for Bulawayo (US$11) and Victoria Falls (US$20) on Saturday, returning 6 am on Sunday. It picks up and drops off at all backpacker hostels.

Sabi Star runs transfers to Troutbeck and Great Zimbabwe from the Holiday Inn for US$21.

Long-distance African buses depart from the Mbare musika in Mbare township, 5km from the centre. There are signs at the terminal indicating destinations. Buses are grouped according to which road they'll be taking out of the city, and most leave hourly for towns throughout the country. You can catch Mutare buses either from Mbare, or Msasa on the Mutare road.

ZUPCO buses leave Mbare for Bulawayo at 8 am and Beitbridge at 7 pm.

For information on international buses from Harare, see the Getting There & Away section of this chapter.

Train The train station is on the corner of Kenneth Kaunda Ave and Second St. Daily trains run to Bulawayo at 9 pm and Mutare at 9.30 pm.

The reservations and ticket office (☎ 786 034) is open from 7 am to 4 pm and from 7 pm to 9.30 pm weekdays, 7 am to 11.30 am and 7 pm to 9.30 pm Saturday, and 6 am to 8 am and 7 pm to 9.30 pm Sunday and public holidays.

Getting Around

To/From the Airport Motorways Express (☎ 573827) has hourly transfers between the city and Harare International Airport. A taxi will cost US$8. The top-end hotels – Meikles, Sheraton, Crowne Plaza and so on – send courtesy vehicles for their guests.

There are no hotel booking facilities at the airport, but there are usually touts waiting for backpackers and currency exchange facilities open whenever international flights arrive.

Bus Harare city buses and commuter minibuses get very crowded. If you're heading out to the suburbs or Mbare, catch them at one of the five central city bus terminals. Theoretically, you can flag them down, but your chances of squeezing on – or even inspiring a driver to stop for you – are inversely proportional to the number of stops you are from the terminus. Fares start at US$0.30.

The five central terminals are Market Square terminus, between Harare and Mbuya Nehanda Sts; Fourth St terminus, on Robert Mugabe Rd between Fourth and Fifth Sts; Angwa St terminus, on the corner of Angwa St and Robson Manyika Ave; Rezende St terminus, on Rezende St between Jason Moyo and Nelson Mandela Aves; Chinhoyi St terminus, on Speke Ave between Cameron and Chinhoyi Sts.

Taxi Taxi stands are found on the corner of First St and Nelson Mandela Ave, on Samora Machal Ave near First St, on Union Ave between Angwa St and Julius Nyerere Way, and in front of large hotels. Official services include Rixi Taxi (☎ 753080), A1 (☎ 703334) and Creamline Taxis (☎ 703333).

Travelling to/from anywhere in the city centre costs from US$1 to US$2, and to the suburbs costs from US$2 to US$3.

AROUND HARARE

Epworth Balancing Rocks

Although there are better examples of balancing rocks all over Zimbabwe, those at Epworth, a mission and former squatter camp 13km south-east of Harare, are probably the most famous. The main attraction is the group known as the Bank Notes, which were catapulted to rock stardom by being featured on Zimbabwe's paper currency.

To get there, take the Epworth bus from the Fourth St terminus and get off at Munyuki shopping centre or the turn-off to Epworth Primary School. From the latter, it's 500m to the park entrance.

Ewanrigg National Park

This small national park, 40km north-east of Harare, consists of an elaborate 40-hectare botanical garden and 200 hectares of woodland. The garden is characterised by an array of prehistoric-looking aloes, cacti and palm-like cycads, and during winter the slopes glow with the brilliant red and yellow blooms of the succulents and the variegated hues of tropical flowers. There's also a stand of bamboo, a herb garden, water garden and arboretum.

Eerily quiet during the week, it's a very popular spot with the Harare crowd on sunny weekends when they come out in droves for picnics, braais, cricket, football and strolls. Entry is US$5 per person.

Take the Shamva bus from Mbare as early in the morning as possible and get off at the Ewanrigg turn-off. It's a 3km walk to the gardens from there.

HARARE TO LAKE CHIVERO

☎ 04

Snake World, 24km from Harare on the Bulawayo road, is a kitsch collection of serpentine sorts. There are harmless varieties as well as baddies such as spitting cobras, gaboon vipers, puff adders, cobras and mambas. It's open from 8.30 am to 5 pm daily.

The **Lion & Cheetah Park** (☎ 27564), Norton, sits on a private estate 24km from Harare off the Bulawayo road. It's the only place in the area where you can see big cats, and it also boasts baboon, crocodile, giraffe, elephant and even a 250-year-old tortoise. It's open from 8 am to 5 pm daily. Walking or hitching is not permitted.

All Bulawayo-bound buses pass these places (see also Organised Tours earlier in this section).

LAKE CHIVERO RECREATIONAL PARK

This 5500-hectare park, 32km south-west of Harare, focuses on the 57-sq-km Lake Chivero (formerly Lake McIlwaine), a reservoir created by the 1952 damming of the Manyame (Hunyani) River. Lake Chivero is all the rage with Harare day-trippers, who love to spend their weekends fishing, boating, partying and braai-ing on its shores.

On the busy northern shore, the **Admiral's Cabin** (☎ 062-27144) has picnic sites and a snack bar. It charges a small entry to the shoreline and has boat and canoe hire.

The **Larvon Bird Garden** (☎ 27564) has over 400 bird species and is useful for familiarising yourself with native species. Larger birds are allowed to roam while waterfowl enjoy the lake. It's open from 9.30 am to 5 pm weekdays and 9 am to 5 pm weekends.

The quieter southern shore is dominated by the 1600-hectare **Chivaro Game Park**, where antelope, zebra, giraffe, and even a couple of well-protected white rhino may be observed. There are also several impressive **rock paintings**. Bushman's Point, at the end of the southern shore drive, has a designated picnic site and walking area within the park. Foreigners pay US$5 for day use and 1½ hour ranger-guided horse safaris cost US$20 per person.

Places to Stay & Eat

Camping is available on the northern shore at the ***National Parks camping ground***, which has a pool and sites with baths, showers, toilets and braai pits. Rates for National Park accommodation include: two-, four- and five-bed lodges for US$12/14.50/18.50; and camping (six people) for US$12. For more details, see under Accommodation in the Facts for the Visitor section earlier in this chapter.

On the southern shore, the ***National Parks rest camp*** has chalets and lodges. Camping isn't permitted. The gates to both the park and the rest camp are locked between 6 pm and 6 am.

Getting There & Away

From Mbare, there's a daily bus to the northern shore. Otherwise, buses run frequently out to the Bulawayo road from where you can get within striking distance of the lake.

Hitchhikers will find it easiest to access the park from the north via Oatlands Rd.

Another route turns off the Bulawayo road at the Shell Turnpike petrol station, 5km north of the Manyame bridge. From there it's just 3km over the ridge to the Hunyani Hills Hotel.

The southern shore isn't connected by road to the northern shore. To get there, take the left turn-off from the Bulawayo road immediately south-west of the Manyame bridge.

To get to the National Park rest camp or Bushman's Point you must pass through the game park, where walking and hitching are prohibited.

DOMBOSHAWA & NGOMAKURIRA

Even without its ancient rock paintings, the Chinamora communal lands would be worthy of a visit just for its scenic value. The stark and colourful lichen-covered domes that characterise the region are intriguing, and there's plenty of walking and rock scrambling opportunities.

Because it's nearer to Harare, Domboshawa is the better-known site. A small museum at the car park has general information and speculation about these Chinamora sites. From there, a well-marked 15-minute walk takes you to **Domboshawa Caves**, where the paintings are concentrated. The site is open until 5 pm; entry costs US$5.

Ngomakurira (Mountain of Drums), is best seen in the afternoon. It's generally agreed that Ngomakurira offers the finest, easily accessible rock paintings in Zimbabwe.

The Chinamora area is also packed with numerous other paintings. For further information and directions to the more obscure sites, see *The Painted Caves* by Peter Garlake.

For Domboshawa, take the city bus from the stop in front of Kingston's Bookshop, opposite African Unity Square, or from along Seventh St. Alternatively, you can get the Bindura via Chinamora bus from Mbare and get off at the turn-off 4km north of Domboshawa village (30km north of Harare), then walk the remaining 1km to the base of the rock. The Bindura bus continues on to the Sasa road turn-off, 2km west of Ngomakurira.

Northern Zimbabwe

Along with eastern Lake Kariba and Mana Pools National Park, the beautiful country north of Harare offers several little-visited gems such as the Mavuradonha Wilderness, the Umfurudzi Safari Area, the middle Zambezi Valley and the sculptors' community at Tengenenge Farm.

Prehistoric rock paintings indicate that north-eastern Zimbabwe has been inhabited for millennia. In the mid-1500s, Fura, a small mountain now known as Mt Darwin, was taken by early Portuguese arrivals to be a corruption of Ophir, and for several centuries Europeans speculated that the Empire of Monomatapa guarded the biblical land of Ophir and the elusive mines of King Solomon. The British who arrived in the late 19th century settled this area because they believed it to be rich in minerals and precious metals.

Later, it attracted others – the defeated Chief Mbare who had ruled from a kopje at present-day Harare, and the charismatic Shona outlaw Mapondera, who died in prison on a hunger strike in 1904 after admitting defeat in his attempts to resist colonial rule.

KARIBA

☎ 061

The name of this impromptu-looking town is derived from *kariwa*, the Shona word for trap. It was originally applied to Kariba Gorge, into which the Zambezi waters were sucked as if into a drainpipe. Now that they're trapped by the dam wall, the metaphor continues to apply and Kariba has also become a trap for tourists.

The Curse of Kariba

For a long time the Batonka (Tonga) people of western Kariba, who are believed to have migrated from Lake Malawi during the 15th or 16th century, lived in a naturally protected enclave below the Zambezi Escarpment. Superimposed international boundaries inflicted the first blow to their culture, but it was the damming of the Zambezi to form Lake Kariba that drove the deepest wound. As construction began, the Tonga called upon Nyaminyami, the fish-headed and serpent-tailed River Zambezi god, to intervene.

Did the god deliver? Well, he had to be annoyed – his wife was trapped on the other side of the dam. On Christmas Eve 1955 the river rose dramatically, sweeping away a pontoon bridge and swamping the cofferdam foundations. Soon after, scorching temperatures stifled work and slowed progress to a crawl. In July 1957 a torrential storm on the upper Zambezi sent floodwaters roaring through the work site, once more damaging the cofferdam. The following March there was yet another climatic anomaly – a once-in-1000-years flood was unleashed, again destroying the cofferdam and destroying a suspension bridge. (In all, 86 project workers died during construction, including those buried alive in wet concrete who remain entombed within the dam wall.)

In 1958 Nyaminyami relented and the project was completed, the waters began to rise over the valleys and 50,000 displaced – and justifiably disgruntled – Tonga were resettled on higher ground.

No sooner had the lake begun to fill than the destructive Kariba weed *(Salvinia molesta)* began choking the lake's surface. Imported amphibious South American grasshoppers countered the problem. However, difficulties continued. In the early 1990s a drought caused water levels to drop so low that there wasn't enough to generate power for both Zimbabwe and Zambia. The rains returned and the lake is now at a reasonable level, but with another dam proposed at Batoka Gorge, it remains to be seen whether the frustrated Nyaminyami will rise in wrath again.

Most Zimbabweans regard Kariba as paradise on earth – it's their greatest watery playground – but in reality this unconsolidated jumble is of little interest. If you can't manage a visit to Matusadona National Park or join the 'beautiful people' at play, don't spend too much time here.

Orientation

Kariba's three-dimensional sprawl leaves people wondering exactly where the town is. In fact, it stretches over 10km of lakeshore between the airport and the Zambian border, and also up the mountain to the cooler and more prestigious Kariba Heights, which disappears into the clouds 600m above the shore.

Information

The Kariba Publicity Association (☎ 2814) at the Kariba Dam Observation Point building can't really help with much, but it does have some Zimbabwe-wide information and good displays on the building of the dam and Operation Noah, the government-sponsored relocation of the area's fauna.

The only bank in town is the Barclays branch in Kariba Heights, although there is a useful ATM at the Total petrol station. Thankfully, there's a post office in Mahombekombe, which saves you the trek up to the one at the Heights.

Kariba Dam Wall

On 17 May 1960, with Britain's Queen Mother officiating, the switch was flipped on the first Kariba generator. Until Egypt's Aswan High Dam was completed in 1971, Kariba was Africa's largest hydroelectric project. The rising waters eventually covered 5200 sq km and held a capacity of 186 billion cubic metres of water.

To visit the Kariba Dam wall, leave your passport at the Zimbabwe immigration and walk onto the hulking concrete mass, which vibrates to the rhythm of the generators that power most of Zimbabwe and Zambia.

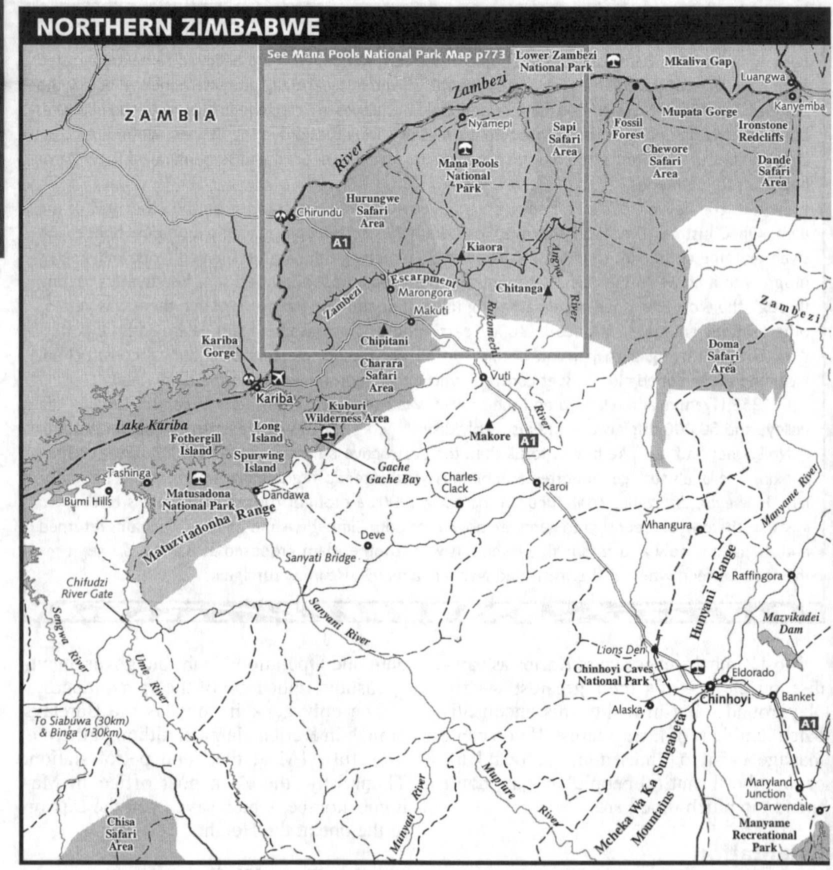

The best view is from the observation point, a short walk uphill from the Shell station, where the Publicity Association has displays with information on the building of the dam, the area and its inhabitants, and on Operation Noah.

Church of Santa Barbara

The small circular Church of Santa Barbara, in Kariba Heights, is dedicated to the patron saint of Italian military engineers, as well as the Virgin Mary and St Joseph (the patron saint of carpenters). Workers from the Italian company that built Kariba Dam built the church in memory of 86 colleagues who died during construction of the dam. A stone plaque lists their names. The open, circular shape of the building represents a cofferdam.

Operation Noah Monument

The rising lake waters caused problems not only for the Tonga people but also for animals trapped on intermediate islands threatened with inundation by the rising Kariba waters.

Word of the crisis prompted the Rhodesian government to assign Rupert Fothergill and a team of 57 wildlife personnel to effect

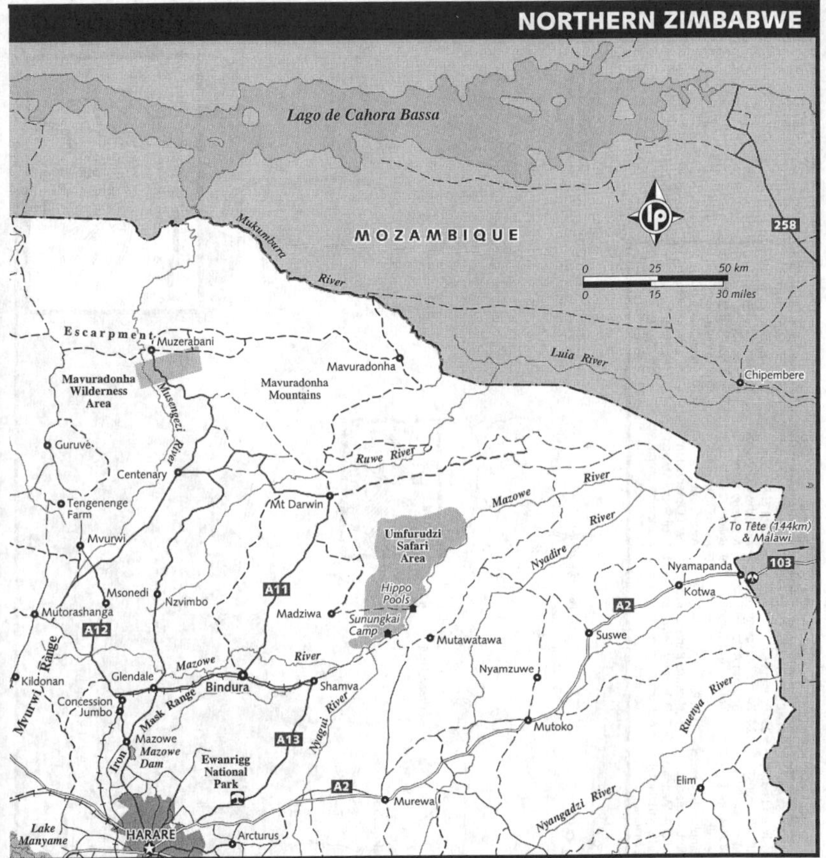

a rescue project. They worked throughout the dry season – from March to December, 1959 – tracking, trapping and relocating over 5000 creatures of at least 35 species, including reptiles (even black mambas!) and small mammals, as well as lion and rhino. The project, dubbed Operation Noah, resulted in artificially dense concentrations of game on the southern shore, particularly at Matusadona National Park. A monument to Operation Noah has been erected at the lake viewpoint in Kariba Heights and the Publicity Association has an interesting display about it.

Boat Charter & Rental

The easiest, least expensive and most straightforward way of cruising on the lake is to hire a boat from the Kariba Breezes Hotel Marina (☎ 2475). A boat for five costs US$18/24.50 for a half/full day, plus fuel (about the same again). The boat comes complete with a driver who should be able to find you a good wildlife viewing spot.

Sail Safaris (☎ 04-339123, fax 339045, @ sailsafaris.co.zw), based at the Cutty Sark, offers a day's sailing on a 9m catamaran for US$25, including lunch. You can lay back and relax or learn a few sailing

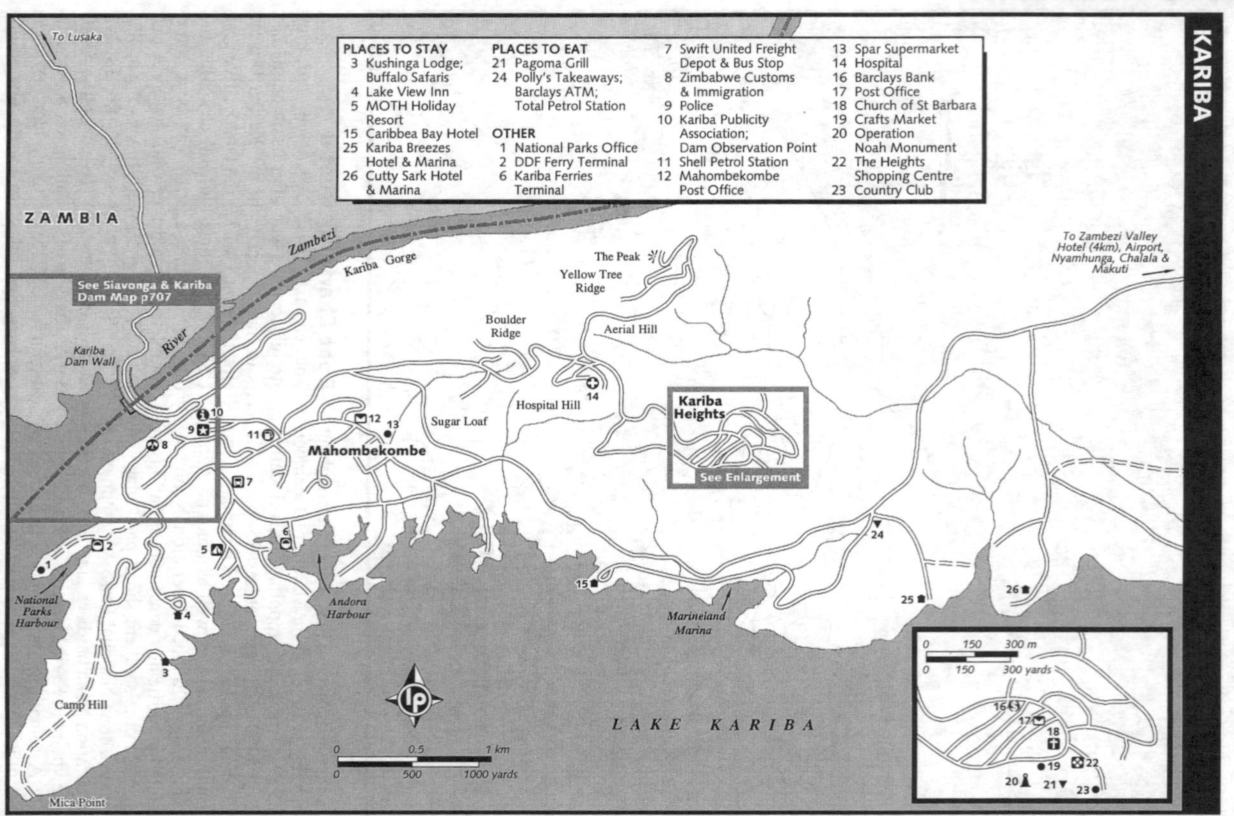
KARIBA
PLACES TO STAY
3 Kushinga Lodge; Buffalo Safaris
4 Lake View Inn
5 MOTH Holiday Resort
15 Caribbea Bay Hotel
25 Kariba Breezes Hotel & Marina
26 Cutty Sark Hotel & Marina
PLACES TO EAT
21 Pagoma Grill
24 Polly's Takeaways; Barclays ATM; Total Petrol Station
OTHER
1 National Parks Office
2 DDF Ferry Terminal
6 Kariba Ferries Terminal
7 Swift United Freight Depot & Bus Stop
8 Zimbabwe Customs & Immigration
9 Police
10 Kariba Publicity Association; Dam Observation Point
11 Shell Petrol Station
12 Mahombekombe Post Office
13 Spar Supermarket
14 Hospital
16 Barclays Bank
17 Post Office
18 Church of St Barbara
19 Crafts Market
20 Operation Noah Monument
22 The Heights Shopping Centre
23 Country Club
To Lusaka
ZAMBIA
Zambezi
River
Kariba Gorge
See Siavonga & Kariba Dam Map p707
Kariba Dam Wall
The Peak
Yellow Tree Ridge
Boulder Ridge
Aerial Hill
Hospital Hill
Sugar Loaf
Mahombekombe
Kariba Heights
See Enlargement
To Zambezi Valley Hotel (4km), Airport, Nyamhunga, Chalala & Makuti
National Parks Harbour
Andora Harbour
Marineland Marina
Camp Hill
Mica Point
LAKE KARIBA
0 0.5 1 km
0 500 1000 yards
0 150 300 m
0 150 300 yards

skills. All-inclusive seven-day hire for four/six persons starts at US$2730/1825.

Organised Tours

Town tours (US$11) with UTC (☎ 2453) PO Box 93, Kariba, depart at 10.30 am from the Cutty Sark Hotel, with pick-ups at Caribbea Bay Hotel and Lake View Inn. Morning or evening wildlife drives in the Charara Safari Area cost US$20.

Simpsons Cruises (☎ 2308) runs day/overnight tours to Matusadona for US$125/150 per person.

Places to Stay – Budget

The most popular place is the convenient ***MOTH Holiday Resort*** *(☎ 2809, PO Box 67)*, a 20-minutes walk from Mahombekombe township. Camping costs US$1 per person in your own tent, or US$1.20 in pre-erected tents. Doubles are US$4 and furnished six-person chalets with cooking facilities are US$10. It also sells braai packs and firewood, and has laundry services and a small reading library. For tents and chalets, bookings are essential during weekends and school holidays; advise them if you're arriving after 6.30 pm.

The friendly ***Kushinga Lodge*** *(☎ 2645, fax 2827, @ buffalo@kariba.harare.iafrica.com)*, near the shore at the western end of town, is a bit remote but it has a pool, bar, and breakfast and dinner braais. Backpacker A-frames are US$12.50 and double self-catering rondavels right on the lake shore are US$27. Camp sites are also available for US$6.

Places to Stay – Mid-Range

The clean, friendly and inexpensive ***Kariba Breezes Hotel*** *(☎ 2433, fax 2767)* is the best mid-range choice, and it's constantly being upgraded. Singles/doubles cost US$45/80, with breakfast. Backpackers also get to stay here, for US$7 per person. If you don't have transport, this is probably the best option – it's got a boat jetty, restaurant, swimming pool and a good lake frontage for wildlife spotting.

The ***Cutty Sark Hotel*** *(☎ 2321, fax 4417, @ indmar@harare.iafrica.com)* at Mopani Bay affords a good view of distant hills. It's a little way out of town, but it's quieter for it. Budget doubles are US$20 while standard/deluxe doubles are US$50/67. There is a plethora of travel agencies, a foreign exchange, wildlife to be spotted and nightly performances of traditional dance. It also offers the option of a lakeside bush dinner for US$13 per person.

The ***Zambezi Valley (ZV) Hotel*** *(☎/fax 2926)*, in Nyamhunga township near the airport, is the opposite of quiet. If you're looking for African-style action and disco music, this is the place. Rooms cost US$18/30, including breakfast.

Places to Stay – Top End

The upmarket hotel here is the ***Caribbea Bay Hotel*** *(☎ 2453, fax 2765)*, which gets nearly as noisy as the ZV Hotel, but here the boozing is Rhodey-style. This sparkling monument to pseudo-Mexican stucco architecture, with its beach, palm trees, tennis courts and casino, fancies itself as being in a faraway tropical paradise. Nonresidents pay US$90/114 for a single/double, with breakfast. A main draw for many is the casino. Monte Carlo or Las Vegas it's not, but it's just as efficient at taking your money. Smart casual dress is strictly enforced.

The ***Lake View Inn*** *(☎ 2411, fax 2413)* offers average accommodation and, as its name would imply, a glorious view of the lake. Nonresidents pay US$79/88, with breakfast.

Places to Eat

The ***Lake View*** offers a pick-up service for those dining in its restaurant – ask your accommodation to give them a call. It has set three-course dinners for US$10 or a la carte for around US$5.50. As the name suggests, you dine on a terrace overlooking the lake.

Pagoma Grill *(☎ 2894)* in Kariba Heights serves up light snacks and grilled dinners in a tasteful setting. If you've made the trek up here, it's well worth enjoying a nice cold beer while savouring the view from its terrace.

A good bet is ***Polly's Takeaways***, at the turn-off to the Kariba Breezes Hotel, where you can eat your burger, pastie, chips, chicken, pizza or ice cream on a shady terrace with lake views.

Hotel dining rooms generally charge in proportion to their room rates. The ***Cutty Sark*** does a good buffet breakfast and it also offers candlelight safari dinners with traditional music and dancing on the lakeshore for US$13 (minimum five people).

For self-catering, there's the ***Spar*** in Mahombekombe; nearby are an inexpensive ***bakery*** and ***butcher***.

Entertainment

The ***Country Club*** in Kariba Heights has a theatre that showcases local talent, and also has an open-air cinema. The Caribbea Bay has a ***casino***. Beyond hotel bars, however, entertainment pickings are slim.

Shopping

All over town you'll find Nyaminyami walking sticks; both the Queen Mother and Pope John Paul II own examples. Also common and worth a look are the beautiful crocheted pieces sold by local women.

The usual array of crafts line the main roads, and there's a small market in the Heights.

Getting There & Away

Air Air Zimbabwe (☎ 2913) and Zimbabwe Express Airlines have daily 45-minute flights between Kariba and Harare (US$35), and Victoria Falls (US$45). Note that for Kariba flights, Air Zimbabwe seems to have rules of its own. Check in at least an hour early; if the pilot is raring to go the plane may be filled with stand-bys and take off early.

Bus Several daily buses link Nyamhunga township with Mbare. Once or twice a week, buses also connect Kariba with Binga via the Siabuwa road, with an occasional branch service south to Gokwe.

UTC do transfers to Harare on demand for US$20 per person (minimum four).

Hitching The road between Harare and Kariba is fairly well travelled, but weekends are the best time for hitching.

Boat Two ferry services link the eastern and western ends of Lake Kariba: Kariba Ferries connects Kariba with Mlibizi, and DDF connects Kariba with Binga.

Kariba Ferries is the more plush and popular of the two. There are no cabins, but passengers get complementary meals and seats that recline into full-length beds – it's not that difficult to imagine you're on a cruise. It sails at 9 am on Monday, Thursday from Kariba, and on Tuesday and Friday from Mlibizi.

Nonresidents pay US$74 one way. Foot passengers are advised to prebook, but with a vehicle you should book two to 12 months in advance. It costs US$51 for an ordinary car and US$71 for a 4WD. For details, contact Kariba Ferries Ltd (☎ 04-65476, 061-2460) PO Box 578, Harare, or Vundla Safaris (☎ 013-3394, fax 4357), Phumula Centre, Victoria Falls.

The more basic DDF ferry (☎ 061-2694) connects Kariba's National Parks Harbour with Binga and Gache Gache Bay. The *Chaminuka* leaves Kariba fortnightly on Thursday at 9 am. The trip takes 2½ days, with stops in Chalala, Sabilobilo, Mackenzie, Sengwe, Chibuyu, Sinamwenda and Chete (which has a small game park).

There is no food is available on board, although there is a cooker to boil water for *sadza* (maize meal porridge). There are no cabins, so passengers either sleep on the boat and cope with the mosquitoes or stay on shore.

On Tuesday at 10 am, the *Nyaminyami* leaves for Chalala via Kings Camp, Tashinga (Matusadona National Park), Musamba, Musango and Bumi Hills, arriving in Chalala at 5 pm the same day and returning to Kariba the following morning. On Wednesday at 10 am, the ferry *Mbuya Nehanda* leaves Kariba for Gache Gache Bay, returning the same afternoon.

Getting Around

To/From the Airport UTC does transfers between the airport and the Lake View, Caribbea Bay and Cutty Sark hotels in town for US$5 per person. It meets all incoming flights.

Bus Buses connect the Swift United Freight Depot with Nyamhunga, near the airport, about every 30 to 60 minutes, following a circuit through Mahombekombe and Kariba Heights.

Taxi Taxi services (☎ 2454) operate from the Caribbea Bay Hotel.

Bicycle Mountain bikes can be hired for US$9 per day at the camping ground or at any of the hotels mentioned here, except for Zambezi Valley.

Hitching Without a vehicle, sprawling up-and-down Kariba may seem intimidating, but most locals are in the same boat and hitching has become the standard transport system. Normally, you shouldn't wait more than a few minutes for a lift from one area of town to another.

KUBURI WILDERNESS

Carved from part of the Charara and Hurungwe safari areas, this recently designated 37,700-hectare wilderness area, south of Kariba, is bounded on the south by Lake Kariba, on the west by Kariba Gorge and on the north by a series of minor gorges. It's a rugged landscape of peaks and watershed harbouring a variety of wildlife, including 67 species of bird and even black rhino.

Entry costs US$1 per person plus US$1 per vehicle, and is valid for as long as you want to stay. The Kuburi headquarters, at the mouth of the Nyanyana River, is open daily from 7 am to 1 pm and 2 to 5 pm.

The ***camping ground*** at Kuburi headquarters has sites for up to 12 people for US$1.50 per person. Alternatively, you can sleep in the ***Kuburi Platform*** game hide for US$5.50 per group of up to 12 people. There's also a small thatched rondavel at the ***Muto River picnic site***, which costs US$5.50 per night. The camp site accommodates 12 people, but the rondavel only has space for six.

The National Park camping ground, ***Nyanyana Camp*** *(☎ 061-2898)*, lies within the wilderness boundary at the mouth of the Nyanyana River. It's 5km down a dirt track from the main Makuti-Kariba road, about 30km from town. Sites have braai pits and access to baths, showers and toilets. For weekends and holidays, prebookings are advised.

Kuburi lies on the main road between Kariba and Makuti, so access is straightforward. All camps are accessible by private vehicle.

MATUSADONA NATIONAL PARK

Those photos you'll see of dead trees before a wild mountain backdrop were taken at Matusadona National Park. The dead trees, of course, are victims of the rising lake waters of the late 1950s, and the mountain backdrop is the Zambezi Escarpment. Matusadona takes in 1407 sq km on the southern shore of Lake Kariba, sandwiched between the Sanyati and Ume Rivers. Much of the wildlife displaced by Lake Kariba eventually settled here, especially on the plains, which provide good crops of torpedo grass. (For more details on making bookings, see the Facts for the Visitor section of this chapter.)

Places to Stay

For booking details of the park's camps and lodges, see under Accommodation in the Facts for the Visitor section of this chapter. Rates for the following National Parks accommodation include: standard camp sites for US$1.50 per person; exclusive camp sites (maximum 12 people) for US$14; and lodges (maximum 12 people) for US$40.

The two National Park camping grounds are ***Sanyati West***, near the mouth of the Sanyati River, and ***Tashinga Camp*** at park headquarters in Tashinga, which also has an airstrip. Both hire camping equipment and Tashinga Camp also offers several pre-erected sleeping shelters. The exclusive camp, ***Changachirere***, on the shore near Spurwing Island, accommodates up to 10 people in one group.

There are also three exclusive chalet camps: ***Ume*** and ***Mbalabala***, on the estuary of the Ume River, and ***Muuyu***, at Elephant Point (not far from Tashinga). Each camp has two six-bed self-catering chalets that are available only for six-day periods.

Along the Siabuwa Road, at the Sanyati Bridge, is the basic ***Sanyati Bridge Camp***, with camping and three self-catering twin rondavels overlooking the Sanyati River. As part of the CAMPFIRE program, it's an excellent place to experience traditional Zimbabwean life. Shona-style meals are available on request.

Getting There & Away

Access to Matusadona is tricky. The buses between Kariba or Karoi and Binga only skirt the southern park boundary and won't get you any closer than 82km from the Tashinga park headquarters. For most of the year you need 4WD for the final bit into Tashinga, as well as for wildlife viewing along park roads. The Matusadona access road turns off the Siabuwa road 150km west of Karoi, from where it's about 10km to the Chifudze River gate into the park.

The crowded DDF ferry *Nyaminyami* goes to Chalala via Tashinga every Monday, but since you're not allowed to walk in the park without a guide, there won't be much to do.

MANA POOLS NATIONAL PARK

Mana Pools, a UNESCO World Heritage Site, is magnificent. Its magic stems from a pervading sense of the wild and natural, its remoteness, and the license to wander on foot (permitted from half an hour after sunrise to half an hour before sunset) according to the dictates of individual courage. The word 'mana' means four, in reference to the four pools around the park headquarters.

Except in the heat of the middle of the day, **Long Pool** is a busy spot. You're almost guaranteed to see hippo and crocodile, as well as zebra, antelope and elephant. It's most crowded at dusk when the entire human population of the park congregates there.

Fishing is allowed at Mana Pools. Visitors may take up to six fish per day from the River Zambezi without a licence. Three-person canoes can be hired for US$3/5 for a half/full day from the park office, but you may need a vehicle to transport the canoes from the office to the river.

Permits

Visitors to Mana Pools National Park should have reserved and paid for a permit (US$20) from the Central Booking Office (☎ 04-706078) in Harare. To get a permit you must say that you have transport into the park; however, most car-rental agencies won't insure (or even allow) their 2WDs on Mana Pools' rough roads. You can pick up the permit in Marongora before 3.30 pm on the day of entry, from where you must get to the ranger's office, near Nyamepi Camp, before 6 pm. En route the permit will be scrutinised no less than four times – at Marongora, the park turn-off, the park boundary and at the park headquarters near Nyamepi Camp – don't even consider trying to sneak past without one. You'll also have to produce it three more times to get out of the park.

Visitors without private vehicles – who are unable to pre-book accommodation – can hitch or take any Kariba- or Chirundu-bound bus to Marongora and hope there's a lift available from the park office there. If park lodges or camp sites are still available – and you have secured a guaranteed lift – the rangers may be able to sort out accommodation and a permit for you. (Hitchhikers can't be added to a driver's permit, so buy a permit valid beyond your intended stay, thus allowing time to find another lift out of the park.)

If the camps are fully booked you can get a day-entry permit for US$10 per person; unfortunately you won't be able to extend this at Nyamepi because no-shows aren't confirmed until 5.30 pm, which is too late to allow you to get back to the gate before the park closes.

If you must wait to enter the park, there's a small ***camp site*** behind the Marongora park office, with braai pits, cold showers and toilets. There's no shop so bring your own food.

Places to Stay

Camping is available from 1 May to 31 October only. Lodges remain open at other times, but access roads to them may be impassable – check before setting out. National

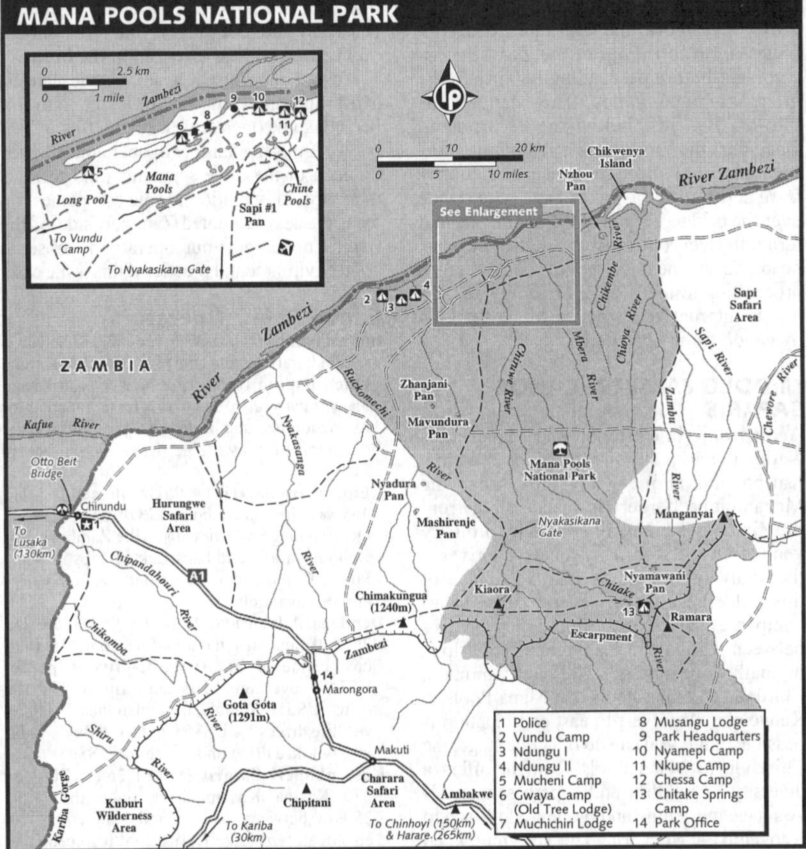

Parks accommodation rates include: camp sites from US$3 to US$8; and four- and eight-bed lodges for around US$17/26.

Most visitors stay at ***Nyamepi Camp***, which has showers, baths, toilets and sinks. Firewood is sold at the office, but campers are asked to bring their own stoves or fuel.

There are also several smaller camp sites. ***Mucheni*** has four sites. ***Chessa Camp***, ***Nkupe Camp*** and ***Gwaya Camp*** or 'Old Tree Lodge'. Each accommodate groups of up to 12 people. ***Ndungu Camp***, 11km west of Nyamepi, has two group sites for 12 people each. ***Vundu Camp*** has sleeping huts for 12 people, a cooking area, a living area and an ablutions block with hot water and showers. There's also ***Chitake Springs Camp***, 50km inland near the Zambezi Escarpment, but it's very remote and is only accessible by 4WD.

The two National Parks lodges, ***Musangu*** and ***Muchichiri***, have eight beds each and cost about twice as much as other Zimbabwe park lodges. They remain very popular – book six months in advance.

There is no shop, restaurant or petrol station in the park. Water should be treated before drinking and fruit is banned.

Getting There & Away

From Marongora, the Chirundu road continues north to the lip of the Zambezi Escarpment before descending 900m into the broad Zambezi Valley. The Mana Pools turn-off lies just below the escarpment. Once past the turn-off gate it's a long, corrugated route through dense and thorny *jesse* scrub to the Nyakasikana gate. Once over the bridge, sign in at the boom gate and turn left. Everyone must check in at the park headquarters near Nyamepi Camp before proceeding to their lodge or camp site.

The alternative access to Mana Pools is by canoe from Chirundu.

MIDDLE ZAMBEZI CANOE SAFARIS

Apart from via Chirundu and Mana Pools National Park, the stretch of river below Kariba and above Kanyemba (near the Mozambique border) is inaccessible from the Zimbabwe highway system by ordinary vehicle. In fact, for many locals, the river *is* the highway system. To take advantage of this wilderness route, several canoe safari companies run two- to nine-day river trips between Kariba and Kanyemba. The trip is normally done in stages: Kariba to Chirundu, Chirundu to Mana Pools and Mana Pools to Kanyemba. Any west to east combination is possible, but if you can do only one stage, the Chirundu to Mana Pools segment offers a diversity of wildlife and superb scenery. If you have more time and money, add Mana to Kanyemba to your trip. The very motivated can go for the entire 10-day Kariba to Kanyemba trip. July to October are peak months for wildlife viewing and although there are plenty of hippo and crocs in the river, run-ins with them are rare.

A canoe trip will usually have a transfer to/from Kariba or Harare included. If you find yourself in Chirundu and need somewhere to stay, there's a camp site, motel and a shop selling staples. Otherwise hitching or catching a bus isn't difficult; buses to Harare leave regularly.

When arranging a Zambezi canoe trip you should shop around. All operators camp on the river banks, but you may not wander more than 50m from the river without a guide licensed to lead foot safaris (your guide should be licensed and experienced in the bush).

All operators use Canadian-style canoes. Most run from April/May to October/November, but some operate year-round. Since Zimbabwe limits the number of operators allowed on each of the three segments (and restricts their days of operation), some companies run from the less regulated Zambian side of the river. Encourage your operator to observe good environmental practice if this is the case.

Canoe Safari Operators

Buffalo Safaris (☎ 061-2645, fax 2827, ⓔ buffalo@kariba.harare.iafrica.com) PO Box 113, Kariba. Offers three to 10-day trips between Kariba and Kanyemba year-round and is recommended for its friendliness and professionalism. Substantial discounts are available from November to March.

Chipembere Safaris (☎ 061-2946, cell 011 711 355 ⓔ chipsaf@zol.co.zw) PO Box 9, Ka-riba. Offers a range of canoeing on the Zambezi, plus walking safaris and backpacking trips in Mana Pools. Combined walking and canoeing trips are also available.

Dendera Adventure Trips (☎ 061-3366, fax 3365, ⓔ dendera@harare.iafrica.com) Has four-day canoeing and wildlife-drive trips for US$495, overnight Matsudona trips for US$185 (plus US$50 transfer). It also has half-day wildlife drives for US$55 and a full day's walking, wildlife drive and cruise for US$95.

Kasambabezi Safaris (☎ 061-2641) PO Box 279, Kariba. Kasambabezi covers the whole 250km between Kariba and Kanyemba and covers eastern Lake Kariba too. It's cheap and especially good if your time is limited.

Safari Par Excellence (☎ 04-720527, fax 722872, ⓔ safpar@harare.iafrica.com) 3rd floor, Travel Centre, Jason Moyo Ave (PO Box 5920), Harare. This large company runs three-to-five-day luxury canoe safaris from the Zambian shore between the mouths of the Kafue and Chikwenga Rivers. Nights are spent at fully equipped tented camps. Alternatively, there's a more basic, less expensive four-day camping safari between Chirundu and Chongwe Falls. It also runs a five-day combination walking and canoeing package through Mana Pools National Park.

Tsoro River Safaris (☎/fax 061-2426, ⓔ kanken@zol.co.zw) Kariva House, Sable Dr, Kariba. This company does canoe safaris from Kariba to Kanyemba and tented safaris in Mana Pools.

CHINHOYI CAVES NATIONAL PARK

Although small, this 'roadside' national park is riddled with limestone and dolomite caves and sinkholes, which have been used for storage and refuge for nearly 1500 years. Sleeping Pool or Chirorodzira (Pool of the Fallen), is so named because locals were cast into the formidable hole by the invading Nguni tribes in the early 19th century. Chirorodzira maintains a constant temperature of 22°C.

In 1887 colonial hunter Frederick Courteney Selous found the area occupied by Chief Chinhoyi, and took the Swiss cheese-like landscape to be the result of ancient mine workings. From Dark Cave, the rear entrance to Chirorodzira, you can look through the sombre shadows to the sunlit waters far below. The effect is magical; the clear water admits light so perfectly that the water line disappears and the pool takes on the appearance of a smoky blue underworld.

The park is open from 6 am to 6 pm year round and entry is US$0.15/0.30 per resident/foreigner.

The ***Caves Motel*** *(☎ 067-2340)* at the park entrance charges US$25/33 for singles/doubles, with breakfast. It also has a restaurant and poolside terrace (visitors can use the pool for US$0.50). The hotel sells petrol. The ***National Park camping ground*** charges US$1.35 per person for camping.

The park entrance is right on the Harare-Chirundu road, 8km north-west of Chinhoyi. From Harare, take any Kariba or Chirundu bus and get off at the Caves Motel.

TENGENENGE FARM

Although it's well off the beaten track, Tengenenge Farm, the remote sculptors' community at the foot of the Great Dyke near Guruve, makes a worthwhile visit. The farm is supported by the sale of artists' works and sponsorship, and is always on the lookout for new talent. Some of the original artists maintain farms at the community while others have established studios nearer their market.

Visitors may stroll through the sculpture gardens, which contain around 17,000 original pieces. Room and board at the farm is expensive for budget travellers, but you can bring your own food and you can always find a camp site in the bush. For information contact Tengenenge Farm, PO Box 169, Mvurwi.

From Harare, follow the Mazowe road to Mazowe Dam, where you should turn left. After 56km turn left again, towards Mvurwi, at a big dome rock. On the road out of town turn right and continue towards Guruve. After 34.5km, 12km south of Guruve, take the right turning signposted for Tengenenge. After 11km you'll run out of tar. Continue for 2km on the gravel and turn left; it's 5km from here to Tengenenge.

There's no public transport to Tengenenge. From Mbare, take the Guruve bus and get off at the Tengenenge turn-off 12km south of Guruve. Unless you're lucky with a lift, you will have to walk the remaining 19km. It's probably not possible to get there from Harare in a single day, although if you contact the farm someone may be able to offer you a lift from Harare.

UMFURUDZI SAFARI AREA

This relatively little known wilderness takes in 76,000 hectares of dry and lonely hills north of the Mazowe River. It is magnificent walking country with lots of wildlife – including elephant, big cats and many others. For longer trips you will need a guide.

The owners of ***Hippo Pools*** *(☎ 04-708843, fax 750619, PO Box 90, Shamva)* have invested a lot of time and millions of dollars creating this budget resort. Idyllically set on the banks of the Mazowe River it's perfect for walks, wildlife drives and rafting. Unfortunately for the owners, they have done their job too well and someone in officialdom has decided they wouldn't mind having a piece of it. At the time of research, entry to the area was blocked, the situation was being monitored by the press and the future of Hippo Pools was uncertain. It's definitely worth calling them to see if they are operating or purely to offer support – it would be a real shame to see this place fold.

In winter, Hippo Pools is accessible by 2WD. From Shamva, head north over the river crossing and turn right towards Madziwa Mine. After 33km turn right into Madziwa village. Just beyond the village shop (which sells staples), turn right down a hill and follow the road to the T-junction, then turn left. After 6km you pass the turn-off to Amms Mine, but keep heading straight, past the national park sign. After 6km you will come to the turn-off to the National Parks office (or the barricade). From this point it's 12km downhill to Hippo Pools.

Sunungukai Camp

The CAMPFIRE-run camp Sunungukai (Welcome and Be Free) lies near Nyagande, beside the Mazowe River. It's quite basic, but is an honest effort by local villagers to bring tourism to this lovely and quiet corner of Zimbabwe; contact CAMPFIRE at the Africa Resources Trust (☎ 04-732625, fax 739163) PO Box HG 690, Highlands, Harare.

A bus marked 'Nyava via Shamva & Mazoe Bridge' leaves from Harare for Mbare musika at around noon and a second bus, 'Nhakiwa via Bindura & Glendale', departs around 4 pm. By car, take the Mutoko road to Murewa and turn left on the tarred road into the Uzumba Maramba Pfungwe communal lands. After 55km, turn left at the Sunungukai signpost and continue for 3km to the Nyagande General Dealer shop, where you turn right. After 1.5km you'll see the camp on your right. You can also take the route via Shamva, but the road along the river may be impassable after rain.

Eastern Highlands

Few first-time travellers to Zimbabwe expect to find anything like the Eastern Highlands, but once they've discovered them, fewer still can get enough. The narrow strip of mountain country that makes up Manicaland, Zimbabwe's easternmost province, isn't the Africa that normally crops up in armchair travellers' fantasies. Homesick colonists have been reminded of Britain, especially the Lake District.

MUTARE

☎ 020

Mutare, Zimbabwe's fourth-largest city, is beautifully situated in a bowl-like valley surrounded by mountains. It has an odd cold-country feel and indeed, some of the hills are cloaked in pine trees and the main route into town is called Christmas Pass.

Umtali, as Mutare was known until Zimbabwean independence in 1980, was originally a white gold-mining settlement near present-day Penhalonga. When Fort Umtali was built further down Penhalonga Valley in 1891 (thanks to a border dispute between the British and Portuguese), the name was commandeered and the new Umtali grew around the fort. In 1896, the town was shifted again, this time to its present location 16km south of the old fort, to accommodate the railway line to Beira. Today, Mutare remains a garrison town.

Information

Tourist Office The well-organised Manicaland Publicity Association (☎ 64711) on Market Square near the corner of Herbert Chitepo St and Robert Mugabe Ave, is one of Zimbabwe's most helpful tourist offices. It's open from 8.30 am to 12.45 pm and 2 to 4 pm weekdays, during which times it offers a book exchange and informal left-luggage facility. Make sure you pick up a copy of the entertaining monthly *Mountain Digest* and check out your immediate future with its bizarre 'Horrorscope'.

Warning

Although the fighting has stopped in Mozambique, the border areas of the Eastern Highlands are still volatile. While the chance of standing on an unexploded land mine is negligible if you keep to well-worn tourist tracks, crime is on the increase. With the close proximity of the Mozambique border it's easy for thieves to mug a tourist and disappear back over the border long before the police have had a chance to respond. Authorities and the local community have made concerted efforts to counter the problem, such as setting up neighbourhood-watch-style programs, which has been effective, but still crime occurs. The best advice is to never walk alone in the area and leave all but the bare essentials somewhere safe (the car probably isn't good enough).

EASTERN HIGHLANDS

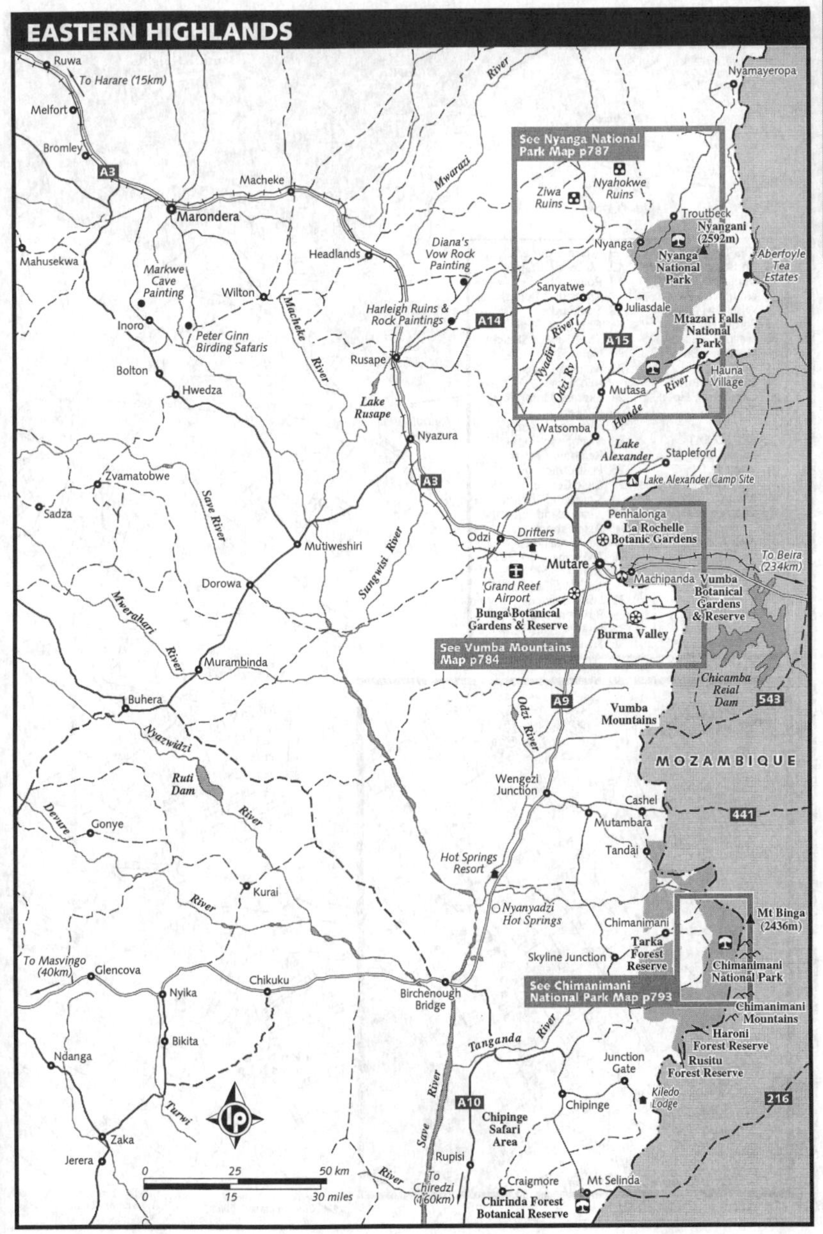

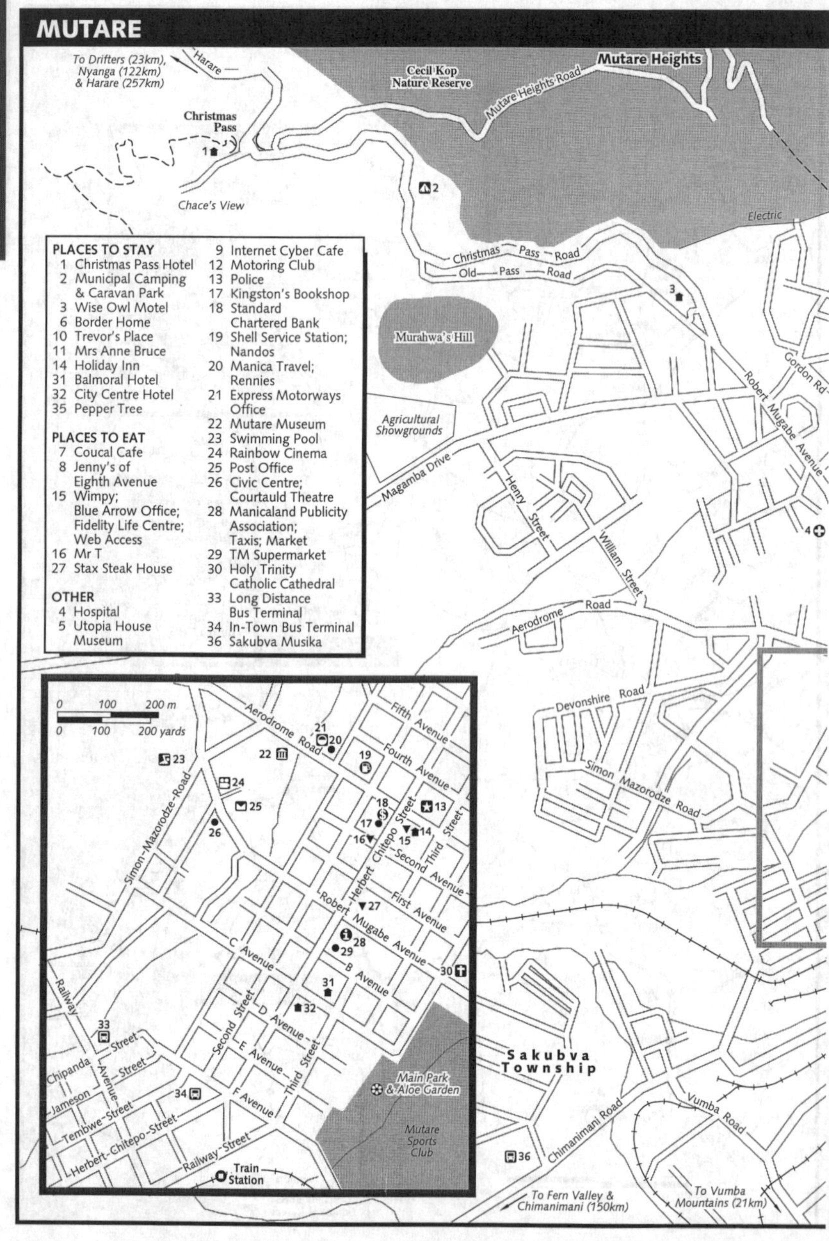
MUTARE
To Drifters (23km), Nyanga (122km) & Harare (257km)
Harare
Mutare Heights
Cecil Kop Nature Reserve
Mutare Heights Road
Christmas Pass
Chace's View
Electric
Christmas Pass Road
Old Pass Road
Murahwa's Hill
Gordon Rd
Robert Mugabe Avenue
Agricultural Showgrounds
Magamba Drive
Henry Street
William Street
Aerodrome Road
Devonshire Road
Simon Mazorodze Road
PLACES TO STAY
1 Christmas Pass Hotel
2 Municipal Camping & Caravan Park
3 Wise Owl Motel
6 Border Home
10 Trevor's Place
11 Mrs Anne Bruce
14 Holiday Inn
31 Balmoral Hotel
32 City Centre Hotel
35 Pepper Tree
PLACES TO EAT
7 Coucal Cafe
8 Jenny's of Eighth Avenue
15 Wimpy; Blue Arrow Office; Fidelity Life Centre; Web Access
16 Mr T
27 Stax Steak House
OTHER
4 Hospital
5 Utopia House Museum
9 Internet Cyber Cafe
12 Motoring Club
13 Police
17 Kingston's Bookshop
18 Standard Chartered Bank
19 Shell Service Station; Nandos
20 Manica Travel; Rennies
21 Express Motorways Office
22 Mutare Museum
23 Swimming Pool
24 Rainbow Cinema
25 Post Office
26 Civic Centre; Courtauld Theatre
28 Manicaland Publicity Association; Taxis; Market
29 TM Supermarket
30 Holy Trinity Catholic Cathedral
33 Long Distance Bus Terminal
34 In-Town Bus Terminal
36 Sakubva Musika
0 100 200 m
0 100 200 yards
Aerodrome Road
Fifth Avenue
Fourth Avenue
Herbert Chitepo Street
Third Street
Second Avenue
First Avenue
Robert Mugabe Avenue
Simon-Mazorodze-Road
C Avenue
B Avenue
D Avenue
E Avenue
F Avenue
Second Street
Third Street
Railway
Chipanda Street
Jameson Street
Avenue
Tembwe Street
Herbert Chitepo Street
Railway Street
Train Station
Main Park & Aloe Garden
Mutare Sports Club
Sakubva Township
Chimanimani Road
Vumba Road
To Fern Valley & Chimanimani (150km)
To Vumba Mountains (21km)

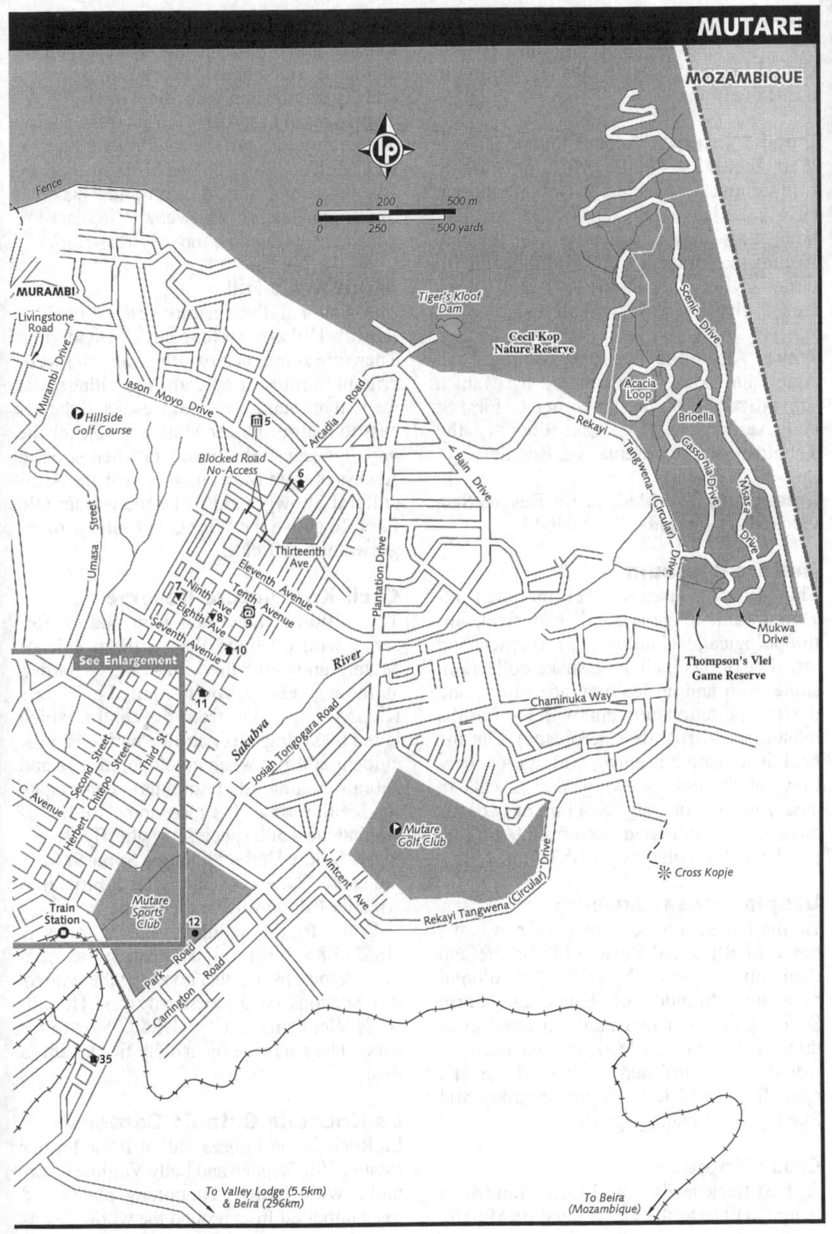
MUTARE
MOZAMBIQUE
0
200
500 m
0
250
500 yards
Fence
MURAMBI
Livingstone Road
Murambi Drive
Jason Moyo Drive
Hillside Golf Course
Umasa Street
Blocked Road No-Access
Arcadia Road
Tiger's Kloof Dam
Cecil Kop Nature Reserve
Scenic Drive
Acacia Loop
Brioella
Cassonia Drive
Msasa Drive
Rekayi Tangwena (Circular) Drive
Bain Drive
Thirteenth Ave
Plantation Drive
Eleventh Avenue
Tenth Avenue
Ninth Ave
Eighth Ave
Seventh Avenue
See Enlargement
Sakubva River
Josiah Tongogara Road
Chaminuka Way
Mukwa Drive
Thompson's Vlei Game Reserve
C Avenue
Herbert Chitepo Street
Second Street
Third St
Mutare Golf Club
Cross Kopje
Vintcent Ave
Rekayi Tangwena (Circular) Drive
Train Station
Mutare Sports Club
Park Road
Carrington Road
To Valley Lodge (5.5km) & Beira (296km)
To Beira (Mozambique)
5
6
7
8
9
10
11
12
35

Money There are plenty of banks and bureaus de change, including one (which should be open outside business hours) at the Holiday Inn.

Email & Internet Access A good place is Web Access (☎ 68603) 5th floor, Fidelity Life Centre; it's open daily. Not only does it have quite fast access for US$2.50 per half hour, it also has a great view over the city. Around the corner at 63-67 Fourth St, the Internet Cyber Cafe (☎ 61367) in Waller's House, charges US$3 per half hour.

Travel Agencies Transport bookings and American Express are handled by Manica Travel (☎ 61809) on the corner of First St and Aerodrome Rd. Next door is the Thomas Cook representative, Rennies.

Emergency The Medical Air Rescue Service (MARS) number is ☎ 64647.

Mutare Museum

The Mutare Museum's well-mounted agglomeration of geological, historical, anthropological, technological, zoological and artistic exhibits include: a snake collection; stone, iron and agricultural-age relics; and the transportation museum (with the world's most unusual flightless aeroplane). Out the back is an active beehive, with a cross section cut for easy viewing, and a walk-in aviary where you may see a bird or two. It's close to the centre and open from 9 am to 5 pm daily; foreigners pay US$2 entry fee.

Utopia House Museum

Utopia House, on Jason Moyo Dr, was the home of Rhys and Rosalie Fairbridge and their son Kingsley (1885–1924), a colonial poet and founder of Fairbridge Farm Schools for homeless and neglected children. It was built in 1897, but has been restored and refurnished in 1920s decor. It's open from 2.30 to 4.30 pm Saturday and Sunday. Foreigners pay US$2.

Cross Kopje

A short track leads from Rekayi Tangwena (Circular) Dr, at the eastern end of Mutare, to the top of the small hill, Cross Kopje, which looks over into Mozambique. The cross on the summit is a memorial to Black Zimbabweans and Mozambicans who died in the WWI campaigns in East Africa. To get there, follow Milner Ave east past the park to Park St, then take a left and carry on one block to Vintcent Ave where you should turn right. This soon turns into Rekayi Tangwena (Circular) Dr, which passes near the foot of Cross Kopje.

Murahwa's Hill

The National Trust nature reserve on Murahwa's Hill is great for a day of wandering. There are some rock paintings and the well-crumbled ruins of an Iron Age village, but the real attractions are the views and the access to nature so near Mutare. Look for the *mujejeje* (rocks that resonate when struck). Access is from Magamba Dr near the Agricultural Showgrounds. The route from Old Pass Rd above the Wise Owl Motel is overgrown and difficult.

Cecil Kop Nature Reserve

The 1700-hectare Cecil Kop Nature Reserve wraps around the northern side of Mutare and abuts the Mozambique border. Without a vehicle, you're limited to Tiger's Kloof Dam, 3.5km from the centre, which is fed by springs. Its zoo-like nature is most evident at 4 pm when antelope, giraffe and zebra – among other animals – congregate for feeding time. It's also home to 200 of Zimbabwe's 500 species of butterfly. To get there, follow Herbert Chitepo St north from the centre. One kilometre after it turns into Arcadia Rd, you'll see the car park.

Entry to the wildlife-viewing area is US$2/0.85 for foreigners/residents; save your receipt as it's also good for the wilderness section (4WD access only) and Thompson's Vlei game reserve (US$0.75 extra for cars). The parks are open daily from 7 am to dusk.

La Rochelle Botanic Gardens

La Rochelle, in Imbeza Valley, is the former estate of Sir Stephen and Lady Virginia Courtauld, with gardens containing plants and trees imported from around the world. It was bequeathed to the nation upon Lady Courtauld's death in 1972. A unique attraction is a guided Braille trail through the garden.

It's open from 8 am to 5 pm daily, and the tearoom serves snacks, light lunches and teas from 9.30 am to 4.30 pm. Foreigners pay US$1 entry. From Mutare, take a Penhalonga bus from the Tembwe St bus terminal, get off at the intersection 6km up the Penhalonga road and walk the remaining 3km.

Organised Tours

For local tours, there's UTC (☎ 64784), based at the Holiday Inn; Green Travellers (☎ 61758, fax 62128); and Mherepere Tours, (☎ 65165) at 91 Herbert Chitepo St. All offer day trips into the surrounding highlands. Green Travellers, bookable through hostels, is cheapest, Mherepere has a cultural slant and UTC caters to a more upmarket clientele.

Places to Stay – Budget

The ***Municipal Camping & Caravan Park*** is unfortunately just metres from the noisy Harare highway near Christmas Pass. Coming from Harare by bus, get off at the summit of Christmas Pass – drivers won't stop on the hill – and walk the 2km downhill to the caravan park. Sites cost US$1.40/0.40 per adult/child.

Mutare also has a clutch of backpackers hostels that appear to be stuck in some kind of time warp. Most central, but a little bit cramped, is ***Mrs Anne Bruce*** *(☎ 63569, 99 Fourth St)*. Beds cost US$3 and meals are available for very reasonable rates.

Trevor's Place *(☎ 64711, @ trevors@hello.com.au, 119 Fourth St)* on the corner of Eighth Ave advertises a free sherry on arrival. It's central with cooking (no meals are provided), laundry and *braai* facilities. Staff won't unlock the gate to let you in until you agree to stay there, but once in it's OK. Dorms cost US$4, doubles are US$8 and camping costs US$2.50 per person.

Slightly larger and a bit further out of town, the calm and friendly ***Border Home*** *(☎ 63346, 3A Jason Moyo Dr)* charges US$2 for camping and US$3 for dorms. There are also several private doubles and cottages in the garden for US$6.50 to US$12. Meals are available (there's a US$0.80 surcharge to use the kitchen facilities) as are laundry facilities, TV lounge and bicycle hire. You can phone for a pick-up.

If you don't have to stay in town, the best choice is ***Drifters*** *(☎ 62964)* backpackers lodge, on a small wildlife reserve 24km west of Mutare. Camping is US$2 per person in provided tents, caravans are US$3, comfortable dorm beds cost US$5, two- or four-bed rooms are US$6.50 per person and double rondavels are US$11. There's a pool and the large bar and restaurant serves meals, including pizzas on Friday night. The easiest way to get here is on a Harare-Mutare bus, which can drop you off en route.

Places to Stay – Mid-Range

If you'd rather bed down in a hotel, the ***Balmoral*** *(☎ 61435)* on C Ave is cheap and cheerful at US$10 per person, with breakfast.

If you're a fitness freak missing out on your daily work-out, consider the ***Pepper Tree*** *(☎ 66509, @ jade@syscom.co.zw, 25 Park Rd, Darlington)* a short way south of the centre. Part of a gym complex, like most places in Mutare it doesn't have a pool, but the tastefully decorated cottages are good value at US$11/13.50, with breakfast.

The ***Wise Owl Motel*** *(☎ 64643, fax 64890)* is quite a way out from the centre on Christmas Pass Rd. Singles/doubles with breakfast cost from US$22/29. It's clean, and if you have a vehicle, it isn't bad.

Places to Stay – Top End

The only top-end accommodation is the ***Holiday Inn*** *(☎ 64431, fax 64466)*, Aerodrome Rd, where standard rooms cost US$123 for foreigners and US$63 for residents. There's also an Apache Spur restaurant, bar, bureau de change, UTC office, coffee shop and small pool here.

Places to Eat

If you wake up starving in the morning, head for the breakfast buffet at the ***Holiday Inn***. The friendly ***Stax Steak House*** *(☎ 62653)* in the First Mutual Centre also serves a mean breakfast – try the backpackers' version, which is the usual bacon and eggs etc, plus a waffle and syrup – great value for less than US$2. It also has the usual steak-house fare, as well as espresso coffee, vegetarian potato burgers, salads and Belgian waffles piled with syrup, cream and smarties.

For lunch or 'real' coffee within a pleasant garden setting, try ***Jenny's of Eighth Avenue*** *(☎ 67764, 139 Herbert Chitepo)*, a nursery and craft shop on the corner of Eighth St, or the slightly more relaxed ***Coucal Cafe*** *(☎ 65509, 111 Second St)*, at the Nyasa Seedcracker Gallery. Both are open from Monday to Saturday for lunch and light snacks.

If you're after some sadza, try the Herbert Chitepo St ***takeaways*** south of Robert Mugabe Ave. For fast food, there's ***Nandos*** *(16 Aerodrome Rd)*; ***Wimpy*** in the Fidelity Life Centre on Herbert Chitepo St and ***Mr T*** *(Bhadella Arcade, 67 Herbert Chitepo St)*; the latter is open until 10 pm Friday and Saturday and isn't bad for ice cream, greasy burgers, chicken, chips and other snacks.

The ***restaurant*** at the Wise Owl Hotel serves up flaming dishes and specialties like deep fried Vumba cheese. There's also a cocktail bar. For something a bit fancier, take a drive out to ***Fantails Restaurant*** *(☎ 62868)* at the Valley Lodge, 6km towards Beira. This place is renowned for its *haute cuisine*, so advance bookings are necessary.

For self-caterers, there's the ***TM supermarket***, which is near the Publicity Association office and a large fruit and vegetable market at Sakubva musika.

Entertainment

A popular spot is the ***Portuguese Club***, which has served as the watering hole of choice for the European players in all recent conflicts in Zimbabwe and Mozambique. It also does meals in the evenings and lunches on weekends, and it even has tablecloths and glasses. For something more local and lively, the ***City Centre Hotel*** sees riotous drinking nightly, with live performances in the beer garden on weekend afternoons.

The ***Rainbow Centre cinema*** shows mostly rubbishy North American films, and the ***Courtauld Theatre*** provides a venue for amateur theatre productions. Both are near the Civic Centre Complex on Robert Mugabe Ave.

Getting There & Away

Bus At 1 pm on Wednesday and Friday and 5 pm on Sunday, Blue Arrow has an express service to Harare (US$11, 4¼ hours); the terminal is at the Holiday Inn. Express Motorways (☎ 63343) has unreliable services from its office to Harare for US$12.50.

The in-town bus terminal is on Chipanda St, between F and Railway Aves. If you're coming from Harare, get off here unless you're heading for Sakubva musika.

For the six-hour trip to Harare (US$5), buses leave hourly between 6 am and 6 pm from both the Chipanda St and Sakubva terminals. There are three buses to Bulawayo (US$8), via Masvingo, leaving between 6 and 7 am.

Hourly buses leave for Juliasdale and Nyanga and cost US$2. There are also daily buses to Birchenough Bridge, Honde Valley, Cashel Valley and Chipinge, and periodic services to Chiredzi, Triangle and Beitbridge.

To Chimanimani, there are five daily buses (via Wengezi). Alternatively, take any Birchenough Bridge bus, get off at Wengezi, hitch to Skyline Junction and then Chimanimani.

Train The easiest (yet longest) way between Harare and Mutare is by overnight train. The service departs from Harare nightly at 9.30 pm, arriving in Mutare at 6 am. From Mutare, it leaves at 9 pm and arrives at 6 am in Harare. The 1st (sleeper)/3rd-class fares are US$8.50/3. The reservations and ticket office in Mutare (☎ 62801) is open from 8 am to 12.30 pm and 2 to 4 pm weekdays.

Getting Around

Urban and local buses run between Sakubva musika and the centre. There are taxi stands at Sakubva musika, the Holiday Inn and the Publicity Association. A1 Taxis can be contacted on ☎ 66195. Green Travellers (☎ 617 58) has bikes for hire.

VUMBA MOUNTAINS

☎ 020

Just 28km south-east of Mutare, the Vumba Mountains are characterised by cool, forested highlands alternating with deep, almost jungled valleys. In Manyika, the name Vumba (or Bvumba as it's often spelt) means 'mist' and you'll probably have the opportunity to determine the name's validity. With its meadows, apple orchards, country gardens and teahouses, the area seems to recreate the British countryside.

Vumba & Bunga Botanical Reserves

The Vumba and Bunga Botanical Reserves are two protected enclaves just over 30km from Mutare. The tiny Bunga Botanical Reserve, which has no facilities, encompasses 39 hectares straddling the Vumba road – it's a bit of a crime spot.

Divided into a botanical garden, with specimens from around the world and wide lawns, and a wild botanical reserve criss-crossed with footpaths through natural bush – the Vumba Botanical Gardens and Reserve has views past several ranges of hills to the tropical lowlands of Mozambique (1000m below). Wildlife includes samango monkeys, unique to the Eastern Highlands, as well as eland, duiker, bushbuck, sable and flashy tropical birds. Watch the forest floor for the odd little elephant shrew, a tiny but ferocious beast that hops like a kangaroo and has long ears and an elongated snout.

The gardens are open from 9 am to 5 pm daily, and the teahouse opens from 10 am to 4 pm Friday to Wednesday. Foreigners/residents pay US$5/2.50 entry; double that for overnight stays. Nonresidents can use the pool and picnic site within the reserve for a small fee.

Burma & Essex Valleys

These two densely populated valleys, nearly 900m lower than Vumba, are accessed by a 70km scenic loop road. Along the partially tarred route, you pass through coffee, banana, tobacco and cotton plantations, and over beautiful forest-laden mountains with views into Mozambique. Essex Valley is like a tiny slice of East Africa, reminiscent of the Kenyan highlands.

A favourite stop is the Crake Valley Farm (☎ 217122) at the 20km point on the Essex Valley road. Famous soft Vumba cheese is produced here, as well as other varieties: peperoni, made with green peppercorns from Chipinge; Zonwe cheddar cheese; and soft Alpine cheese. Tours and samples (US$0.40) are available from 10 am to 3 pm Monday to Saturday.

Chinyakwaremba (Leopard Rock)

The Chinyakwaremba (Sitting-Down Hill) monolith, also known as Leopard Rock, may be easily climbed via a signposted track from Vumba Rd about 2km east of the Vumba Botanical Reserve turn-off. The views from the top are excellent.

Activities

Even if you've never held a **golf** club in your life, don't miss out on a round at the Leopard Rock Hotel. The grounds are superb with stunning vistas; budget travellers may never afford to play on this class of course again. Caddies (US$1.35 plus tip) are compulsory and in some cases essential, and there's also a dress code (shirts with collar, though the authorities can be pretty relaxed about this). Nine/18 holes will cost US$5/10 unless you're a Leopard Rock or local-hotel guest, student or senior, in which case you'll get a discount. Club hire is available for US$3/6.

There are a couple of **horse-riding** options: the Vumba Basket Shoppe (☎ 68193), which charges US$4 per hour (Tuesday to Sunday); or Campbell-Masons (☎ 210310) near Leopard Rock.

Foreign/resident **birdwatching** enthusiasts can do a 2½ hour guided walk with Seldomseen Birdwatching (☎ 215115) for US$3.30/2. You should book in advance.

Places to Stay

Camping & Hostels The *camping ground* and *caravan park* in the Vumba Botanical Reserve have good amenities, as well as a prime setting and swimming pool. Camping

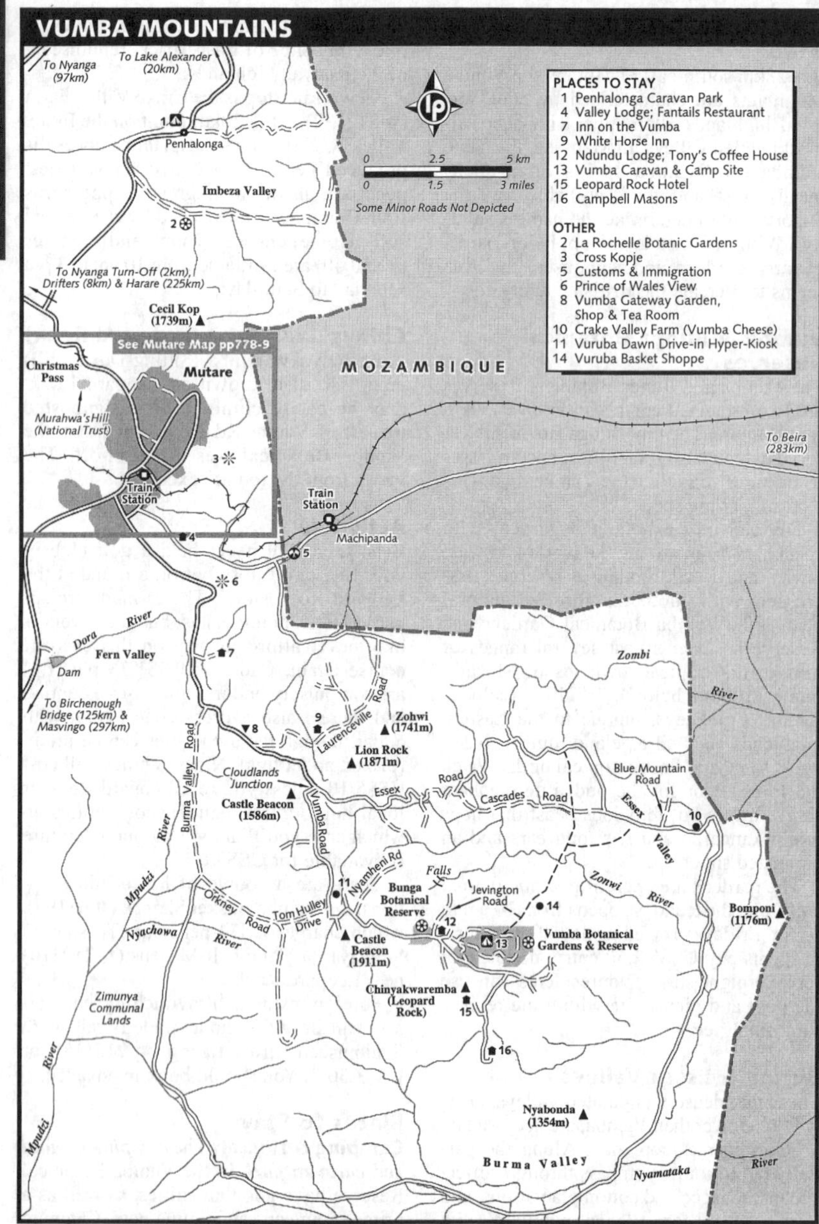
VUMBA MOUNTAINS
PLACES TO STAY
1 Penhalonga Caravan Park
4 Valley Lodge; Fantails Restaurant
7 Inn on the Vumba
9 White Horse Inn
12 Ndundu Lodge; Tony's Coffee House
13 Vumba Caravan & Camp Site
15 Leopard Rock Hotel
16 Campbell Masons
OTHER
2 La Rochelle Botanic Gardens
3 Cross Kopje
5 Customs & Immigration
6 Prince of Wales View
8 Vumba Gateway Garden, Shop & Tea Room
10 Crake Valley Farm (Vumba Cheese)
11 Vuruba Dawn Drive-in Hyper-Kiosk
14 Vuruba Basket Shoppe
0 2.5 5 km
0 1.5 3 miles
Some Minor Roads Not Depicted
To Nyanga (97km)
To Lake Alexander (20km)
Penhalonga
Imbeza Valley
To Nyanga Turn-Off (2km), Drifters (8km) & Harare (225km)
Cecil Kop (1739m)
See Mutare Map pp778-9
Christmas Pass
Mutare
Murahwa's Hill (National Trust)
Train Station
MOZAMBIQUE
To Beira (283km)
Train Station
Machipanda
Dora River
Fern Valley
Dam
To Birchenough Bridge (125km) & Masvingo (297km)
Burma Valley Road
Laurenceville Road
Zohwi (1741m)
Lion Rock (1871m)
Cloudlands Junction
Castle Beacon (1586m)
Vumba Road
Essex Road
Cascades Road
Blue Mountain Road
Essex Valley
Zombi River
Mpudzi River
Orkney Road
Tom Hulley Drive
Nyamheni Rd
Falls
Jevington Road
Bunga Botanical Reserve
Zonwi River
Bomponi (1176m)
Nyachowa River
Castle Beacon (1911m)
Vumba Botanical Gardens & Reserve
Chinyakwaremba (Leopard Rock)
Zimunya Communal Lands
River
Mpudzi
Nyabonda (1354m)
Burma Valley
Nyamataka River

costs US$1.40/0.70 for adults/children and nonguests can cool off in the pool for US$0.40.

A 10-minute walk from Vumba Botanical Reserve is the ***Ndundu Lodge*** *(☎ 63777, @ ndundulodge@yahoo.com)*, an imaginatively decorated three-tiered house with a superb view into Mozambique. There's a cosy lounge with a great music selection, a well-stocked bar fridge, home-cooked meals and self-catering facilities, all in such a relaxing atmosphere that you won't want to leave. Beds cost from US$5 in a two-bed dorm to US$9.50 in a deluxe double; camping costs US$6 per person. The lodge does pick ups from the Manicaland Publicity Association around noon on Monday, Wednesday and Friday.

Holiday Cottages You'll find a number of holiday cottages and guesthouses scattered through the region. You can pick up the latest listings and contact details from the Manicaland Publicity Association in Mutare.

Hotels Vumba hotels are struggling to outcharm their competition, yet each fills a different niche. Nearest to Mutare is the ***Inn on the Vumba*** *(☎/fax 67449)*. Families are welcomed and there's a swimming pool and playground for the kids. Standard singles/doubles with a mountain view cost US$36/53. There's also two self-catering cottages for up to four people costing US$66 for two, plus US$13 per extra adult. Meals, including favourites like roast beef and Yorkshire pudding, are included in the price.

More exclusive is the elegant ***White Horse Inn*** *(☎ 60138, fax 60325)*, set in a deep valley amid trees and gardens with a pool and croquet course. Each room is pleasantly (if ostentatiously) trimmed in a different floral theme, reminiscent of an English country B&B. Rooms cost US$29/ 43, with breakfast. Carrying the Anglo theme even further, there's also a garden cottage, which affords more privacy. Nonguests may also enjoy its fine cuisine and well-stocked wine cellar, light snacks or simply a drink. In the evening, guests must dress for dinner – no jeans or T-shirts.

Below the flanks of Chinyakwaremba (Leopard Rock), the ***Leopard Rock Hotel*** *(☎ 60115, fax 61165, @ lrock@syscom.co.zw)*, with vast lawns and lavish gardens, is modelled on a French chateau. It was built of stone by Italian prisoners of war during WWII, and in 1953 the British Queen Mother stayed on a royal visit. It was destroyed in 1978 during the Second Chimurenga, but has been renovated and boasts the usual facilities plus a casino and a world-class 18-hole golf course. The reception area has an awesome wall of glass, behind which a rainforest poses against a bare rock face, pulling gazes away from the gaudy opulence all around. Foreigners pay from US$140/160 (residents pay US$55/64), for a room by the casino, to US$275/310 (US$102) for a presidential suite.

Places to Eat

At the turn-off to the Vumba Botanical Reserve is ***Tony's Coffee House***, which more than justifies the trip out here – it has a huge selection of specialty tea and coffee, and the cakes definitely deserve the hype. You can buy very basic staples at the local shop, 500m west of the gardens turn-off. There are ***teahouses*** at the Vumba Basket Shoppe and botanical reserve, and unless fully booked-out, local hotels offer lunches, dinners and light snacks.

Shopping

In Vumba, roadside carving vendors give way to kids selling tablecloths, aprons and hankies embroidered with women at toil. For other Vumba specialities – pickles, honey, Vumba cheese, biltong, coffee and protea flowers – go to the Vumba Dawn Drive-In Hyper-Kiosk at the 21km peg of the Vumba road.

Getting There & Away

Without a vehicle, access to the Vumba area is quite limited. From Mutare's Chipanda St bus terminal, there's a bus to Leopard Rock at 8 am and 3 pm on Friday, Saturday and Sunday, returning just over an hour later. There are also daily buses doing the Essex and Burma Valley circuit. For day-trip information, see Organised Tours under Mutare.

NYANGA NATIONAL PARK

☎ 129

The 33,000-hectare Nyanga National Park is a scenically distinct enclave in the Eastern Highlands. Cecil Rhodes fell in love with it, and as only he could have done, bought it for his own residence. Not surprisingly the park, like the entire country, acquired his name; it's still sometimes referred to as Rhodes Inyanga. The African name, Nyanga, means Shaman's Horn.

Nyanga Dam was the site of the Rhodes estate homestead, which stands beside the small artificial lake that once bore his name, surrounded by English gardens and imported European hardwoods. Near the National Park lodges is the National Parks office (☎ 8274), open from 7 am to 6 pm daily.

The Nyanga Publicity Association (☎ 8435), housed in Nyanga library, has local information; it's open from 8 am to 1 pm and 2 to 4 pm Monday to Thursday and 9 am to 4 pm Saturday.

Rhodes Museum

In the Rhodes Museum, in Cecil Rhodes' old stables, one would expect devotion to the coloniser himself, but it also dedicates space to black African history, the struggles of the Second Chimurenga and the good works of Zimbabwean war hero and philanthropist Rekayi Tangwena. It's open Tuesday to Sunday.

Brighton Beach

Between the Nyanga Dam complex and the Nyangombe camping ground is a natural wide spot below a cascade in the Nyangombe River. There's a sandy beach, unofficially known as Brighton Beach, a green lawn, changing rooms and bilharzia-free swimming – if you're prepared to brave the chilly mountain water.

Nyangombe Falls

Just outside the park's western boundary, the Nyangombe River tumbles over terraced stacks of cuboid boulders and plunges into a steep but shallow gorge. The whole thing may remind you more of an abstractly sculpted fountain than a work of nature. Once you've seen the upper falls, which are depicted on all the brochures and postcards, have a look downstream, where there's a higher and louder single drop into a deep river pool. Stay off the rocks near the falls; the moss makes them hazardously slippery.

Pit Structures

The reconstructed pit structures near Nyanga Dam may put the architecture of the many pit structures dotted around Nyanga into perspective. The most plausible explanation is that they were used as corrals for small livestock and were entered through dark, narrow tunnels; the animals were kept in by pales extending through the floor of the family hut that was built on a level stone platform above the tunnel. Smaller stone platforms surrounding the pit were probably used as foundations for grain-storage huts.

Chamowera Fort

This fort is a pleasant 6km hike up the Nyangombe River from Nyanga Dam; follow the well-defined path along the north bank (or drive from the Troutbeck road). Like Nyangwe Fort, it's one of a series of similar structures stretching across the Nyanga region. Although they resemble defence structures, it's more likely they served as simple lookouts. Local sources have suggested that sentries posted in these hilltop structures, which are mutually visible on clear days, communicated by blowing on spiral kudu horns.

Nyangwe Fort

Nyangwe Fort is the best preserved of the Nyanga structures. The main enclosure, full of storage-hut platforms and partially overgrown with aloes and msasa trees, is surrounded by five smaller fort-like enclosures. Nyangwe is a 2km walk along a driveable road from Nyangwe Dam.

World's View

World's View is perched atop the Troutbeck Massif, on a precipice 11km up the winding mountain road from Troutbeck. As its name implies, this National Trust site affords a broad view across northern Zimbabwe. You

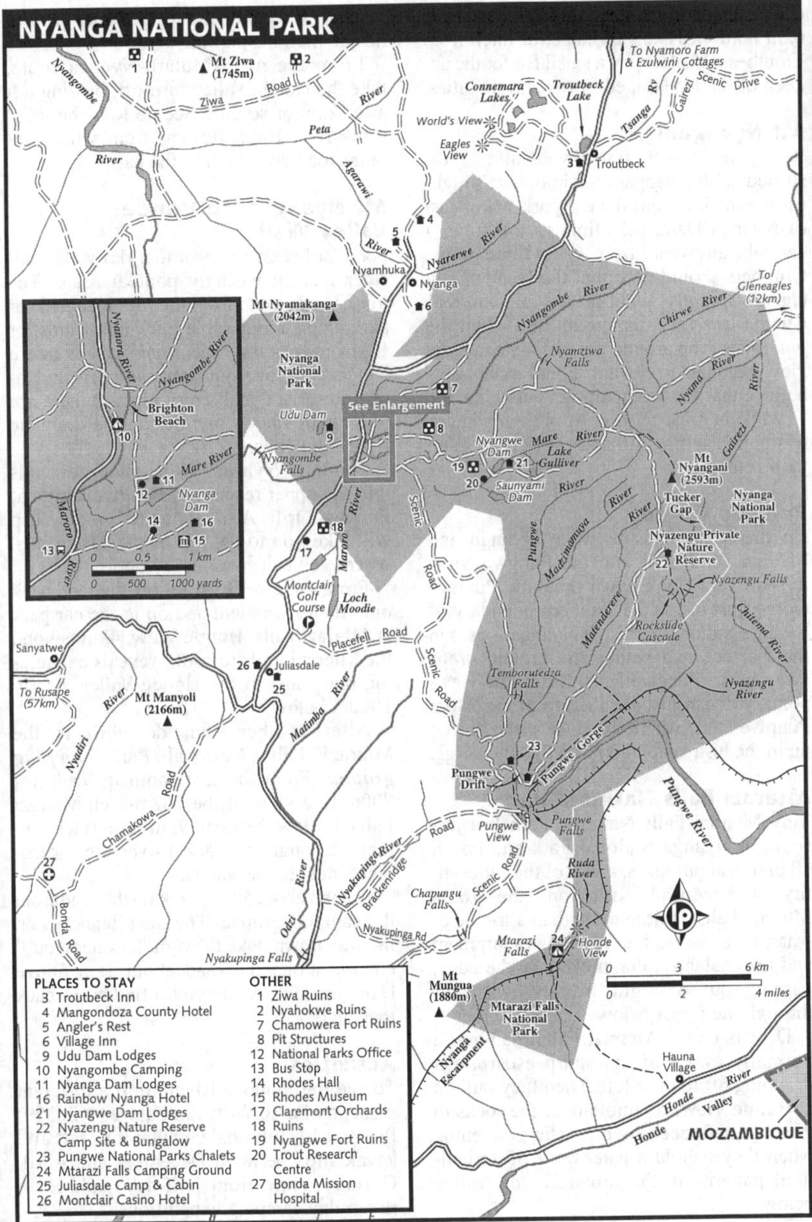

NYANGA NATIONAL PARK
Mt Ziwa (1745m)
Ziwa Road
Peta River
Nyangombe River
Agarawi River
To Nyamoro Farm & Ezulwini Cottages
Connemara Lakes
Troutbeck Lake
Scenic Drive
World's View
Eagles View
Tsanga Rv
Gairezi
Troutbeck
Nyarerwe River
Nyamhuka
Nyanga
Mt Nyamakanga (2042m)
Nyanga National Park
Nyangombe River
To Gleneagles (12km)
Chirwe River
Nyamziwa Falls
Nyama River
See Enlargement
Udu Dam
Nyangombe Falls
Nyangwe Dam
Mare River
Lake Gulliver
Saunyami Dam
Mt Nyangani (2593m)
Tucker Gap
Nyanga National Park
Nyazengu Private Nature Reserve
Nyazengu Falls
Rockslide Cascade
Chitema River
Pungwe River
Madzimamuya River
Matenderere River
Scenic Road
Maroro River
Montclair Golf Course
Loch Moodie
Placefell Road
Sanyatwe
To Rusape (57km)
Juliasdale
Mt Manyoli (2166m)
Matimba River
Nyadiri River
Temborutedza Falls
Nyazengu River
Pungwe Gorge
Pungwe Drift
Pungwe View
Pungwe Falls
Pungwe River
Ruda River
Chamakowa Road
Bonda Road
Odzi River
Nyakupinga River
Brackenridge Road
Nyakupinga Rd
Nyakupinga Falls
Chapungu Falls
Mtarazi Falls
Honde View
Mt Mungua (1880m)
Mtarazi Falls National Park
Nyanga Escarpment
Hauna Village
Honde Valley
Honde River
MOZAMBIQUE
0 3 6 km
0 2 4 miles
Nyanora River
Brighton Beach
Mare River
Nyanga Dam
Maroro River
0 0.5 1 km
0 500 1000 yards
PLACES TO STAY
3 Troutbeck Inn
4 Mangondoza County Hotel
5 Angler's Rest
6 Village Inn
9 Udu Dam Lodges
10 Nyangombe Camping
11 Nyanga Dam Lodges
16 Rainbow Nyanga Hotel
21 Nyangwe Dam Lodges
22 Nyazengu Nature Reserve Camp Site & Bungalow
23 Pungwe National Parks Chalets
24 Mtarazi Falls Camping Ground
25 Juliasdale Camp & Cabin
26 Montclair Casino Hotel
OTHER
1 Ziwa Ruins
2 Nyahokwe Ruins
7 Chamowera Fort Ruins
8 Pit Structures
12 National Parks Office
13 Bus Stop
14 Rhodes Hall
15 Rhodes Museum
17 Claremont Orchards
18 Ruins
19 Nyangwe Fort Ruins
20 Trout Research Centre
27 Bonda Mission Hospital

can get there on the steep footpath beginning 6km north of Nyanga village, or hitch from Troutbeck. Visitors pay a small fee for the upkeep of the landscaped lawns and facilities.

Mt Nyangani

Rising to 2593m, flat-topped and myth-shrouded Mt Nyangani is Zimbabwe's highest mountain. From the car park 14km east of Nyanga Dam, the climb to the summit can take anywhere from 1½ to three hours. Climbers should note that the weather can change abruptly; wind-driven rain can render the trip very unpleasant and when the *guti* mists drop around the marshy peak, the view becomes irrelevant. Local inhabitants believe that the mountain devours hikers.

Walkers must register at park headquarters before setting off, and check back in on their return.

Pungwe Gorge

On the back roads between Nyanga and Mtarazi Falls, pull into the Pungwe View turn-off for a look down dramatic Pungwe Gorge, just inside the southern boundary of Nyanga National Park. Mt Nyangani rises in the distance and below, the ground drops away to the Pungwe River. From the viewpoint, you can just see the top of the 240m Pungwe Falls, where the river is swallowed up in the lush vegetation that fills the gorge.

Mtarazi Falls National Park

Tiny Mtarazi Falls National Park lies just south of Nyanga National Park and is, for all practical purposes, a part of the same entity. The central attraction, the 762m Mtarazi Falls, is little more than a trickle of water that reaches the lip of the escarpment and nonchalantly plummets over the edge, passing out of sight in long cascades through the forest below.

Drivers on the Mtarazi Falls road aren't normally aware of the sharp escarpment dropping off to their left. Then they pull up at **Honde View**, scramble over the rocks to the edge and receive a dramatic awakening when they behold a patchwork of agricultural patterns in the broad Honde Valley below.

There is a national-park ***camping ground*** beside the falls parking area.

From the main Mutare-Nyanga route, take the Honde Valley turn-off, bearing left after 2km or so onto Scenic Rd. The falls' turn-off is 16km further, from where another road goes 7km to the car park.

Mt Nyangani to Honde Valley Walk

For a fairly easy three- or four-day **walk**, consider this increasingly popular route. The track heads south from the Mt Nyangani car park along a motorable track that winds for 12km over grassy hills, then widens into a better road. Entering Nyazengu Private Nature Reserve (small entry charge) there are two ***camp sites*** – one beside the dramatic **Nyazengu Falls**.

South of Nyazengu the route descends into the upper reaches of **Pungwe Gorge** at Pungwe Drift. A one-hour return side trip will take you to the top of the 240m falls, where you can swim in icy pools.

From Pungwe Drift, follow the road back onto the escarpment and on to the car park at **Mtarazi Falls**. **Honde View**, 4km beyond the Mtarazi Falls turn-off, reveals an enticing panorama of the Honde Valley, nearly 1000m below.

After another 3km downhill is the Mtarazi Falls National Park ***camping ground***. From there, a footpath leads for 700m to a view of the 762m-high Mtarazi Falls. Follow the steep 9km farm track (actually a tangle of tracks) over the escarpment into Honde Valley.

It starts about 500m back up the road from the camping ground. The track branches on the way down; take the right fork and you'll emerge along the road about 1km above **Hauna** village, where you'll find buses back to Mutare.

Activities

To see the Pungwe River from a different angle, try Far & Wide Zimbabwe (☎ 26329) PO Box 14, Juliasdale, which runs **raft and kayak trips** between December and April. Options range from half-day paddles to seven-day camping expeditions.

The national park has **horse riding**, **boats** for hire and trout **fishing** available.

Places to Stay & Eat

You can stay either within the national park or in one of the towns that flank the park.

Juliasdale For chilling out in the mellow mountain air, budget travellers love ***Juliasdale Camp & Cabin*** *(☎ 8202)*. It has garden camp sites and simple cabins accommodating up to four people.

The four-star ***Montclair Casino Hotel*** *(☎ 2441, fax 2447, e montclai@pci.co.zw)* has luxurious trappings; casino, tennis courts, swimming pool, croquet, horse riding, golf and so on. Foreigners pay US$43/50 for singles/doubles, half-board.

There are ***restaurants*** and ***bars*** at all the hotels. The ***takeaway*** at Juliasdale petrol station bakes excellent chicken pies, and between Juliasdale and Nyanga the ***Claremont Orchard Shop*** sells Nyanga trout and apples.

Nyanga The ***Angler's Rest*** *(☎ 8436, fax 9713)* on Anglers Rest Rd, about a 30-minute walk north of Nyanga village, has a swimming pool; dorms cost US$4 and doubles US$14 (US$16.50 with cooking facilities).

The basic ***Village Inn*** *(☎ 8336, fax 335)*, at the end of a country lane in Nyanga village, offers singles/doubles with bath and meals for US$26/50.

If you'd like to take in the scenery but are sick of the pseudo-British places, try the ***Mangondoza Country Hotel*** a few kilometres north of Nyanga village. There's a bar and veranda from where you can watch the locals go about their business. Rooms with breakfast cost US$7/13.

The ***Rochdale shop*** in Nyanga village sells groceries, and the market ***food stalls*** by the bus terminal in Nyamhuka township provide another option.

Nyanga National Park The ***Nyangombe Camping & Caravan Site*** lies between the Nyangombe River and the highway. It's full of big pine woods and has nice hot showers, baths, braai pits and toilets.

You'll find cosy ***National Park lodges*** (for booking details, see under Accommodation in Facts for the Visitor section) at Udu Dam, Nyanga Dam and Nyangwe Dam, all close to the main park service area. (For example, three- and five-bed lodges cost from US$11/13.) At Pungwe Drift, near the southern extreme of the park, are two remote ***lodges*** (five-bed lodge for US$18.50) and a ***camping ground***.

The ***Rainbow Nyanga Hotel*** *(☎ 377, fax 477, e rtzhotel@omnizim.com)*, with its tropical veranda and well-kept gardens, was once the big man's home. Rooms cost US$26/42, half board.

Troutbeck The ***Troutbeck Sun*** *(☎ 8305, fax 474)*, founded by Irishman Major Robert McIlwaine, sits at an altitude of 2000m. The food is 100% typically English – cream teas, Yorkshire puddings and game pies – with the atmosphere and weather to match. Tradition has it that the log fire roaring in the main hall has been burning since the hotel was founded in 1950! There's tennis, swimming, shooting, squash courts, a golf course, a private lake for trout fishing, lawn bowls and stables. Rooms cost US$115/128, including breakfast.

Shopping

A surprising highlight is the Zuwa Weaving Cooperative (☎ 8293), behind Nyanga post office, which sells sturdy wool and cotton blankets and rugs, and mohair scarves. It's open Monday to Saturday. The name Zuwa means either Day or Sun.

Nyamhuka township, the terminal for buses to/from Mutare, Rusape and Harare, has a couple of shops and stalls, a shabby 'crafts village' and a relaxed atmosphere.

Getting There & Away

All buses go via Juliasdale and terminate in Nyanga, Nyamhuka or Troutbeck. The national park bus stop is right in front of the Nyangombe camping ground.

Daily services from Mbare to Juliasdale and Nyanga (Nyamhuka township) leave at 6 am. In Harare, catch the bus from the corner of Glenara and Robert Mugabe Rds, or flag it down on the Mutare road. The fare is US$5. Alternatively, take a Rusape bus and connect there with hourly services to Juliasdale and Nyanga. From Mutare's Chipanda St terminal, buses depart for Juliasdale and Nyanga hourly.

Zimbabwe Sun Hotels' Sabi Star runs transfers between Harare and the Troutbeck Sun for US$21.

For day trips to Nyanga, see Organised Tours under Mutare.

CHIMANIMANI

☎ 126

Chimanimani village is enclosed by green hills on three sides, and opens on the fourth side to the dramatic wall of the Chimanimani Mountains.

The name Chimanimani is derived from the Manyika word for a place that must be passed single file, presumably referring to the narrow gap where the Msapa River flows. Chimanimani National Park is covered in the next section.

The friendly and helpful Chimanimani Tourist Association (☎ 2294) PO Box 75, Chimanimani, sells the *Milkmaps Guides*, detailing walks around the village and national park (US$0.75) and topographical sheets of Chimanimani National Park. It's open from 9 am to 1 pm and 2 to 5 pm Friday to Wednesday (9 am to 1 pm Sunday). The bank opens from 8 am to 2.30 pm on Monday, Tuesday, Thursday, 8 am to 1 pm Wednesday, and 8 to 11 am Saturday.

Internet facilities are available at the Blue Moon, which is also a bar, opposite the Chimanimani Hotel entrance.

Things to See

The 18-sq-km **Chimanimani Eland Sanctuary** was established to protect antelope, which found it difficult to resist young shoots of maize and coffee and pine saplings in the surrounding agricultural and timber lands. The odd thing about the Eland Sanctuary is the conspicuous absence of eland. Apparently, there were flaws in the sanctuary concept and they were all poached, presumably by Mozambican insurgents. You may, however, see waterbuck or baboon, and perhaps even a duiker, klipspringer or the odd zebra.

You can walk or drive around **Nyamzure** (also known as Pork Pie Hill, for obvious reasons). From town, turn left at the T-junction north of the post office, then right at the first opportunity. From there, it's 5km uphill to the base of Nyamzure, where a well-defined track leads to the summit, with spectacular views all around.

In a lush setting 6km from Chimanimani, **Bridal Veil Falls** is a slender 50m drop on the Nyahodi River. The road in is rough and winding, but it's an easy and pleasant walk and a super spot for a picnic. There is a US$5 entry fee and there's a camping area.

Activities

A whole range of activities in and around Chimanimani (including the national park), such as **walking**, **mountain-biking**, **rafting**, **birdwatching** and **cultural tours**, can be arranged through Mahobahoba (MH2) Tours (☎ 2701) PO Box 200, Chimanimani.

The bottle shop hires out camping and trekking equipment.

Horse-riding trips around Chimanimani village are available for US$7 per hour. For information, contact Tempé (☎ 2496) or the Frog & Fern Cottages (☎ 2294). Advance bookings and some riding experience are required.

Two week *djembe* **drum workshops** allow you to build your own drum. The course costs US$250, including all materials, accommodation, transfers and tools – ask at the Msasa Cafe.

The **Chimanimani Country Club** (☎ 2266) offers tennis, table tennis, snooker, squash, a swimming pool and, of course, golf, against a fabulous mountain backdrop.

Places to Stay & Eat

The most popular budget place is ***Heaven Lodge*** *(☎/fax 2701)*, 300m towards the national park. It's a cosy place with constant activity and a superb view. You can choose between dorms or double A-frames for US$8 per person, and camping costs US$5.50 per person. The 1st-floor dorm is over the bar and dining area so can be a tad noisy. Delicious meals include vegetarian

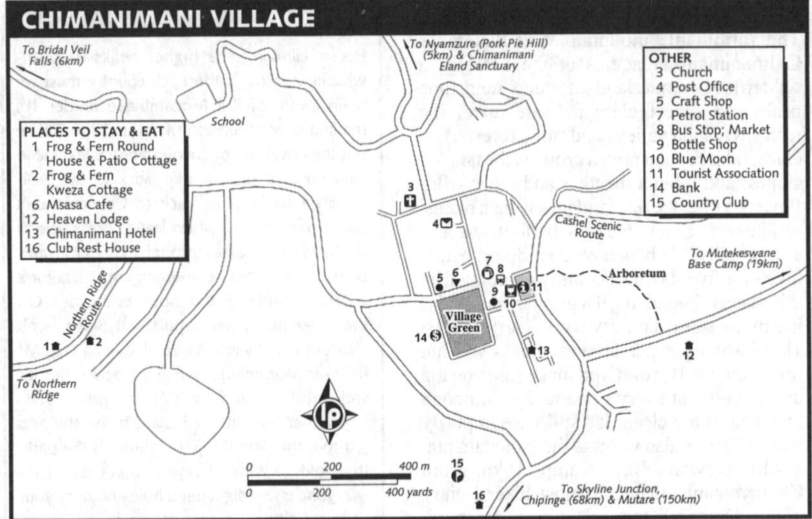

choices and it does transfers to the national park for US$3/4 one way/return; guides are also available and there's a card phone.

Another budget option is the quiet and friendly ***Club Rest House*** *(☎ 2266)* at the Country Club, 500m towards Skyline Junction. Huts in the car park cost from US$5; there's no cooking facilities, but the Rest House does meals and the bar is a great place to hear all the local gossip.

In the heights on the Northern Ridge Route is the ***Frog & Fern Cottages*** *(☎ 2294)*. The four architecturally distinct cottages have stunning views. Rates start at US$18 per person and guests have use of the common lounge, dining room and kitchen facilities.

The ***Chimanimani Hotel*** *(☎ 2511, fax 2515)* is a faded colonial wonder, surrounded by gardens, a pool, casino, minigolf course and fine mountain views. Rooms complete with fireplaces, balconies and big antique bathtubs cost US$24/39 for singles/doubles – ask for a mountain view. Camping is permitted for US$2 per person on the spacious hotel lawns, surrounded by flower-filled gardens. The hotel's dining room serves meals and buffets of inconsistent quality, but the prices are suitably low.

Msasa Cafe will cheer those looking for something healthy and wholesome. It serves up lasagne, Mexican fare, smoothies and real coffee. It's open for lunch and dinner daily. This is also the place to ask about drum workshops.

A couple of small ***shops*** in the village sell essential groceries, and the ***market*** has an impressive selection of fresh vegetables and fruit. Delicious soft Chimanimani cheese, which is good for mountain hikes, is available from the ***bottle shop***, ***Frog & Fern Cottages*** and ***Heaven Lodge***.

Getting There & Away

There are daily buses from Mutare, leaving Sakubva between 5.30 am and 1 pm. From Chimanimani buses to Mutare depart between 4.45 am and 5 pm. There are also buses to Masvingo (via Wengezi) and Chipinge (between 8 and 9 am). To get to Harare, board a Mutare bus and change there.

Hitching to/from Mutare isn't especially good, and will probably entail a series of short lifts from Mutare. The route in from Chipinge is normally easier than from Wengezi Junction.

CHIMANIMANI NATIONAL PARK

The formidable mountain wall that faces Chimanimani village is at the heart of a wilderness wonderland of steep sandstone peaks and towers, clear and safe swimming rivers, savanna valleys and stone forests. Orchids, hibiscus and protea grow on the tangled slopes, and lobelia, heather and other wildflowers carpet the intermittent savanna plains.

The park, accessible only by foot, is a hikers' paradise. Whether you're doing a day hike or a five-day backcountry camping trip, this place is bound to get a grip on you. Walking in the sun is hot, dry work; carry at least 1L of water per person and, unless you are following the Bundi River, make sure you top up the bottle at every opportunity. Although the streams are clean, it's still wise to purify water. There's also water at the mountain hut.

Mutekeswane Base Camp, 19km from Chimanimani village, is most hikers' entry point. There's a ranger's office, car park, camping ground with hot showers and braais, and a welcome tuck shop with cold drinks. Visitors must report to the ranger's office and pay fees before proceeding into the park. See the boxed text 'Warning' for information.

Corner

This park off-shoot, which juts into Mozambique, is connected to the main body of the park by a 10km-long and approximately 300m-wide swathe along the international boundary. The highlight is probably the narrow *chimanimani* through the constricted Msapa River Gap, which gave its name to the entire region. You can camp anywhere in Corner, but firewood collection is prohibited.

Corner is accessible by vehicle from Chimanimani along the Cashel Scenic Route via Martin Forest Reserve and the village of Chikukwa. You can reach Chikukwa on a daily bus that leaves Chimanimani in the early evening (and returns early the next morning), but from there you have a good 10km walk into Corner. Park fees are collected by rangers who greet you on arrival.

Places to Stay & Eat

If you've had to walk to Mutekeswane, you'll probably wind up spending a night there. ***Camping***, hot baths and showers are available; there's no electricity, so bring a torch.

Overlooking the Bundi Valley, across the first range of peaks, two to three hours walk from Mutekeswane, is a classic stone ***mountain hut*** with bed frames, propane cooking rings and cold showers. It comfortably sleeps 20 to 30 people, but foreigners pay US$3 per person, so it remains empty most of the time.

Fortunately, the Bundi Valley is riddled with ***caves*** and rock overhangs, which make ideal camp sites. The most accessible caves lie near the valley's northern end and fill up quickly. North Cave, a 30 minute walk from the mountain hut, overlooks a waterfall and opens onto views of the highest peaks. Above the waterfall is a pool, good for a cold swim, and Red Wall Cave lies 10 minutes further on.

A similar distance down the valley from the hut is Digby's Waterfall Cave, where the river provides a swimming hole; beyond that is Peter's House Cave. Further along, 1km north of Southern Lakes and two hours from the hut, is Terry's Cave, which is divided into two rooms by an artificial stone wall. It's east of the river and not easily found, but there's a faint track leading up to it.

Warning

Hikers climbing the higher peaks or bushwhacking through the back country must remain aware of the Mozambique border. It's marked only at Skeleton Pass and the Saddle but the possibility of encountering unexploded land mines makes it risky. Stick to the well-travelled tracks. The track to Chimanimani's southern extremes, which leaves Zimbabwe at the Saddle and passes through 8km of Mozambique territory before re-emerging at Dragon's Tooth, is dangerous and should be avoided. On the other hand, the popular Mt Binga climb also loops briefly into Mozambique (in fact, Mt Binga is Mozambique's highest peak), but it's well travelled and doesn't present risks.

Another less sinister hazard is the shit and loo rolls that line the paths through the park. It should go without saying: don't ruin it for everyone else – dig a deep hole and bury your daily ablutions.

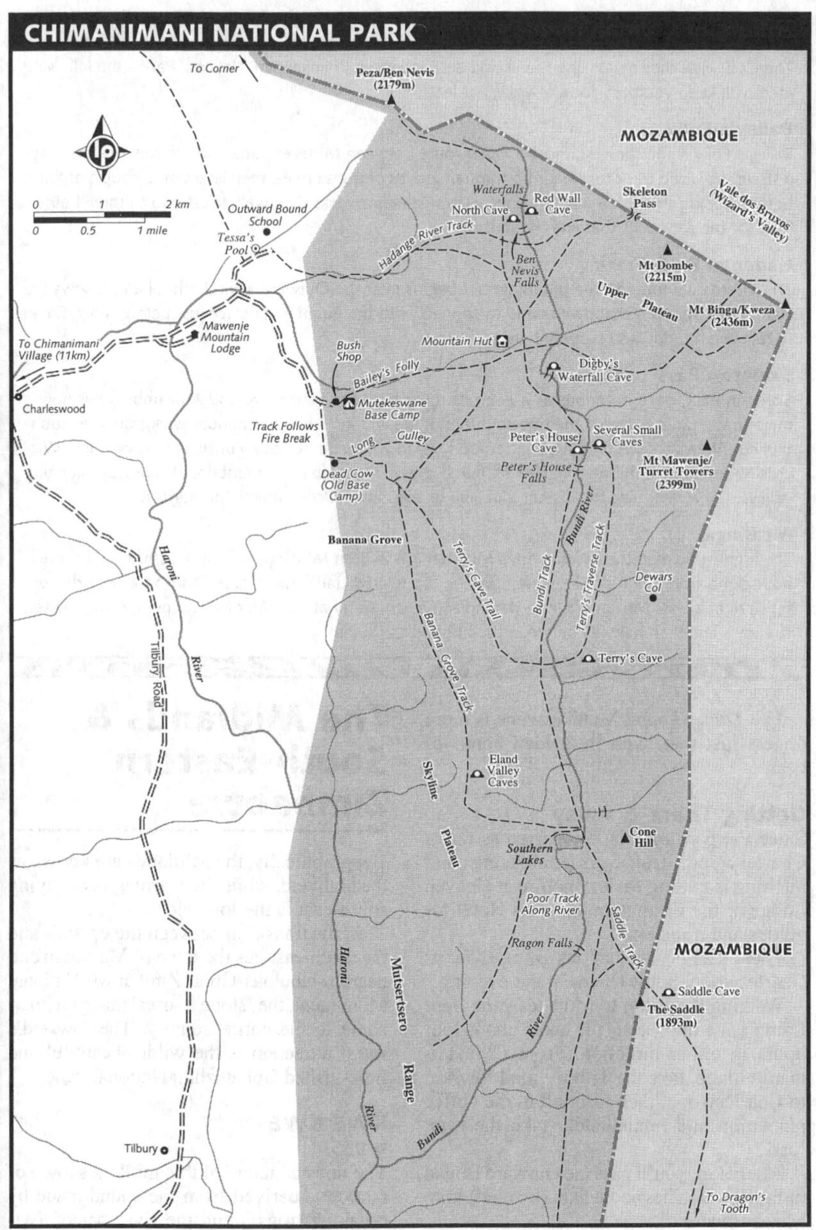
CHIMANIMANI NATIONAL PARK
To Corner
Peza/Ben Nevis (2179m)
MOZAMBIQUE
0 1 2 km
0 0.5 1 mile
Outward Bound School
Tessa's Pool
Waterfalls
North Cave
Red Wall Cave
Skeleton Pass
Vale dos Bruxos (Wizard's Valley)
Hadange River Track
Ben Nevis Falls
Mt Dombe (2215m)
Upper Plateau
Mt Binga/Kweza (2436m)
Mawenje Mountain Lodge
To Chimanimani Village (11km)
Mountain Hut
Bush Shop
Bailey's Folly
Digby's Waterfall Cave
Charleswood
Mutekeswane Base Camp
Track Follows Fire Break
Long Gulley
Several Small Caves
Peter's House Cave
Peter's House Falls
Mt Mawenje/ Turret Towers (2399m)
Dead Cow (Old Base Camp)
Banana Grove
Haroni
Terry's Cave Trail
Bundi River
Bundi Track
Terry's Traverse Track
Dewars Col
Tilbury Road
River
Banana Grove Track
Terry's Cave
Eland Valley Caves
Skyline Plateau
Cone Hill
Southern Lakes
Poor Track Along River
Saddle Track
Ragon Falls
MOZAMBIQUE
Haroni
Mutsertsero Range
Saddle Cave
The Saddle (1893m)
River
River
Bundi
Tilbury
To Dragon's Tooth

Hiking In Chimanimani

There's a wide choice of hiking routes and destinations in Chimanimani National Park – the following ideas will keep you busy for a few days at least.

Bailey's Folly

Bailey's Folly is the shortest, most popular route between Mutekeswane and the mountain hut. It's a straightforward track that leads up through groves of msasa trees, then levels off a couple of times before passing through a magnificent forest of standing rocks. The walk takes two to three hours – look for the rock piles that line the route.

Hadange River Track

This alternative route to the mountain hut begins near the Outward Bound school and follows the Hadange River up a shadowy ravine to connect with the Bundi River track just below North Cave. It gets very muddy and slippery here.

Skeleton Pass

Skeleton Pass, once notorious as a guerrilla route between Zimbabwe and Mozambique, is now a major trade route between the two countries. It lies within an easy 40-minute walk from the mountain hut. Views are best in the late afternoon, when you're treated to an unsurpassed view into Wizards Valley and range after range of fluted green Mozambican mountains divided by plunging valleys. On a clear day, the distant blue line of the Indian Ocean meets the horizon.

Mt Binga

The highest point in the Chimanimani Mountains is 2436m Mt Binga, which is a stiff two- to three-hour climb from the hut. The view from the top is predictably spectacular, and on a clear day extends right across Mozambique to the Indian Ocean. Carry at least 1L of water per person; the last stream is less than halfway between the hut and the summit.

The *Tuck Shop* at Mutekeswane is more or less just that, with the added bonus of beer.

Getting There & Away

Since the park road is now tarred as far as Charleswood, traffic is increasing and hitching is getting easier. Inquire at Heaven Lodge or the Chimanimani Arms Hotel for guides and transfers.

There's an occasional bus going as far as Charleswood, but it leaves in the evening.

Walking the 19km to Mutekeswane Base Camp isn't unpleasant; it takes about four hours in either direction. From Chimanimani village, take the Tilbury road for 9km to Charleswood, then turn left at the coffee plantation and immediately take the right fork.

After 5km, you'll pass the Outward Bound turn-off, which lies about 5km (by road) from Mutekeswane.

The Midlands & South-Eastern Zimbabwe

Geographically, the Midlands are known as the highveld, while the warmer, lower-lying south-east is the lowveld.

At the transition between the uplands and the south-east lies the town of Masvingo and nearby, fabulous Great Zimbabwe National Monument, the 'stone houses' that gave their name to the entire country. The lowveld's finest attraction is the wildly beautiful and little-visited Gonarezhou National Park.

KWE KWE

☎ 055

The unusual name of this midlands town of 60,000 is derived from the sound made by croaking frogs along the river banks. Evi-

Hiking In Chimanimani

Southern Lakes

Little more than wide-spots in a U-turn bend of the Bundi River, the vegetation-murky pools known as Southern Lakes make a nice lunch spot or a passable camp site. The obvious mountain rising to the east is Mt Mawenje, also known as Turret Towers.

The Saddle

The Saddle, at 1893m, is another pass into Mozambique. To get there, cross the Bundi River between the first and second Southern Lakes and walk north along the river until you reach a steep track heading up the slope. From there, it's about an hour to the top.

Banana Grove & Long Gully

These two routes up to the first level of peaks begin south of Mutekeswane. The Banana Grove Track is a gentler, but longer, ascent than Bailey's Folly. The lush, rocky ravine known as Long Gully is steeper, but leads to Digby's Waterfall Cave.

Both routes begin at Mutekeswane. Descend steeply from the southern side of the road, about 250m west of the ranger's office. At the bottom, slop your way through the small swamp, then follow the up-and-down fire swathe to the old base camp enigmatically known as Dead Cow. Here the track turns sharply to the left and winds upward.

At the fork above Dead Cow, you can choose between the two routes; the left one ascends Long Gully and the right one climbs to Banana Grove.

The Banana Grove route is most often used by hikers returning to Mutekeswane via the Southern Lakes. Coming from the mountain hut along the Bundi River, watch on your right as you approach the first Southern Lake and you'll see the red-earth track climbing steeply from the main river route before levelling off. Allow at least seven hours to walk from the mountain hut to Mutekeswane via Southern Lakes and Banana Grove.

dence of the value of the region's gold production can be found throughout the district.

The friendly and worthwhile **National Museum of Gold Mining** provides a fascinating introduction to commercial gold-mining in Zimbabwe, past and present. You're greeted by a working scale model of the Globe & Phoenix mine, which can be heard grinding away nearby. The Paper House, Zimbabwe's first prefabricated building, is also here.

The museum is open from 9 am to 5 pm daily; foreigners pay US$2/1 for adults/children which includes a guided tour. It's at the end of First Ave, signposted from the main road.

Places to Stay & Eat

The friendly three-star ***Golden Mile Motel*** *(☎ 3711, fax 3120)*, 2km south of town on the Bulawayo road, has rooms for US$42, and there's a nice poolside bar, nightclub and restaurant.

Several remote farms have opened their doors to budget travellers. Most people head for ***Mopani Park Farm*** *(☎ 27822)*, deep in the bush 49km from Kwe Kwe. Eight properties have been combined to create a large nature reserve and mecca for riding enthusiasts.

There are plenty of horses, suitable for experienced and novice riders. Camping is US$1, dorms are US$2 and doubles cost US$10; breakfast/lunch/dinner are an additional US$2/1/4. Bush rides cost US$5 per hour or you can join in a game of polocrosse (a mix of polo and lacrosse) for US$6. Overnight rhino safaris on horseback cost US$125 and overnight walking trips are US$70. Transfers from town are available; call ☎ 2625.

There's plenty of takeaways in town, including a ***Wimpy*** just opposite the mosque.

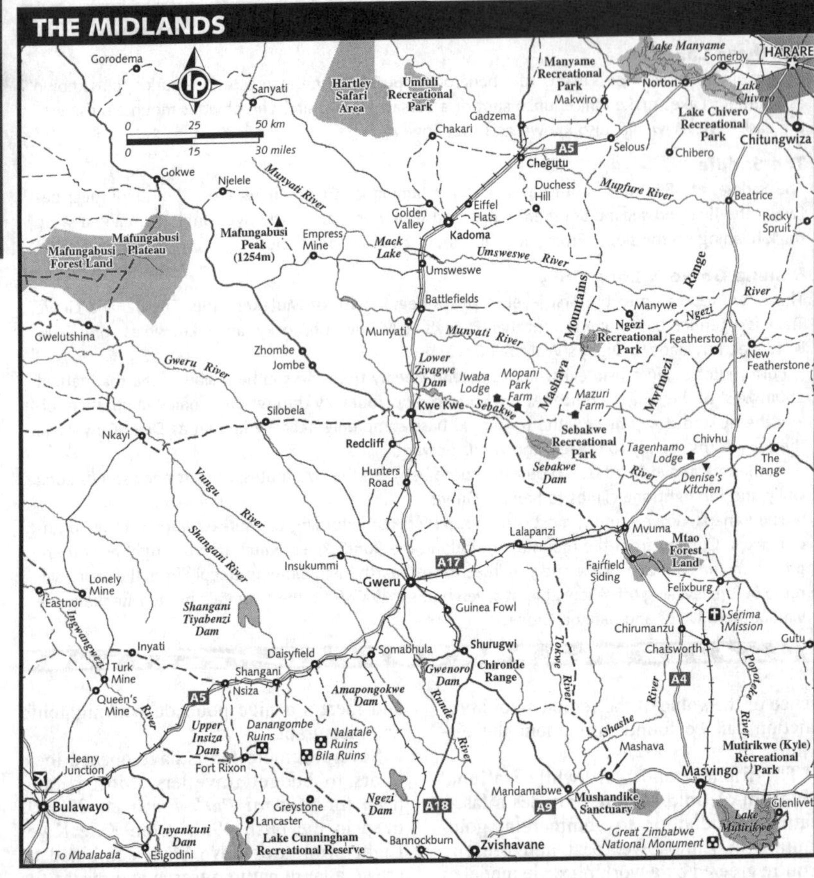

Getting There & Away

Blue Arrow buses to Harare (US$5.50) and Bulawayo (US$11) stop at Golden Mile Motel (11.05 am Thursday, 6.35 pm Monday). Local bus services run from the market behind the mosque. Trains between Harare and Bulawayo stop at Kwe Kwe in the small hours of the morning; call ☎ 2327 for details.

GWERU

☎ 054

Gweru, with a population of 105,000, isn't a travellers' destination by any means, but most pass through it at some stage.

The Gweru Publicity Association (☎ 226) in the City Hall on the corner of Eighth St and Robert Mugabe St is open from 8 am to 4.30 pm weekdays.

The informative **Midlands Museum** is devoted to the evolution of Zimbabwe's military and police history and technology, from the earliest tribal wars, through the Rhodesian years to modern Zimbabwe. It's open from 9 am to 5 pm daily; foreigners pay US$2 entry.

The **Boggie Memorial Clock Tower** can't be missed, mainly because it blocks Gweru's two main streets. It was erected by Mrs Jeannie

Boggie in 1937, as a memorial to her husband, Major WJ Boggie, as well as 'all colonial pioneers and their beasts of burden'.

Places to Stay & Eat

The green ***Caravan Park*** *(☎ 2929)* fronts the sports club, about 500m from the centre on the Bulawayo road. Camping costs US$1 plus US$0.65 per person. Check in at the cocktail bar in the sports club.

The three-star ***Fairmile Motel*** *(☎ 4144)* also on the Bulawayo road, avoids any bland pretences. Standard singles/doubles cost US$33/41. Another good choice is the ***Pamusha Lodge Guest House*** *(☎ 3535, 73 Kopje Rd)* which has rooms for US$20/27 with shared bath and US$22/31 with private bath.

Catering to passing travellers is the ***Dutch American Style Coffee House*** on Fifth St. Are you brave enough to ask for the blue job special? Next door, the ***Waldorf Cafe*** has a bakery and serves more African fare. There's also the usual cast of fast food places.

Getting There & Away

All buses between Harare and Bulawayo stop in Gweru. African buses use the Kudzenayi terminal near the market on Robert Mugabe St between Second and Third Sts. Blue Arrow buses stop at the Fairmile Motel on the Bulawayo road. Book express services through Manica Travel (☎ 23316), in the First Mutual Centre, on the corner of Robert Mugabe St and Fifth St.

Rail services between Harare and Bulawayo stop at Gweru in the early morning hours; call ☎ 3711 for information.

NALATALE & DANANGOMBE

Nalatale (also spelt Nalatela or Nalatele) rates among the best of Zimbabwe's 150 walled ruins. A simple structure on a remote granite hilltop, it enjoys a commanding view across the hills, plains and kopjes of **Somabhula Flats**. (On one hill, Wadai, visible across the flats, is a large colony of nesting **Cape vultures**. It's the most northerly colony of this protected species.) The main feature, a decorated wall, exhibits in one collection all the primary decorative wall patterns found in Zimbabwe: chevron, chequer, cord, herringbone and ironstone.

The ruins are well signposted. Coming from the north, turn south off the Gweru-Bulawayo road at the Daisyfield Siding. From the south, turn east from Shangani and follow the gravel road approximately 27km to the signposted left turn-off. The site is 1km uphill from the parking area.

Commonly known as Dhlo Dhlo (approximate pronunciation: 'hshlo hshlo'), Danangombe isn't as lovely or as well preserved as Nalatale, but it does remain quiet and unspoilt.

Originally a royal retreat under the Torwa dynasty, after the Torwa were defeated by the Changamires, it became the Rozwi administrative centre. The most interesting feature is a crumbling enclosure formed partially by natural boulders. The whole thing is overgrown by wandering tree roots and sheltered by large trees. Relics of Portuguese origin have been uncovered by amateur treasure hunters (such as a priest's ring, a leg-iron, a cannon and gold jewellery), but Danangombe's past largely remains a mystery. It's postulated that Portuguese traders were held captive there by the ruling *mambo*, possibly for assisting revolutionaries in the destruction of Khami (see Around Bulawayo later in this chapter). After the Ndebele invasions of the 1830s, the site was abandoned. It was rediscovered by white settlers after the 1893 Ndebele uprising.

Danangombe lies a well-signposted 22km from Shangani, or less from Nsiza via Fort Rixon.

There are no facilities at either site, but it is possible to rough camp.

MASVINGO

☎ 139

Masvingo, with a population of 40,000, emits a clean and routine small-town laziness. Mucheke township, 2km away, is vibrant Africa, with as lively a market as you can imagine. The name Masvingo, which was adopted after Zimbabwean independence, is derived from *rusvingo*, the Shona word for 'walled-in enclosures', in reference to the nearby Great Zimbabwe.

Historically, Masvingo prided itself on being the first white settlement in Zimbabwe (a fact that few other people cared about one way or another). The pioneer column of the British South Africa Company (BSAC), under Frederick Courteney Selous, moved through Lobengula's stronghold in Matabeleland and across the dry lowveld to the cooler plateaus. In August 1890, the column paused at a spot now known as Clipsham Farm, a few kilometres south of present-day Masvingo, to establish Fort Victoria and construct a rude mud fortification. However, a drought two years later forced the removal of the settlement to a more amenable location between the Shagashe and Mucheke Rivers, where a new, more permanent fort was built.

Information

The friendly Masvingo Publicity Association (☎ 62643) on Robert Mugabe St, is open from 8 am to 1 pm and 2 pm to 4.30 pm weekdays, and 9 am to noon Saturday. It distributes a good map of the area with tourist listings.

The town has plenty of banks (with ATMs), a post office and a hospital. On Robert Mugabe St is the One Stop Tourist Shop, which combines an accommodation service, Internet access, bureau de change and curio shop. It's open during business hours Monday to Saturday. The best bookshop in town is the Mambo Press Bookshop on Josiah Tongorara Ave.

Things to See

The Italian-style **Church of St Francis of Assisi** was constructed between 1942 and 1946 by Italian POWs; the interior holds the remains of 71 of their compatriots who died in Zimbabwe between 1942 and 1947. The simulated mosaics in the apse were the work of an Italian engineer, while the wall murals were completed 10 years later by Masvingo artists. To get to the church, go 3km east towards Mutare, take the left turn and then turn immediately left again. Just in front of the military barracks, turn left yet again; you'll see the church 100m away.

The small **Shagashe Game Park** lies 10km towards Harare.

Places to Stay

Masvingo's ***Caravan Park*** *(☎ 62431)*, with green lawns and a riverside setting, charges US$2.50 per person, but there's no security.

On the way to Great Zimbabwe (via the old road, and near the river), ***Sundowners*** *(☎ 62718, @ sunbird@mvo.samara.co.zw)* is a great place to unwind before tackling the ruins; in fact it encourages this by offering a free guided tour for those staying two nights. Dorms cost US$5 and private rooms US$7 per person, and a hearty dinner around a big table is US$3. It also offers camping (US$2), Internet access, a bar and town transfers.

Another great spot with the advantage of a pool is the friendly ***Clovelly Lodge*** *(☎ 64751)* off Glyntnor Rd, which is nestled among the gum trees 4km west of the centre. Comfortable dorms cost US$8 per person and doubles are US$20, including breakfast and family-style dinners. Transfers from town are included and horse riding is available from US$5 per hour.

More central, but also more basic, is ***Backpackers Rest*** *(☎ 63960)*, in the Escher-like Dauth building. The ***Paw Paw Lodge*** *(☎ 65231, 18 Kirton Rd)* and the ***Titambire Lodge*** *(☎ 62475, 14 Kirton Rd)* near the Publicity Association, are small and basic. All three offer dorms for US$4 and doubles for US$16. The first two serve meals on request.

The ***Chevron Hotel*** *(☎ 62054)* on the main road charges US$30/39 for singles/doubles, with breakfast. The nicer ***Flamboyant Motel*** *(☎ 53085, fax 52899)* has rooms with bath and breakfast for US$40/54. There's a pool, restaurants and bars; a dress code is enforced after 6 pm.

Places to Eat

The best eatery is the ***Garden Cafe***, behind Roselli Gallery (39 Hughes St), which has daily lunch specials, including vegetarian dishes. It's open from 8.30 am to 4.30 pm weekdays, and 8.30 am to 1 pm Saturday.

The ***Tea Cosy Snack Bar***, at Meikles Department Store on Robert Mugabe St, serves tea, cakes and pastries. The takeaways at the ***petrol stations*** are best for snacks. Kyle Shell also has a ***Spar Market***, open from 7 am to 8 pm daily.

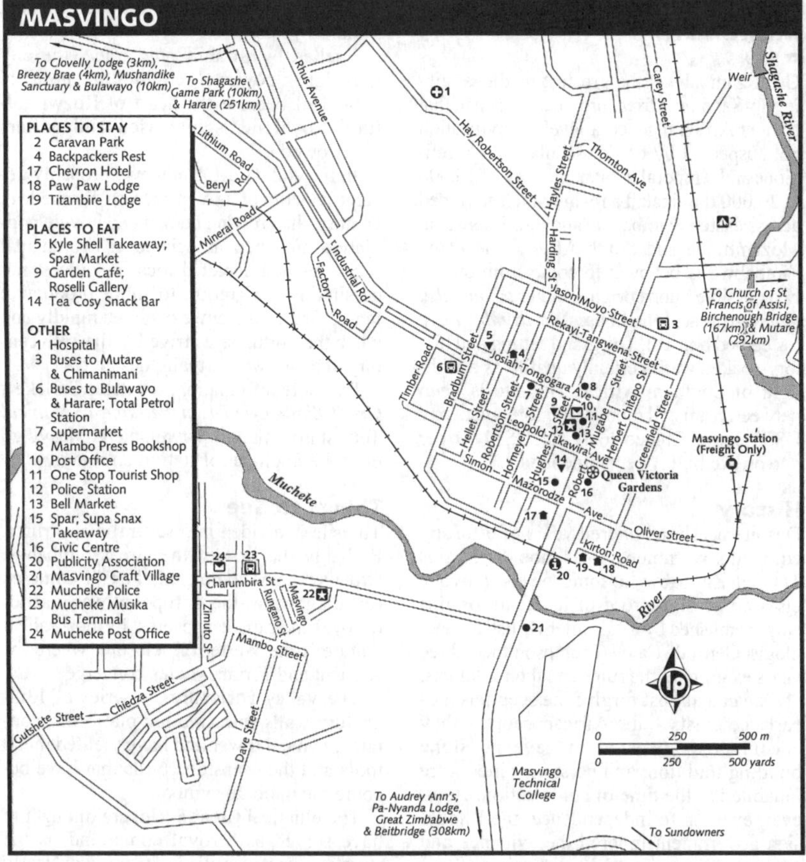

There are restaurants and takeaway joints situated all over town, serving the usual chicken, burgers, chips and deep-fried snacks. The terrace in front of the ***Chevron Hotel*** (see Places to Stay) is great for a snack and a drink, and other hotel dining rooms are also OK.

For self-caterers, there's the ***supermarket*** on Josiah Tongogara Ave.

Getting There & Away

Air Zimbabwe (☎ 04-794481 in Harare) flies between Masvingo and Harare on Monday, Wednesday and Friday.

Long-distance African buses use the Mucheke *musika* terminal, 1.5km south-west of the town centre. Access is by bus or taxi. All buses to Mucheke also stop in the town centre. Buses to and from Harare depart on the hour between 6 am and 5 pm, and there are several daily services to both Bulawayo and Mutare.

Buses between Harare and Jo'burg all pass through Masvingo. Most use the Shell petrol station at the Great Zimbabwe turn-off as their terminal. For details, see South Africa in the main Getting There & Away section of this chapter.

GREAT ZIMBABWE NATIONAL MONUMENT

☎ 139

Great Zimbabwe, the greatest medieval city in sub-Saharan Africa, provides evidence that ancient Africa reached a level of civilisation not suspected by earlier scholars. As a religious and temporal capital, this city of 10,000 to 20,000 dominated a realm which stretched across eastern Zimbabwe and into Botswana, Mozambique and South Africa. The name Zimbabwe is believed to come from one of two possible Shona origins; either *dzimba dza mabwe* (great stone houses) or *dzimba woye* (esteemed houses). The grand setting and history-soaked walls certainly qualify as a highlight of Southern Africa. The site is open between 6 am and 6 pm daily; foreigners pay US$5 entry. Guided tours for US$1.50 per person are highly recommended.

History

Despite nearly a hundred years of effort by colonial governments to ascribe the origins of Great Zimbabwe to someone else (anyone else) conclusive proof of its Bantu origins was established by 1932, after British archaeologist Gertrude Caton-Thompson spent three years examining the ruins and their artefacts.

One can almost forgive the scepticism of early colonists – the African peoples they encountered appeared to have no stone building tradition, and no stone cities were inhabited at the time of colonisation. However, even up to independence, the Rhodesian government ignored the evidence and supported fantasies of foreign origins.

Outside influences did, however, play a role in the development of Great Zimbabwe. Swahili traders were present along the Mozambique coast from the 10th century, and trade goods – Chinese porcelain, Persian crockery and beads and Indian trinkets – have turned up there. Outsiders undoubtedly had an influence.

What became the Great Zimbabwe site was first occupied in the 11th century. The settlers are thought to have comprised several scattered groups that recognised the safety of numbers. Construction of the Hill Complex commenced in the 13th century; the remainder was built over the next hundred years.

Fuelled by Swahili gold trade, the city grew into a powerful religious and political capital; it became the heart of Rozwi culture. Royal herds increased and coffers overflowed.

In the end, Great Zimbabwe probably became a victim of its own success. By the 15th century, the growing human and bovine population and their associated environmental pressures had depleted local resources, necessitating emigration to more productive lands. Great Zimbabwe declined rapidly and when the Portuguese arrived in the 16th century, the city was virtually deserted.

For more information, see Peter Garlake's *Great Zimbabwe Described and Explained.* Tourist information is available in Masvingo or at the Shell petrol station en route.

Things to See

The site is divided into several major ruins. Probably the first of the Great Zimbabwe structures to be completed, the **Hill Complex** (once known as the Acropolis) was a series of royal and ritual enclosures. Its most salient feature is the Western Enclosure, where the Ancient and Terrace routes converge.

The **Valley Enclosures**, a series of 13th-century walls and *daga* hut platforms, contain a conical tower and have yielded metal tools and the soapstone birds that have become the national symbol.

The elliptical **Great Enclosure**, thought to have served as a royal compound, is the structure most identified with the site. Nearly 100m across and 255m in circumference, it's the largest ancient structure in sub-Saharan Africa. The mortarless walls rise 11m and, in places, are 5m thick. The greatest source of speculation is the 10m-high **Conical Tower**, a solid and apparently ceremonial structure, which probably has phallic significance.

Leading north-east from the Conical Tower is the narrow 70m-long **Parallel Passage**. It may have been a means of moving from the North Entrance to the Conical Tower without being detected by those within the enclosure. It may also have been that the construction skills of the builders had im-

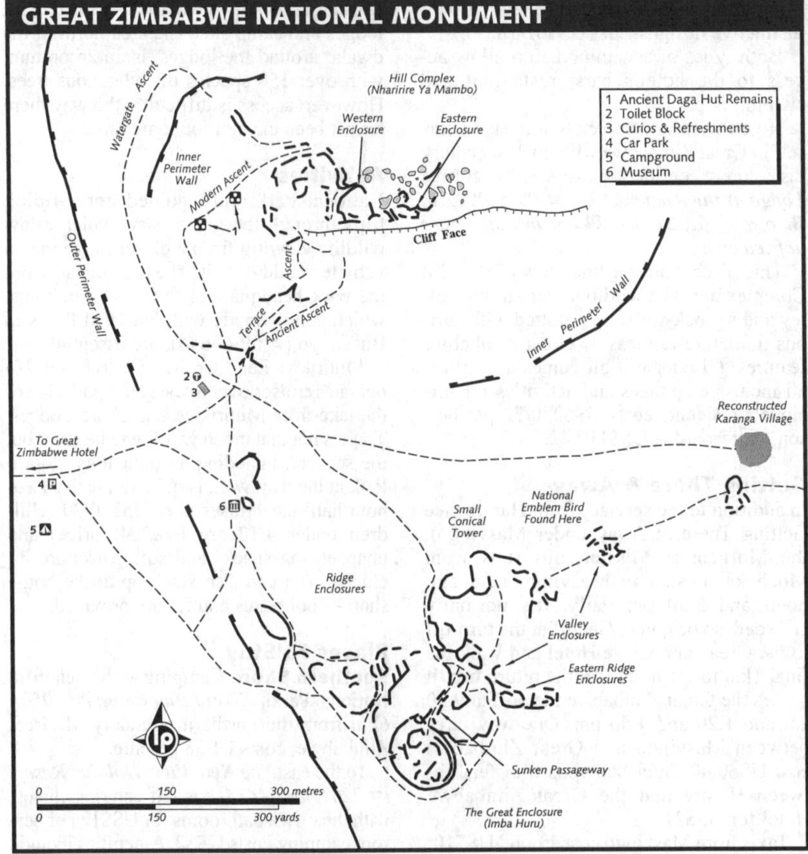

proved so dramatically over time that they decided to rebuild the entire wall in a superior manner. The outside wall of the Parallel Passage, perhaps the most architecturally advanced structure in Great Zimbabwe, is 6m thick at the base and 4m thick at the top, with each course of stone tapering to add stability to the 11m-high wall. This stretch is capped by three rings of decorative chevron patterns.

The site **museum**, open from 8 am to 4.30 pm daily, houses most of the Great Zimbabwe archaeological finds. For most, the soapstone Zimbabwe birds, which were probably Rozwi dynasty totems, are the highlight. Other exhibits of interest include porcelain and glass goods brought by Swahili traders.

Places to Stay & Eat

Campers have the chance to bed down at the ***National Museums & Monuments Campground*** (*☎ 7052*), within sight of the Hill Complex. It also has beds in two large dorms for US$3, which you will probably have sole use of.

The ***Great Zimbabwe Hotel*** (*☎ 64713, fax 64884*) charges foreigners US$126/158 for singles/doubles, including a good buffet breakfast. Self-contained lodges, closer to the ruins themselves and reflecting their distinctive designs, cost US$62/78.

Both types of accommodation allow access to the hotel's bars, restaurant and swimming pool.

If you want to completely immerse yourself in Great Zimbabwe with no 21st century distractions, consider the exotic and exclusive ***Lodge at the Ancient City*** *(☎ 09-540922 in Bulawayo, fax 229088, @ touchwld@harare.iafrica.com)*.

This place enjoys a fine view of the Hill Complex across a wild boulder-strewn valley and its rocky hillside is dotted with curious miniature replicas of Great Zimbabwe features. Of course it all comes at a price: all-inclusive cottages and activities for foreigners/residents costs US$250/72 per person; half-board is US$119/42.

Getting There & Away

In addition to the services from Harare (see Getting There & Away under Masvingo), the Morgenster Mission bus runs from Mucheke musika in Masvingo at 8 am, noon and 3.30 pm daily. It's normally crowded, so be quick. Get off at the turn-off to the Great Zimbabwe Hotel and walk the final 1km to the hotel. On the return trip, it passes the Great Zimbabwe turn-off at 9.20 am and 1.20 and 4.50 pm. One-way fares between Masvingo and Great Zimbabwe cost US$0.40. Sabi Star runs transfers between Harare and the Great Zimbabwe Hotel for US$21.

Taxis from Masvingo cost around US$10; call ☎ 63453.

MUTIRIKWE (KYLE) RECREATIONAL PARK

☎ 039

A 305m-wide dam wall blocks the impressive Mutirikwe Gorge, forming Lake Mutirikwe. Completed in 1961, in the early 1990s, after nearly a decade of drought, it shrank to 1% of its capacity. Although the rains eventually came, and currently the lake is pretty full, lowveld irrigation projects continue to suffer.

The Mutirikwe Game Park hosts more species of antelope than any other park in Zimbabwe. Walking is permitted only around Mushagashe Arm near the National Park lodges and camp site. The area north of the dwala, around the lodges, is an arboretum, with over 150 species of indigenous trees. However, access is difficult – the way there hasn't been cleared for some time.

Activities

National Parks runs guided **horse-riding trips** through the game park, which allow **wildlife viewing** from a closer range than a vehicle would permit. The trips depart from the park headquarters. Advance bookings, which can be made with National Parks in Bulawayo (☎ 09-63646), are essential.

Mutirikwi Lake Cruises (☎ 011-209516) operates **cruises** over to the game-park side of the lake from Mutirikwe Lakeshore Lodges. There's not that much wildlife to be seen, but the scenery, including an obligatory stop to look at the dam wall, is quite dramatic. Two-hour/half-day cruises cost US$10/20 (children under 4/12 are free/half price) and unappetising snacks and soft drinks are included. You can also stock up at the bottle shop – cool boxes and ice are provided.

Places to Stay

Southern Shore Camping at the beautiful National Parks' ***Sikato Bay Camp*** *(☎ 7050)*, 6km from the northern boundary of Great Zimbabwe, costs US$8 per site.

To the east, the ***Kyle View Holiday Resort*** *(☎ 7202, fax 64484)* has self-catering chalets with their own bathrooms for US$12 per person; camping costs US$2. Amenities include a swimming pool, tennis courts and a relaxed restaurant and pub.

Mutirikwe Lakeshore Lodge *(☎ 64878)* has two-storey self-catering rondavels (six people maximum), which look like the kind of place a faerie would come home to after a hard day at the end of the garden. Singles/doubles are good value at US$13/15.50. Economy rooms cost US$11/13.50 and camping US$2 per person. There's a swimming pool, shop, and a pub and bottle shop.

The ***Inn on Great Zimbabwe*** *(☎ 64879, fax 65083, @ nj@mvo.samara.co.zw)* is recommended for its friendly, homely atmosphere. Head 200m east of Kyle View Holiday

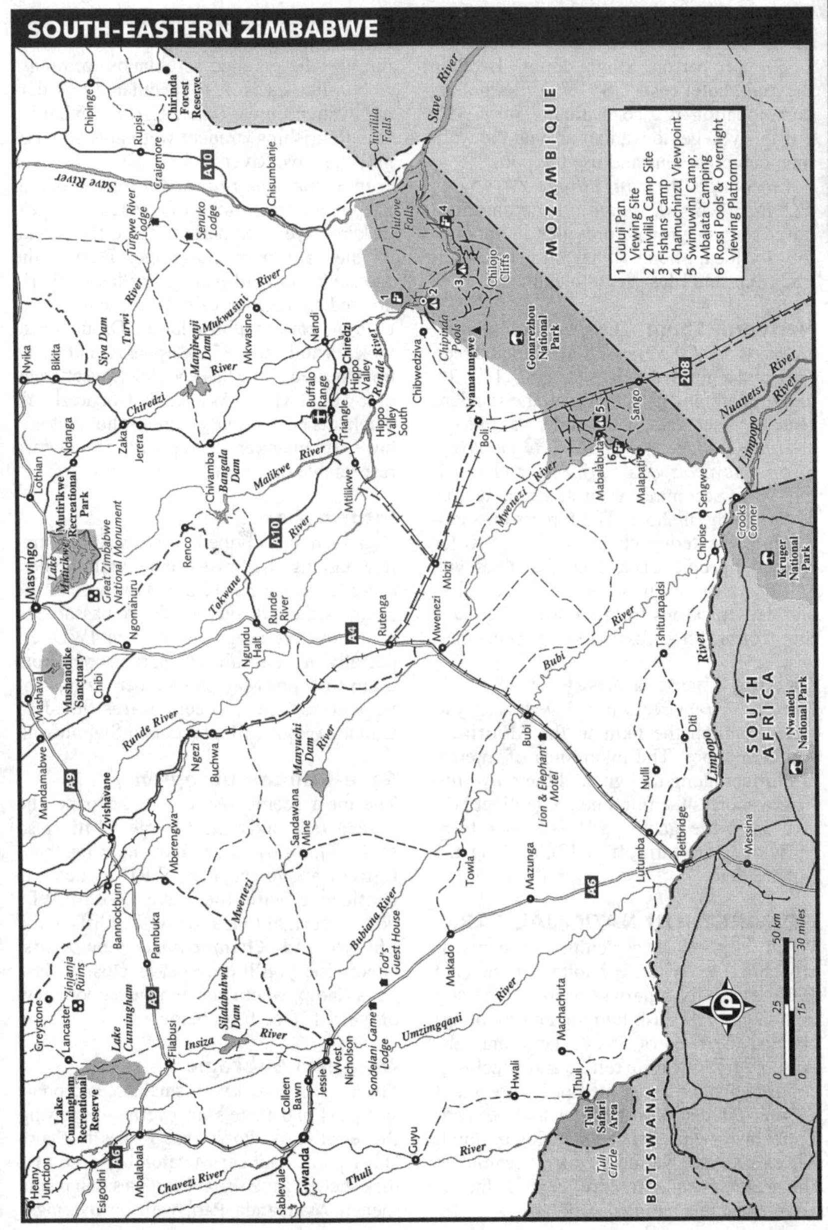
SOUTH-EASTERN ZIMBABWE
1 Guluji Pan Viewing Site
2 Chivilila Camp Site
3 Fishans Camp
4 Chamuchinzu Viewpoint
5 Swimuwini Camping; Mbalata Camping
6 Rossi Pools & Overnight Viewing Platform
MOZAMBIQUE
SOUTH AFRICA
BOTSWANA
Chipinge
Chirinda Forest Reserve
Rupisi
Craigmore
Chisumbanje
Chivilila Falls
Save River
Turgwe River Lodge
Senuko Lodge
Clutove Falls
Chilojo Cliffs
Chipinda Pools
Gonarezhou National Park
Nyika
Bikita
Siya Dam
Turwi River
Mukwasini River
Mkwasine
Nandi
Manjirenji Dam
Chiredzi River
Chiredzi
Hippo Valley
Buffalo Range
Triangle
Hippo Valley South
Runde River
Chibwedziva
Nyamatungwe
Boli
Sango
Mabalauta
Malapati
Nuanetsi River
Limpopo River
Lothian
Ndanga
Zaka
Jerera
Chivamba
Bangala Dam
Malikwe River
Mtilikwe
Mwenezi River
Mutirikwe Recreational Park
Lake Mutirikwe
Great Zimbabwe National Monument
Masvingo
Renco
Tokwane River
Runde River
Ngomahuru
Mbizi
Chipise
Sengwe
Crooks Corner
Kruger National Park
Mashava
Mushandike Sanctuary
Chibi
Ngundu Halt
Rutenga
Mwenezi
Bubi River
Tshiturapadsi
Mandamabwe
Zvishavane
Ngezi
Buchwa
Manyuchi Dam
Bubi
Lion & Elephant Motel
Diti
Nulli
Nwanedi National Park
Mberengwa
Sandawana Mine
Mwenezi
Towla
Mazunga
Lutumba
Beitbridge
Messina
Greystone
Lancaster
Zinjanja Ruins
Bannockburn
Pambuka
Bubiana River
Tod's Guest House
Makado
Machachuta
Lake Cunningham
Lake Cunningham Recreational Reserve
Filabusi
Insiza River
Silalabuhwa Dam
Sondelani Game Lodge
West Nicholson
Umzimgwani River
Jessie
Colleen Bawn
Hwali
Thuli
Tuli Safari Area
Tuli Circle
Heany Junction
Esigodini
Mbalabala
Chavezi River
Sablevale
Gwanda
Thuli River
Guyu
A10
A4
A9
A6
208
0 25 50 km
0 15 30 miles

Resort and it's on the hillside to the right, facing the lake. Self-catering chalets cost US$13 per person. Single/double B&B in the main hotel costs US$36/53. Budget accommodation is also available for US$7. For this you get to wander around the well-manicured gardens and use the pool.

Chesvingo African Village *(☎ 65793, PO Box 773, Masvingo)*, a community-based tourism project, provides an opportunity for local Shona villagers to share their traditions and lifestyle with campers.

Northern Shore The ***National Parks' camp*** *(☎ 62913)* offers self-contained three-, five- and eight-bed lodges for US$11/17/26, and the camping ground has all the standard features – showers, baths and braai pits.

Hippo Lodge *(☎/fax 63659, ⓔ glenlivt@mvo.samara.co.zw)* has friendly and excellent-value accommodation in a remote area of the northern shore. The three stone-and-thatch self-catering chalets cost US$40 for up to four people. Backpackers' doubles with half board (or use of self-catering facilities) and daily pick-ups from the Masvingo One Stop Tourist Shop cost US$10 per person.

Getting There & Away

Once you're at Great Zimbabwe, it's easy to walk or hitch the 6km to the Mutirikwe southern shore. The main sites of interest are further along though, and the only public transport is the infrequent Glenlivet bus. Access to the game park, is easier from Masvingo; the turn-off is 13km along the Mutare road.

GONAREZHOU NATIONAL PARK

When large-scale agriculture began encroaching on wildlife habitat in the late 1960s, tsetse-fly control measures (involving both large-scale bush-burning and shooting) claimed the lives of 55,000 large animals. Pressure for a wildlife refuge and poaching-control corridor along the border grew and a scenic 5000-sq-km chunk of south-eastern Zimbabwe – virtually an extension of South Africa's Kruger National Park – became the Gonarezhou Game Reserve. In 1975, the reserve became a national park.

The landscapes are impressive; the broad Mwenezi, Save and Runde Rivers wind through the parched scrublands forming a ribbon-like oasis. It is speculated that during wetter times, when Great Zimbabwe was flourishing, traders were able to navigate the Save River as far as Chivilila Falls.

In Shona, *Gona-re-zhou* means Abode of Elephant, and some of Africa's largest tuskers have lived here. It's also the habitat of the rare nyala antelope. During the Mozambican civil war, guerrillas regularly crossed the border to escape pursuers and used the park as a bush larder. Drought also took its toll, and 750 elephants had to be translocated to the Save Valley Conservancy or to South Africa. As a result, Gonarezhou's elephants bear a grudge against humans and have a cantankerous reputation – keep a respectable distance.

Information

Gonarezhou is divided into two administrative regions: the Save-Runde, with the best wildlife, in the north; and Mwenezi in the south. Although some roads are passable to cars, most are rough and require 4WD, especially in the south. The park is open from 6 am to 6 pm May to October. From November to April, access is restricted to Chipinda Pools, Mbalauta and Swimuwini.

Save-Runde Subregion

The most scenic section of the park, the rugged red sandstone Chilojo Cliffs (also spelt Tjolotjo), rise like a Rajasthani fortress above the Runde River, near its confluence with the Save. With 4WD, you'll get right to the top of the cliffs at the **Chilojo and Chamuchinzu viewpoints**. Otherwise, you'll only get as close as **Fishans Camp**, where you'll have a good view of the cliff face from below.

Mwenezi Subregion

Mwenezi is dotted with small, scenic pools and pans and there's an overnight viewing shelter at **Rossi Pools** (see Places to Stay). Other pools include: **Mwatomba**, deep in a rock shelter; **Mukokwani**, with a small picnic shelter; **Manyanda Pan**, with an overnight platform; and **Makonde**, overlooked by Wright's Tower, used for wildlife viewing.

The large oxbow lake, **Majinji Pan**, lies just outside the park west of the Mwenezi River. It once attracted thousands of water-loving birds, but increased siphoning of the Runde and Save Rivers for lowveld irrigation is causing it to dry up.

Organised Tours

From May to October, during the full moon, groups of up to six can join four-day ranger-guided wildlife walks through Mwenezi for US$40 for the first day and US$15 per day thereafter. Overnight camps are made within sight of permanent water holes, making for excellent wildlife viewing.

The best way to see the park is on foot and Khangela Safaris (see Organised Tours in the main Getting Around section earlier in this chapter) runs fabulous backpacking safaris, as well as a series of day walks from semipermanent camps. Scheduled trips last from six to 10 days and run at least monthly, but custom safaris are also available.

Places to Stay

Bookings for the following places can be made with National Parks in Bulawayo (☎ 09-63646), and rates include: camp sites from US$1.50 to US$3 per person; and three- and five-bed chalets for US$3.50/8.

The most accessible camp site in the Save-Runde subregion is idyllic ***Chipinda Pools***, 63km from Chiredzi along a badly corrugated but easily passable gravel road. All camp sites have shelters and braais, and overlook the vegetation-lined pools that teem with hippo. Further upstream is ***Chinguli Camp***. Both these camps have showers and flush toilets, and in the dry season both are accessible without 4WD.

More primitive exclusive camps are strung along the Runde River. With the exception of Fishans Camp, you can reach them only with 4WD.

In the Mwenezi subregion, the nicest camp is ***Swimuwini Camp*** (Place of Baobabs), which overlooks Buffalo Bend in the Mwenezi River. It's accessible in a 2WD and offers both camping and chalets. It's also a haunt of elephant and lion, and the small pond frequently attracts thirsty nyala. The more basic ***Mbalauta Camping & Caravan Site*** has five camp sites and an ablutions block. Two wildlife-viewing hides – Rossi Pools and Manyanda Pan – serve as exclusive camps.

The nearest ***grocery stores*** and other places for supplies, are at Rutenga and Chiredzi.

Bulawayo

☎ 09

Zimbabwe's intriguing second city (population 900,000) was originally called *Gu-Bulawayo* (Killing Place), from the Mzilikazi's Thabas Indunas (Hill of Chiefs) executions, although today it also styles itself as the 'City of the Kings'.

History

Following the Ndebele settlement with Rhodes, an uneasy peace came into effect; foreigners moved into Bulawayo and the BSAC assumed control over all Matabeleland. The colonists laid out the grid for a 'new improved' Bulawayo and proceeded to scour the surrounding countryside in search of its rumoured mineral deposits.

On 1 June 1894, Dr Leander Starr Jameson climbed onto a soapbox outside the Maxim Hotel bar and casually announced the city's founding to a gathering of boozy revellers. There was little pomp and ceremony: 'I don't think we want any talk about it', he said. 'I make the declaration now. There is plenty of whisky and soda inside, so come in.' This little event provided cause for Bulawayo's extensive centenary celebrations in 1994.

Orientation

Most of the population live in the high-density suburbs west of the industrial sector and north-west of the centre. This has left central Bulawayo resembling a middle-sized, Midwest American town. African-oriented businesses and less expensive shops are to be found around Lobengula St.

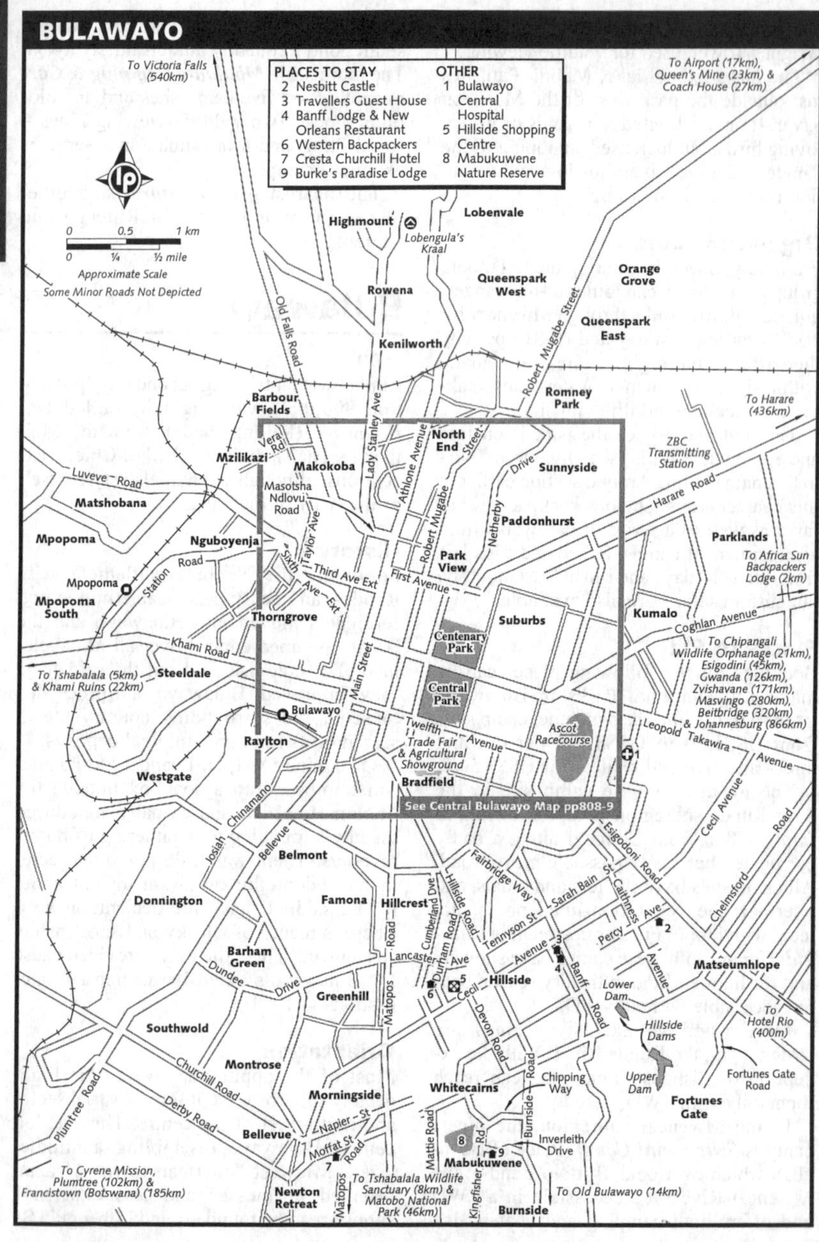
BULAWAYO
PLACES TO STAY
2 Nesbitt Castle
3 Travellers Guest House
4 Banff Lodge & New Orleans Restaurant
6 Western Backpackers
7 Cresta Churchill Hotel
9 Burke's Paradise Lodge
OTHER
1 Bulawayo Central Hospital
5 Hillside Shopping Centre
8 Mabukuwene Nature Reserve
To Victoria Falls (540km)
To Airport (17km), Queen's Mine (23km) & Coach House (27km)
0 0.5 1 km
0 ¼ ½ mile
Approximate Scale
Some Minor Roads Not Depicted
Highmount
Lobengula's Kraal
Lobenvale
Rowena
Queenspark West
Orange Grove
Queenspark East
Kenilworth
Old Falls Road
Robert Mugabe Street
Romney Park
Barbour Fields
To Harare (436km)
ZBC Transmitting Station
North End
Vera Rd
Makokoba
Mzilikazi
Lady Stanley Ave
Athlone Avenue
Sunnyside
Luveve Road
Matshobana
Masotsha Ndlovu Road
Robert Mugabe
Netherby Drive
Harare Road
Paddonhurst
Mpopoma
Nguboyenja
Taylor Ave
Parklands
Station Road
Sixth Ave Ext
Third Ave Ext
First Avenue
Park View
To Africa Sun Backpackers Lodge (2km)
Mpopoma
Mpopoma South
Thorngrove
Suburbs
Kumalo
Coghlan Avenue
Khami Road
Centenary Park
To Chipangali Wildlife Orphanage (21km), Esigodini (45km), Gwanda (126km), Zvishavane (171km), Masvingo (280km), Beitbridge (320km) & Johannesburg (866km)
To Tshabalala (5km) & Khami Ruins (22km)
Steeldale
Main Street
Central Park
Bulawayo
Ascot Racecourse
Leopold Takawira Avenue
Twelfth Avenue
Raylton
Trade Fair & Agricultural Showground
Westgate
Bradfield
See Central Bulawayo Map pp808-9
Cecil Avenue
Road
Chinamano
Josiah
Bellevue
Belmont
Esigodoni Road
Fairbridge Way
Chelmsford
Sarah Bain St
Caithness
Cumberland Dve
Hillside Road
Donnington
Famona
Hillcrest
Durham Road
Tennyson St
Percy Ave
Avenue
Barham Green
Road
Lancaster Ave
Matopos
Banff
Matseumhlope
Dundee Drive
Hillside
Lower Dam
Greenhill
Cecil
Devon Road
Road
To Hotel Rio (400m)
Southwold
Hillside Dams
Montrose
Churchill Road
Burnside Road
Chipping Way
Upper Dam
Fortunes Gate Road
Whitecairns
Fortunes Gate
Morningside
Plumtree Road
Derby Road
Mattie Road
Napier St
Bellevue
Moffat St
Road
Inverleith Drive
Kingfisher Rd
Mabukuwene
To Cyrene Mission, Plumtree (102km) & Francistown (Botswana) (185km)
To Tshabalala Wildlife Sanctuary (8km) & Matobo National Park (46km)
Matopos
Newton Retreat
To Old Bulawayo (14km)
Burnside

Information

Tourist Offices Bulawayo's reliable Publicity Association (☎ 60867, fax 60868, ⓔ Bulawayo@telconet.co.zw) PO Box 861, Bulawayo, is on the City Hall car park between Eighth Ave and Leopold Takawira Ave. It distributes accommodation lists and the free *Bulawayo This Month*, which has a city plan. It's open from 8.30 am to 4.45 pm weekdays, and 8.30 am to noon Saturday.

The friendly National Parks booking office (☎ 63646), on Eleventh Ave near Lobengula St, is open from 8 am to 4 pm weekdays.

Immigration Office The Department of Immigration Control (☎ 65621), next to the National Parks booking office on Eleventh Ave, is open from 7.45 am to 1 pm and 2 to 4.45 pm weekdays.

Money All banks change major foreign currencies and travellers cheques. Out of banking hours, try the train station or Banfords in the Bulawayo Centre.

Post & Communications On the corner of Eighth Ave and Main St, the GPO (☎ 62535) has an efficient poste restante. Public coin telephones are found inside, while cardphones are on the Leopold Takawira Ave side. Faxes can be sent or received at the GPO (fax 78053).

Email & Internet Access AfriNet Surfing (☎ 70324, ⓔ secbird@harare.iafrica.com), in the Bulawayo Centre, is open from 9 am to 6 pm weekdays, 9 am to 1 pm Saturday. Matabele Sports Tours on Leopold Takawira Ave also has Internet access for US$4.50 per hour.

Travel Agencies Sunshine Tours & Travel (☎ 67791, fax 74832, ⓔ sunshine@acacia.samara.co.zw) and Eco Logical Safaris (☎ 540590, fax 61189, ⓔ cbristow@acacia.samara.co.zw), both in the Bulawayo Centre, can arrange accommodation, safaris etc.

Camping Equipment Eezee Kamping, on George Silundika St between Ninth and Tenth Aves, is probably the best outdoors shop in Zimbabwe, which isn't saying much.

Laundry You'll find an automatic laundrette (☎ 64171), on the corner of Fife St and Tenth Ave; it's open from Monday to Saturday.

Emergency For nonemergency police calls, dial ☎ 72516. The best-equipped and most accessable hospital is Bulawayo Central (☎ 72111) on St Lukes Ave, Kumalo, a suburb near the Ascot racecourse. The Medical Air Rescue Service (MARS) number is ☎ 60351.

Dangers & Annoyances Bulawayo is more laid-back than Harare, but women should avoid remote corners of Centenary and Central parks and noone should walk alone between the city centre and the Municipal Caravan Park & Camp Site after dark – some call this the most dangerous spot in Zimbabwe.

Museum of Natural History

Bulawayo's Museum of Natural History (☎ 751797) in Centenary Park merits at least half a day's exploration. Nearly every type of wildlife indigenous to Zimbabwe and Southern Africa is represented – birds, antelope, predators, fish, reptiles and even (they claim) the world's second-largest stuffed elephant. One room is dedicated entirely to bugs. In all, 75,000 specimens are on display.

Historical displays deal with both African and European cultures, arts and artefacts. An artificial mine explains extraction methods and has rock and mineral specimens. The museum captions, with their blatant colonial bent, are almost antiquities themselves, but they do offer a very simplistic introduction to Southern Africa.

The museum is open from 9 am to 5 pm daily except Christmas and Good Friday. Foreigners/residents pay US$2/1 entry. It has wheelchair access and there's a canteen-style kiosk serving food and drinks.

Railway Museum

The Railway Museum houses a collection of historic steam locomotives, old railway offices and buildings, passenger carriages and a model of an historic station with period furnishings. Don't miss Cecil Rhodes' opulent private carriage, which dates from the 1890s.

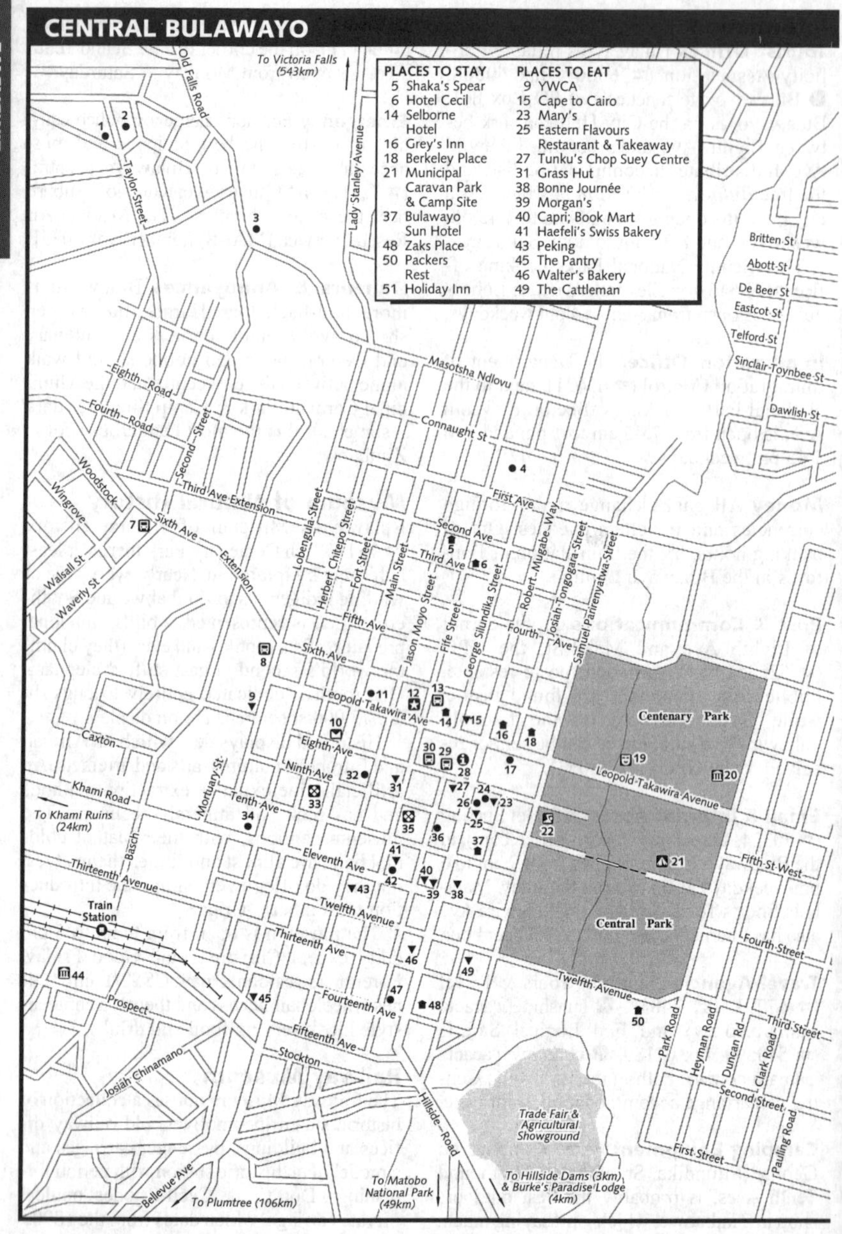
CENTRAL BULAWAYO
PLACES TO STAY
5 Shaka's Spear
6 Hotel Cecil
14 Selborne Hotel
16 Grey's Inn
18 Berkeley Place
21 Municipal Caravan Park & Camp Site
37 Bulawayo Sun Hotel
48 Zaks Place
50 Packers Rest
51 Holiday Inn
PLACES TO EAT
9 YWCA
15 Cape to Cairo
23 Mary's
25 Eastern Flavours Restaurant & Takeaway
27 Tunku's Chop Suey Centre
31 Grass Hut
38 Bonne Journée
39 Morgan's
40 Capri; Book Mart
41 Haefeli's Swiss Bakery
43 Peking
45 The Pantry
46 Walter's Bakery
49 The Cattleman
To Victoria Falls (543km)
Old Falls Road
Taylor Street
Lady Stanley Avenue
Britten St
Abott St
De Beer St
Eastcot St
Telford St
Sinclair-Toynbee St
Dawlish St
Masotsha Ndlovu
Connaught St
Eighth Road
Fourth Road
Second Street
Woodstock
Wingrove
Third Ave Extension
Sixth Ave Extension
Walsall St
Waverly St
Lobengula Street
Herbert Chitepo Street
Fort Street
Main Street
Jason Moyo Street
Fife Street
George Silundika Street
Robert Mugabe Way
Josiah Tongogara Street
Samuel Parirenyatwa Street
First Ave
Second Ave
Third Ave
Fourth Ave
Fifth Ave
Sixth Ave
Leopold Takawira Ave
Eighth Ave
Ninth Ave
Tenth Ave
Eleventh Ave
Twelfth Avenue
Thirteenth Ave
Fourteenth Ave
Fifteenth Ave
Centenary Park
Leopold Takawira Avenue
Central Park
Fifth St West
Fourth Street
Twelfth Avenue
Third Street
Second Street
First Street
Park Road
Heyman Road
Duncan Rd
Clark Road
Pauling Road
Caxton
Khami Road
To Khami Ruins (24km)
Mortuary St
Basch
Thirteenth Avenue
Train Station
Prospect
Stockton
Josiah Chinamano
Bellevue Ave
To Plumtree (106km)
Hillside Road
To Matobo National Park (49km)
Trade Fair & Agricultural Showground
To Hillside Dams (3km), & Burke's Paradise Lodge (4km)

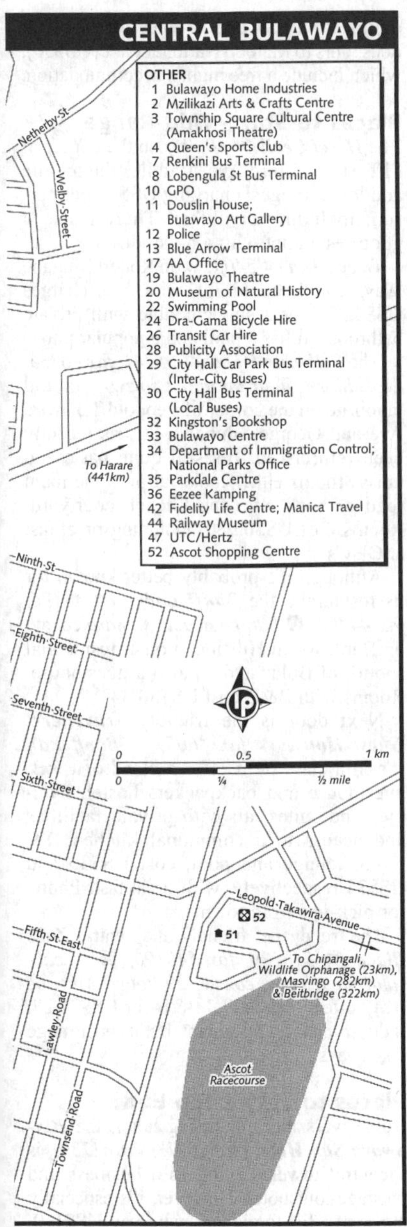

The museum is open from 8.30 am to 4 pm Tuesday, Wednesday and Friday, and noon to 5 pm Saturday and Sunday. Entry is just US$0.15.

Douslin House & Bulawayo Art Gallery

The imposing Douslin House, on the corner of Main St and Leopold Takawira Ave, is one of Bulawayo's finest colonial buildings. Completed in 1900, it was originally known as the Willoughby building, after the mining and ranching firm that occupied it. In 1956, the building was taken over by African Associated Mines and given the riveting name of Asbestos House. In 1980 it was purchased by the Bulawayo Art Gallery and the name changed in honour of its architect, William Douslin.

The gallery is open from 10 am to 5 pm Tuesday to Sunday; entry is US$0.55/0.15 for foreigners/residents, but free on Sunday.

Mzilikazi Arts & Crafts Centre

The Mzilikazi Arts & Crafts Centre (☎ 67245), established in 1963 to provide art training, is a Bulawayo highlight. The concentration of artistic ability in this institution, which seems more like a museum than a school (indeed, there is a small museum, with recent students' work), is amazing. Free tours are conducted from 8.30 am to 12.30 pm and 2 to 4 pm weekdays.

Take the Mpilo or Barbour Fields (marked BF) bus from the Lobengula St terminus and get off at either the centre or the Mzilikazi Primary School.

Organised Tours

United Touring Company (UTC; ☎ 61402) runs half-day city tours (US$11), as well as half-day excursions to the Khami Ruins (US$21) and Chipangali Wildlife Orphanage (US$17). Half/full-day tours of Matobo National Park cost US$45/55.

Mzingeli Tours (☎ 79178, fax 79182) at 133 Leopold Takawira Ave does full-day city tours with a cultural slant – it includes Old Bulawayo kraal, the high-density suburbs, the Mzilikazi Arts & Crafts Centre and the Amakhosi Theatre (see Entertainment).

Special Events

The Zimbabwe International Trade Fair, held in April/May, gives Bulawayo an excuse to party.

Places to Stay – Budget

The ***Municipal Caravan Park & Campsite*** *(☎ 63851)* on Caravan Way, just a 10-minutes walk from the centre, is *the* place for overlanders. It's clean and well guarded, with hot showers and baths. Sites cost US$1.20/2.60 per tent/caravan plus US$1.20 per person. Basic chalets are US$6 per person and hired caravans cost US$9. Don't even consider walking here after dark.

Close to the centre is the friendly and secure ***Berkeley Place*** *(☎ 67701, 71 Josiah Tongogara St)*. Beds cost US$9 per person, including breakfast. It has no bar or pool, but you can't beat the location, and it has a great craft shop where you can browse without being hassled to buy.

Shaka's Spear *(☎ 41686, 4 Baron Flats)* on the corner of Second Ave and Jason Moyo St is central and has dorms for US$2 and doubles for US$5. This price includes access to cooking and laundry facilities, a bar, pool table, dart board, library, luggage store and TV.

In Burnside (about 4.5km south of the centre) is the friendly, secure and quiet ***Burke's Paradise Lodge*** *(☎ 46481, fax 64576, e mfsburke@harare.iafrica.com, 11 Inverleith Dr)*. Dorms cost US$4.50 per person, including use of the pool, barbecue, videos, laundry and cooking facilities. Pick-ups and transfers to and from town are free and it really does feel like you're a guest in someone's house.

A short walk from the city centre is ***Packers Rest*** *(☎ 71111, fax 71124, e acacia .samara.co.zw, 1 Oak Ave, Suburbs)*. It's a small place with limited facilities, but it does offer free email. Dorm places cost US$5 and doubles US$20; there's a kitchen with basic supplies for sale.

The ***Western Backpackers*** *(☎ 44100, e tourzim@telconet.co.zw, 5 Nottingham Rd, Hillcrest)* lies 600m off Hillside Rd and offers a bar, pool table, swimming pool and braai. It has a friendly and lively atmosphere, with dorms for US$4 and doubles for US$9. It does tours to Matobo National Park (US$50), which include a free night's accommodation.

Places to Stay – Mid-Range

The ***Hotel Cecil*** *(☎ 60295)* on the corner of Fife St and Third Ave straddles the middle and lower ranges, charging US$15 per person, including breakfast. There's also a good restaurant with a noisy disco.

Grey's Inn *(☎ 540318)* on Robert Mugabe Way, near Leopold Takawira Ave, charges US$22/26 for a single/double with private bathroom. It has a pool and a popular pub.

The ***Selborne Hotel*** *(☎ 65741, fax 76335, e selborne@africaonline.co.zw)*, an old favourite on the corner of Leopold Takawira Ave and George Silundika St, has recently been refurbished. It's still quite basic and noisy; rooms either look out onto the main road or back onto the kitchen courtyard. Rooms cost US$65/80, including breakfast at Olav's.

Although it's probably better known for its restaurant, the ***Banff Lodge*** *(☎ 43176, fax 44402, e banff@acacia.samara.co.zw)* on Banff Rd in Hillside, a quiet residential suburb of Bulawayo, is also a guesthouse. Rooms with B&B cost US$30/34.

Next door is the friendly ***Travellers' Guest House*** *(☎/fax 46059, 2 Banff Rd)*. It's in a class by itself – a blend of B&B, guesthouse and backpackers hostel. Doubles and suites, all with private facilities and access to a communal kitchen, TV room, lounge and pool, cost US$30 and US$35 respectively, with breakfast. Phone for pick-ups from town.

The trendy yet friendly and central ***Zaks Place*** *(☎ 540129, fax 540190, e zaksplace@ telconet.co.zw, 129 Robert Mugabe Way)* offers 'executive' B&B for US$21/28. It doesn't have a restaurant, but it can arrange takeaways.

Places to Stay – Top End

Bulawayo's most imposing hotel, the ***Bulawayo Sun Hotel*** *(☎ 540273, fax 61739)*, is a central tower serving as a business and package-tour hotel. However, it's especially expensive for foreigners, who pay US$110/

170 for a single/double. On the fringe of the city, the ***Holiday Inn*** *(☎ 72464, fax 76227, @ byoholinn@zimsun.co.zw)* charges US$110 for standard rooms and US$330 for suites.

For a foray into decadence, consider the luxurious ***Nesbitt Castle*** *(☎ 42726, fax 41864, @ castle@acacia.samara.co.zw, 6 Percy Ave, Hillside)*, a cross between a medieval castle and an English country estate. It was built at the turn of the century by a former mayor.

Amenities include sauna, gymnasium, library, pool and billiard table. For suite-like doubles, you'll pay US$316, with dinner and a champagne breakfast. Advance bookings are essential.

Places to Eat

Restaurants One of the city's nicest restaurants is the ***Capri*** *(☎ 68639)* on the corner of Eleventh Ave and George Silundika St. Authentically Italian, with murals on the wall and a fountain in the corner, the food complements the decor. It opens daily for lunch and dinner.

Almost a prerequisite for those on the overland trail, the ***Cape to Cairo*** *(☎ 72387)* on the corner of Leopold Takawira Ave and George Silundika St is a tasteful colonial-theme restaurant/bar specialising in game dishes. It's open for lunch and dinner weekdays and in the evening on Saturday.

For Chinese food, the best choice is ***Peking*** *(☎ 60646)* on Jason Moyo St, where tasty renditions of Sichuan and Cantonese fare are served. It's open for lunch on weekdays and for dinner Monday to Saturday.

Morgan's *(☎ 79404)* in the Ramji Centre on Eleventh Ave offers bar meals as well as a la carte beef, chicken, seafood, pork and vegetarian choices. It's open from Monday to Saturday for lunch and dinner.

The ***Cattleman*** *(☎ 76086)* on the corner of Josiah Tongogara St and Twelfth Ave is a local favourite. Lots of restaurants have kudu heads on the wall, but here, a reproachful bovine looks over people being served tender steaks by cowboys. It's open daily for lunch and dinner.

Haute cuisine in Bulawayo comes in the form of the ***Maison Nic*** *(☎ 61884)* on Main St, near Fourth Ave, or the ***New Orleans*** *(☎ 43176)* at the Banff Lodge, Banff Rd in Hillside. The Maison Nic serves organic food and is very good and not prohibitively expensive. The New Orleans serves continental and Cajun cuisine (in as much as it can be reproduced in Zimbabwe). Advance bookings are recommended for both.

Olav's *(☎ 65741)* in the Selborne Hotel has a Norwegian chef, and continental and fresh dishes are priced around the US$6 mark.

Cafe society has arrived in Bulawayo with the air-con ***Cafe Baku*** in the Bulawayo Centre. Complete with artworks on the wall it serves up average pasta, filled baguettes and a medley of drinks. It's open until late and there's live music on the weekends – don't forget your black T-shirt.

Breakfast, Lunch & Snacks You'll find wholemeal bread, doughnuts, European-style cakes, pies, pastries and good coffee at ***Haefeli's Swiss Bakery***, on Fife St between Tenth and Eleventh Aves. It's open daily from breakfast until late. Also recommended is ***Walter's Bakery*** *(☎ 61071, 124 Robert Mugabe Way)*.

The aptly named ***Grass Hut*** on Fife St will remind you that you're in Africa until the menu arrives with the usual English breakfast options. It also has an enormous selection of sandwiches and grills.

Bulawayo has a range of takeaway places. ***Eastern Flavours*** *(☎ 74617)* on the corner of Robert Mugabe Way and Ninth Ave is one of the best. Herbivores can also fill up on their burgers, curries etc.

Chinese is the speciality at the frankly named ***Tunku's Chop Suey Centre*** *(☎ 72828)* on Eighth Ave, between Robert Mugabe Way and George Silundika St. For traditional Zimbabwean fare, try the ***Pantry*** on Fifteenth Ave, between Main and Fort Sts. It's open from 5 am to 3 pm.

The clean ***YWCA*** *(☎ 60185)* on Lobengula St is open to nonguests for lunch between 12.30 and 3 pm. For around US$1, you'll get a filling plate of sadza ladled over with the relish of the day, normally some sort of beef stew.

The Portuguese-owned ***Bonne Journée*** *(☎ 64839, 105 Robert Mugabe Way)* between Tenth and Eleventh Aves specialises in ice cream as well as steaks, burgers, omelettes, *peri-peri* chicken, and standard snacks such as chips and hot dogs.

Another place for sweet treats is ***Mandy's Coffee Shop*** *(112 Josiah Tongogara St)*. It's great for goodies such as chocolate cake, quiche, biscuits, muffins and coffee, and also does pub lunches and salads. The popular ***Mary's*** *(☎ 76721)*, opposite the medical centre on Eighth Ave, serves pizza, Greek specialities and chicken and beef dishes, as well as sweet snacks and coffee. It's wise to book for lunch.

Light pub meals are available at the ***Old Vic Pub*** at the Bulawayo Sun Hotel. The serene ***Ester's*** in the Bulawayo Art Gallery is also popular for its pastas, salads and teas.

Self-Catering For cheap fruit and vegetables, the best place is ***Makokoba Market***, beyond the Renkini bus terminal. For refined tastes, the ***supermarket*** at the Ascot shopping centre is probably the best stocked in town.

Entertainment

Bars & Clubs The ***Alabama***, around the side and underneath the Bulawayo Sun Hotel, is a pleasant and normally crowded bar with live and diverse jazz styles. It's open until late.

Joe's Place *(☎ 77460)* on the corner of George Silundika St and Eleventh Ave is a sports bar with pool tables to attract the backpacker crowd. ***Sneaky's Sports Bar***, on the 1st floor of the Parkade Centre (on the corner of Fife St and Ninth Ave), has TV screens and a dance floor.

For an Anglo-Zimbabwean atmosphere, try the ***Old Vic Pub*** in the Bulawayo Sun, or the ***Knight's Arms*** in the Holiday Inn Hotel. Another decent bar is ***Morgan's*** (see Places to Eat). Young Rhodeys hang out at ***Harleys' Pub*** *(☎ 62081)* at the showgrounds. Be careful here after dark.

On Friday, the public bar at the ***Cresta Churchill*** has live music and, if a well-known name is being featured, it can be fabulous.

Cinemas in Bulawayo have a good choice of quality cinema. The best are the ***Kine 600*** and ***Elite 400*** on Robert Mugabe Way between Tenth and Eleventh Aves, and the ***Rainbow Vistarama*** on Fife St between Eleventh and Twelfth Aves. The ***Bulawayo Art Gallery*** occasionally sponsors lunchtime films – inquire at the gallery or the Bulawayo Publicity Association.

Alliance Française *(☎ 70245, 61 Heyman Rd, Suburbs)* screens subtitled French films several times monthly.

Theatre & Dance The ***Bulawayo Theatre*** *(☎ 65393)*, in Centenary Park, stages dramatic productions and occasionally hosts visiting troupes. The fabulous African-oriented ***Amakhosi Theatre*** stages productions of local interest and organises the annual Inxusa Festival, which involves both national and international theatre, music and film productions, and workshops.

Contact the Bulawayo Publicity Association (☎ 60867) for information on current productions or consult the *Daily Chronicle*.

Shopping

Along the Fife St footpath at Town Hall Square, souvenir hawkers, needle-workers, artists and flower vendors display their wares. For an interesting selection of African beadwork, go to Buhlaluse, in the Tshabalala suburb about 6km from the centre near the Khami road.

Across the lawn from the Mzilikazi Arts & Crafts Centre is Bulawayo Home Industries, where artisans weave rugs and produce domestic arts. Originally set up for widows, divorcees, abandoned and elderly women with no other means of support, it now pays for itself. It's open from 9 am to 4 pm weekdays.

Getting There & Away

Air Air Zimbabwe (☎ 72051) and Zimbabwe Express (☎ 04-705923 in Harare) connect Bulawayo to all major airports in the country, with several flights daily to and from Harare and roundabout daily connections to Kariba, Victoria Falls and Hwange National Park. The charter airline United Air Services has nonstop flights between Bulawayo and Kariba. Book through Air Zimbabwe.

Bus Blue Arrow (☎ 65548, fax 65549) runs at least one coach daily to Harare (US$18) via either Chivhu or Kwe Kwe. It also has services to Victoria Falls (US$19) at 7.30 am Monday and Saturday, and 2.30 pm Sunday. The terminal is in Unifreight House at 73a Fife St.

Translux (☎ 66528, fax 78347) has a daily service, leaving from the Blue Arrow office, to Victoria Falls at 11.30 am on Tuesday and Friday. Another service leaves for Johannesburg (Jo'burg) at 5 pm and buses to Victoria Falls leave at 11.30 am on Tuesday and Friday. They return from Victoria Falls at 6.30 pm on Thursday and Sunday.

The long-distance African bus terminal is Renkini on the Sixth Ave Extension, opposite the Mzilikazi police station. Domestic buses travel to Beitbridge, Harare, Mutare and Masvingo. Every morning, buses depart from Entumbane for Hwange and Victoria Falls. Additional buses to Masvingo leave from the Lobengula St terminus. They all depart daily when full, starting around 6 or 7 am.

Train The train reservations and ticket offices (☎ 322210) are open from 7 am to 8.50 pm weekdays, 7 am to 2 pm weekends, and 6 to 8 pm public holidays.

The daily trains between Bulawayo and Harare depart at 9 pm in both directions, arriving before 7 am the following day. To Hwange and Victoria Falls, the service departs at 7 pm, arriving at Dete (Hwange National Park) at 1.30 am and Victoria Falls at 7 am. The train from Victoria Falls also departs at 7 pm, passes Dete at 12.45 am and arrives in Bulawayo at 7.05 am. The sleeper/economy class fares to Harare or Victoria Falls are US$15/5.

There's also a service to Chiredzi at 9.30 pm for US$8/6/3 in 1st/2nd/economy class.

Getting Around

To/From the Airport The Air Zimbabwe bus runs between the Bulawayo Sun Hotel and the airport (26423), about 7km north of town. Taxis cost at least US$7 each way.

Bus Bulawayo has two suburban bus terminals. The City Hall terminal (☎ 67172), on Eighth Ave between Robert Mugabe Way and George Silundika Sts, serves the more affluent northern, eastern and southern suburbs. The published timetable is often inaccurate but there is an information booth.

The Lobengula St terminal (☎ 74059) on the corner of Lobengula St and Sixth Ave serves the high-density suburbs west and south-west of the centre.

Car You can rent a vehicle at Transit Car Hire, on the corner of Twelfth Ave and Robert Mugabe Way.

Taxi Rixi Taxi (☎ 60666 or ☎ 61933) and Skyork's (☎ 72454) are reliable.

Bicycle Dra-Gama's (☎ 72739), near the corner of Eighth Ave and Josiah Tongogara St, has bicycle hire for US$5 per day. It's open from 8 am to 5 pm daily.

AROUND BULAWAYO

Tshabalala Wildlife Sanctuary

This small sanctuary, 10km south of Bulawayo, was established on the former landholding of Fairburn Usher, a British sailor who arrived in 1883, and his Ndebele wife, one of Lobengula's daughters. There are no predators, so it's perfect for a day of relaxing, **walking** or **horse riding**. Take a picnic lunch and plan to spend a full day here.

The sanctuary is open from 6 am to 6 pm in the summer and 8 am to 5 pm in winter. Foreigners pay US$10 entry and horse riding is US$10 per hour. No bikes or motorcycles are allowed. Contact National Parks (☎ 09-63646) in Bulawayo .

The Kezi bus from the Renkini bus terminal in Bulawayo passes Tshabalala, and the Matobo Rd bus from City Hall Terminal can drop you at Retreat, 3km from the entrance. Hitching from Bulawayo isn't bad, but you'll have to get out of the congested area first.

Chipangali Wildlife Orphanage

☎ 09

Chipangali (☎ 229646) was founded in 1973 as a centre for the rearing of orphaned animals and the caring of injured, illegally captured or sick animals. The idea is to release them into the wild when they're able to cope, but some are inevitably destined for a life of captivity. The large walk-through aviaries house both large raptors and smaller birds. There's a display area with all kinds of preserved animal foetuses, including a perfectly formed elephant. It's open from 10 am to 5 pm Tuesday to Sunday but the gates close at 4.30 pm. The staff feed the animals at 3.30 pm on Tuesday, Thursday and Sunday. Entry is US$5/2.50 for adults/children.

If you can't bear to leave the already abandoned orphans, you can stay in a basic hut for US$10/5.50 for foreigner/resident. Camping costs US$2/3.

Chipangali lies 24km east of Bulawayo and 200m from the Masvingo road. You can get here on an Esigodini bus from the Renkini terminal. Hitching is best from beyond Ascot shopping centre.

Khami Ruins

Khami, a UNESCO World Heritage Site, isn't as expansive as the Great Zimbabwe ruins, but this crumbled 40-hectare city remains more or less as it was when its inhabitants fled the fire that destroyed it. It was built by the Torwa dynasty in the 16th century. In the late 17th century, Torwa was apparently absorbed by the larger Rozwi state, which arrived from the north and conquered the ruling Changamire dynasty, burning and levelling the capital Khami and replacing it with Danangombe, 100km to the north-east.

At the northern end of the ruins is the **Hill Complex**, which served as the royal enclosure. There are several hut platforms here and Khami's greatest concentration of stone walling. At the northern end of the Hill Complex is an odd platform with a stone Dominican cross, reputedly placed there by an early Portuguese missionary.

The scattered ruins of southern Khami contain several interesting sites; the **Vlei Platforms**, near the museum, are believed to have served as cattle kraals. Near the dam wall, a *mujejeje* (rock) rings like a bell when struck. The beautifully decorated 6m-high, 68m-long retaining wall of the **Precipice Platform**, just east of the dam, bears a chequerboard design along its entire length.

For more information, pick up *A Trail Guide to the Khami National Monument*, which is sold at the museum. Khami is open from 8 am to 5 pm daily; entry is US$2/1 for adults/children.

There are no buses along the little-travelled Khami road, so most travellers hire bicycles in Bulawayo and pedal the flat 22km to the ruins. Just head out on Eleventh Ave beyond Lobengula St and follow the signposted route. A taxi should cost around US$9.

MATOBO NATIONAL PARK

You need not be in tune with any alternative wavelength to sense that the Matobo Hills are one of the world's power places. Dotted around the park are a wealth of ancient San paintings and old grain bins, where Lobengula's warriors once stored their provisions. Some hidden niches still shelter clay ovens, which were used as iron smelters in making the infamous *assegais* (spears), used against the colonial hordes.

Some peaks, such as Shumba Shaba, Shumba Sham, Imadzi (Bald One), Efifi and Silozwane, are now considered sacred, and locals believe that even to point at them will bring misfortune. Hidden in a rock cleft is the Ndebele's **sacred rain shrine Njelele,** where people still pray to Mwali. During the recent devastating drought, even government officials came to pull some strings here.

With the history comes a superb array of **wildlife**. You may have the chance to see the African hawk eagle *(Hieraaetus spilogaster)* or the rare Cape eagle owl *(Bubo capensis)*. Matobo is also home to the world's greatest concentration of nesting sites of the black eagle *(Aquila verreauxii)*.

The **Whovi Game Park** portion of Matobo offers a variety of wildlife, but is best known for its zealously guarded population of both white and black rhino.

Maleme Dam

Maleme Dam, the park headquarters, is the busiest part of Matobo. Here you'll find lodges, chalets, a general store, the main

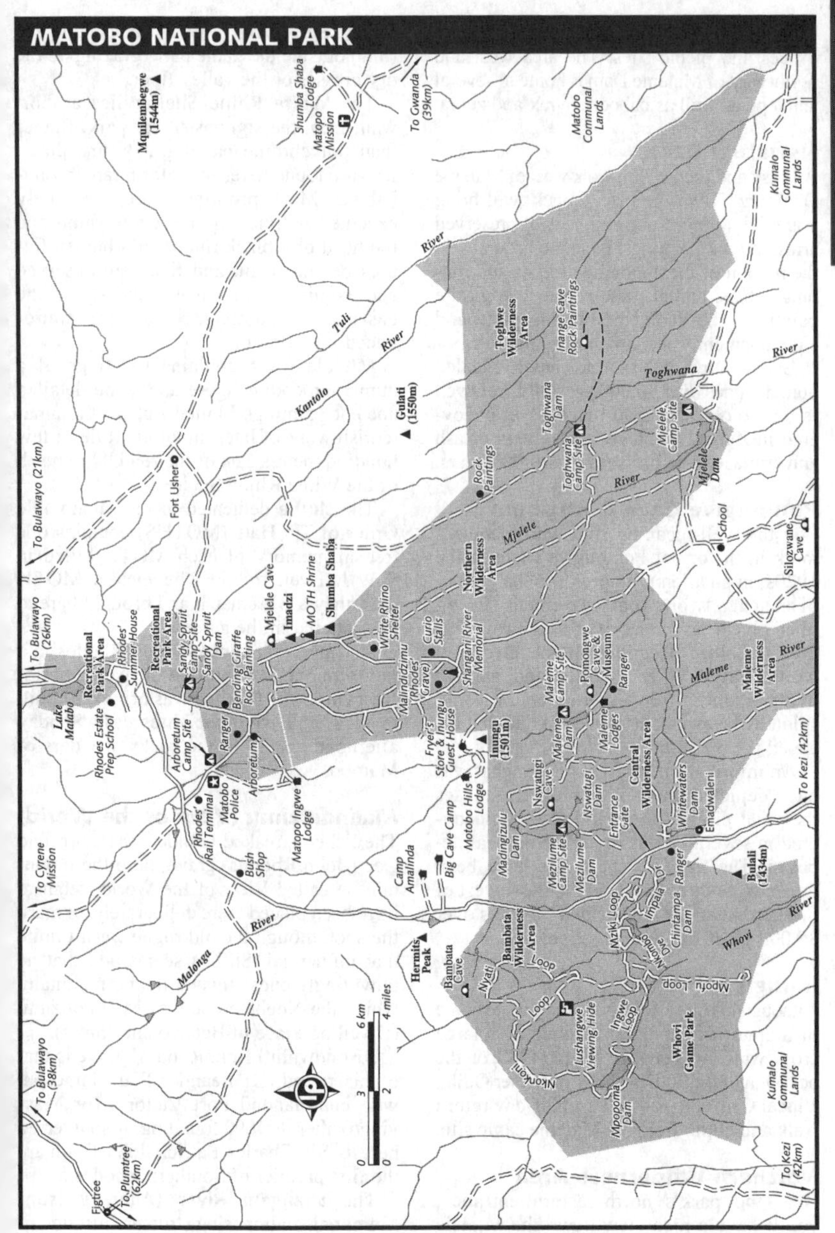
MATOBO NATIONAL PARK
To Bulawayo (21km)
To Bulawayo (26km)
To Bulawayo (38km)
To Cyrene Mission
Figtree
To Plumtree (62km)
Lake Malabo
Recreational Park Area
Rhodes Estate Prep School
Rhodes' Summer House
Sandy Spruit Camp Site
Sandy Spruit Dam
Arboretum Camp Site
Ranger
Bending Giraffe Rock Painting
Arboretum
Rhodes' Rail Terminal
Matobo Police
Matopo Ingwe Lodge
Bush Shop
Malonga
River
Mjelele Cave
Imadzi
MOTH Shrine
Shumba Shaba
White Rhino Shelter
Malindidzimu (Rhodes' Grave)
Curio Stalls
Shangani River Memorial
Fryer's Store & Inungu Guest House
Inungu (1501m)
Motobo Hills Lodge
Big Cave Camp
Camp Amalinda
Hermits Peak
Bambata Cave
Nyati
Bambata Wilderness Area
Loop
Lushangwe Viewing Hide
Nkonkoni
Ingwe Loop
Mpopoma Dam
Whovi Game Park
Mpofu Loop
Nkombo Dwe
Mziki Loop
Impala Dr
Chintampa Dam
Ranger
Bulali (1434m)
Whovi
River
Kumalo Communal Lands
To Kezi (42km)
Madingizulu Dam
Mezilume Camp Site
Mezilume Dam
Nswatugi Cave
Nswatugi Dam
Entrance Gate
Central Wilderness Area
Whitewaters Dam
Emadwaleni
Maleme Dam
Maleme Camp Site
Maleme Lodges
Pomongwe Cave & Museum
Ranger
Maleme
River
Maleme Wilderness Area
To Kezi (42km)
Northern Wilderness Area
Mjelele
River
Rock Paintings
School
Silozwane Cave
Mjelele Dam
Mjelele Camp Site
Toghwana Camp Site
Toghwana Dam
Toghwana
River
Inange Cave Rock Paintings
Toghwe Wilderness Area
Kumalo Communal Lands
Matobo Communal Lands
To Gwanda (39km)
Fort Usher
Kantolo
River
Tuli
River
Gulati (1550m)
Mquilembegwe (1544m)
Shumba Shaba Lodge
Matopo Mission
0 3 6 km
0 2 4 miles

camping ground, horse stables, the ranger's offices and picnic sites. The area west and north-west of Maleme Dam is home to several antelope as well as baboon, hyrax and zebra.

Nswatugi Cave

An easy and scenic 7km walk west of Maleme Dam, and 200m up a steep track, will bring you to Nswatugi Cave and its well-preserved array of rock paintings. Note the accuracy in the motion of the galloping giraffes and running zebras, and also the perspective giraffe paintings, the kudu, the hunting party and eight apparently sleeping human figures.

Excavations at Nswatugi have revealed human bones over 40,000 years old, believed to be the oldest human remains yet uncovered in Zimbabwe. Overlying layers of ash and artefacts date back around 10,000 years.

Pomongwe Cave & Museum

Pity the well-meaning soul who made his mark in history at Pomongwe Cave in the 1920s; in an attempt to preserve the gallery of ancient artwork from the elements, he applied glycerine shellac over all the cave figures – before ascertaining the effects it would have. Where giraffe and ancient hunters once trod, there remain only splotchy brown stains and one kudu that escaped the brush-off.

An information board explains what was once depicted and a new museum houses the great piles of tools and pottery uncovered in several levels of archaeological deposits. The most recent layers have been dated to about 6500 BC while the lowest of these excavations has yielded artefacts over 35,000 years old. Entry is free.

Inungu

Although it's outside the park, the granite dome of Inungu is a landmark, topped by a large cross, which was erected in June 1982, on the occasion of the 70th birthday of Father Odilo, a local Catholic priest. It's a half-day return walk and climb from the Maleme camp site.

Northern Wilderness Area

Near the park's north-eastern entrance, you'll have a nice view down the Mjelele Valley. Surprisingly, it's not unusual to see rhino outside the game park, grazing on the dry grasses of the valley floor.

The **White Rhino Shelter** lies a short walk from the signposted car park. Rather than polychrome paintings, outline drawings are found here; an art form rare in Zimbabwe. Most prominent are the finely executed outlines of five white rhino and the head of a black rhino, with human figures behind them, and five well-observed and exquisitely drawn wildebeest. On the basis of this painting, rhino were reintroduced into Matobo.

Mjelele Cave contains paintings of a human-crocodile figure and some detailed ancient paintings blotted out by the amateurish work of later imitators. It lies a few hundred metres east of the road, 8km north of the White Rhino Shelter.

The **shrine** dedicated to the Memorable Order of Tin Hats (MOTHS) contains one tree in memory of each MOTH killed in WWII. Even today, whenever a MOTH dies, they are cremated and brought here to be scattered in the garden.

Not much remains of Cecil Rhodes' old **rail terminal**, 2km outside the park's north-west entrance. The line was originally built to give Bulawayo socialites easy Sunday afternoon access to the rocky wonders of Matobo.

Malindidzimu (View of the World)

The lichen-streaked boulders that surround Cecil John **Rhodes' grave**, atop the mountain he called View of the World, seem to have been placed there deliberately, to mark the spot, though the old rogue wasn't quite that influential. Still, it seems odd that he unwittingly chose this particular mountain, which the Ndebele knew as Malindidzimu (Dwelling Place of Benevolent Spirits).

Just downhill from Rhodes' grave is that of his friend, Dr Leander Starr Jameson, who commanded Fort Victoria (or Masvingo) after its 1890 founding. Also interred here is Sir Charles Patrick John Coghlan, the first premier of Southern Rhodesia.

The **Shangani River (Allan Wilson) Memorial**, an imposing structure just down-

They Just Won't Let Leaping Lizards Lie

Even if you have no interest in Rhodes, or his mates, it's worth the climb up to his grave for the view. Also up there is a prolific lizard population – females are grey-green and males are rainbow-coloured – skittering over gravestones and equally colourful lichen-encrusted rocks.

For many years a park attendant has entertained tourists with the tricks he got lizards to perform in return for food. Unfortunately the original 'Lizard Man' passed away in 1999. While the news is sad, for another park attendant it was his big break. Having spent years patiently standing in the wings, this 'understudy Lizard Man' has stepped right into the dead man's shoes and certainly the lizards don't seem to have noticed the difference.

hill from Rhodes' Grave, was erected in 1904 to the memory of Allan Wilson and the 33 soldiers of his Shangani River Patrol. The entire troupe was wiped out by the forces of General Mtjaan and his 30,000 Ndebele warriors, of whom more than 400 were slain by the patrol's superior firepower. Mistakenly believing that Lobengula's *impies* (spear-carrying 'soldiers') had committed acts of war against the British at Fort Victoria, the patrol had been sent in pursuit of the fleeing king. Lobengula himself conceded that their battle was bravely fought.

A display at the bottom of the hill outlines highlights of Rhodes' life and career.

Whovi Game Park

In addition to a full complement of antelope, zebra, giraffe and other species (except elephant), Whovi enjoys a relatively healthy population of white rhino, and lucky visitors may even spot the more elusive black rhino. What's more, the scenery, with Matobo's most precarious and imaginative pinnacles and boulder stacks, is as good as the wildlife. Gates are open between 6 am and 6 pm. You must stay in your vehicle (unless you're with a guide); the speed limit is 40km/h.

Toghwe Wilderness Area

This remote eastern third of Matobo is the wildest wilderness area. It combines parts of the scenic Mjelele and Toghwana Valleys, both of which have secluded camp sites, as well as Inange Cave and its fine collection of rock paintings. Roads are rough with some very steep bits and low-slung cars may have problems. After rains, low-lying stretches may become impassable without 4WD.

Atop a dwala dome, **Inange Cave** is a four- to six-hour, 14km-return walk from the Toghwana camping ground. It's worth the effort, for inside is one of Zimbabwe's most complex and well-executed **cave paintings**. Mixed herds of African animals march in confused profusion across the walls, interspersed with hunters and geometric and stylised designs. Most of the 7km route to Inange is marked by green-painted arrows and small rock cairns, and although it can become confusing as it passes over a series of nearly identical ridges and valleys, you shouldn't have problems getting there.

Organised Tours

Many lodges in Bulawayo organise and recommend tours to Matobo for about US$40 to US$60. A recommended company is Black Rhino Safaris (☎/fax 09-41662, @ blckrhino@hotmail.com), which treats the job as a labour of love. Its staff have likely spent more time at Matobo than anyone else, yet their enthusiasm remains infectious. Nine-hour day tours cost US$55, including lunch and a wildlife drive in Whovi.

Other operators include Adventure Travel (☎ 09-66525, @ advtvl@acacia.samara.co.zw), which will almost certainly provide an entertaining tour; and UTC (☎ 09-61402).

Activities

Guided 1½-hour **horse-riding trips** are available from the National Parks rangers at Whitewaters (near the Whovi Game Park entrance). Advance booking with the rangers is essential.

Places to Stay & Eat

Most campers wind up at Maleme Dam, so it can get quite crowded on weekends and holidays – these are the easiest times to hitch a ride but maybe not the most pleasant to actually *be* there. Maleme has National Parks ***camp sites***, chalets and lodges, including two luxury lodges; the ***Black Eagle*** and ***Fish Eagle***, which afford a boulder-studded hilltop vista. Advance bookings are essential.

There are also several other camp sites. At the northern entrance is ***Sandy Spruit Camp Site***, which is too near the highway, but convenient if you're arriving late. ***Toghwana Camp Site*** and ***Mjelele Camp Site*** are both very nice, but access can be difficult. Near the arboretum entrance in the north of the park is the very civilised ***Arboretum Camp Site*** and there's also the small ***Mezilume Camp Site***.

The Bulawayo Publicity Association and travel agencies can provide listings and book accommodation around the park perimeter (see the Bulawayo section).

Apart from the hotels and lodges, there are no restaurants in the Matobo Hills. The only supplies are at the basic ***shop*** at Maleme Dam and at ***Fryer's Store***, 6km upstream from Maleme Dam or 10km along the road.

Some drinking water in the park is treated – look for designated drinking taps. If you're unsure, boil or treat water before drinking; note that all park water contains bilharzia.

Getting There & Away

Whatever you may be told, taxis aren't permitted in the park. Hitching is slow, but hitchers always arrive eventually, and since there are several camping grounds around the park perimeter, you need only reach the proximity to be within walking distance.

Guided tours are recommended, and if you want to explore further after the tour, most companies will drop you at Maleme Dam and pick you up on another day.

Alternatively, you can take the Kezi bus from Renkini bus terminal in Bulawayo and get off at one of the three Matobo turn-offs. An option is to hire bicycles in Bulawayo and carry them on the bus (cyclists aren't permitted in the Whovi Game Park).

Getting Around

You are allowed to walk and cycle around the park (with the exception of the Whovi Game Park). There's also horse riding available. Make sure you take plenty of water with you.

Western Zimbabwe

With Zimbabwe's major attractions – Victoria Falls and Hwange National Park – and a few minor ones, western Zimbabwe looms big on most travellers' Southern African itineraries. Naturally, Hwange and 'the Falls', as they're known locally, are the main draw, but there are also other wonderful places: western Lake Kariba, a wild version of its eastern counterpart, with unique Tonga culture; and remote Chizarira, Zimbabwe's wildest and arguably most beautiful national park.

HWANGE NATIONAL PARK

☎ 018

Although Hwange is Zimbabwe's most accessible and wildlife-packed park, it's not overcrowded and most safari vehicles stick to short loop drives within 10km of Hwange Main Camp. The best time for wildlife viewing is September and October when animals congregate around the water holes (most of which are artificially filled by way of petrol-powered pumps). When the rains come and the rivers are flowing, successful viewing requires more diligence, as the animals spread across the park's 14,650 sq km seeking a bit of trunk and antler room.

History

The park sits near the edge of the Kalahari Desert, and although it was once home to nomadic families of San people, the area was considered by other groups to be too hot, dry and sandy for permanent habitation. Originally, wildlife spread across the region during the rainy season, then retreated to the Zambezi Valley during the dry season.

During the 19th century, the area served as a hunting reserve for the Ndebele kings. When Europeans arrived on the scene, they too set about over-hunting it.

Because it was unsuitable for farming, Hwange was accorded national park status in 1929, to provide a wildlife-viewing venue for tourists en route to Victoria Falls. Settlers created 60 artificial watering holes fed by underground water and so, by the 1970s, Hwange had one of the densest concentrations of wildlife in Africa.

Park information and sketchy photocopied maps are available at the Main, Sinamatella and Robins camp ranger offices. Photosafari publishes the *Tourist Map of Hwange National Park*, which shows the main routes and 4WD tracks.

Hwange Main Camp & 10 Mile Drive

Hwange Main Camp has most park services, including ranger headquarters, a shop and petrol station. However, during South African school holidays, it begins to resemble a metropolis.

All that many visitors experience of Hwange is the 10 Mile Drive, a convenient loop around the most wildlife-packed part of the national park, which can be easily completed in a two-hour wildlife drive.

The highlight is Nyamandhlovu Pan, which features the high-rise Nyamandhlovu

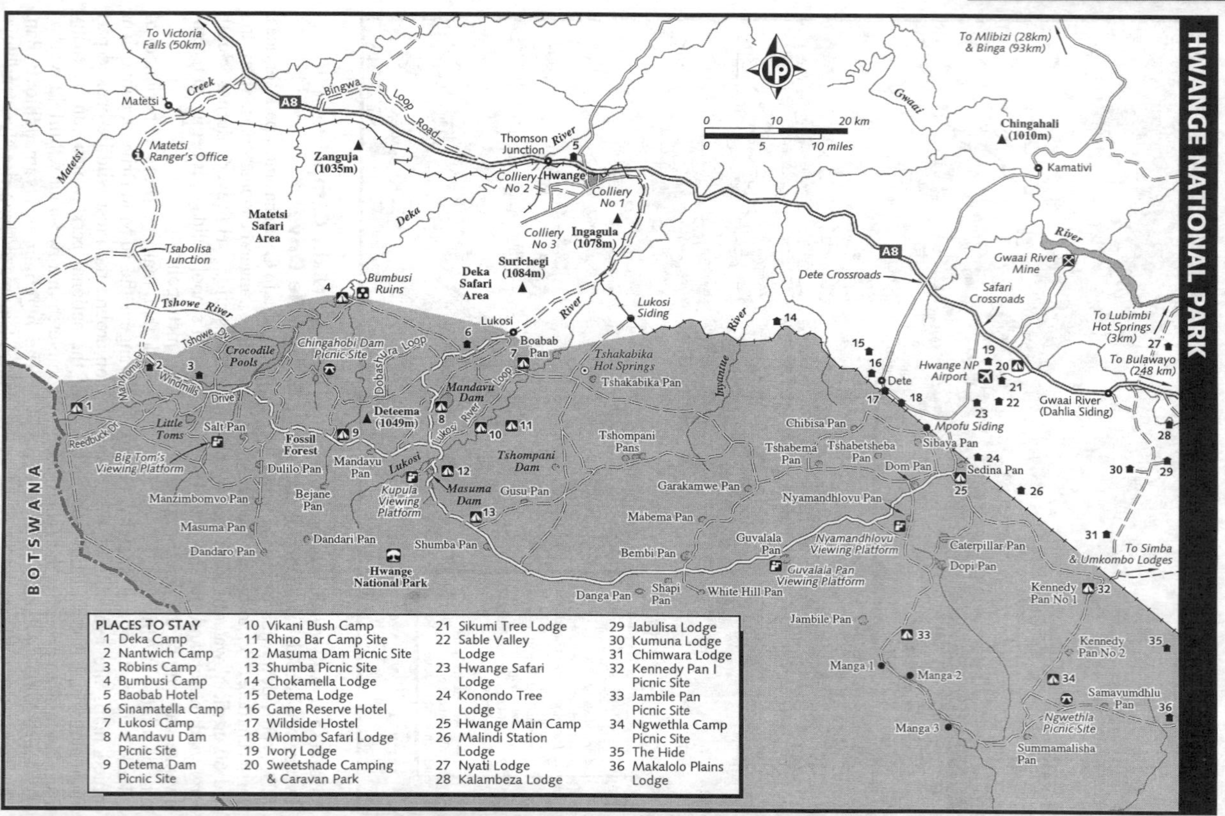
HWANGE NATIONAL PARK
PLACES TO STAY
1 Deka Camp
2 Nantwich Camp
3 Robins Camp
4 Bumbusi Camp
5 Baobab Hotel
6 Sinamatella Camp
7 Lukosi Camp
8 Mandavu Dam Picnic Site
9 Detema Dam Picnic Site
10 Vikani Bush Camp
11 Rhino Bar Camp Site
12 Masuma Dam Picnic Site
13 Shumba Picnic Site
14 Chokamella Lodge
15 Detema Lodge
16 Game Reserve Hotel
17 Wildside Hostel
18 Miombo Safari Lodge
19 Ivory Lodge
20 Sweetshade Camping & Caravan Park
21 Sikumi Tree Lodge
22 Sable Valley Lodge
23 Hwange Safari Lodge
24 Konondo Tree Lodge
25 Hwange Main Camp
26 Malindi Station Lodge
27 Nyati Lodge
28 Kalambeza Lodge
29 Jabulisa Lodge
30 Kumuna Lodge
31 Chimwara Lodge
32 Kennedy Pan I Picnic Site
33 Jambile Pan Picnic Site
34 Ngwethla Camp Picnic Site
35 The Hide
36 Makalolo Plains Lodge
To Victoria Falls (50km)
To Mlibizi (28km) & Binga (93km)
To Lubimbi Hot Springs (3km)
To Bulawayo (248 km)
To Simba & Umkombo Lodges
A8
Matetsi
Creek
Matetsi Ranger's Office
Matetsi Safari Area
Zanguja (1035m)
Bingwa Loop Road
Tsabolisa Junction
Tshowe River
Tshowe Dr
Manhoma Dr
Reedbuck Dr
Deka
Deka Safari Area
Thomson Junction
River
Hwange
Colliery No 1
Colliery No 2
Colliery No 3
Ingagula (1078m)
Surichegi (1084m)
Lukosi
Lukosi Siding
Kamativi
Chingahali (1010m)
Gwaai
Gwaai River Mine
Safari Crossroads
Dete Crossroads
Dete
Mpofu Siding
Hwange NP Airport
Gwaai River (Dahlia Siding)
Bumbusi Ruins
Deteema (1049m)
Chingahobi Dam Picnic Site
Dobashura Loop
Crocodile Pools
Fossil Forest
Little Toms
Salt Pan
Big Tom's Viewing Platform
Windmills Drive
Mandavu Dam
Lukosi River Loop
Masuma Dam
Kupula Viewing Platform
Tshompani Dam
Tshakabika Hot Springs
Tshakabika Pan
Boabab Pan
Hwange National Park
Shumba Pan
Dandari Pan
Dandaro Pan
Masuma Pan
Manzimbomvo Pan
Dulilo Pan
Bejane Pan
Mandavu Pan
Gusu Pan
Tshompani Pans
Mabema Pan
Bembi Pan
Danga Pan
Shapi Pan
White Hill Pan
Garakamwe Pan
Guvalala Pan
Guvalala Pan Viewing Platform
Nyamandhlovu Pan
Nyamandhlovu Viewing Platform
Tshabema Pan
Tshabetsheba Pan
Chibisa Pan
Jambile Pan
Dom Pan
Sibaya Pan
Sedina Pan
Caterpillar Pan
Dopi Pan
Manga 1
Manga 2
Manga 3
Kennedy Pan No 1
Kennedy Pan No 2
Ngwethla Picnic Site
Samavumdhlu Pan
Summamalisha Pan
Inyantue
BOTSWANA
0 10 20 km
0 5 10 miles

Viewing Platform overlooking a popular water hole.

From the Main Camp office, two-hour ranger-guided walks to the wildlife-viewing hide at Sedina Pan depart at 6.30 and 10 am and 4 pm. For two or three nights around each full moon, Main Camp rangers lead two-hour convoys into the park to see what's brewing.

Ngwethla Loop

Ngwethla is accessible to any vehicle via the Kennedy pans; the greatest concentrations of animals are around Ngwethla picnic site. The Kennedy pans are magnificent, especially at dusk, when elephant pack into the water to bathe and frolic.

Sinamatella Camp

Sinamatella Camp sits atop a 50m mesa with a commanding 50km panorama. By day, you'll see buffalo and antelope in the grassy patch below the camp, but it's at nighttime that Sinamatella really comes alive. Vicious little honey badgers skitter around the restaurant looking for hand-outs and even invade the chalets if given half a chance.

Once you've bedded down, expect to be haunted by the contented roaring of lions and the disconcerting howling of hyaenas at the foot of the hill, along with a host of unidentified screeches, thumps and bumps.

Amenities include a ranger office, museum display, craft shop, basic supplies, petrol, restaurant and pub.

Leave Main Camp before noon to get there.

Activities

Ranger-escorted walks are available for groups of up to six people; a popular **walk** is cross-country from Sinamatella camp to Mandavu Dam and back.

The UTC (☎ 04-770623, fax 770641 in Harare), with an office at the Hwange Safari Lodge, offers two-hour **wildlife cruises** around the 10 Mile Drive several times daily from the lodge or Main Camp. Touch the Wild (☎ 09-540 922, fax 229 088 in Bulawayo, @ ttw@acacia.samara.co.zw) runs two-hour/full-day wildlife drives for US$48/154 but, as the prices would indicate, it caters mainly for prebooked package tours. However, if you have a local in your group you may be able to get local rates.

Khangela Safaris (☎ 09-49733 in Bulawayo) has two to eight-day trips through the park's back country for US$130 per day, including meals.

Places to Stay & Eat

For contact details of the following places to stay, see Accommodation in the Facts for the Visitor section earlier in this chapter. Rates for National Park accommodation include: camp sites for US$8 per site; two- and four-bed lodges for US$11/17; two- and four-bed cottages for US$8/11; and two- and four-bed chalets for US$5.50.

Hwange Main Camp has a camping ground, pub, restaurant, cottages and lodges. The shop is open daily from 8 to 10 am, noon to 2 pm and 4 to 7 pm. At ***Sinamatella***, accommodation includes camping, chalets, cottages and lodges.

Robins and ***Nantwich*** camps, west of Sinamatella, are in prime lion, cheetah and hyaena country. Robins Camp also has a sparsely stocked shop, a restaurant and bar. You can take guided day-walks and overnight trips with armed game scouts. Nantwich has two-bedroom lodges, each accommodating up to six people, but there are no other facilities.

Leave Main Camp before noon to get to either camp. Other camp sites are ***Bumbusi Camp***, ***Lukosi***, ***Vikari*** and ***Rhino Bar***. Note that safari operators often have these sites booked in advance, so you should try and do the same.

The enclosed public picnic sites at ***Shumba***, ***Mandavu Dam***, ***Masuma Dam***, ***Ngwethla***, ***Jambile***, ***Kennedy Pan I*** and ***Detema Dam*** are available to groups of up to eight people as exclusive camps. Lion are frequently seen around Shumba (Lion); Mandavu has a nice big expanse of water; and Kennedy Pan I has hordes of elephant at night. Ngwethla is situated in an area of heavy wildlife concentration. Masuma Dam is a great site; you can spend the night listening to belching hippos and trumpeting elephants.

Camps and lodges, especially in the luxury range, are sprouting like mushrooms around Hwange. Travel agents and the Bulawayo Publicity Association have listings.

Getting There & Away

Air Air Zimbabwe (☎ 018-393) and Zimbabwe Express Airlines (☎ 04-705923 in Harare) fly to Hwange National Park from Harare via Kariba and/or Victoria Falls daily.

Southern Cross Aviation (☎ 013-4618 in Victoria Falls) offers charter flights and safari camp transfers from Hwange.

There are no taxis serving the airport but UTC vehicles meet incoming flights and provide transfers to and from the Hwange Safari Lodge or Main Camp.

Bus Basically, any bus between Bulawayo and Victoria Falls can drop you at the Safari Crossroads. A better choice is Ajay's Motorways, which drops you at the Hwange Safari Lodge, or Blue Arrow, which stops at the Miombo Safari Lodge and Dete.

Train The train between Bulawayo and Victoria Falls passes Dete far too early in the morning to be a real option.

Getting Around

The park speed limit is 40km/h, so don't try to see the entire park in a single day. If you're booked into a camp, however, and don't turn up before the gates close, a search will be conducted and once you're located, you'll have to foot the bill for the rangers' time and efforts.

Petrol is available at Hwange Safari Lodge, Main Camp and Sinamatella Camp.

VICTORIA FALLS

☎ 013

An awestruck David Livingstone, upon first seeing the world-famous Victoria Falls (Mosi-ou-Tunya), wrote in his journal 'on sights as beautiful as this, angels in their flight must have gazed'. The Falls, 1.7km wide, drop between 90 and 107m into the Zambezi Gorge. An average of 550,000 cubic metres of water plummet over the edge every minute, but during the floods from March to May, it can be up to 10 times this amount. The Falls are one of the world's great attractions, and miles and miles of film and videotape are gobbled by cameras here every year.

The town of Victoria Falls (just a short distance from the waterfall that gives it its name) was built on tourism and has developed into an archetypal tourist trap. This town, and the area, is often known simply as Vic Falls. Fortunately, the star attraction – Victoria Falls itself – is safely cordoned off by a jungle of its own creation. To walk along the paths through the spray-generated rainforests flanking the gorge, you'd never suspect the existence of anything other than the monumental waterfall that's giving you such a good soaking.

Information

Tourist Offices The Victoria Falls Publicity Association (☎ 4202), adjacent to the town's camping ground, distributes local advertising and sells town maps and booklets. It's open from 8 am to 1 pm and 2 to 5 pm weekdays, and 8 am to 1 pm Saturday.

Backpackers Bazaar (☎ 2189, fax 2208, ⓔ backpack@africaonline.co.zw), in the Vic Falls Centre, offers good and as unbiased information as you'll get on activities, transport and accommodation.

The National Parks and Wildlife office distributes information only.

Money The banks are lined up in the post office car park and all charge the same 1% commission. Some bureaus de change in town offer better rates – shop around.

Post & Communications The post office can get incredibly busy, and you may have to wait up to an hour just to buy stamps. Many hotel gift shops also sell stamps.

If you've bought handicrafts and need to post them home, it's worth popping over to Livingstone in Zambia, where parcel rates are considerably lower.

To dial Livingstone you don't need the international code – simply dial 8, then the local number.

Email & Internet Access The Internet Village on the 1st floor of Sopers Arcade has Internet access from 7 am to 10 pm daily for US$5 per 30 minutes.

The Zambezi Internet Cafe is in Shop 6 of the Zambezi Centre. Access costs US$5/2.80 per 30 minutes for foreigners/residents.

Medical Services If you need medical attention, try the Victoria Falls Surgery (☎ 3356) on West Dr. It's open from 9 am to 5 pm weekdays, and weekend mornings. The MARS number is ☎ 4646.

Victoria Falls Park

Before setting off for the Falls, prepare yourself for a good soaking from the spray. Protect your camera equipment and wrap cash and valuables in plastic. Also wear waterproofs or clothing that won't create a scandal when soaked.

Entry to the park is US$10/0.15 for foreigners/residents; plan your visit properly because they won't let you back in once you exit. The park is open from 6.30 am to 6 pm daily (8 pm on full-moon nights).

If possible, see if you can be at the Falls during a full moon. You will be treated to a breathtaking sight – the spray is almost luminous and, where the rainbow was during the day, you'll see a lunar rainbow. Once in a lifetime experience I reckon!

Lisa Burman

Once you reach the rim, a network of surfaced tracks takes you to a series of viewpoints. One of the most dramatic is **Cataract View**, the westernmost point, which requires climbing down a steep stairway into (and out of) the gorge.

Another track, the aptly named **Danger Point**, has terraces of slippery moss-covered rocks and a sheer and unfenced 100m drop-off, which conspire to rattle your nerves as you approach the stunning and frightening view into the first gorge. During low water, look for tentative foreigners on the Zambian side building up the courage to jump into a rock pool on the rim of the main Falls. From Danger Point, you can follow a side track for a view over the gracefully precarious **Zambezi Bridge**. It's now a favourite vantage point for locals, who gather to watch insane foreigners launching themselves off the bridge on giant rubber bands.

While walking through the rainforests, note the profusion of unusual species growing in this unique little enclave – ebony, ferns, fig trees and a variety of lianas and flowering plants. Also, watch for bushbuck, which may be seen browsing right up to the lip of the gorge.

Along the Zambezi

The walk along the River Zambezi above the Falls is excellent and packed with wildlife. Unfortunately, the top of the Falls is now fenced in as part of the Rainforest Reserve. To get to the river from town, head towards the reserve and turn left onto Zambezi Drive. Once you see the river, leave the road and follow the track which leads north to the **Big Tree**, a massive baobab with a 20m circumference. If you're keen, from here you can continue along the river almost as far as the Zambezi National Park, from where you can follow the road back into town. If you've had enough, jump back onto Zambezi Drive and follow it as it loops back towards the centre.

Don't take walks along the river too lightly; you may see warthog, crocodile, hippo, antelope and even elephant, buffalo and lion. Avoid walking too close to the riverbank – there are plenty of crocs here and they can appear from nowhere without warning.

Falls Craft Village

In this fortified mock-up of traditional Zimbabwean lifestyles, you'll see ethnic huts, prefabricated in their area of origin and moved to the village. You can also watch craftspeople at work and consult with a *nganga*, who can let you in on your future – if you really want to know it. What they won't mention is that you're destined to exit the place through an immense curio shop.

The village (☎ 4309) is open from 9.30 am to 4.30 pm Monday to Saturday and 9 am to 12.30 pm Sunday. Tours are held at 9.30 am, and there's a live traditional dance production from 6.30 to 8.30 pm nightly. Entry is US$5/2 for adults/children.

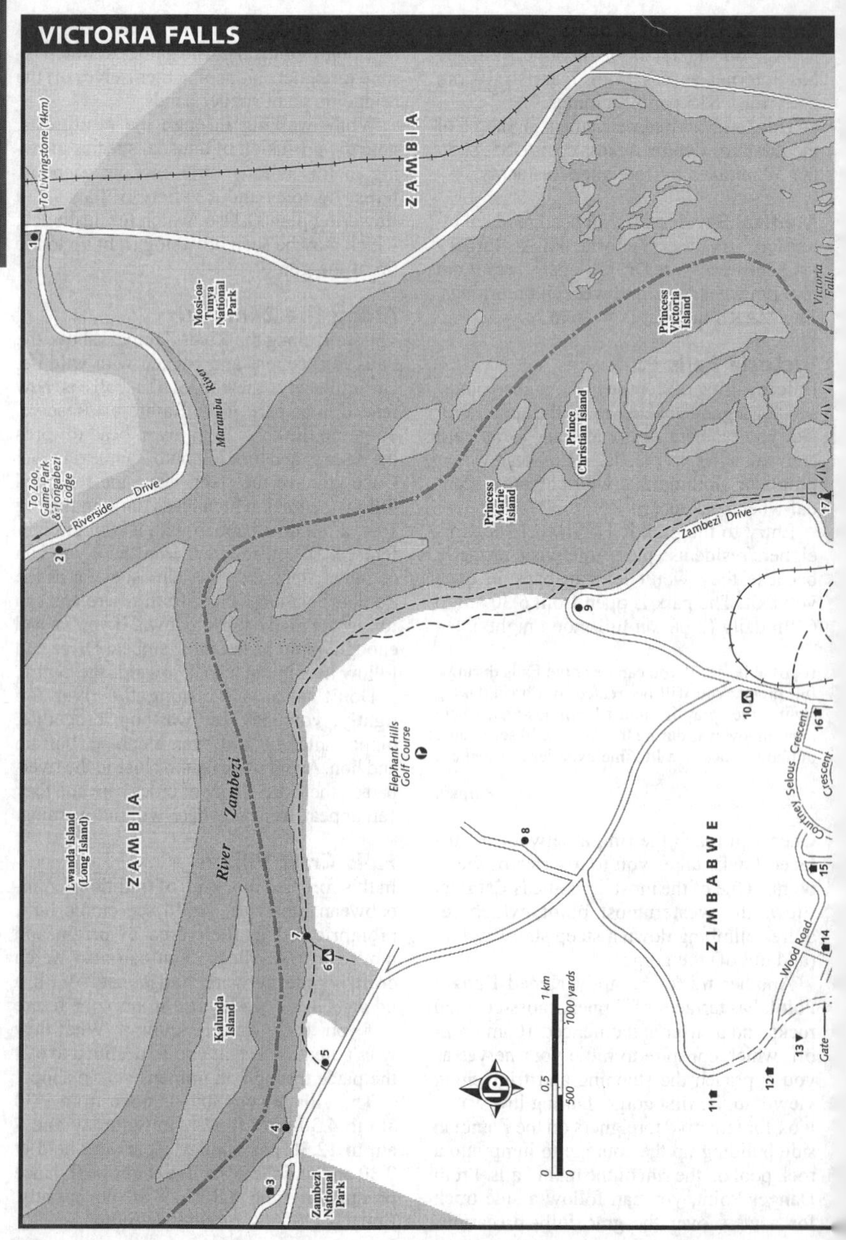
VICTORIA FALLS
ZAMBIA
To Livingstone (4km)
Mosi-oa-Tunya National Park
Maramba River
To Zoo, Game Park & Tongabezi Lodge
Riverside Drive
Princess Victoria Island
Victoria Falls
Prince Christian Island
Princess Marie Island
Zambezi Drive
Elephant Hills Golf Course
Lwanda Island (Long Island)
ZAMBIA
River Zambezi
Kalunda Island
Zambezi National Park
ZIMBABWE
Courtney Selous Crescent
Wood Road
Gate
0
0.5
1 km
0
500
1000 yards

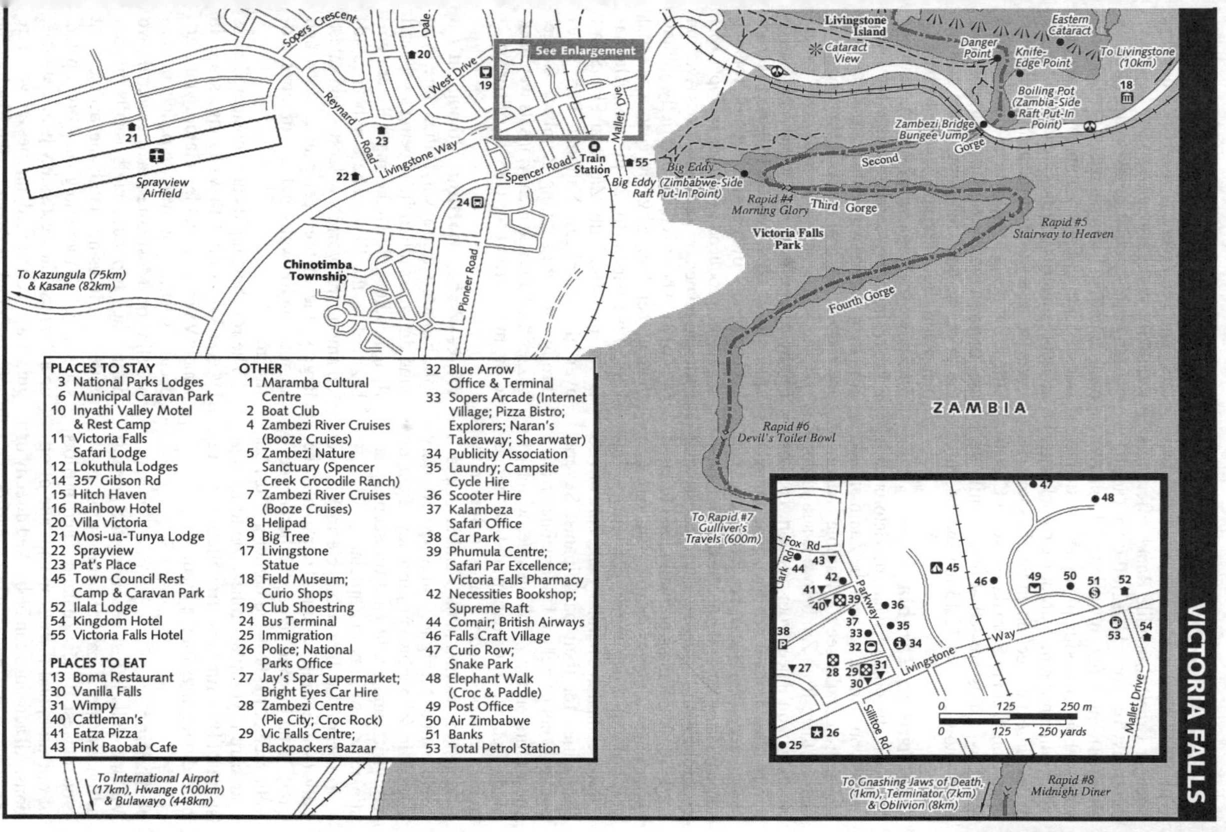
VICTORIA FALLS
ZAMBIA
Livingstone Island
Cataract View
Danger Point
Knife-Edge Point
Eastern Cataract
Boiling Pot (Zambia-Side Raft Put-In Point)
To Livingstone (10km)
Zambezi Bridge Bungee Jump
Second Gorge
Third Gorge
Fourth Gorge
Rapid #4 Morning Glory
Rapid #5 Stairway to Heaven
Rapid #6 Devil's Toilet Bowl
To Rapid #7 Gulliver's Travels (600m)
To Gnashing Jaws of Death (1km), Terminator (7km) & Oblivion (8km)
Rapid #8 Midnight Diner
Victoria Falls Park
Big Eddy
Big Eddy (Zimbabwe-Side Raft Put-In Point)
See Enlargement
Mallet Dve
Train Station
Spencer Road
West Drive
Dale
Sopers Crescent
Reynard Road
Livingstone Way
Pioneer Road
Chinotimba Township
Sprayview Airfield
To Kazungula (75km) & Kasane (82km)
To International Airport (17km), Hwange (100km) & Bulawayo (448km)
Fox Rd
Clark Rd
Parkway
Livingstone Way
Sillitoe Rd
Mallet Drive
0 125 250 m
0 125 250 yards
PLACES TO STAY
3 National Parks Lodges
6 Municipal Caravan Park
10 Inyathi Valley Motel & Rest Camp
11 Victoria Falls Safari Lodge
12 Lokuthula Lodges
14 357 Gibson Rd
15 Hitch Haven
16 Rainbow Hotel
20 Villa Victoria
21 Mosi-ua-Tunya Lodge
22 Sprayview
23 Pat's Place
45 Town Council Rest Camp & Caravan Park
52 Ilala Lodge
54 Kingdom Hotel
55 Victoria Falls Hotel
PLACES TO EAT
13 Boma Restaurant
30 Vanilla Falls
31 Wimpy
40 Cattleman's
41 Eatza Pizza
43 Pink Baobab Cafe
OTHER
1 Maramba Cultural Centre
2 Boat Club
4 Zambezi River Cruises (Booze Cruises)
5 Zambezi Nature Sanctuary (Spencer Creek Crocodile Ranch)
7 Zambezi River Cruises (Booze Cruises)
8 Helipad
9 Big Tree
17 Livingstone Statue
18 Field Museum; Curio Shops
19 Club Shoestring
24 Bus Terminal
25 Immigration
26 Police; National Parks Office
27 Jay's Spar Supermarket; Bright Eyes Car Hire
28 Zambezi Centre (Pie City; Croc Rock)
29 Vic Falls Centre; Backpackers Bazaar
32 Blue Arrow Office & Terminal
33 Sopers Arcade (Internet Village; Pizza Bistro; Explorers; Naran's Takeaway; Shearwater)
34 Publicity Association
35 Laundry; Campsite Cycle Hire
36 Scooter Hire
37 Kalambeza Safari Office
38 Car Park
39 Phumula Centre; Safari Par Excellence; Victoria Falls Pharmacy
42 Necessities Bookshop; Supreme Raft
44 Comair; British Airways
46 Falls Craft Village
47 Curio Row; Snake Park
48 Elephant Walk (Croc & Paddle)
49 Post Office
50 Air Zimbabwe
51 Banks
53 Total Petrol Station

Zambezi Nature Sanctuary

With 5000 crocodiles of all sizes, the former Spencer Creek Crocodile Ranch offers lots of crocs for your US$2.80/0.85 (adults/children) entry fee. It screens informative videos about crocodile lifestyles and there's a crocodile museum, tearoom, cat enclosure, aviary, insect collection and curio shop. It's open from 8 am to 5 pm daily except Christmas Day. Lions are fed at 4 pm while the crocs chow down at 11.15 am and 3.45 pm.

Day Trips to Zambia

You've really only seen half of Victoria Falls unless you also see it from the Zambian side (for more details, see the Zambia chapter). Getting there from Zimbabwe is straightforward, but you'll need your passport. The border is open from 6 am to 8 pm, and you should get an early start because queues can sometimes be long. If you need a short-visit visa for Zambia, they're issued on the spot for US$10. Officials normally aren't fussed about onward tickets or sufficient funds. If you go with a day tour organised in Zimbabwe, companies normally take care of visa formalities for their participants. Several backpackers hostels in Livingstone arrange short tours on the Zambian side, which include free accommodation and do not require a visa (see under Places to Stay in the Livingstone section in the Zambia chapter).

Note that foreigners may export only Z$500 in Zimbabwean currency, even on day visits, and credit card transactions are subject to a 5% tax in Zambia.

You can also hire a bicycle in Victoria Falls (see Getting Around, later in this section). If taking one across the border, keep your receipt to show the border guards, but take care if you plan to head on to Livingstone (11km further); travellers have reported muggings on the road.

Activities

Victoria Falls is fast becoming the greatest adrenalin-sports capital-cum-tourist playground, west of New Zealand. There are lots of operators and there's no shortage of options. All activities can be booked directly or through agents and accommodation, and should include visa and park fees, all transfers and emergency medical coverage should the worst happen.

Many of the activities take place (and can be arranged) in Livingstone, on the Zambian side of Victoria Falls. Zambian-based operators organising activities are covered in the Livingstone section of the Zambia chapter. Often, the deals are better on the Zambian side (you get more action for your money, or the price includes tempting offers such as meals and beer), but you have to be back in Zimbabwe by 8 pm, which can make things a bit rushed. Also, Zambia has far fewer laws than Zimbabwe to protect the Zambezi and the wildlife that makes it their home.

Flight of the Angels The name of this 10- to 15-minute buzz over the Falls comes from Livingstone's overworked quote. Today's angels are produced in Kansas by Piper Aircraft and owned by Southern Cross Aviation (☎ 4618). The privilege of briefly joining them in their Falls Skyview costs a celestial US$50 per person for 25 minutes. Alternatively, the 40-minute Zambezi Sky Safari over the Zambezi National Park flies through the zigzagging Zambezi Gorge, buzzes the Falls and then wings its way back to the main airport for US$70 per person.

White-Water Rafting Although it's a splash-out in more ways than one, you shouldn't miss the thrill of being swept and flung headlong down the angry River Zambezi below the Falls. The Zambezi rapids are among the world's wildest – and safest, largely due to the deep water, steep and smooth canyon walls and lack of rocks midstream.

The roughest rapids are considered class IV and V (on the I to VI ratings scale, in which VI is unrunnable). Before you start, decide whether you want to paddle or simply cling on. Most rafters take a swim or two during their trip, but there's usually one raft with a guide using stabilising paddles that stays upright. If you do go in – don't panic, operators use the best safety gear available, guides are well trained, injuries are very rare and – although it doesn't seem like it at the

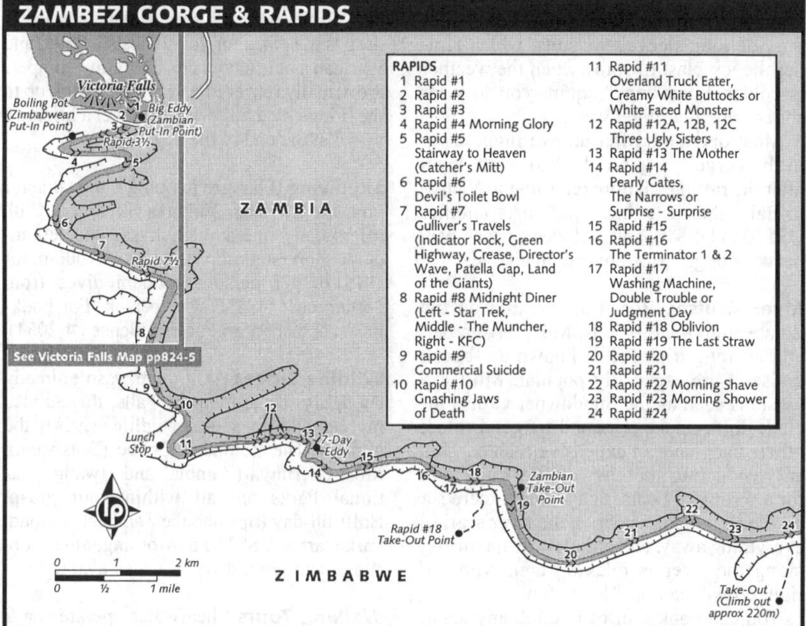

time – when you're dragged under, you will pop up eventually.

The main rafting operators in Victoria Falls are Shearwater (☎ 4471, e shearadv@zol.co.zw), Safari Par Excellence (☎ 2054) and Frontiers (☎ 5800). Most operators (including the Zambians) have booking offices along Parkway.

Prices are more or less standardised. For a full-day's rafting, you'll pay around US$100 if you 'put in' (launch your raft) on the Zimbabwean side – a bit less if you put in on the Zambian side. Most companies run daily trips when the water is high enough. When the water is very low, the rapids are too rocky and dangerous for rafting.

High-water runs through Rapids 11 to 18 (or 23), which are relatively mundane and can be done between 1 July and 15 August, though in high rainfall years they may begin as early as mid-May. Wilder low-water runs operate from roughly 15 August to late December, taking in the winding 22km from rapids four to 18 (or 23) if you put in on the Zimbabwe side, and from Rapids one to 18 (or 23) if you put in on the Zambian side.

The put-in points are Big Eddy (Zimbabwean side) and the Boiling Pot (Zambian side), which is just about as near as you can get to the Falls in a raft, and not possible to reach if you put in on the Zimbabwean side.

If you wish to continue to Rapid 23, make it clear when booking, or they may pull out at Rapid 18 (known as Oblivion). All operators walk around Rapid 9, which is affectionately nicknamed Commercial Suicide. The day is exhausting but it's the walk out of the gorge that's the killer. Reserve some energy for the climb as the steps (in reality, a ladder made of tree branches) are precarious – a cold drink waiting at the top is a welcome incentive to keep you going. The drinking continues into the evening as video footage of your day's adventures is shown at an appropriate hostel.

In warm seasons, you can go rafting in shorts and T-shirt, but don't forget to protect yourself from sunburn. Some companies provide long-sleeved wetsuits, which temper the icy blast of spray when the weather is colder. Some may require you to wear shoes, which will get wet.

Most operators offer an overnight camp in the gorge – a good place to wind down after the rafting – before returning to Victoria Falls the next day. This costs another US$30 to US$40, and includes a beach barbecue. Longer trips are also available.

River Cruises Boat trips are run on the Zambezi above the Falls. Most have a bar, and evening trips (often known as 'booze cruises') are especially popular. Most excursions such as the Sundowner Cruise include drinks in the price and are good value; others may have an expensive cash bar. It's easy enough to spot the wildlife – just look for a throng of boats, that's unless there's a particularly boozy boat on the river scaring everything away. Nevertheless, just cruising along the river is relaxing and, with the right crowd, can be a lot of fun.

You can book cruises through any agent in Victoria Falls. Priced between US$12 and US$25 they usually include drinks, food and pick-up and drop-off. It's probably worth paying a little bit extra for better food, more attentive service and chequered tablecloths.

Shearwater runs an interesting and more exclusive variation on the booze cruise, where a small group travels in comfortable canoes, complete with paddlers, who also mix drinks and pass around picnic food, while you simply enjoy the scenery and evening serenity.

Canoeing & Kayaking It's a lot of fun to paddle around the wide, mostly smooth river above the Falls, exploring islands and shooting mini-rapids. All companies charge roughly the same rates. Half/full-day trips are US$65/85. One/two/three-night trips, which operate from 1 April to 15 October, cost US$240/330/390.

Bungee Jumping If you have the desire to launch yourself from one of the world's highest commercial bungee jumps, then the Zambezi Bridge with its spectacular Falls backdrop is the place for you. It costs US$95, and you can book anywhere. Dangling jumpers are actually retrieved and dragged back up to the bridge by a guy who must feel a bit like a yo-yo at the end of the day.

Skydiving If bungee jumping is too tame for you, the Zambezi Vultures Skydivers Club offers daily one-day skydiving courses, including one static-line jump from 1000m, for US$110 per person. Tandem dives from 2500m cost US$160 per person. For bookings, contact Safari Par Excellence (☎ 2054).

Wildlife Drives As if there wasn't already enough to do around the Falls, there's also myriad wildlife, adding wildlife drives to the options. The Zambezi, Chobe (Botswana), Mosi-oa-Tunya (Zambia) and Hwange National Parks are all within your grasp. Half/full-day trips into the Zambezi National Park start at US$35/85. Morning, afternoon, sunset and night drives are also available.

Walking Tours Shearwater operates half/full-day walking tours on the banks of the Zambezi above the Falls for US$50/100, including food and transfers. Overnight trips are US$145. These can also be combined with a canoe trip, and are an ideal way to immerse yourself in the natural surroundings.

Steam Train The *Victoria Falls Safari Express* (☎ 4682, @ Fallsexp@mail.pci.co.zw) allows rail buffs to enjoy a morning, afternoon tea or moonlight dinner train ride to Zambia to Livingstone aboard a 1st-class coach from 1900 pulled by a 1922 Class 10 steam locomotive. Fares for the daily trip start at US$40 for an hour-long journey, to US$110 for the dinner run – don't forget your passport.

Horse & Elephant Rides Zambezi Horse Trails has daily two/three-hour novice or experienced rides for US$45/65 through a game reserve. Overnighters can be arranged. For information, contact Safari Par Excellence (☎ 2054).

Places to Stay

Accommodation in Victoria Falls is on the increase, although it can still be hard to find – reservations are advisable. Local elephants have discovered there's food aplenty to be had in town and they especially like wandering through camping areas at night. Almost impossible to hear until they're upon you they will gently avoid humans; but even so, security guards will probably alert you to the fact they're around.

Places to Stay – Budget

Camping The ***Town Council Rest Camp & Caravan Park*** *(☎ 4210, fax 4308)* on Livingstone Way, smack in the centre of town, is spacious but still gets crowded with tents and overland trucks. Camping costs US$2.80 per person and beds in not-too-pleasant dorms are US$5. Chalets cost US$4.80 per person, with bedding and cooking equipment. Six-bed cottages cost US$5.80 per person. It has a cloakroom where you can leave stuff but it's not too secure. The town laundry is within the grounds, and service washes only are available.

For more solitude, and a Zambezi setting, try the out-of-town ***Municipal Caravan Park***. Rates are the same as those at the Council Rest Camp, but there are no dorms or chalets.

The ***Inyathi Valley Motel & Rest Camp*** *(☎ 2345, 011-607034, 951 Parkway)* is a large, green camping ground, a short way out of town. Camping costs US$2.80 per site plus US$2 per person (children under 12 receive a 50% discount). They also have self-contained cabins for US$11 per person, including some that are nonsmoking.

Hostels The nicest backpacker option is ***357 Gibson Rd*** *(☎ 2179, e colourgem@iafrica.com)*, which has a lovely communal attic dorm and A-frame doubles for US$10 per person. Camping is US$5 per person. There's a large and homey lounge (with TV) in an open sided A-frame, an honesty bar fridge, pool, games room and lockers.

Closest to town and a bit more frenetic, ***Club Shoestring*** *(cell ☎ 011 800 731, 12 West Dr)* is a one-minute walk from the centre. Beds in colourful dorms are US$9, although if there's two of you it's worth shelling out the extra US$1 each for a private bath. There's a bar, lockers, kitchen, pool and a chill-out veranda. Camping is available for US$4 per person.

Further down West Dr, ***Pat's Place*** *(☎ 4375)* is much more basic, and a little bit cramped, with dorms for US$4 or doubles for US$14. A little bit better is ***Hitch Haven*** *(cell ☎ 011 405946, 332 Wood Rd)* with camping/dorms for US$2.90/6.60 per person. There's a small bar, which should refresh you for the walk into town.

Places to Stay – Mid-Range

The least expensive hotel is ***Sprayview*** *(☎ 4344)* on Livingstone Way, which has singles/doubles for US$45/60 in a pleasant garden setting. Ordinary meals are served by the pool terrace and there's a couple of bars and a disco.

A favourable alternative is ***Villa Victoria*** *(☎ 4386, 165 Courteney Selous Crescent)*. Quiet, comfortable rooms with private/shared bath cost US$20 per person/room. Guests have access to a pool, lounge, braai and self-catering facilities.

The ***Mosi-ua-Tunya Lodge*** *(☎ 4336, fax 4639, e moslodge@telcovic.co.zw)* has two self-catering thatched cottages containing doubles/triples/quads for US$60/70/80. There's no bar but it does have a pool, games room, lounge and TV room.

Places to Stay – Top End

Ilala Lodge *(☎ 4737, fax 4740, e ilalazws@coldfire.dnet.co.zw, 411 Livingstone Way)* is central with a pleasant natural decor, sunny terrace bar, pool and restaurant. The green lawns and nearby bushland create a natural atmosphere. Singles/doubles start at US$200/286. There's also a casino and a soundproof disco on site.

The historic four-star ***Victoria Falls Hotel*** *(☎ 4751, fax 4586, e zimsuncro@zimsun.co.zw)* is a lovely old place and when you step off the train and pass through the Edwardian train station, it provides a fitting climax to the grand colonial illusion. It oozes atmosphere, and its setting above the

Second Zambezi Gorge is nothing short of spectacular. For rooms, foreigners pay from US$335/372.

The Great Zimbabwe-styled ***Kingdom Hotel*** *(☎ 4275, fax 4782, e kingdom@kingdom.zimsun.co.zw)* dominates Livingstone Way. The punters seem to like it despite the inflated room rates (from US$68/228 for residents/foreigners) and its plastic appearance – funnily enough Michael Jackson is rumoured to have invested in it. The centre of the hotel is an open area of ornamental pools and lawns connected by wooden bridges. There's a couple of restaurants and bars and a massive swimming pool – it's worth stopping by for a meal, drink, swim or look.

The ***Victoria Falls Safari Lodge*** *(☎ 3201, fax 3205, e saflodge@saflodge.co.zw)* is an immense and beautifully designed place with sunset views and an ecological theme. Room rates for foreigners are US$268/358 in the high season.

Colourful and upmarket two/three-bedroom lodges in the adjacent ***Lokuthula Lodges*** *(☎ 4714, fax 4792, e lokuthula@saflodge.co.zw)* cost from US$160/210. Each lodge, with airy open-plan architecture, accommodates up to six/eight people.

Places to Eat

For a good-value breakfast, try ***Naran's Takeaways*** in Sopers Arcade. Its 'campers breakfast' is steak, bacon, egg, toast and chips for US$2. Open for lunch and snacks, you can't beat its vegetarian specialities, including great curries and samosas. Also in Sopers Arcade, ***Pizza Bistro*** *(☎ 4396)* serves pizzas, crepes, pasta and baked spuds and also does deliveries until 9 pm. Next door, the ***Explorer's Bar*** has a full restaurant of its own serving up bar snacks and meals.

Pink Baobab Cafe does tea, coffee, fresh juice, a daily lunch special and a range of snacks – crepes, potato salad, baked spuds, filled rolls and the like. It's got shaded garden seating complete with its own waterfall.

On Parkway is ***Eatza Pizza***, a takeaway that does pizza and fried snacks. It's open daily from 10 am to midnight.

All the hotels/lodges offer buffet breakfasts, lunches and dinners. The ***Ilala Lodge*** has a dinner buffet for US$7 and an oriental restaurant. The ***Rainbow Hotel*** has traditional entertainment by its pool while dinner is served. The evening braai at the ***Victoria Falls Hotel*** is highly recommended and will satisfy even the biggest appetite. Overlooking the Zambezi Bridge, a meal, afternoon tea or just a drink at this place will prove a highlight. The nostalgic Livingstone Room has a live dance band.

Boma *(☎ 3201)* at Lokuthula Lodges is consistently recommended. For US$17 (under 10s, US$5.50) you get a four-course African buffet, including game and local cuisine – sadza, rice, salad, potatoes, bread and sauces. A Ndebele choir performs in the background. Vegetarian meals and free pick-ups from the big hotels are also available.

For self-catering, the well-stocked ***Jay's Spar Supermarket*** is open until 6 pm Monday to Saturday. At other times you may find what you want at the ***7-Eleven***. There's also ***Ceres*** green grocer in Sopers Arcade and a decent butcher in Chinotimba township.

Wimpy fries up the usual fastfood. There's a ***Subway*** between Jay's Spar and the Shell petrol station and ***Pie City***, in the Zambezi Centre, is popular. The clean ***Vanilla Falls*** dishes up excellent ice cream and frozen yoghurt.

Entertainment

Vic Falls is definitely a party town with overlanders and five-star tourists celebrating their victory over the Zambezi, gravity, wild creatures and everything else dangerous. There are plenty of bars, casinos, traditional dancing and a whole range of booze cruises available (see River Cruises earlier).

Bars, Discos & Casinos Until early evening, the ***beer hall*** in Chinotimba township, near the bus terminal, is good for some local action. The big-hotel bars offer toned-down live music, often pseudo-African 'banana boat' revues and insipid marimba muzak.

The most popular bar is the ***Explorers Travellers Club*** *(☎ 4468)* in Sopers Arcade, which is loud, hot and sweaty with plenty of six-pack-stomached guides strutting around.

Adrenalin pumped tourists straight off the raft compete for dancing room on the tables and it's a fun place to let off some steam. There's a US$1.10 cover charge, but tell them you're eating and they should let you off.

The competing ***Croc & Paddle*** *(☎ 3450)* tucked away in the Elephant Walk complex is a bit more civilised but still gets those rafters. Being open sided it's a lot less sweaty and there's a view over the parkland leading to the Falls where scavenging baboons offer side entertainment. It also has TV screens and game dishes.

The beauty of ***Croc Rock*** is that you can check out the clientele before you go in. Catering to a more local crowd, it has a low-level outdoor bar area, which you can look onto from above. There's also an indoor nightclub area with TV screens where Mark from Sweden entertains on ladies' night.

Once the pubs close, the crowds invariably head to the ***Downtime Night Club*** (US$2.50 cover charge), beneath Ilala Lodge, which stays open 'til late (or early!). The music is aimed at travellers and includes recent western hits, pop anthems and disco divas.

Casinos can be found in the ***Great Enclosure*** (next to the Kingdom Hotel), the ***Ilala Lodge*** and the ***Elephant Hills*** hotels.

Traditional Dancing The ***Falls Craft Village*** *(☎ 4309)* stages a traditional dancing performance at dusk (around 7 pm) for US$3.50, as does the ***Elephant Hills*** for a pricier US$11.00. The ***Rainbow Hotel*** and ***Boma*** also have traditional dancing accompanying dinner.

Shopping

When Victoria Fall's first white settler, Percy Clark, opened his curio shop in 1903, little would he have realised that the town would become one of the world's biggest tourist traps. Nowadays street vendors, touts (usually offering ganga) and craft stores all vie with each other for the tourist dollar. The streets are lined with gimmicky curio shops, including the Victoria Falls Aquarium, with Zimbabwean freshwater creatures fed daily at 2 pm; Soper's Curios, which has been in business since 1911 and still has a crocodile in its pool; and the Zambezi Taxidermy Snake Park where snakes are milked. Regional specialties you'll find here include Tonga stool seats with their roughly carved wooden bases. Another favourite is a rafting souvenir, most companies will offer you their T-shirts for up to US$30; a good alternative is a Zambezi Lager T-shirt from Jay's Spar for US$10.50.

The area behind the post office is the place to go for crafts. There's something for everyone, from women's cooperatives to upmarket boutiques. Elephant Walk is a swanky shopping complex with coffee shop, tourist information, classy shops and a bar. There are also galleries in the area and it's worth having a look around just to appreciate the pieces on display.

Getting There & Away

Air Air Zimbabwe (☎ 4316) and Zimbabwe Express Airlines (☎ 04-705923 in Harare) both fly at least daily between Victoria Falls and Harare; some flights go via Kariba and Hwange National Park.

Bus The terminal for African buses to Hwange town, Dete Crossroads, Safari Crossroads and Bulawayo is near the market, on Pioneer Rd in Chinotimba township (but they also make a stop near the Sprayview Hotel on Livingstone Rd). There are normally three to five buses daily, departing when full. Blue Arrow buses to Bulawayo (US$19) leave its office at 7.30 am Saturday and Monday, and 2.30 pm Sunday.

Shoestring Shuttle (☎ 011-800713) has a 6 am bus for Bulawayo (US$11) and Harare (US$20) on Saturday, returning at 6 am on Sunday. They pick-up and drop-off at all backpackers hostels.

Translux has services between Victoria Falls and Bulawayo with connections to Jo'burg. They leave on Thursday and Sunday at 6.30 pm. From Bulawayo, they depart at 11.30 am on Tuesday and Friday. Book through the UTC (☎ 61402). UTC does transfers to Hwange for US$29 per person.

Route 49 and the Baz Bus terminate here on their long rides up from South Africa.

For more information, see the Getting Around the Region chapter.

Train Until the early 1990s, a romantic highlight of a Zimbabwe trip was riding the steam train to Victoria Falls; now everything is diesel. Trains leave Bulawayo and Victoria Falls at 6.30 pm daily. The 1st/2nd-class sleeper fare is US$8.60/7.30. Economy class costs US$2.60.

The booking office (☎ 391) is open from 7 am to noon and 2 to 4 pm weekdays and 7 to 10 am weekends (the ticket office is open until 6.15 pm daily).

Taxi To get to Mlibizi for the ferry to Kariba, you'll have to charter a taxi, which should cost around US$25 per person. It may be worth sticking some notices up to find someone to share with you.

Hitching The road between Bulawayo and Victoria Falls isn't exactly busy, but you'd have to be very unlucky not to find something.

Getting Around

The Victoria Falls airport is 20km out of town along the Bulawayo road. A shuttle bus between the airport and town, connecting with all arriving and departing flights, costs US$3.

Midnight Taxis (☎ 4290) is a reputable company; taxis between town and Zambia should cost US$9.

Anyone aged over 18 with a driving licence can hire a 50cc motor scooter from the guy opposite the Phumula Centre on Parkway. You'll pay around US$7/10 per half/full day, with unlimited kilometres. The Shell petrol station, behind Jay's Spar, is open 24 hours.

You can hire mountain bikes from Baobab Cafe or between the camping ground and Parkway for US$5.50/8.50 per half/full day.

ZAMBEZI NATIONAL PARK

The 56,000-hectare Zambezi National Park consists of 40km of River Zambezi frontage and a spread of wildlife-rich inland mopane forest and savanna. The park office is open from 6 am to 6.30 pm.

Horse riding (US$44 for 2½ hours), wildlife drives and wildlife walks are available through operators in Victoria Falls (see that section). Visitors may only walk on their own between the riverbank picnic areas Nos 1 to 25, near the park's eastern boundary.

The lodges on the riverbank at the park entrance each have two bedrooms, a living area and veranda. There are also three fishing camps, ***Mpala-Jena***, ***Kandahar*** and ***Sansimba***, all beautifully located along the river, and five exclusive camps. Visitors may camp overnight at the remote ***Chamabonda Wildlife-Viewing Platform***, near the southern end of the park. ***Chundu 1*** and ***Chundu 2***, between Mpala-Jena and Sansimba, occupy a lovely stretch of riverbank. ***Chamunzi*** is on the bank, 40km west of the park entrance and ***Siamunungu*** is 7km west of Chamunzi. Each has a limit of 12 people. For bookings and contact information, see under Accommodation in the Facts for the Visitor section earlier in this chapter.

WESTERN LAKE KARIBA

The western half of Lake Kariba bears little resemblance to its eastern counterpart (see the Northern Zimbabwe section earlier in this chapter), and is characterised by wilderness outposts, traditional Tonga culture and wild rolling hills.

Binga

☎ 055

The most interesting western Kariba settlement, Binga was constructed expressly as a government administrative centre, with the purpose of resettling the Tonga people displaced by the rising Lake Kariba waters. Binga wanders sparsely from the shore to the hills, and without a vehicle, getting around entails some dry and exhausting walks. However, it's a good place to look for Tonga crafts, including decorative stools, headrests and drums.

Beyond the smoking of *mbanje* (cannabis), traditional Tonga culture appears to be sadly and permanently disappearing into history. The government is trying to absorb the Tonga into mainstream Zimbabwe by providing schools and medical services. Any images of a utopian Kathmandu-by-the-Lake are largely unfounded.

Chibwatatata Hot Springs, long considered a 'power place' by the Tonga, once served as a rain-making site. A less violent spring nearby provides naturally heated water for the rest camp's swimming pool. It's also used as a laundry and bath, and has become polluted.

Chilangililo Cooperative *(☎ 015-563)*, a novel and successful tourism concept, is the brainchild of anthropologist Dr Peta Jones. Her interests included promoting donkeys as transport and encouraging production of quality local crafts; sadly she's retired. The project continues and visitors have the chance to meet local people and sample traditional Tonga foods. Very basic sleeping huts cost US$4 per person.

The ***Kulizwe Lodge*** *(☎ 286, Private Bag 5701, Binga)* has two/three/four person self-catering chalets for US$11/15/17 and camping for US$0.80 per person. It also has boats for hire and sells firewood.

Now that the Binga road is tarred, hitching isn't too difficult. You'll have the most luck on Saturday morning.

Getting There & Away There's a bus service that travels between Bulawayo and Harare via Binga, Siabuwa and Karoi, which involves an overnight in Siabuwa (camping only). The bus from Binga to Bulawayo leaves at 5 am from the market, beside the beer hall. For Victoria Falls, get off this bus at Dete Crossroads and hitch or catch a westbound bus. You can also catch the ferry from Kariba (see that entry in the Northern Zimbabwe section earlier in this chapter).

Mlibizi

☎ 055

Unless they're fishing, most travellers spend just one night at Mlibizi, either arriving or connecting with the Kariba-bound lake ferry. At the ferry terminal is the mid-range ***Mlibizi Zambezi Resort*** *(☎ 272)*, where double chalets cost US$125 and camp sites are about US$2 per person.

Further along is the more affordable ***Mlibizi Hotel & Safari Camp*** *(☎/fax 271)*, which bills itself as 'the best place to do nothing'. A simple bungalow costs US$25/41.50. Garden villas with six-bed dorms cost US$20 per person. It has a bar, restaurant and pool.

Taxi transfers from Victoria Falls cost around US$25 per person, but beware of unlicensed taxi drivers quoting good rates. They will probably demand more than you agreed on when you get there. You can also take the Binga bus (there are one or two daily) from Dete Crossroads; get off at the Mlibizi turn-off and walk the hot 15km into Mlibizi.

Chizarira National Park

The name of this magnificent 192,000-hectare park is derived from the Tonga word *chijalila* (closed off or barrier). Although access is difficult, Chizarira is Zimbabwe's most scenic park. It sits along the Zambezi Escarpment, and comprises steep green gorges, a high plateau region (great for hiking) and the lovely Busi River flood plain, bearing a strong resemblance to Mana Pools. The main draws are its wild and remote nature and rich wildlife populations.

The best way to explore the park is by walking tour (see Organised Tours in the main Getting Around section of this chapter). You can choose between backpacking safaris, in which you carry everything, or walking safaris, where daily forays are made from semipermanent base camps. Khangela Safaris (☎ 09-49733) in Bulawayo offers trips from $US130 per person per day, including transport, guide and meals .

Places to Stay & Eat Chizarira has no services, so all supplies – food, spares, camping equipment, fuel etc – must be carried in.

National Parks has several exclusive camps (for contact and booking details, see Accommodation in the Facts for the Visitor section of this chapter), including the plush ***Kaswiswi***; the dramatic ***Mucheni*** overlooking Mucheni Gorge; ***Mobola***, beside the Mucheni River; and ***Busi***, amid the acacias on a flood plain. Water is available only at the Mabola and Kaswiswi camps. At Busi, water must be obtained elephant-style by digging for it in the riverbed. Rates for National Parks accommodation ranges from camp sites for US$0.80 per site to six-bed lodges for US$17.

Getting There & Away Without a 4WD, you can resign yourself to joining a tour; hitching is strictly forbidden and the national park doesn't receive enough visitors to make it worthwhile anyway. Petrol is available at Binga and sporadically at Siabuwa.

Language

AFRIKAANS

Although Afrikaans has been closely associated with the ethnic identity of the Afrikaners, it is also spoken as a first language by many coloureds. Ironically, it was probably first used as a common language by the polyglot coloured community of the Cape and passed back to whites by nannies and servants. Around six million people speak the language, roughly half of whom are Afrikaners and half of whom are coloureds. It wasn't recognised as one of the country's official languages until 1925; before then it was officially regarded as a dialect of Dutch.

Afrikaans is phonetically consistent, and words are generally pronounced the way they are spelt, with the characteristic guttural emphasis and rolled 'r' of Germanic languages. The following pronunciation guide is not complete, but it does include the more difficult sounds.

a	as the 'u' in 'pup'
e	as in hen
i	as the 'e' in 'angel'
o	as in 'fort', or as the 'oy' in 'boy'
u	as the 'e' in 'angel' but with lips pouted
r	a rolled 'rr' sound
aai	as the 'y' in 'why'
ae	as 'ah'
ee	as in 'deer'
ei	as the 'ay' in 'play'
ie	as the 'ee' in 'need'
oe	as the 'oo' in 'loot'
oë	as the 'oe' in 'doer'
ooi	as the 'oi' in 'oil', preceded by 'w'
oei	as the 'ooey' in 'phooey', preceded by 'w'
tj	as the 'ch' in 'chunk'

South African English

English has undergone some changes during its time in South Africa. Quite a few words have changed meaning, new words have been appropriated from other languages and, thanks to the influence of Afrikaans, a distinctive accent has developed. British rather than US practice is followed in grammar and spelling. In some cases, British words are preferred to their US equivalent (eg, 'lift' not 'elevator', 'petrol' not 'gas'). In South African English, repetition for emphasis is common: something that burns you is 'hot hot'; fields after the rains are 'green green'; a crowded minibus with no more room is 'full full' and so on. See the glossary at the back of this book for some examples.

Greetings & Civilities

Hello.	*Hallo.*
Goodbye.	*Totsiens.*
Good morning.	*Goeie môre.*
Good afternoon,	*Goeie middag.*
Good evening.	*Goeie naand.*
Good night.	*Goeie nag.*
Please.	*Asseblief.*
Thank you.	*Dankie.*
You're welcome.	*Dis 'n plesier.*
How are you?	*Hoe gaan dit?*
Good, thank you.	*Goed, dankie.*
Pardon.	*Ekskuus.*
Excuse me.	*Verskoon my.*

Useful Words & Phrases

Yes.	*Ja.*
No.	*Nee.*
What?	*Wat?*
How?	*Hoe?*
How many/much?	*Hoeveel?*
Where?	*Waar?*
Do you speak ...?	*Praat u ... ?*
English	*Engels*
Afrikaans	*Afrikaans?*
I only understand a little Afrikaans.	*Ek verstaan net 'n bietjie Afrikaans.*
Where are you from?	*Waarvandaan kom u?*
from ...	*van ...*
overseas	*oorsee*
daughters	*dogters*
sons	*seuns*

husband	*eggenoot*
wife	*vrou*
father	*pa*
mother	*ma*
brother	*broer*
sister	*suster*
sir/madam	*meneer/mevrou*
emergency	*nood*
bad	*sleg*
nice/good/pleasant	*lekker*
cheap	*goedkoop*
expensive	*duur*
party/rage	*jol*

Getting Around

arrival	*aankoms*
departure	*vertrek*
ticket	*kaartjie*
one way	*enkel*
return	*retoer*
to	*na*
from	*van*
travel	*reis*

Around Town

art gallery	*kunsgalery*
at the corner	*op die hoek*
avenue	*laan*
bank	*bank*
building	*gebou*
church	*kerk*
city	*stad*
city centre	*middestad*
enquiries	*navrae*
exit	*uitgang*
information	*inligting*
left	*links*
office	*kantoor*
pharmacy/chemist	*apteek*
police	*polisie*
police station	*polisiestasie*
post office	*poskantoor*
right	*regs*
road	*pad, weg*
rooms	*kamers*
station	*stasie*
street	*straat*
tourist bureau	*toeristeburo*
town	*dorp*
traffic light	*robot*

In the Country

bay	*baai*
beach	*strand*
car	*kar*
caravan park	*woonwapark*
field/plain	*veld*
ford	*drift*
freeway	*vrymaak*
game reserve	*wildtuin*
highway	*snelweg*
hiking trail	*wandelpad*
lake	*meer*
marsh	*vlei*
mountain	*berg*
point	*punt*
river	*rivier*
road	*pad*
track	*spoor*
utility/pick-up	*bakkie*

Food & Drink

barbecue	*braai/braaivleis*
beer	*bier*
bread	*brood*
cheese	*kaas*
chicken	*hoender*
cup of coffee	*koppie koffie*
dried, salted meat	*biltong*
farm sausage	*boerewors*
fish	*vis*
fruit	*vrugte*
glass of milk	*glas melk*
hotel bar	*kroeg*
meat	*vleis*
pork	*varkvlies*
steak	*biefstuk*
tea	*tee*
vegetables	*groente*
water	*water*
wine	*wyn*

Time & Days

When?	*Wanneer?*
am	*vm*
pm	*nm*
soon	*nou-nou*
today	*vandag*
tomorrow	*môre*
yesterday	*gister*
daily	*daagliks*
weekly	*weekblad*
public holiday	*openbare vakansiedag*

Monday	*Maandag (Ma)*
Tuesday	*Dinsdag (Di)*
Wednesday	*Woensdag (Wo)*
Thursday	*Donderdag (Do)*
Friday	*Vrydag (Vr)*
Saturday	*Saterdag (Sa)*
Sunday	*Sondag (So)*

Numbers

1	*een*
2	*twee*
3	*drie*
4	*vier*
5	*vyf*
6	*ses*
7	*sewe*
8	*agt*
9	*nege*
10	*tien*
11	*elf*
12	*twaalf*
13	*dertien*
14	*veertien*
15	*vyftien*
16	*sestien*
17	*sewentien*
18	*agtien*
19	*negentien*
20	*twintig*
21	*een en twintig*
30	*dertig*
40	*veertig*
50	*vyftig*
60	*sestig*
70	*sewentig*
80	*tagtig*
90	*negentig*
100	*honderd*
1000	*duisend*

CHICHEWA

Chichewa is the national language of Malawi and is also a very close relative of the Nyanja language spoken in Zambia – the two are mutually intelligible. It is a complex language: word prefixes and suffixes change according to context, so one single word cannot always be given for its English equivalent. The most common forms are given here, but do remember that although these words and phrases may not be 'proper' Chichewa, you will be understood. Most Malawians and Zambians will be pleased to hear even a few words spoken by a foreigner.

Getting it Right

The actual title of several Southern African languages can cause confusion for visitors. For example, in Malawi the language of the Chewa people is Chichewa. Likewise, the language of the Basotho people (from Lesotho) is SeSotho. Usually, the prefixes (in these cases 'Chi' and 'Se') simply mean 'language', but they're only used when actually speaking that language. When speaking English the prefixes are usually dropped. To say 'I find it difficult to learn isiZulu' is like saying 'I find it easy to speak Français'. However, Chichewa usually retains the prefix whatever language you're speaking.

Following are the the current official English designations for the predominant languages of Southern Africa (with their indigenous titles in brackets):

Chichewa, Ndebele (Sindebele), North Sotho (SeSotho sa Lebowa), South Sotho (SeSotho), Swati (SiSwati), Tsonga (Xitsonga), Tswana (SeTswana), Venda (Tshivenda), Xhosa (isiXhosa), Zulu (isiZulu)

Greetings & Civilities

Bambo literally means 'father' but is a polite way to address any Malawian man. The female equivalent is *amai* or *mai*. *Mazungu* means 'white person', but is not a derogatory term.

Hello.	*Moni.*
Hello, anybody in?	*Odi.* (ie, when knocking on door, or calling at gate)
Come in/Welcome.	*Lowani.*
How are you?	*Muli bwanji?*
I'm fine.	*Ndili bwino.*
And you?	*Kaya-iwe?* (to one person) *Kaya inu?* (to several people)
Please.	*Chonde.*
Thank you/Excuse me.	*Zikomo.*

Tumbuka & Yao in Malawi

The two other principal indigenous languages of Malawi are Tumbuka (in the north) and Yao (in the south). Nearly all Tumbuka and Yao people also speak Chichewa, and many speak English as well. Nevertheless, a few simple words in Tumbuka and Yao will be most welcome.

English	Tumbuka	Yao
Hello.	*Yewo.*	*Quamboni.*
How are you?	*Muliwuli?*	*Iliwuli?*
Fine.	*Nilimakola.*	*Ndiri chenene.*
And you?	*Manyi imwa?*	*Qualinimye?*
Goodbye.	*Pawemi.*	*Siagara gani ngwaula.*
Thank you (very much).	*Yewo (chomene).*	*Asante (sana).*
What's your name?	*Zinolinu ndimwenjani?*	*Mwe linachi?*
My name is ...	*Zinalane ndine ...*	*Une linaliangu ...*
Where are you from?	*Mukukhalankhu?*	*Ncutama qua?*
I'm from ...	*Nkhula khu ...*	*Gutama ku ...*

Thank you very much.	*Zikomo kwambile/ kwambiri.*
Good/Fine/OK.	*Chabwino.*
Good night.	*Gonani bwino.*
Goodbye.	*Tsala bwino.* (lit: 'stay well', when leaving)
Goodbye.	*Pitani bwino.* (lit: 'go well', when staying)

Useful Words & Phrases

Yes.	*Inde.*
No.	*Iyayi.*
I don't understand.	*Sindikunva.*
What's your name?	*Dzina lako ndani?*
Where are you going?	*Ukupita kuti?*
I'm going to Blantyre.	*Ndikupita ku Blantyre.*
What is this?	*Ndi chiani?*
What is that? (far away)	*Icho ndi chiani?*
Where?	*Kuti?*
Here.	*Pano.*
Over there.	*Uko.*
Why?	*Chifukwa?*
How much?	*Ntengo bwanji/ Ndalama zingati?*
enough/finish	*bas*
many	*zambile*
I'm tired.	*Ndatopa.*
I want ...	*Ndifuna ...*
I don't want ...	*Sindifuna ...*
to buy	*kugula*
to eat	*kudya*
to sleep	*kugona*
Men (toilets)	*Akuma*
Women (toilets)	*Akazi*

Food & Drink

Bring me ...	*Mundi passe ...*
bread	*buledi*
chicken	*nkhuku*
coffee	*khofi*
eggs	*mazira*
fish	*somba*
fruit (one)	*chipasso*
fruits (many)	*zipasso*
lake perch	*chambo*
meat	*nyama*
milk	*mkaka*
potatoes	*batata*
tea	*ti*
vegetables	*mquani*
water	*mazi*

In restaurants *nsima* is a stiff maize porridge eaten with a sauce of meat, beans or vegetables.

Time

today	*lero*
tomorrow (early morning)	*m'mara*
tomorrow	*mara*
yesterday	*dzulo*

Numbers

Chichewa speakers talking together will normally use English for numbers and prices. Similarly, time is nearly always expressed in English.

1	*chimonzi*
2	*ziwili*
3	*zitatu*
4	*zinayi*
5	*zitsano*

NDEBELE (Zimbabwe)

The Ndebele language of Zimbabwe is spoken primarily in Matabeleland in the western and south-western parts of the country. It's derived from the Zulu group of languages and is not mutually intelligible with Shona.

You could assume that the Ndebele of South Africa (also known as Southern Ndebele) and that of Zimbabwe are the same language, but the truth is that the two are quite distinct. See the boxed text 'The Other Ndebele' for some useful phrases in the South African variety.

Pronunciation

Ndebele was first written using phonetic English transliteration, so most letters are pronounced as they would be in English. The major exceptions are the 'clicks', made by drawing the tongue away from the front teeth (dental), slapping it on the roof of the mouth (palatal) or drawing it quickly sideways from the right upper gum (lateral). Each of the clicks have four different variants: voiced, aspirated, nasal and aspirated nasal. For interest only – non-native speakers rarely get the hang of this – the following table outlines standard transliterations for each of these sounds:

	voiced	aspirated	nasal	aspirated nasal
dental	gc	ch	nc	ngc
palatal	gq	qh	nq	ngq
lateral	gx	xh	nx	ngx

Other Ndebele differences of note include:

o	as in 'or'
b	pronounced implosively, ie, taking air into the mouth through the lips
th	aspirated, as the 't' in 'too'
m	before a word-initial consonant, it's pronounced as a light hum
n	before a word-initial consonant, it's a hum with an 'n' sound

Greetings & Civilities

Hello. (initial)	*Sawubona/Salibonani.*
Hello. (reply)	*Yebo.*
Welcome.	*Siyalemukela.*
Good morning.	*Livukenjani.*
Good afternoon.	*Litshonile.*
Good evening.	*Litshone njani.*
How are you?	*Linjani/Kunjani?*
I'm well.	*Sikona.*
Goodbye.	*Lisale kuhle.* (when staying)
Goodbye.	*Uhambe kuhle.* (when leaving)
Yes.	*Yebo.*
No.	*Hayi.*
Please.	*Uxolo.*
Thank you.	*Siyabonga kakulu.*
What's your name?	*Ibizo lakho ngubani?*
My name is ...	*Elami igama ngingu ...*
I'm from ...	*Ngivela e ...*
sir/madam	*umnimzana/inkosikazi*
boy/girl	*umfana/inkazana*

Useful Words & Phrases

I'd like ...	*Ngicela ...*
How much?	*Yimalini?*
Where is the (station)?	*Singapi (isiteshi)?*
What time is it?	*Yisikhati bani?*
today	*lamhla*
tomorrow	*kusasa*
yesterday	*izolo*
Men (toilets)	*Amadoda*
Women (toilets)	*Abafazi*
friend	*mngane*
small/large	*okuncane/ncinyane*
market/shop	*imakethe/isitolo*

When does the ... leave?	*Izawuhamba nini ...?*
bus	*bhasi*
car	*imoto*
train	*isitimela*

Food & Drink

beef	*nkomo*
beer	*utshwala*
bread	*isinkwa*
butter	*ibatha*
chicken	*nkukhu*
coffee	*ikofi*
eggs	*amaqanda*
fish	*ininhlanzi*
fruit	*izithelo*
ground nuts	*amazambane*
maize	*umbila*
maize porridge	*sadza*
meat	*inyama*
milk	*ucago*
potatoes	*amagwili*
salt	*isaudo*
sugar	*ushukela*
tea	*itiye*
vegetables	*mbhida*
water	*amanzi*

Animals

baboon	*ndwangu*
buffalo	*nyathi*
dog	*nja*
elephant	*ndhlovu*
giraffe	*ntundla*
goat	*mbuzi*
hippopotamus	*mvubu*
horse	*ibhiza*
hyaena	*mpisi*
impala	*mpala*
leopard	*ngwe*
lion	*silwane*
monkey	*nkawu*
rabbit	*mvundla*
rhinoceros	*ubhejane*
warthog	*ungulube yeganga*
zebra	*ndube*

The 'Other' Ndebele

The Ndebele language of South Africa is spoken in the country's north-eastern region. It shares many linguistic features with North Sotho but is not mutually intelligible with the Ndebele language spoken in Zimbabwe. Here are a few phrases that may prove useful:

Hello.	*Lotsha.*
Goodbye.	*Khamaba kuhle/ Sala kuhle.*
Yes.	*I-ye.*
No.	*Awa.*
Please.	*Ngibawa.*
Thank you.	*Ngiyathokaza.*
What's your name?	*Ungubani ibizo lakho?*
My name is ...	*Ibizo lami ngu ...*
I come from ...	*Ngibuya e ...*

Days

Monday	*umbulo*
Tuesday	*olwesibili*
Wednesday	*ngolwesithathu*
Thursday	*ngolwesine*
Friday	*ngolwesihlanu*
Saturday	*ngesabatha*
Sunday	*ngesonto*

Numbers

1	*okukodwa*
2	*okubili*
3	*okutathu*
4	*okune*
5	*okuyisihlanu*
6	*okuyisithupha*
7	*okuyisikhombisa*
8	*okuyisitshiyangalo mbila*
9	*okuyisitshiyangalo lunye*
10	*okuli tshumi*

NORTH SOTHO

North Sotho is spoken in the north-eastern provinces of South Africa.

Hello.	*Thobela.*
Goodbye.	*Sala gabotse.*
Yes.	*Ee.*
No.	*Aowa.*
Please.	*Ke kgopela.*
Thank you.	*Ke ya leboga.*
What's your name?	*Ke mang lebitso la gago?*
My name is ...	*Lebitso laka ke ...*
I come from ...	*Ke bowa kwa ...*

PORTUGUESE

Portuguese is a Romance language (ie, one closely derived from Latin), and the official language in Mozambique.

Note that Portuguese uses masculine and feminine word endings, usually '-o' and '-a' respectively – to say 'thank you', a man will therefore say *obrigado*, a woman, *obrigada*. These differences are noted in this guide by the abbreviations 'm' and 'f' respectively.

Pronunciation

The following list should give you a rough idea of pronunciation, but listening to how local people speak will be your best guide.

ã	as the 'an' in 'fan' plus the '-ng' sound at the end of the word 'sing'
ão	as the 'ow' in 'how'
é	as the 'e' in 'whey'
ç	as the 'c'in 'celery'
c	as the 'k' in 'kit'
ch	as the 'sh' in 'shake'
h	usually silent; sometimes as in 'hot'
m	often silent; nasalises the preceding vowel
s	as in 'sun' when word-initial; as 'sh' before **c**, **f**, **p**, **q** or **t**; as in 'pleasure' before **b**, **d**, **g**, **l**, **m**, **n**, **r** and **v**
qu	as in 'queen' or as the 'k' in 'kiosk'
x	as the 'sh' in 'shake'
z	as 'jz' when word-final; elsewhere as 'sz'

Greetings & Civilities

Good morning.	*Bom dia.*
Good afternoon.	*Boa tarde.*
Good evening.	*Boa noite.*
Goodbye.	*Adeus/Ciao.*
See you later.	*Até mais logo.*
How are you?	*Como está?*
I'm fine, thank you.	*Muito bem, obrigado/a.* (m/f)
friend	*amigo/a* (m/f)
What's your name?	*Como se chama?*
Please.	*Por favor.*
Thank you.	*Obrigado/a.* (m/f)
No problem.	*Não faz mal.*
You're welcome.	*De nada.*
Excuse me. (sorry)	*Desculpe.*

Useful Words & Phrases

Yes.	*Sim.*
No.	*Não.*
I don't understand.	*Não compreendo.*
I don't speak Portuguese.	*Não falo Português.*
Would you write it down, please?	*Escrever, por favor.*
When?	*Quando?*
Where?	*Onde?*
No/Never/Nothing.	*Nada.*
Do you have/ Is there ...?	*Tem ...?*
How much is it?	*Quanto custa?*
May I?	*Com/Dá licença?*

all	*todo/s* (sing/plural)
here	*aqui*
cheap	*barato*
expensive	*caro*
very/too expensive	*muito caro*
on the left	*à esquerda*
on the right	*à direita*
perhaps	*talvez*
today	*hoje*
tomorrow	*amanhã*
yesterday	*ontem*
Women (toilets)	*Senhoras*
Men (toilets)	*Senhors*
Customs	*Alfândega*

Getting Around

avenue	*avenida*
beach	*praia*
beach road/ esplanade	*marginal*
corner	*esquina*
house	*casa*
National Highway	*Estrada Nacional*
road/street	*rua*
square	*praça*
town	*vila*

bus	*bus/machimbombo*
converted passenger truck	*chapa/chapa-cem*
ticket	*bilhete*
train	*comboio*
How many kilometres to ...?	*Quantos kilometros até ...?*

Accommodation & Food

hotel	*hotel/pousada*
cheap hotel	*pensão*

Emergencies – Portuguese

Help!	*Socorro!*
Call the police!	*Chame a polícia!*
Call a doctor!	*Chame um médico!*
I've been robbed.	*Fui roubado/a.*
Go away!	*Deixe-me em paz!*
I'm lost.	*Estou perdido/a.*

Is there a ... available?	*Tem um ... ?*
room	*quarto*
single/double	*simple/duplo*
room for married couples	*casal*
bed	*cama*
toilet/bathroom	*casa da banho*
market	*mercado*
restaurant	*restaurante*
snack bar	*quiosque*
street food stall	*barraca*
menu (a set meal)	*menu*
breakfast	*pequeno almoço*
lunch	*almoço*
supper	*jantar*
bill	*conta*
receipt	*recibo*

beer	*cerveja*
bread	*pão*
chicken	*frango/galinha*
chips/fries	*batatas fritas*
crayfish	*lagostim*
eggs	*ovos*
fish	*peixe*
fruit	*fruta*
lobster	*lagosta*
meat	*carne*
mineral water	*agua mineral*
potatoes	*batatas*
prawn	*camarão*
rice	*arroz*
salt	*sal*
scrambled eggs	*ovos mexidos*
squid (calamari)	*lulas*
steak	*bife*
steak sandwich	*prego*
sugar	*açucar*
tea	*chá*
vegetables	*legumes*
water	*agua*

Numbers

1	*um/uma*
2	*dois/duas*
3	*três*
4	*quatro*
5	*cinco*
6	*seis*
7	*sete*
8	*oito*
9	*nove*
10	*dez*
50	*cinquenta*
100	*cem*
500	*quinhentos*
1000	*mil*

SHONA

Shona is an amalgamation of several Bantu languages. It's spoken almost universally in the central and eastern parts of Zimbabwe. The 'high' dialect, the one used in broadcasts and other media, is Zezuru, which is indigenous to the Harare area.

Although most urban Zimbabweans have at least a little knowledge of English, many rural dwellers' English vocabulary is limited, so it helps to know a few words and phrases in Shona or Ndebele (see the 'Ndebele – Zimbabwe' section in this chapter). Even those Zimbabweans who speak English well will be pleasantly surprised to hear a foreigner attempt to speak a few words in the indigenous languages.

If two translations are given for the same word or expression in the following section, the first is used when speaking to one person, the second with more than one.

Pronunciation

Shona, like Ndebele, was first written down by phonetic English transliteration, so most letters are pronounced as they would be in English. Differences of note are:

dya	pronounced 'jga', as near to one syllable as possible
tya	this one is 'chka', said quickly
sv	try saying 's' with your tongue near the roof of your mouth
zv	like the 's-v' sound in 'is very'

m before a word-initial consonant, it's pronounced as a light hum
n before a word-initial consonant, it's a hum with an 'n' sound

Greetings & Civilities

Hello. (initial)	*Mhoro/Mhoroi.*
Hello. (reply)	*Ahoi.*
Welcome.	*Titambire.*
How are you?	*Makadii/Makadi-ni?*
I'm well.	*Ndiripo.*
Good morning.	*Mangwanani.*
Good afternoon.	*Masikati.*
Good evening.	*Manheru.*
Goodbye.	*Chisarai zvakanaka.* (when staying)
Goodbye.	*Fambai zvakanaka.* (when leaving)
Please.	*Ndapota.*
Thank you.	*Ndatenda/Masvita.*

Useful Words & Phrases

Yes.	*Ehe.*
No.	*Aiw.*
What's your name?	*Unonzi ani zita rako?*
My name is ...	*Ndini ...*
I'm from ...	*Ndinobva ku ...*
sir/madam	*changamire/ mudzimai*
boy/girl	*mukomana/ musikana*
I'd like ...	*Ndinoda ...*
How much?	*I marii?*
Where is the (station)?	(*Chiteshi) chiri kupi?*
What time is it?	*Dzavanguvai?*
today	*nhas*
tomorrow	*mangwana*
yesterday	*nezuro*
Men (toilets)	*Varume*
Women (toilets)	*Vakadz*
friend	*shamwari*
small/large	*diki/guru*
market/shop	*musika/chitoro*

What time does the ... leave?	*... richaynda rihni?*
bus	*ehazi*
car	*motokari*
train	*chitima*

Food & Drink

beef	*mombe*
beer	*doro/whawha*
bread	*chingwa*
butter	*bhat*
chicken	*huku*
coffee	*kofi*
eggs	*mazai*
fish	*hove*
fruit	*michero*
ground nuts	*nzungu*
maize	*chibage*
maize porridge	*sadza*
meat	*nyama*
milk	*mukaka*
potatoes	*mbatatisi*
salt	*muny*
sugar	*shuga*
tea	*ti*
vegetables	*muriwo*
water	*mvura*

Animals

baboon	*gudo*
buffalo	*nyati*
dog	*imbwa*
elephant	*nzou*
giraffe	*twiza*
goat	*mbudzi*
hippopotamus	*mvuu*
horse	*bhiza*
hyena	*bere*
impala	*mhara*
leopard	*mbada*
lion	*shumbai*
monkey	*bveni*
rabbit	*tsuro*
rhinoceros	*chipembere*
warthog	*njiri*
zebra	*mbiz*

Days

Monday	*muvhuro*
Tuesday	*chipiri*
Wednesday	*chitatu*
Thursday	*china*
Friday	*chishanu*
Saturday	*mugovera*
Sunday	*svondo*

Numbers

1	*potsi*
2	*piri*
3	*tatu*
4	*ina*
5	*shanu*
6	*tanhatu*
7	*nomwe*
8	*tsere*
9	*pfumbamwe*
10	*gumi*

SOUTH SOTHO

South Sotho is spoken by Basotho people in Lesotho. In South Africa it's spoken in the Free State, North-West Province and Gauteng. It's useful to know some words and phrases if you're planning to visit Lesotho, especially if you want to trek in remote areas.

Hello.	*Dumela.*
Greetings.	*Lumela.*
Peace.	*Khotso.*

Lumela and *khotso* will usually be followed by a title, eg, *Khotso, 'me* (lit: mother; said to an older woman). Other titles are:

to an older man	*ntate* (lit: father)
to a young man	*abuti* (lit: brother)
to a young woman	*ausi* (lit: sister)
Yes	*Ee.*
No.	*Tjhee.*

There are three possible ways to say 'How are you?':

How are you?	*O kae?* (sg) *Le kae?* (pl)
How do you live?	*O phela joang?* (sg) *Le phela joang?* (pl)
How did you get up?	*O tsohele joang?* (sg) *Le tsohele joang?* (pl)

The responses are:

I'm here.	*Ke teng.* (sg) *Re teng.* (pl)
I live well.	*Ke phela hantle.* (sg) *Re phela hantle.* (pl)
I got up well.	*Ke tsohile hantle.* (sg) *Re tsohile hantle.* (pl)

These questions and answers are quite interchangeable, eg, someone could ask you *O phela joang?* and you could answer *Ke teng.*

When trekking, people always ask *Lea kae?* (Where are you going?) and *O tsoa kae?* or the plural *Le tsoa kae?* (Where have you come from?).

When parting, use the following expressions:

Stay well.	*Sala hantle.* (sg) *Salang hantle.* (pl)
Go well.	*Tsamaea hantle.* (sg) *Tsamaeang hantle.* (pl)

'Thank you' is *kea leboha* (pronounced 'keya lebowah'). The herd boys often ask for *chelete* (money) or *lipompong* (sweets), pronounced 'dee-pom-pong'. If you want to say 'I don't have any', the answer is *ha dio* (pronounced 'ha dee-oh').

SWATI

Swati is one of two official languages in Swaziland (the other is English). It's very similar to Zulu, and the two languages are mutually intelligible. Swati is a tone language (changes of pitch within words determine their meaning), and there are also some clicks to contend with.

Yebo is often said as a casual greeting. It is the custom to greet everyone you meet. Often you will be asked *U ya phi?* (Where are you going?).

Hello. (to one person)	*Sawubona.* (lit: 'I see you')
Hello. (more than one person)	*Sanibona.*
How are you?	*Kunjani?*
I'm fine.	*Kulungile.*
Goodbye. (when leaving)	*Sala kahle.* (lit: 'stay well')
Goodbye. (when staying)	*Hamba kahle.* (lit: 'go well')
Please.	*Ngicela.*
I thank you.	*Ngiyabonga.*
We thank you.	*Siyabonga.*
Yes.	*Yebo.* (also an all-purpose greeting)
No.	(click) *Cha.*
Sorry.	*Lucolo.*

What's your name?	*Ngubani libito lakho?*
My name is ...	*Libitolami ngingu ...*
I'm from ...	*Ngingewekubuya e ...*
How much?	*Malini?*
Is there a bus to ...?	*Kukhona ibhasi yini leya ...?*
When does it leave?	*Isuka nini?*
today	*lamuhla*
tomorrow	*kusasa*
yesterday	*itolo*
morning	*ekuseni*
afternoon	*entsambaba*
evening	*kusihlwa*
night	*ebusuku*

TSONGA

Tsonga is spoken in South Africa (north of Hluhluwe in Kwa-Zulu-Natal) and in Mozambique.

Hello.	*Avusheni.* (morning)
	Inhelekani. (afternoon)
	Riperile. (evening)
Goodbye.	*Salani kahle.*
Yes.	*Hi swona.*
No.	*A hi swona.*
Please.	*Nakombela.*
Thank you.	*I nkomu.*
What's your name?	*U mani vito ra wena?*
My name is ...	*Vito ra mina i ...*
I come from ...	*Ndzihuma e ...*

TSWANA

Tswana is widely spoken throughout Botswana and in parts of South Africa (in the eastern areas of Northern Cape, in the North-West Province and in western Free State). There are clear similarities in vocabulary between Tswana and the two Sotho languages, and the speakers of each can generally understand one another.

The letters of the Tswana alphabet represent similar sounds to their English counterparts, except that **g** is pronounced as 'h' or, more accurately, as a strongly aspirated 'g', and **th** is pronounced as a slightly aspirated 't', as in 'tip'.

The greetings *dumêla mma* or *dumêla rra* are considered compliments and Batswana people appreciate their liberal usage. When addressing a group, say *dumêlang*.

Another useful phrase, which is normally placed at the end of a sentence or conversation is *go siame*, meaning the equivalent of 'all right, no problem'.

Greetings & Civilities

Hello.	*Dumêla mma/rra.* (to woman/man)
Hello.	*Dumêlang.* (to group)
Hello!	*Ko ko!* (hailing person from your door)
Come on in!	*Tsena!*
How's it going?	*O kae?*
I'm fine.	*Ke teng.* (informal)
How are you?	*A o tsogile?* (lit: 'How did you wake up?')
Did you get up well?	*A o sa tsogile sentle?*
Yes, I woke up well.	*Ee, ke tsogile sentle.*
How are you?	*O tlhotse jang?* (afternoon)
I'm fine.	*Ke tlhotse sentle.*
Goodbye.	*Tsamayo sentle.* (when staying)
Goodbye.	*Sala sentle.* (when leaving)
Please.	*Tsweetswee.*
Thank you.	*Kea itumela.*
OK/No problem.	*Go siame.*

Useful Words & Phrases

Yes.	*Ee.*
No.	*Nnyaa.*
Do you speak ...?	*A o bua se ...?*
Where are you from? (birthplace)	*O tswa kae?*
I'm from ...	*Ke tswa kwa ...*
Where do you live?	*O nna kae?*
I live in ...	*Ke nna kwa ...*
Where are you going?	*O ya kae?*
What's your name?	*Leina la gago ke mang?*
My name is ...	*Leina la me ke ...*
How do I get to ...?	*Tsela ... e kae?*
Where is the train station/hotel?	*Seteseine/hotele se kai?*

Is it far?	*A go kgala?*
What would you like?	*O batla eng?*
I'd like ...	*Ke batla ...*
Cheers!	*Pula!*
bread	*borotho*
food	*dijo*
mealies (corn cobs)	*bogobe*
meat	*nama*
milk	*mashi*
water	*metsi*

VENDA

Venda is spoken in the north-eastern region of South Africa's Northern Province.

Hello.	*Ndi matseloni.* (morning)
	Ndi masiari. (afternoon)
	Ndi madekwana (evening)
Goodbye.	*Kha vha sale zwavhudi.*
Yes.	*Ndi zwone.*
No.	*A si zwone.*
Please.	*Ndikho u humbela.*
Thank you.	*Ndo livhuwa.*
What's your name?	*Zina lavho ndi nnyi?*
My name is ...	*Zina langa ndi ...*
I come from ...	*Ndi bva ...*

XHOSA

Xhosa is the language of the people of the same name. It's the dominant indigenous language in Eastern Cape in South Africa, although you'll meet Xhosa speakers throughout the region.

It's worth noting that *bawo* is a term of respect used when addressing an older man.

Hello.	*Molo.*
Goodbye.	*Sala kakuhle.*
Goodnight.	*Rhonanai.*
Yes.	*Ewe.*
No.	*Hayi.*
Please.	*Nceda.*
Thankyou.	*Enkosi.*
Do you speak English?	*Uyakwazi ukuthetha siNgesi?*
Are you well?	*Uphilile na namhlanje?*
Yes, I'm well.	*Ewe, ndiphilile kanye.*
Where are you from?	*Uvela phi na okanye ngaphi na?*
I'm from ...	*Ndivela ...*
When will we arrive?	*Siya kufika nini na?*
The road is good.	*Indlela ilungile.*
The road is bad.	*Indlela imbi.*
I'm lost.	*Ndilahlekile.*
Is this the road to ...?	*Yindlela eya ... yini le?*
Would you show me the way to ...?	*Ungandibonisa na indlela eye ...?*
How much is it?	*Idla ntoni na?*
day	*usuku*
week	*iveki*
month (moon)	*inyanga*
east	*empumalanga*
west	*entshonalanga*

ZULU

Zulu is spoken in South Africa by the people of the same name. As with several other Nguni languages, Zulu uses a variety of clicks, which are very hard to reproduce without practice. Many people don't try (the 'Kwa' in KwaZulu is a click), although it's worth the effort, if only to provide amusement for your listeners. To ask a question, add *na* to the end of a sentence.

Hello.	*Sawubona.*
Goodbye.	*Sala kahle.*
Please.	*Jabulisa.*
Thank you.	*Ngiyabonga.*
Yes.	*Yebo.*
No.	*Cha.*
Where does this road go?	*Iqondaphi lendlela na?*
Which is the road to ...?	*Iphi indlela yokuya ku ...?*
Is it far?	*Kukude yini?*
left	*ekhohlo*
right	*ekumene*
food	*ukudla*
water	*amanzi*
lion	*ibhubesi*
rhino (black)	*ubhejane*
rhino (white)	*umkhombe*
snake	*inyoka*

Glossary

Although English is widely spoken in most Southern African countries, native speakers from Australasia, North America and the UK will notice many words that have developed different meanings locally. There are also many unusual terms that have been borrowed from Afrikaans, Portuguese or indigenous languages. This Glossary includes many of these particular 'Afro-English' words, as well as other general terms and abbreviations that may not be understood.

In African English, repetition for emphasis is common: something that burnt you would be 'hot hot'; fields after the rains are 'green green'; a crowded minibus with no more room is 'full full', and so on.

For more useful words and phrases in local languages, see the Language chapter.

ablutions block – found at camping grounds and caravan parks: a building that contains toilets, showers and washing-up area; also known as an amenities block
af – derogatory reference to a black person, as bad as 'nigger' or 'abo'
ANC – African National Congress
apartheid – 'separate development of the races'; a political system in which peoples are segregated according to skin colour
ASL – above sea level
ATVs – all terrain vehicles

baas – boss; subservient address reserved mainly for white males
babalass – a hangover (mainly Zimbabwe)
bakkie – (pronounced 'bukkie') utility or pick-up truck
barchan dunes – migrating crescent-shaped sand dunes
bashas – thatched A-frame chalets (mainly Zimbabwe)
BDF – Botswana Defence Forces
bhundu – the bush, the wilderness
bilharzia – water-borne disease caused by minute worms which are passed on by freshwater snails
biltong – dried and salted meat that can be made from just about anything from eland or ostrich, to mutton or beef
bioscope – a cinema
bobotie – traditional Malay dish; delicately flavoured curry with a topping of beaten egg baked to a crust, served with stewed fruits and chutney
boer – farmer in Afrikaans; (cap) an earlier name for the Afrikaner people
boerewors – a spicy Afrikaner sausage of varying consistency
bogobe – sorghum porridge, a staple food in Botswana
boma – in Zambia, Malawi and some other countries, this is a local word for 'town'. In East Africa the same word means 'fortified stockade'. It's not an indigenous African word, and may be derived from the colonial term BOMA (British Overseas Military Administration), applied to any government building, such as offices or forts.
braai – a barbecue; a Southern African institution, particularly among whites
BSAC – British South Africa Company; led by Cecil Rhodes, this company was hugely influential in shaping Southern Africa in colonial times
buppies – black yuppies

camião – truck (Mozambique)
camping ground – area where tents can be pitched and caravans parked
camp site – an individual pitch at a camping ground
casal – room for married couples (Mozambique)
cassper – SADF (now SANDF) armoured vehicle; also used as slang for hippo
CBD – Central Business District; this rather scientific-sounding abbreviation is commonly used where other English speakers might say city centre or downtown area
CDM – Consolidated Diamond Mines
cell phone – mobile phone (mobile phone – cordless phone)
chapa – converted passenger truck or mini-van (Mozambique)

chibuku – local style mass-produced beer, stored in tanks served in buckets, or available in takeaway cartons (mostly in Zimbabwe and Malawi) and plastic bottles known as *scuds*. It's good for a quick euphoria and a debilitating *babalass*.
chiperone – damp misty weather which affects southern Malawi
Comrade (or Cde) – a Marxist title used mainly by the media, referring to black Zimbabweans, especially government officials
coupé – two-person compartment on a train

daga hut – a traditional African round house consisting of a wooden frame, mud and straw walls and thatched roof (mainly Zimbabwe)
dagga – (pronounced dacha) South African term for grass, marijuana
dambo – area of grass, reeds or swamp alongside a river course
dhow – ancient Arabic sailing vessel
difaqane – forced migration by several Southern African tribes in the face of Zulu aggression; also *mfecane*
djembe – a type of hand drum
donga – steep-sided gully caused by soil erosion
donkey boiler – a watertank positioned over a fire and used to heat water
dorp – a small country settlement
drankwinkel – literally 'drink shop'; a Namibian or South African off-licence
drift – a river ford; most are normally dry
dumpi – smallest size of beer bottle (see also *pint* and *quart*)
Dutchman – term of abuse for a white person of Afrikaner descent

eh – (pronounced to rhyme with hay) all purpose ending to sentences, even very short ones such as 'Thanks, eh.'

fathom – nautical measurement equal to six feet (1.83m)
flotty – a hat for canoe safaris, with a chinstrap and a bit of cork in a zippered pocket to ensure that it floats in case of a capsize
4WD – four-wheel drive; also written 4x4
Frelimo – Frente pela Libertação de Moçambique, or Mozambique Liberation Front

game – formally used for any animal hunted, now means larger mammals
gap it – make a quick exit
Gemütlichkeit – German appreciation of comfort and hospitality
GMA – Game Management Area (Zambia)
GPS – global positioning system
guti – dank, drizzly weather that can afflict Zimbabwe's Eastern Highlands in winter

half-bus – a bus with about 30 seats – to distinguish it from big buses or minibuses (Malawi)
Homelands – self-governing black states which were part of the apartheid regime's plan for a separate black and white South Africa

IMF – International Monetary Fund
inselbergs – isolated ranges and hills; literally 'island mountains'
Izzit? – rhetorical question that most closely translates as 'Really?' and is used without regard to gender, person or subject number. Therefore, it could mean 'Is it?', 'Are you?', 'Is he?', 'Are they?', 'Is she?', 'Are we?' etc. Also 'How izzit?, for 'How's it going?' etc.

jesse – dense, thorny scrub, normally impenetrable to humans
jol –party, both verb and noun
jukskei – this Afrikaner game is something like horseshoe-tossing but uses items associated with trek wagons
just now – refers to some time in the future but implies a certain degree of imminence; it could be half an hour from now or two days from now, ie, 'at the appropriate time'

kaffir – derogatory term for a black person
kapenta – an anchovy-like fish caught in Lake Kariba and favoured by Zimbabweans *(Limnothrissa mioda)*
karakul – variety of Central Asian sheep, which produce high-grade wool and pelts; raised in Namibia and parts of Botswana
kerk – church
kloof – a ravine or small valley
koeksesters – small doughnuts dripping in honey; very gooey and figure-enhancing
konditorei – German pastry shops

kopje – (pronounced and sometimes spelt 'koppie') an isolated hill or rocky outcrop, which translates from Afrikaans as 'little hill'
kraal – Afrikaans for the Portuguese word 'curral'; an enclosure for livestock or hut village, especially one surrounded by a stockade

larney – posh, smart, high quality
lekker – (pronounced lak-ker) very good, sweet, enjoyable or tasty
location – another word for township, more usually in rural situations

machibombo – large bus (Mozambique)
make a plan – 'sort it out'; refers to anything from working through a complicated procedure to circumventing bureaucracy
Malawi shandy – nonalcoholic drink made from ginger beer, Angostura bitters, orange or lemon slices, soda and ice
marimba – African xylophone, made from strips of resonant wood with various-sized gourds for sound boxes
matola – pick-up or van carrying passengers (Malawi)
mbanje – cannabis (Zimbabwe)
mbira – thumb piano; it consists of 22 to 24 narrow iron keys mounted in rows on a wooden sound board
mealie meal or **mielie pap** – maize porridge; staple for indigenous African people
mielies – cooked cobs of maize
mfecane – see *difaqane*
miombo – dry open woodland, also called *Brachystegia* woodland
mokoro (s), **mekoro** (pl) – dugout canoe used in the Okavango Delta; it is propelled by a poler who stands in the stern
mopane worms – the caterpillar of the moth Gonimbrasiabelina, eaten as a delicacy, mostly in Zimbabwe
murunge – see *muzungu*
mushe – (pronounced mush-ie) good (mostly in Zimbabwe)
musika – a market outside the town centre; also called *renkini* in Ndebele (Zimbabwe)
muzungu – white person, especially in Zambia and Malawi, also *muzungo*, or *murunge* in Zimbabwe

não faz mal – 'no problem' in Portuguese
nartjie – (pronounced 'narchie') South African tangerine
now now – not the present moment, but pretty soon after it; sometime sooner than 'just now'
NWR – Namibia Wildlife Resorts

oke – bloke, guy (mainly South Africa)
omuramba (s), **omiramba** (pl) – fossil river channel in northern Namibia and north-western Botswana
oshana – dry river channel in northern Namibia and north-western Botswana

padrão – tribute to a royal patron, erected by early Portuguese navigators along the African coast
pan – dry flat area, often seasonal lake-bed
participation safari – a type of safari – clients cook their own meals, pitch their own tent etc; generally the cost of these safaris is lower than all-inclusive tours
peg – milepost
peri peri – ultra-hot pepper-based sauce that usurps the flavour of your *sadza ne nyama* (*mielie* with meat *relish*)
pint – small bottle of beer or can of oil (or similar) usually around 300ml to 375ml (not necessarily equal to a British or US pint)
plus-minus – meaning 'about'; this scientific/mathematical term has entered common parlance, particularly among non-English-as-a-first-language speakers in South Africa, eg, 'the bus will come in plus-minus 10 minutes'
pondo – 'pound', occasionally used in Botswana to refer to two pula
praça – town square (Mozambique)
pronking – leaping, as done by several species of antelope, apparently for sheer fun
pula – the Botswanan currency; meaning 'rain' in Tswana
pungwe – all night drinking and music party (Zimbabwe)
quart – about (but not necessarily exactly) twice the size of a pint

relish – sauce of meat, vegetables, beans etc eaten with nsima, nshima or *mealie meal*
Renamo – Resistência Nacional Moçambicana, or Mozambique National Resistance

renkini – see *musika*
Rhodey – a normally derogatory term for a white Zimbabwean; roughly the same as 'ocker' or 'redneck' in Australia and the US
robot – traffic light
rondavel – round, African-style hut
rooibos – literally 'red bush' in Afrikaans; herbal tea that reputedly has therapeutic qualities
rubber duck – inflatable boat
rusks – solid bits of biscuit-like bread made edible by immersion in coffee or tea

SADF – South African Defence Force (now renamed SANDF South African National Defence Force)
sadza – maize meal porridge (Zimbabwe)
sangoma – witchdoctor; herbalist
scud – plastic bottle
seif dunes – prominent linear sand dunes, as found in the central Namib Desert
self-catering – term applied at camps, with many different meanings. Sometimes all that's provided is a kitchen and stove, while you bring food, utensils – maybe even water and firewood – and do the cooking yourself. In other places, everything is provided, including a fully equipped kitchen, staffed by cooks; you just bring your food – they prepare it to your instructions (and wash up).
shame! – an expression of commiseration
shebeen – an illegal township drinking establishment (South Africa)
slasher – hand tool with a curved blade used to cut grass or crops, hence 'to slash' means 'to cut grass'
Sperrgebiet – forbidden area; alluvial diamond region of south-western Namibia
spruit – a little streambed, which rarely contains any water
squaredavel – see *rondavel* and work out the rest
stiffy – computer disc
SWAKARA – South-West Africa Karakul (sheep)
SWAPO – South-West African People's Organisation

tackies – trainers, tennis shoes, gym shoes
Tonkies – derogatory word for members of the Batonka tribe, and for anybody/thing basic, simple or 'gone bush'
township – high-density black residential area outside a central city or town
toy toy – jubilant dance
tsotsi – hoodlum, thief
TWOGs – acronym for 'Third World groupies', used by white Zimbabweans in reference to foreigners who travel to underdeveloped countries and consciously sink to the lowest level of local society

UNESCO – United Nations Education, Scientific and Cultural Organisation
UNIP – United National Independence Party (Zambia)
UNITA – União pela Independência Total de Angola (National Union for the Total Independence of Angola)
upshwa – see *xima*

van der Merwe – archetypal Boer country bumpkin who is the butt of jokes throughout Southern Africa
veld – open grassland (pronounced 'felt'); variations: lowveld, highveld, bushveld, strandveld, panveld
vlei – (pronounced 'flay') any low open landscape, sometimes marshy
VSO – Volunteer Service Overseas

wag 'n bietjie – Afrikaans name for the buffalo thorn tree; literally 'wait-a-bit'
watu – dugout canoe; also known as *mokoro*
WWF –World Wide Fund for Nature

xima (or **upshwa**) – maize or cassava based staple, usually served with a sauce of beans, vegetables or fish (Mozambique)

ZANLA – Zimbabwe African National Liberation Army
ZANU – Zimbabwe African National Union
ZAPU – Zimbabwe African Peoples' Union
ZAR – Zuid-Afrikaansche Republiek (South African Republic)
ZIPRA – Zimbabwe Peoples' Revolutionary Army
ZIPU – Zimbabwe People's Army
zol – see *dagga*
ZUM – Zimbabwe Unity Movement

LONELY PLANET

You already know that Lonely Planet produces more than this one guidebook, but you might not be aware of the other products we have on this region. Here is a selection of titles which you may want to check out as well:

Read this First: Africa
ISBN 1 86450 066 2

South Africa, Lesotho & Swaziland
ISBN 1 86450 322 X

Mozambique
ISBN 1 86450 108 1

Watching Wildlife Southern Africa
ISBN 1 86450 035 2

Namibia
ISBN 1 74059 042 2

East Africa
ISBN 0 86442 676 3

Songs to an African Sunset
ISBN 0 86442 472 8

Malawi
ISBN 1 86450 095 6

Cape Town
ISBN 0 86442 759 X

Cape Town City Map
ISBN 1 86450 076 X

Southern Africa Road Atlas
ISBN 1 86450 101 4

Healthy Travel Africa
ISBN 1 86450 050 6

Zimbabwe
ISBN 1 74059 043 0

Botswana
ISBN 1 74059 041 4

Zambia
ISBN 1 74059 045 7

Available wherever books are sold.

Lonely Planet Guides by Region

Lonely Planet is known worldwide for publishing practical, reliable and no-nonsense travel information in our guides and on our Web site. The Lonely Planet list covers just about every accessible part of the world. Currently there are 16 series: Travel guides, Shoestring guides, Condensed guides, Phrasebooks, Read This First, Healthy Travel, Walking guides, Cycling guides, Watching Wildlife guides, Pisces Diving & Snorkeling guides, City Maps, Road Atlases, Out to Eat, World Food, Journeys travel literature and Pictorials.

AFRICA Africa on a shoestring • Botswana • Cairo • Cairo City Map • Cape Town • Cape Town City Map • East Africa • Egypt • Egyptian Arabic phrasebook • Ethiopia, Eritrea & Djibouti • Ethiopian Amharic phrasebook • The Gambia & Senegal • Healthy Travel Africa • Kenya • Malawi • Morocco • Moroccan Arabic phrasebook • Mozambique • Namibia • Read This First: Africa • South Africa, Lesotho & Swaziland • Southern Africa • Southern Africa Road Atlas • Swahili phrasebook • Tanzania, Zanzibar & Pemba • Trekking in East Africa • Tunisia • Watching Wildlife East Africa • Watching Wildlife Southern Africa • West Africa • World Food Morocco • Zambia • Zimbabwe, Botswana & Namibia
Travel Literature: Mali Blues: Traveling to an African Beat • The Rainbird: A Central African Journey • Songs to an African Sunset: A Zimbabwean Story

AUSTRALIA & THE PACIFIC Aboriginal Australia & the Torres Strait Islands •Auckland • Australia • Australian phrasebook • Australia Road Atlas • Cycling Australia • Cycling New Zealand • Fiji • Fijian phrasebook • Healthy Travel Australia, NZ & the Pacific • Islands of Australia's Great Barrier Reef • Melbourne • Melbourne City Map • Micronesia • New Caledonia • New South Wales • New Zealand • Northern Territory • Outback Australia • Out to Eat – Melbourne • Out to Eat – Sydney • Papua New Guinea • Pidgin phrasebook • Queensland • Rarotonga & the Cook Islands • Samoa • Solomon Islands • South Australia • South Pacific • South Pacific phrasebook • Sydney • Sydney City Map • Sydney Condensed • Tahiti & French Polynesia • Tasmania • Tonga • Tramping in New Zealand • Vanuatu • Victoria • Walking in Australia • Watching Wildlife Australia • Western Australia
Travel Literature: Islands in the Clouds: Travels in the Highlands of New Guinea • Kiwi Tracks: A New Zealand Journey • Sean & David's Long Drive

CENTRAL AMERICA & THE CARIBBEAN Bahamas, Turks & Caicos • Baja California • Belize, Guatemala & Yucatán • Bermuda • Central America on a shoestring • Costa Rica • Costa Rica Spanish phrasebook • Cuba • Cycling Cuba • Dominican Republic & Haiti • Eastern Caribbean • Guatemala • Havana • Healthy Travel Central & South America • Jamaica • Mexico • Mexico City • Panama • Puerto Rico • Read This First: Central & South America • Virgin Islands • World Food Caribbean • World Food Mexico • Yucatán
Travel Literature: Green Dreams: Travels in Central America

EUROPE Amsterdam • Amsterdam City Map • Amsterdam Condensed • Andalucía • Athens • Austria • Baltic States phrasebook • Barcelona • Barcelona City Map • Belgium & Luxembourg • Berlin • Berlin City Map • Britain • British phrasebook • Brussels, Bruges & Antwerp • Brussels City Map • Budapest • Budapest City Map • Canary Islands • Catalunya & the Costa Brava • Central Europe • Central Europe phrasebook • Copenhagen • Corfu & the Ionians • Corsica • Crete • Crete Condensed • Croatia • Cycling Britain • Cycling France • Cyprus • Czech & Slovak Republics • Czech phrasebook • Denmark • Dublin • Dublin City Map • Dublin Condensed • Eastern Europe • Eastern Europe phrasebook • Edinburgh • Edinburgh City Map • England • Estonia, Latvia & Lithuania • Europe on a shoestring • Europe phrasebook • Finland • Florence • Florence City Map • France • Frankfurt City Map • Frankfurt Condensed • French phrasebook • Georgia, Armenia & Azerbaijan • Germany • German phrasebook • Greece • Greek Islands • Greek phrasebook • Hungary • Iceland, Greenland & the Faroe Islands • Ireland • Italian phrasebook • Italy • Kraków • Lisbon • The Loire • London • London City Map • London Condensed • Madrid • Madrid City Map • Malta • Mediterranean Europe • Milan, Turin & Genoa • Moscow • Munich • Netherlands • Normandy • Norway • Out to Eat – London • Out to Eat – Paris • Paris • Paris City Map • Paris Condensed • Poland • Polish phrasebook • Portugal • Portuguese phrasebook • Prague • Prague City Map • Provence & the Côte d'Azur • Read This First: Europe • Rhodes & the Dodecanese • Romania & Moldova • Rome • Rome City Map • Rome Condensed • Russia, Ukraine & Belarus • Russian phrasebook • Scandinavian & Baltic Europe • Scandinavian phrasebook • Scotland • Sicily • Slovenia • South-West France • Spain • Spanish phrasebook • Stockholm • St Petersburg • St Petersburg City Map • Sweden • Switzerland • Tuscany • Ukrainian phrasebook • Venice • Vienna • Wales • Walking in Britain • Walking in France • Walking in Ireland • Walking in Italy • Walking in Scotland • Walking in Spain • Walking in Switzerland • Western Europe • World Food France • World Food Greece • World Food Ireland • World Food Italy • World Food Spain **Travel Literature:** After Yugoslavia • Love and War in the Apennines • The Olive Grove: Travels in Greece • On the Shores of the Mediterranean • Round Ireland in Low Gear • A Small Place in Italy

Lonely Planet Mail Order

Lonely Planet products are distributed worldwide.They are also available by mail order from Lonely Planet, so if you have difficulty finding a title please write to us. North and South American residents should write to 150 Linden St, Oakland, CA 94607, USA; European and African residents should write to 10a Spring Place, London NW5 3BH, UK; and residents of other countries to Locked Bag 1, Footscray, Victoria 3011, Australia.

INDIAN SUBCONTINENT & THE INDIAN OCEAN Bangladesh • Bengali phrasebook • Bhutan • Delhi • Goa • Healthy Travel Asia & India • Hindi & Urdu phrasebook • India • India & Bangladesh City Map • Indian Himalaya • Karakoram Highway • Kathmandu City Map • Kerala • Madagascar • Maldives • Mauritius, Réunion & Seychelles • Mumbai (Bombay) • Nepal • Nepali phrasebook • North India • Pakistan • Rajasthan • Read This First: Asia & India • South India • Sri Lanka • Sri Lanka phrasebook • Tibet • Tibetan phrasebook • Trekking in the Indian Himalaya • Trekking in the Karakoram & Hindukush • Trekking in the Nepal Himalaya • World Food India **Travel Literature:** The Age of Kali: Indian Travels and Encounters • Hello Goodnight: A Life of Goa • In Rajasthan • Maverick in Madagascar • A Season in Heaven: True Tales from the Road to Kathmandu • Shopping for Buddhas • A Short Walk in the Hindu Kush • Slowly Down the Ganges

MIDDLE EAST & CENTRAL ASIA Bahrain, Kuwait & Qatar • Central Asia • Central Asia phrasebook • Dubai • Farsi (Persian) phrasebook • Hebrew phrasebook • Iran • Israel & the Palestinian Territories • Istanbul • Istanbul City Map • Istanbul to Cairo • Istanbul to Kathmandu • Jerusalem • Jerusalem City Map • Jordan • Lebanon • Middle East • Oman & the United Arab Emirates • Syria • Turkey • Turkish phrasebook • World Food Turkey • Yemen **Travel Literature:** Black on Black: Iran Revisited • Breaking Ranks: Turbulent Travels in the Promised Land • The Gates of Damascus • Kingdom of the Film Stars: Journey into Jordan

NORTH AMERICA Alaska • Boston • Boston City Map • Boston Condensed • British Columbia • California & Nevada • California Condensed • Canada • Chicago • Chicago City Map • Chicago Condensed • Florida • Georgia & the Carolinas • Great Lakes • Hawaii • Hiking in Alaska • Hiking in the USA • Honolulu & Oahu City Map • Las Vegas • Los Angeles • Los Angeles City Map • Louisiana & the Deep South • Miami • Miami City Map • Montreal • New England • New Orleans • New Orleans City Map • New York City • New York City City Map • New York City Condensed • New York, New Jersey & Pennsylvania • Oahu • Out to Eat – San Francisco • Pacific Northwest • Rocky Mountains • San Diego & Tijuana • San Francisco • San Francisco City Map • Seattle • Seattle City Map • Southwest • Texas • Toronto • USA • USA phrasebook • Vancouver • Vancouver City Map • Virginia & the Capital Region • Washington, DC • Washington, DC City Map • World Food New Orleans **Travel Literature**: Caught Inside: A Surfer's Year on the California Coast • Drive Thru America

NORTH-EAST ASIA Beijing • Beijing City Map • Cantonese phrasebook • China • Hiking in Japan • Hong Kong & Macau • Hong Kong City Map • Hong Kong Condensed • Japan • Japanese phrasebook • Korea • Korean phrasebook • Kyoto • Mandarin phrasebook • Mongolia • Mongolian phrasebook • Seoul • Shanghai • South-West China • Taiwan • Tokyo • Tokyo Condensed • World Food Hong Kong • World Food Japan **Travel Literature:** In Xanadu: A Quest • Lost Japan

SOUTH AMERICA Argentina, Uruguay & Paraguay • Bolivia • Brazil • Brazilian phrasebook • Buenos Aires • Buenos Aires City Map • Chile & Easter Island • Colombia • Ecuador & the Galapagos Islands • Healthy Travel Central & South America • Latin American Spanish phrasebook • Peru • Quechua phrasebook • Read This First: Central & South America • Rio de Janeiro • Rio de Janeiro City Map • Santiago de Chile • South America on a shoestring • Trekking in the Patagonian Andes • Venezuela **Travel Literature**: Full Circle: A South American Journey

SOUTH-EAST ASIA Bali & Lombok • Bangkok • Bangkok City Map • Burmese phrasebook • Cambodia • Cycling Vietnam, Laos & Cambodia • East Timor phrasebook • Hanoi • Healthy Travel Asia & India • Hill Tribes phrasebook • Ho Chi Minh City (Saigon) • Indonesia • Indonesian phrasebook • Indonesia's Eastern Islands • Java • Lao phrasebook • Laos • Malay phrasebook • Malaysia, Singapore & Brunei • Myanmar (Burma) • Philippines • Pilipino (Tagalog) phrasebook • Read This First: Asia & India • Singapore • Singapore City Map • South-East Asia on a shoestring • South-East Asia phrasebook • Thailand • Thailand's Islands & Beaches • Thailand, Vietnam, Laos & Cambodia Road Atlas • Thai phrasebook • Vietnam • Vietnamese phrasebook • World Food Indonesia • World Food Thailand • World Food Vietnam

ALSO AVAILABLE: Antarctica • The Arctic • The Blue Man: Tales of Travel, Love and Coffee • Brief Encounters: Stories of Love, Sex & Travel • Buddhist Stupas in Asia: The Shape of Perfection • Chasing Rickshaws • The Last Grain Race • Lonely Planet ... On the Edge: Adventurous Escapades from Around the World • Lonely Planet Unpacked • Lonely Planet Unpacked Again • Not the Only Planet: Science Fiction Travel Stories • Ports of Call: A Journey by Sea • Sacred India • Travel Photography: A Guide to Taking Better Pictures • Travel with Children • Tuvalu: Portrait of an Island Nation

Index

Abbreviations

B – Botswana
GP – Game Park
GR – Game Reserve
L – Lesotho
Mal – Malawi
Moz – Mozambique
N – Namibia
NP – National Park
RP – Recreational Park
SA – South Africa
Swa – Swaziland
WG – Wildlife Guide
WR – Wildlife Reserve
Zam – Zambia
Zim – Zimbabwe

Text

Bold indicates maps.

C

Bold indicates maps.

Bold indicates maps.

Bold indicates maps.

N

Bold indicates maps.

Bold indicates maps.

T

Bold indicates maps.

X

Y

Z